Photographs of British Algæ.

Cyanotype Impressions.

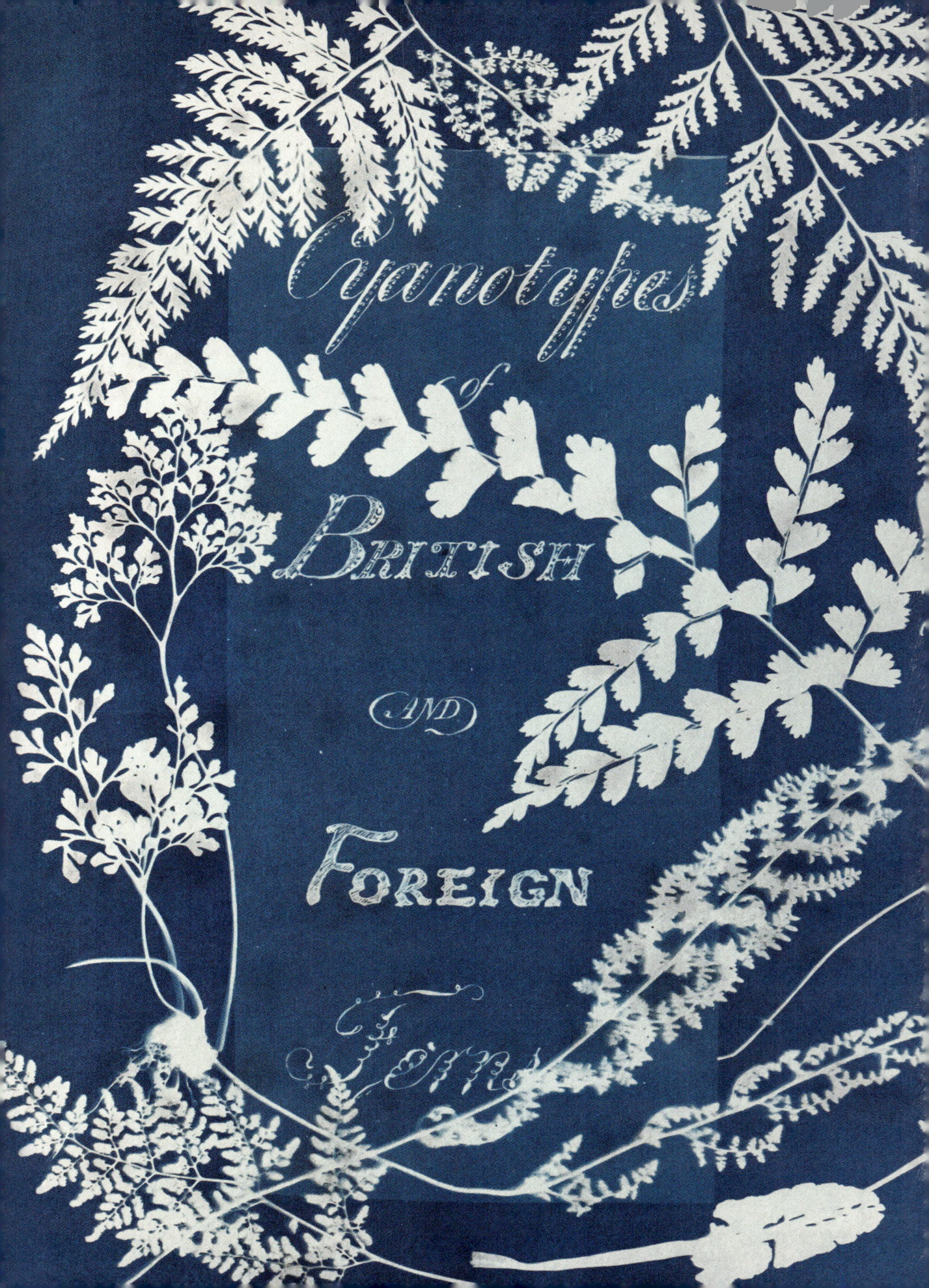
Cyanotypes
of
British
and
Foreign
Ferns

Peter Walther (Ed.)

Anna Atkins
Cyanotypes

Directed and produced by Benedikt Taschen

The copies used for printing belong to the

New York Public Library
J. Paul Getty Museum, Los Angeles
Metropolitan Museum of Art, New York
Rijksmuseum, Amsterdam
Natural History Museum, London

TASCHEN

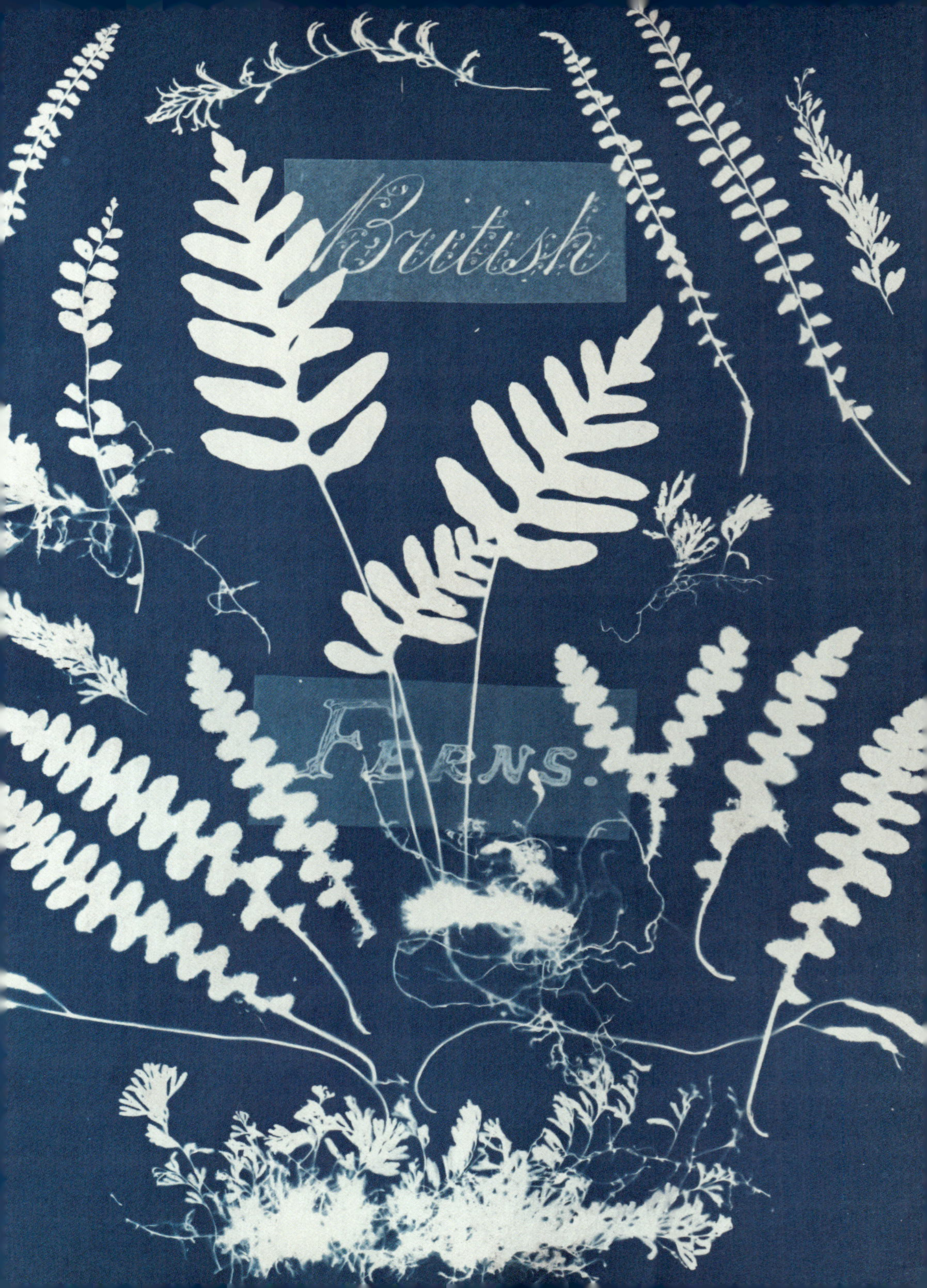
British
Ferns.

Contents

Green Folder.
Mrs. Atkins's British Algæ
CATALOGUED
by
M.F.H.
DRAWING ROOM
Grille Cupb'd
2
Mrs Atkins's
British
Algæ

Anna Atkins – a Pioneer of Early Photography

Halstead Place

During the reign of Queen Victoria (1819–1901), Halstead Place, a manor house south-east of London in the county of Kent, was set in an idyllic park, surrounded by elm trees. The front of the house overlooked open countryside. In fine weather it was here that wooden shelves were erected, designed to hold contact printing frames containing botanical specimens neatly close together. Algae and ferns were pressed under glass and exposed to the sun for up to 15 minutes, during which the sunlight traced the plants' outlines on to paper coated with light-sensitive chemicals. Between 1843 and 1853 some 10,000 images were created. This open-air photographic laboratory was the workplace of Anna Atkins (1799–1871), whose creativity and determination we can thank for one of the most extraordinary accomplishments in the early history of photography.

Following the Second World War, Halstead Place lay in ruins and was demolished in 1952. In the decades after Anna Atkins' death, her photographic legacy, similarly, threatened to be forgotten. However, in recent years, recognition of her pioneering achievements has steadily grown. Critically acclaimed exhibitions and publications, inspired by the research of the photographic historian Larry Schaaf, have introduced the work of the botanist and photographer to a much wider public.

This book offers an overview of Anna Atkins' photographic oeuvre. It includes her two major works, *British Algae* (1843–1853) and *Cyanotypes of British and Foreign Ferns* (1853), the latter of which was produced in collaboration with her friend Anne Dixon (1799–1865). The importance of these volumes is hard to overestimate, for they are milestones in the history of science and media. Even so, independent of their historic importance, the filigree forms of the algae and ferns, interwoven against the blue background of the cyanotype, have created images of timeless aesthetic appeal.

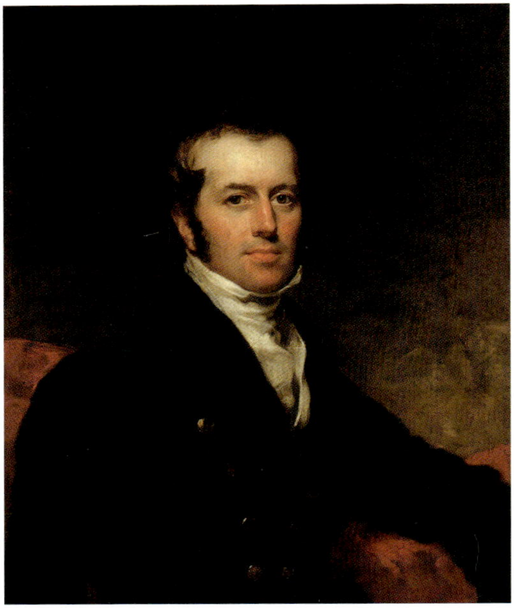

Background and Childhood

It was her father, John George Children, who had the strongest influence on young Anna Atkins. When he died at Halstead in 1852, Anna wrote a book in his memory in which she paid tribute to his achievements as a scientist. At the same time, her descriptions offer an insight of the world into which she was born.

John George Children (1777–1852) was the only son of a landowner and banker (ill. p. 8). His mother died a few days after giving birth. His father, Anna's grandfather, was a man interested in things technical and artistic, who also wrote poetry. He never remarried following his wife's death, but devoted himself to bringing up his son. Young John George had a private tutor before moving on to Eton and, in 1794, continued to Queens' College, Cambridge. There he initially read theology, but his studies were interrupted when he fell in love with Hester Anna Holwell. In 1798, when barely of age, the couple were married and a year later their daughter Anna was born.

John George Children planned to return to Cambridge and resume his studies, but the death of his wife only months after the birth of their daughter left him a widower at the age of 23. Tragically, the fate of the father was repeated in the life of the son. Similarly, Anna's lifelong bond with her father was particularly intense, even though she rarely saw him face-to-face in her early years. In 1800, he travelled with friends to Lisbon. In the spring of 1802 he visited a cousin in the USA, before undertaking adventurous expeditions into the Canadian wilderness. Then, on his return in 1803, he joined the West Kent Militia to help ward off attack on England by Napoleon's troops.

Two years later, Children left the army to devote himself to his scientific work. His main interests were mineralogy and chemistry. These years brought with them friendly relationships with many eminent scientists of the period, among them the chemist Humphry Davy (1778–1829), one of the pioneers in the field of electrochemistry. He often came to visit the Childrens at their home in Tonbridge, Kent, where Anna got to know him. Since around 1800, he had experimented with photosensitive material. He made contact copies of leaves, but never managed to fix them.

In 1807 Children was elected a Fellow of the Royal Society, and two years later, he married for the second time. However, after only eight months this marriage also ended with the death of his wife. Children found solace in his research. At Ferox Hall in Tonbridge, where Anna grew up, her father and grandfather set up a laboratory where they used a huge galvanic battery, containing 4,300 litres of acid, for their experiments with gunpowder. Children encouraged his teenage daughter's scientific interests by giving her a series of private lessons on the basics of chemistry.

From 1811 onwards, Anna grew up with Anne, a girl of the same age whose father was a friend of her father's. Born in 1799, Anne Austen was a second cousin of the novelist Jane Austen. When Anne's mother died – her father was an army officer stationed in Portugal – Children took their daughter into his own family. When Anna mentioned Anne in her father's biography, she added that she was "considered by Mr Children almost as a daughter, and ... to his real daughter had been from childhood as dear as a sister."

Children's carefree life – at least from a material point of view – came to an end in 1816, when his father's bank went bankrupt. He was obliged to take up a post as librarian at the British Museum Library. He had long since made a name for himself as a scientist, having served as Secretary of the Royal Society and a member of numerous scientific societies across the country, as well as editor of a zoological journal, and contributor to many scientific publications.

In September 1818 Children visited the site of the Battle of Waterloo, where three years before Napoleon had suffered a devastating defeat. Anna, now 19 years old, accompanied him on the journey. In England there had arisen a notorious veneration of the elm tree which, during the Battle of Waterloo, had served as the victorious Duke of Wellington's command post. Souvenir hunters had chopped almost all the branches from the elm, which meant Anna and her father only saw the scrawny skeleton of the once majestic tree.

Children bought the tree and shipped it to England, where the wood was used to make various items of furniture. Among them was a chair built by Thomas Chippendale the Younger (1749–1822) for King George IV (1762–1830), which still stands in Windsor Castle, as well as a desk used by Children himself and later handed down to Anna Atkins. Anna's 1818 drawing of the Waterloo battlefield and what remained of the Waterloo Elm are among the early demonstrations of her artistic talents (ill. p. 15).

In 1822 Children was appointed assistant keeper of the British Museum's natural history collection. The following year, his translation from French of Jean-Baptiste de Lamarck's (1744–1829) book *The Genera of Shells* was published. The publication was accompanied by 30 plates with 240 illustrations of molluscs. The drawings that served as prototypes for these illustrations were the work of his daughter, Anna (ill. pp. 18/19).

Page 6
Clothbound cover of Volume I of the Herschel copy of *British Algae*, 1849–1851
Leineneinband des Herschel-Exemplars der *British Algae*, Band I
Reliure en toile de l'exemplaire Herschel des *British Algae*, Volume I
21 × 27 cm (8 ¼ × 10 ⅝ in.)
New York Public Library

Benjamin Rawlinson Faulkner, **John George Children**, 1826
Oil on canvas, 76.2 × 63.5 cm (30 × 25 in.)
London, National Portrait Gallery

A Love of Botany

In 1825 Anna married John Pelly Atkins (1790–1872), a prosperous merchant, Sheriff of Kent, and a close friend of her father's. Some of the time the couple resided at Halstead Place, but they also maintained a home in London, thus enabling Anna's close relationship with her father to continue. Her father-in-law had made his fortune as a trader and plantation owner in Jamaica and Bermuda. As a respected businessman, he chaired various trade organizations and was for a time Lord Mayor of London. Eleven of his 14 children died, Anna's husband being his only surviving male descendant. The Atkins' own marriage was to remain childless. At Halstead Place, the rural manor, they enjoyed a prosperous way of life. John Pelly Atkins was devoted to extending their fine art collection, which already included paintings by Correggio, Caravaggio and Bruegel. Also, with his interest in the sciences, he encouraged his wife's ambitions. In 1847, Queen Victoria appointed him Sheriff of Kent.

In 1837 Anne Austen, the friend whom Anna said she loved like a sister, was also married (ill. p. 56). Her husband, Henry Dixon (1798–1870), belonged to the Childrens' circle of friends. Anne moved with him to Ferring, a little village set right on the English Channel, where Dixon was the vicar of St Andrew's Church. Henry Dixon came from a family with interests in literature and science. His father was a poet and amateur botanist, and one of his brothers was both physician and geologist, with a wife who was a talented artist. Contact between the Atkins, Children and Dixon families remained regular, with only short intervals in between visits.

Now married, Anna broadened her interests in botany. In 1835, she began by creating a herbarium. She collected, dried, and flattened samples and, when her friends went travelling, she asked them to bring her back plants from the places where they had stayed. Her particular interest was in British algae. However, she was not content with simply collecting and assembling examples, and was also interested in botanical classification techniques.

In an era of masculine domination, botany was one of the few disciplines open to women as a field of scientific activity. Thanks to her father, Anna came to know many leading scientists among his circle of friends and acquaintances. As Secretary of the Royal Society, Children enjoyed privileged access to the very latest scientific knowledge discussed at society meetings, in which he allowed his daughter to participate.

Such knowledge offered a new, methodical view of the world which laid the foundations of the technological advances during this early phase of the Industrial Revolution. This progress became noticeable in people's daily lives. They saw how transport (through steamship and railroad travel) and communication (via electrical telegraph) accelerated. Major research expeditions at the beginning of the century, such as those made by Alexander von Humboldt (1769–1859) across Central and South America (1799–1804) and the overland journey of Meriwether Lewis (1774–1809) and William Clark (1770–1838) across the western United States (1804–1806), together unleashed an obsession with collection and categorization.

Unknown artist, **Anna Children**, ca. 1820
Pencil on paper
Kent, Nurstead Court Archives

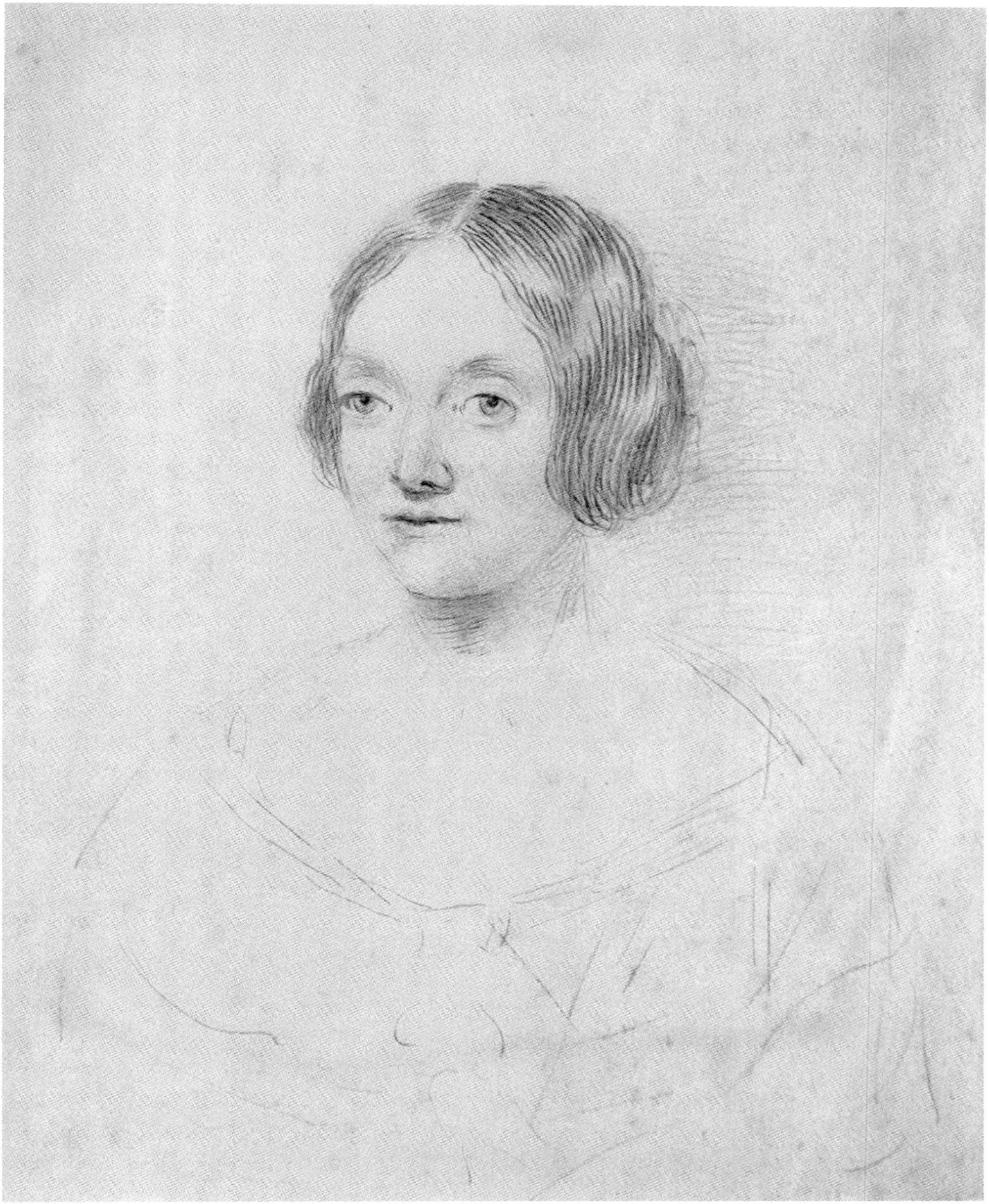

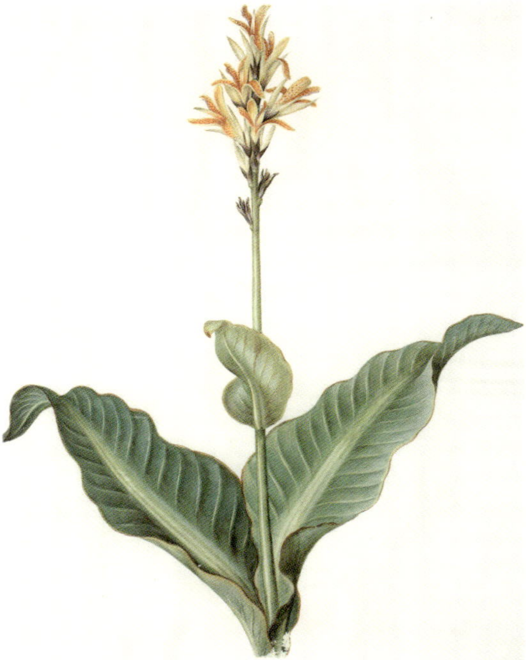

Hans Simon Holtzbecker
Canna indica
Gouache, 50.5 × 38.5 cm (19 7⁄8 × 15 1⁄8 in.)
From: *Gottorfer Codex*, 1649–1659
Copenhagen, Den Kongelige Kobberstiksamling

As a discipline so well equipped to adapt to a newly established approach to scientific knowledge, botany attracted increasing interest thanks to its exemplary way of offering terminology that could be used by encyclopaedia compilers throughout the world. In his book *Species Plantarum*, published in 1753, Carolus Linnaeus (1707–1778) offered a system for naming plant species, thereby paving the way for the categorization still in use today. *Canna indica* was the first plant to be listed in Linnaeus' *Species Plantarum*, which continues to provide a valid classification with a two-part name (ill. p. 12). Numerous books with systematic lists of plants followed, in addition to elaborately designed volumes with botanical illustrations. These books seemed simultaneously to serve and promote the interest in botany that had become fashionable among the upper classes.

In 1839, Anna Atkins was admitted to the newly founded Botanical Society of London, of which her father was vice-president. For Children, it was a year that marked a private and professional turning point. After 20 years together, his third wife died. He retired from his position at the British Museum and soon afterwards moved to live with his daughter and son-in-law at Halstead Place.

On 7 January 1839 the photographic process of Louis Jacques Mandé Daguerre (1787–1851), the French painter and inventor of the diorama, was presented to a session of the Académie des Sciences in Paris. It was an event that triggered hectic activity among Europe's scientific communities. Particularly in France, Britain and Germany, researchers were simultaneously attempting to fix impressions of light on light-sensitive material. Spurred on by Daguerre's announcement, they now disclosed their own findings on various photographic methods.

In England it was a good friend of Children's, William Henry Fox Talbot (1800–1877, ill. p. 20), who on 31 January 1839 presented his paper, *Some Account of the Art of Photogenic Drawing*, to the Royal Society. By March of the same year, at a meeting of the Botanical Society in London, there was the first small exhibition showing images produced "by the photogenic process of Mr Talbot". The earliest years of the art of photography saw the development of calotype, a process invented by Talbot which was used to create images of the amateur botanist's favourite subjects: leaves and moss.

Talbot, Herschel and Cyanotypes

On 21 February 1839 when Talbot presented in person his research and his specimens to the Royal Society – the session was chaired by Children – details of Daguerre's invention were as yet unknown. Talbot was convinced that Daguerre's methods were identical to his own. In fact, the daguerreotype and Talbot's calotype process differed in more than details. Daguerre's use of a polished metal sheet resulted in vibrant, sharp images which left Talbot's paper prints a long way behind. However, daguerreotypes were expensive, unique pieces, while Talbot's negative process belonged to the future, allowing as it did the reproduction of photographic images. Talbot kept Children up to date on his progress and sent him samples of his calotypes. In September 1841 Children asked the miniature portrait painter Henry Collen (1797–1879), a friend of Talbot's and the first person to be licensed by the latter as a professional calotypist, to take his portrait using the camera (ill. p. 16). Printed on salt paper, on which today only the tracing of the outline is visible, it is among the oldest surviving calotype portraits.

Even so, Children was not only interested in results, but also in the calotype process, which in its early days was still associated with many uncertainties. He wrote to the inventor telling him that he and his daughter would themselves adopt the method and that he had already ordered a camera for Anna from the optician Andrew Ross (1798–1859). Unfortunately, no photos taken by Anna Atkins' camera have survived, in contrast to an ironic poem by her father which recounted the failure to take a calotype portrait.

In 1841, the same year in which Anna and her father were experimenting with the calotype process, there appeared *A Manual of the British Algae* by the Irish algae specialist William Henry Harvey (1811–1866, ill. p. 30). By the age of 15, Harvey had already gathered extensive knowledge of algae, and in 1838 he published the first scientific description of the fauna of South Africa. Although he was a gifted artist whose publications occasionally included his own illustrations, his book on British algae was without visuals. He himself recommended readers to consult Mary Wyatt's (1789–1871) book entitled *Algae Danmonienses or Dried Specimens of Marine Plants* (1834–1840).

Anna Atkins used *A Manual of the British Algae* as a prototype for the classification and description of her plant specimens. At the same time, she looked for a way to enhance Harvey's book with pictures of the plants he described. Talbot's calotype process proved to be too complicated for such purposes. More stable and simpler was a process which Talbot's friend John Herschel (1792–1871, ill. p. 34) was to develop the following year.

Herschel was a scientist whose interests ranged far and wide. He was an astronomer, mathematician, chemist and philosopher, who also studied botany. During their stay in South Africa, he and his wife, Margaret (1810–1884), produced between 1834 and 1838 an album with botanical illustrations of the flora of the Cape of Good Hope (ill. p. 36). He used a camera lucida to draw the plants' outlines while his wife added details and colour to the drawings. Back in England in 1838, he resumed close contact with Talbot, encouraging him to push ahead with his photochemical research.

Inspired by Daguerre's announcement in January 1839, Herschel concentrated on photochemical issues. He had sent a letter to Harvey, the algae specialist, in which some of the pages had been coated with an emulsion containing silver so that plants might be photographed. In September 1839 he succeeded in fixing an image of his father's 40-foot telescope on to glass (ill. p. 35). He also worked alongside Henry Collen to produce calotypes using Talbot's process. However, his most decisive step towards the advancement of photography was the development of a photochemical process which simplified fixing the action of light in an unprecedented way, namely the invention of the cyanotype process.

The process was so easy to master that it soon became a leisure activity in the Herschel family. It only needed two chemicals which, in subdued light, were spread over a backing paper with a paint brush or sponge. Objects were arranged on the prepared paper and exposed to sunlight, only becoming visible when the salt loaded with iron was washed away. The longer the paper was exposed to the sun, the deeper the blue to which the illuminated areas turned, while the covered areas stayed white, creating a negative image of the object.

Herschel not only invented the cyanotype process, he also coined the terms "negative" and "positive" to describe photographic images, and was also credited with introducing the word "photography". In an article he immediately sent to Children, the inventor outlined the new photochemical process. Perhaps this was how Anna learnt about its invention. It might have been during one of Herschel's frequent visits to Halstead Place – the two families had become friends – that she first heard the word "cyanotype". In any case, learning about this process enabled Anna Atkins to bring together her botanical interests and her artistic inclinations for practical purposes.

British Algae

When Anna Atkins had begun producing cyanotypes of algae, she chronicled her endeavours in one of her few surviving letters. In October 1843, in a letter to her friend Sophia Bliss, she wrote: "I have lately taken in hand a rather lengthy performance, encouraged by my father's opinion that it will be useful – it is the taking photographical impressions of all (that I can procure) of the British algae and confervae, many of which are so minute that accurate drawings of them are very difficult to make."

Even though cyanotype as a photographic process was much easier to handle than calotype, there were still many questions to be answered: What paper was most suitable? For how long did light-sensitive coating keep? What exposure time led to which result? Unfortunately, Anna Atkins' precise modus operandi was never recorded, but contemporary descriptions of copying techniques and indications provided by the material itself gave some idea.

Anna Atkins, ***The Waterloo elm***, 1818 / ***Die Waterloo-Ulme*** / ***L'orme de Waterloo***
Pencil and chalk on paper, 37.5 × 27.5 cm (14 ¾ × 10 ⅞ in.)
London, Royal Collection Trust

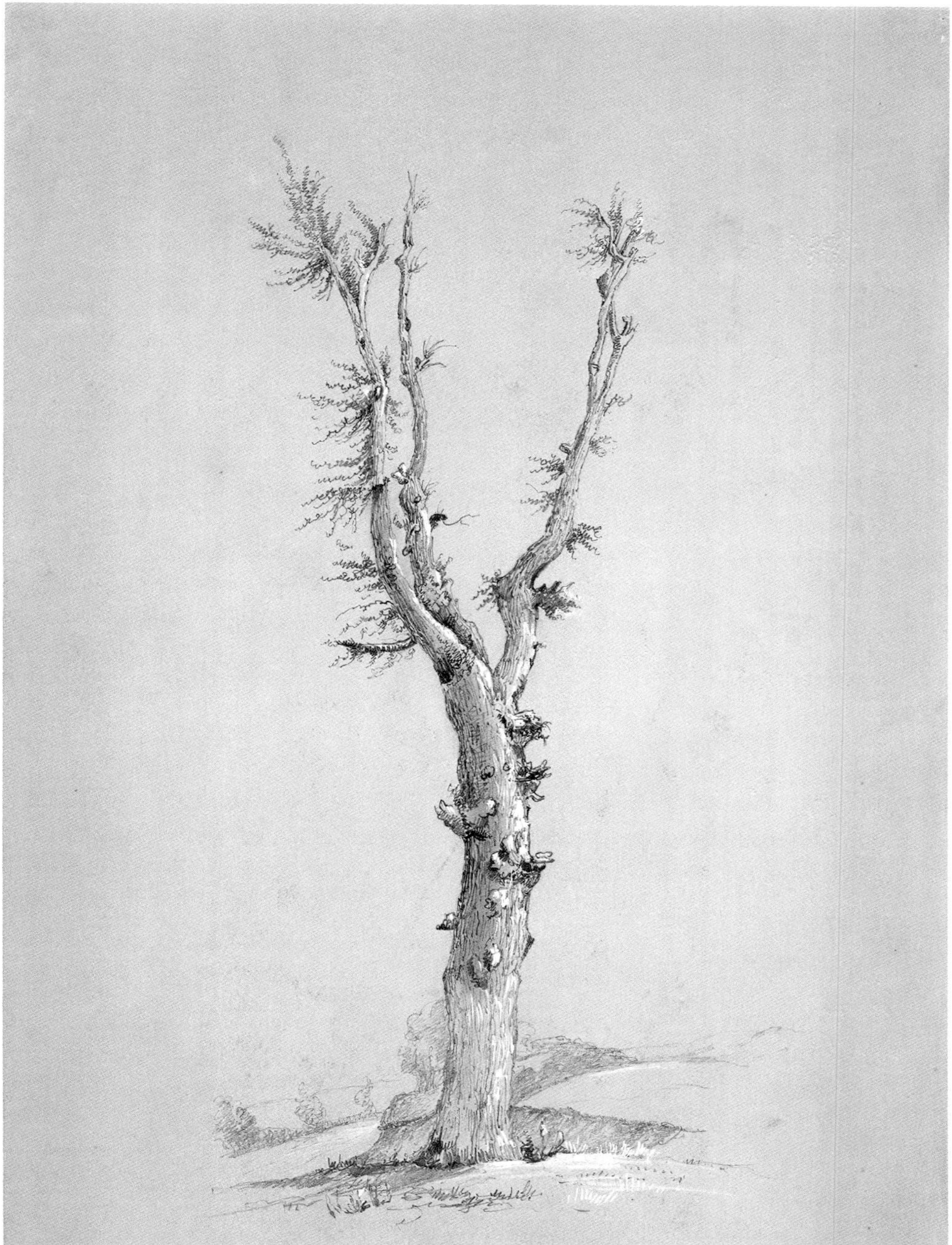

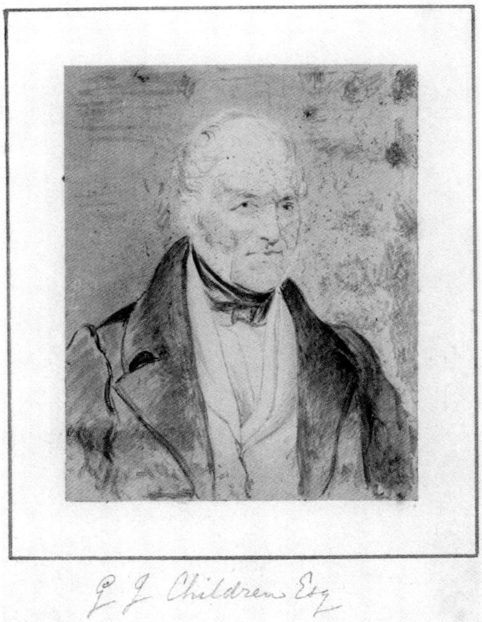

For her photographs, Atkins – like Talbot and nearly all British photographers in the pioneer age of the medium – used writing paper branded "J. Whatman, Turkey Mill". As early as Part 1 of the album, the company's watermark showing the years 1842 and 1843 could be found on single sheets (ill. p. 46). The paper's surface, absorbency, colour, weight, and strength all played a role in deciding whether it increased the quality of the picture. Small holes on the edge of the cyanotypes suggest that after Atkins prepared the sheets, then washed and dried them, she had attached them to a wall.

Anna Atkins herself had collected and dried most of the plants included in *British Algae.* At harvest time, the algae were immediately rinsed in water, then taken home where she used dissecting forceps and camelhair brushes to remove extraneous matter, before finally pressing and drying them. Since the backs of many of Atkins' images are pale blue in colour, we can assume that she did not always sensitize the paper with a brush or sponge. Instead, she immersed it in chemical solutions. To create a cyanotype, Atkins placed the plants on to the suitably prepared paper set into a copy frame, which she then covered with a glass plate so as to guarantee the closest possible contact with the support surface. The result was a lavishly detailed outline image. Areas only partly permeable to light appeared brighter in the image than those fully exposed, while denser algae were less distinctly visible.

Alongside the specimen, a label showing the name of the plant was placed on the paper. The label indicating the plant's name was first dipped in oil to make it transparent, so that when exposed to the light only the script remained. Depending on the weather and the intensity of the sun the copy frames were left in the sun for between five and 15 minutes. After a time, the paper would turn a yellowish green colour which, after the sheets were rinsed in water, turned a more or less intense blue.

Anna Atkins gave her cyanotypes serial numbers. Even when she examined the plant numerous times, there were some noticeable differences between specimens belonging to the same series. Before each exposure, the algae were rearranged on the prepared paper. Sometimes they appeared in reverse in the image, but at other times they seemed to have moved only a short distance. The intensity of the blue varied from one species to another.

October 1843 saw the publication of around 15 copies of the first volume of *British Algae*, which Anna Atkins dedicated to her father. In a foreword, she reflected on the reasons why she had produced the book. "The difficulty of making accurate drawings of objects so minute as many of the algae has induced me to avail myself of Sir John Herschel's beautiful process of cyanotype, to obtain impressions of the plants themselves, which I have much pleasure in offering to my botanical friends."

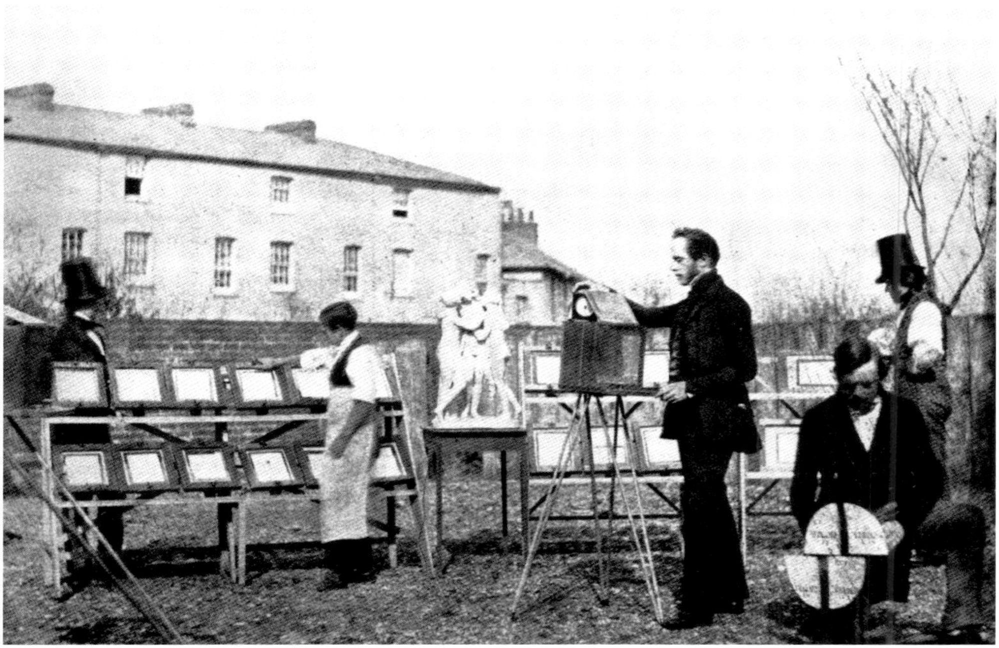

The first editions of the album were sent to the Royal Society, Herschel, Talbot, the mineralogy and photo pioneer Robert Hunt (1807–1887) and the book collector Thomas Phillips (1792–1872). The British Museum, the Linnean Society of London and the botanical gardens in London and Edinburgh were similarly honoured. A further volume of *British Algae* was published in February of the following year. In the subsequent years leading up to the spring of 1849, a total of ten volumes, each containing 12 prints were produced, which Atkins sewed together by hand. The recipients were responsible for collating and binding the sections together.

Atkins' practice of delivering and exchanging individual prints, the reordering of parts, and the transition from dealing with tiny plants to assembling prints spreading across three volumes, did cause confusion, however. To this day, just under 20 complete collections of *British Algae* are known to exist, so it is not always clear whether one is dealing with plates from the same volume, or a different one.

Henry Collen
Portrait of John George Children, ca. 1841 / **Porträt John George Children** / **Portrait de John George Children**
Salt paper print from a calotype negative, 9 × 7.1 cm (3 ½ × 2 ¾ in.)
Bradford, National Science and Media Museum

Commercial reproduction of calotypes by William Henry Fox Talbot and Nicolaas Henneman, 1846
Kommerzielle Reproduktion von Kalotypien durch William Henry Fox Talbot und Nicolaas Henneman
Reproduction commerciale de calotypes par William Henry Fox Talbot et Nicolaas Henneman
Salted paper print from paper negative, 18.1 × 22 cm (7 ⅛ × 8 ⅝ in.)
Los Angeles, J. Paul Getty Museum

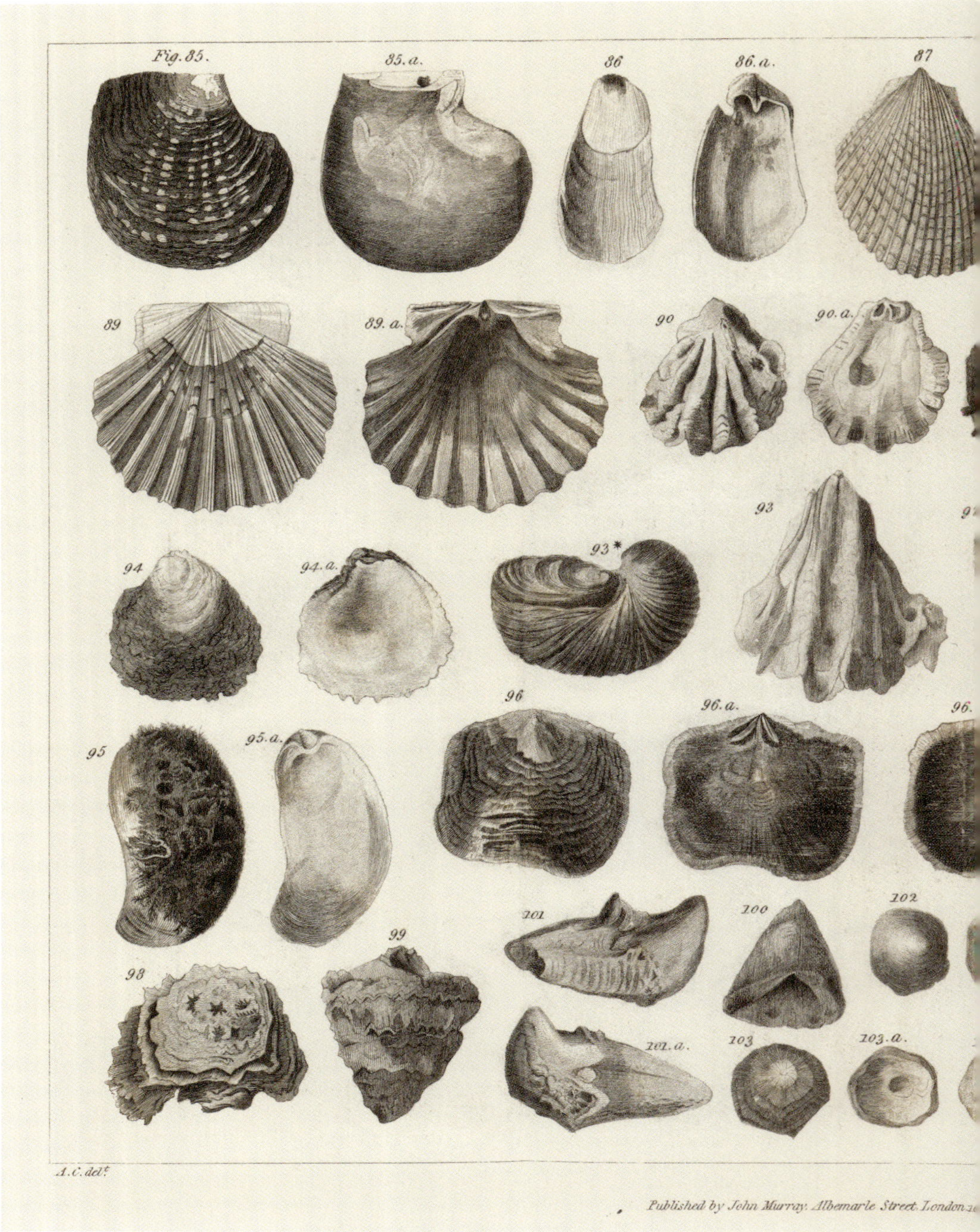
Fig. 85.
85. a.
86
86. a.
87
89
89. a.
90
90. a.
93
94
94. a.
93*
96
96. a.
95
95. a.
101
100
102
99
98
101. a.
103
103. a.
A. C. delᵗ.
Published by John Murray, Albemarle Street, London

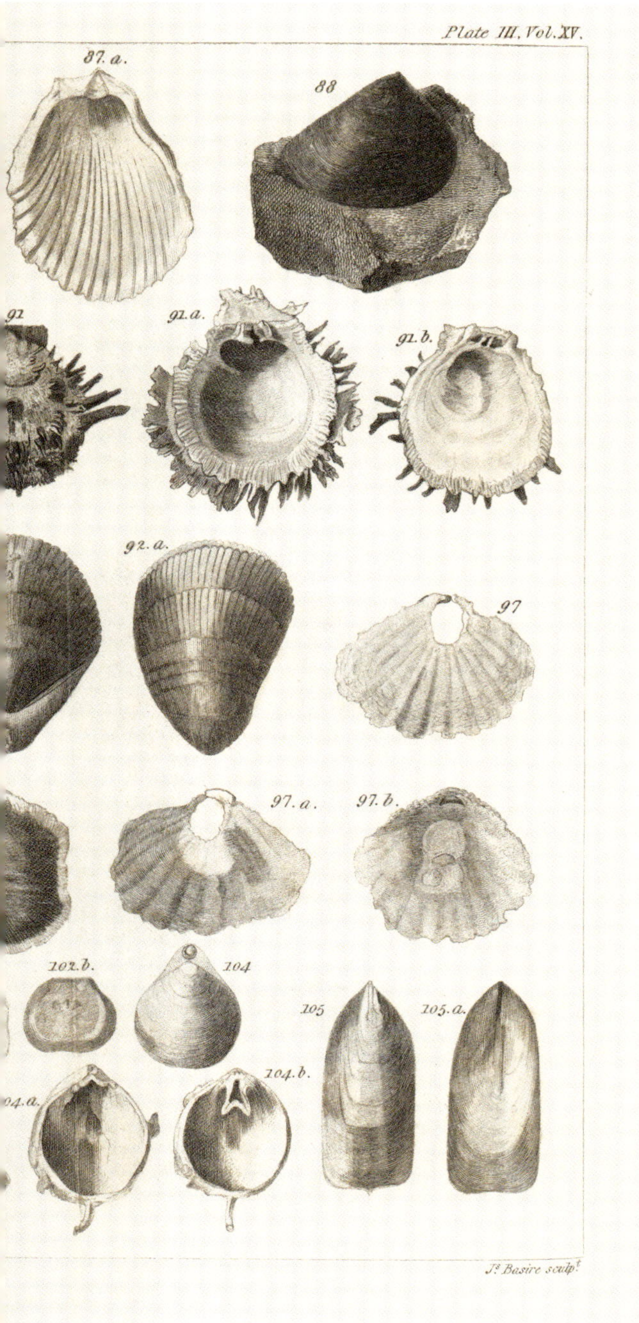

James Basire, after Anna Atkins
Engraving of Atkins' illustrations for Lamarck's *The Genera of Shells* / Stich von Atkins Illustrationen für Lamarcks *The Genera of Shells* / Burin d'après les illustrations dessinées par Atkins pour l'ouvrage de Lamarck *The Genera of Shells*
From: *The Quarterly Journal of Science, Literature, and the Arts*, vol. 15, no. 29, 1823, plate 3
New York Public Library

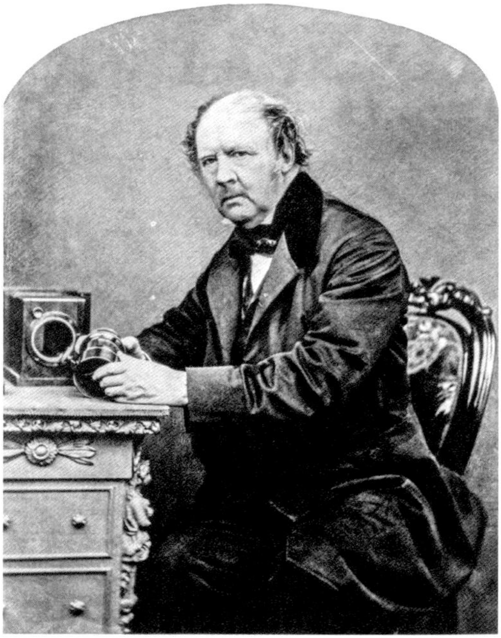

No copy of a book looked the same as another. In some cases, plates delivered separately were never correctly matched. Sometimes recipients would follow Anna Atkins' instructions and exchanged and rearranged plates to their own satisfaction. In one case, even the same plates belonging to different sets and volumes, without taking account of the table of contents, were rearranged and bound together in alphabetical order. This meant it was impossible to correctly number the plates as listed. Counting the different images delivered to different destinations, in some 15 copies of *British Algae*, Anna Atkins exposed more than 450 cyanotypes of various specimens of algae. The sheer scale of this venture made it the most significant application of the cyanotype process.

Little is known of how the recipients of Anna Atkins' gift reacted. Talbot reciprocated by sending a copy of *The Pencil of Nature*, the first commercially published book to be illustrated with photographs (ill. p. 49). The list of addressees confirms that Atkins did not only send the book as a token of friendship. She also wanted it to help to draw attention to a practice that both served as a scientific tool and opened up new methods in applying photographic techniques in the world of publishing.

The Twilight Years

Even before Anna Atkins could finish *British Algae*, she was struck by a cruel blow of fate. New Year's Day 1852 saw the sudden death of her father, John George Children, who had lived at Halstead Place with the Atkins family since 1839. Standing by Anna in her grief was Anne Dixon, her friend since childhood. For decades the two couples had remained in close touch. Anne and her husband had also remained childless. During these months, work on *British Algae* was suspended. Helped by Anne and her husband, Anna went through her father's papers, which reached back across three generations. In his memory, she wanted to write his biography. The book, only intended for family and friends, was published in spring 1853 (ill. p. 54). It revealed that, in addition to her scientific interests and artistic inclinations, Atkins had considerable literary talent.

Already in 1852, Anna Atkins had anonymously published a three-volume novel entitled *The Perils of Fashion.* There soon followed a second book, *The Colonel* (1853). The protagonists in both novels were idealized images of her father. It appears that during his lifetime she had no wish to emerge as an author, since both extensive books (each with 900 pages) must have been started long before Children's death. Some years later, Atkins published two more novels, again anonymously: *Murder Will*

Out (1859) and *A Page from the Peerage* (1863). These were favourably received by critics, although the author did not achieve continued literary success.

In the summer of 1853 Anna Atkins went back to work on *British Algae*, completing the third and last volume in November of the same year. It can be assumed that she was already working with Anne Dixon, who had for years shared her interest in botany. It was not long before they jointly produced two collections of cyanotypes, in which ferns from among domestic and foreign fauna were photographed.

Cyanotypes of British and Foreign Ferns (1853), the second album to be printed here in this edition, was a gift from Anne to her 19-year-old nephew, Henry Dixon, a photography enthusiast. The change in the choice of specimens to be photographed from algae to ferns coincided with the arrival in Britain of so-called fern fever. For almost half a century until the end of the Victorian era, the fixation with ferns became a trend that permeated many areas of everyday life, from art to the décor of public and domestic spaces. Anna herself became fascinated with ferns, not least on her journeys to Ireland between 1851 and 1861. Today it is no longer possible to determine who had played which part in the compilation of *Cyanotypes of British and Foreign Ferns*. Worth noting are the 25 plates with ferns from Jamaica appearing in the book's foreign section, which presumably had something to do with John Pelly Atkins' overseas collections.

Cyanotypes of British and Foreign Flowering Plants and Ferns (1854), on which the two women also collaborated, was more freely designed than its forerunner (ill. p. 57). With this publication, they seem to have aimed at producing something artistic and ornamental, rather than a scientific document. For a long time the work was privately owned. Following an auction in 1981, it was taken apart and sold sheet by sheet. Today the 160 plates are scattered far and wide.

A further collaborative album – another gift for Anne's nephew Henry – was dated 1861. As well as plates from earlier works such as *British Algae*, it also contained images of ferns, feathers and lace. One of the leaves bore Anna Atkins' handwriting showing the watermark for the year 1856, suggesting that Atkins had worked on the production of cyanotypes for years after the completion of *British Algae*.

After the death of her friend Anne in March 1865, Anna Atkins abandoned her systematic study of botany and donated her herbarium to the British Museum. Her life was increasingly overshadowed by illness, with two nurses living permanently in the house. In a letter to her cousin, Anna spoke of her approaching end and how she worried how her husband would cope if she were to die soon.

In the final months of 1870, Anna Atkins received some surprising correspondence from Sir John Herschel. The polymath had translated Schiller's philosophical poem *The Walk* into English. In his letter Herschel recalled how almost three decades ago he had invented cyanotype to copy his own handwriting. Now he was sending a copy of the poem as a gift to his friend of so many years, Anna Atkins. She had used, most extensively and consistently, the process of the cyanotype with its technical and artistic possibilities. Herschel died in May 1871 and was buried in Westminster Abbey, only a few steps away from the resting place of Isaac Newton (1643–1727). Anna Atkins died only weeks later, on 9 June 1871, at the age of 72, and was buried at Halstead.

John Moffat, **William Henry Fox Talbot**, 1864
Photograph

Life Thereafter

John Pelly Atkins survived his wife for little over a year, a time in which he put together in her memory an album of her most artistic works. Following the death of the childless couple, Halstead Place was taken over by relatives. Knowledge of Anna Atkins' pioneering achievements was lost. During her lifetime there had been no exhibitions, no celebrations, no public demonstrations of cyanotypes. In contemporary publications her achievements were reported only twice, and her identity was never revealed.

Decades later, one reference attracted the attention of the Scottish photographic historian and book collector William Lang Jr (1846–1913). An article by Talbot entitled "On Photography Without the Use of Silver", appearing in 1864, referred to "a lady, some years ago, photographed the entire series of British seaweeds, and most kindly and liberally distributed the copies to persons interested in botany and photography." Lang, who was also President of the Glasgow and West of Scotland Amateur Photographic Association, had spent years searching for these cyanotypes until, in 1888, he was able to purchase a copy of *British Algae* that had once belonged to Robert Hunt.

The following year, Anna Atkins' cyanotypes could be seen publicly for the first time, at an exhibition in Glasgow organized by Lang, who assumed that the initials "A. A.", with which she signed her foreword to *British Algae*, stood for "Anonymous Amateur". In a letter, the botanist James Britten (1846–1924) was able to confirm the identity of the photographer in question. Lang wrote frequent contributions to scientific journals and showed Atkins' work at two more exhibitions, first in Glasgow in 1896 and then in London in 1903. Thereafter, her work once more sank into obscurity.

Not until Larry Schaaf embarked on his research had Anna Atkins' cyanotypes been rediscovered. Now, she is prominently represented in all major reference works on the history of photography. Since 1997, a little blue plaque fixed to the wall of Halstead Place's gatehouse, which still stands, has been serving as a reminder of the work of the groundbreaking photographer. Anna Atkins was the first to explore the technical and aesthetic possibilities of photographic book illustration, producing a body of work which, even now, continues to arouse fascination in the clarity, serenity and beauty of these natural forms when they are photographed.

Anna Atkins, ***Siliquaria anguina***
From: Jean-Baptiste Lamarck, *The Genera of Shells*, trans. J. C. Children, 1822–1824
London, Natural History Museum

Page 24
Anna Atkins and Anne Dixon, ***Cypripedium***
From: *Cyanotypes of British and Foreign Flowering Plants and Ferns*, 1854
Cyanotype, 25.9 × 20.2 cm (10 ¼ × 8 in.)
Los Angeles, J. Paul Getty Museum

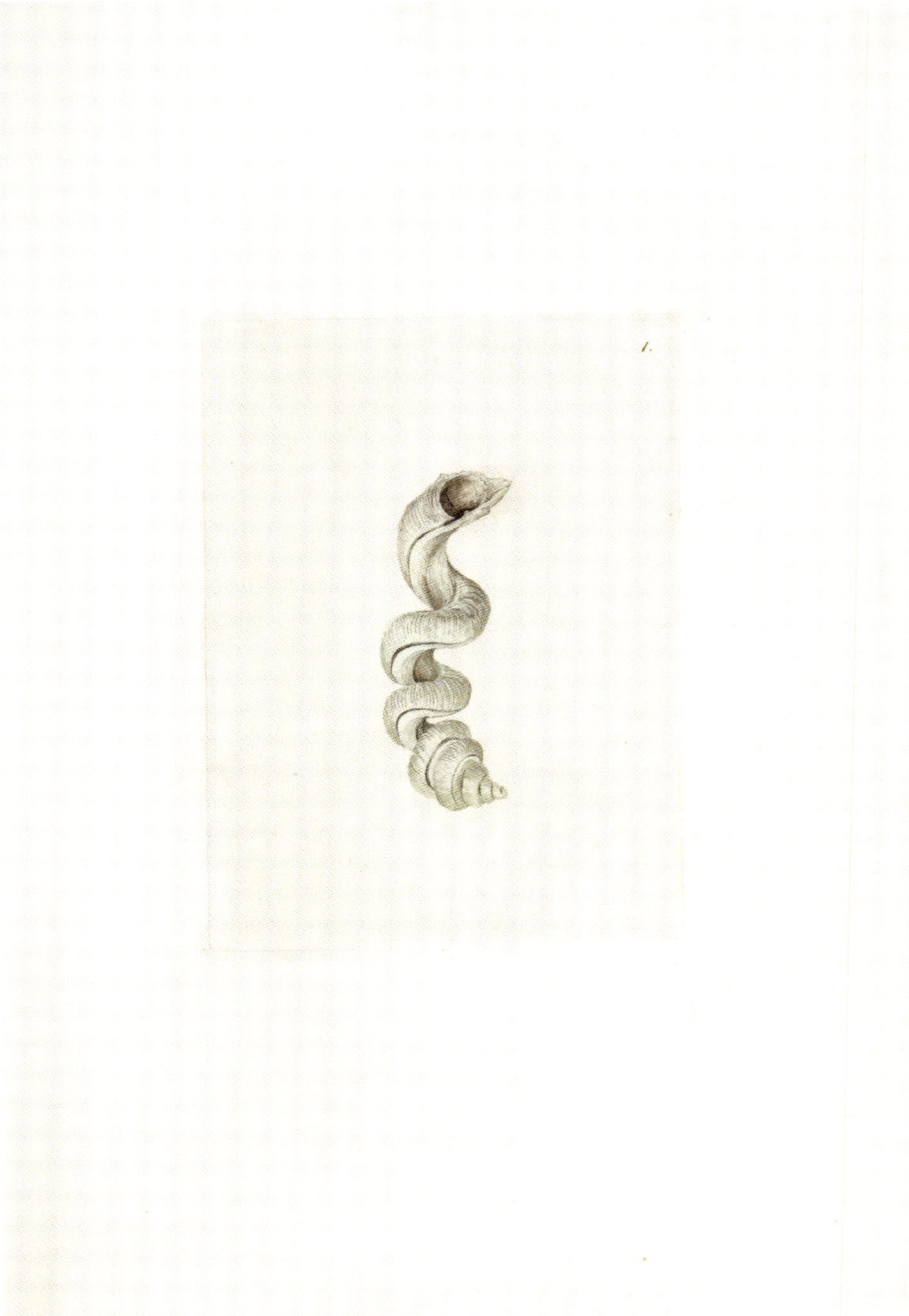

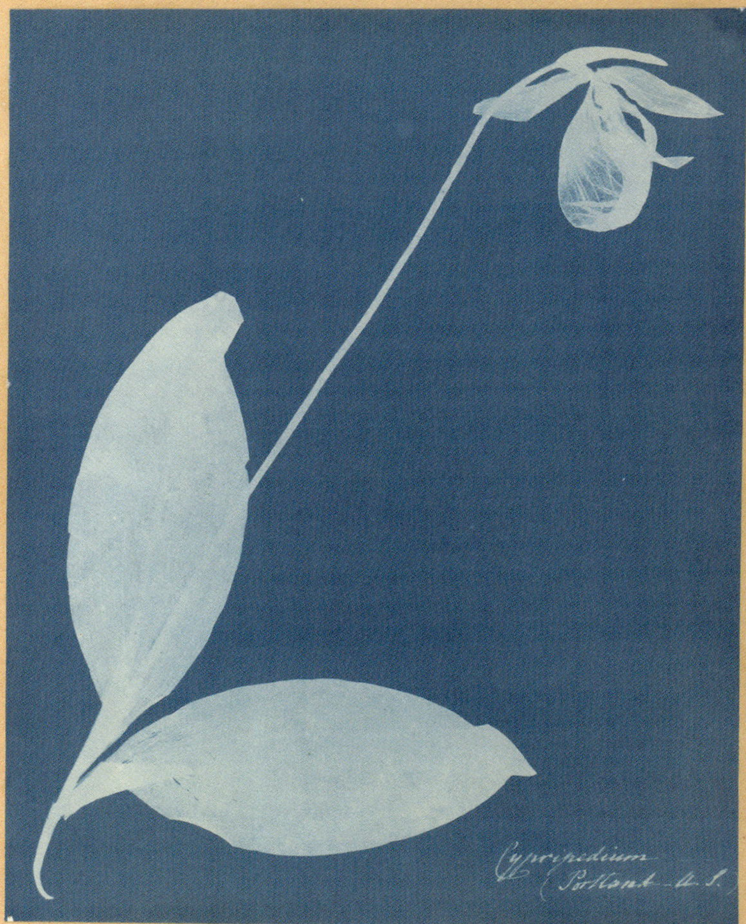
Cypripedium
(Portland – U. S.)

Anna Atkins – eine Pionierin der frühen Fotografie

Halstead Place

Das Landhaus Halstead Place in der Grafschaft Kent südöstlich von London lag in viktorianischer Zeit inmitten eines idyllischen, mit Ulmen bestandenen Parks. Vor dem Haus öffnete sich der Park zur freien Landschaft. Hier waren bei gutem Wetter hölzerne Gestelle aufgebaut, auf denen dicht an dicht Kopierrahmen mit botanischen Präparaten lagen. Bis zu 15 Minuten wurden die unter Glas gepressten Algen und Farne der Sonne ausgesetzt. Das Licht hielt die Umrisse der Pflanzen auf einem fotochemisch beschichteten Papier fest. Auf diese Weise entstanden in den Jahren von 1843 bis 1853 annähernd 10.000 Bilder. Betrieben wurde dieses fotografische Freiluftlabor von einer Frau: Anna Atkins (1799–1871). Ihrer Kreativität und Beständigkeit verdanken wir ein Werk, das zu den außergewöhnlichsten Zeugnissen der frühen Fotografiegeschichte gehört.

Halstead Place verfiel nach dem Zweiten Weltkrieg zur Ruine und wurde 1952 abgerissen. Auch das fotografische Erbe von Anna Atkins drohte nach ihrem Tod in Vergessenheit zu geraten. Doch in den vergangenen Jahren ist die Bewunderung für ihre Pionierleistungen stetig gewachsen. Ausgehend von den Forschungen des Fotohistorikers Larry Schaaf ist in vielbeachteten Ausstellungen und Publikationen ein breites Publikum mit den Arbeiten der Botanikerin und Fotografin bekannt geworden.

Der vorliegende Band bietet einen Überblick über das fotografische Schaffen von Anna Atkins. Er enthält ihre beiden Hauptwerke, das Album *British Algae* (1843–1853) und die gemeinsam mit ihrer Freundin Anne Dixon (1799–1865) angefertigten *Cyanotypes of British and Foreign Ferns* (1853). Die Bedeutung dieser Alben ist kaum zu überschätzen, sie sind Marksteine der Wissenschafts- und Mediengeschichte. Doch unabhängig von ihrem geschichtlichen Wert verleihen die filigranen Formen der Algen und Farne auf dem blauen Hintergrund der Cyanotypien den Bildern einen ästhetischen Reiz, der von zeitloser Geltung ist.

Herkunft und Jugend

Die entscheidenden Prägungen empfängt Anna Atkins in ihrer Jugend von ihrem Vater. Als John George Children 1852 in Halstead stirbt, widmet Anna seinem Andenken ein Buch, in dem sie sein Wirken als Wissenschaftler würdigt. Ihre Schilderungen geben zugleich auch einen Einblick in die Welt, in die sie hineingeboren wurde.

John George Children (1777–1852) ist der einzige Sohn eines Landeigners und Bankiers (Abb. S. 8). Seine Mutter stirbt wenige Tage nach seiner Geburt. Der Vater, Annas Großvater, pflegt technische und künstlerische Interessen und schreibt Verse. Er heiratet nach dem Tod seiner Frau nicht wieder, sondern widmet sich der Erziehung seines Sohnes. Der junge Children bekommt einen Privatlehrer, besucht die Schule in Eton und studiert ab 1794 am Queens' College in Cambridge, wo er zunächst eine theologische Laufbahn anstrebt. Doch die Liebe zu Hester Anna Holwell lässt ihn sein Studium unterbrechen. 1798, gerade volljährig, heiraten die beiden, im Jahr darauf wird ihre Tochter Anna geboren.

John George Children plant, sein Studium in Cambridge fortzusetzen, doch nur Monate nach der Geburt ihrer Tochter stirbt seine Frau. So ist er mit 23 Jahren Witwer. Auf tragische Weise wiederholt sich das Schicksal des Vaters im Leben des Sohns. Es bewirkt zugleich, dass Annas Bindung an ihren Vater zeitlebens von besonderer Intensität ist, selbst wenn sie ihn während ihrer ersten Lebensjahre selten zu Gesicht bekommt. Er reist 1800 mit Freunden nach Lissabon, besucht im Frühjahr 1802 einen Cousin in den USA, unternimmt abenteuerliche Ausflüge in die kanadische Wildnis und schließt sich nach seiner Rückkehr 1803 einem Regiment in Kent an, um die Bedrohung Englands durch napoleonische Truppen abwehren zu helfen.

Nach zwei Jahren quittiert Children den Militärdienst und widmet sich fortan der wissenschaftlichen Arbeit. Sein Interesse gilt vor allem der Mineralogie und Chemie. Während dieser Jahre entstehen freundschaftliche Beziehungen zu vielen bedeutenden Wissenschaftlern seiner Zeit, etwa zum Chemiker Humphry Davy (1778–1829), der zu den Wegbereitern der modernen Elektrochemie gehört. Er kommt häufig zu den Childrens nach Tonbridge in der Grafschaft Kent, wo auch Anna ihn kennenlernt. Davy hat bereits um 1800 mit lichtempfindlichem Material experimentiert. Er stellt Kontaktkopien von Blättern her, jedoch gelingt es ihm nicht, die Ergebnisse zu fixieren.

1807 wird Children als Fellow in die Royal Society gewählt, zwei Jahre später heiratet er ein zweites Mal. Doch nach nur acht Monaten endet auch diese Ehe mit dem Tod seiner Frau. Children flüchtet sich in seine Forschungen. In Ferox Hall in Tonbridge, wo Anna aufwächst, betreiben Vater und Großvater ein Labor, in dem sie an einer gigantischen galvanischen Batterie – sie enthält 4.300 Liter Säure – und mit Schießpulver experimentieren. Children fördert das wissenschaftliche Interesse seiner Tochter, indem er der Heranwachsenden in einer Reihe von Privatlektionen die Grundlagen der Chemie vermittelt. In den Jahren ab 1811 wächst Anna gemeinsam mit Anne auf, der gleichaltrigen Tochter eines Freundes ihres Vaters. Anne Austen ist eine Cousine zweiten Grades der Schriftstellerin Jane Austen. Als Annes Mutter stirbt – ihr Vater ist als Offizier in Portugal stationiert –, nimmt Children die Tochter seines Freundes in seiner Familie auf. In der Biographie, die Anna später über ihren Vater schreibt, erwähnt sie, ihr Vater hätte Anne „beinahe wie eine Tochter angesehen", ihr selbst sei sie „seit der Kindheit so lieb wie eine Schwester" gewesen.

Das – zumindest in materieller Hinsicht – sorgenfreie Leben Childrens als Privatgelehrter endet 1816, als die Bank seines Vaters Bankrott geht. Er ist gezwungen, eine Stellung als Bibliothekar an der British Museum Library anzunehmen. Längst hat er sich einen Namen als Wissenschaftler gemacht. Er ist einer der Sekretäre der Royal Society und Mitglied zahlreicher wissenschaftlicher Gesellschaften des Landes, Herausgeber einer zoologischen Zeitschrift und Autor von Beiträgen für zahlreiche wissenschaftliche Journale.

Im September 1818 besucht Children das Schlachtfeld von Waterloo, wo drei Jahre zuvor Napoleon vernichtend geschlagen worden war. Die neunzehnjährige Anna begleitet ihn auf dieser Reise. In England war ein skurriler Kult um eine Ulme entstanden, die dem siegreichen Herzog von Wellington während der Schlacht von Waterloo als Kommandoposten diente. Anna und ihr Vater bekommen von dem einst stattlichen Baum nur noch ein kümmerliches Gerippe zu sehen, da sich Souvenirjäger über die Ulme hergemacht und beinahe alle Äste abgesägt haben.

Children kauft den Baum, lässt ihn nach England verladen und das Holz zu verschiedenen Möbeln verarbeiten. Dazu gehört ein Stuhl, den Thomas Chippendale jr. (1749–1822) für König George IV. (1762–1830) herstellt und der heute noch in Schloss Windsor steht, sowie ein Arbeitstisch, den Children selbst nutzt und der später in den Besitz von Anna Atkins übergeht. Die Zeichnung, die

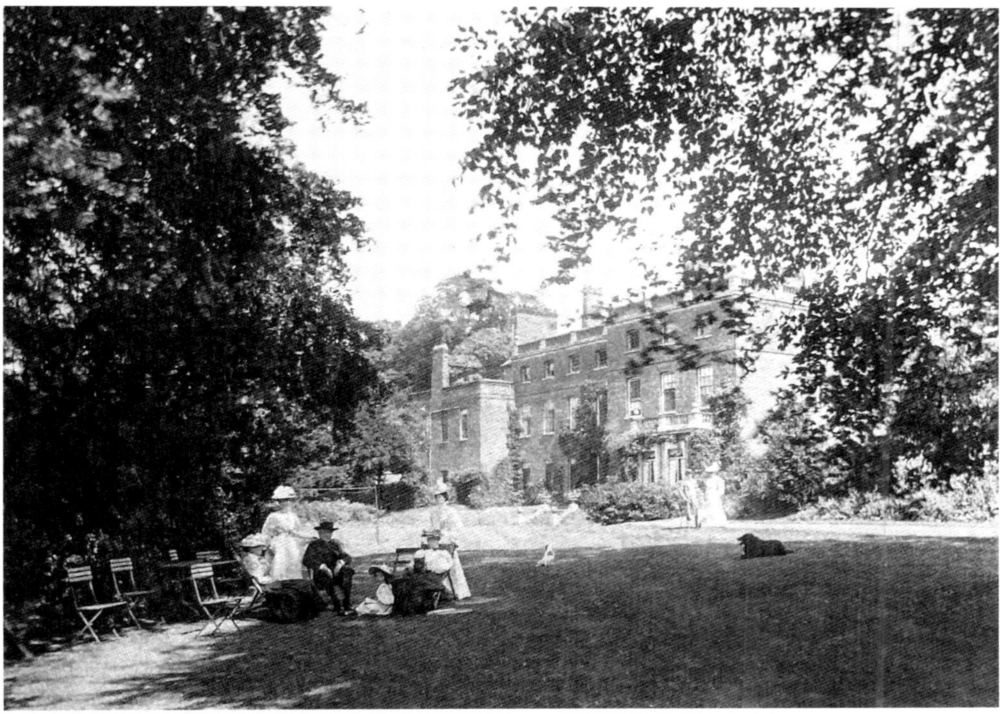

The back of Halstead Place with the Burnaby-Atkins family, ca. 1890
Die Rückseite von Halstead Place mit der Burnaby-Atkins-Familie
Halstead Place côté jardin, avec la famille Burnaby-Atkins
Photograph. Kent, Nurstead Court Archives

Anna 1818 auf dem Schlachtfeld von Waterloo von den Resten der Waterloo-Ulme anfertigt, gehört zu den frühen Proben ihrer künstlerischen Begabung (Abb. S. 15).

Als Children 1822 zum zweiten Leiter der naturhistorischen Sammlung am British Museum berufen wird, lässt er in einer Artikelserie seine Übersetzung von Jean-Baptiste de Lamarcks (1744–1829) Buch über die Systematisierung von Muscheln drucken. Beigegeben sind der Veröffentlichung dreizehn Tafeln mit über 240 Abbildungen von Muscheln. Die Vorlagen für diese Illustrationen hat seine Tochter Anna gezeichnet (Abb. S. 18/19).

Die Liebe zur Botanik

1825 heiratet Anna den wohlhabenden Kaufmann und Landrat John Pelly Atkins (1790–1872), einen engen Freund ihres Vaters. Das Paar lebt zeitweise in Halstead Place, unterhält aber auch eine Wohnung in London. So bleibt Anna in engem Austausch mit ihrem Vater. Ihr Schwiegervater ist als Händler und Plantagenbesitzer auf Jamaika und den Bermudas vermögend geworden. Als angesehener Geschäftsmann stand er verschiedenen Handlungsvereinigungen vor und war eine Zeitlang Lord Mayor von London. Elf seiner vierzehn Kinder sind gestorben, Annas Mann ist der einzige überlebende männliche Nachkomme. Die Ehe der jungen Atkins' selbst bleibt kinderlos. Im Landhaus Halstead Place pflegt man einen gehobenen Lebensstil. Um die Erweiterung der Gemäldesammlung, zu der Bilder von Correggio, Caravaggio und Brueghel gehören, kümmert sich John Pelly Atkins selbst. Er ist aber auch wissenschaftlich interessiert und unterstützt die Ambitionen seiner Frau. 1847 wird er von Königin Victoria (1819–1901) zum Sheriff of Kent ernannt.

1837 heiratet auch Annas schwesterliche Freundin Anne Austen (Abb. S. 56). Ihr Mann, Henry Dixon (1798–1870), gehört zum Freundeskreis der Childrens. Sie zieht zu ihm in den kleinen Ort Ferring in Sussex direkt an der Kanalküste, wo Dixon als Vikar an der St. Andrew's Church tätig ist. Henry Dixon stammt aus einer Familie, die literarisch und wissenschaftlich interessiert ist, sein Vater ist Dichter und Hobby-Botaniker, einer seiner Brüder Mediziner und Geologe und dessen Frau eine talentierte Künstlerin. Der Kontakt zwischen den Familien Atkins, Children und Dixon bleibt rege, man besucht sich regelmäßig und in kurzen Abständen.

Anna baut in den Jahren ihrer Ehe ihre botanischen Interessen aus. Um 1835 beginnt sie mit der Anlage eines Herbariums. Sie sammelt, trocknet und presst Präparate und bittet Freunde, ihr von Reisen Proben von Pflanzen mitzubringen. Besonders interessiert sie sich für die heimischen Algen. Doch belässt sie es nicht beim Sammeln und Zusammenstellen, sondern beschäftigt sich auch mit den unterschiedlichen botanischen Ordnungssystemen.

Die Botanik gehört in dieser Zeit zu den wenigen Disziplinen, die in einer männlich dominierten Umwelt auch Frauen als Feld wissenschaftlicher Betätigung offensteht. Durch die Vermittlung ihres Vaters wird Anna mit vielen bedeutenden Wissenschaftlern aus dessen Freundes- und Bekanntenkreis bekannt. Als Sekretär der Royal Society hat Children zudem einen privilegierten Zugang zu den neuesten wissenschaftlichen Erkenntnissen, die in den Sitzungen der Gesellschaft verhandelt werden, und lässt seine Tochter daran teilhaben.

Es ist ein neuer, sachlich-systematisierender Blick auf die Welt, der die Grundlagen des technischen Fortschritts in dieser frühen Phase der Industrialisierung legt. Der Fortschritt wird für die Zeitgenossen im Alltag spürbar, sie erleben, wie sich der Verkehr durch Dampfschiffe und Eisenbahnen

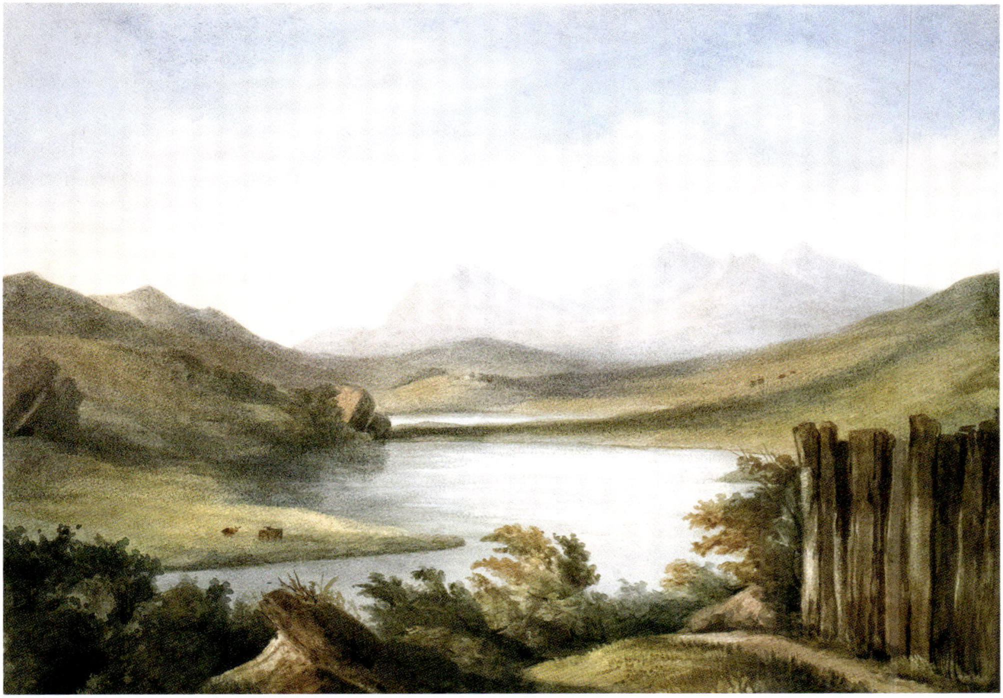

Anna Atkins, **Snowdon as seen from the guesthouse at Capel Curig**, undated
Der Snowdon, vom Gasthaus Capel Curig aus gesehen / Le mont Snowdon vu de l'auberge de Capel Curig
Watercolour, dimensions unknown
Private collection

und die Kommunikation durch elektrische Telegrafen beschleunigt. Die großen Forschungsreisen vom Beginn des Jahrhunderts wie Alexander von Humboldts (1769–1859) Expeditionen durch Mittel- und Südamerika (1799–1804) oder die nordamerikanische Überlandexpedition von Meriwether Lewis (1774–1809) und William Clark (1770–1838) in den Jahren 1804–1806 lösen eine Euphorie des Sammelns und Systematisierens aus.

Zur Leitdisziplin für eine neue Organisation des Wissens avanciert die Botanik, indem sie modellhaft ein stabiles Bezeichnungsgerüst für die enzyklopädische Aneignung der Welt zur Verfügung stellt. Bereits 1753 führt Carl von Linné (1707–1778) in seinem Buch *Species Plantarum* ein System zur Benennung von Pflanzenarten ein, das wegweisend für alle bis heute gängige Taxonomien wird. *Canna indica* ist die erste Pflanze, die in Linnés *Species Plantarum* in der bis heute gültigen binären Nomenklatur mit einem zweiteiligen Namen benannt wurde (Abb. S. 12). Eine Vielzahl von Büchern mit systematischen Aufzählungen von Pflanzen folgt. Daneben erscheinen häufig aufwendig gestaltete Bände mit botanischen Illustrationen. Diese Bücher bedienen und befördern zugleich die in gehobenen Ständen zur Mode gewordene Beschäftigung mit der Botanik.

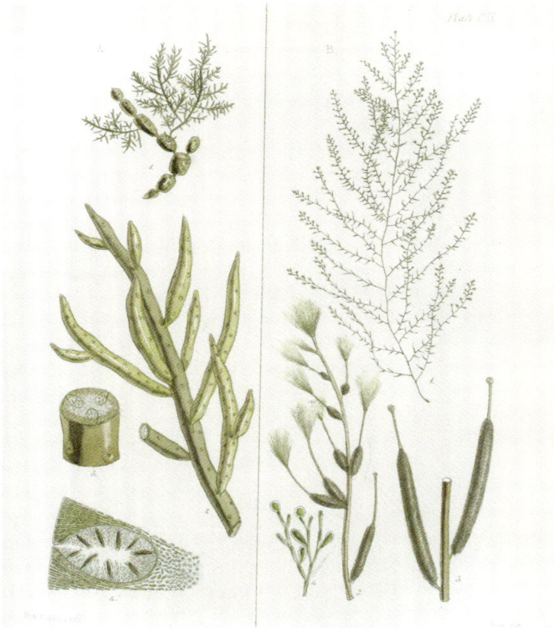

1839 wird Anna Atkins in die gerade gegründete Botanical Society of London aufgenommen, deren Vizepräsident ihr Vater ist. Für Children markiert dieses Jahr einen familiären und beruflichen Einschnitt. Nach 20 gemeinsamen Jahren in dritter Ehe stirbt seine Frau. Er verabschiedet sich von seiner Tätigkeit am British Museum in den Ruhestand und zieht wenig später zu Tochter und Schwiegersohn nach Halstead Place.

Als am 7. Januar 1839 der französische Dioramen-Maler und Erfinder Louis Jacques Mandé Daguerre (1787–1851) auf einer Sitzung der Académie des sciences in Paris sein fotografisches Verfahren vorstellen lässt, löst das eine hektische Betriebsamkeit im europäischen Wissenschaftsbetrieb aus. Vor allem in Frankreich, Großbritannien und Deutschland arbeiteten zahlreiche Forscher parallel an Versuchen, die Eindrücke des Lichts auf lichtempfindlichem Material zu fixieren. Angetrieben von der Ankündigung Daguerres, melden sie jetzt ihren Anspruch auf die verschiedenen fotografischen Verfahren an.

In England ist es ein guter Bekannter von Children, der am 31. Januar 1839 seinen *Bericht über die Kunst der Photogenen Zeichnung* vor der Royal Society verlesen lässt: William Henry Fox Talbot (1800–1877, Abb. S. 20). Schon im März desselben Jahres wird auf einem Treffen der Botanical Society in London eine erste kleine Ausstellung mit Bildern präsentiert, die „nach dem fotogenetischen Prozess von Mr. Talbot" hergestellt wurden. Auf diesen Kalotypien sind die Lieblingsmotive des Hobby-Botanikers Talbot in jenen frühen Jahren der Fotografie zu sehen: Blätter und Moose.

Talbot, Herschel und die Cyanotypie

Als Talbot am 21. Februar 1839 seine Forschungen und Proben in der Royal Society persönlich vorstellt – die Sitzung wird von Children geleitet –, sind von der Erfindung Daguerres noch keine Einzelheiten bekannt. Talbot lebt in dem Glauben, Daguerres Verfahren sei mit dem seinen identisch. Tatsächlich jedoch unterscheiden sich die Daguerreotypie und Talbots Kalotypie nicht nur in Details.

William Henry Harvey, ***Notheia anomala, Sporochnus stylosus***, 1855
Lithographs
From: *The botany of the Antarctic voyage of H.M. discovery ships Erebus and Terror in the years 1839–1843*, London, 1844
Massachusetts, Marine Biological Library, Woods Hole Oceanographic Institution

Die Abbildungen Daguerres bieten auf einer polierten Metallplatte eine Schärfe und Dynamik, die von den Papierabzügen Talbots bei weitem nicht erreicht werden. Aber es sind teure Unikate, während dem Negativ-Verfahren von Talbot die Zukunft gehört, weil es die Vervielfältigung der aufgenommenen Bilder erlaubt.

Talbot hält Children über die Fortschritte seiner Arbeit auf dem Laufenden und sendet ihm Arbeitsproben seiner Kalotypien zu. Im September 1841 lässt sich Children von dem Porträtmaler Henry Collen (1797–1879) mit der Kamera porträtieren (Abb. S. 16). Collen ist ein Freund Talbots und dessen erster Lizenznehmer. Der Abzug auf Salzpapier, auf dem heute fast nur noch die Nachzeichnung der Umrisse zu erkennen ist, zählt zu den ältesten noch erhaltenen Kalotypie-Porträts.

Doch Childrens Interesse gilt nicht allein den Ergebnissen, sondern auch der Praxis der Kalotypie, die in ihrer Frühzeit noch mit zahlreichen Unwägbarkeiten verbunden ist. Dem Erfinder schreibt er, seine Tochter und er würden sich das Verfahren zu eigen machen, er habe für Anna bereits eine Kamera beim Optiker Andrew Ross (1798–1859) bestellt. Leider sind keine Aufnahmen von Anna Atkins mit der Kamera überliefert. Dagegen hat sich ein ironisches Gedicht ihres Vaters erhalten, in dem es um das Scheitern beim Aufnehmen eines Kalotypie-Porträts geht.

1841, im gleichen Jahr, in dem Anna und ihr Vater mit der Kalotypie experimentieren, erscheint *A Manual of the British Algae* des irischen Algenforschers William Henry Harvey (1811–1866, Abb. S. 30). Harvey hatte bereits mit 15 Jahren ein umfangreiches Wissen über Algen angesammelt und 1838 eine erste wissenschaftliche Beschreibung der Fauna Südafrikas vorgelegt. Obwohl er selbst ein begabter Zeichner ist und seinen Veröffentlichungen auch vereinzelt eigene Illustrationen beigibt, erscheint sein Buch über die britischen Algen ohne Abbildungen. Er selbst empfiehlt, Mary Wyatts (1789–1871) mit getrockneten Algenpflanzen versehenes Werk *Algae Danmonienses* (1834–1840) zu Rate zu ziehen.

Anna Atkins dient das *Manual of British Algae* als Vorlage bei der Systematisierung und Bezeichnung ihrer pflanzlichen Präparate. Zugleich aber sucht sie nach einem Weg, das Kompendium Harveys mit Bildern der darin beschriebenen Pflanzen zu ergänzen. Talbots Kalotypie erweist sich für diese Zwecke als zu aufwendig. Stabiler und simpler ist ein Verfahren, das Talbots Freund John Herschel (1792–1871, Abb. S. 34) im Jahr darauf entwickelt.

Herschels wissenschaftliche Interessen sind vielfältig, er ist Astronom, Mathematiker, Chemiker, Philosoph und beschäftigt sich auch mit Botanik. Während seines Aufenthalts in Südafrika stellt er 1834–1838 gemeinsam mit seiner Frau Margaret (1810–1884) ein Album mit botanischen Illustrationen der Flora am Kap der Guten Hoffnung zusammen (Abb. S. 36). Er zeichnet die Umrisse der Pflanzen mit einer Camera lucida, die ihm als Kopierhilfe dient, während seine Frau die Details ergänzt und die Zeichnungen koloriert. 1838 zurück in England, steht er im engen Austausch mit Talbot und ermuntert ihn, seine fotochemischen Forschungen voranzutreiben.

Angeregt durch die Ankündigung Daguerres im Januar 1839, beschäftigt sich Herschel auch selbst mit fotochemischen Fragen. Überliefert hat sich sein Brief an den Algenforscher Harvey, in dem Herschel Teile des Papiers mit einer silberhaltigen Emulsion bestrich, um darauf Pflanzen abzulichten. Im September 1839 gelingt es ihm, das Abbild eines 12 Meter langen Teleskops auf Glas zu fixieren (Abb. S. 35). Er arbeitet auch mit Henry Collen zusammen und fertigt Kalotypien nach dem

Verfahren Talbots an. Den wichtigsten Impuls für die Entwicklung der Fotografie gibt er jedoch mit der Ausarbeitung eines fotochemischen Verfahrens, das die Fixierung von Lichteindrücken auf bisher ungekannte Weise vereinfacht: mit der Erfindung der Cyanotypie.

Das Verfahren ist so leicht zu beherrschen, dass es bald zur Freizeitbeschäftigung in der Familie Herschel wird. Benötigt werden nur zwei Chemikalien, die in dunkler Umgebung mit einem Pinsel oder einem Schwamm auf eine Papierunterlage aufzubringen sind. Legt man ein Objekt auf den präparierten Bogen und setzt man beides dem Sonnenlicht aus, zeichnen sich Umrisse des Objekts latent auf dem Blatt ab. Sichtbar werden sie erst nach dem Auswaschen der eisenhaltigen Salze. Je länger das Papier der Sonne ausgesetzt wird, desto tiefer färben sich die belichteten Stellen blau, während die abgedeckten Stellen weiß bleiben. So entsteht ein negatives Abbild des Objekts.

Herschel ist nicht nur Erfinder der Cyanotypie, auf ihn gehen auch die Begriffe „Positiv" und „Negativ" für die entsprechenden fotografischen Abbilder zurück. Ebenso wird ihm die Schöpfung des Worts „Fotografie" zugeschrieben. In einem Beitrag, den er umgehend Children zusendet, beschreibt der Erfinder den neuen fotochemischen Prozess. Womöglich erhält Anna auf diesem Weg Kenntnis davon. Es kann aber auch sein, dass sie bei einem der häufigen Besuche der Herschels in Halstead – beide Familien sind befreundet – erstmals mit der Cyanotypie in Berührung gekommen ist. Jedenfalls ist mit diesem Verfahren das Bindeglied gefunden, das es Anna Atkins erlaubt, ihre botanischen Interessen mit ihren ästhetischen Neigungen und ihren praktischen Absichten zusammenzuführen.

British Algae

Wann Anna Atkins damit begonnen hat, Cyanotypien von Algen herzustellen, geht aus einem der wenigen von ihr überlieferten Briefe hervor. Im Oktober 1843 schreibt sie ihrer Freundin Sophia Bliss: „Ich habe kürzlich ein ziemlich langwieriges Vorhaben in Angriff genommen, ermutigt durch die Meinung meines Vaters, dass es nützlich sein würde – es geht um die Aufnahme von fotografischen Eindrücken aller britischen Algae und Confervae, soweit ich sie beschaffen kann, von denen viele so winzig sind, dass genaue Zeichnungen von ihnen nur sehr schwierig anzufertigen sind."

Auch wenn das fotografische Verfahren der Cyanotypie deutlich einfacher zu handhaben ist als das der Kalotypie, waren anfänglich zahlreiche Fragen zu klären: Welches Papier eignet sich am besten? Wie lange ist die lichtempfindliche Beschichtung haltbar? Welche Belichtungszeit führt zu welchem Ergebnis? Leider ist Anna Atkins' genaues Vorgehen nicht überliefert, aber aus der zeitgenössischen Beschreibung von Kopiertechniken und aus Anhaltspunkten, die das Material selbst hergeben, lässt sich auf ihre Technik schließen.

Atkins nutzt für ihre Aufnahmen – wie auch Talbot und beinahe alle britischen Fotografen in der Pionierzeit des Mediums – Schreibpapier der Marke „J. Whatman, Turkey Mill". Bereits im Teil 1 des Albums finden sich einzelne Blätter mit Wasserzeichen der Firma, datiert auf die Jahre 1842 und 1843 (Abb. S. 46). Die Oberfläche des Papiers, seine Saugfähigkeit, seine Farbe, sein Gewicht und seine Stärke spielen mit, wenn es um die Qualität der Abbildung geht. Kleine Löcher am Rand der Cyanotypien deuten darauf hin, dass Atkins die Blätter nach dem Präparieren und dann wieder nach dem Auswaschen zum Trocknen an eine Wand geheftet hat.

Ein Großteil der Pflanzen, die im Album *British Algae* präsentiert werden, hat sie selbst gesammelt und getrocknet. Beim Ernten werden die Algen bereits im Wasser gereinigt, dann zu Hause mit

Präparierzange und Kamelhaarpinsel von Fremdkörpern befreit und schließlich gepresst. Da viele der Bilder von Atkins auch auf der Rückseite einen leichten Blauton zeigen, ist anzunehmen, dass sie das Papier nicht in jedem Fall mit Pinsel oder Schwamm, sondern häufig auch durch Eintauchen in die Chemikalien sensibilisiert hat. Für die Anfertigung der Cyanotypien drapiert Atkins die Pflanzen auf das präparierte Papier, das in einem Kopierrahmen liegt, und deckt es mit einer Glasplatte ab, um einen möglichst engen Kontakt zur Auflagefläche herzustellen. So entsteht eine detailreiche Umrisszeichnung. Stellen, die für das Licht teildurchlässig sind, erscheinen auf dem Bild heller als die vollständig dem Licht ausgesetzten Bereiche. Algen, die ein größeres Volumen haben, verlieren in der Abbildung an Schärfe.

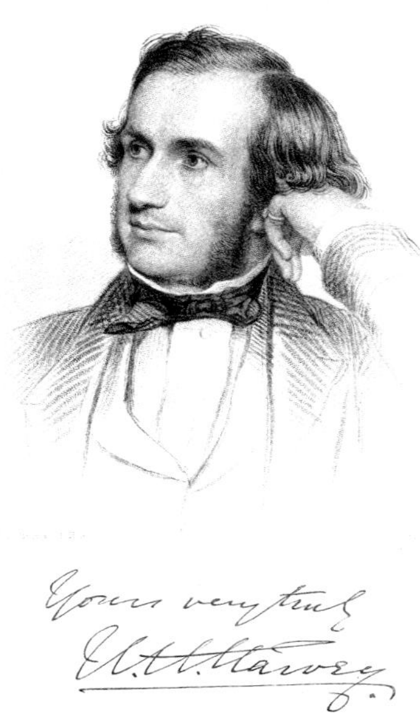

Zusammen mit dem Präparat wird ein Label auf dem Papier platziert. Das Etikett mit dem Namen der Pflanze wird zuvor in Öl getränkt und transparent gemacht, sodass bei der Belichtung lediglich die Schrift ausgespart bleibt. Je nach Wetter und Sonnenintensität liegen die Kopierrahmen zwischen 5 und 15 Minuten in der Sonne. Das Papier nimmt nach einiger Zeit eine gelbgrüne Färbung an, die nach dem Wässern des Blatts in ein mehr oder weniger intensives Blau umschlägt.

Anna Atkins stellt ihre Cyanotypien als serielle Unikate her. Wenn sie auch jede Pflanze etliche Male ablichtet, gibt es zwischen den Exemplaren derselben Serie teilweise gravierende Unterschiede. Die Algen werden vor jeder Belichtung neu auf dem Papier angeordnet. Manchmal erscheinen sie in der Abbildung seitenverkehrt, manchmal aber nur geringfügig verschoben. Auch die Intensität des Blaus variiert in den unterschiedlichen Exemplaren.

Im Oktober 1843 ist der erste Teil des Albums *British Algae*, den sie ihrem Vater widmet, in einer Auflage von etwa 15 Exemplaren fertiggestellt. In einem Vorwort geht Atkins auf ihre Motive bei der Herstellung des Albums ein: „Die Schwierigkeit, genaue Zeichnungen von winzigen Objekten wie Algen und Confervae anzufertigen, hat mich veranlasst, Sir John Herschels wunderschönes Verfahren der Cyanotypie zu nutzen, um Eindrücke von den Pflanzen selbst zu gewinnen, die ich gerne meinen botanischen Freunden präsentieren möchte."

Die ersten Exemplare des Albums gehen an die Royal Society, an Herschel, Talbot, an den Mineralogen und Fotopionier Robert Hunt (1807–1887) und an den Büchersammler Thomas Phillips

Francis Holl (after Frederic William Burton), **William Henry Harvey**, undated
Copper engraving, 16 × 12 cm (6 ¼ × 4 ¾ in.)
London, Wellcome Collection

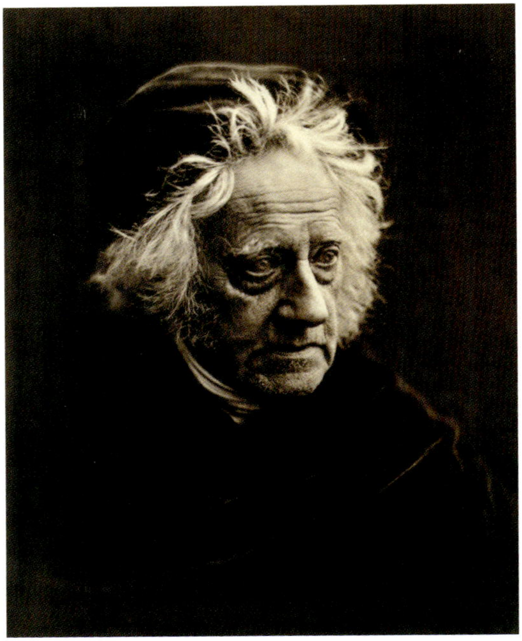

Julia Margaret Cameron, **John Herschel**, 1867
Photograph, 31.8 × 24.9 cm (12 ½ × 9 ¾ in.)
Los Angeles, J. Paul Getty Museum

John Herschel
The 40-foot telescope, built by his father William Herschel and his aunt Caroline Herschel, 1839
Das 40-Fuß-Teleskop, das von seinem Vater William Herschel und seiner Tante Caroline konstruiert wurde
Le « Télescope de 40 pieds » construit par son père William Herschel et sa tante Caroline
Photograph on glass, Ø 9.2 cm (3 ⅝ in.)
Oxford, Museum of the History of Science

(1792–1872). Auch das British Museum, die Linnean Society of London und die botanischen Gärten in London und Edinburgh werden bedacht. Bereits im Februar des kommenden Jahres ist ein weiterer Teil der *British Algae* fertiggestellt, und nun erscheinen in den kommenden Jahren bis zum Frühjahr 1849 insgesamt zehn Teile mit jeweils zwölf Bildtafeln. Atkins näht die Tafeln der einzelnen Teile zu Heften zusammen. Die Empfänger sind für das Kollationieren und Binden der Einzellieferungen selbst verantwortlich.

Ihr Konzept der Lieferungen und des Austausches einzelner Tafeln, der Neusortierung der Teile und des Übergangs von der kleinteiligen Struktur der Teile zu einer Konfektionierung des Werks in drei Bänden sorgt allerdings für Konfusion. Knapp zwanzig unterschiedlich vollständige Sammlungen der *British Algae* sind bis heute bekannt, wobei nicht immer klar ist, ob es sich um Teile eines Albums derselben Provenienz oder um unterschiedliche Alben handelt.

Kein Album sieht dabei aus wie das andere. In einigen Fällen blieben die Teillieferungen ungebunden, manchmal folgten die Empfänger den Anweisungen von Anna Atkins zum Austausch und zur Neusortierung von Tafeln, dann wieder gingen sie eigene Wege. In einem Fall wurden sogar sämtliche Tafeln der verschiedenen Teile und Bände, ohne die einzelnen Inhaltsverzeichnisse zu berücksichtigen, neu geordnet und alphabetisch eingebunden. Daher lässt sich auch keine verlässliche Zahl zur beabsichtigten Anzahl der Bildtafeln angeben. Zählt man die an verschiedenen Orten überlieferten Bilder zusammen, so hat Anna Atkins für das in einer Auflage von etwa fünfzehn Exemplaren gefertigte Album *British Algae* über 450 Cyanotypien verschiedener Algen belichtet. Allein der Umfang dieser Produktion macht sie zur bedeutendsten Anwenderin der Cyanotypie überhaupt.

Wenig weiß man darüber, wie die Empfänger die Geschenke von Anna Atkins aufgenommen haben. Talbot revanchiert sich für den ersten Teil der *British Algae* mit einem Exemplar von *The Pencil of Nature* (Abb. S. 49), dem ersten kommerziell publizierten Buch, das mit Fotografien ausgestattet war. Die Liste der Adressaten spricht dafür, dass es Atkins mit der Herstellung und dem Versand der Alben nicht nur um ein Zeichen der Verbundenheit mit ihren Freunden ging. Sie wollte zugleich die Aufmerksamkeit auf ein Werk lenken, das nicht nur als wissenschaftliches Hilfsmittel nützlich war, sondern bei der Anwendung fotografischer Verfahren in Publikationen auch neue Wege wies.

Die späten Jahre

Noch bevor Anna Atkins die *British Algae* fertigstellen kann, ereilt sie ein Schicksalsschlag. Am Neujahrstag 1852 stirbt unerwartet John George Children, ihr Vater, der seit 1839 bei der Familie Atkins in Halstead gelebt hat. In ihrer Trauer steht ihr Anne Dixon bei, ihre Freundin aus der Kindheit. Die Familien haben über die Jahrzehnte engen Kontakt gehalten, auch die Ehe von Anne ist kinderlos geblieben. In diesen Monaten ruht die Arbeit an den *British Algae*. Anna sieht gemeinsam mit Anne und ihrem Mann die Papiere ihres Vaters durch, die über drei Generationen zurückreichen. Sie möchte ihm mit einer Biographie ein bleibendes Andenken setzen. Das Buch, lediglich für die Familie und die Freunde gedacht, erscheint im Frühjahr 1853 (Abb. S. 54). Es zeugt davon, dass Atkins neben ihren wissenschaftlichen Interessen und ihren ästhetischen Neigungen auch ein ausgeprägtes literarisches Talent besitzt.

Anna Atkins hat bereits 1852 anonym den dreibändigen Roman *The Perils Of Fashion* veröffentlicht, wenig später folgt ein zweiter, *The Colonel* (1853). Die Protagonisten in beiden Romanen sind nach dem Idealbild ihres Vaters gezeichnet. Es scheint, dass Anna zu dessen Lebzeiten nicht als Autorin hervortreten wollte, denn die beiden umfangreichen Bücher (jeweils um die 900 Seiten) müssen während eines längeren Zeitraums vor Childrens Tod entstanden sein. In späteren Jahren erscheinen, wiederum anonym, zwei weitere Romane von Atkins, *Murder Will Out* (1859) und *A Page From The Peerage* (1863). Sie werden von der Kritik wohlwollend aufgenommen, ohne dass die Autorin dauerhaft schriftstellerischen Erfolg verbuchen kann.

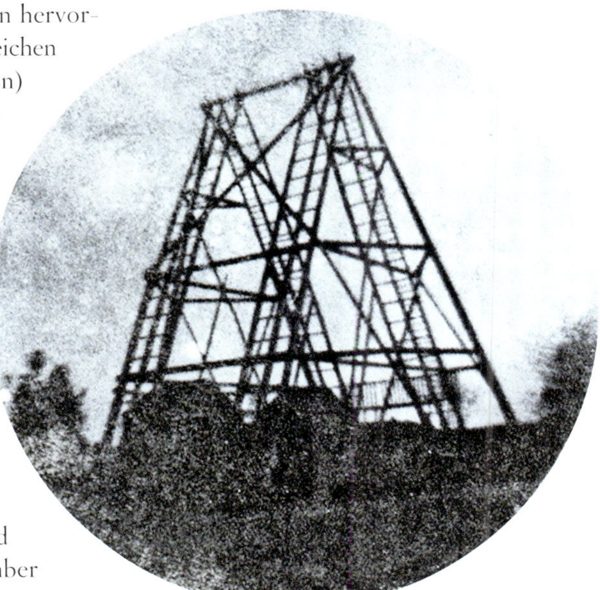

Im Sommer 1853 nimmt Anna Atkins die Arbeit an den *British Algae* wieder auf und schließt den dritten und letzten Band des Albums im November desselben Jahres ab. Vermutlich arbeitet sie

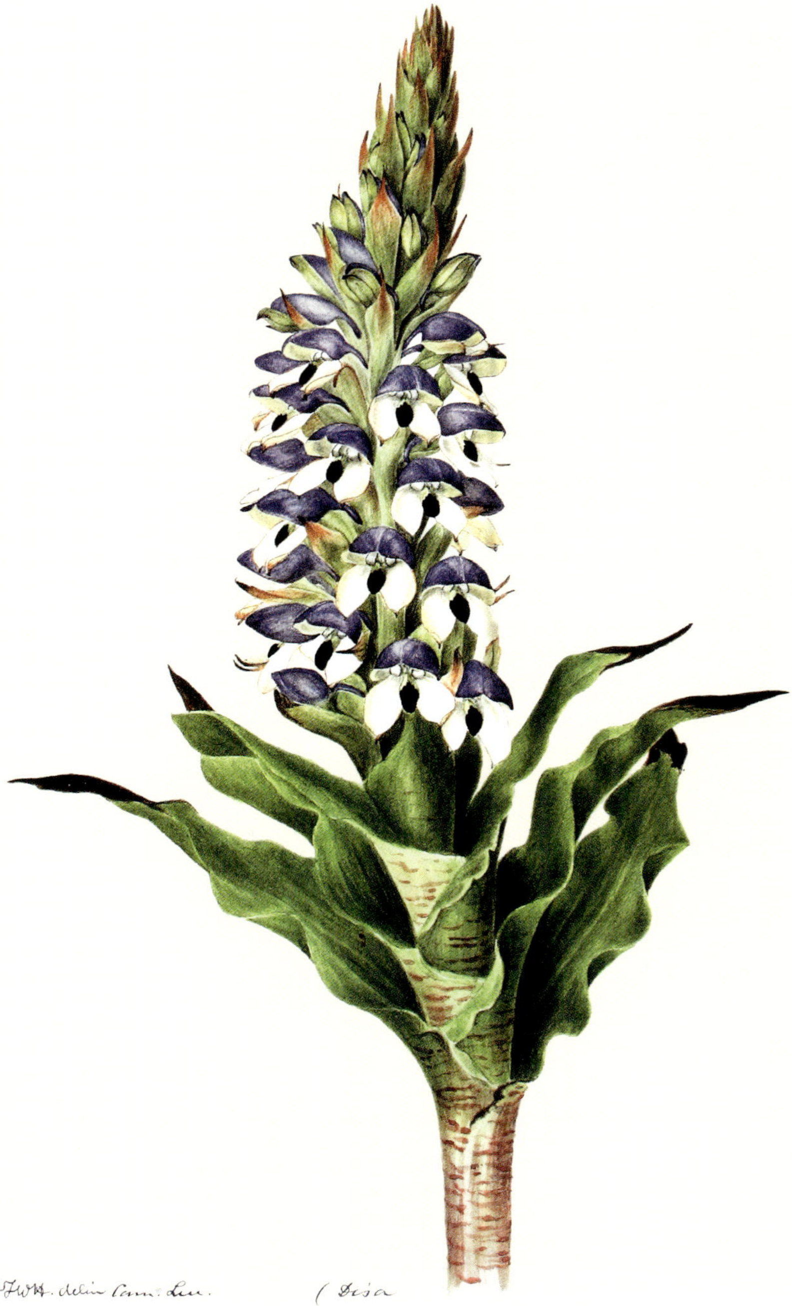
(Disa

dabei bereits mit ihrer Freundin Anne Dixon zusammen, die schon länger ihre botanischen Interessen teilt. Nur wenig später fertigen beide gemeinsam zwei Sammlungen mit Cyanotypien an, in denen Farngewächse der heimischen und ausländischen Fauna abgelichtet sind.

Das Album *Cyanotypes of British and Foreign Ferns* (1853), das zweite der hier abgedruckten Alben, ist ein Geschenk von Anne Dixon an ihren fotografieinteressierten neunzehnjährigen Neffen Henry Dixon (1824–1883). Der Wechsel in der Auswahl der abgelichteten Präparate von den Algen zu den Farnen fällt mit dem Aufkommen des „Farnfiebers" in Großbritannien zusammen. Für beinahe ein halbes Jahrhundert, bis zum Ende des Viktorianischen Zeitalters, wird die Beschäftigung mit Farnen zu einer Modeerscheinung, die in viele Bereiche des Alltags eindringt – von der Kunst bis hin zum Dekor im öffentlichen Raum und zur privaten Inneneinrichtung. Auch Anna beschäftigt sich fortan mit Farnen, zuletzt auf ihren Reisen nach Irland 1851–1861. Wer welchen Anteil an der Zusammenstellung der *Cyanotypes of British and Foreign Ferns* hatte, ist heute nicht mehr feststellbar. Bemerkenswert sind die 25 Tafeln mit Farnen aus Jamaika, die den Teil mit ausländischen Farnen in dem Album ausmachen. Sie stehen vermutlich im Zusammenhang mit den überseeischen Besitzungen von John Pelly Atkins.

Das ebenfalls in Zusammenarbeit der beiden Freundinnen entstandene Album *Cyanotypes of British and Foreign Flowering Plants and Ferns* (1854, Abb. S. 57) ist im Vergleich zu den vorangegangenen freier in der Gestaltung. Die Freundinnen scheint in diesem Fall weniger ein wissenschaftlich-dokumentarischer als ein ästhetisch-dekorativer Impuls geleitet zu haben. Das Album befand sich lange in Privatbesitz. Nach einer Auktion 1981 wurde es zerlegt und blattweise verkauft. Heute sind die 160 Tafeln in alle Richtungen verstreut.

Ein weiteres gemeinsames Album – gleichfalls ein Geschenk für Anne Dixons Neffen Henry – ist auf das Jahr 1861 datiert. Neben einigen Tafeln aus älteren Werken wie den *British Algae* finden sich in ihm auch Abbildungen von Farnen, Federn und Spitzen. Eines der Blätter, das die Handschrift von Anna Atkins trägt, enthält als Wasserzeichen die Jahreszahl 1856, was darauf hindeutet, dass sie sich noch Jahre nach Fertigstellung der *British Algae* mit der Anfertigung von Cyanotypien beschäftigt hat.

Nach dem Tod ihrer Freundin Anne Dixon im März 1865 gibt Anna Atkins die systematische Beschäftigung mit der Botanik auf und übereignet ihr Herbarium dem British Museum. Das Leben der Atkins' wird zunehmend von Krankheit überschattet, im Haus leben ständig zwei Krankenschwestern. In einem Brief an ihren Cousin spricht Anna offen über ihr nahes Ende und macht sich Sorgen darum, was mit ihrem Mann passiert, sollte sie eher sterben.

In den letzten Monaten des Jahres 1870 erhält Anna Atkins überraschend Post von Sir John Herschel. Der Universalgelehrte hat Schillers Ideengedicht *Der Spaziergang* übersetzt. Um seine Handschrift zu kopieren, besann sich Herschel auf die von ihm beinahe drei Jahrzehnte zuvor erfundene Cyanotypie. Einen Abzug des Gedichts schenkt er seiner langjährigen Freundin Anna Atkins. Sie hat das Verfahren der Cyanotypie mit seinen technischen und künstlerischen Möglichkeiten am

Margaret and John Herschel, ***Disa cornuta***
Watercolour over pencil, camera lucida drawing, 32.7 × 23.8 cm (12 7/8 × 9 3/8 in.)
From: *Flora Herscheliana*, 1834–1838
Johannesburg, Brenthurst Library

ausgiebigsten und konsequentesten genutzt. Herschel stirbt im Mai 1871, er wird in Westminster Abbey nur ein paar Schritte entfernt von der Ruhestätte Isaac Newtons (1643–1727) beigesetzt. Anna Atkins stirbt nur Wochen später am 9. Juni 1871 mit 72 Jahren und wird in Halstead begraben.

Nachleben

John Pelly Aktins überlebt seine Frau um ein reichliches Jahr. Während dieser Zeit stellt er im Andenken an sie ein Album ihrer künstlerischen Arbeiten zusammen. Nach dem Tod des kinderlosen Paars wird das Anwesen Halstead Place von einer verwandten Familie übernommen. Das Wissen um die Pionierleistungen von Anna Atkins geht verloren. Zu ihren Lebzeiten gab es keine Ausstellungen, keine Würdigung, keine öffentlichen Präsentationen der Cyanotypien. In zeitgenössischen Publikationen wurden ihre Leistungen lediglich zwei Mal erwähnt, ohne jedoch ihren Namen zu nennen.

Eine dieser Erwähnungen erregt Jahrzehnte später die Aufmerksamkeit des schottischen Fotohistorikers und Buchsammlers William Lang jr. (1846–1913). Talbot hatte in einem Artikel *Über Fotografie ohne den Gebrauch von Silber* (1864) über Herschels Cyanotypie geschrieben und dabei von „einer Dame" berichtet, die „vor einigen Jahren eine ganze Reihe britischer Seegräser fotografiert und Abzüge davon freundlich und großzügig an Botanik- und Fotografieinteressierte verteilt" habe. William Lang, der auch Präsident der Glasgow Photographic Association ist, sucht jahrelang nach diesen Cyanotypien, bis es ihm 1888 gelingt, das Exemplar der *British Algae* aus dem einstigen Besitz von Robert Hunt zu erwerben.

Im Jahr darauf sind die Cyanotypien von Anna Atkins zum ersten Mal in einer von William Lang organisierten Ausstellung in Glasgow öffentlich zu sehen. Die von ihr in der Vorrede der *British Algae* genutzten Initialen „A. A." deutet der Fotohistoriker als „Anonymous Amateur". Durch einen Hinweis des Botaniker James Britten (1846–1924) kann die Identität der Fotografin jedoch geklärt werden. Lang schreibt verschiedene Beiträge für Fachzeitschriften und zeigt die Arbeiten von Atkins auf weiteren Ausstellungen 1896 in Glasgow und 1903 in London. Danach gerät ihr Werk erneut in Vergessenheit.

Erst die Forschungen von Larry Schaaf haben in jüngster Zeit die Cyanotypien von Anna Atkins wieder ans Licht gebracht. Inzwischen ist sie prominent in allen bedeutenden Nachschlagewerken zur Fotografiegeschichte vertreten. Seit 1997 erinnert auch eine kleine blaue Plakette am stehengebliebenen Torhaus von Halstead Place an das Wirken der Fotografiepionierin. Anna Atkins hat als Erste überhaupt die technischen und ästhetischen Möglichkeiten der fotografischen Buchillustration erkundet und in einem Werk veranschaulicht, das bis heute durch die Klarheit, Ruhe und Schönheit der abgelichteten Naturformen fasziniert.

Primula veris
Leaf from Anna Atkins' herbarium, undated, 23 × 43 cm (9 × 16 7/8 in.)
London, Natural History Museum

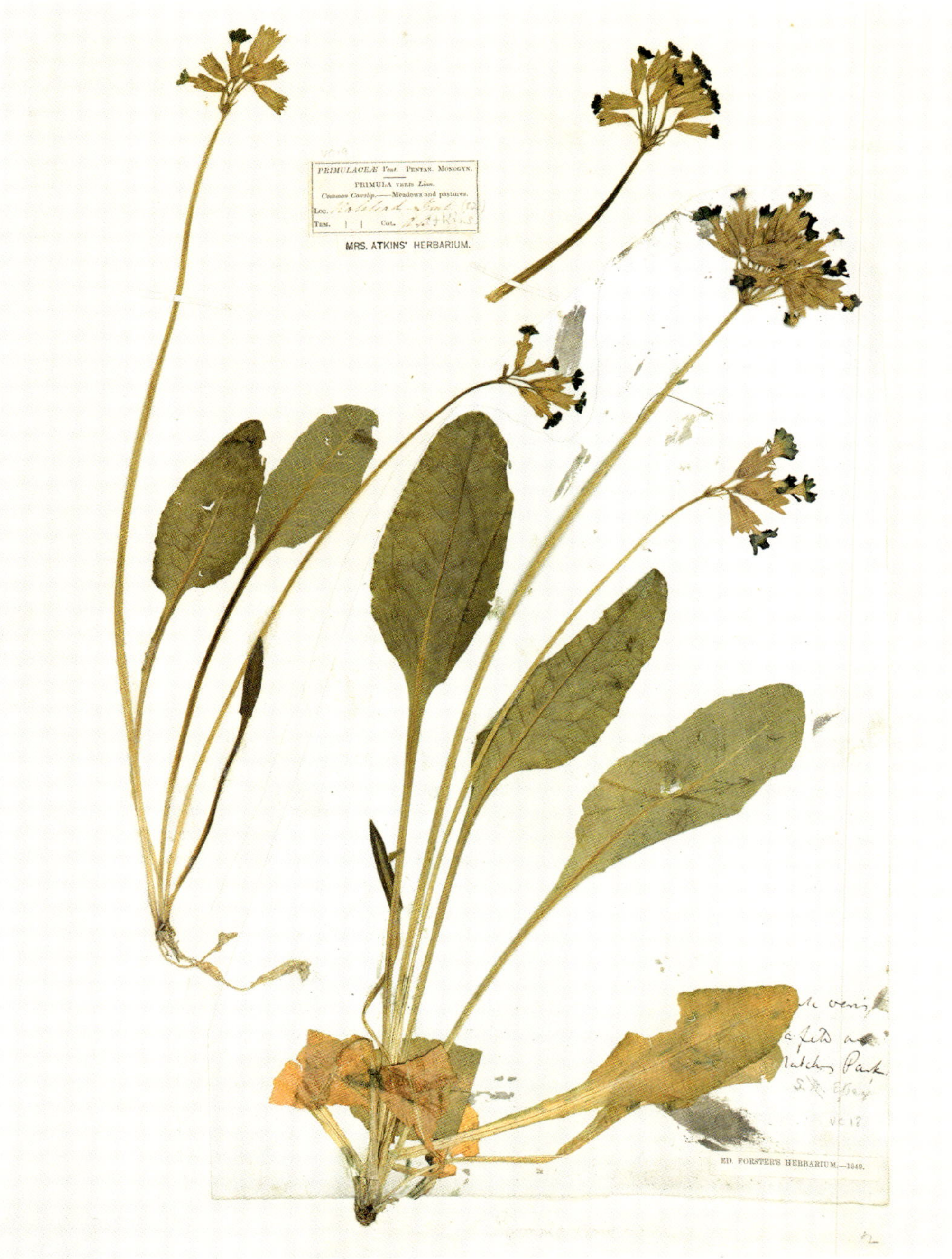
PRIMULACEÆ Vent. PENTAN. MONOGYN.
PRIMULA VERIS Linn.
Common Cowslip.——Meadows and pastures.
Loc.
Tem. | | Col.
MRS. ATKINS' HERBARIUM.
ED. FORSTER'S HERBARIUM.—1849.

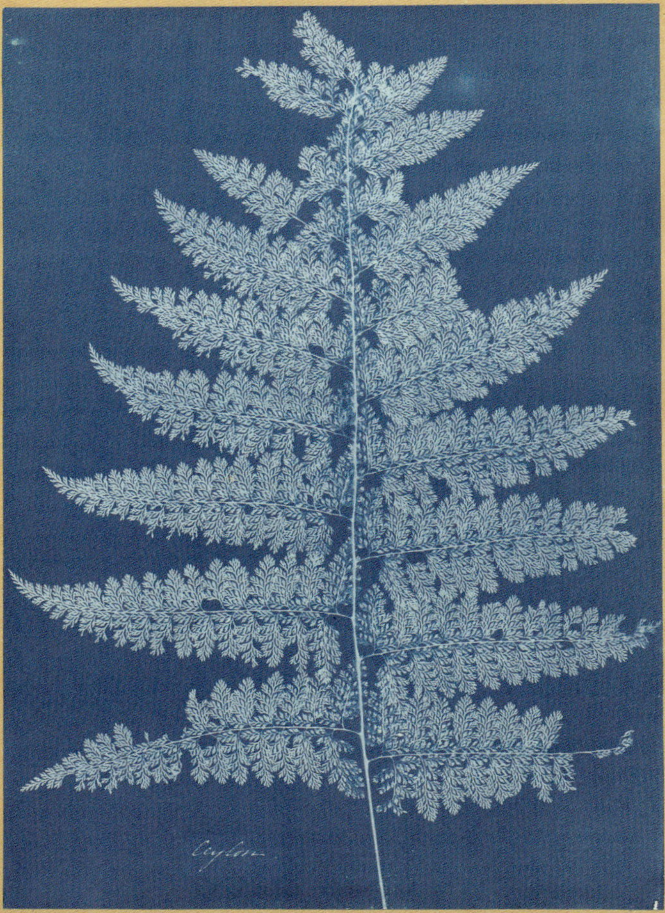
Ceylon

Anna Atkins – une pionnière des débuts de la photographie

Halstead Place

À l'époque victorienne, le manoir de Halstead Place, dans le comté du Kent, au sud-est de Londres, est entouré d'un parc idyllique planté d'ormes. Devant la propriété, le parc s'ouvre sur un vaste paysage. Par beau temps, l'on y installe des tréteaux de bois sur lesquels sont disposés en rangs serrés des châssis-presses contenant des préparations botaniques. Les algues et les fougères pressées sous verre sont exposées au soleil pour une durée maximale d'une quinzaine de minutes. La lumière du soleil fixe les contours des plantes sur une feuille de papier enduite d'une solution photochimique. Entre les années 1843 et 1853, quelque 10 000 images ont ainsi été réalisées selon cette technique. Ce labo photo à ciel ouvert est dirigé par une femme : Anna Atkins (1799–1871). Nous devons à sa créativité et à sa persévérance une œuvre qui compte parmi les témoignages les plus singuliers des tout premiers temps de l'histoire de la photographie.

Après la Seconde Guerre mondiale, Halstead Place se délabre jusqu'à menacer ruine. La propriété est démolie en 1952. Après la mort d'Anna Atkins, son héritage photographique menace également de sombrer dans l'oubli. Mais au cours de ces dernières années, l'admiration pour ses réalisations pionnières n'a cessé de grandir. Partant des recherches de l'historien de la photographie Larry Schaaf, des expositions et des publications très remarquées ont fait connaître les travaux de la botaniste et photographe à un large public.

Le présent ouvrage propose une vue d'ensemble de l'œuvre photographique d'Anna Atkins. Il contient ses deux ouvrages principaux, l'album *British Algae* (1843–1853) et le recueil *Cyanotypes of British and Foreign Ferns* (1853) réalisé en collaboration avec son amie Anne Dixon (1799–1865). L'importance de ces albums ne saurait guère être surestimée. Il s'agit en effet de pierres miliaires de l'histoire des sciences et des médias. Mais indépendamment de leur valeur historique, les formes filigranes des algues et des fougères épargnées sur fond bleu confèrent aux images un charme esthétique résolument intemporel.

Origines et jeunesse

C'est de son père qu'Anna Atkins reçoit les impressions décisives de ses jeunes années. En 1852, quand John George Children meurt à Halstead, Anna consacre à son père un livre de souvenirs dans lequel elle rend hommage à son action scientifique. En même temps, ses évocations livrent un aperçu du monde qui l'a vu naître.

John George Children (1777–1852) est l'unique fils d'un propriétaire terrien et banquier (ill. p. 8). Sa mère décède quelques jours après sa naissance. Son père, le grand-père d'Anna, cultive des intérêts scientifiques et artistiques. Après la mort de sa femme, il ne se remarie pas et se consacre à l'éducation de son fils. Le jeune Children reçoit un précepteur, suit les cours de l'école d'Eton, et à partir de 1794, des études au Queens' College à Cambridge, où il vise d'abord une carrière de théologien. L'amour qu'il éprouve pour Hester Anna Holwell l'amène toutefois à interrompre ses études. En 1798, tout juste majeurs, tous deux se marient. L'année suivante voit naître leur fille Anna.

John George Children a le projet de poursuivre ses études à Cambridge, mais quelques mois seulement après la naissance d'Anna, sa femme meurt. Il se retrouve alors veuf à l'âge de 23 ans. Le destin tragique du père se reproduit ainsi dans la vie du fils. Ceci a en même temps pour conséquence que le lien qui lie Anna à son père sera d'une intensité particulière pendant toute sa vie, même si pendant ses premières années, elle ne le voit guère. De fait, en 1800, Children voyage à Lisbonne avec des amis ; en 1802, il rend visite à un cousin aux États-Unis, d'où il entreprend des expéditions aventureuses dans les terres sauvages du Canada. À son retour en 1803, il rejoint un régiment dans le Kent pour aider à repousser la menace que les troupes napoléoniennes font peser sur l'Angleterre.

Deux ans plus tard, Children quitte le service militaire et consacre désormais son temps à l'activité scientifique. Ses intérêts portent avant tout sur la minéralogie et la chimie. Durant ces années, il tisse des liens amicaux avec nombre de grands scientifiques de son temps, notamment avec le chimiste Humphry Davy (1778–1829), pionnier de l'électrochimie moderne. Celui-ci rend fréquemment visite aux Children dans le comté de Kent, où Anna fait également sa connaissance. Vers 1800, Davy avait déjà mené des expériences avec des matériaux photosensibles, réalisant des copies-contact de feuillets sans parvenir toutefois à en fixer les résultats.

En 1807, Children est élu *fellow* de la Royal Society. Deux ans plus tard, il se remarie, mais après huit mois, ce second mariage se termine à nouveau par le décès de sa femme. Children se réfugie dans ses recherches. Dans la demeure de Ferox Hall, à Tonbridge, où grandit Anna, le père et le grand-père possèdent un laboratoire dans lequel ils mènent des expériences avec une gigantesque batterie galvanique – elle contient 4 300 litres d'acide – et sur la poudre à canon. Children soutient les intérêts scientifiques de la jeune Anna en l'initiant aux bases de la chimie à travers une série de cours particuliers.

Après 1811, Anna grandit avec la fille d'une amie de son père. Née en 1799, Anne Austen, cousine issue de germains de l'écrivaine Jane Austen, a le même âge qu'Anna. À la mort de la mère d'Anne – son père officier est stationné au Portugal –, Children accueille la fille de son ami dans sa famille. Dans la biographie qu'Anna écrira plus tard sur son père, elle évoque le fait que celui-ci « considérait Anne presque comme sa propre fille », et qu'elle lui avait été, à elle-même, « aussi chère qu'une sœur depuis l'enfance ».

La vie insouciante – matériellement du moins – de Children en qualité de savant privé, s'achève en 1816 quand la banque de son père fait faillite. Children est alors contraint d'accepter un poste de bibliothécaire à la British Museum Library. Il s'est depuis longtemps fait un nom en tant que scientifique. Il est un des secrétaires de la Royal Society, membre de nombreuses sociétés scientifiques du pays, directeur de publication d'une revue de zoologie et contributeur de nombreuses publications scientifiques.

En septembre 1818, Children visite le champ de bataille de Waterloo, où Napoléon a subi une cuisante défaite trois ans plus tôt. Anna âgée de 19 ans l'accompagne pendant ce voyage. En Angleterre, un culte dérisoire s'est constitué autour d'un orme ayant servi de poste de commandement au duc de Wellington, vainqueur de Waterloo. Les chasseurs de souvenirs ont jeté leur dévolu sur l'orme et en ont scié presque toutes les branches, de sorte qu'Anna et son père ne trouvent plus là qu'un piteux squelette de l'arbre autrefois imposant.

Children achète l'arbre, le fait transporter en Angleterre et en fait transformer le bois en plusieurs meubles. En font partie un fauteuil fabriqué par Thomas Chippendale Junior (1749–1822) pour le roi George IV (1762–1830), et qui se trouve aujourd'hui encore au château de Windsor, ainsi qu'une table de travail utilisée personnellement par Children. Cette table passe plus tard à Anna Atkins. Le dessin des restes de l'orme de Waterloo qu'Anna réalise en 1818 sur le champ de bataille de Waterloo compte parmi les jeunes essais de son talent d'artiste (ill. p. 15).

En 1822, quand Children est nommé sous-directeur du département d'histoire naturelle au British Museum, il fait imprimer dans une série d'articles sa traduction du livre de Jean-Baptiste de Lamarck (1744–1829) sur la classification des coquillages. Cette publication est accompagnée de 13 planches montrant plus de 240 illustrations de coquillages. Les dessins qui servent de modèles à ces illustrations sont de la main de sa fille Anna (ill. p. 18/19).

L'amour de la botanique

En 1825, Anna épouse le riche marchand et sheriff John Pelly Atkins (1790–1872), un proche ami de son père. Le couple vit temporairement à Halstead Place, mais possède aussi un appartement à Londres. Anna reste ainsi en contact étroit avec son père. Le beau-père d'Anna a fait fortune comme marchand et propriétaire de plantations en Jamaïque et aux Bermudes. Homme d'affaires en vue, il est président de plusieurs sociétés marchandes et a été un temps lord-maire de Londres. Onze de ses quatorze enfants sont morts, le mari d'Anna est le seul descendant mâle survivant. Le mariage des jeunes Atkins reste lui-même sans enfants. Au manoir d'Halstead Place, l'on vit dans l'aisance. John Pelly Atkins s'occupe personnellement de l'agrandissement de la collection de peintures, qui compte des œuvres de Corrège, Caravage et Brueghel. Mais il nourrit aussi des intérêts scientifiques et soutient les ambitions de sa femme. En 1847, la reine Victoria (1819–1901) le nomme High Sheriff of Kent.

En 1837, Anne Austen, la sœur d'adoption et amie d'Anna, se marie à son tour (ill. p. 56). Son époux, Henry Dixon (1798–1870), fait partie du cercle d'amis des Children. Anne s'installe chez son mari à Ferring, petit village du Sussex situé sur le littoral de la Manche, où Dixon est actif en qualité de vicaire à la St. Andrew's Church. Henry Dixon est issu d'une famille qui cultive des intérêts littéraires et scientifiques. Son père est poète et botaniste amateur, un de ses frères est médecin et géologue, l'épouse de

Page 40
Anna Atkins and Anne Dixon, ***Ceylon/Fern***
From: *Cyanotypes of British and Foreign Flowering Plants and Ferns*, 1854
Cyanotype, 34.8 × 24.7 cm (13 ¾ × 9 ¾ in.)
Los Angeles, J. Paul Getty Museum

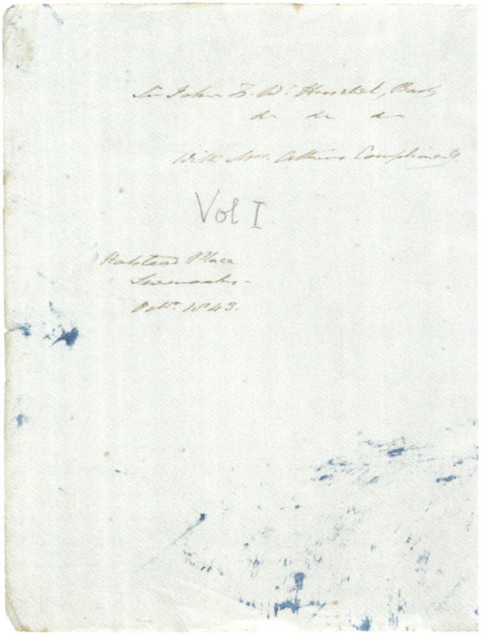

ce dernier est une artiste talentueuse. Le contact entre les familles Atkins, Children et Dixon reste vivace, l'on se rend visite régulièrement.

Pendant les années de son mariage, Anna développe ses intérêts botaniques. Vers 1835, elle se lance dans la création d'un herbier. Elle cueille, sèche et presse des préparations et demande à des amis de lui rapporter des spécimens de plantes de leurs voyages. Elle s'intéresse tout particulièrement aux algues de son pays. Elle ne se borne pas toutefois à collecter et à composer, mais étudie aussi les différents systèmes de classification botaniques.

Dans un environnement dominé par les hommes, la botanique est alors un des rares champs d'activité scientifique ouverts aux femmes. Grâce à l'entremise de son père, Anna fait la connaissance de nombreux scientifiques de renom appartenant à son cercle d'amis et de relations. En qualité de secrétaire de la Royal Society, Children a en outre un accès privilégié aux dernières découvertes scientifiques, qui sont présentées et débattues lors des séances de la Société, séances auxquelles il fait participer sa fille.

Il s'agit d'un regard sur le monde inédit, sobrement classificateur, qui jette les bases du progrès technique en cette phase précoce de l'ère industrielle. Pour les contemporains, le progrès se fait sentir quotidiennement : ils voient s'accélérer les transports avec l'apparition des bateaux à vapeur et du chemin de fer, et la communication grâce au télégraphe électrique. Les grands voyages d'exploration du début du siècle comme ceux d'Alexandre de Humboldt (1769–1859) en Amérique Centrale et du Sud (1799–1804) ou l'expédition de Meriwether Lewis (1774–1809) et William Clarck (1770–1838) à travers le continent nord-américain (1804–1806), déclenchent une activité euphorique de collection et de classification.

La botanique accède au statut de discipline maîtresse pour une nouvelle organisation des connaissances en offrant une structure de dénominations solide pour l'appropriation encyclopédique du monde. En 1753, Carl von Linné (1707–1778) avait introduit un système de désignation des types de plantes qui allait ouvrir la voie à toutes les taxinomies aujourd'hui courantes. *Canna indica* est la première plante désignée par un double nom dans les *Species Plantarum* de Linné selon la nomenclature

Inside cover of Volume I of the Herschel copy of *British Algae*, 1849–1851
Vorsatz des Leineneinbands des Herschel-Exemplars der *British Algae*, Band I
Contregarde supérieure de l'exemplaire Herschel des *British Algae*, Volume I
21 × 27 cm (8 ¼ × 10 ⅝ in.). New York Public Library

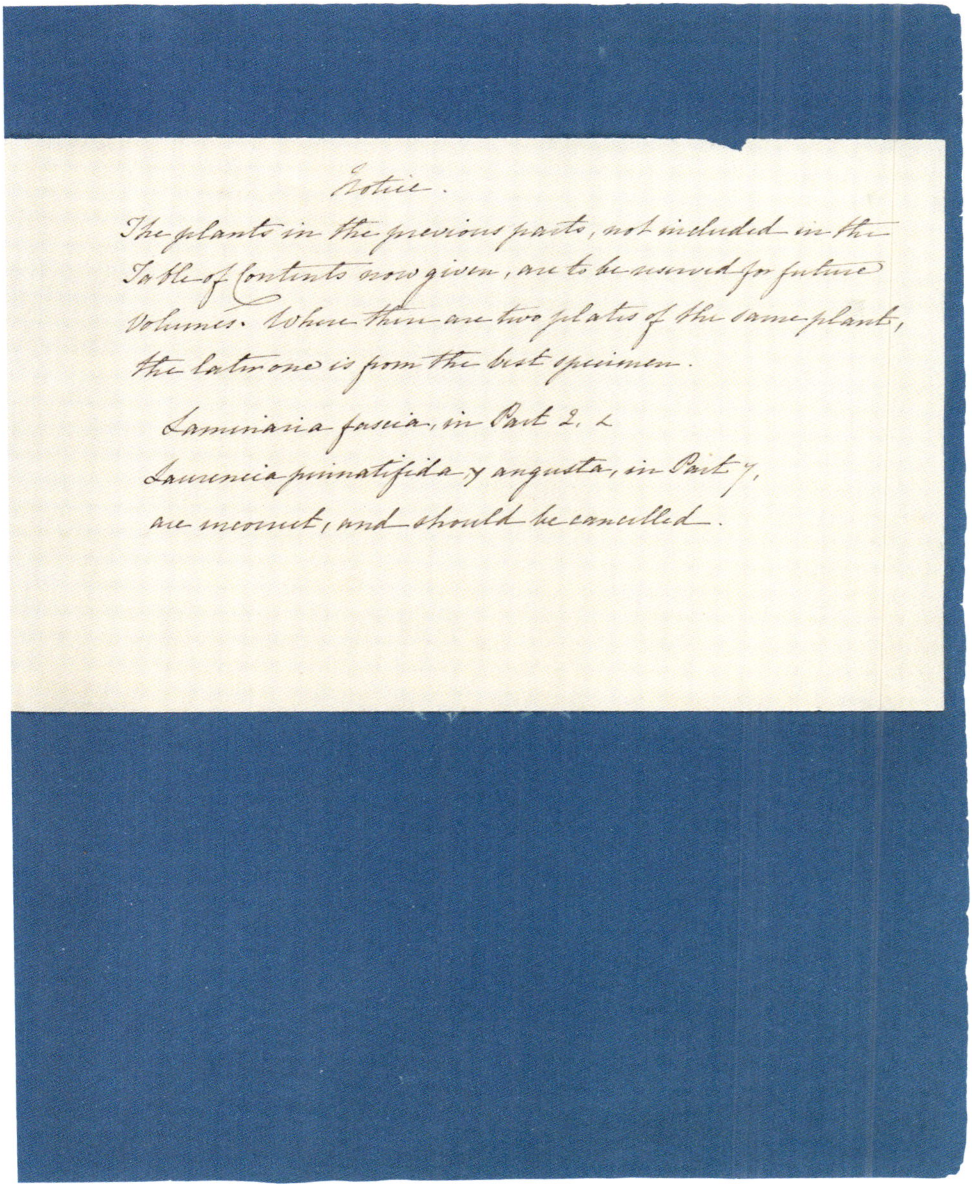

Notice.

The plants in the previous parts, not included in the Table of Contents now given, are to be reserved for future Volumes. Where there are two plates of the same plant, the later one is from the best specimen.

Laminaria fascia, in Part 2. &
Laurencia pinnatifida γ angusta, in Part 7,
are incorrect, and should be cancelled.

Anna Atkins, **Note regarding the arrangement of the plates in the album created for John Herschel**, 1850
Notiz mit Hinweisen zur Kollationierung der Tafeln in dem für John Herschel bestimmten Album
Note avec des indications pour le collationnement des planches dans l'album destiné à John Herschel
From: *British Algae*, vol. 1, 1843. 21 × 27 cm (8 ¼ × 10 ⅝ in.). New York Public Library

binominale encore en vigueur aujourd'hui (ill. p. 12). S'ensuivra un grand nombre de publications présentant des énumérations systématiques des plantes. Parallèlement sont souvent publiés des volumes richement dotés d'illustrations botaniques. Ces ouvrages nourrissent et encouragent l'intérêt pour la botanique, très en vogue dans les hautes sphères de la société.

En 1839, Anna Atkins est accueillie au sein de la toute jeune Botanical Society of London, dont son père est vice-président. Pour Children, cette année marque une profonde césure professionnelle et familiale. Après 20 ans de vie commune, sa troisième épouse décède. Il se retire alors de ses activités au British Museum et s'installe peu après auprès de sa fille et de son gendre à Halstead Place.

Le 7 janvier 1839, quand le peintre de dioramas français et inventeur Louis Jacques Mandé Daguerre (1787–1851) fait présenter son procédé photographique lors d'une séance de l'Académie des sciences à Paris, il déclenche une poussée d'activisme subite au sein du monde scientifique européen. Surtout en France, en Grande-Bretagne et en Allemagne, de nombreux chercheurs menaient déjà des recherches pour parvenir à fixer les impressions lumineuses sur un matériau photosensible. Stimulés par l'annonce de Daguerre, ces chercheurs proclament à leur tour leurs revendications de paternité sur les différents procédés photographiques.

En Angleterre, c'est une bonne connaissance de Children, William Henry Fox Talbot (1800–1877, ill. p. 20), qui fait lire le 31 janvier 1839 à la Royal Society son « Some Account of the art of Photogenic

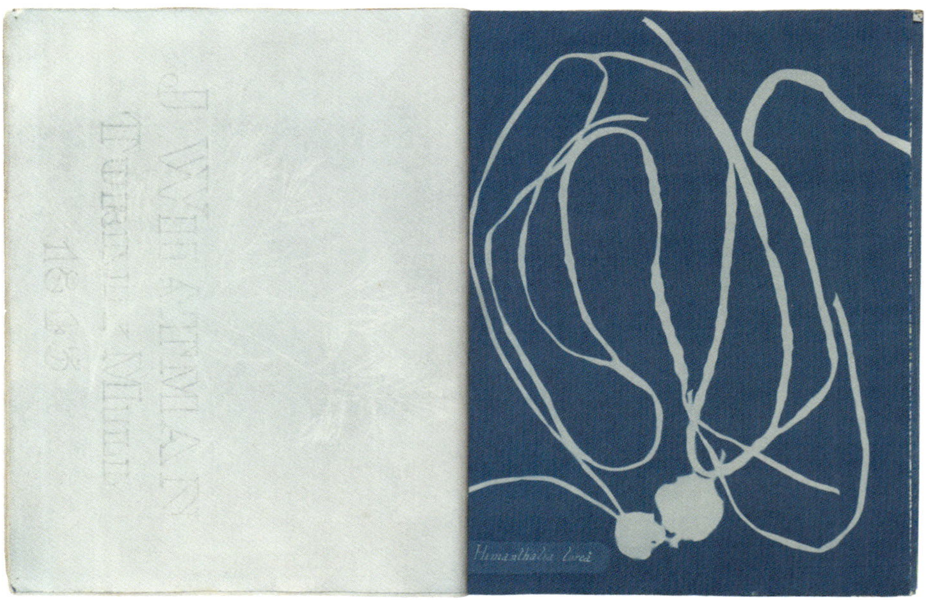

Back of page showing J. Whatman's watermark
Rückseite mit Wasserzeichen der Firma J. Whatman / Verso avec filigrane de la firme J. Whatman
From: *British Algae*, Part I, 1843. 42 × 27 cm (16 ½ × 10 ⅝ in.)
Los Angeles, J. Paul Getty Museum

Drawing ». Dès le mois de mars de la même année, une première petite exposition est ensuite présentée lors d'une réunion de la Botanical Society à Londres, avec des images réalisées « selon le procédé photogénique de Mr. Talbot ». Ces calotypes montrent les motifs de prédilection du botaniste amateur Talbot en ces tout premiers temps de la photographie : des feuilles et des mousses.

Talbot, Herschel et le cyanotype

Le 21 février 1839, quand Talbot présente personnellement ses recherches et ses exemples à la Royal Society – la séance est dirigée par Children –, aucun détail de l'invention de Daguerre n'est encore connu. Talbot vit dans la croyance que le procédé de Daguerre et le sien sont identiques. Concrètement, le daguerréotype et le calotype de Talbot ne diffèrent pas seulement sur des points de détail. Sur une plaque de métal poli, les images de Daguerre possèdent une précision et une dynamique que n'atteignent pas, beaucoup s'en faut, les tirages sur papier de Talbot. Mais il s'agit de coûteuses pièces uniques, tandis que l'avenir appartient au procédé négatif de Talbot, qui permet la duplication des clichés.

Talbot tient Children au courant de l'avancement de ses recherches et lui fait parvenir des exemples de ses calotypes. En septembre 1841, Children se fait portraiturer à l'aide d'un appareil par le peintre portraitiste Henry Collen (1797–1879), un ami et premier concessionnaire de Talbot (ill. p. 16). Le tirage sur papier salé, qui ne montre aujourd'hui guère plus que les contours repassés par le portraitiste, compte parmi les plus anciens portraits au calotype encore conservés.

Cela dit, l'intérêt de Children ne porte pas seulement sur les résultats, mais aussi sur la pratique du calotype, dont les débuts sont encore affectés de bien des impondérables. Il écrit à l'inventeur que sa fille et lui-même travaillent à s'approprier le procédé, et qu'il a d'ores et déjà commandé un appareil auprès de l'opticien Andrew Ross (1798–1859). Malheureusement, aucun cliché réalisé par Anna Atkins à l'aide d'un appareil ne nous est parvenu. Un poème ironique de son père a, en revanche, été conservé, dans lequel il est question d'une tentative manquée de portrait au calotype.

En 1841, l'année même où Anna et son père mènent des expériences sur le calotype, paraît le *Manual of the British Algae* du chercheur irlandais William Henry Harvey (1811–1866, ill. p. 30). Harvey avait acquis de vastes connaissances sur les algues dès l'âge de 15 ans et, en 1838, il avait présenté une première description scientifique de la faune d'Afrique du Sud. Bien qu'étant lui-même un dessinateur talentueux qui enrichit ponctuellement ses publications de dessins de sa main, son livre sur les algues paraît sans illustrations. Harvey lui-même recommande de consulter les *Algae Danmonienses* (1834–1840) de Mary Wyatt (1789–1871), un ouvrage accompagné d'algues séchées.

Si le *Manual of British Algae* lui sert de modèle pour la classification et la dénomination de ses préparations botaniques, Anna Atkins cherche aussi à compléter le compendium d'Harvey par des images des plantes qui y sont décrites. Le calotype de Talbot s'avère trop onéreux pour une telle entreprise. Plus stable et plus simple est un procédé que John Herschel (1792–1871, ill. p. 34), un ami des Children, développe en 1842.

Les intérêts scientifiques de John Herschel couvrent un champ très vaste. Il est astronome, mathématicien, chimiste, philosophe, et s'intéresse aussi à la botanique. Pendant son séjour en Afrique du Sud en 1834–1838, il a compilé avec sa femme Margaret (1810–1884) un album d'illustrations botaniques de la flore du cap de Bonne-Espérance, copiant les contours des plantes à l'aide d'une chambre claire, tandis que sa femme complète les détails et colorie les dessins (ill. p. 36). De retour en Angleterre en 1838, il est en contact étroit avec Talbot, qu'il encourage à progresser dans ses recherches photochimiques.

Stimulé par la communication de Daguerre en janvier 1839, Herschel travaille lui-même sur des questions photochimiques. Dans une lettre adressée à l'algologue Harvey, laquelle a été conservée, il déclare recouvrir des parties d'une feuille papier avec une émulsion argentique pour y reproduire des plantes. En septembre 1839, il parvient à fixer sur verre l'image d'un télescope de 12 mètres de long (ill. p. 35). Il travaille aussi avec Henry Collen et réalise des calotypes selon le procédé de Talbot. Herschel va toutefois donner une impulsion décisive au développement de la photographie en mettant au point un procédé photochimique qui simplifie la fixation d'impressions lumineuses d'une manière jusqu'alors inédite : le cyanotype.

Ce procédé est si simple à maîtriser qu'il devient bientôt une activité de loisirs au sein de la famille Herschel. Il ne requiert que deux substances chimiques qui doivent être appliquées sur un support de papier au pinceau ou à l'éponge, en environnement obscurci. Lorsqu'on pose un objet sur la feuille préparée et qu'on expose le tout à la lumière solaire, les contours de l'objet se dessinent de manière latente sur la feuille et apparaissent une fois la feuille rincée des solutions de sels ferriques. Plus le papier est insolé longtemps, plus les parties exposées se colorent d'un bleu profond, les parties occultées par l'objet restant blanches. Ainsi voit le jour une image de l'objet en négatif.

Herschel n'est pas seulement l'inventeur du cyanotype, on lui doit aussi les termes « positif » et « négatif » désignant les images photographiques correspondantes. C'est aussi à lui qu'on attribue l'invention du mot « photographie ». Dans une contribution qu'il transmet immédiatement à Children, l'inventeur décrit le nouveau procédé photochimique. C'est vraisemblablement par cette voie qu'Anna en a pris connaissance. Mais il se peut aussi qu'elle soit entrée pour la première fois en contact avec le cyanotype lors d'une des nombreuses visites des Herschel à Halstead Place – les deux familles sont liées d'amitié. En tout état de cause, ce procédé fournit le trait d'union qui lui permet de lier ses intérêts botaniques à ses penchants scientifiques et à ses projets pratiques.

British Algae

Le moment où Anna Atkins a commencé à produire des cyanotypes d'algues a été relaté dans l'une de ses rares lettres qui ont été conservées. En octobre 1843, elle écrit à son amie Sophia Bliss : « Voici peu, je me suis attelée à un projet de longue haleine, encouragée par l'avis de mon père selon lequel celui-ci serait fort utile – il s'agit de la fixation d'impressions photographiques de toutes les algues et conferves, pour autant que je puisse me les procurer, dont beaucoup sont si minuscules qu'il est très difficile d'en réaliser des dessins précis. »

Même si le procédé photographique du cyanotype est beaucoup plus simple à mettre en œuvre que le calotype, de nombreuses questions attendent encore de recevoir la bonne réponse : quel est le papier le mieux indiqué ? combien de temps la couche photosensible reste-t-elle stable ? quelle durée d'insolation produit quel résultat ? La procédure exacte suivie par Anna Atkins n'est malheureusement pas connue, mais la description contemporaine des techniques de copie et certains repères fournis par le matériau lui-même, permettent de reconstituer la technique utilisée.

Pour ses clichés, Anna Atkins – tout comme Talbot et presque tous les photographes britanniques de l'époque pionnière du médium – utilise du papier à lettres de la marque « J. Whatman, Turkey

William Henry Fox Talbot
Title page / Titelblatt / Page de titre
From: *The Pencil of Nature*, London, 1844
New York Public Library

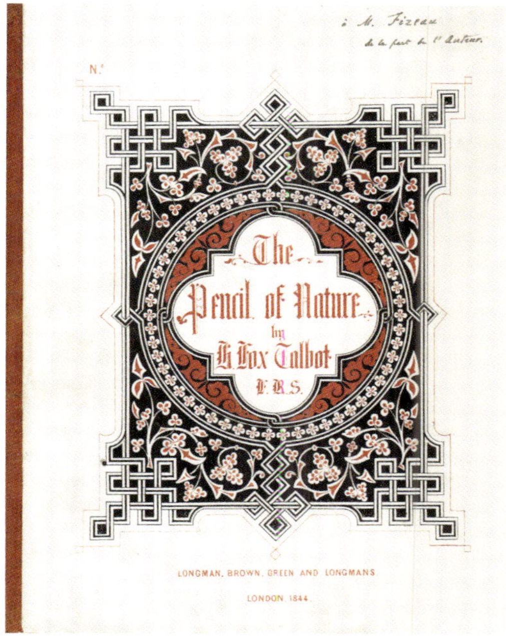

Mill ». Dès la première partie de l'album, on trouve différentes feuilles présentant le filigrane de la firme daté des années 1842 et 1843 (ill. p. 46). La surface du papier, son pouvoir absorbant, ses couleurs, poids et épaisseur jouent sur la qualité de la reproduction. De petites perforations pratiquées en bordure des cyanotypes indiquent qu'Atkins a accroché les feuilles au mur pour les faire sécher, tant après leur préparation qu'après leur rinçage.

Une grande partie des plantes présentées dans l'album *British Algae* ont été personnellement collectées et herborisées par Atkins. Au moment de leur cueillette, les algues subissent déjà un premier nettoyage dans l'eau ; à domicile, elles sont ensuite débarrassées de tout corps étranger à l'aide de la pince à préparation et du pinceau en poils de chameau, et pour finir pressées et séchées. Dans la mesure où nombre de ses illustrations présentent un ton bleuté au verso, on peut supposer qu'Anna Atkins n'a pas toujours sensibilisé le papier au pinceau ou à l'éponge, mais souvent aussi en l'immergeant dans la solution chimique. Pour la réalisation des cyanotypes, Atkins étale les plantes à même le papier préparé fixé dans un châssis-presse, et recouvre le tout d'une plaque de verre pour assurer un contact aussi étroit que possible avec le support. Il en résulte un dessin de contour détaillé. Les parties translucides apparaissent plus claires dans l'image que les parties exposées à la lumière directe du soleil. Les algues présentant un volume plus important perdent en précision dans la reproduction.

Une étiquette est en outre placée sur le papier avec la préparation. Elle indique le nom de la plante et a préalablement été rendue transparente en la plongeant dans un bain d'huile, de sorte qu'au moment de l'insolation, seule l'écriture est épargnée. Selon la météorologie et l'intensité du rayonnement solaire, les châssis-presses sont exposés au soleil pendant une durée allant de 5 à 15

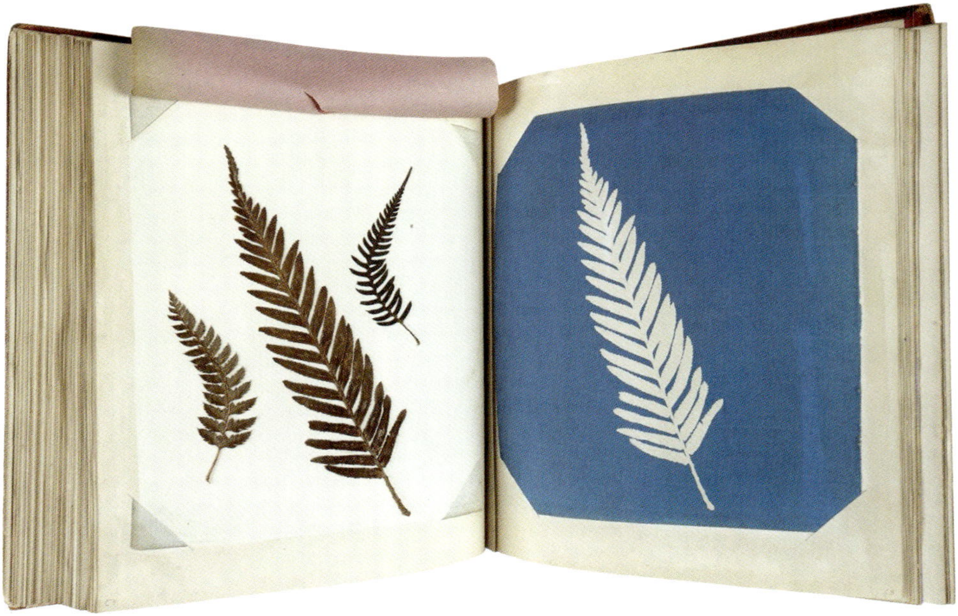

Album with cyanotypes and dried ferns from different locations, ca. 1843
Album mit Cyanotypien und getrockneten Farnen aus unterschiedlichen Gegenden
Album de cyanotypes et de fougères séchées de diverses régions
Bradford, National Science and Media Museum

Anacamptis morio, Leaf from Anna Atkins' herbarium, 1852
London, Natural History Museum

minutes. Après un moment, le papier prend une teinte jaune-vert qui vire à un bleu plus ou moins intense après rinçage.

Anna Atkins produit ses cyanotypes comme des pièces uniques réalisées en série. Même si chaque plante est insolée plusieurs fois, on relève des différences parfois importantes entre les exemplaires d'une même série. Les algues sont réarrangées sur le papier avant chaque insolation. Parfois, elles apparaissent inversées dans la reproduction, parfois seulement légèrement déplacées. L'intensité du bleu varie, elle aussi d'un exemplaire à l'autre.

Au mois d'octobre 1843, la première partie de l'album *British Algae*, qu'Anna Atkins dédie à son père, est achevée en 15 exemplaires. Dans son préambule, Atkins aborde les motifs lors de la réalisation de l'album : « La difficulté de réaliser des dessins précis d'objets aussi minuscules que des algues et des conferves m'a amenée à utiliser le merveilleux procédé de Sir John Herschel, le cyanotype, afin d'en tirer, à partir des plantes elles-mêmes, des clichés que j'ai le plaisir d'offrir à mes amis botanistes. »

Les premiers exemplaires vont à la Royal Society, à Herschel, à Talbot, au minéralogiste et pionnier de la photographie Robert Hunt (1807–1887) et au bibliophile Thomas Phillips (1792–1872). Le British

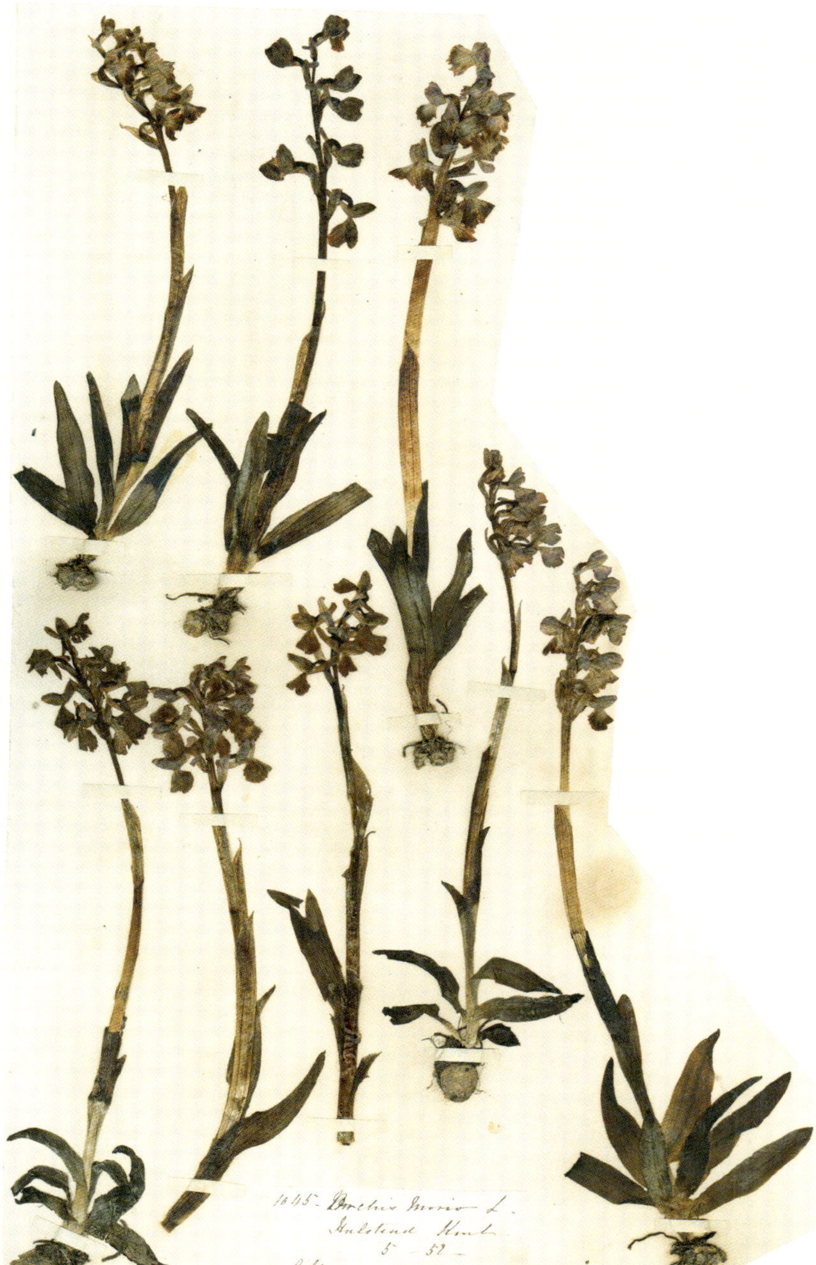

Museum, la Linnean Society of London et les jardins botaniques de Londres et d'Édimbourg reçoivent également un exemplaire. Dès le mois de février de l'année suivante, une nouvelle partie des *British Algae* est achevée. Au cours des années suivantes et jusqu'au printemps 1849 seront produites en tout et pour tout dix parties comptant chacune 12 planches. Atkins coud les planches des différentes parties en fascicules. Les destinataires sont ensuite chargés du collationnement et de la reliure des livraisons.

Sa conception des livraisons et de l'échange de certaines planches, du nouveau tri des parties et le passage d'une structure divisée en parties à une suite en trois volumes seront il est vrai source de confusion. À ce jour se sont fait connaître une petite vingtaine de recueils plus ou moins complets des *British Algae*, sachant qu'il n'est pas toujours clair au cas par cas s'il s'agit de parties d'un album de même provenance ou d'albums différents.

Aucun album ne présente de ce fait le même aspect qu'aucun autre. Dans quelques cas, les livraisons partielles n'ont pas été reliées, d'autres fois, les destinataires ont suivi les indications d'Anna Atkins pour intervertir et reclasser les planches, tandis que d'autres ont suivi leur propre idée. Dans un cas, l'intégralité des planches des différentes parties et volumes a même été réorganisée et reliée par ordre alphabétique, sans tenir compte des différentes tables des matières. Il est donc impossible de donner une indication fiable sur le nombre de planches prévu. Si l'on fait le compte des images connues en divers endroits, pour l'album *British Algae* produit en une série d'environ 15 exemplaires, Anna Atkins a insolé plus de 450 cyanotypes d'algues différentes. La seule étendue de cette entreprise fait de son auteure la créatrice de cyanotypes la plus productive de l'histoire.

L'on ne sait que peu de choses sur la manière dont les destinataires ont reçu les cadeaux d'Anna Atkins. Talbot a répondu à la première partie des *British Algae* par un exemplaire du *Pencil of Nature*, premier livre illustré de photographies publié commercialement (ill. p. 49). La liste des destinataires suggère qu'avec sa production et son envoi des albums, Atkins n'entendait pas seulement donner un signe d'affection à ses amis. Elle voulait aussi attirer l'attention sur un ouvrage qui n'était pas seulement utile en tant qu'outil de travail scientifique, mais qui ouvrait aussi de nouvelles perspectives à l'application de procédés photographiques dans des publications.

Les années tardives

Avant même qu'Anna Atkins ait pu achever la production des *British Algae*, elle est frappée par un coup du sort. Le jour de l'an 1852, son père John George Children, qui vivait à Halstead auprès de la famille Atkins depuis 1839, décède de manière inattendue. Anna est assistée dans son deuil par son amie d'enfance Anne Dixon. Pendant des décennies, les familles des deux amies sont restées en contact étroit. Le mariage d'Anne est également resté sans enfants. Durant quelques mois, le travail sur les *British Algae* est interrompu. Anna passe en revue avec Anne et son mari les papiers de son père, qui remontent à plus de trois générations. En sa mémoire, elle souhaite écrire sa biographie. Ce livre conçu pour le seul cercle familial et amical paraît au printemps 1853 (ill. p. 54). Il montre qu'à côté de ses intérêts scientifiques, Anna Atkins est aussi douée d'un indéniable talent littéraire.

Dès 1852, Atkins avait déjà fait paraître à titre anonyme *The Perils of Fashion*, roman en trois volumes qu'elle avait fait suivre un peu plus tard d'un deuxième livre, *The Colonel* (1853). Les personnages des deux œuvres sont conçus sur le modèle idéal de son père. Il semble qu'Anna n'ait pas voulu se faire connaître comme écrivaine de son vivant, car ces deux titres de grande envergure

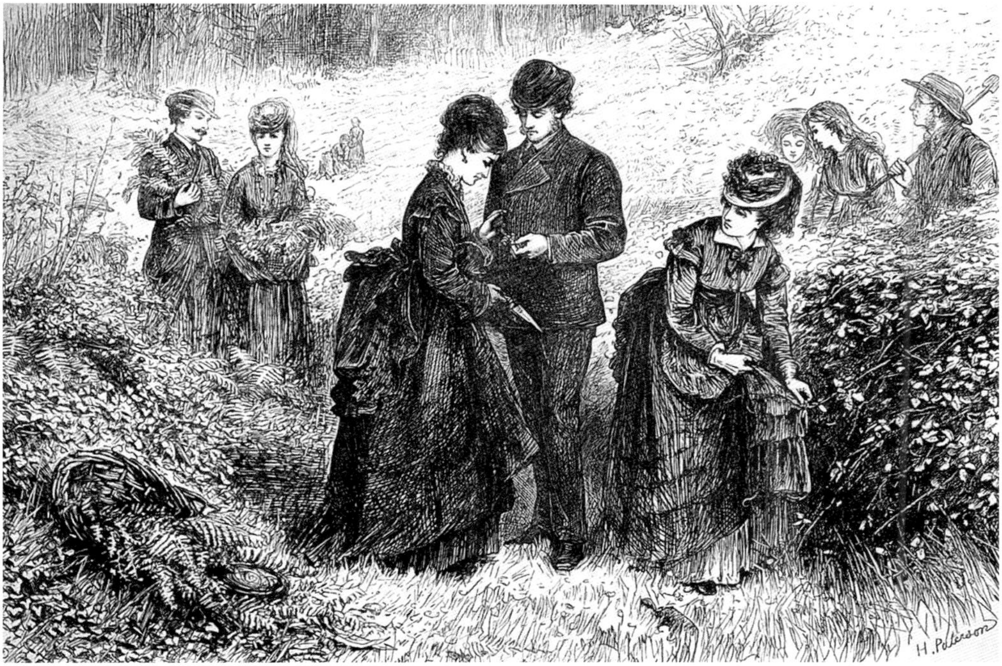

H. Paterson (Helen Paterson Allingham)
Gathering ferns / Beim Farnsammeln / La Cueillette de fougères
From: *The Illustrated London News*, 1 July 1871
San Francisco, Kahle/Austin Foundation

(chacun compte environ 900 pages) ont dû être rédigés sur une assez longue période de temps avant la mort de Children. Dans les années tardives, Anna Atkins fera encore paraître – encore une fois anonymement – deux autres romans, *Murder Will Out* (1859) et *A Page From The Peerage* (1863). Ces œuvres sont bien accueillies par la critique, sans que leur auteure puisse compter sur un succès littéraire durable.

À l'été 1853, Anna Atkins reprend son travail sur les *British Algae* et achève le troisième volume de l'album en novembre de la même année. Probablement travaille-t-elle déjà en parallèle avec son amie Anne Dixon, qui partage depuis longtemps déjà ses intérêts pour la botanique. Ce n'est qu'un peu plus tard que les deux amies vont compiler deux recueils de cyanotypes dans lesquels sont reproduites des fougères d'Angleterre et étrangères.

L'album *Cyanotypes of British and Foreign Ferns* (1853), deuxième des albums reproduits dans le présent ouvrage, est un cadeau d'Anne Dixon à Henry Dixon (1824–1883), son neveu âgé de 19 ans et passionné de photographie. Le changement dans le choix des préparations reproduites – des algues aux fougères – coïncide avec la « ptéridomanie » qui sévit alors en Grande-Bretagne. Pendant presque un demi-siècle et jusqu'à la fin de la période victorienne, l'engouement pour les fougères devient un

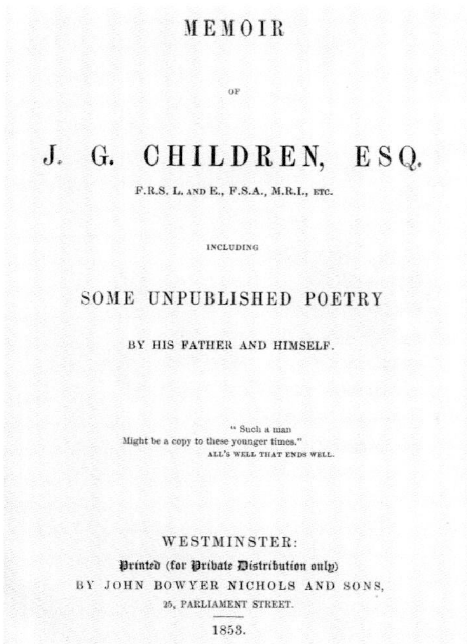

MEMOIR

OF

J. G. CHILDREN, ESQ.

F.R.S. L. AND E., F.S.A., M.R.I., ETC.

INCLUDING

SOME UNPUBLISHED POETRY

BY HIS FATHER AND HIMSELF.

"Such a man
Might be a copy to these younger times."
ALL'S WELL THAT ENDS WELL.

WESTMINSTER:
Printed (for Private Distribution only)
BY JOHN BOWYER NICHOLS AND SONS,
25, PARLIAMENT STREET.

1853.

Anna Atkins
Title page / Titelblatt / Page de titre
From: *Memoir of J. G. Children, Esq.*, London, 1853
Provo, Utah, Brigham Young University

phénomène de mode qui investit bien des domaines de la vie quotidienne – de l'art aux décorations de l'espace public en passant par les aménagements intérieurs. Anna s'intéresse à son tour aux fougères, et ce jusqu'à ses voyages tardifs en Irlande entre 1851 et 1861. La part de chacune des deux amies dans la compilation des *Cyanotypes of British and Foreign Ferns* ne peut plus être reconstituée aujourd'hui. Remarquables sont les 25 planches de fougères de Jamaïque dans la partie « Fougères étrangères » de l'album. Sans doute sont-elles liées aux propriétés que John Pelly Atkins possède outre-mer.

Comparativement aux précédents, l'album *Cyanotypes of British and Foreign Flowering Plants and Ferns* (1854, ill. p. 57), également réalisé comme un travail collaboratif des deux amies, dénote une plus grande liberté dans la forme. Ici, les deux amies semblent avoir été guidées par une impulsion moins scientifique et documentaire qu'esthétique et décorative. L'album s'est longtemps trouvé dans une collection privée. Après une vente publique en 1981, il a été démembré et vendu feuille à feuille. Les 160 planches en sont aujourd'hui dispersées aux quatre vents.

Un autre album réalisé en commun – à nouveau un cadeau pour Henry, le neveu d'Anne Dixon – est daté de 1861. À côté de quelques planches issues de précédents ouvrages comme les *British Algae*, on y trouve des reproductions de fougères, de plumes et de dentelles. L'une des feuilles, qui porte l'écriture manuscrite d'Anna Atkins, présente en filigrane l'année 1856, ce qui indique que des années après l'achèvement des *British Algae*, Anna a encore travaillé à la production de cyanotypes.

Après la mort de son amie Anne Dixon en mars 1865, Anna Atkins met un terme à toute activité systématique en botanique et fait don de son herbier au British Museum. La vie des Atkins est peu à peu assombrie par la maladie – au manoir vivent à demeure deux infirmières. Dans une lettre adressée

Anna Atkins, 1861
Photograph
Yorkshire, The Royal Photographic Society

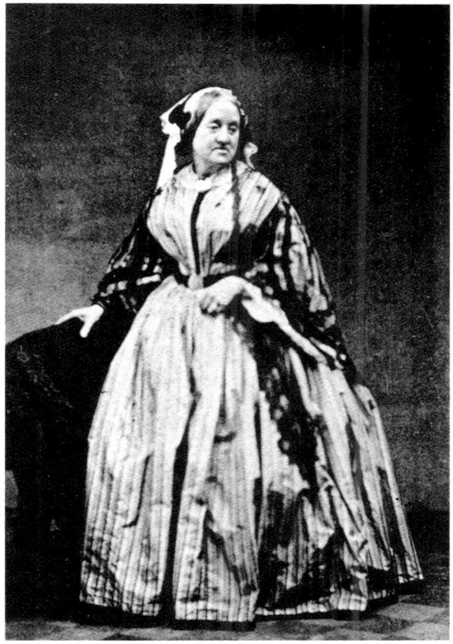

à son cousin, Anna évoque ouvertement sa fin proche et ses inquiétudes sur ce qui adviendrait de son mari si elle venait à décéder avant lui.

Dans les derniers mois de l'année 1870, Anna Atkins reçoit de façon tout à fait inattendue un courrier de Sir John Herschel. Le savant universel a traduit le poème philosophique de Schiller *La Promenade*. Pour réaliser des copies de son manuscrit, il s'est souvenu de la cyanotypie qu'il a inventée presque trente ans plus tôt. Il envoie en présent une copie du poème à son amie de longue date Anna Atkins. Elle est la personne qui a exploité le plus abondamment et de la manière la plus suivie le procédé cyanotypique et ses possibilités techniques et artistiques. Herschel meurt en mai 1871, il est honoré d'une tombe à l'abbaye de Westminster, à quelques pas de celle d'Isaac Newton (1643–1727). Anna Atkins meurt quelques semaines plus tard, le 9 juin 1871, à l'âge de 72 ans, elle est inhumée à Halstead.

Postérité

John Pelly Atkins survit un peu plus d'un an à sa femme. Pendant le temps qui lui reste à vivre, il compile en sa mémoire un album de ses travaux artistiques. Après la mort du couple resté sans enfants, la propriété d'Halstead est reprise par une autre branche de la famille. La conscience des travaux pionniers d'Anna Atkins se perd. De son vivant, aucune exposition, aucun hommage, aucune présentation officielle des cyanotypes. Dans les publications de l'époque, son œuvre n'est évoqué en tout et pour tout que deux fois, sans la moindre mention de son nom.

Des années plus tard, une de ces évocations éveille l'attention de l'historien de la photographie écossais et bibliophile William Lang Junior (1846–1913). Dans un article « Sur la photographie sans

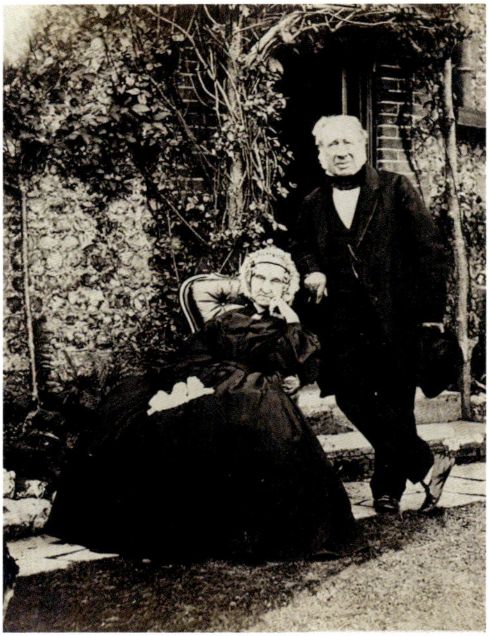

l'utilisation d'argent » (1864), Talbot avait décrit la cyanotypie de Herschel et parlé dans ce contexte d'« une dame qui a photographié voici quelques années toute une série d'herbes marines britanniques et en a généreusement distribué à titre amical des tirages à des amateurs de botanique et de photographie ». William Lang, qui est aussi président de la Glasgow Photographic Association, cherche ces cyanotypes pendant des années. En 1888, il parvient finalement à acquérir l'exemplaire des *British Algae* qu'Anna Atkins avait offert à Robert Hunt.

L'année suivante, les cyanotypes d'Anna Atkins sont présentés pour la première fois au public dans le cadre d'une exposition organisée à Glasgow par William Lang. L'historien interprète les initiales « A. A. » dont Anna Atkins signe son préambule comme « Anonymous Amateur ». Grâce à une information du botaniste James Britten (1846–1924), l'identité de la photographe pourra néanmoins être élucidée. Lang écrit plusieurs contributions pour des revues spécialisées et présente les travaux d'Atkins dans d'autres expositions – en 1896 à Glasgow et en 1903 à Londres –, après quoi l'œuvre d'Anna Atkins sombre à nouveau dans l'oubli.

Il faudra attendre les recherches de Larry Schaaf pour que les cyanotypes d'Anna Atkins revoient la lumière. Aujourd'hui, leur auteure est représentée en place éminente dans tous les ouvrages de référence sur l'histoire de la photographie. Depuis 1997, une petite plaque bleue, apposée sur le pavillon d'entrée resté intact à Halstead Place, rappelle l'action de la pionnière de la photographie. Anna Atkins a été la première à explorer les possibilités techniques et esthétiques de l'illustration photographique de livres et les a visualisées dans une œuvre qui fascine jusqu'à ce jour par la clarté, la paix et la beauté des formes naturelles qui y sont reproduites.

Anne Dixon and her husband, the Reverend Henry Dixon, outside the vicarage at Ferring, 1863
Anne Dixon und ihr Mann, Reverend Henry Dixon, vor dem Pfarrhaus in Ferring
Anne Dixon et son mari le révérend Henry Dixon, devant la maison du pasteur à Ferring
Albumen print, 11 × 8.5 cm (4 ¼ × 3 ¼ in.)
Sussex, Ferring History Group

Anna Atkins and Anne Dixon, ***Spiraea aruncus (Tyrol)***
From: *Cyanotypes of British and Foreign Flowering Plants and Ferns*, 1854
Cyanotype, 35.1 × 24.6 cm (13 ⅞ × 9 ¾ in.)
Los Angeles, J. Paul Getty Museum

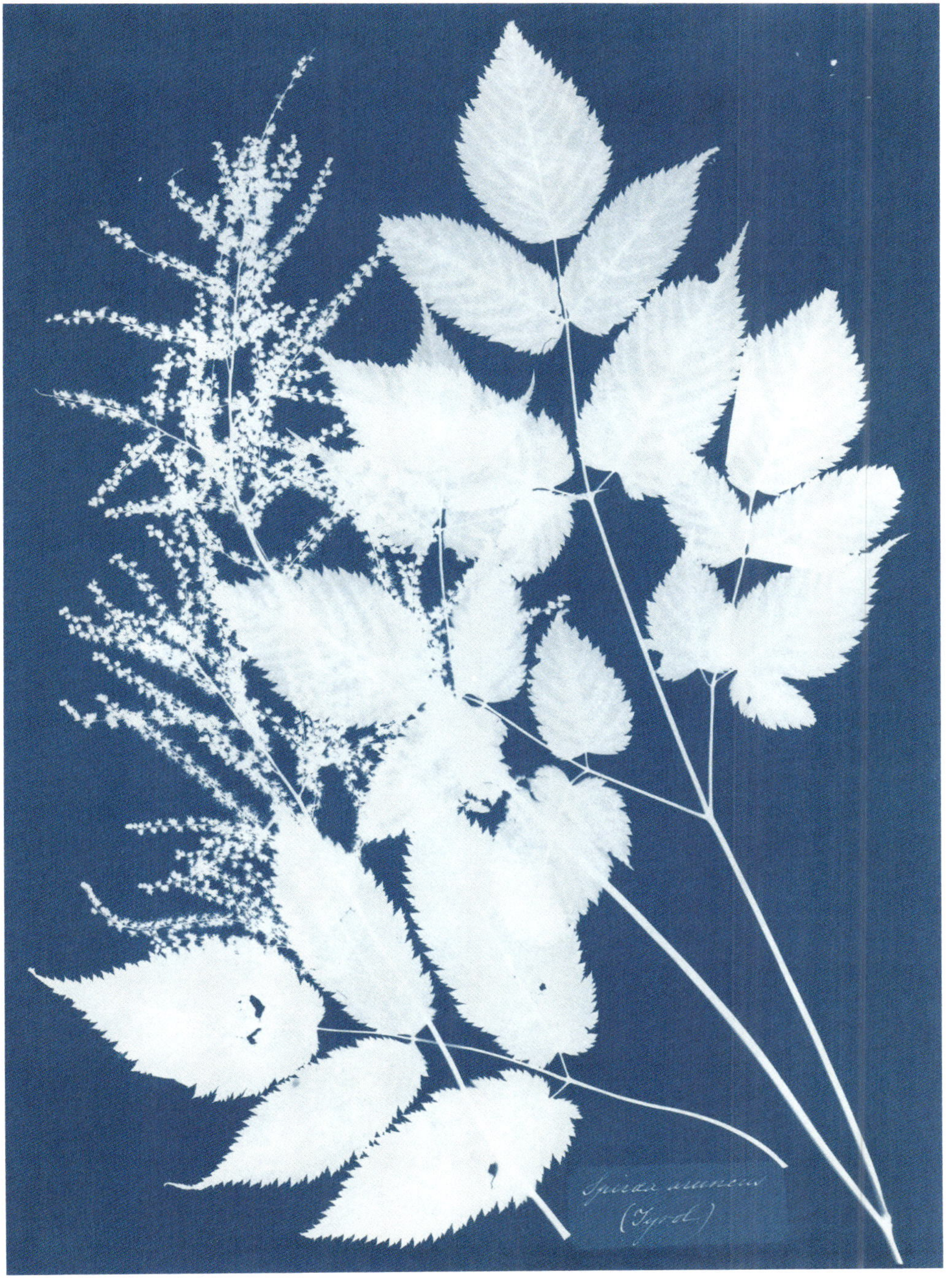
Spiraea aruncus
(Tyrol)

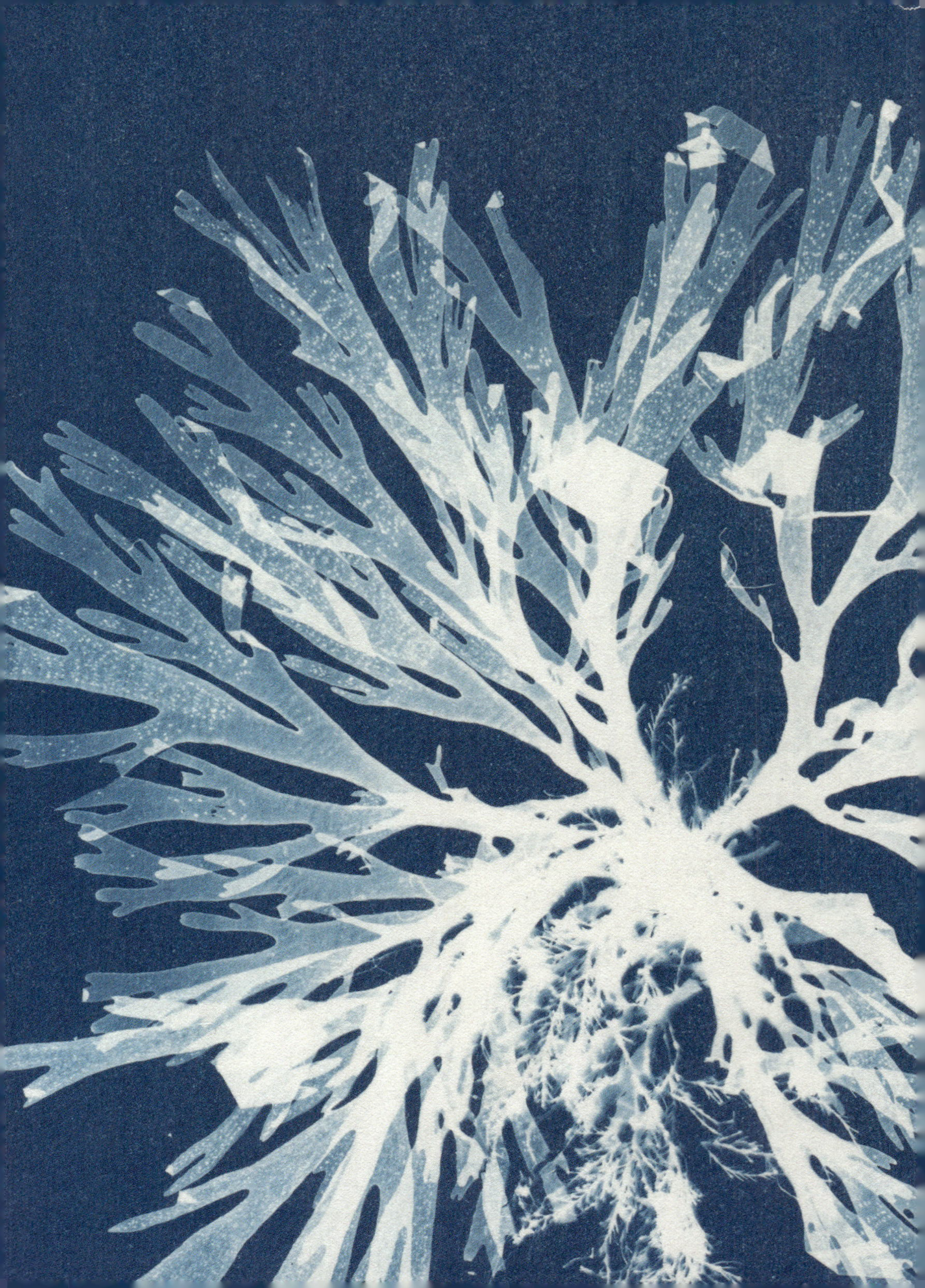

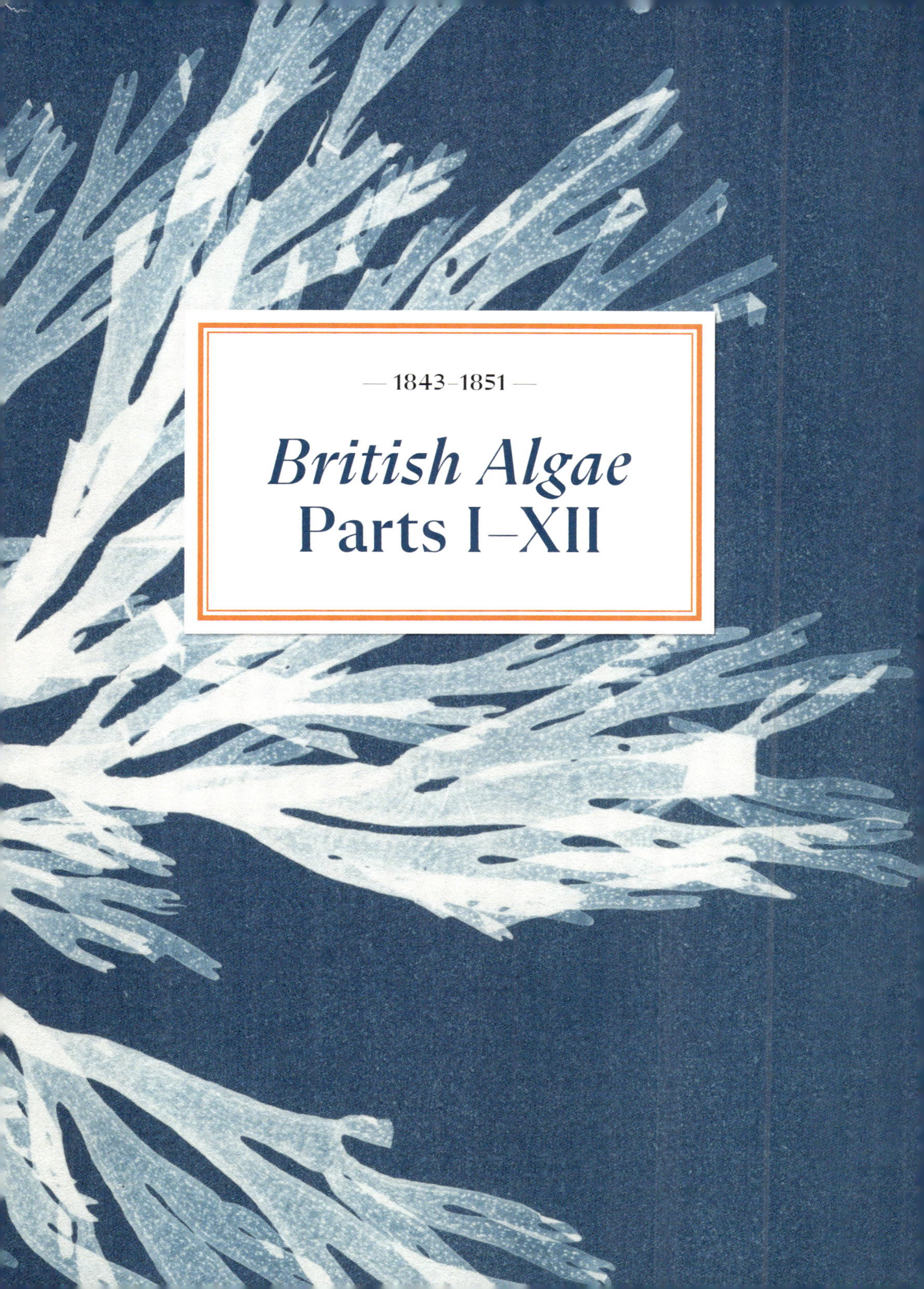

— 1843–1851 —

British Algae
Parts I–XII

Photographs

of

British Algæ.

Cyanotype Impressions.

To

my dearest Father

this attempt

is affectionately inscribed.

The difficulty of making accurate drawings of objects so minute as many of the Algæ and Confervæ, has induced me to avail myself of Sir John Herschel's beautiful process of Cyanotype, to obtain impressions of the plants themselves, which I have much pleasure in offering to my botanical friends.

I hope that *in general* the impressions will be found sharp and well defined, but in some instances (such as the Fuci) the thickness of the specimens renders it impossible to press the glass used in taking Photographs sufficiently close to them to ensure a perfect representation of every part. Being however unwilling to omit any species to which I had access, I have preferred giving such impressions as I *could* obtain of these thicker objects, to their entire omission. — I take this opportunity of returning my thanks to the friends who have allowed me to use their collections of Algæ on this occasion. —

The names refer to Harvey's "Manual of British Algæ". — I have taken the Tribes and Species in their proper order when I was able to do so, but in many cases I have been compelled to make long gaps, from the want of the plants that should have been next inserted, and in this first number I have intentionally departed from the systematic arrangement, that I might give specimens of very various characters as a sample.

A. A.

Part 1.

Contents.

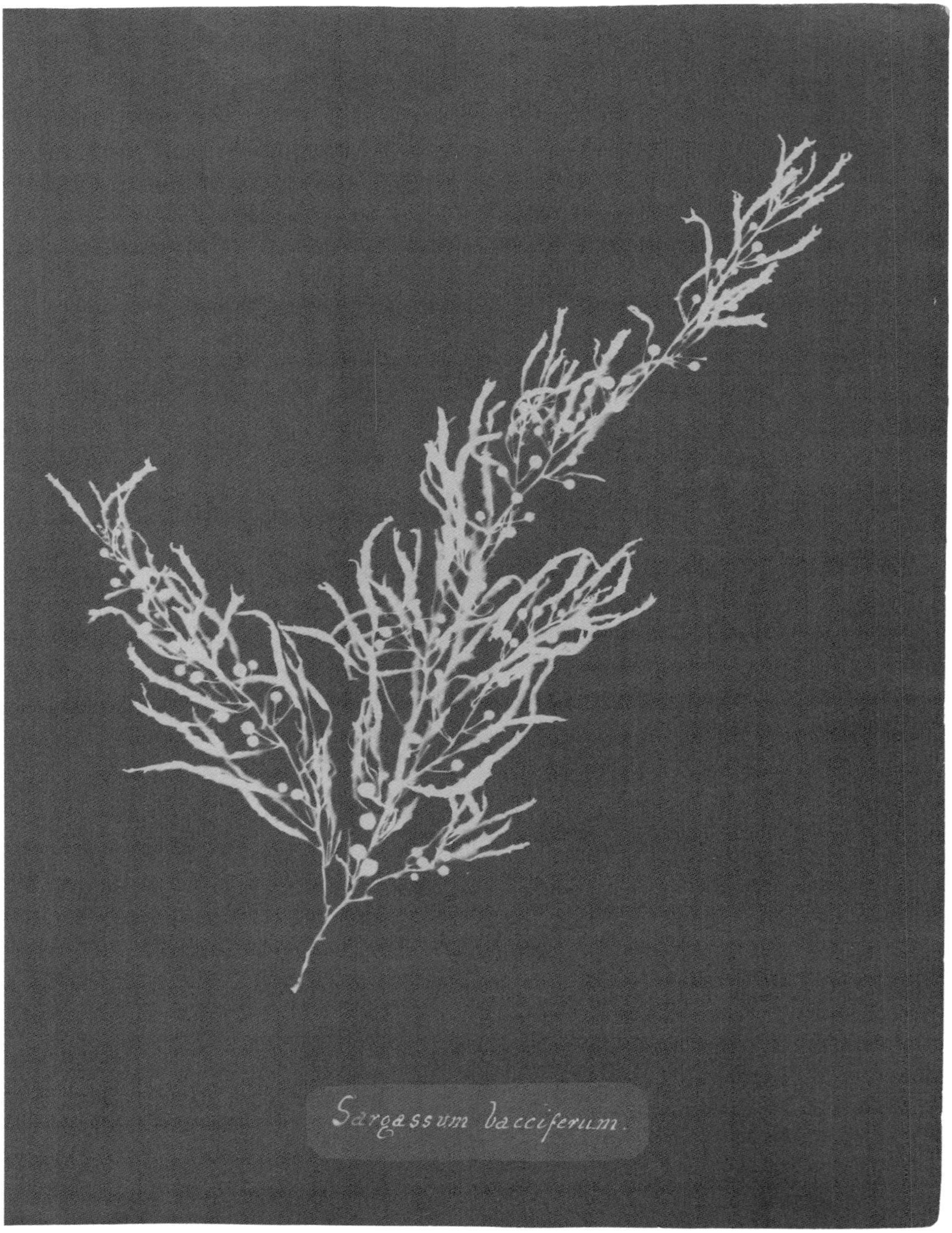

Plate 1. *Sargassum bacciferum*

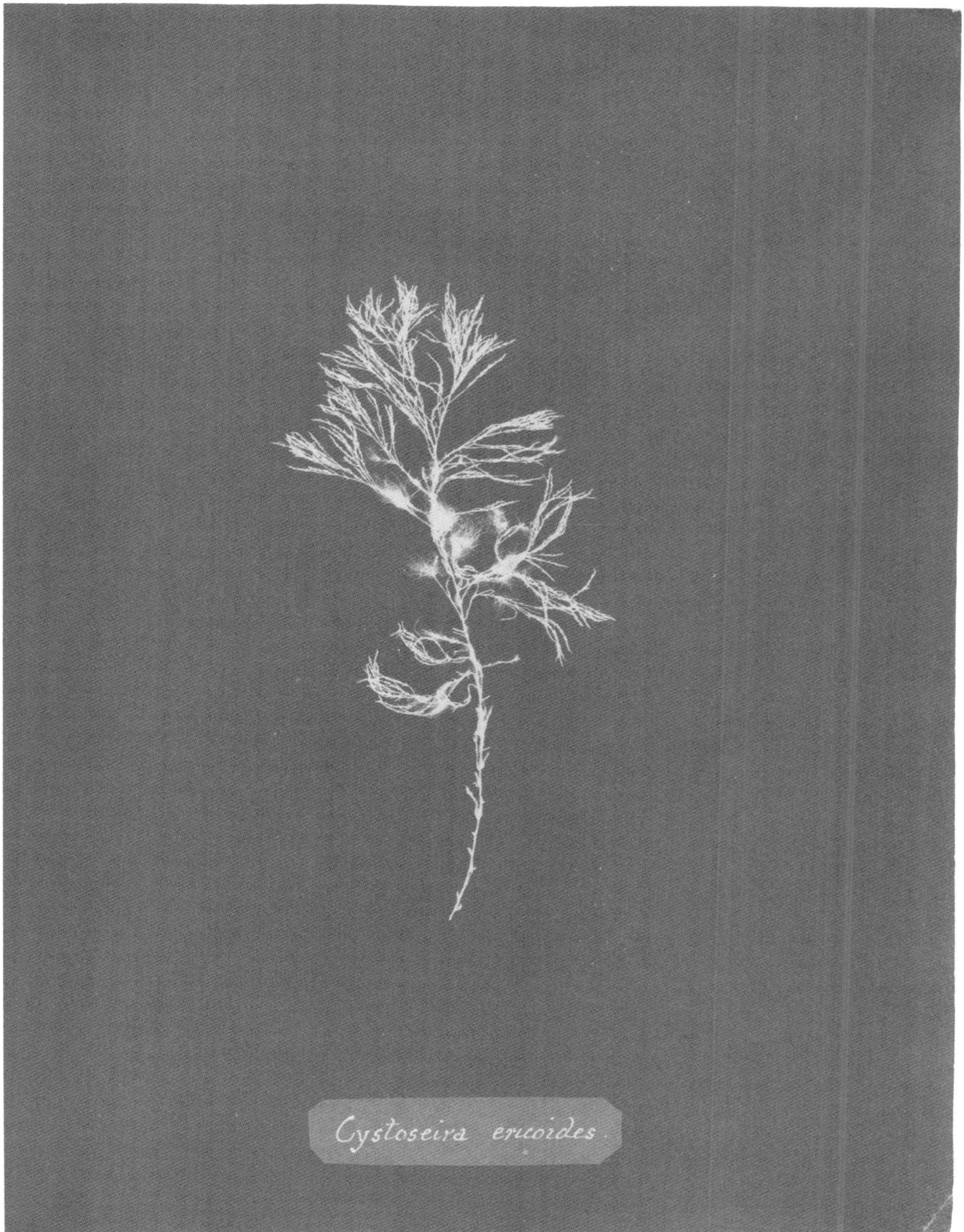

Plate 2. *Cystoseira ericoides*

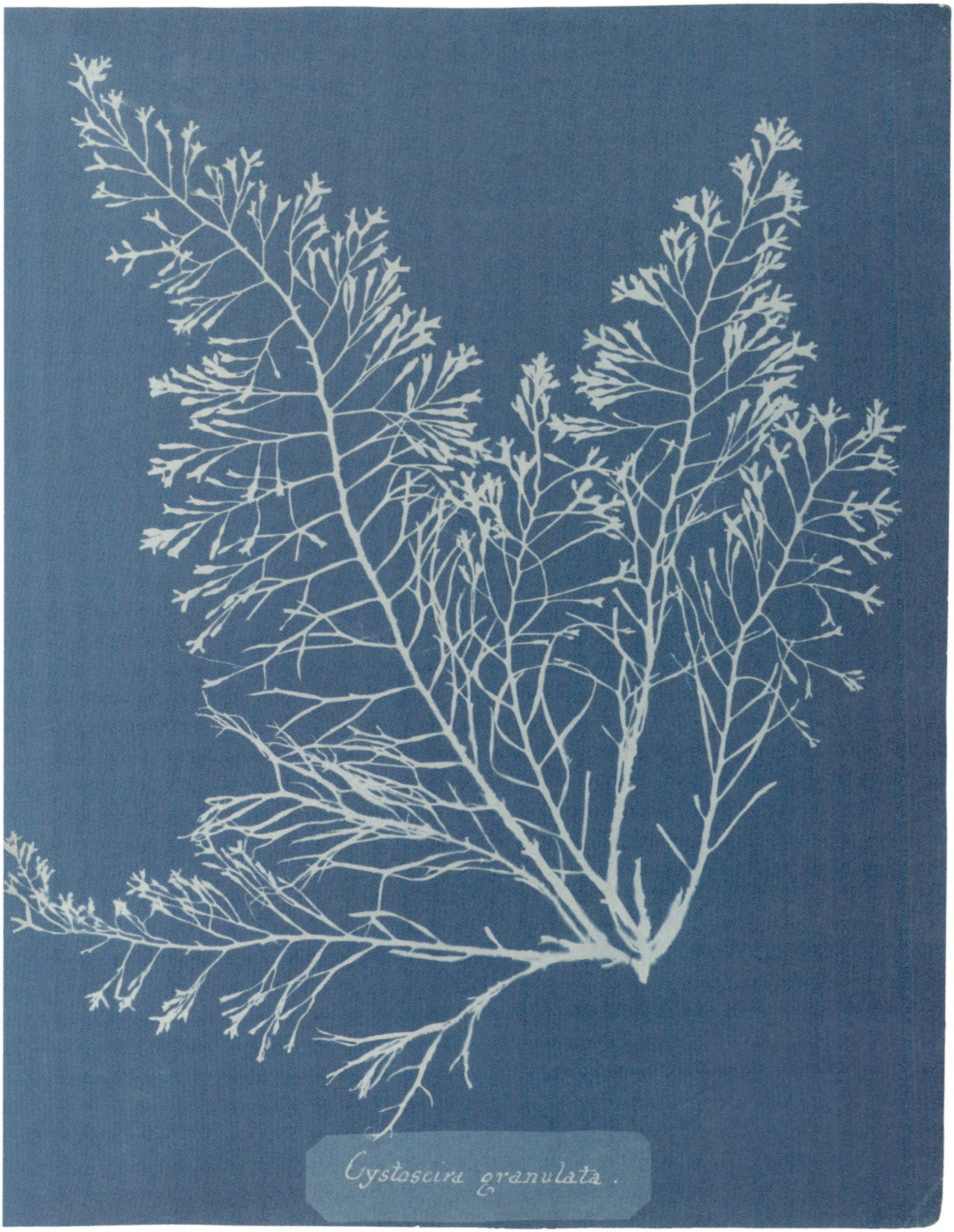

Plate 3. *Cystoseira granulata*

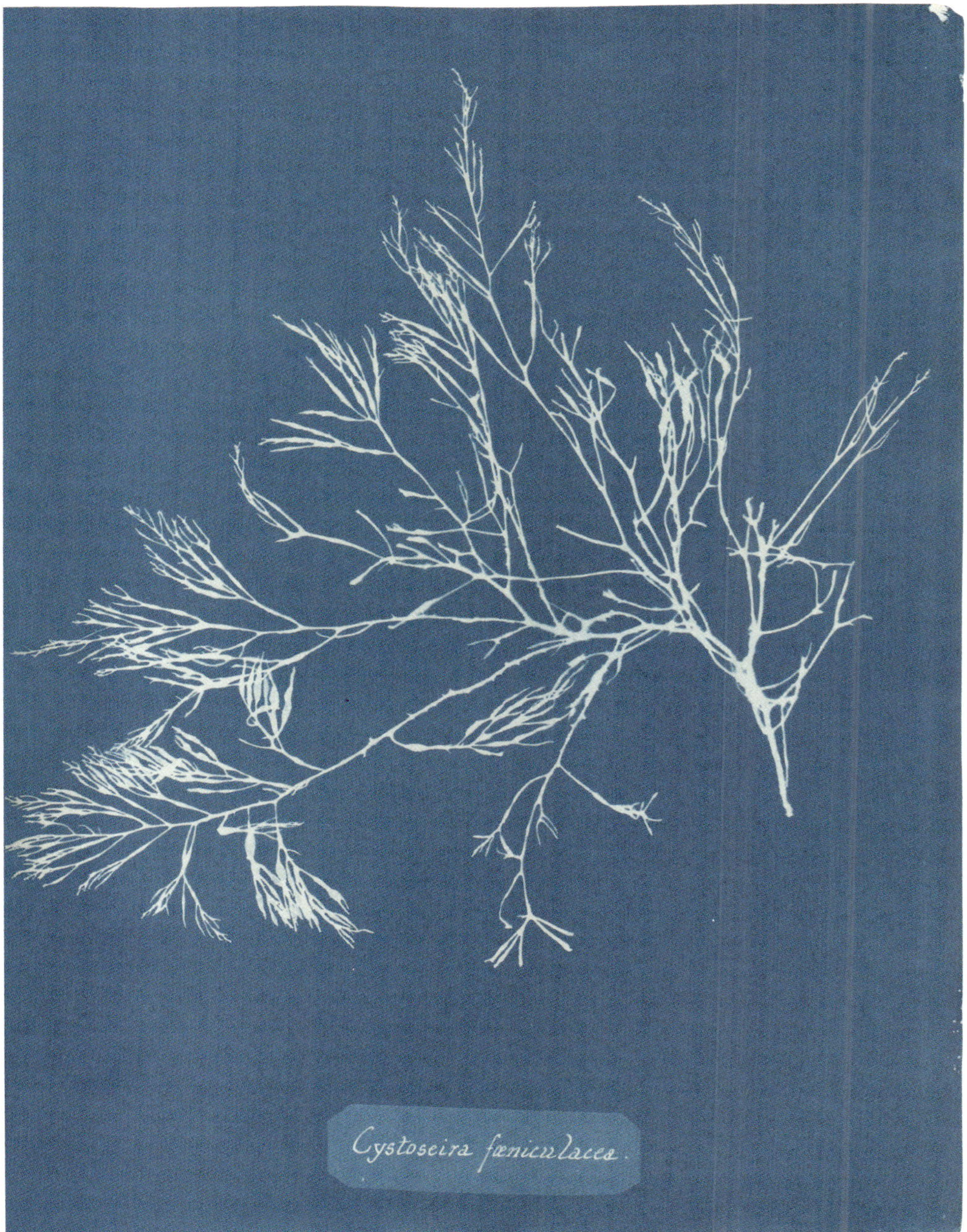

Plate 4. *Cystoseira foeniculacea*

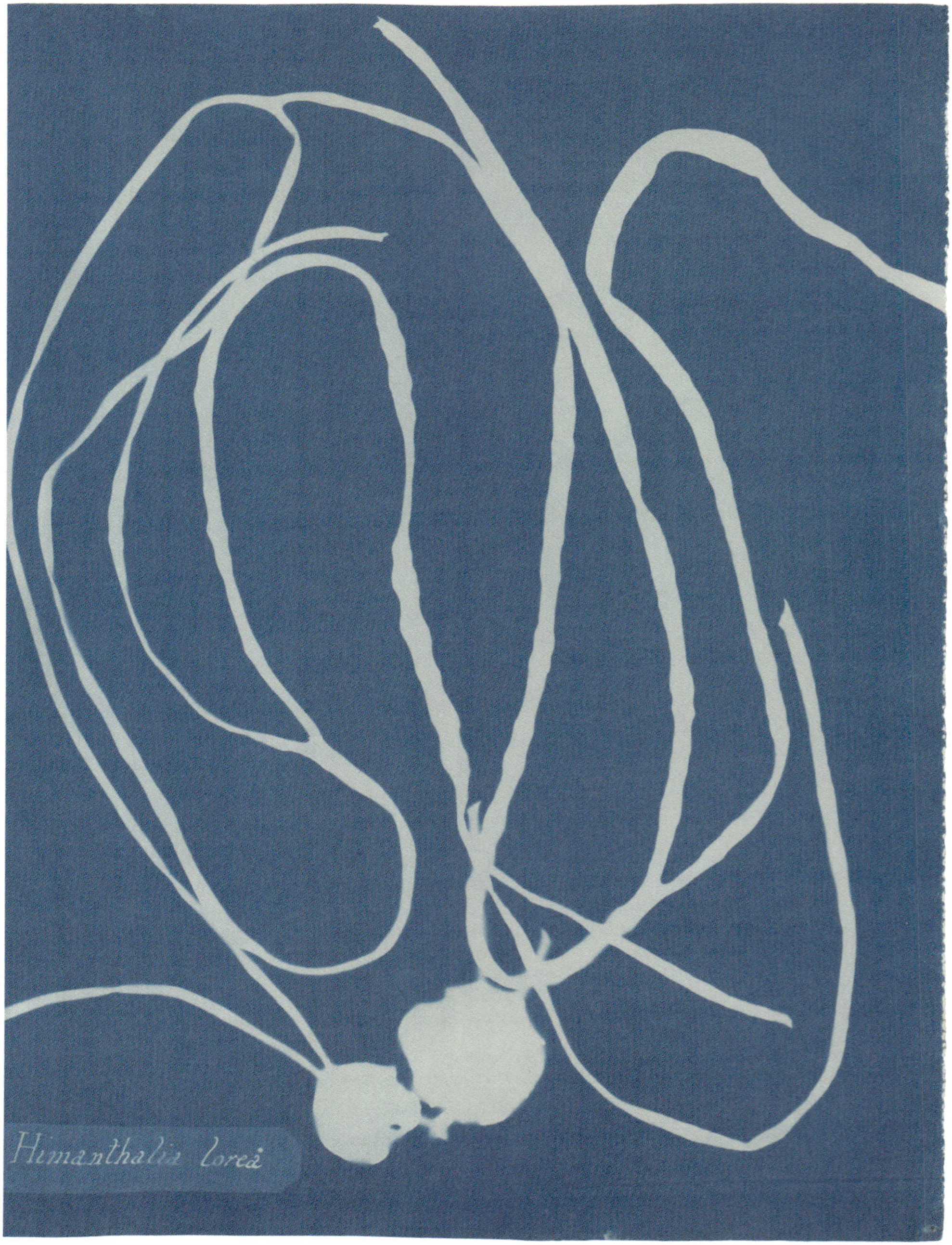

Plate 5. *Himanthalia lorea*

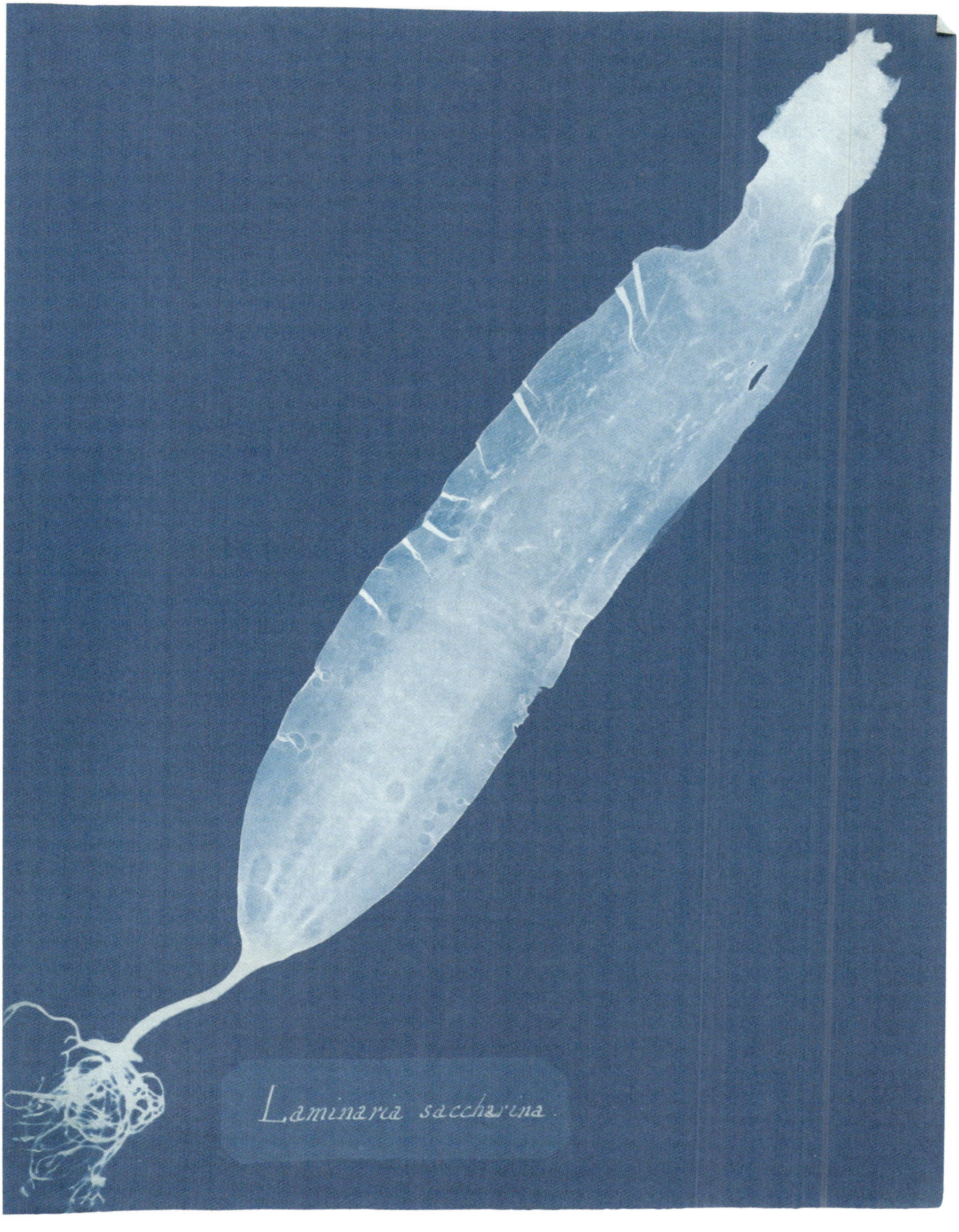

Plate 6. *Laminaria saccharina*

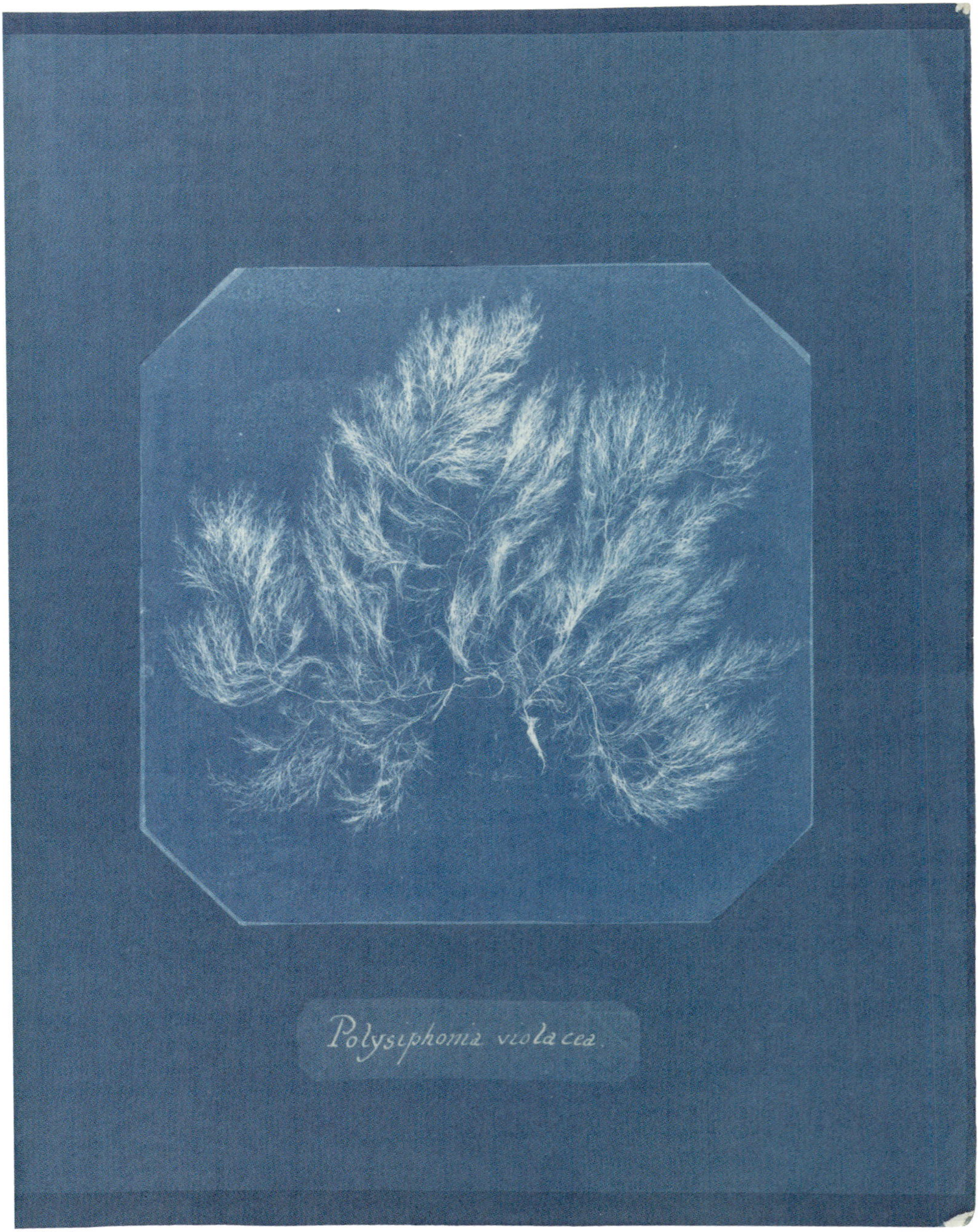

Plate 7. *Polysiphonia violacea*

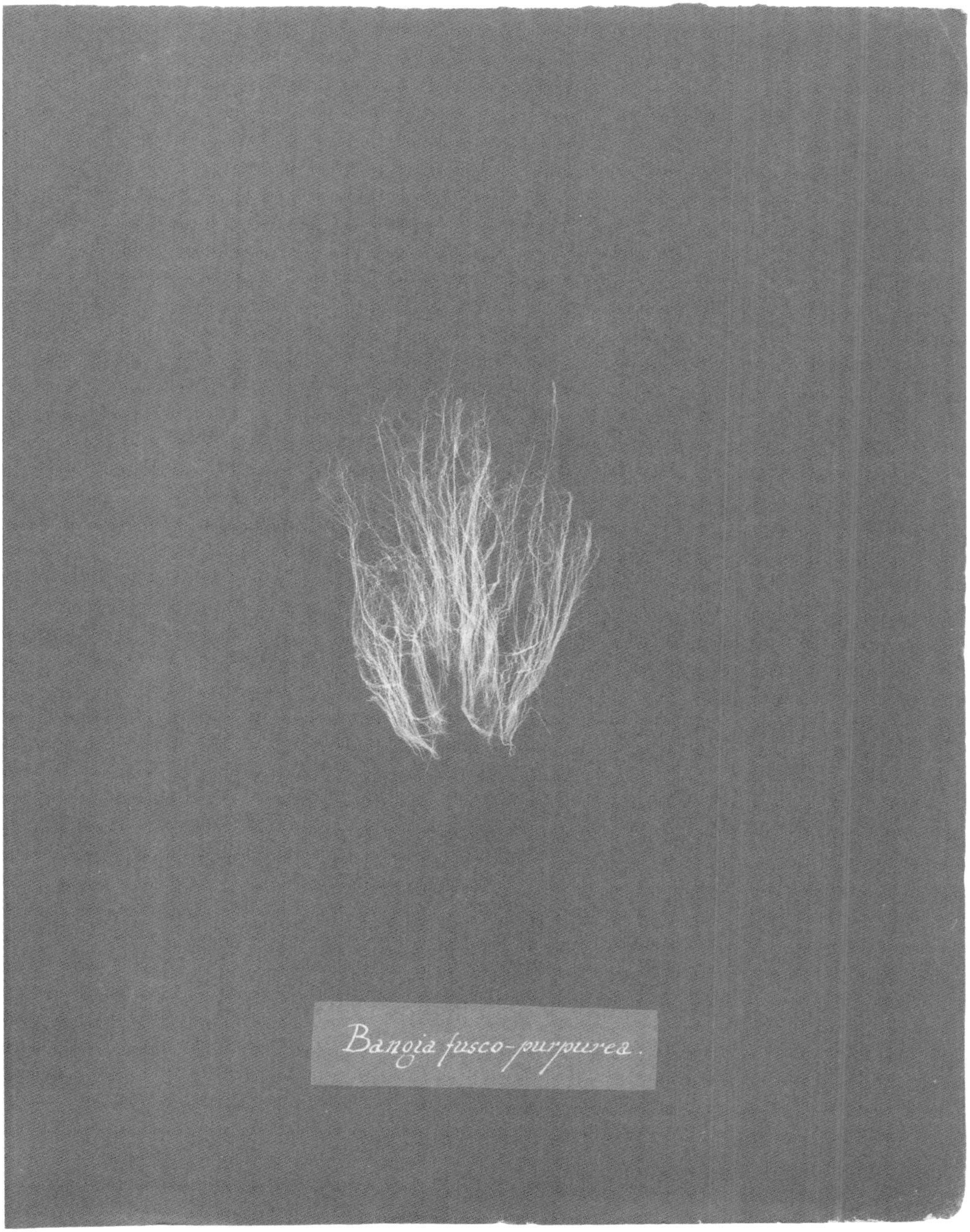

Plate 8. *Bangia fusco-purpurea*

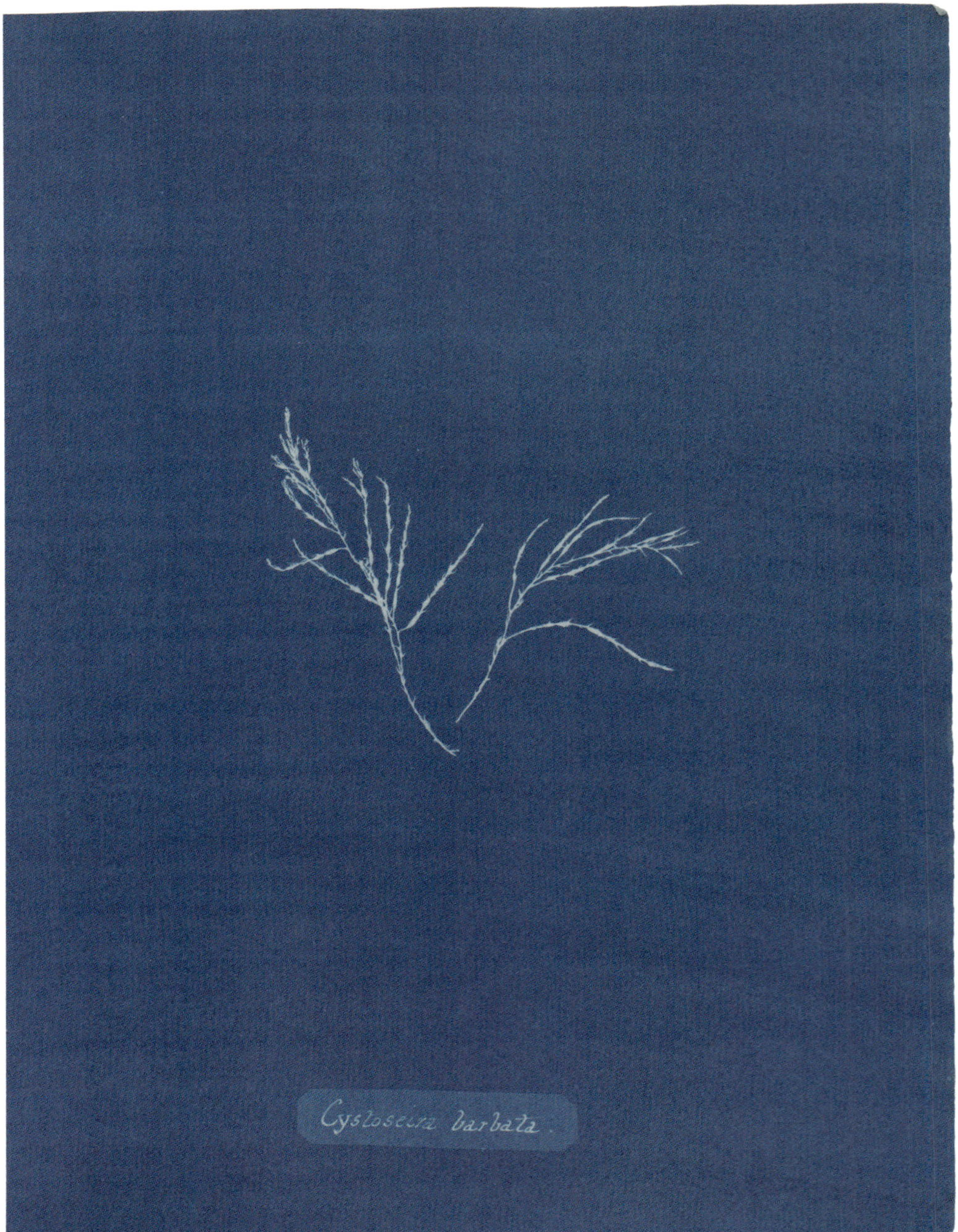

Plate 9. *Cystoseira barbata*

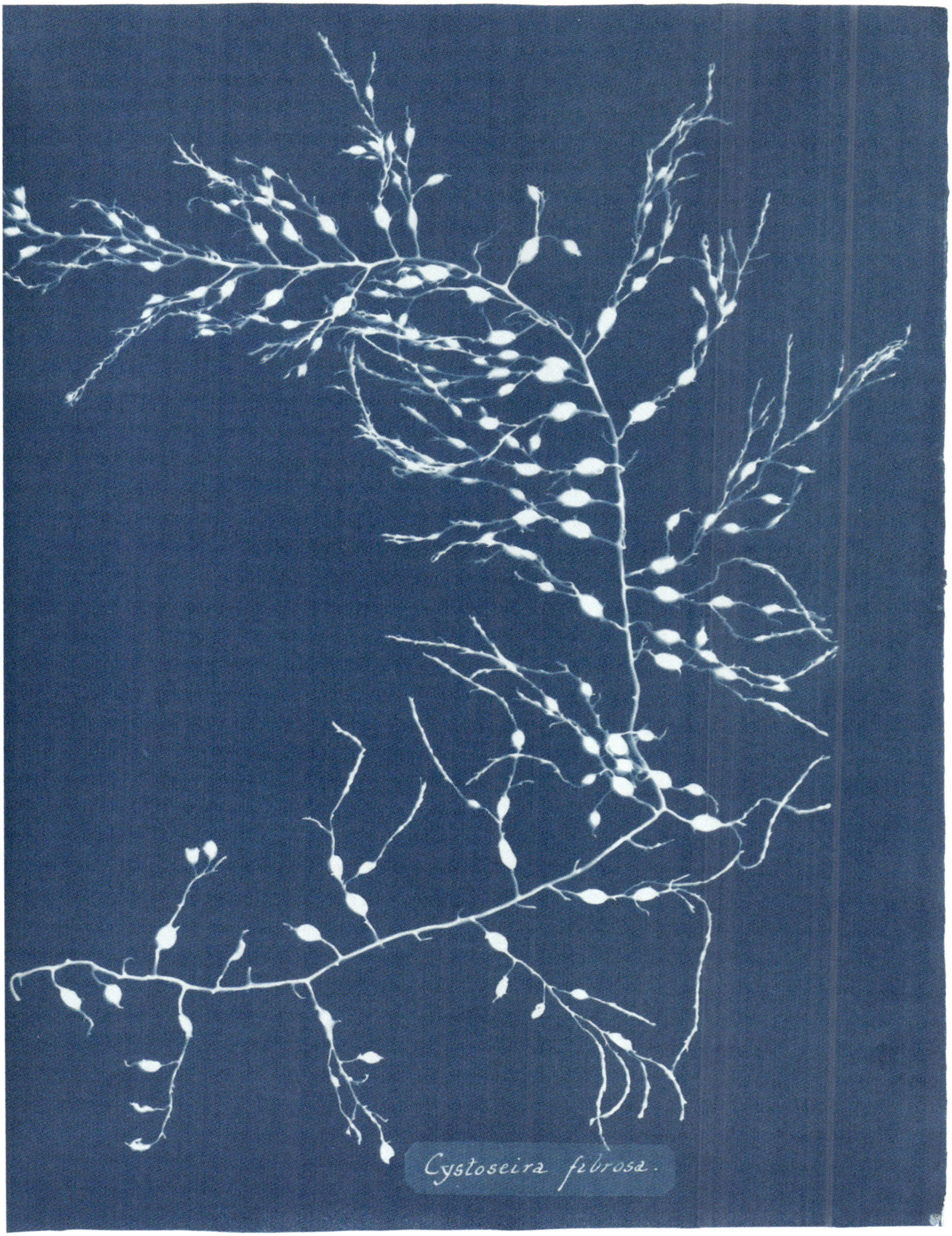

Plate 10. *Cystoseira fibrosa*

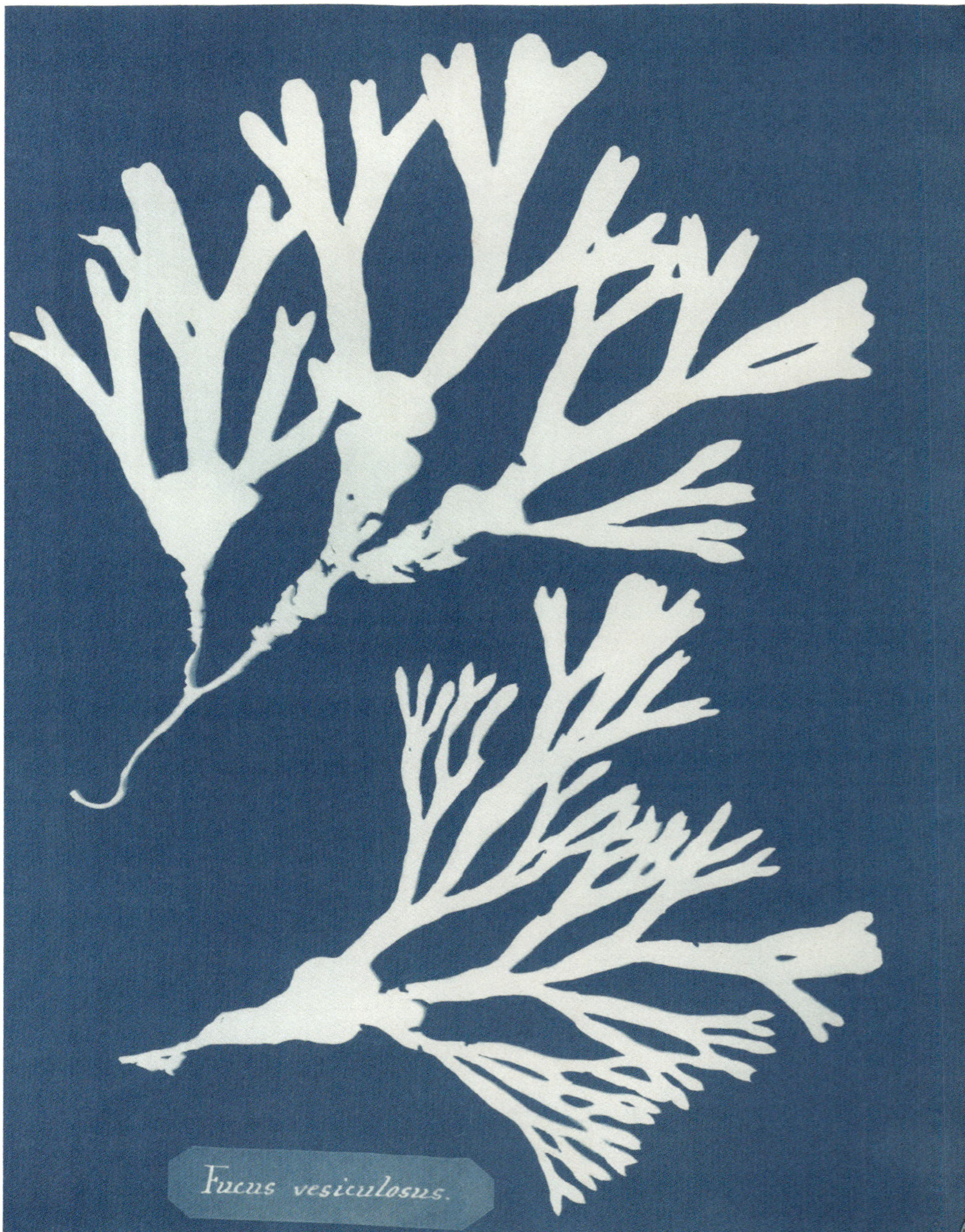

Plate 11. *Fucus vesiculosus*

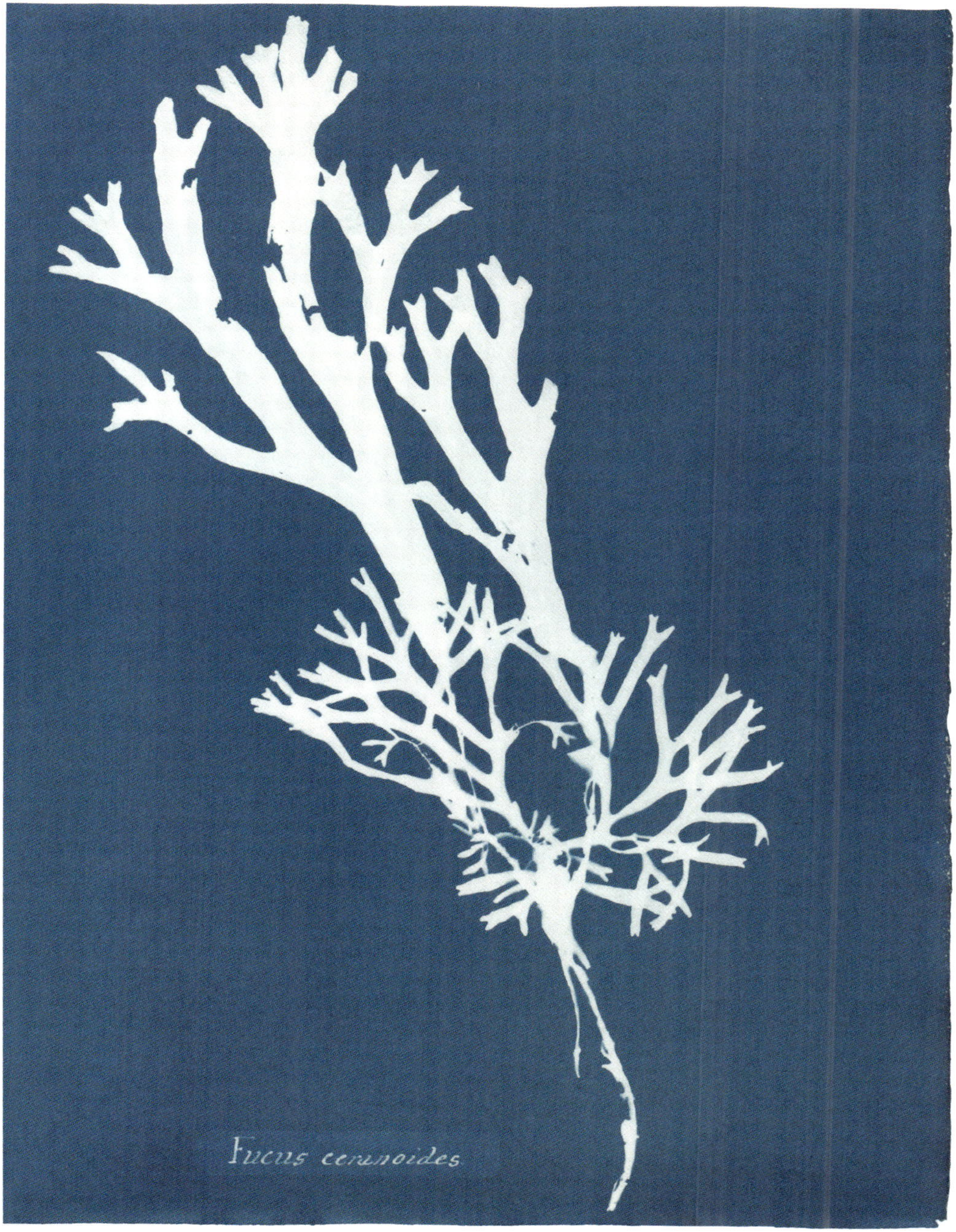

Plate 12. *Fucus ceranoides*

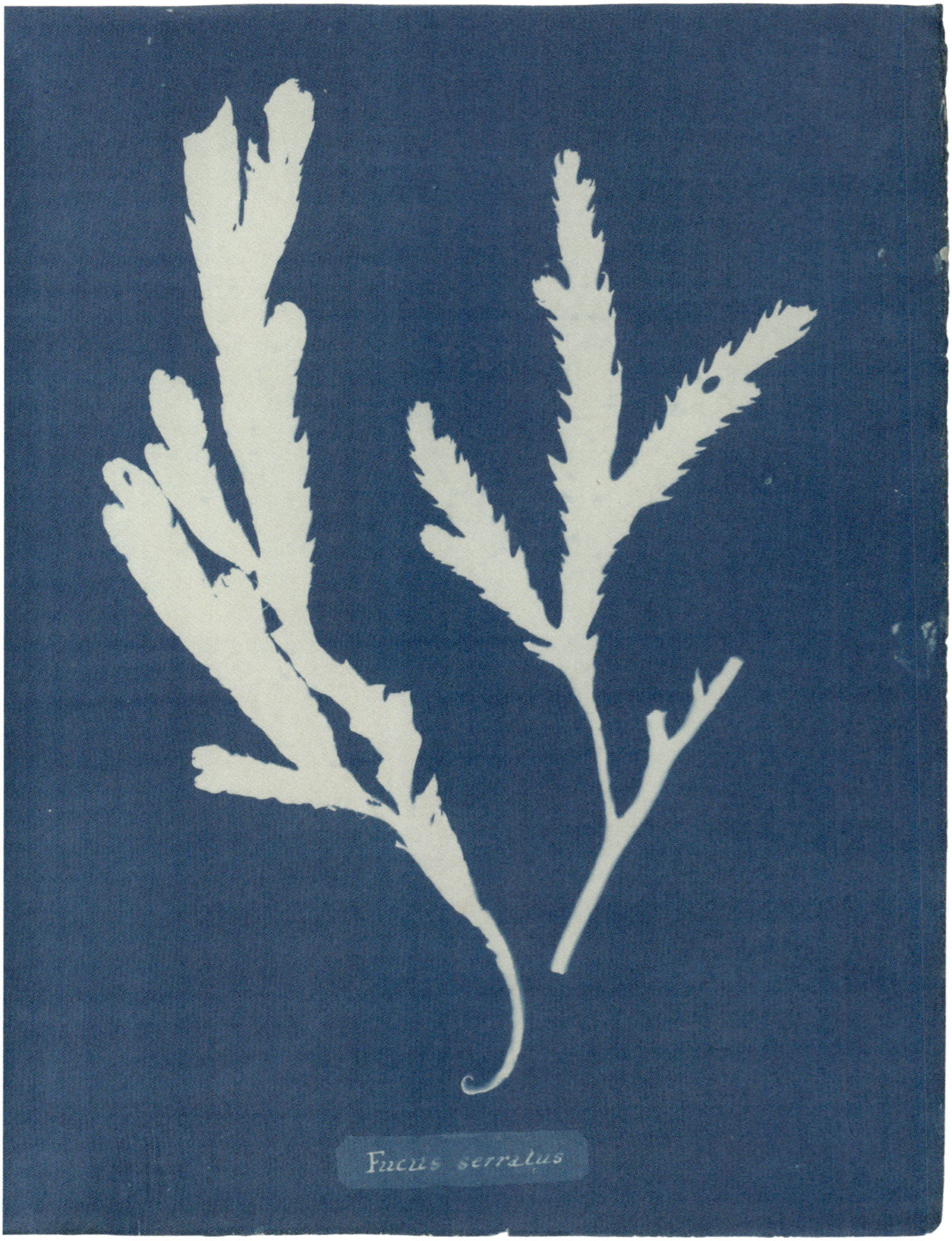

Plate 13. *Fucus serratus*

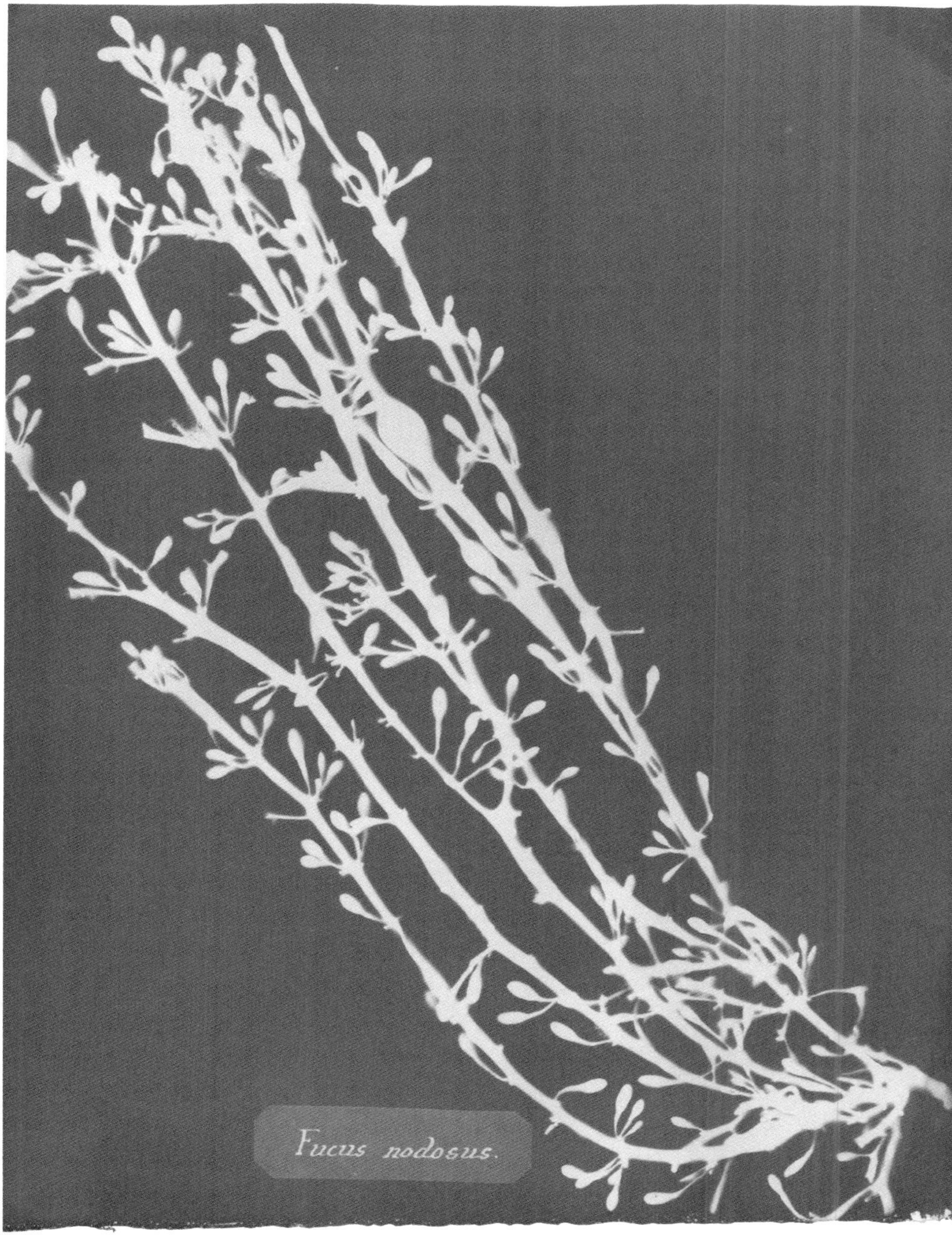

Plate 14. *Fucus nodosus*

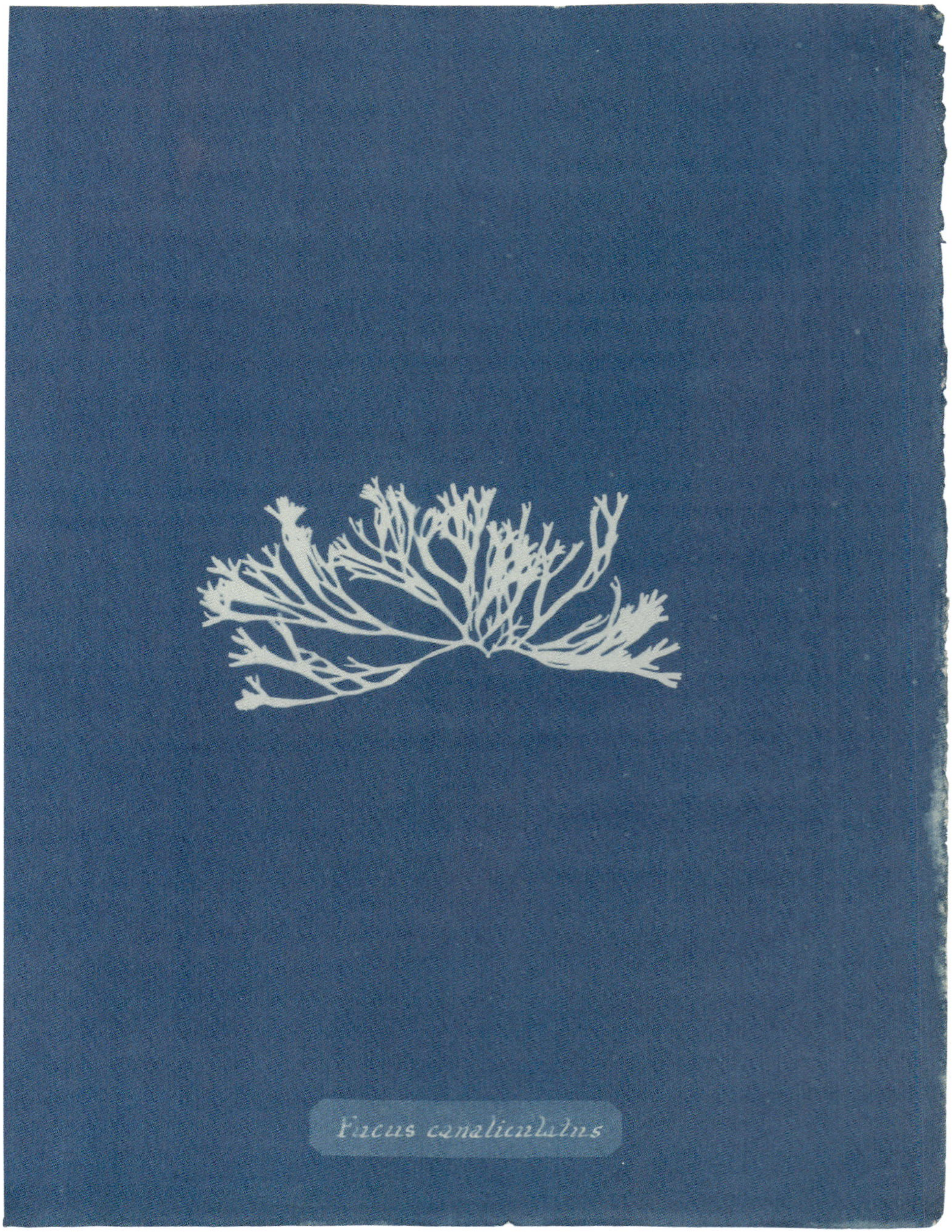

Plate 15. *Fucus canaliculatus*

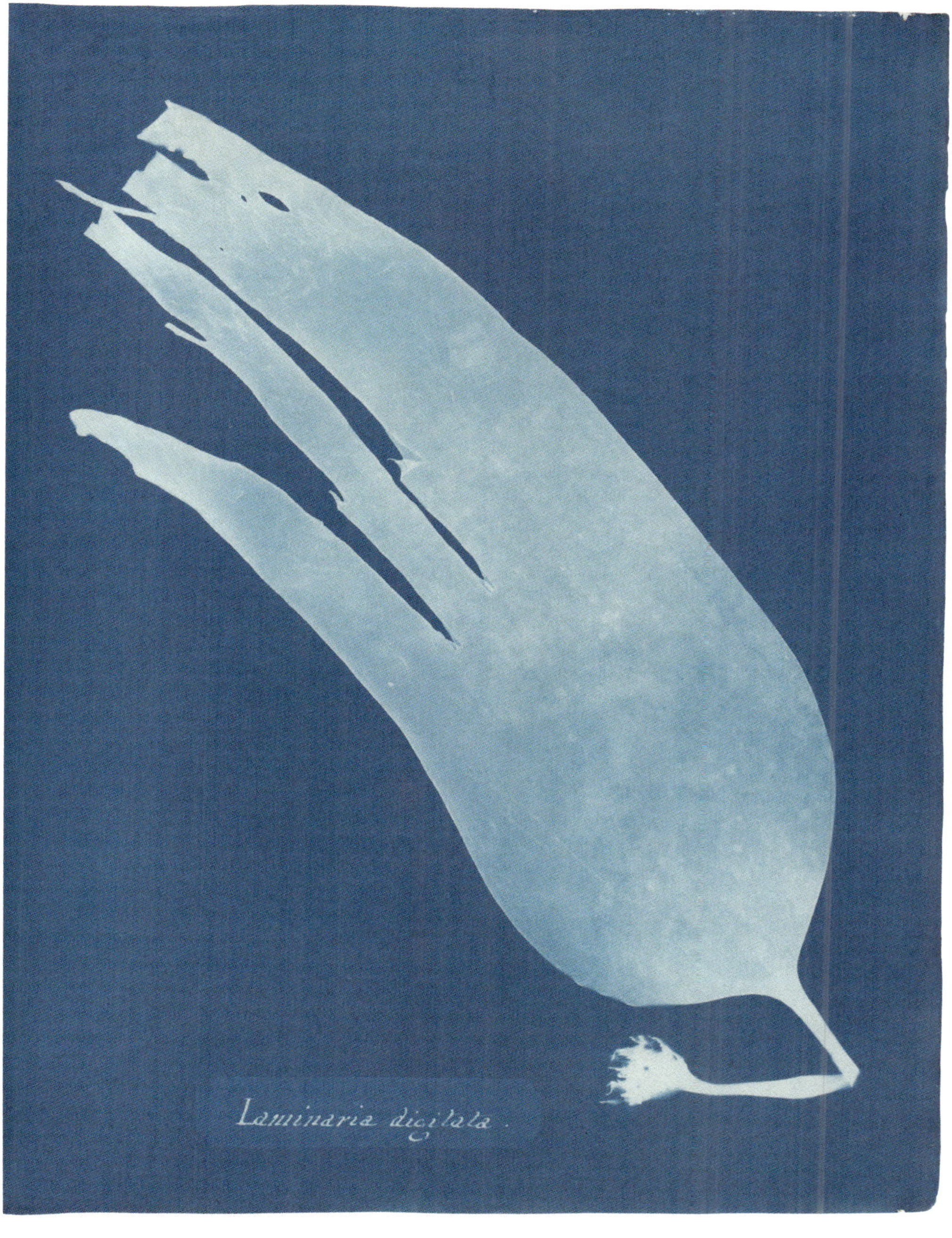

Plate 17. *Laminaria digitata*

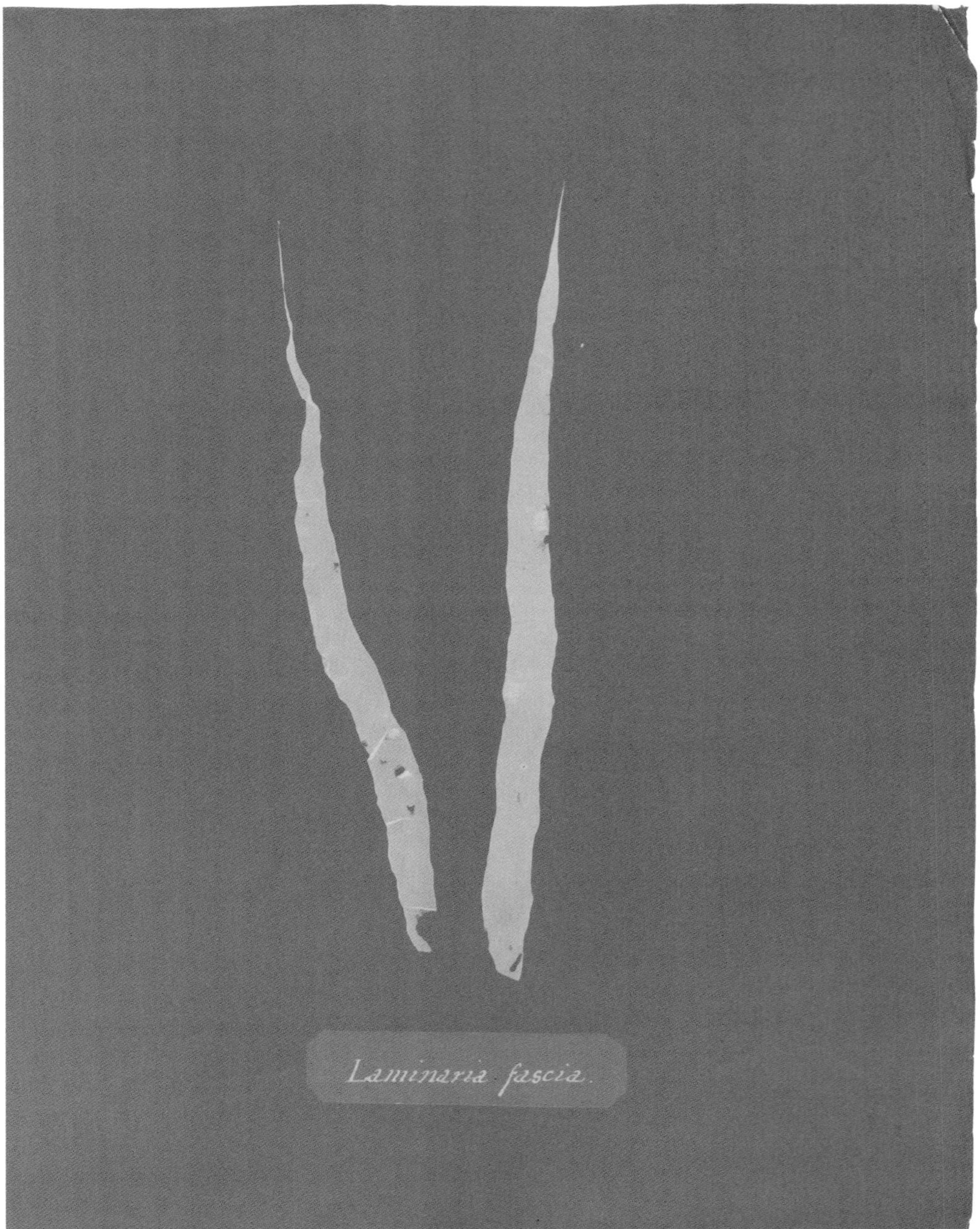

Plate 18. *Laminaria fascia*

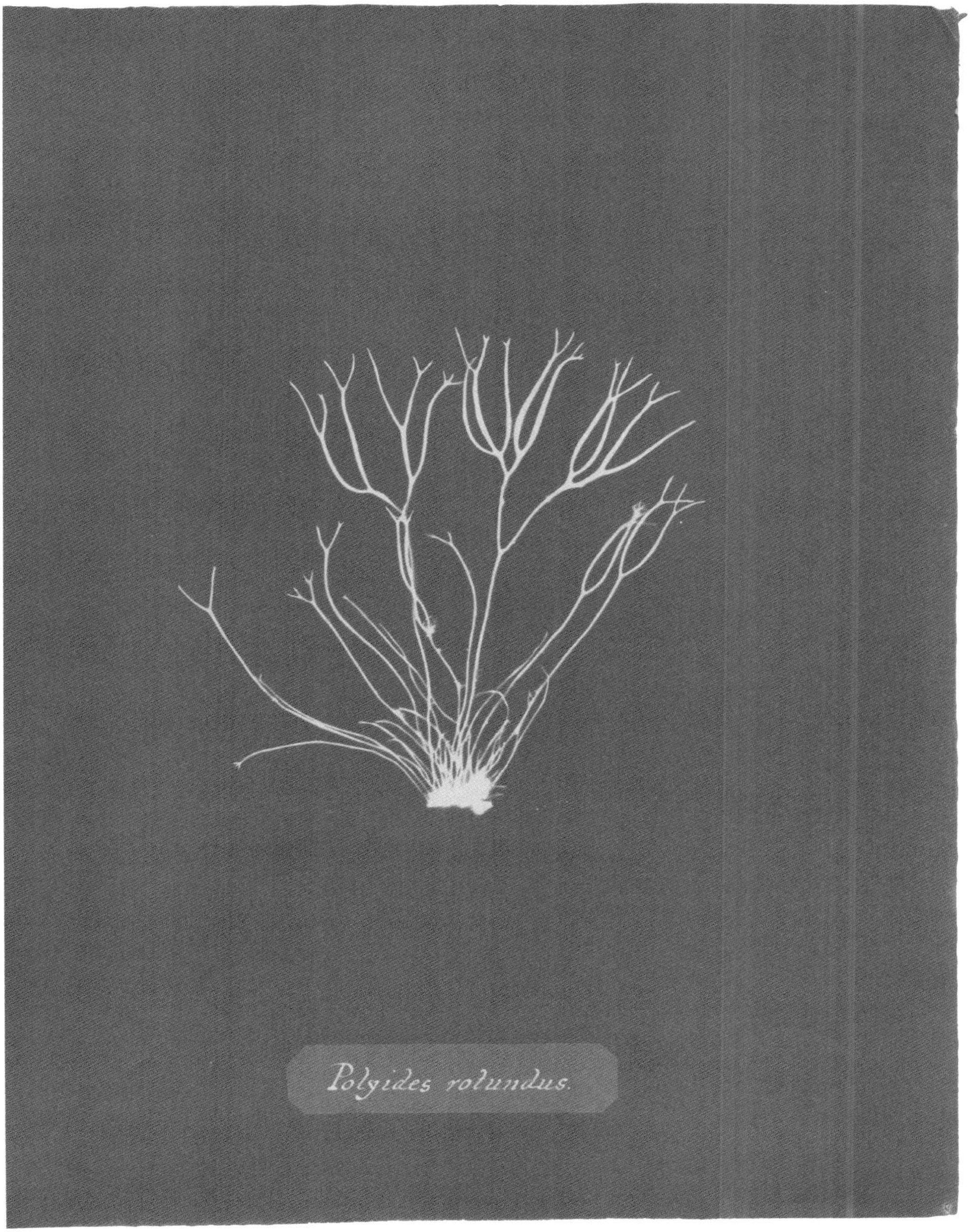

Plate 19. *Polyides rotundus*

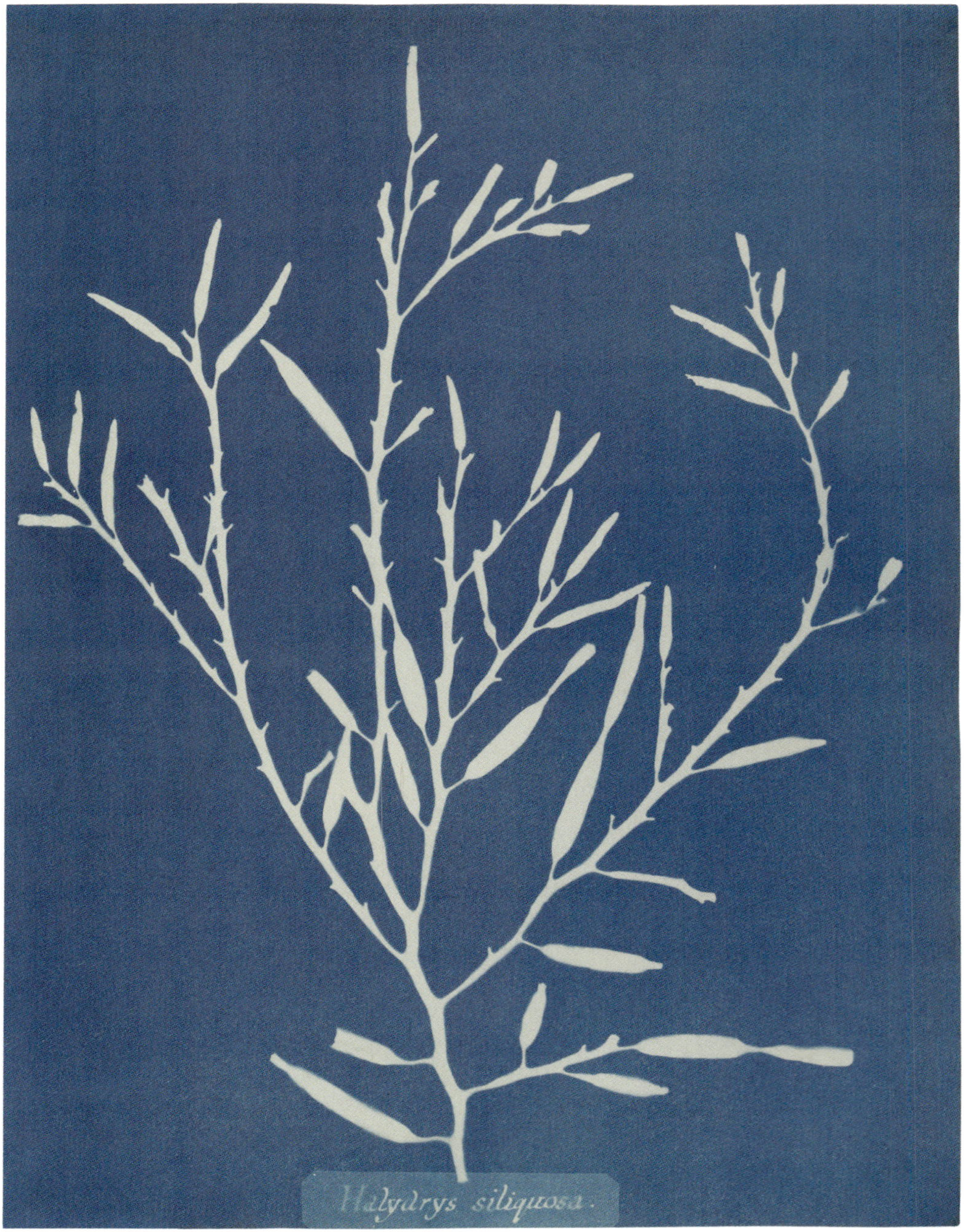

Plate 21. *Halydrys siliquosa*

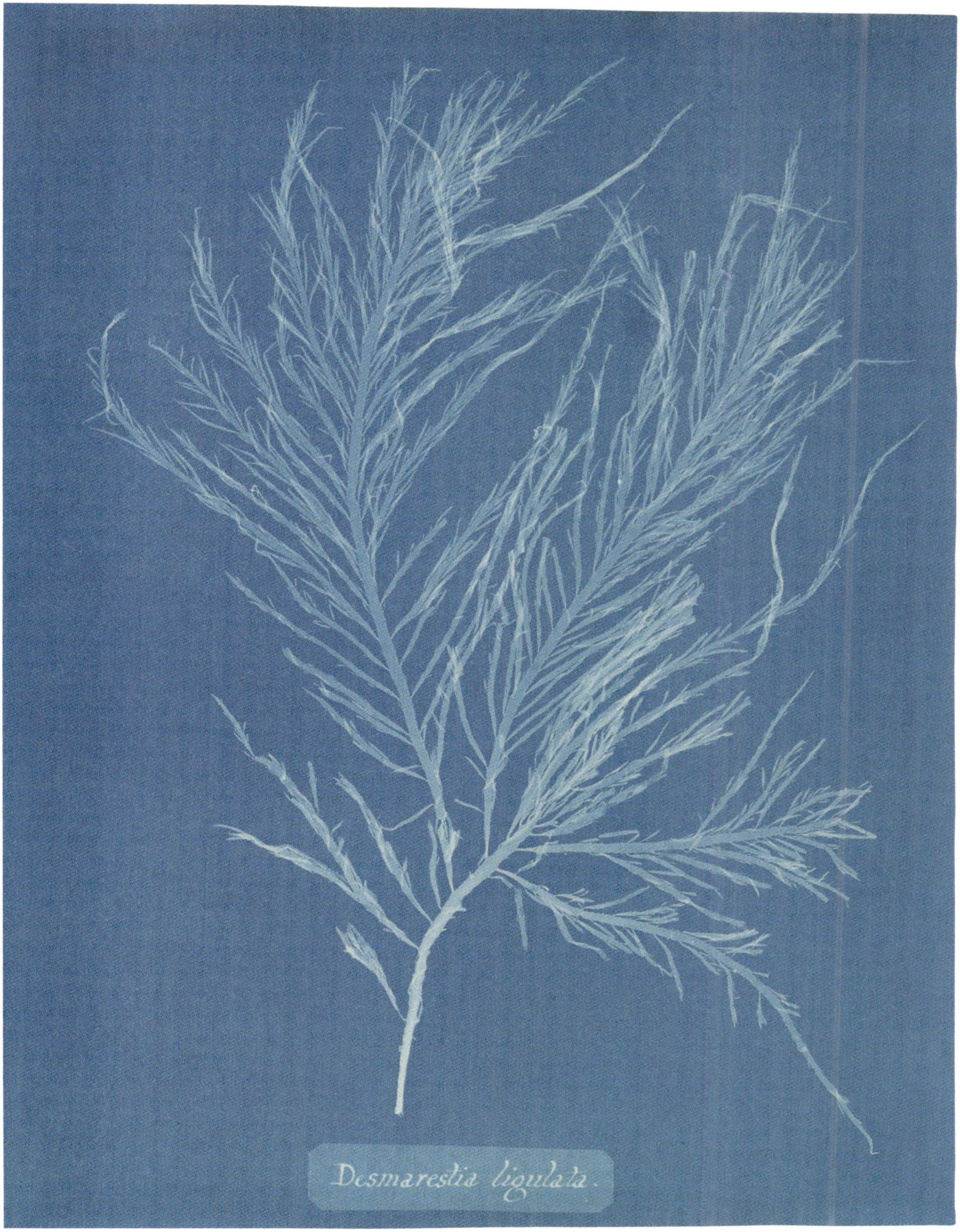

Plate 22. *Desmarestia ligulata*

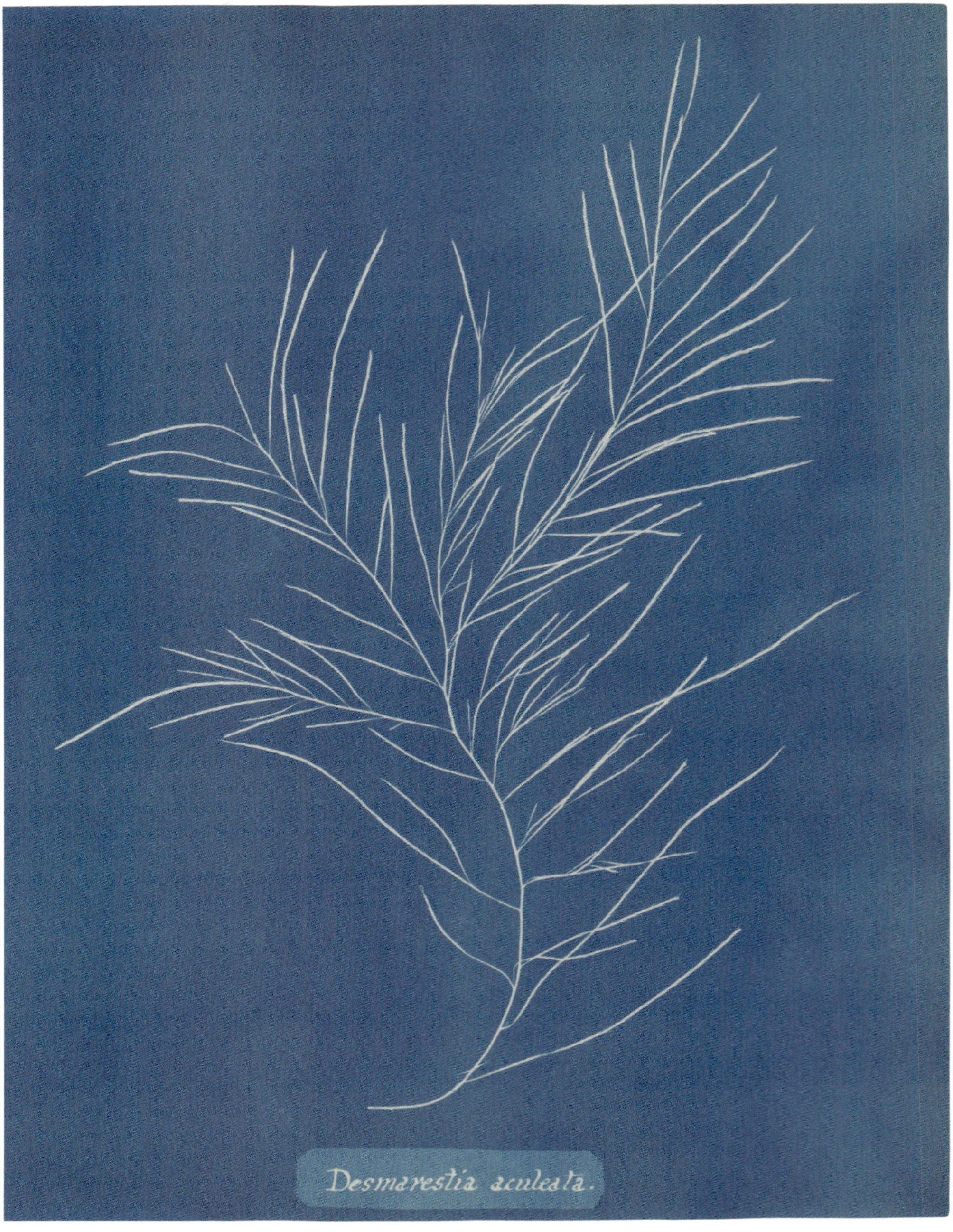

Plate 23. *Desmarestia aculeata*

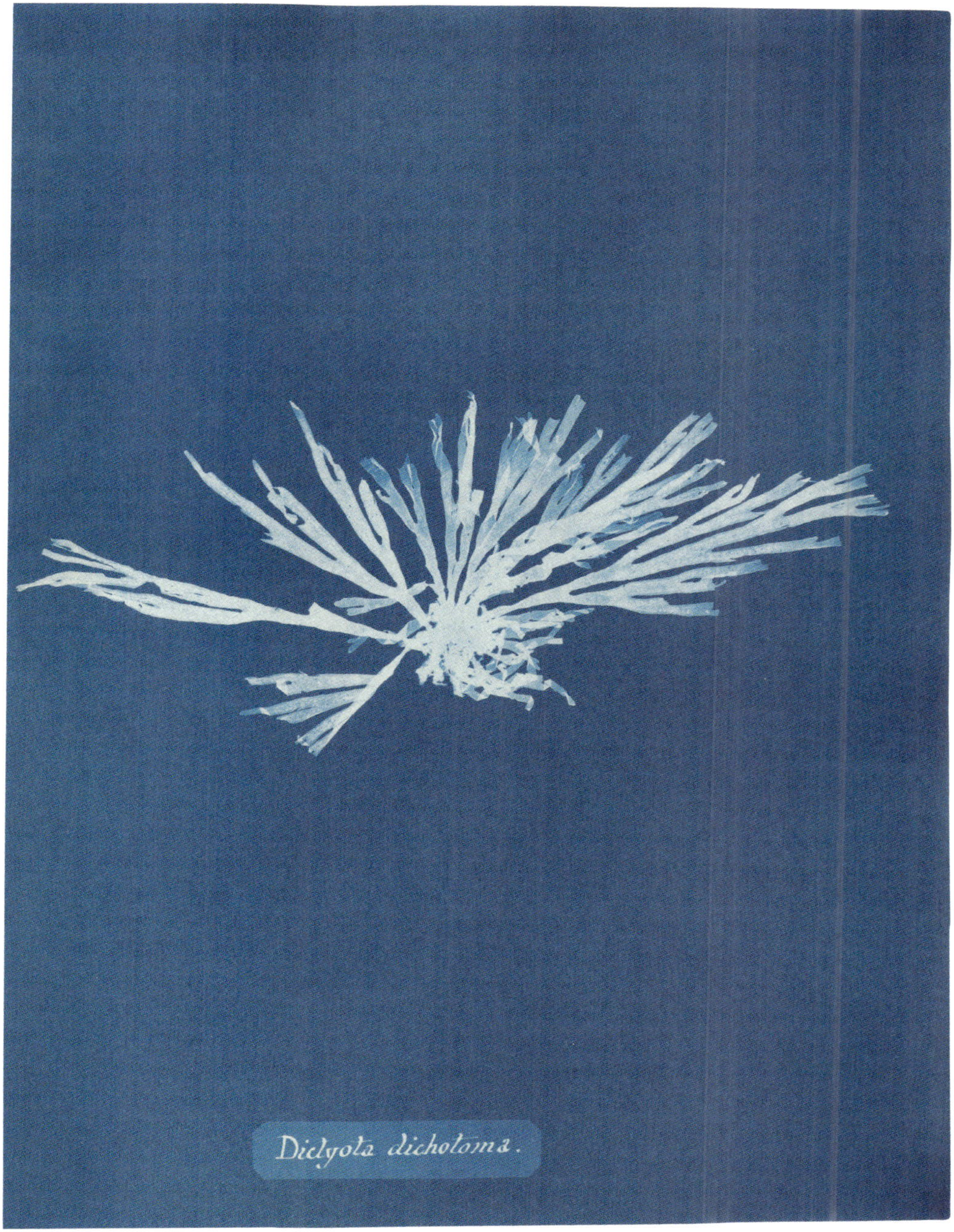

Plate 24. *Dictyota dichotoma*

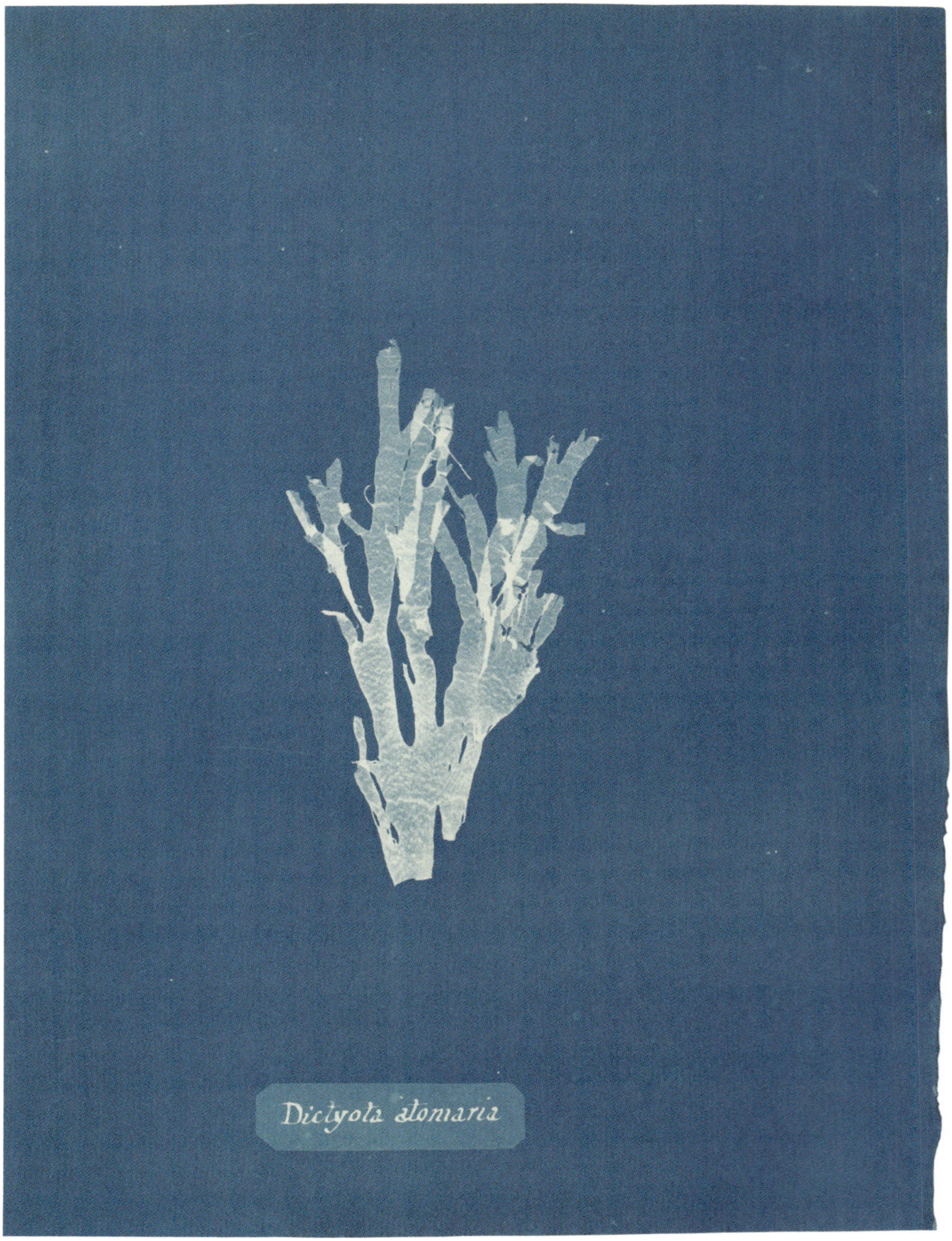

Plate 25. *Dictyota atomaria*

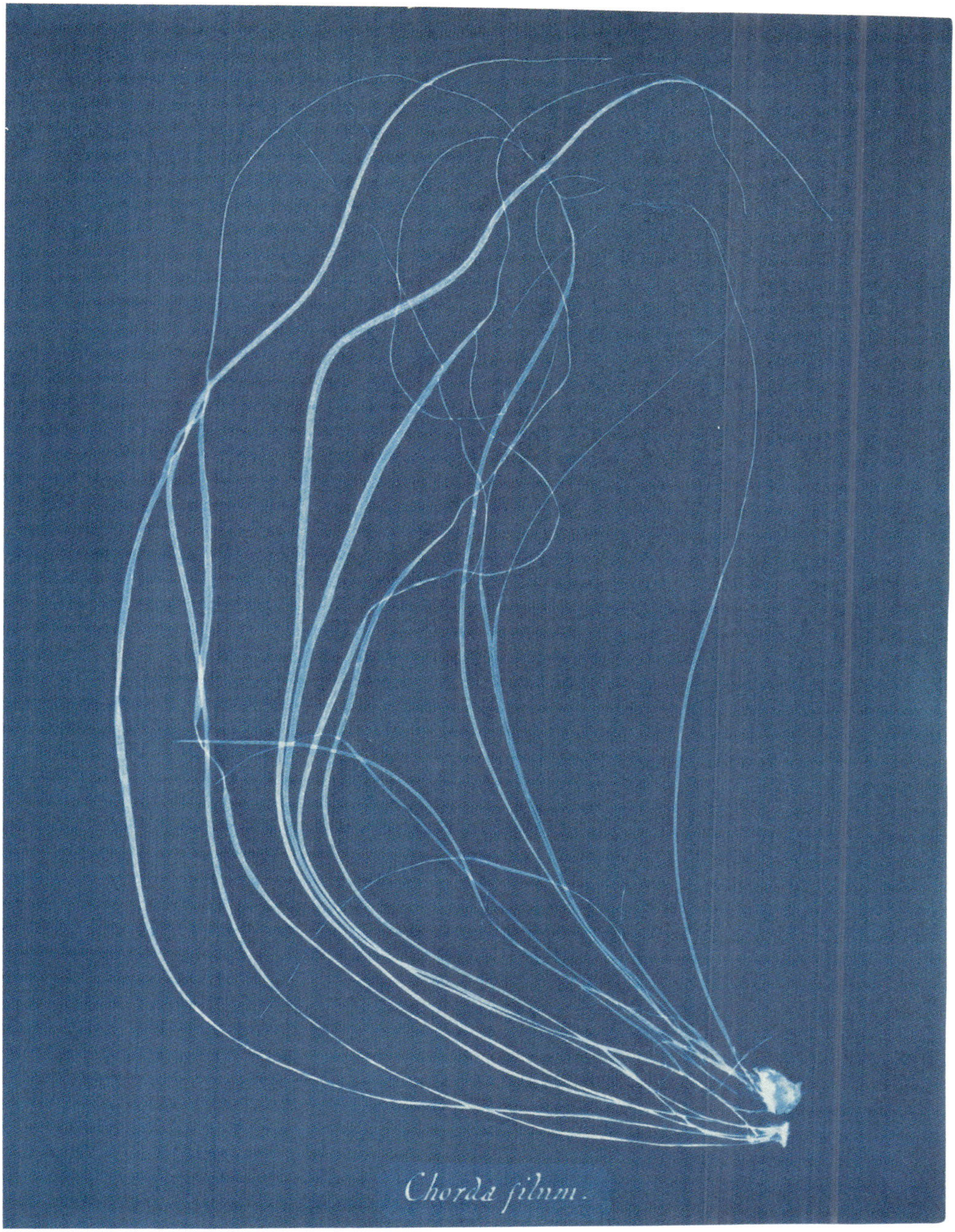

Plate 27. *Chorda filum*

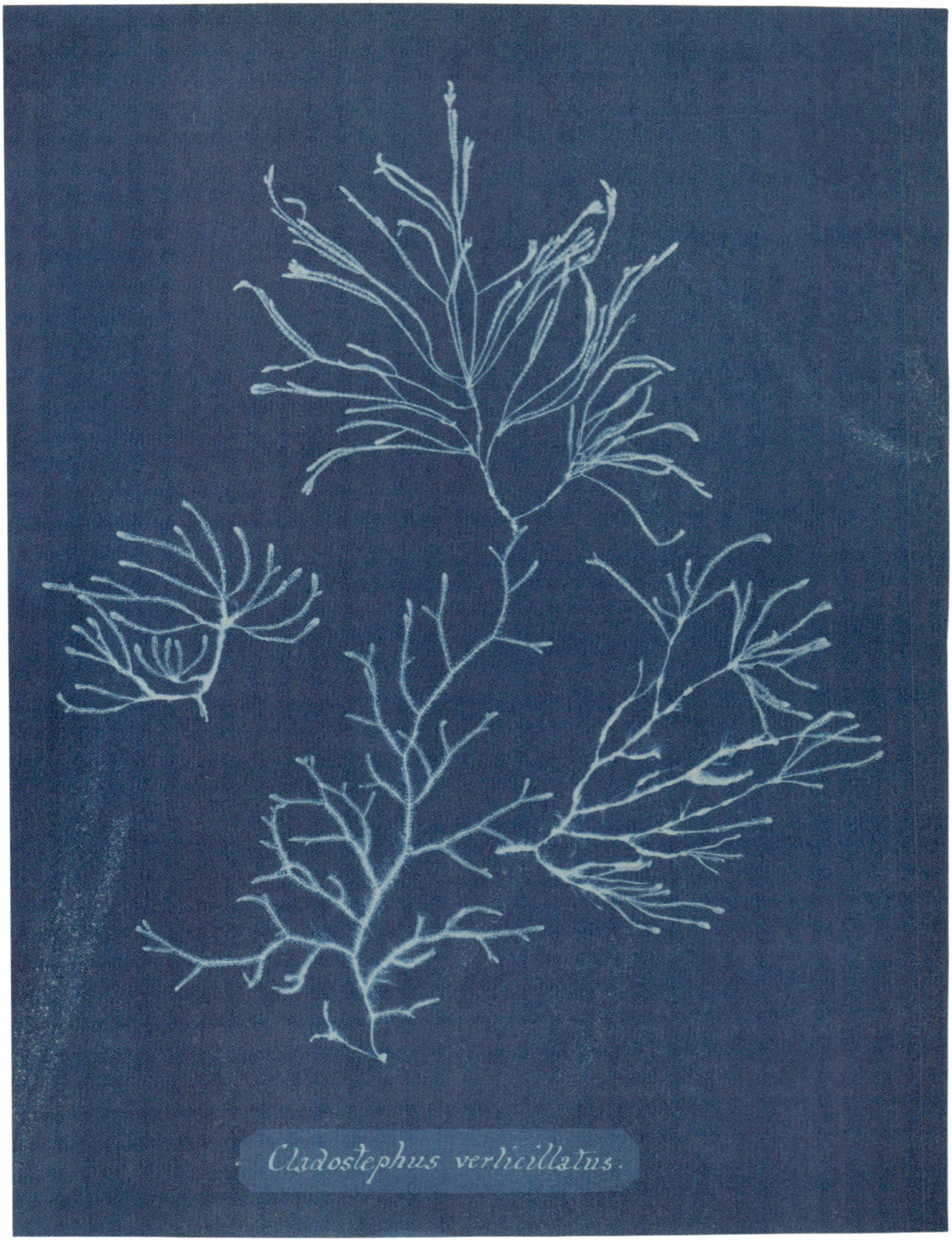

Plate 28. *Cladostephus verticillatus*

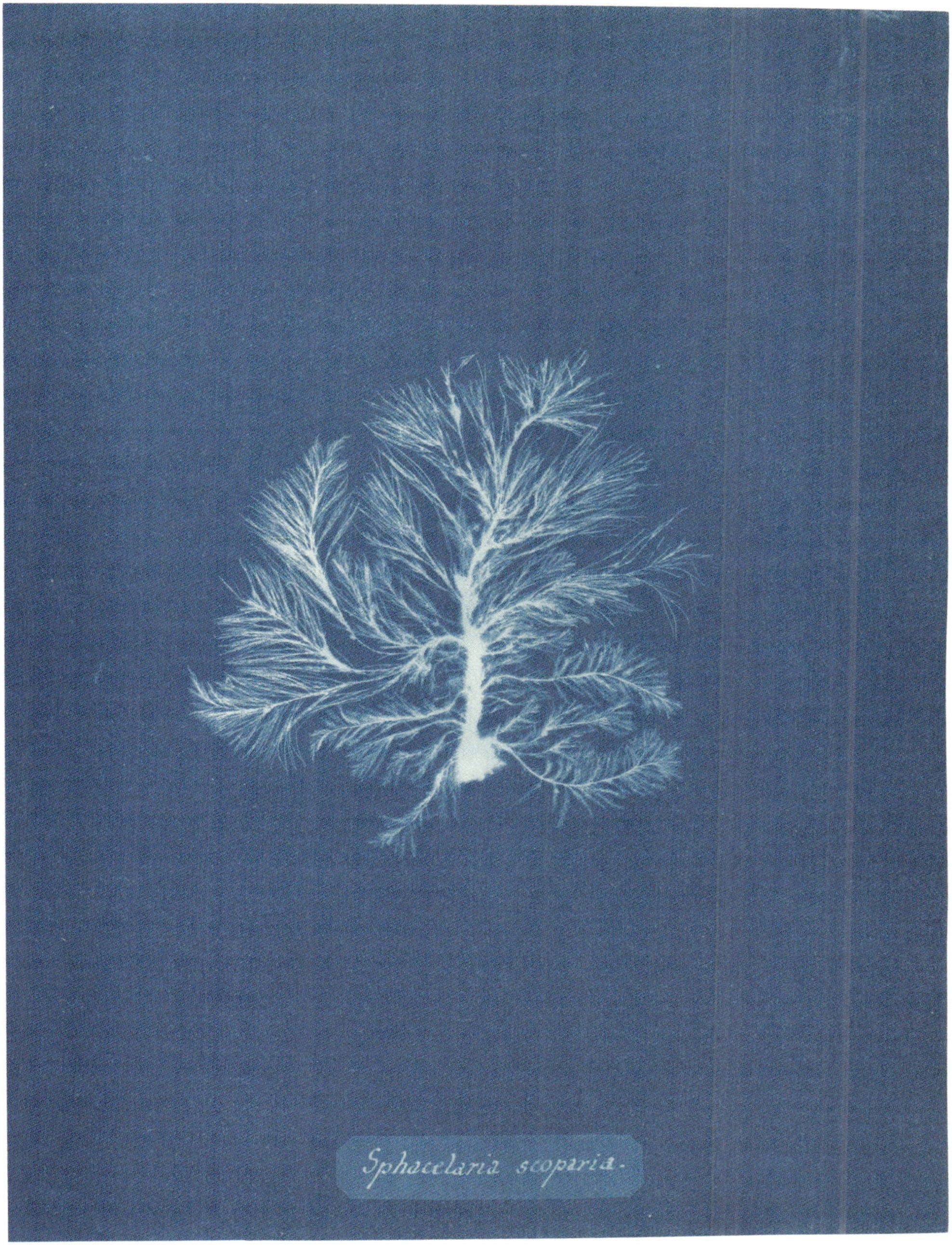

Plate 31. *Sphacelaria scoparia*

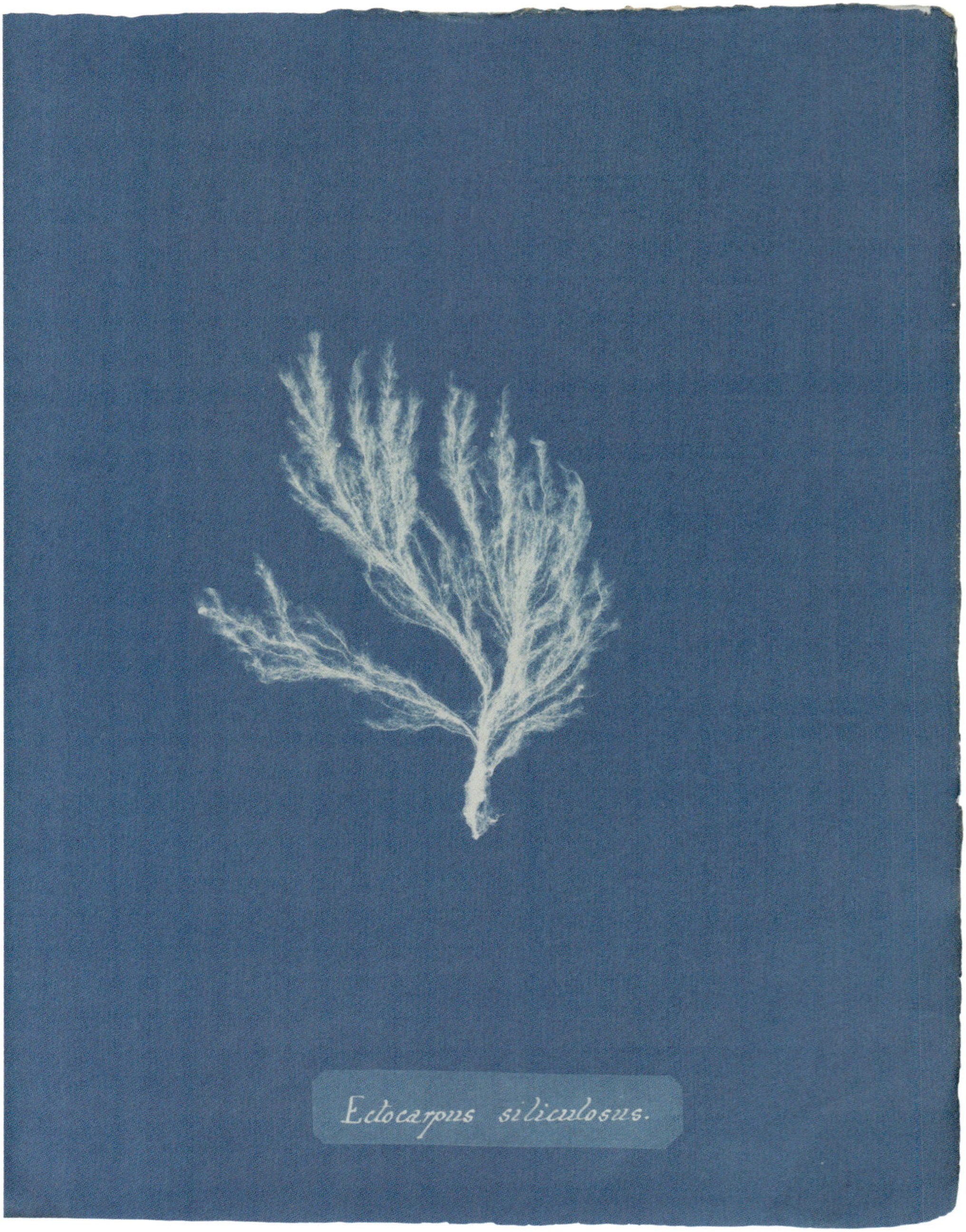

Plate 35. *Ectocarpus siliculosus*

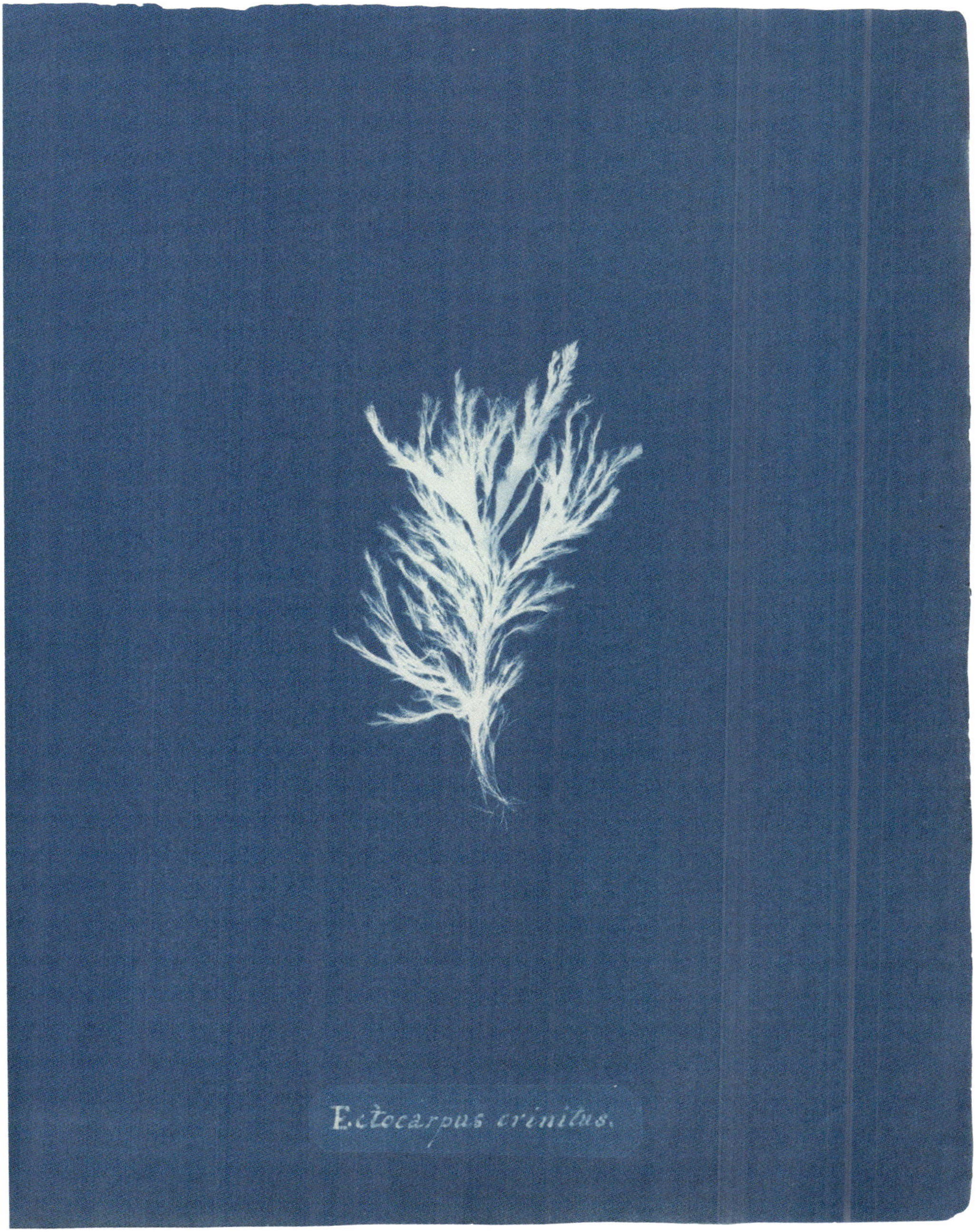

Plate 36. *Ectocarpus crinitus*

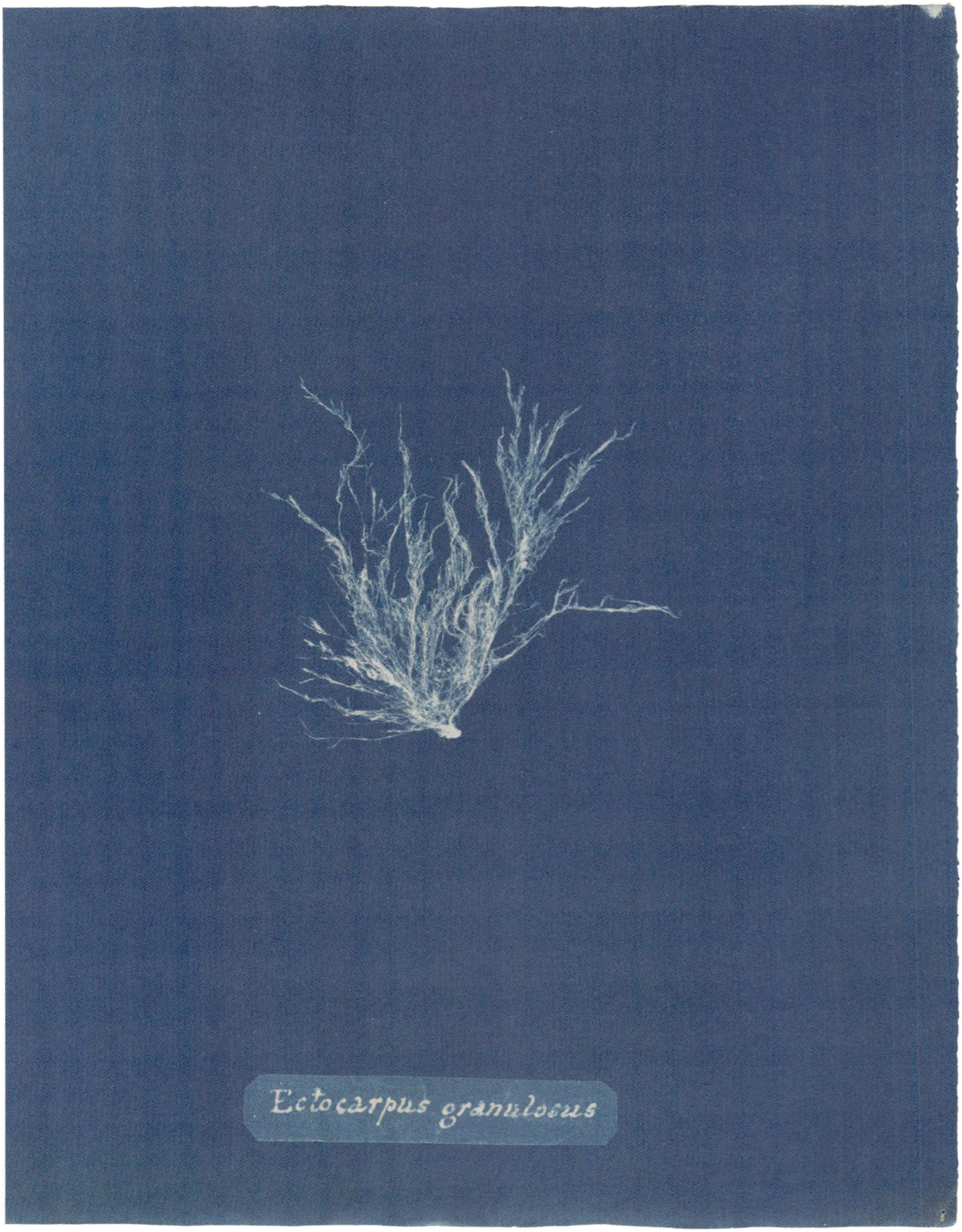

Plate 37. *Ectocarpus granulosus*

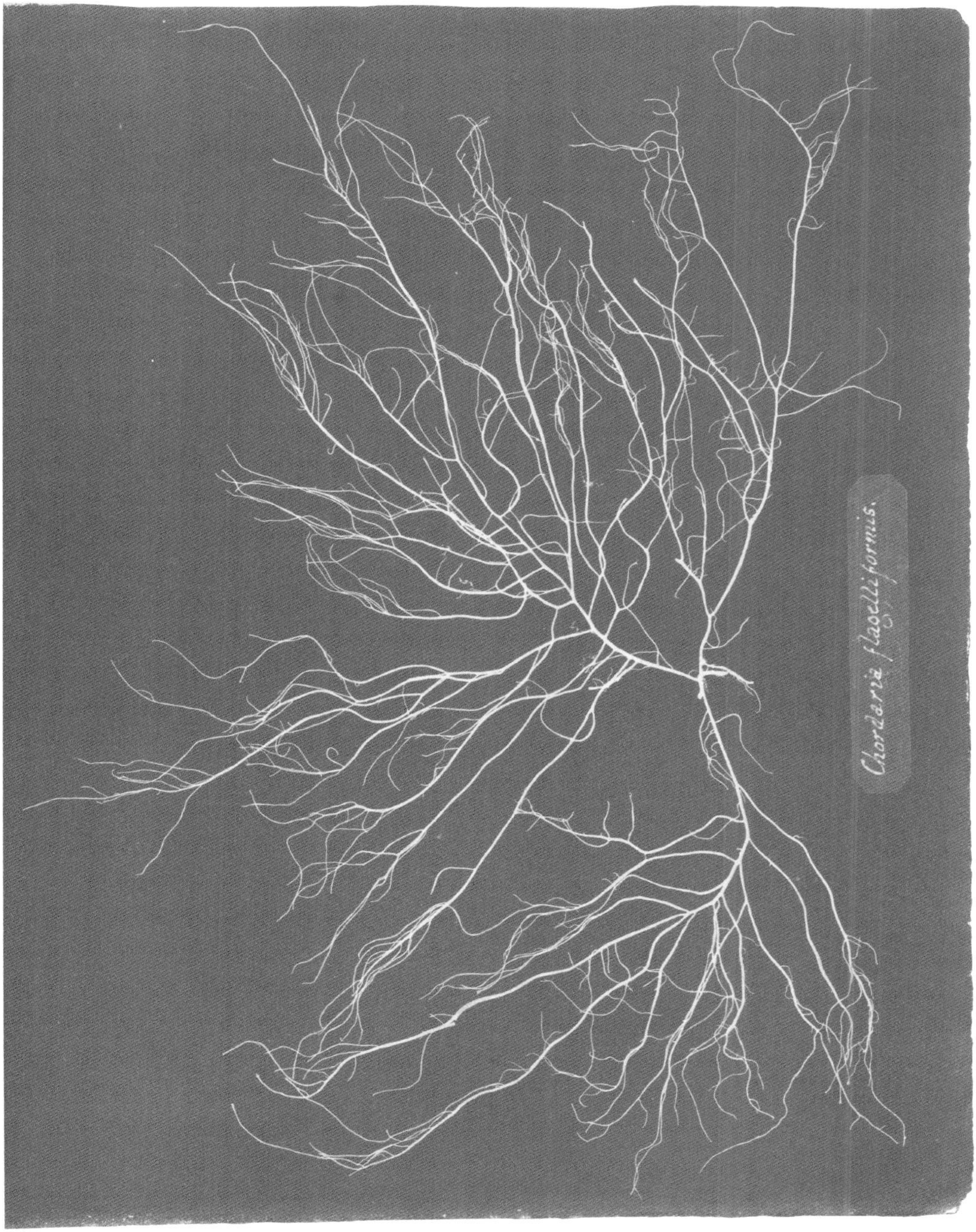

Plate 40. *Chordaria flagelliformis*

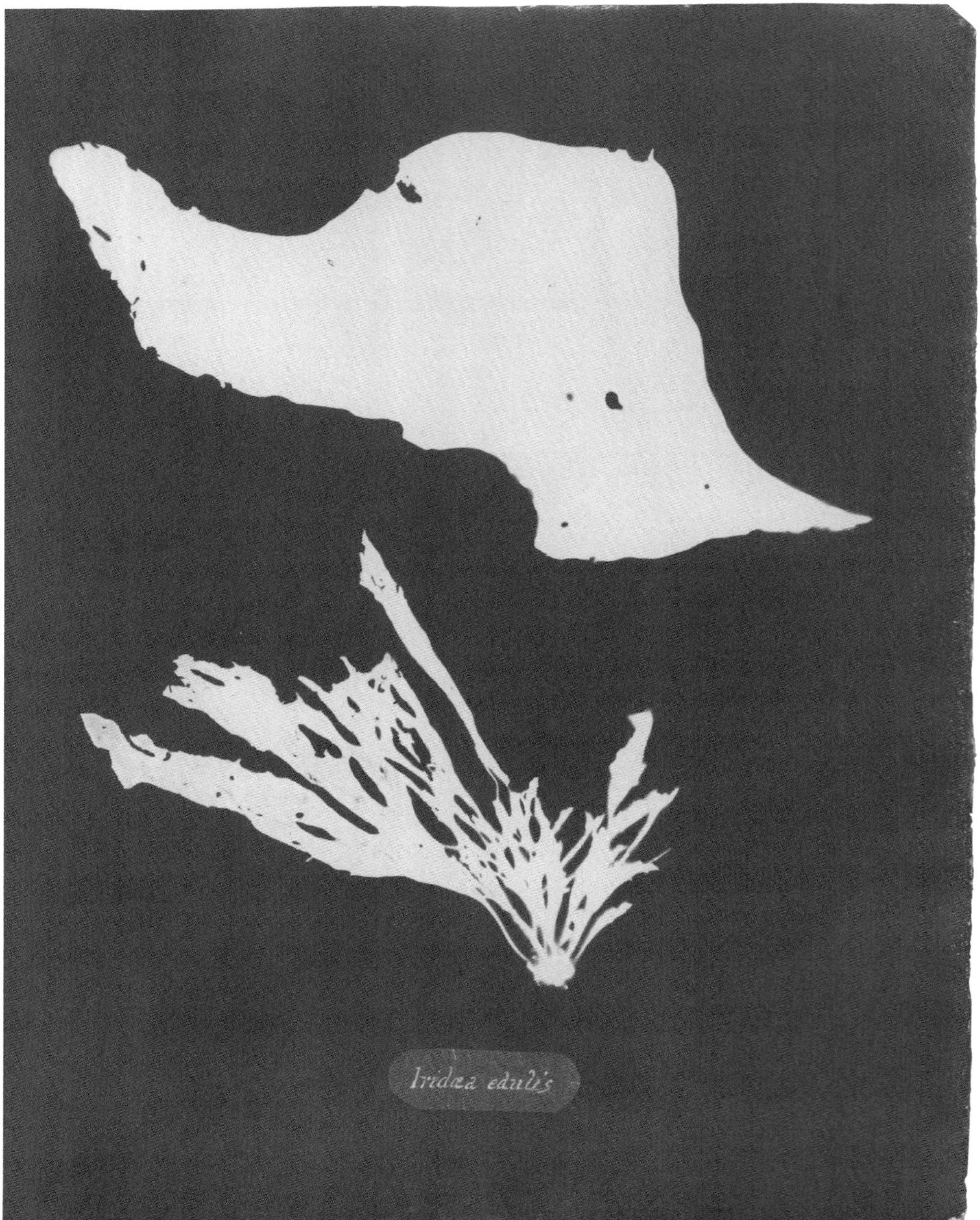

Plate 43. *Iridaea edulis*

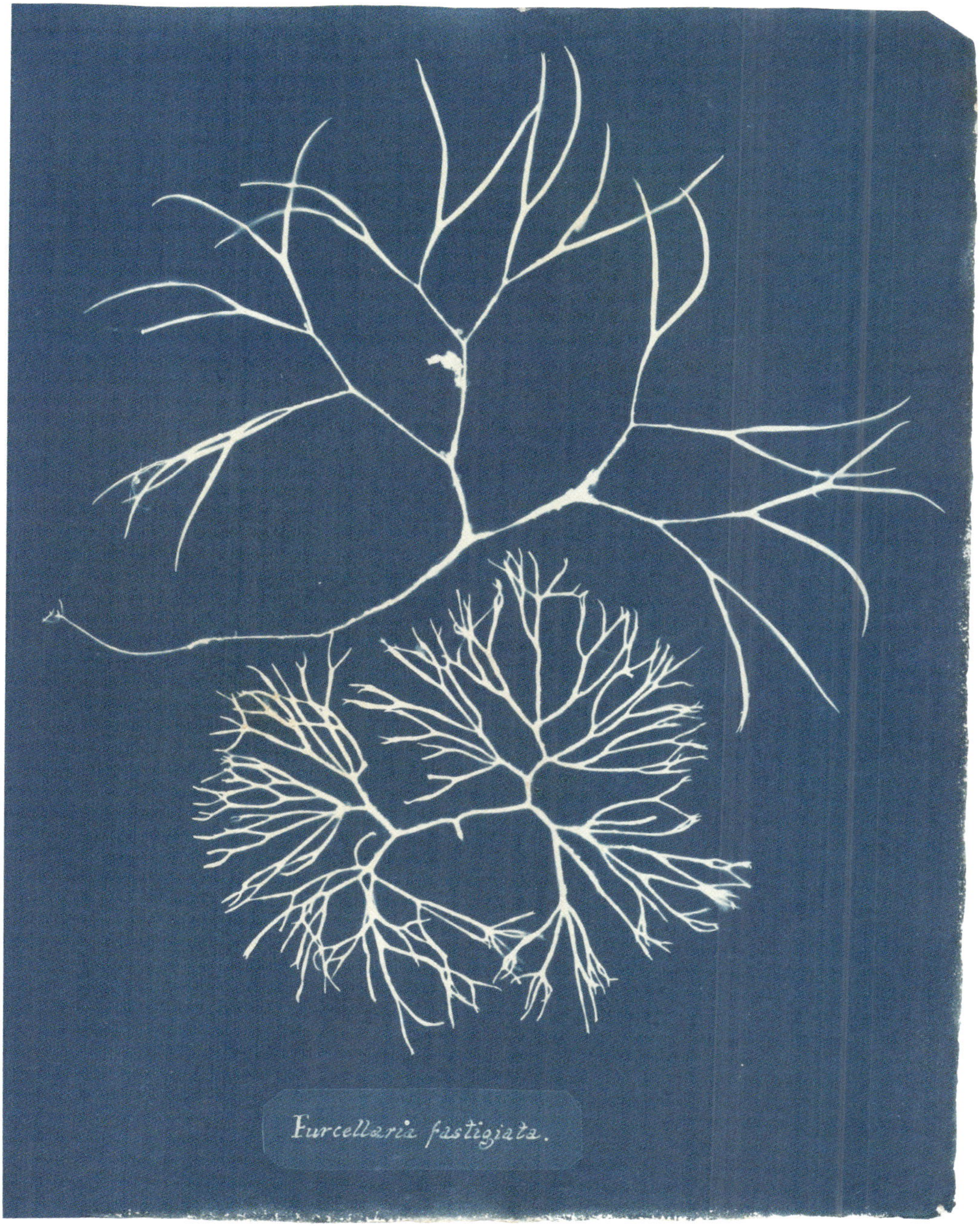

Plate 44. *Furcellaria fastigiata*

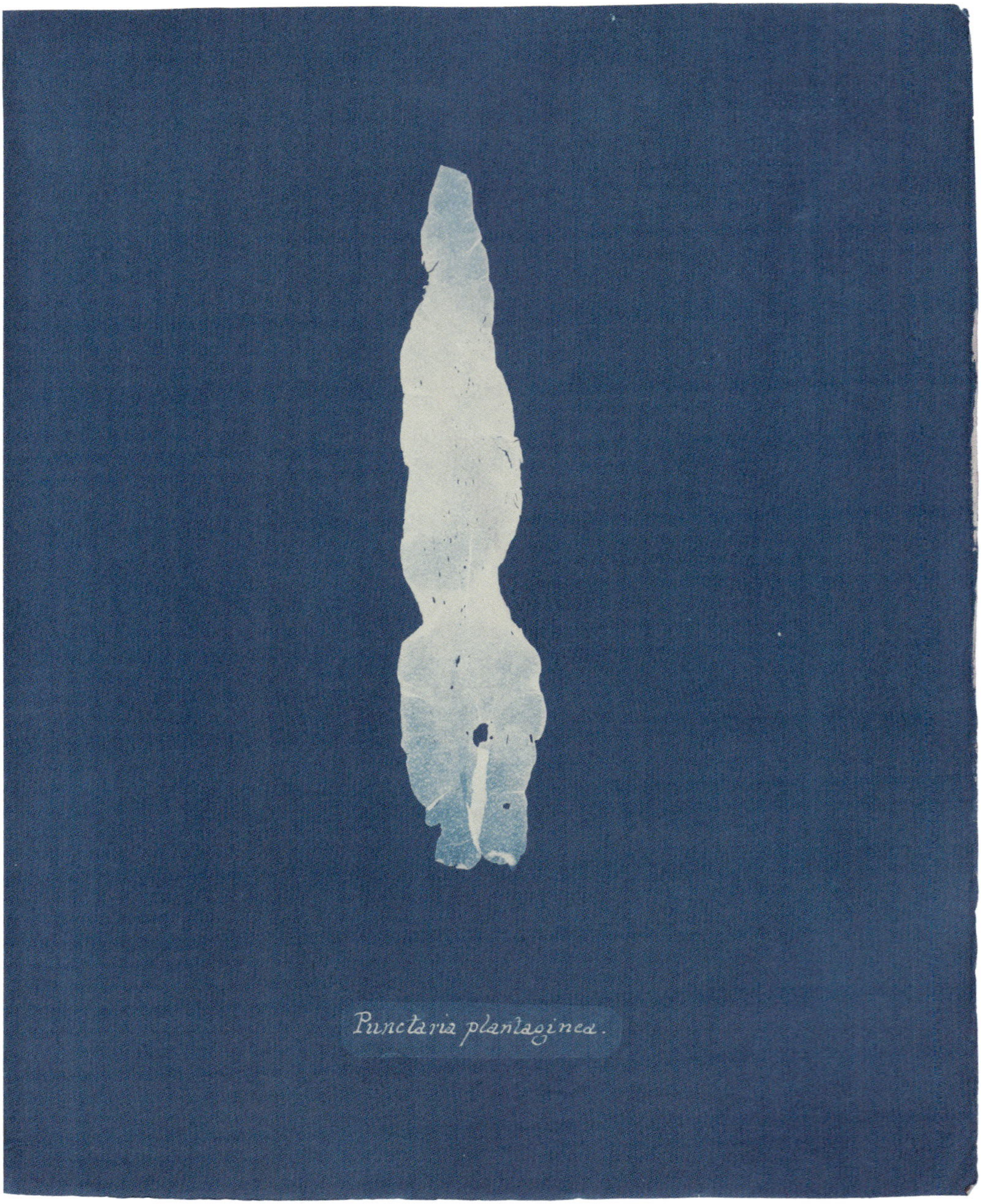

Plate 45. *Punctaria plantaginea*

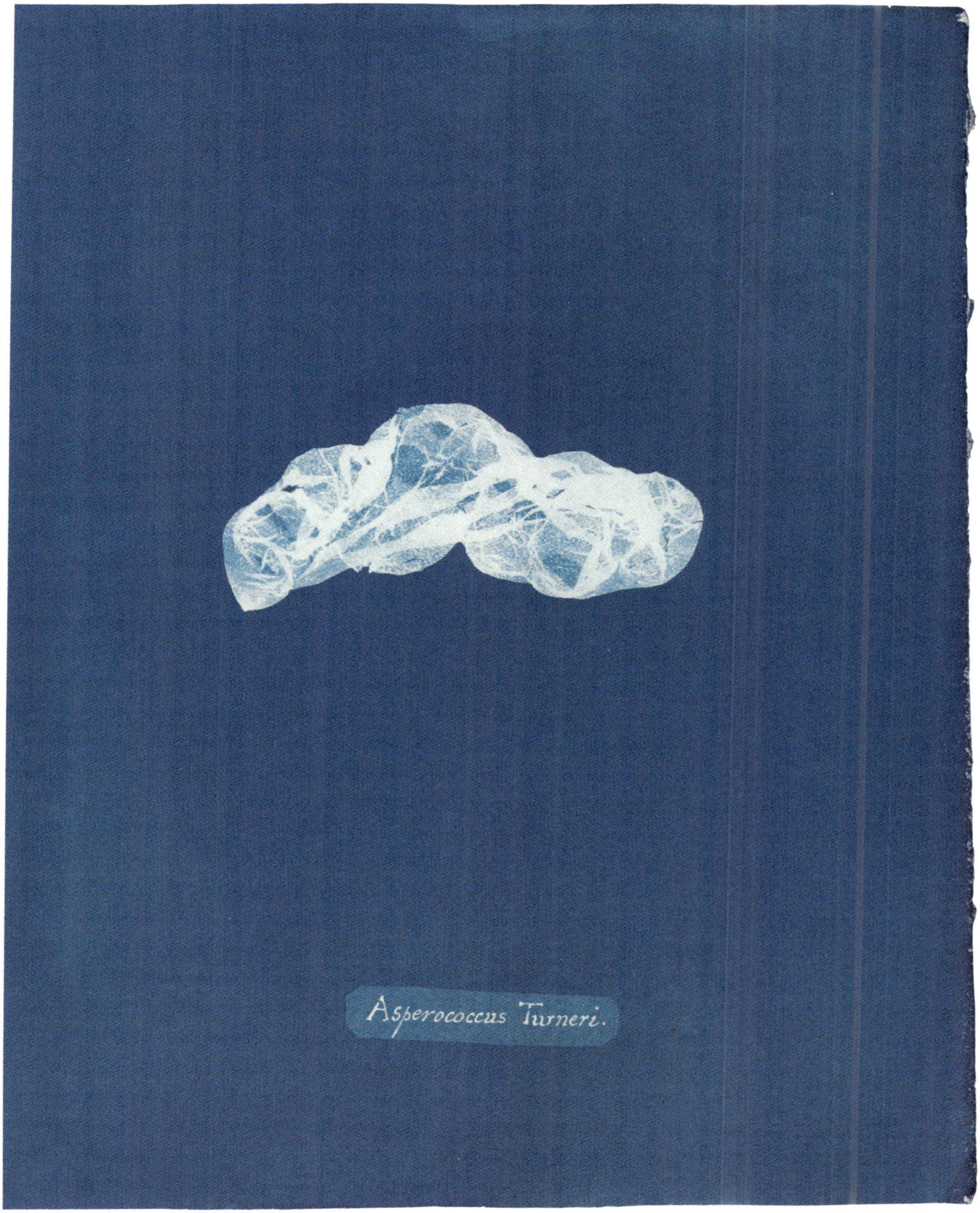

Plate 46. *Asperococcus turneri*

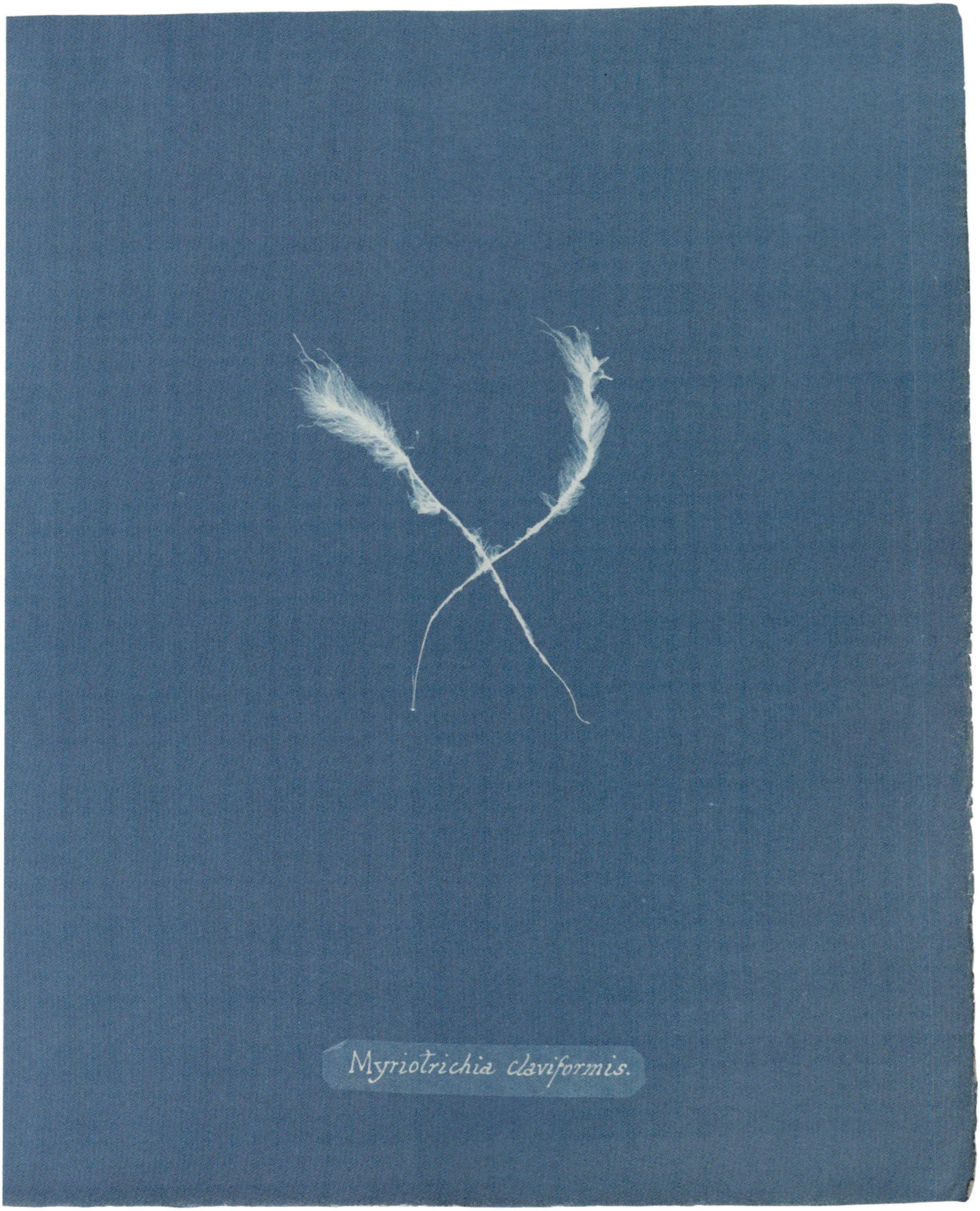

Plate 47. *Myriotrichia claviformis*

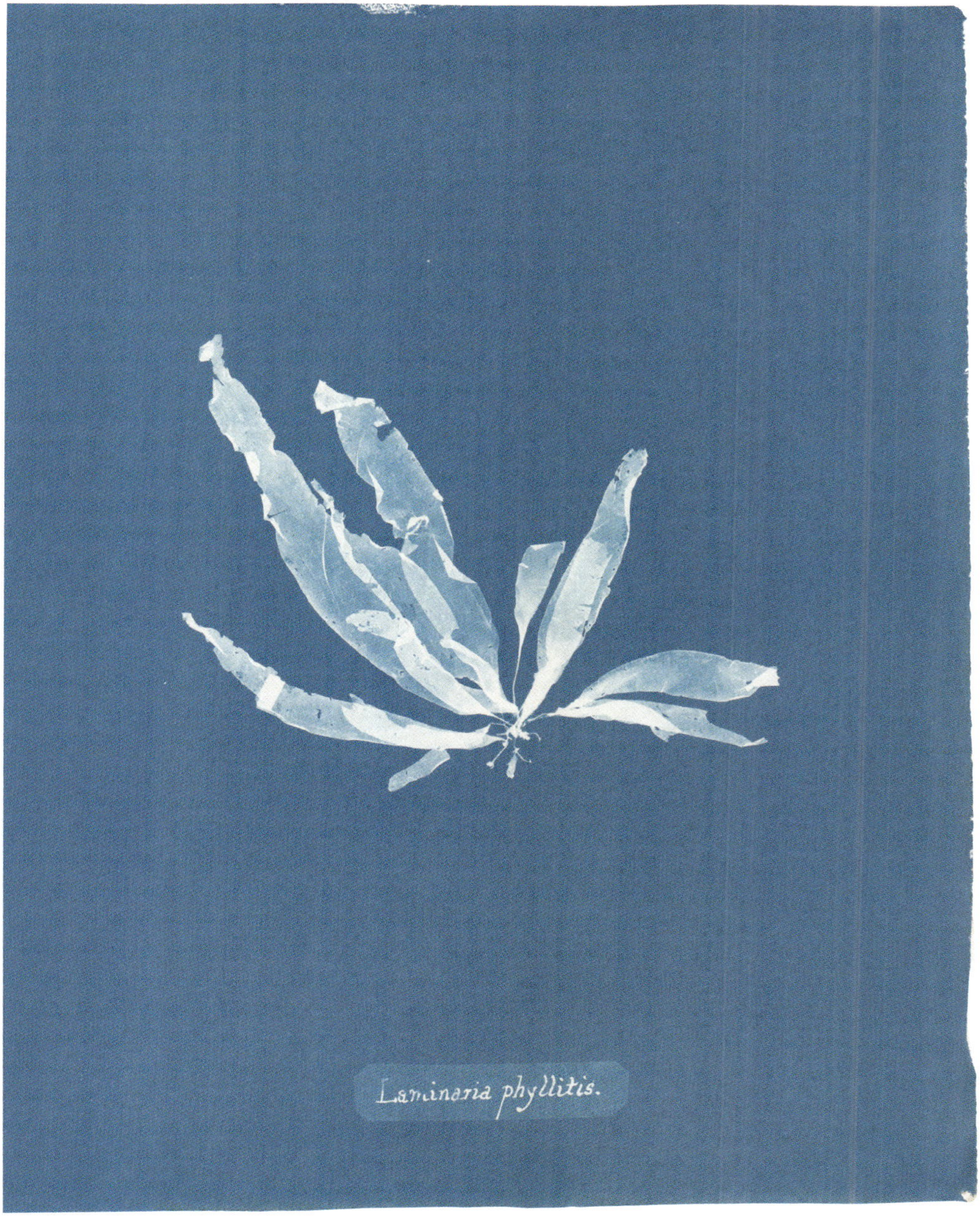

Plate 48. *Laminaria phyllitis*

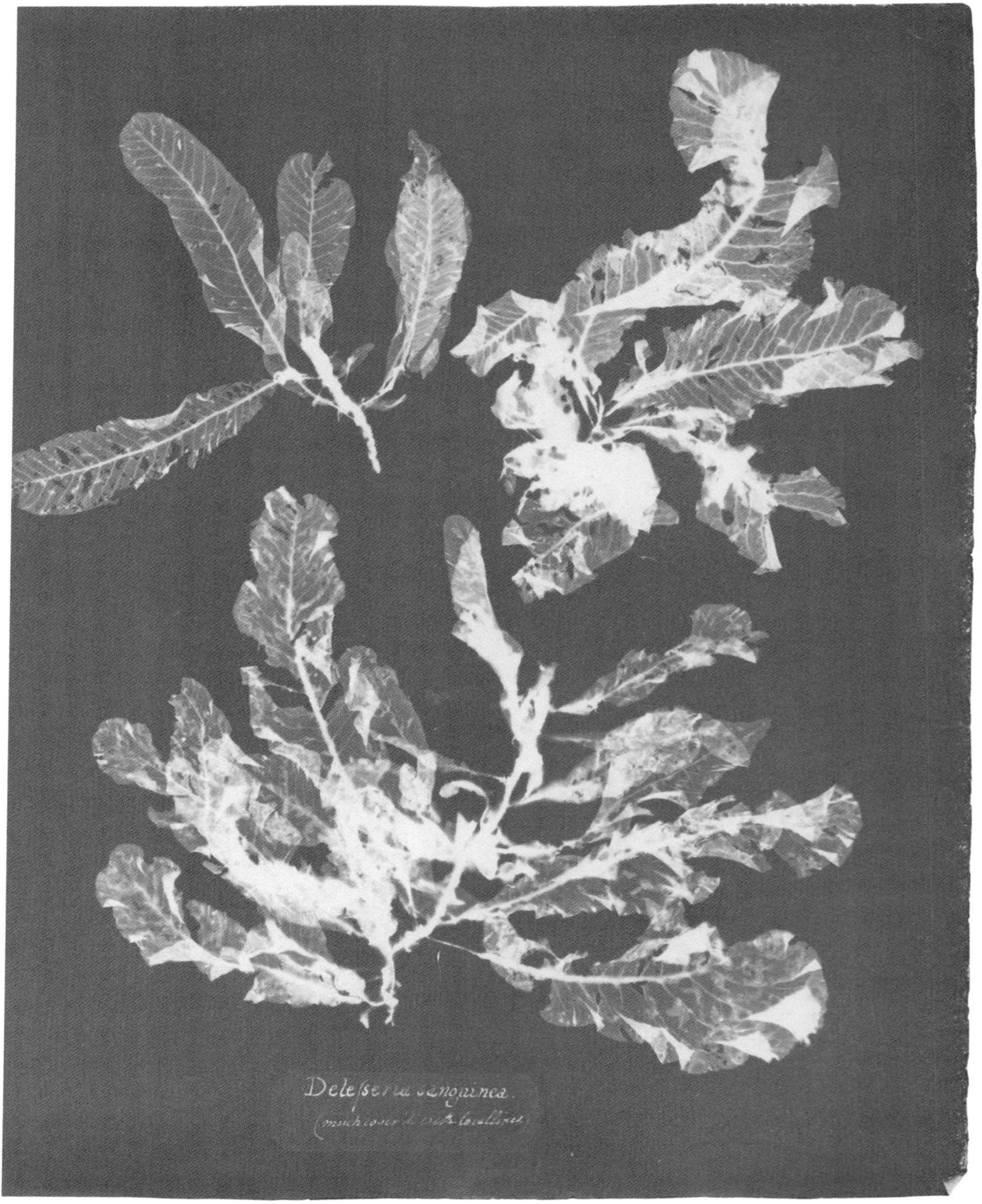

Plate 49. *Delesseria sanguinea* (much covered with Corallines)

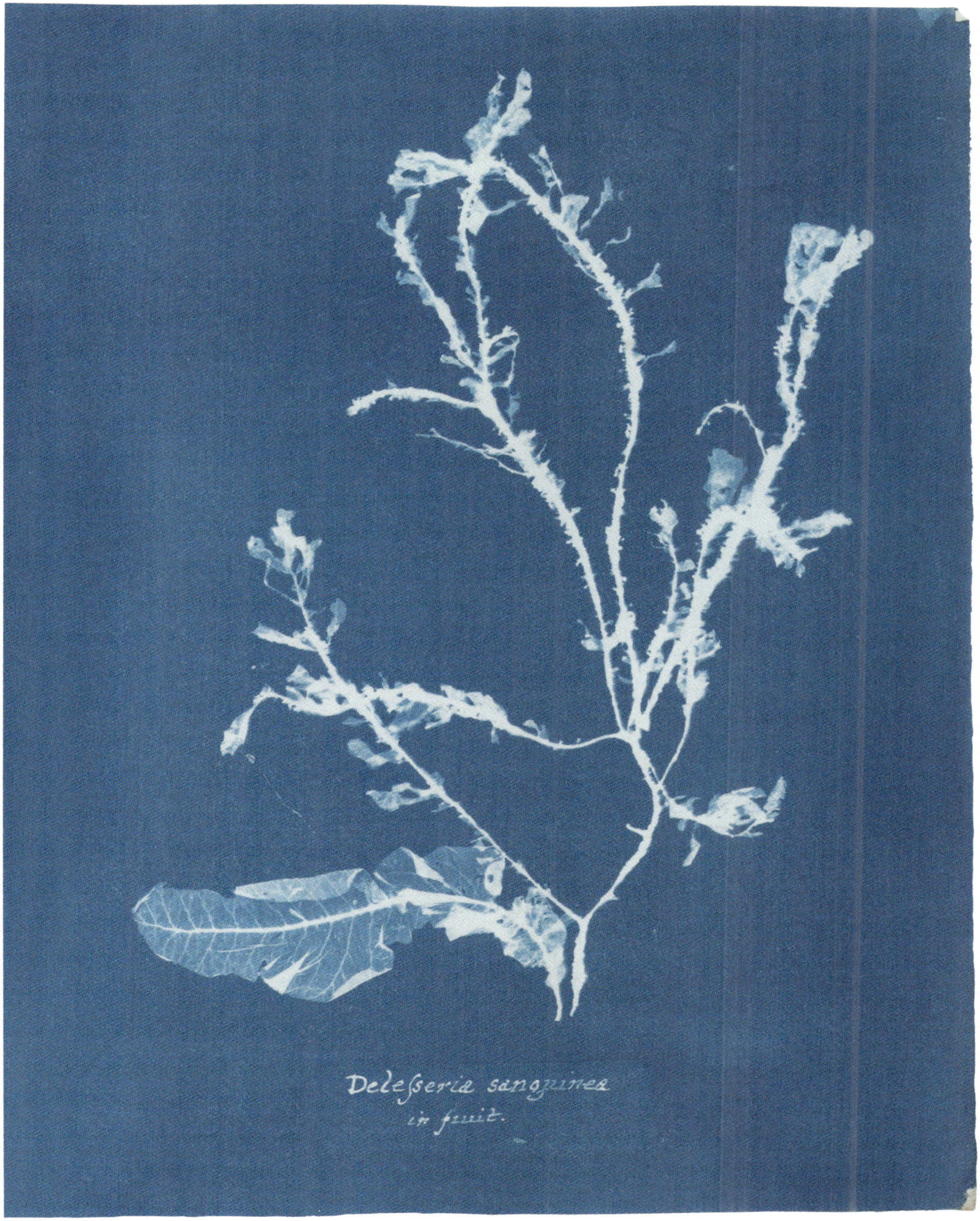

Plate 50. *Delesseria sanguinea* in fruit

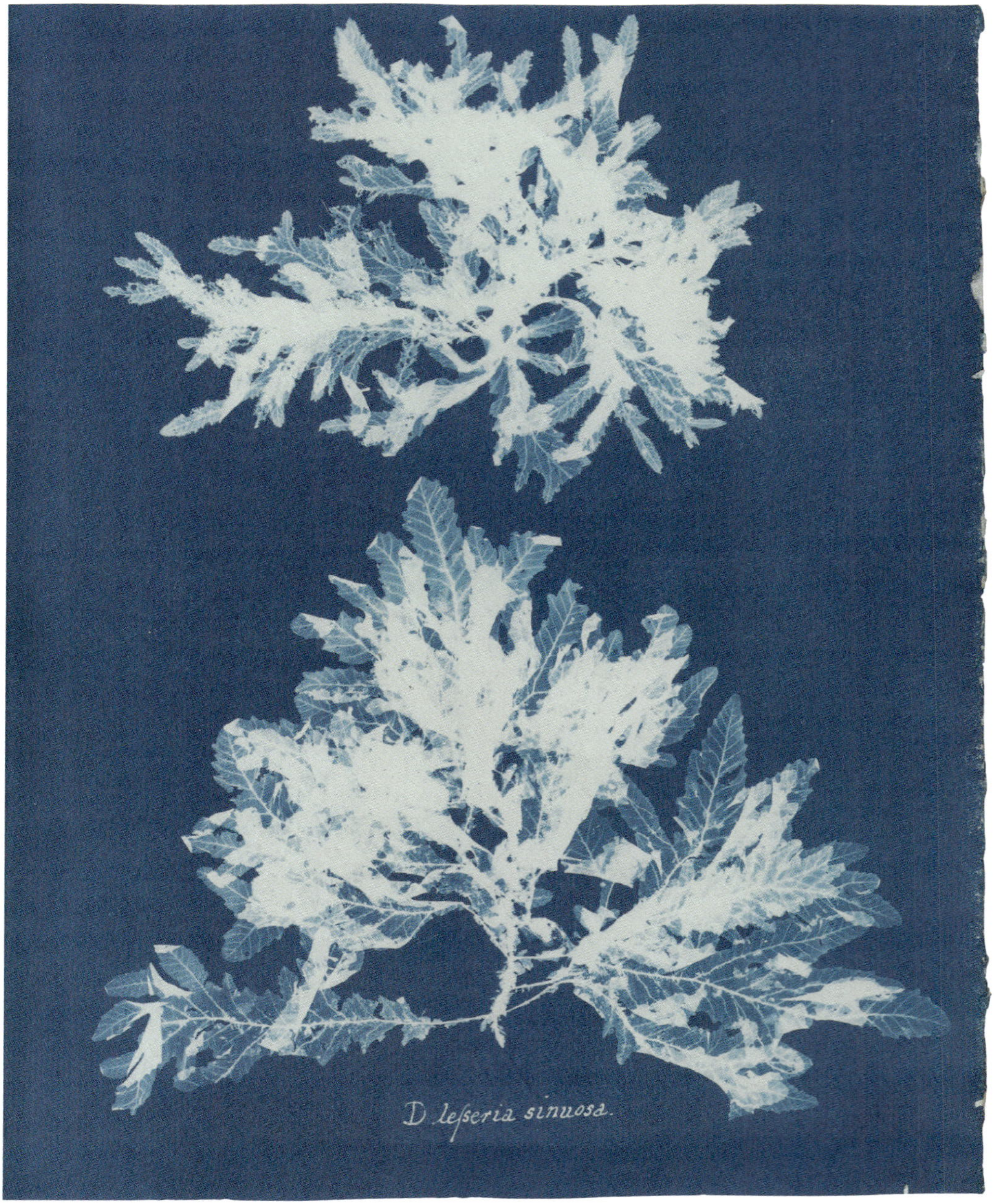

Plate 51. *Delesseria sinuosa*

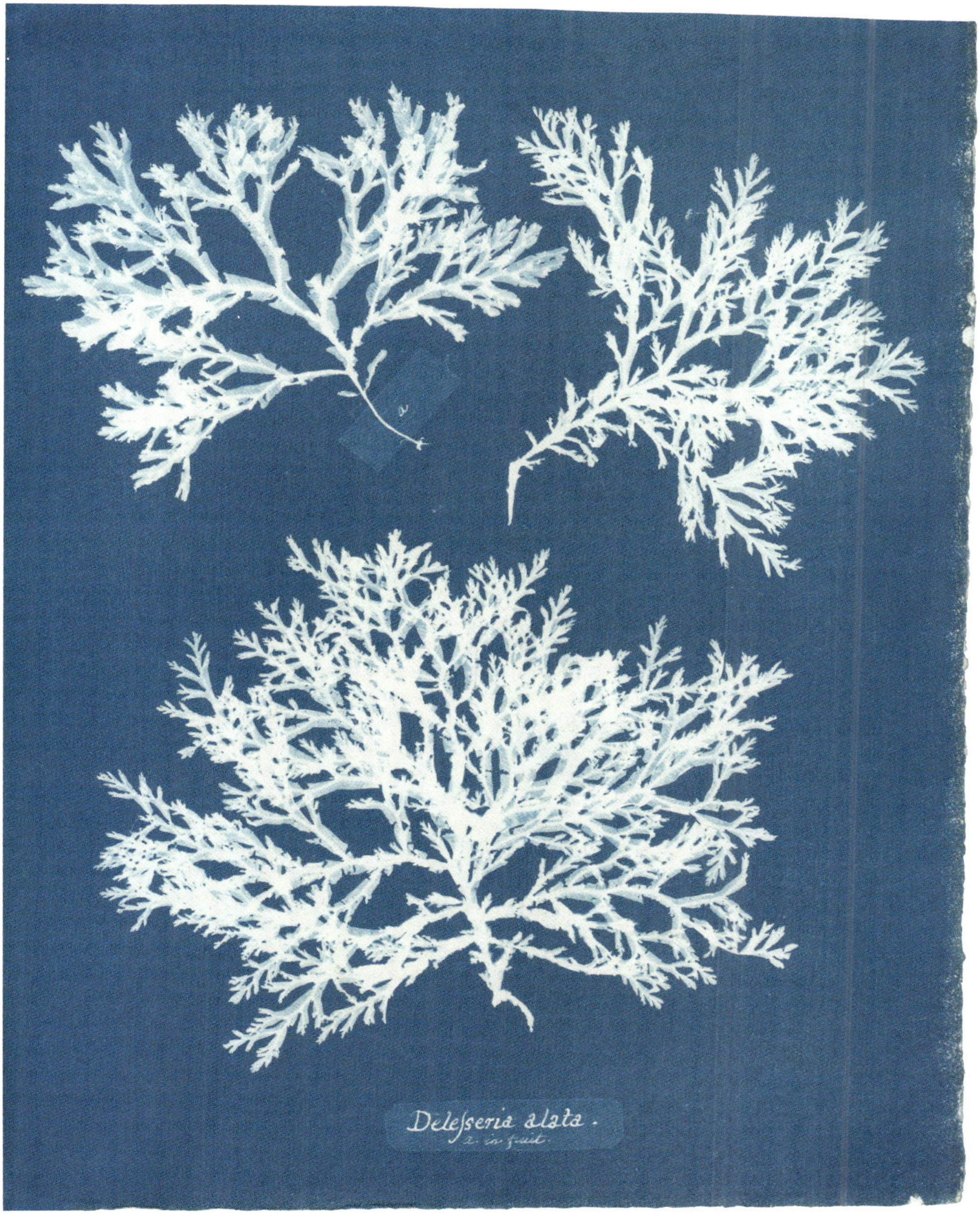

Plate 52. *Delesseria alata a.* in fruit

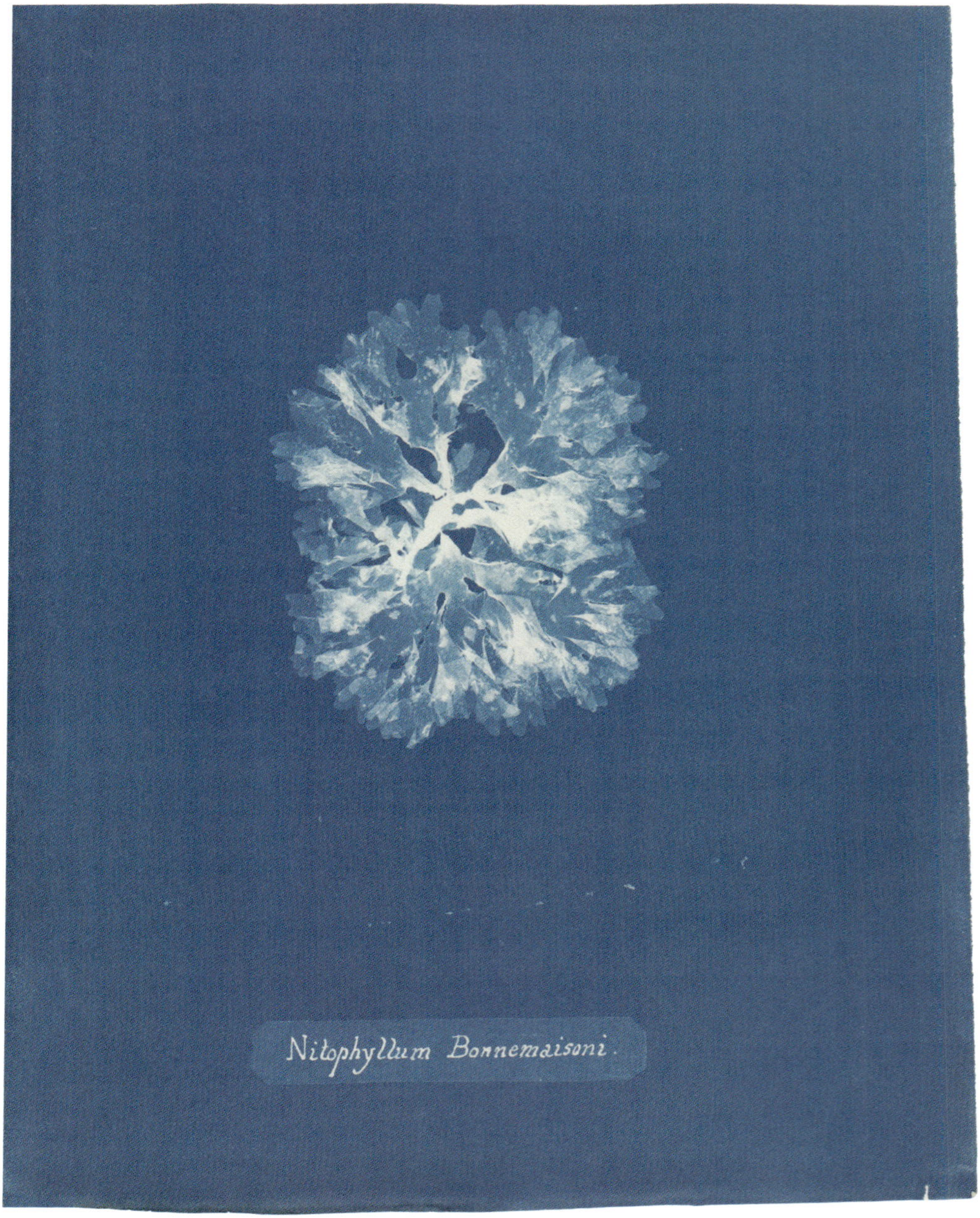

Plate 55. *Nitophyllum bonnemaisoni*

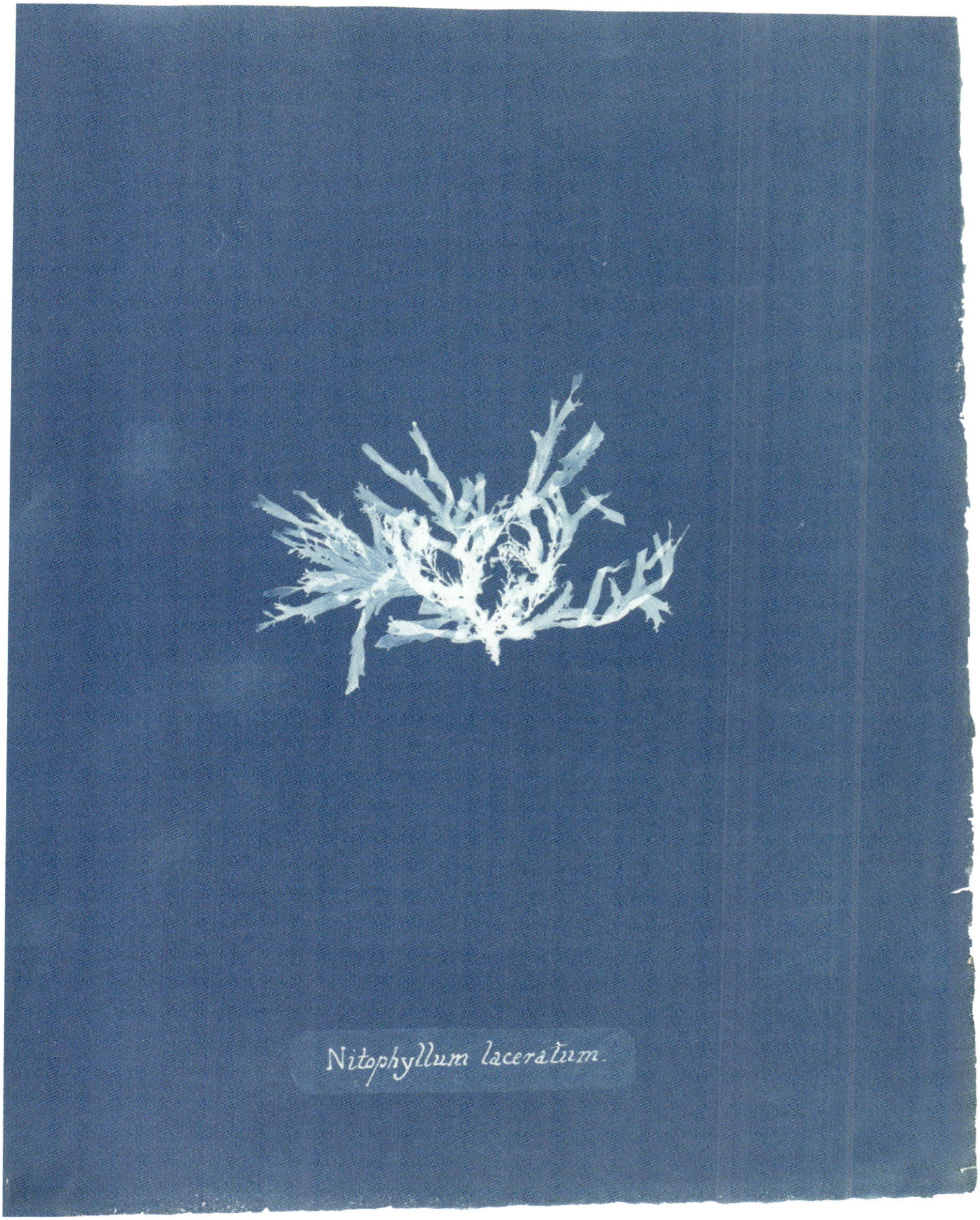

Plate 56. *Nitophyllum laceratum*

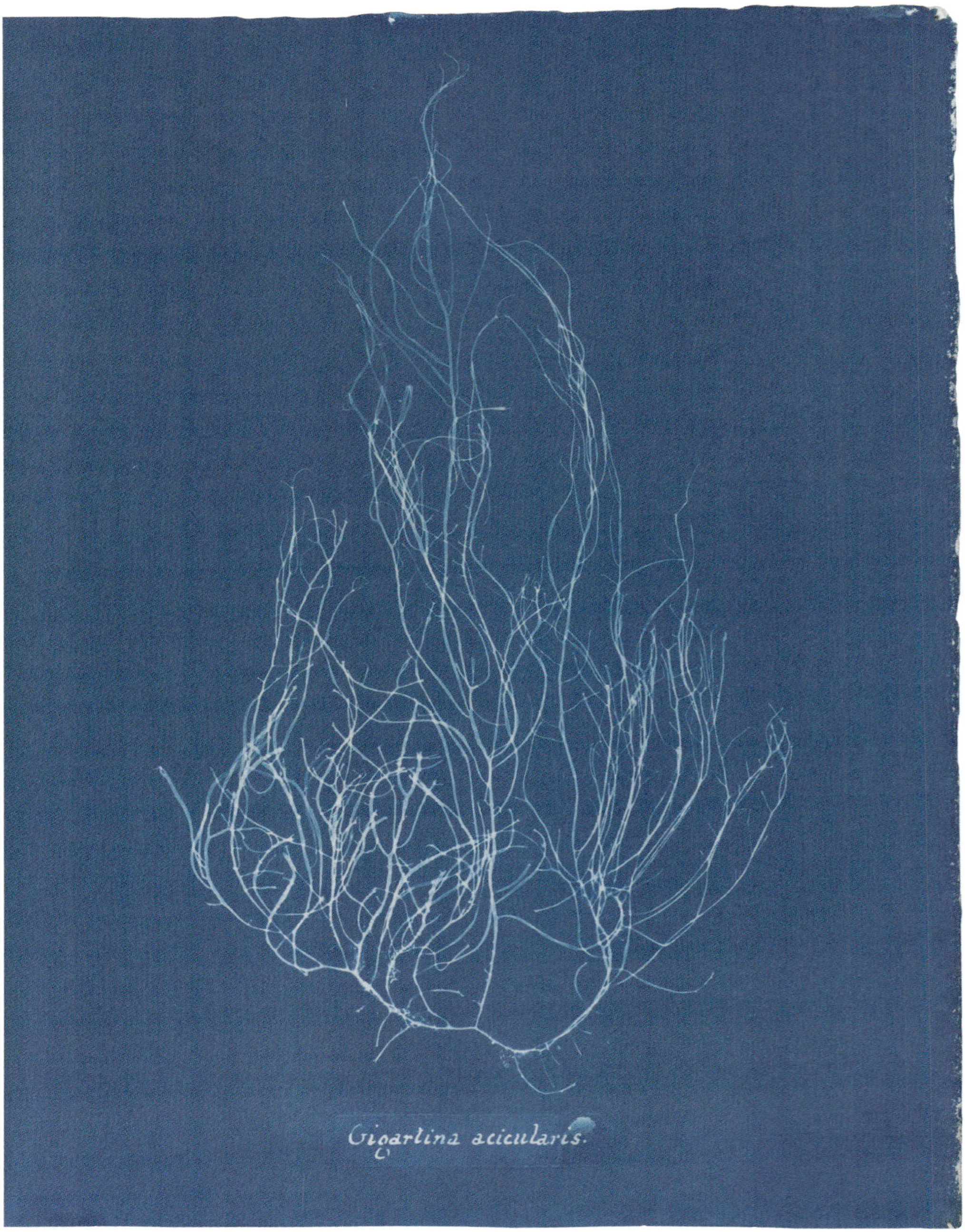

Plate 59. *Gigartina acicularis*

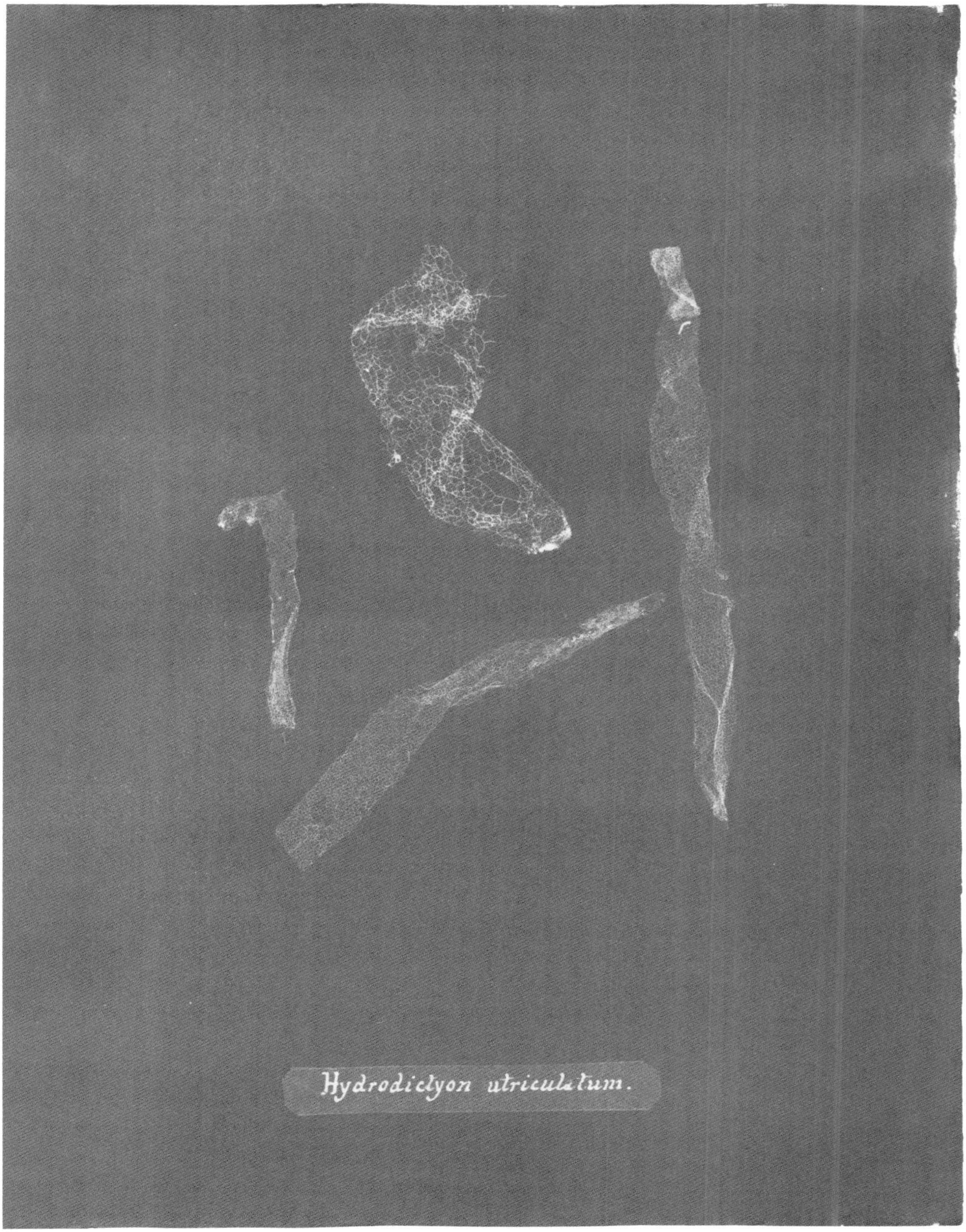

Plate 60. *Hydrodictyon utriculatum*

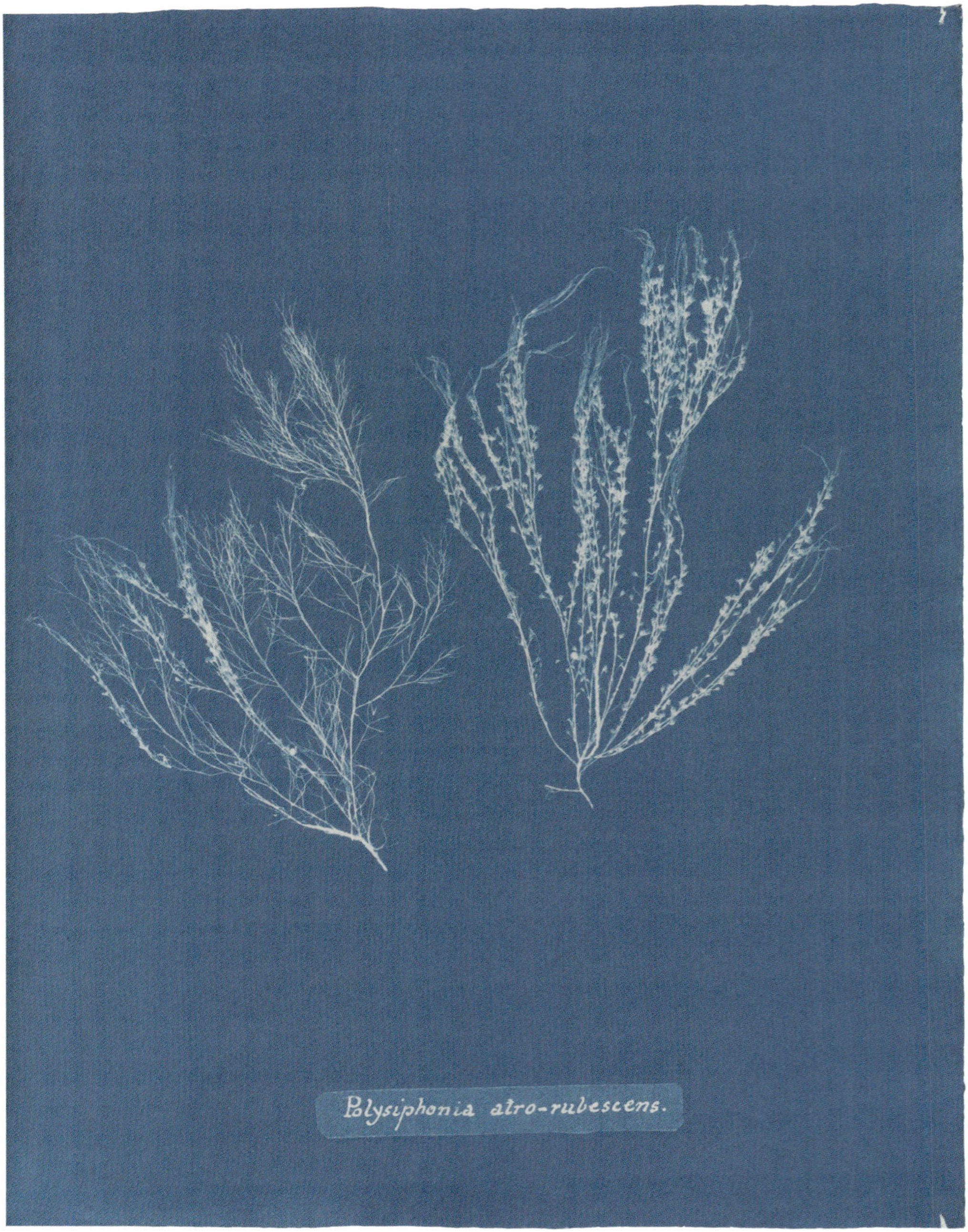

Plate 61. *Polysiphonia atro-rubescens*

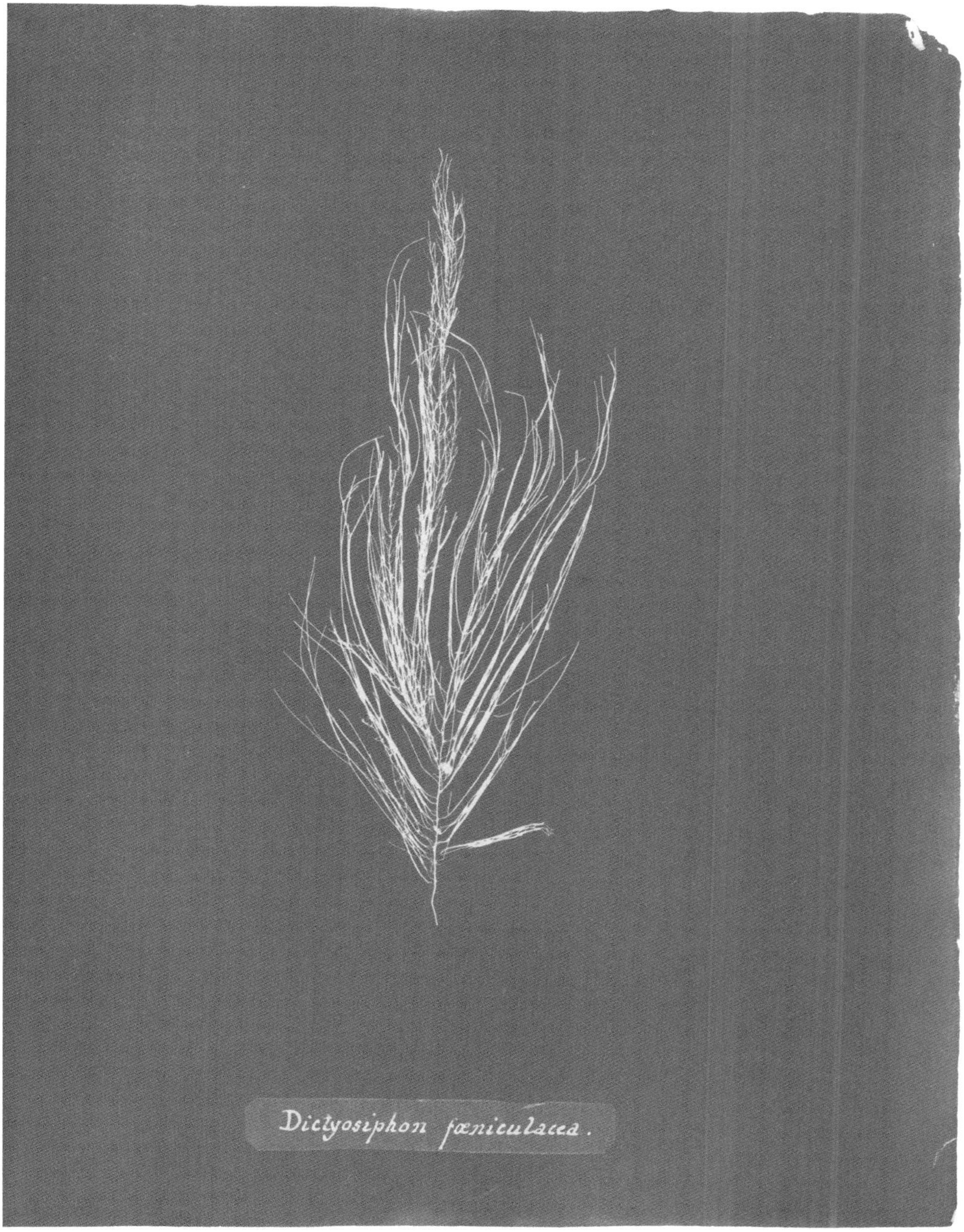

Plate 62. *Dictyosiphon faeniculacea*

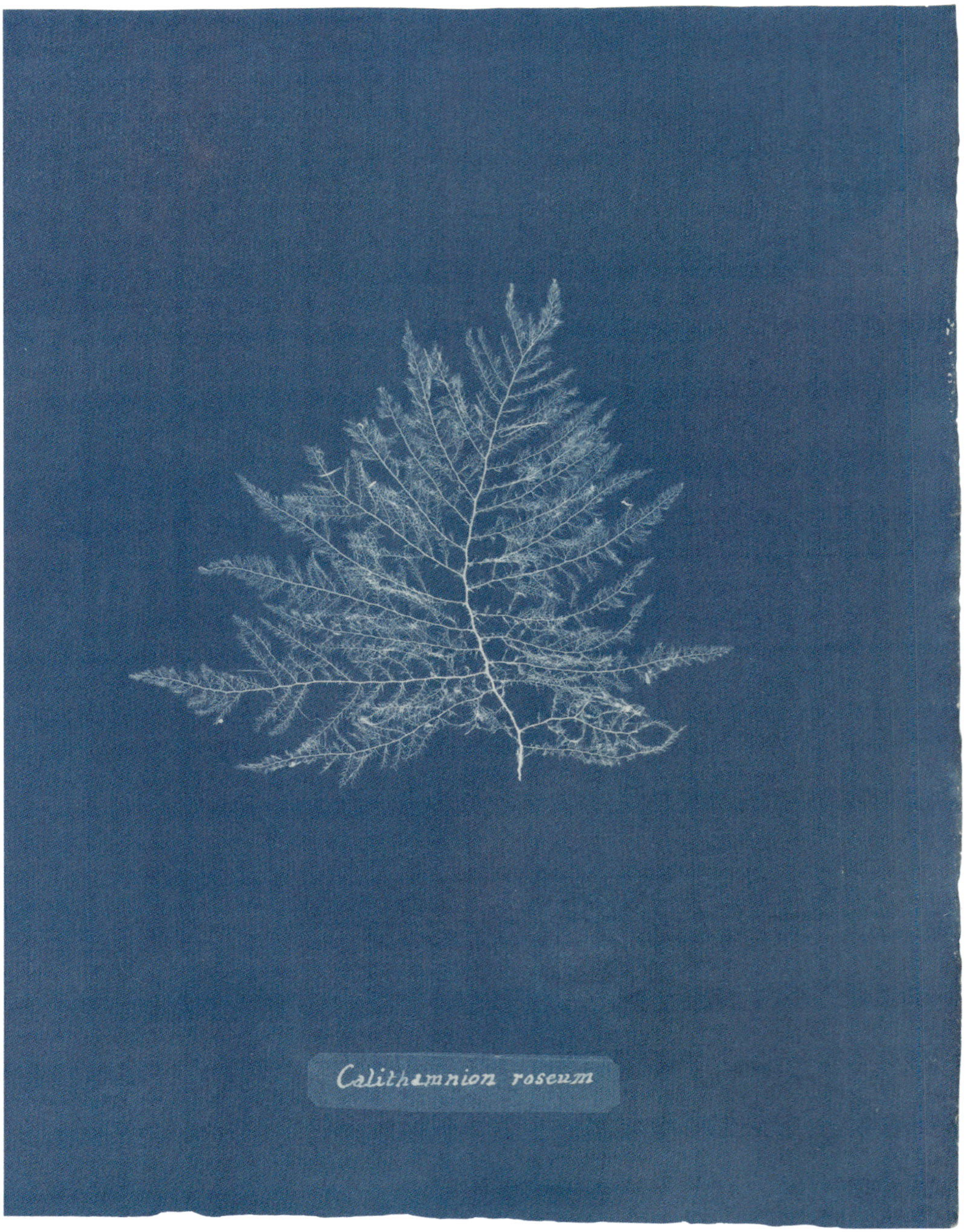

Plate 63. *Ca[l]lithamnion roseum*

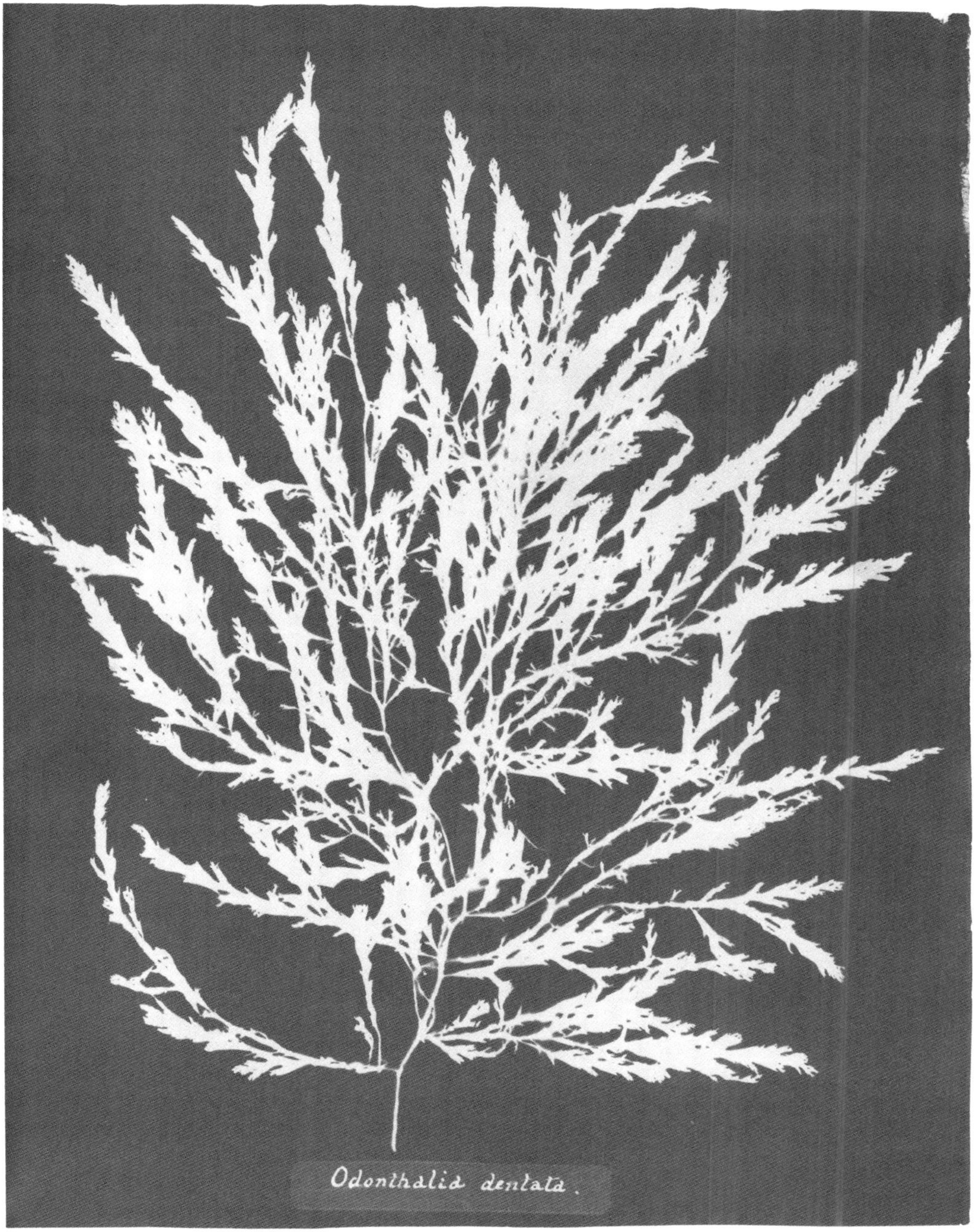

Plate 64. *Odonthalia dentata*

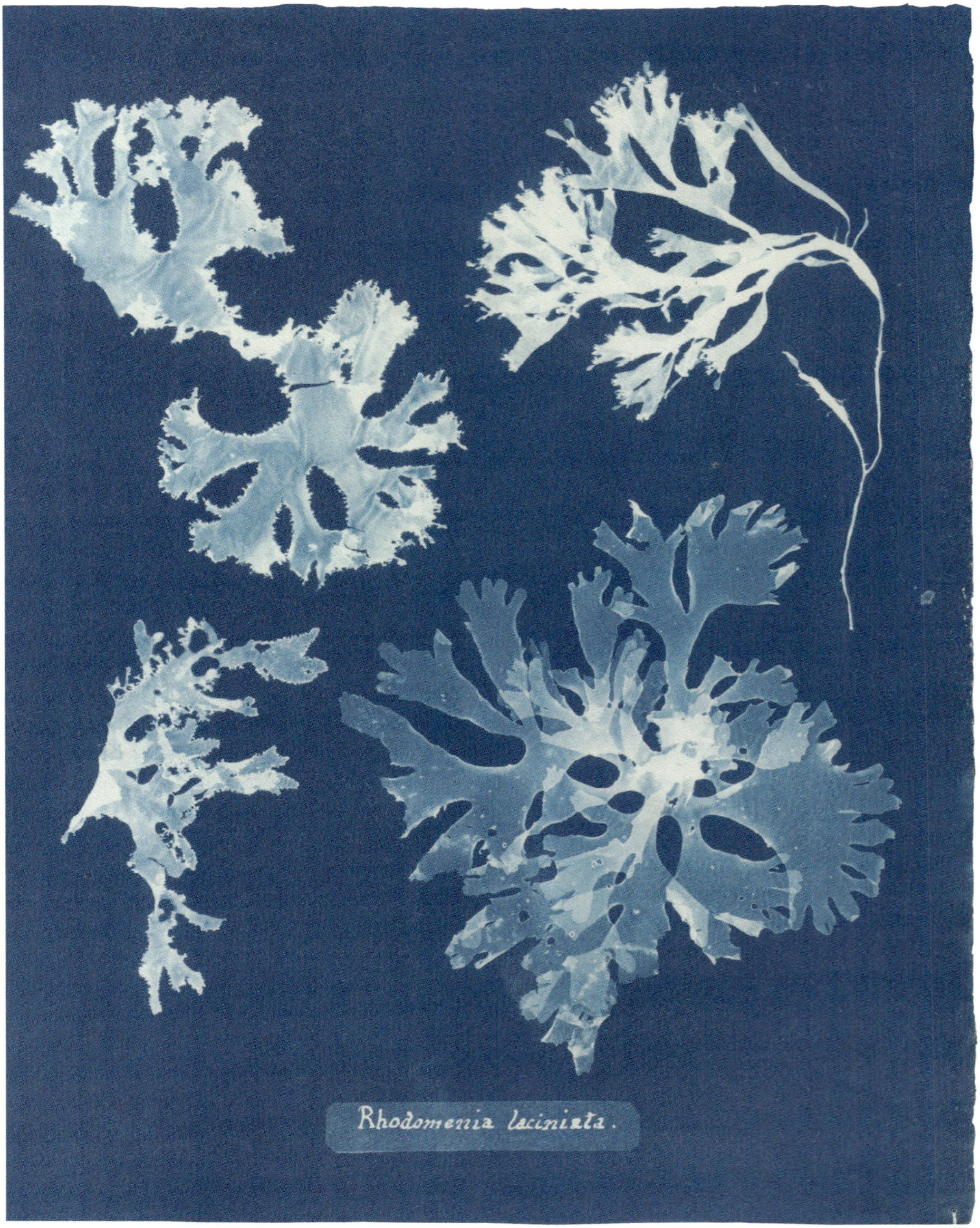

Plate 65. *Rhodomenia laciniata*

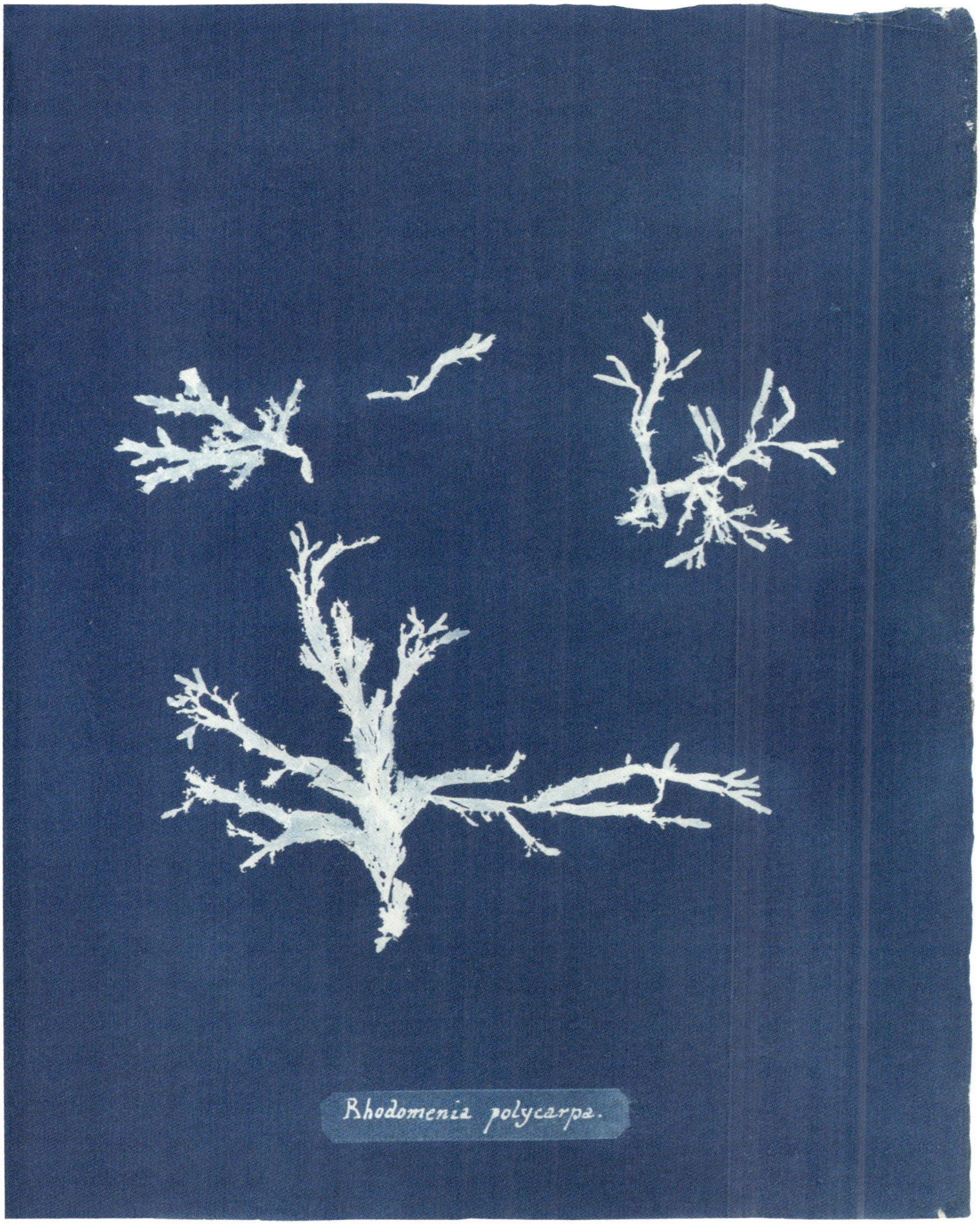

Plate 66. *Rhodomenia polycarpa*

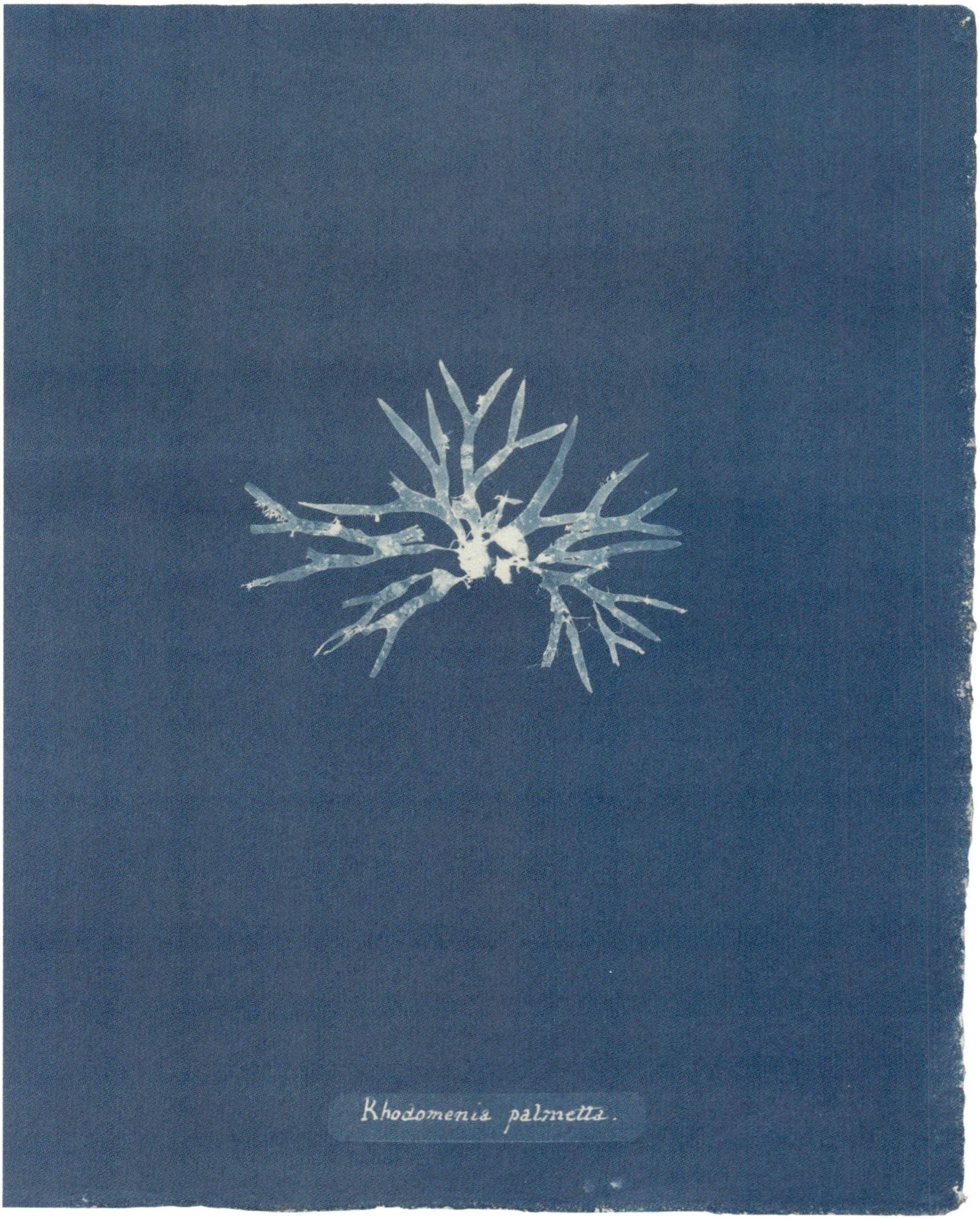

Plate 67. *Rhodomenia palmetta*

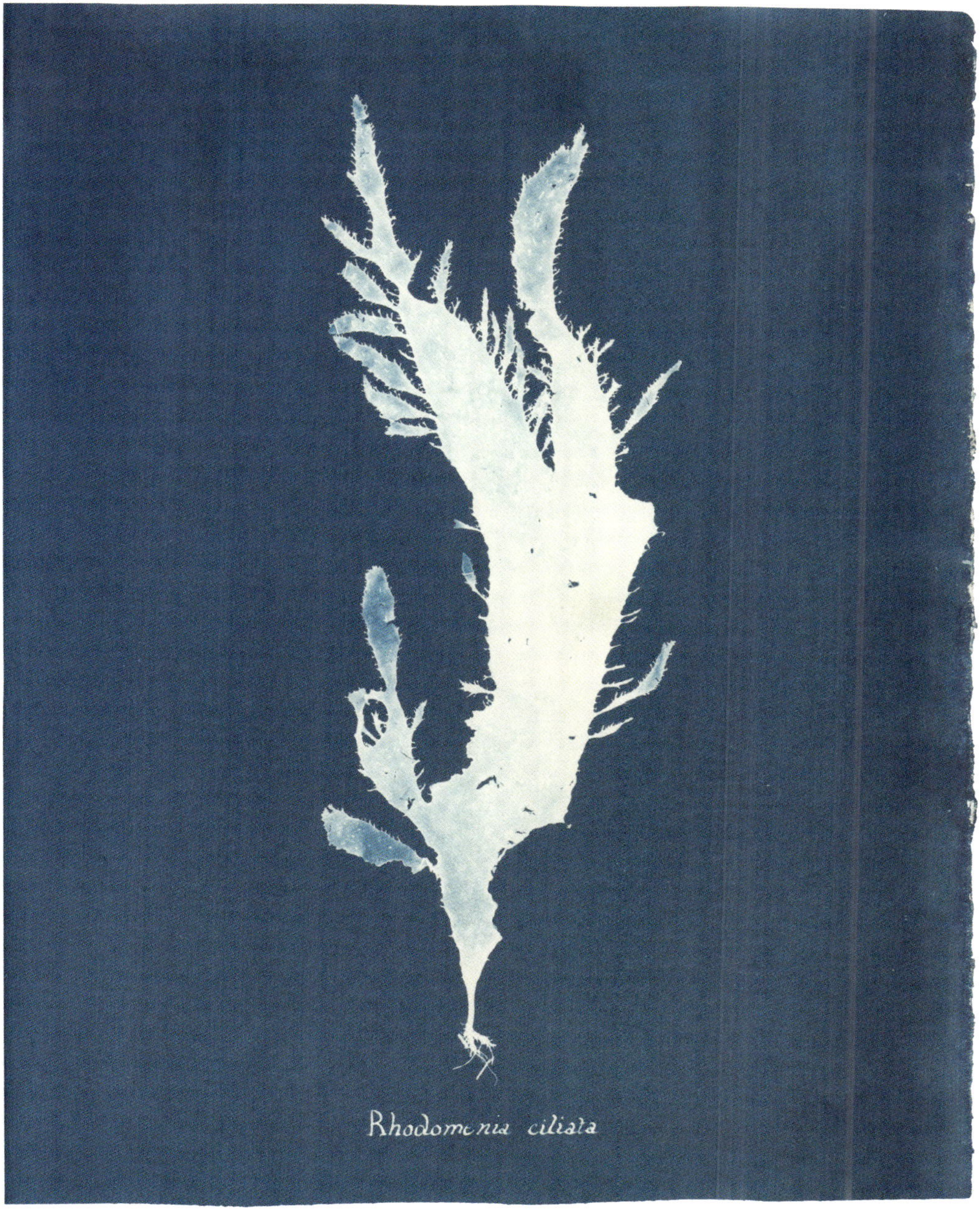

Plate 68. *Rhodomenia ciliata*

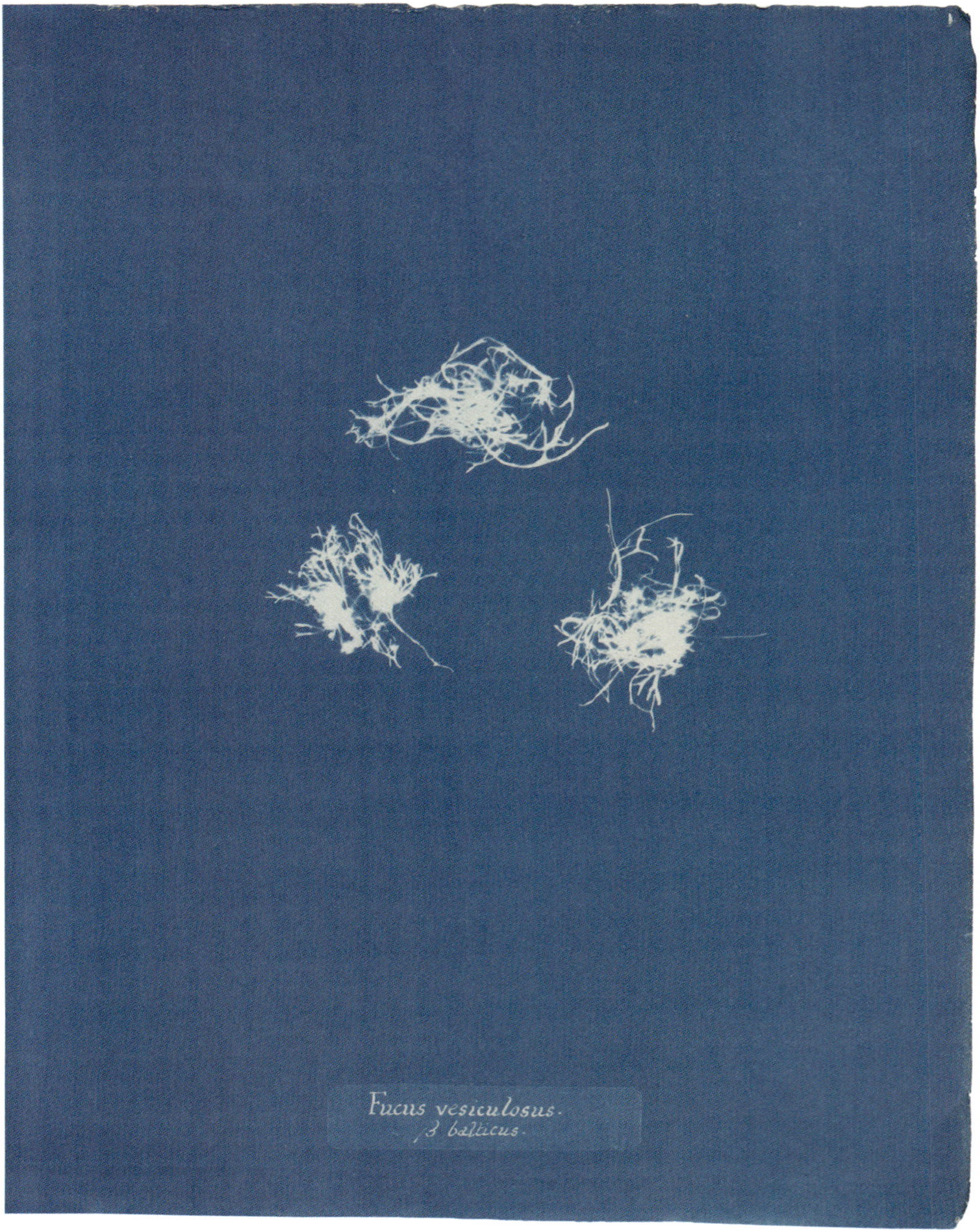

Plate 69. *Fucus vesiculosus* β *balticus*

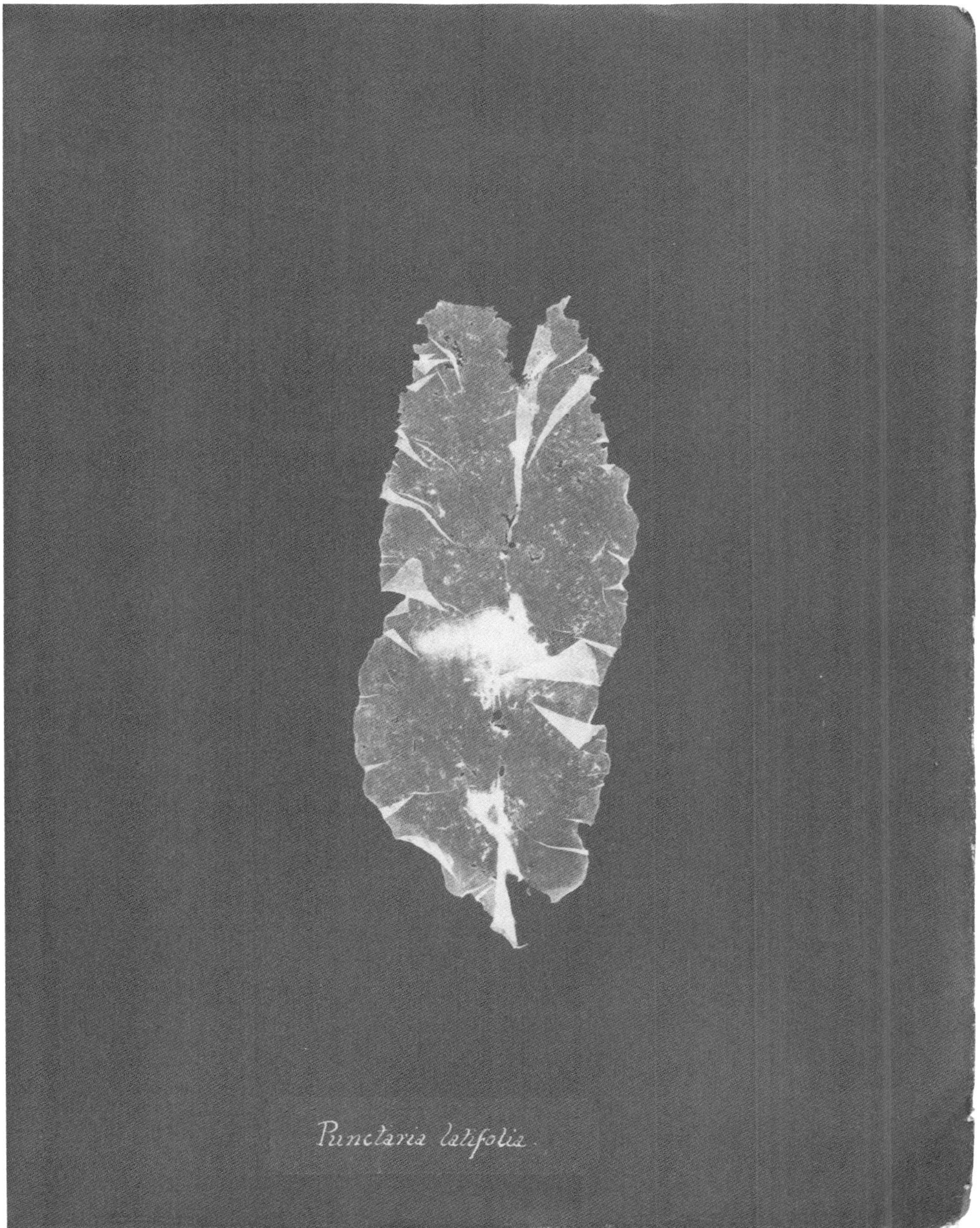

Plate 70. *Punctaria latifolia*

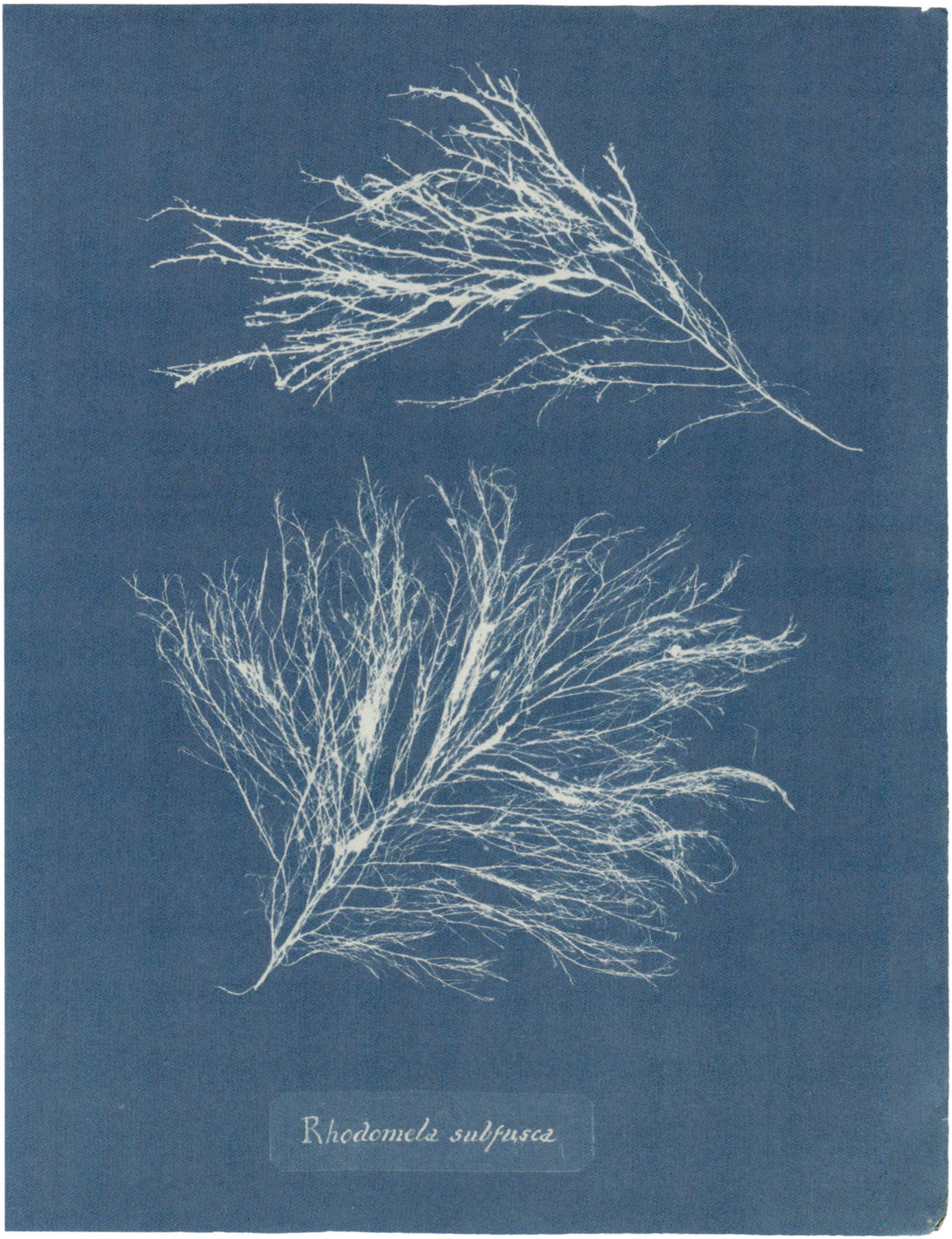

Plate 71. *Rhodomela subfusca*

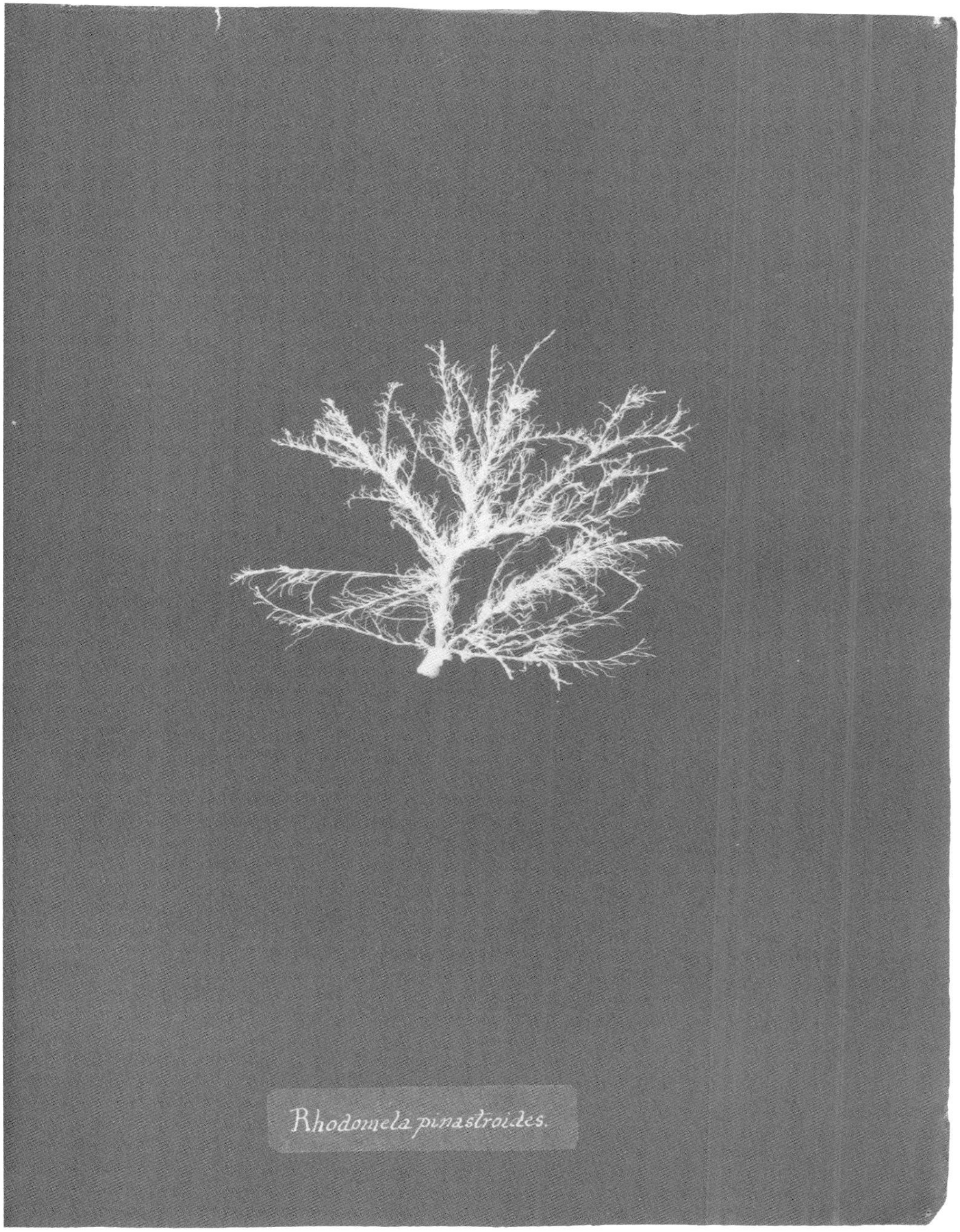

Plate 72. *Rhodomela pinastroides*

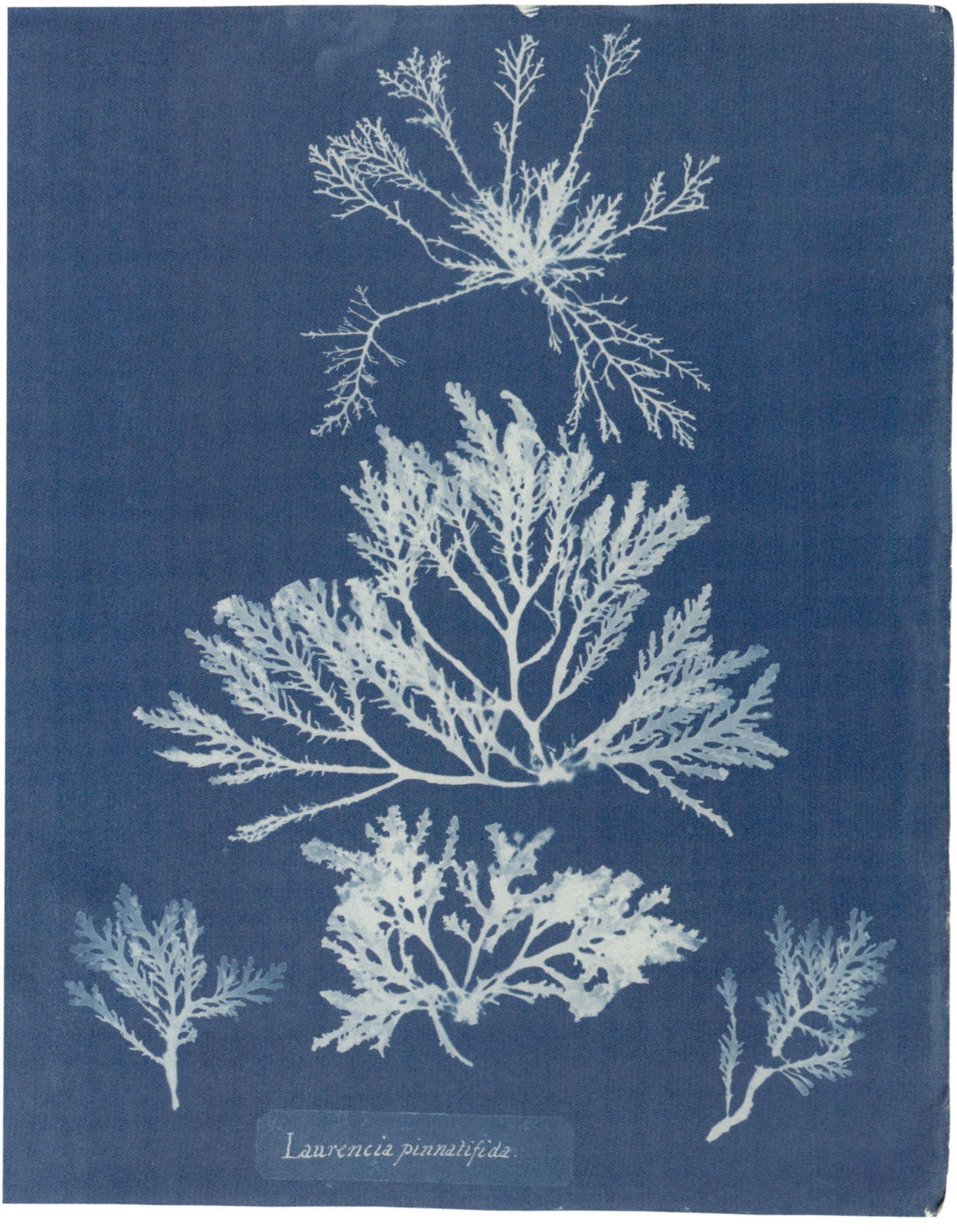

Plate 73. *Laurencia pinnatifida*

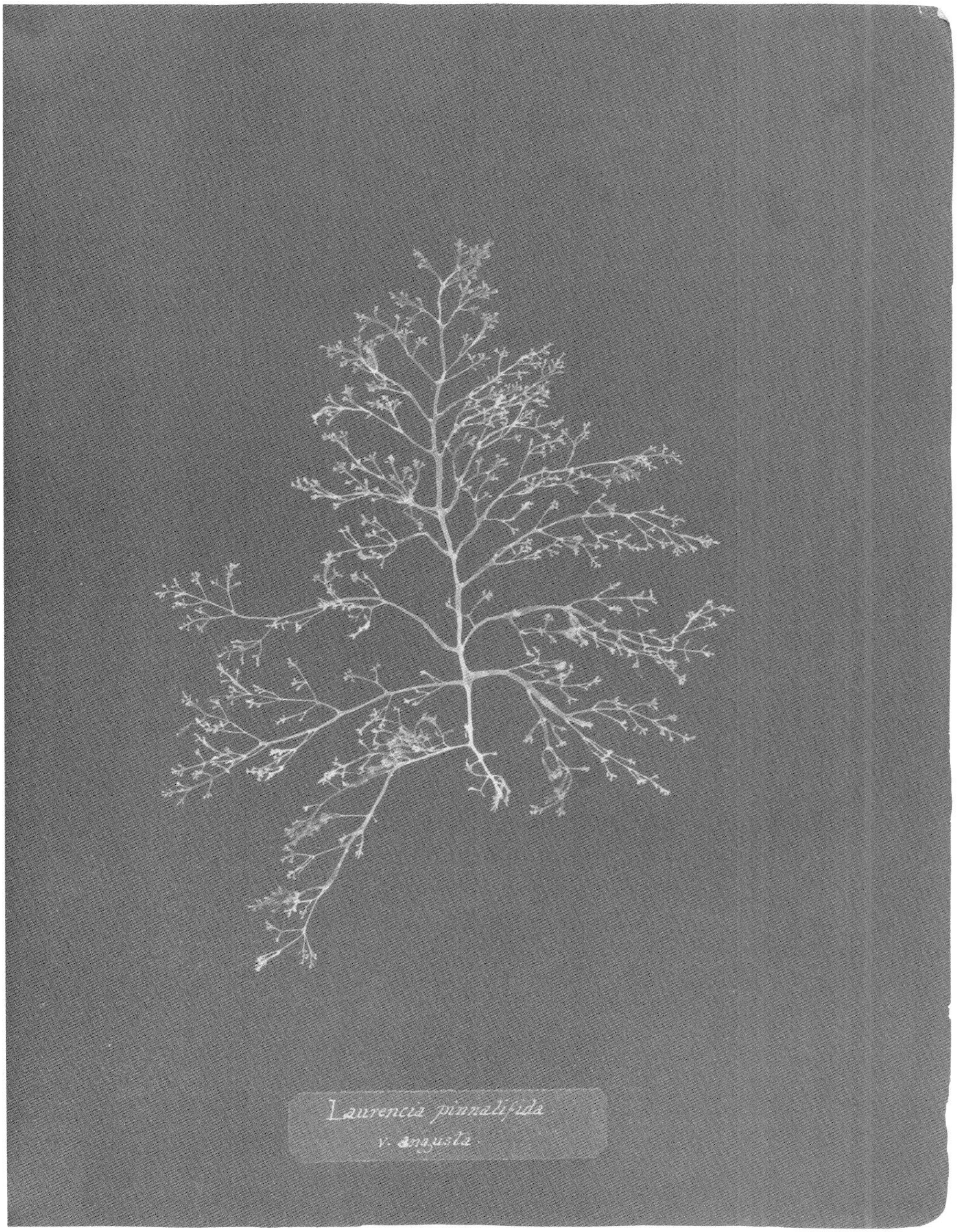

Plate 74. *Laurencia pinnatifida* v. *angusta*

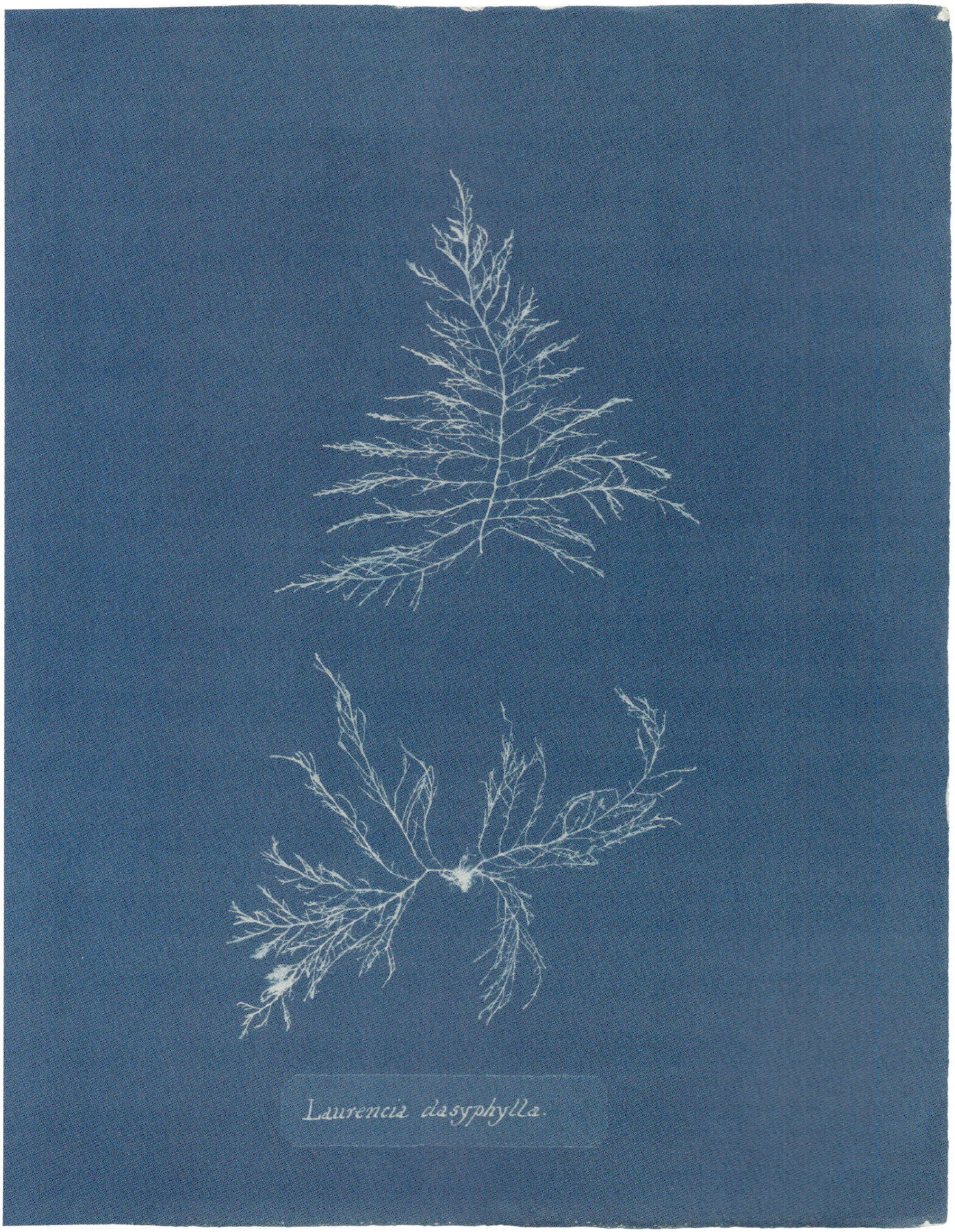

Plate 75. *Laurencia dasyphylla*

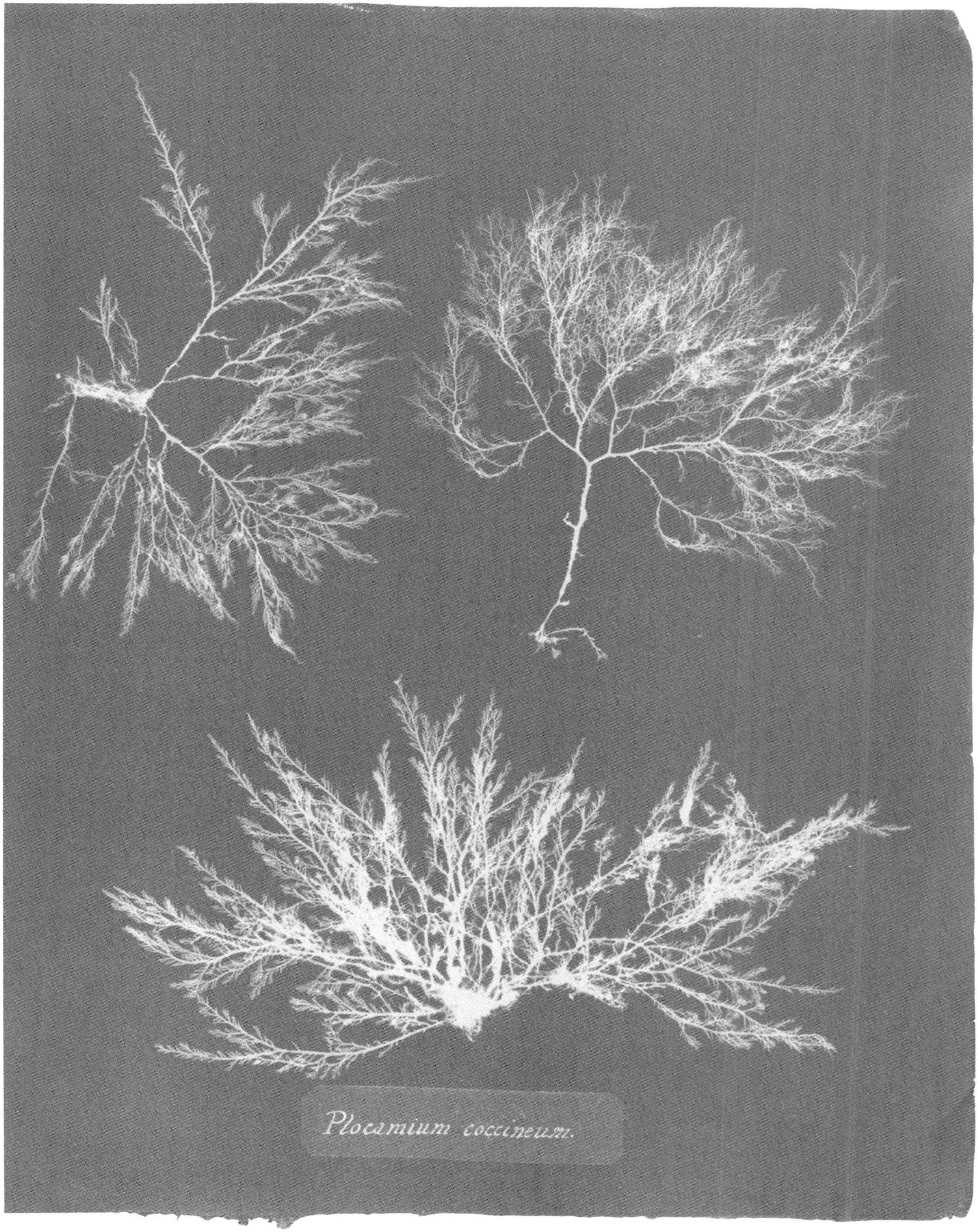

Plate 76. *Plocamium coccineum*

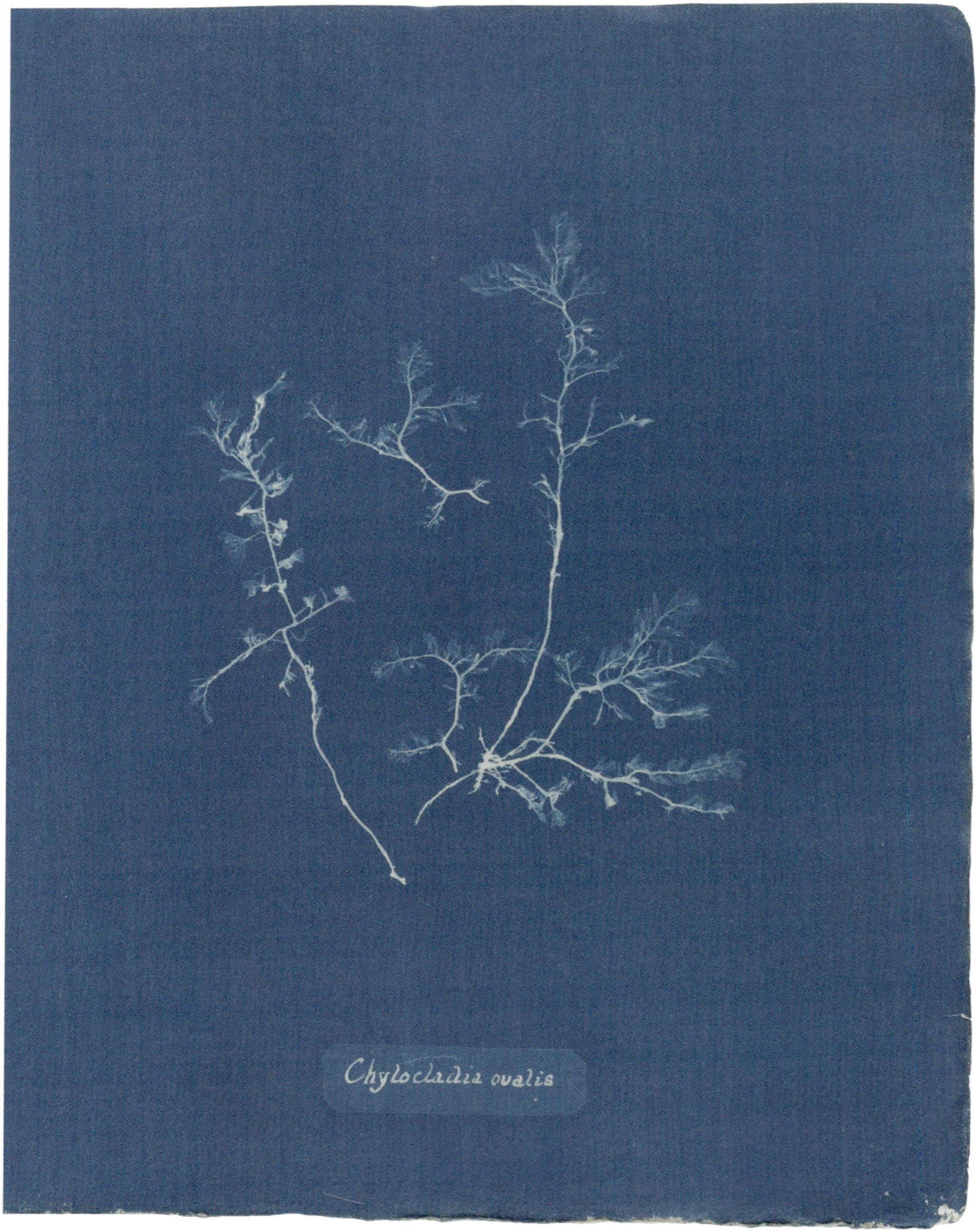

Plate 77. *Chylocladia ovalis*

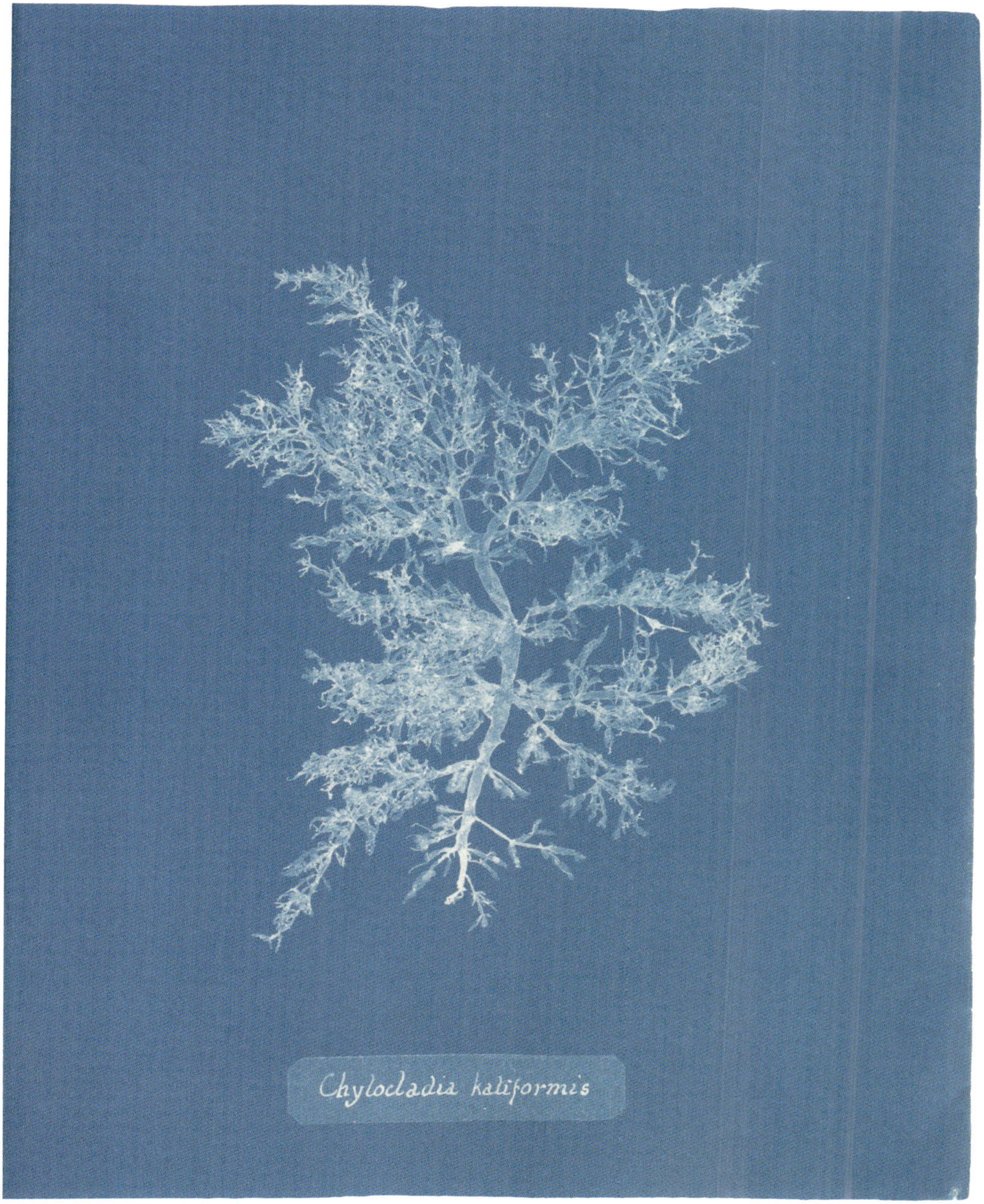

Plate 78. *Chylocladia kaliformis*

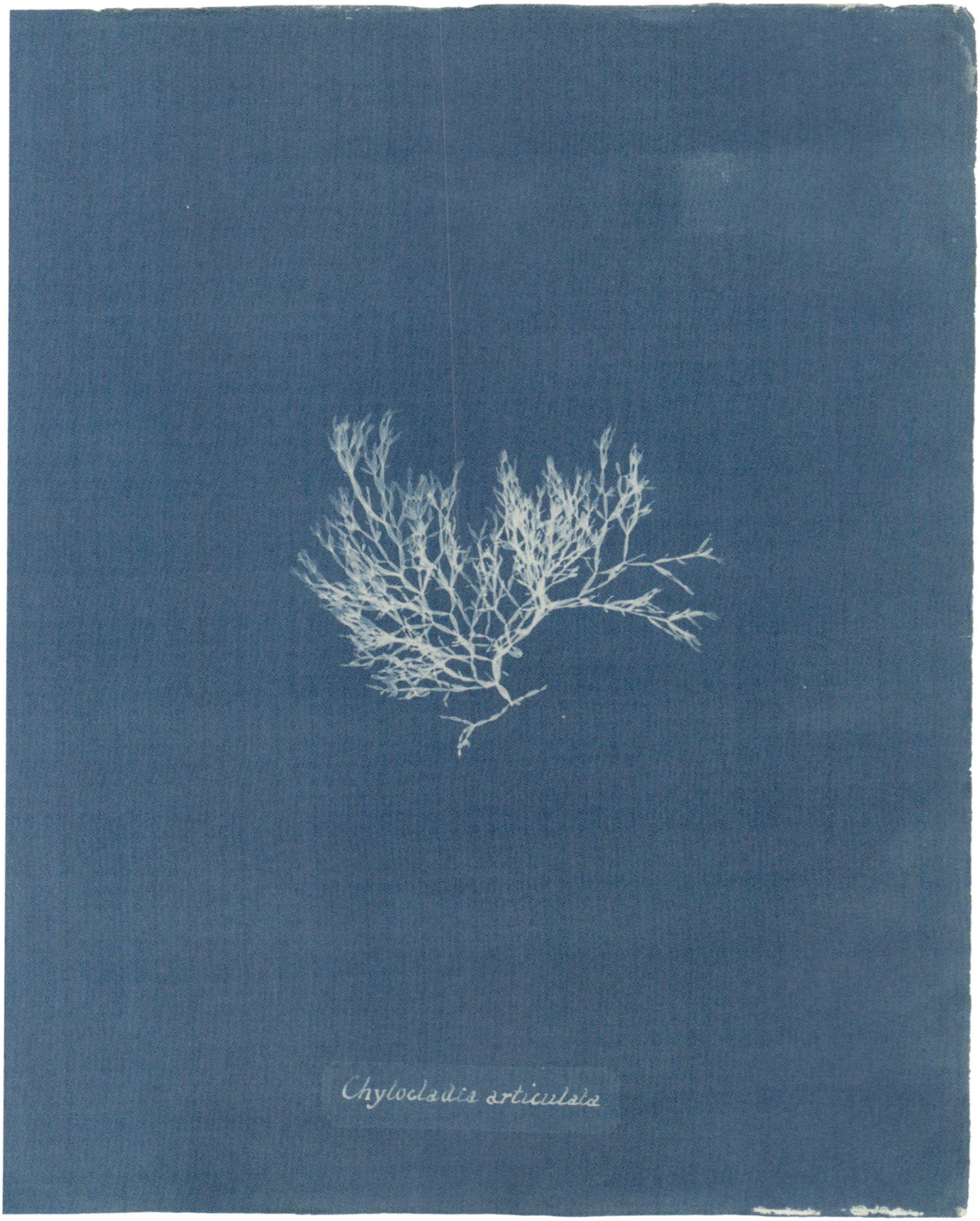

Plate 79. *Chylocladia articulata*

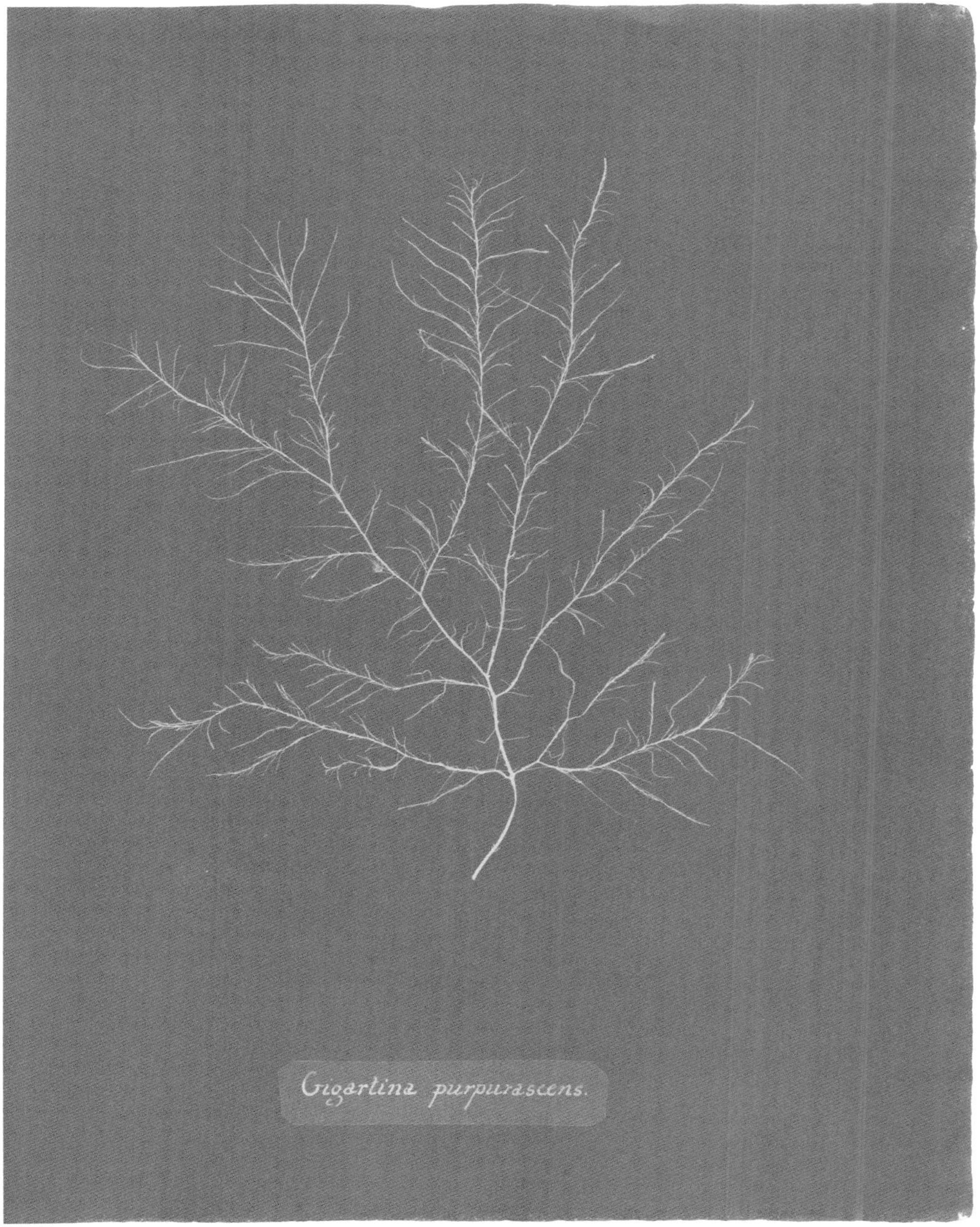

Plate 80. *Gigartina purpurascens*

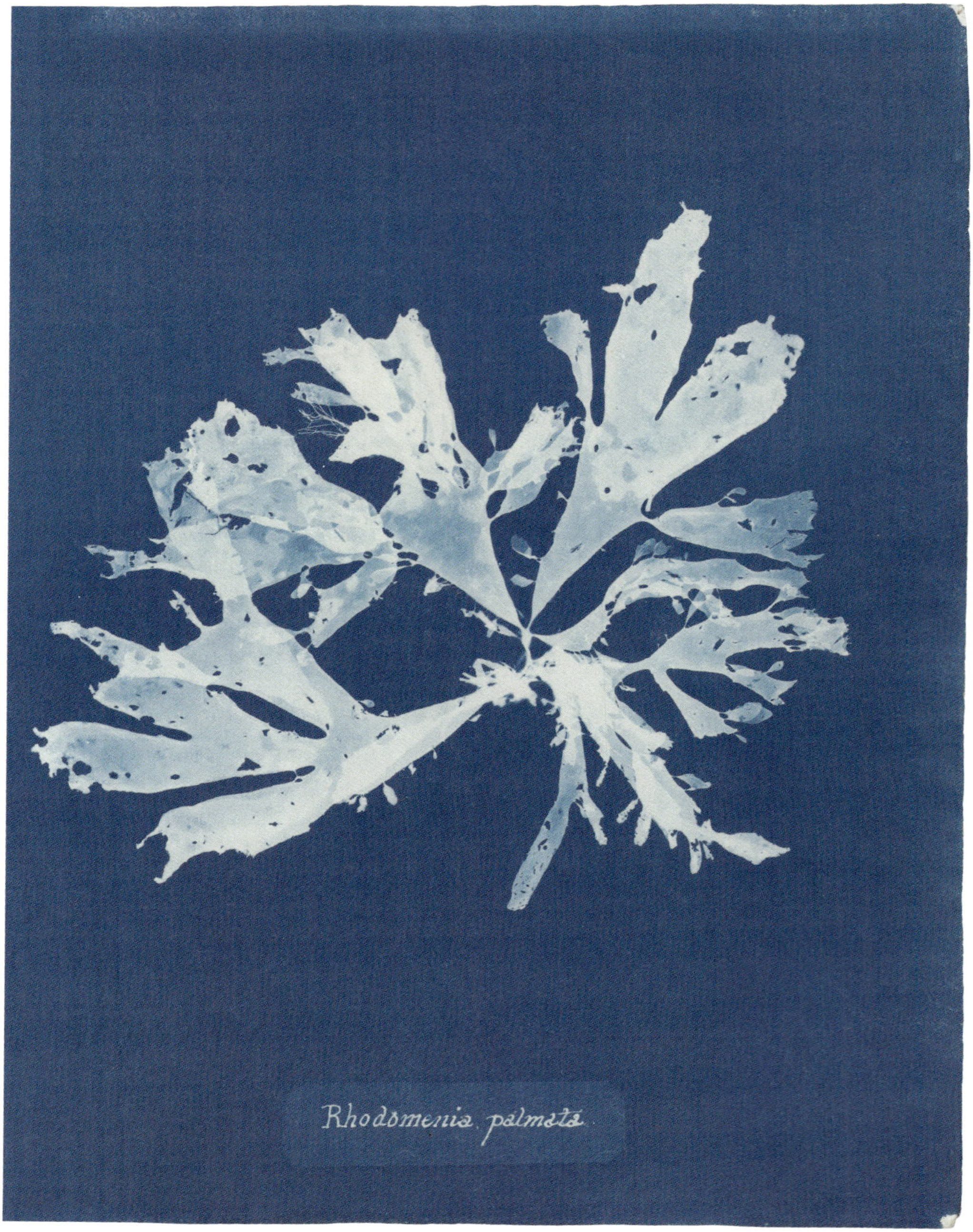

Plate 81. *Rhodomenia palmata*

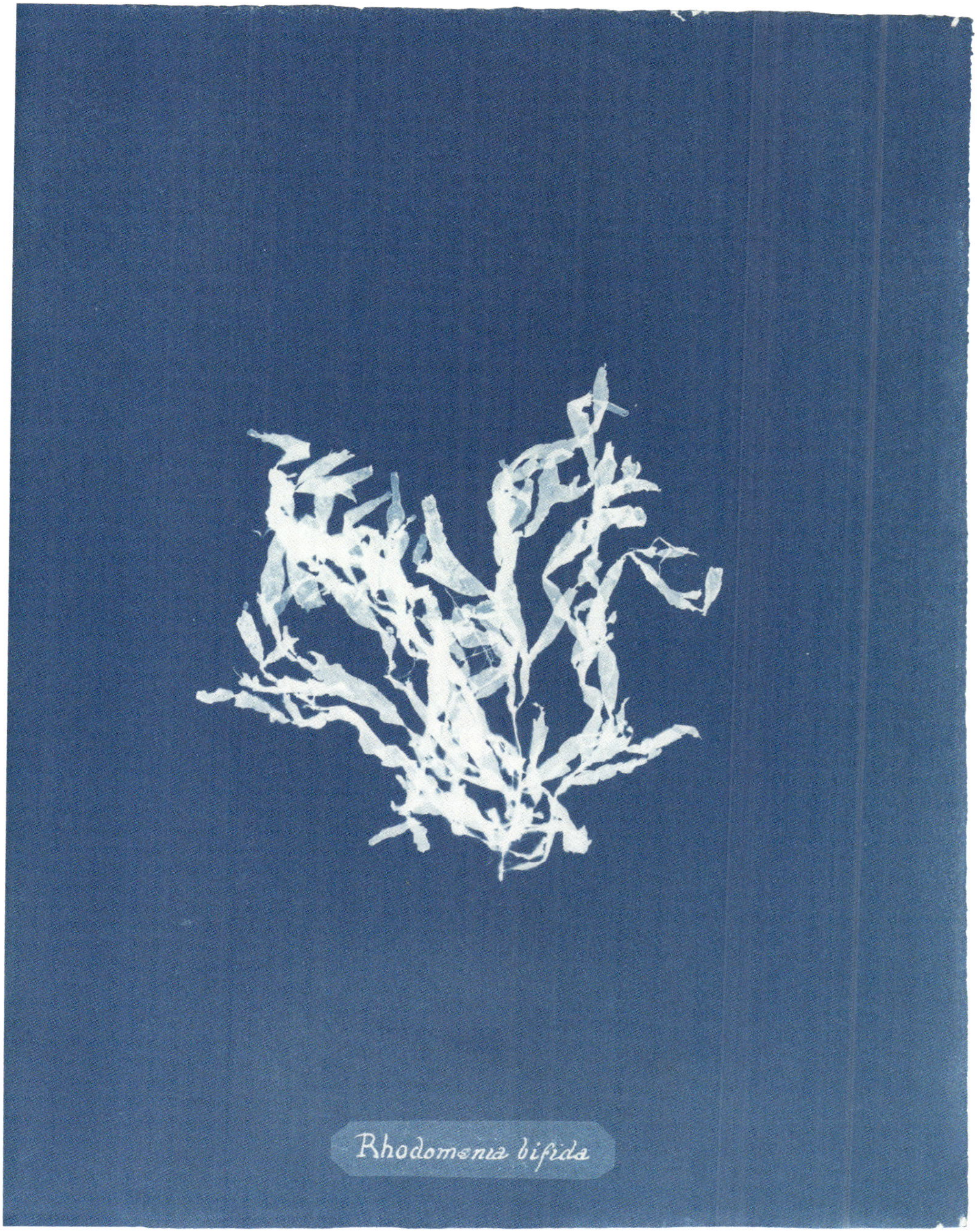

Plate 82. *Rhodomenia bifida*

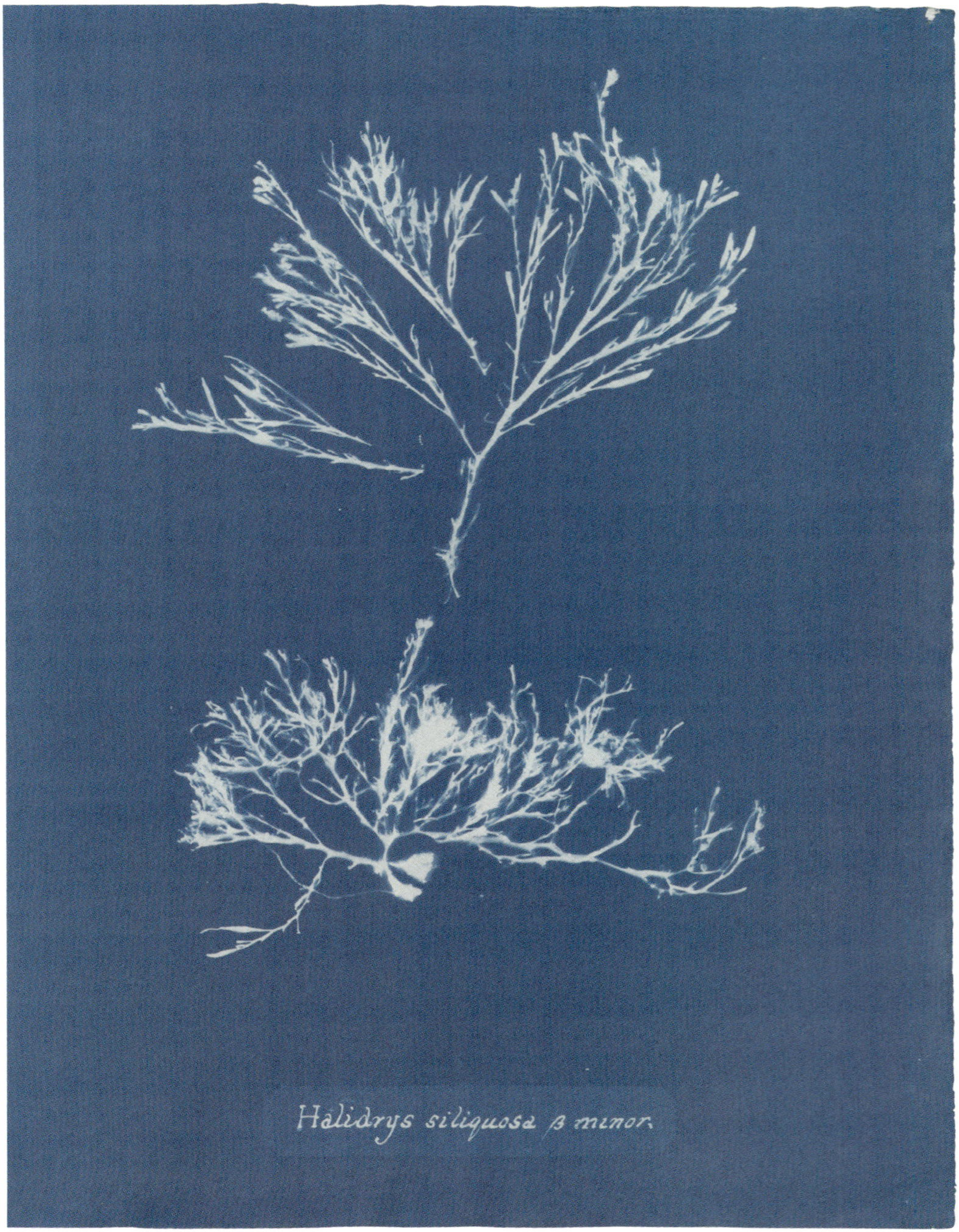

Plate 83. *Halidrys siliquosa* β *minor*

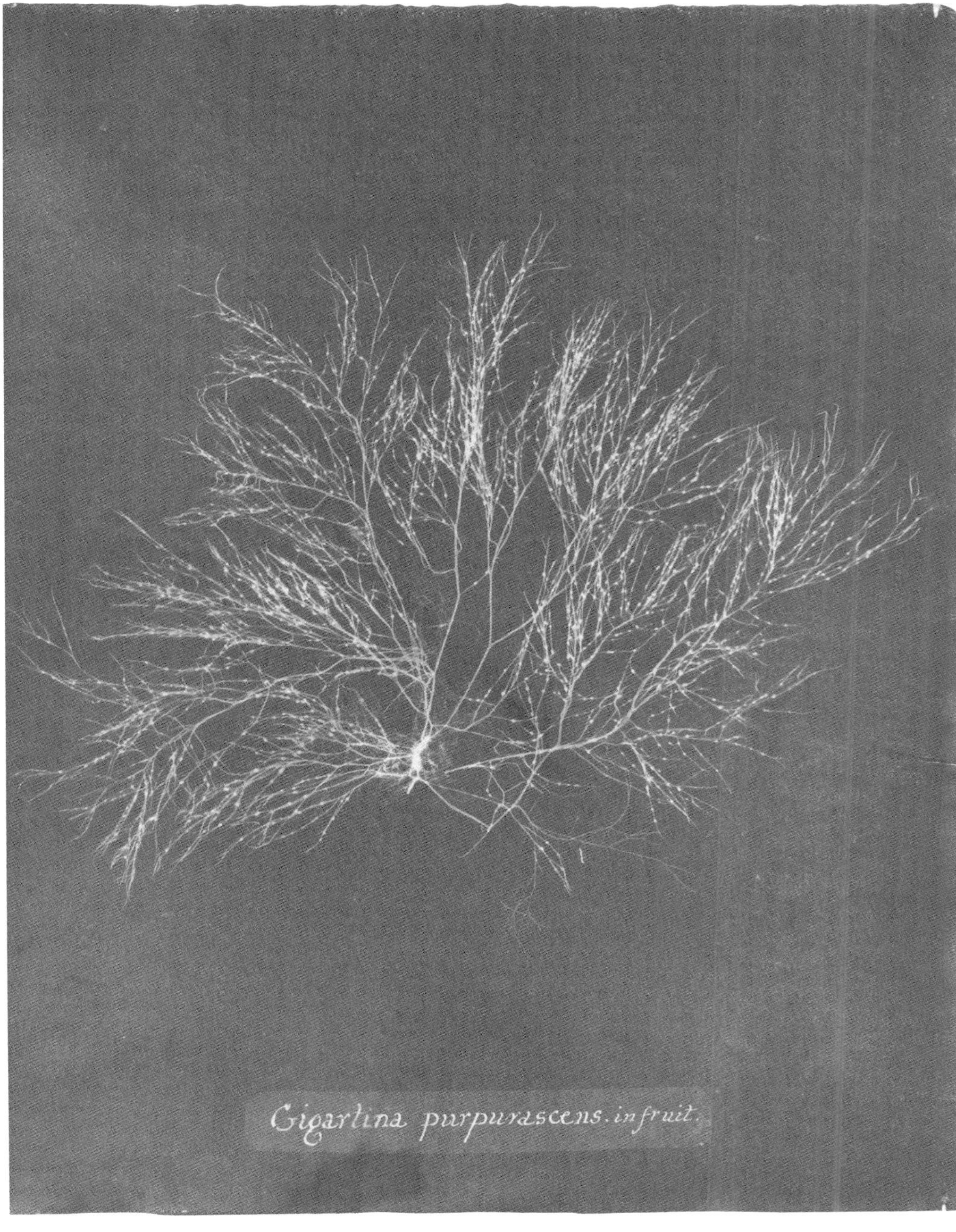

Plate 84. *Gigartina purpurascens* in fruit

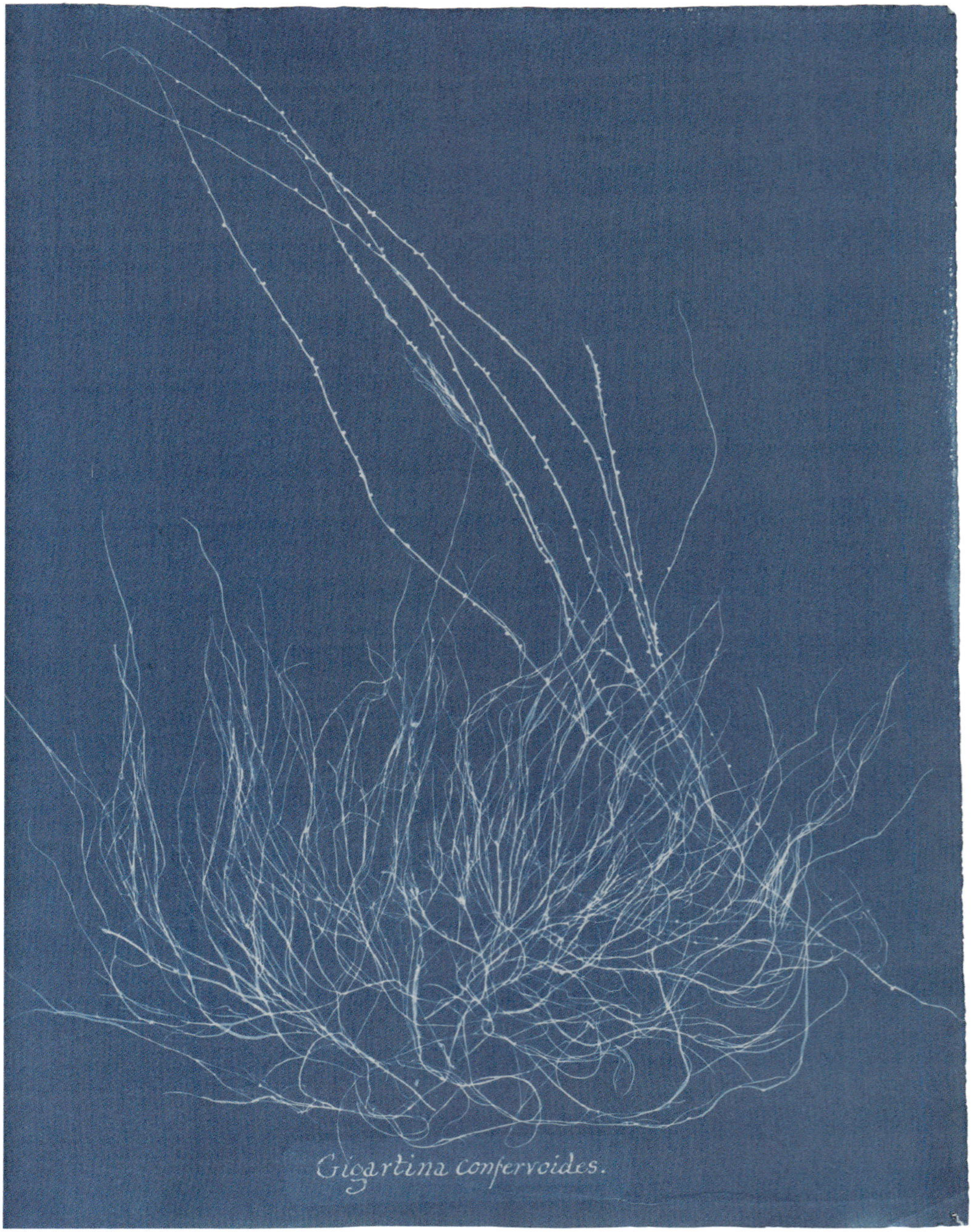

Plate 85. *Gigartina confervoides*

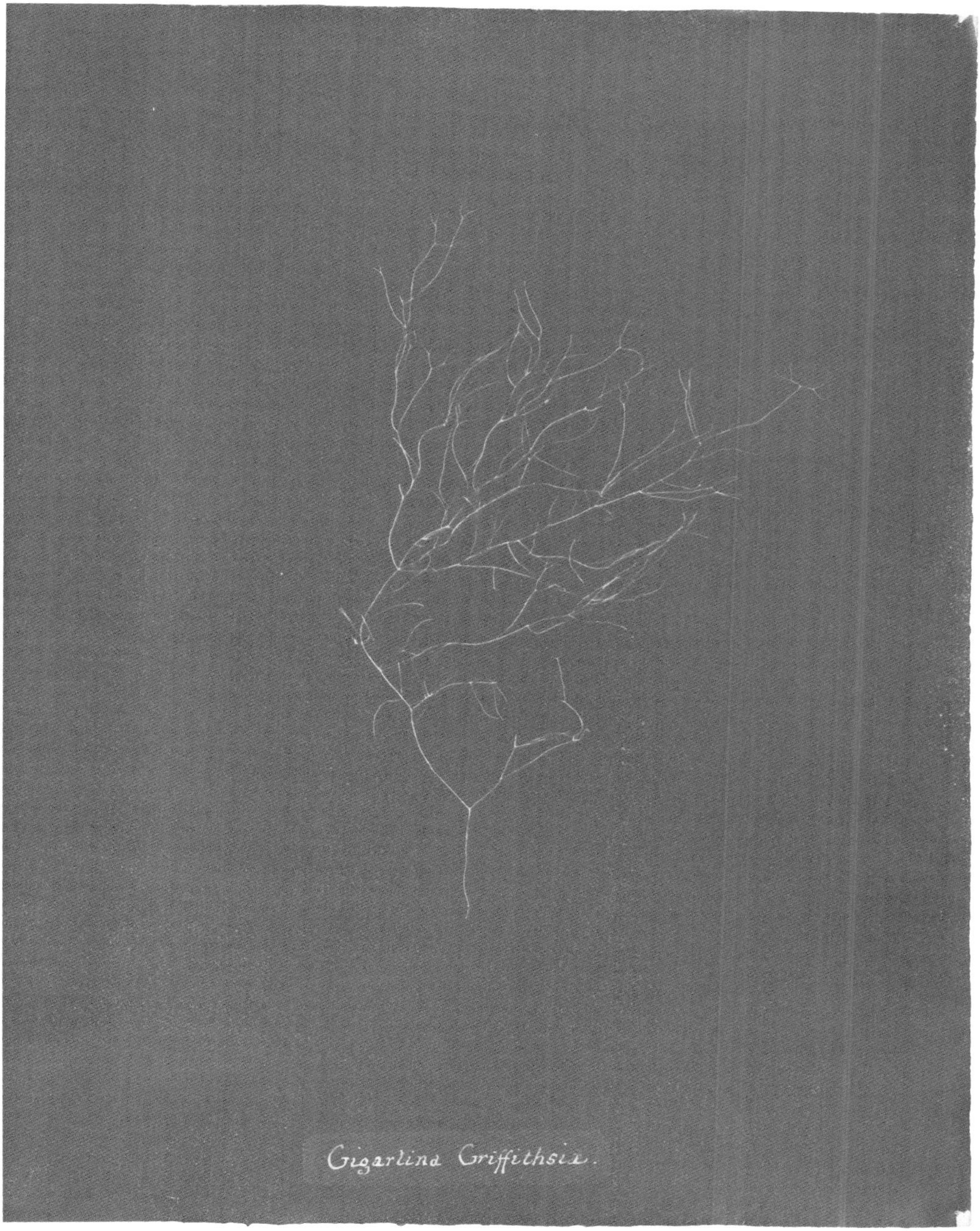

Plate 86. *Gigartina griffithsiae*

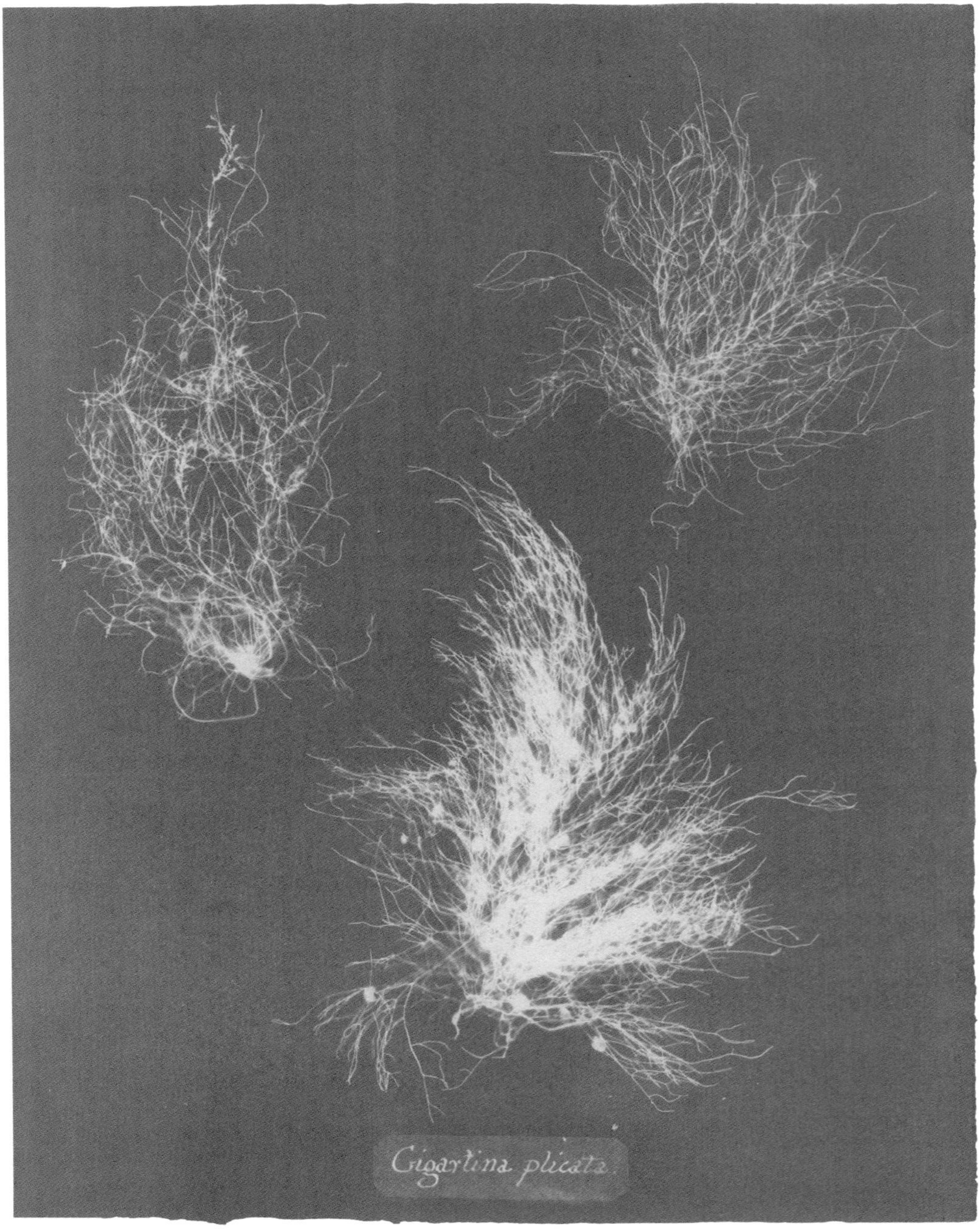

Plate 87. *Gigartina plicata*

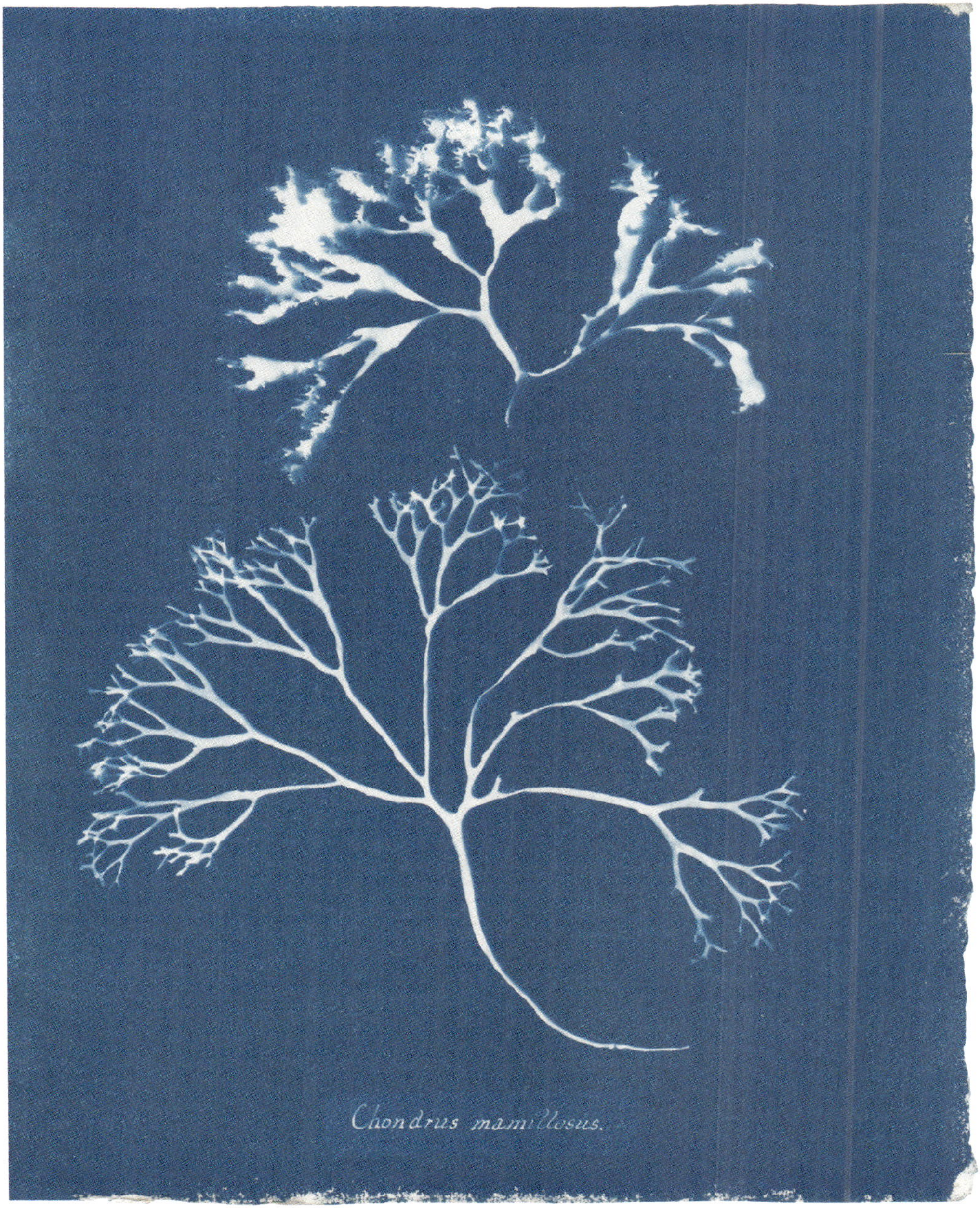

Plate 88. *Chondrus mamillosus*

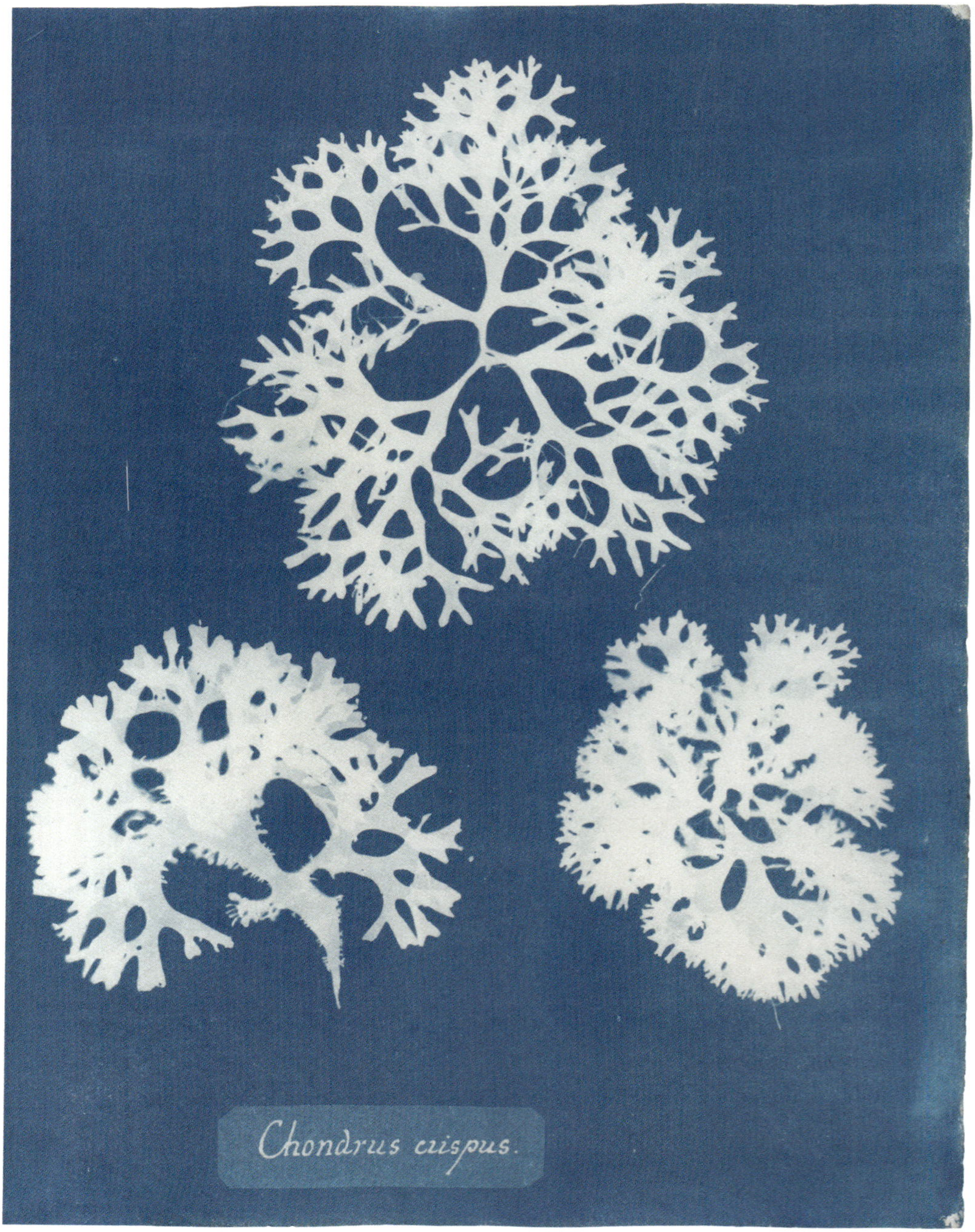

Plate 89. *Chondrus crispus*

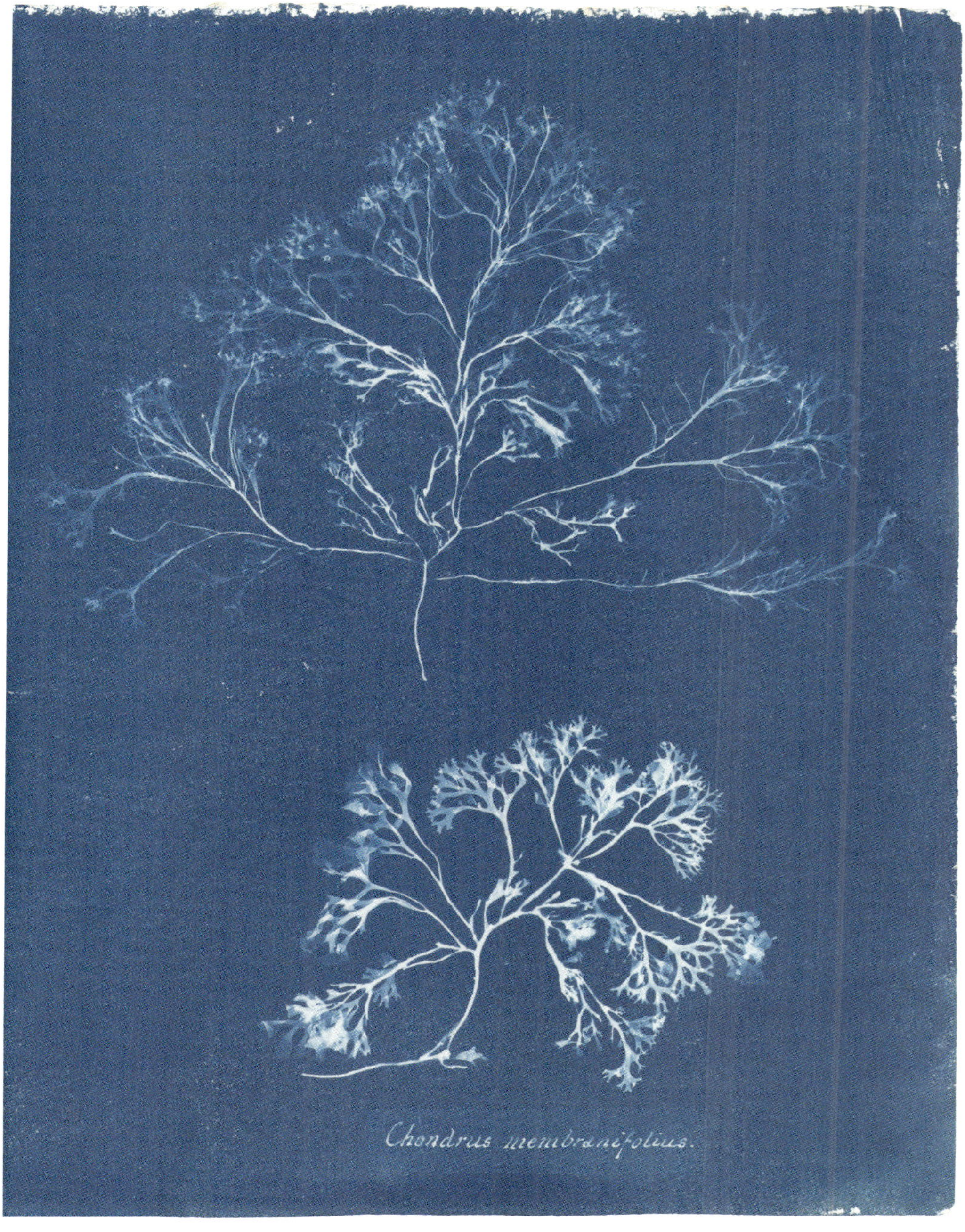

Plate 92. *Chondrus membranifolius*

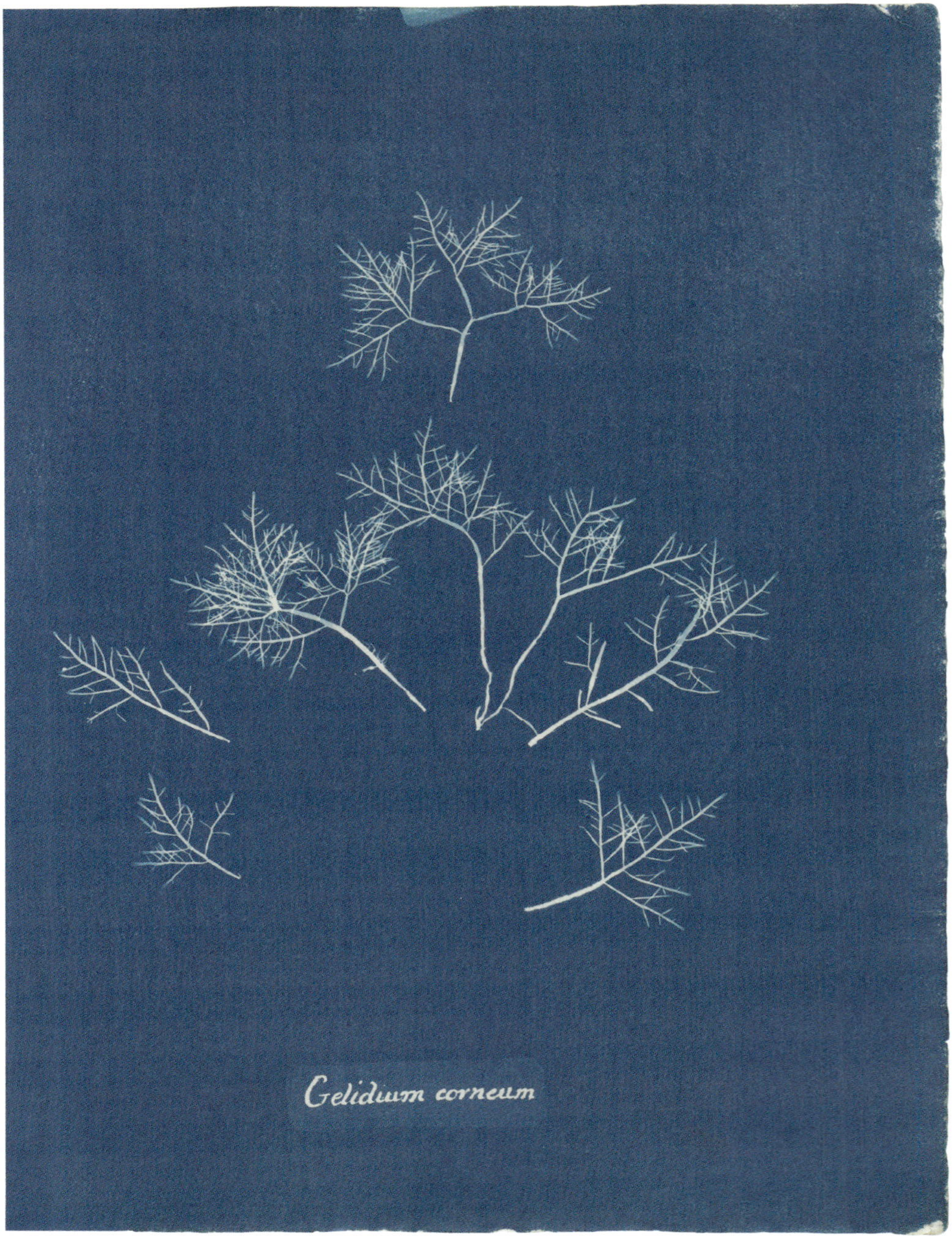

Plate 93. *Gelidium corneum*

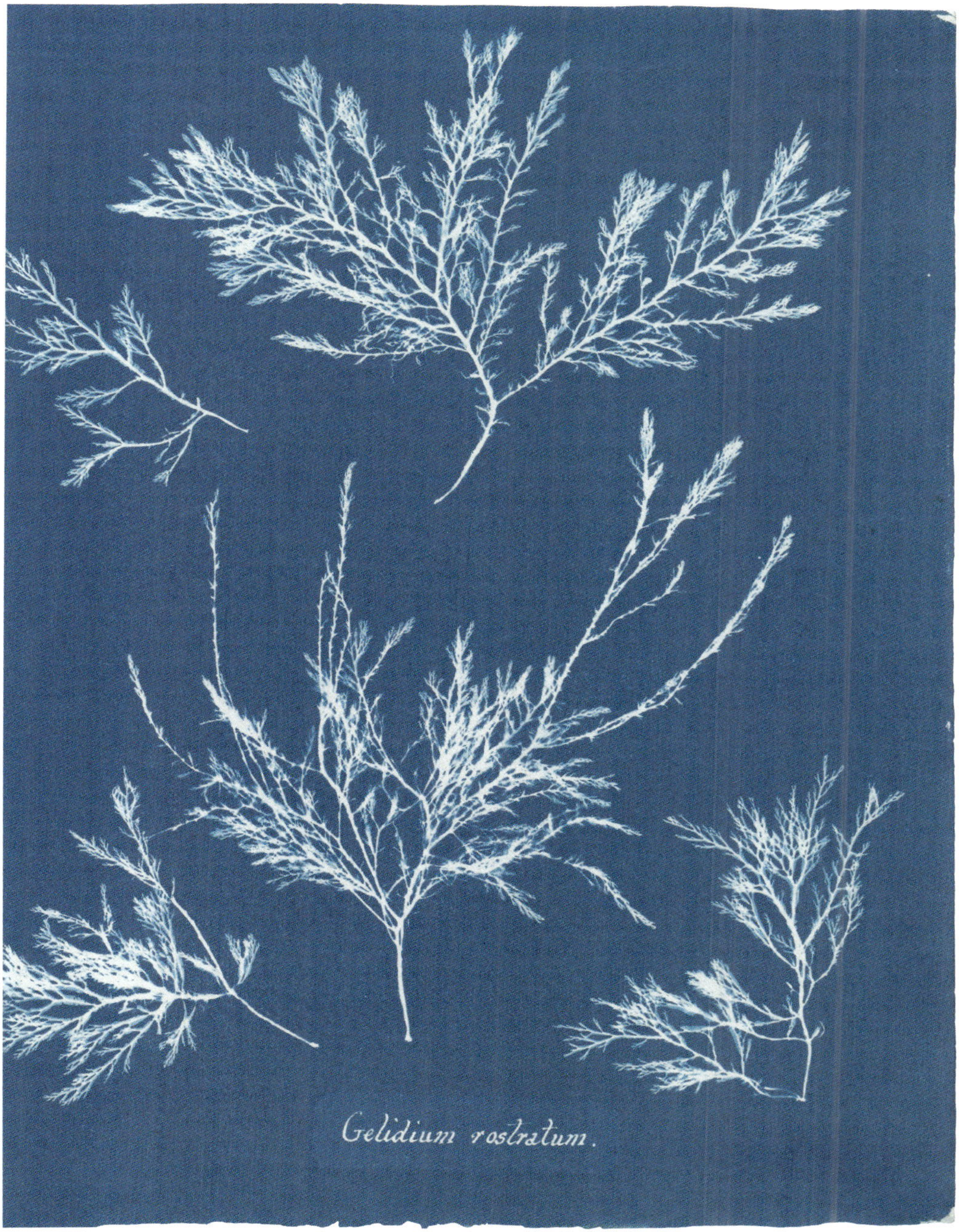

Plate 94. *Gelidium rostratum*

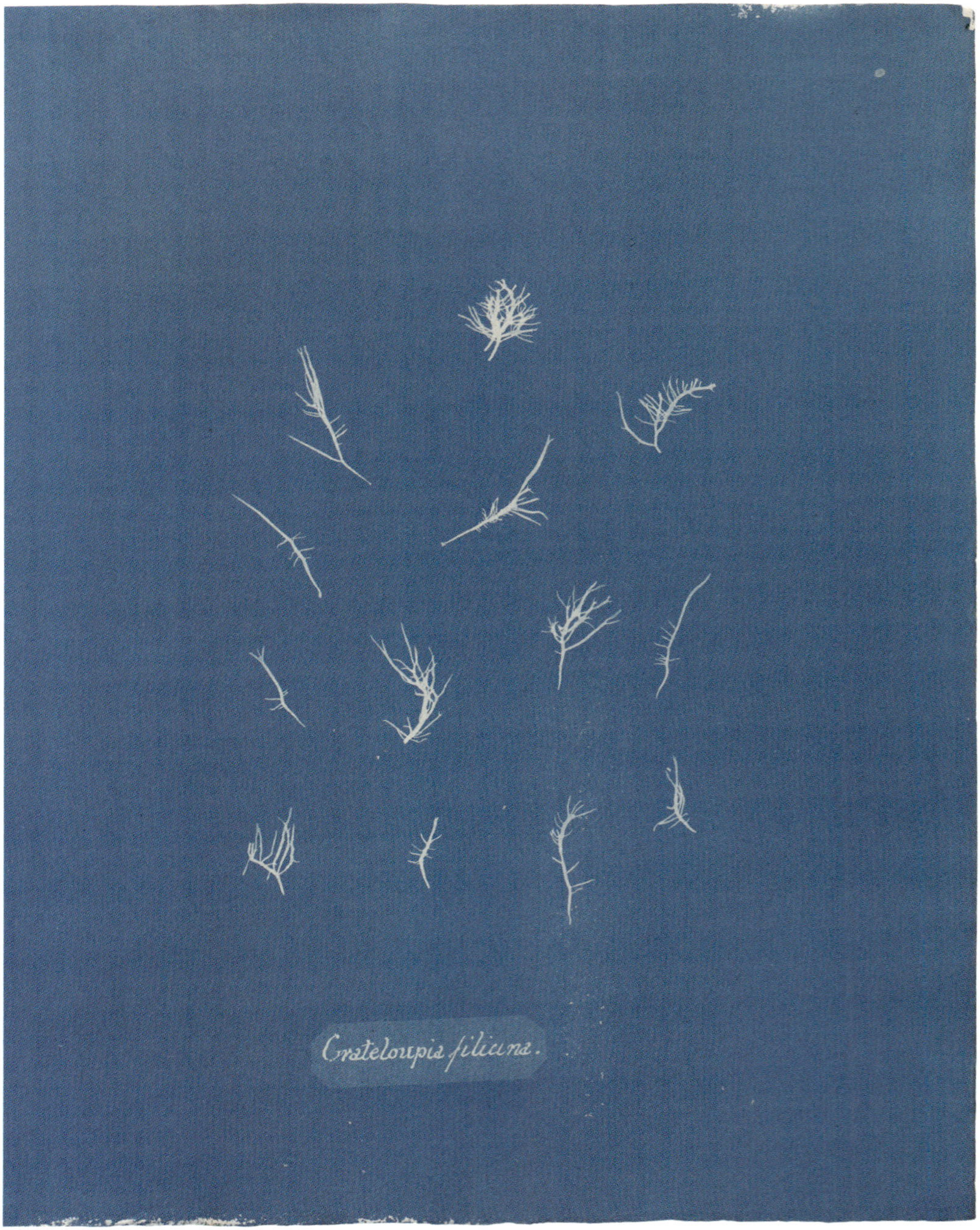

Plate 95. *Grateloupia filicina*

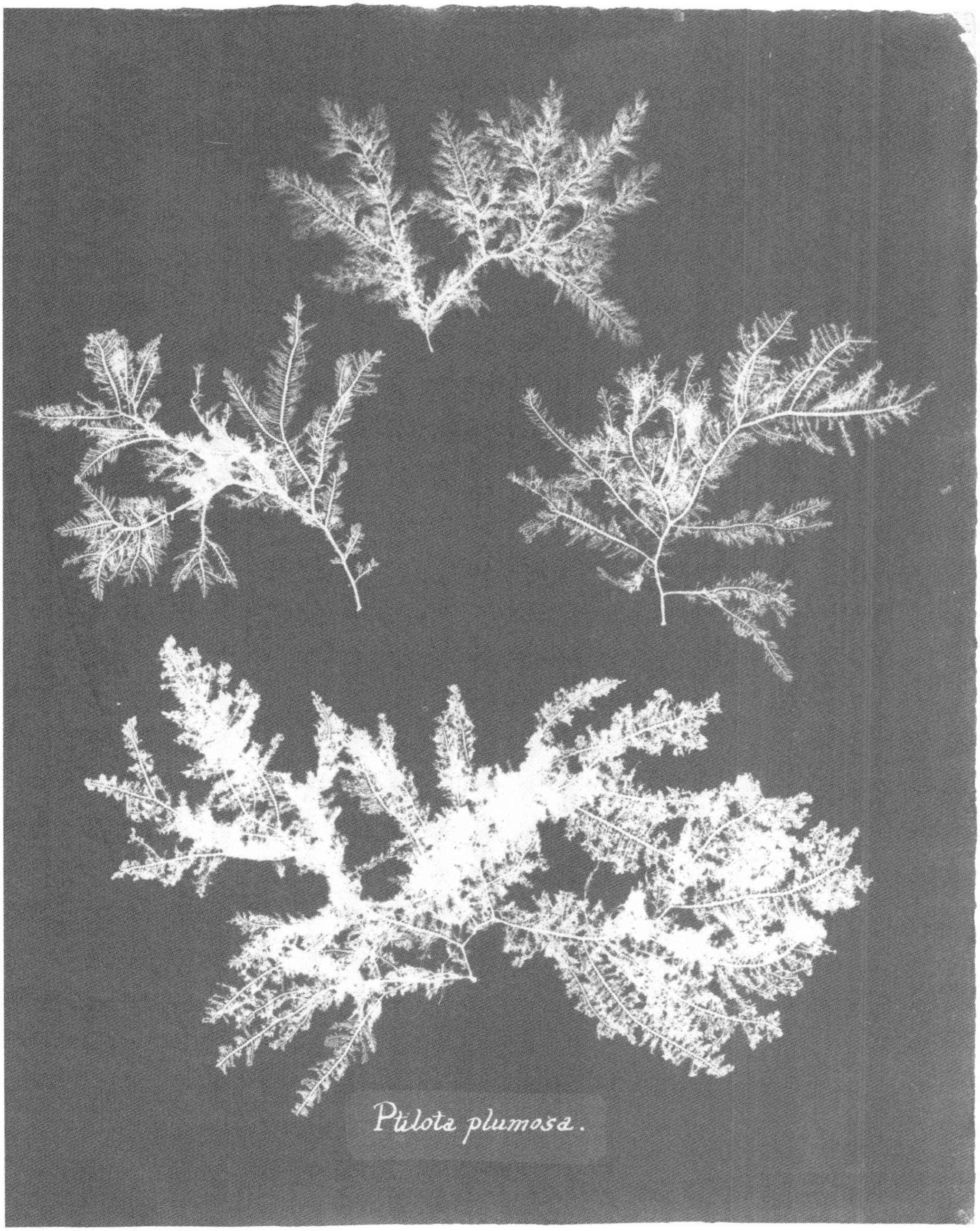

Plate 96. *Ptilota plumosa*

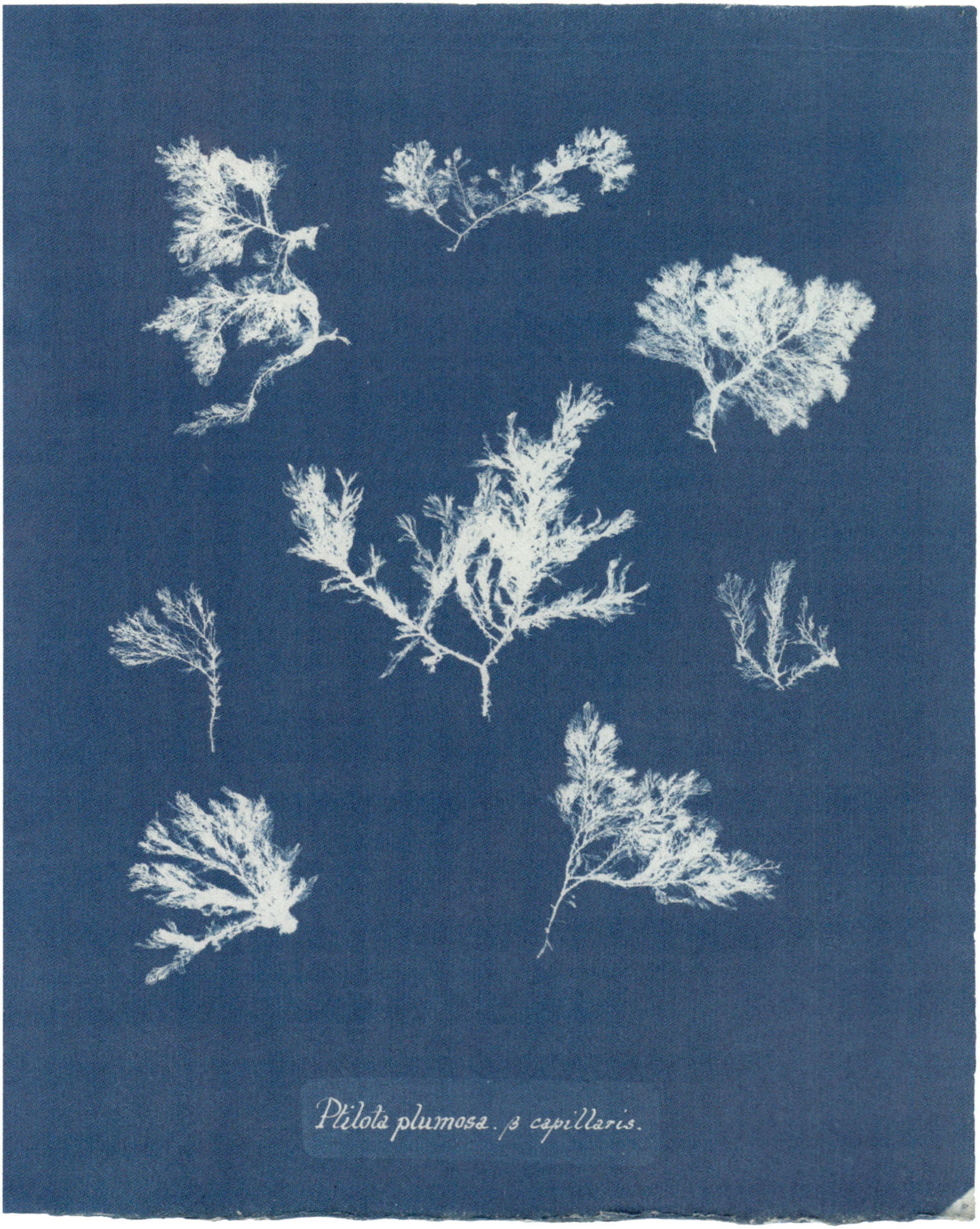

Plate 97. *Ptilota plumosa* β *capillaris*

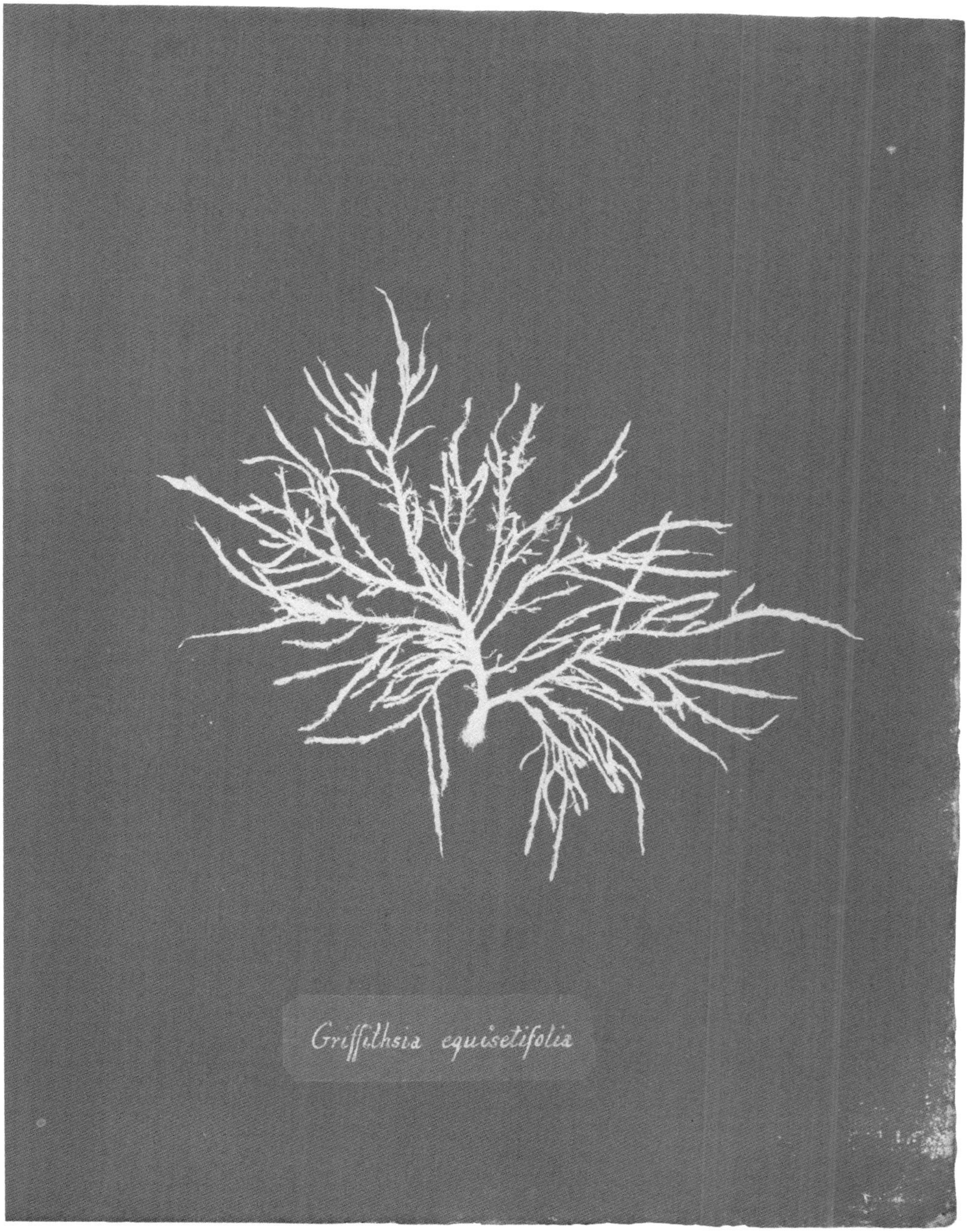

Plate 98. *Griffithsia equisetifolia*

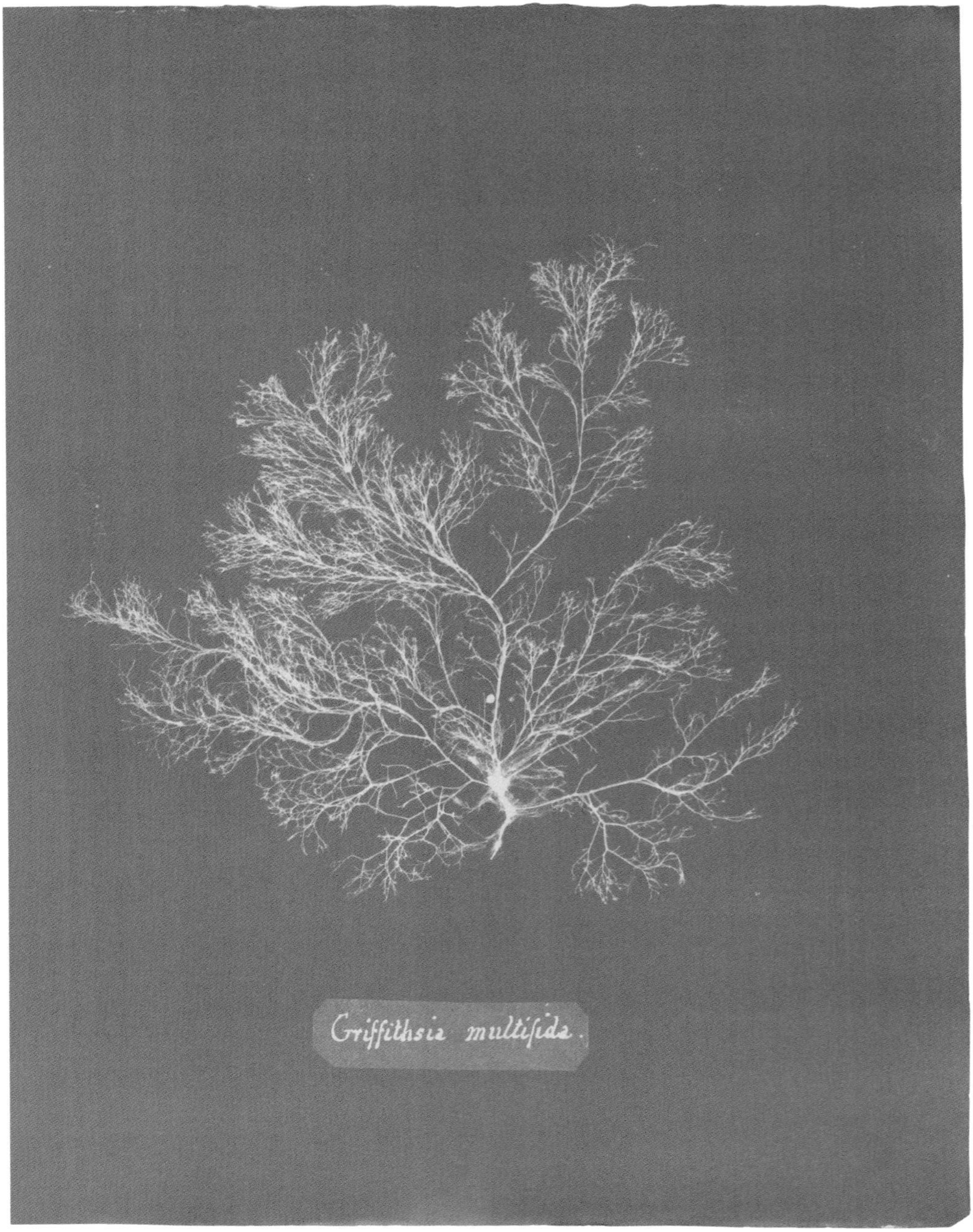

Plate 99. *Griffithsia multifida*

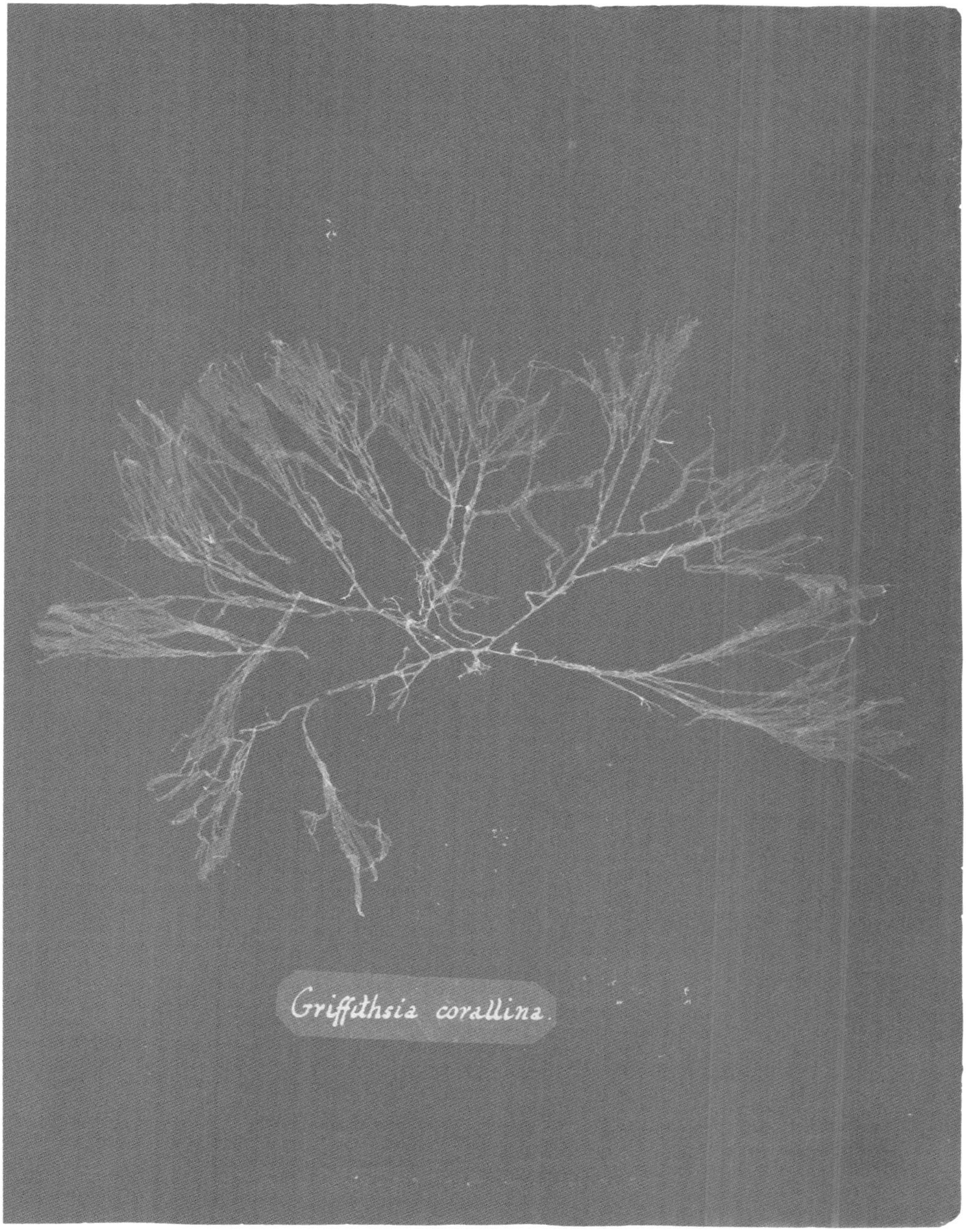

Plate 100. *Griffithsia corallina*

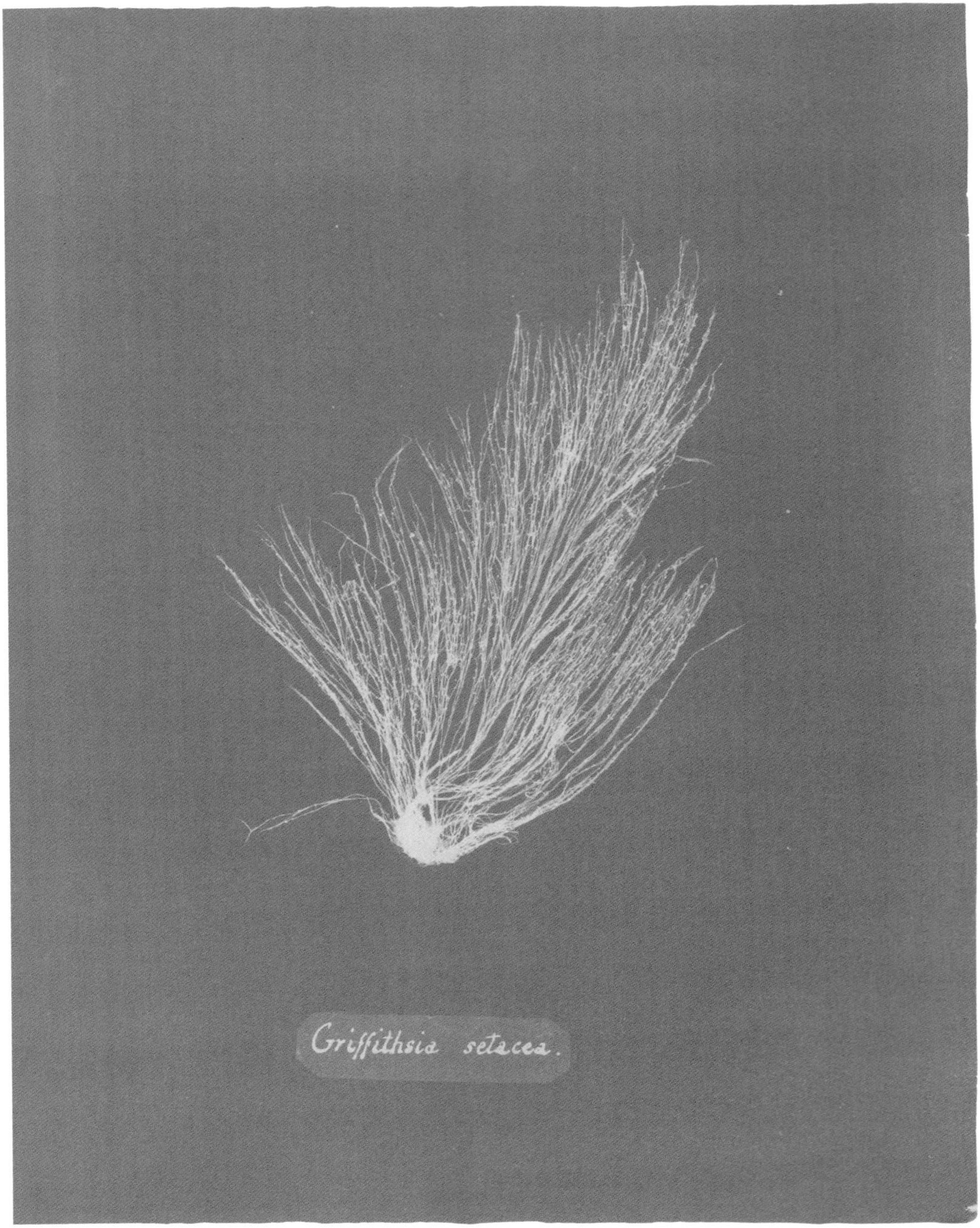

Plate 101. *Griffithsia setacea*

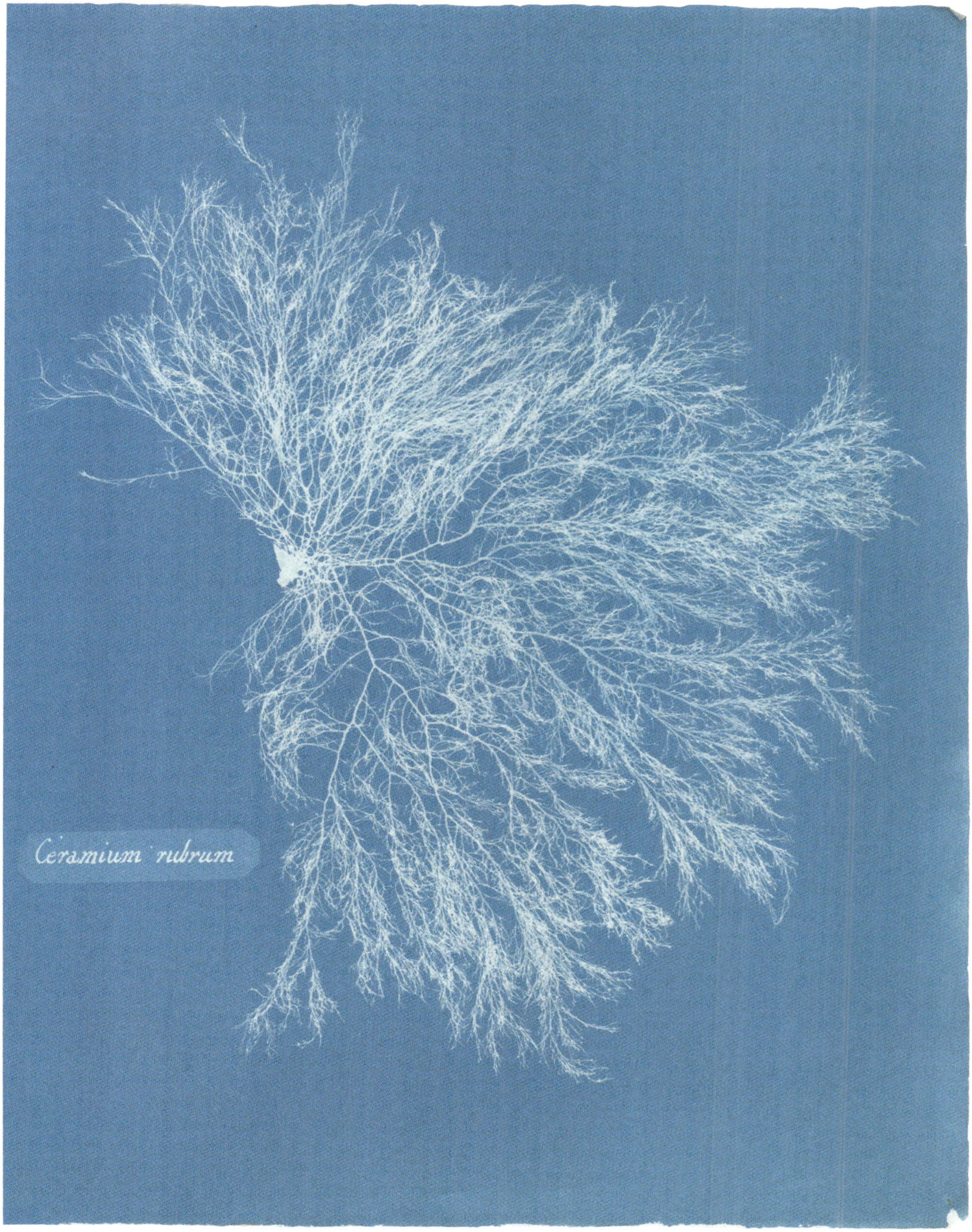

Plate 102. *Ceramium rubrum*

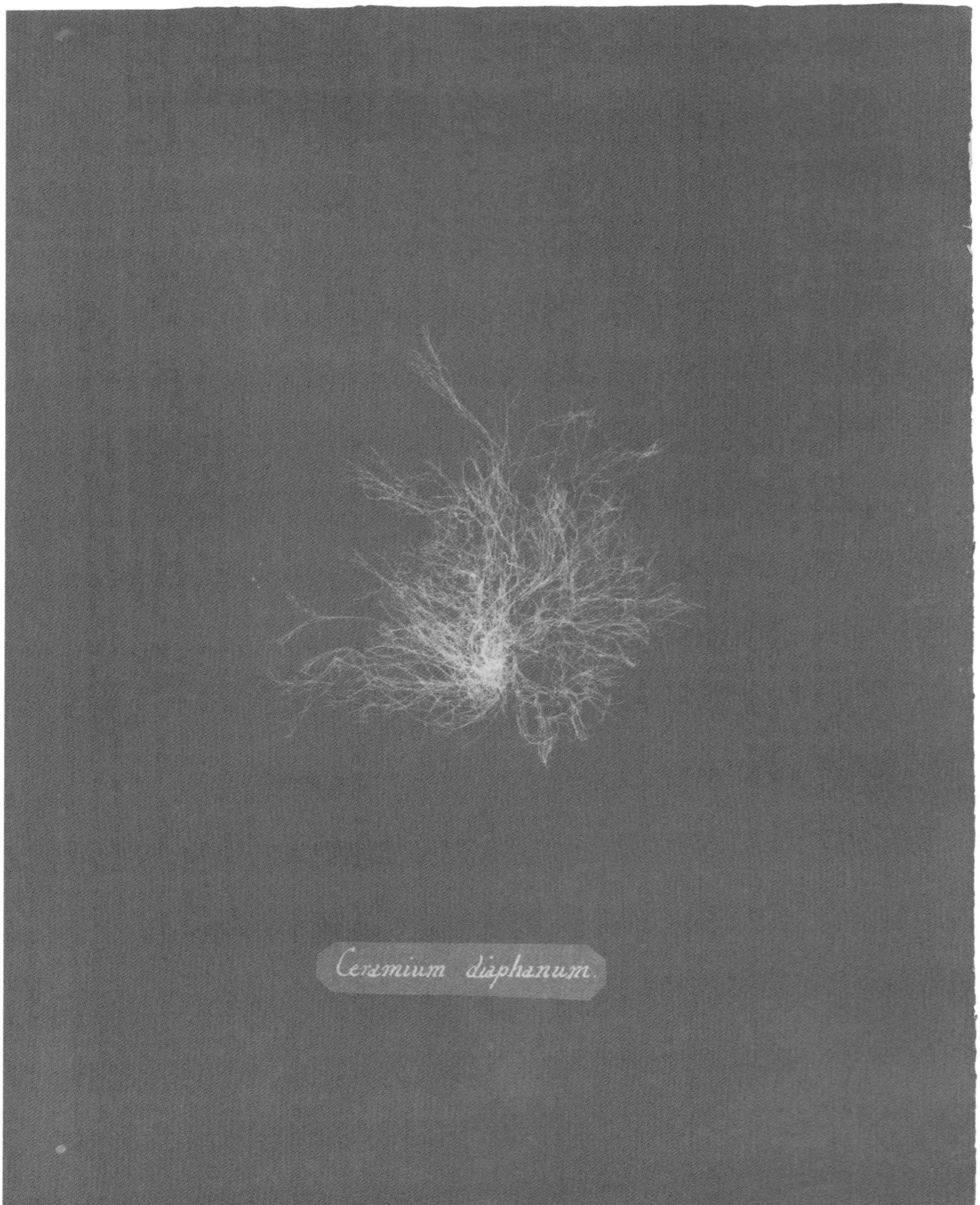

Plate 103. *Ceramium diaphanum*

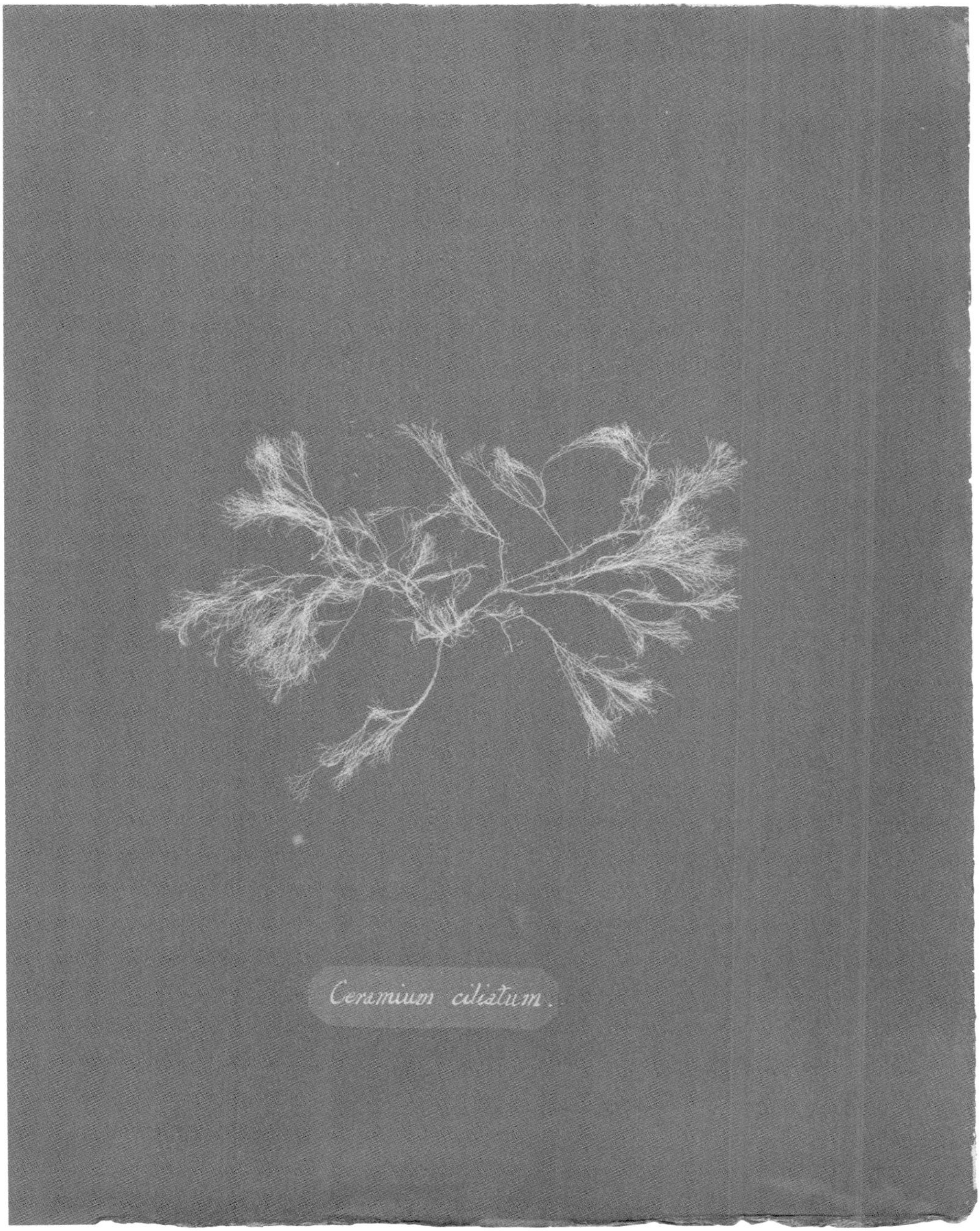

Plate 104. *Ceramium ciliatum*

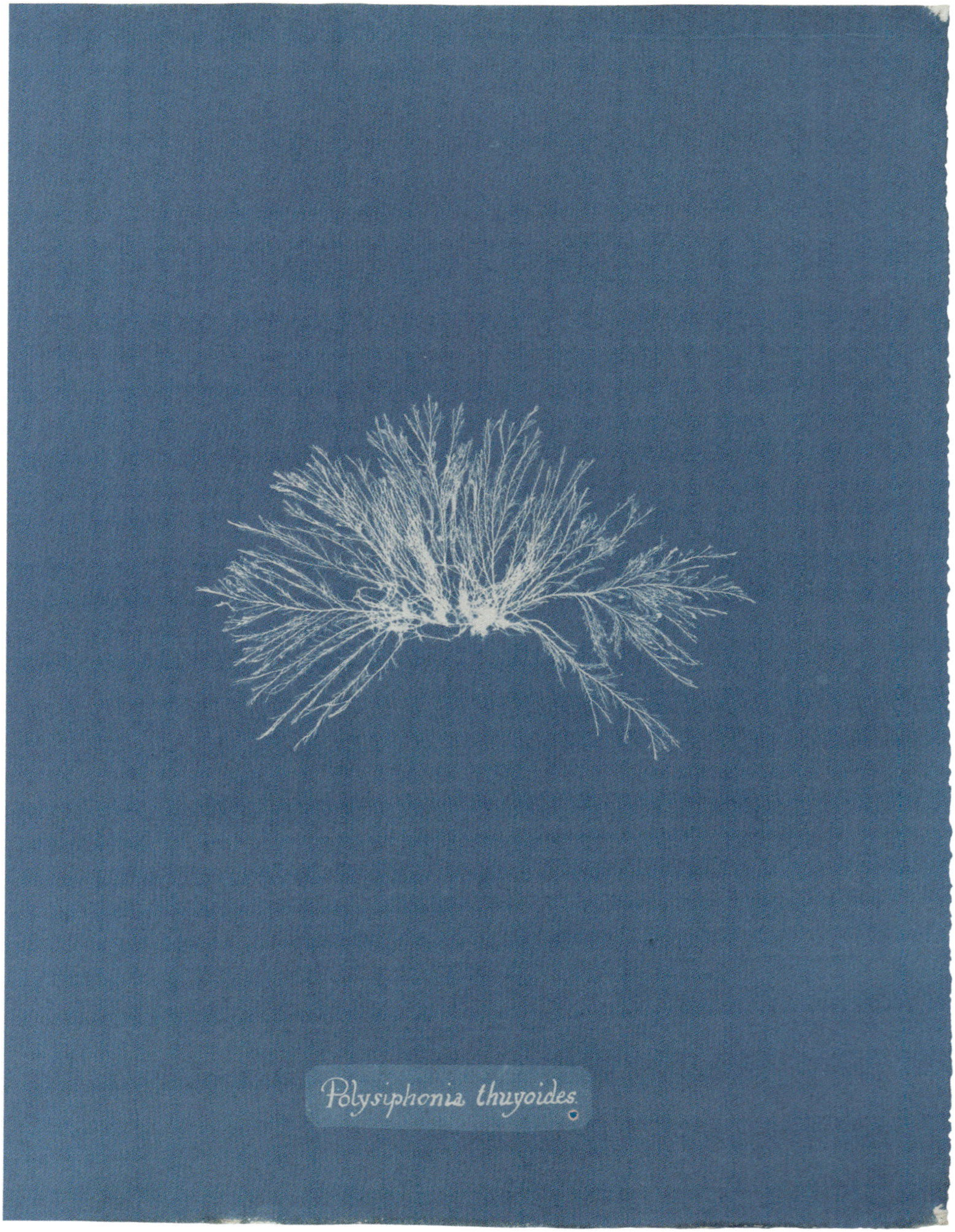

Plate 107. *Polysiphonia thuyoides*

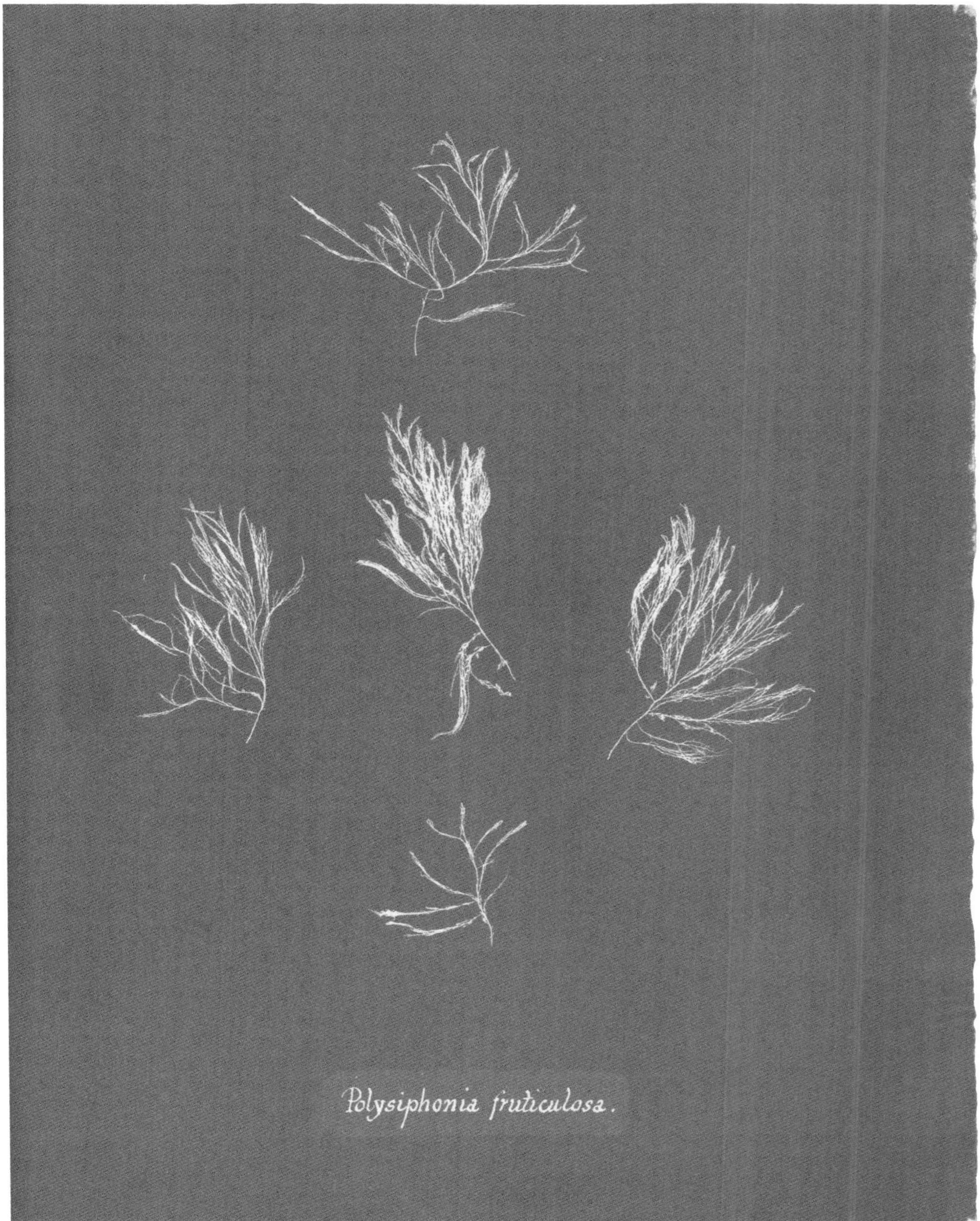

Plate 108. *Polysiphonia fruticulosa*

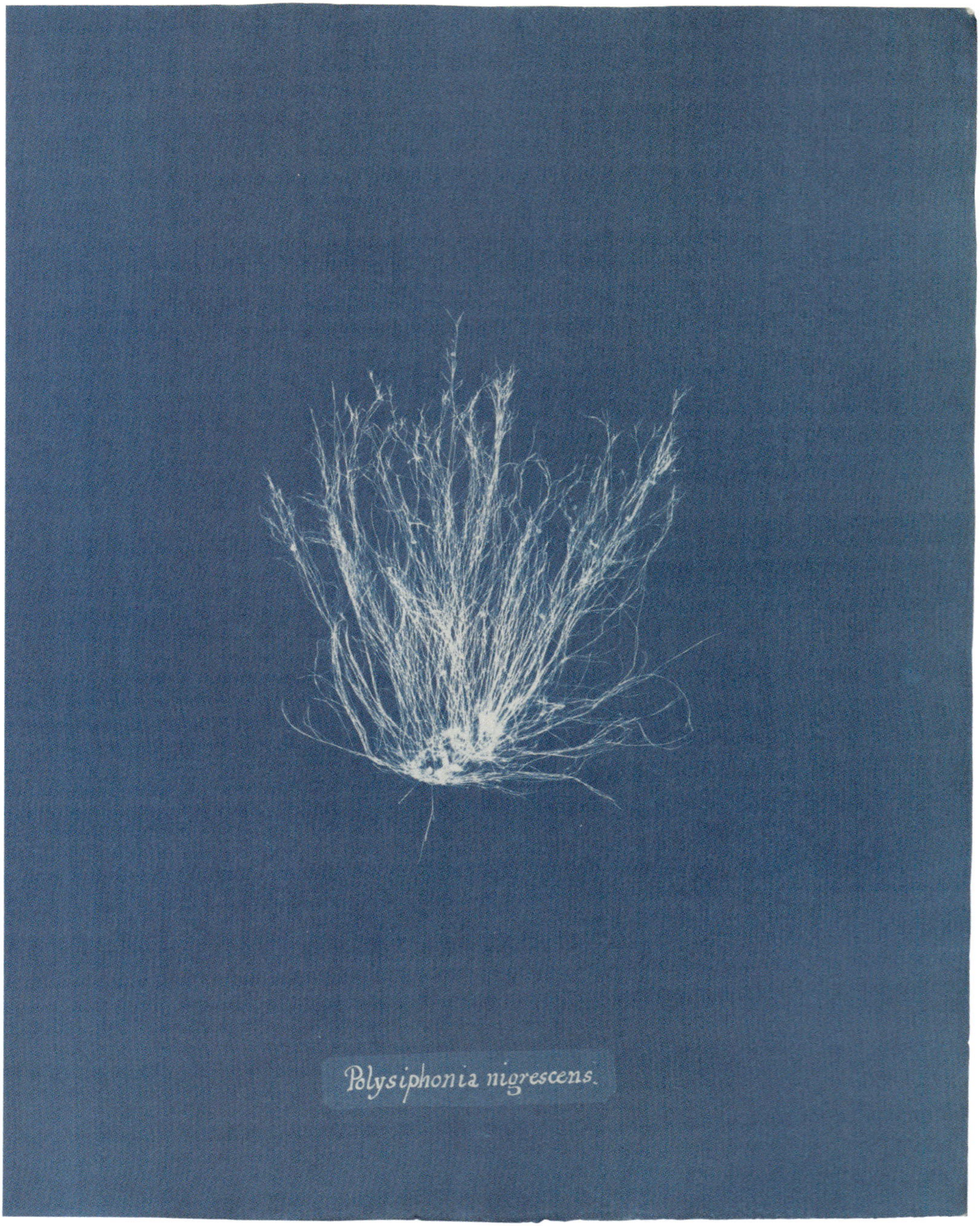

Plate 110. *Polysiphonia nigrescens*

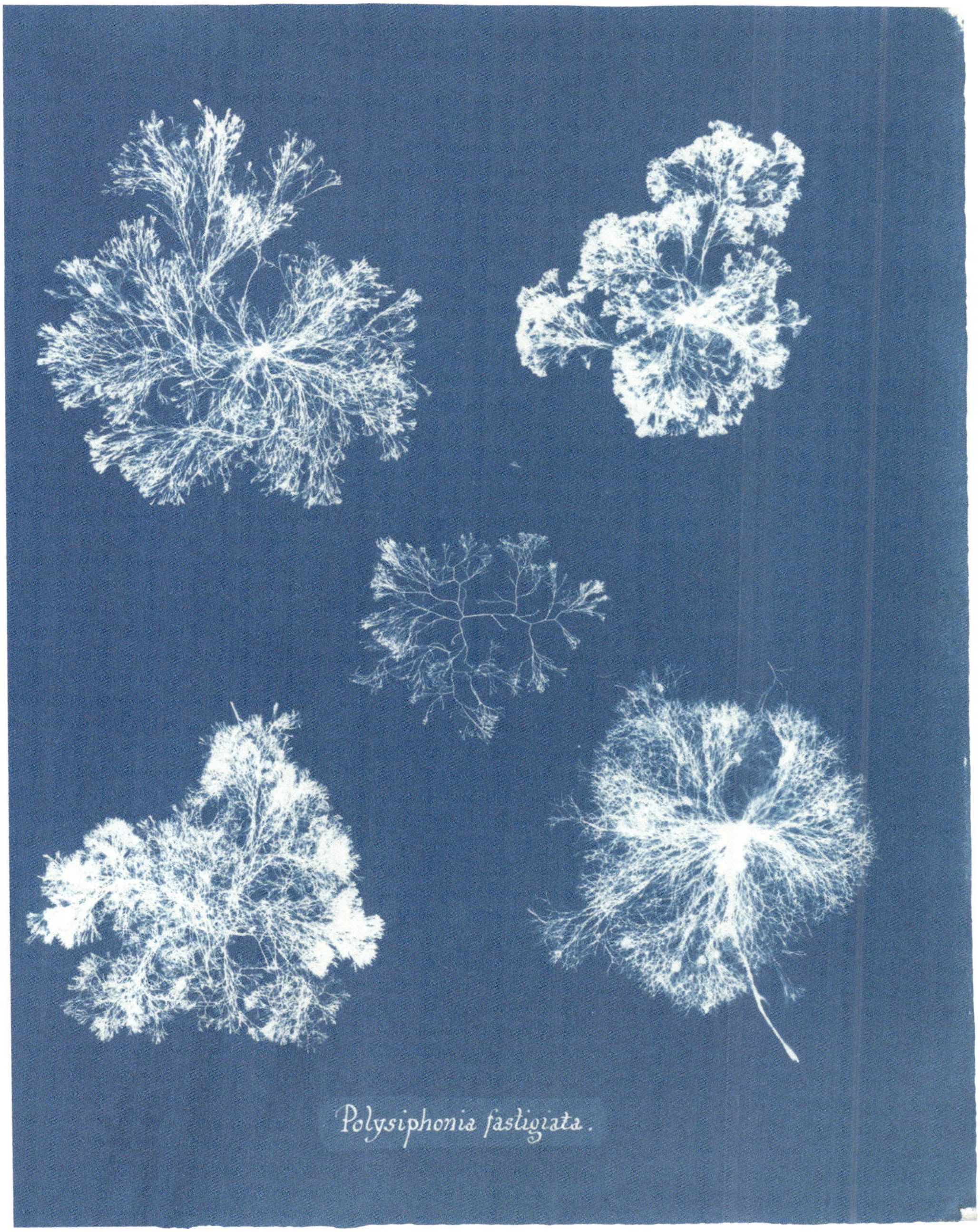

Plate 111. *Polysiphonia fastigiata*

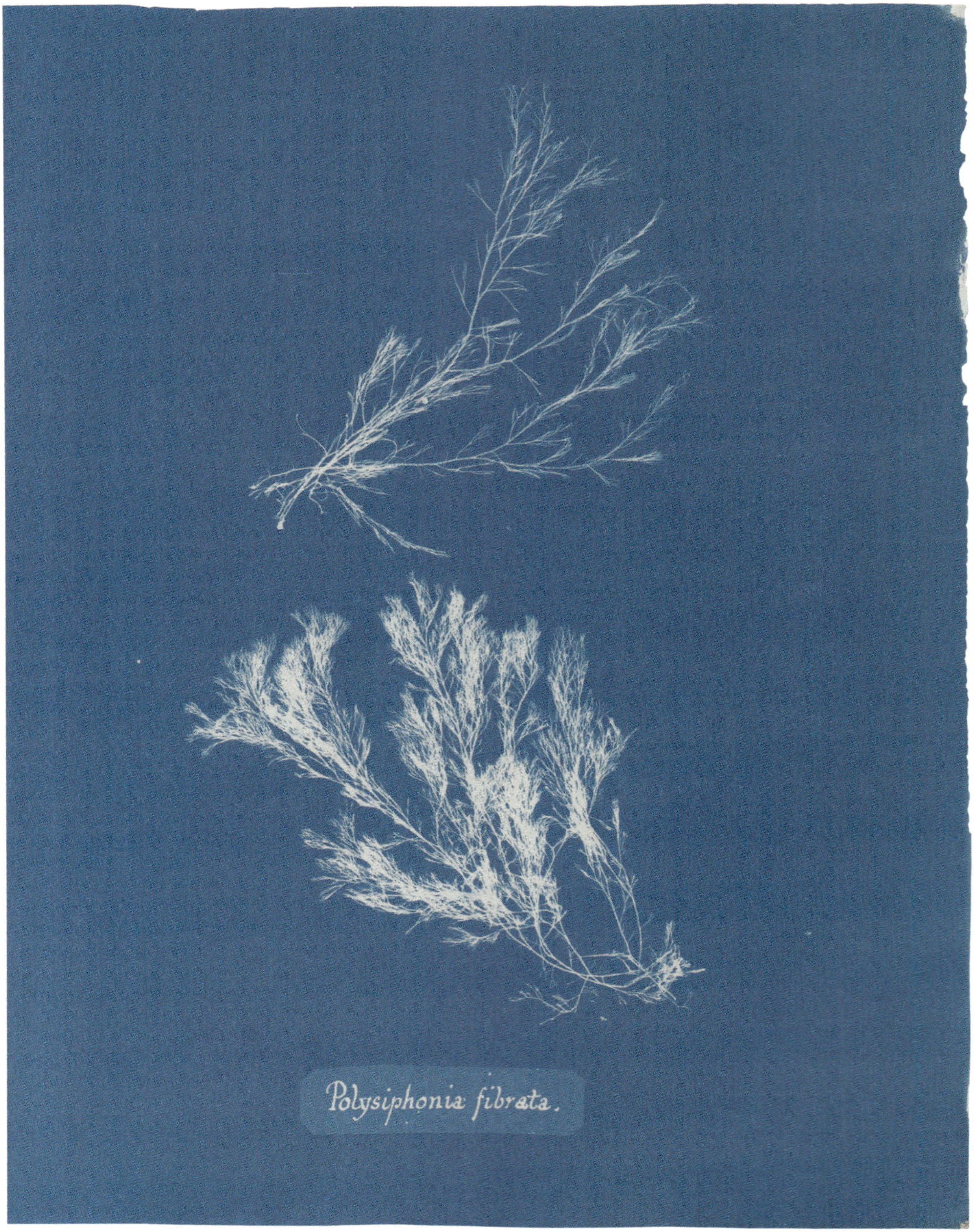

Plate 113. *Polysiphonia fibrata*

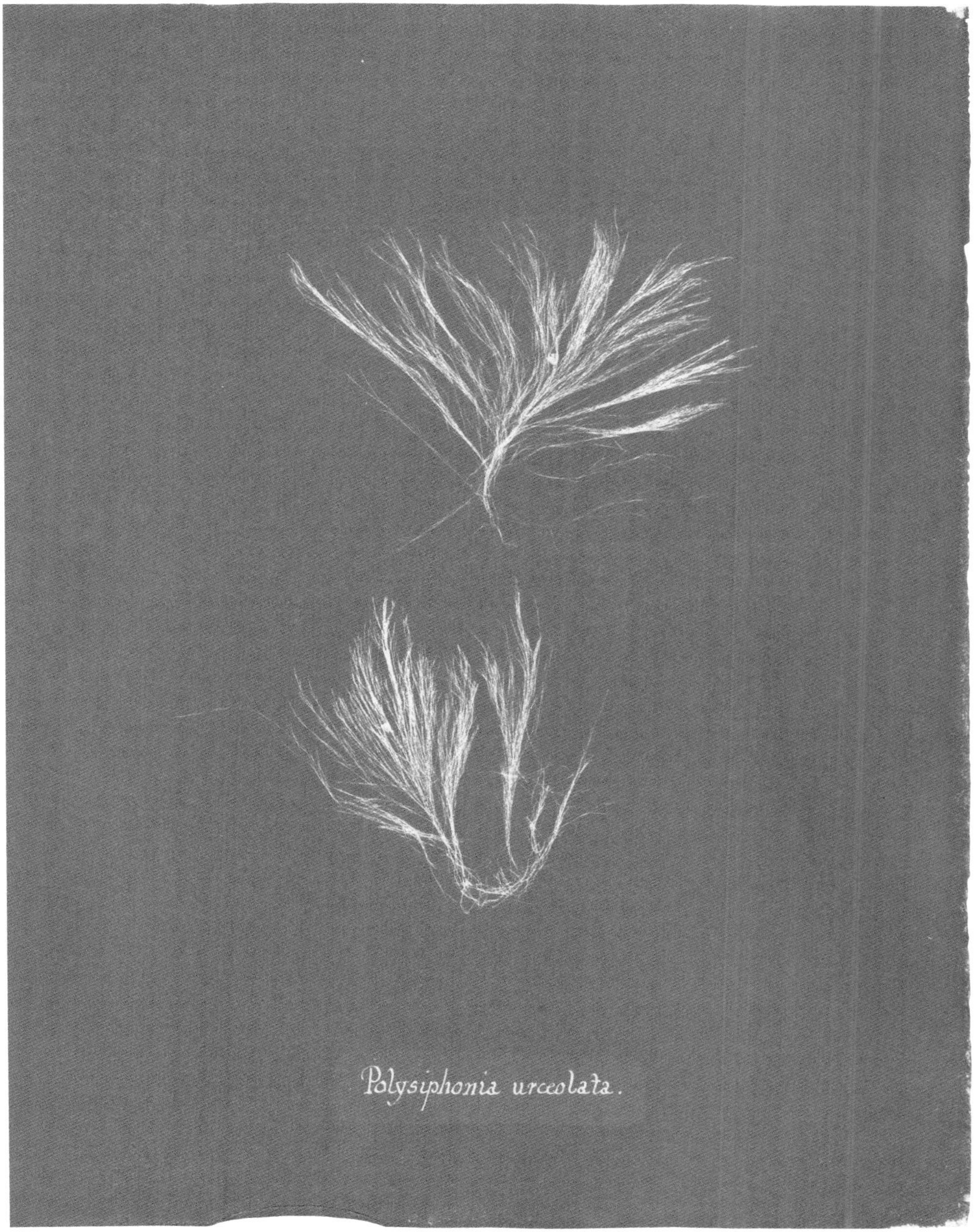

Plate 114. *Polysiphonia urceolata*

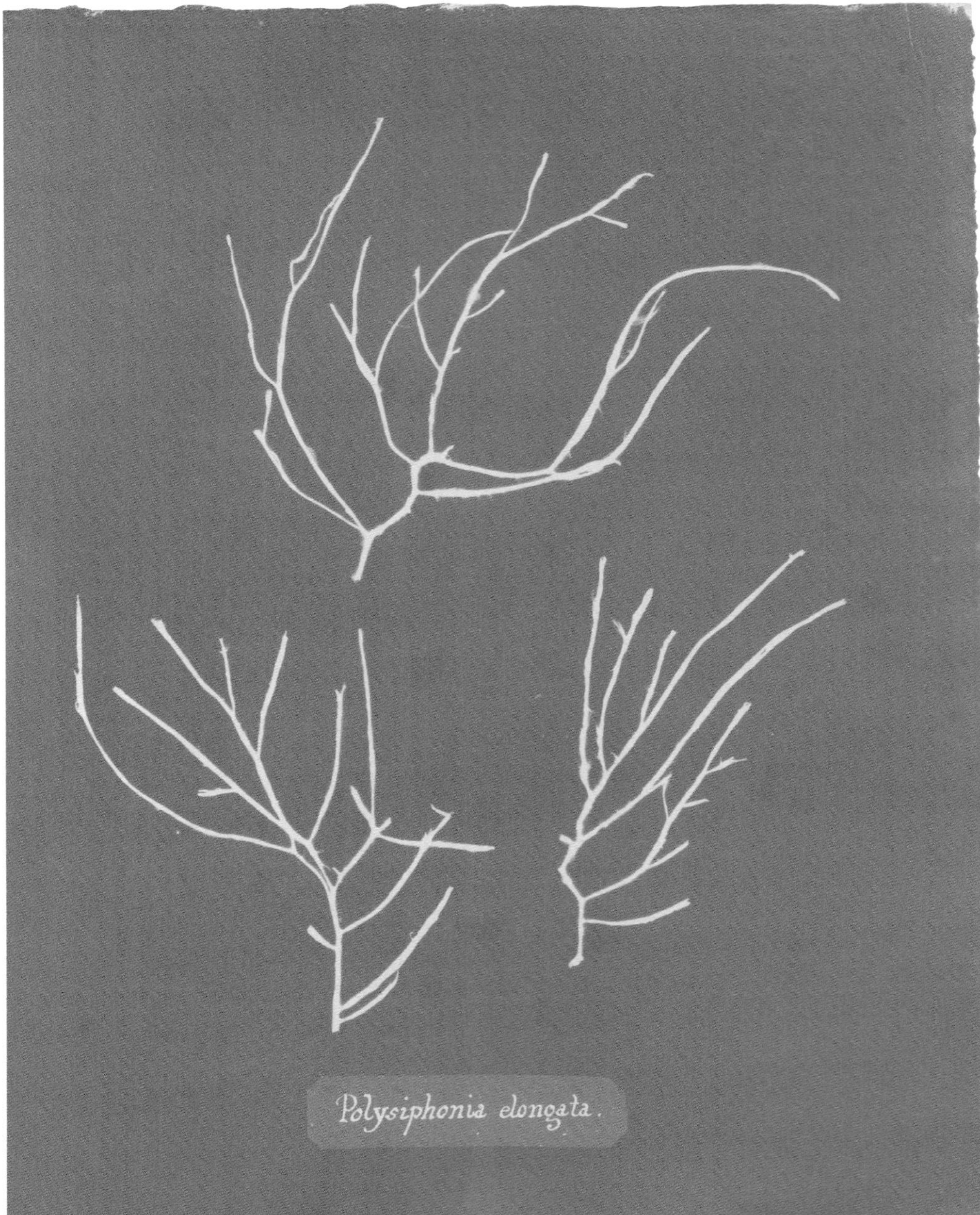

Plate 115. *Polysiphonia elongata*

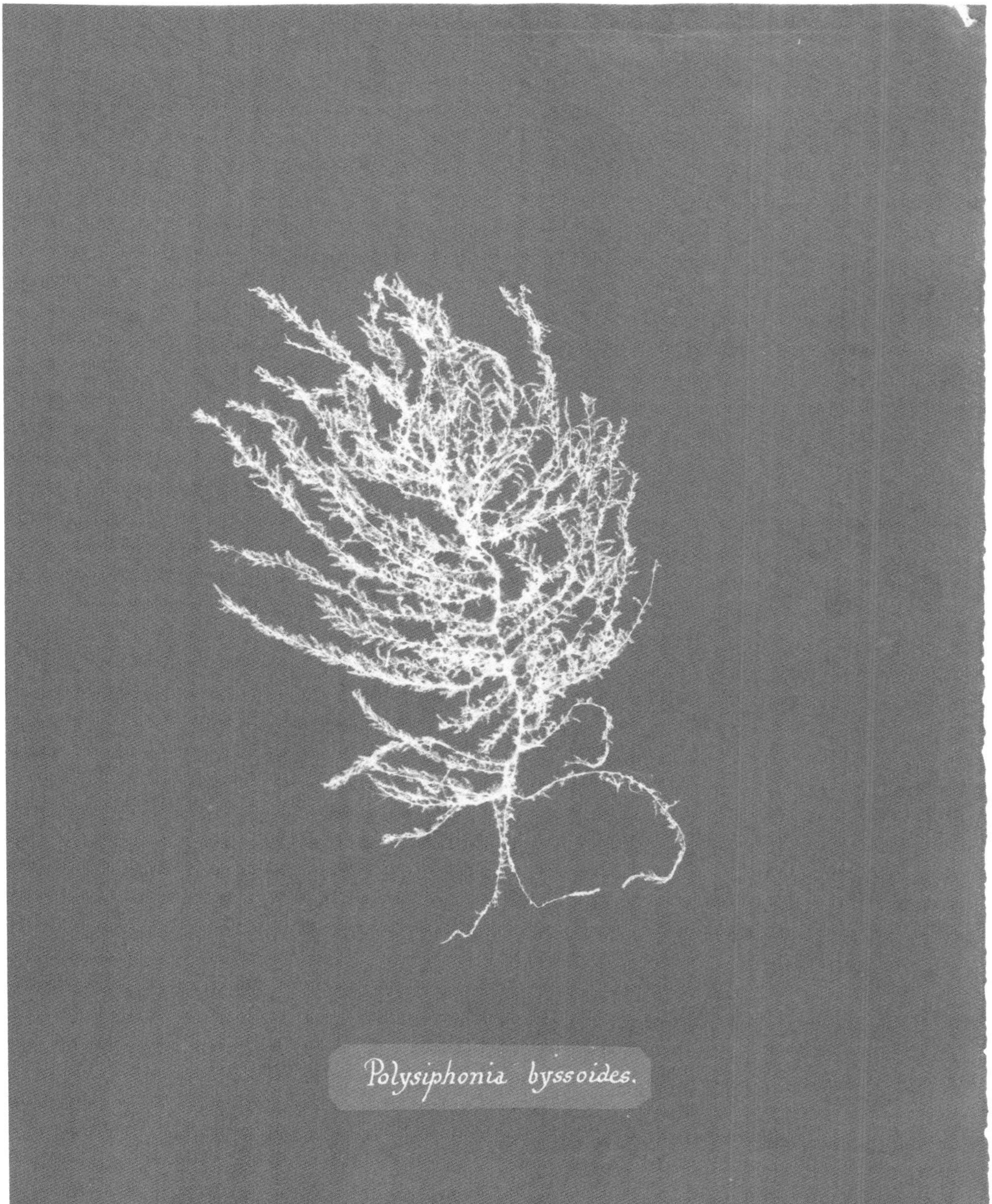

Plate 116. *Polysiphonia byssoides*

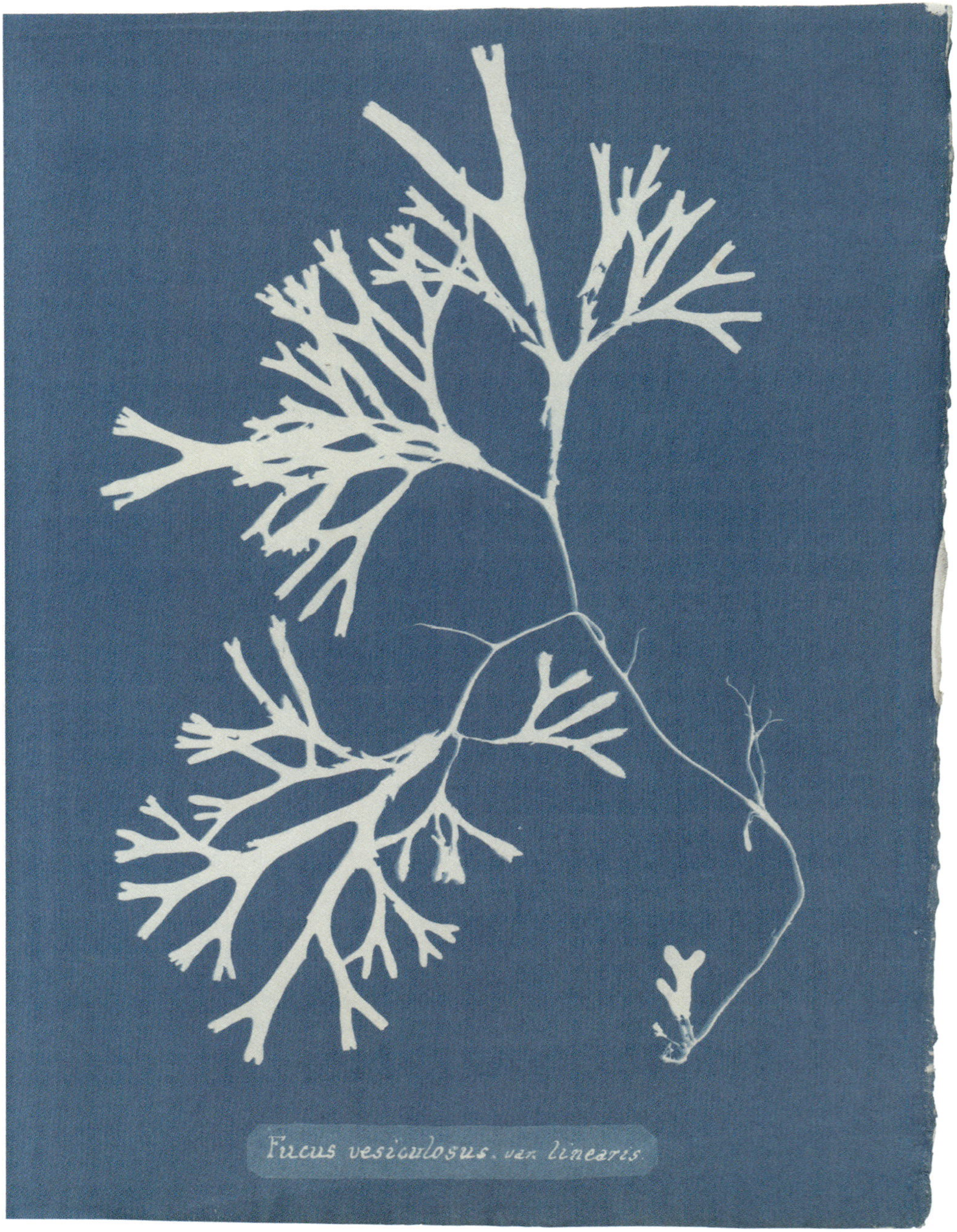

Plate 117. *Fucus vesiculosus* var. *linearis*

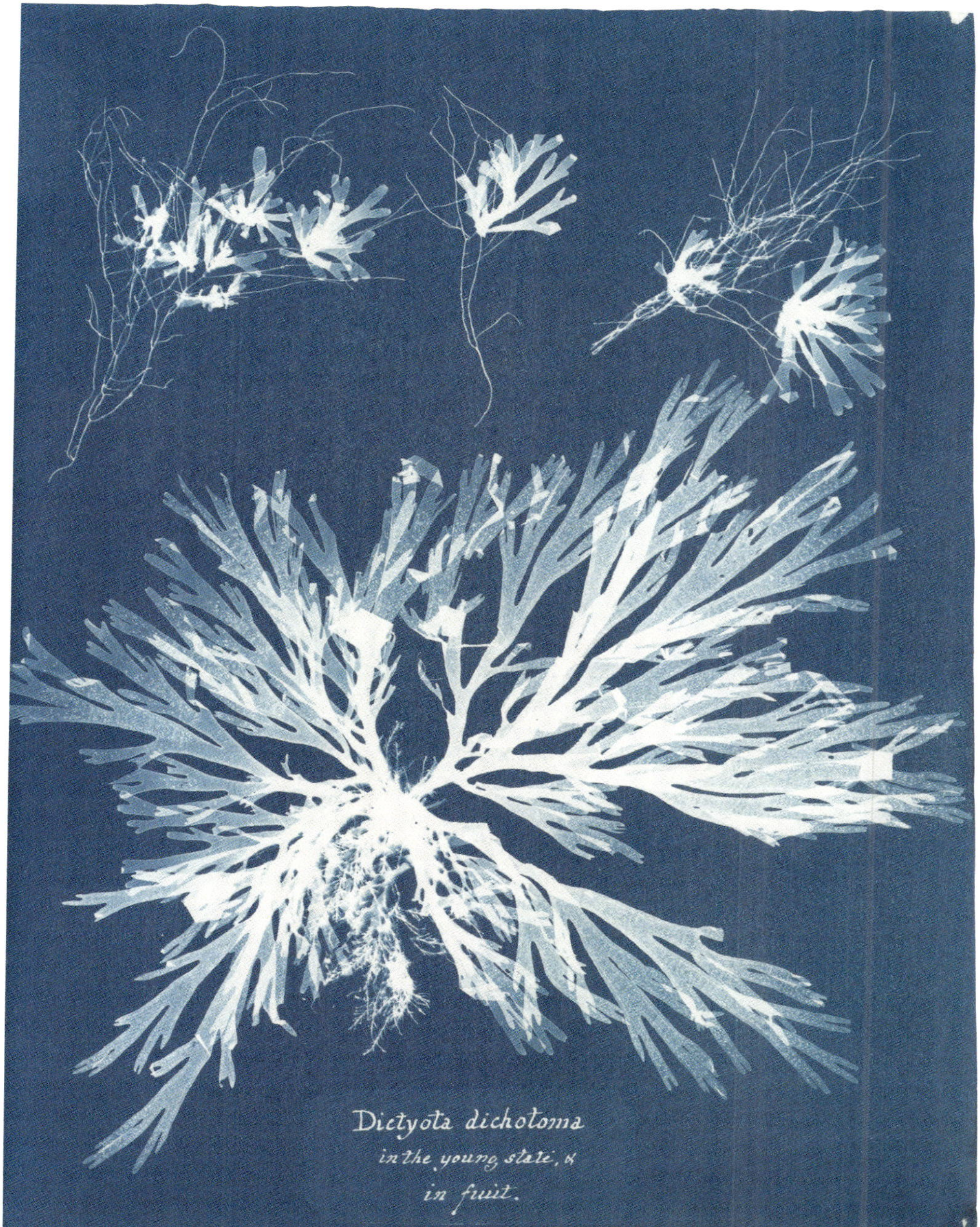

Plate 118. *Dictyota dichotoma*, in the young state, and in fruit

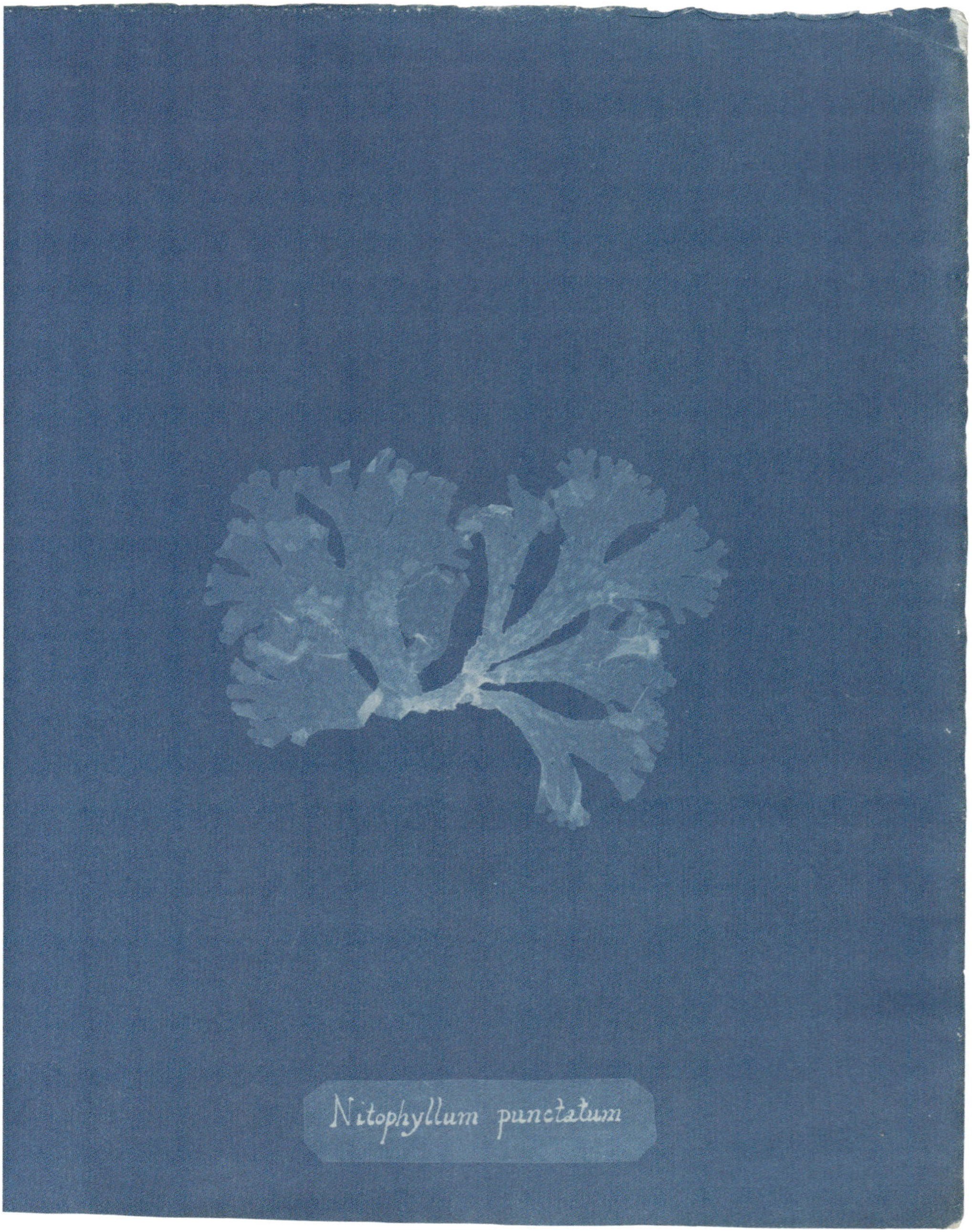

Plate 119. *Nitophyllum punctatum*

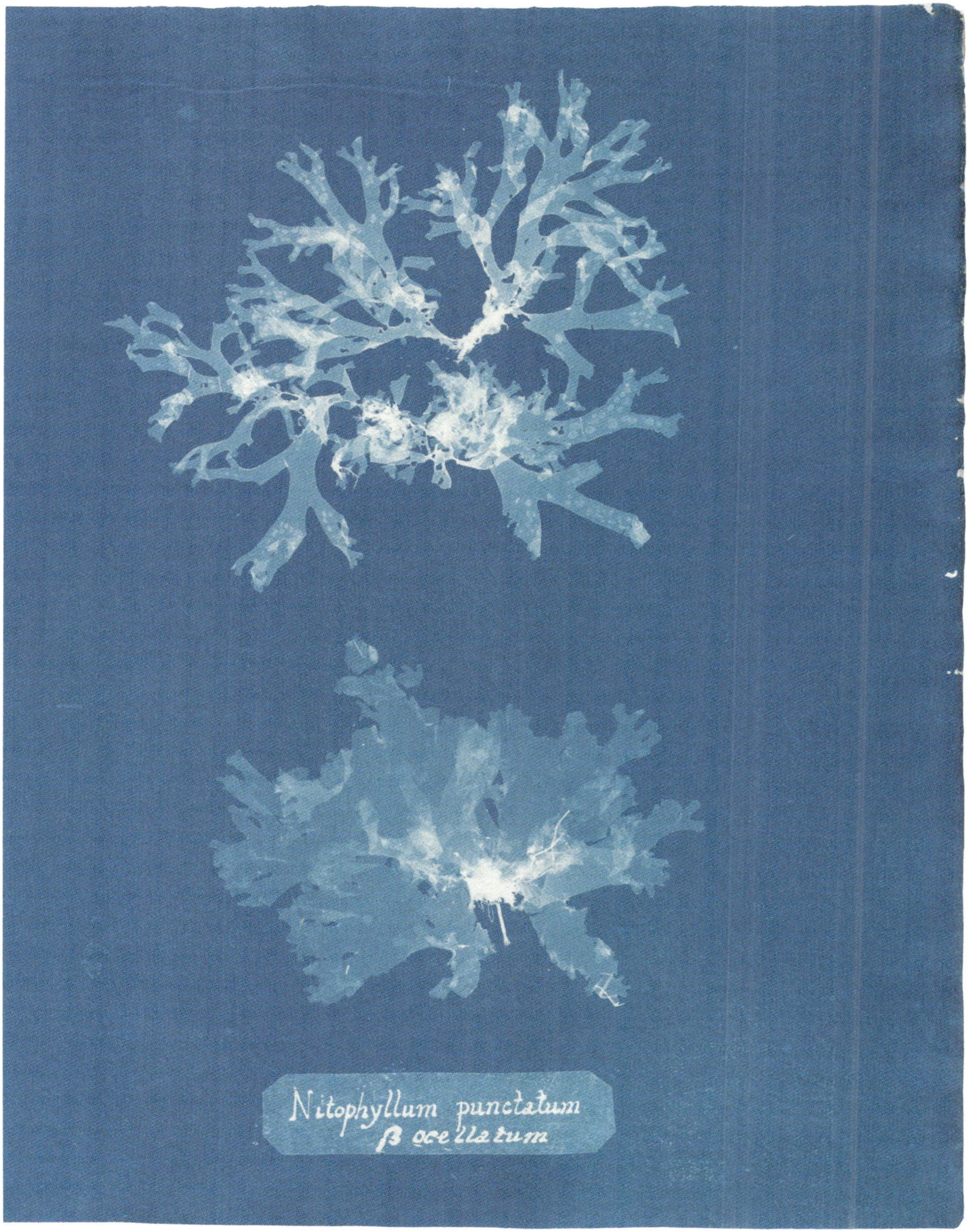

Plate 120. *Nitophyllum punctatum* β *ocellatum*

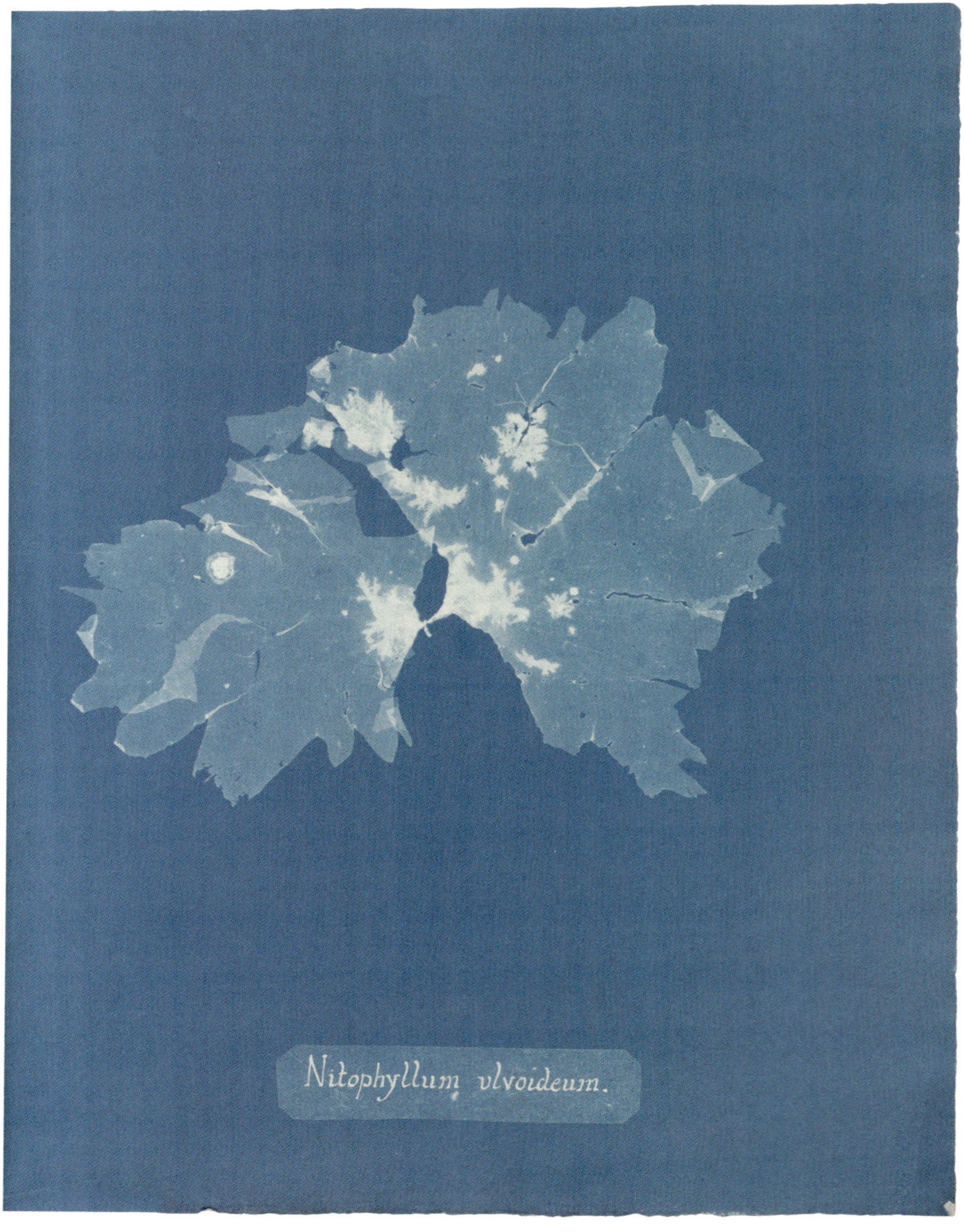

Plate 121. *Nitophyllum ulvoideum*

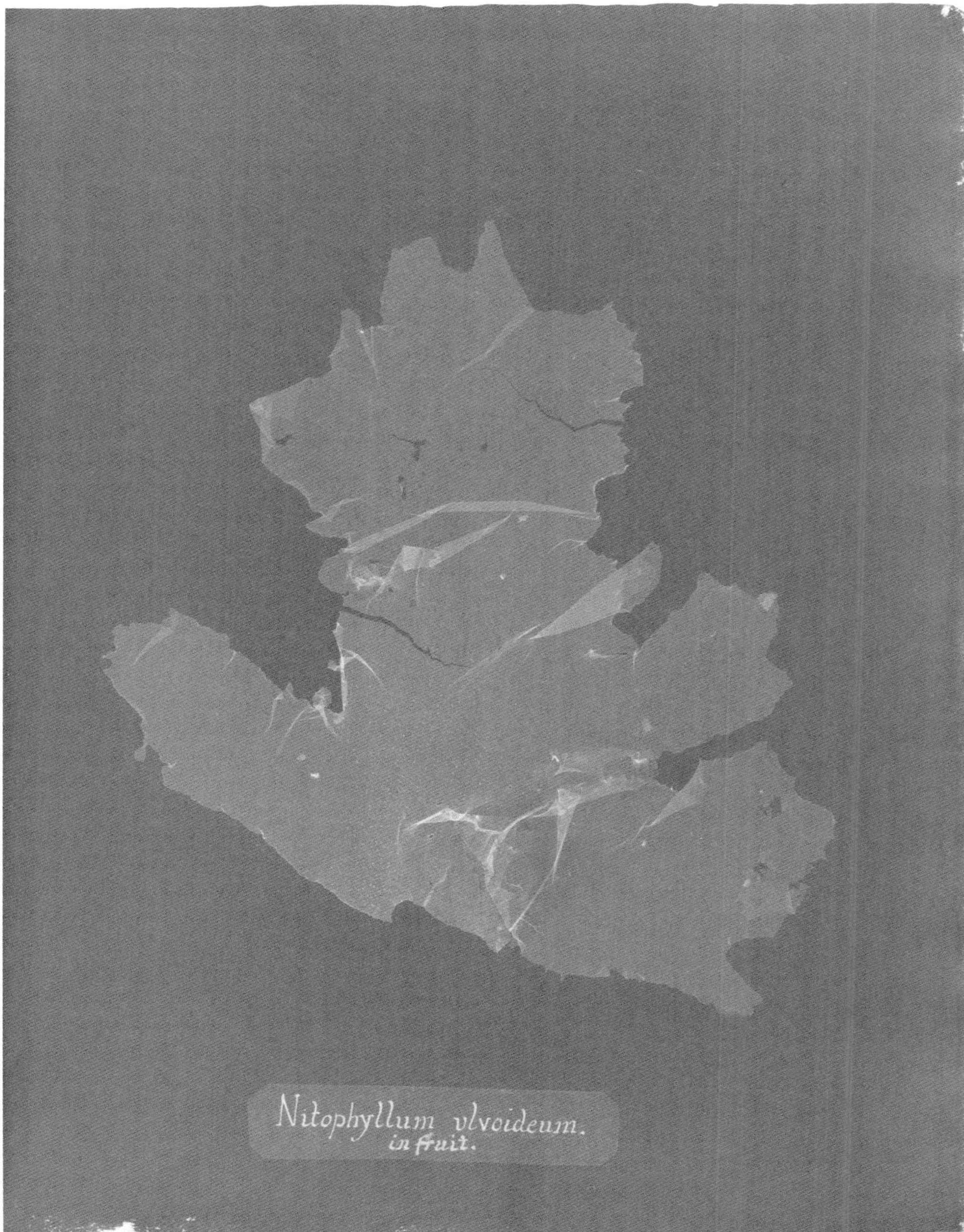

Plate 122. *Nitophyllum ulvoideum* in fruit

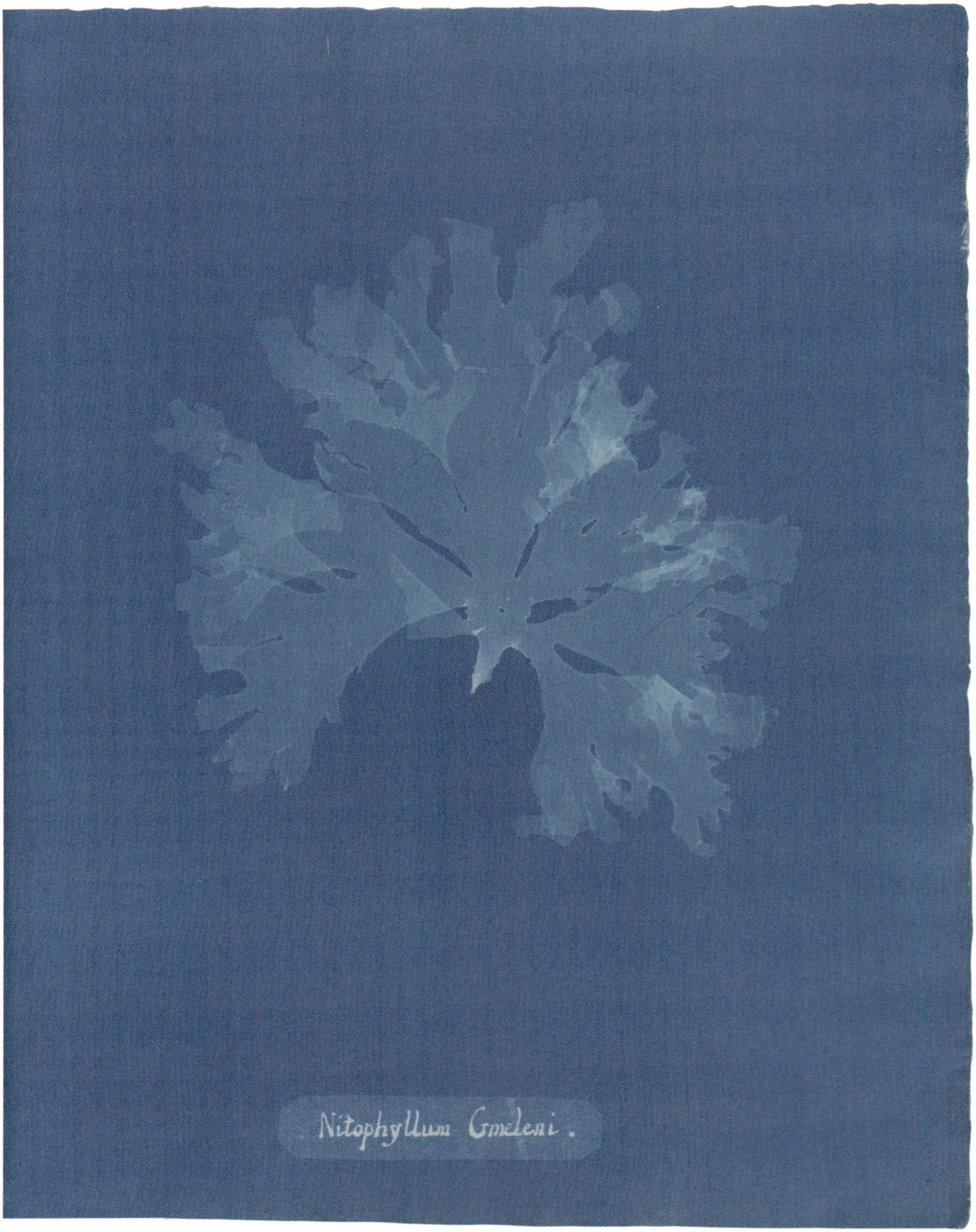

Plate 123. *Nitophyllum gmeleni*

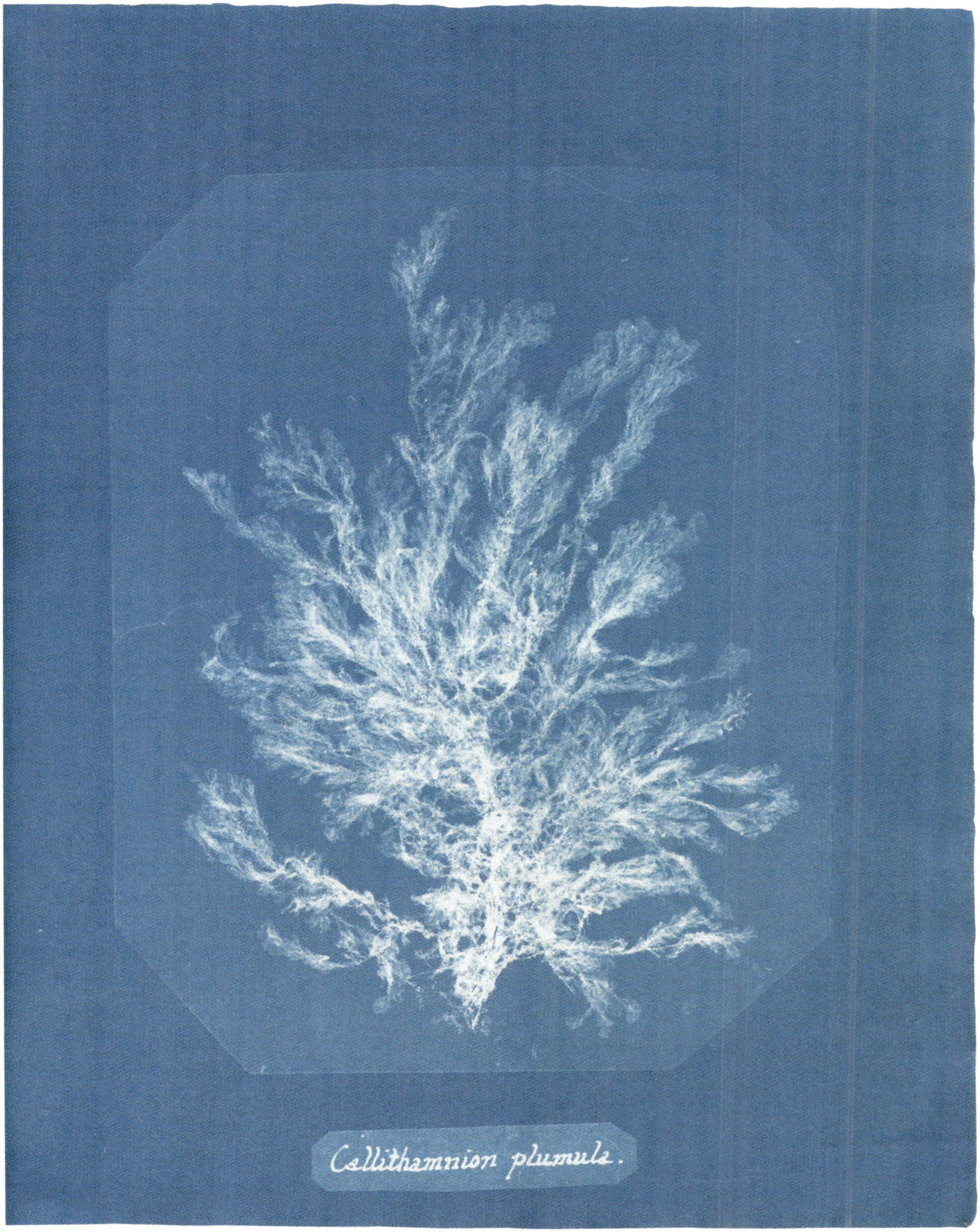

Plate 124. *Callithamnion plumula*

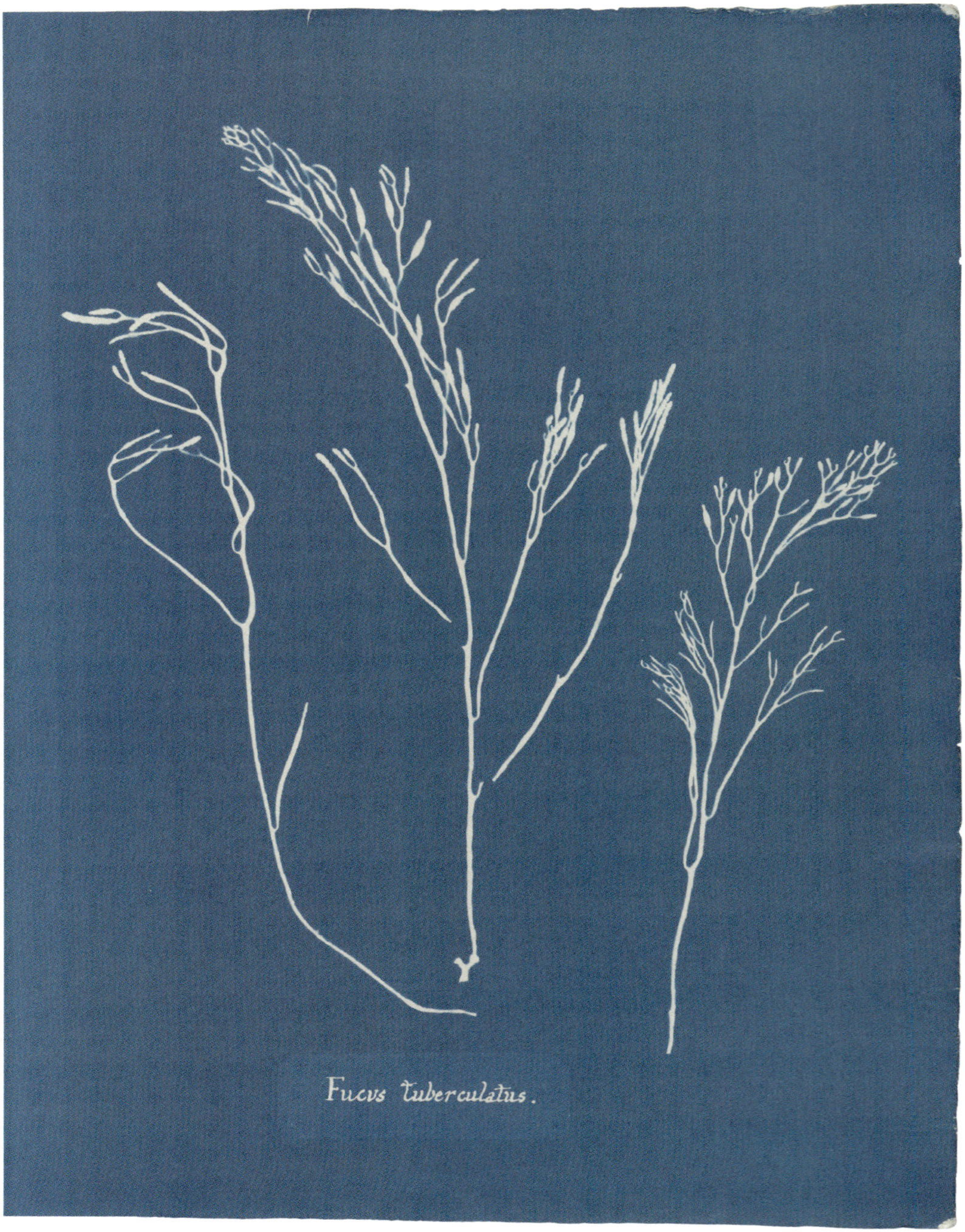

Plate 129. *Fucus tuberculatus*

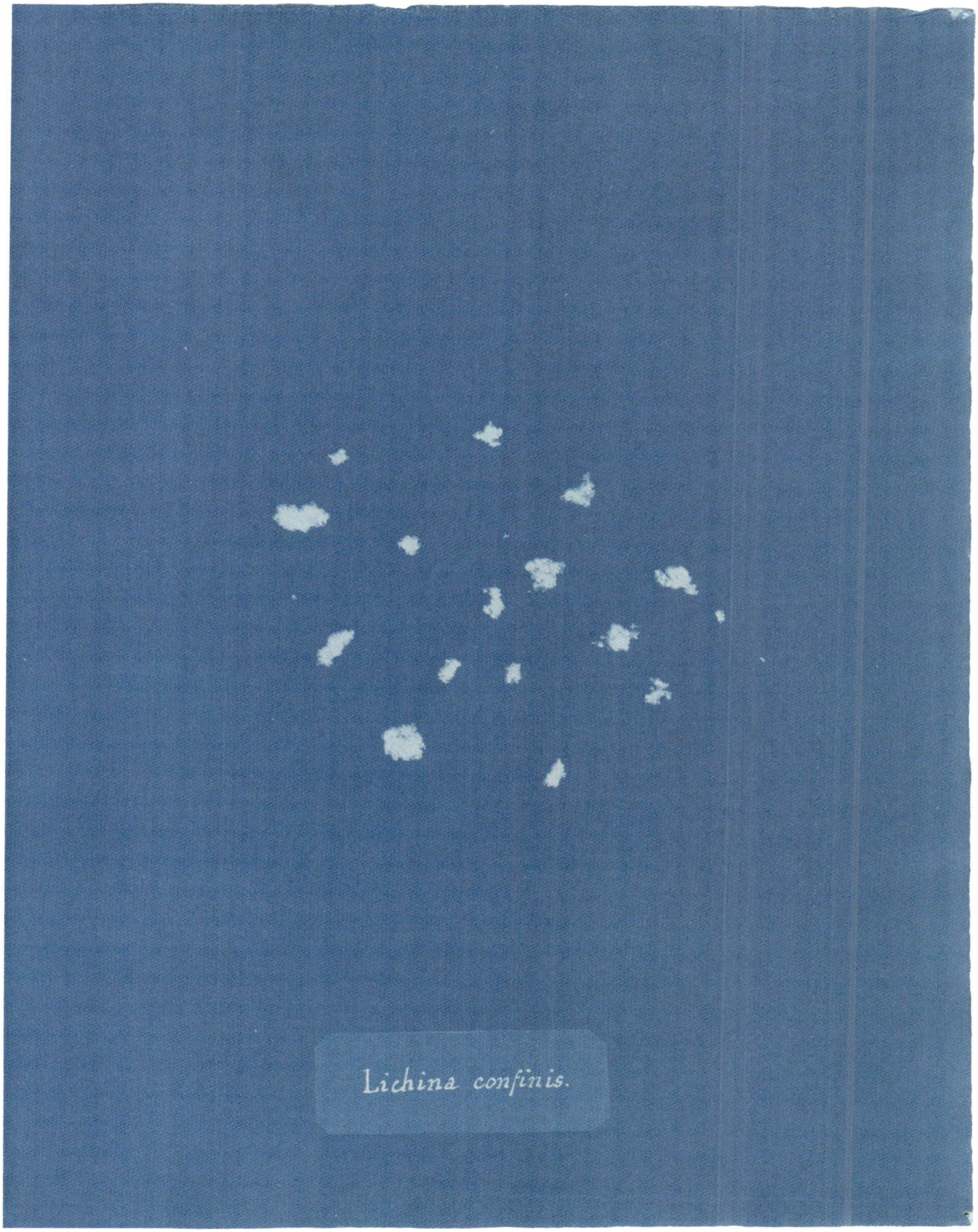

Plate 130. *Lichina confinis*

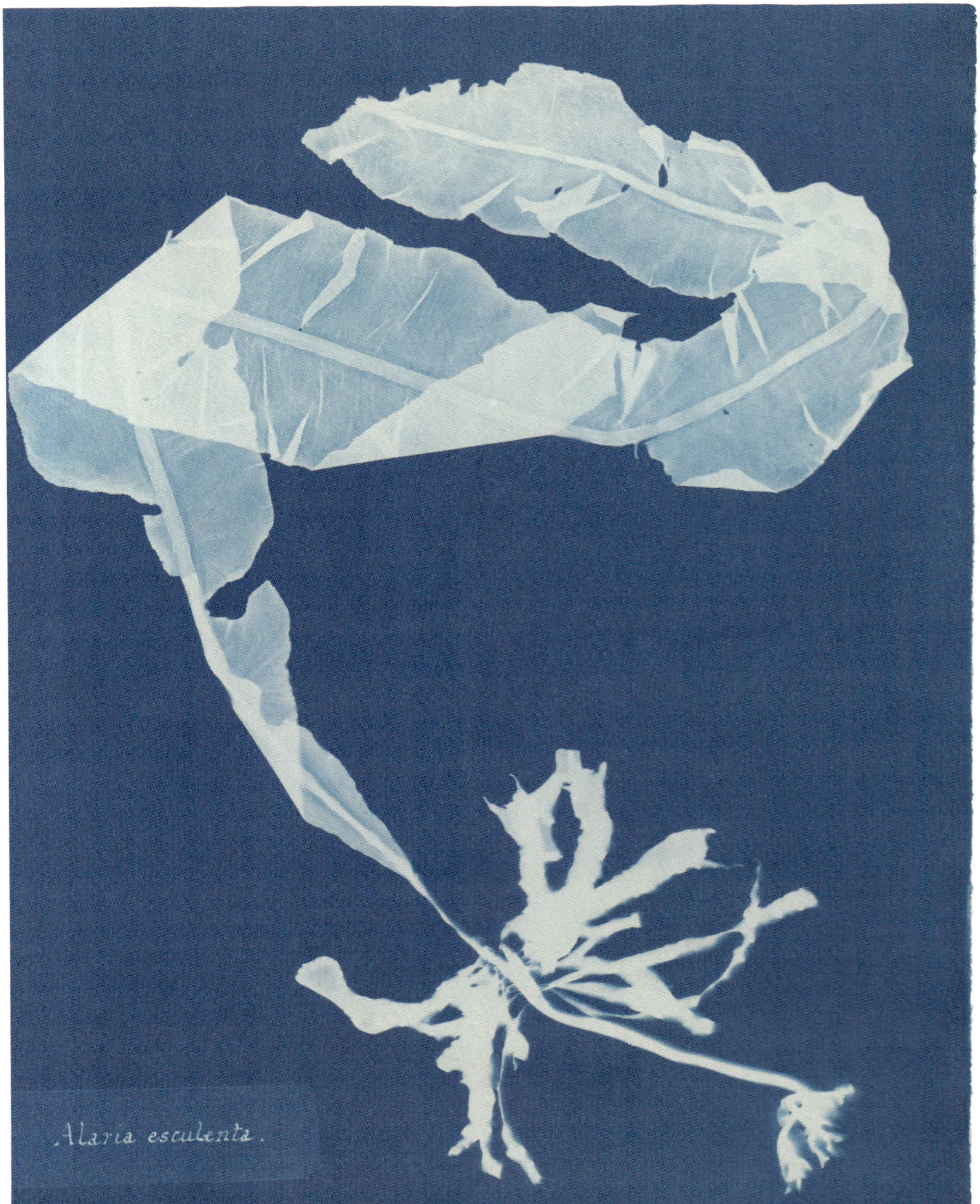

Plate 131. *Alaria esculenta*

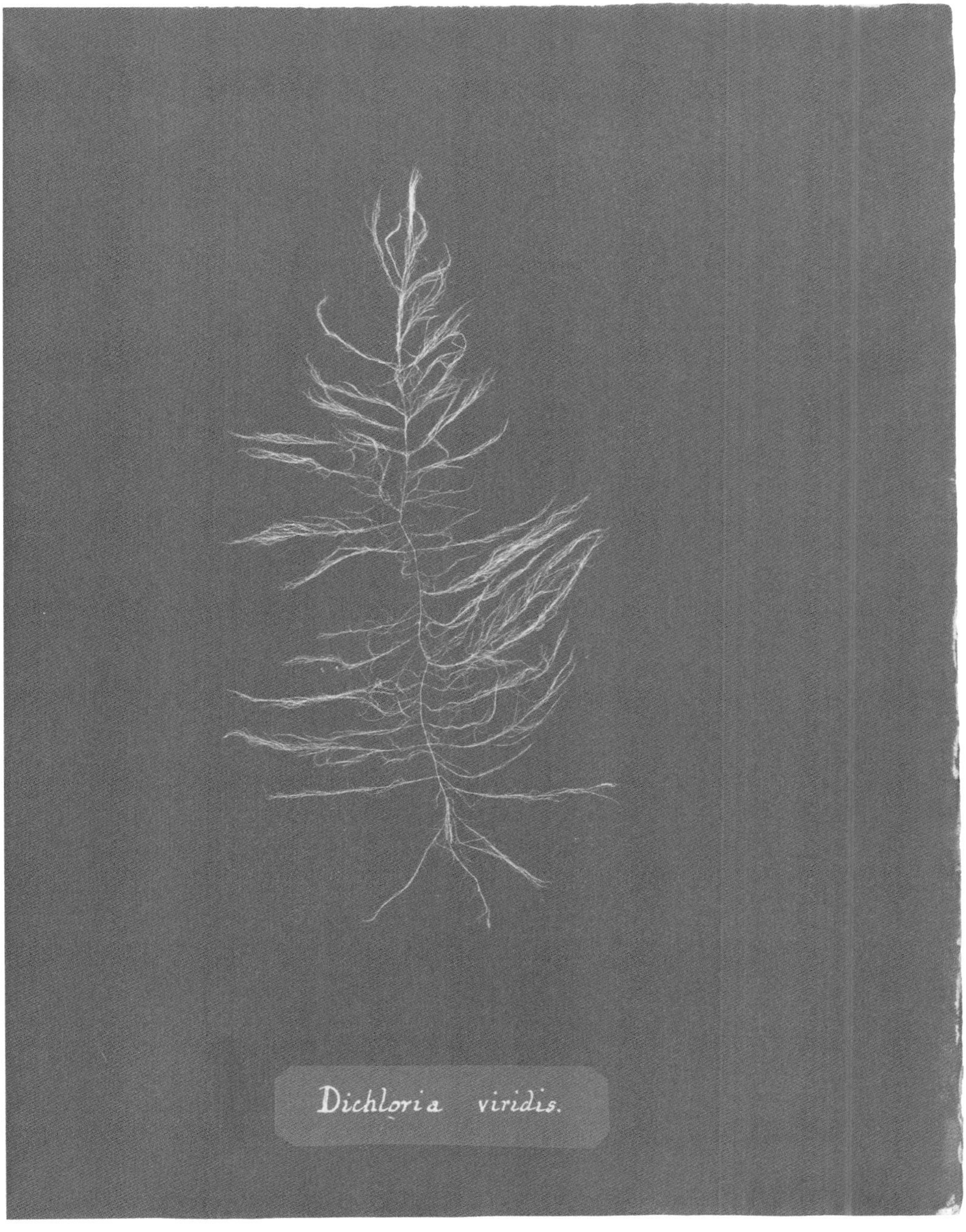

Plate 132. *Dichloria viridis*

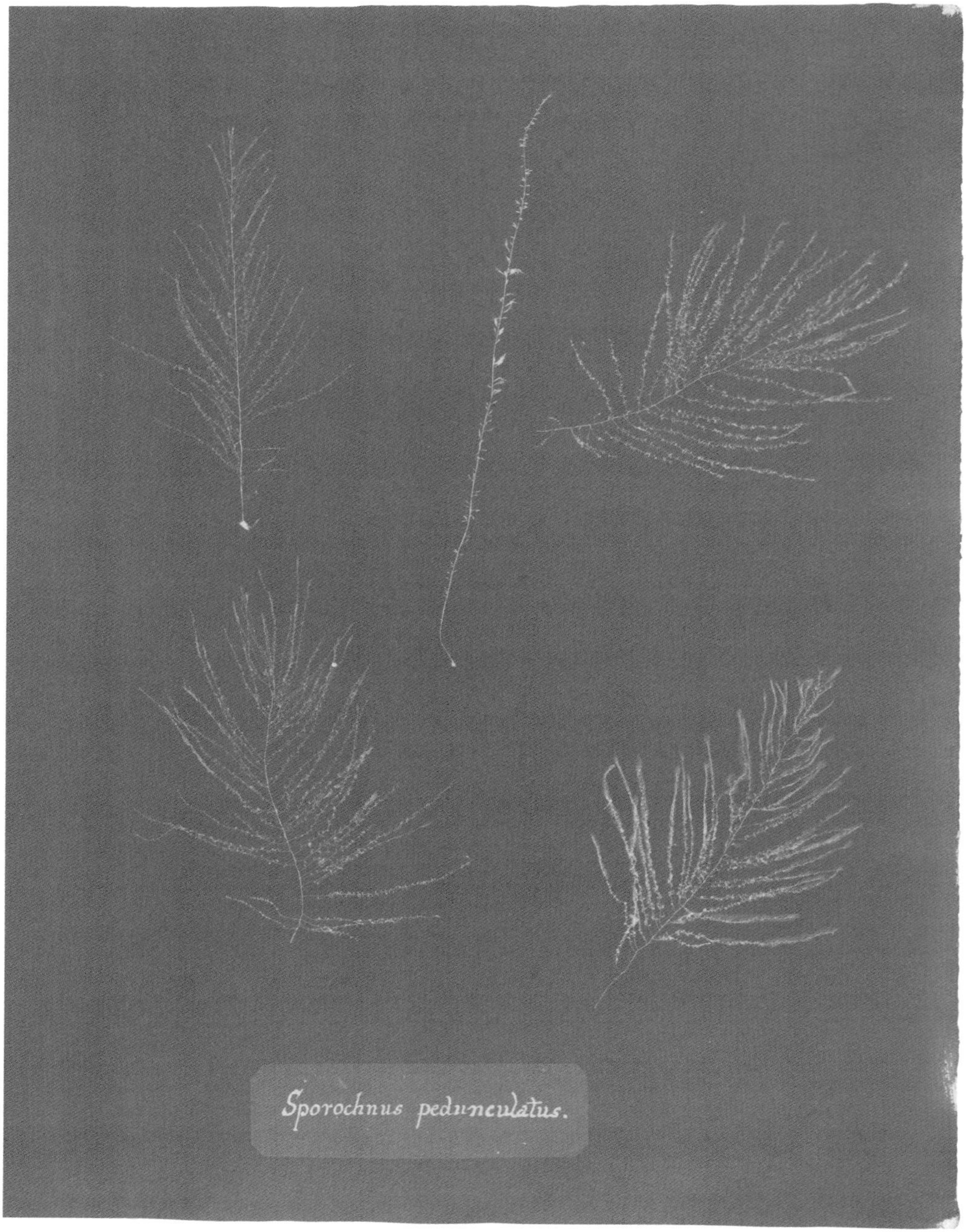

Plate 133. *Sporochnus pedunculatus*

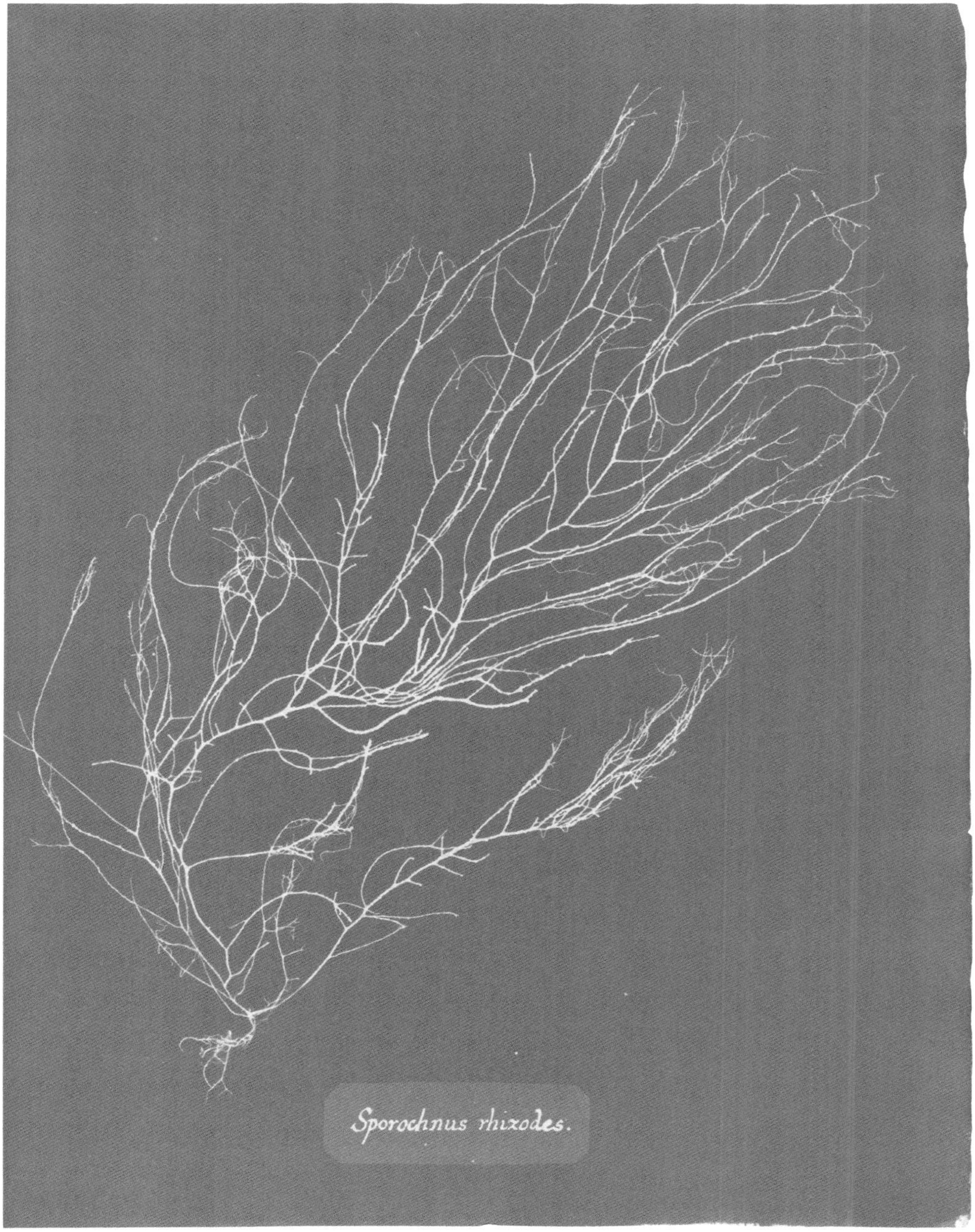

Plate 134. *Sporochnus rhizodes*

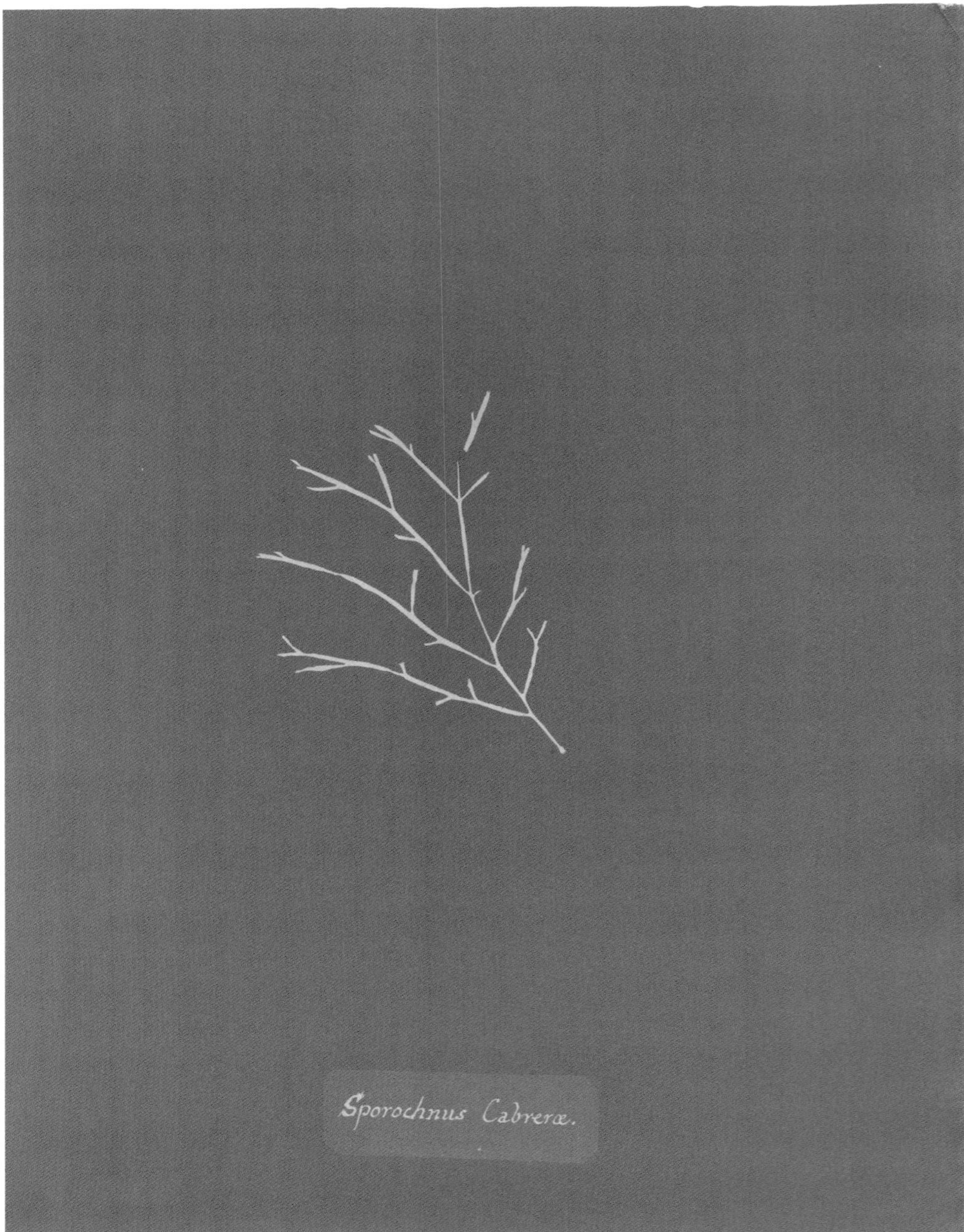

Plate 135. *Sporochnus cabrerae*

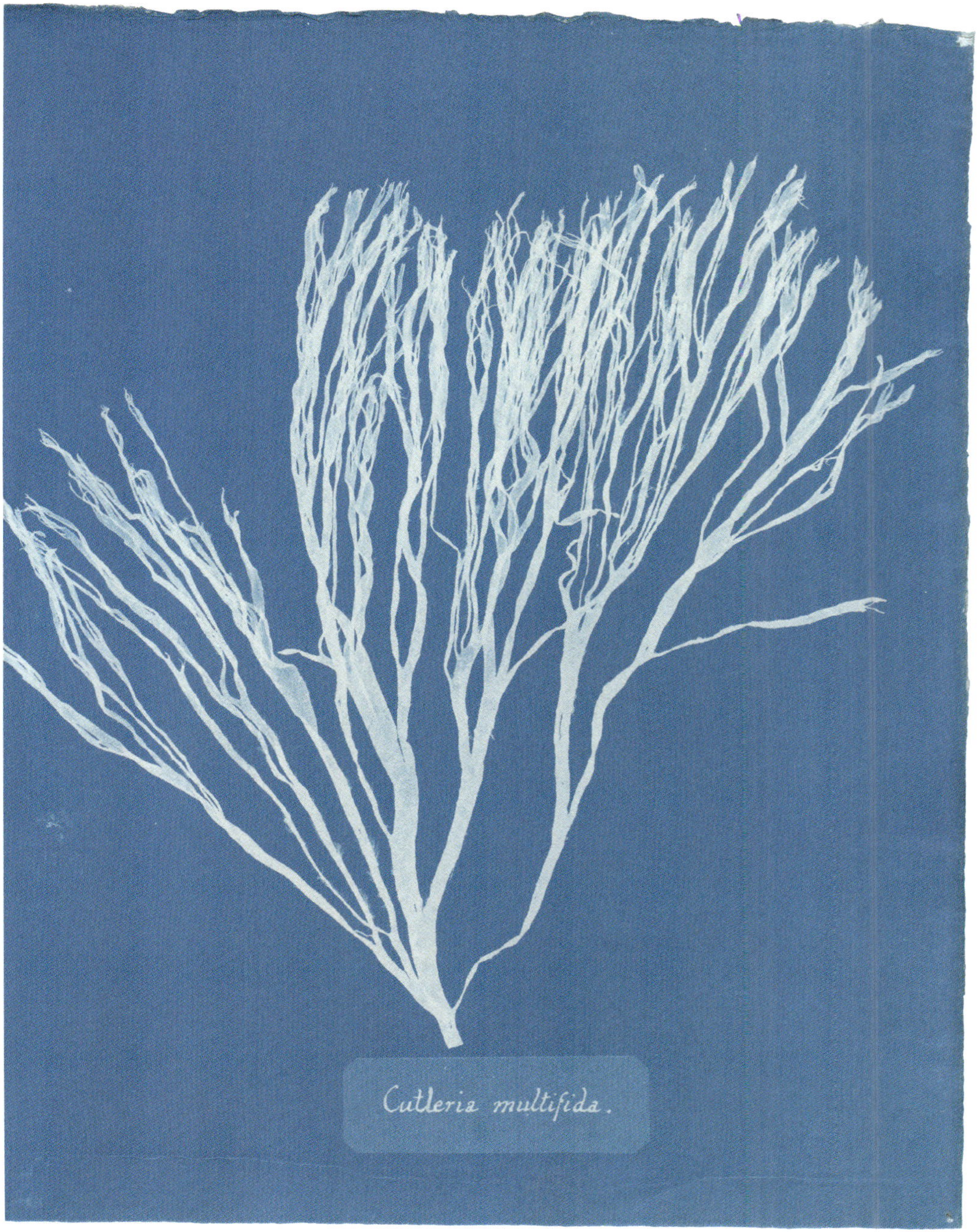

Plate 136. *Cutleria multifida*

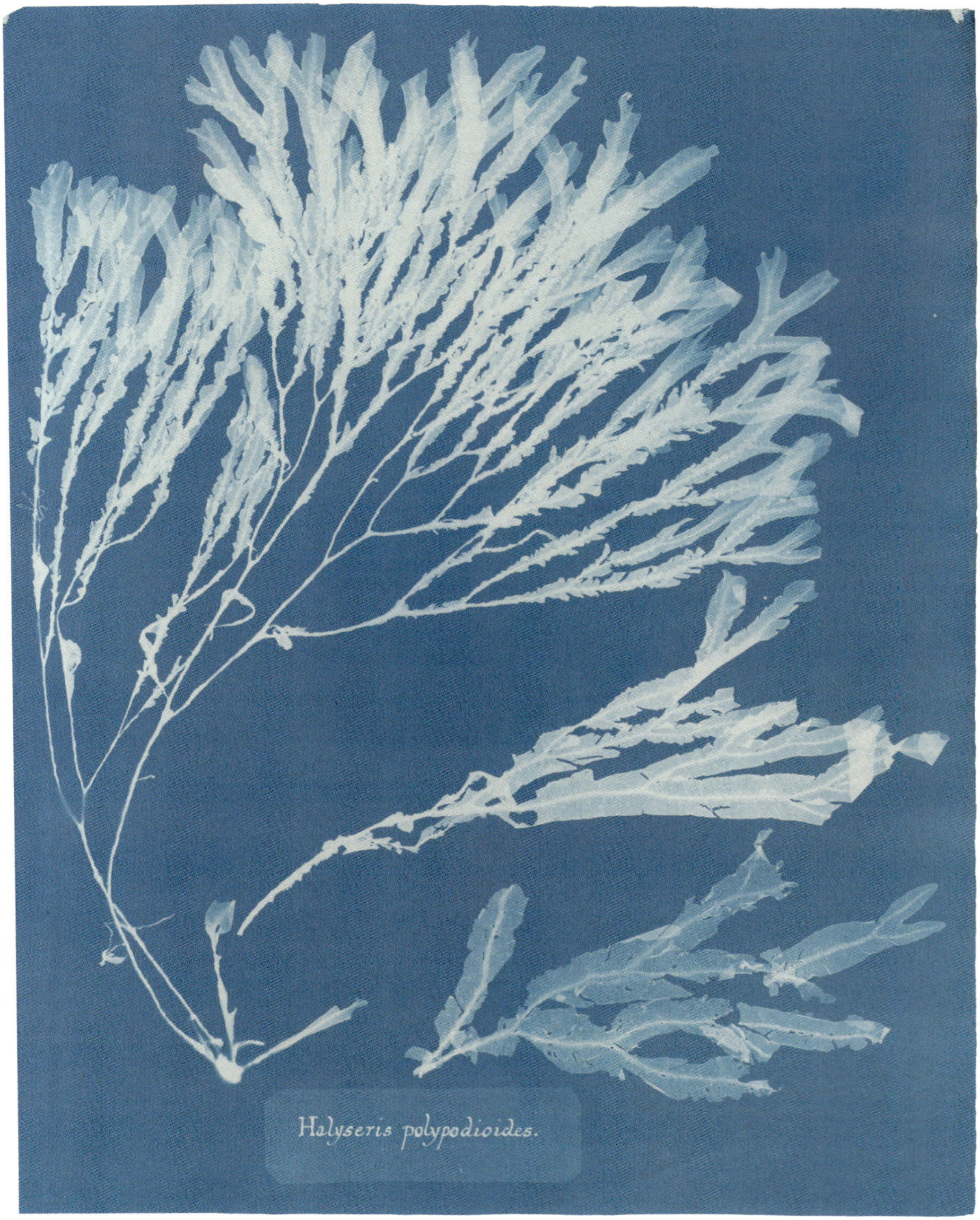

Plate 137. *Halyseris polypodioides*

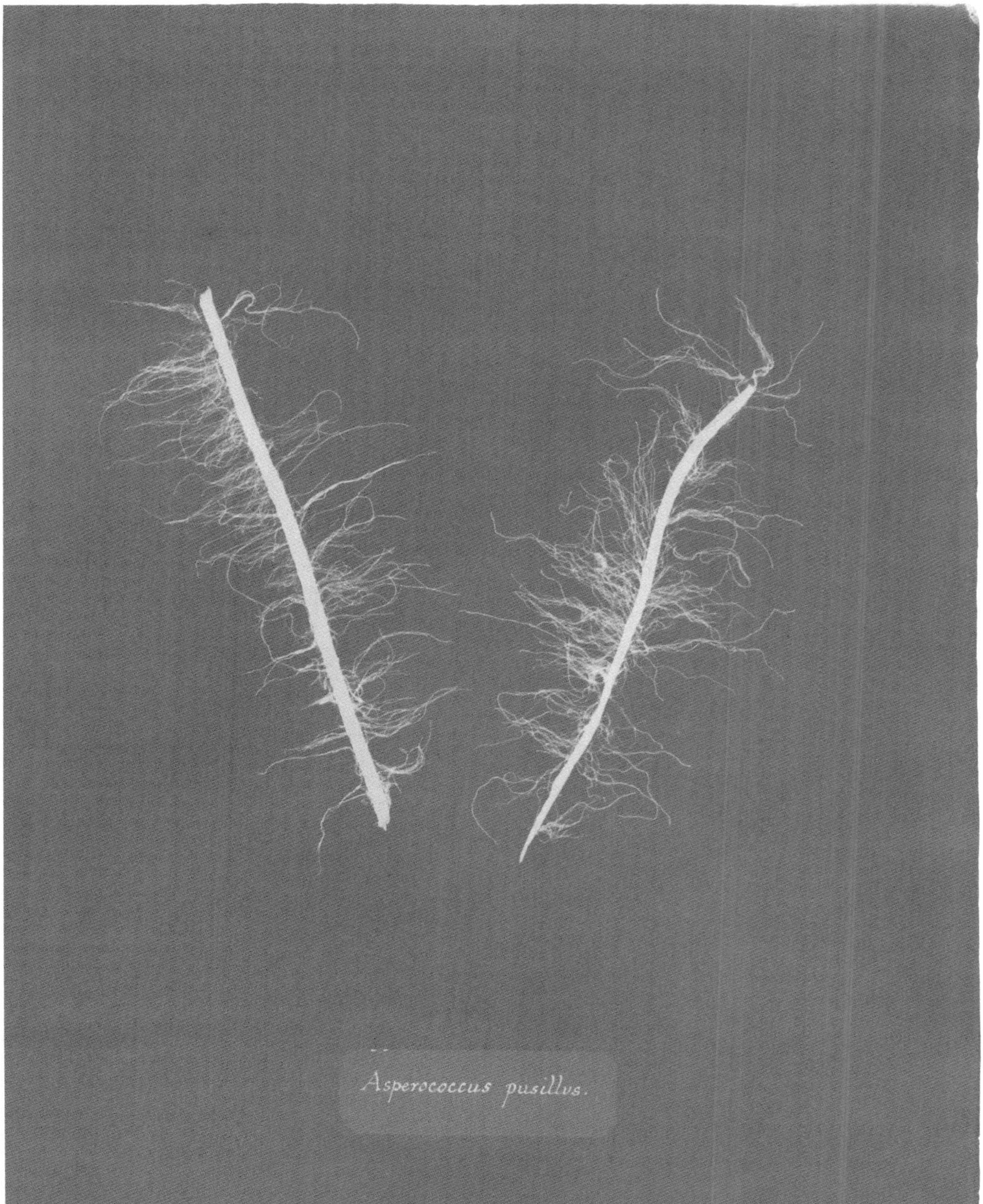

Plate 138. *Asperococcus pusillus*

Botanophilia and Fern Fever

The diversion of a large percentage of the bourgeoisie towards an interest in botany, otherwise known as "botanophilia", was a phenomenon rooted in the spirit of the European Enlightenment. Its beginnings dated back to somewhere around 1740, although it peaked in the first half of the 19th century, between 1800 and 1840. While the design of the aristocracy's gardens was based on a need to flaunt their wealth, their middle-class contemporaries regarded the world of plants as a source of knowledge, insight and learning.

Plants were arranged in order, then described, examined and identified. Interest was no longer directed towards exotic and costly specimens, but specifically at plants found in the neighbouring countryside, where they grew "wild and untamed". The study of the great outdoors, according to the tenet of Enlightenment thought, would help the free human being draw closer to the light and the truth. At this point in time, the modern systematics of the period still saw plants as "sleeping, dreaming beings", who in some vague and preconscious way, could breathe, love and feel.

In the early 19th century, "botanizing" meant more than merely collecting and classifying plants. It also included mapping their geography, as well as studying plant anatomy and discovering new species. Botany was still a self-taught discipline, undertaken without being put to any specific practical use. Nevertheless, as an auxiliary science for medicine and agriculture, it provided the basis for a variety of practical applications.

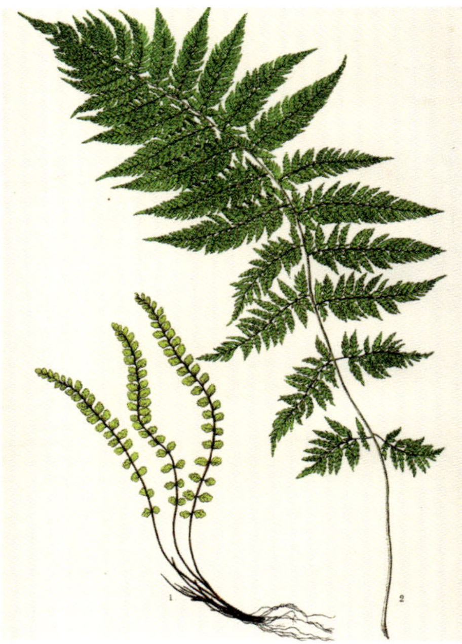

At first, many pharmacists, doctors, theologians, sometimes even soldiers and entrepreneurs, went on botanical excursions and expeditions. Later, botany became part of a teaching programme designed to suit a wide circle of young men and women. Educationists saw botanizing as a means of underpinning both memory and judgement. Those who dissected and compared the individual parts of plants were exercising their powers of observation. At the same time the activity awakened an understanding of the usefulness and sheer beauty of the many forms of plant life. The study of nature could also lead to compassion towards others, championing the revival of things spiritual, to which time spent in the open air also contributes, it was argued.

Botanizing could play a part in any walk, not only in the countryside but also in the city or public gardens. It became possible to join an organized trip or excursion focused on botany. A variety of botanical textbooks, covering countryside botany and regional flora, were published in large numbers, mostly based on Linnaeus' binomial nomenclature. Since, as a rule, textbooks and guide books were not illustrated, plants were identified by external features, such as the number and configuration of stamens.

One of botanizing's central cultural techniques was to create a herbarium. This served as a store of knowledge, often handed down from one generation to the next as an inventory or extendable field guide, but also as visual evidence of a person's own botanical achievements. It would not only record the name of the plant, but also the place and time at which it was found. Ideally, the herbarium could be seen as a reflection of the garden where plants were collected in summer and nostalgically remembered in winter.

From the outset, botanizing was a communal activity. Major cities in England, France, Germany, and the USA saw the foundation of botanical societies and associations, which often published journals or magazines. There were "botanical festivities", such as exhibitions, award ceremonies, plant exchange networks, and plant markets. Increased mapping of flora was reflected in the spread of information supplied from rural areas. Facts were gathered by both amateurs and academics. Magazines contained requests for rare plants to be sent, while in "Botanical Letters" columns, nature-lovers shared their knowledge with a large community of like-minded people.

From the beginning, women contributed to botanical research in a variety of ways. Not only did they collect, arrange and examine specimens under the microscope and carry out experiments, they also read scientific literature in detail, attended lectures by botanists, corresponded with naturalists, and wrote their own books on botany. The production of plant illustrations was regarded as a specifically female domain. The botanist Catharina Helena Dörrien (1717–1795), whose works date from the early days of botanophilia, created more than 1,400 watercolours of plants, together with descriptions.

Women's work often flowed unnamed into the publications of their male contemporaries. The earliest botanists wrote in Latin, the study of which was not included in civic education programmes designed for women. It was not long before the arrival of botany classes specifically for women, delivered in their respective native language. By around 1850, mapping of native plants was coming to an end and new species were seldom discovered. Botany was becoming increasing institutionalized and simply regarded as an academic discipline. As a result the widespread interest in botanophilia narrowed down to a botanical science of interest only to men.

Francis George Heath
Athyrium filix-femina Victoriae
From: *The Fern World*, London, 1877
London, Wellcome Collection

A particularly British demonstration of the love of plants, which later found followers in the USA, was an enthusiasm for ferns, mostly shared by women. What became known as "fern fever" began with the invention of the Wardian case in 1829. This forerunner of the modern terrarium was originally designed to protect exotic plants being shipped from overseas to Europe. Soon, however, these miniature greenhouses could be found in the households of many amateur botanists. Gardening grew from a hobby for the rich to a passion for the larger middle class.

Their reproduction from spores, their decorative value, and the fact that they had not yet been researched to the same extent as flowering plants, made ferns the ideal choice for botanical experiments. So began a real frenzy for tracking them down. Often excursions led to Britain's underdeveloped northern and western regions, where ferns were abundant. Accidents occasionally occurred on the hunt for new species on rough terrain. One which has been passed down is the tragic case of Jane Myers. In 1867, the young woman fell 170 feet to her death when she attempted to pick a fern from the edge of a cliff.

Ferns were the prevailing decorative motif of the Victorian era, featured on clothing, furniture, tableware, chandeliers, business cards and even gravestones. Wrought-iron gates, candelabra and fireguards took on the shape of ferns. The plants themselves were indispensable adornments in living and dining rooms, or concert halls, theatres, and hospitals. At the height of fern fever, tea parties were abandoned in favour of organized fern-picking outings. Rare specimens attracted high prices, while there were even cases of fern robbery.

Fern collecting was one of the few hobbies to transcend class barriers. Labourers, clerks, farmers, and aristocrats were equally enthusiastic about collecting and cultivating ferns. Only with the death of Queen Victoria in 1901 did fern fever dwindle. Until then, the passion for collecting ferns had led to a dramatic depopulation of native species. Fern fever had accelerated a development that began with botanophilia. As a broadening of our cultural heritage and an unpretentious addition to our desire for a modest sense of luxury, we have inherited a resident botanic companion, the potted plant.

H. Briscoe
An ornamental Wardian case for the home / Ziergefäß für ein Wardian Case / Caisses de Ward décoratives
From: Shirley Hibberd, *Rustic Adornments for Homes of Taste*, London, 1870
Berkeley, University of California Library

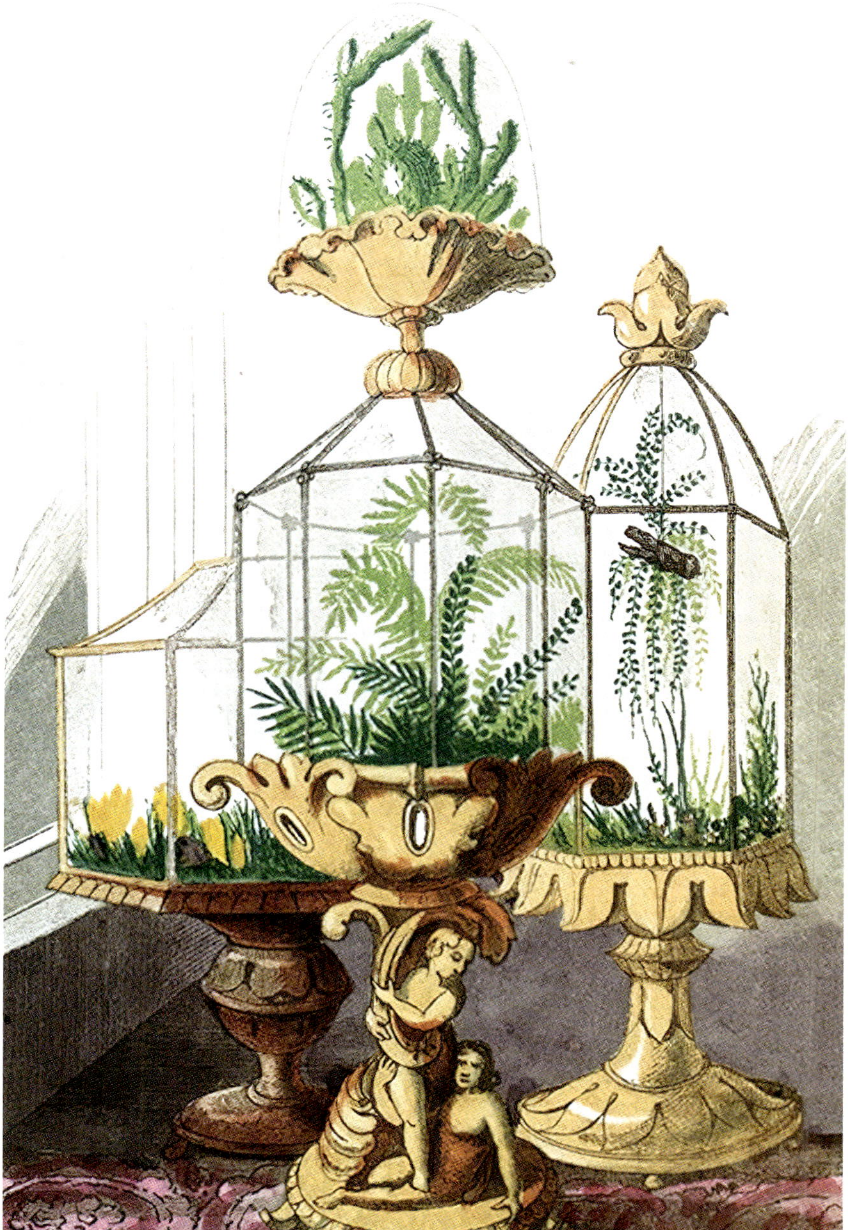

Botanophilie und Farnfieber

Die Hinwendung einer breiten bürgerlichen Schicht zur Beschäftigung mit der Botanik, die Botanophilie, ist ein Phänomen, das im Geist der europäischen Aufklärung wurzelt. Ihre Anfänge reichen bis in die Zeit um 1740 zurück, ihr eigentlicher Höhepunkt liegt jedoch in der ersten Hälfte des 19. Jahrhunderts, etwa in den Jahren 1800 bis 1840. Während es dem Adel bei der Gartengestaltung vor allem um die Befriedigung eines Repräsentationsbedürfnisses geht, entdeckt das Bürgertum die Welt der Pflanzen in dieser Zeit als Wissens-, Erkenntnis- und Bildungsfeld.

Die Pflanzen werden geordnet, beschrieben, untersucht und bestimmt. Interessant ist nicht mehr nur das exotische und kostbare Exemplar, sondern vor allem die in der heimischen Natur in ihrer wilden, „ungezähmten" Gestalt wachsende Pflanze. Im Studium der freien Natur, so der aufklärerische Gedanke, komme der freie Mensch dem Licht und der Wahrheit näher. Eine moderne Systematik verträgt sich in dieser Zeit noch mit dem Verständnis der Pflanze als „schlafendes, träumendes Wesen", das im Vorbewussten lebe, atme, liebe und empfinde.

„Botanisieren" bedeutet im frühen 19. Jahrhundert mehr als nur das Sammeln und Herbarisieren von Pflanzen. Es geht auch um die Kartierung der Pflanzengeographie, um das Studium der pflanzlichen Anatomie und die Entdeckung neuer Arten. Noch ist die Botanik eine autodidaktische Disziplin, die nicht auf einen bestimmten praktischen Nutzen gerichtet ist. Als Hilfswissenschaft für Medizin und Landwirtschaft liefert sie jedoch die Grundlagen für eine Vielzahl von neuen Anwendungen.

Zunächst sind es vielfach Apotheker, Ärzte, Theologen, manchmal auch Soldaten und Kaufmänner, die Exkursionen und botanische Reisen unternehmen. Später wird die Botanik als Teil einer pädagogischen Bewegung zum Betätigungsfeld für einen breiten Kreis von jungen Männern und Frauen. Der pädagogische Wert des Botanisierens wird in der Stärkung des Gedächtnisses und der Urteilskraft gesehen. Wer die einzelnen Teile der Pflanzen zergliedert und vergleicht, übt seine Beobachtungsgabe. Zugleich entsteht ein Gefühl für die Zweckmäßigkeit und Schönheit der vielgestaltigen pflanzlichen Lebewesen. So hat die Beschäftigung mit der Natur auch positive Effekte für die Herzensbildung und dient der Regeneration seelischer Kräfte, wozu auch die Bewegung an frischer Luft beiträgt.

Auf jedem Spaziergang kann man botanisieren, bei jedem Aufenthalt in der Natur, aber auch in der Stadt oder im Garten. Es werden spezielle botanische Reisen und Exkursionen organisiert. Beim

Charles Sillem Lidderdale
The fern gatherer, 1877 / **Die Farnsammlerin** / **La Cueilleuse de fougères**
Oil on canvas, 76 × 53 cm (29 7/8 × 20 7/8 in.)
Private collection

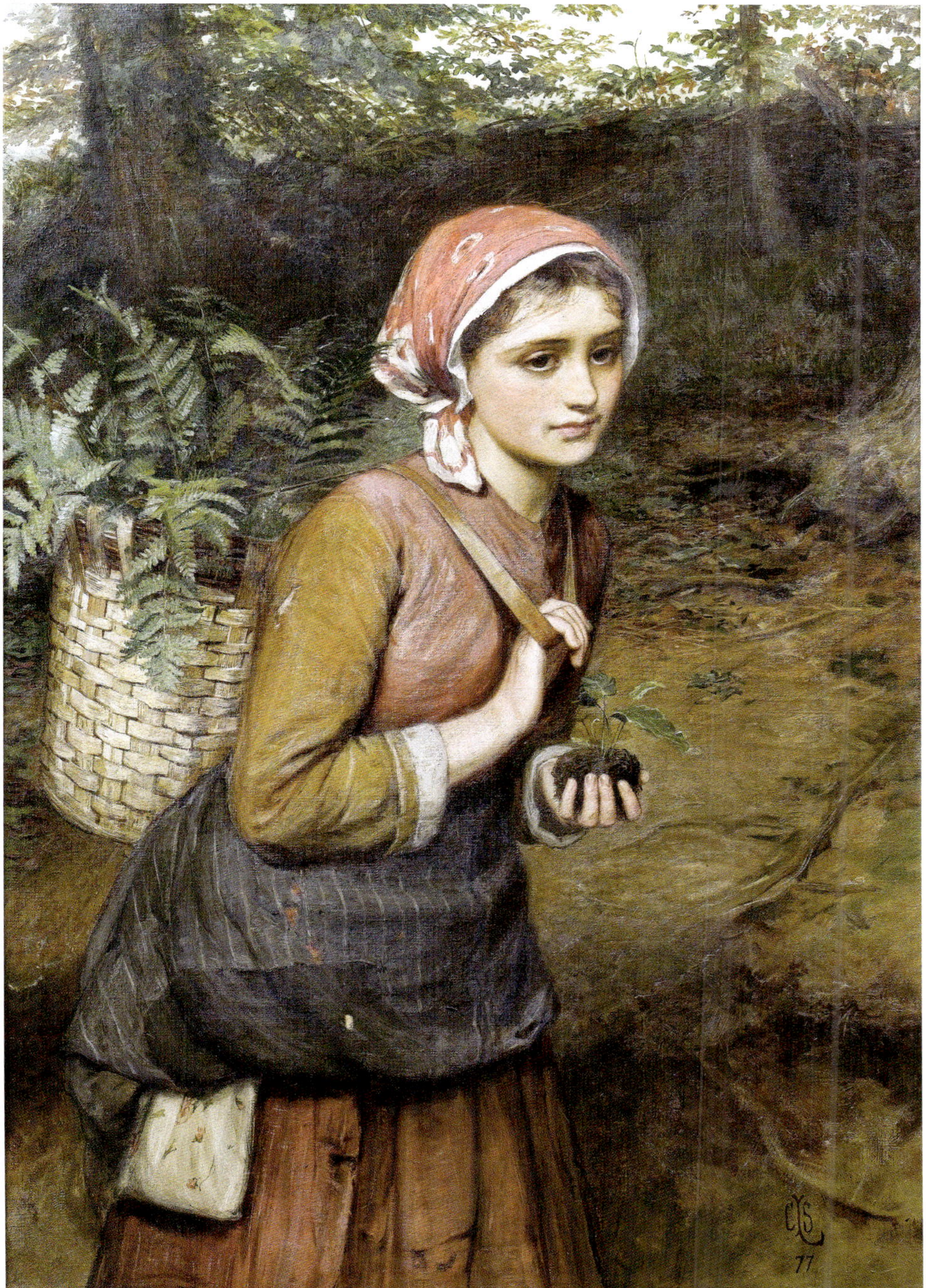

Sammeln der Pflanzen soll nicht auf Schönheit, sondern auf Vollständigkeit geachtet werden. Eine Vielzahl von Botaniklehrbüchern, von Länderbotaniken und Regionalfloren erscheint in großen Auflagen. Die meisten von ihnen gehen von der Linné'schen Nomenklatur aus. Da die Lehr- und Handbücher in der Regel nicht illustriert sind, muss die Pflanze durch äußere Merkmale wie etwa die Anzahl und Anordnung der Staubfäden bestimmt werden.

Eine zentrale Kulturtechnik des Botanisierens ist das Anlegen eines Herbariums. Es dient als Wissensspeicher, der häufig über Generationen weitergegeben wird, als Findmittel, als erweiterbares Bestimmungsbuch, aber auch als visuelles Zeugnis für die eigenen botanischen Leistungen. Aufgezeichnet werden nicht nur der Name der Pflanze, sondern auch Fundort und Fundzeit. Das Herbarium ist im Idealfall ein Spiegelbild des Gartens, das geeignet ist, die im Sommer gesammelten Pflanzen im Winter ins Gedächtnis zurückzurufen.

Botanisieren ist von Beginn an ein kollektives Unternehmen. Vor allem in England, Frankreich, Deutschland und den USA entstehen in den großen Städten botanische Vereine und Gesellschaften, die häufig auch Journale oder Magazine herausgeben. Es gibt „botanische Geselligkeiten", Ausstellungen, Preisverleihungen, Tauschbörsen und Pflanzenmärkte. Die zunehmende Kartierung der Flora spiegelt sich in regionalen Floren und Länderbotaniken. Sie entstehen als Gemeinschaftswerke von Amateuren und Gelehrten. In Zeitschriften wird um Einsendung seltener Pflanzen gebeten, in „botanischen Briefen" teilen Naturfreunde ihr Wissen mit einer großen Gemeinde Gleichgesinnter.

Frauen wirken von Beginn an auf vielfältige Weise in der botanischen Forschung mit. Sie sammeln, ordnen, mikroskopieren und experimentieren nicht nur, sondern beschäftigen sich mit botanischer Fachliteratur, besuchen botanische Vorlesungen, korrespondieren mit Naturforschern und verfassen selbst botanische Bücher. Als spezifisch weibliche Domäne gilt die Anfertigung von Pflanzenillustrationen. So hinterlässt die Botanikerin Catharina Helena Dörrien (1717–1795), deren Wirken in die Frühzeit der Botanophilie fällt, mehr als 1.400 Pflanzenaquarelle und -beschreibungen.

Häufig fließt die Arbeit von Frauen ungenannt in die Publikationen ihrer Männer ein. Da die meisten frühen Botaniken in lateinischer Sprache geschrieben sind, deren Erwerb nicht zum bürgerlichen Bildungsprogramm für Frauen gehört, erscheinen bald spezielle Botaniken für Frauen in den jeweiligen Landessprachen. Um 1850 ist die Kartierung heimischer Pflanzen nahezu abgeschlossen, neue Pflanzenarten werden kaum noch entdeckt. Zunehmend institutionalisiert und akademisiert sich die Botanik. Damit wird die breite Bewegung der Botanophilie verengt auf eine botanische Wissenschaft, die vor allem den Männern vorbehalten ist.

Eine spezifisch britische Ausprägung der Pflanzenliebe, die in ihrer Spätzeit auch Anhänger in den USA fand, war die vor allem von Frauen getragene Begeisterung für Farngewächse. Das sogenannte „Farnfieber" nimmt seinen Ausgangspunkt in der Erfindung des Wardian-Case um 1829. Dieser Vorläufer des modernen Terrariums diente zunächst dem Schutz exotischer Pflanzen, die aus Übersee nach Europa eingeführt wurden. Bald jedoch stehen solche miniaturisierten Treibhäuser im Haushalt vieler Amateurbotaniker. Das Gärtnern wird aus einem Hobby für Reiche zu einer Leidenschaft für die breite Mittelschicht.

Ihre Reproduktion aus Sporen, ihr dekorativer Wert und der Umstand, dass sie noch nicht im gleichen Maß wie Blühpflanzen erforscht sind, macht die Farne zu idealen Objekten für botanische Experimente. Eine regelrechte Jagd auf Farngewächse beginnt. Häufig führen die Ausflüge in die schlecht erschlossenen nördlichen und westlichen Teile Großbritanniens, wo Farne am reichhaltigsten vorkommen. Auf der Jagd nach neuen Arten im unwegsamen Gelände kommt es gelegentlich zu Unfällen. Überliefert ist der tragische Fall von Jane Myers, einer jungen Frau, die im Jahr 1867 50 Meter tief in den Tod stürzt, als sie am Rand eines Felsens ein Farngewächs auflesen will.

Farne bilden das beherrschende Dekor im Viktorianischen Zeitalter. Sie finden sich auf Kleidern, Möbeln, Geschirr, Visitenkarten und sogar auf Grabsteinen. Gusseiserne Tore, Kronleuchter und Kamingitter nehmen die Form von Farnen an. Die Pflanzen selbst sind nicht wegzudenken aus den Wohn- und Esszimmern, aus Konzertsälen, Theatern oder Krankenhäusern. Auf dem Höhepunkt des Farnfiebers werden Teepartys zugunsten von Farnexkursionen gegeben und seltene Exemplare zu hohen Preisen gehandelt, es gibt sogar Fälle von Farndiebstahl.

Das Farnsammeln ist eines der wenigen Hobbys, das die Klassenbarrieren überwindet. Arbeiter und Angestellte, Landwirte und Aristokraten begeistern sich gleichermaßen für das Sammeln und Kultivieren der Farne. Erst mit dem Tod von Königin Victoria 1901 klingt das Farnfieber ab. Bis dahin hat die Sammelleidenschaft der Farnbegeisterten zu einer dramatischen Entvölkerung heimischer Arten geführt. Das Farnfieber hat eine Entwicklung beschleunigt, die mit der Botanophilie begann: Aus der Pflanze wird, als Kultur- und Luxuselement, ein Mitbewohner der Menschen, die Zimmerpflanze.

Botanophilie et ptéridomanie

L'intérêt d'une large couche de la bourgeoisie pour la botanique, la « botanophilie », est un phénomène qui plonge ses racines dans l'esprit européen des Lumières. Ses débuts remontent à 1740 environ et son apogée se situe toutefois dans la première moitié du XIXe siècle, entre 1800 et 1840 environ. Alors que la création de jardins relève avant tout de la satisfaction d'un besoin de représentation de la noblesse, la bourgeoisie découvre le monde des plantes comme champ de connaissances, de réflexion et de culture.

Les plantes sont classées, décrites, analysées, déterminées. L'intérêt ne porte plus seulement sur le spécimen exotique et rare, mais en premier lieu sur la plante qui pousse dans la nature autochtone, sous sa forme sauvage, « non domestiquée ». Par l'étude au sein de la nature, telle est l'idée des Lumières, l'homme libre se rapproche de la lumière et de la vérité. À l'époque, une classification moderne est encore compatible avec la perception de la plante comme d'un « être dormant, rêvant », qui vit, respire, aime et ressent dans un état préconscient.

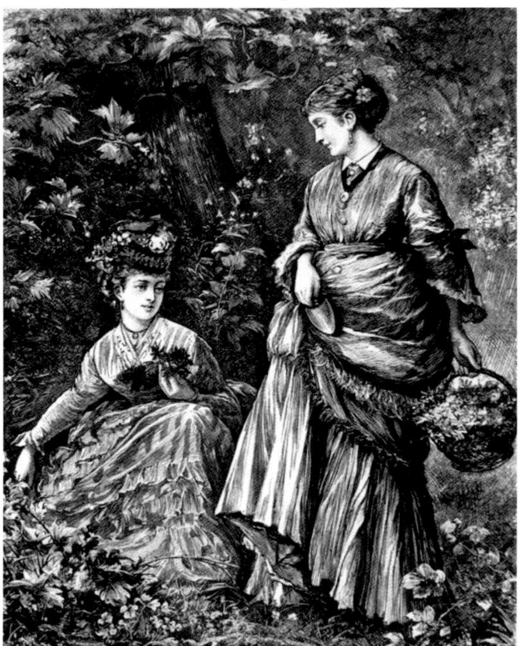

Au début du XIXe siècle, l'activité botanique dépasse la simple cueillette et herborisation des plantes. Elle vise aussi la cartographie de la flore, l'étude de l'anatomie des plantes et la découverte de nouvelles espèces. La botanique est encore une discipline autodidacte ; elle est pratiquée sans recherche utilitaire particulière. En tant que science auxiliaire de la médecine et de l'agriculture, elle jette néanmoins les bases d'un grand nombre de nouvelles applications pratiques.

Aux premiers temps, ce sont souvent des pharmaciens, des médecins, des théologiens, parfois aussi des soldats et des marchands qui entreprennent des voyages et des excursions botaniques. Plus tard, la botanique, s'inscrivant dans un mouvement pédagogique, devient le champ d'activité d'un large cercle de jeunes hommes et femmes. La valeur pédagogique de l'activité botanique est vue dans le développement de la mémoire et de la faculté de jugement. Une personne qui démembre et compare les différentes parties des plantes exerce sa faculté d'observation. En même temps se développe une perception sensible de l'utilité et de la beauté des êtres vivants multiformes que sont les plantes. Ainsi, l'intérêt pour la nature a aussi des effets positifs sur la noblesse de cœur et favorise la régénération des forces de l'âme, à quoi contribue en outre l'activité en plein air.

Toute promenade, tout séjour dans la nature, mais aussi en ville ou au jardin, donnent l'occasion de botaniser. Des voyages et des excursions botaniques spécifiques sont organisés. La cueillette des plantes ne doit pas s'attacher à la beauté, mais viser l'exhaustivité. Un grand nombre de traités, de botanique nationale et de flore régionale paraissent en grand tirage. La plupart s'appuient sur la nomenclature élaborée par Linné. Dans la mesure où les manuels et les guides ne sont généralement pas illustrés, la plante doit être déterminée par des caractéristiques extérieures comme le nombre et la disposition des étamines.

Une pratique centrale de l'activité botanique est la création d'un herbier. L'herbier sert de réservoir de connaissances, il est souvent légué de génération en génération en tant qu'outil de recherche ou de détermination pouvant être étendu, mais aussi comme témoignage visuel des réalisations botaniques personnelles. Y sont consignés non seulement le nom de la plante, mais aussi l'endroit et la date à laquelle elle a été trouvée. Idéalement, l'herbier est une image miroir du jardin qui, durant la saison hivernale, permet à son propriétaire de se remettre en mémoire les plantes collectées pendant l'été.

Dès les débuts de la botanophilie, l'activité botanique est une entreprise collective. C'est surtout dans les grandes villes d'Angleterre, de France, d'Allemagne et des États-Unis que voient le jour des associations et des sociétés botaniques qui publient souvent des journaux ou des magazines. L'on organise des « rencontres botaniques », des expositions, des remises de prix, des bourses d'échange et des marchés aux plantes. La cartographie croissante de la végétation se reflète dans des flores régionales et des botaniques nationales qui voient le jour sous forme d'ouvrages collectifs d'amateurs et de savants. Des revues sollicitent l'envoi de plantes rares, et dans des « lettres botaniques », les amoureux de la nature partagent leurs connaissances avec une forte communauté d'amateurs nourrissant les mêmes intérêts.

Dès le début, les femmes collaborent de multiples manières à la recherche botanique. Elles ne se contentent pas de collecter, classer, analyser au microscope et expérimenter, mais s'intéressent à la littérature spécialisée, assistent à des conférences de botanique, correspondent avec des naturalistes et s'illustrent comme auteures d'ouvrages de botanique. Est considéré comme un domaine spécifiquement féminin la réalisation d'illustrations de plantes. Ainsi, la botaniste Catharina Helena Dörrien (1717–1795), dont la période d'activité coïncide avec les premiers temps de la botanophilie, a laissé plus de 1 400 aquarelles et descriptions de plantes.

Le travail des femmes entre fréquemment dans les publications de leurs maris sans être cité. Dans la mesure où la plupart des botanique des premiers temps sont rédigées en latin, dont l'apprentissage

Henry Woods
Fern gatherers, 1872 / **Farnsammlerinnen** / **Cueilleuses de fougères**
From: *The Graphic*, 7 September 1872
New York Public Library

ne fait pas partie du programme culturel bourgeois dispensé aux femmes, des botaniques particulières dédiées aux femmes paraissent bientôt dans les différentes langues nationales. Vers 1850, la cartographie des plantes autochtones est largement achevée, et l'on ne découvre plus guère d'espèces nouvelles. Progressivement, la botanique s'institutionnalise et s'académise. Le vaste mouvement botanophile se voit alors réduit à une science botanique essentiellement réservée aux hommes.

Une version spécifiquement britannique de l'amour des plantes, qui aura aussi des adeptes aux États-Unis en sa phase tardive, a été l'engouement pour les fougères, surtout partagé par les femmes. La « ptéridomanie », tel est son nom, prend son essor avec l'invention, vers 1829, de la caisse de Ward. Ce précurseur du terrarium moderne est surtout destiné à protéger les plantes exotiques introduites en Europe en provenance des pays d'outre-mer. Mais bientôt, ce genre de serres miniaturisées se retrouve dans les demeures de bien des amateurs de botanique. D'un passe-temps pour les riches, jardiner devient une passion pour une large classe moyenne.

Leur reproduction par dissémination de spores, leur valeur décorative et le fait qu'elles ne sont pas encore aussi bien connues que les plantes à fleurs, font des fougères des objets idéaux pour réaliser des expériences botaniques. Une véritable chasse aux fougères commence. Souvent, les excursions conduisent les amateurs dans les parties mal connues du nord et de l'ouest de la Grande-Bretagne, où les fougères sont le plus nombreuses. Dans la chasse aux nouvelles espèces en terrain difficile, des accidents se produisent parfois. L'on connaît ainsi le cas tragique de Jane Myers : en 1867, cette jeune femme fit une chute mortelle de 50 mètres en voulant cueillir une fougère qui poussait au bord d'une falaise.

Les fougères deviennent l'élément décoratif dominant de la période victorienne. Elles se retrouvent sur les vêtements, les meubles, la vaisselle, les cartes de visite, et même sur des pierres tombales. Les portails en fonte, les lustres et les pare-feux de cheminée prennent des formes de fougères. Les plantes elles-mêmes sont omniprésentes dans les salons, les salles à manger, les salles de concert, les théâtres et les hôpitaux. À l'apogée de la ptéridomanie, des *tea parties* sont organisées au profit d'excursions sur le thème des fougères, et les exemplaires rares se négocient à prix d'or – l'on a même connaissance de vols de fougères.

La cueillette de fougères est un des rares passe-temps qui dépasse les différences de classes. Ouvriers et employés, agriculteurs et aristocrates se passionnent tout autant pour la collecte et la culture des fougères. La ptéridomanie ne va décroître qu'avec la mort de la reine Victoria en 1901. Entre-temps, la passion de collectionner des fougères a aussi accéléré une évolution qui avait commencé avec la botanophilie : en tant qu'élément de culture et de luxe, la plante se transforme en cohabitant avec les humains et devient la plante d'intérieur.

W. H. Fitch
Polypodium calcareum; Woodsia ilvensis
Lithograph
From: Thomas Moore, *A Popular History of the British Ferns and the Allied Plants*, London, 1851
University of Toronto Library, Gerstein Science Information Centre

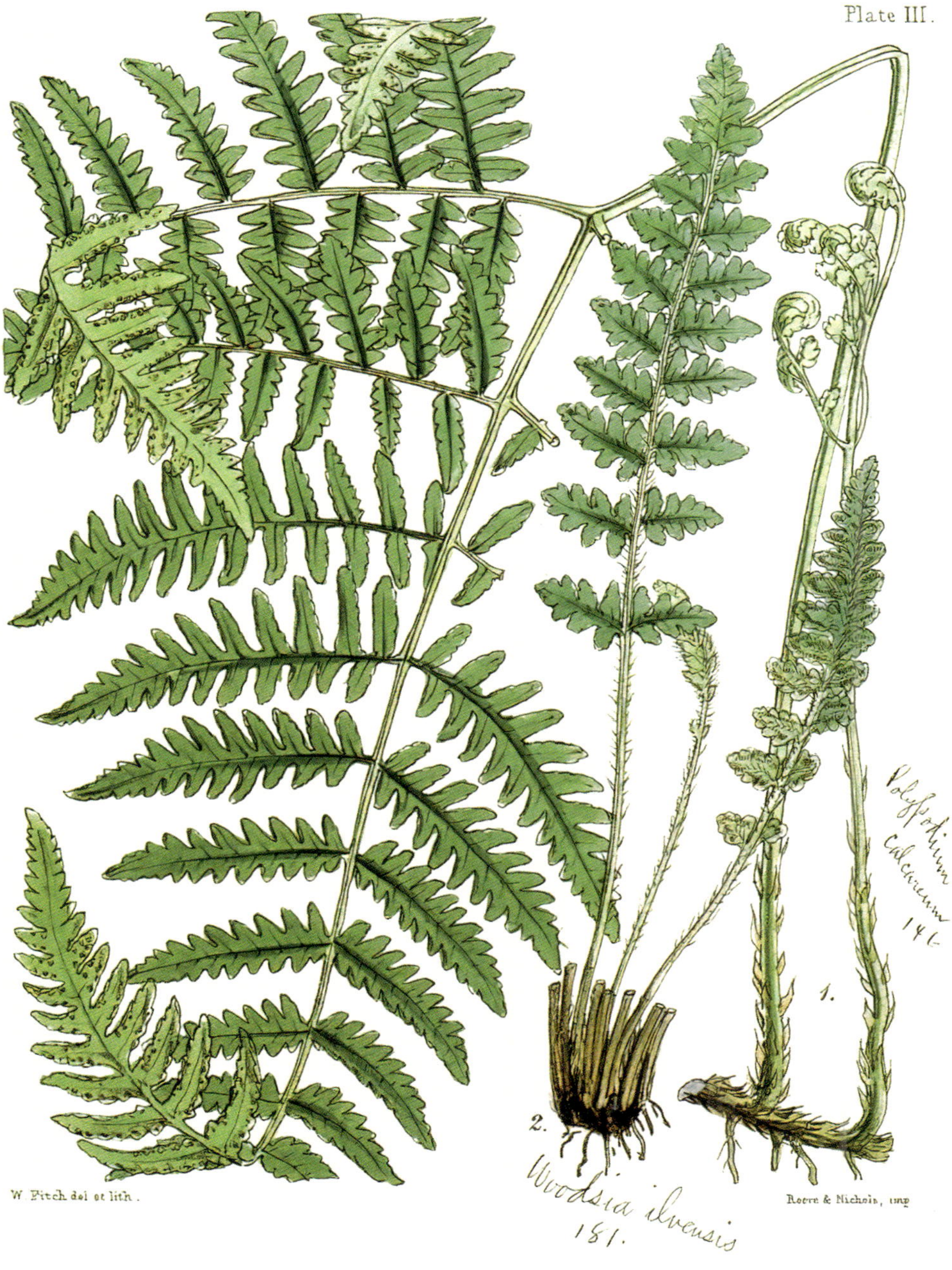
Plate III.
Polypodium Calcareum 146
1.
2.
W. Fitch del et lith.
Woodsia ilvensis 181.
Reeve & Nichols, imp

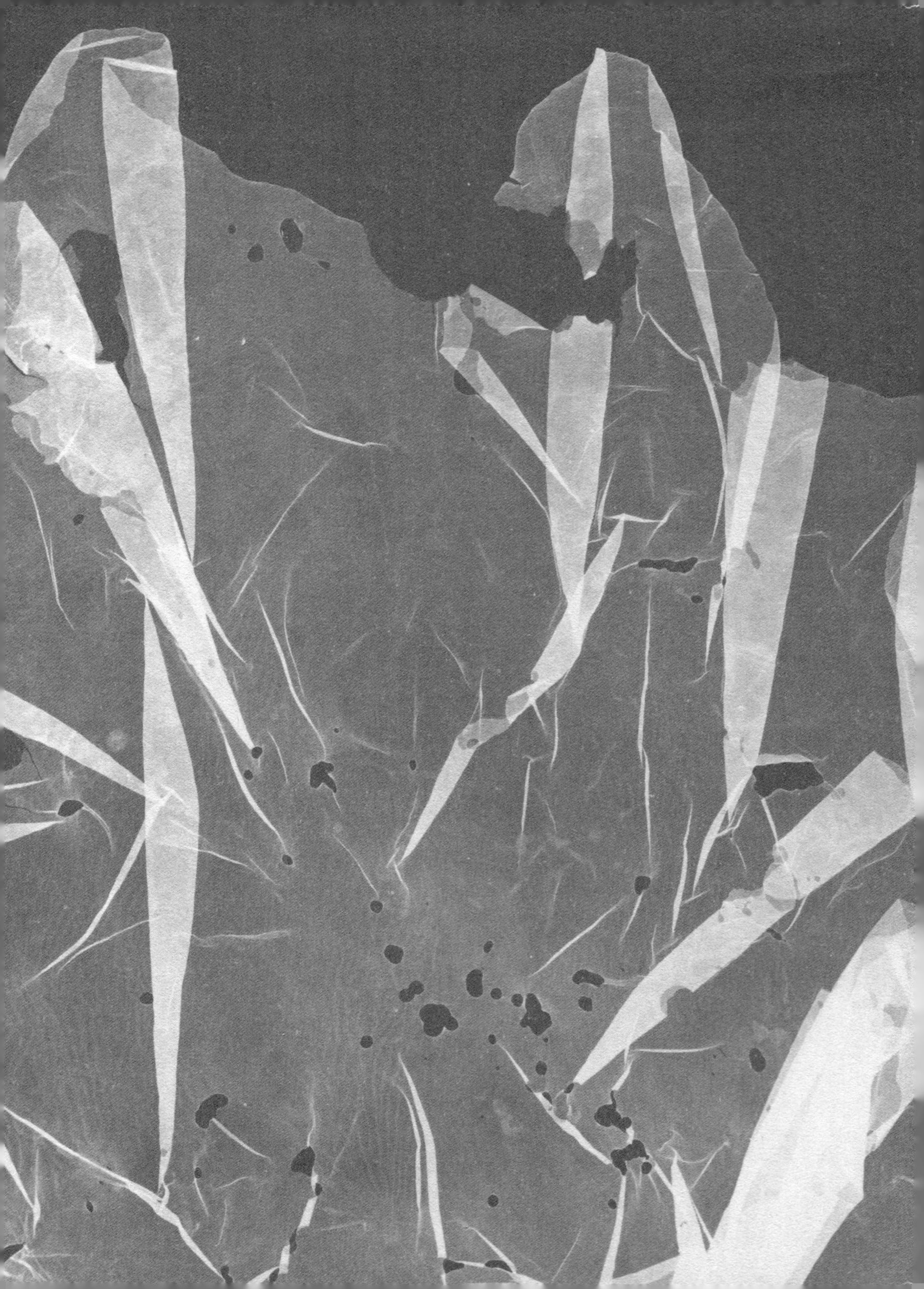

— 1849–1853 —

British Algae Volumes I–III

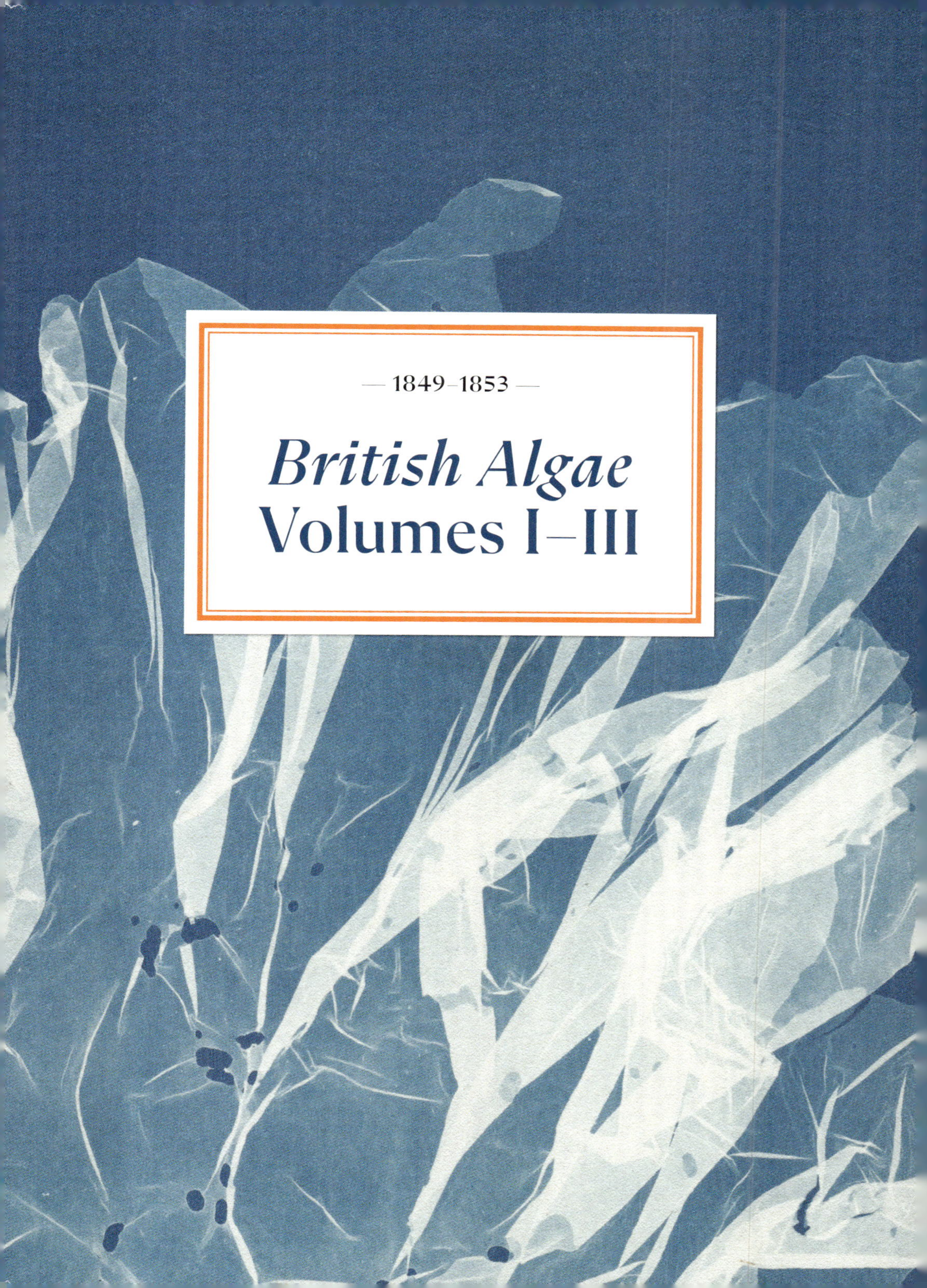

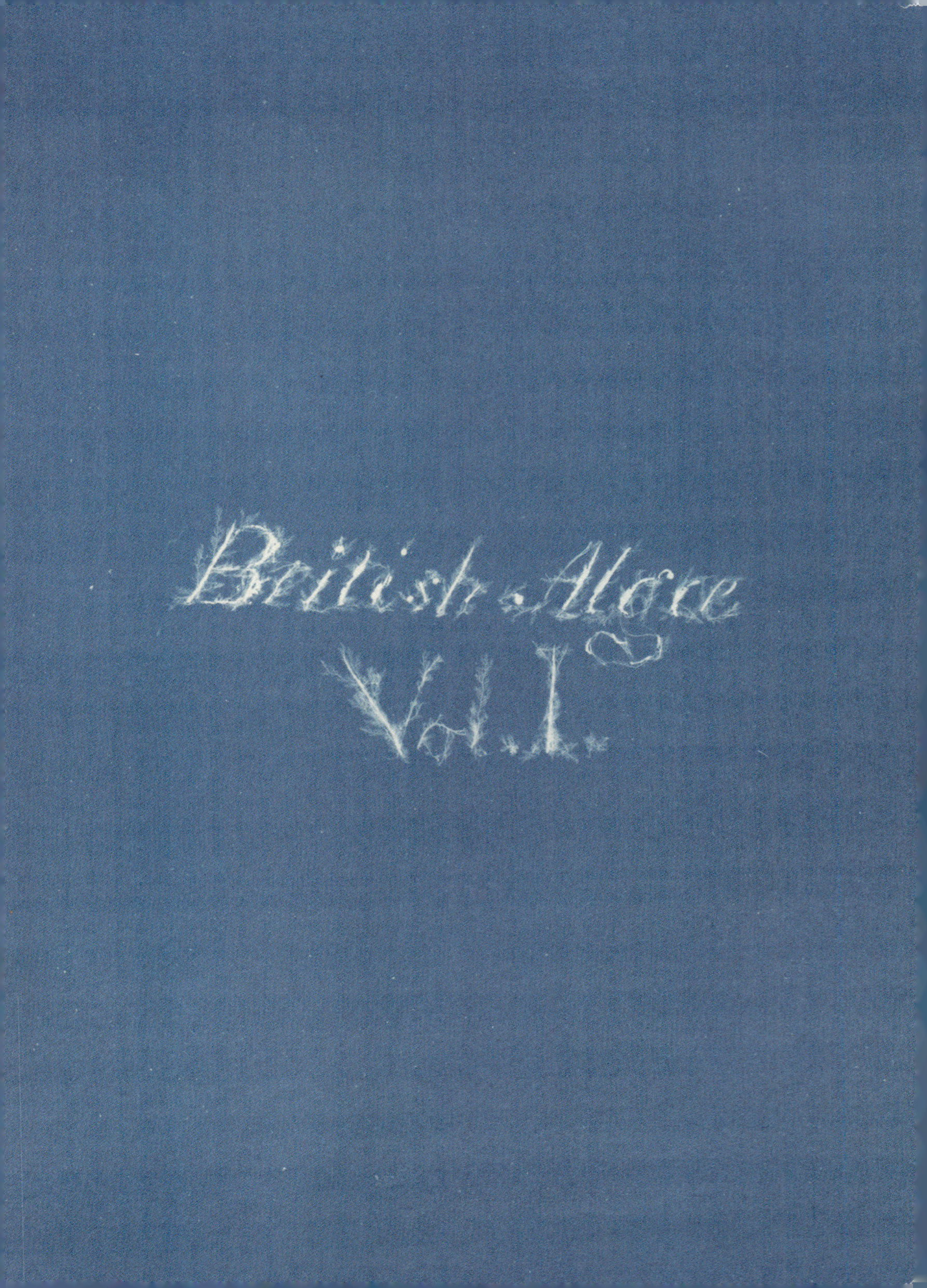
British Algae
Vol. I.

Contents.

Vol. I.

* S. plumosum, (newly found on the British coast.)

SPH: radicans, Harv.
cirrhosa. Ag.
velutina, Grev.

ECTOCARPUS, Lyngb.

littoralis, Lyngb.

siliculosus, Lyngb.

fasciculatus, Harv.

tomentosus, Lyngb.

crinitus, Carm.

pusillus, Harv.

granulosus, Ag.

sphærophorus, Carm.

brachiatus, Harv.

Mertensii, Ag.

MYRIOTRICHIA. Harv.

clavæformis, Harv.

filiformis, Harv.

CHORDARIA. Ag.

flagelliformis, Ag.

HELMINTHOCLADIA. Harv.

vermicularis, Harv.

Griffithsiana, Grev.

virescens, Carm.

CORYNEPHORA. Ag.

marina, Ag.

MESOGLOIA, Ag.

multifida, Ag.

M. Hudsoni, Ag.

purpurea, Harv.

coccinea, Ag.

moniliformis, Griff.

GLOIOSIPHONIA, Carm.

capillaris, Carm.

NACCARIA, Endl.

Wigghii, Endl.

CATENELLA. Grev.

Opuntia. Grev.

DUMONTIA. Lamour.

filiformis, Grev.

HALYMENIA, Ag.

ligulata, Ag. & vars.

furcellata. (2 plates.) Ag.

IRIDÆA, Bory.

edulis, Bory.

POLYIDES, Ag.

rotundus. Grev.

FURCELLARIA, Lamour.

fastigiata, Lamour.

DELESSERIA, Lamour.

sanguinea, Lamour.

sinuosa, Lamour.

alata, Lamour.

Hypoglossum, Lamour.

D. ruscifolia, Lamour.

angustissima. Griff.

NITOPHYLLUM. Grev.

punctatum, Grev.

ulvoideum, Hook.

Bonnemaisoni, Grev.

Gmelini, Grev.

laceratum. Grev. & vars.

RHODOMENIA. Grev.

bifida, Grev.

laciniata, Grev.

polycarpa, Grev.

Palmetta, Grev.

ciliata, Grev.

jubata, Grev.

palmata, Grev.

sobolifera, Grev.

reniformis, Hook.

PLOCAMIUM, Lamour.

coccineum. Lyngb.

MICROCLADIA, Grev.

glandulosa, Grev.

ODONTHALIA, Lyngb.

dentata, Lyngb.

RHODOMELA. Ag.

lycopodioides, Ag.

R. subfusca, Ag.
pinastroides, Ag.
scorpioides, Ag.
BONNEMAISONIA. Ag.
asparagoides, Ag.
LAURENCIA. Lamour.
pinnatifida, Lamour. and varieties.
obtusa, Lamour.
dasyphylla, Lamour.
tenuissima, Lamour.
CHYLOCLADIA, Grev.
clavellosa, Hook.
ovalis, Hook.
kaliformis, Hook.
parvula, Hook.
articulata, Hook.

C. reflexa,
GIGARTINA, Lamour.
purpurascens, Lamour.
confervoides, Lamour.
erecta, Hook.
compressa, Hook.
pistillata, Lamour.
acicularis, Lamour.
Teedii, Lamour.
Griffithsiæ, Grev.
plicata, Lamour.
CHONDRUS, Stack.
mamillosus, Grev.
crispus, Lyngb.
norvegicus, Lamour.
membranifolius, Grev.

C. Brodiæi, Grev.
PHYLLOPHORA, Grev.
rubens, Grev.
SPHÆROCOCCUS, Stack.
coronopifolius, Ag.
GELIDIUM, Lamour.
corneum, Lamour. & vars.
cartilagineum, Grev.
rostratum, Griff.
GRATELOUPIA. Ag.
filicina, Ag.
PTILOTA, Ag.
plumosa, Ag.
sericea.

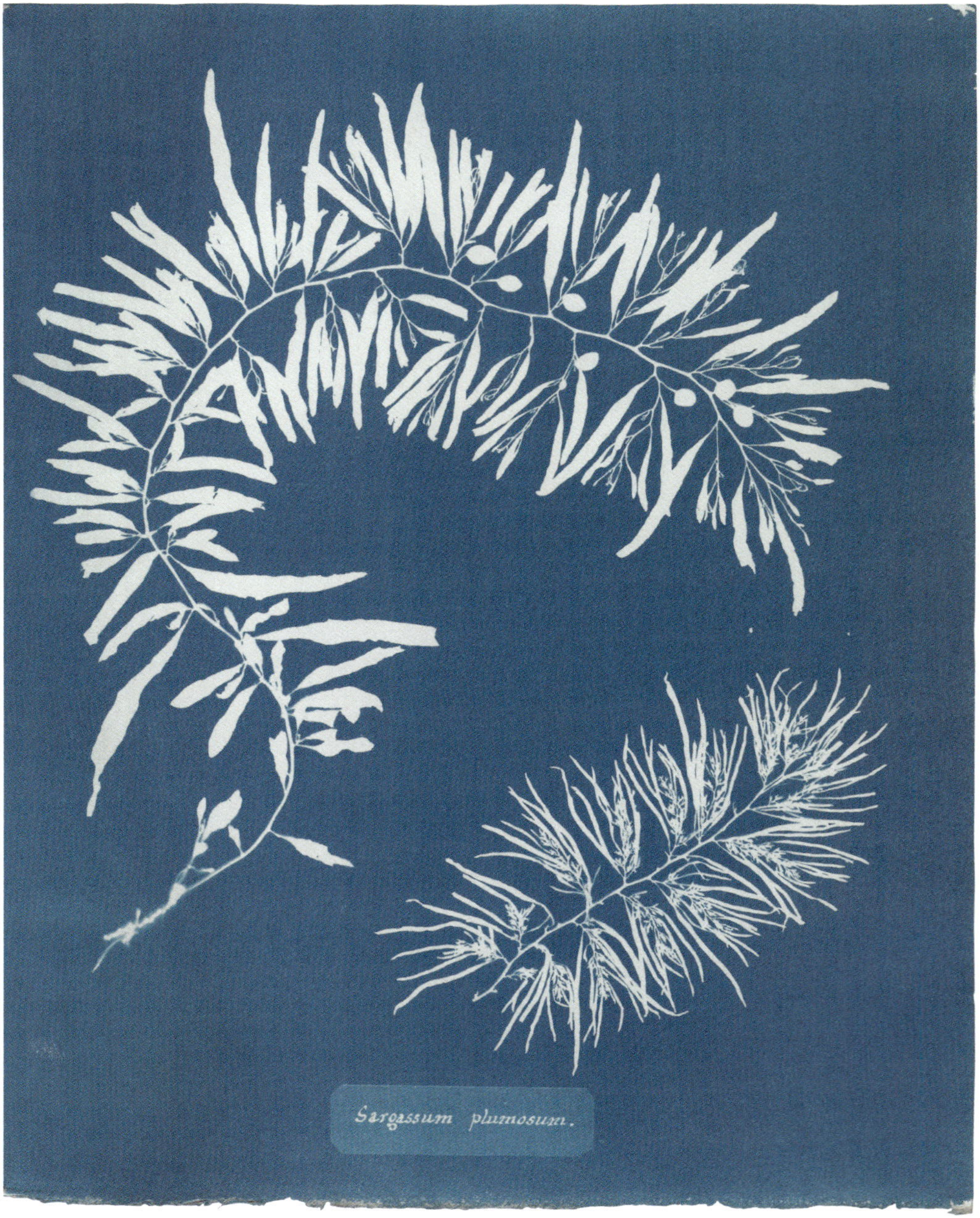

Plate 142. *Sargassum plumosum*

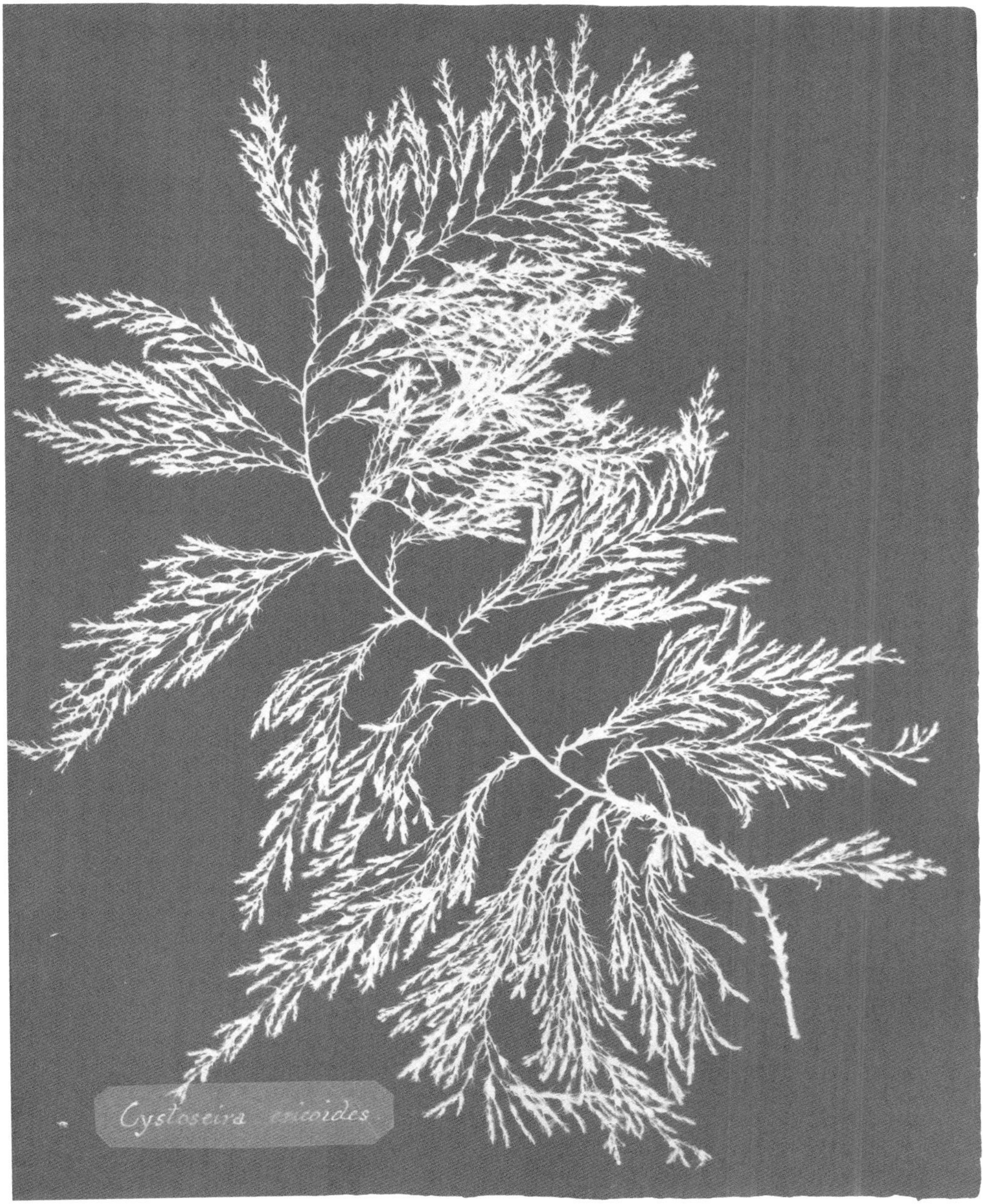

Plate 143. *Cystoseira ericoides*

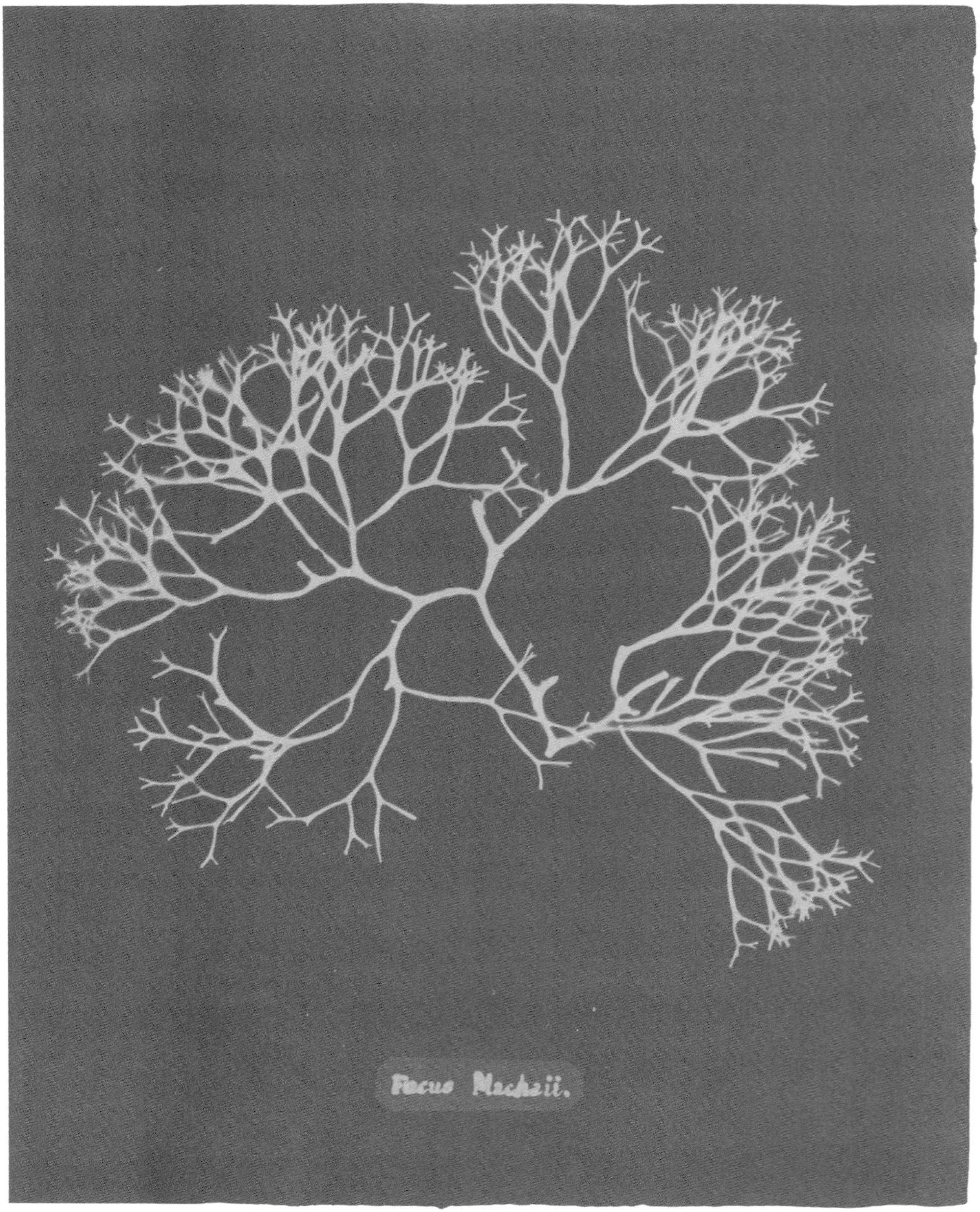

Plate 144. *Fucus machaii*

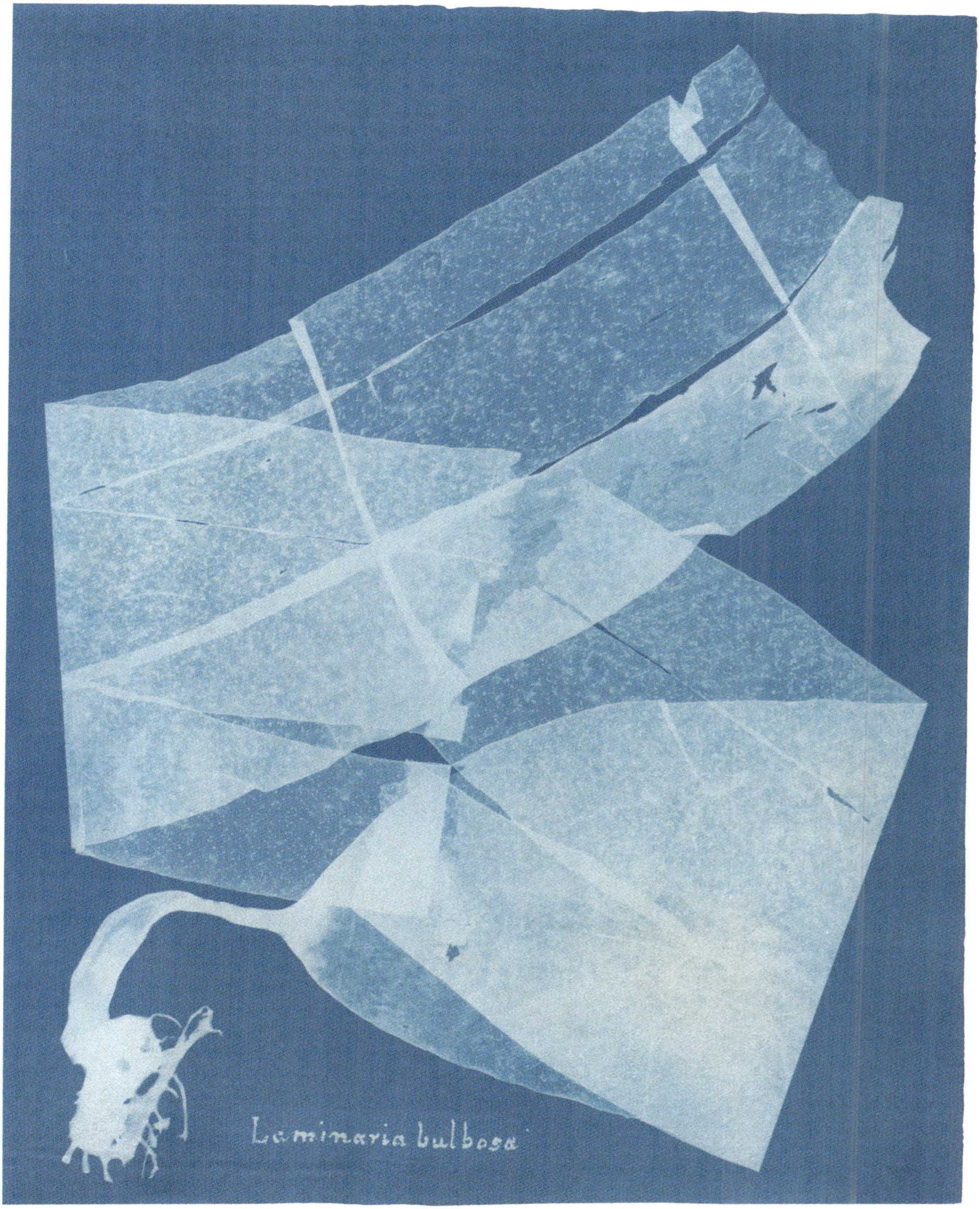

Plate 145. *Laminaria bulbosa*

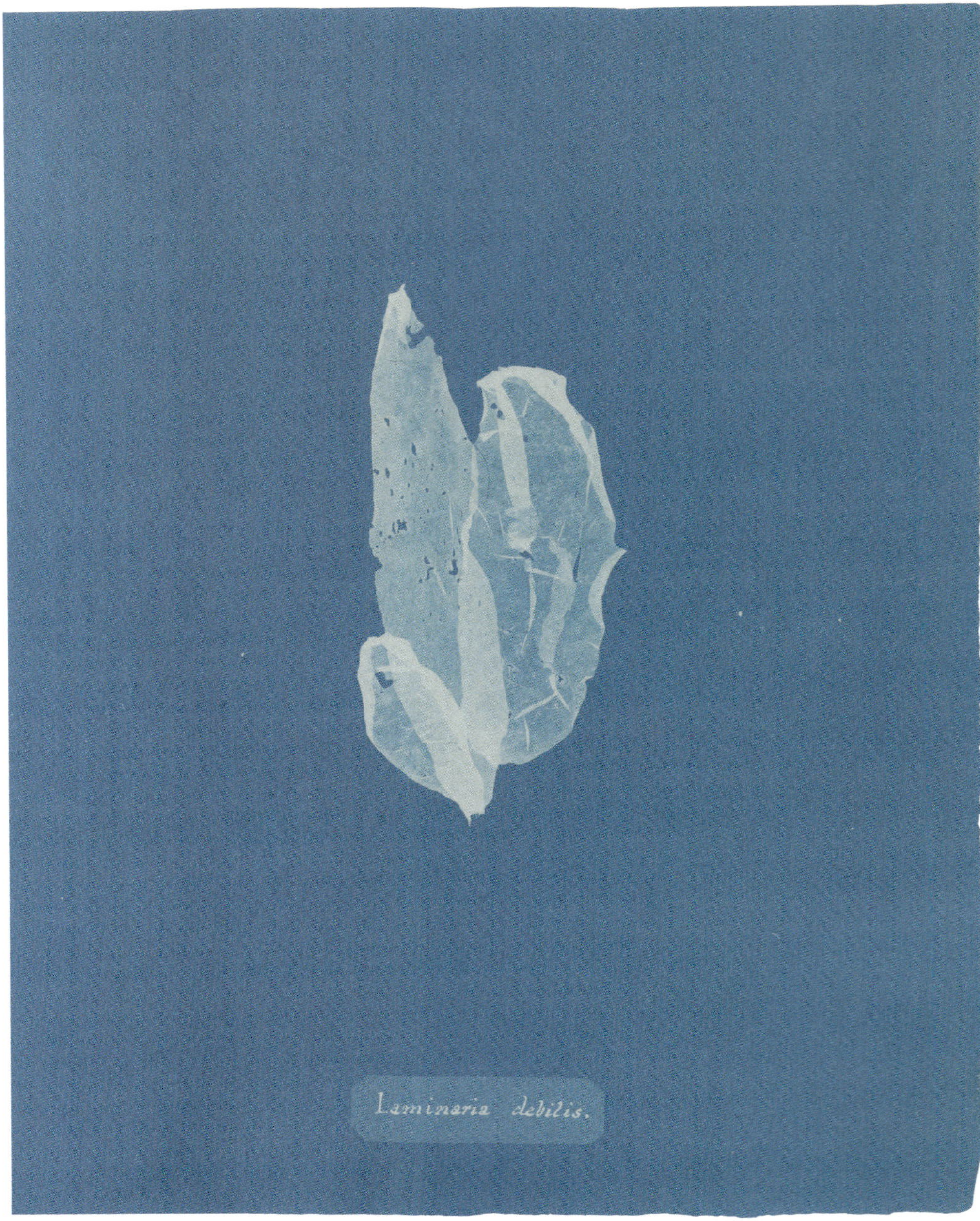

Plate 146. *Laminaria debilis*

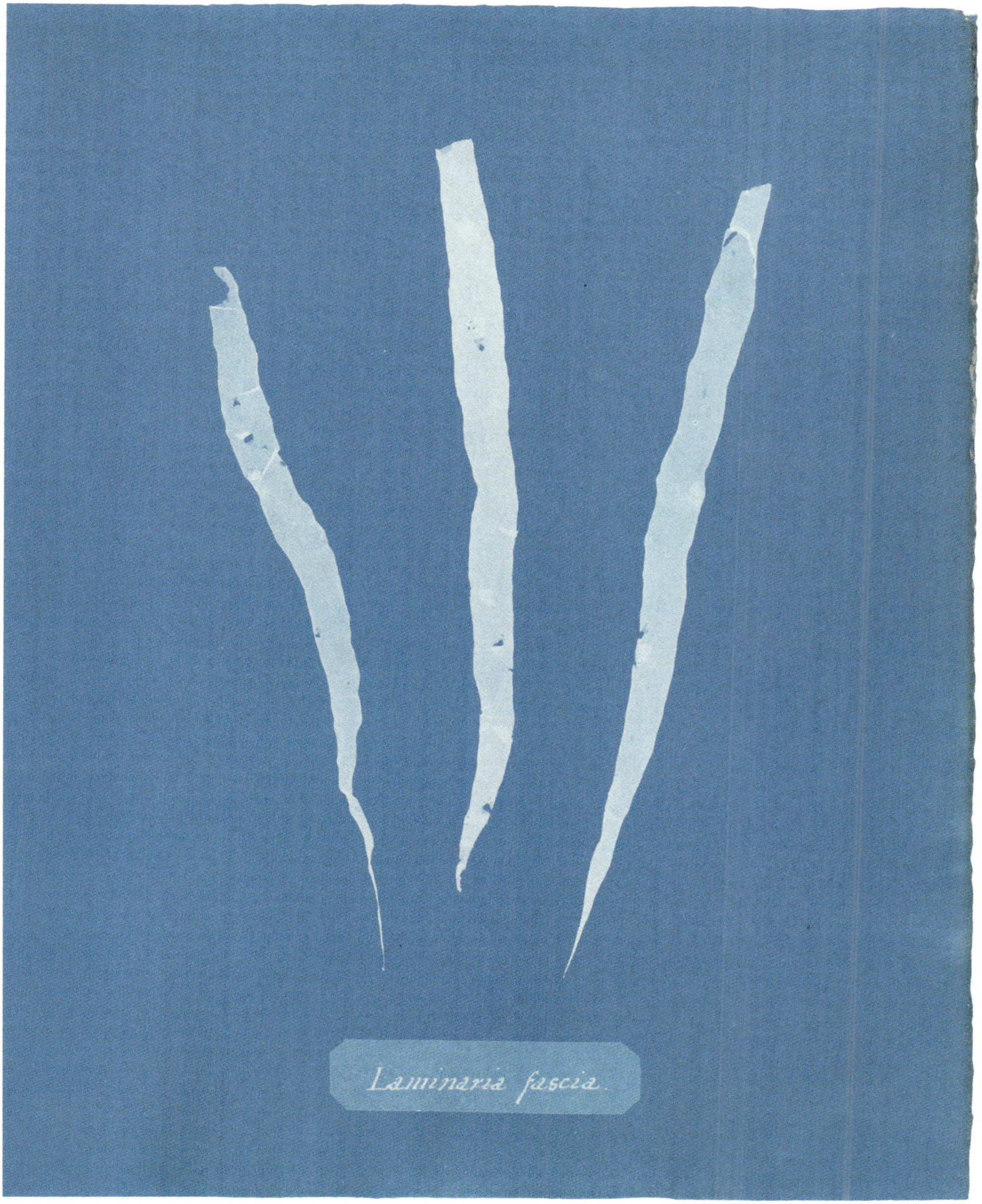

Plate 147. *Laminaria fascia*

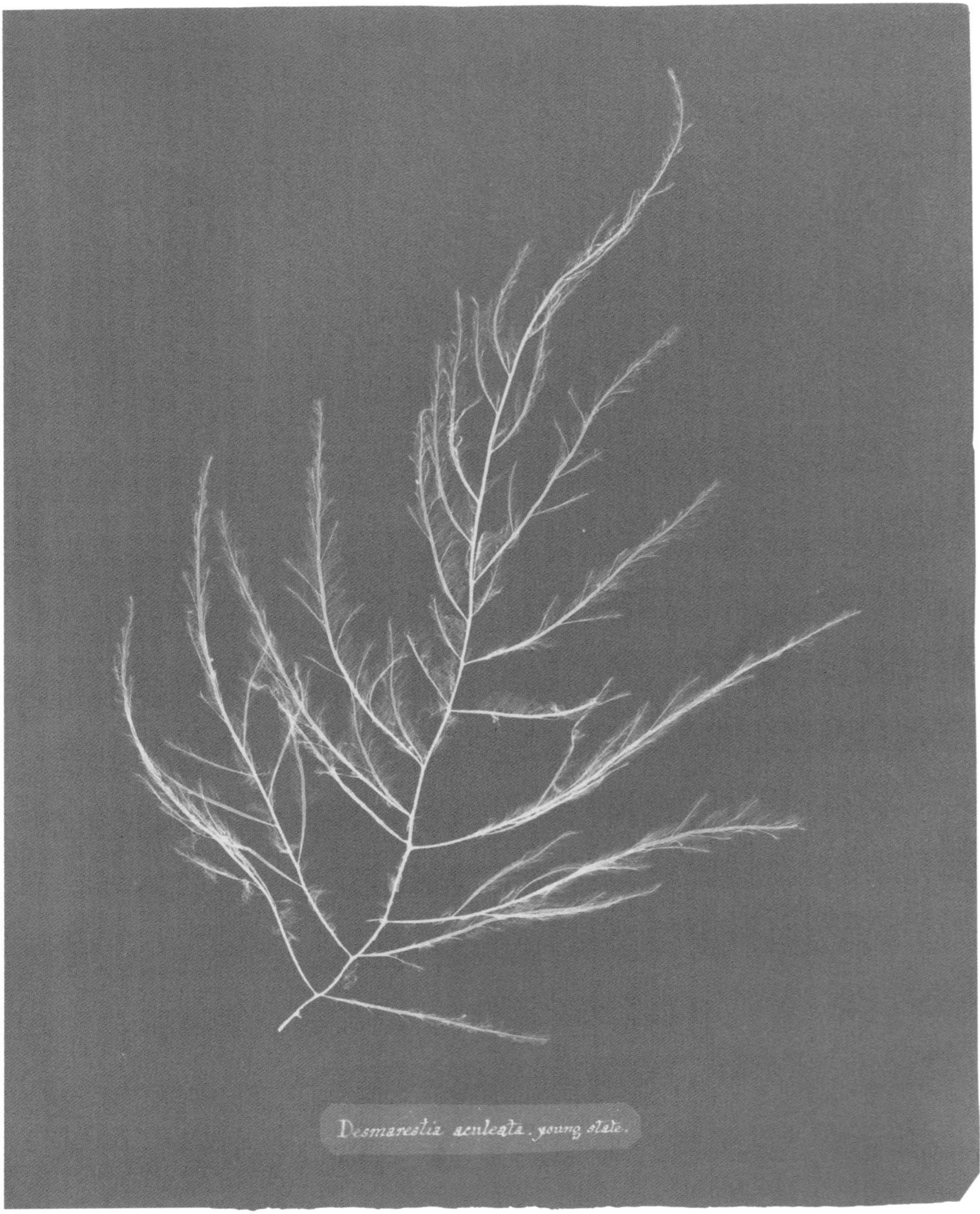

Plate 148. *Desmarestia aculeata*, young state

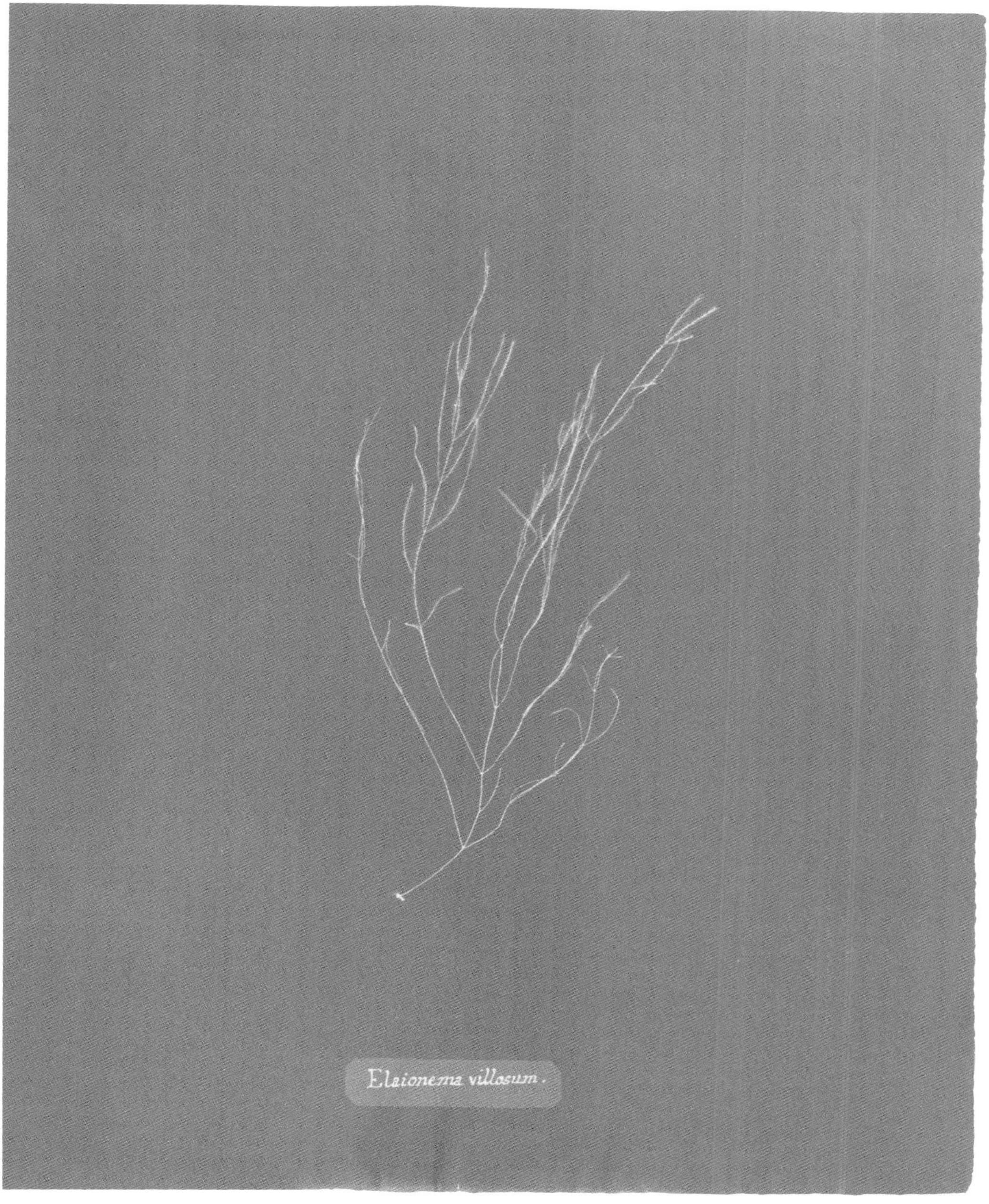

Plate 149. *Elaionema villosum*

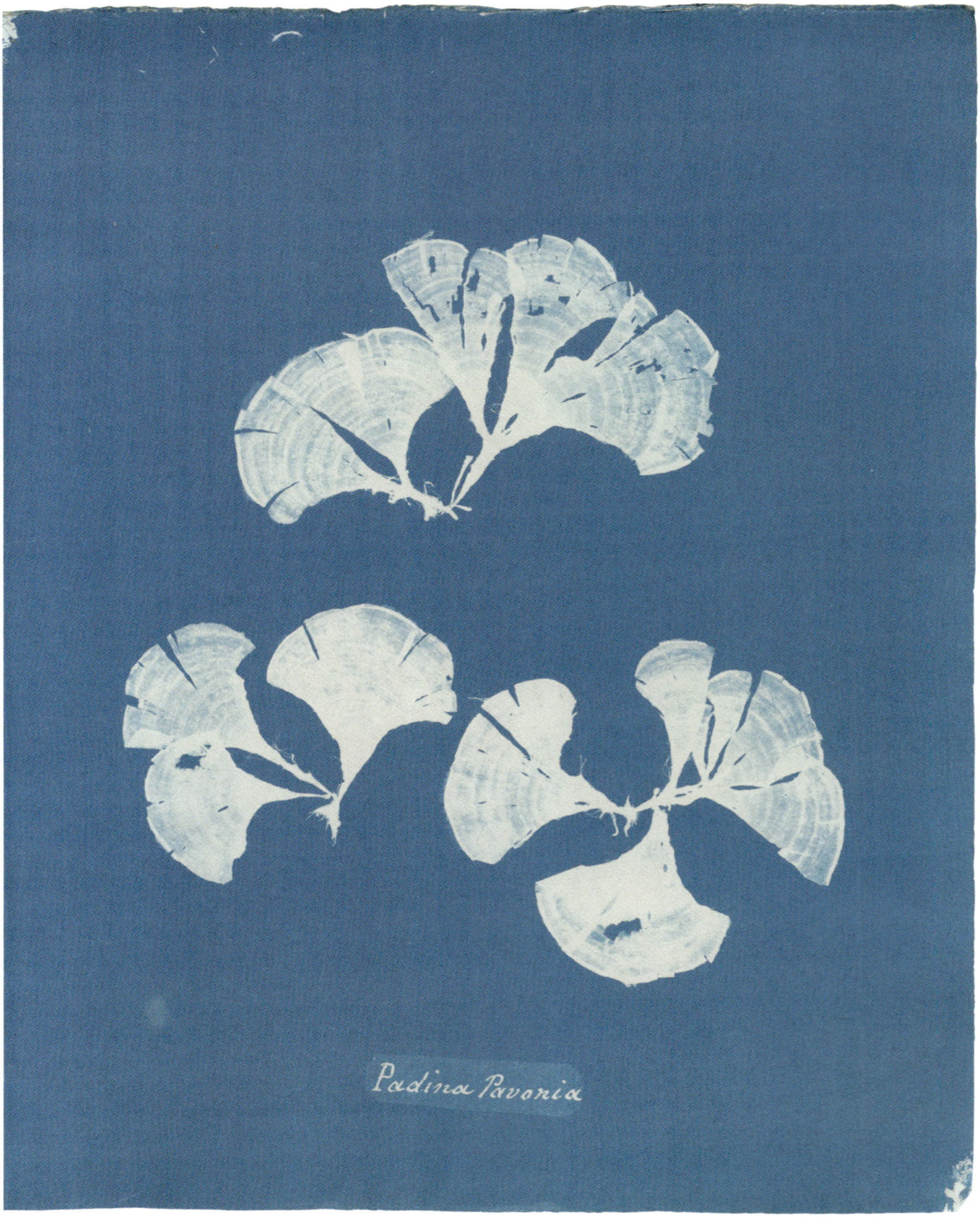

Plate 150. *Padina pavonia*

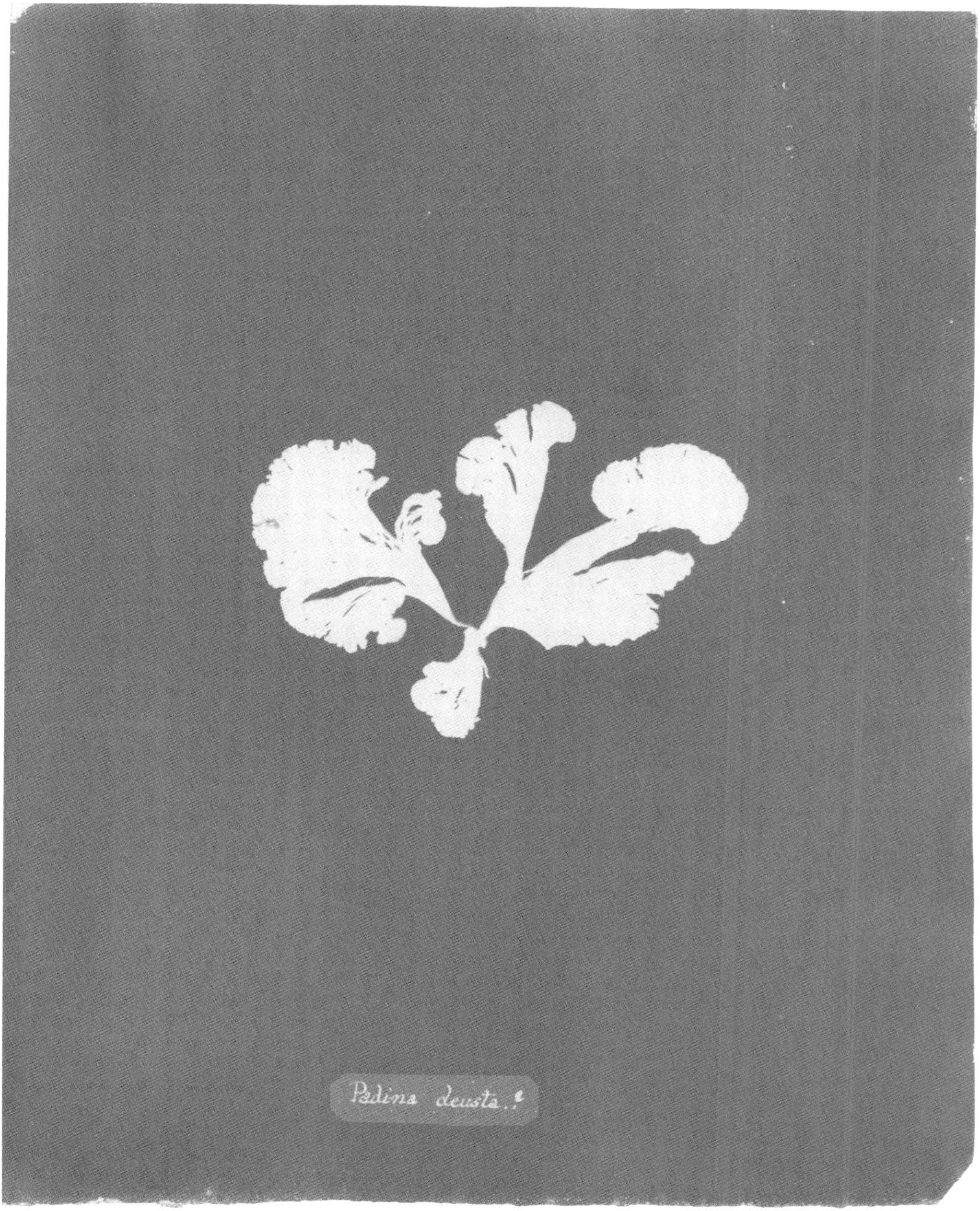

Plate 151. *Padina deusta*

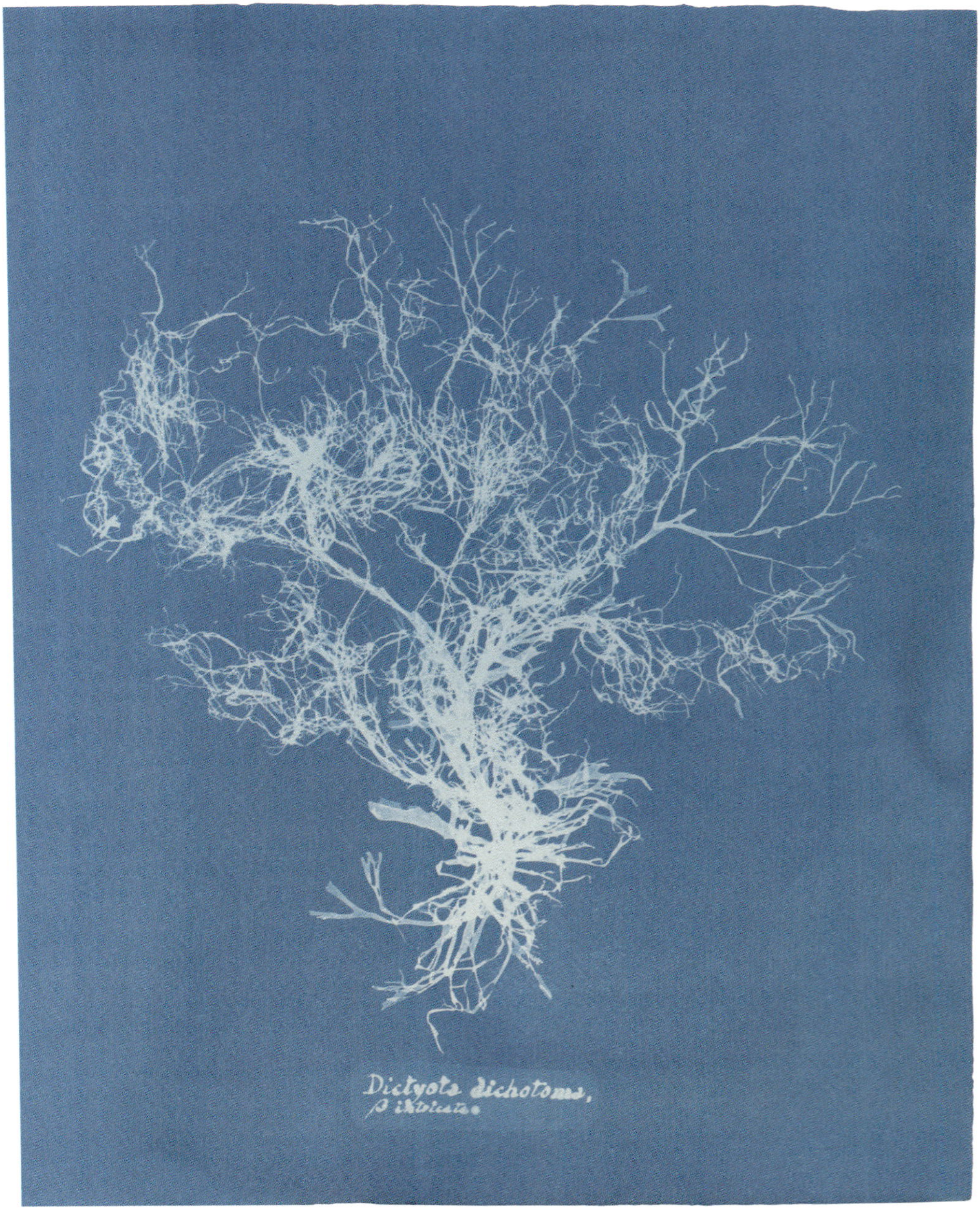

Plate 152. *Dictyota dichotoma,* β *intricata*

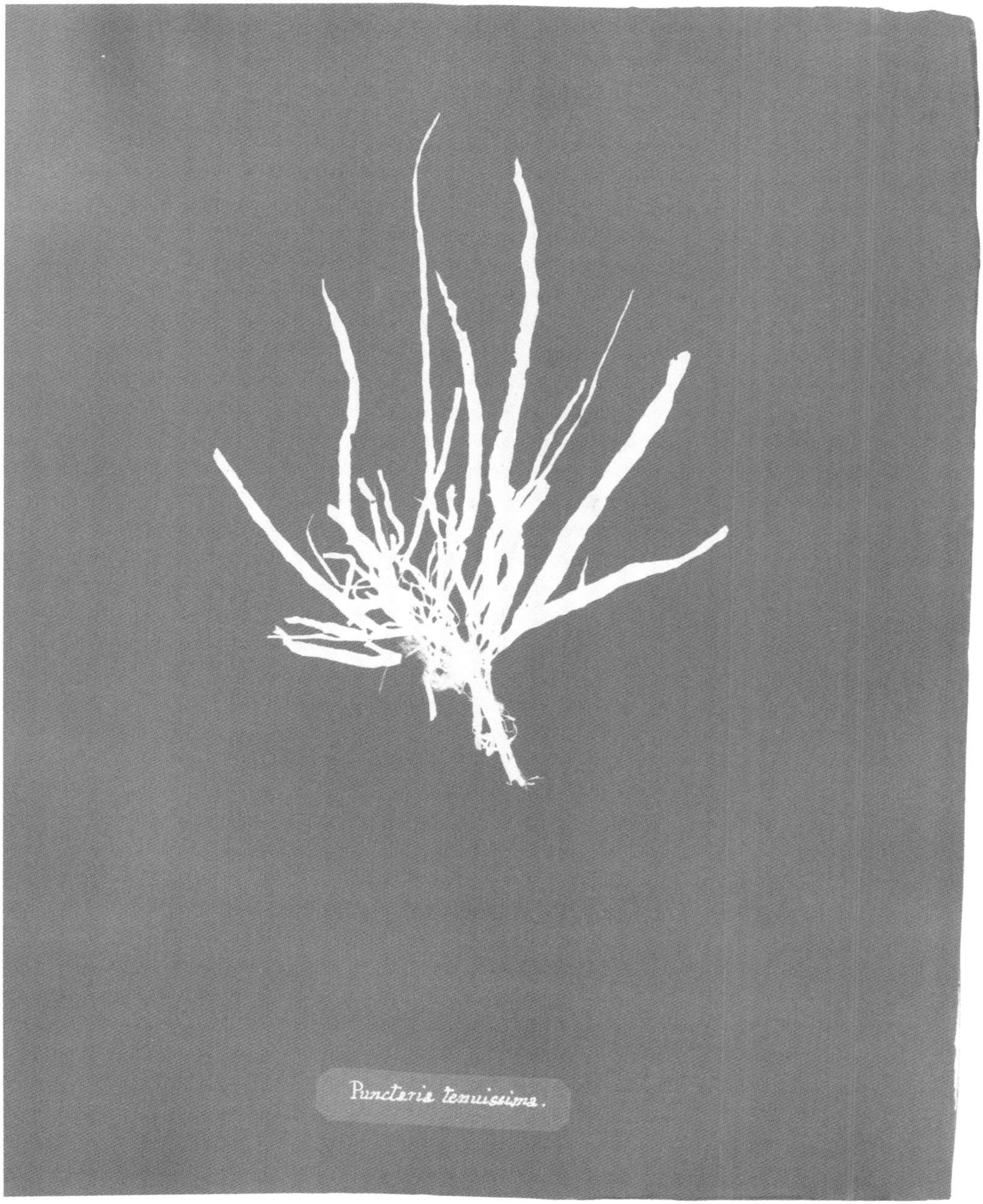

Plate 153. *Punctaria tenuissima*

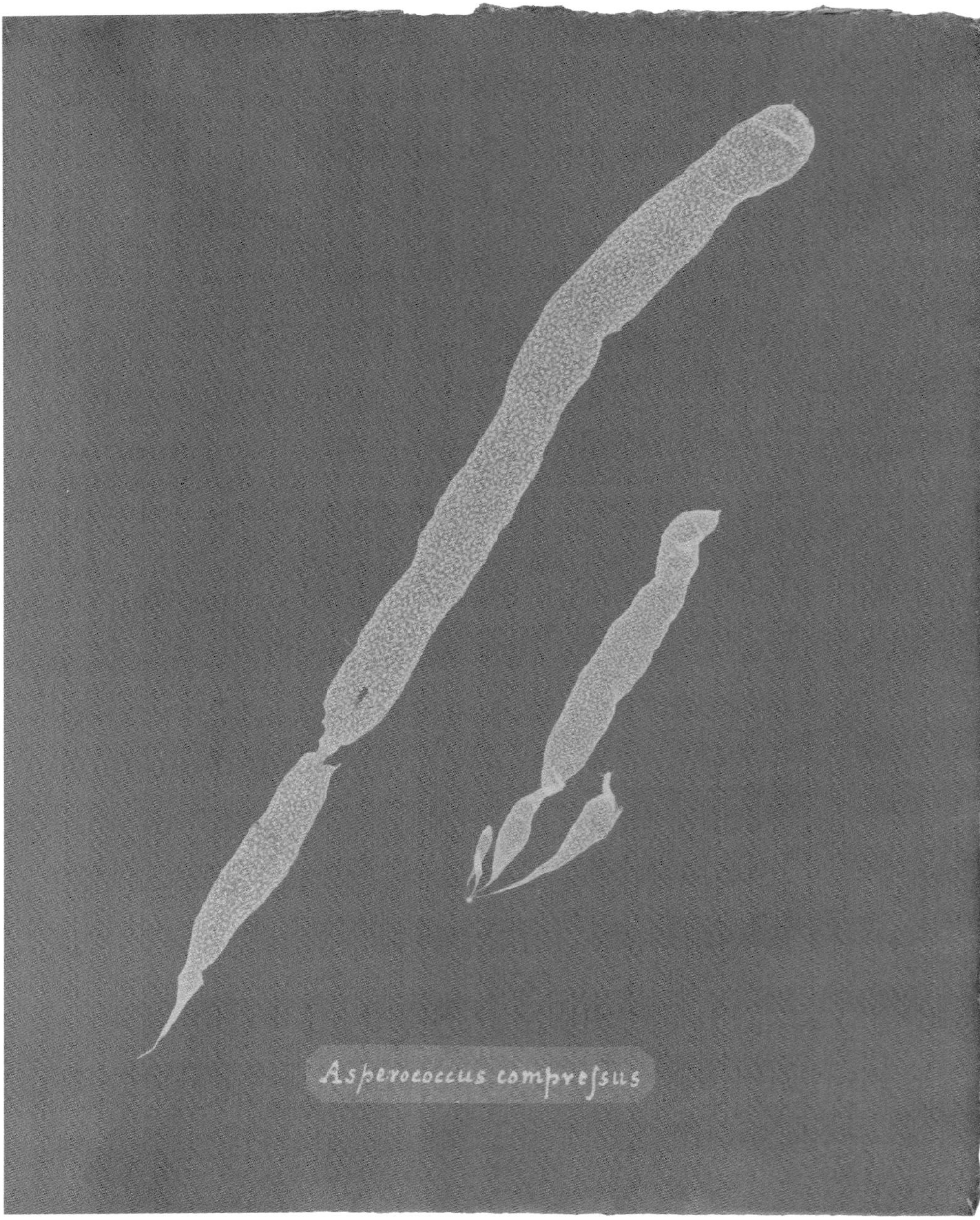

Plate 154. *Asperococcus compressus*

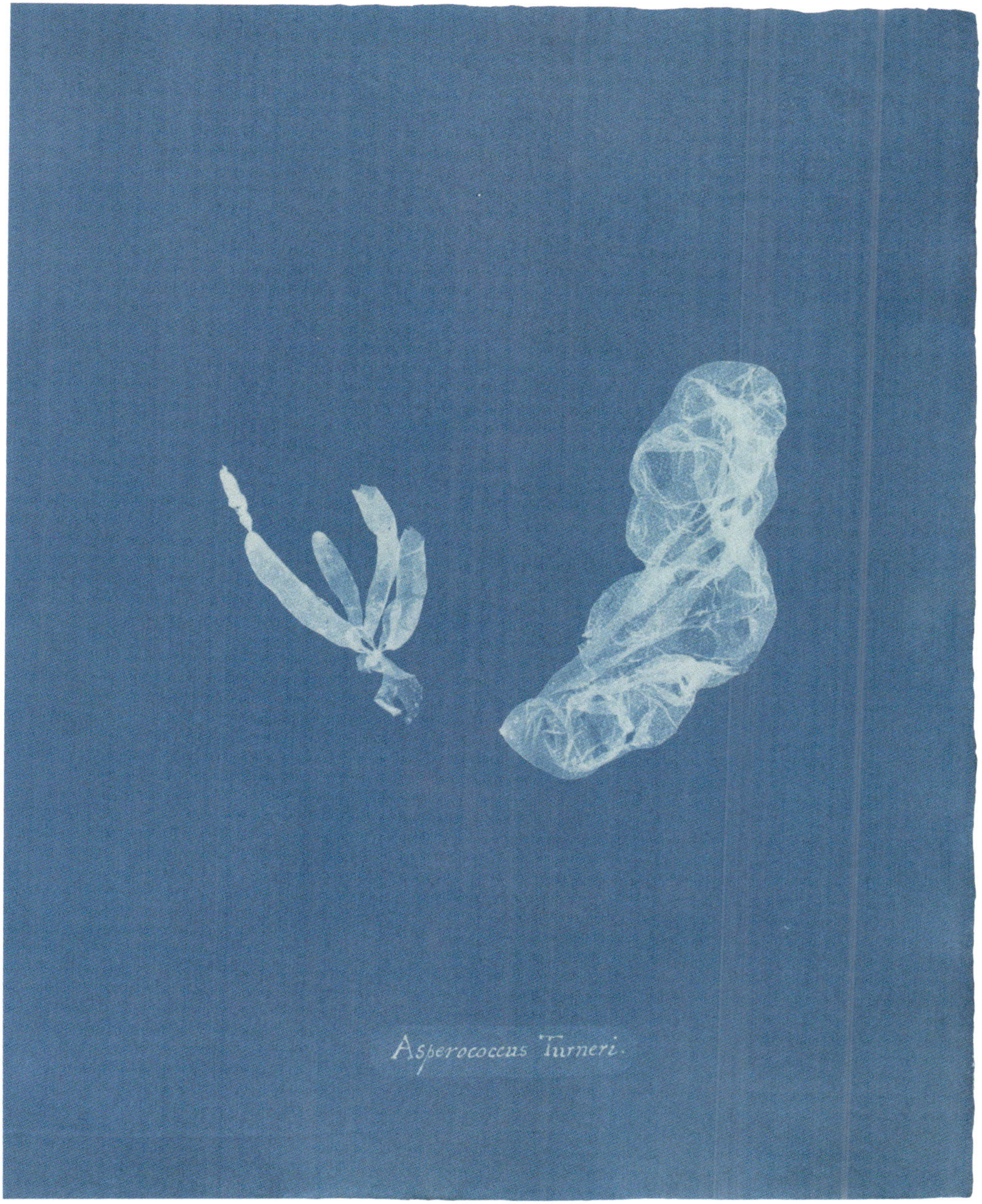

Plate 155. *Asperococcus turneri*

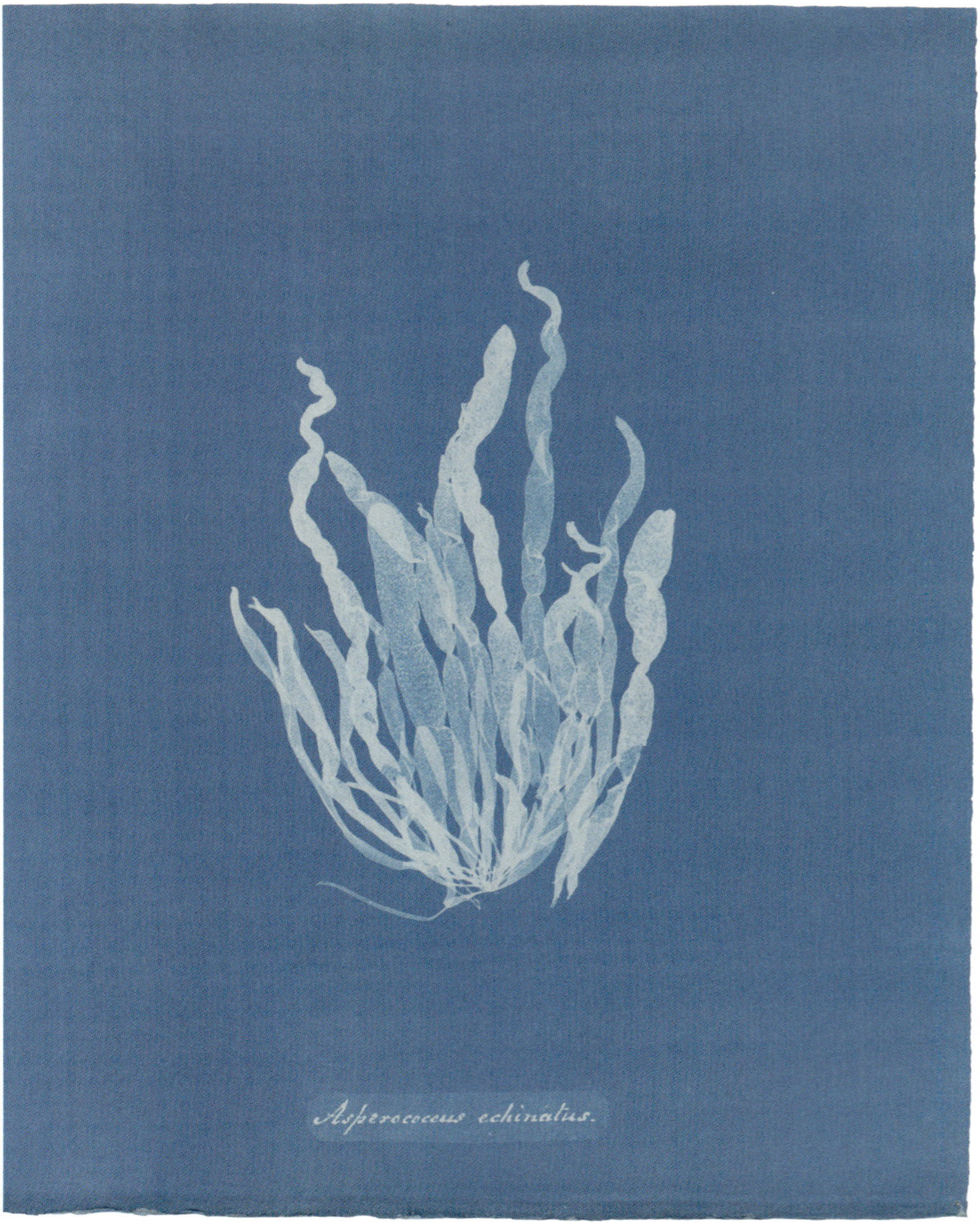

Plate 156. *Asperococcus echinatus*

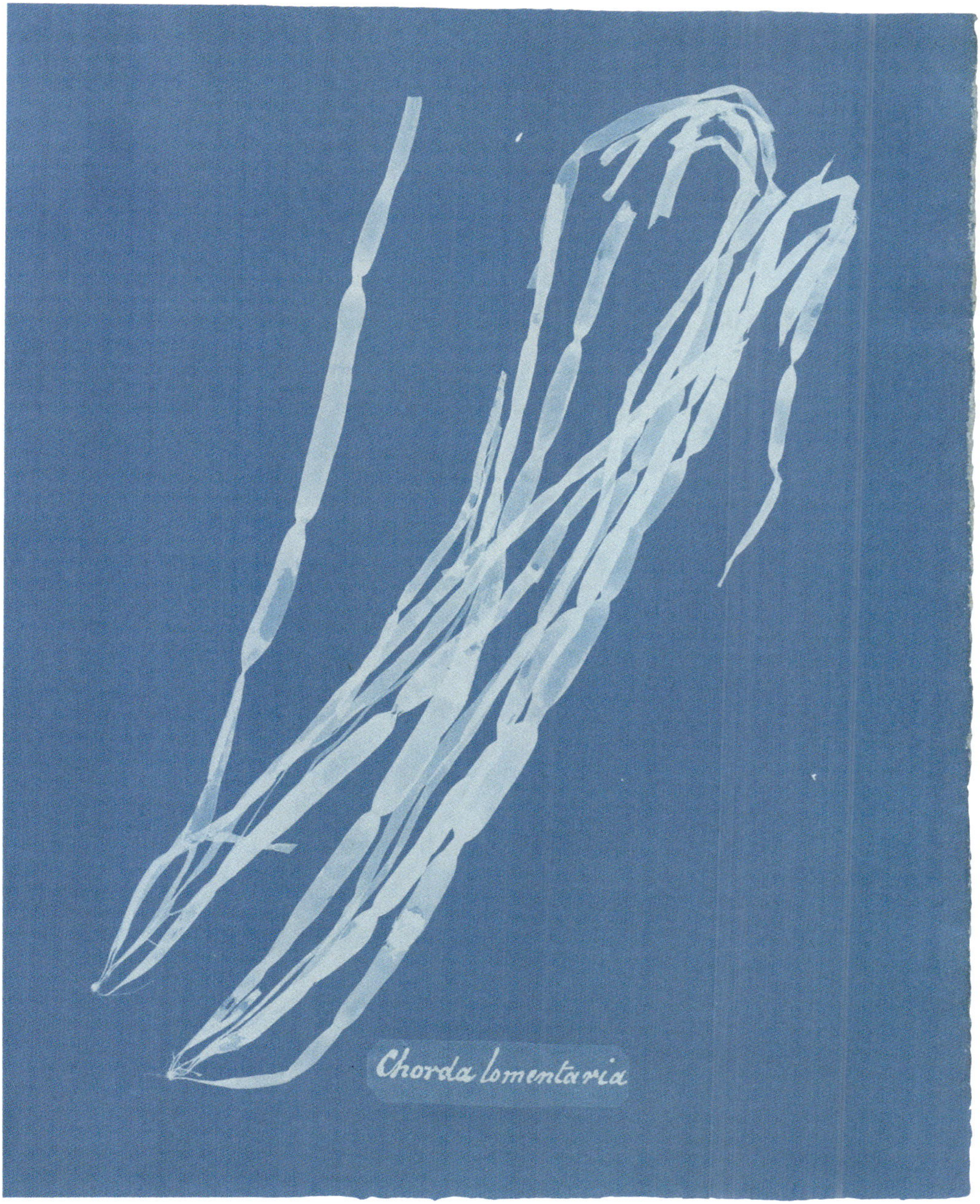

Plate 157. *Chorda lomentaria*

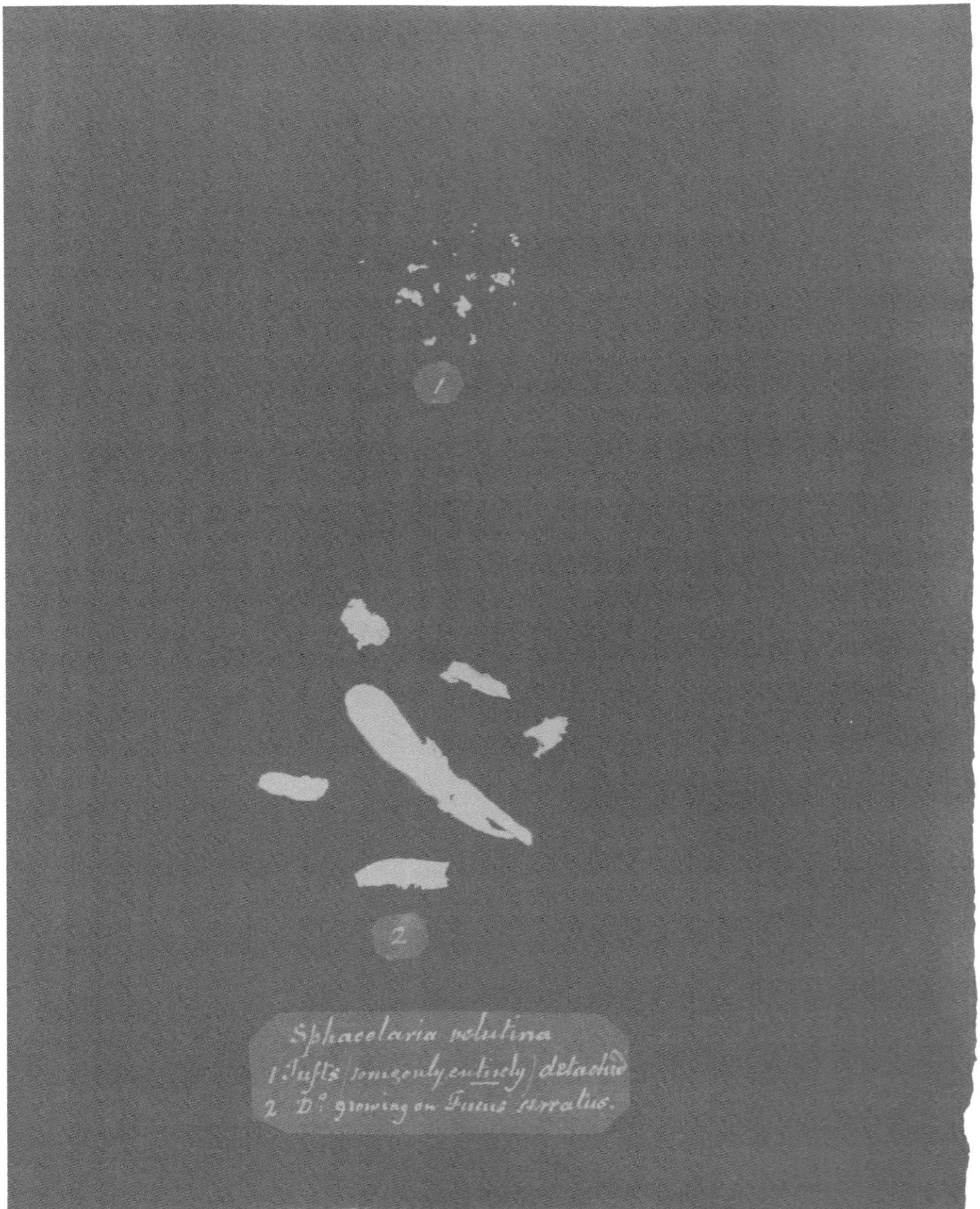

Plate 158. *Sphacelaria velutina*: 1. Tufts (some only entirely) detached; 2. [Tufts] growing on *Fucus serratus*

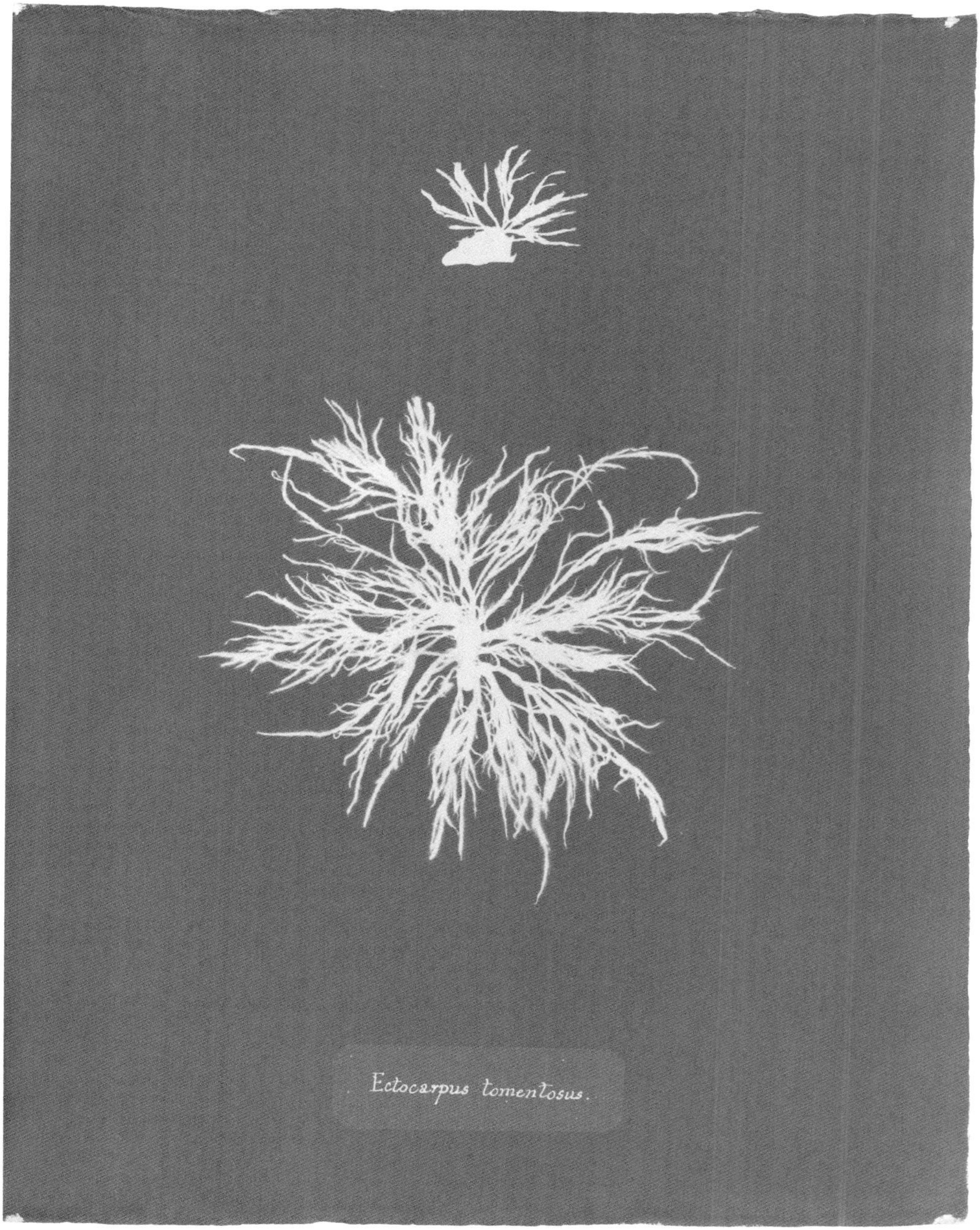

Plate 159. *Ectocarpus tomentosus*

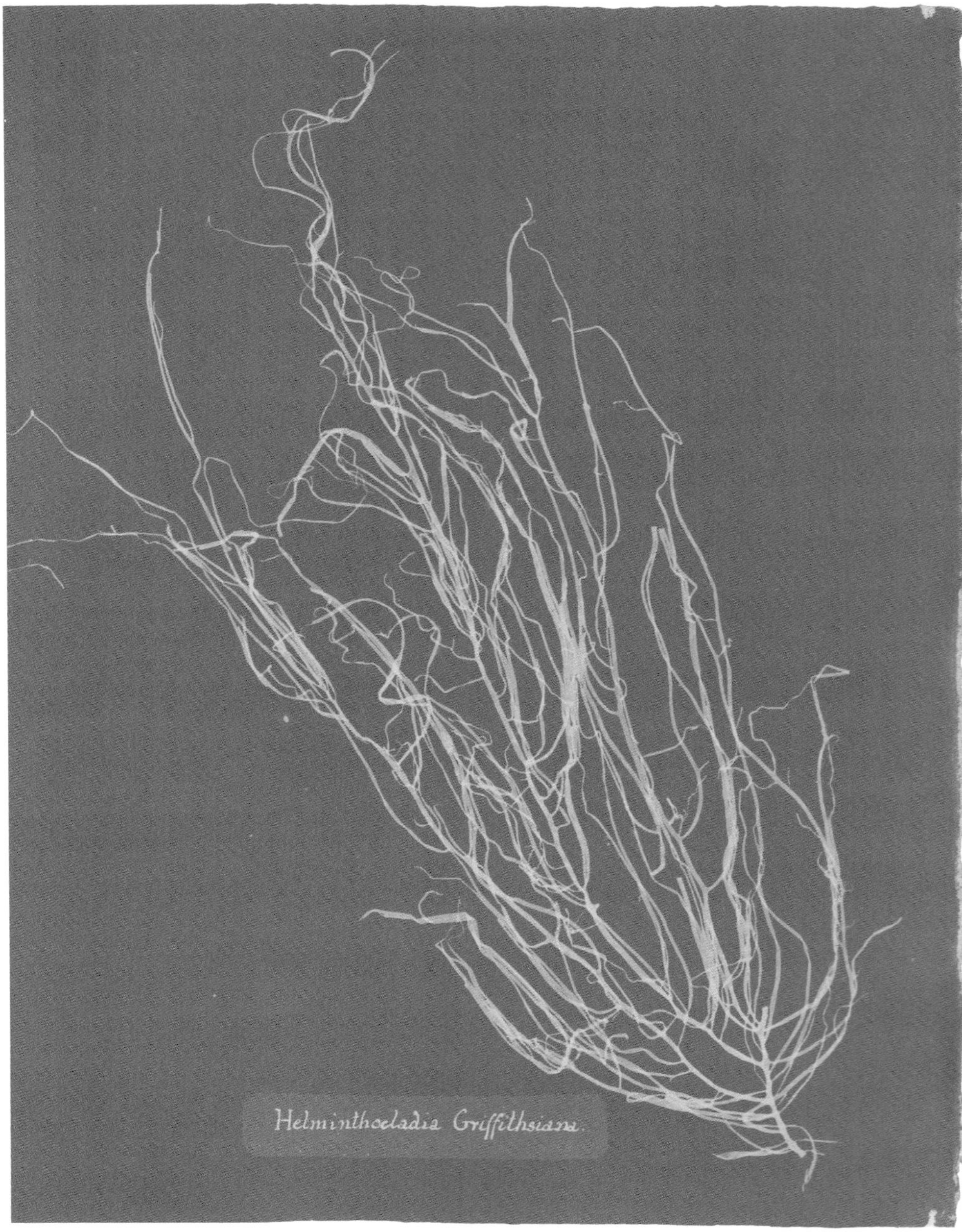

Plate 164. *Helminthocladia griffithsiana*

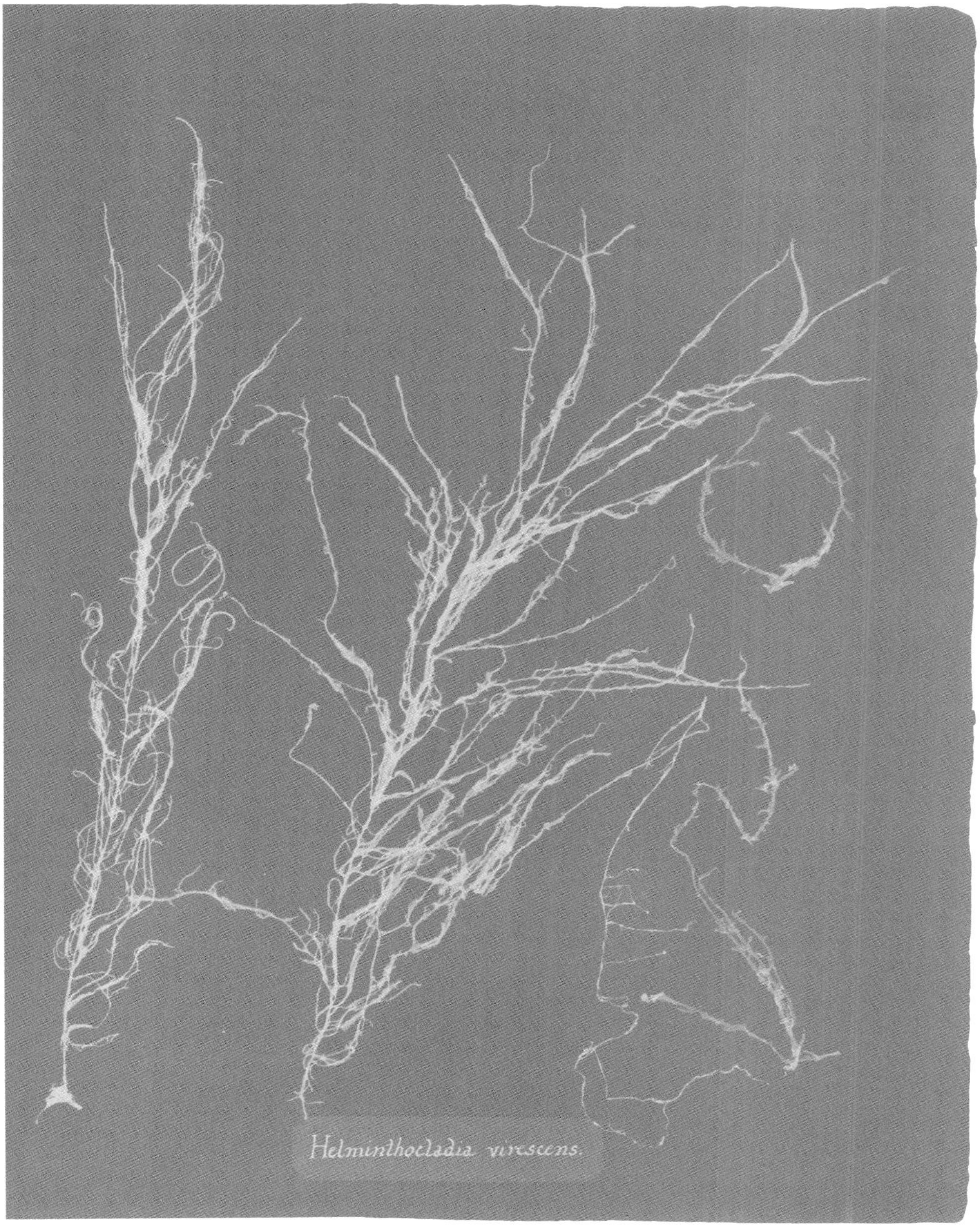

Plate 165. *Helminthocladia virescens*

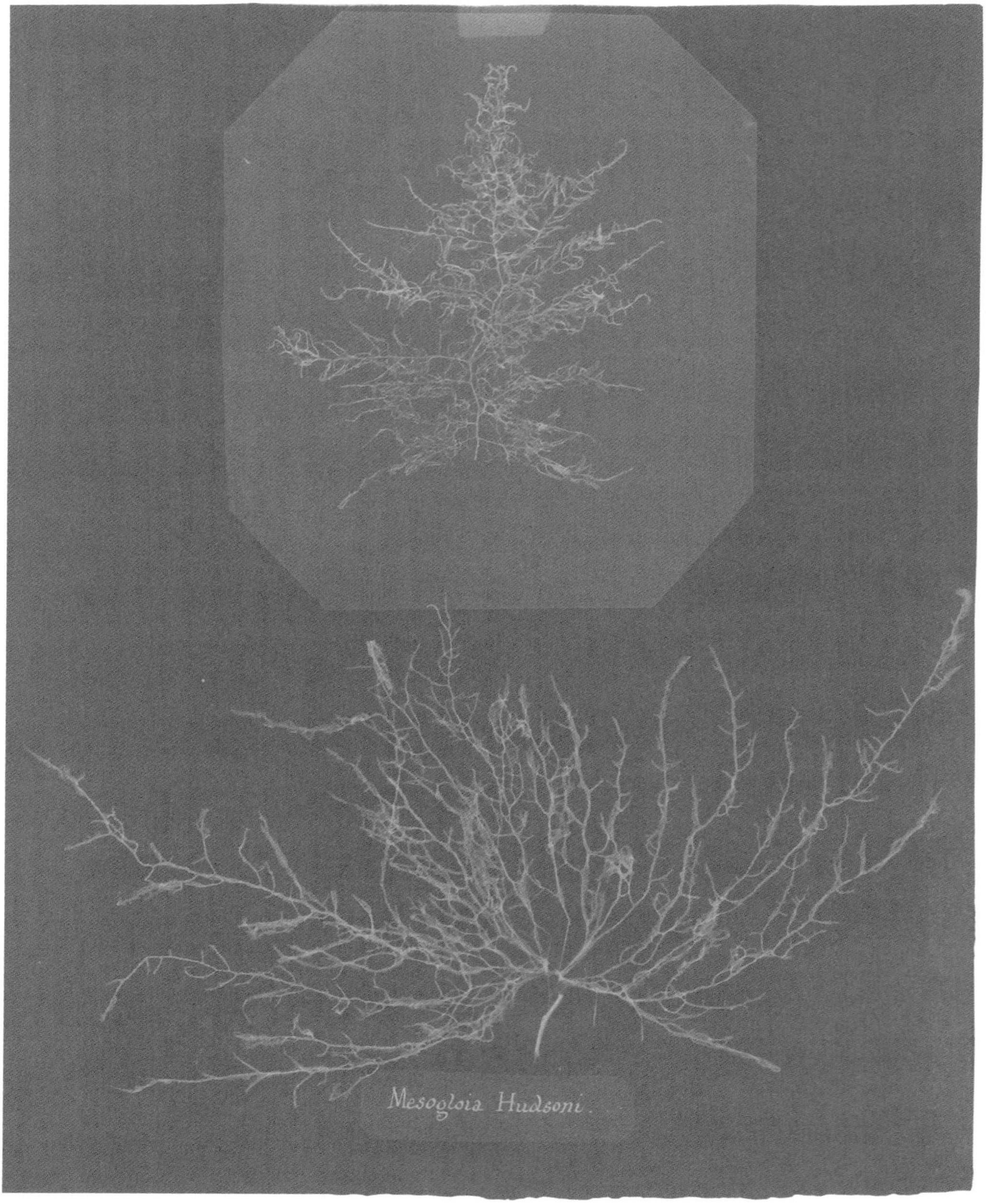

Plate 168. *Mesogloia hudsoni[i]*

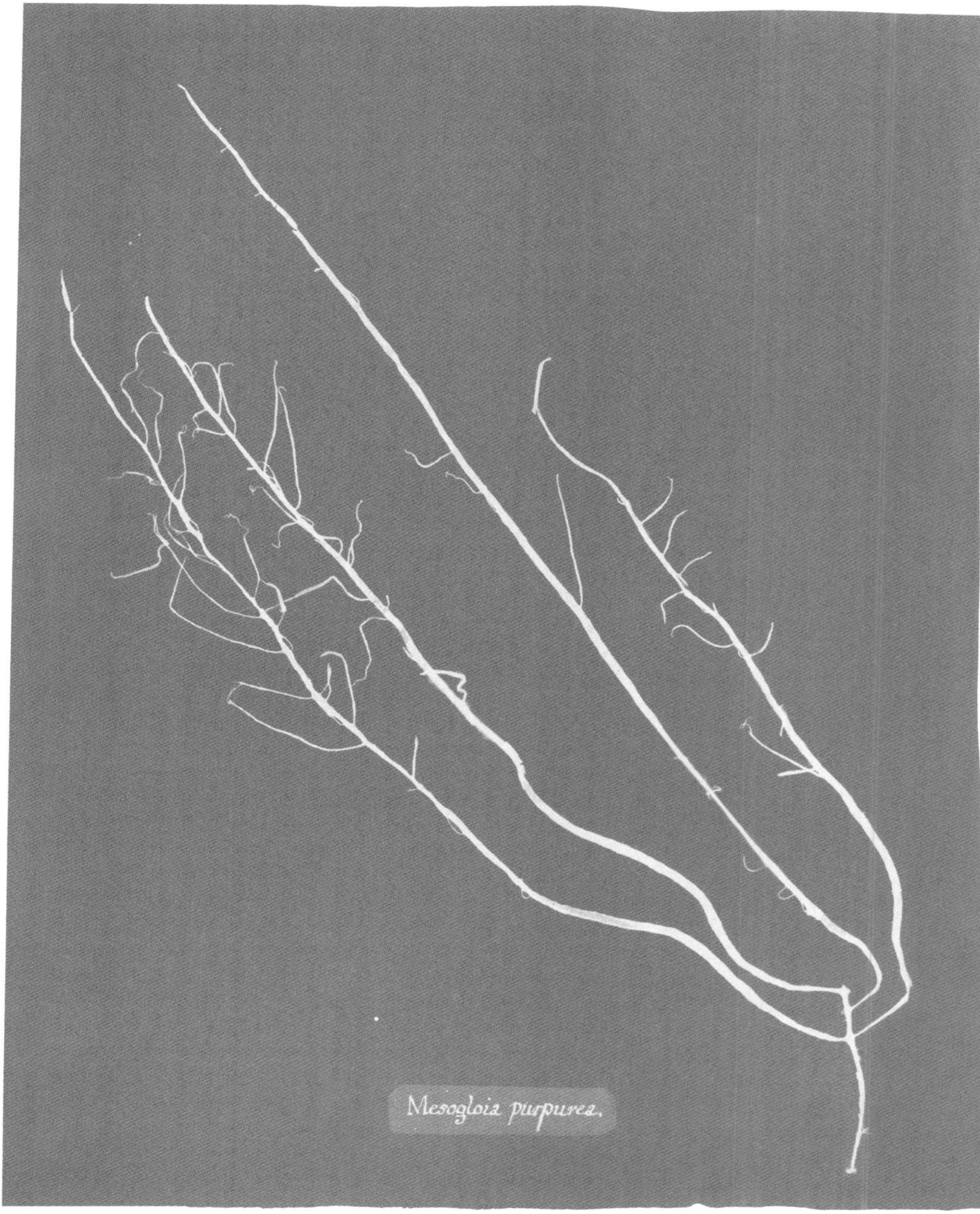

Plate 169. *Mesogloia purpurea*

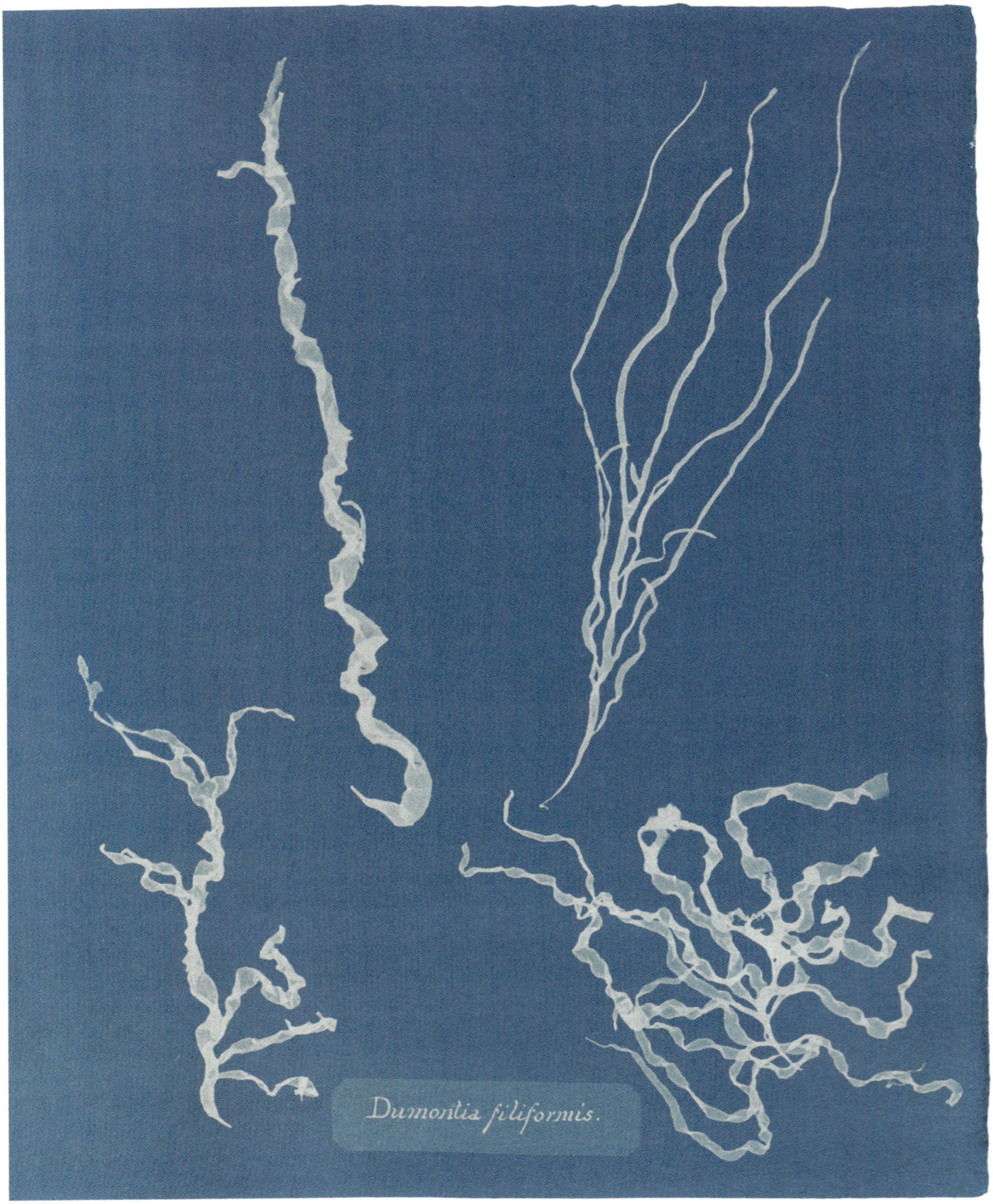

Plate 174. *Dumontia filiformis*

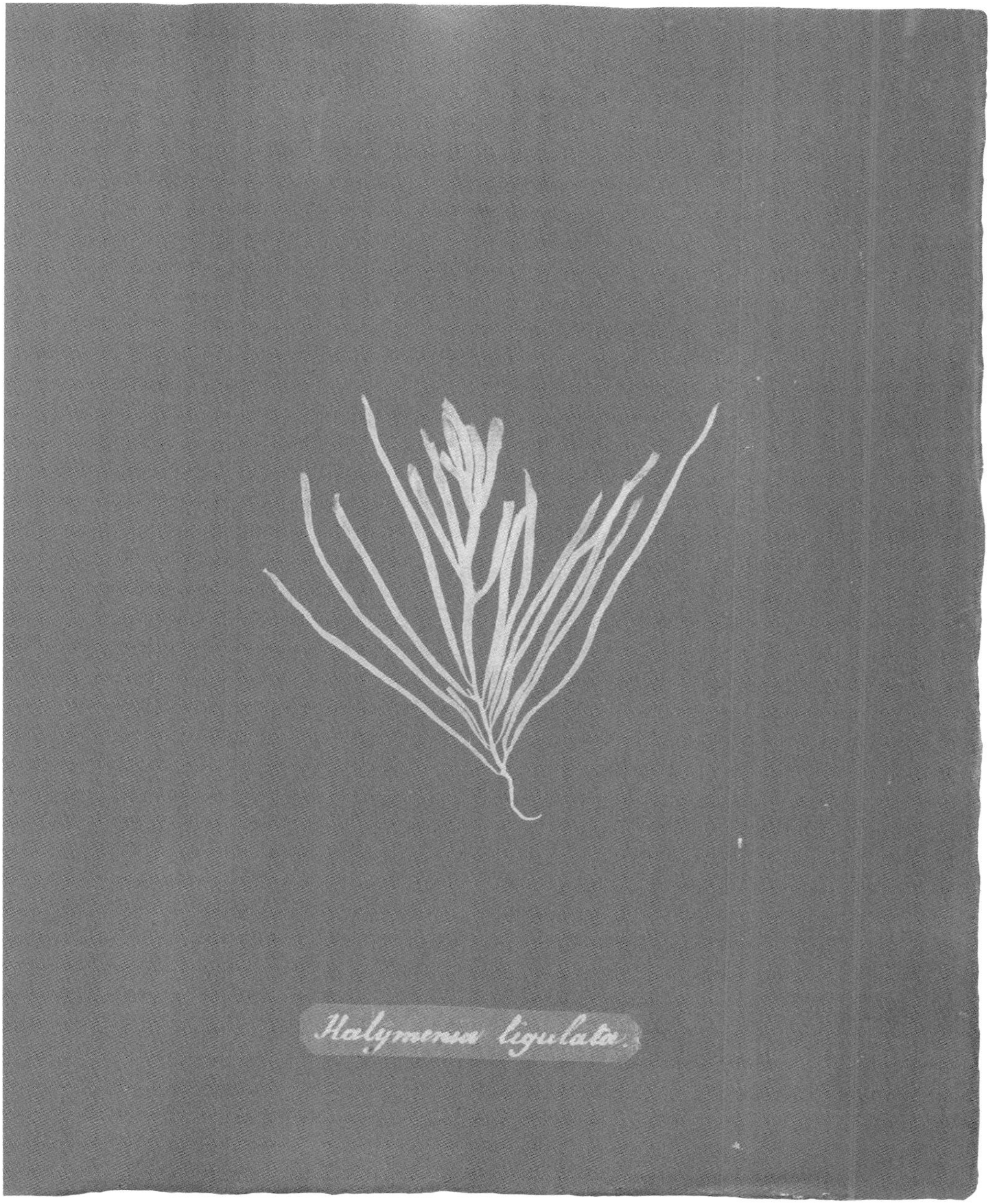

Plate 175. *Halymenia ligulata*

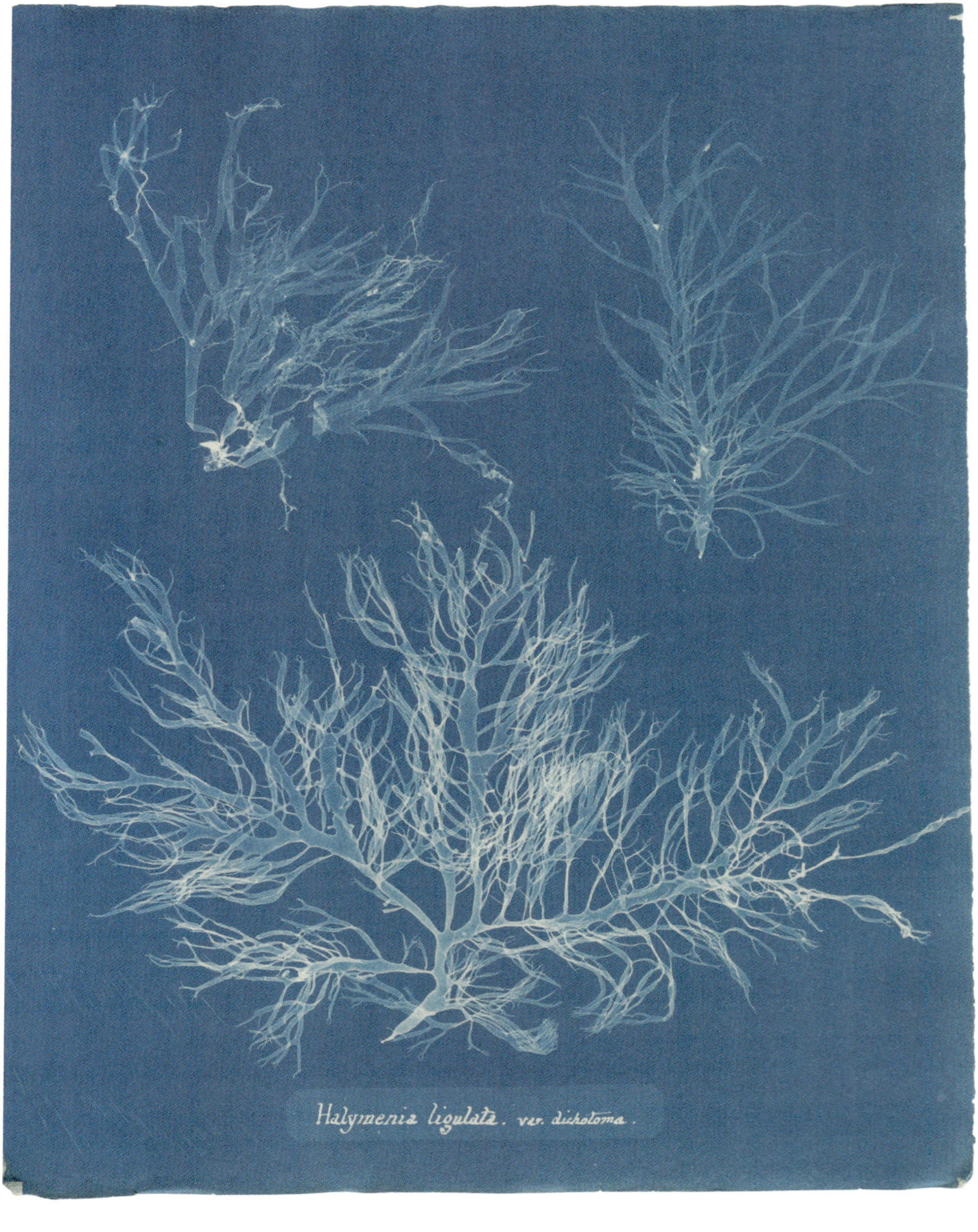

Plate 176. *Halymenia ligulata* var. *dichotoma*

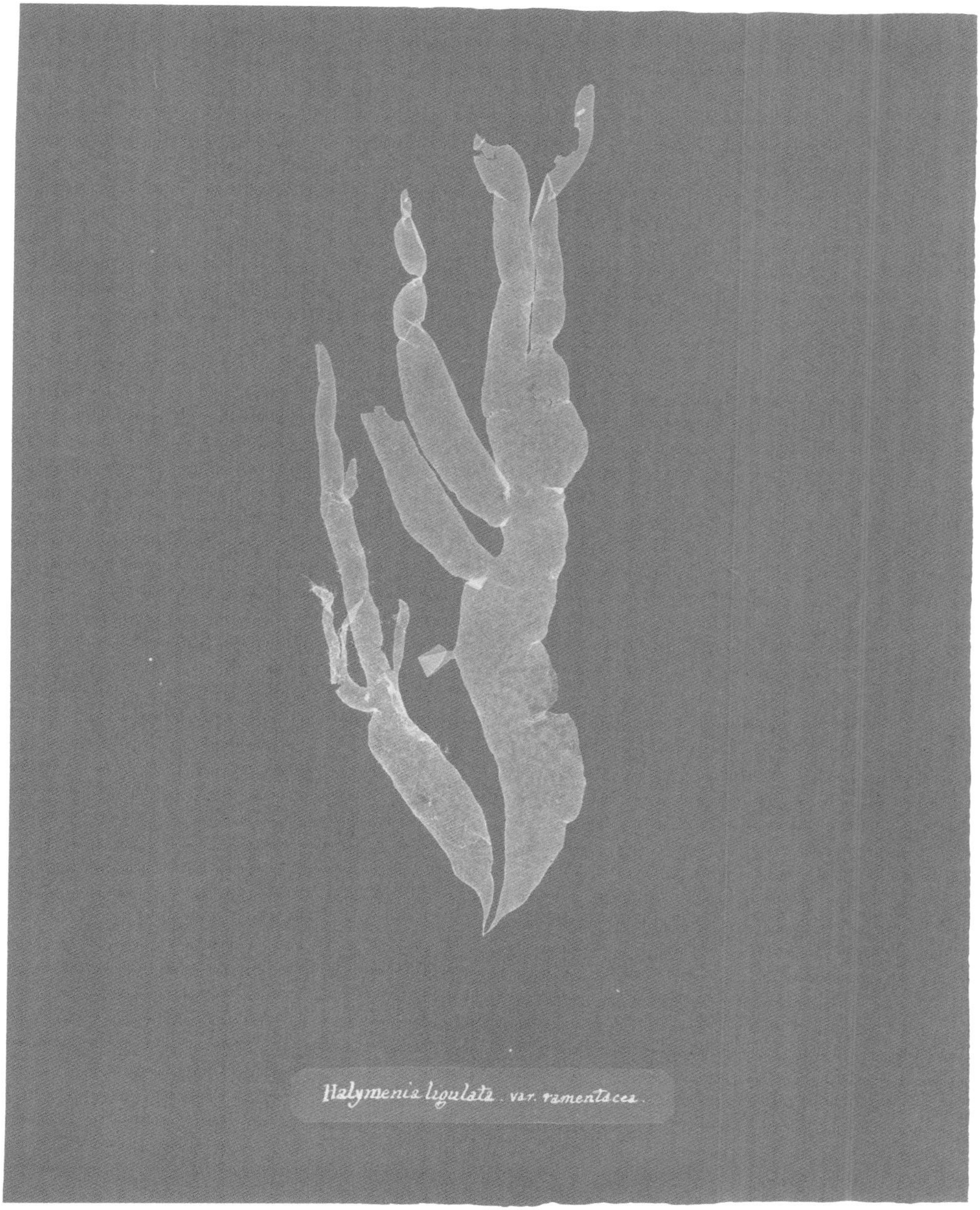

Plate 177. *Halymenia ligulata* var. *ramentacea*

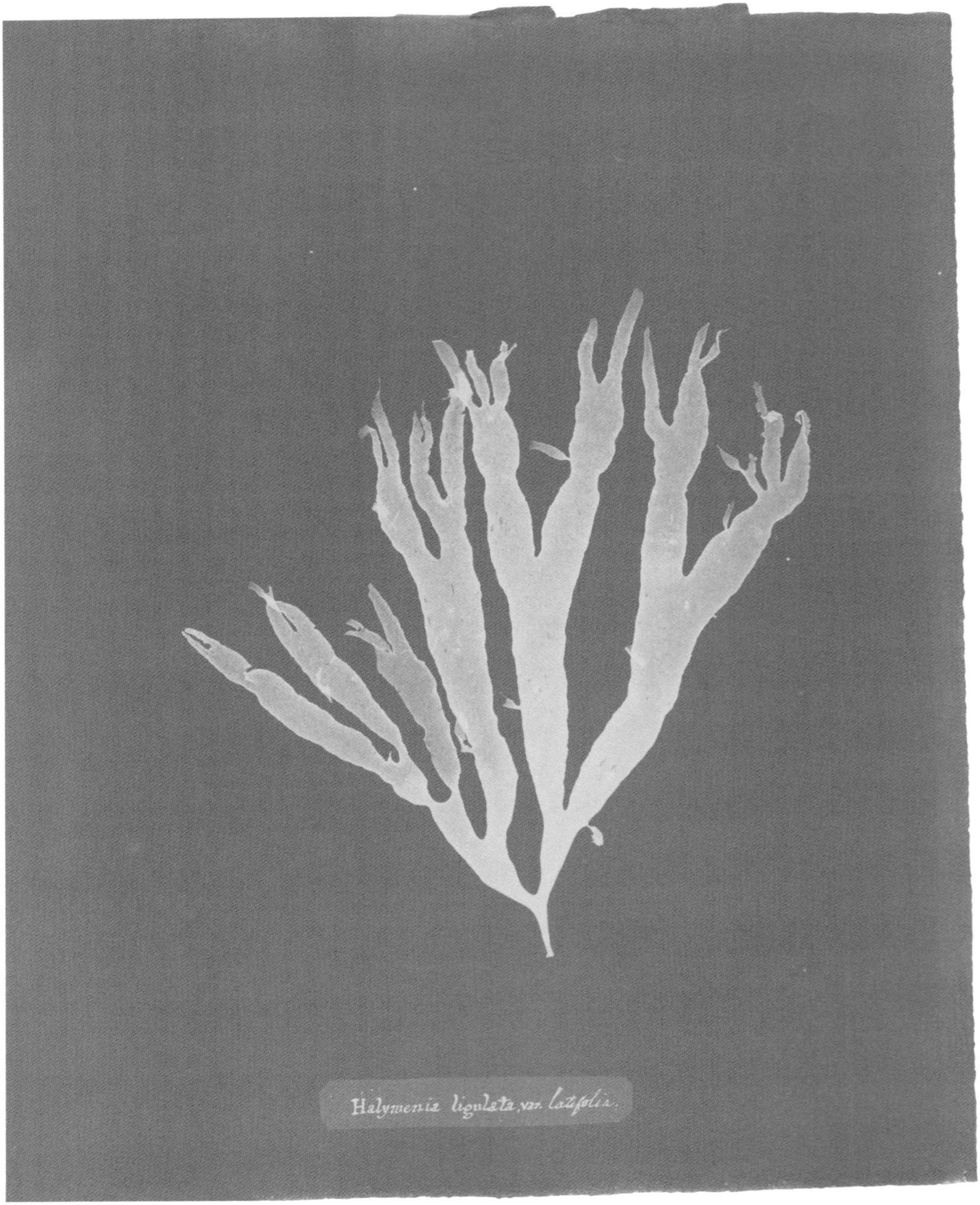

Plate 178. *Halymenia ligulata* var. *latifolia*

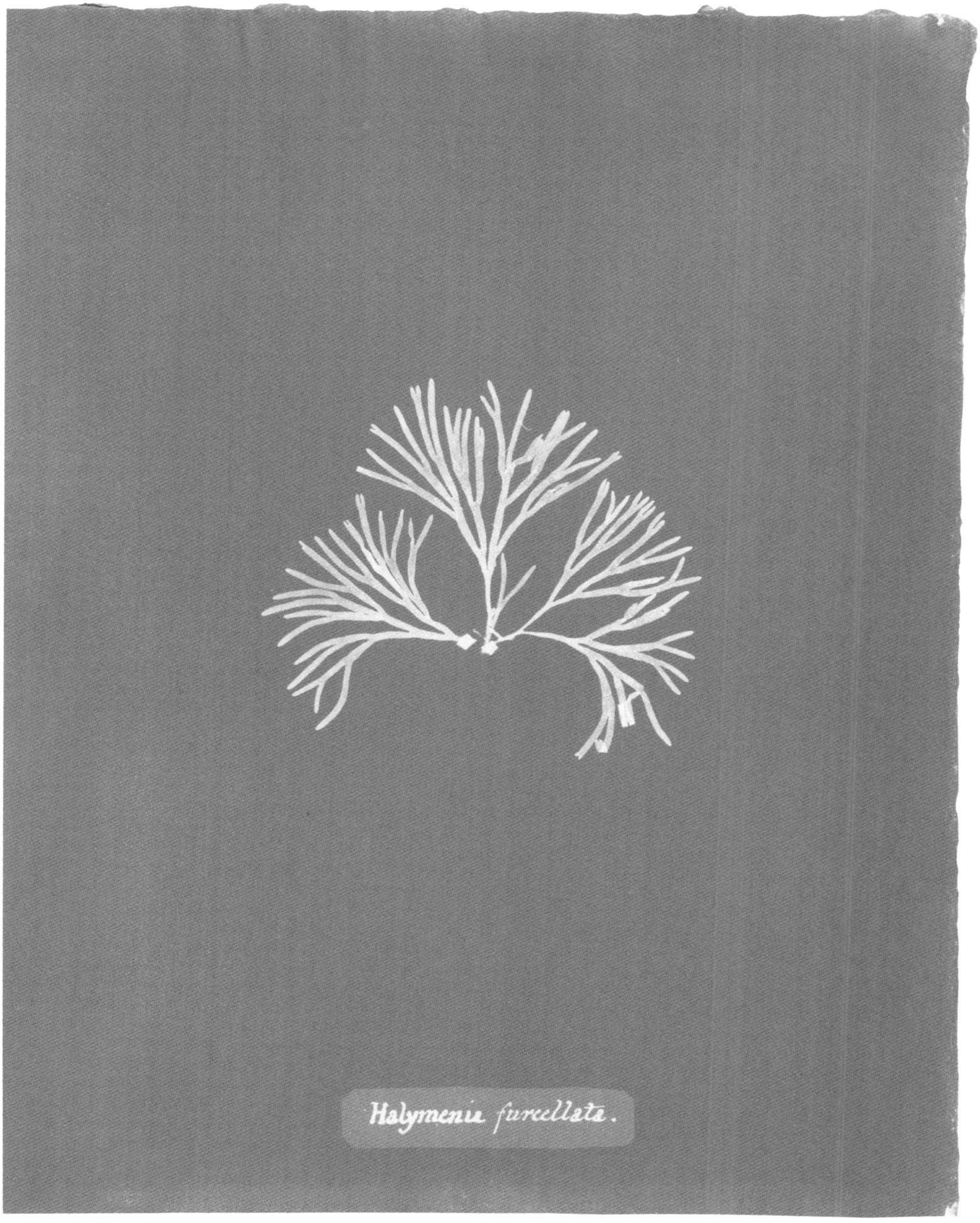

Plate 179. *Halymenia furcellata*

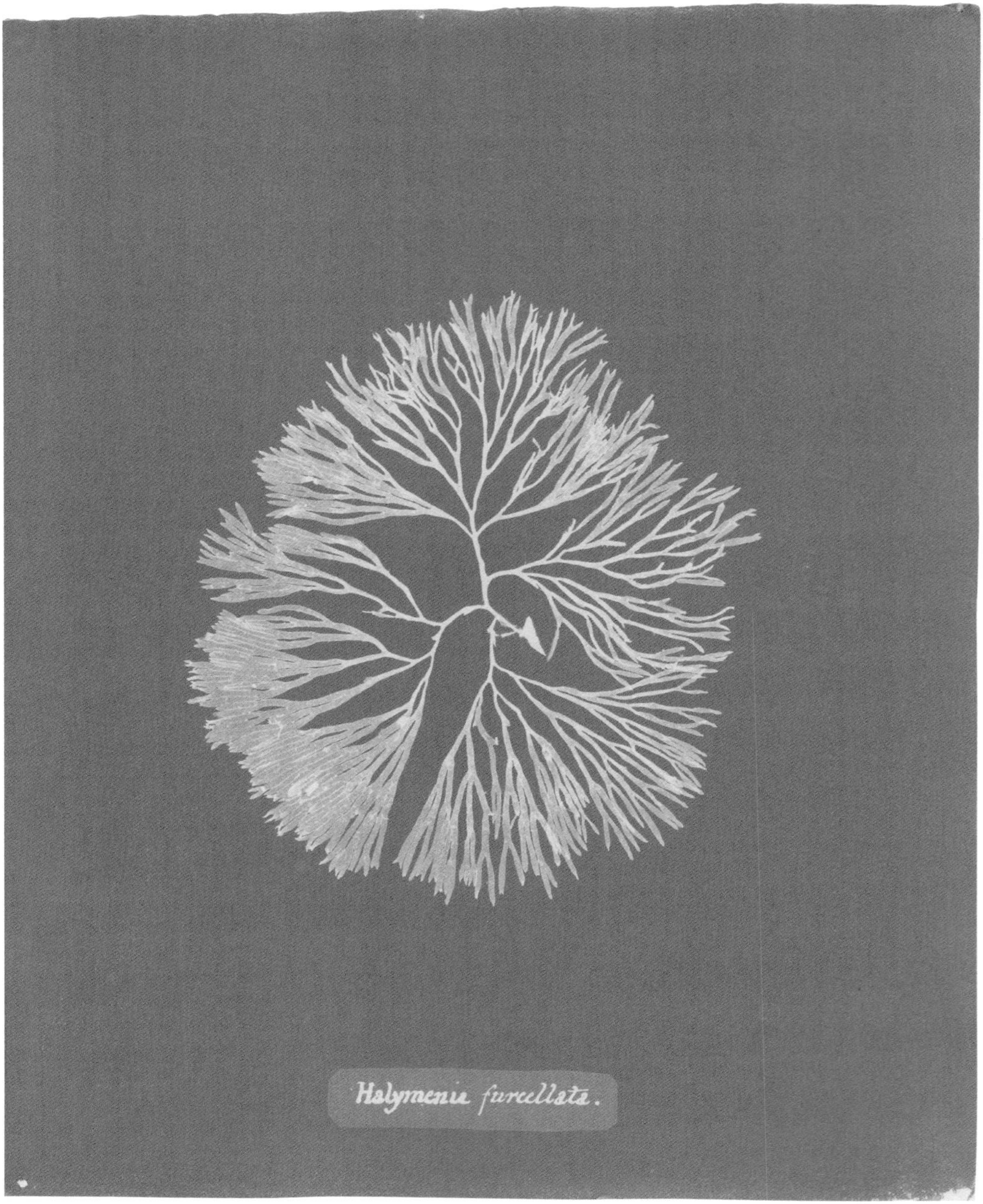

Plate 180. *Halymenia furcellata*

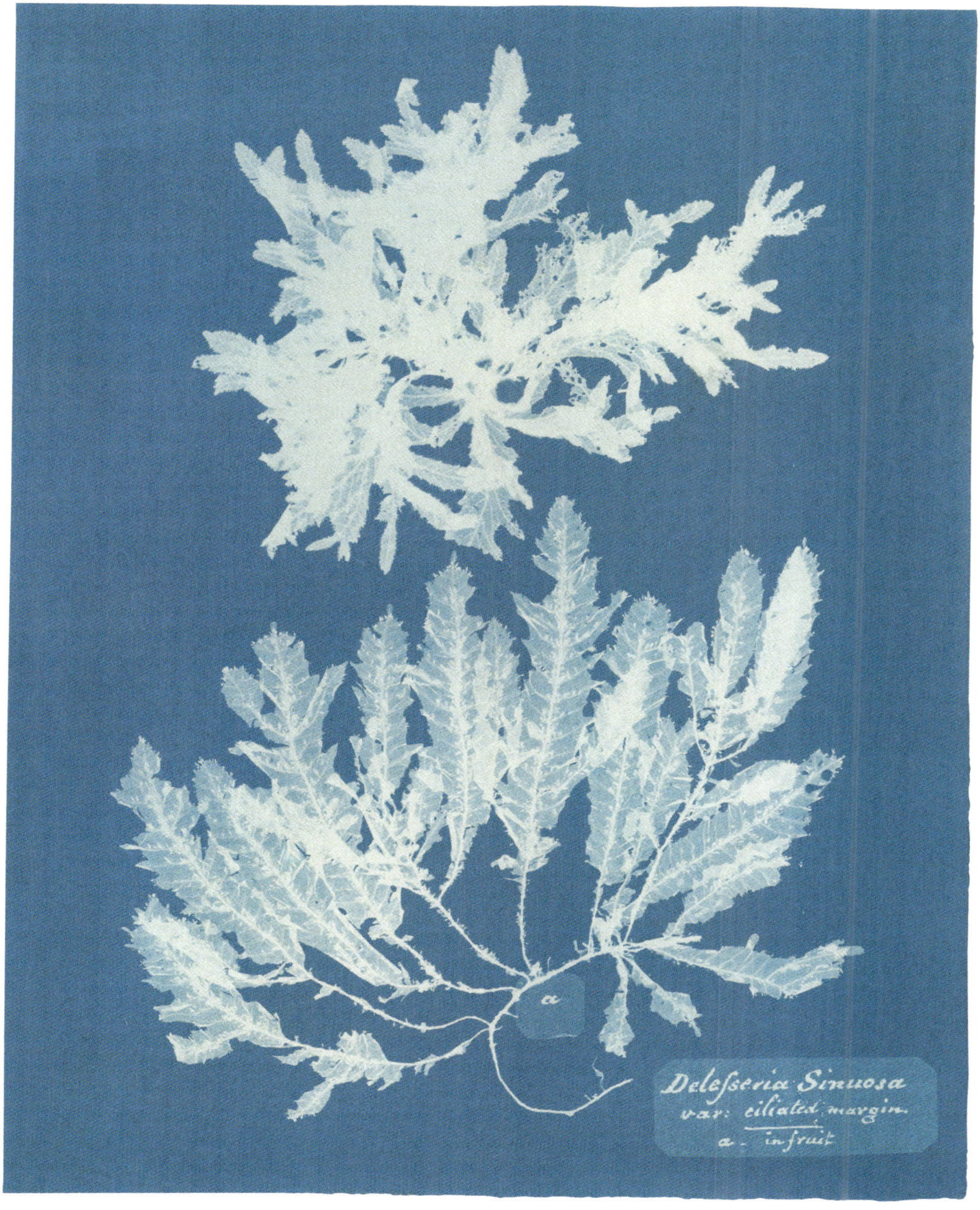

Plate 181. *Delesseria sinuosa* var. ciliated margin, a. in fruit

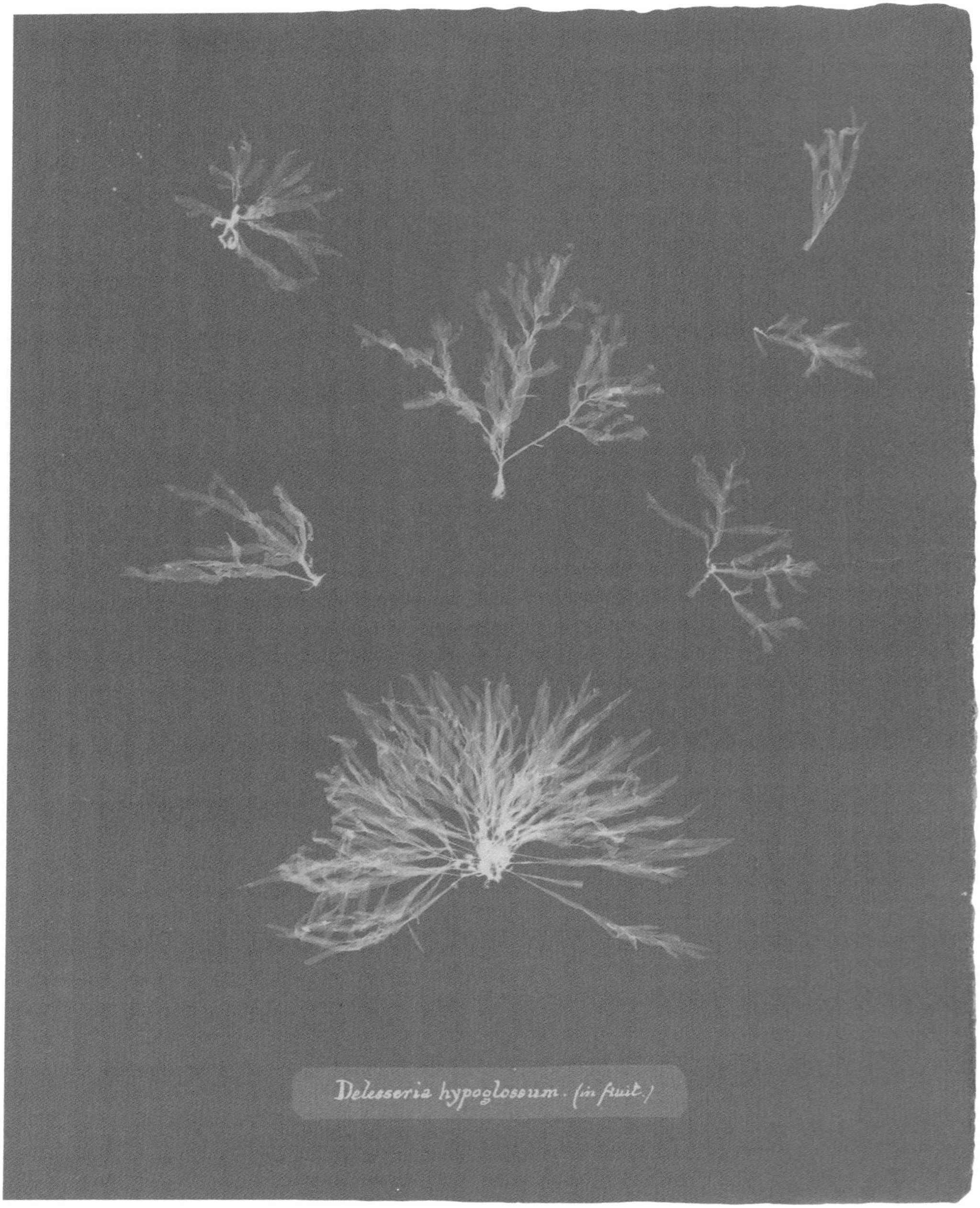

Plate 182. *Delesseria hypoglossum* (in fruit)

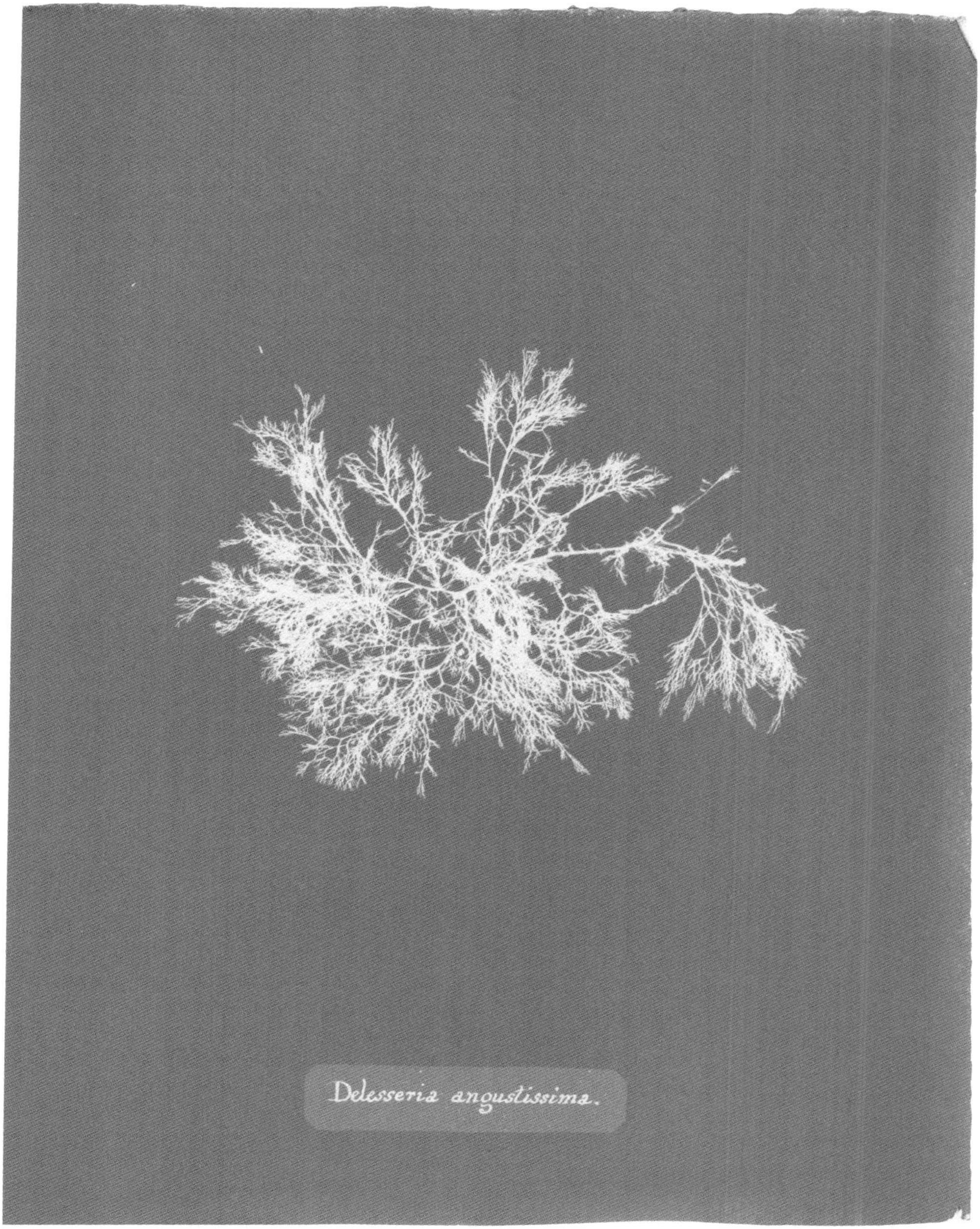

Plate 183. *Delesseria angustissima*

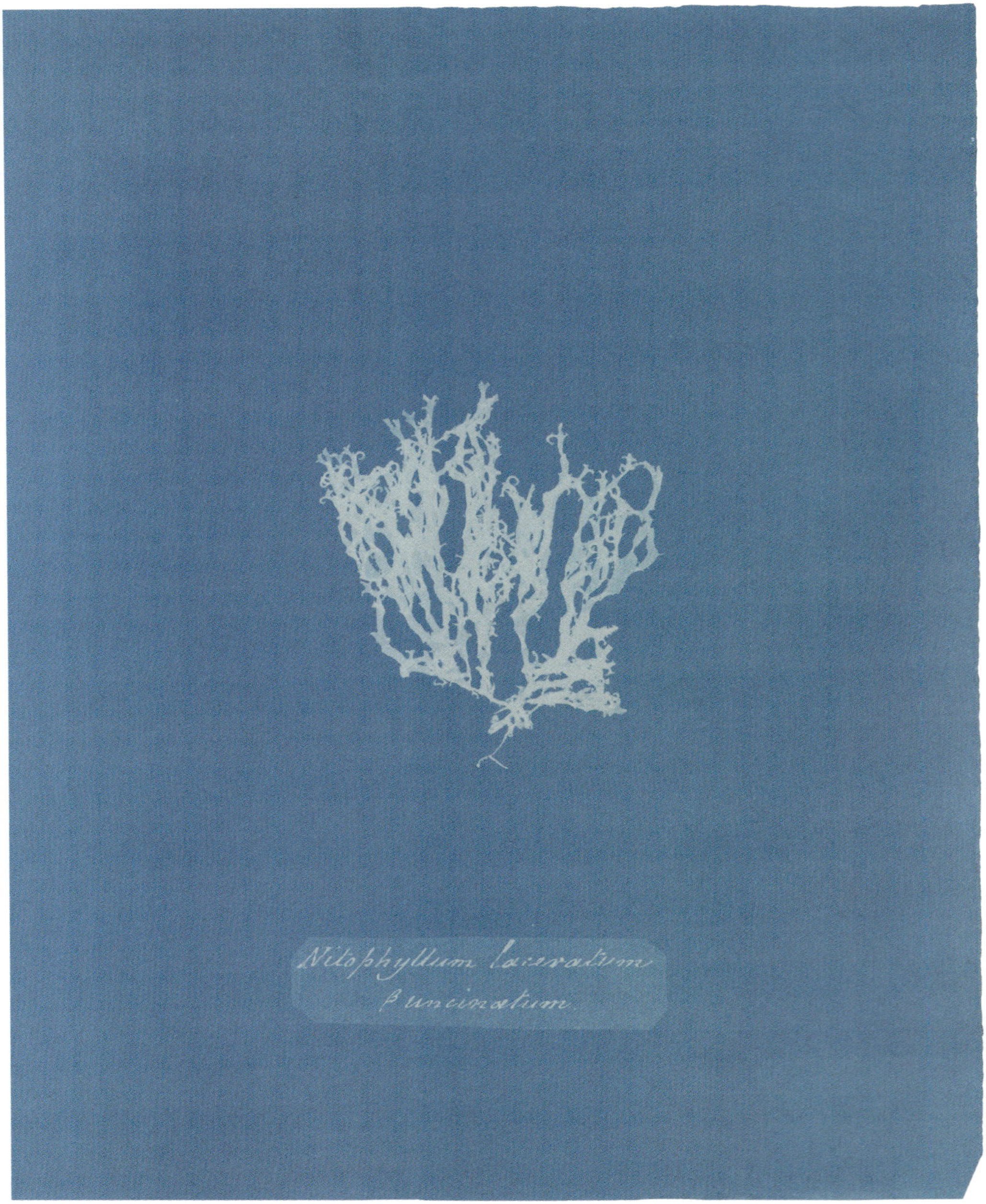

Plate 184. *Nitophyllum laceratum* β *uncinatum*

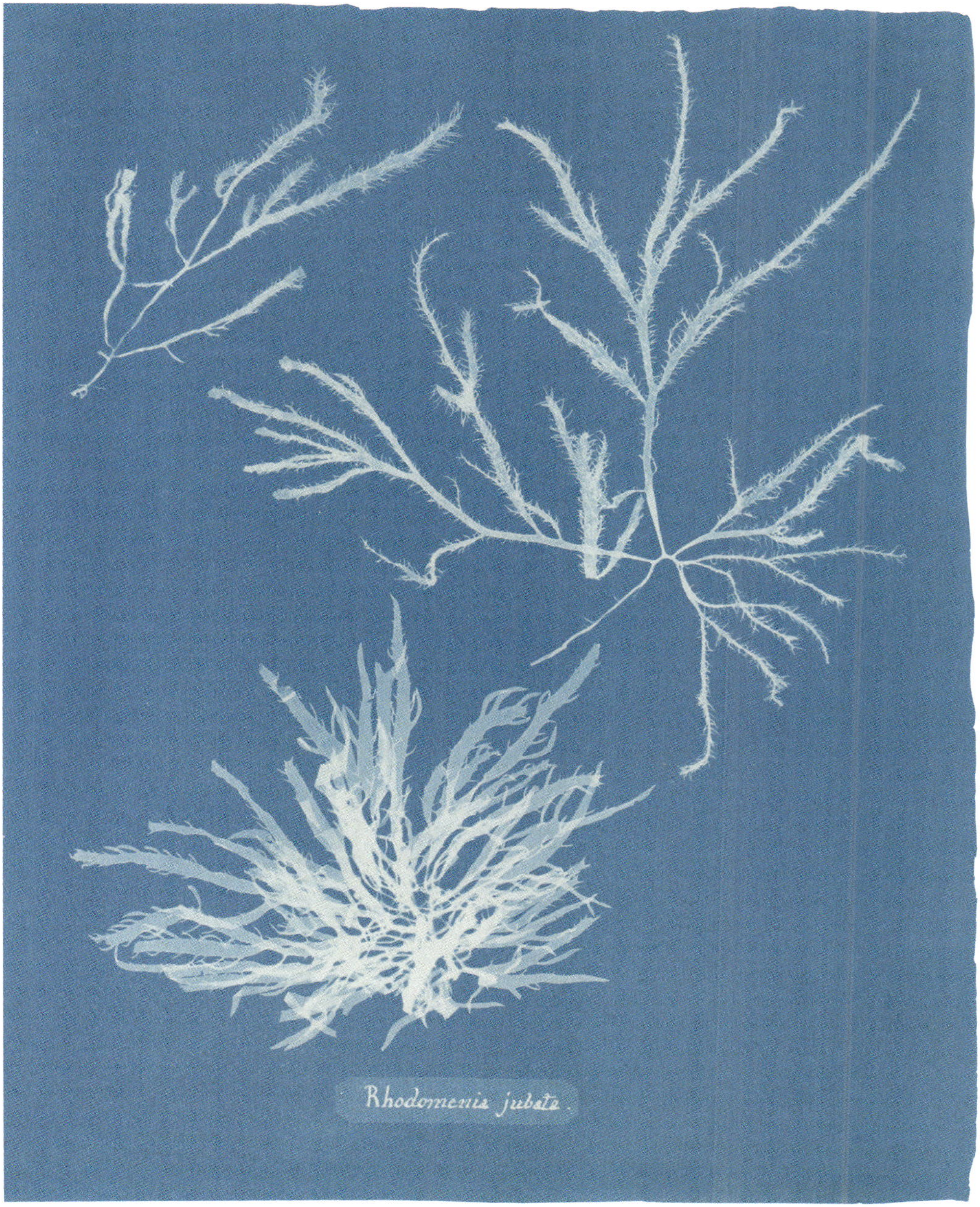

Plate 185. *Rhodomenia jubata*

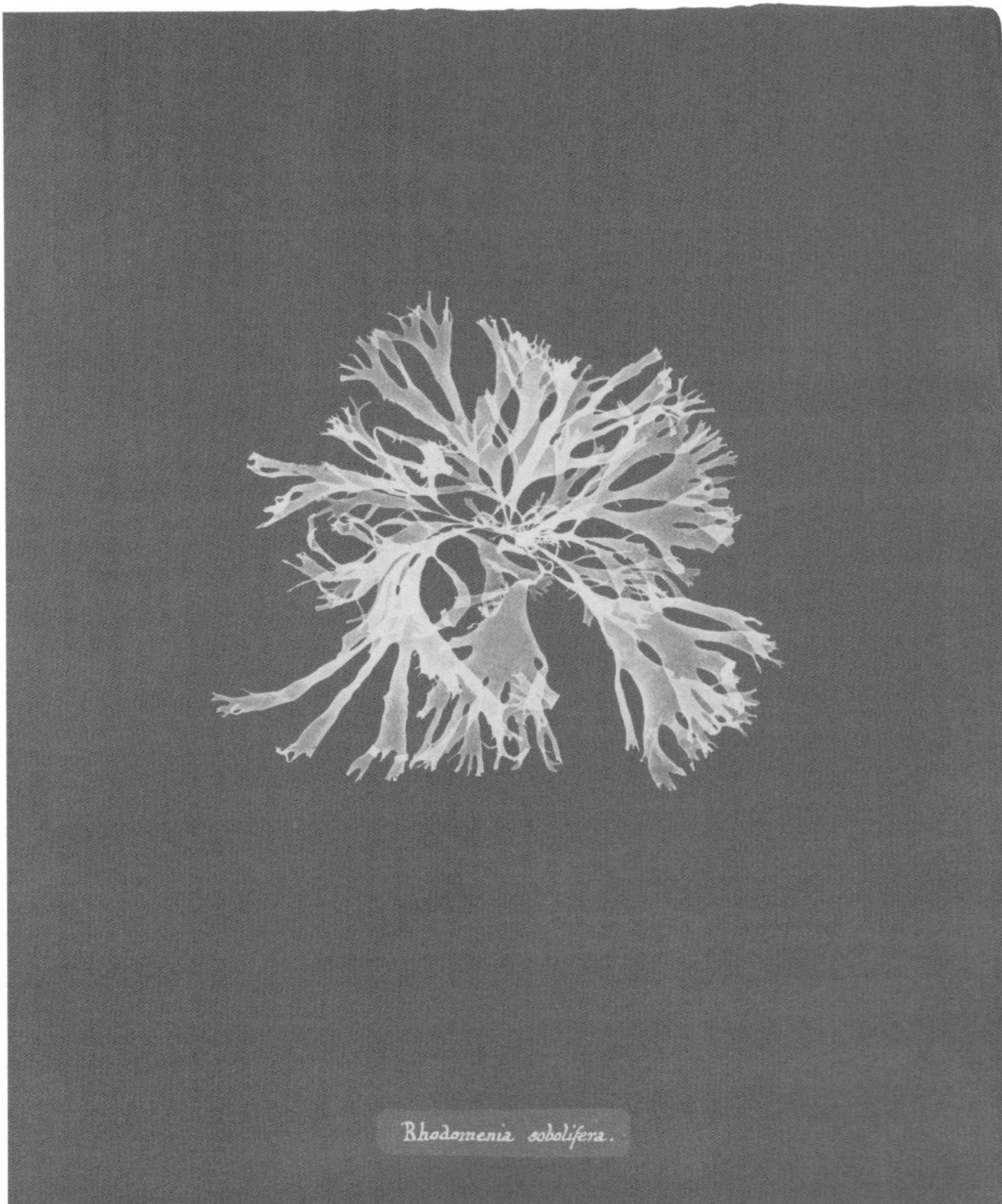

Plate 186. *Rhodomenia sobolifera*

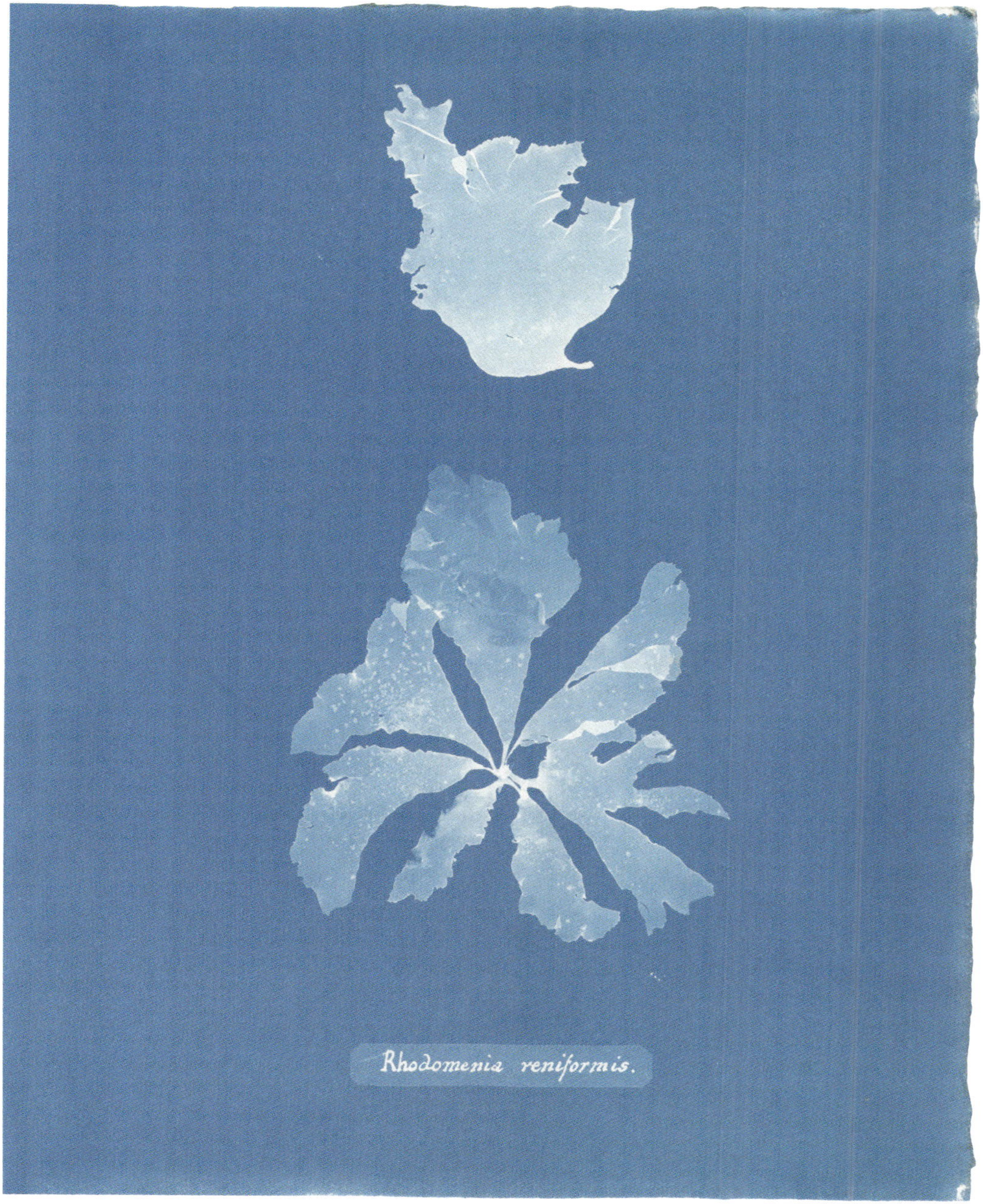

Plate 187. *Rhodomenia reniformis*

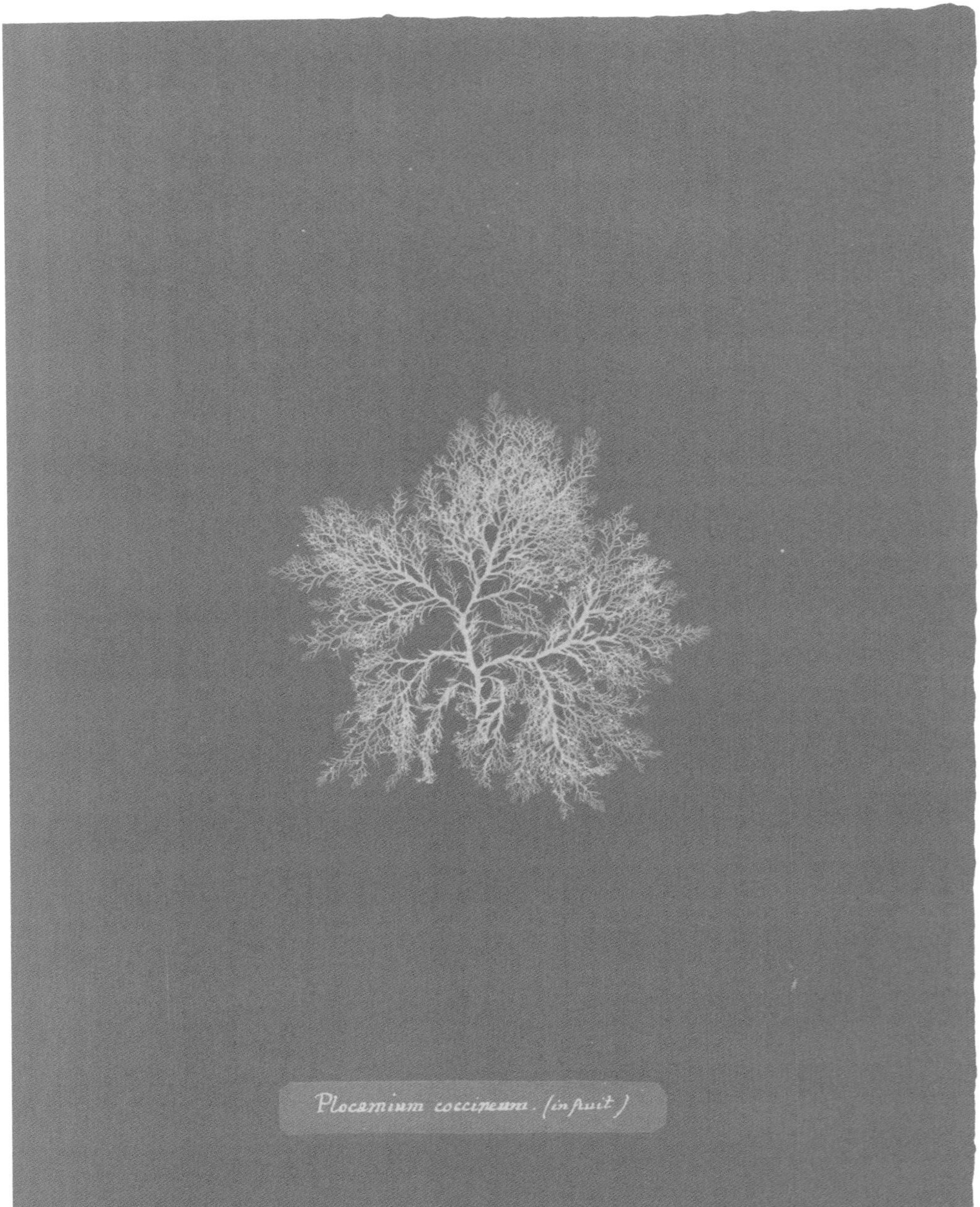

Plate 188. *Plocamium coccineum* (in fruit)

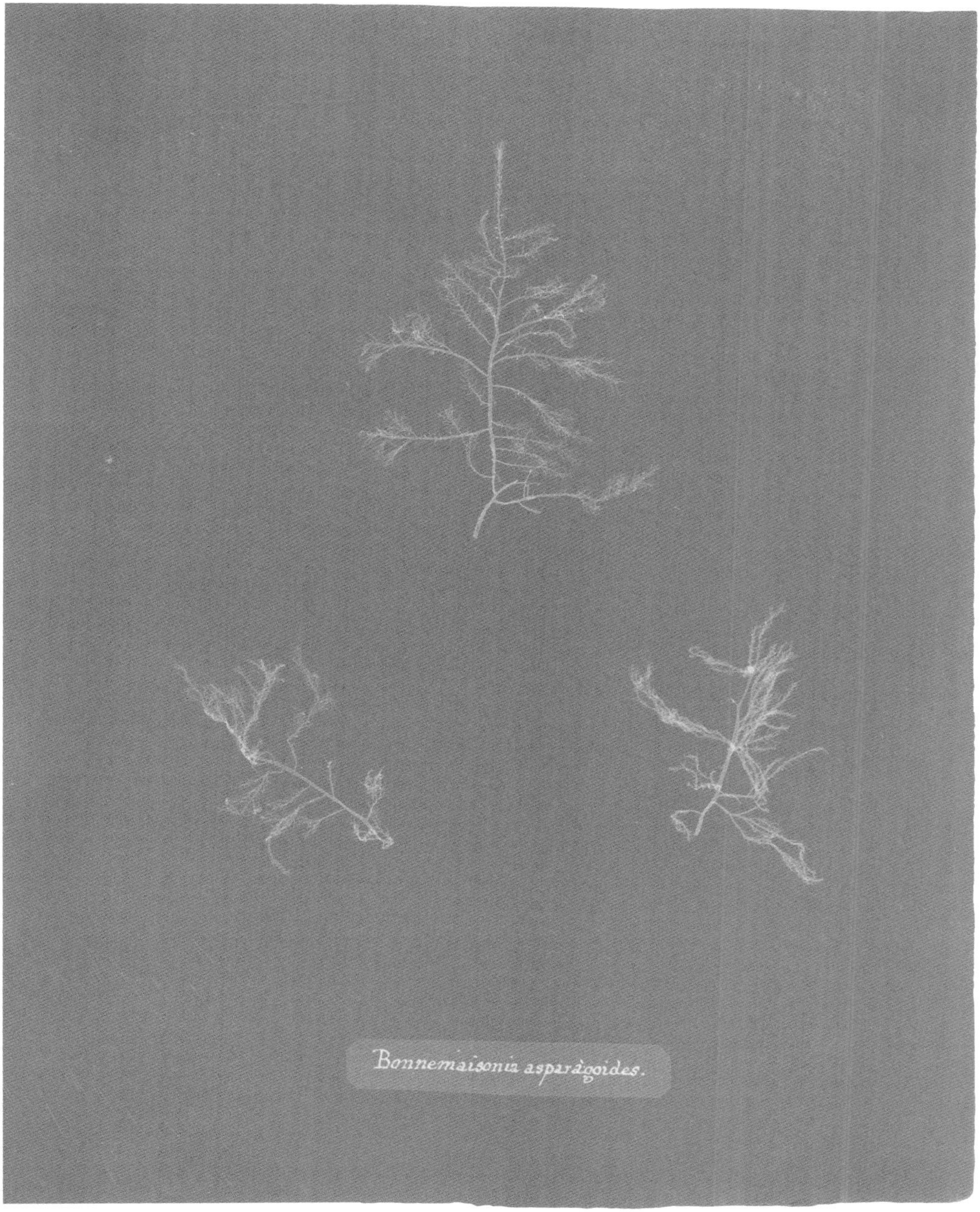

Plate 192. *Bonnemaisonia asparagoides*

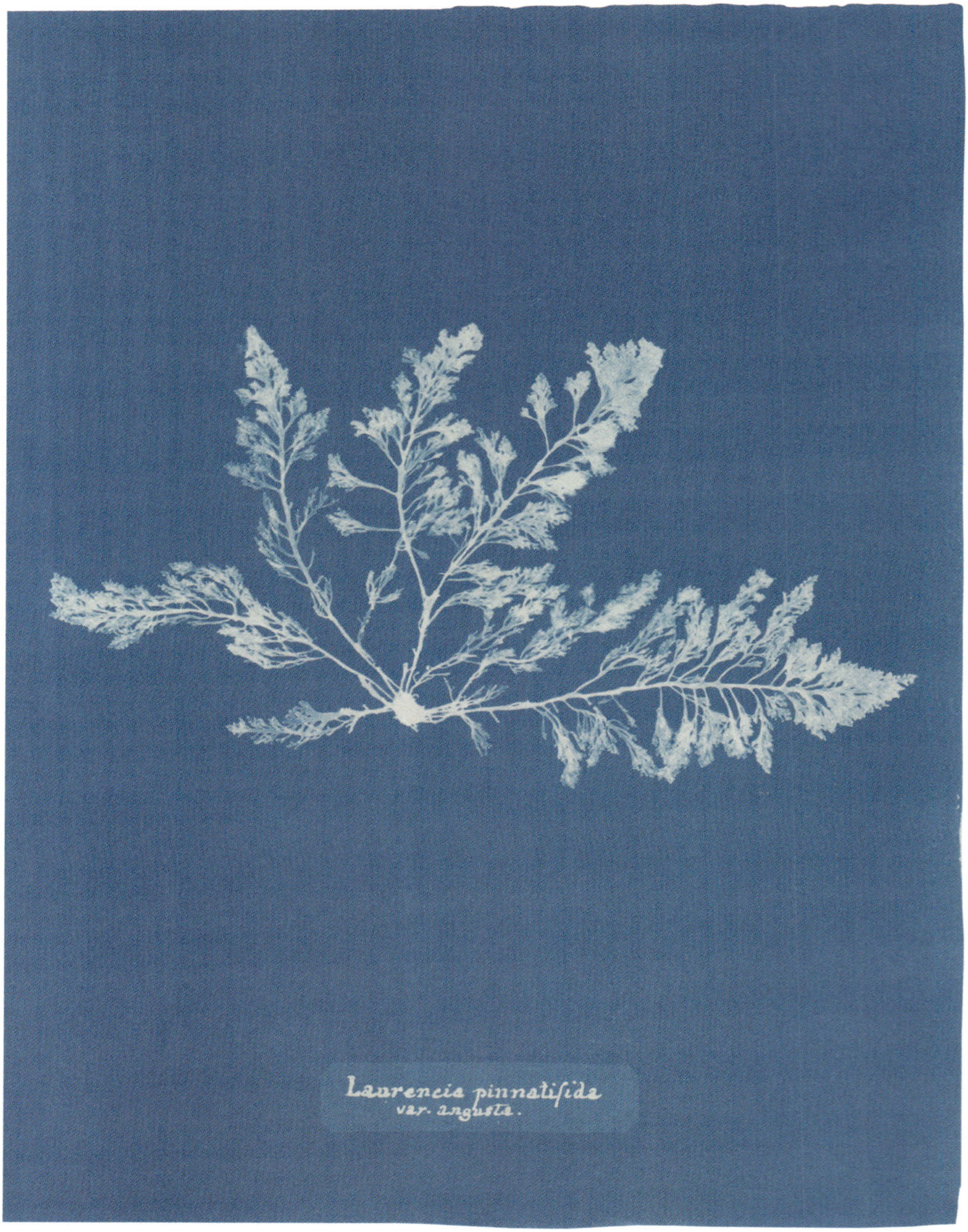

Plate 193. *Laurencia pinnatifida* var. *angusta*

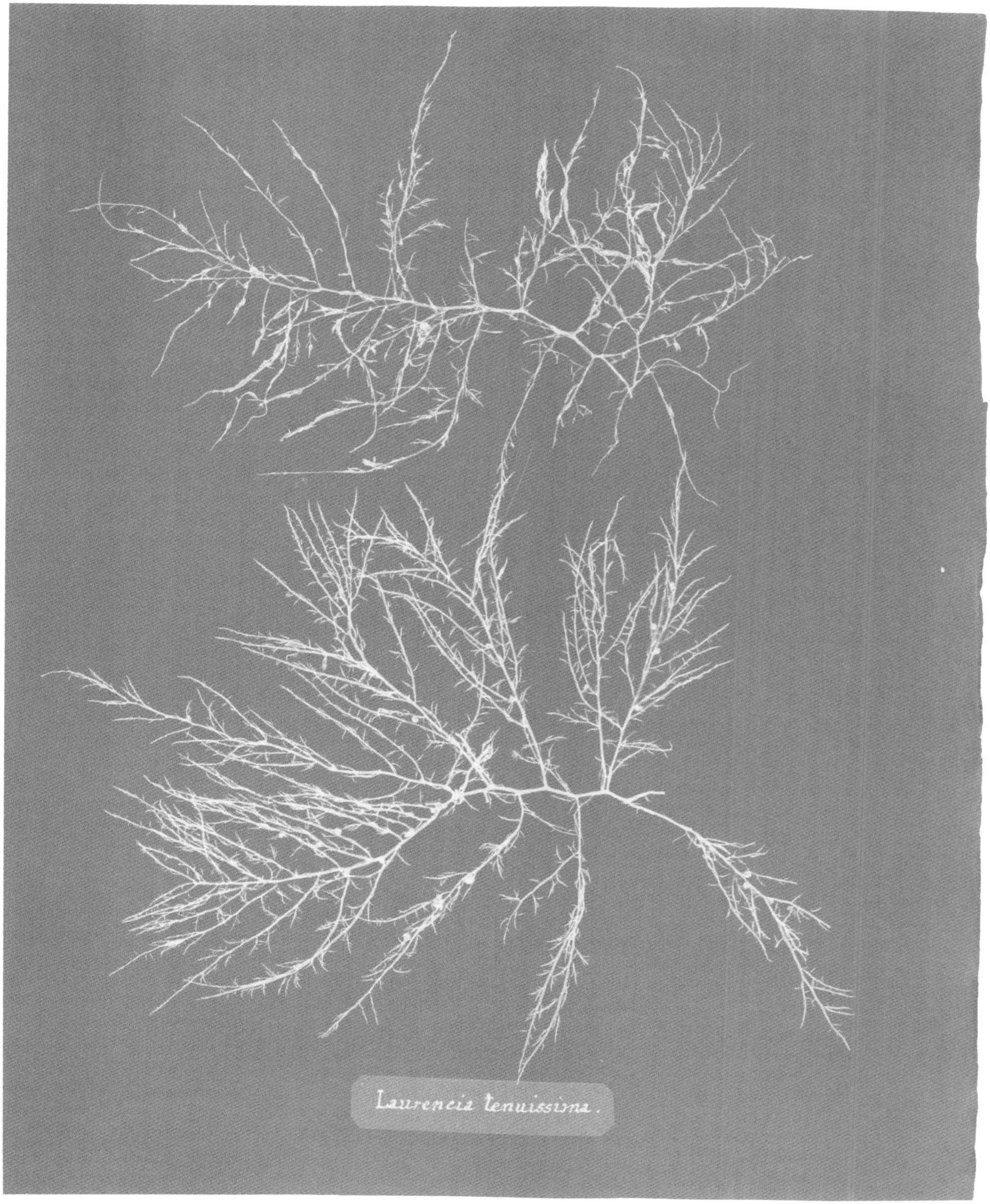

Plate 195. *Laurencia tenuissima*

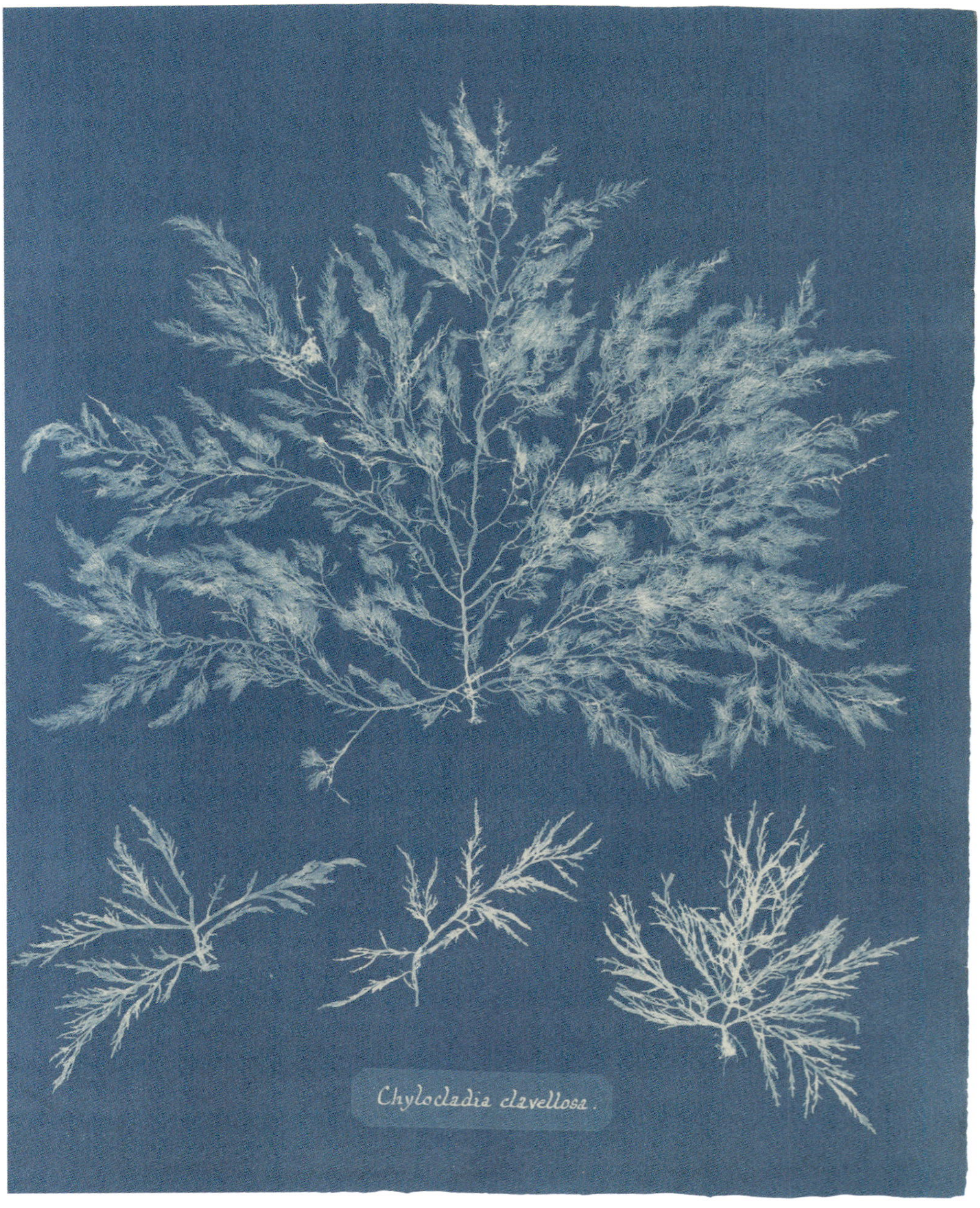

Plate 196. *Chylocladia clavellosa*

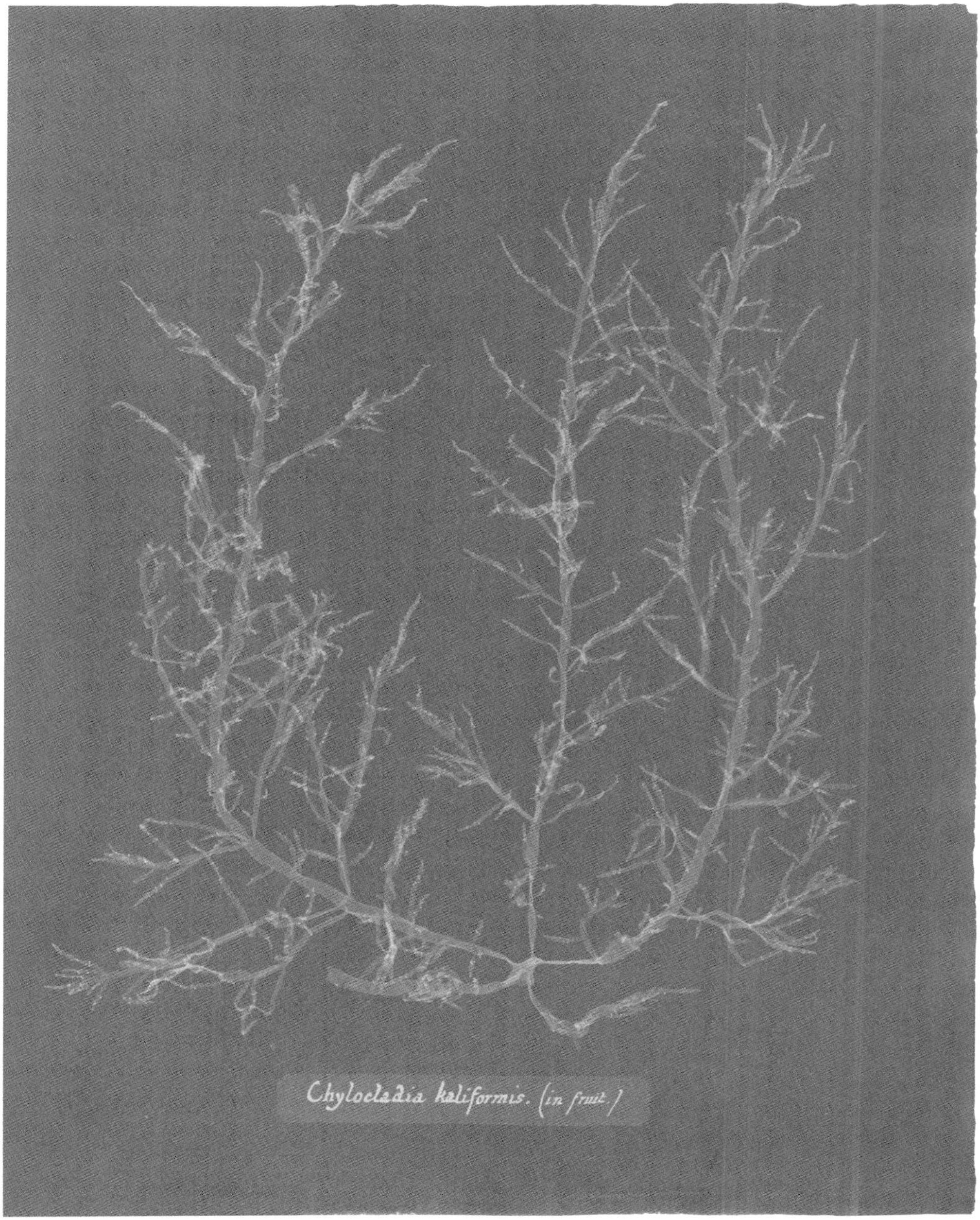

Plate 197. *Chylocladia kaliformis* (in fruit)

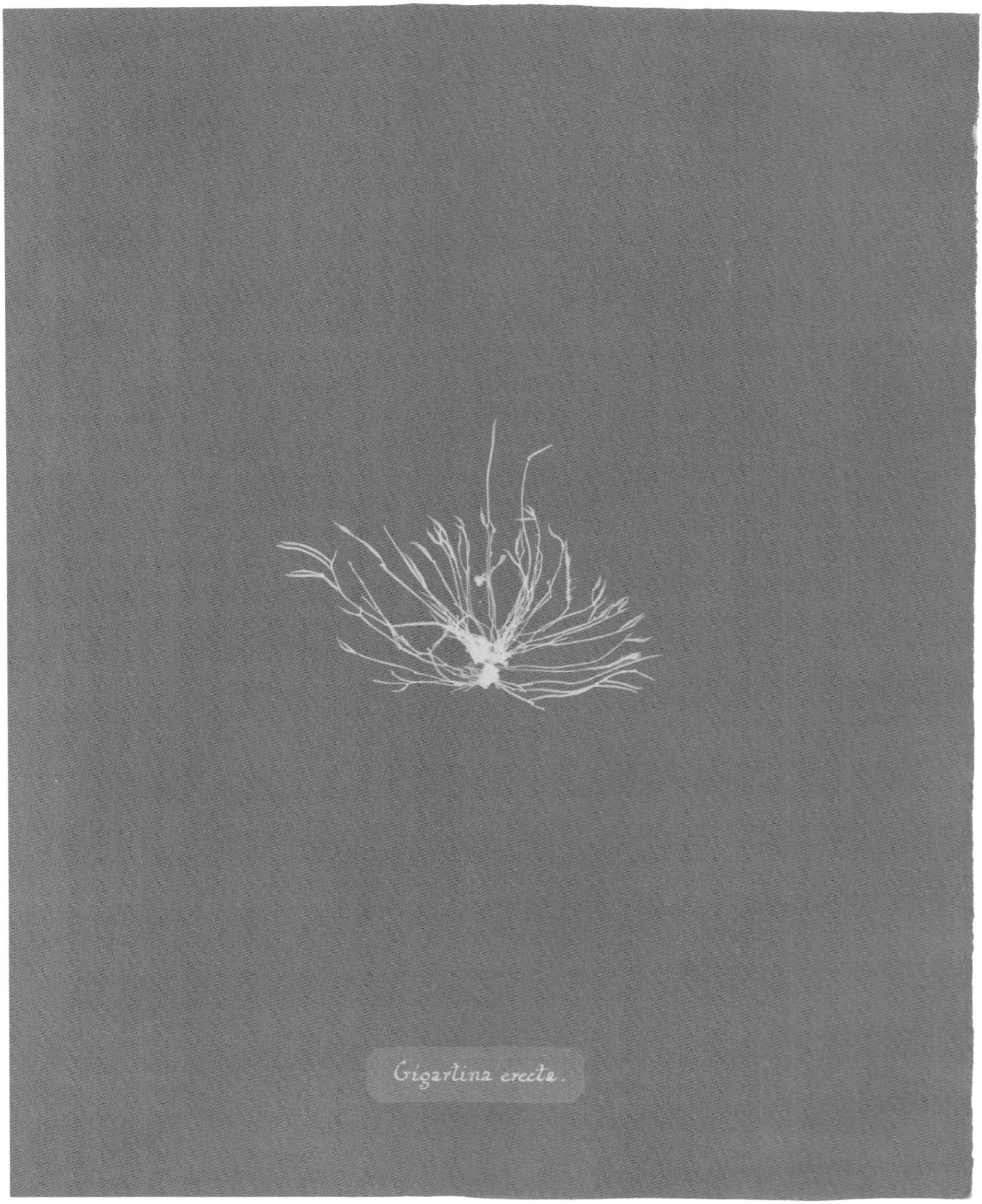

Plate 200. *Gigartina erecta*

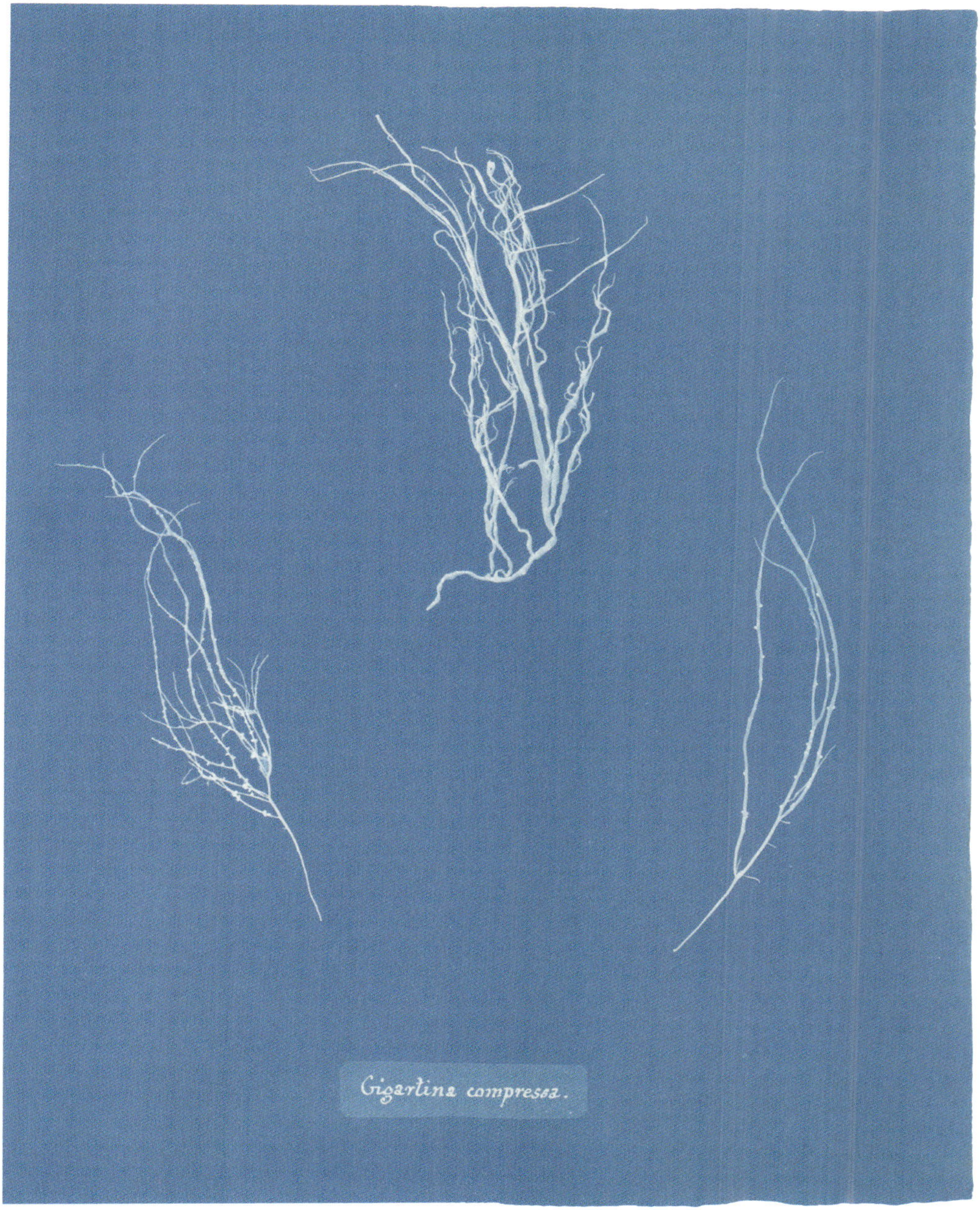

Plate 201. *Gigartina compressa*

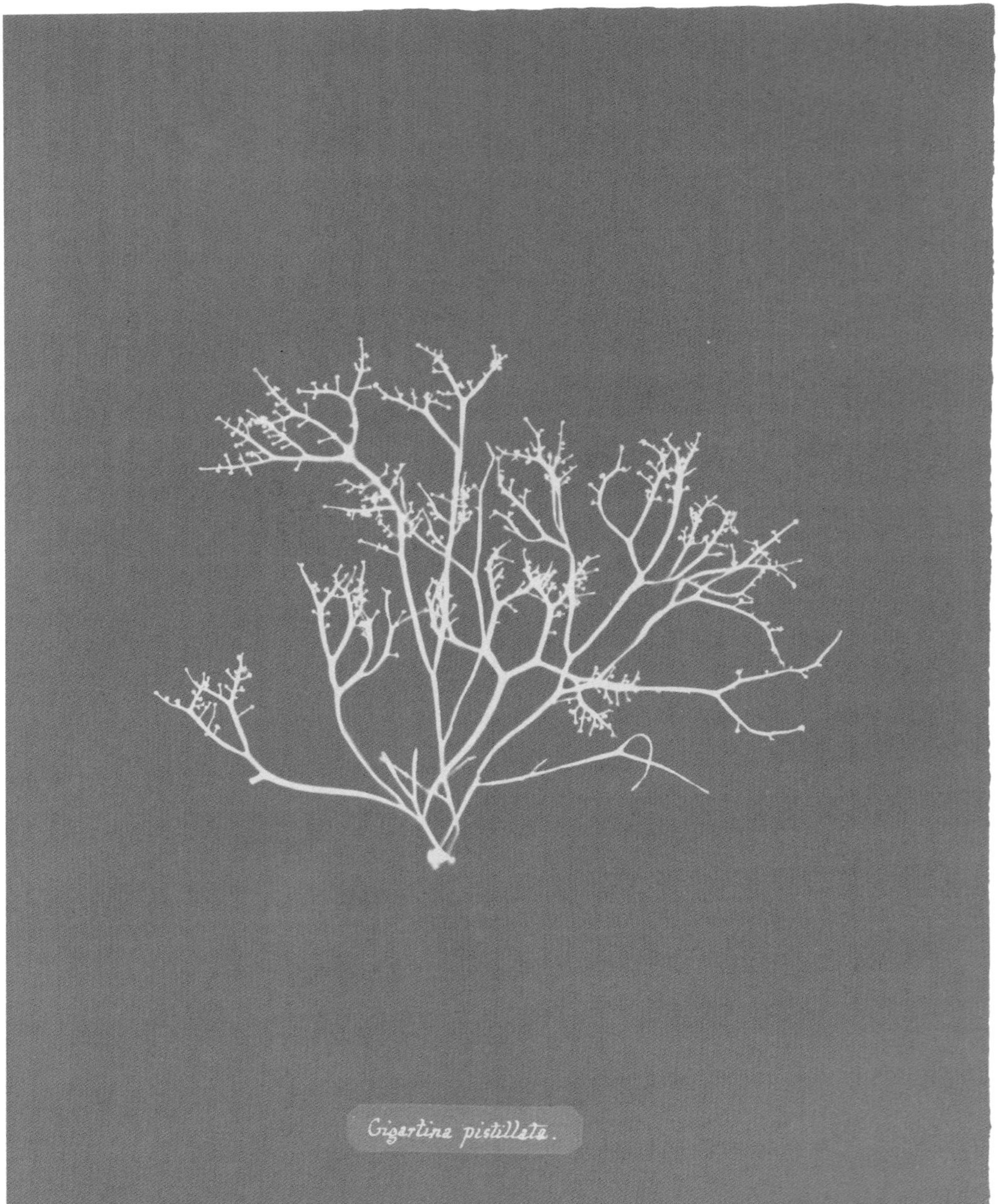

Plate 202. *Gigartina pistillata*

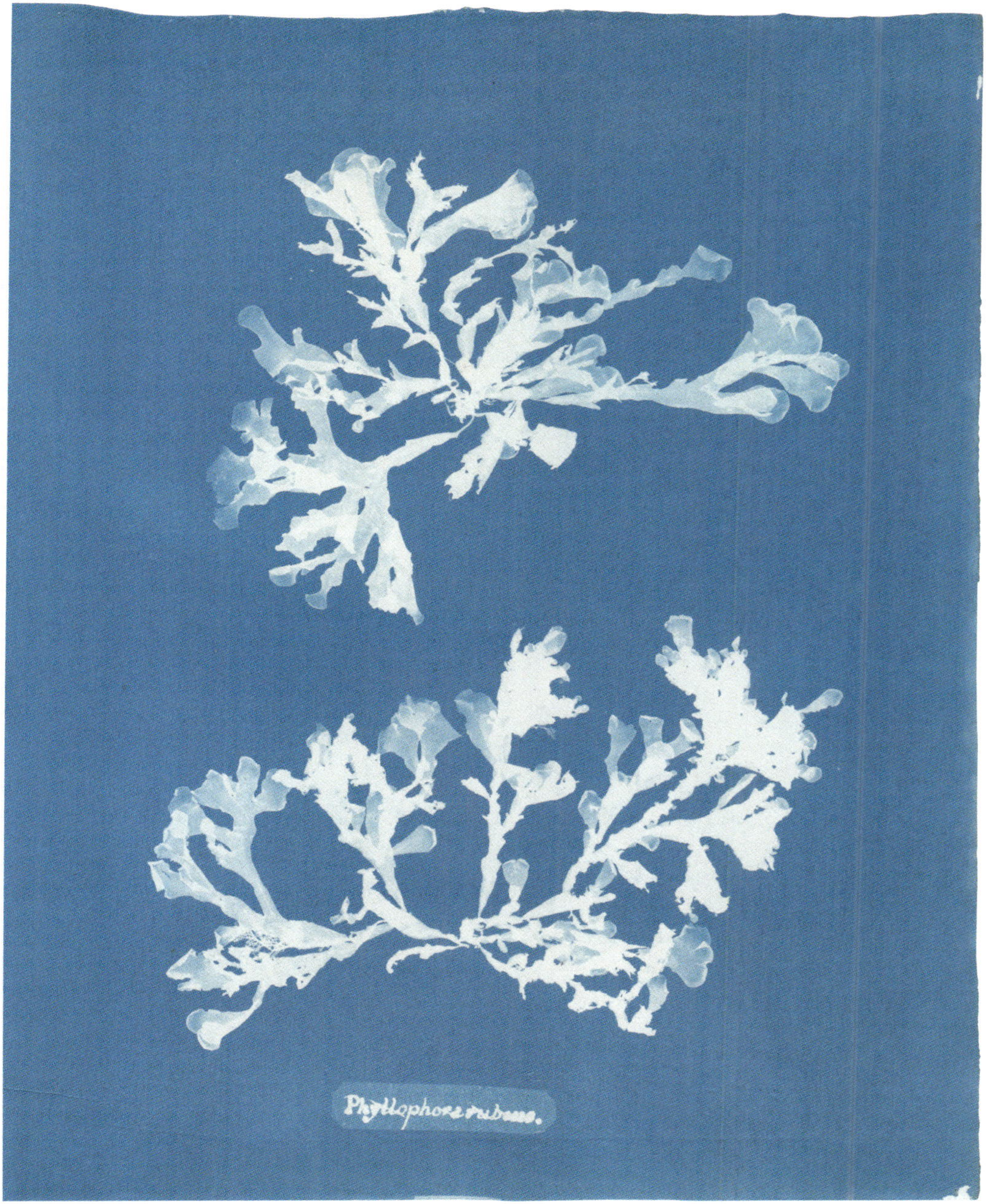

Plate 205. *Phyllophora rubens*

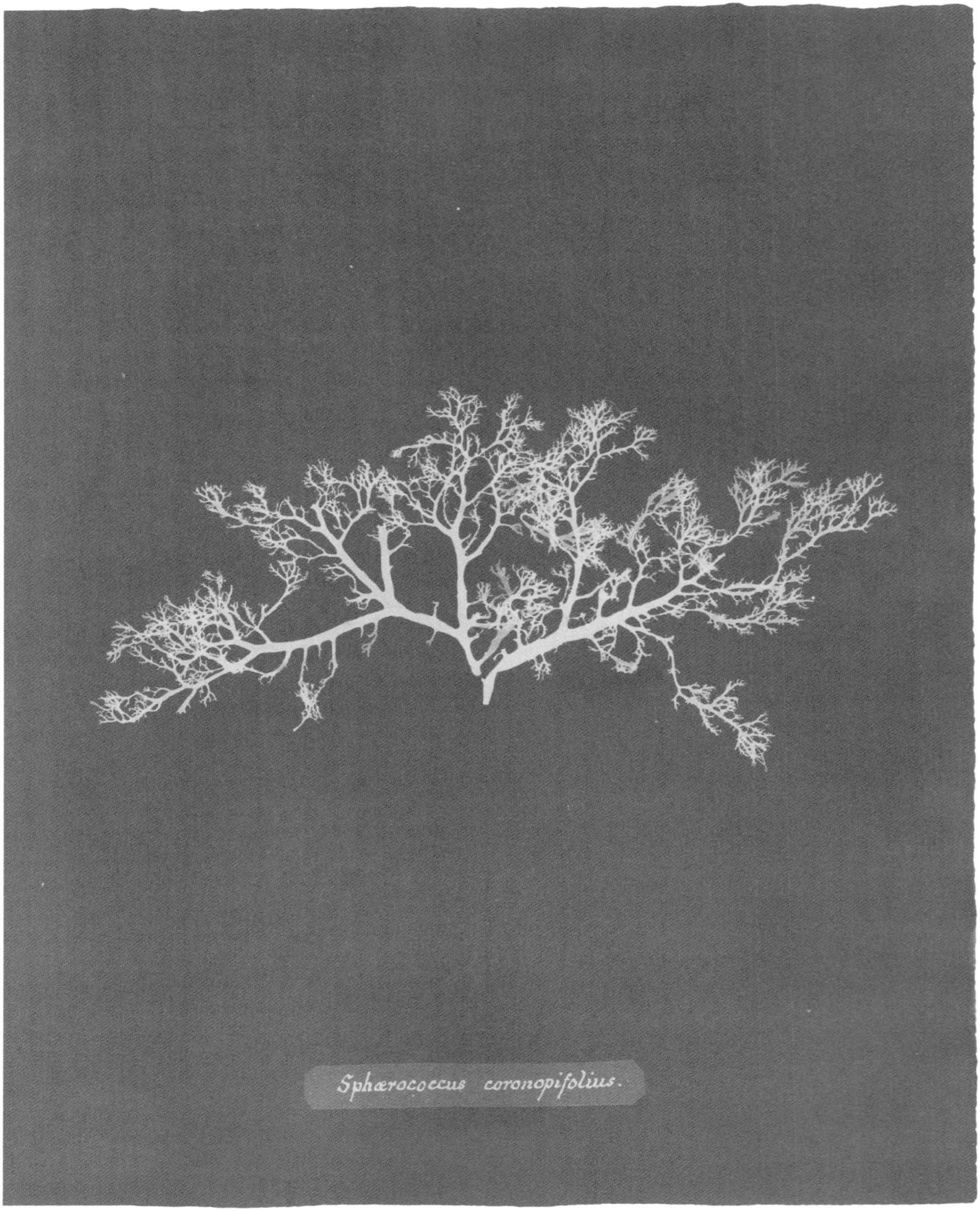

Plate 206. *Sphaerococcus coronopifolius*

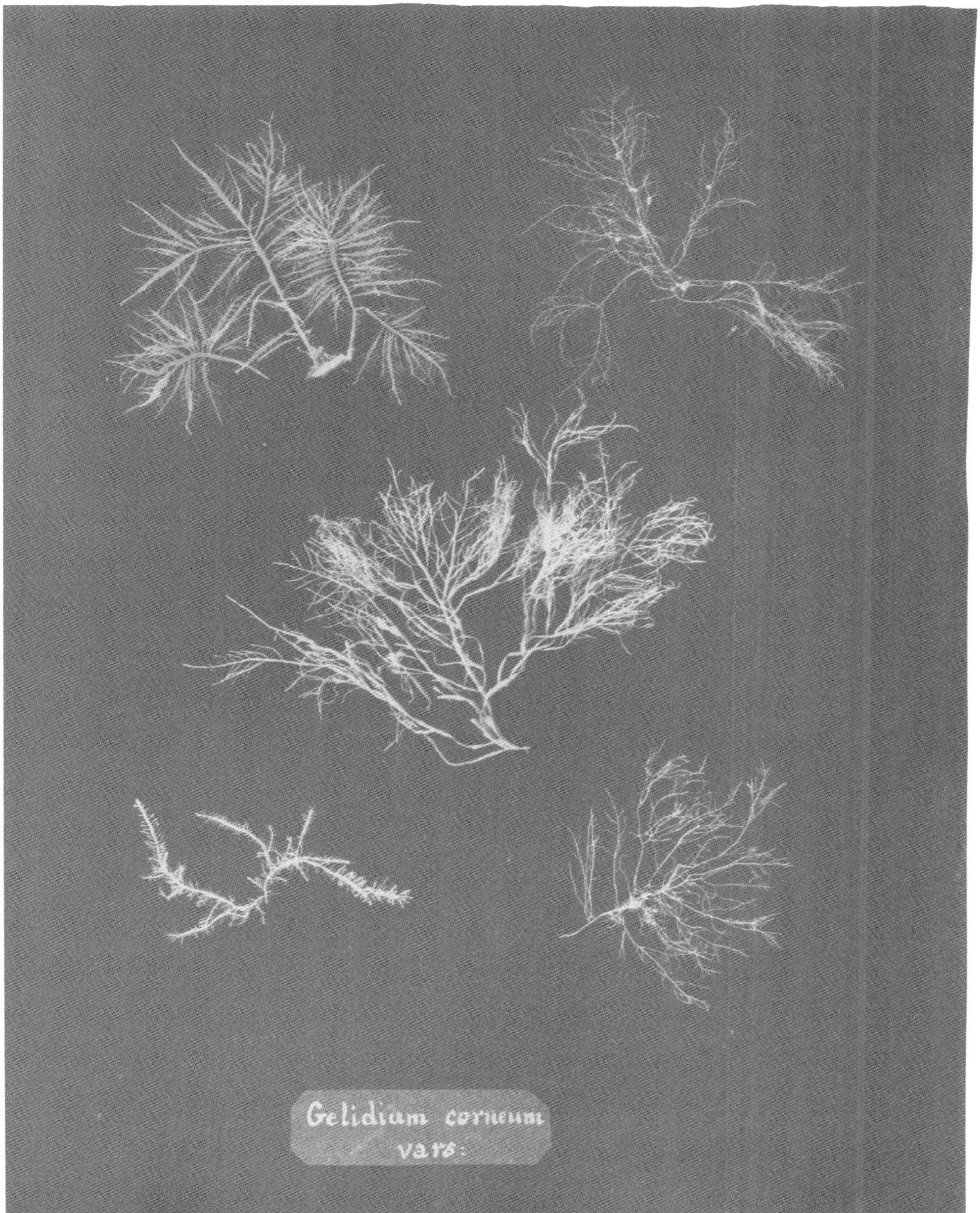

Plate 207. *Gelidium corneum* vars.

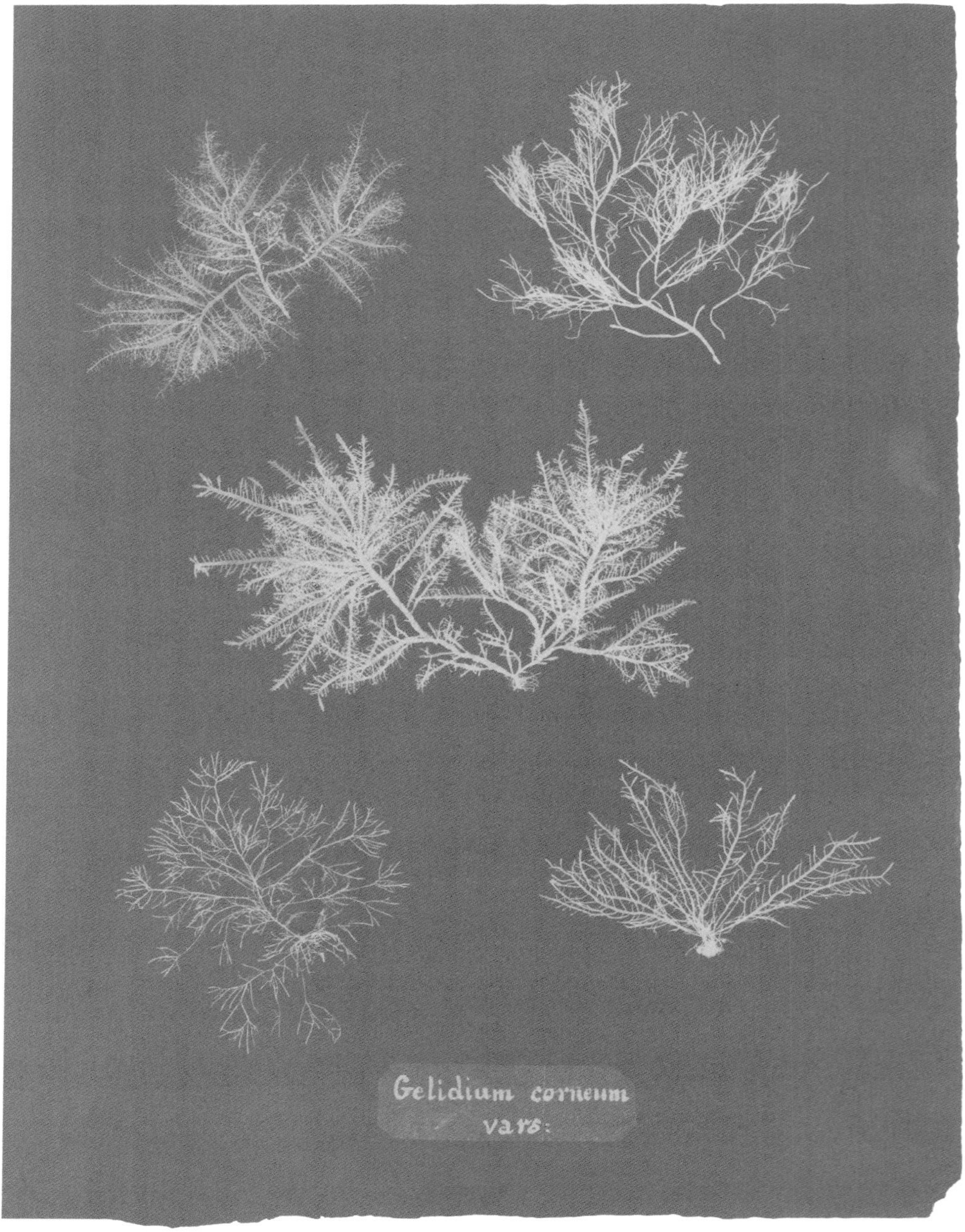

Plate 208. *Gelidium corneum* vars.

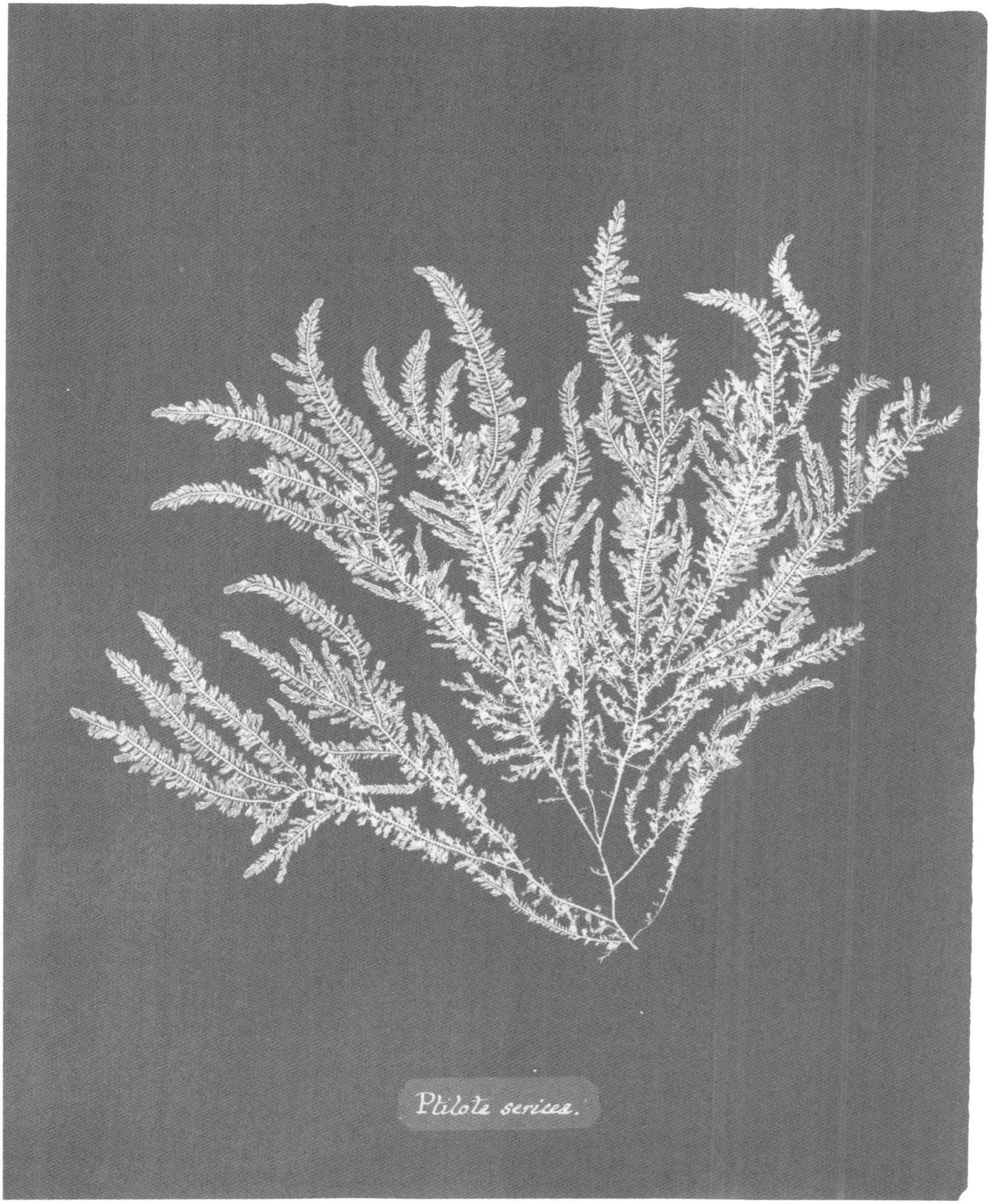

Plate 210. *Ptilota sericea*

Cyanotype

The year 1839 witnessed the birth of photography. In January, Louis Jacques Mandé Daguerre introduced his daguerreotype process in Paris. Shortly afterwards, William Henry Fox Talbot presented his "Photogenic Drawings" in London. In 1842, John Herschel introduced a third photographic process. Unlike its forerunners, it was not based on the light sensitivity of silver compounds, but on the sensitivity of iron salt to the ultraviolet parts of the spectrum.

In his attempts to produce colour photographs, Herschel made a chance discovery: if a material is coated with a certain iron compound and exposed to the sun, it turns blue. The dye fixing the latent images is known as "Berlin blue" or "Prussian blue". As early as 1706 Johann Jacob Diesbach in Berlin had succeeded in producing the pigment which occurs naturally in this form. Until then, painters had given the colour blue, which they claimed had a calming effect, a place of honour on the colour spectrum, as it was available only in the expensive form of ultramarine. The synthetic pigment called "Berlin blue" had excellent colour fastness, high opacity and long colour stability.

Cyanotypes from the pioneering age of photography are still well preserved, while most early calotypes have faded. In addition, cyanotypes were easy to produce and the source material was cheap. However, the process also had a definite disadvantage. Iron salts were far less sensitive to light than silver compounds. This meant that the cyanotype was not suitable for direct exposure to the camera. However, it was ideal for producing photograms and contact copies, where there were no problems with prolonged exposure time.

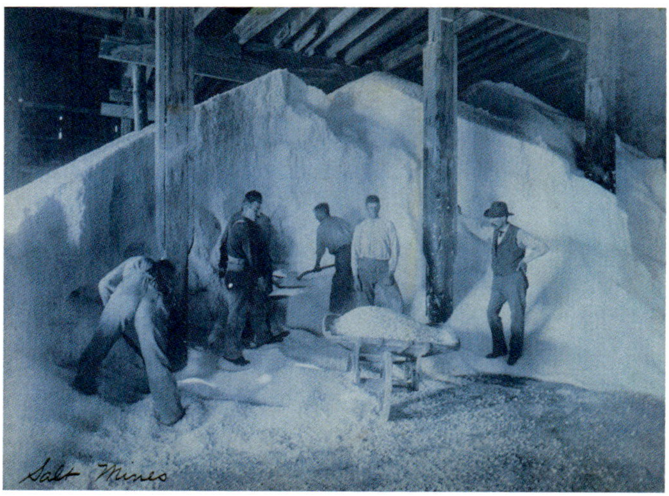

During the first three decades of the process, the only people to use it were Herschel himself and members of his family, as well as Anna Atkins and Anne Dixon. With some 800 different plant images and probably more than 10,000 copies, it was Atkins, sometimes in collaboration with her friend, who was by far the most productive user of cyanotype. As well as these albums and individual examples of cyanotypes produced by the Herschel family and their friends, before long there emerged another indication of how they might be used. In 1843, an album of unknown origin appeared in which dried ferns were shown alongside their corresponding cyanotype images.

As well as using the cyanotype for botanical illustration, Herschel had soon recognized – and made use of – its potential for reproducing writing and drawing. However, not until after his death in 1871 was the commercial use of cyanotypes seen as a low-cost copying method for plans and architectural drawings. In 1875, Marion & Co in London advertised ready-prepared paper under the brand name of the "Ferro-Prussiate-Process". It was placed in a simple frame with the sun as the light source. In its modernized version – with electrically generated light and copy cylinder – this method of reproduction was still in operation in the 1950s, by which time it was known as "blueprint". It was cost effective, posed hardly any toxicity hazards and was usable on many different surfaces.

By the 1870s cyanotype's advantages had increased to the extent that it could be used to copy less light-resistant silver prints, for example by the British engineer Washington Teasdale (1830–1903), the French painter Henri Le Secq (1818–1882), as well as the American photojournalist Frances Benjamin Johnston (1864–1952). Others availing themselves of cyanotype's advantages included Henry Peter Bosse (1844–1903), who from 1883 to 1892 produced topographic and documentary studies during the development of the Mississippi River. The method was popular because it still succeeded without laboratory equipment and even under adverse conditions. During a 1910 expedition, the American ethnologist Edward S. Curtis (1868–1952) produced numerous prints from negatives. Many of the studies of animals in motion by Eadweard Muybridge (1830–1904) were made as cyanotype prints.

For art galleries and museums, however, it was a long time before they considered that cyanotype might be of any interest. They saw the process more as a technical aid that might be of practical use. In this vein the British military commander of the South African town of Mafeking (present-day Mahikeng) in 1900 ordered the use of cyanotype in the production of banknotes and stamps. At the same time in the USA cyanotype images were sold in large numbers as postcards. Not until experiments carried out by Paul Burty Haviland (1880–1950), a member of the circle surrounding Alfred Stieglitz (1864–1946), was cyanotype artistically rehabilitated. Haviland consciously used the medium's tonal range and its coarse grain structure for female nudes and portraits. Like Haviland, Joseph Keiley (1869–1914), who also belonged to the Stieglitz circle, produced impressive portraits as cyanotype prints. In 1949 Susan Weil (b. 1930) persuaded her artist friend Robert Rauschenberg (1925–2008), to experiment with cyanotype. The results were full-body nudes lit in the studio by ultraviolet lamps. One of Rauschenberg's cyanotypes was chosen by Edward Steichen (1879–1973) for the 1951 MoMA exhibition *Abstraction in Photography*.

The interest in cyanotype as artistic technique has steadily increased since the 1970s. Often the pioneering achievements of Anna Atkins and Anne Dixon would lend inspiration to artists such as Barbara Ciurej (b. 1956) and Lindsay Lochman (b. 1952), who interweave cyanotype plant patterns

Frances Benjamin Johnston
In a salt mine, ca. 1893 / **In einer Salzmine** / **Dans une mine de sel**
Cyanotype, 18.4 × 24.5 cm (7 ¼ × 9 ⅝ in.)
Washington, D.C., Library of Congress

with their portraits of women. Similarly, the art books of Jesseca Ferguson (b. 1949) take the reader right back to the time when cyanotype was invented. Her works' melancholic style owes a great deal to visual quotes that refer back to the 19th century's forward-looking, scientifically inspired ideas of progress.

Other works of art, no less influenced by the tradition of Atkins and Dixon, include *Floral Blueprints* by Alexander Hamilton (b. 1950), whose cyanotypes offer beguiling views of his plants' internal structure. In 1993, after suffering a stroke that led to extensive blindness, John Dugdale (b. 1960) dedicated himself to 19th-century photographic techniques. In his photographs of male nudes, he pushes the limits of the cyanotype's blurry potential so as to create sensitive portraits. The British photographer Nick Veasey (b. 1962) uses the process to produce a series of his own X-ray photos.

The currently increasing popularity of the process is witnessed by various exhibitions, such as those in Worcester, Massachusetts (2016), or Mülheim an der Ruhr, Germany (2019), dedicated exclusively to cyanotype. To tackle the technology, numerous resources come into play. Paper, textiles or wood are used in differing sizes and formats. At the same time imagery and pictorial techniques range from graphic abstract to ornamental and figurative, from simple photogram via contact copy to montage and collage. Today, while the old photographic process of cyanotype is no longer regarded as a necessity, it still survives and continues to be seen as a medium of artistic exploration.

Edward S. Curtis
Native American mother and child of the Arapaho tribe, 1910
Mutter und Kind aus dem Volk der Arapaho / Une mère et un enfant du peuple arapaho
Cyanotype, 19.9 × 15 cm (7 ⅞ × 5 ⅞ in.)
Los Angeles, J. Paul Getty Museum

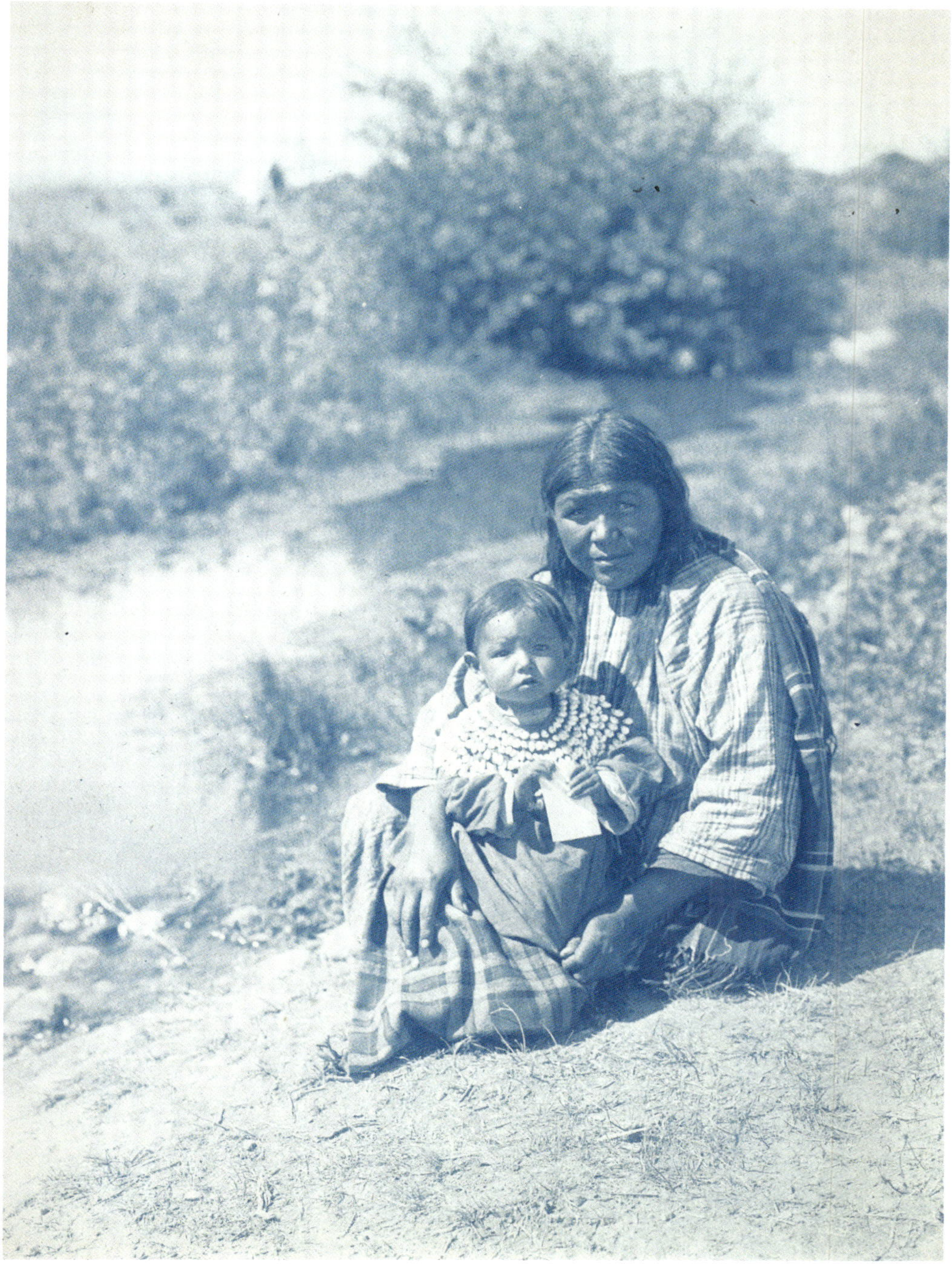

Die Cyanotypie

Das Jahr 1839 gilt als Geburtsjahr der Fotografie. Im Januar stellt Louis Jacques Mandé Daguerre in Paris die Daguerreotypie vor, wenig später präsentiert William Henry Fox Talbot seine „fotogenischen Zeichnungen“ in London. 1842 entwickelt John Herschel ein drittes fotografisches Verfahren: die Cyanotypie. Sie beruht, anders als ihre Vorgänger, nicht auf der Lichtempfindlichkeit von Silberverbindungen, sondern auf der Sensibilität von Eisensalz für die ultravioletten Anteile des Lichts.

Bei seinen Versuchen, farbige Fotografien herzustellen, macht Herschel eine zufällige Entdeckung: Setzt man ein mit einer bestimmten Eisenverbindung beschichtetes Material der Sonne aus, färbt es sich beim Fixieren mit einfachem Wasser blau. Der Farbstoff, der beim Fixieren des latenten Bildes entsteht, ist „Berliner Blau“ (auch „Preußischblau“). Bereits 1706 war es Johann Jacob Diesbach in Berlin gelungen, das Pigment herzustellen, das in dieser Form in der Natur nicht vorkommt. Bis dahin nahm die Farbe Blau, der eine beruhigende Wirkung zugesprochen wird, für die Maler einen Ehrenplatz im Spektrum der Farben ein, da sie nur als teuer zu beschaffendes Ultramarin verfügbar war. Das synthetische Pigment „Berliner Blau“ hat eine hervorragende Farbechtheit, hohes Deckvermögen und ist lange farbstabil.

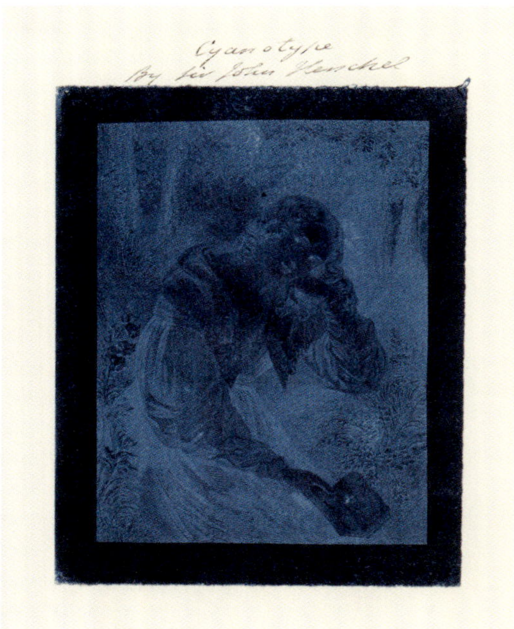

So sind Cyanotypien aus der Pionierzeit der Fotografie auch heute häufig noch gut erhalten, während die frühen Kalotypien zumeist stark ausgeblichen sind. Hinzu kam, dass die Cyanotypie einfach zu handhaben und das Ausgangsmaterial günstig war. Diesen Vorteilen stand jedoch ein entscheidender Nachteil gegenüber: Die Eisensalze reagieren weit weniger empfindlich auf das Licht als Silberverbindungen. Deshalb ist die Cyanotypie für die direkte Belichtung mit der Kamera nicht geeignet. Ideal ist sie jedoch für die Herstellung von Fotogrammen und Kontaktkopien, bei denen eine lange Belichtungsdauer unproblematisch ist.

In den ersten drei Jahrzehnten wird das Verfahren beinahe nur von Herschel, seinen Familienmitgliedern sowie von Anna Atkins und Anne Dixon genutzt. Mit etwa 800 unterschiedlichen Motiven von Pflanzen und vermutlich über 10.000 Kopien ist Atkins, teilweise gemeinsam mit ihrer Freundin, die bei weitem produktivste Anwenderin der Cyanotypie. Neben diesen Alben und einzelnen Exemplaren von Cyanotypien aus dem Umkreis der Herschel-Familie ist aus der Frühzeit des Verfahrens lediglich ein weiteres Anwendungsbeispiel überliefert, ein Album unbekannter Herkunft von 1843, in dem getrocknete Farne ihren entsprechenden Cyanotypie-Abbildern gegenüberstellt sind.

Neben dem Nutzen der Cyanotypie für die botanische Illustration hat Herschel bereits früh ihr Potenzial für die Vervielfältigung von Schrift und Zeichnungen erkannt und genutzt. Doch erst nach seinem Tod 1871 beginnt die kommerzielle Verwertung der Cyanotypie als günstiges Verfahren zum Kopieren von Plänen und Konstruktionszeichnungen. 1875 bietet die Londoner Firma Marion & Co fertig präparierte Papiere unter dem Titel „Ferro-Prussiat" an. Man nutzt anfangs einfache Kopierrahmen, als Lichtquelle dient die Sonne. In seiner modernisierten Variante – mit elektrisch erzeugtem Licht und Kopierzylinder – wird diese Art der Reproduktion als „Blaupause" noch bis in die 1950er-Jahre praktiziert, denn sie ist kostengünstig, birgt kaum toxische Gefahren und ist auf vielen Oberflächen anwendbar.

Die Vorteile der Cyanotypie werden seit den 1870er-Jahren auch zunehmend für das Kopieren von weniger lichtbeständigen Silberabzügen genutzt, u. a. vom britischen Bauingenieur Washington Teasdale (1830–1903), vom französische Künstler Henri Le Secq (1818–1882) oder auch von der amerikanischen Fotojournalistin Frances Benjamin Johnston (1864–1952). In diese Reihe gehören auch die Cyanotypien von Henry Peter Bosse (1844–1903), der in den Jahren von 1883 bis 1892 topographische und dokumentarische Studien beim Ausbau des Mississippi angefertigt hat. Beliebt ist die Methode, weil sie ohne Laborausrüstung auch unter ungünstigen Bedingungen zum Erfolg führt. So fertigt der amerikanische Ethnologe Edward S. Curtis (1868–1952) auf einer Exkursion um 1910 zahlreiche Abzüge von Negativen an. Auch von den chronofotografischen Arbeiten Eadweard Muybridges (1830–1904) sind zahlreiche Cyanotypie-Kopien überliefert.

Für kunst- und museumswürdig gilt die Cyanotypie jedoch lange Zeit nicht. Sie wird eher als technisches Hilfsmittel angesehen und in den Bereich praktischer Nutzanwendung verwiesen. So verwendet der britische Militärkommandant der südafrikanischen Stadt Mafikeng (heute: Mahikeng) um 1900 das Verfahren, um Geldscheine und Briefmarken herstellen zu lassen. In den USA werden zur gleichen Zeit Cyanotypien in hohen Auflagen als Postkarten vertrieben. Künstlerisch rehabilitiert wird die Cyanotypie erst mit den Experimenten von Paul Burty Haviland (1880–1950), der zum Kreis um Alfred Stieglitz (1864–1946) gehört. Haviland nutzt bewusst den geringen Tonwertumfang und die grobe Kornstruktur des Mediums für stimmungsvolle weibliche Akte und Porträts. Wie Haviland gehört auch Joseph Keiley (1869–1914) zum Kreis um Stieglitz. Von ihm

John Herschel
Portrait of a young woman, ca. 1842 / **Porträt einer jungen Frau** / **Portrait d'une jeune femme**
Cyanotype, 10.2 × 7.8 cm (4 × 3 1/8 in.)
Los Angeles, J. Paul Getty Museum

stammen eindrucksvolle Porträtaufnahmen als Cyanotypie-Abzüge. 1949 regt Susan Weil (geb. 1930) ihren Künstlerfreund Robert Rauschenberg (1925–2008) zur Beschäftigung mit der Cyanotypie an. Es entstehen Ganzkörper-Akte, die im Atelier mit einer UV-Lichtlampe ausbelichtet werden. Eine der Cyanotypien Rauschenbergs wird von Edward Steichen (1879–1973) für die MoMA-Ausstellung *Abstraction in Photography* (1951) ausgewählt.

Das Interesse an der Cyanotypie als künstlerischer Technik wächst seit den siebziger Jahren stetig. Häufig wirken die Pionierleistungen von Anna Atkins und Anne Dixon als Anregung, wie etwa bei Barbara Ciurej (geb. 1956) und Lindsay Lochman (geb. 1952), die in ihren Cyanotypien Pflanzenmuster in die Silhouette von Frauenporträts montieren. Auch in den Kunstbüchern Jesseca Fergusons (geb. 1949) findet man Rückbezüge auf die Entstehungszeit der Cyanotypie. Ihren melancholischen Charakter verdanken die Arbeiten vor allem Bildzitaten, die sich auf den naturwissenschaftlich inspirierten Fortschrittsgedanken des 19. Jahrhundert beziehen.

Nicht weniger stehen die *Floral Blueprints* von Alexander Hamilton (geb. 1950) in der Tradition von Atkins und Dixon. Hamilton gelingt es in seinen Cyanotypien, faszinierende Ansichten von den Binnenstrukturen seiner pflanzlichen Objekte zu präsentieren. John Dugdale (geb. 1960) wendet sich 1993, nachdem ein Schlaganfall zu seiner weitgehenden Erblindung geführt hat, intensiv den fotografischen Techniken des 19. Jahrhunderts zu. In seinen Fotografien mit männlichen Akten reizt er das Potenzial der Cyanotypie zur Unschärfe für die Schaffung sensibler Porträts aus. Auch der britische Fotograf Nick Veasey (geb. 1962) nutzt das Verfahren und stellt eine Reihe von Cyanotypien seiner Röntgenfotografien her.

Von der gewachsenen Popularität der Technik in der Gegenwart zeugen verschiedene Ausstellungen etwas in Worcester, Massachusetts, (2016) oder in Mülheim an der Ruhr (2019), die ausschließlich der Cyanotypie gewidmet sind. Bei der Beschäftigung mit der Technik kommen zahlreiche Materialien ins Spiel: Papier, Stoff oder Holz werden in unterschiedlicher Größe und Format genutzt. Auch Bildsprache und Bildtechnik reichen vom Grafisch-Abstrakten bis zum Ornamentalen und Figürlichen, vom schlichten Fotogramm über die Kontaktkopie bis zu Montagen und Collagen. So bleibt das alte fotografische Verfahren der Cyanotypie, nachdem es nicht mehr an einen Gebrauchszweck gebunden ist, als Medium künstlerischer Auseinandersetzung bis heute lebendig.

Joseph Keiley, **Has No Horses**, 1902
Cyanotype, 20.6 × 15.9 cm (8 ⅛ × 6 ¼ in.)
Los Angeles, J. Paul Getty Museum

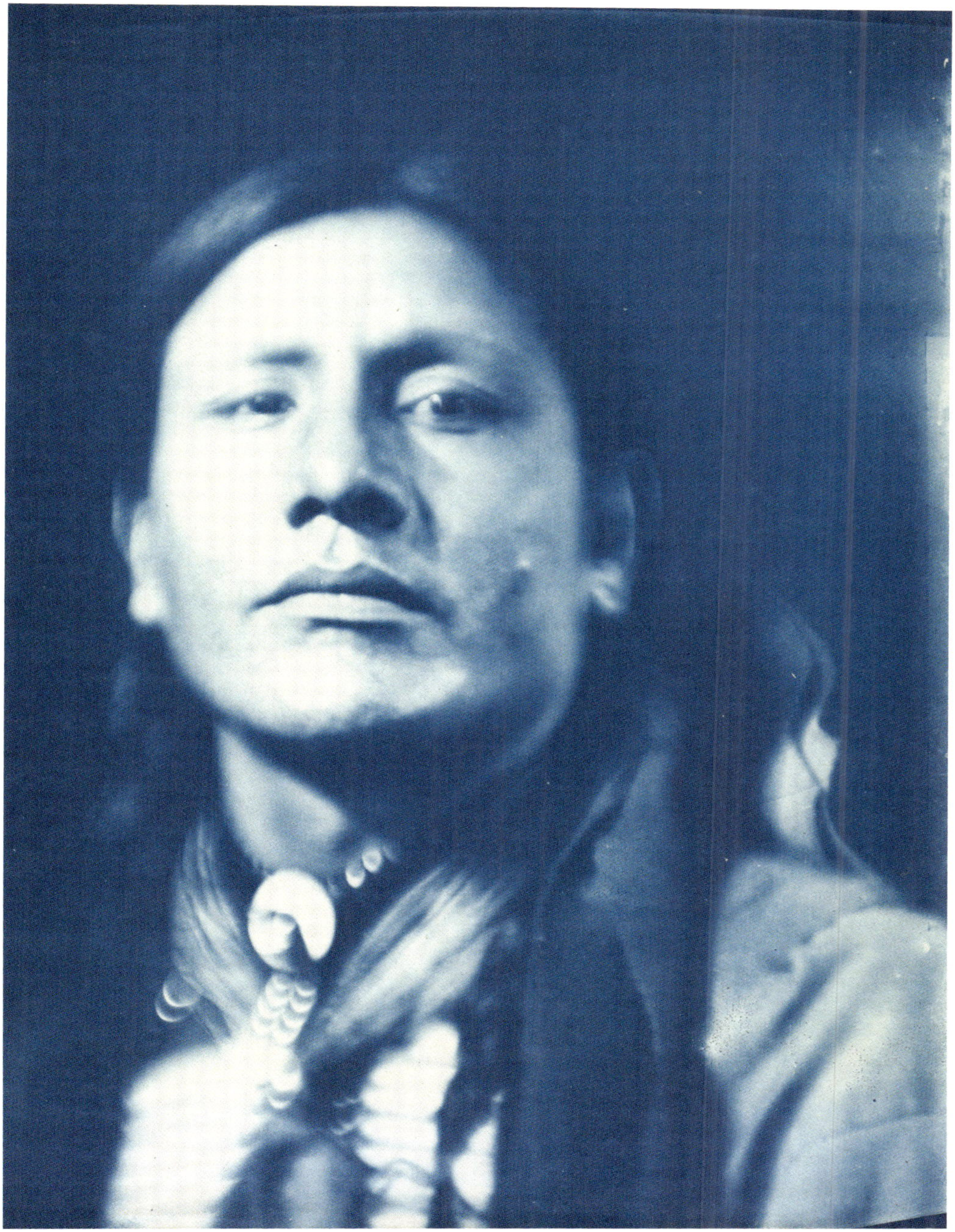

Le cyanotype

L'année 1839 est considérée comme l'année de naissance de la photographie. En janvier, Louis Jacques Mandé Daguerre expose la technique du daguerréotype à Paris. Peu après, William Henry Fox Talbot présente à Londres ses « dessins photogéniques ». En 1842, John Herschel met au point un troisième procédé photographique : le cyanotype. À la différence de ses prédécesseurs, le cyanotype ne repose pas sur la photosensibilité de telle ou telle solution argentique, mais sur la sensibilité des sels ferriques au rayonnement ultraviolet de la lumière.

Dans ses tentatives de produire des photographies en couleurs, Herschel fait une découverte fortuite : lorsqu'on insole un matériau enduit d'un certain composé ferrique, il se teinte en bleu par simple fixation au rinçage à l'eau. La substance chromatique qui apparaît lorsqu'on fixe l'image latente, est le « Berliner Blau » ou bleu de Prusse. Dès 1706, Johann Jacob Diesbach était parvenu à Berlin à produire ce pigment inexistant sous cette forme dans la nature. Le bleu, auquel on attribue une action apaisante, occupait jusqu'alors une place prééminente dans le spectre chromatique du peintre, car il était seulement disponible sous forme du très onéreux bleu outremer. Le pigment synthétique dit « bleu de Prusse » possède une excellente solidité chromatique, un haut pouvoir couvrant et une grande stabilité dans la durée.

C'est ce qui fait que les cyanotypes de l'époque pionnière de la photographie sont souvent encore bien conservés aujourd'hui, alors que les premiers calotypes ont pour la plupart fortement pâli. À cela s'ajoute le fait que le procédé était simple à mettre en œuvre et que le matériau de base était bon marché. Ces avantages étaient toutefois contrebalancés par un inconvénient de poids : les sels ferriques sont beaucoup moins sensibles à la lumière que les composés argentiques. C'est pourquoi la cyanotypie se prête mal à l'exposition directe de l'appareil photographique. Elle est en revanche idéale pour réaliser des photogrammes et des tirages contacts, pour lesquels une longue durée d'exposition ne pose pas de problème.

Pendant les trois premières décennies, le procédé est presque exclusivement employé par Herschel, les membres de sa famille, Anna Atkins et Anne Dixon. Avec quelque 800 motifs de plantes et vraisemblablement plus de 10 000 tirages, Atkins, en partie en collaboration avec son amie, est de loin la créatrice de cyanotypes la plus productive de l'histoire. À côté de ces albums et de cyanotypes isolés réalisés dans l'entourage de la famille Herschel, l'on ne connaît aux premiers temps du procédé qu'un seul autre champ d'application : un album d'origine inconnue datant de 1843, dans lequel des fougères séchées sont placées en regard de leurs copies en cyanotype.

Indépendamment de l'utilité du procédé dans le domaine de l'illustration botanique, Herschel en a reconnu et utilisé très tôt le potentiel pour la duplication d'écrits et de dessins. C'est toutefois seulement après sa mort en 1871 que débute l'exploitation commerciale du cyanotype en tant que procédé bon marché permettant de copier des plans d'architecture et des dessins industriels. En 1875 à Londres, la firme Marion & Co propose un papier préparé sous l'appellation « Ferro-Prussiate ». Au début, on se sert de simples châssis-presses, la source lumineuse étant le soleil. Dans sa version modernisée – avec lumière électrique et tambour copieur – ce genre de reproduction sera encore pratiqué jusqu'aux années 1950 sous le nom de « photocalque bleu » ou « bleu », car il est bon marché, ne recèle guère de dangers en termes de toxicité et peut être utilisé sur de nombreux supports.

À partir des années 1870, les avantages de la cyanotypie sont aussi exploités de plus en plus souvent pour la copie des tirages argentiques, moins stables à la lumière, notamment par l'ingénieur britannique Washington Teasdale (1830–1903), l'artiste français Henri Le Secq (1818–1882) ou la photojournaliste américaine Frances Benjamin Johnston (1864–1952). Il convient encore d'ajouter à cette liste les cyanotypes de Henry Peter Bosse (1844–1903), auteur d'études topographiques et documentaires réalisées de 1883 à 1892 dans le cadre des travaux de viabilisation du Mississippi. La méthode est particulièrement appréciée parce qu'elle donne d'excellents résultats sans faire appel à des équipements laborantins et dans des conditions même difficiles. Lors d'une expédition menée vers 1910, l'ethnologue américain Edward S. Curtis (1868–1952) réalise ainsi de nombreux tirages de négatifs. Mais un grand nombre de tirages de cyanotypes ont aussi été réalisés dans le cadre des travaux chronophotographiques d'Eadweard Muybridge (1830–1904).

Reste que le cyanotype est encore loin d'être considéré comme une technique digne de l'art et des musées. Il est plutôt vu comme un moyen technique auxiliaire et demeure confiné dans le domaine des applications pratiques. Vers 1900, le commandant militaire britannique de la ville de Mahikeng, dans l'actuelle Afrique du Sud, utilise ainsi le procédé pour faire imprimer des billets de banque et des timbres-poste. À la même époque, des cyanotypes sont diffusés en grands tirages aux États-Unis sous forme de cartes postales. Le cyanotype ne reçoit ses lettres de noblesse dans l'art qu'avec les expérimentations de Paul Burty Haviland (1880–1950), qui fait partie du cercle d'Alfred Stieglitz (1864–1946). Haviland exploite délibérément l'échelle de tons réduite et la forte granularité du médium pour des nus féminins et des portraits chargés d'ambiance. Joseph Keiley (1869–1914) fait lui aussi partie du cercle de Stieglitz. Il est l'auteur d'impressionnants portraits tirés en cyanotype. En 1949, Susan Weil (1930–) pousse son ami artiste Robert Rauschenberg (1925–2008) à s'intéresser au procédé. Des nus voient alors le jour qui sont insolés à l'atelier à l'aide d'une lampe à rayons ultra-violets. Un des cyanotypes de Rauschenberg sera choisi par Edward Steichen (1879–1973) pour son exposition *Abstraction in Photography*, présentée au MoMA en 1951.

L'intérêt pour le cyanotype en tant que technique artistique grandit depuis les années 1970. Souvent, les travaux pionniers d'Anna Atkins et Anne Dixon jouent un rôle déclencheur, comme pour Barbara Ciurej (1956–) et Lindsay Lochman (1952–), qui intègrent des motifs végétaux dans la silhouette de portraits féminins réalisés en cyanotype. Dans les livres d'art de Jesseca Ferguson (1949–), on trouve également des références aux premiers temps du cyanotype. Ses œuvres doivent surtout leur caractère mélancolique à des citations iconographiques renvoyant à l'idée de progrès d'inspiration scientifique du XIXe siècle.

Les *Floral Blueprints* d'Alexander Hamilton (1950–) s'inscrivent également dans la tradition d'Atkins et Dixon. Dans ses cyanotypes, Hamilton parvient à présenter des vues fascinantes des structures intérieures de ses sujets végétaux. En 1993, après une attaque d'apoplexie qui l'a laissé quasiment aveugle, John Dugdale (1960–) se tourne intensivement vers les techniques photographiques du XIXe siècle. Dans ses photographies de nus masculins, il exploite à l'extrême la tendance au flou du cyanotype pour la création de portraits sensibles. Le photographe Nick Veasey (1962–) se sert lui aussi du procédé et réalise une série de cyanotypes à partir de ses photographies aux rayons X.

Plusieurs expositions dédiées exclusivement au cyanotype, notamment à Worcester, Massachusetts (2016) ou à Mülheim an der Ruhr (2019), témoignent de la popularité croissante de cette technique à l'époque contemporaine. Le travail avec le médium fait appel à de nombreux matériaux : papier, tissu ou bois sont utilisés dans des tailles et des formats variables. Le langage et la technique iconographiques vont du domaine graphique et abstrait à l'ornemental et au figuré, du sobre photogramme au montage et au collage en passant par le tirage contact. Désormais délié de son ancienne fonction utilitaire, l'ancien procédé photographique du cyanotype vit aujourd'hui en tant que médium artistique.

Robert Rauschenberg, Susan Weil
Untitled (double Rauschenberg), ca. 1950
Ohne Titel (double Rauschenberg) / **Sans titre (double Rauschenberg)**
Cyanotype, 209.6 × 92.1 cm (82 ½ × 36 ¼ in.)
New York, Robert Rauschenberg Foundation

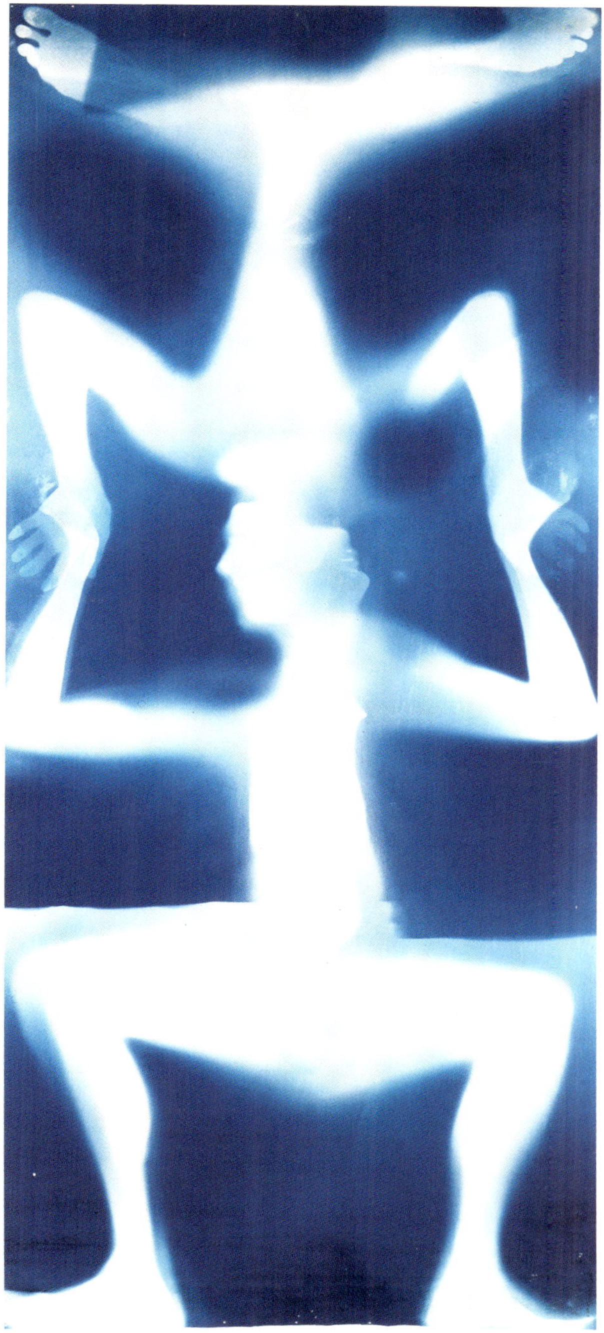

British Algæ,

Vol. II.

Contents.
Vol. II.

CALLITHAMNION
versicolor, Harv.
spongiosum, Harv.
pedicellatum, Dillw.
Turneri, Dillw.
Pluma, Dillw.
repens, Lyng.
Rothii, L.
floridulum, Dillw.
Daviesii, Sm.
secundatum, Harv.
sphærospermum,
TRENTEPOHLIA, Ag.
pulchella, Ag. & var.
LEMANIA, Bory.
fluviatilis, Ag.
BATRACHOSPERMUM, Roth.
vagum, Ag.
moniliforme, Ag.
atrum, Harv.
THOREA, Bory.
ramosissima, Bory.
BULBOCHÆTE, Ag.
setigera, Ag.
DRAPARNALDIA, Bory.
plumosa, Ag.
glomerata, Ag.

D. tenuis, Ag.
nana,
elongata.
CHÆTOPHORA, Ag.
endivæfolia, Ag.
pisiformis, Ag.
MYRIONEMA, Grev.
strangulans, Grev.
CONFERVA, Ag.
ericetorum, Roth.
purpurascens, Carm.
alpina, Bory.
bombycina, Ag.
floccosa, Ag.
zonata, Web. et Mohr.
fontinalis, Ag.
vesicata, Ag.
rivularis, Linn.
capillaris, L.
polita, Harv.
dissiliens, Dill.
Linum, Ag.
crassa, Ag.
tortuosa, Dillw.
implexa, Dillw.
ulothrix, Lyng.
arenosa, Carm.

CONF. melagonium, W. et M.
ærea, Dill.
fucicola, Velley.
flaccida, Dillw.
scutulata, Sm.
carnea, Dillw.
crispata, Roth.
flavescens, Roth.
fracta, Fl. Dan.
glomerata, Linn.
ægagropila, L.
Brownii, Dillw.
pellucida, Huds.
rectangularis, Griff.
Hutchinsiæ, Dillw.
diffusa, Roth.
rupestris, L.
læte-virens, Dillw.
flexuosa, Dillw.
gracilis, Griff.
refracta, Ag.
albida, Huds.
lanosa, Roth.
uncialis, Ag.
glaucescens, Griff.
arcta, Dillw.
æruginosa, Huds.
Casparyi.

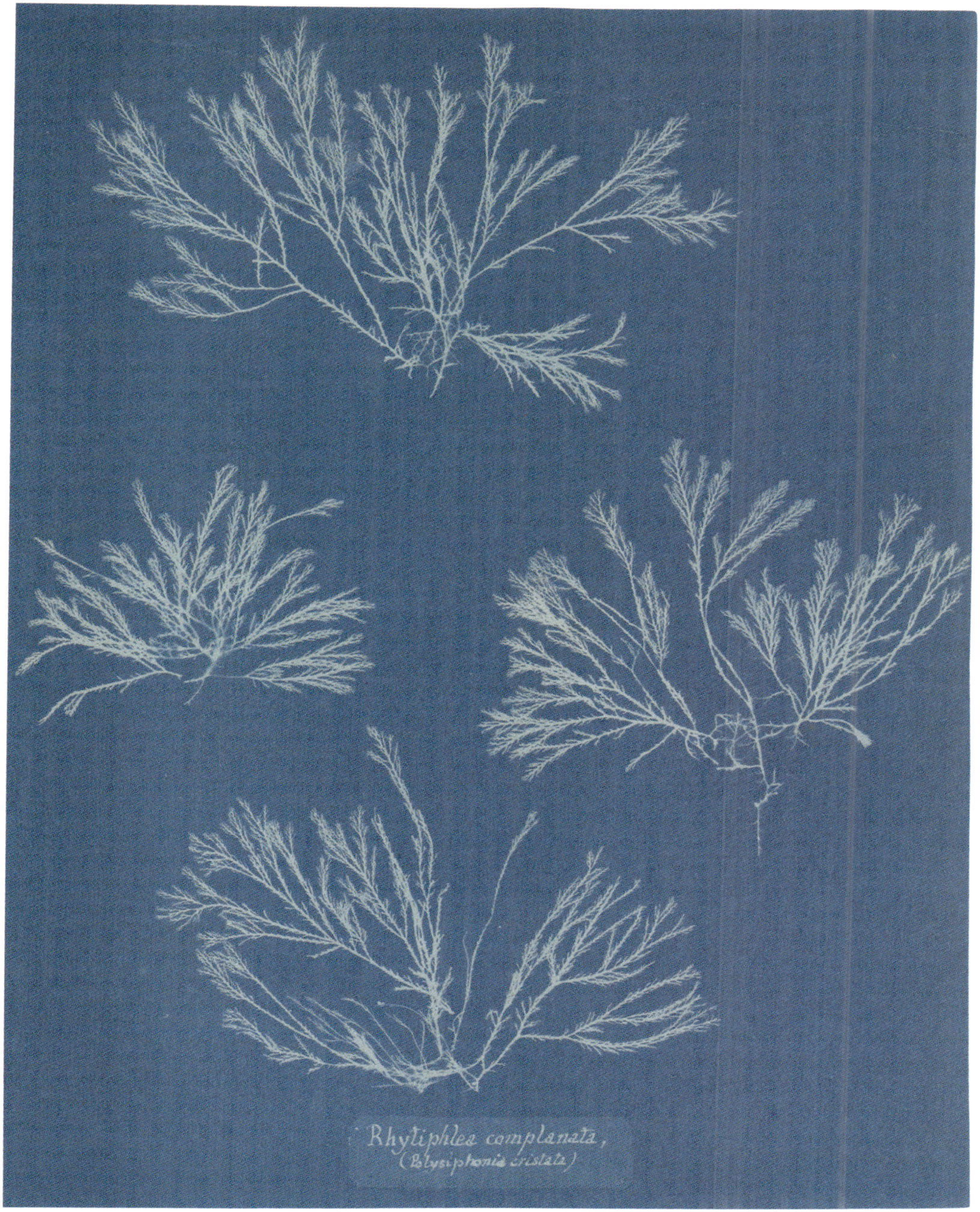

Plate 211. *Rhytiphlea complanata (Polysiphonia cristata)*

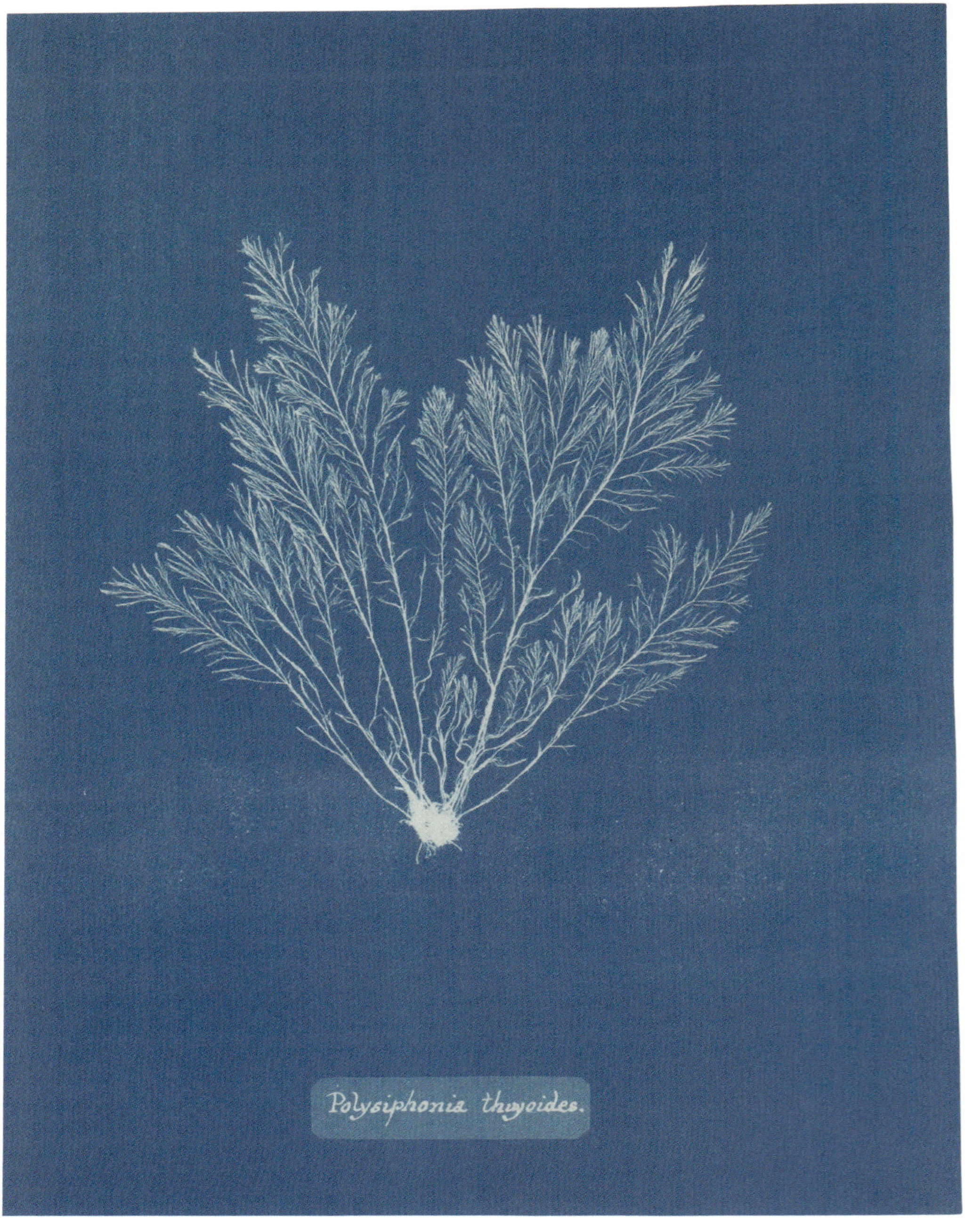

Plate 212. *Polysiphonia thuyoides*

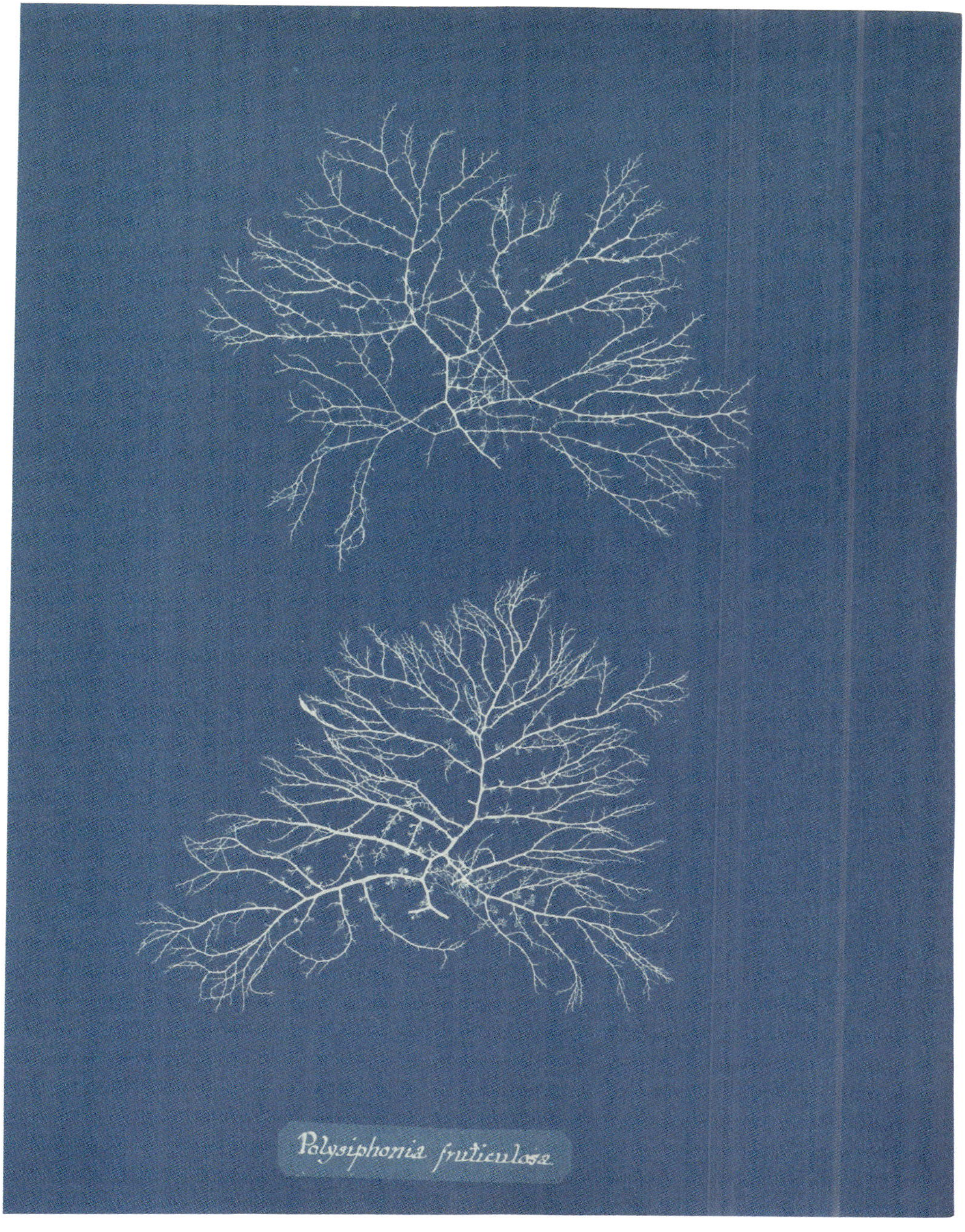

Plate 213. *Polysiphonia fruticulosa*

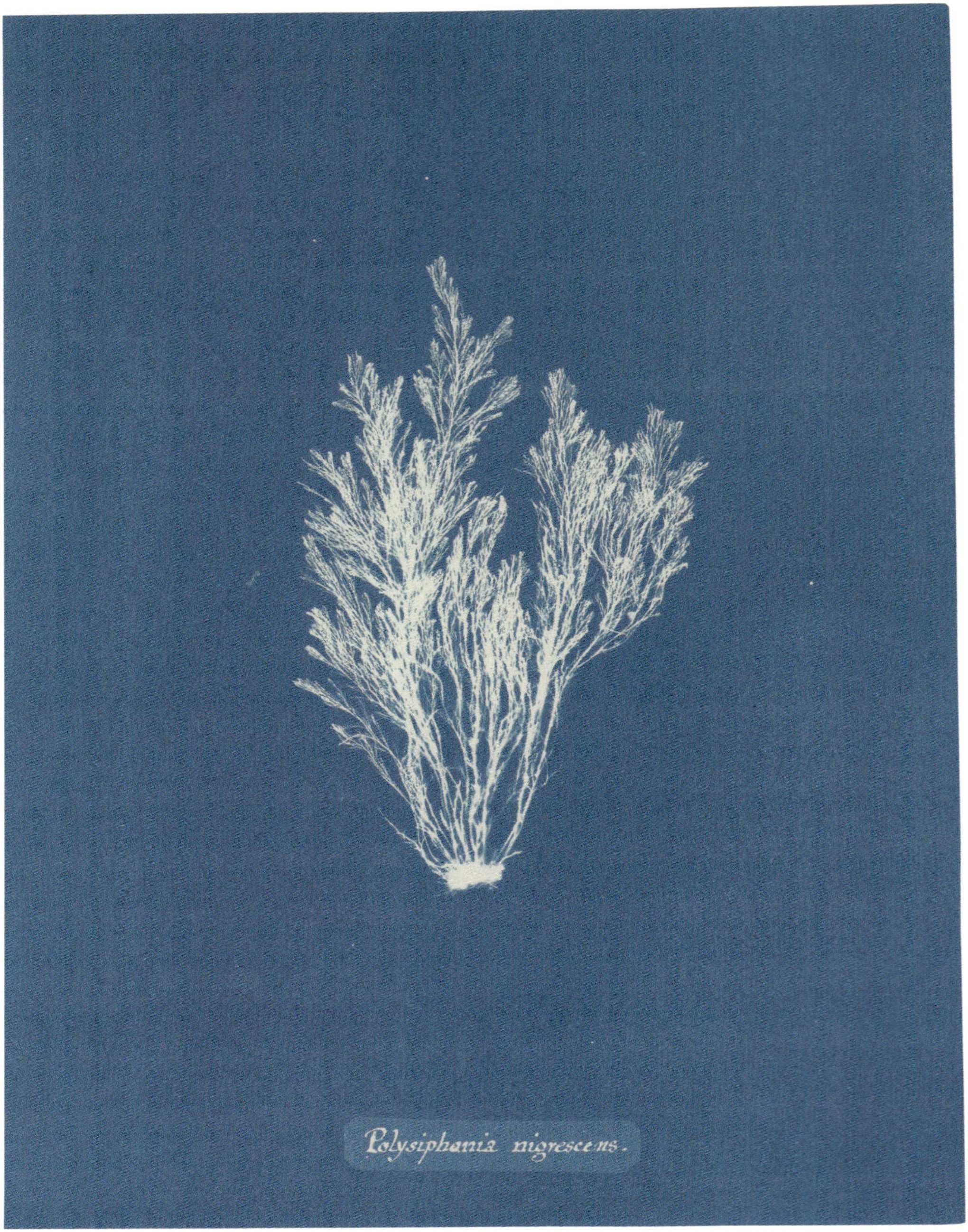

Plate 215. *Polysiphonia nigrescens*

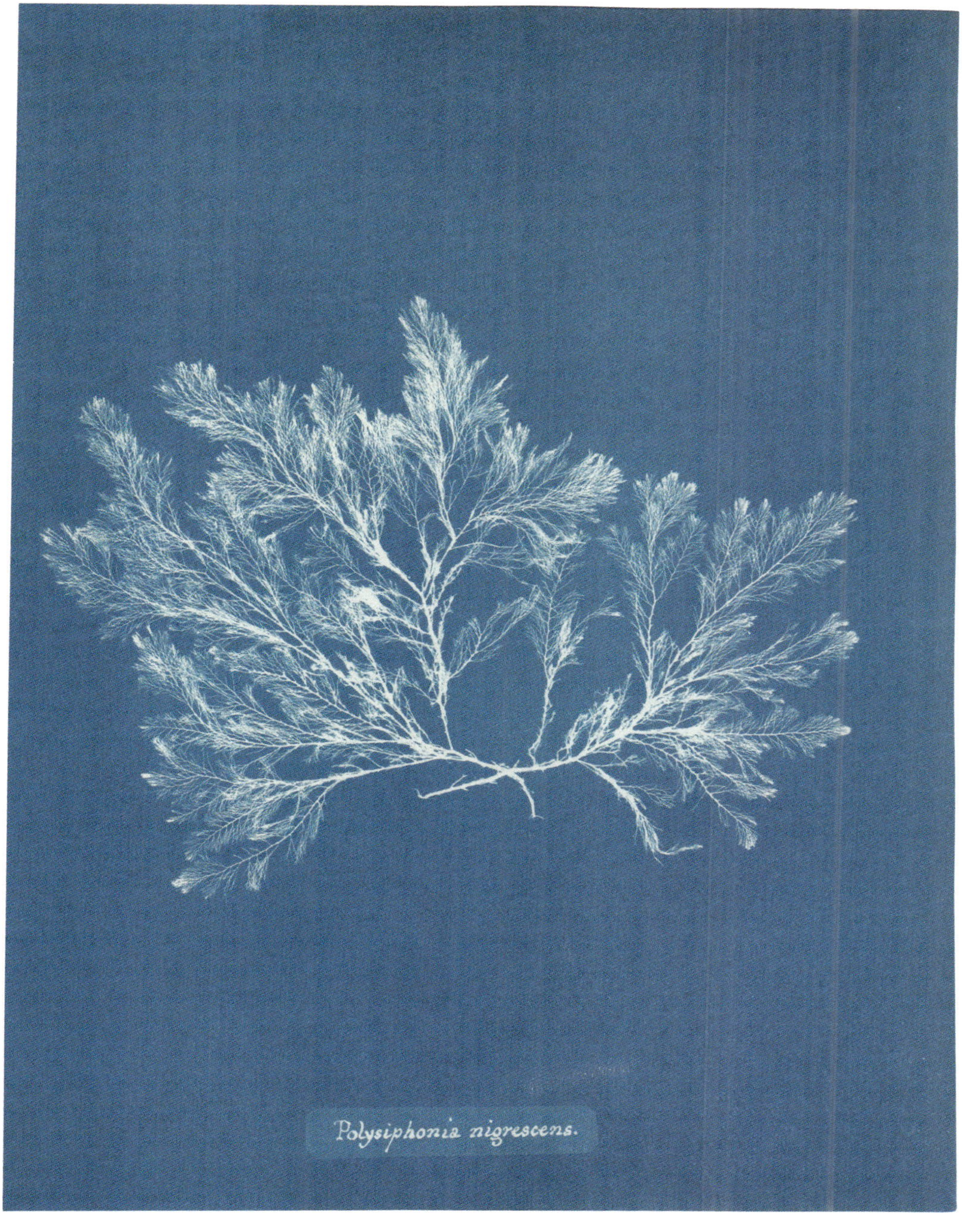

Plate 216. *Polysiphonia nigrescens*

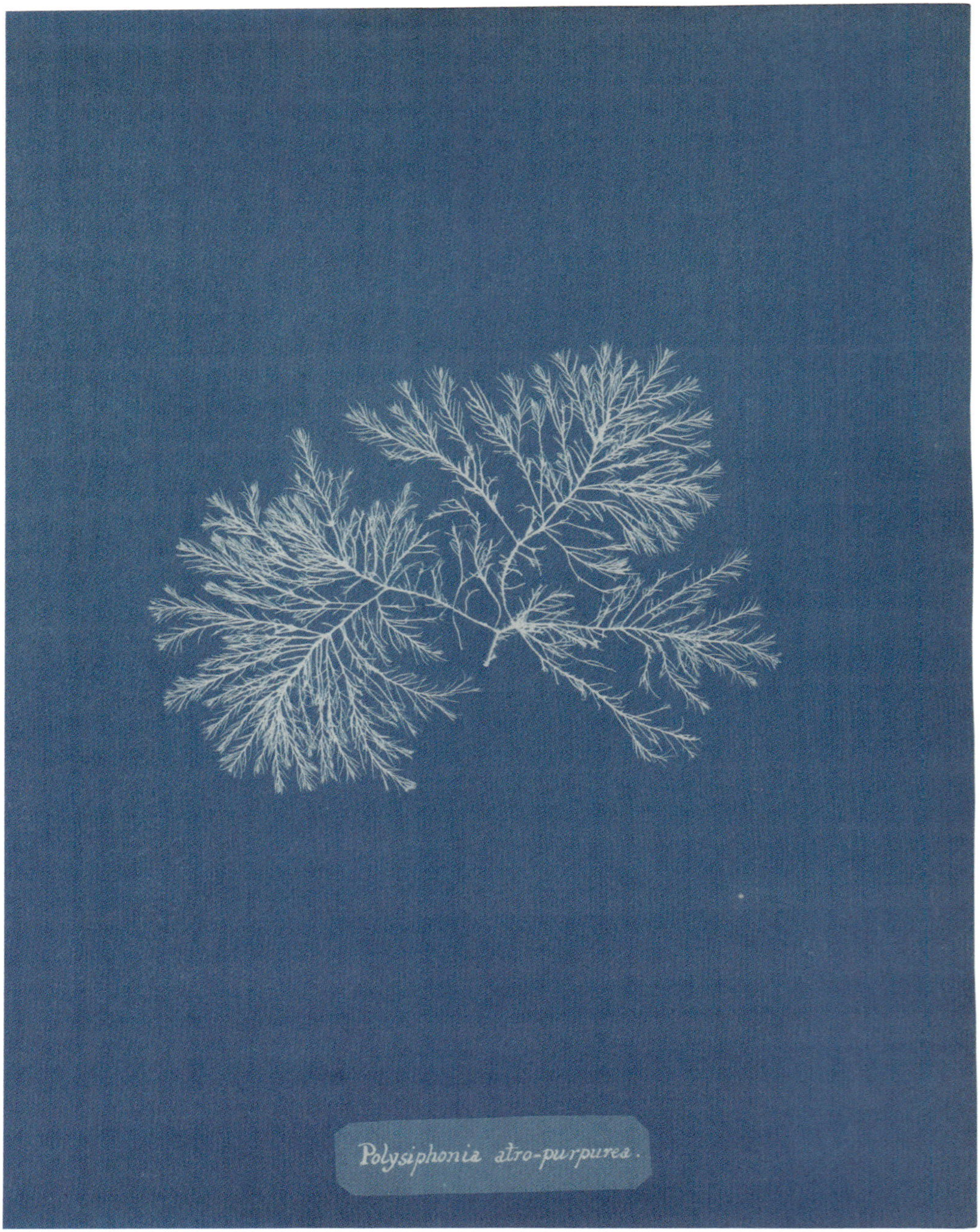

Plate 217. *Polysiphonia atro–purpurea*

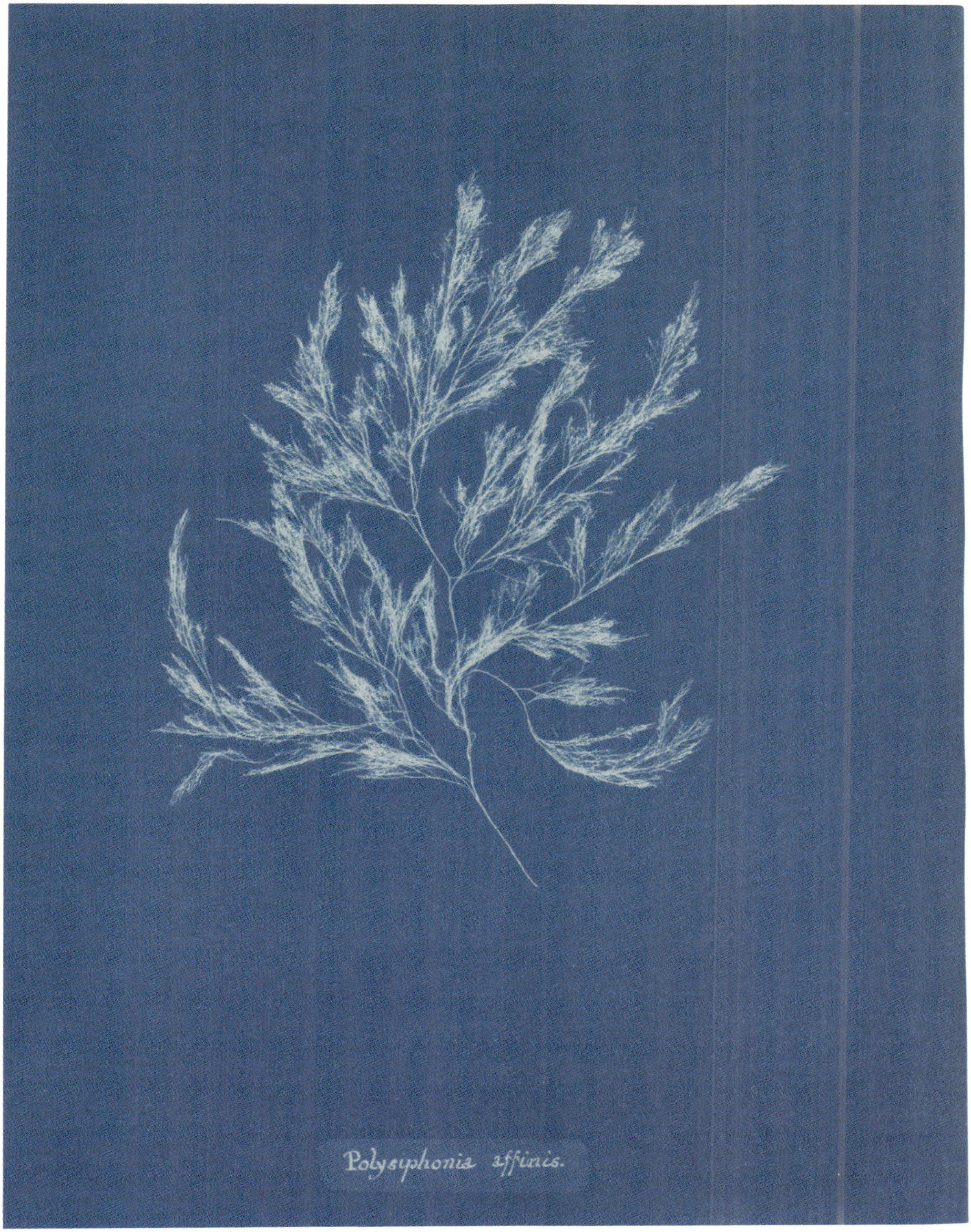

Plate 218. *Polysiphonia affinis*

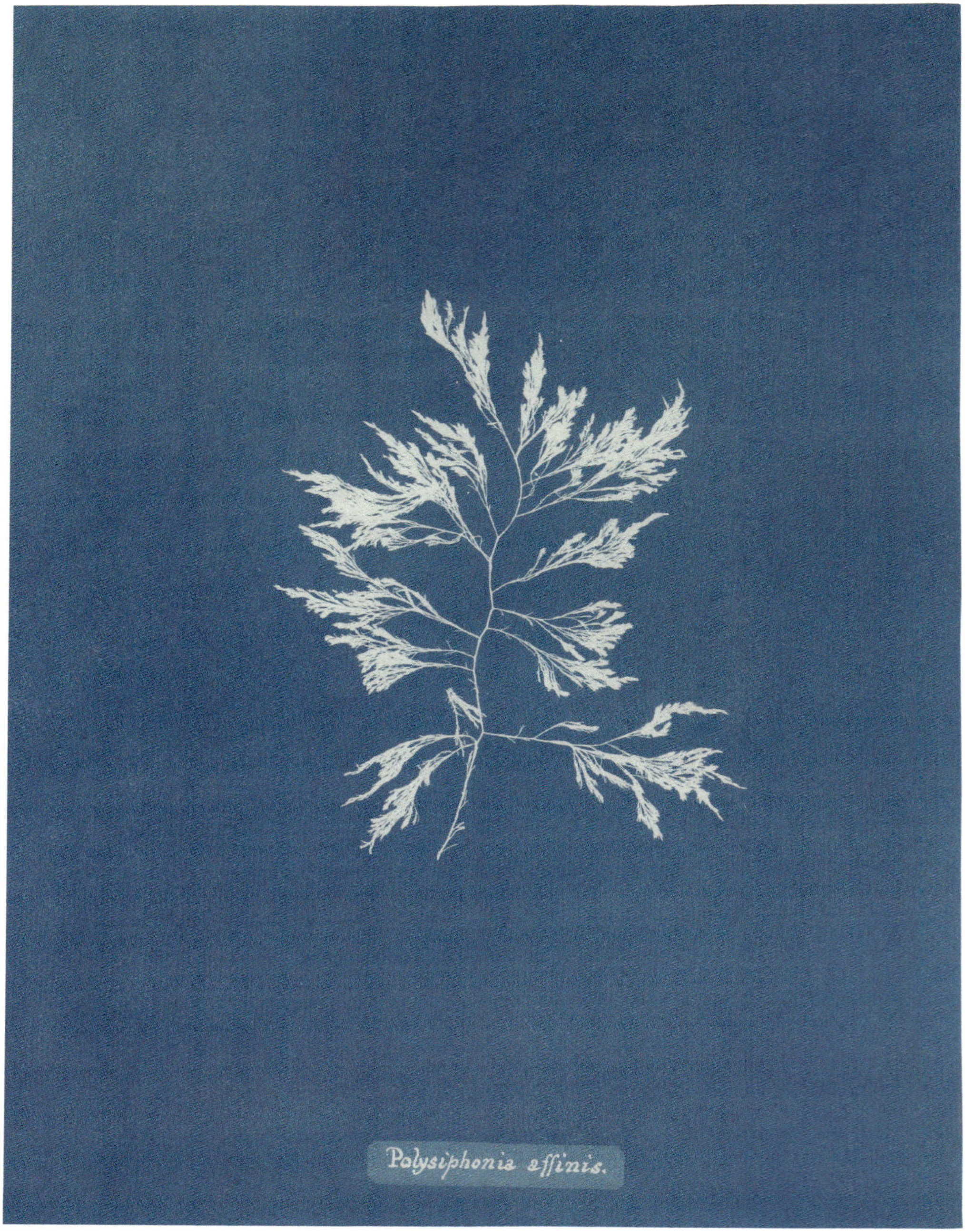

Plate 219. *Polysiphonia affinis*

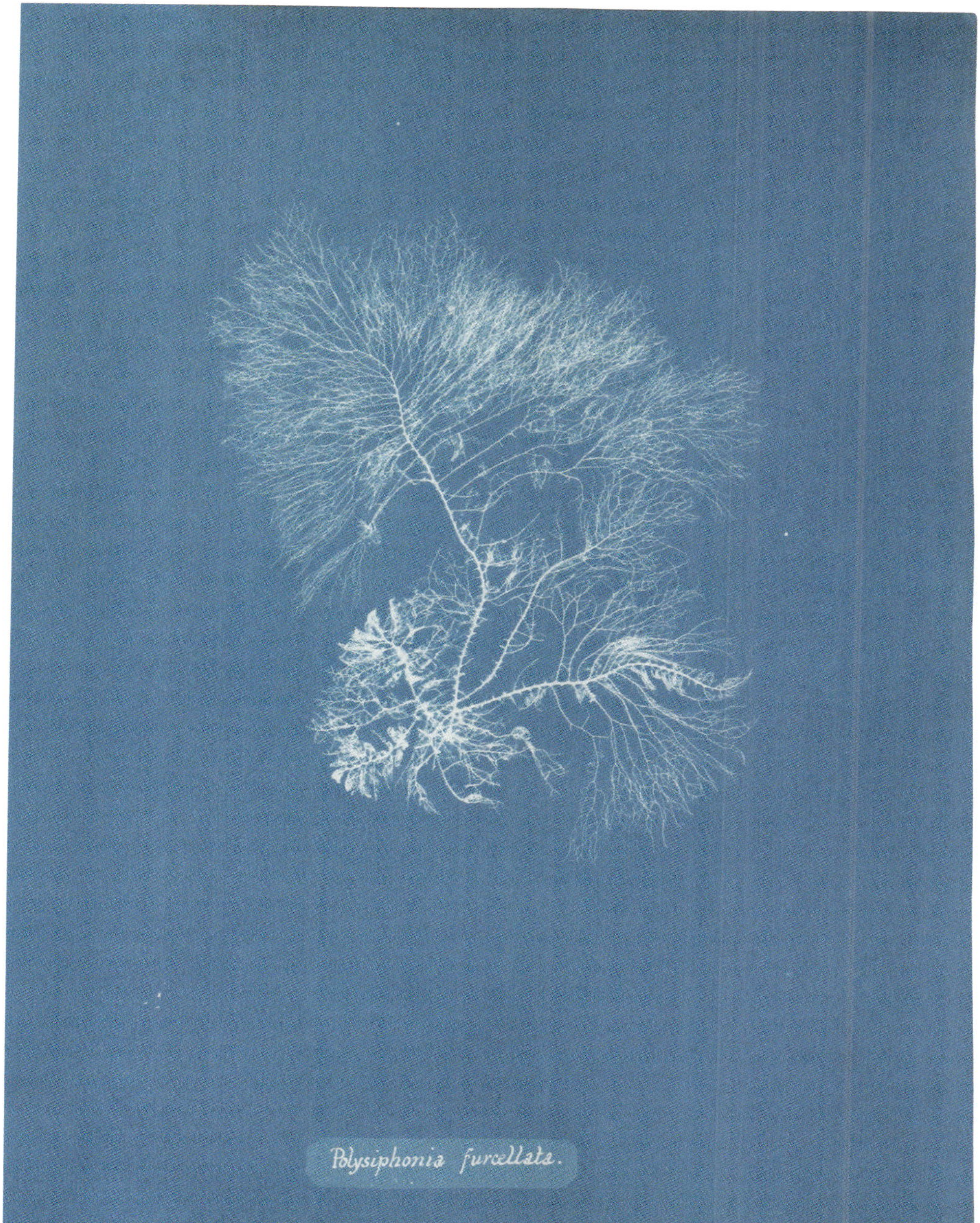

Plate 220. *Polysiphonia furcellata*

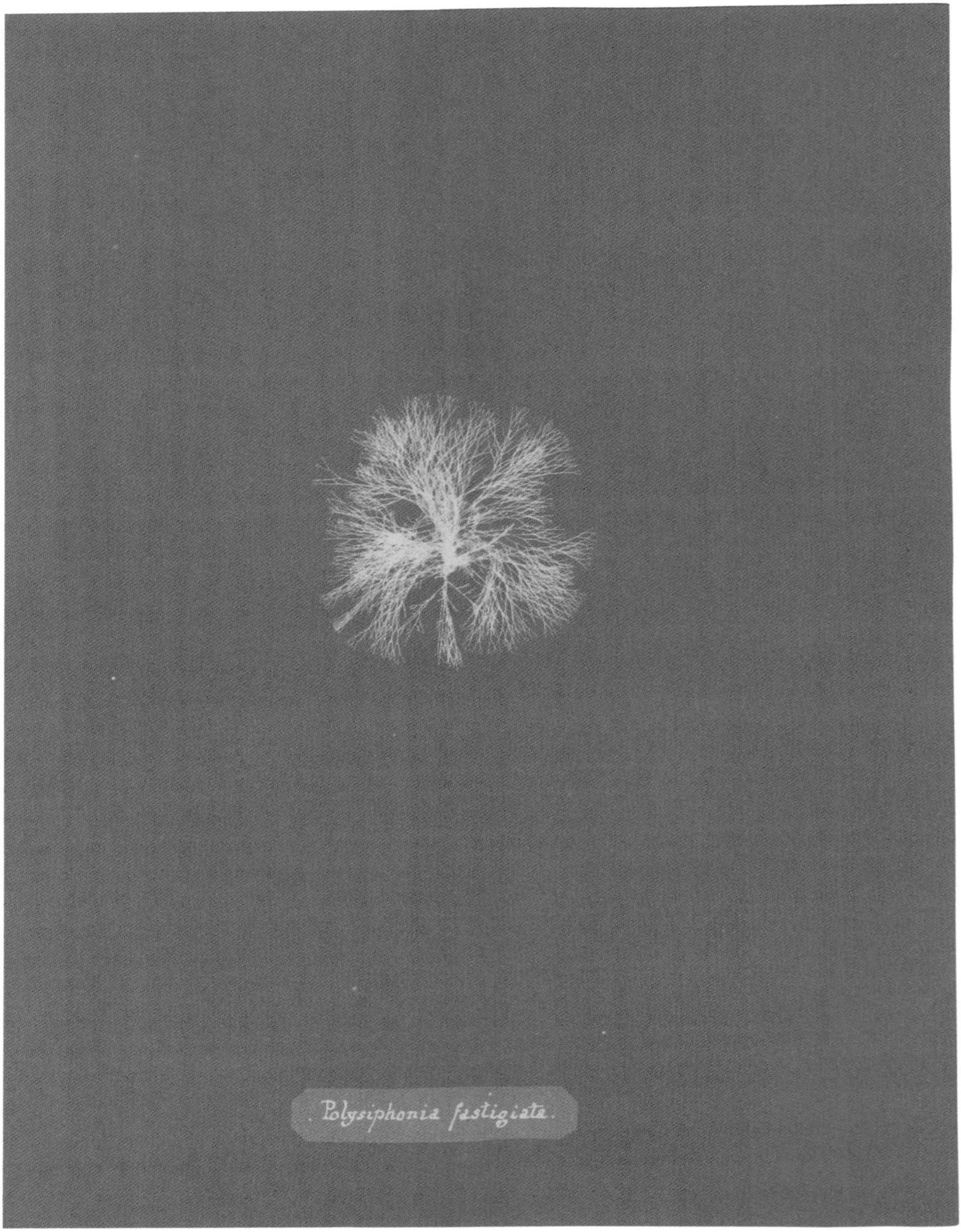

Plate 221. *Polysiphonia fastigiata*

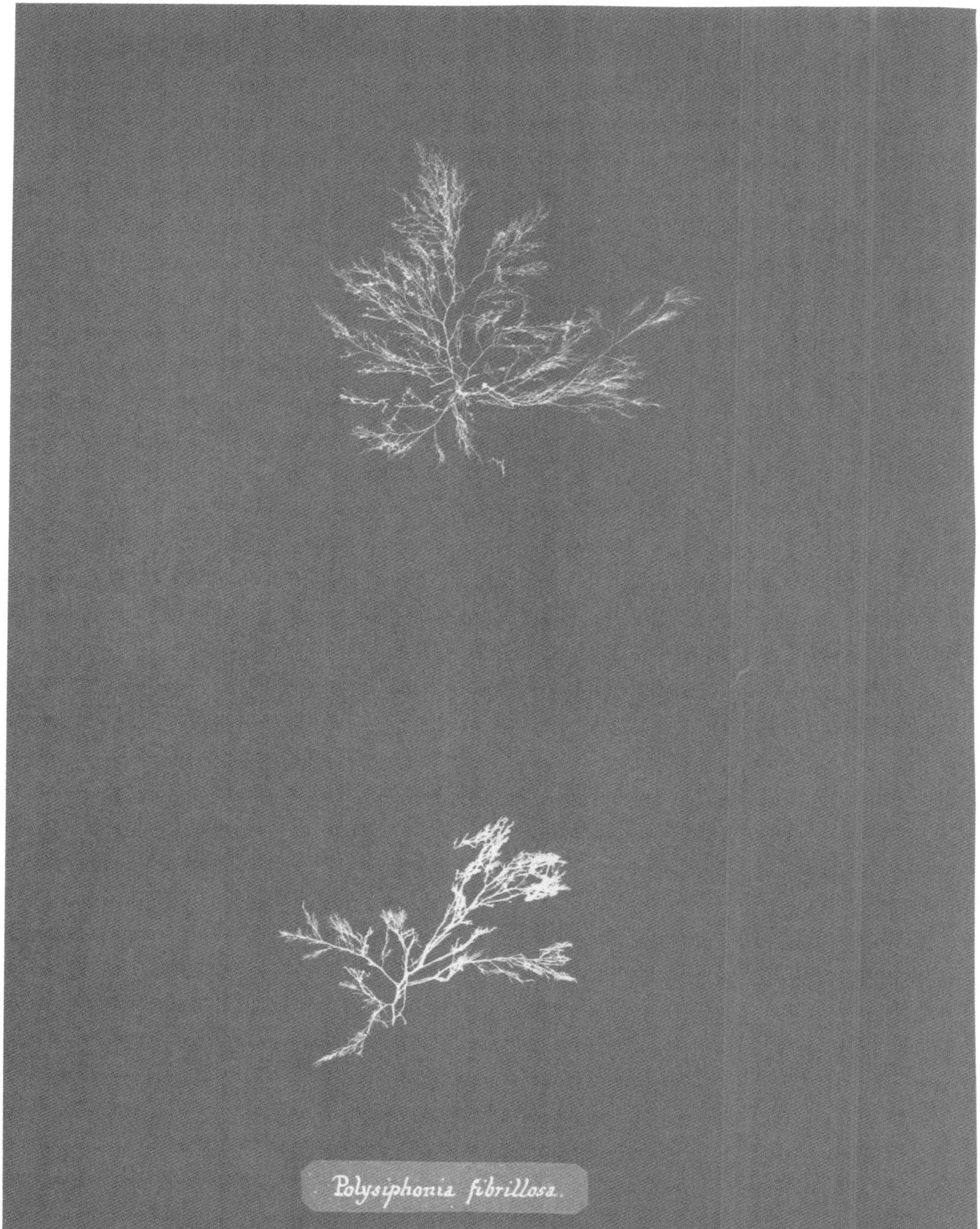

Plate 222. *Polysiphonia fibrillosa*

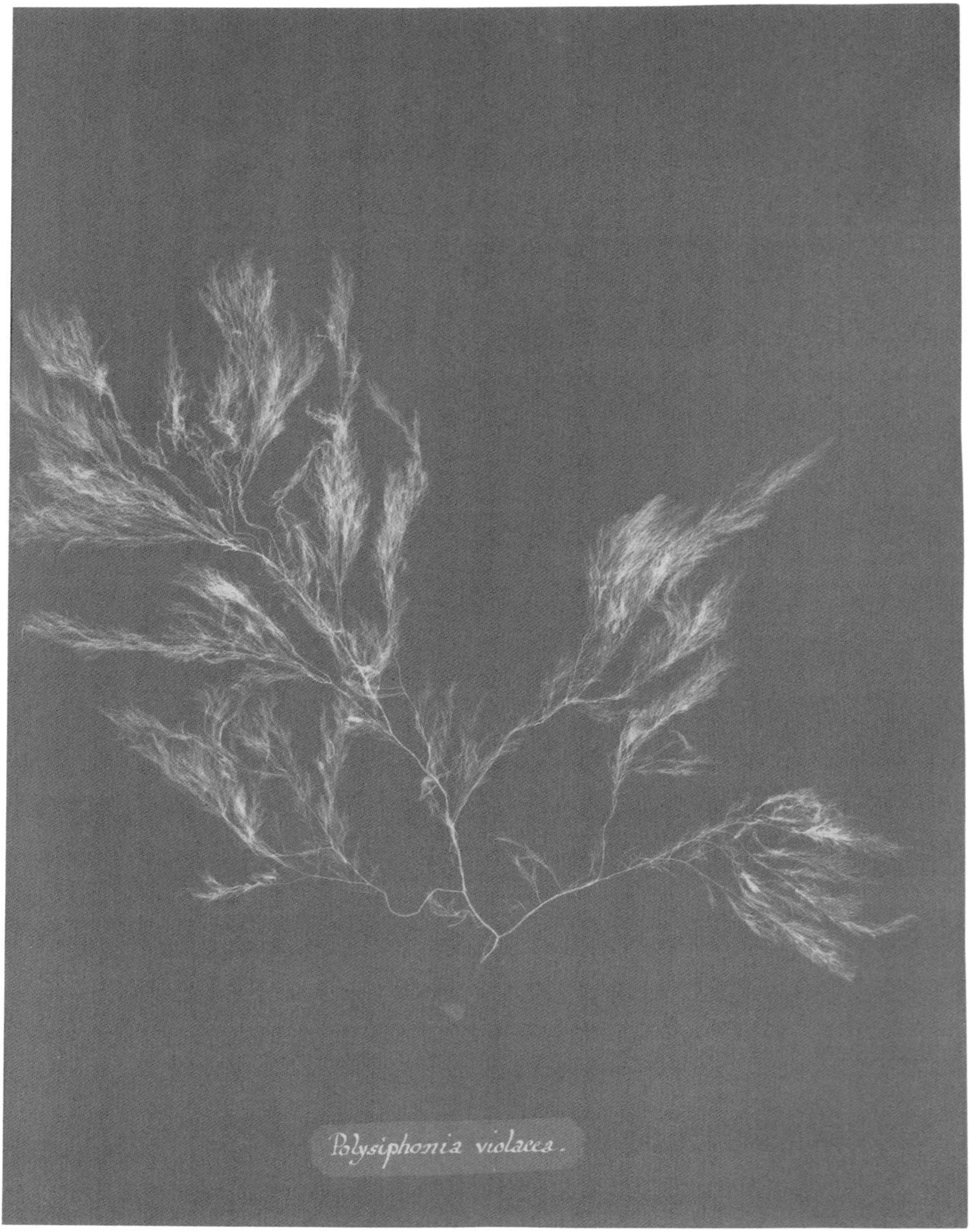

Plate 223. *Polysiphonia violacea*

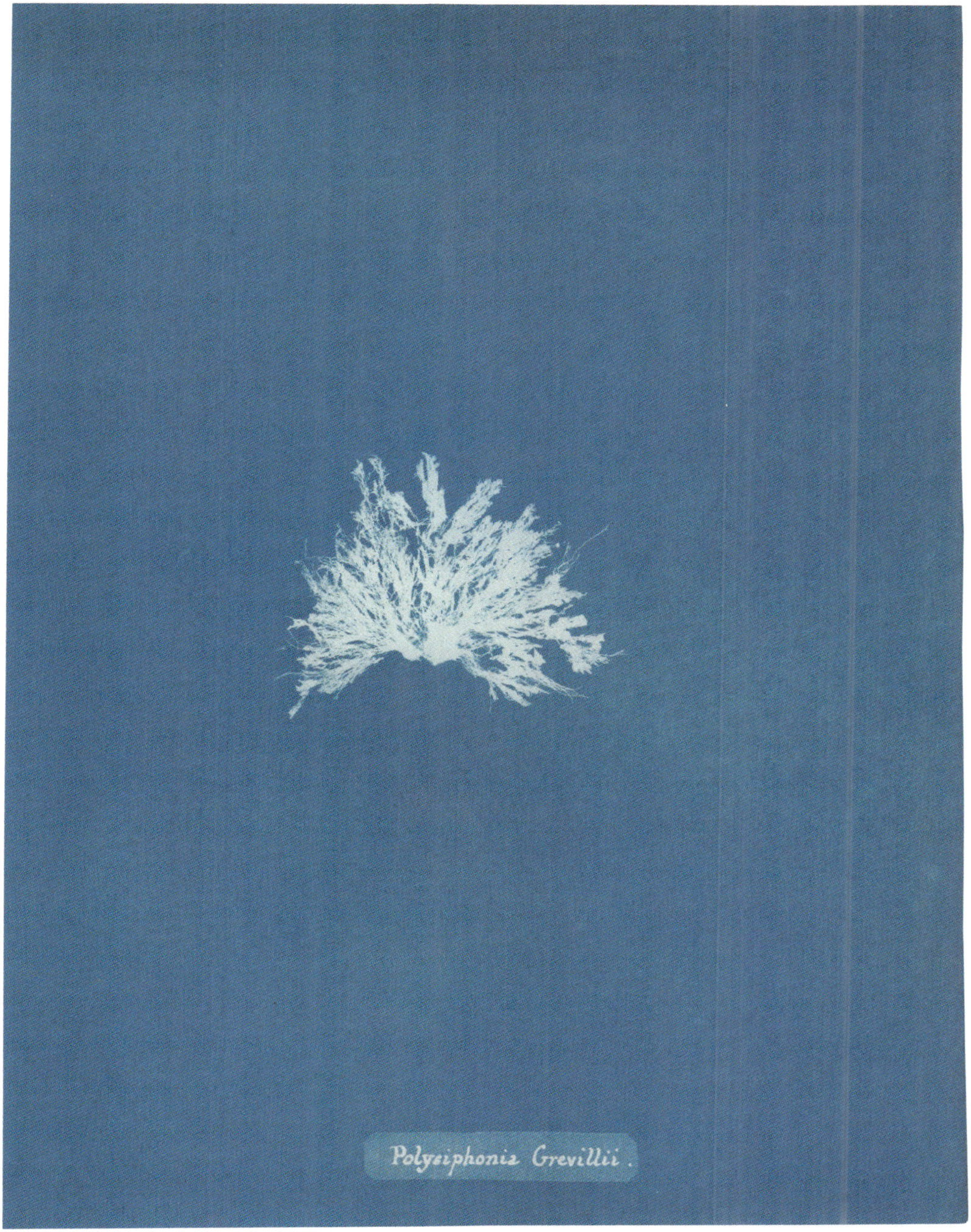

Plate 224. *Polysiphonia grevillii*

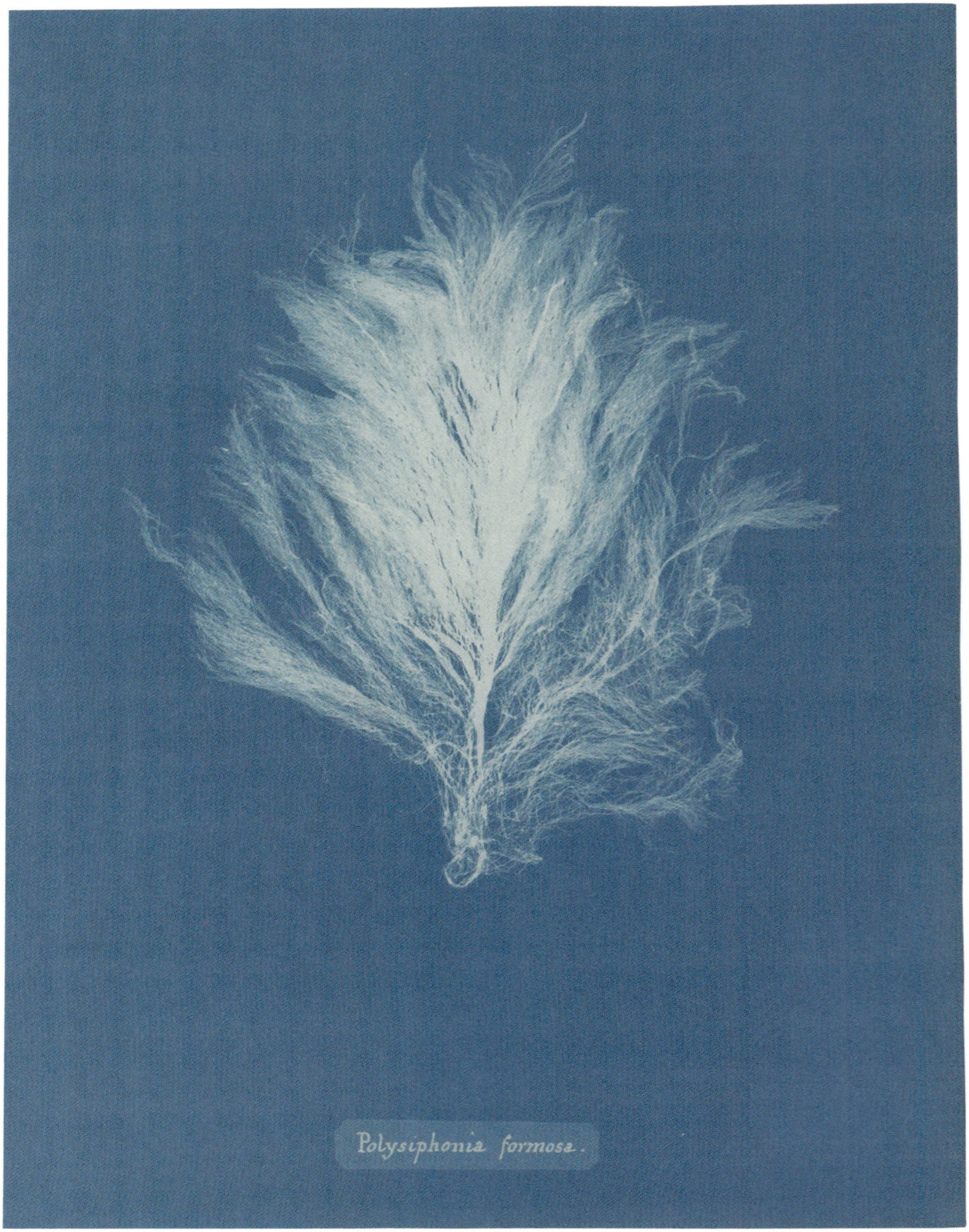

Plate 227. *Polysiphonia formosa*

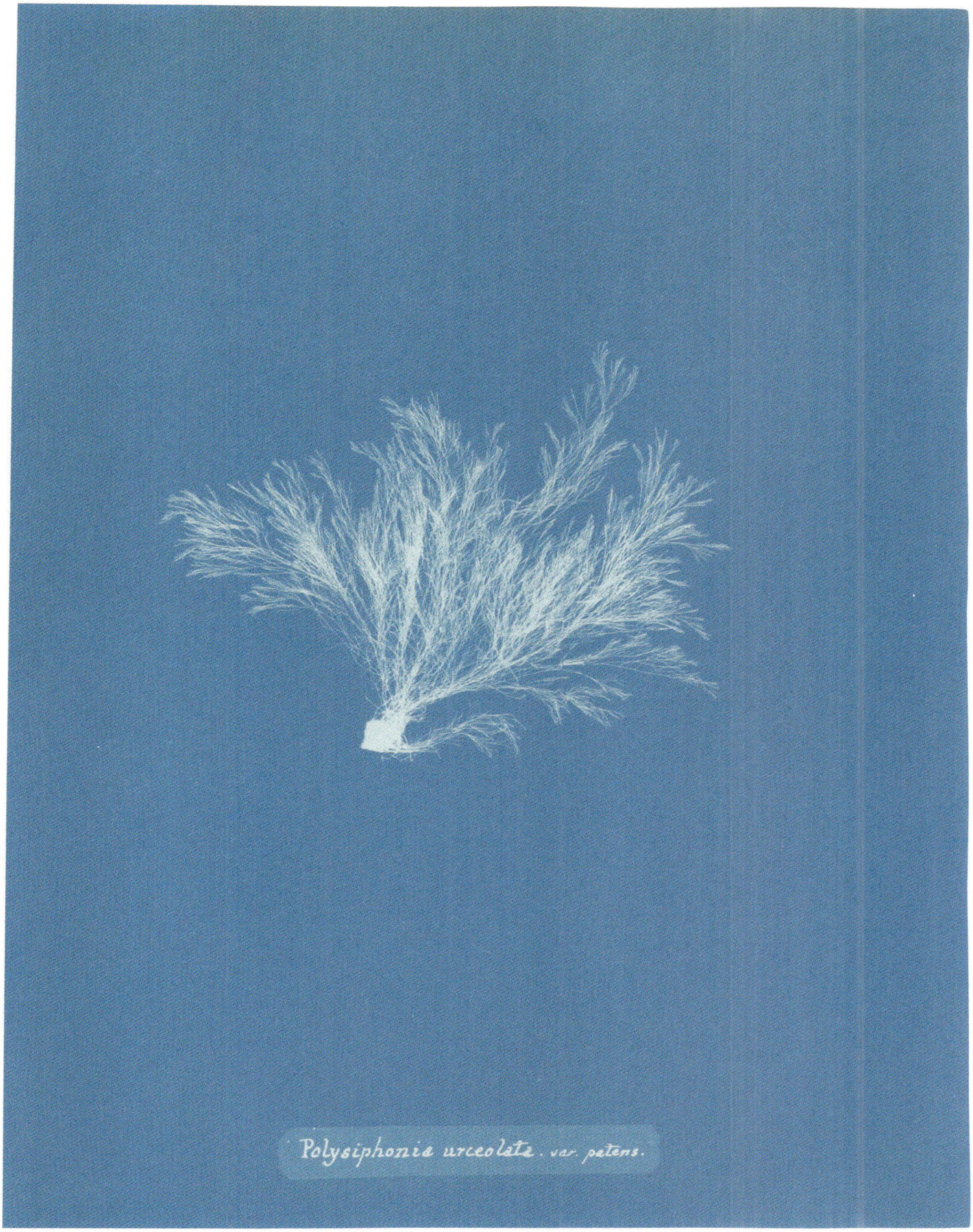

Plate 228. *Polysiphonia urceolata.* var. *patens*

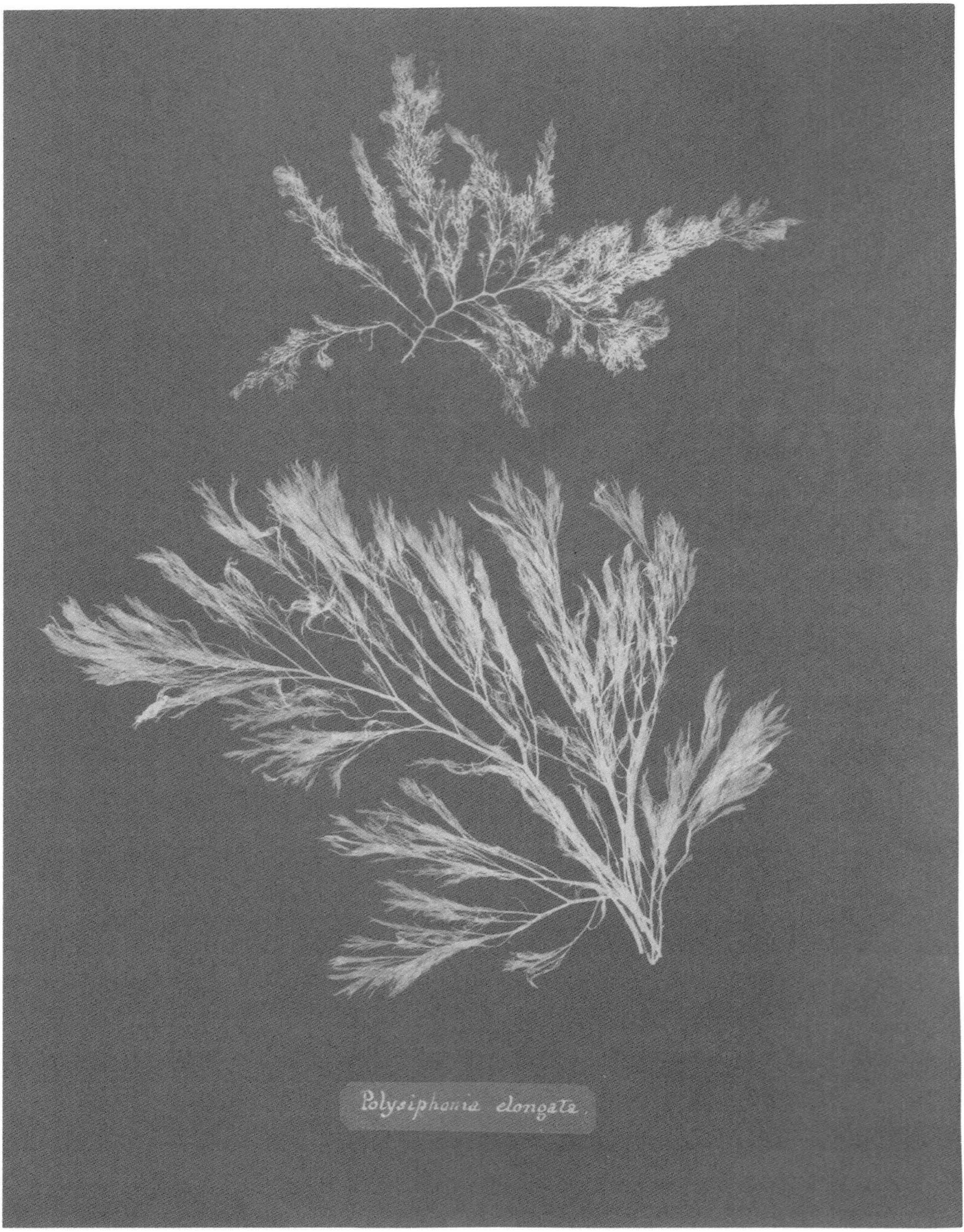

Plate 229. *Polysiphonia elongata*

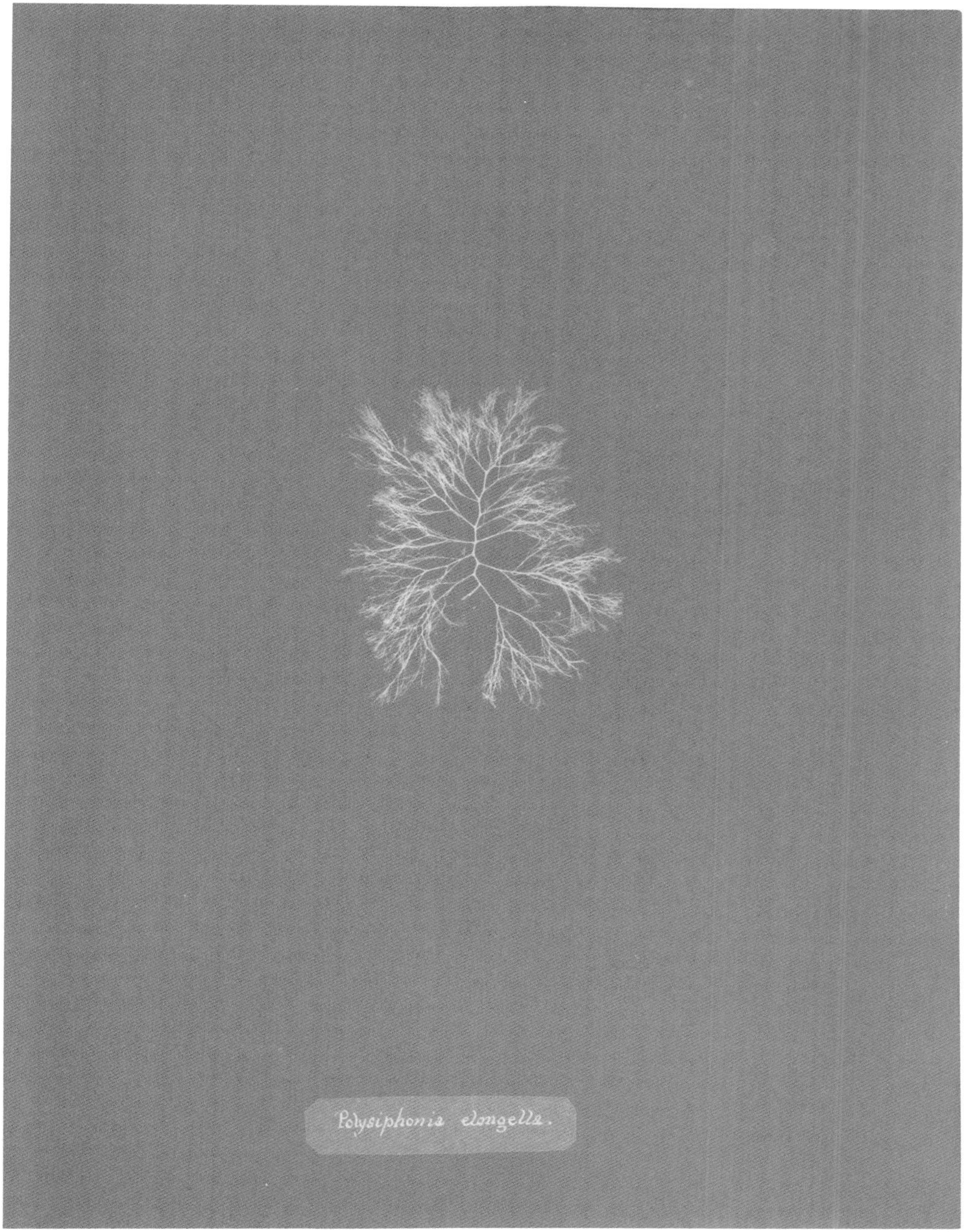

Plate 230. *Polysiphonia elongella*

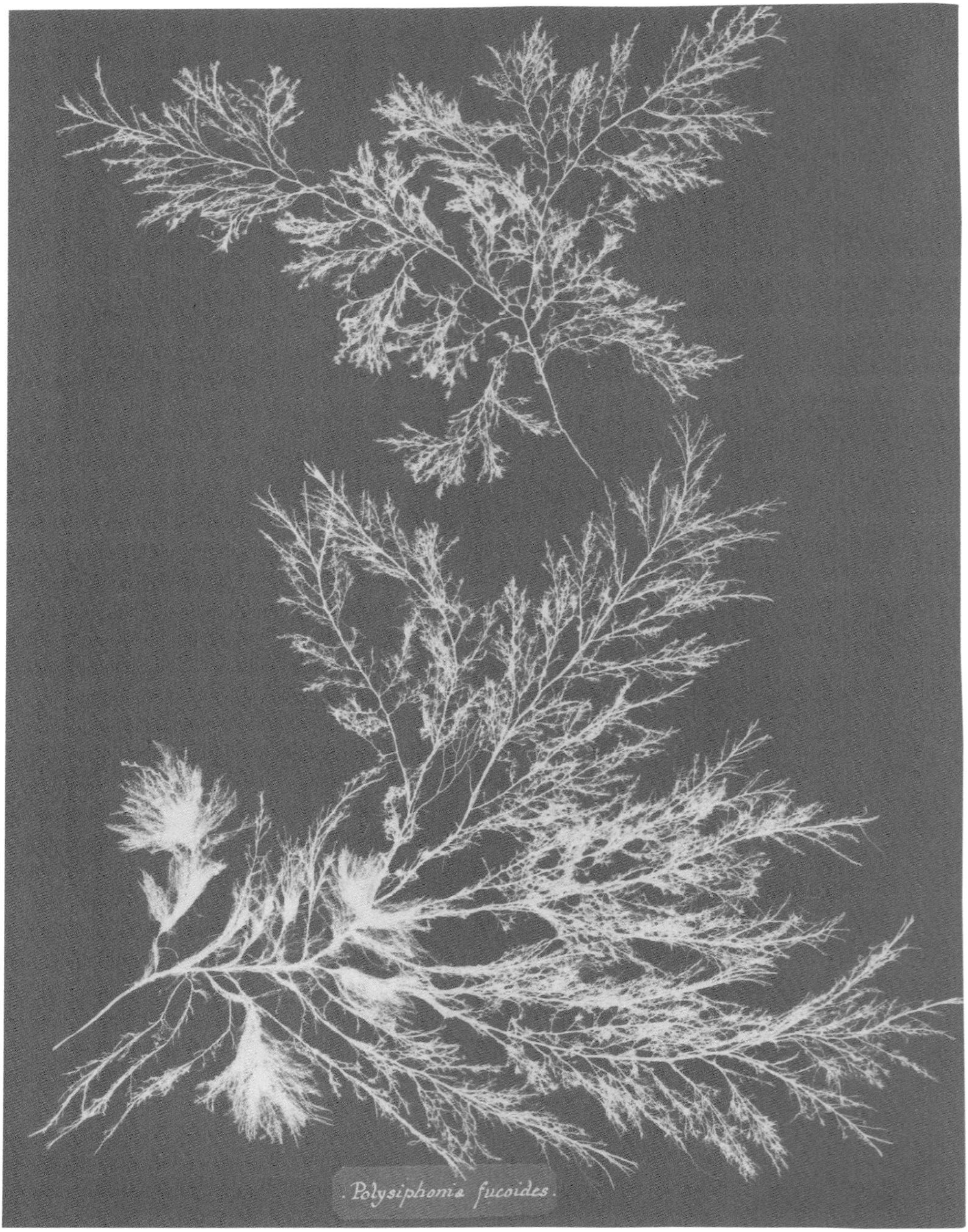

Plate 231. *Polysiphonia fucoides*

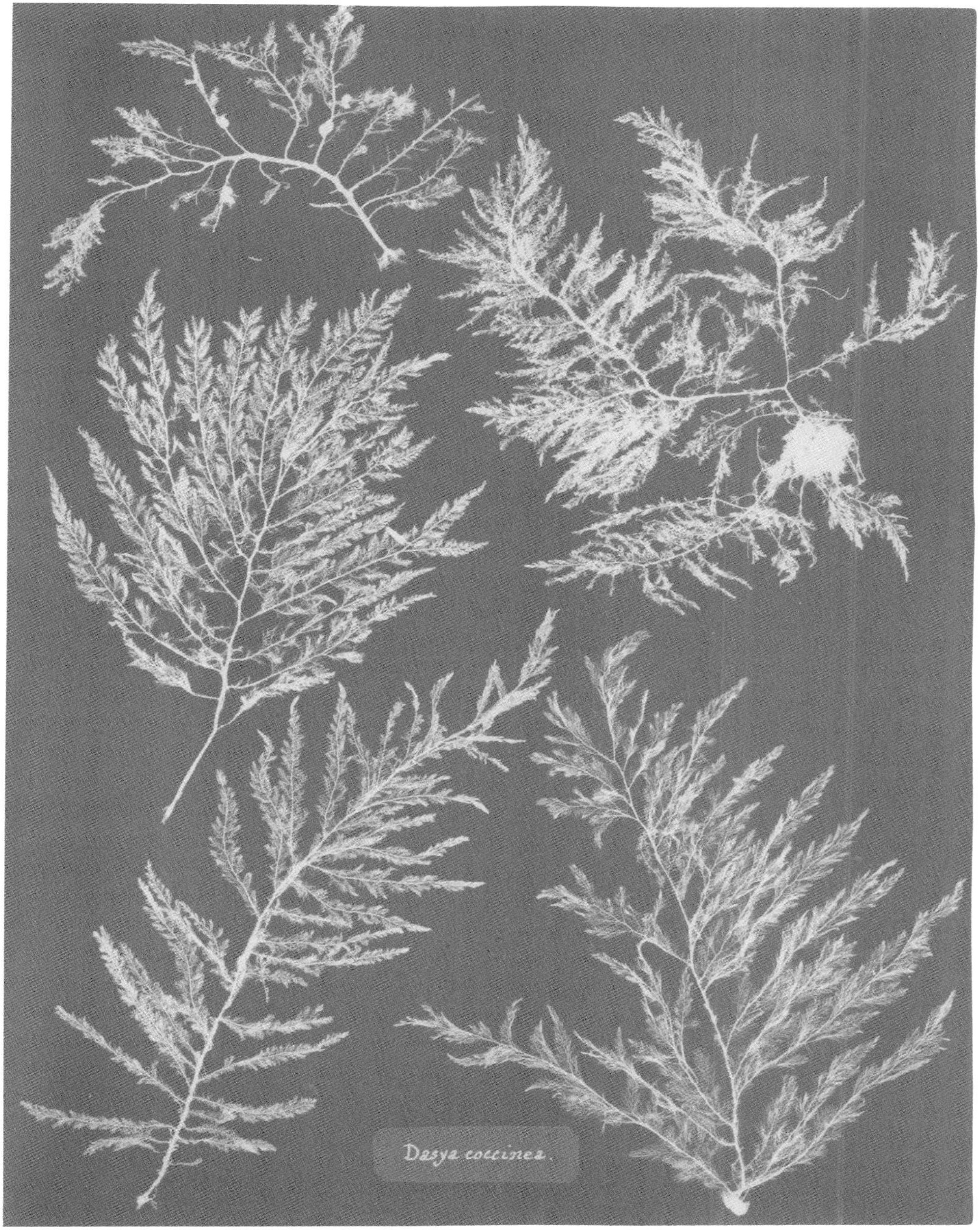

Plate 234. *Dasya coccinea*

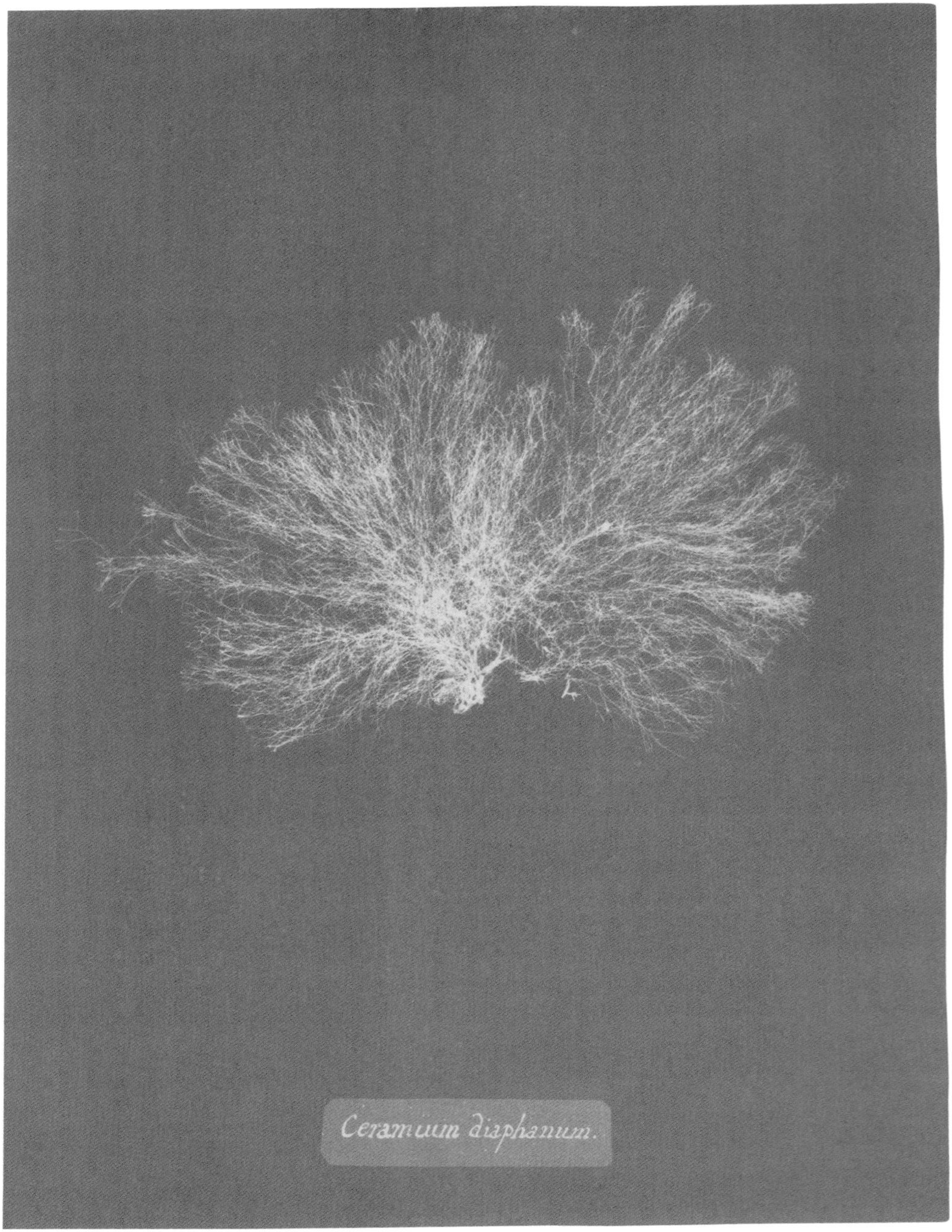

Plate 237. *Ceramium diaphanum*

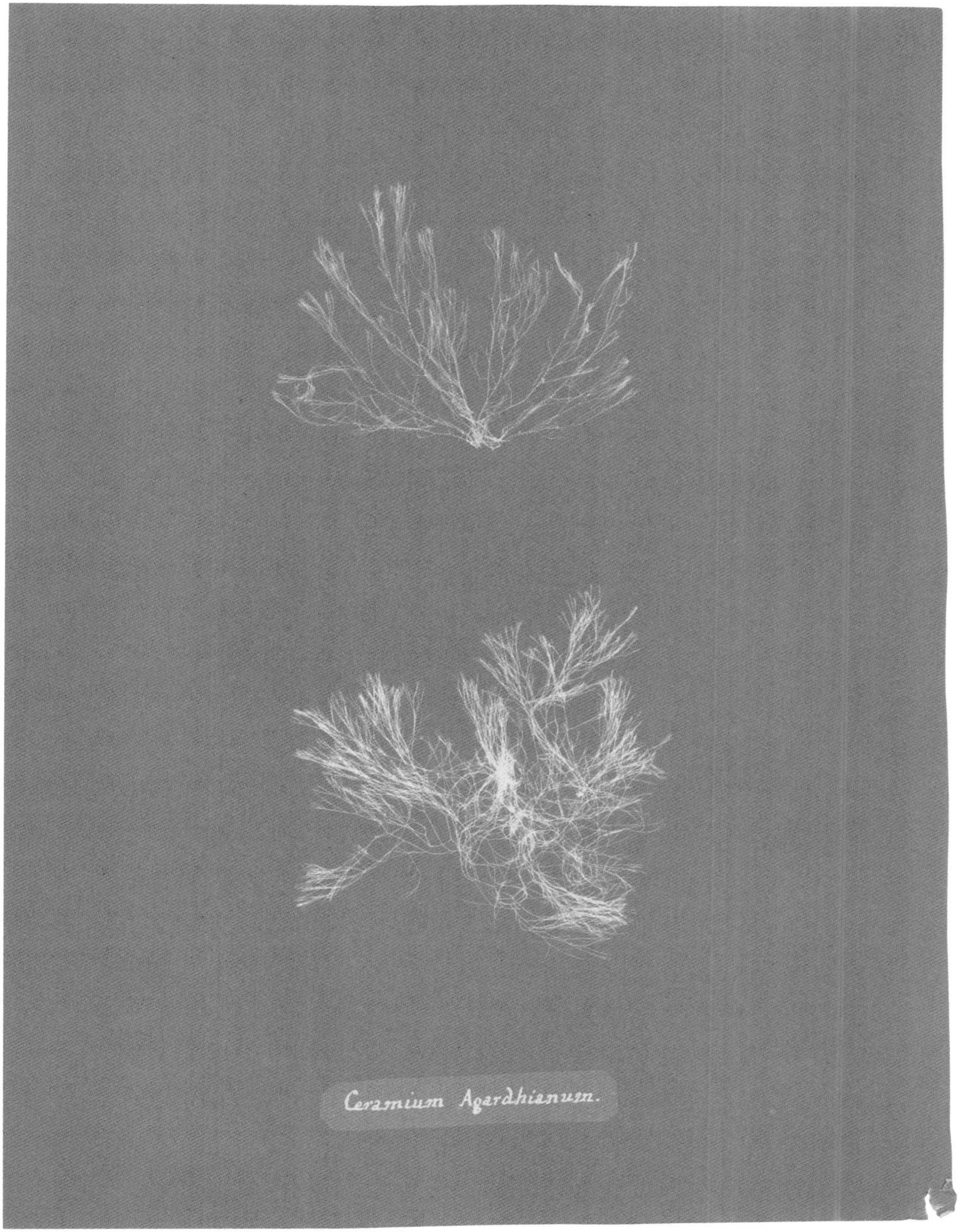

Plate 239. *Ceramium agardhiarum*

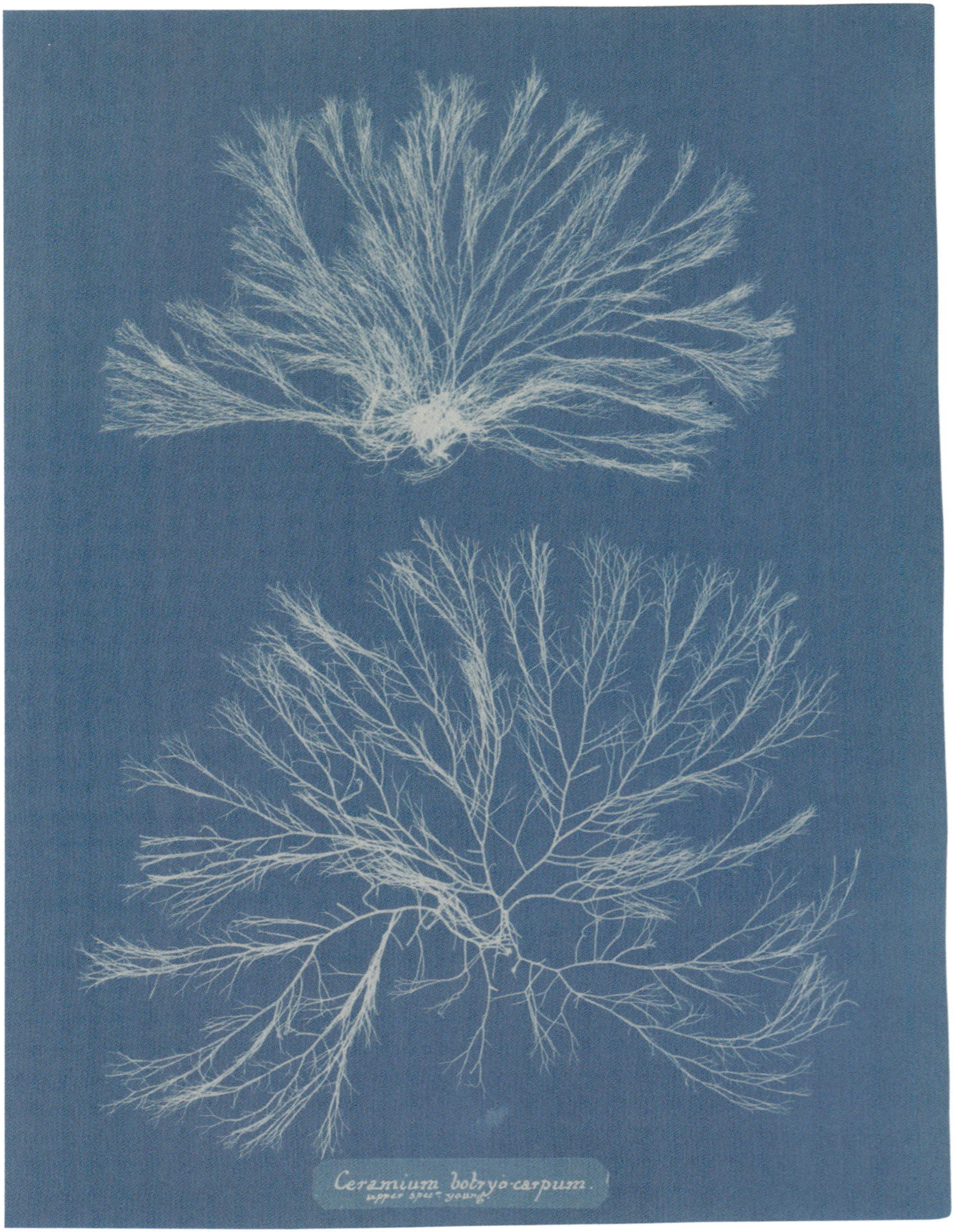

Plate 241. *Ceramium botryocarpum*, upper spec[ime]n young

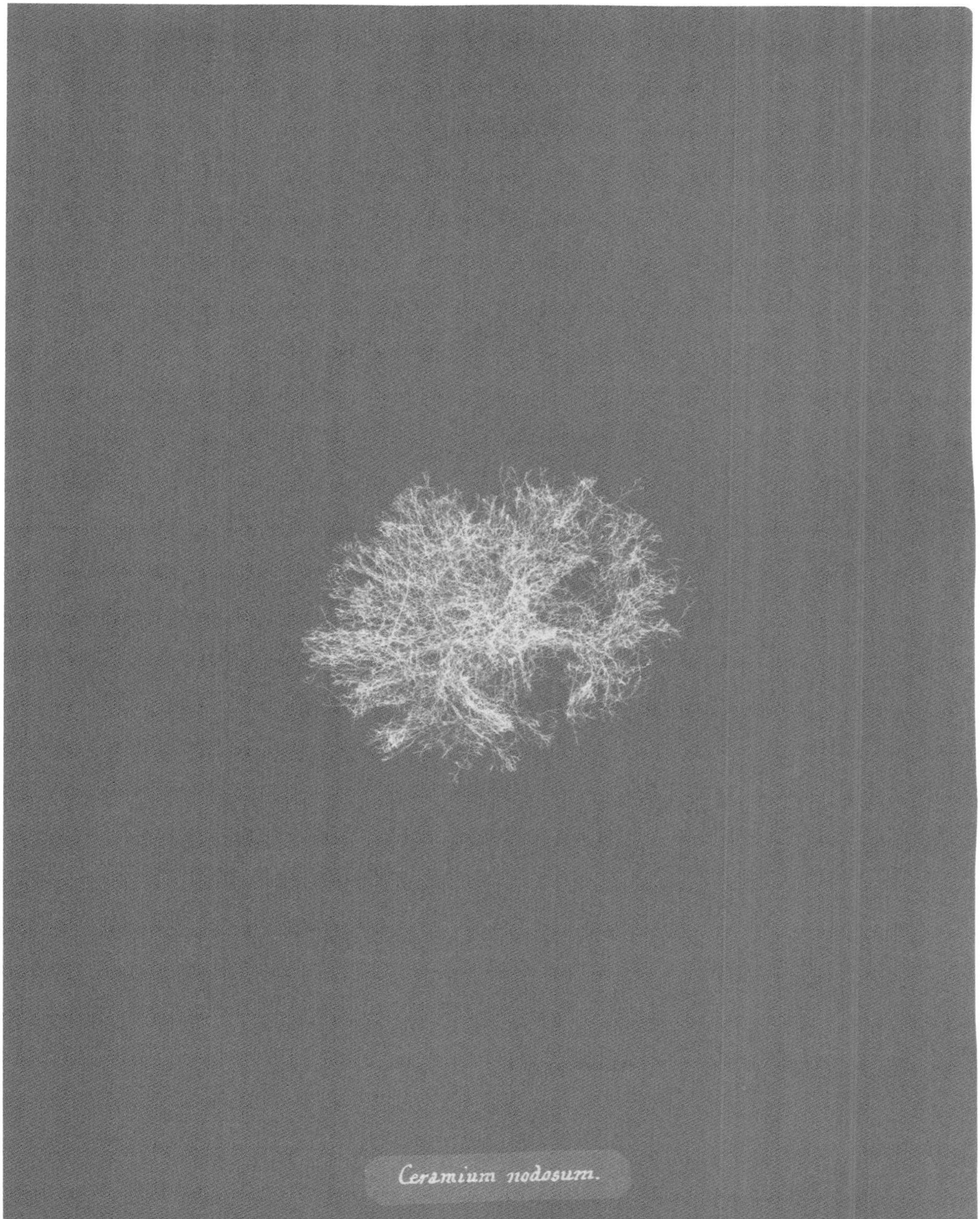

Plate 242. *Ceramium nodosum*

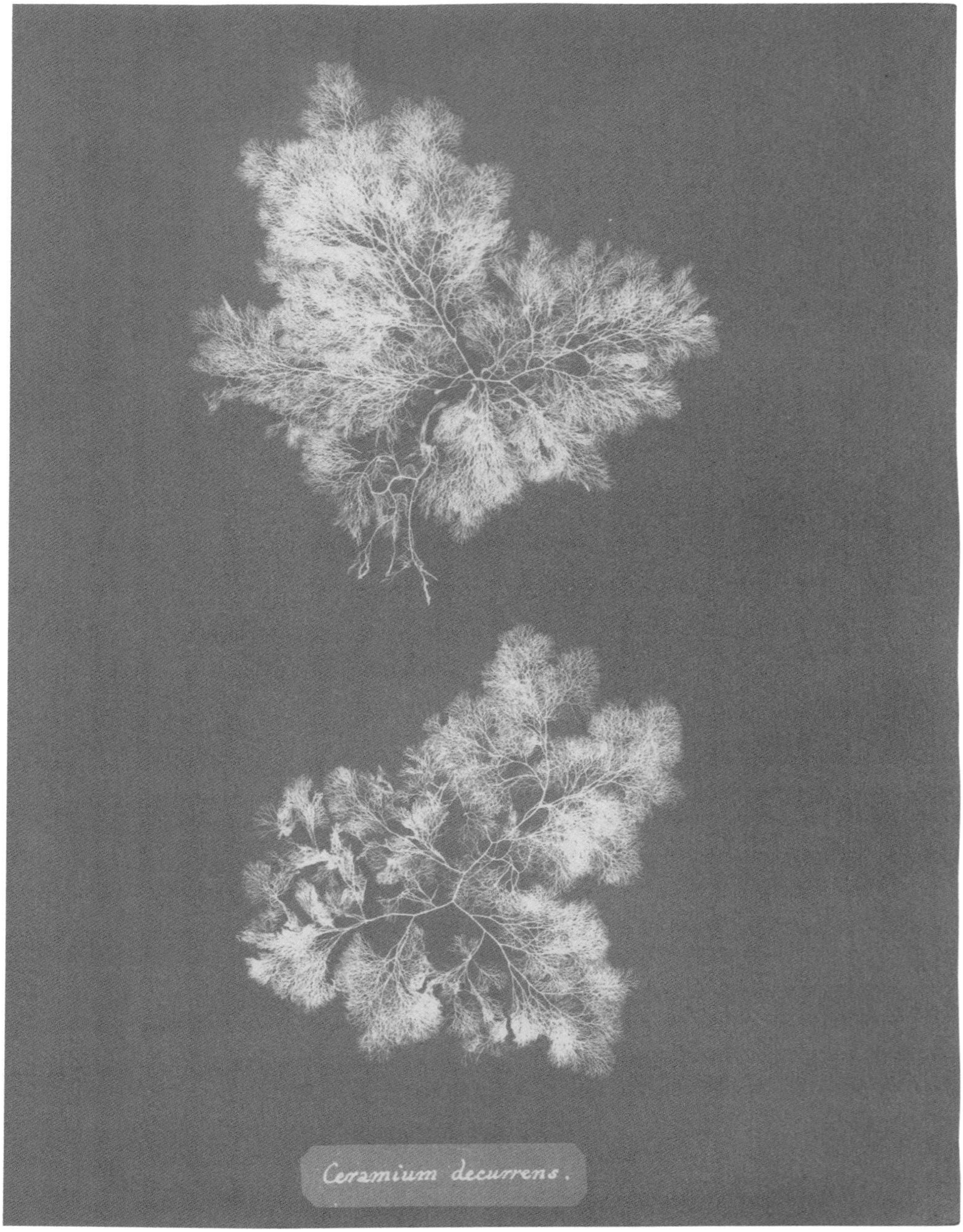

Plate 245. *Ceramium decurrens*

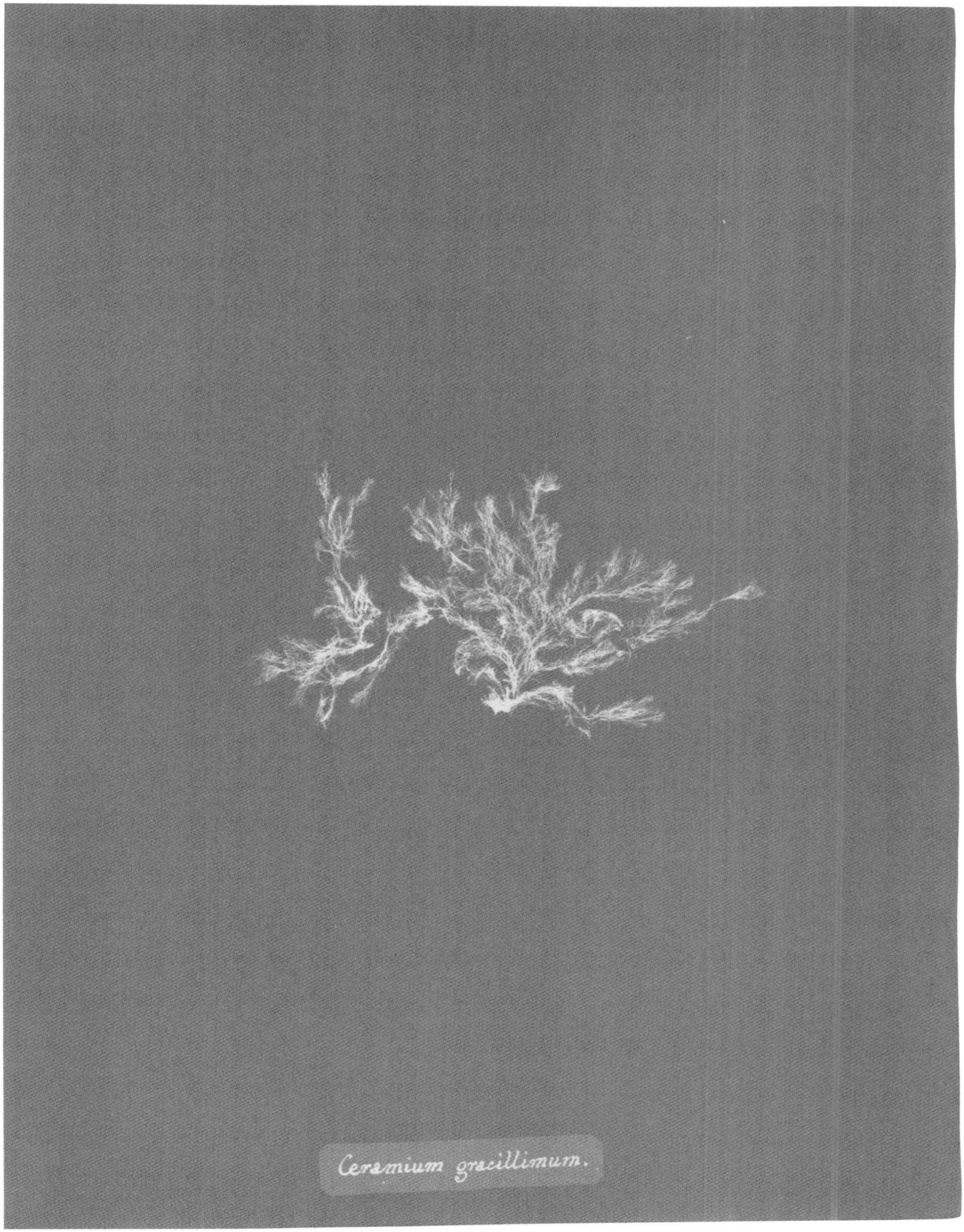

Plate 246. *Ceramium gracillimum*

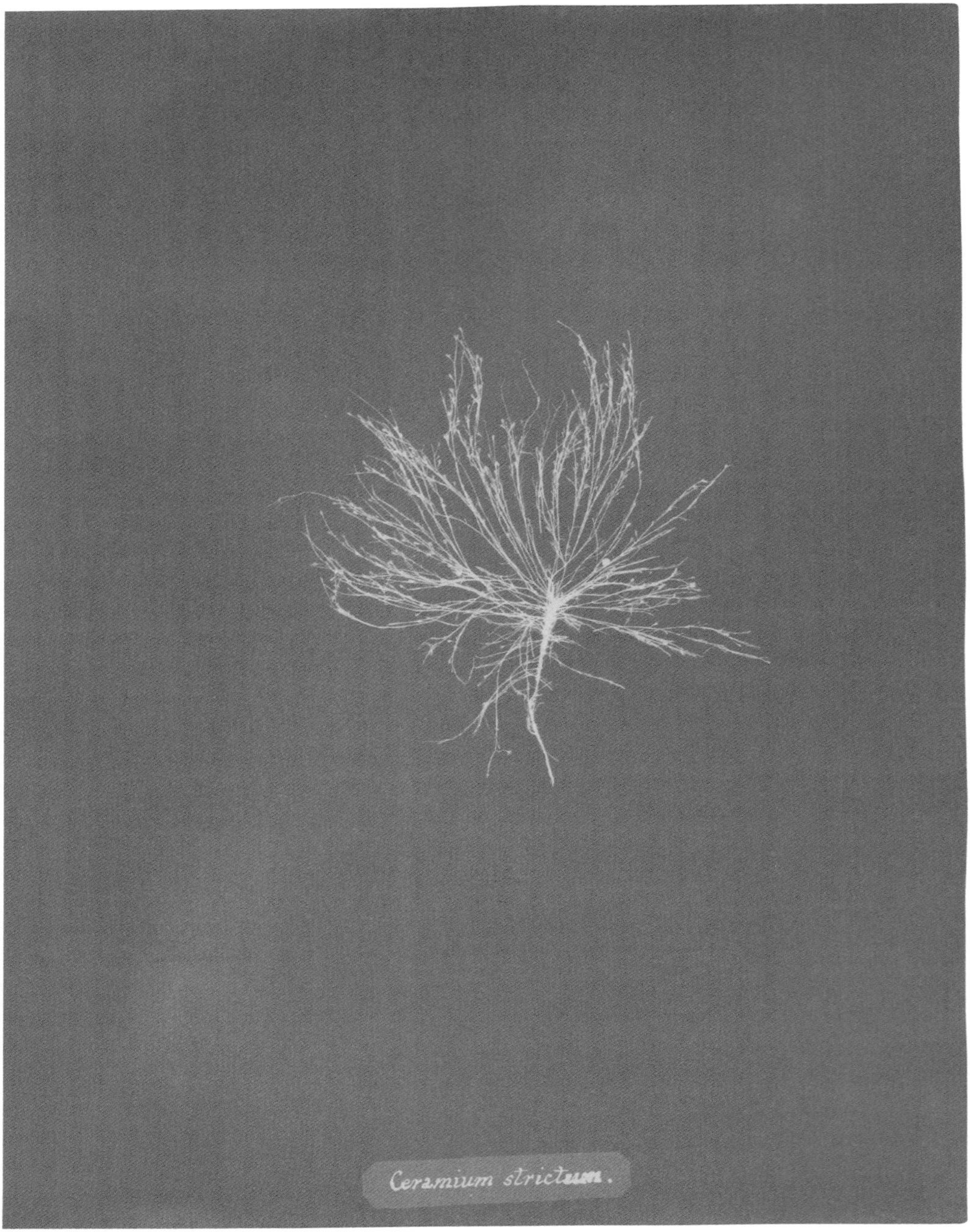

Plate 247. *Ceramium strictum*

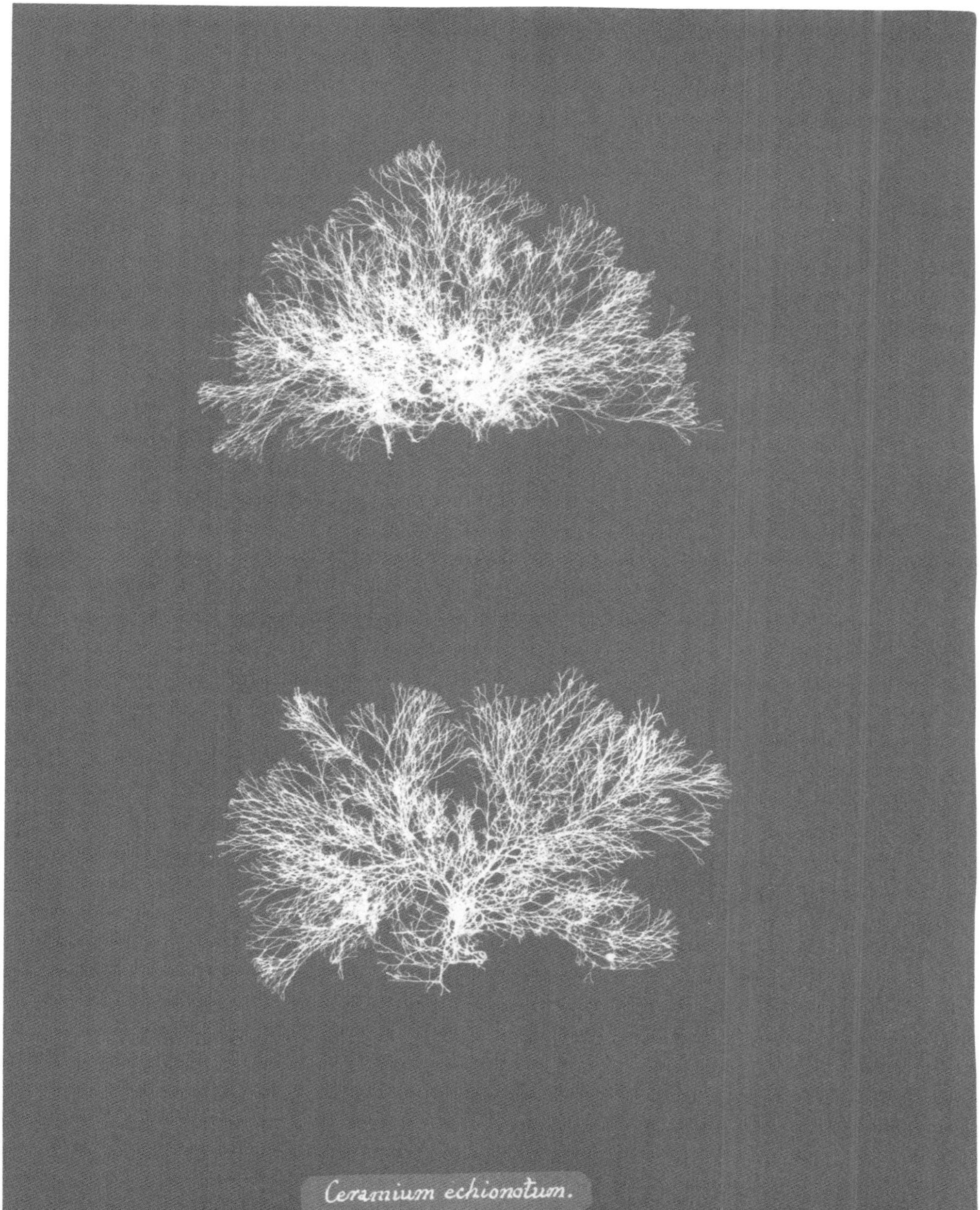

Plate 248. *Ceramium echionotum*

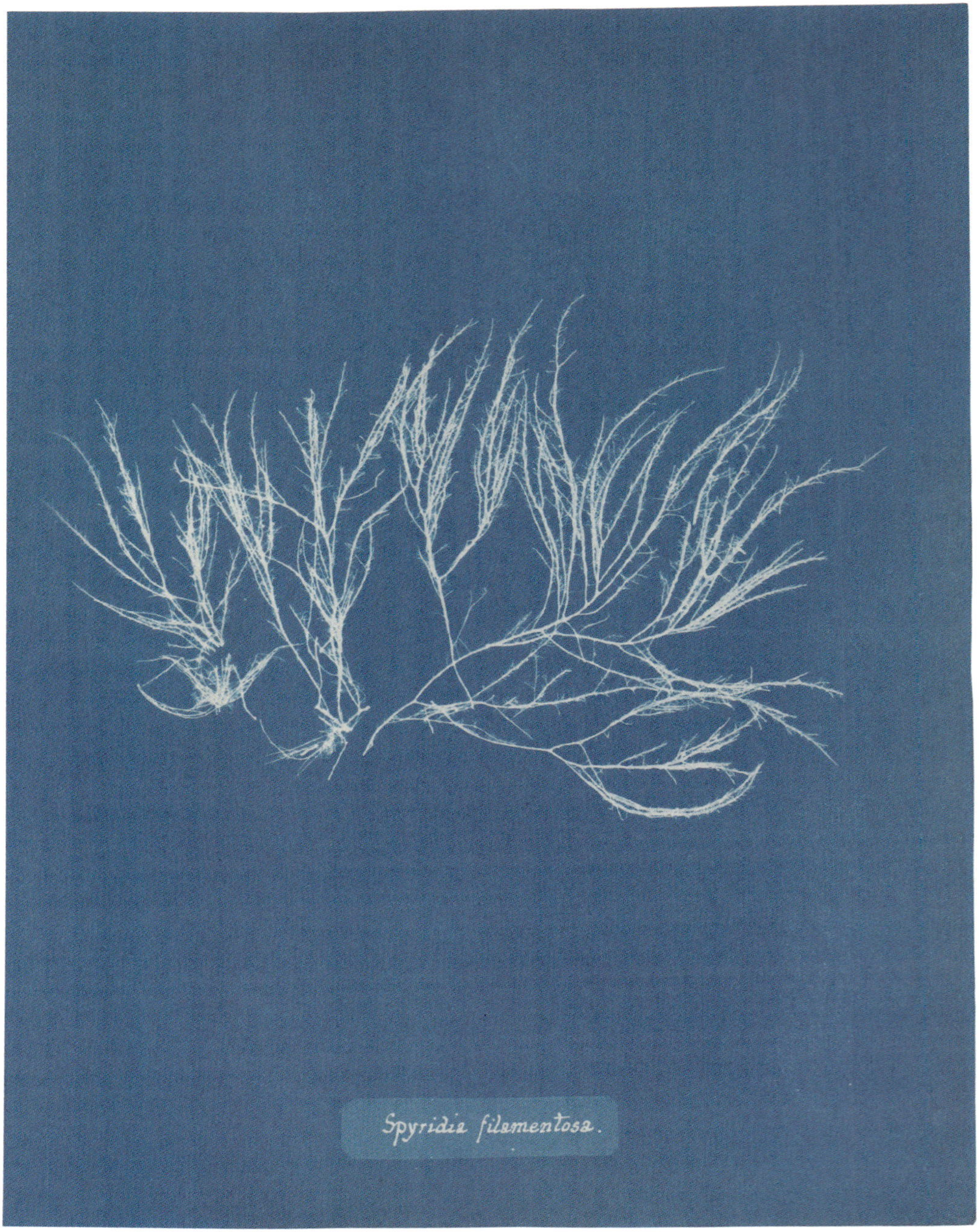

Plate 249. *Spyridia filamentosa*

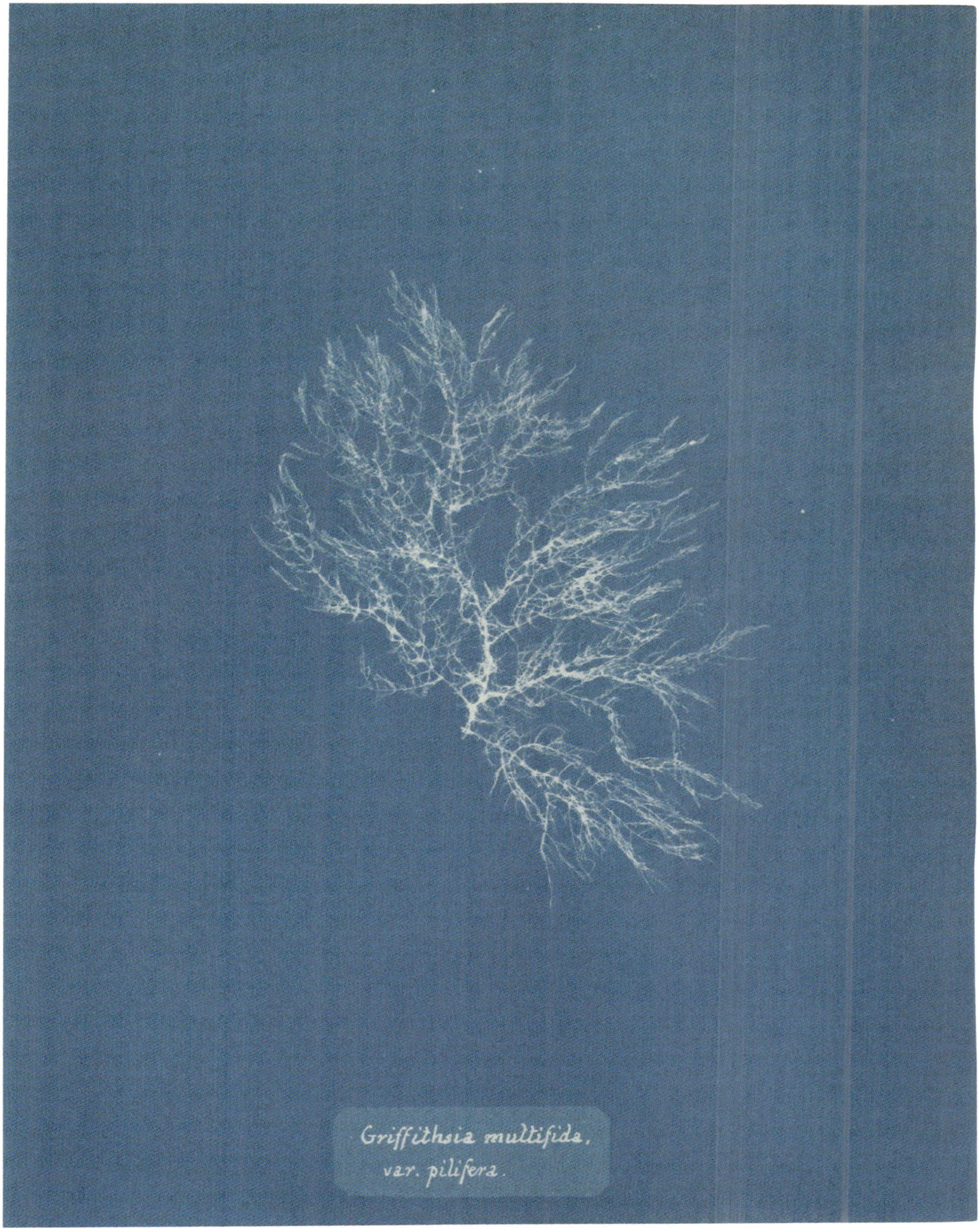

Plate 250. *Griffithsia multifida,* var. *pilifera*

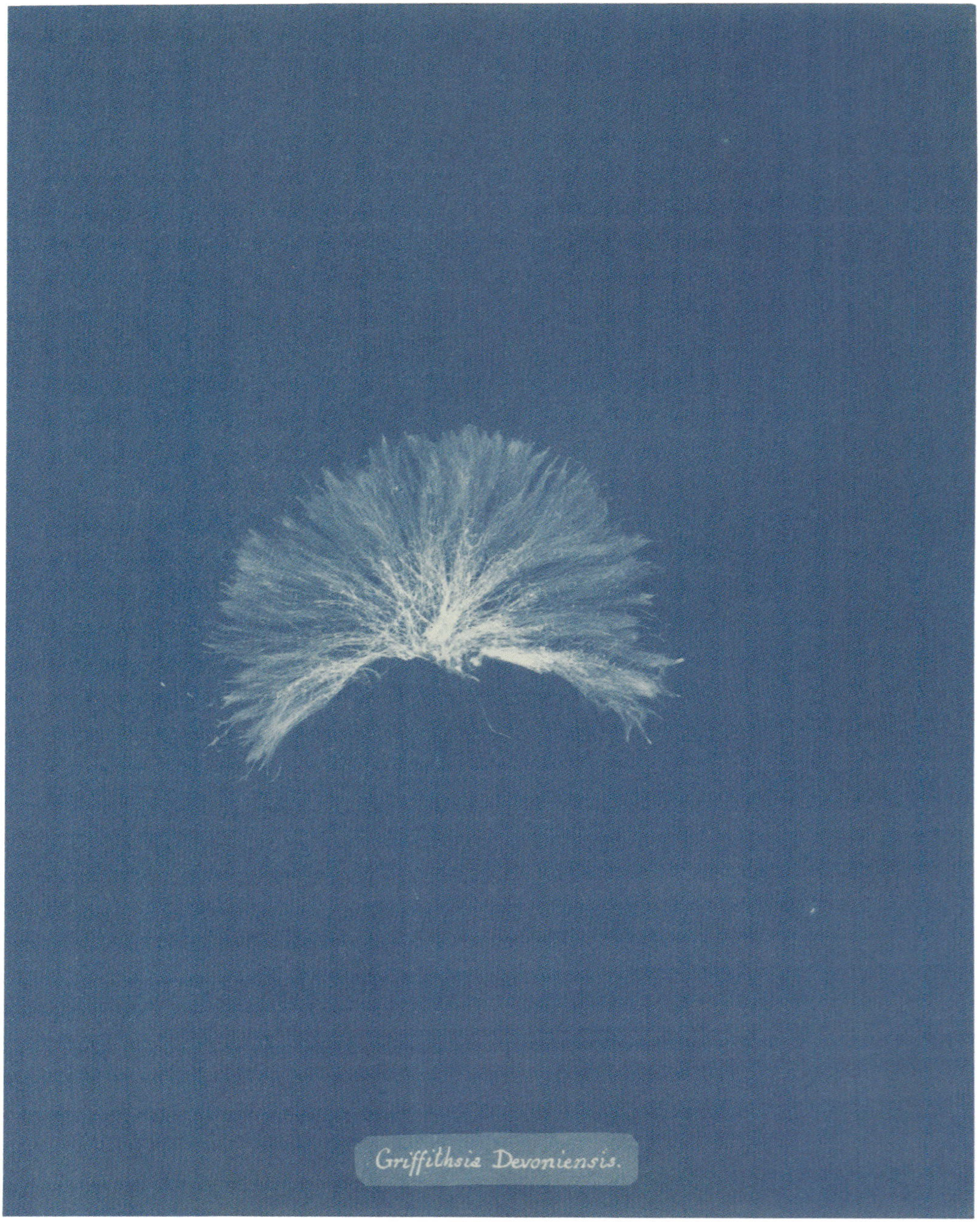

Plate 252. *Griffithsia devoniensis*

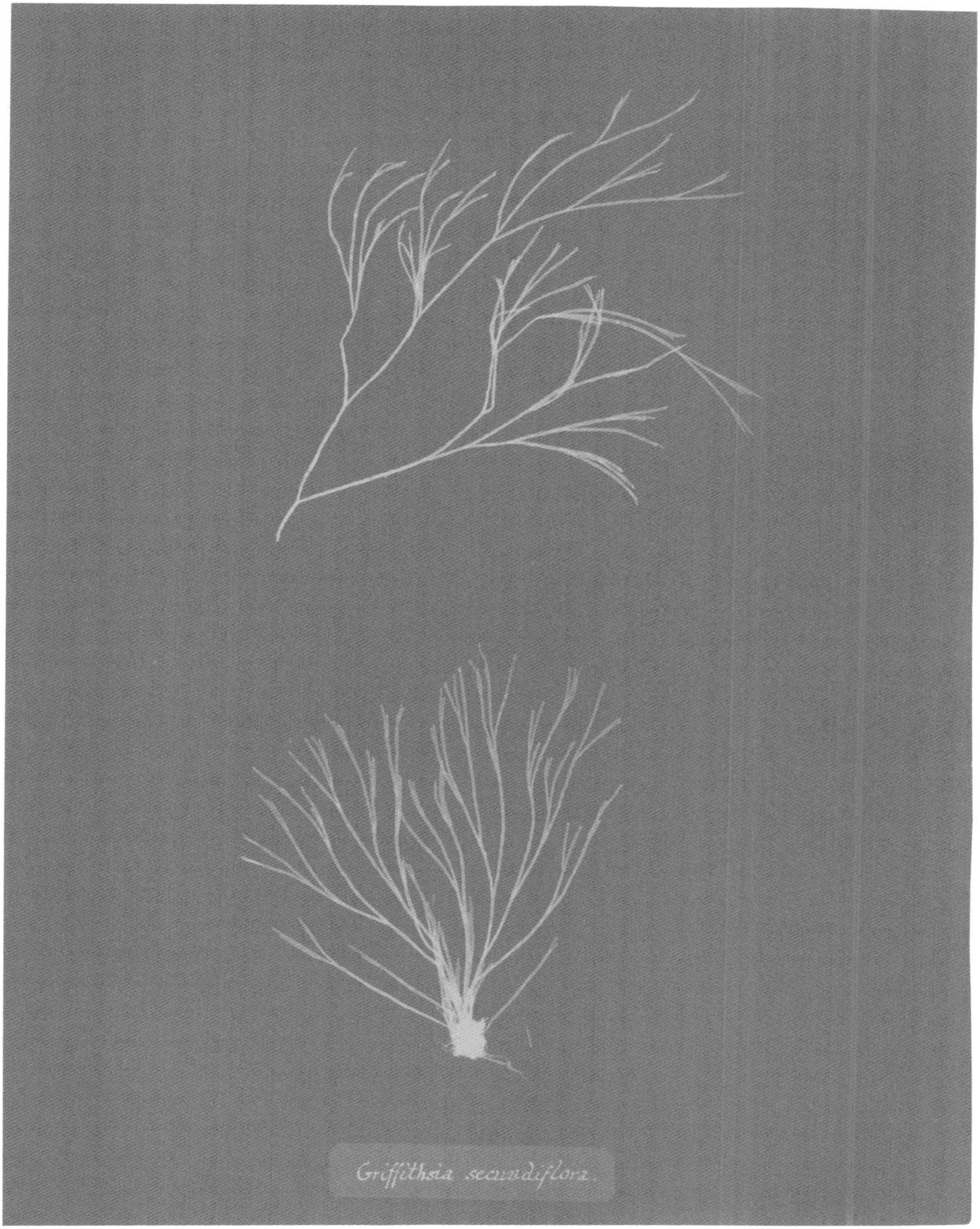

Plate 253. *Griffithsia secundiflora*

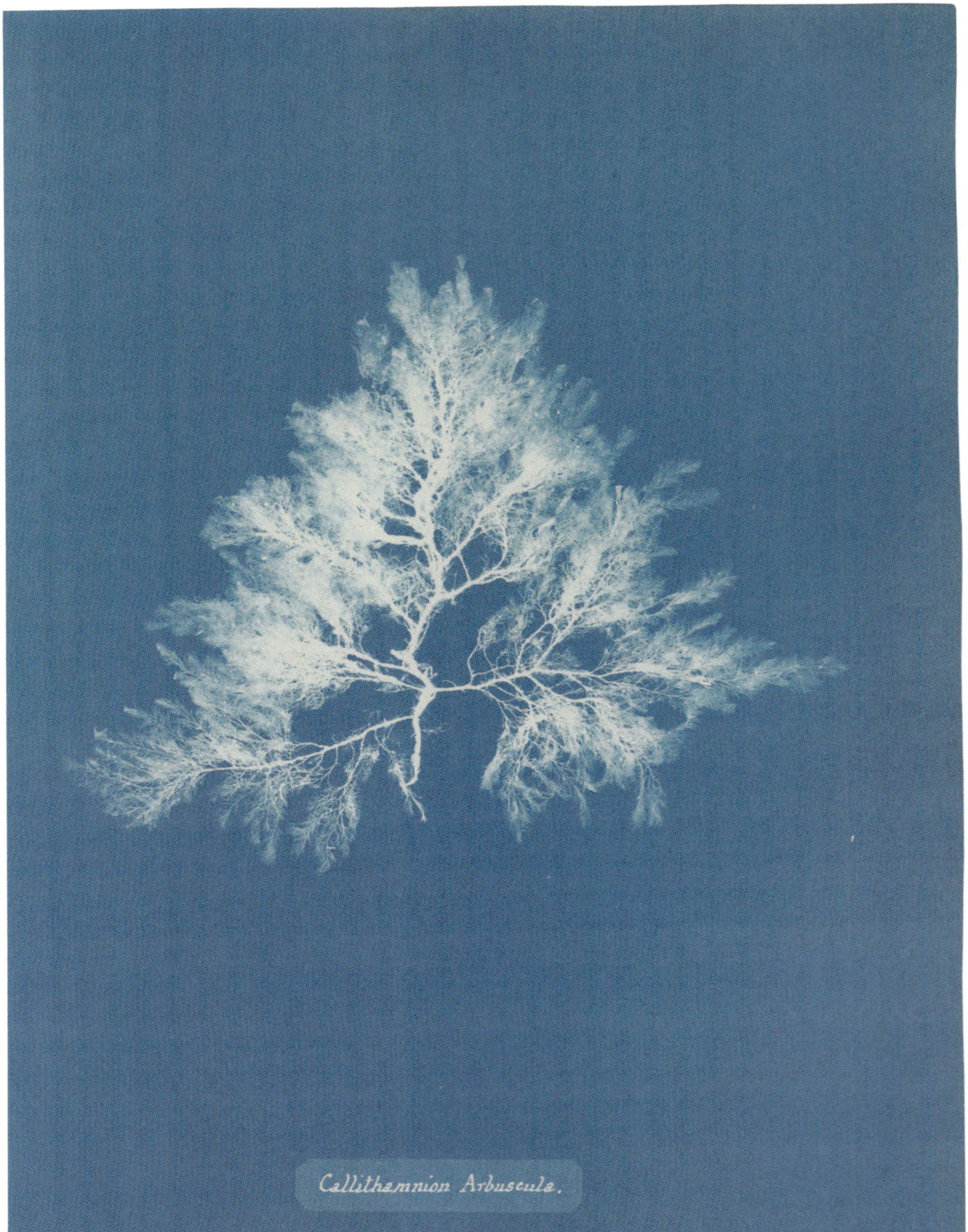

Plate 256. *Callithamnion arbuscula*

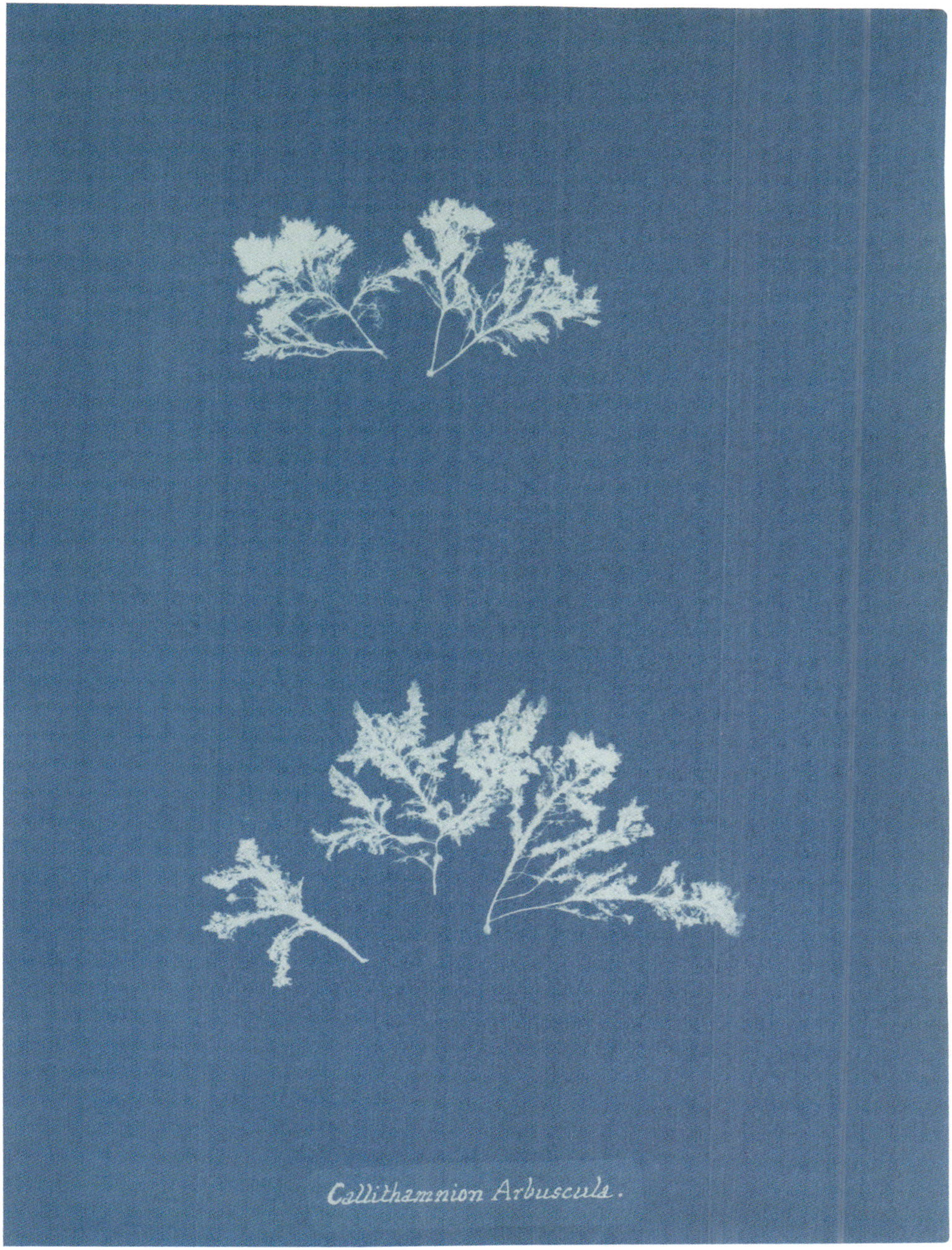

Plate 257. *Callithamnion arbuscula*

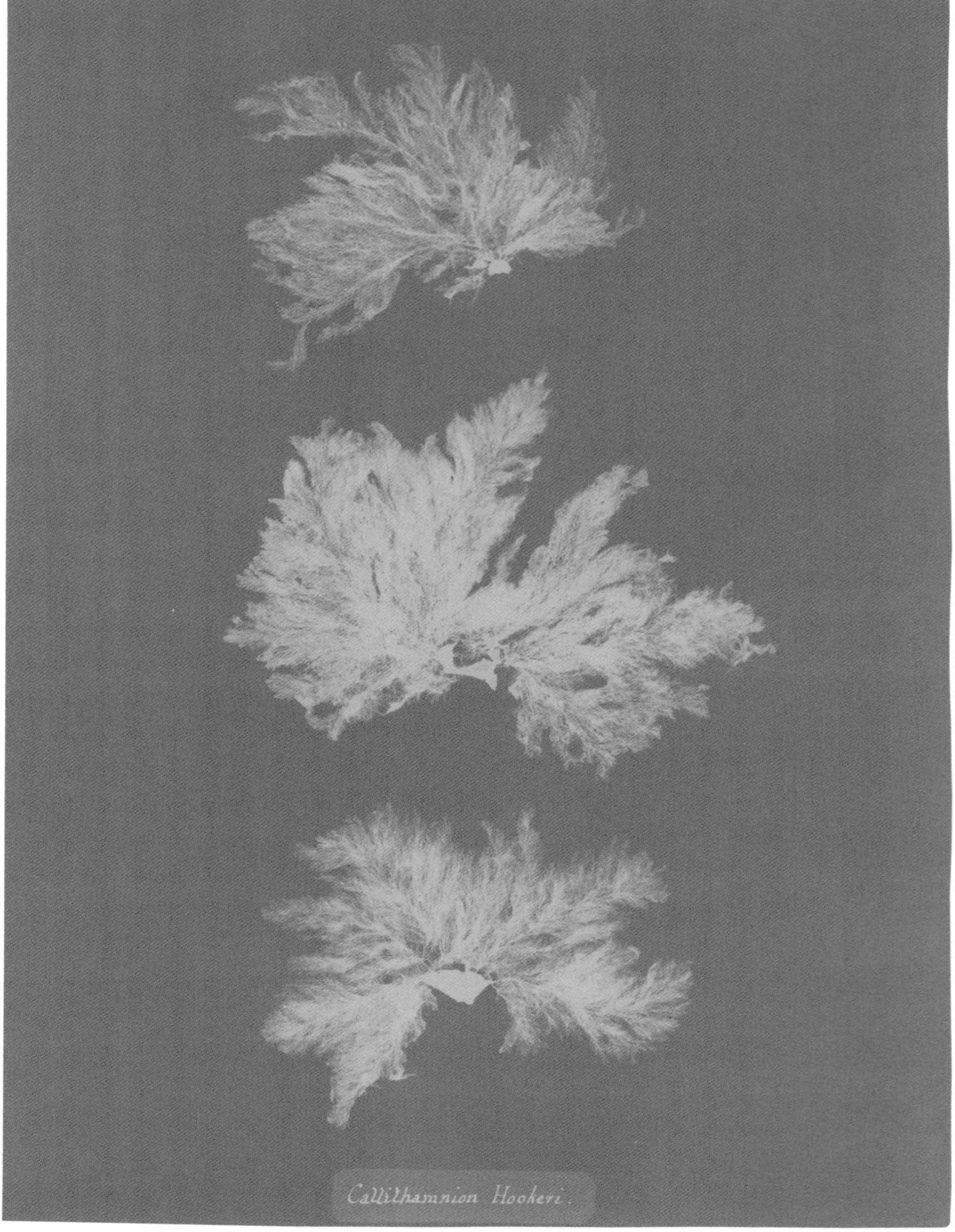

Plate 258. *Callithamnion hookeri*

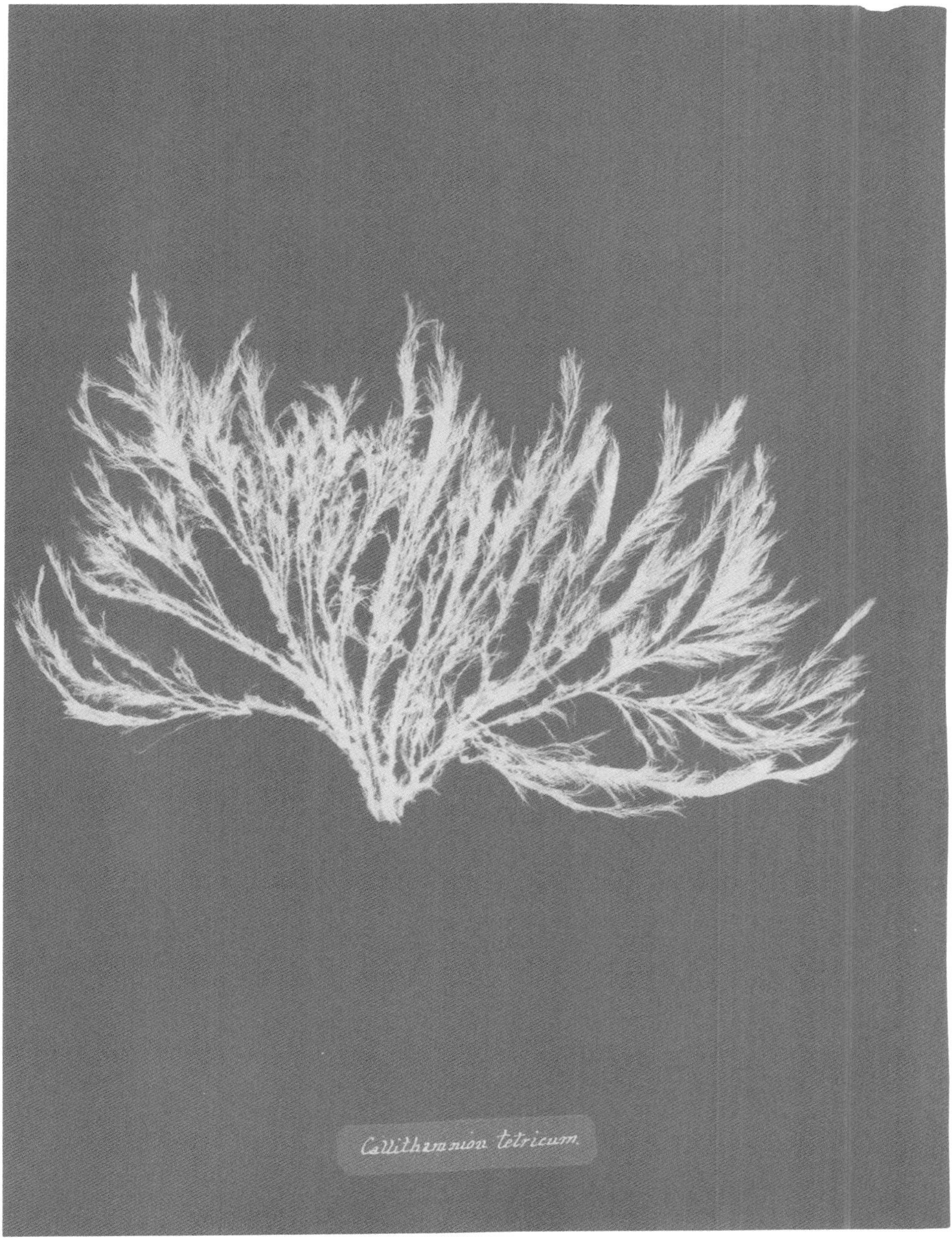

Plate 261. *Callithamnion tetricum*

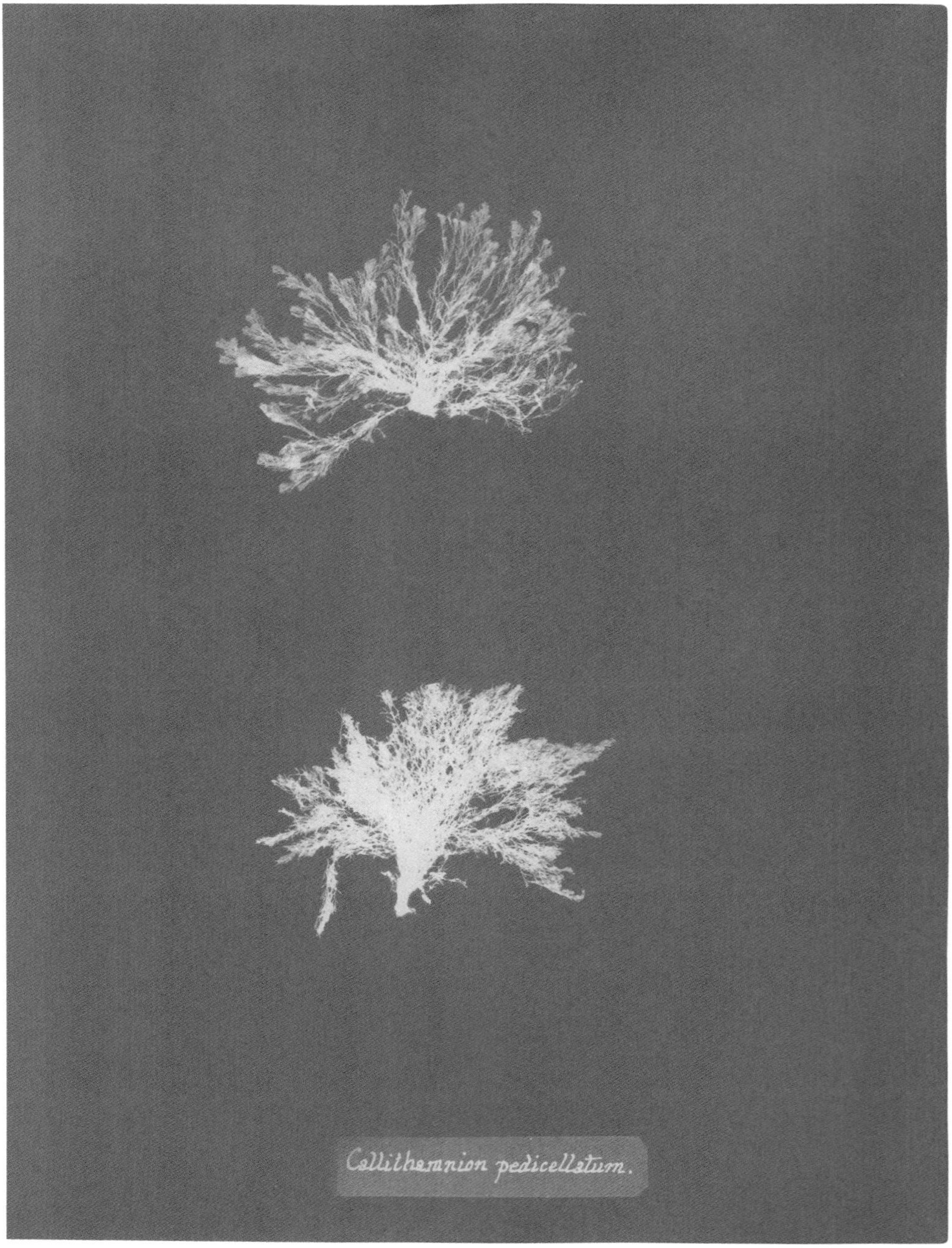

Plate 269. *Callithamnion pedicellatum*

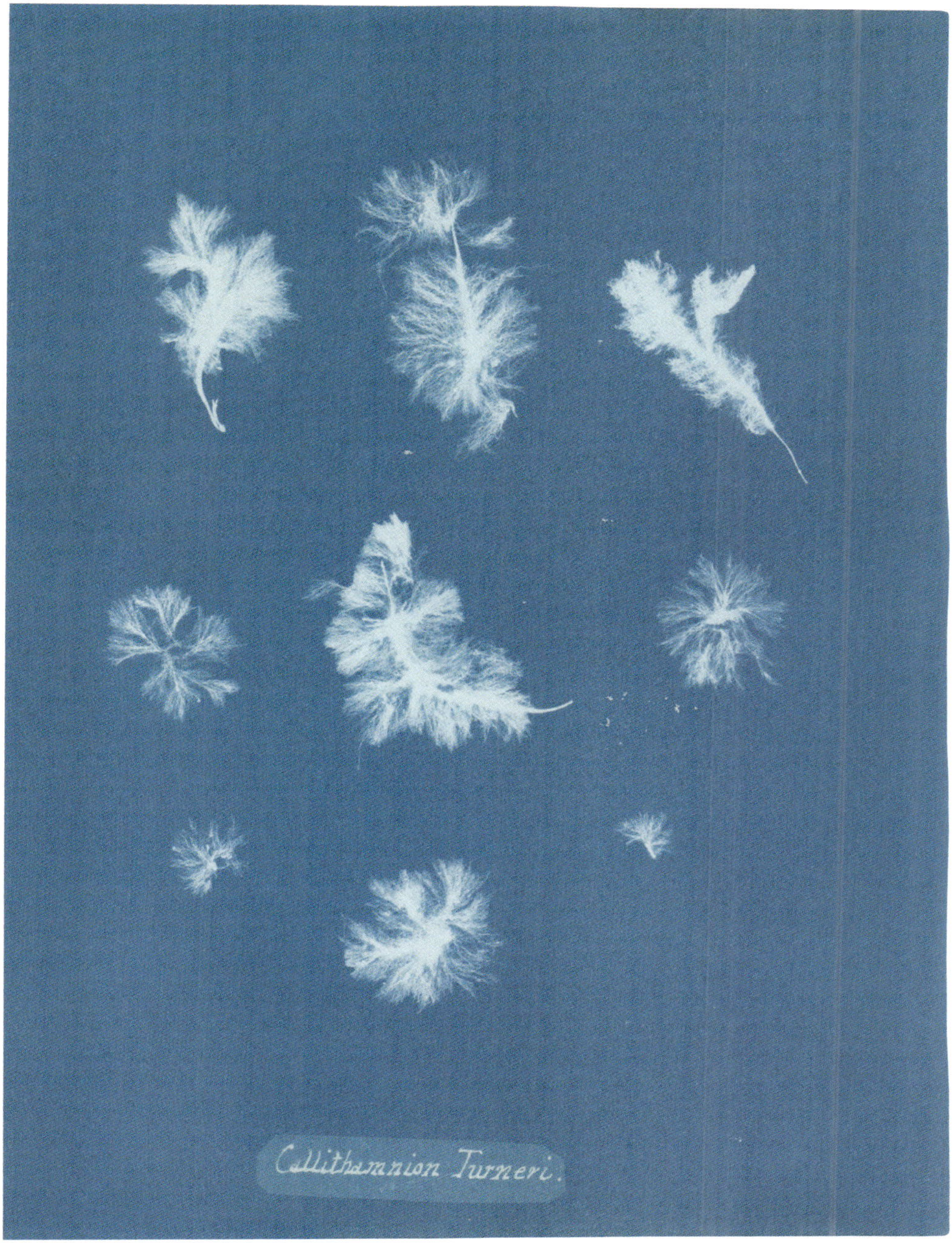

Plate 270. *Callithamnion turneri*

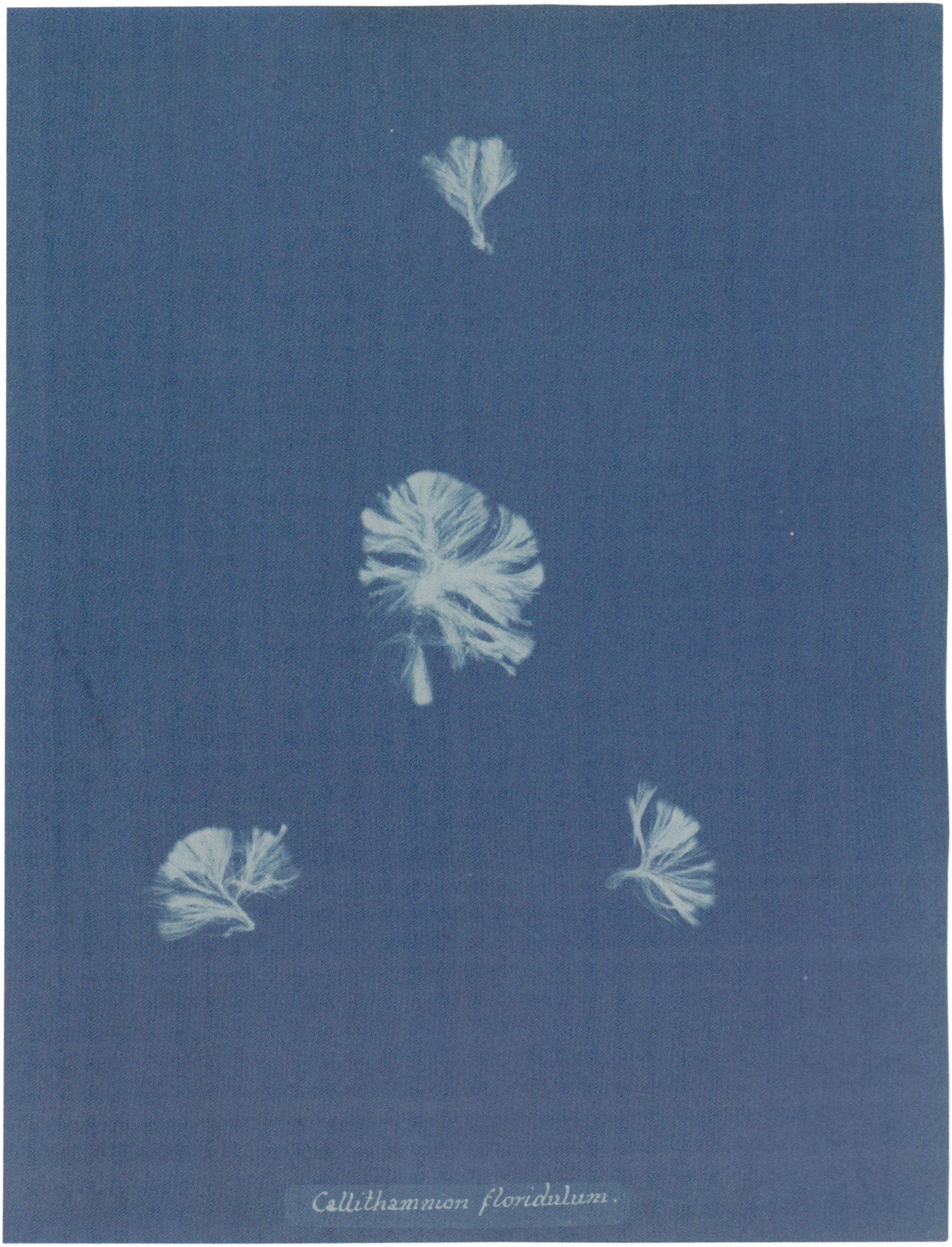

Plate 273. *Callithamnion floridulum*

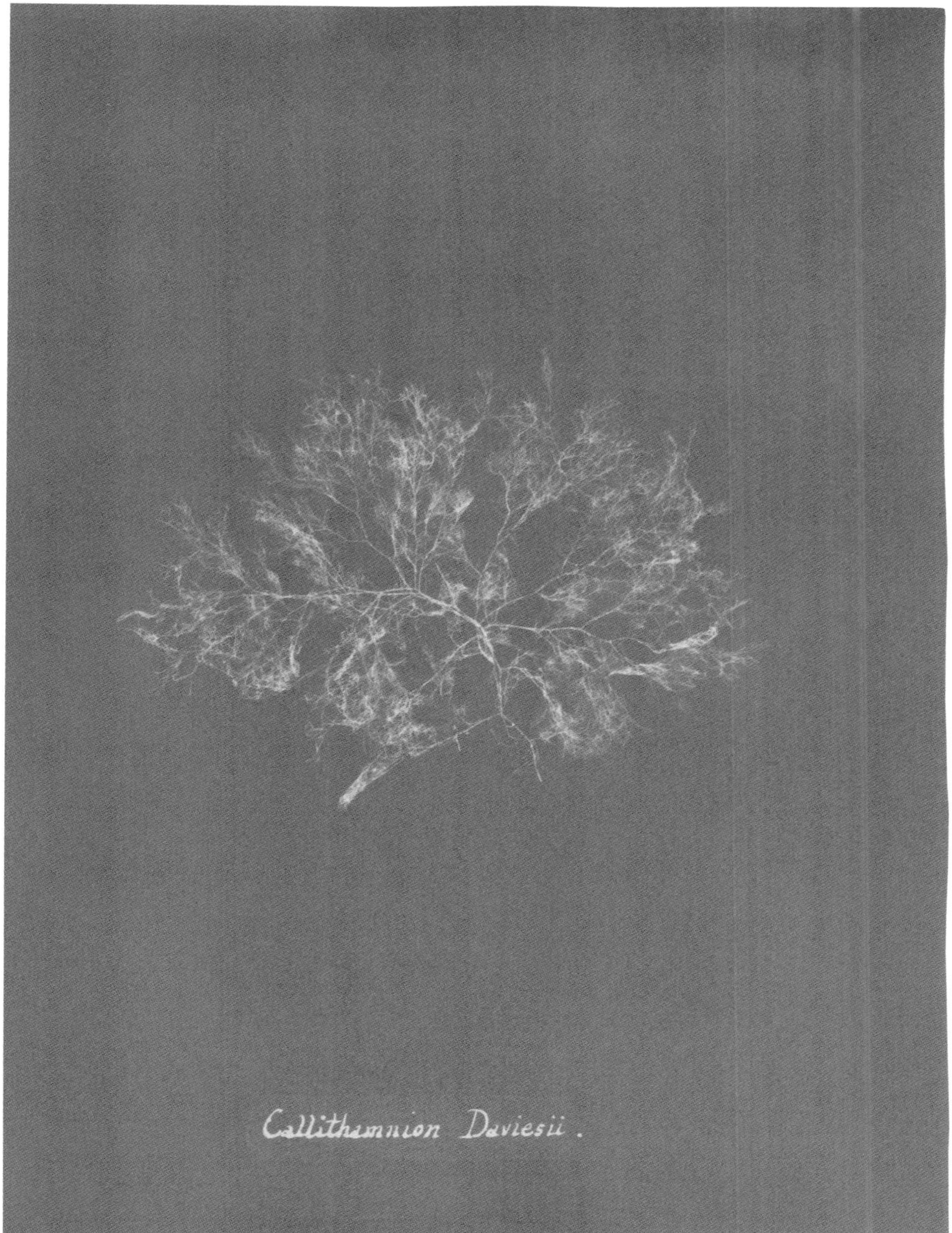

Plate 274. *Callithamnion daviesii*

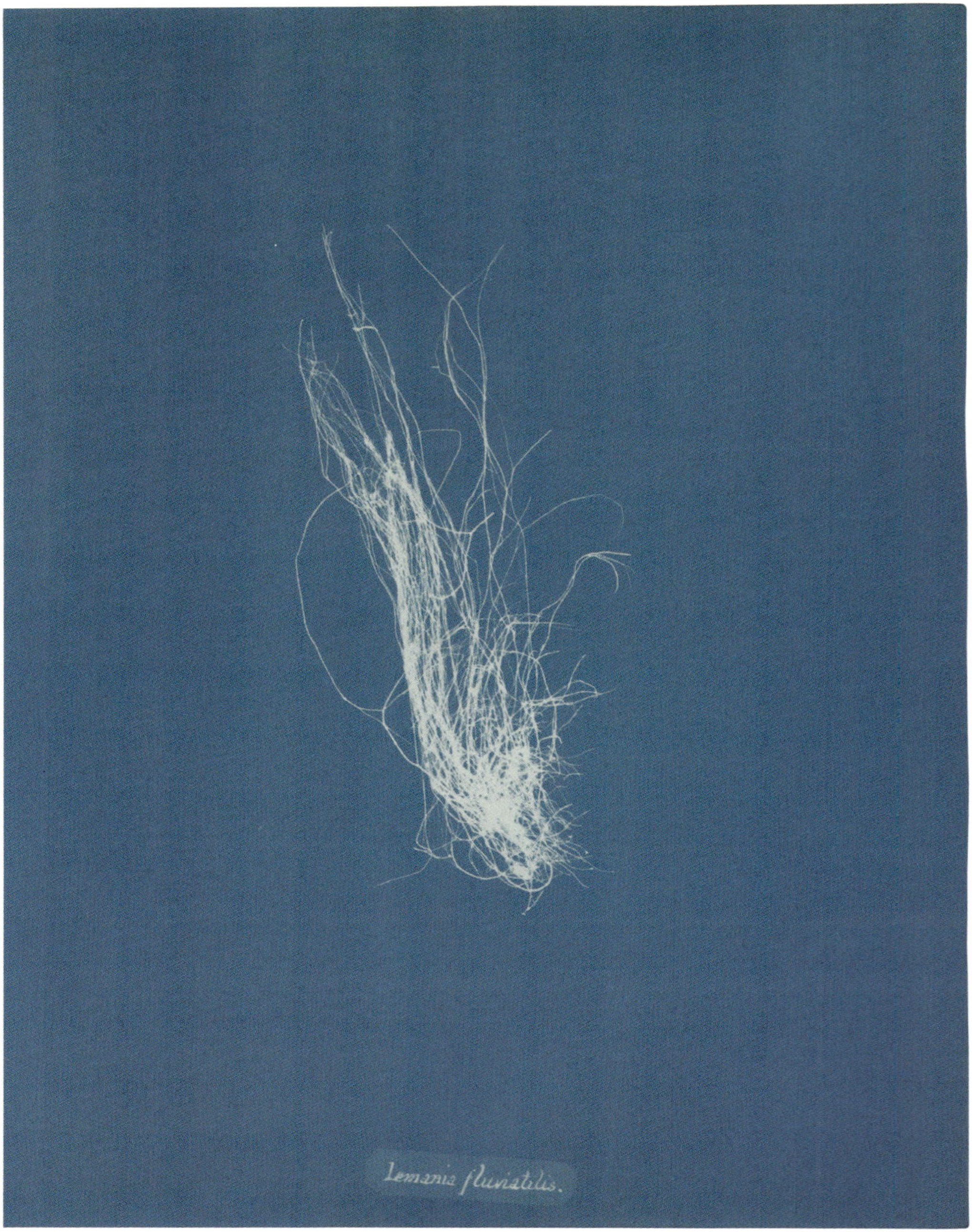

Plate 278. *Lemanea fluviatilis*

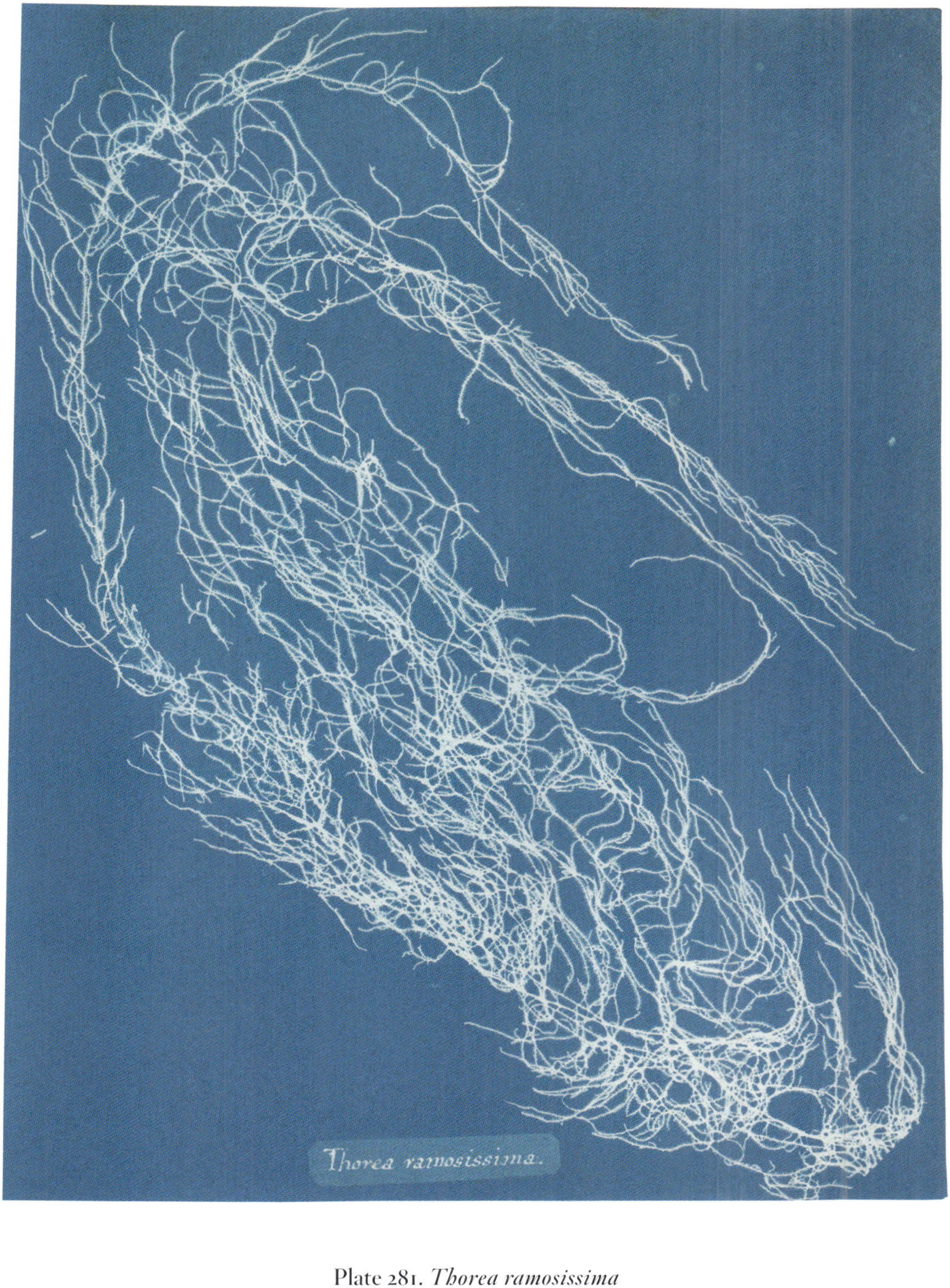

Plate 281. *Thorea ramosissima*

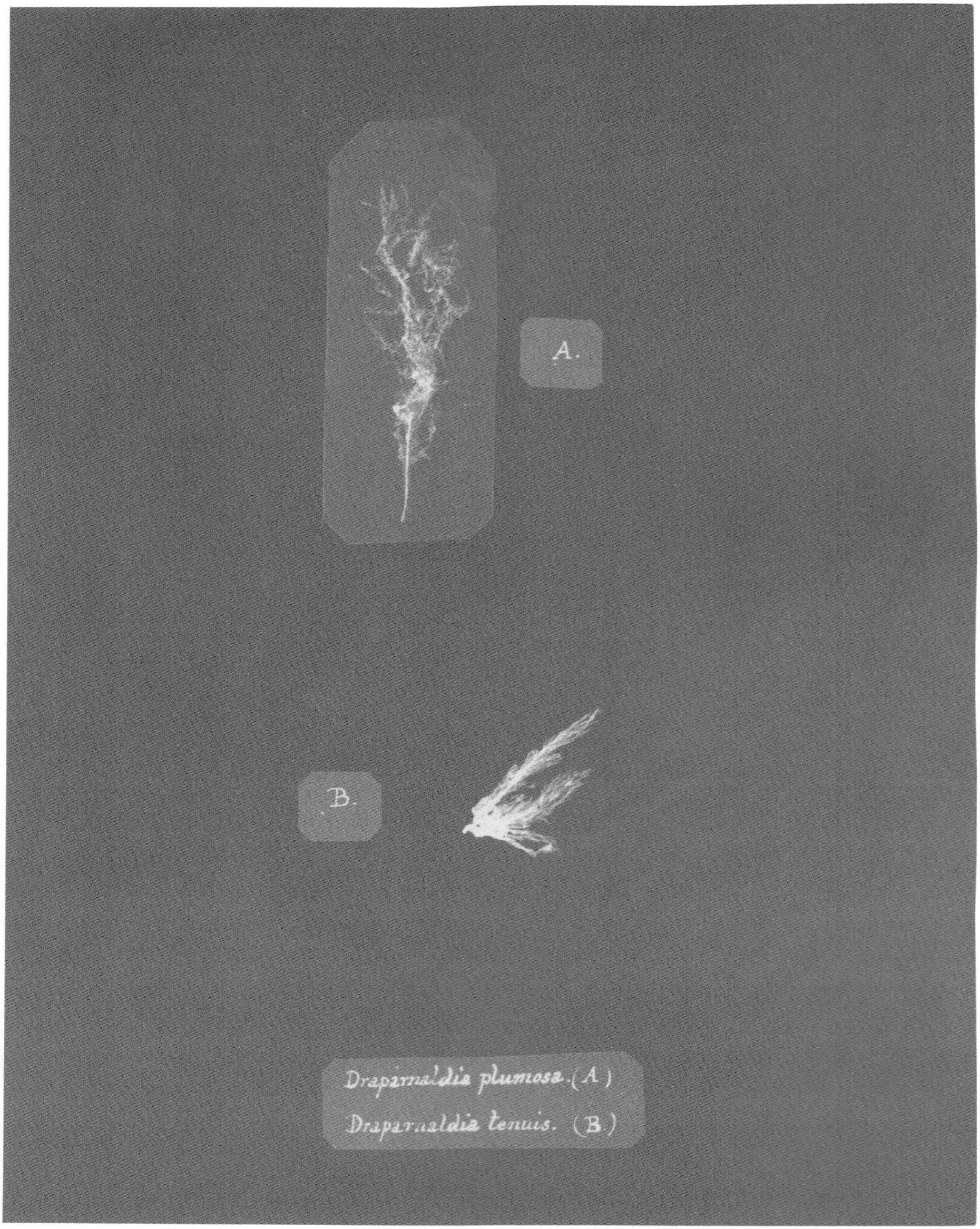

Plate 283. *Draparnaldia plumosa* (A), *Draparnaldia tenuis* (B)

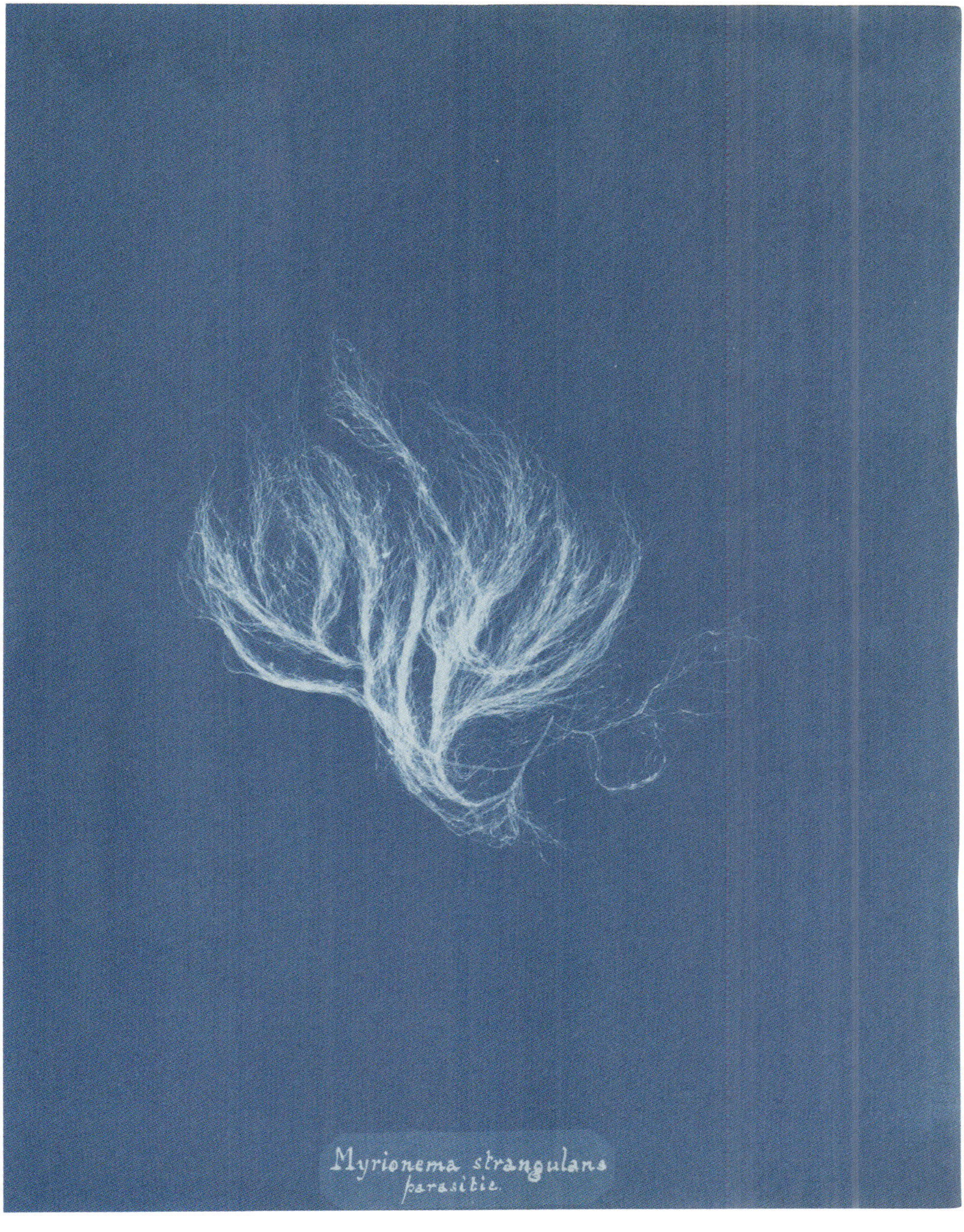

Plate 289. *Myrionema strangulans*, parasitic

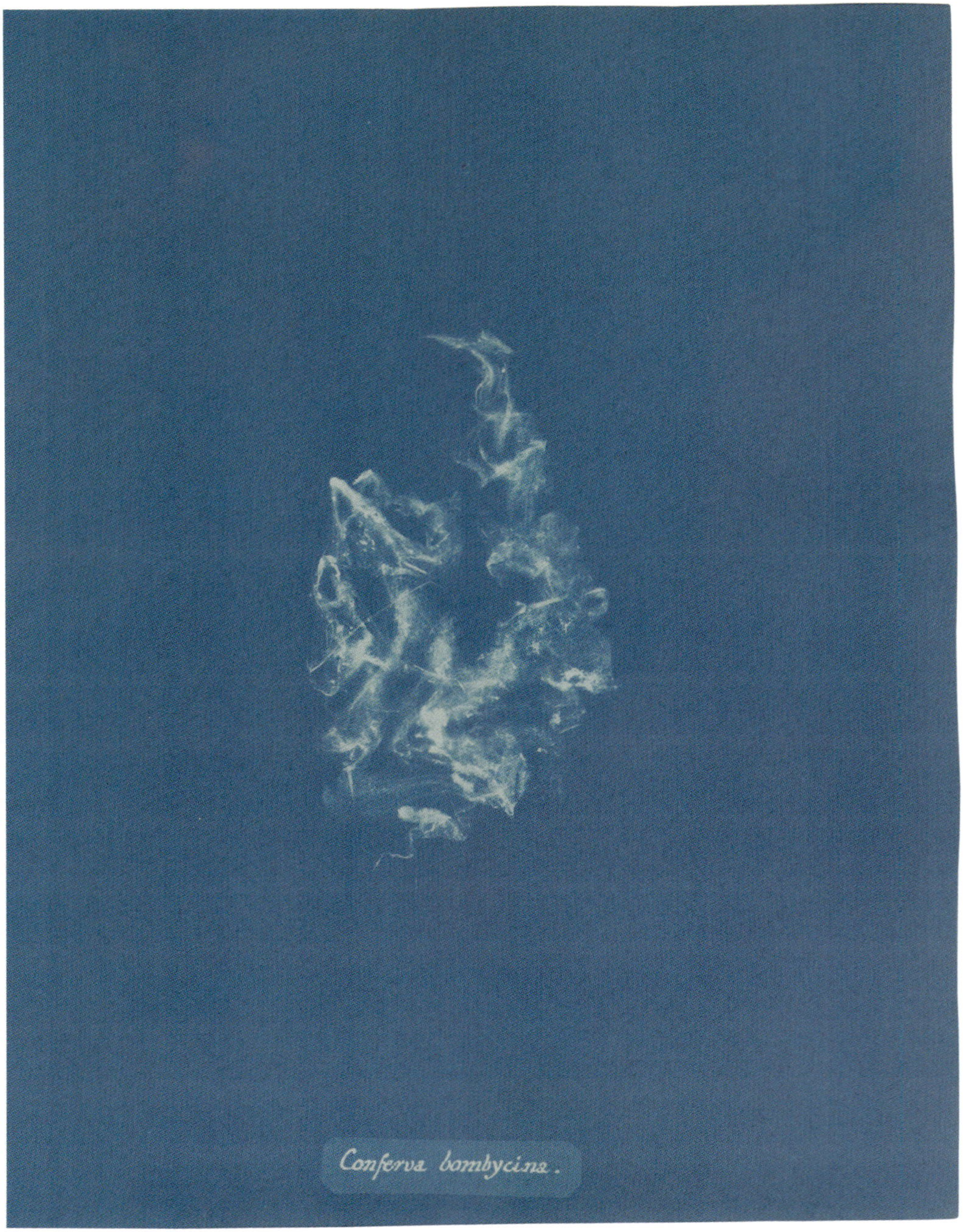

Plate 293. *Conferva bombycina*

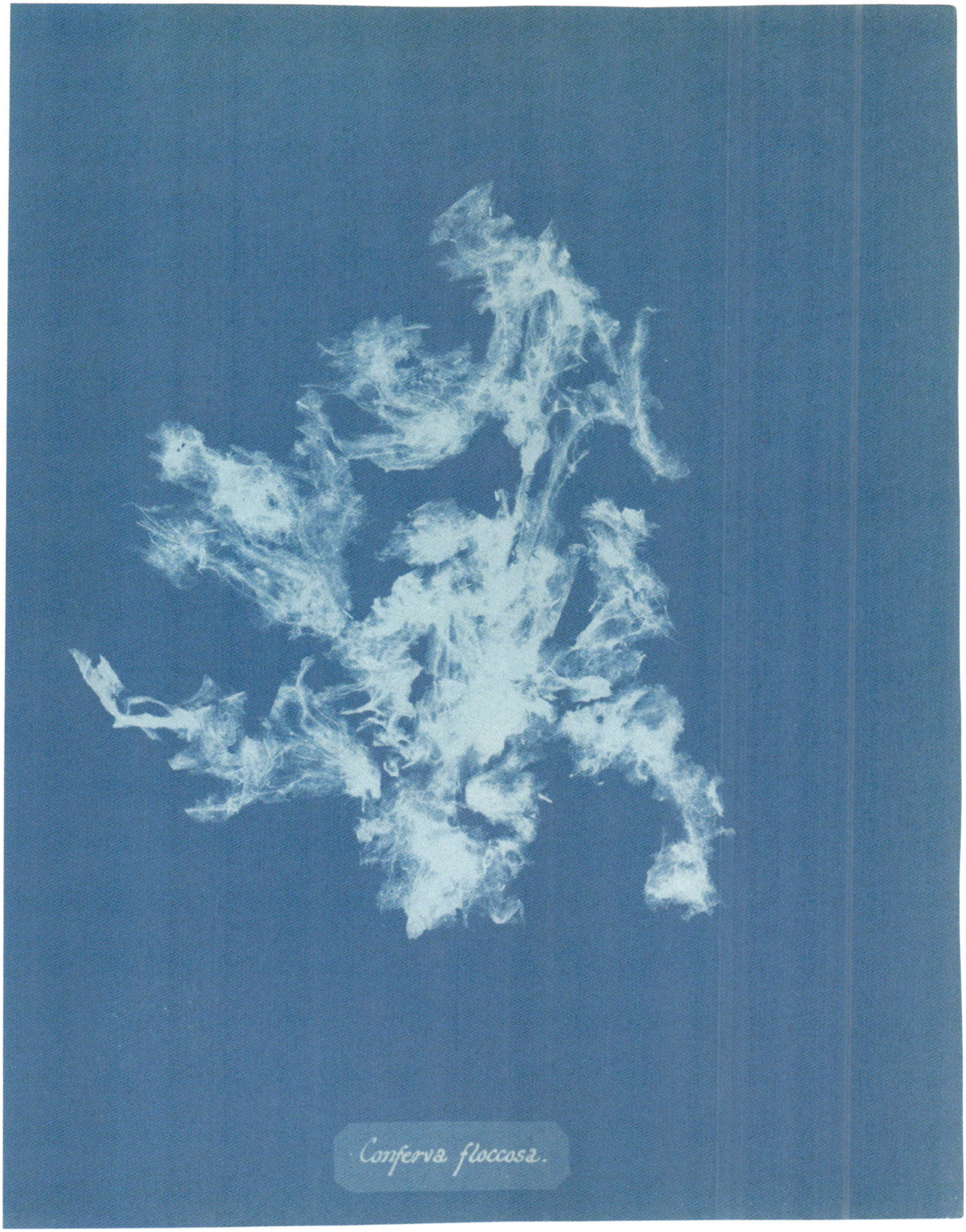

Plate 294. *Conferva floccosa*

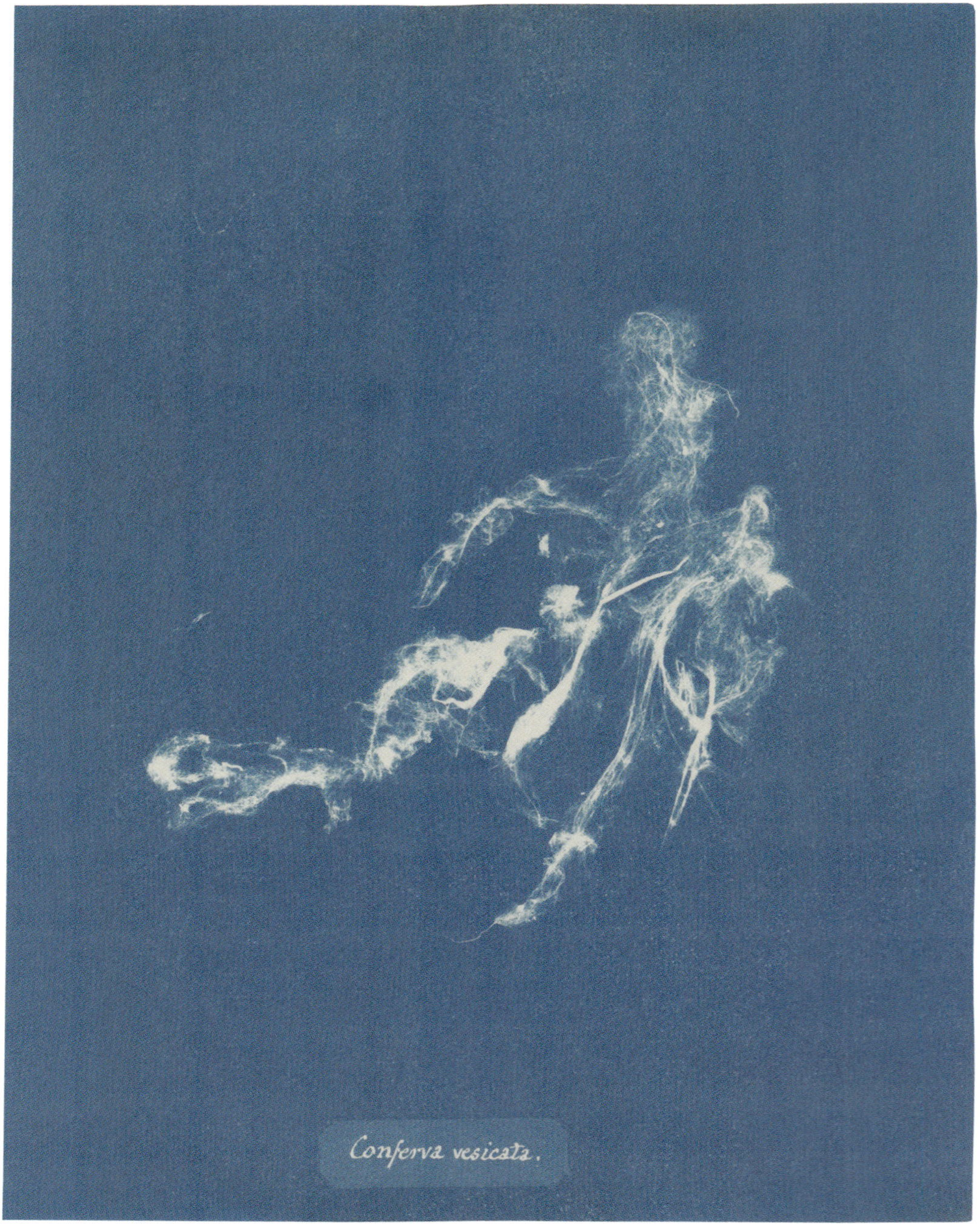

Plate 297. *Conferva vesicata*

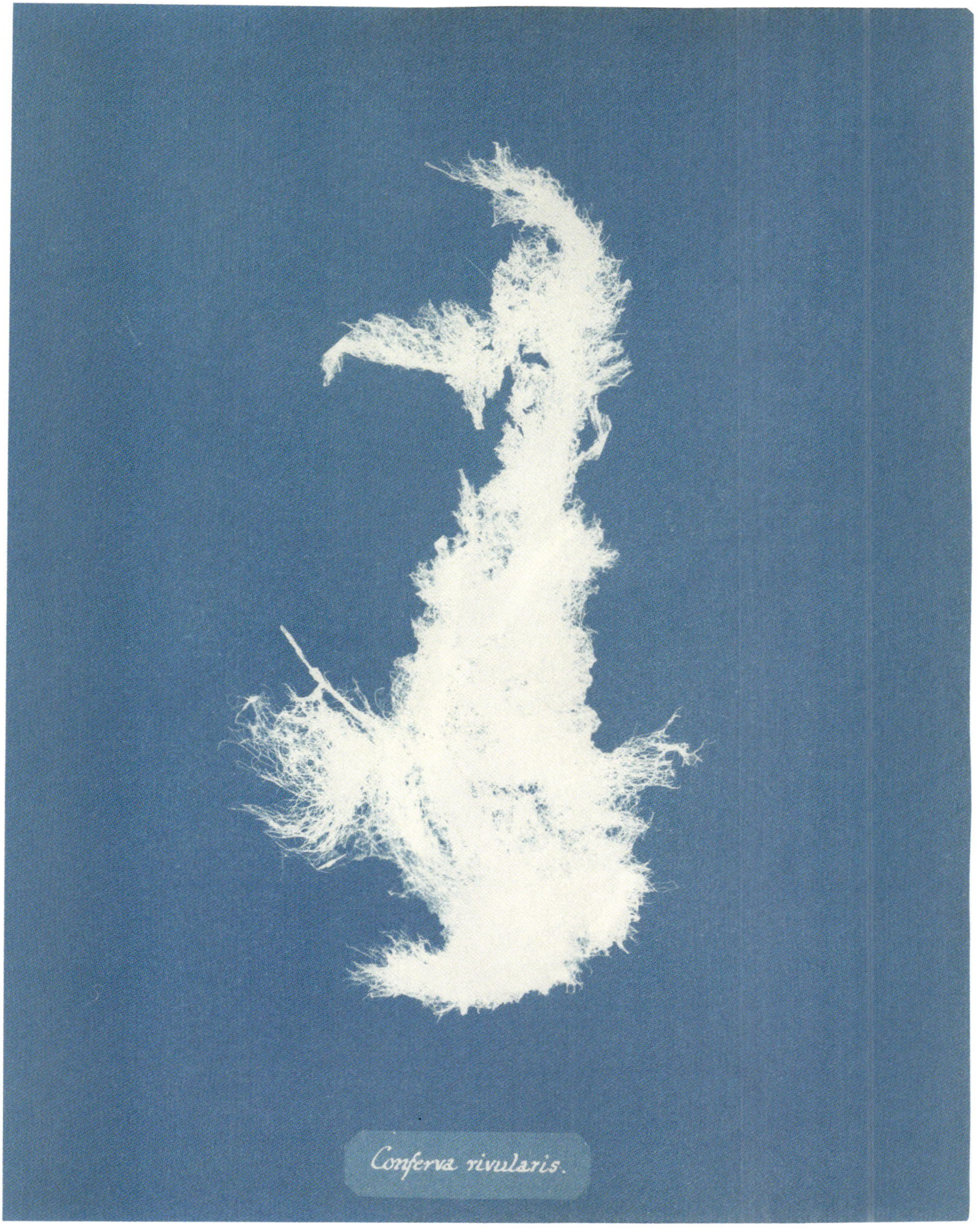

Plate 298. *Conferva rivularis*

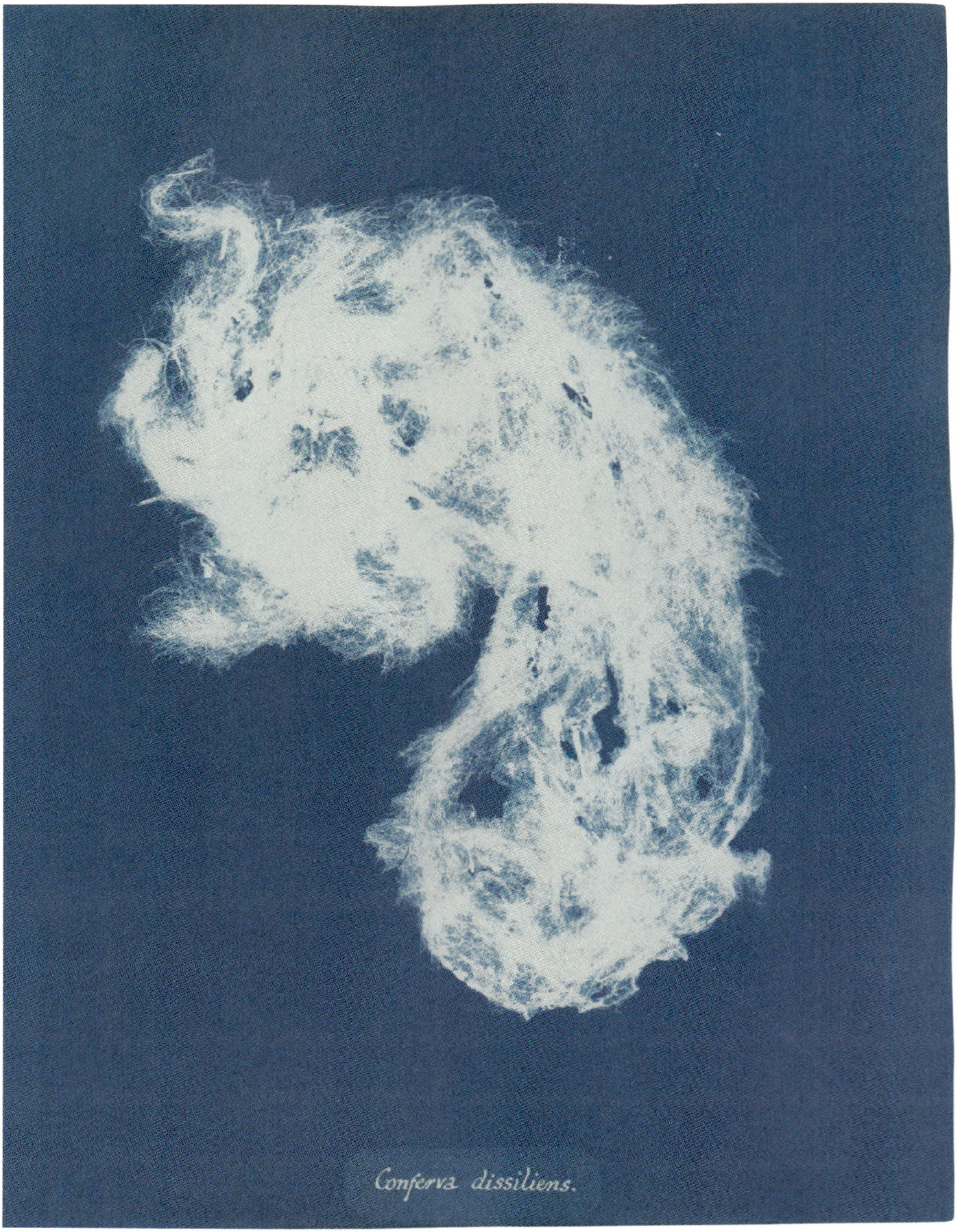

Plate 301. *Conferva dissiliens*

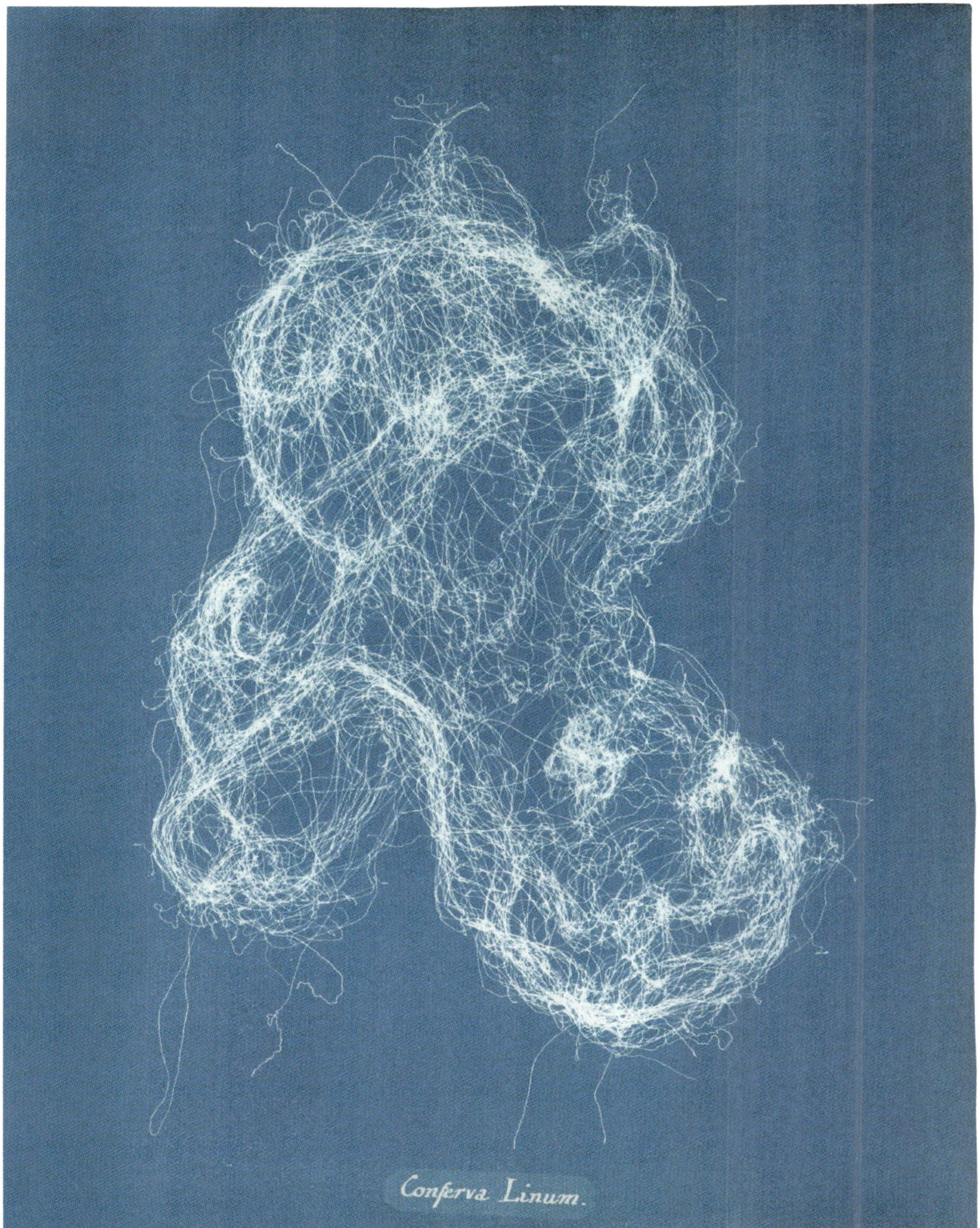

Plate 302. *Conferva linum*

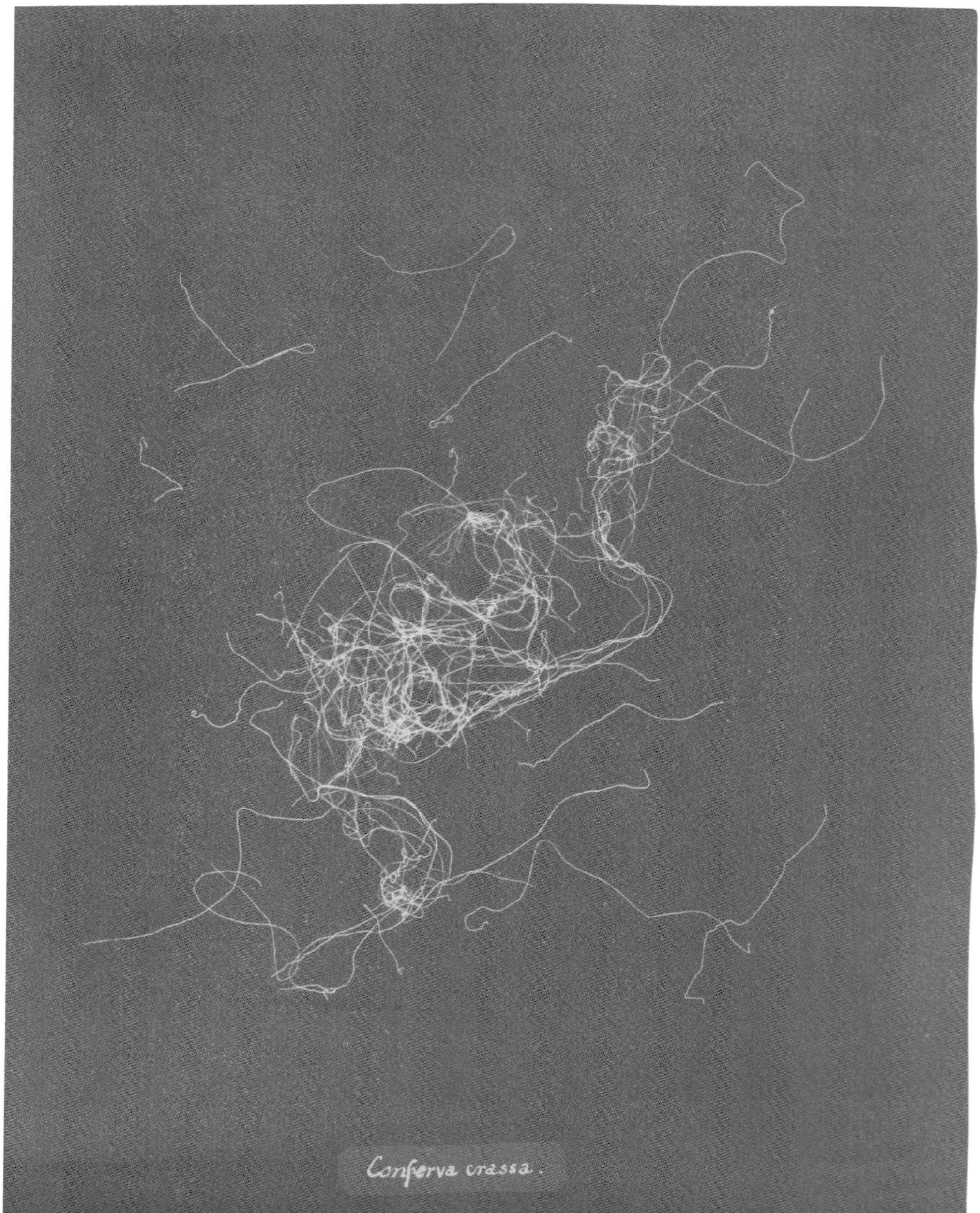

Plate 303. *Conferva crassa*

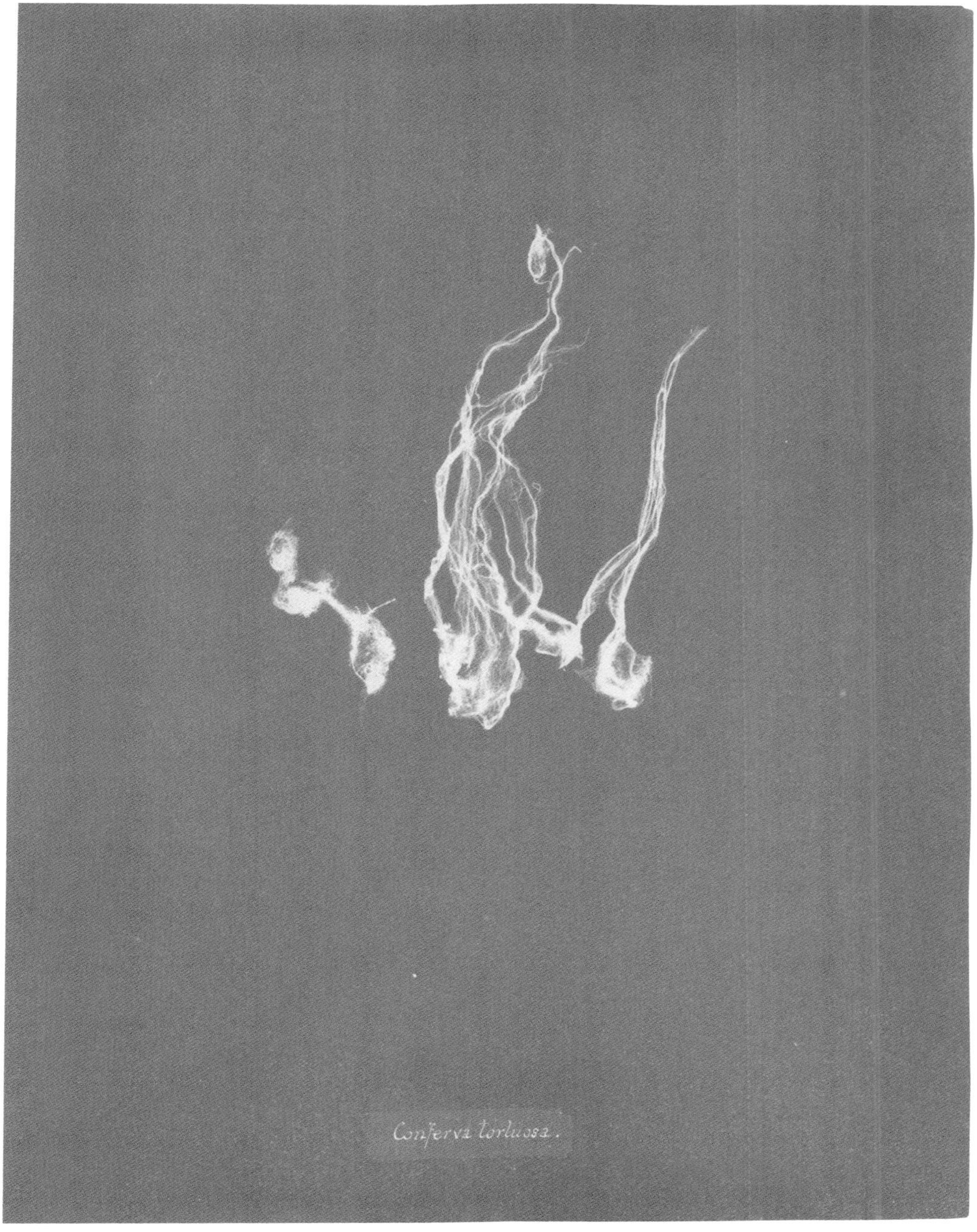

Plate 304. *Conferva tortuosa*

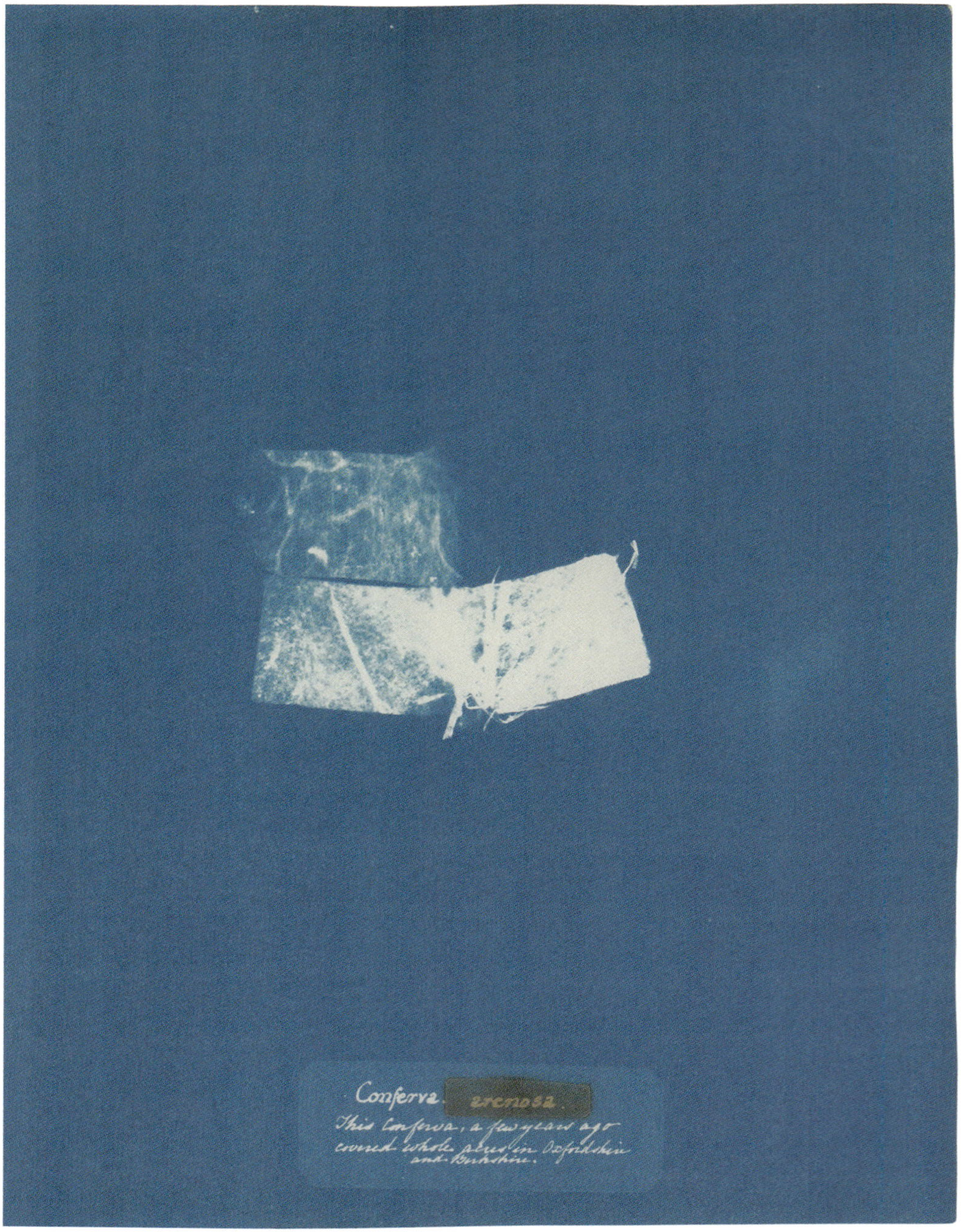

Plate 307. *Conferva arenosa*, this *conferva* a few years ago covered whole areas in Oxfordshire and Berkshire.

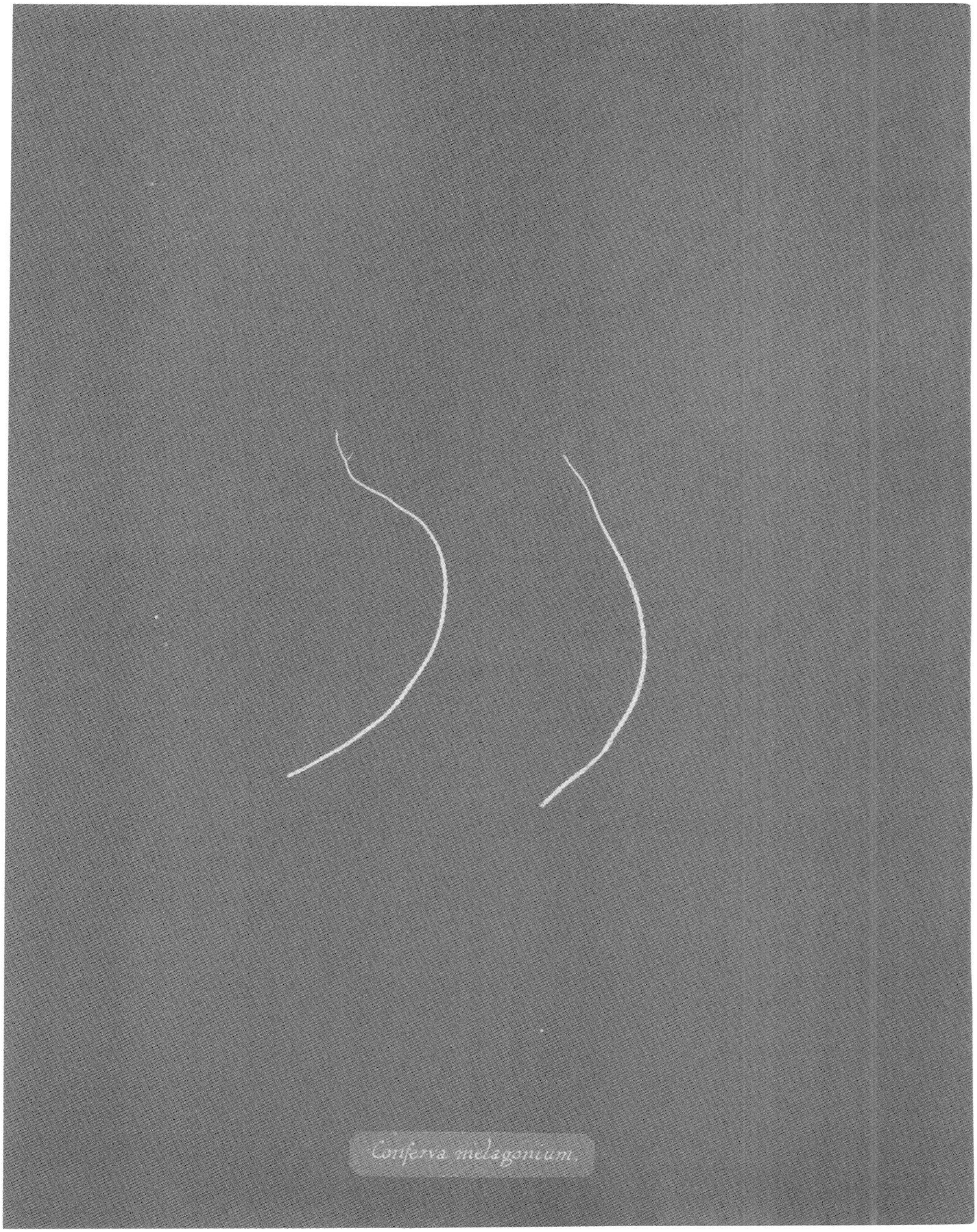

Plate 308. *Conferva melagonium*

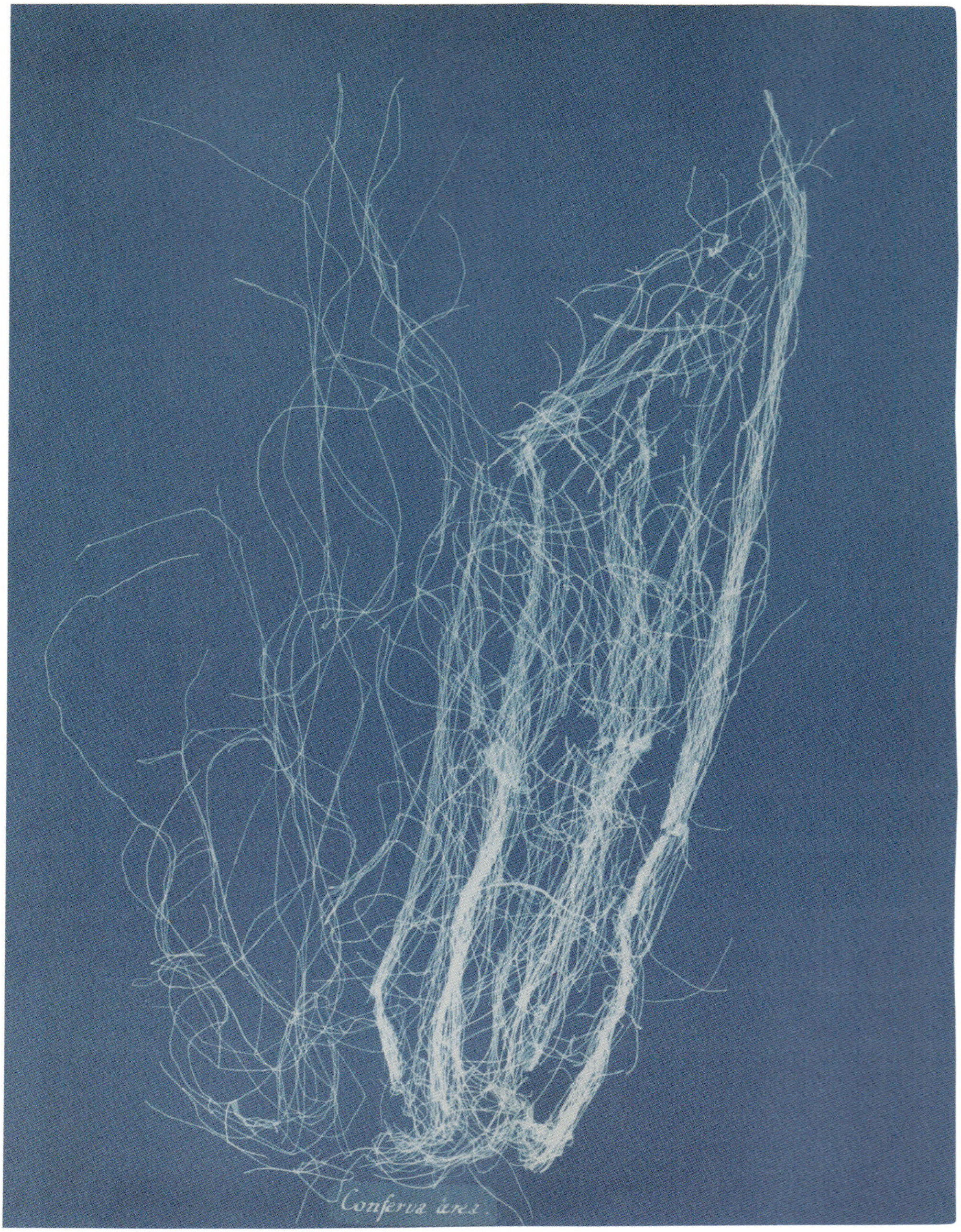

Plate 309. *Conferva aerea*

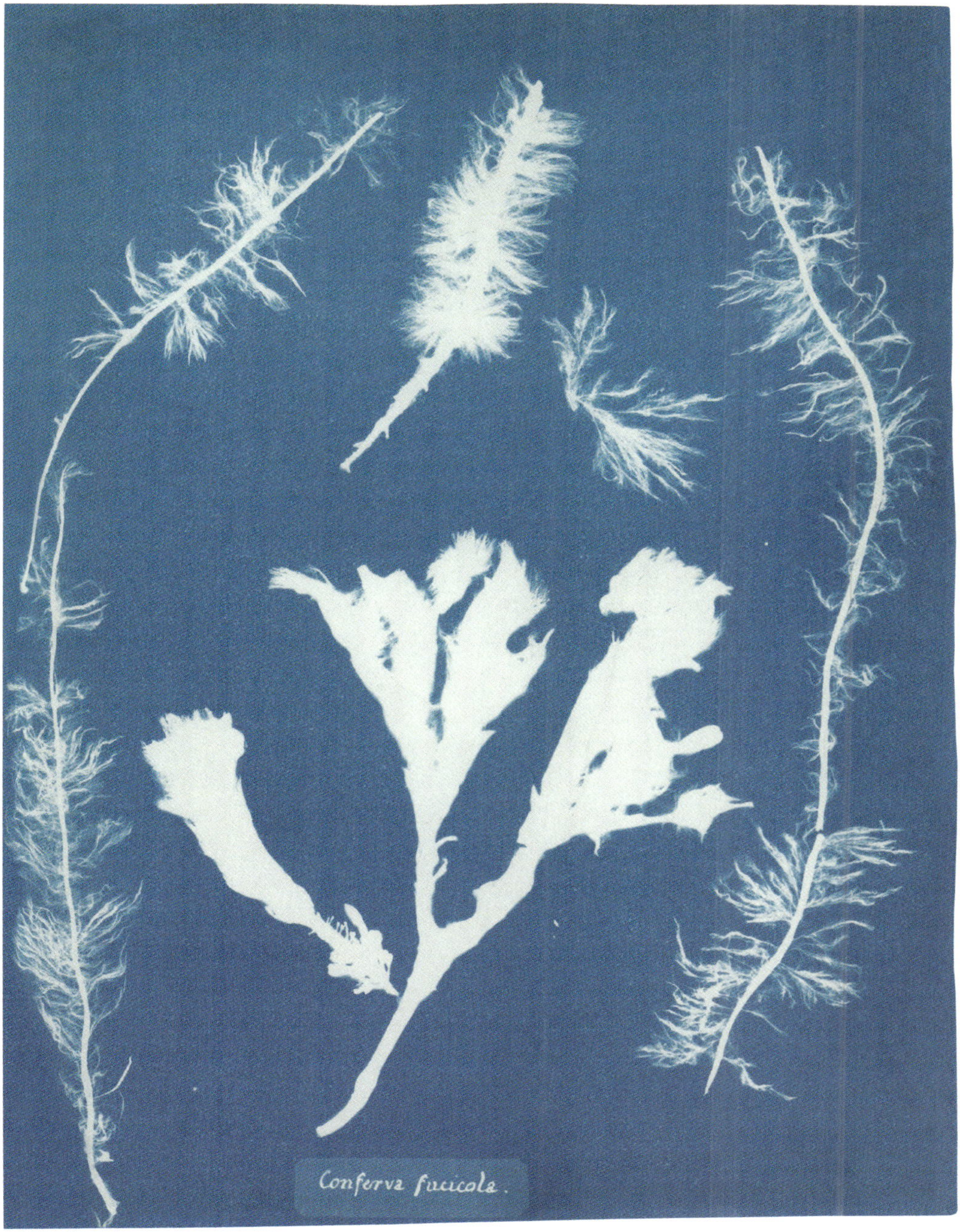

Plate 310. *Conferva fucicola*

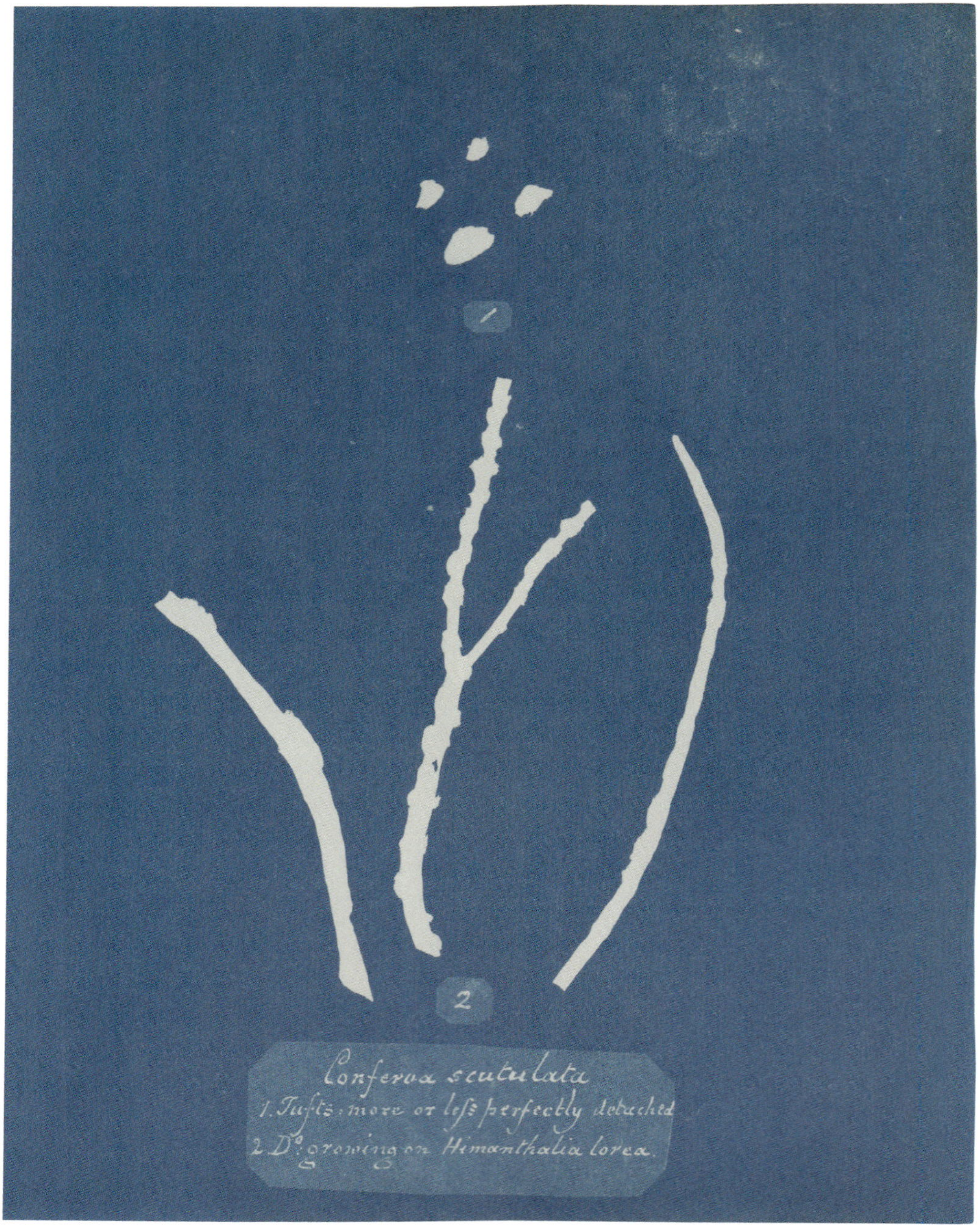

Plate 312. *Conferva scutulata*, 1. Tufts more or less perfectly detached, 2. D[itt]o growing on *Himanthalia lorea*

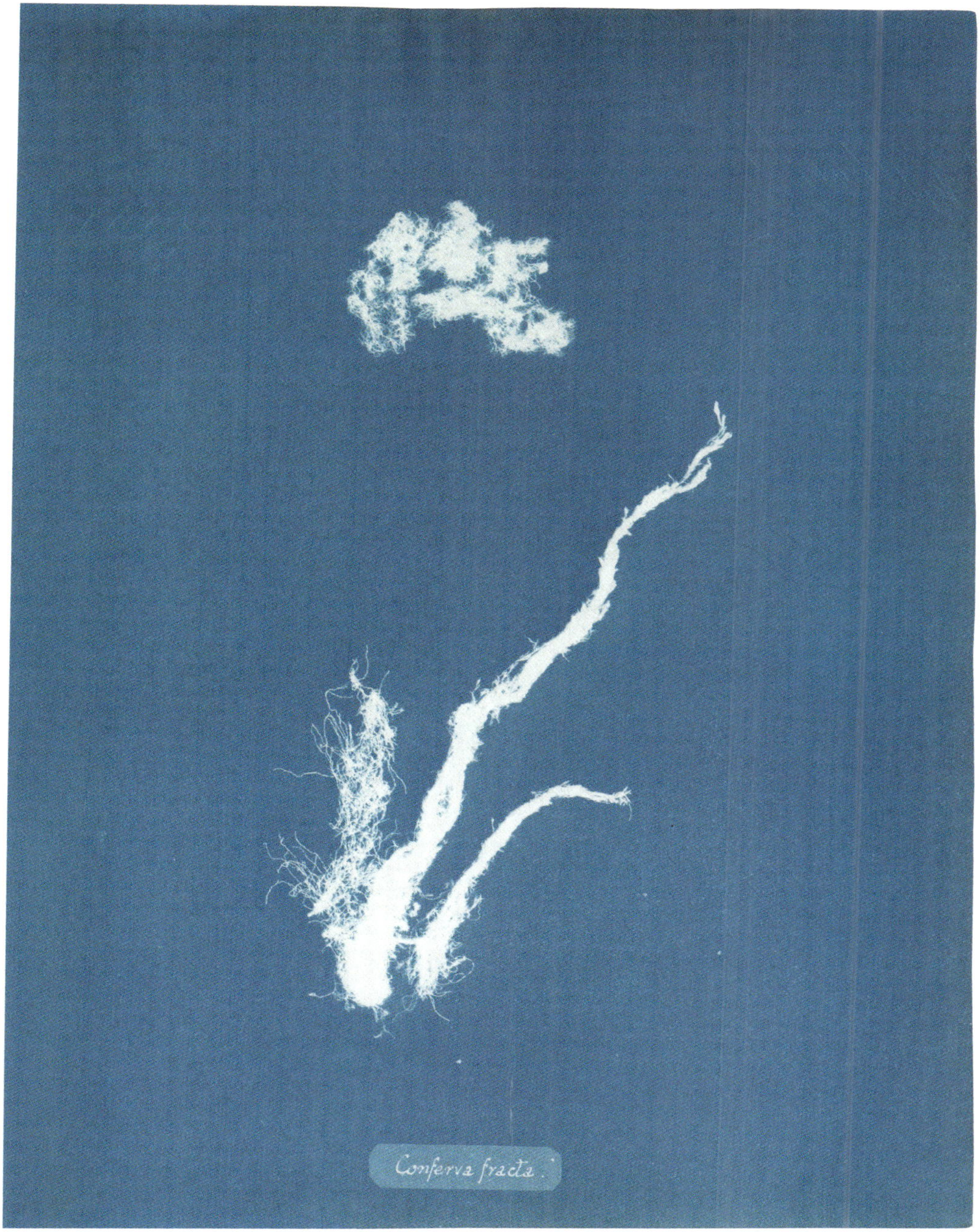

Plate 316. *Conferva fracta*

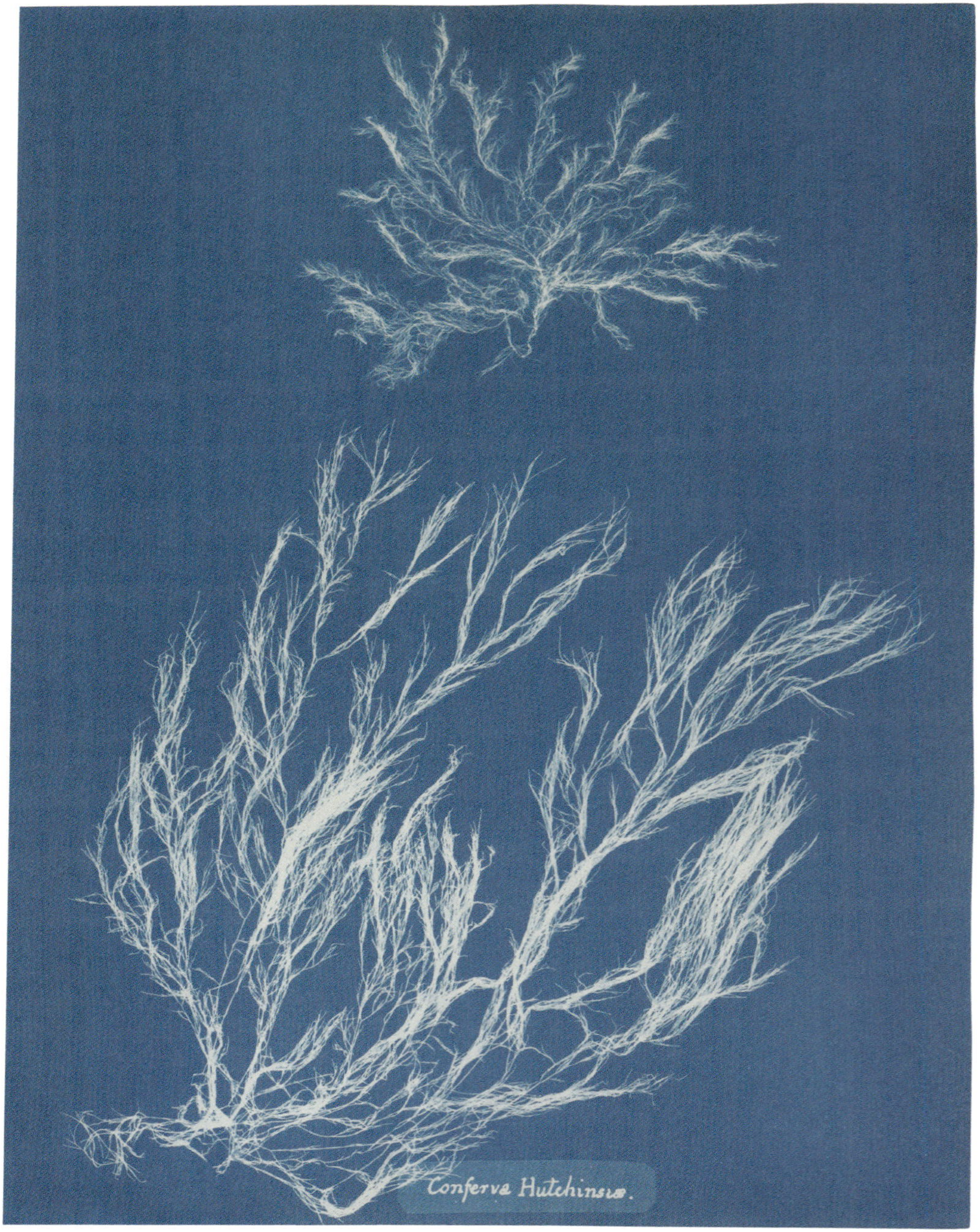

Plate 323. *Conferva hutchinsus*

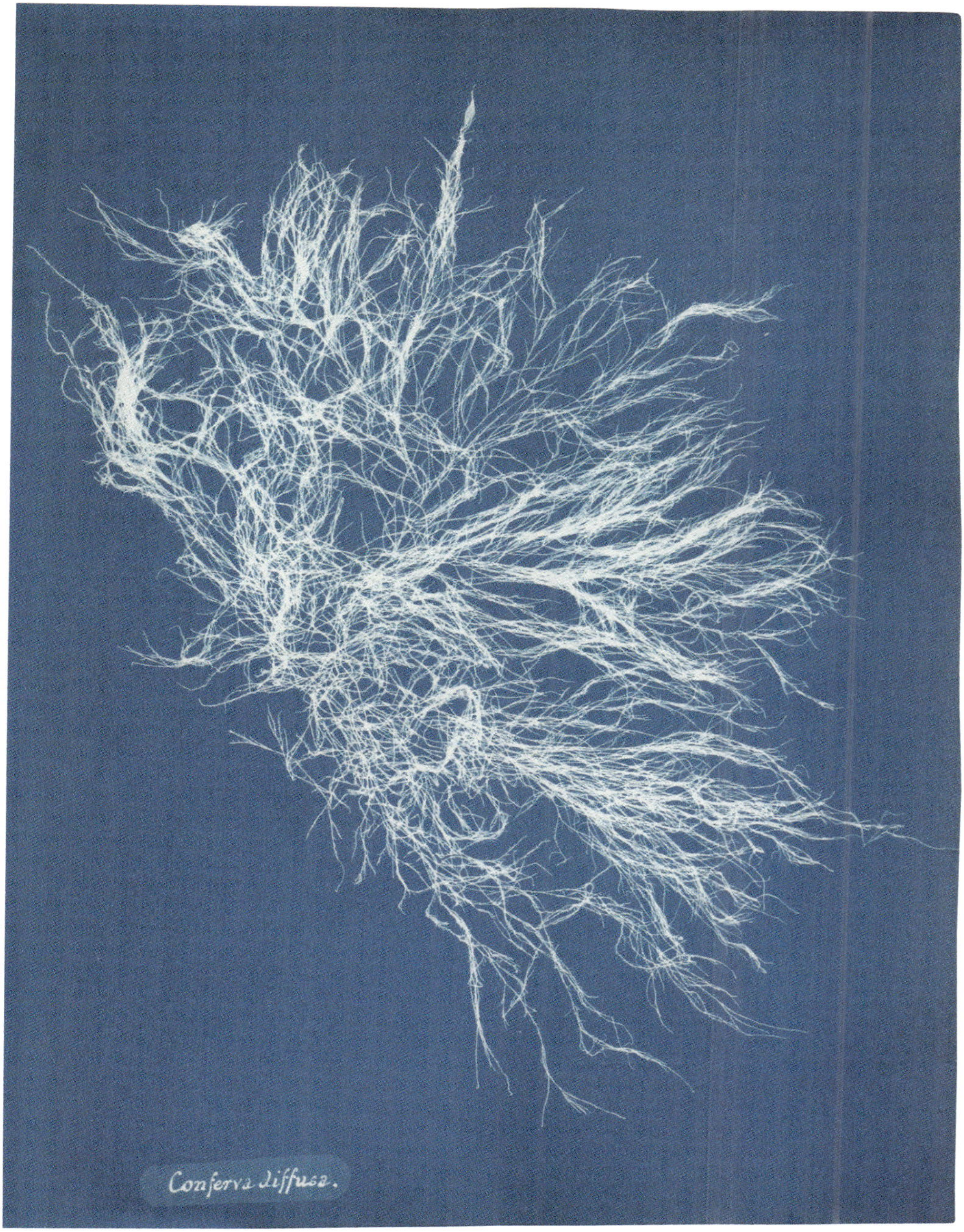

Plate 324. *Conferva diffusa*

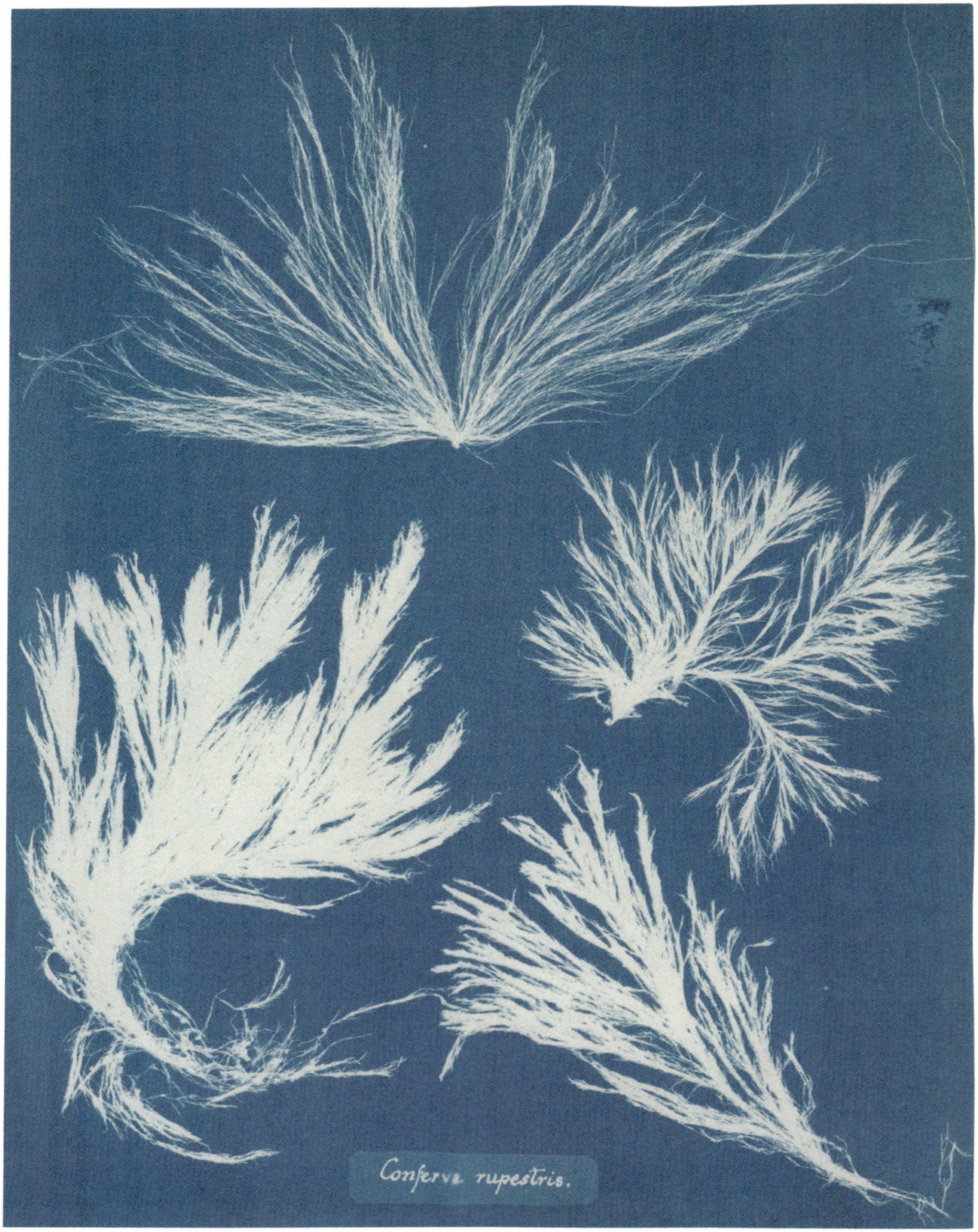

Plate 325. *Conferva rupestris*

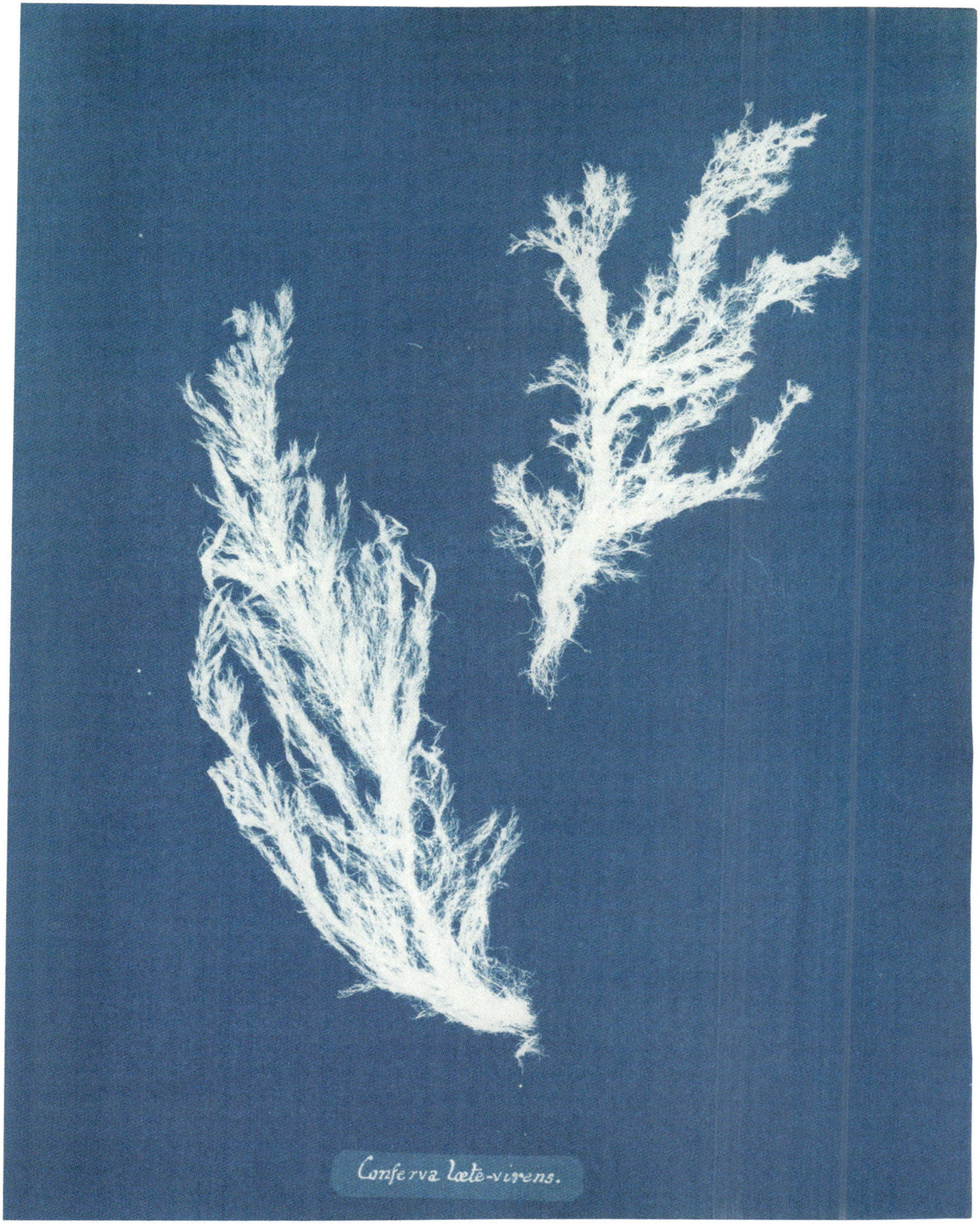

Plate 326. *Conferva laete-virens*

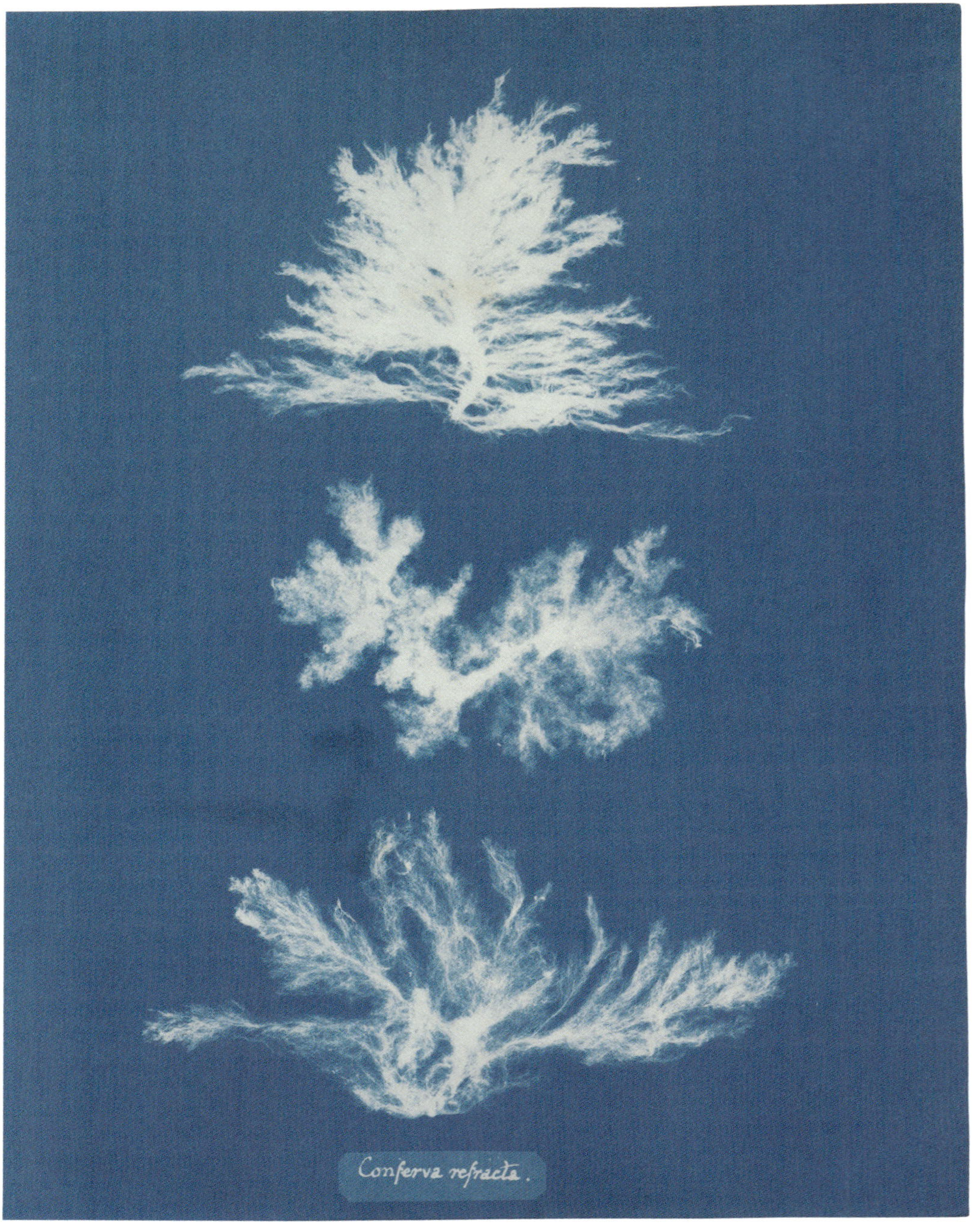

Plate 329. *Conferva refracta*

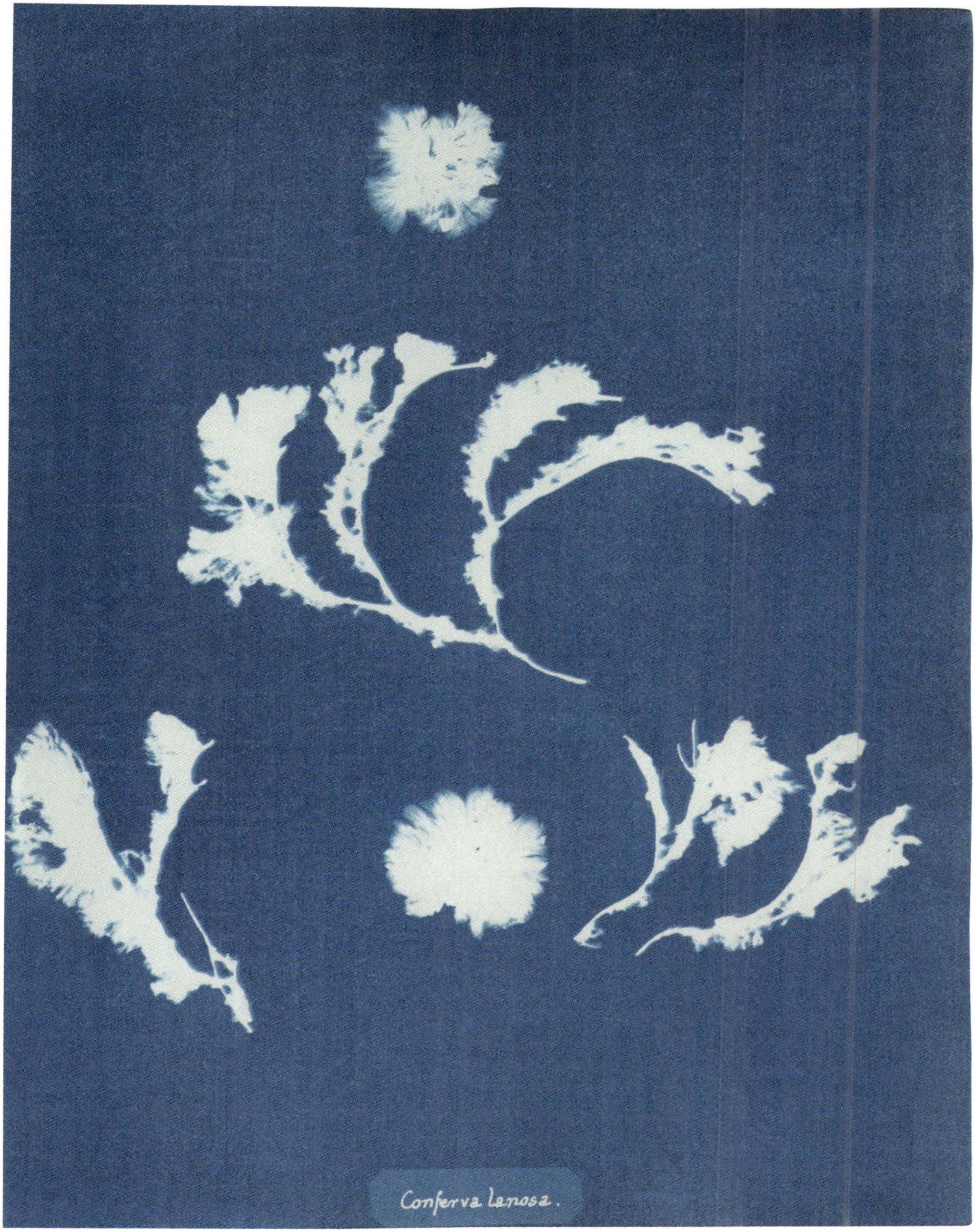

Plate 331. *Conferva lanosa*

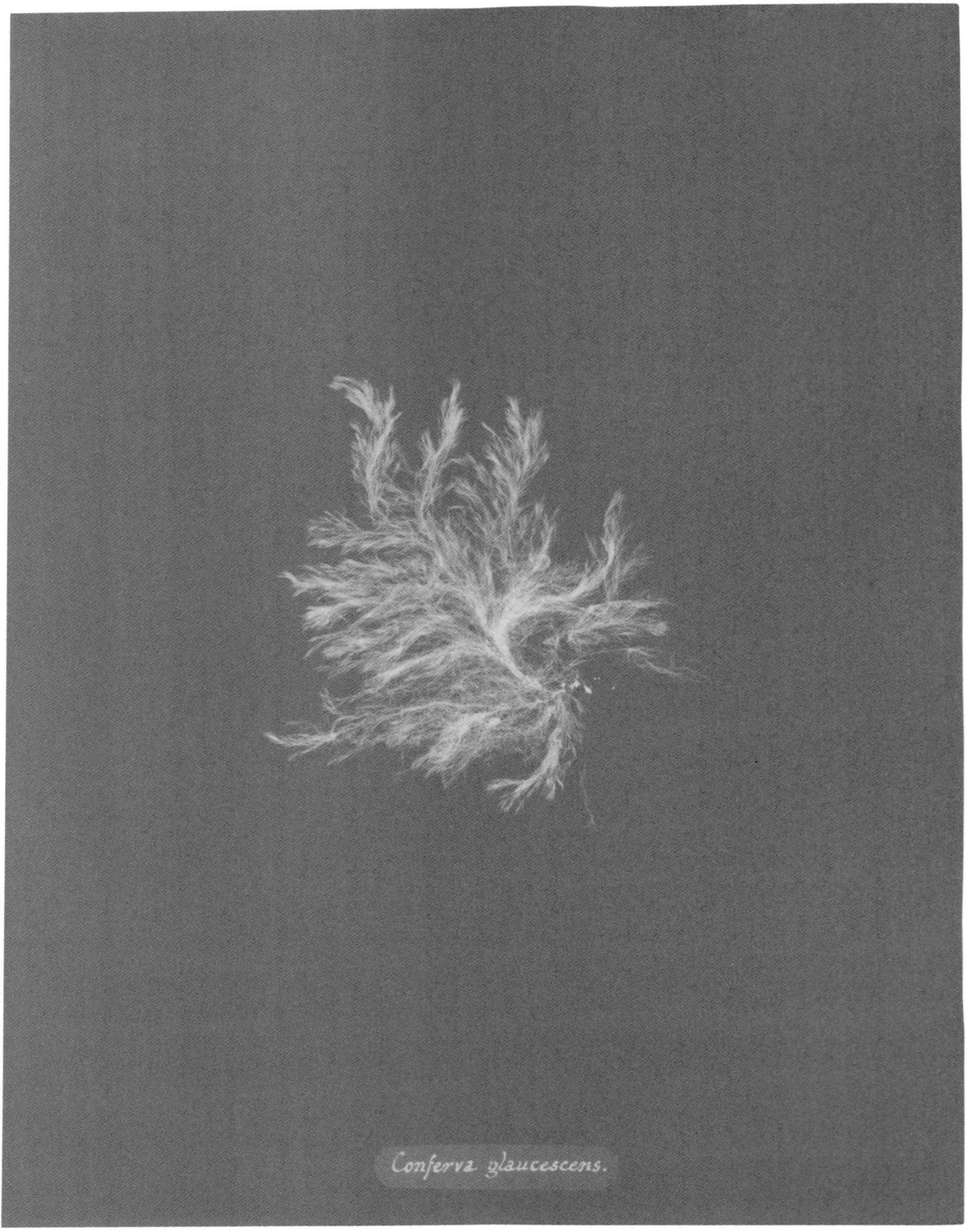

Plate 333. *Conferva glaucescens*

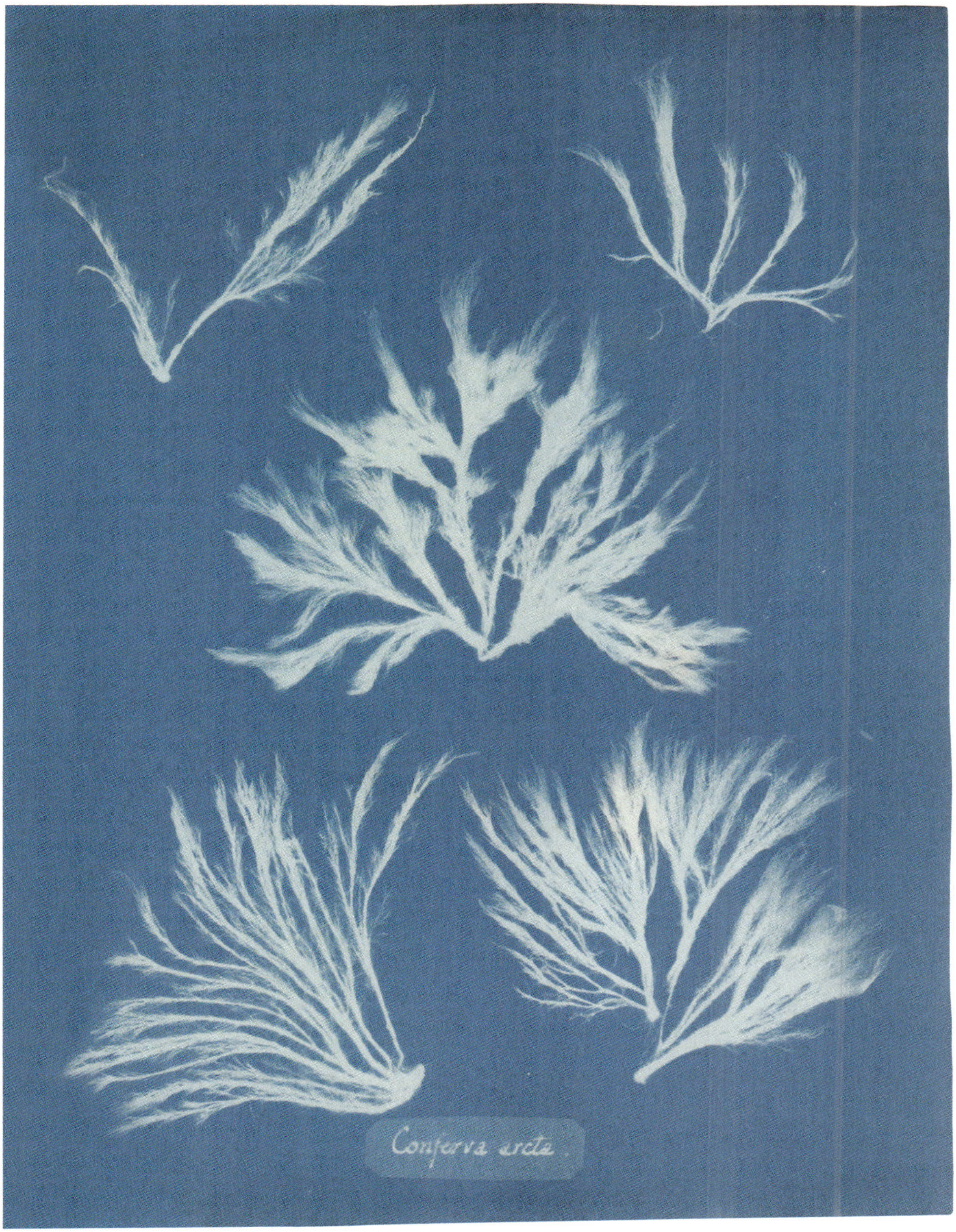

Plate 334. *Conferva arcta*

Photography without a Camera: The Photogram

A photographic image created without a camera is called a photogram. The subject is usually a flat object, placed against a background of sensitized carrier material and directly exposed to light. As early as 1802, the chemist Humphry Davy and the photographic pioneer Thomas Wedgwood (1771–1805) – both of whom were British – experimented with paper and leather coated with silver nitrate. They made pictures of leaves and insects' wings but found them impossible to fix. Sunlight served as a light source. In 1834, William Henry Fox Talbot succeeded for the first time in producing photograms of plants, leaves and lace and making them permanently visible. Unique features of the photogram are its reversed tonal values, which means they produce negatives. If the object is opaque, the image is no more than an outline. As well as paper, leather and textiles, glass and celluloid film also make good carrier material.

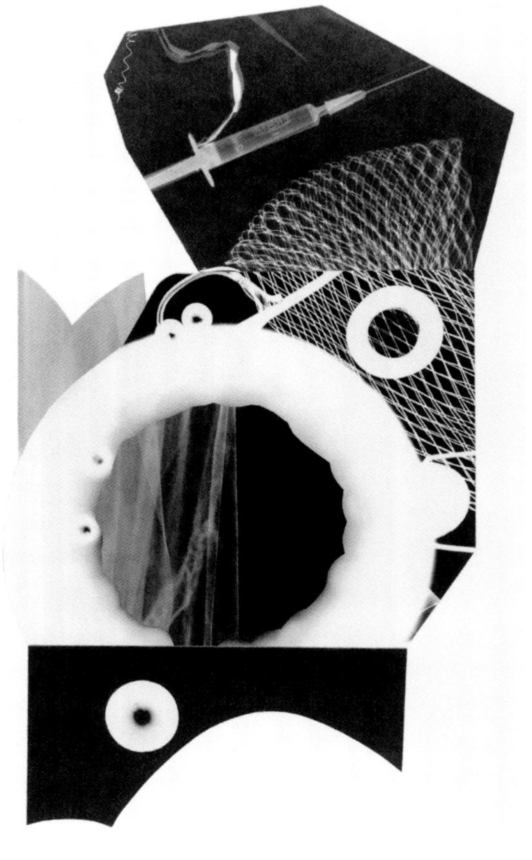

In the early days of photography, there were various proposals to use the term "photography", which had been coined by John Herschel, to designate only the process itself, and to call the result a "photogram" (analogous to the terms "telegraphy" and "telegram"). Even so, this term to describe all photochemically generated images, produced with or without a camera, did not yet become part of the everyday vernacular. The word "photogram" as we understand it dates back to László Moholy-Nagy (1895–1946), who used this technique in the 1920s.

It is indisputable that producing photograms is part of the photographic process. But are photograms actual photographs, or merely a preliminary stage, a special discipline within photography? This depends on whether the use of a camera and the creation of a perspective image are considered essential properties of the medium. In early photographic history, no distinction was made between pictures taken with or without a camera. On 25 January 1839, at the Royal Institute in London, Talbot presented the world's first photographic exhibition, where images taken using a camera obscura were displayed alongside "photogenic drawings" of pressed flowers, leaves and pieces of lace.

Early in 1839, the London art dealers Ackermann & Co. brought out a set, which included a pamphlet, accompanied by chemicals and apparatus to enable amateur enthusiasts to create photogenic drawings. By that time, Talbot had come to recognize the importance of photography both in the reproduction of existing works of art or to create botanical specimens. The French photographer Hippolyte Bayard (1801–1887) experimented with photograms to reproduce images of patterned fabrics, feathers and etchings. John Herschel's invention of cyanotype made photograms simpler to create. In those early days in the history of photography, photograms were mostly used in the company of the family or friends of Talbot and Herschel. The situation was the same with the cyanotypes of Anna Atkins and Anne Dixon.

Nevertheless, it was not long before photograms came to be seen as a technical preliminary stage in camera photography. Their manufacture required very little equipment and they were soon regarded as little more than a pastime, especially suited to women. Instructions in books on photography and illustrations in magazines made the photogram a popular product. Just like silhouettes, most photograms showing botanic images were collected, glued in albums and given as gifts.

In 1919, the Loheland School for Physical Education, Agriculture and Crafts was founded in the German state of Hesse. Influenced by the emerging *Lebensreform* (Life reform) movement, the school admitted only women. It was here, thanks to the work of Bertha Günther, that the photogram underwent a renaissance as an art form. At the Bauhaus, László Moholy-Nagy was inspired by Günther's photograms to initiate his own research of the medium, in which he extended the means of artistic expression through multiple exposures and projecting light from a distance. Likewise, in 1919 the painter Christian Schad (1894–1982) took everyday objects, as well as handwritten pages and torn up newspapers, to build a picture on light-sensitive paper. In his photogram collages, Man Ray (1890–1976) created graphically engaging patterns by superimposing varying types of shape. At the same time, his works also had a major impact on the photomontages of George Grosz (1893–1959) and John Heartfield (1891–1968). Strongly influenced by Bauhaus photography, the photographer Marta Hoepffner (1912–2000) and the painter Rolf Cavael (1898–1979) developed their own approaches to the medium.

While the photograms produced by the Czech photographer Jaroslav Rössler (1902–1990) were mostly composed of abstract spatial forms, Jaromir Funke (1896–1945), another representative of the Czech avant-garde, worked with a variety of focal planes. In 1941, under the title *How to make a*

Christian Schad
Schadographie no. 115, 1975
Photograph, 36.7 × 21.8 cm (14 ½ × 8 ⅝ in.)
Museum der Stadt Aschaffenburg

photogram, the Museum of Modern Art in New York organized a travelling exhibition celebrating the first century of the medium. The photograms on show inspired new works, among them the full-body images by Robert Rauschenberg and the "photogenics" of the photographer Lotte Jacobi (1896–1990), characterized by large-scale blurred spaces.

Seven decades after the first overview exhibition in New York, London's Victoria & Albert Museum staged the exhibition *Shadow Catchers,* offering an overview of camera-less photographs by contemporary artists including Floris Neusüss (1937–2020), Pierre Cordier (1933–2024), Susan Derges (b. 1955), Garry Fabian Miller (b. 1957), and Adam Fuss (b. 1961). Thanks to technological advances, new imaging techniques and the possibilities of manipulating digital image data, the boundaries between the medium of the photogram and closely linked art forms are more permeable. However, it seems to be precisely the reduction of graphic means of expression that makes the photogram a continually enticing medium of artistic exploration.

Man Ray, **Rayographie no. 6**, 1922
From: *Champs délicieux*, Paris, 1922
Gelatin silver print
Paris, Musée national d'Art moderne, Centre Pompidou

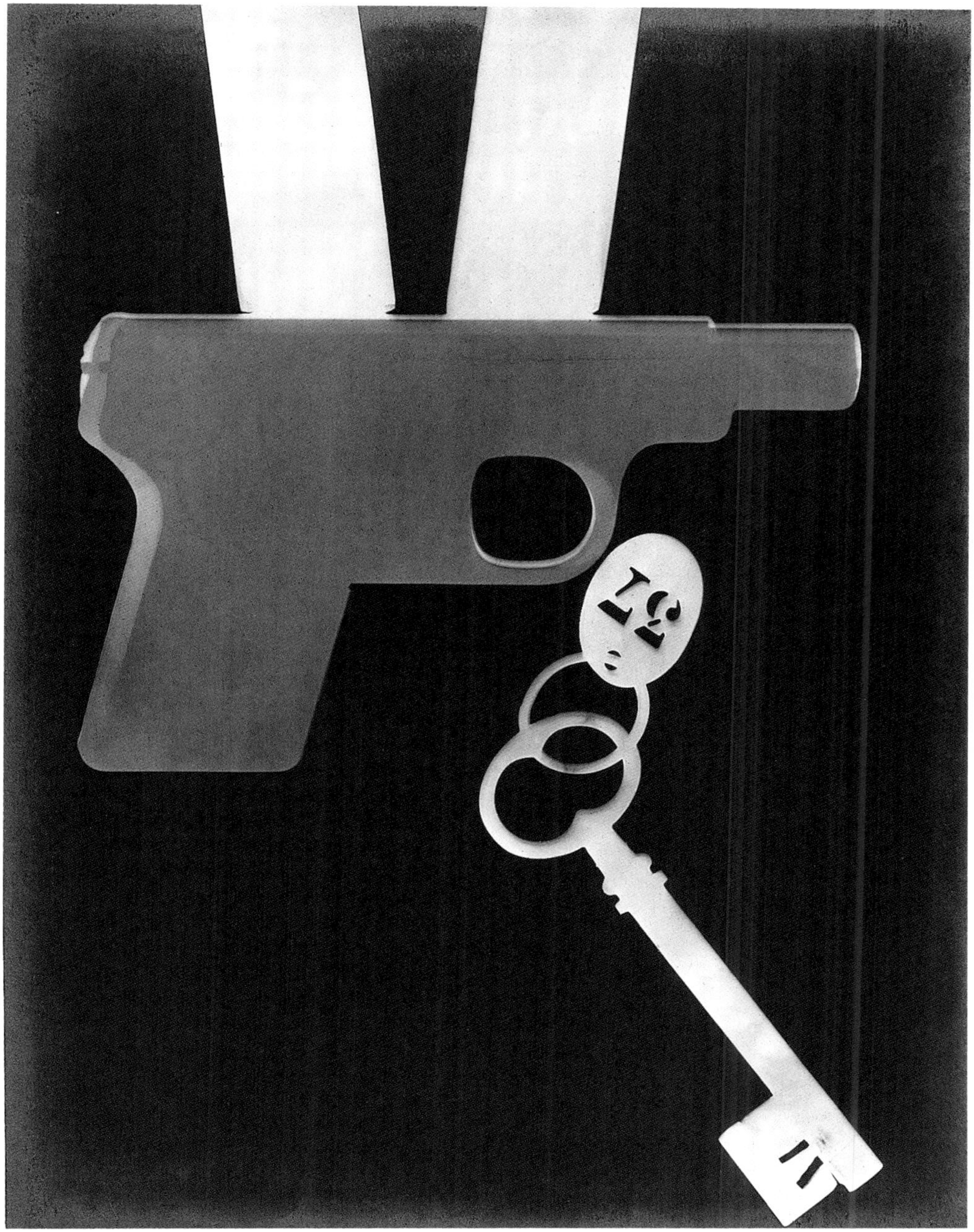

Fotografieren ohne Kamera: Das Fotogramm

Die Abbildung von zumeist flachen Objekten vor dem Hintergrund eines sensibilisierten Trägermaterials durch direktes Einwirken von Licht nennt man Fotogramm. Bereits ab 1802 experimentieren die britischen Chemiker Humphry Davy und Thomas Wedgwood (1771–1805) mit silbernitratbeschichtetem Papier und Leder. Sie fertigen Bilder von Blättern und Insektenflügeln an, die allerdings noch nicht fixiert werden können. Als Lichtquelle dient die Sonnenstrahlung. Henry Fox Talbot gelingt es um 1834 erstmals, Fotogramme von Pflanzen, Blättern und Spitzen dauerhaft sichtbar zu machen. Die Fotogramme sind Unikate mit umgekehrten Tonwerten, also Negativbilder. Wenn das Objekt lichtundurchlässig ist, reduziert sich die Abbildung auf ein einfaches Umrissbild. Als Trägerschicht für das Fotogramm kann neben Papier, Leder und Stoff auch Glas oder Zelluloidfilm dienen.

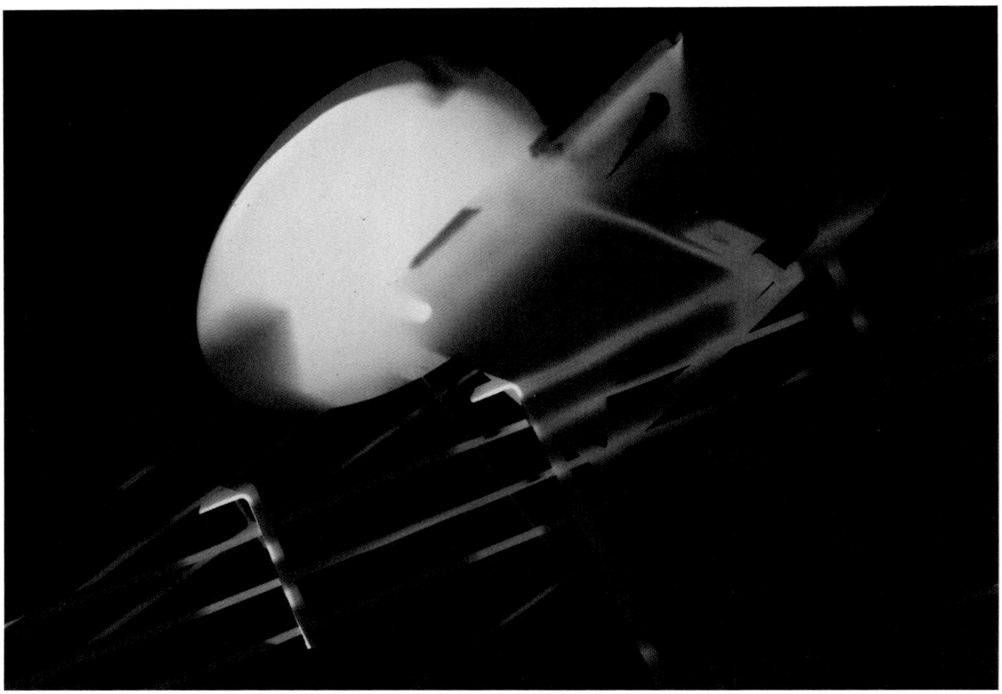

In der Frühzeit der Fotografie gibt es verschiedentlich Vorschläge, den auf John Herschel zurückgehenden Begriff der Fotografie nur für das Verfahren selbst zu nutzen, das Ergebnis aber „Fotogramm" zu nennen (analog zu den Begriffen „Telegrafie" und „Telegramm"). Diese Bezeichnung für alle fotochemisch erzeugten Bilder, ob mit oder ohne Kamera entstanden, setzt sich im Sprachgebrauch jedoch nicht durch. Der Begriff „Fotogramm" in unserem heutigen Verständnis geht auf László Moholy-Nagy (1895–1946) zurück, der diese Technik in den 1920er-Jahren für sich entdeckt.

Dass die Herstellung von Fotogrammen zu den fotografischen Verfahren gehört, ist unumstritten. Sind Fotogramme aber auch Fotografien oder nur eine Vorstufe, eine Sonderform der Fotografie? Dies hängt davon ab, ob man das Mitwirken einer Kamera und die Entstehung eines perspektivischen Abbilds zu den Grundeigenschaften des Mediums zählt. In der Frühzeit der Fotografiegeschichte wird jedoch nicht unterschieden zwischen Bildern, die mit oder ohne Kamera entstanden sind. Die erste Fotoausstellung weltweit wird am 25. Januar 1839 in der Royal Institution in London von Talbot präsentiert. Dort sind neben Aufnahmen mit der Camera obscura auch „fotogenische Zeichnungen" von gepressten Blumen, Blättern oder Spitzenmuster zu sehen.

Bereits zu Beginn des Jahres 1839 bringt die Londoner Kunsthandlung Ackermann & Co. ein Set mit Chemikalien und Geräten heraus, das die Herstellung „fotogenischer Zeichnungen" durch Laien ermöglichen soll. Zu dieser Zeit sieht Talbot selbst die grundlegende Bedeutung der Fotografie in der Reproduktion künstlerischer Vorlagen oder in der Abbildung botanischer Präparate. Auch der französische Fotografiepionier Hippolyte Bayard (1801–1887) experimentiert mit Fotogrammen und bildet Stoffmuster, Federn und Radierungen ab. Die Erfindung der Cyanotypie durch John Herschel 1842 vereinfacht die Handhabung von Fotogrammen. In den ersten Jahren der Fotografiegeschichte entstehen sie häufig im Familien- und Freundesumfeld von Talbot und Herschel, wozu auch die Cyanotypien von Anna Atkins und Anne Dixon gehören.

Bald jedoch gelten Fotogramme nur noch als eine technische Vorstufe der Kamerafotografie. Ihre Herstellung, die weitgehend ohne Apparaturen auskommt, wird als nützlicher Zeitvertreib vornehmlich für Frauen angesehen. Anleitungen in Büchern zur Fotografie und Bildbeispiele in Zeitschriften machen die Herstellung von Fotogrammen populär. Ähnlich wie Schattenrisse werden zumeist Fotogramme mit botanischen Motiven in Alben geklebt, gesammelt und verschenkt.

Im Umfeld einer 1919 im hessischen Loheland gegründeten anthroposophischen Reformschule für Frauen erlebt das Fotogramm mit den Arbeiten von Bertha Günther eine Renaissance als Kunstform. Ihre Fotogramme regen László Moholy-Nagy am Bauhaus zu eigenen Versuchen mit dem Medium an, bei denen er die Mittel des künstlerischen Ausdrucks durch Mehrfachbelichtungen und Projektionen von Licht aus der Distanz ausweitet. Gleichfalls 1919 komponiert der Maler Christian Schad (1894–1982) Alltagsgegenstände zusammen mit Schrift und ausgerissenen Zeitungsteilen zu Bildern auf lichtempfindlichem Papier. In den Fotogramm-Collagen von Man Ray (1890–1976) entstehen durch Überlagerung unterschiedlicher Formen grafisch reizvolle Muster. Mit seinen Arbeiten übt er großen Einfluss auf die Fotomontagen von George Grosz (1893–1959) und John Heartfield (1891–1968) aus.

László Moholy-Nagy, **Untitled**, 1927 / **Ohne Titel** / **Sans titre**
Silver gelatin photogram, 17.8 × 23.9 cm (7 × 9 3/8 in.)
The Art Institute of Chicago, Julien Levy Collection, Gift of Jean and Julien Levy

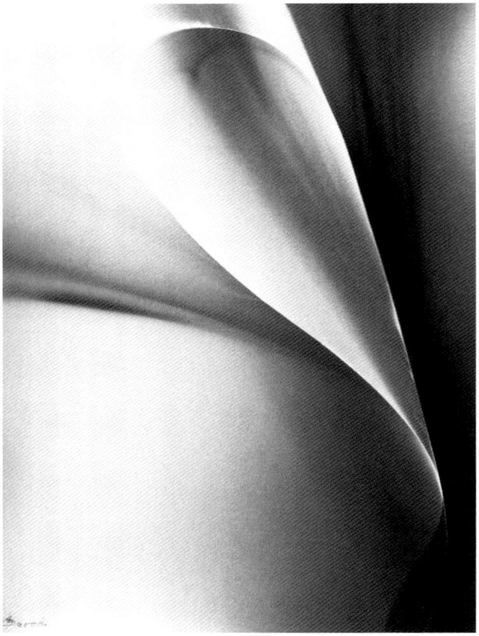

Angeregt von der Bauhaus-Fotografie, nutzen auch die Fotografin Marta Hoepffner (1912–2000) und der Maler Rolf Cavael (1898–1979) das Medium für sich.

Während die Fotogramme des tschechischen Fotografen Jaroslav Rösslers (1902–1990) zumeist abstrakt-räumliche Formen zeigen, arbeitet Jaromir Funke (1896–1945), ein weiterer Exponent der tschechischen Avantgarde, mit verschiedenen Schärfeebenen. 1941 wird im Museum of Modern Art in New York unter dem Titel *How to make a photogram* eine Bestandsaufnahme aus dem ersten Jahrhundert des Mediums präsentiert. Die hier gezeigten Fotogramme regen neue Arbeiten an, zu denen auch die Ganzkörper-Bilder von Robert Rauschenberg oder die durch großflächige Unschärfe charakterisierten *Photogenics* der Fotografin Lotte Jacobi (1896–1990) gehören.

Sieben Jahrzehnte nach der ersten Überblicksausstellung in New York zeigt das Victoria & Albert Museum in London in der Ausstellung *Shadow Catchers* einen Überblick mit Arbeiten kameraloser Fotografie von zeitgenössischen Künstlern wie Floris Neusüss (1937–2020), Pierre Cordier (1933–2024), Susan Derges (geb. 1955), Garry Fabian Miller (geb. 1957) und Adam Fuss (geb. 1961). Durch die technische Entwicklung, durch neue bildgebende Verfahren und die Manipulationsmöglichkeiten digitaler Bilddaten sind die Grenzen zwischen dem Medium Fotogramm und benachbarten Kunstformen heute durchlässig geworden. Es scheint jedoch gerade die Reduktion der grafischen Ausdrucksmittel zu sein, die das Fotogramm als Medium künstlerischer Auseinandersetzung weiterhin attraktiv macht.

Lotte Jacobi
Photogenic, Untitled, ca. 1947 / **Photogenic, Ohne Titel** / **Photogenic, Sans titre**
University of New Hampshire, Lotte Jacobi Collection

La photographie sans appareil : le photogramme

La reproduction d'objets généralement plats sur la toile de fond d'un support rendu photosensible par l'action directe de la lumière, s'appelle le photogramme. Dès 1802, les chimistes britanniques Humphry Davy et Thomas Wedgwood (1771–1805) menaient des expériences sur du papier et du cuir au nitrate d'argent. Ils réalisent alors des images de feuilles et d'ailes d'insectes, mais ne peuvent encore les fixer. La source lumineuse utilisée est le soleil. Vers 1834, Henry Fox Talbot parvient pour la première fois à visualiser durablement des photogrammes de plantes, de feuilles et de dentelles. Les photogrammes sont des pièces uniques présentant des valeurs tonales inversées, en d'autres termes, des images négatives. Lorsque l'objet est opaque, la reproduction se limite à une simple silhouette. Comme support du photogramme peuvent également être utilisés du cuir ou du tissu, ou encore du verre ou de la pellicule celluloïde.

Aux premiers temps de la photographie, différentes propositions ont été avancées pour réserver le terme « photographie », qui remonte à John Herschel (1792–1871), au seul procédé, et appeler le résultat « photogramme » (par analogie avec les termes « télégraphie » et « télégramme »). Cette dénomination appliquée à toutes les images produites par procédé photochimique, que ce soit avec ou sans appareil, ne s'imposera pas. Tel que nous l'entendons aujourd'hui, le terme « photogramme » remonte à László Moholy-Nagy (1895–1946), qui découvrit cette technique pour son propre usage dans les années 1920.

S'il est unanimement admis que le photogramme fait partie des procédés photographiques, la question se pose de savoir si les photogrammes sont eux aussi des photographies, ou s'ils ne sont qu'un stade préalable, une forme particulière de la photographie ? La réponse dépend de ce que l'on considère ou non l'utilisation d'un appareil photo et la création d'une image en perspective comme des propriétés intrinsèques du médium. Toutefois, au tout début de l'histoire de la photographie, la distinction entre images réalisées avec ou sans appareil n'existe pas encore. Lors de la première exposition de photographies de l'histoire présentée par Talbot le 25 janvier 1839 à la Royal Institution de Londres, on pouvait aussi voir, à côté des clichés réalisés à la chambre noire, des « dessins photogéniques » de fleurs, de feuilles ou de motifs de dentelle pressés.

Dès le début de l'année 1839, le marchand d'art londonien Ackermann & Co propose à la vente un kit de produits chimiques et d'appareils devant permettre à des amateurs de créer des « dessins photogéniques ». À l'époque, Talbot lui-même voit l'importance fondamentale de la photographie dans la reproduction de modèles artistiques ou la représentation de préparations botaniques. Le pionnier français de la photographie Hippolyte Bayard (1801–1887) expérimente avec des photogrammes et reproduit des motifs textiles, des plumes et des eaux-fortes. En 1842, l'invention du cyanotype par Herschel va simplifier la création de photogrammes. Pendant les premières années de l'histoire de la photographie, les cyanotypes voient souvent le jour dans le contexte familial et amical de Talbot et Herschel, dont font aussi partie Anna Atkins et Anne Dixon.

Mais bientôt, le photogramme n'est plus considéré que comme une étape technique vers la photographie avec appareil. La création de photogrammes, qui se passe largement de tout appareil, est considérée comme un passe-temps utile, surtout pour les femmes. Des modes d'emplois dans des livres sur la photographie et des exemples d'images dans les revues popularisent la création de photogrammes. Un peu comme les silhouettes en papier, les photogrammes montrant des motifs botaniques sont collés dans des albums, collectionnés et offerts en cadeau.

Dans le contexte d'une école anthroposophique créée en 1919 à Loheland, dans la Hesse, le photogramme va connaître une renaissance en tant que forme artistique grâce à Bertha Günther, dont les productions dans ce domaine incitent László Moholy-Nagy à réaliser ses propres essais au Bauhaus. Dans le cadre de ces essais, Moholy-Nagy va étendre les moyens d'expression artistique du photogramme par des expositions multiples et des projections lumineuses distantes. Également en 1919, le peintre Christian Schad (1894–1982) réalise sur papier photosensible des compositions d'objets quotidiens combinés avec des écritures et des journaux déchirés. Dans les photogrammes-collages de Man Ray (1890–1976), des motifs graphiquement attrayants apparaissent grâce à la superposition de différentes formes. Ses œuvres exercent une forte influence sur les photomontages de George Grosz (1893–1959) et John Heartfield (1891–1968). Inspirés par la photographie du Bauhaus, la photographe Marta Hoepffner (1912–2000) et le peintre Rolf Cavael (1898–1979) utilisent le médium dans leur pratique artistique.

Alors que les photogrammes du photographe tchèque Jaroslav Rössler (1902–1990) sont généralement caractérisés par des formes abstraite et spatiales, Jaromir Funke (1896–1945), autre artiste de l'avant-garde tchèque, travaille sur différents niveaux de netteté. En 1941, le Museum of Modern Art de New York présente un tour d'horizon du premier siècle du médium sous le titre *How to make a photogram*. Les photogrammes présentés dans cette exposition vont inspirer de nouveaux travaux, au nombre desquels comptent notamment les images de corps entiers réalisées par Robert Rauschenberg ou encore les « photogenics » de la photographe Lotte Jacobi (1896–1990), caractérisés par leurs grandes surfaces floues.

Sept décennies après le premier tour d'horizon présenté à New York, le Victoria & Albert Museum de Londres présente dans l'exposition *Shadow Catchers* un panorama d'œuvres de photographie sans appareil réalisées par des artistes contemporains comme Floris Neusüss (1937–2020), Pierre Cordier (1933–2024), Susan Derges (1955–), Garry Fabian Miller (1957–) et Adam Fuss (1961–). Avec les évolutions techniques, les nouveaux procédés de génération d'images et les possibilités de manipulation des données numériques de l'image, les frontières entre le photogramme et les médiums artistiques apparentés sont aujourd'hui devenues poreuses. Il semble néanmoins que ce soit justement la réduction des moyens d'expression graphiques qui continue de rendre le photogramme attractif en tant que médium dans la pratique de l'art.

William Henry Fox Talbot, **Arrangement of botanical specimens**, 1839
Arrangement botanischer Präparate / **Arrangement de spécimens botaniques**
Photogenic drawing negative, 22.4 × 18.4 cm (8 ⅞ × 7 ¼ in.)
Los Angeles, J. Paul Getty Museum

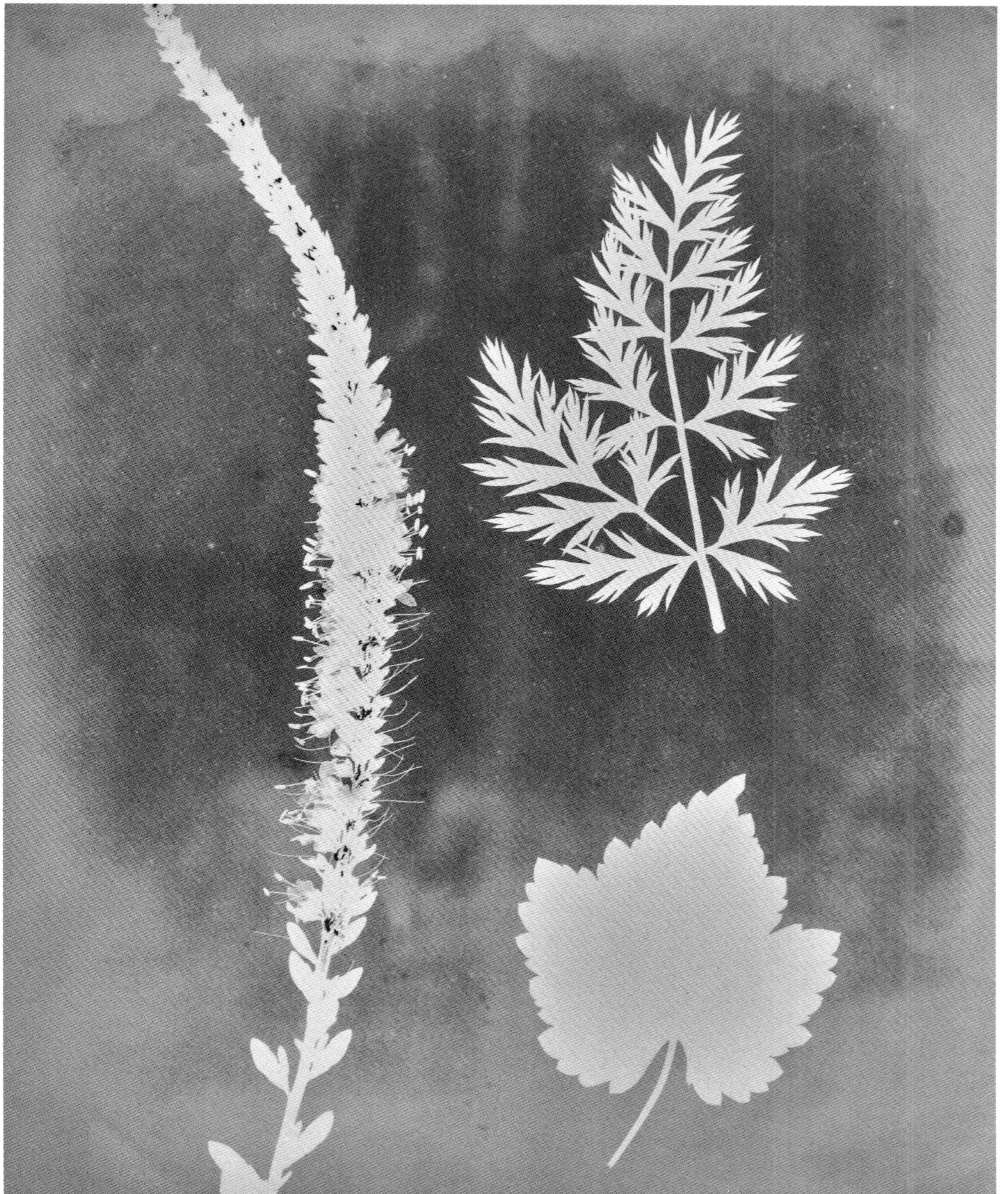

British Algæ,

Vol. III.

Contents.

Vol. III.

Errata.

Vol. 1.

Cystoseira barbata should be granulata (mere scraps of it)
.... fæniculacea .. .. d°
Dichloria viridis – .. .. Ectocarpus littoralis
Padina deusta .. Zonaria variegata (a W. Ind. species)
Rhodomela lycopodiodes – if correct, is not characteristic.

Vol. 2.

Polysiphonia thuyoides – large specimen is P. nigrescens.
.. .. spinulosa, is P. simulans
.... atropurpurea .. Rhodomela subfusca (young)
.... furcellata .. Bostrychia Montagnei, var. (not British)
.... Grevillii – is probably the remains of fibrata
.... fibrata .. Ceramium rubrum.
.... stricta is P. urceolata.
Ceramium strictum is Griffithsia setacea.
Griffithsia multifida – the smaller specimen only is correct.
Callithamnion purpurascens is C. polyspermum.
Conferva implexa is C. ærea – curled up.
C. .. colothrix – is implexa.
C. pellucida – the lower specimen only correct.

APPENDIX.

Contents.

Notice

Should any of the plants which are omitted, or of which the impressions are from poor specimens, be obtained, a supplementary part may at some future time, be added to this work. A. A.

H. P. Sep. 1859.

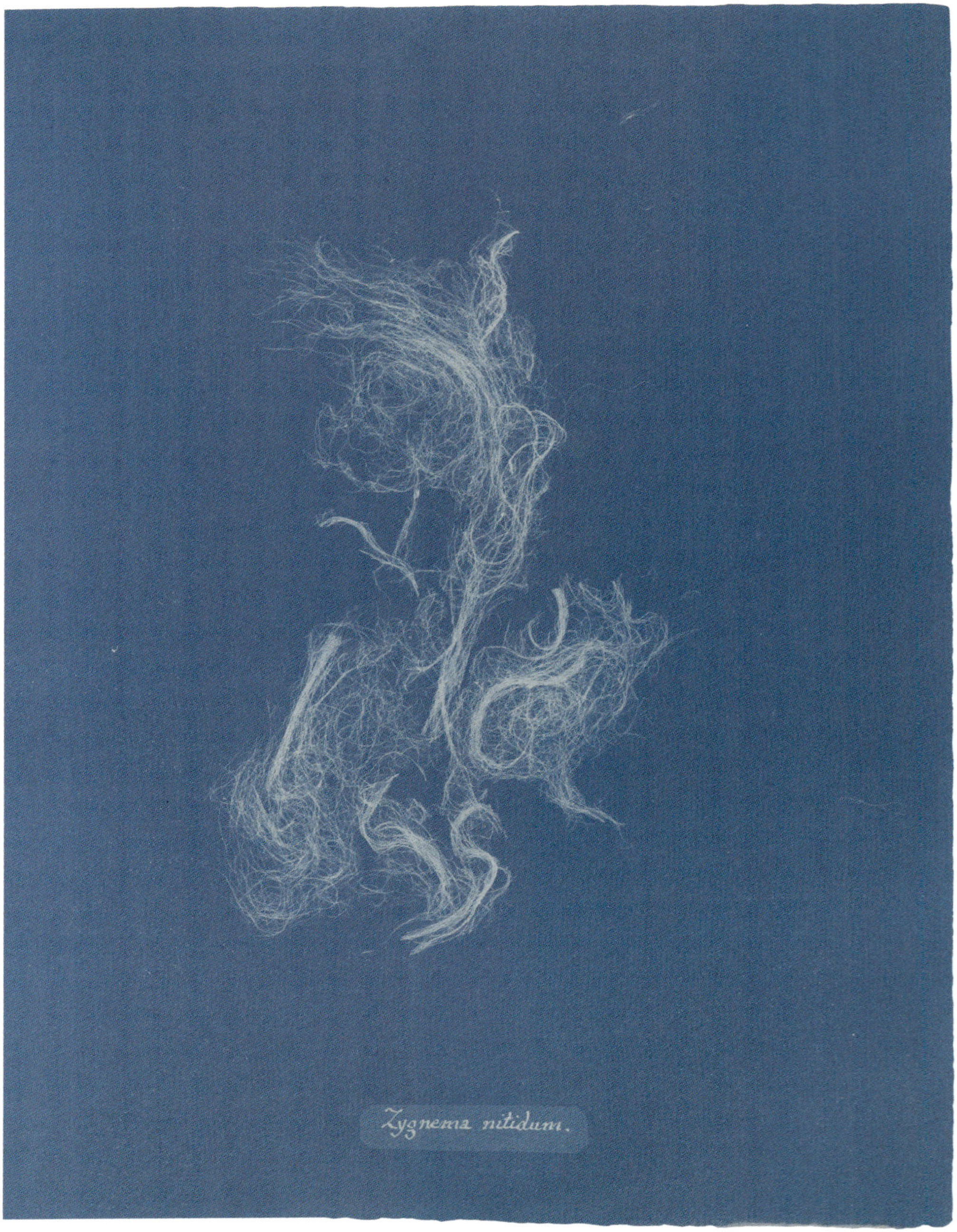

Plate 336. *Zygnema nitidum*

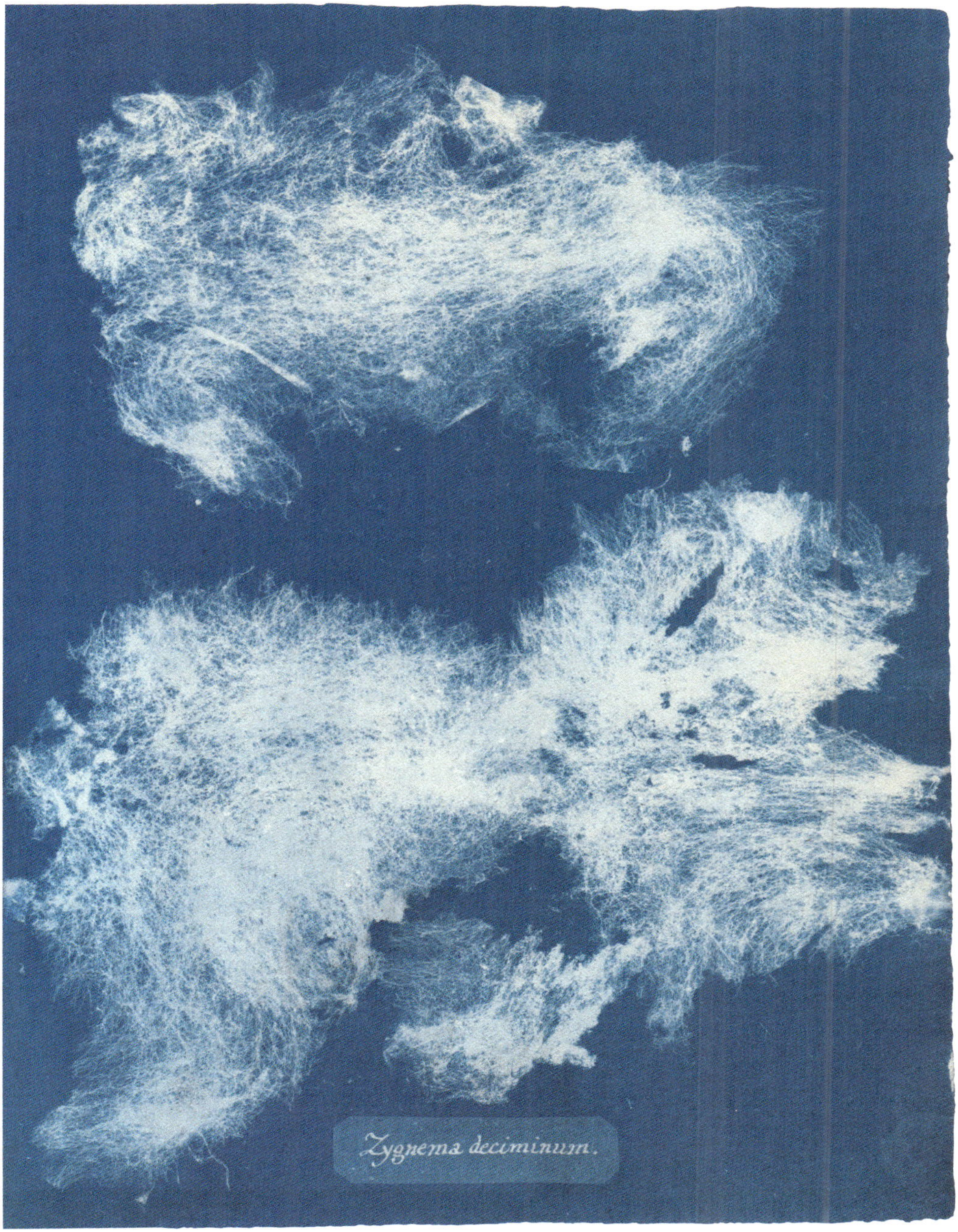

Plate 337. *Zygnema deciminum*

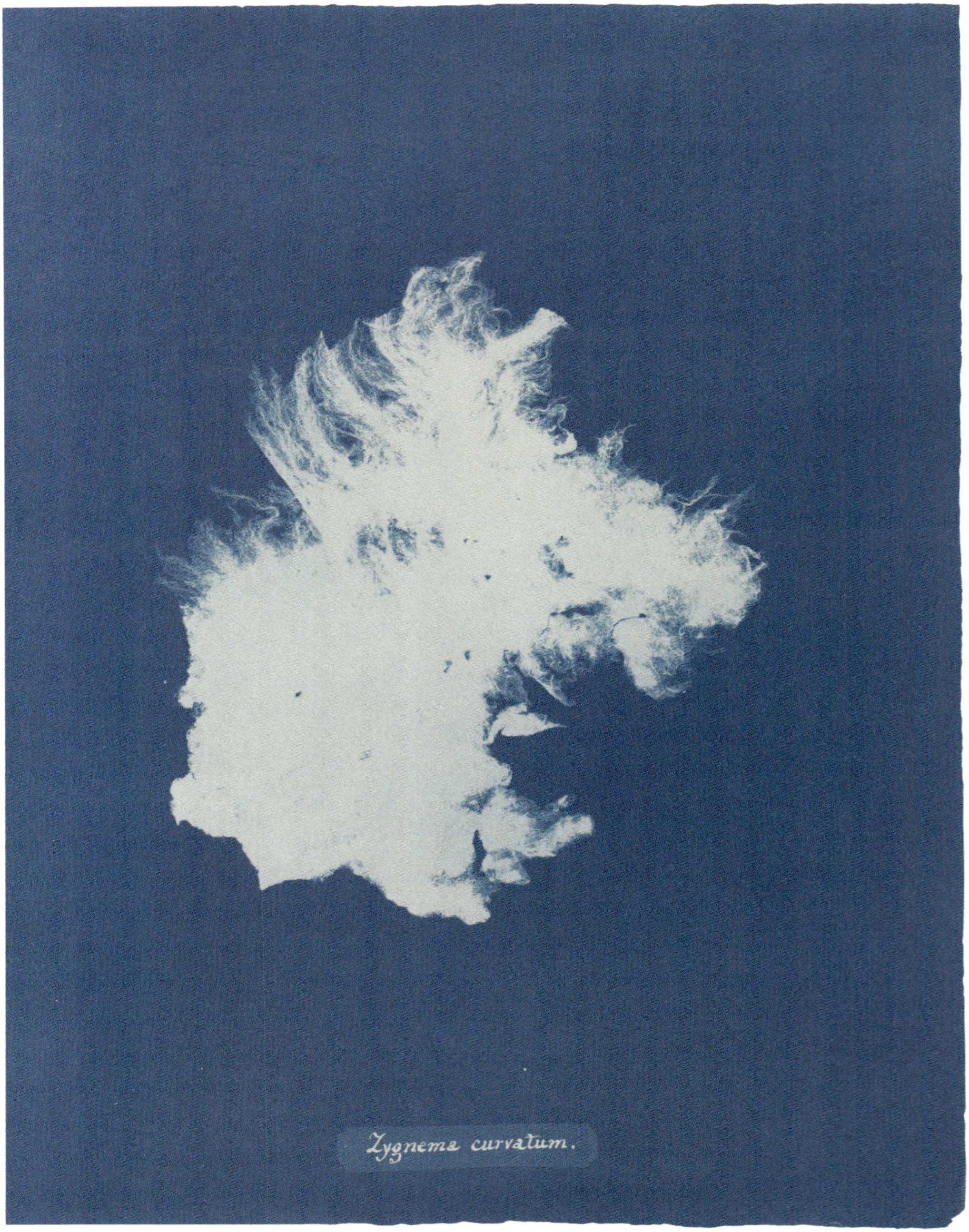

Plate 338. *Zygnema curvatum*

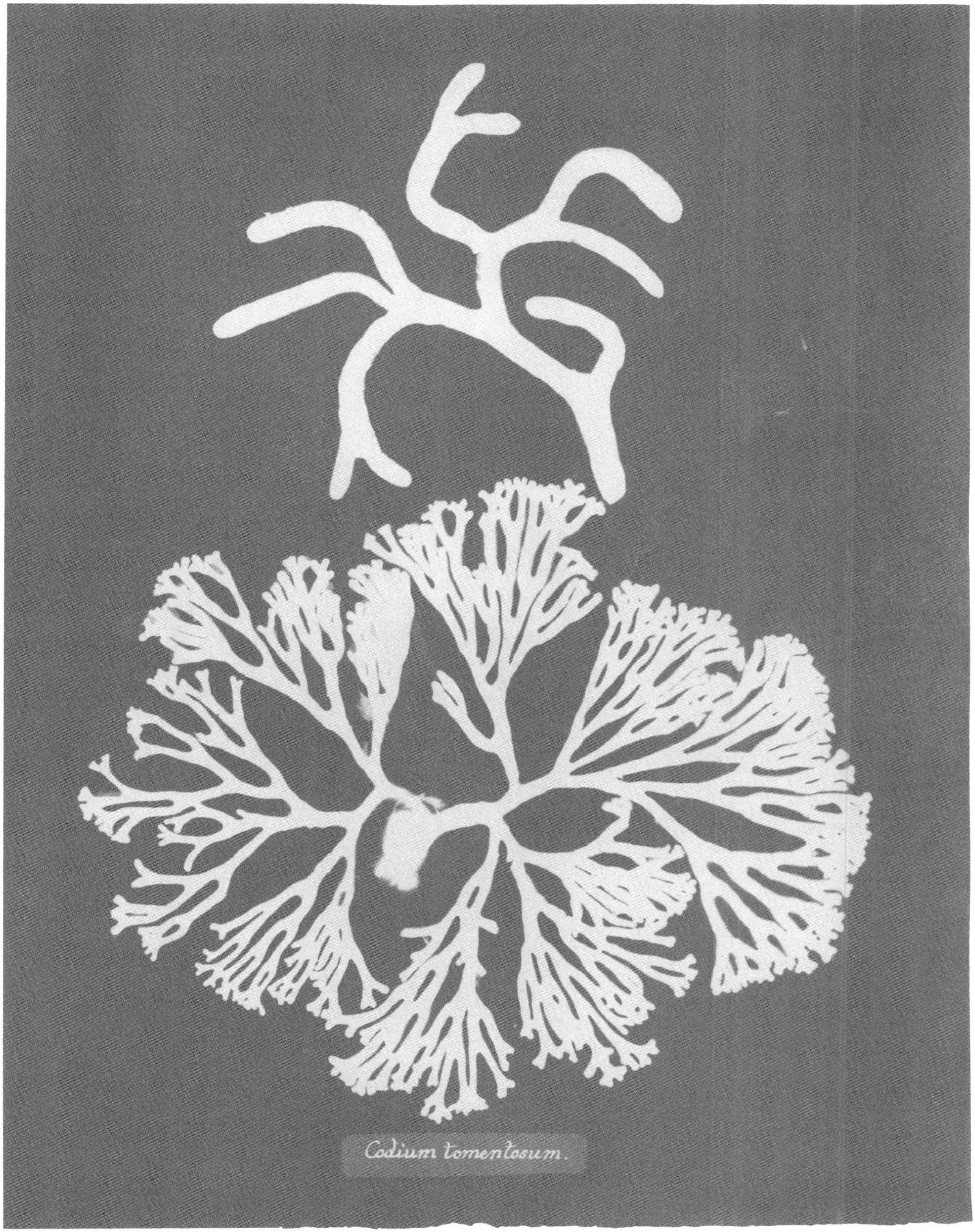

Plate 340. *Codium tomentosum*

Plate 341. *Codium bursa*

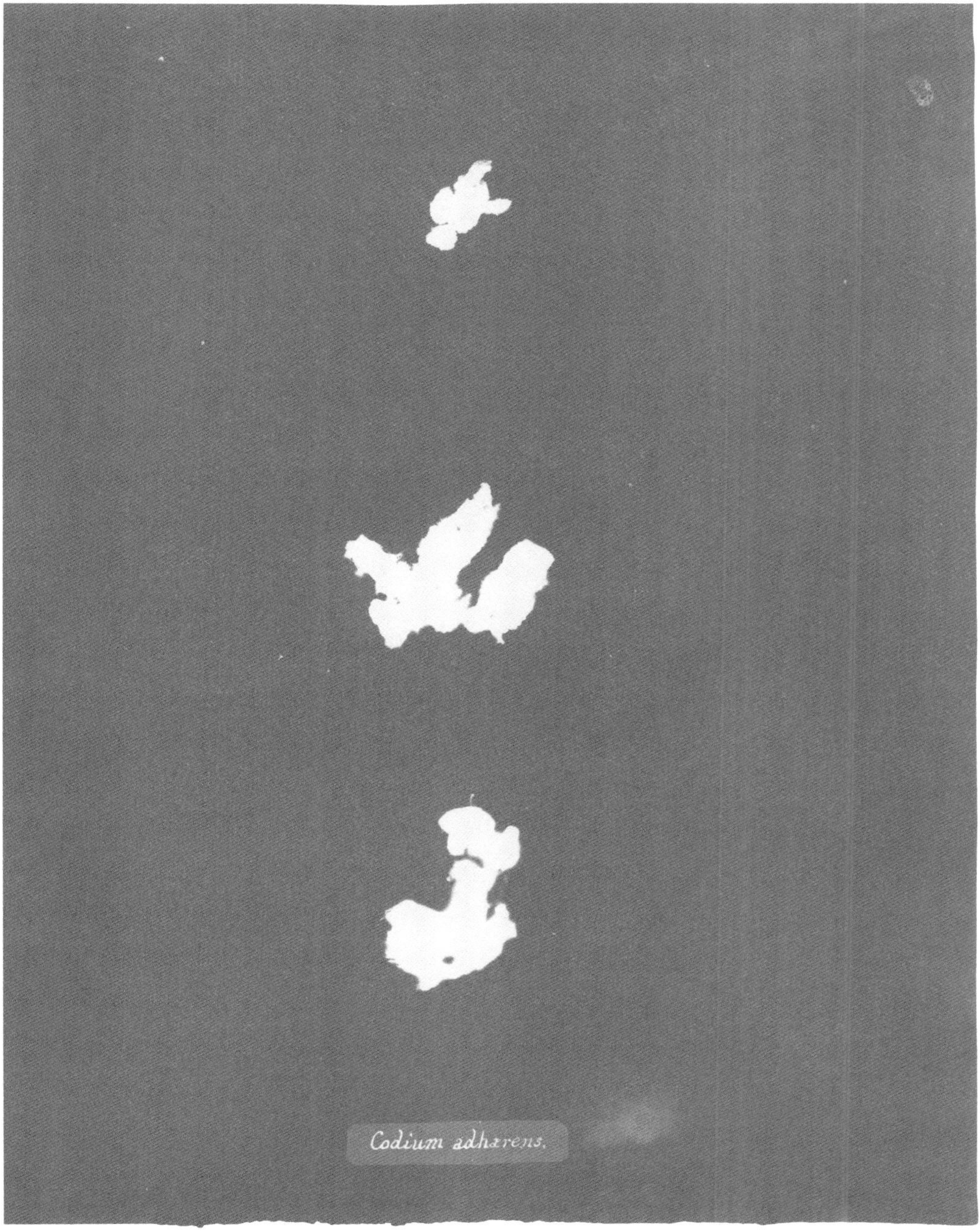

Plate 342. *Codium adhaerens*

Plate 343. *Codium amphibium*

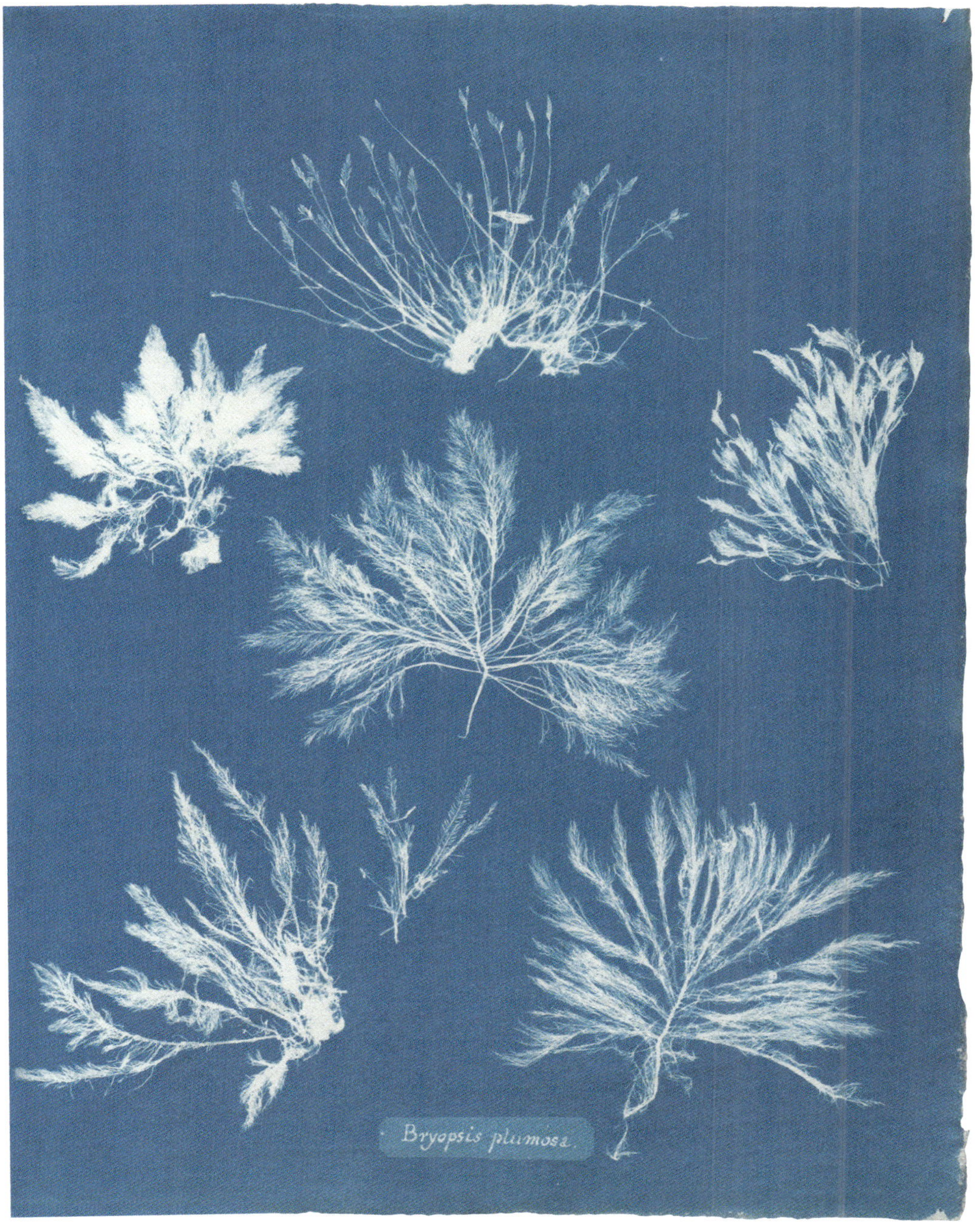

Plate 344. *Bryopsis plumosa*

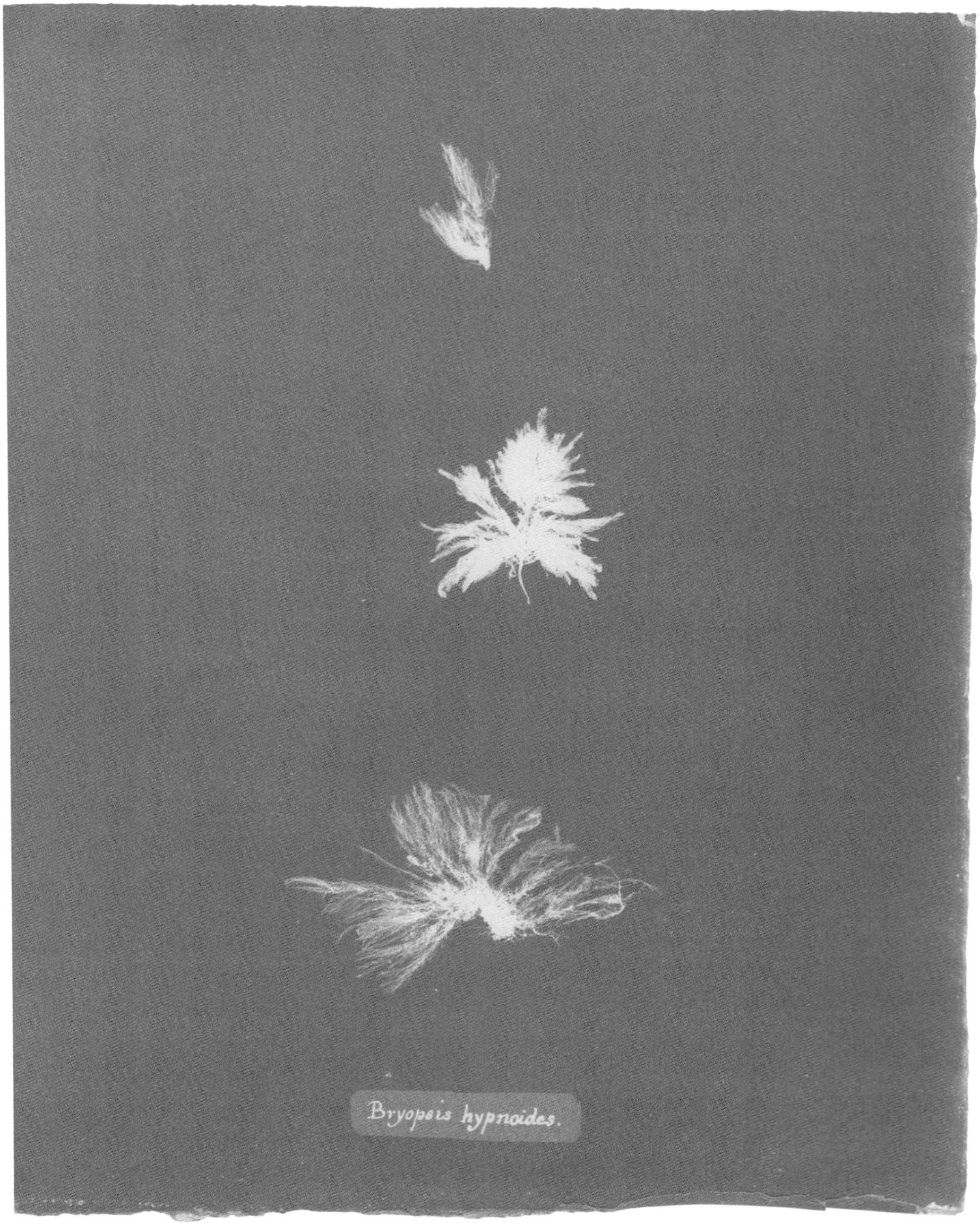

Plate 345. *Bryopsis hypnoides*

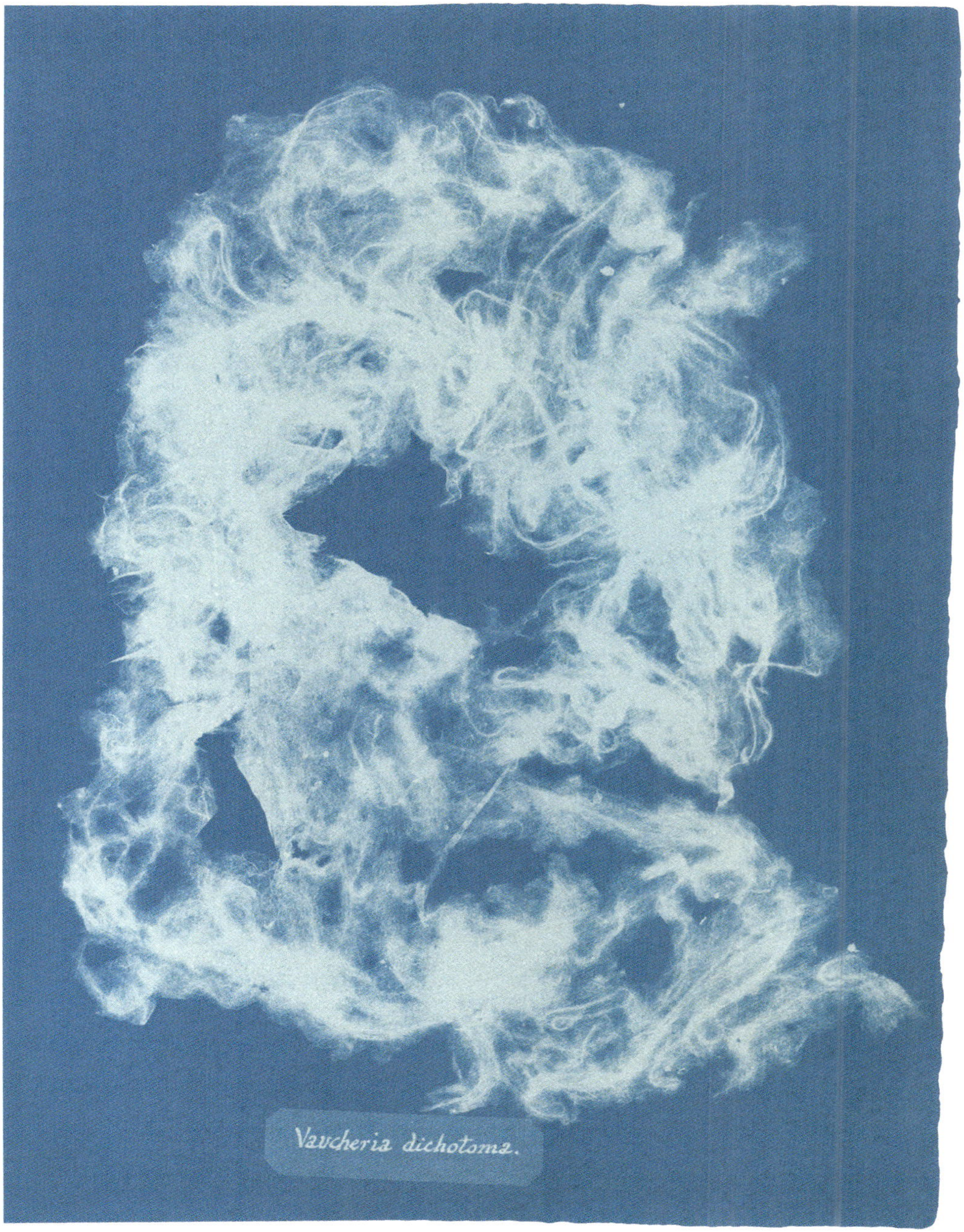

Plate 346. *Vaucheria dichotoma*

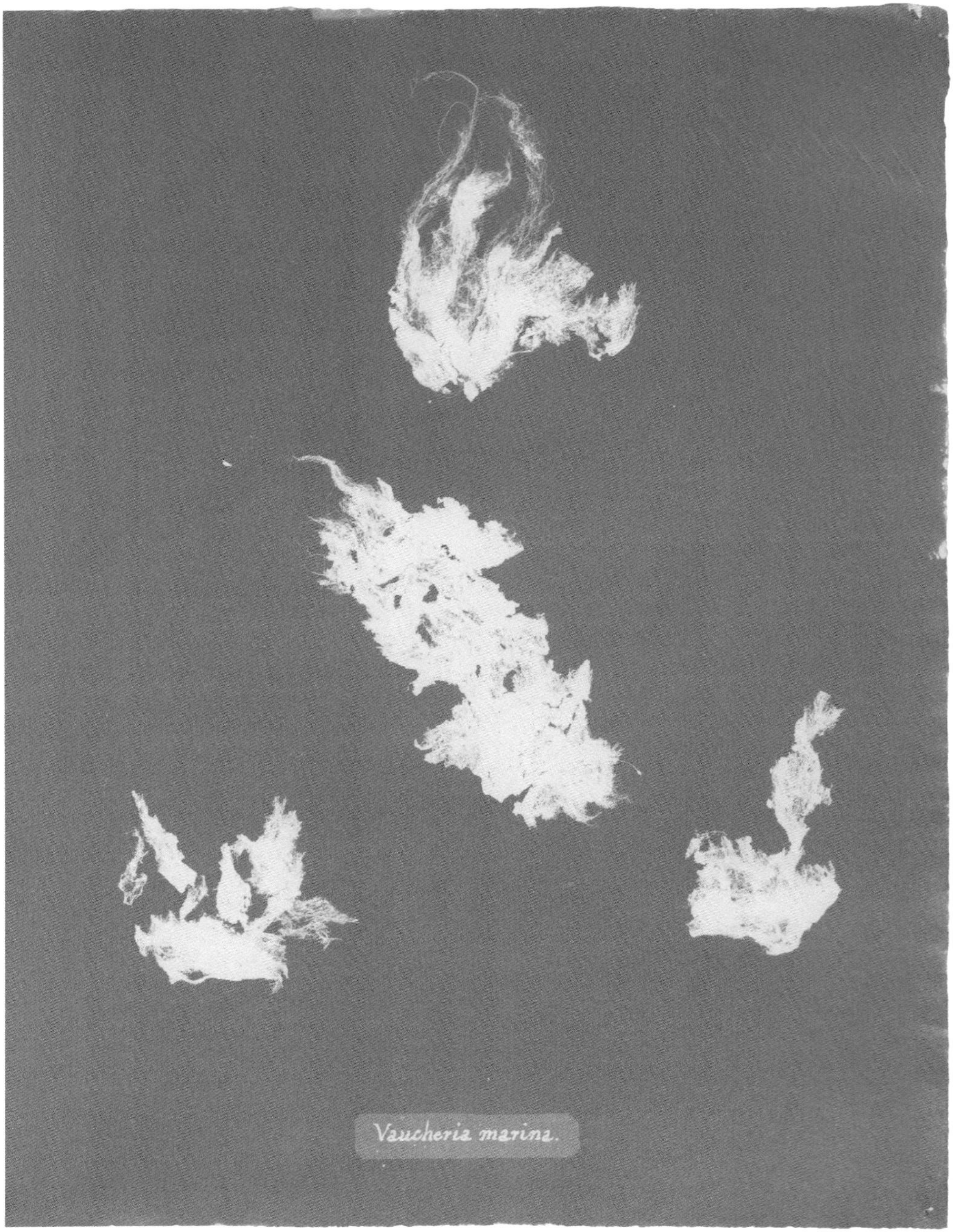

Plate 347. *Vaucheria marina*

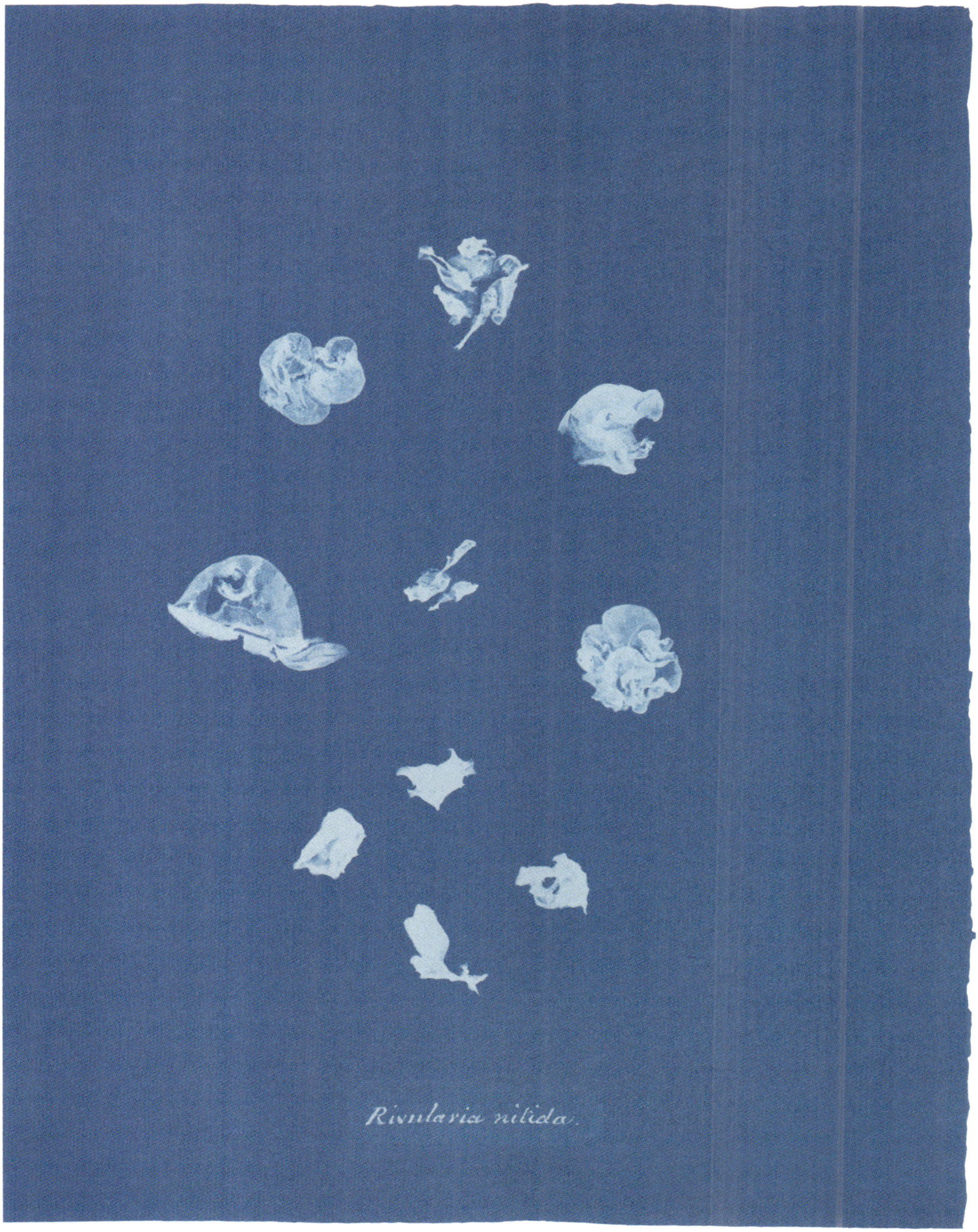

Plate 350. *Rivularia nitida*

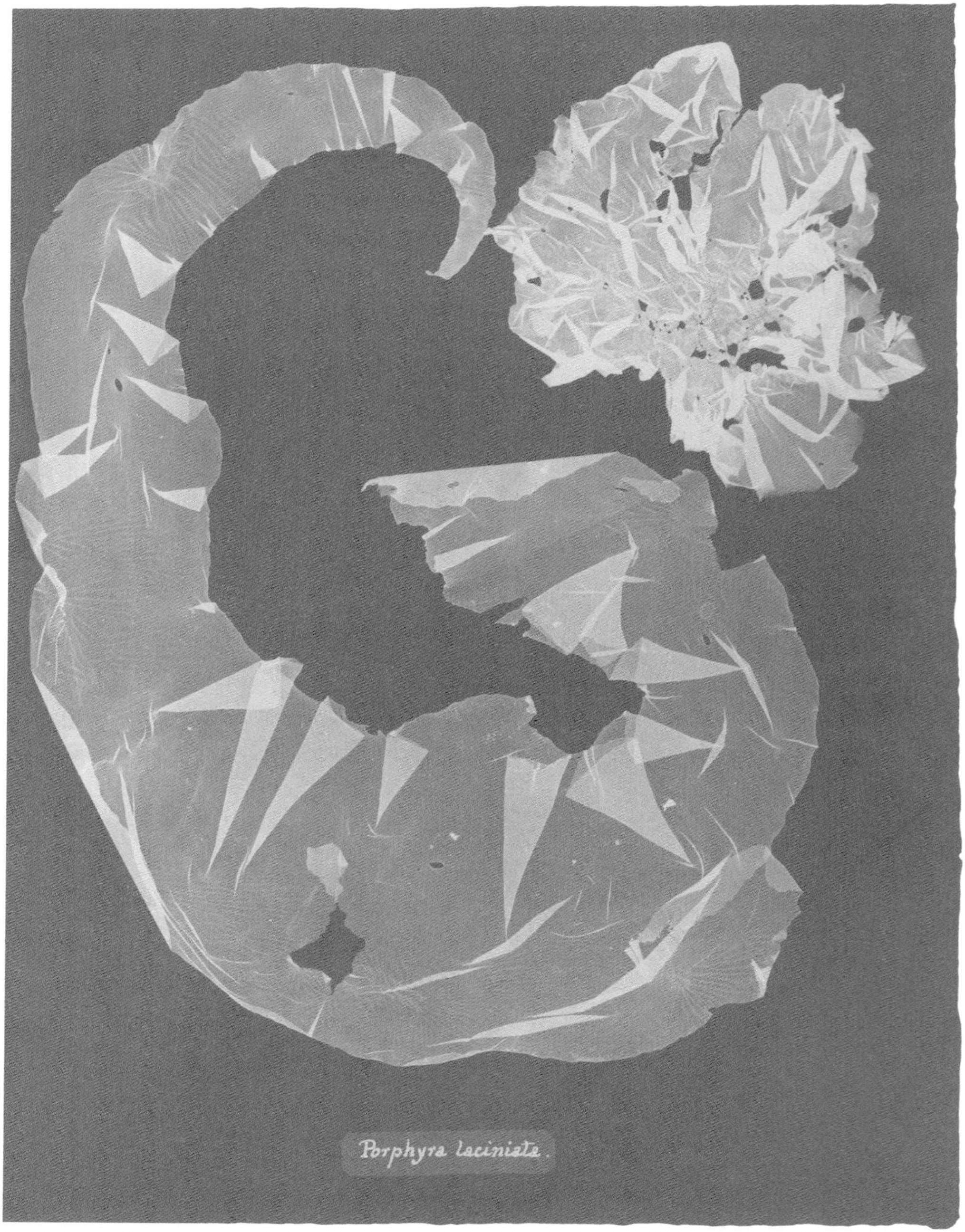

Plate 359. *Porphyra laciniata*

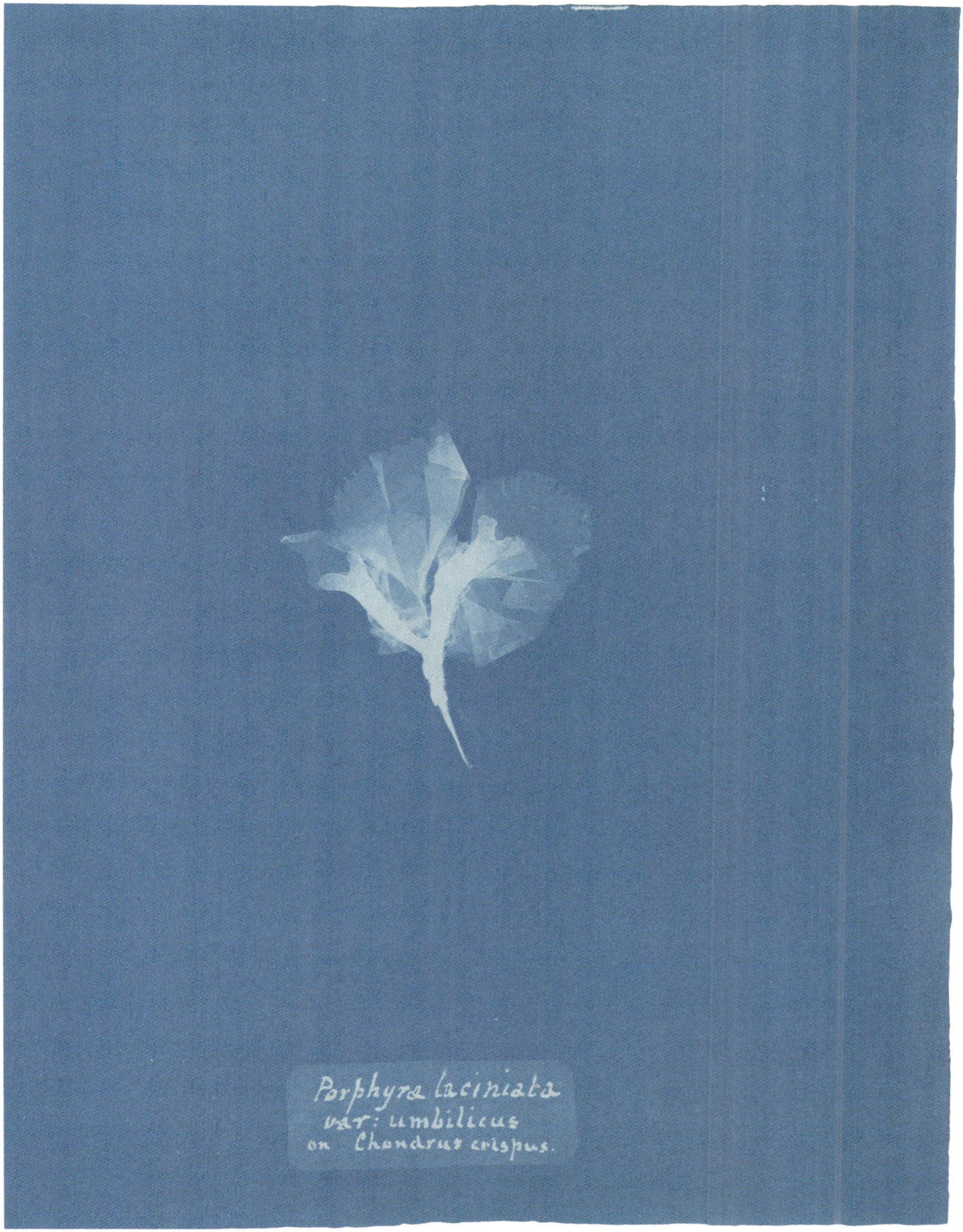

Plate 360. *Porphyra laciniata* var. *umbilicus* or *Chondrus crispus*

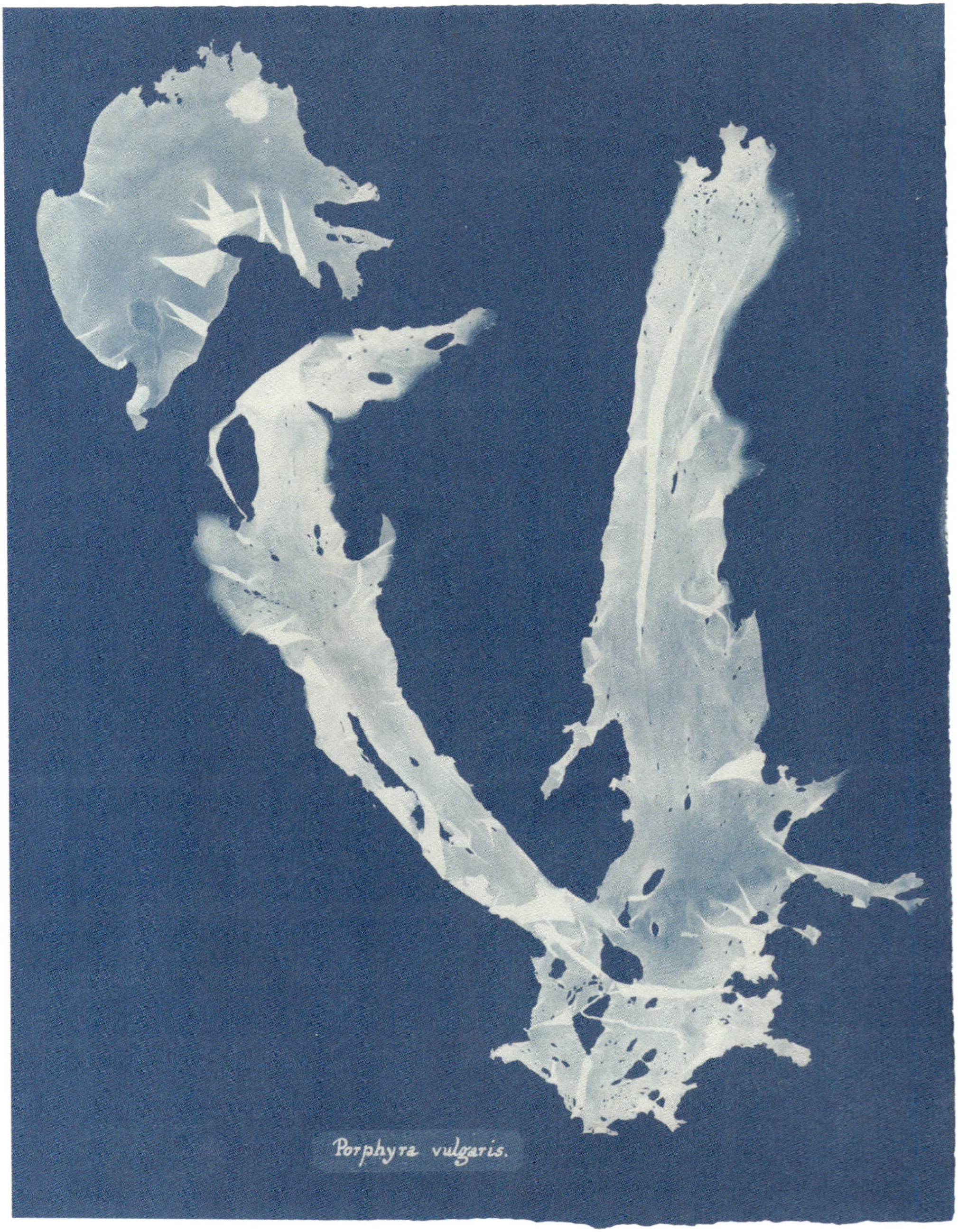

Plate 361. *Porphyra vulgaris*

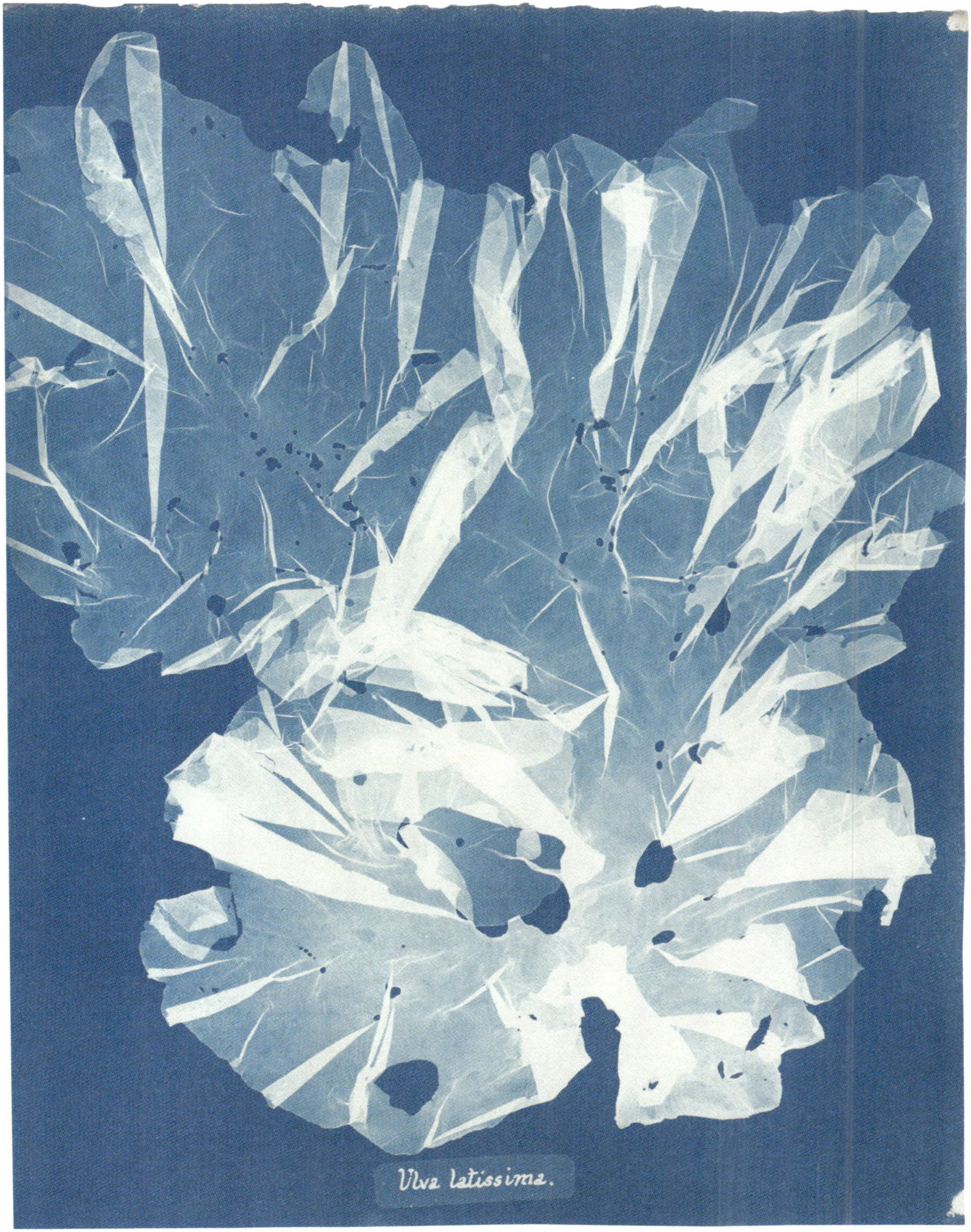

Plate 362. *Ulva latissima*

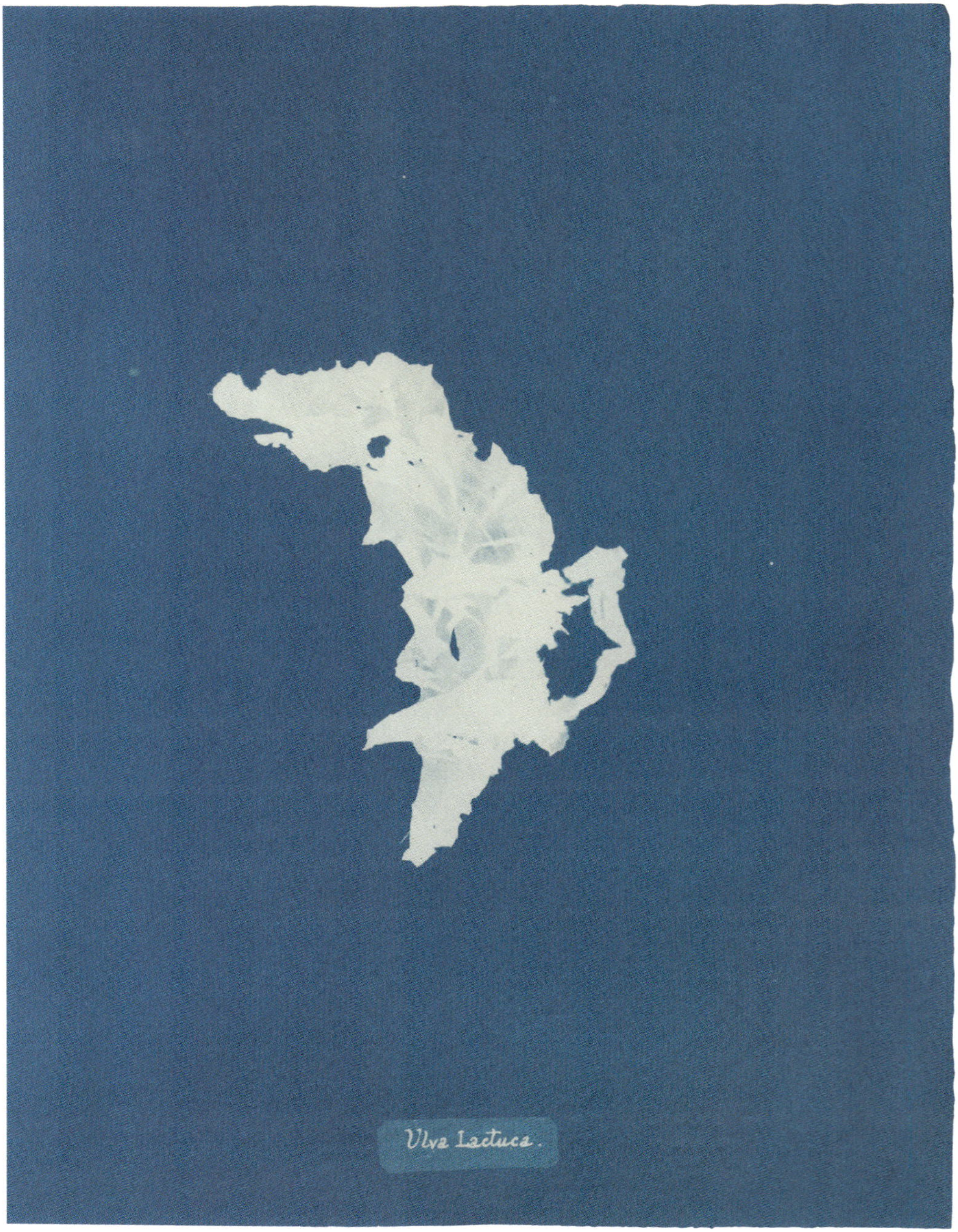

Plate 363. *Ulva lactuca*

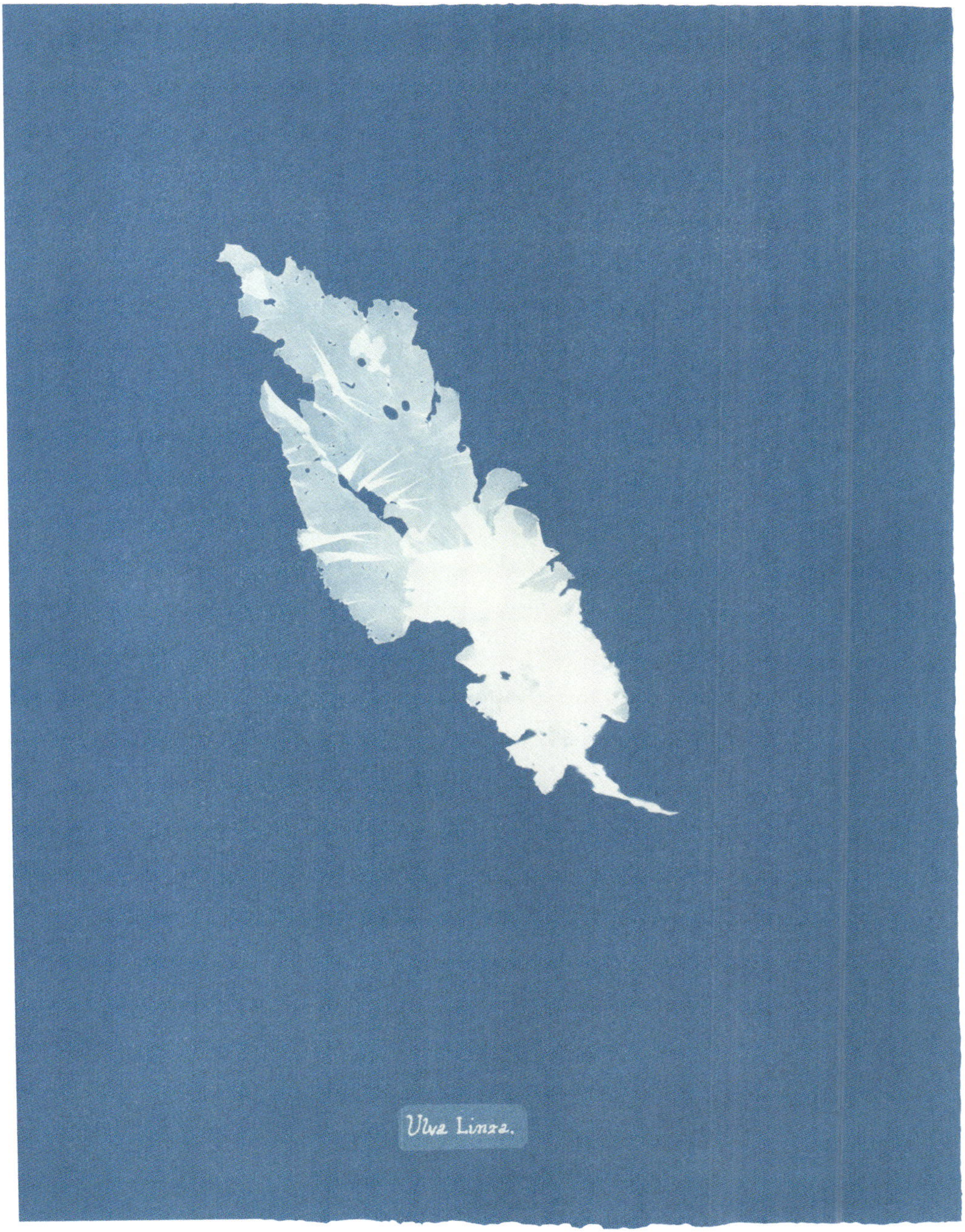

Plate 364. *Ulva linza*

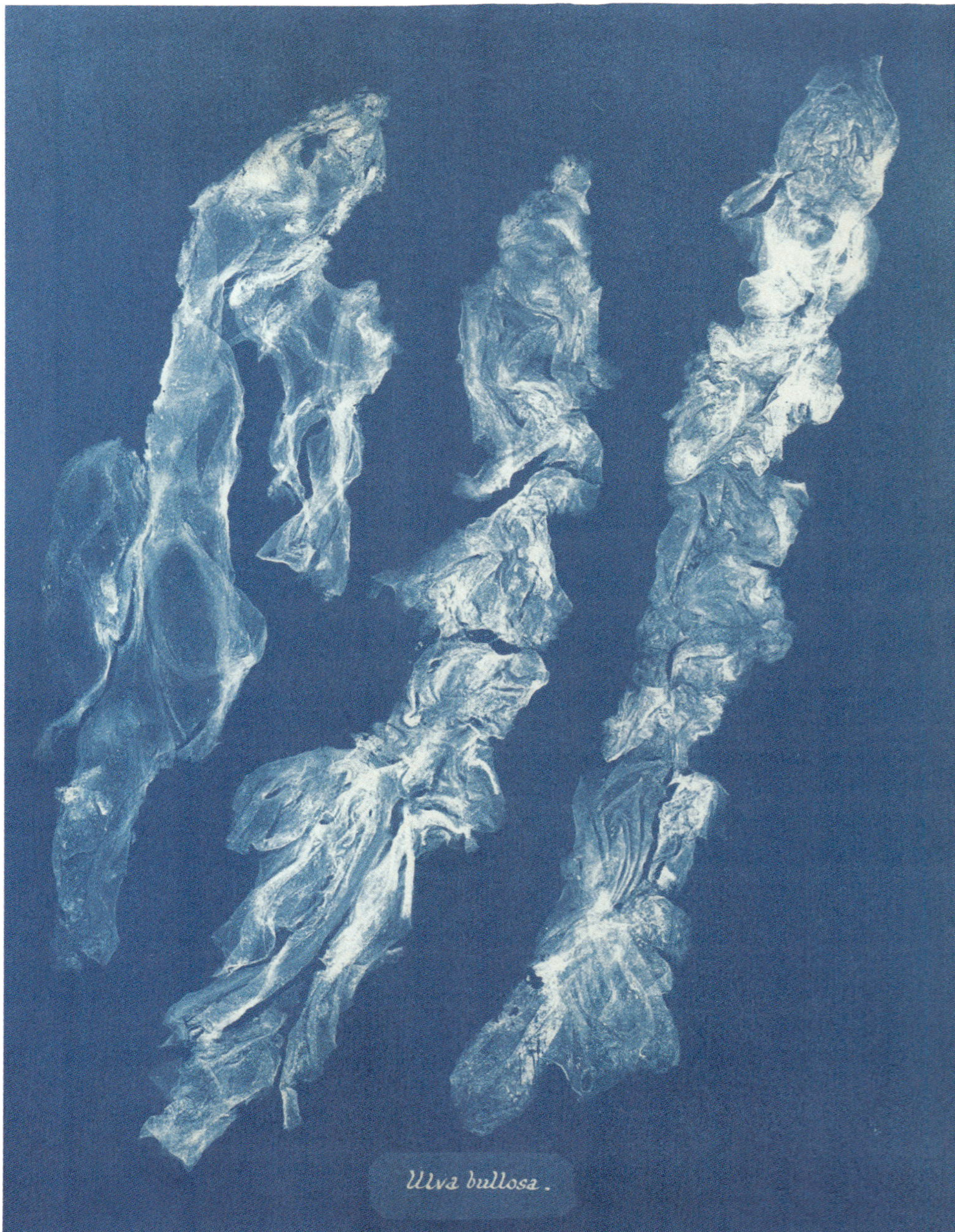

Plate 365. *Ulva bullosa*

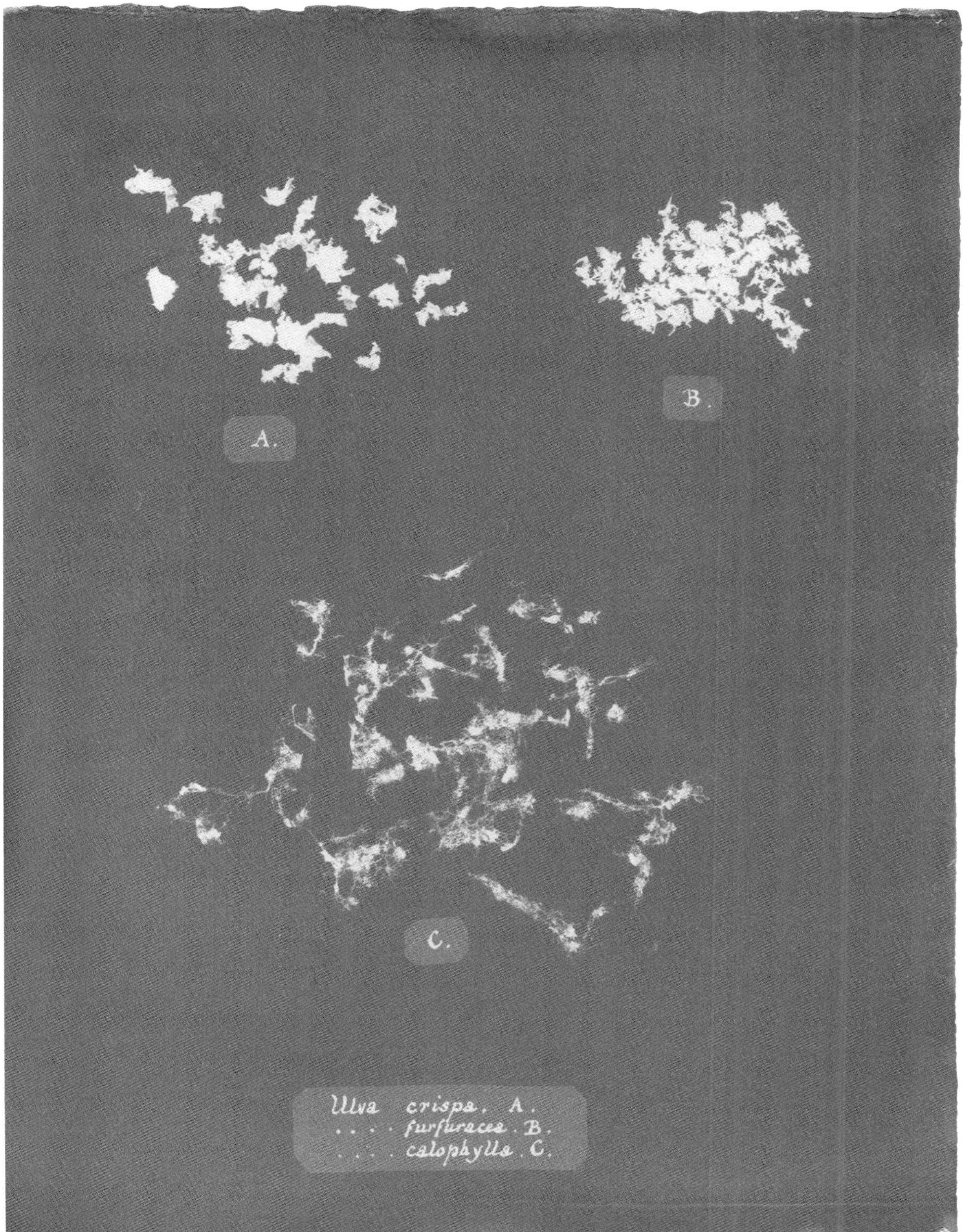

Plate 366. *Ulva crispa*, A; *Ulva furfuracea*, B; *Ulva calophylla*, C

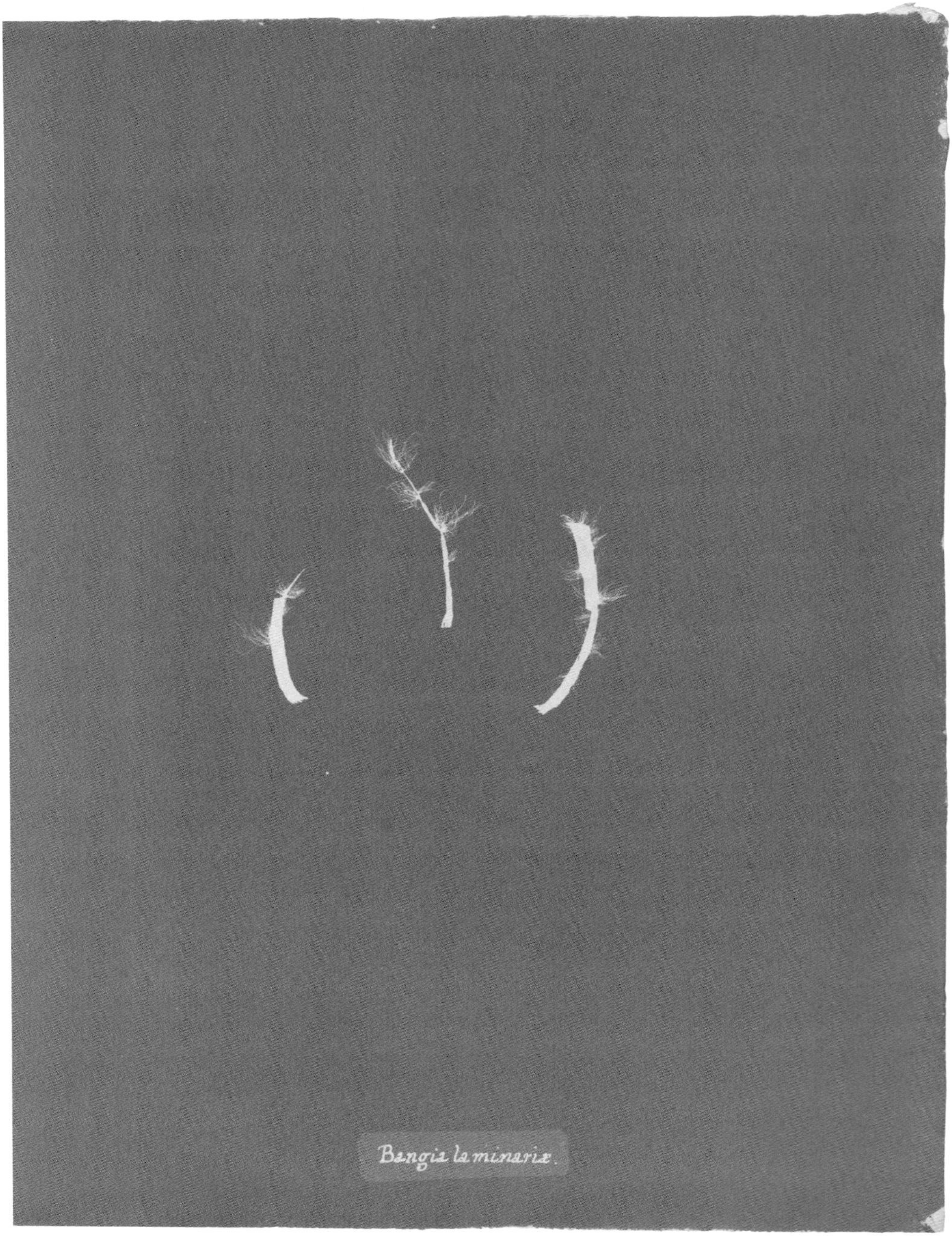

Plate 367. *Bangia laminariae*

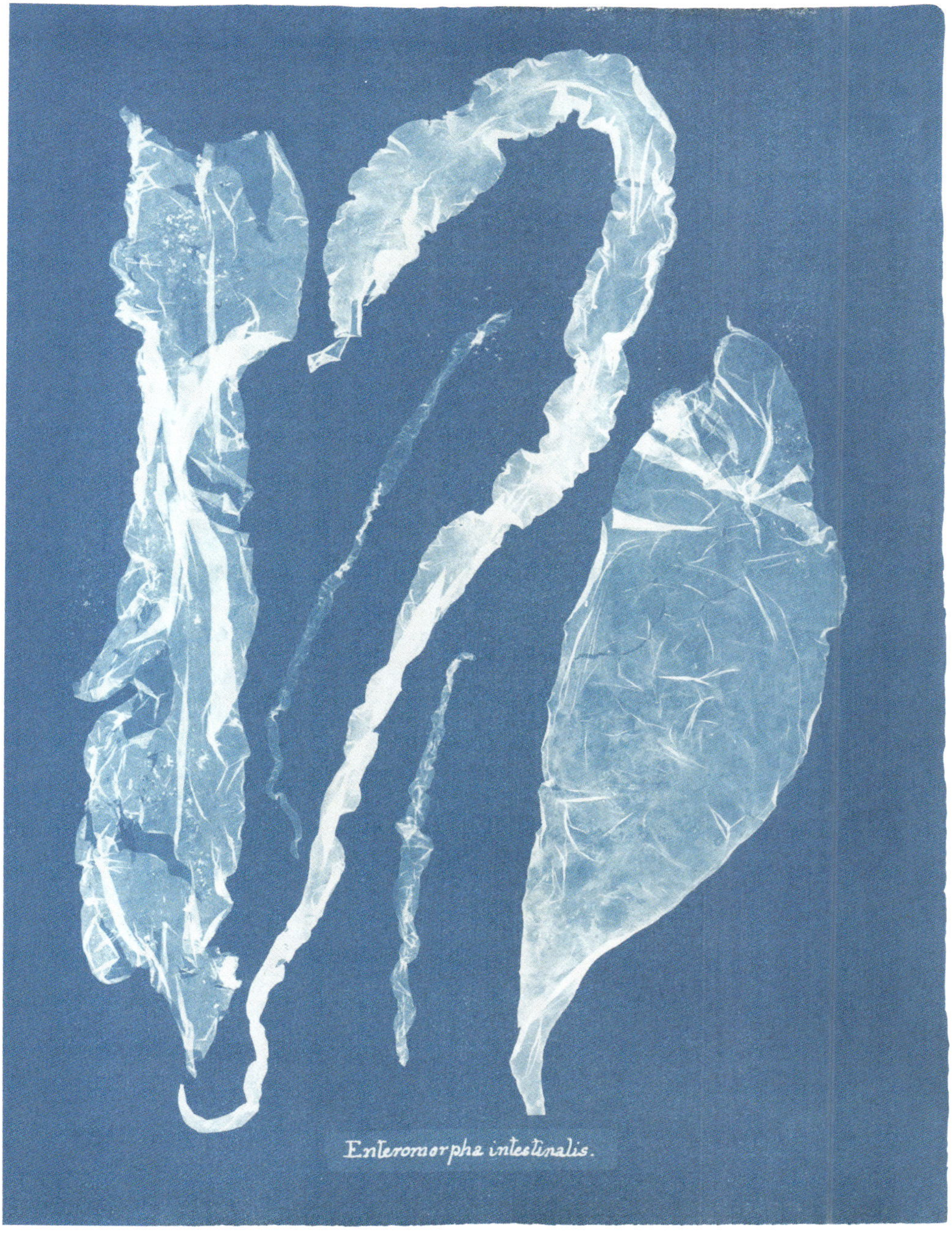

Plate 368. *Enteromorpha intestinalis*

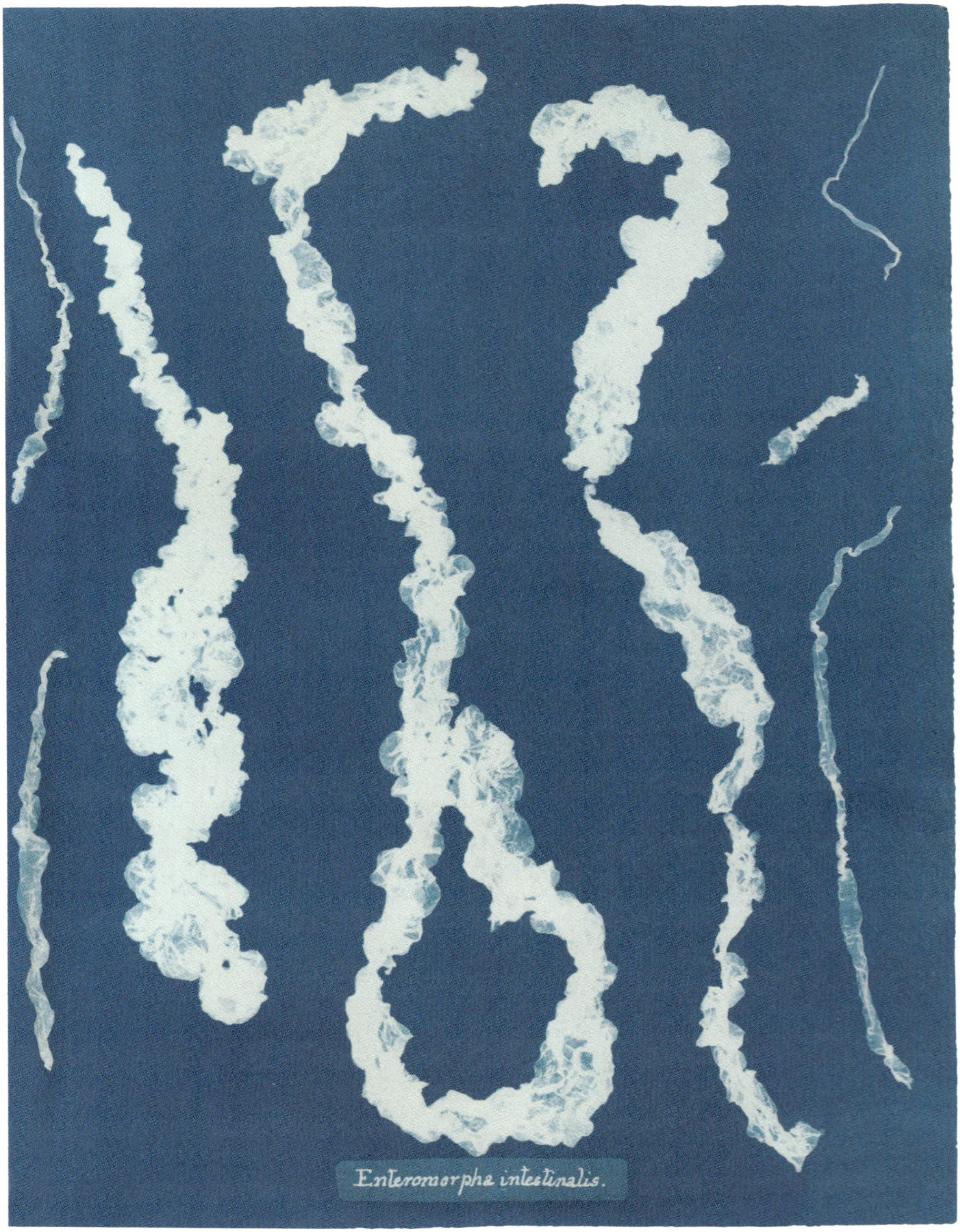

Plate 369. *Enteromorpha intestinalis*

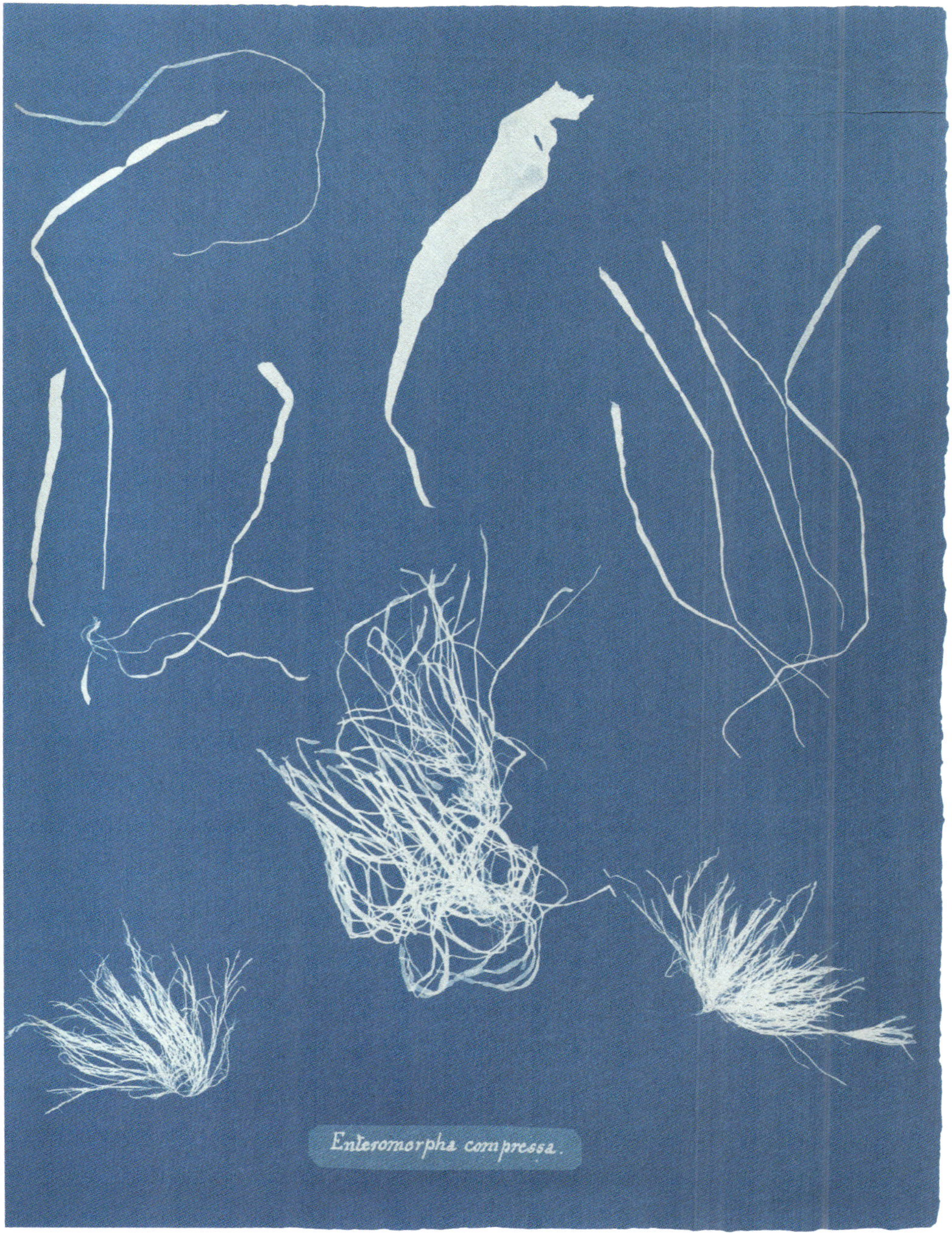

Plate 370. *Enteromorpha compressa*

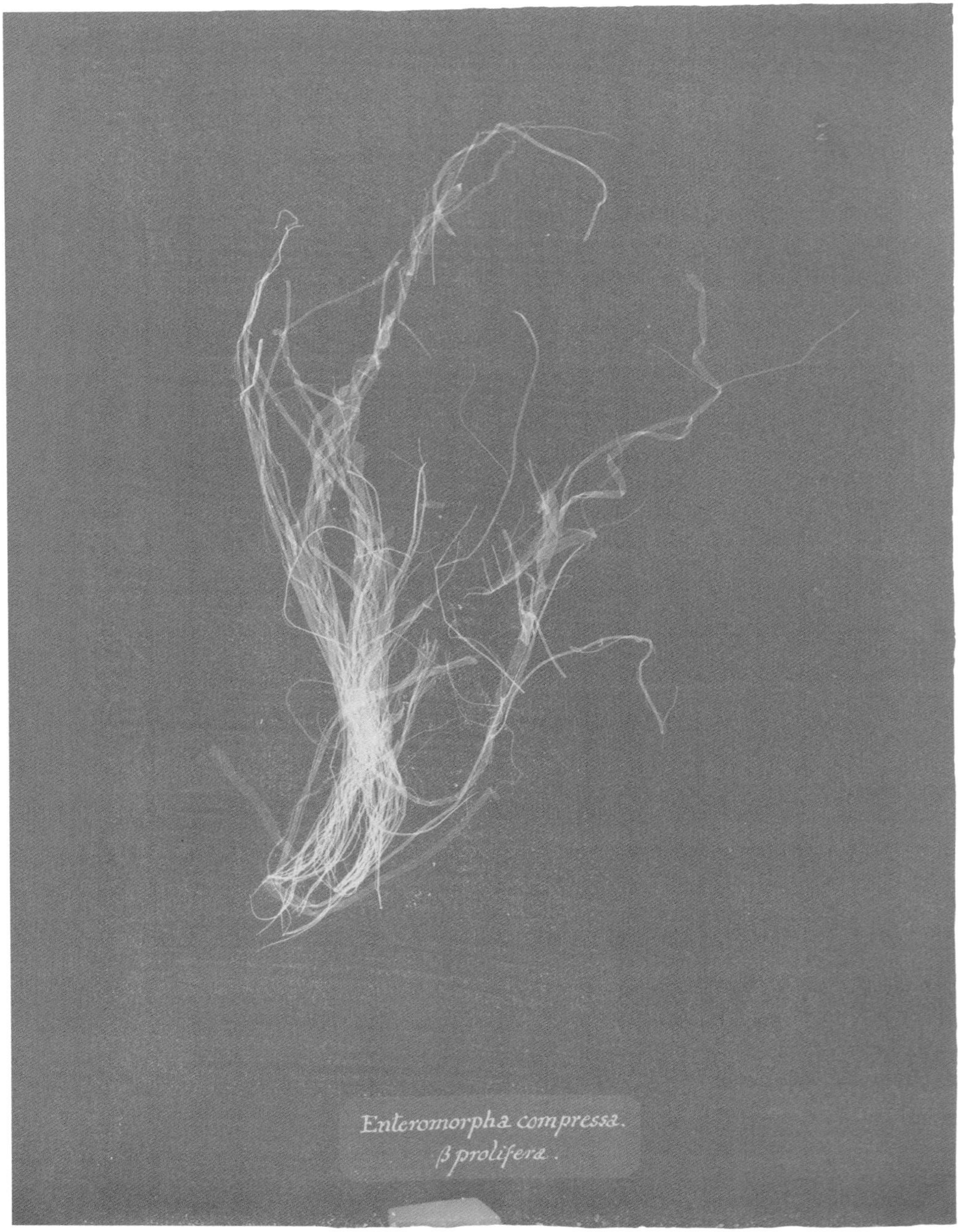

Plate 371. *Enteromorpha compressa* β *prolifera*

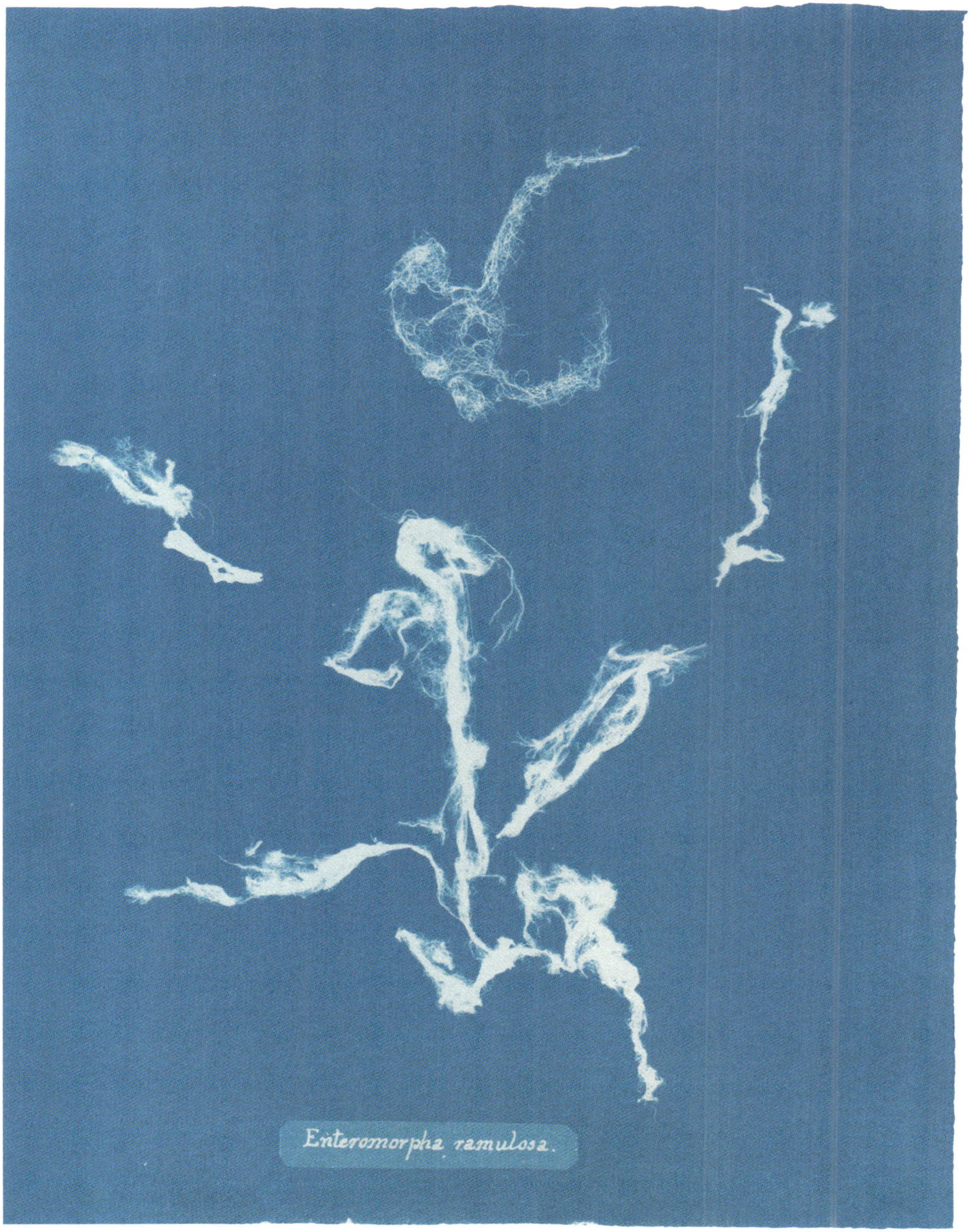

Plate 374. *Enteromorpha ramulosa*

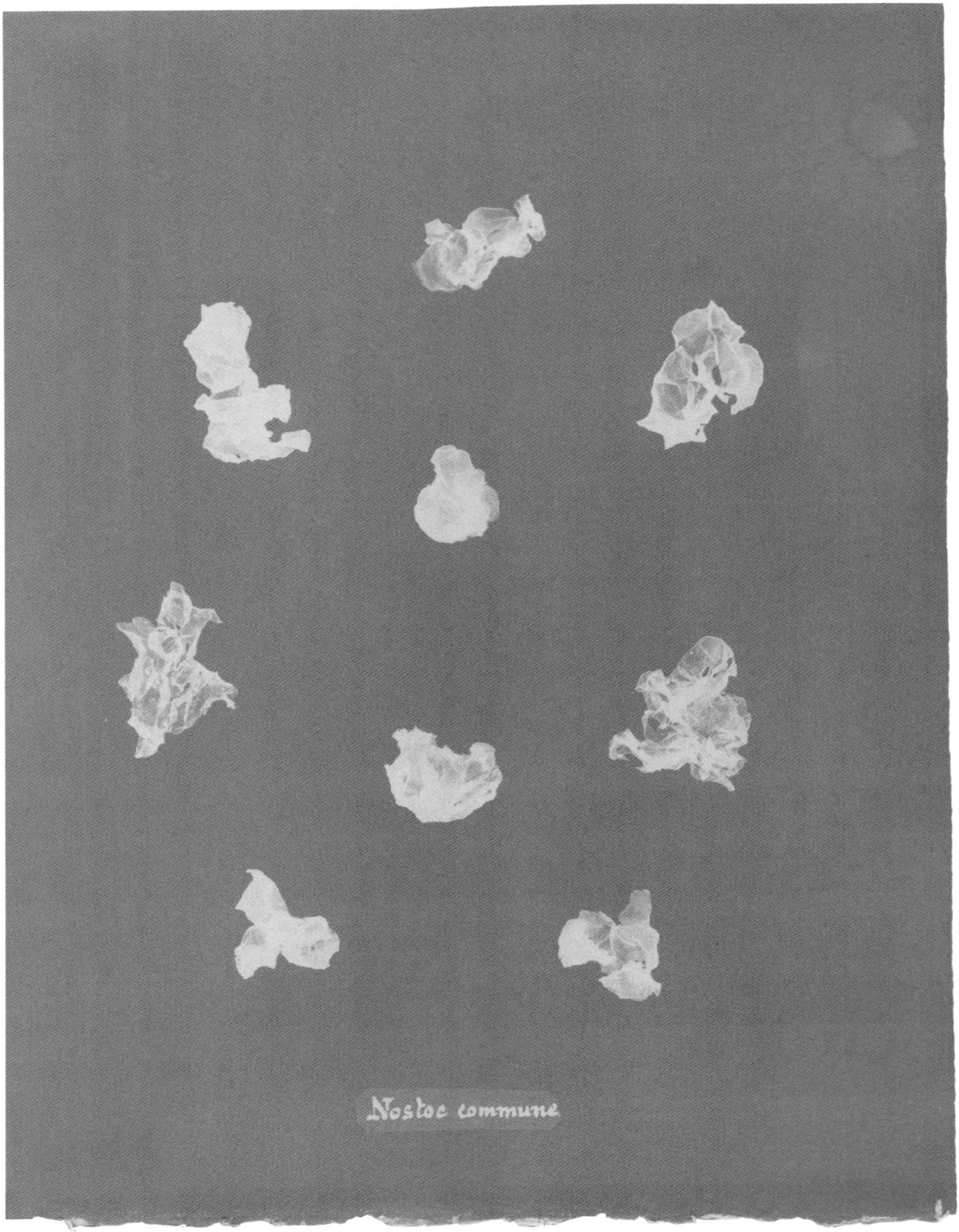

Plate 375. *Nostoe commune*

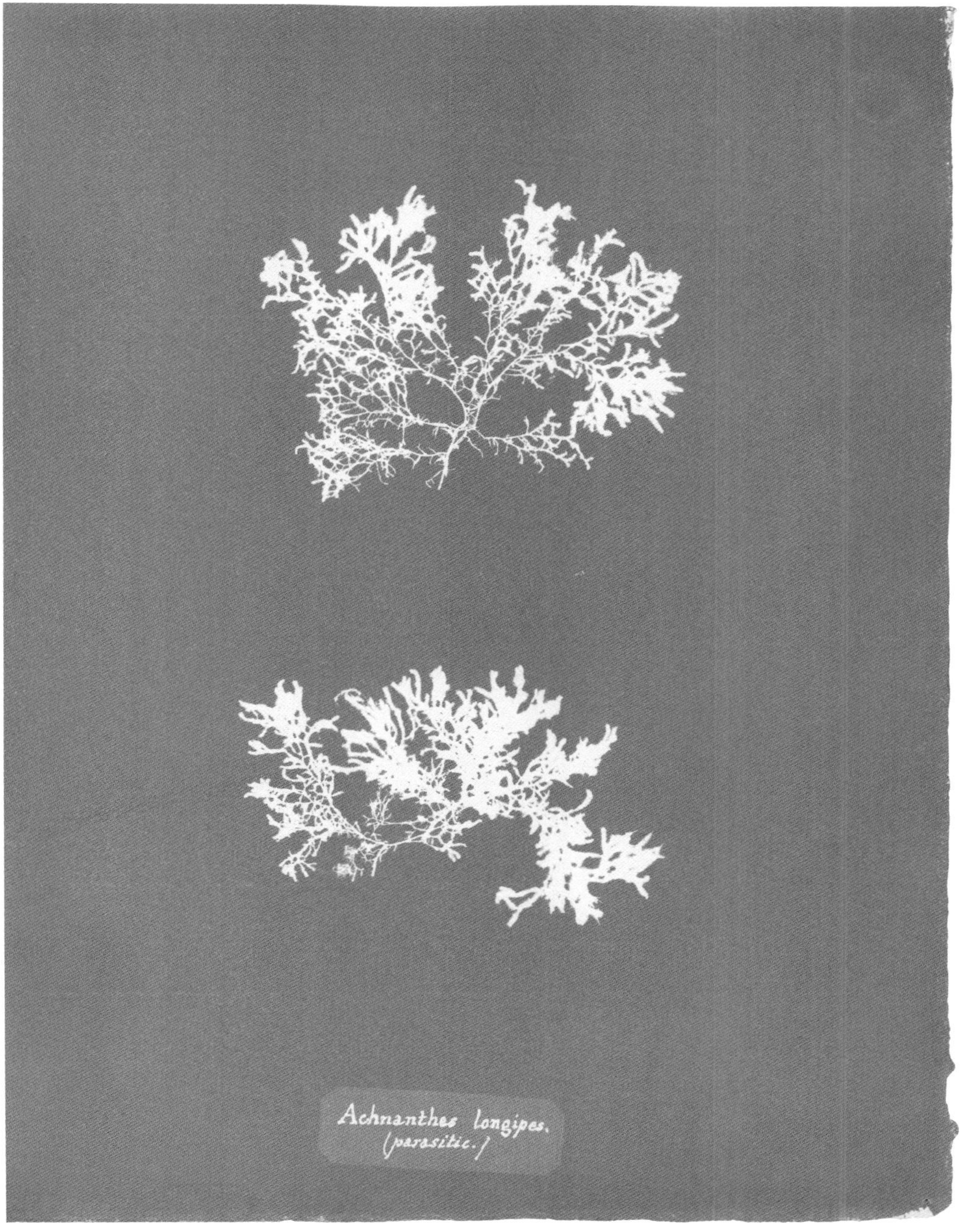

Plate 376. *Achnanthes longipes* (parasitic)

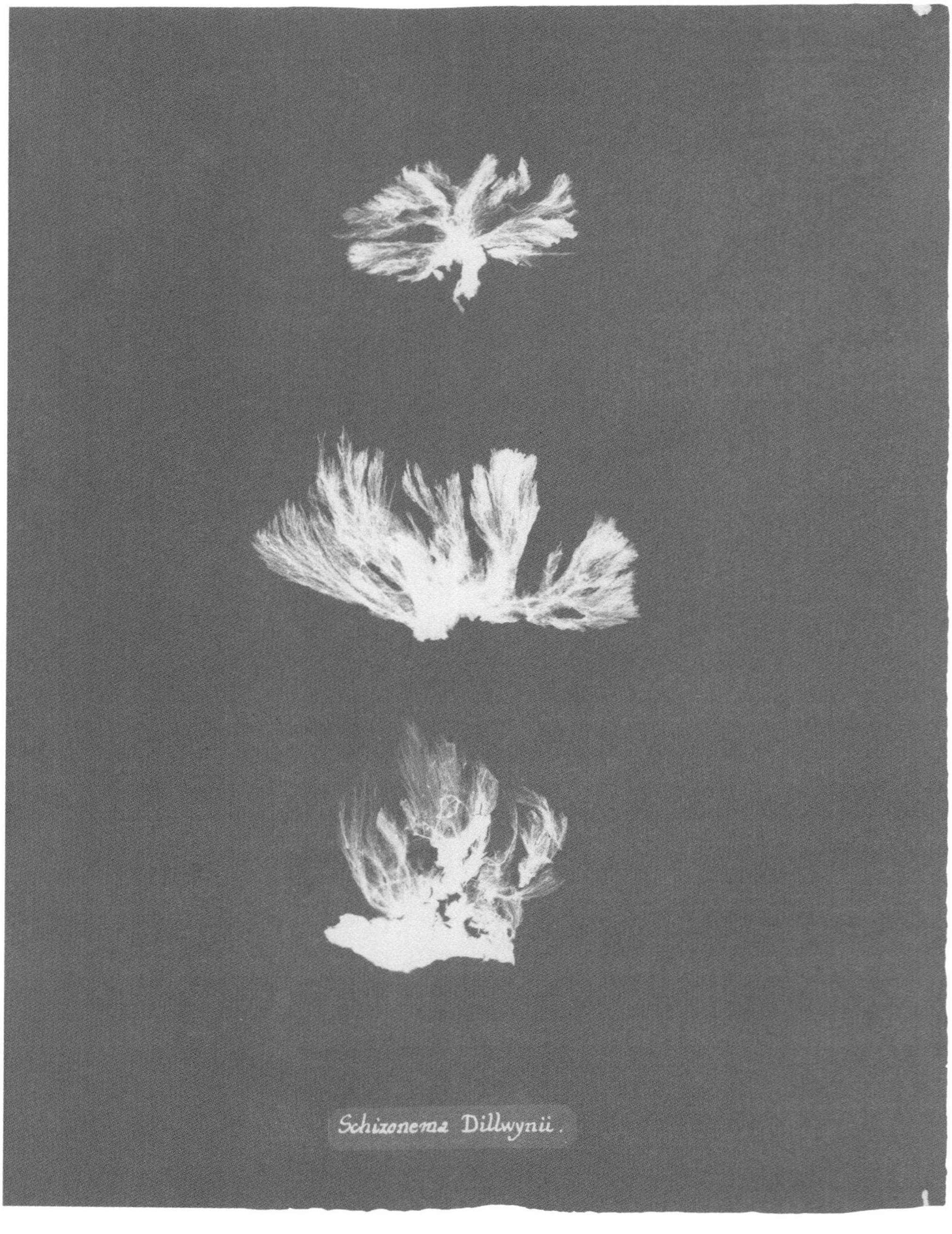

Plate 384. *Schizonema dillwynii*

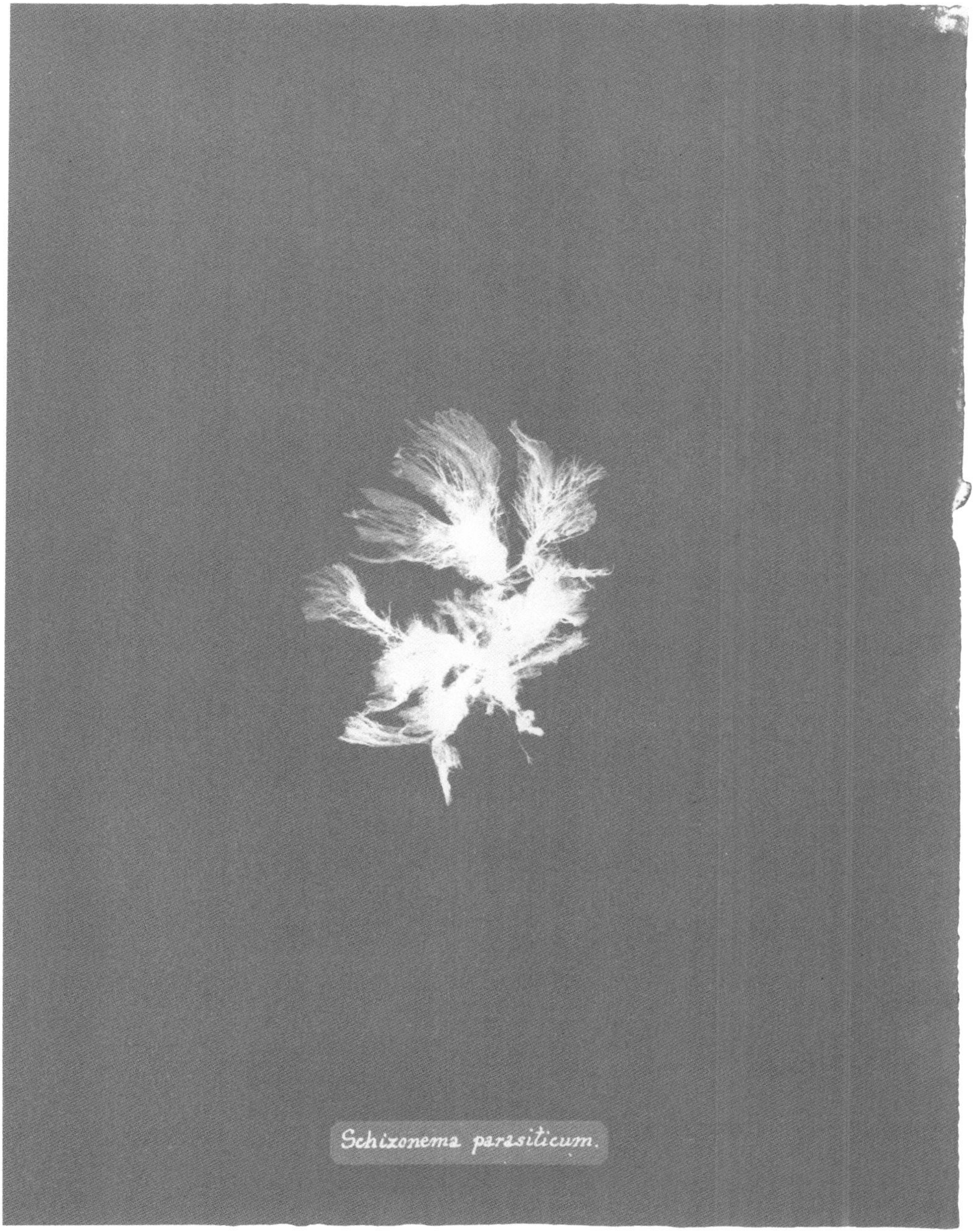

Plate 386. *Schizonema parasiticum*

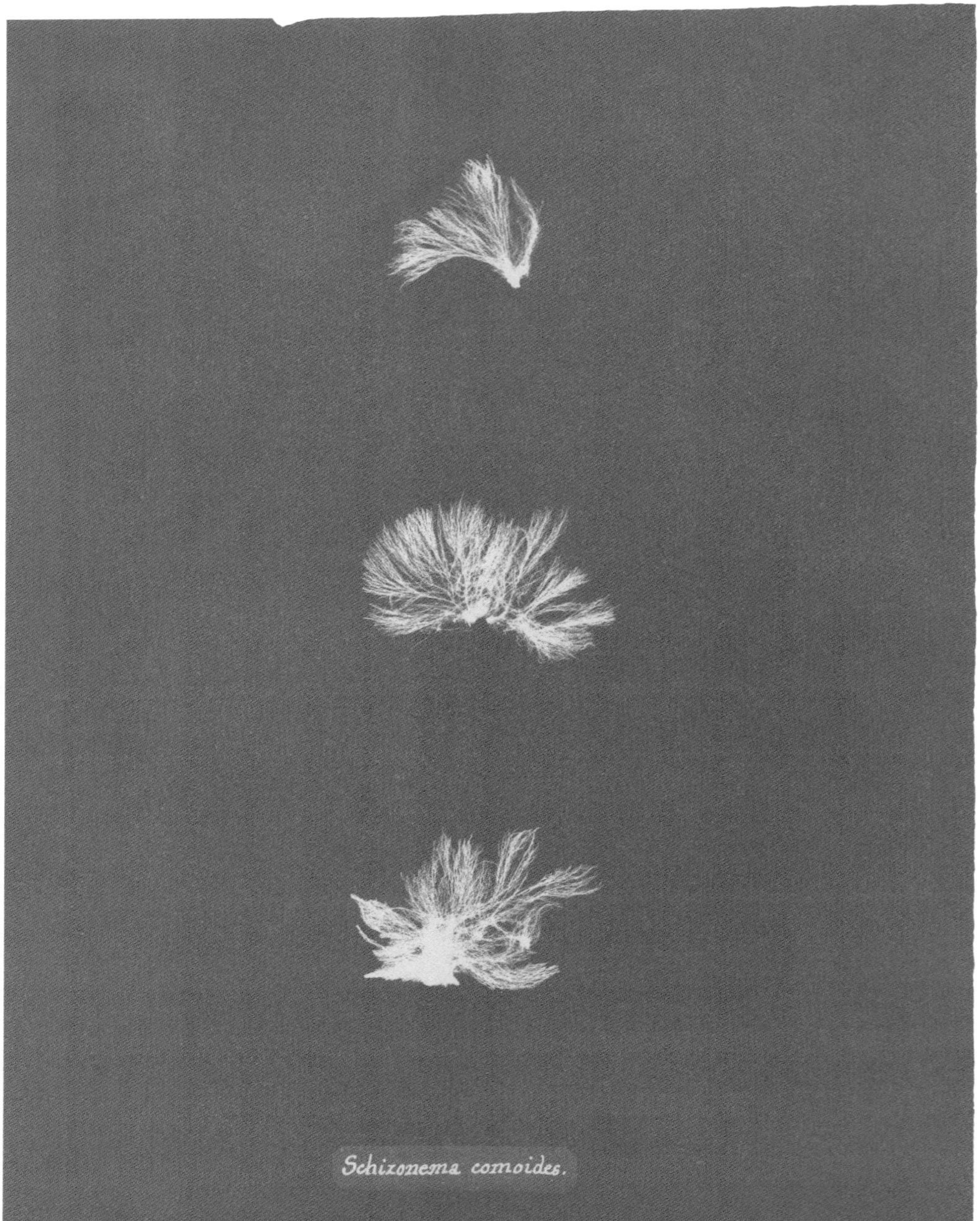

Plate 387. *Schizonema comoides*

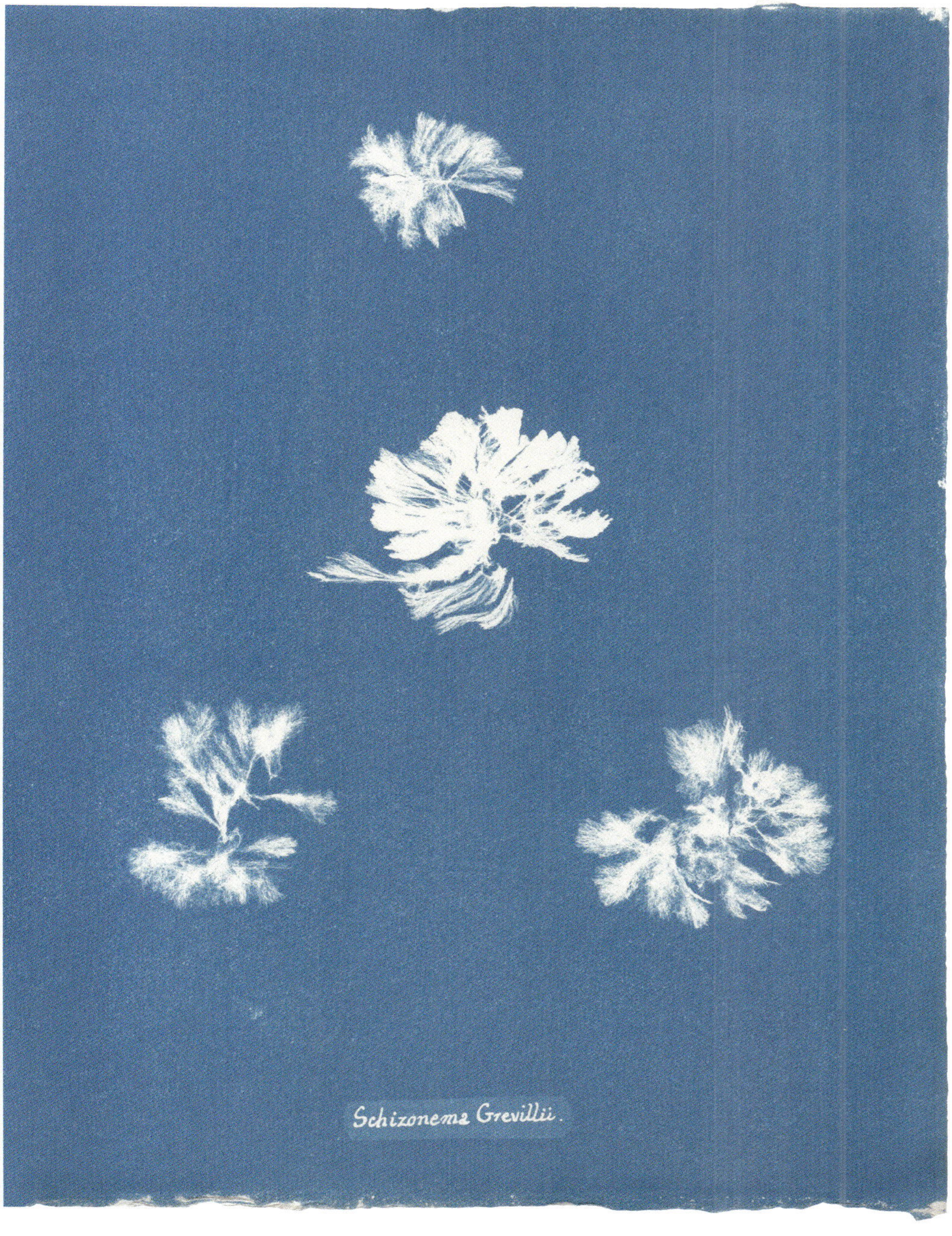

Plate 388. *Schizonema grevillii*

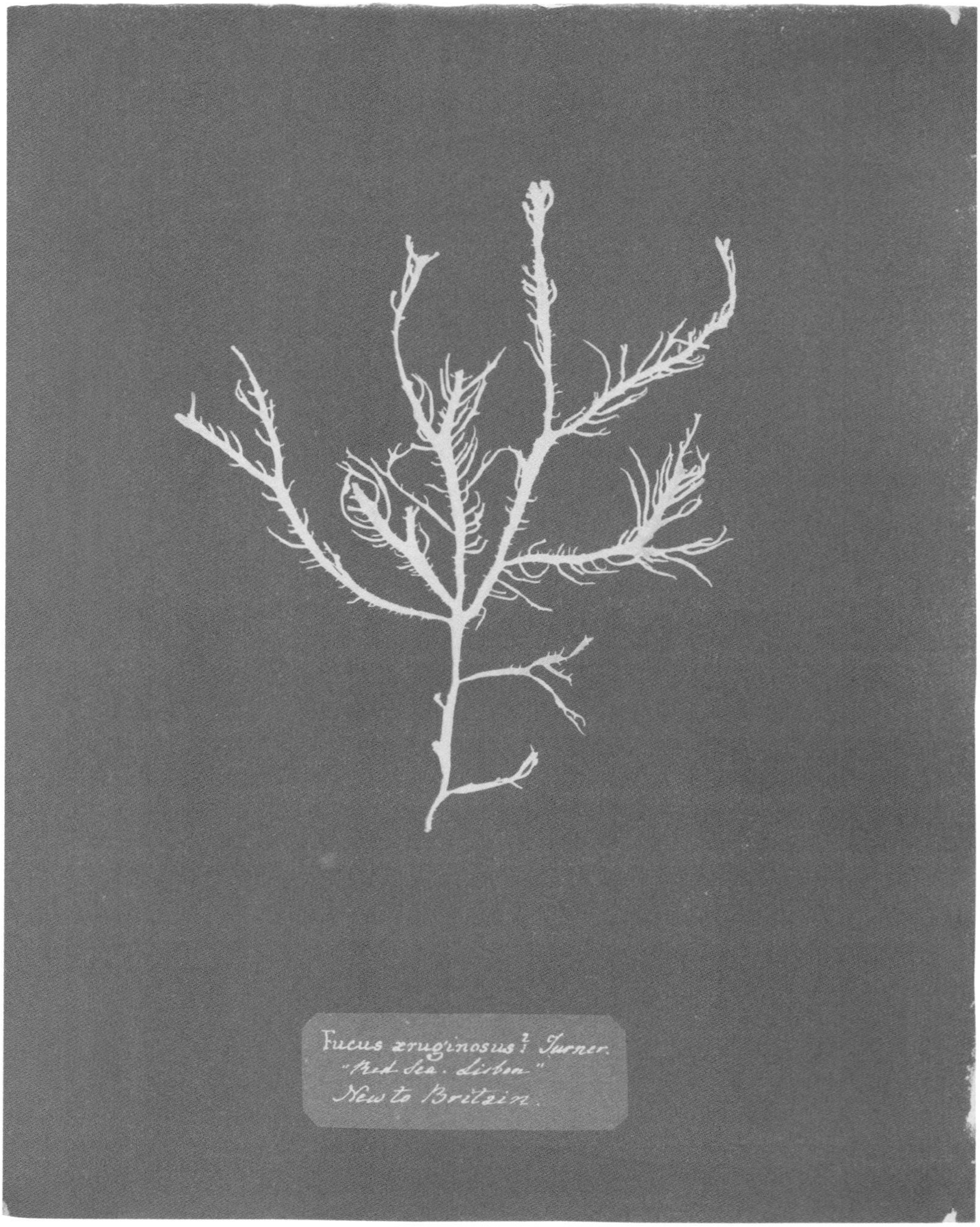

Plate 390. *Fucus aruginosus?* Turner. "Red Sea, Lisbon." New to Britain

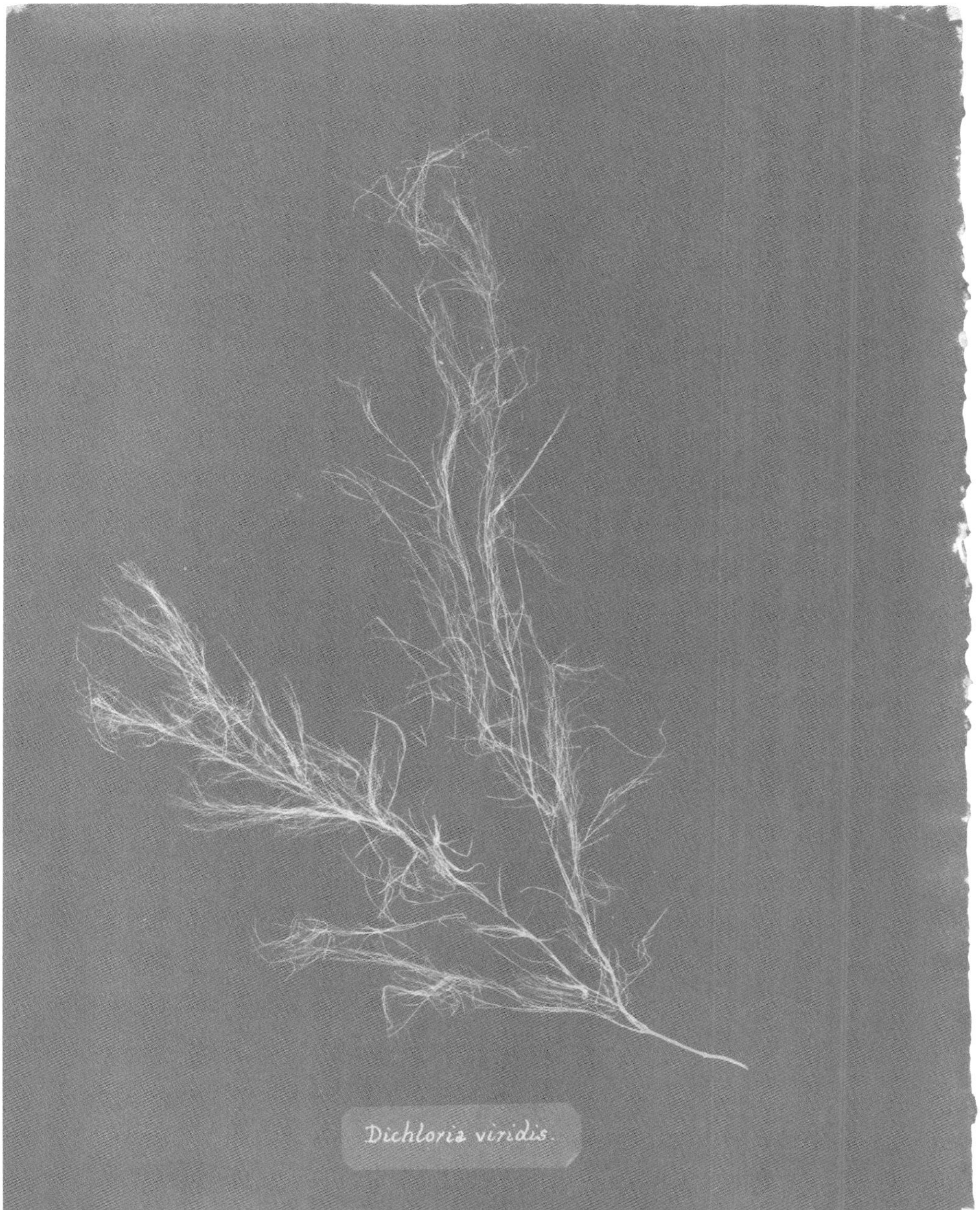

Plate 391. *Dichloria viridis*

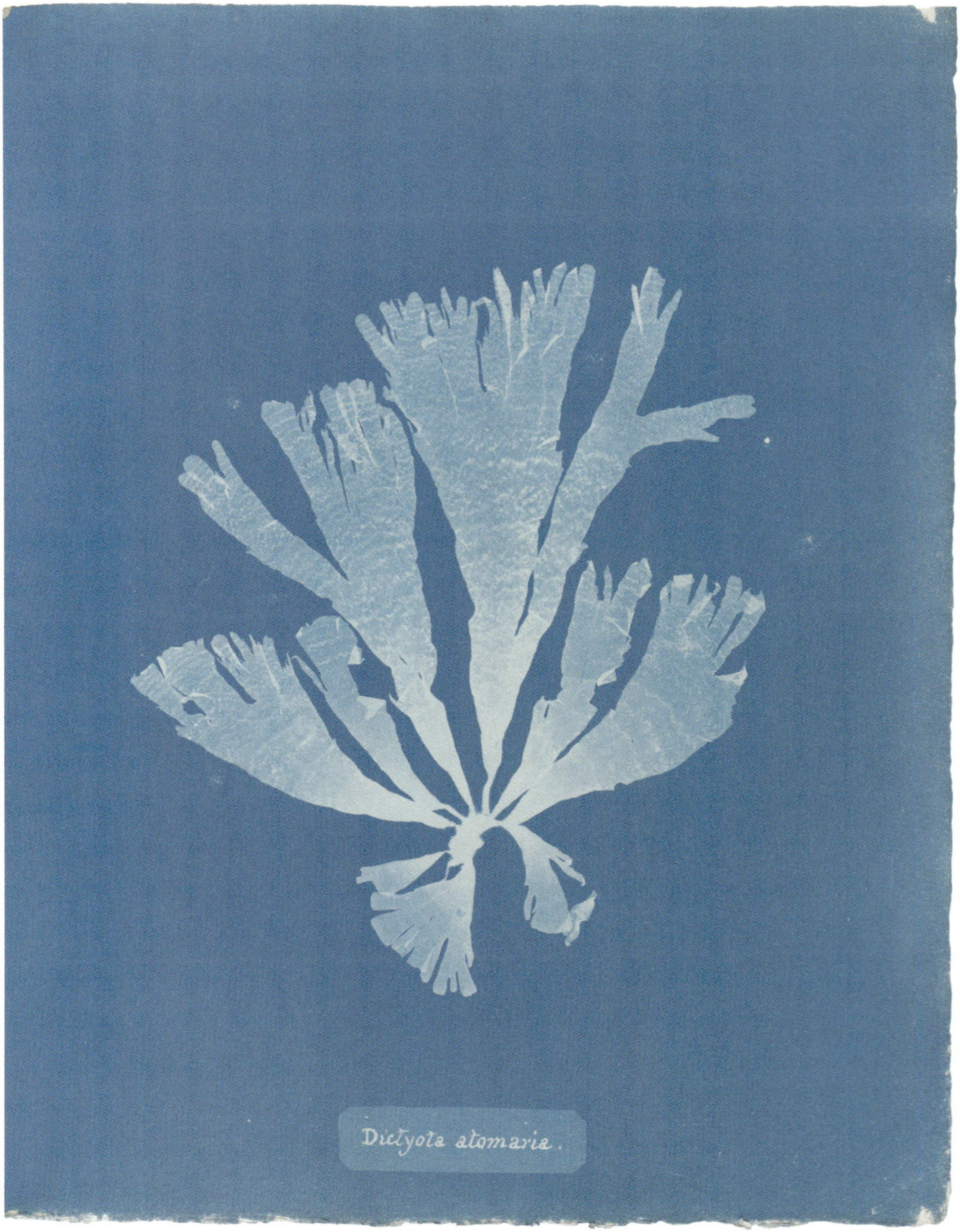

Plate 394. *Dictyota atomaria*

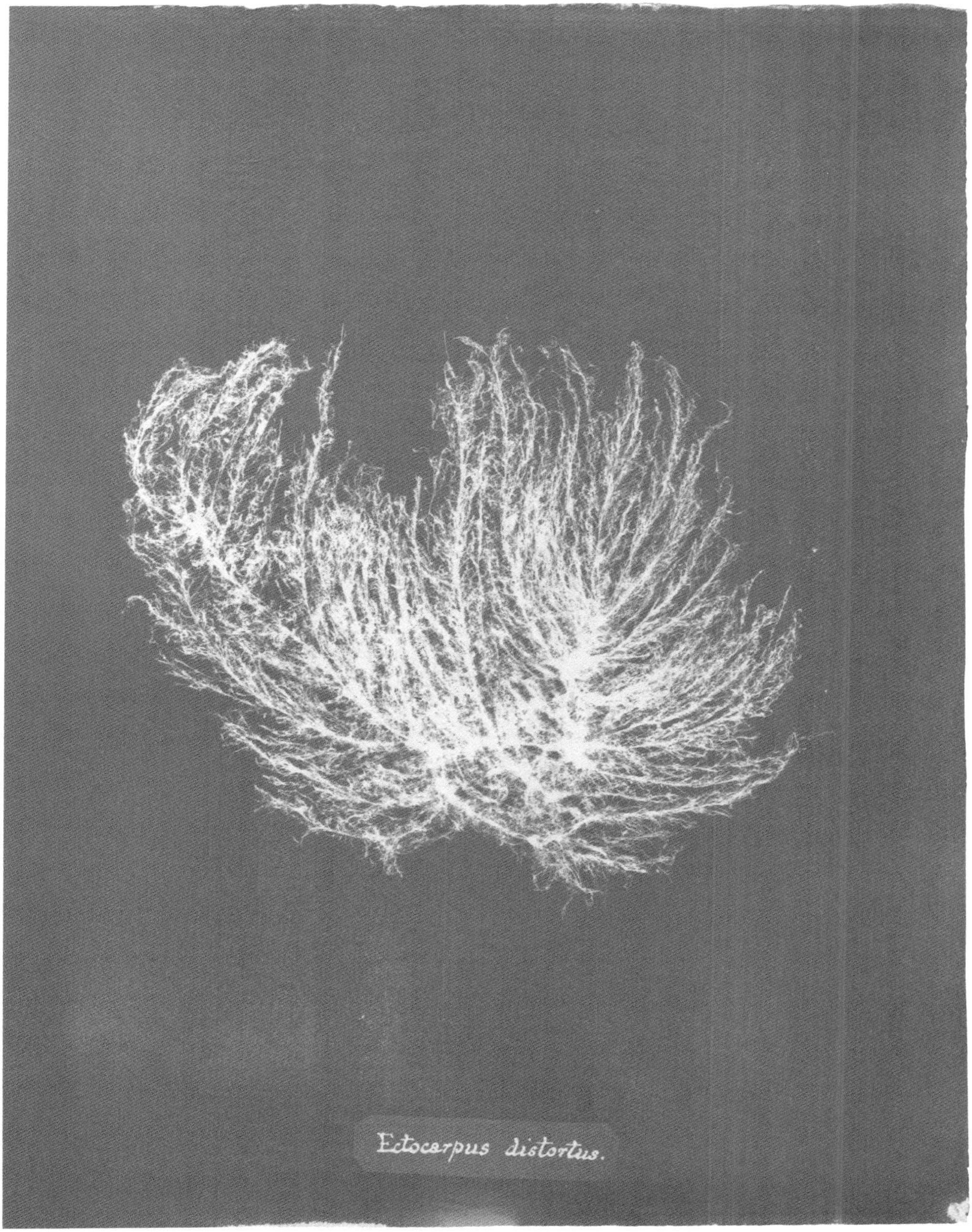

Plate 395. *Ectocarpus distortus*

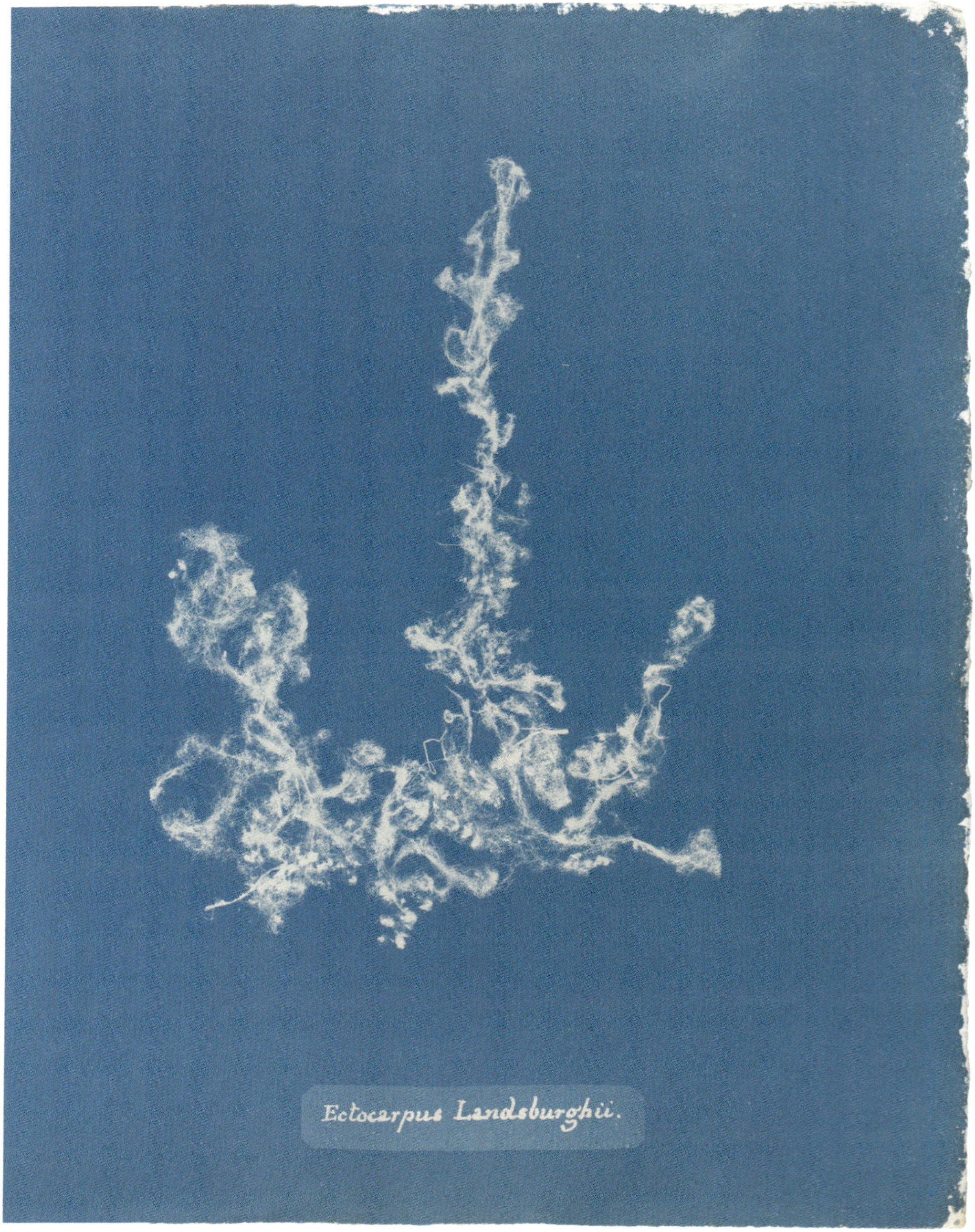

Plate 397. *Ectocarpus landsburghii*

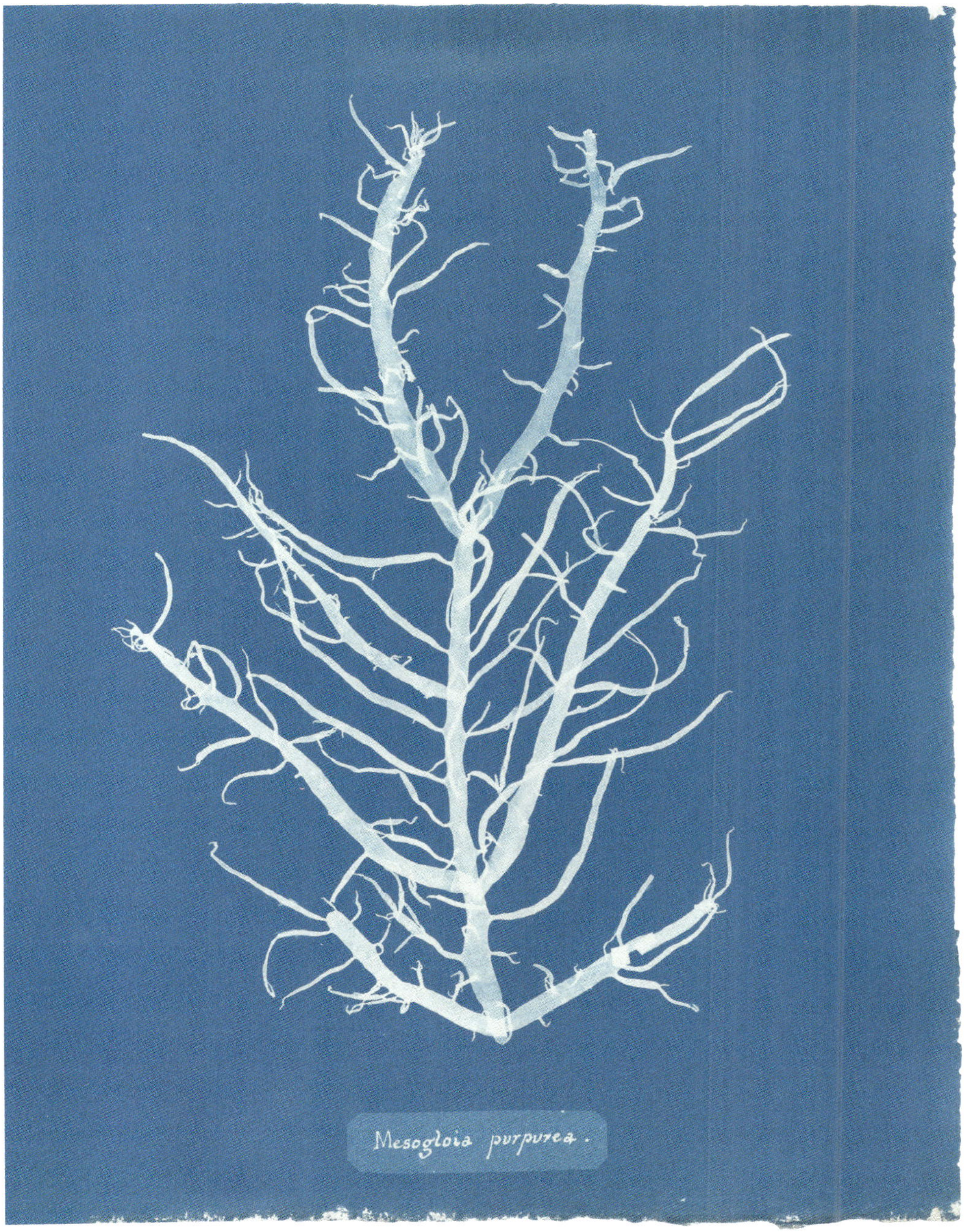

Plate 398. *Mesogloia purpurea*

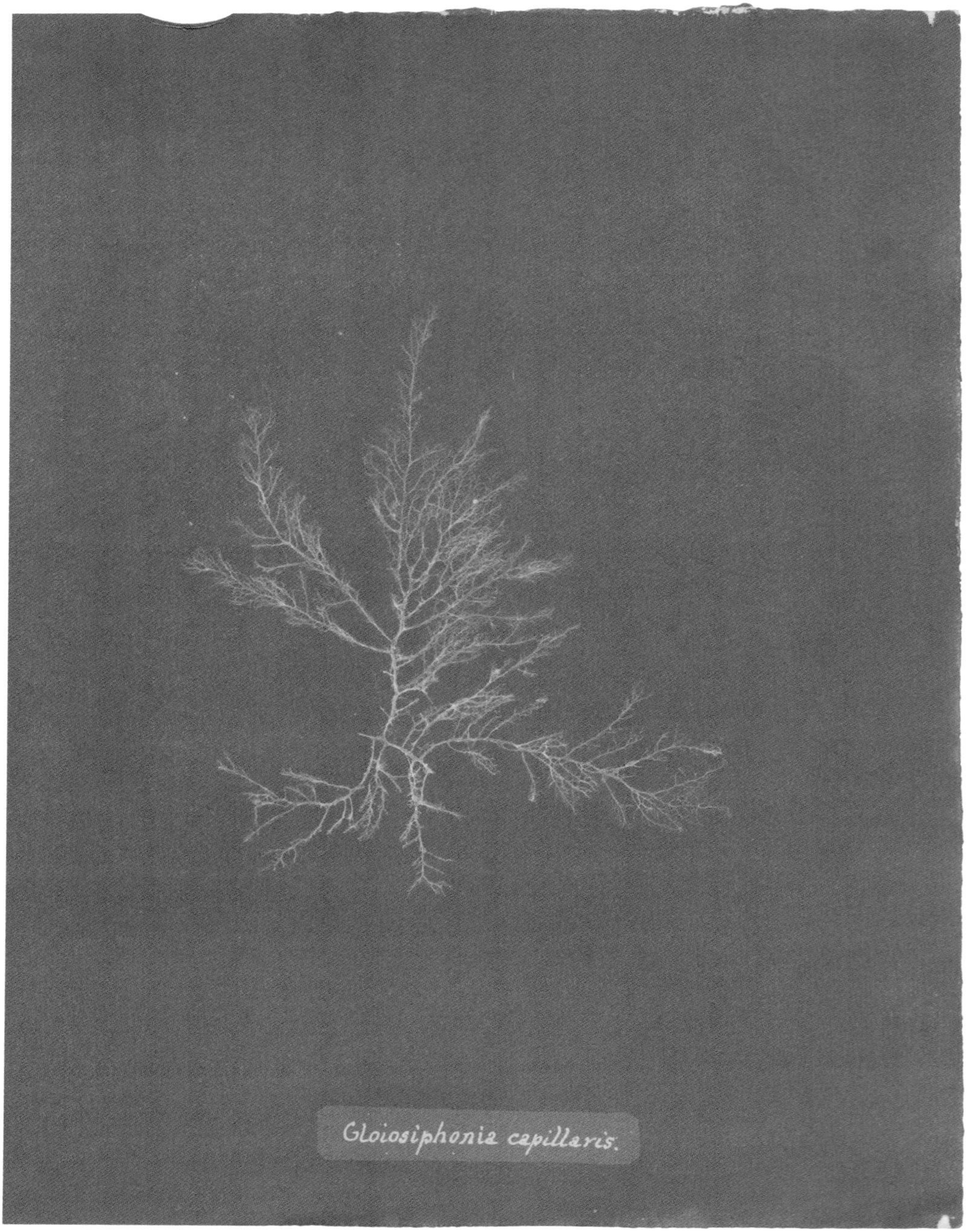

Plate 399. *Gloiosiphonia capillaris*

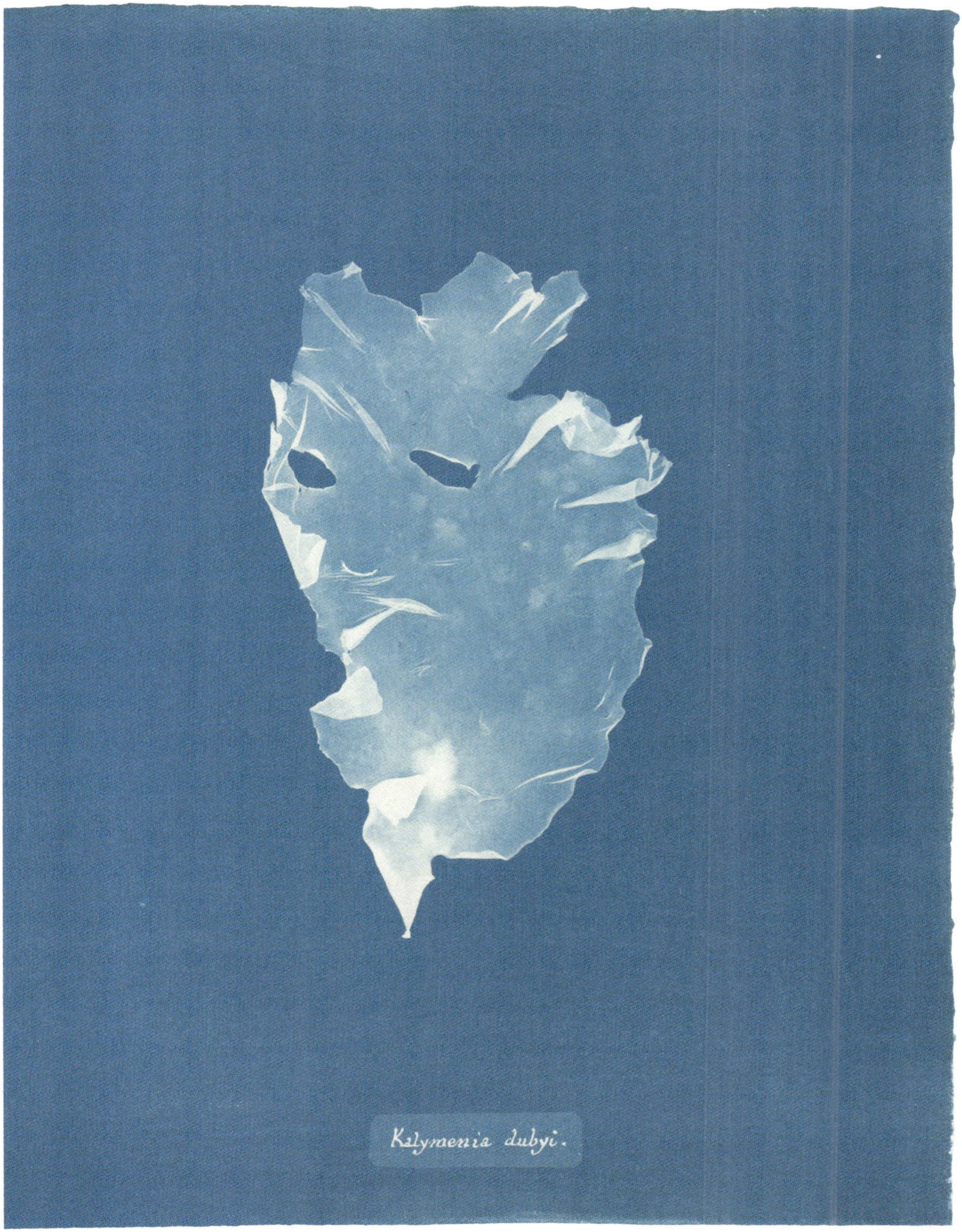

Plate 400. *Kalymenia dubyi*

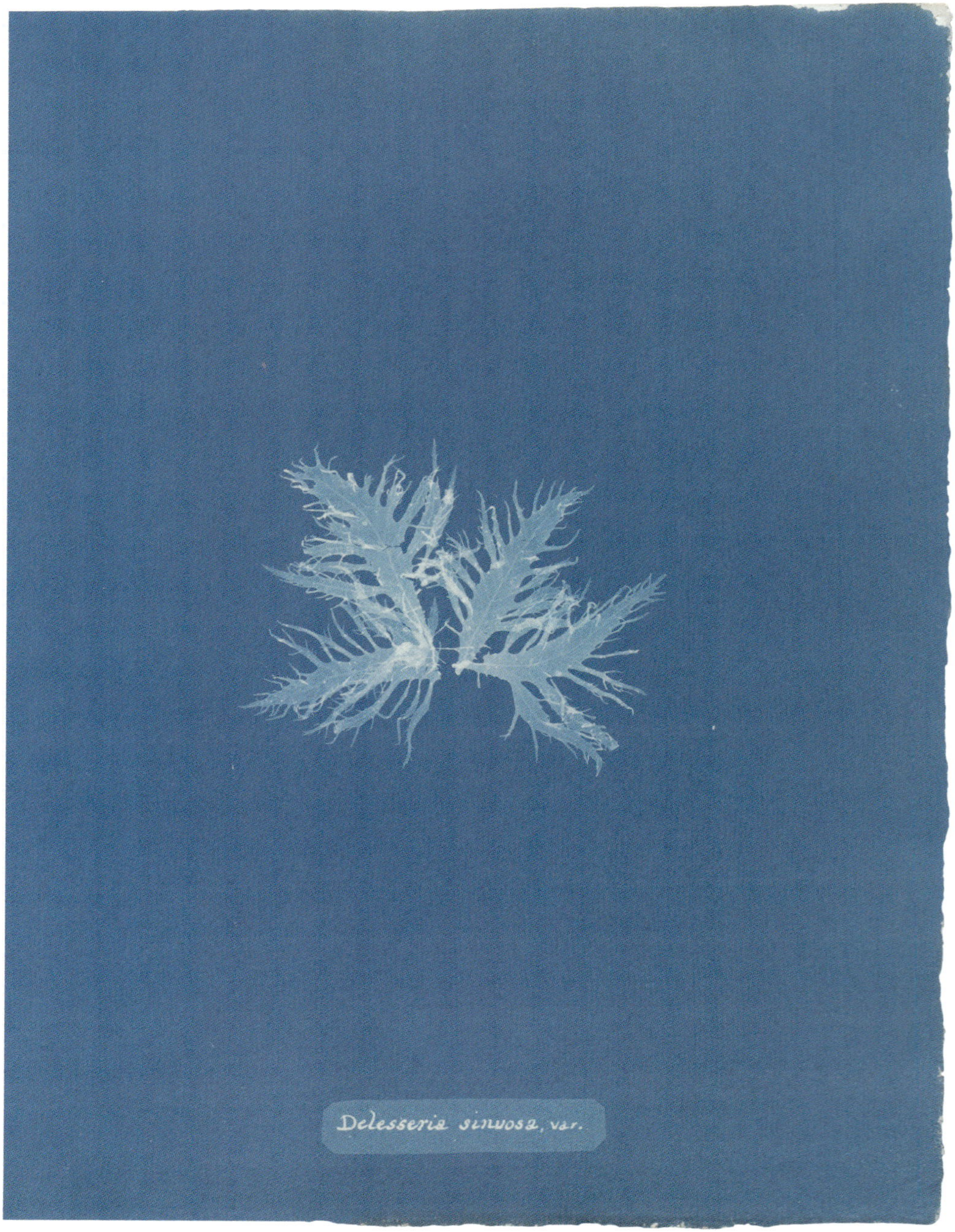

Plate 401. *Delesseria sinuosa,* var.

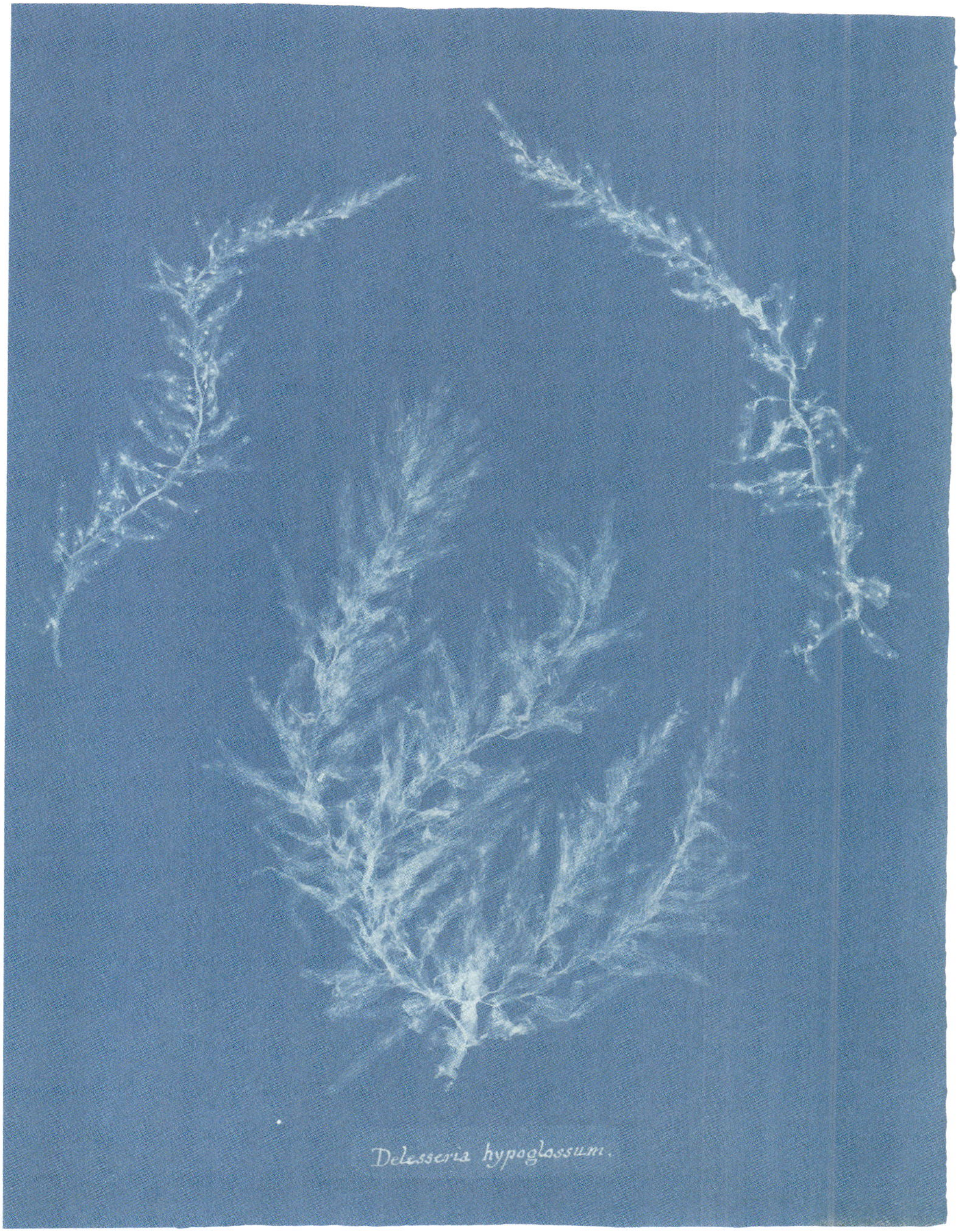

Plate 402. *Delesseria hypoglossum*

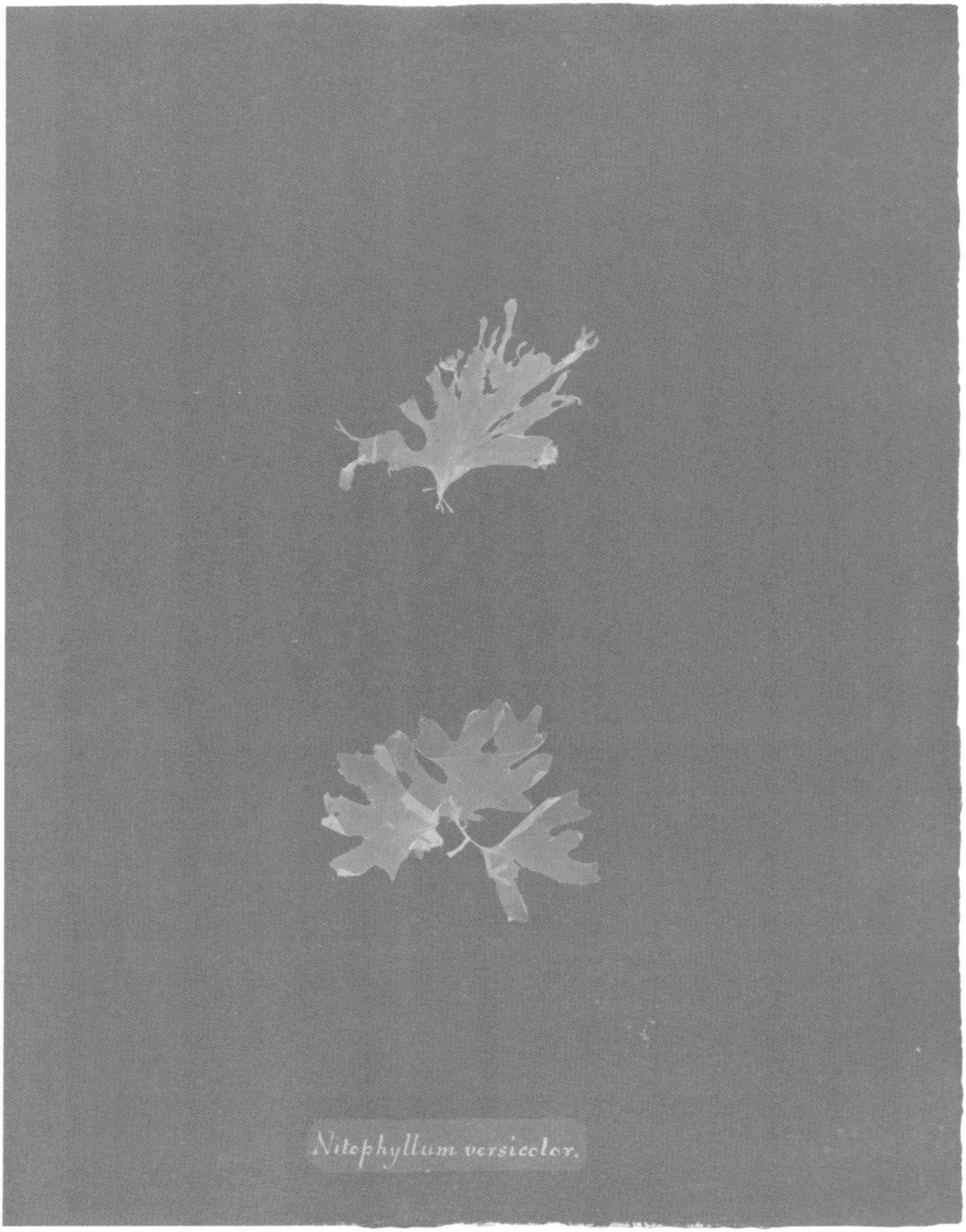

Plate 403. *Nitophyllum versicolor*

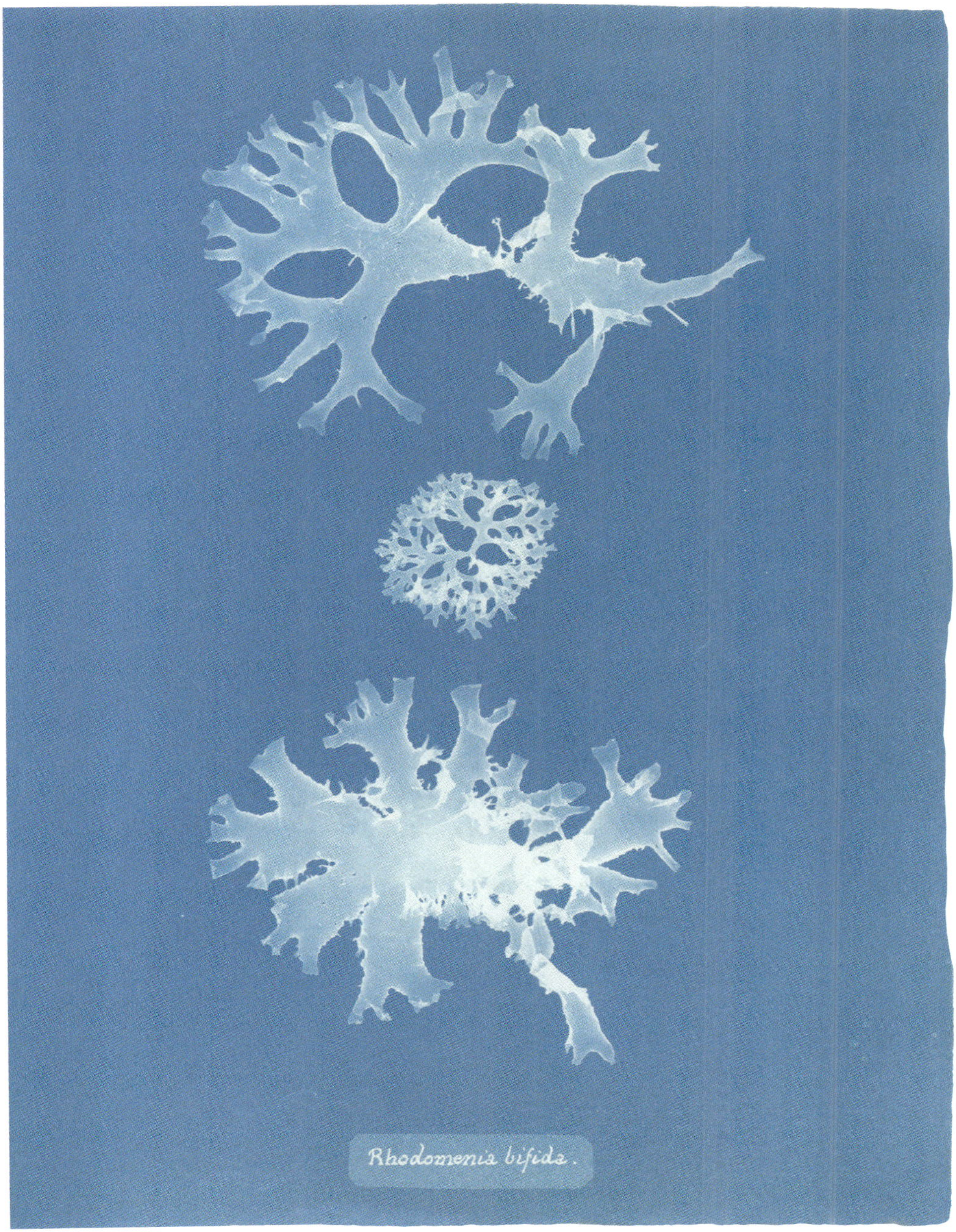

Plate 404. *Rhodomenia bifida*

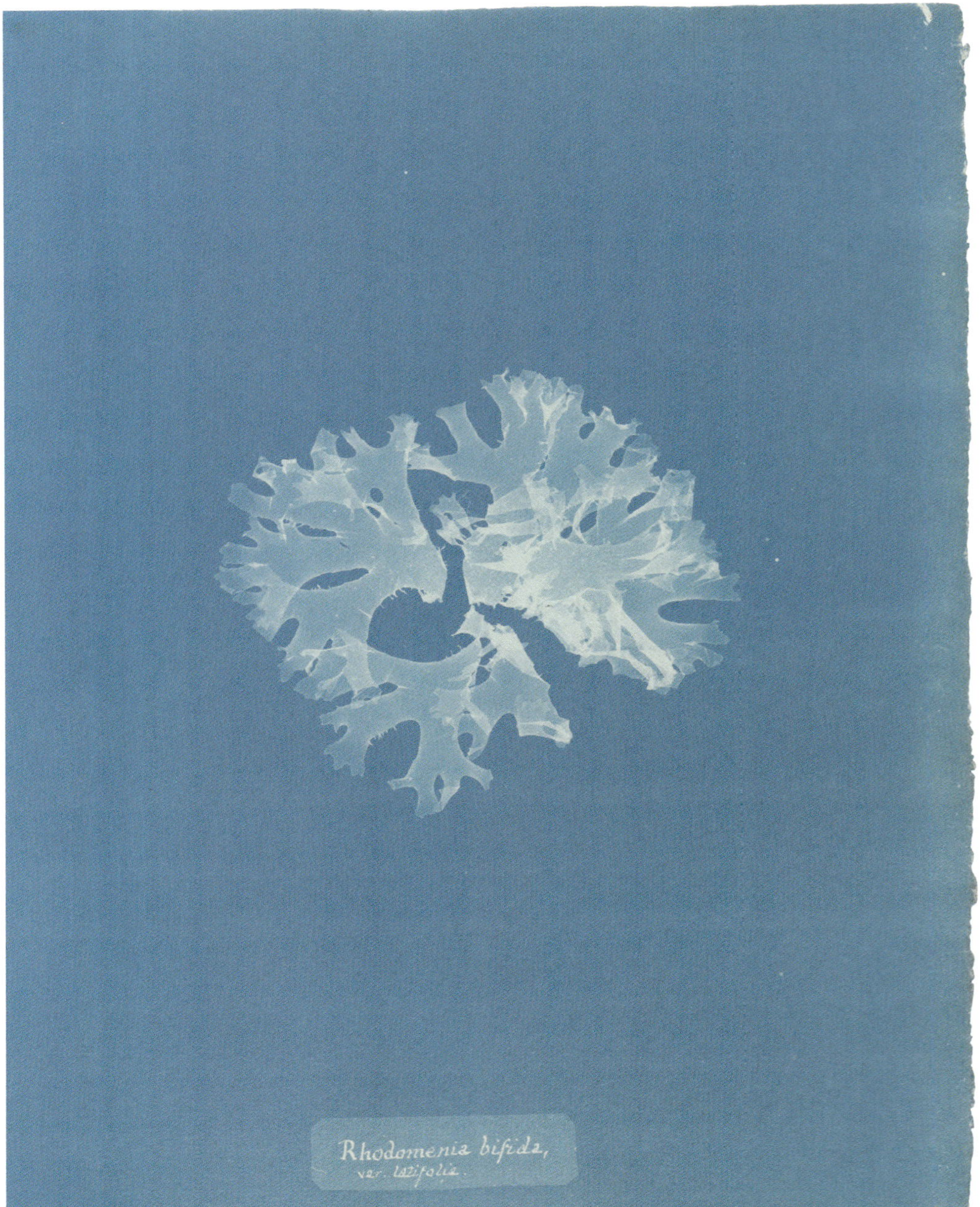

Plate 405. *Rhodomenia bifida,* var. *latifolia*

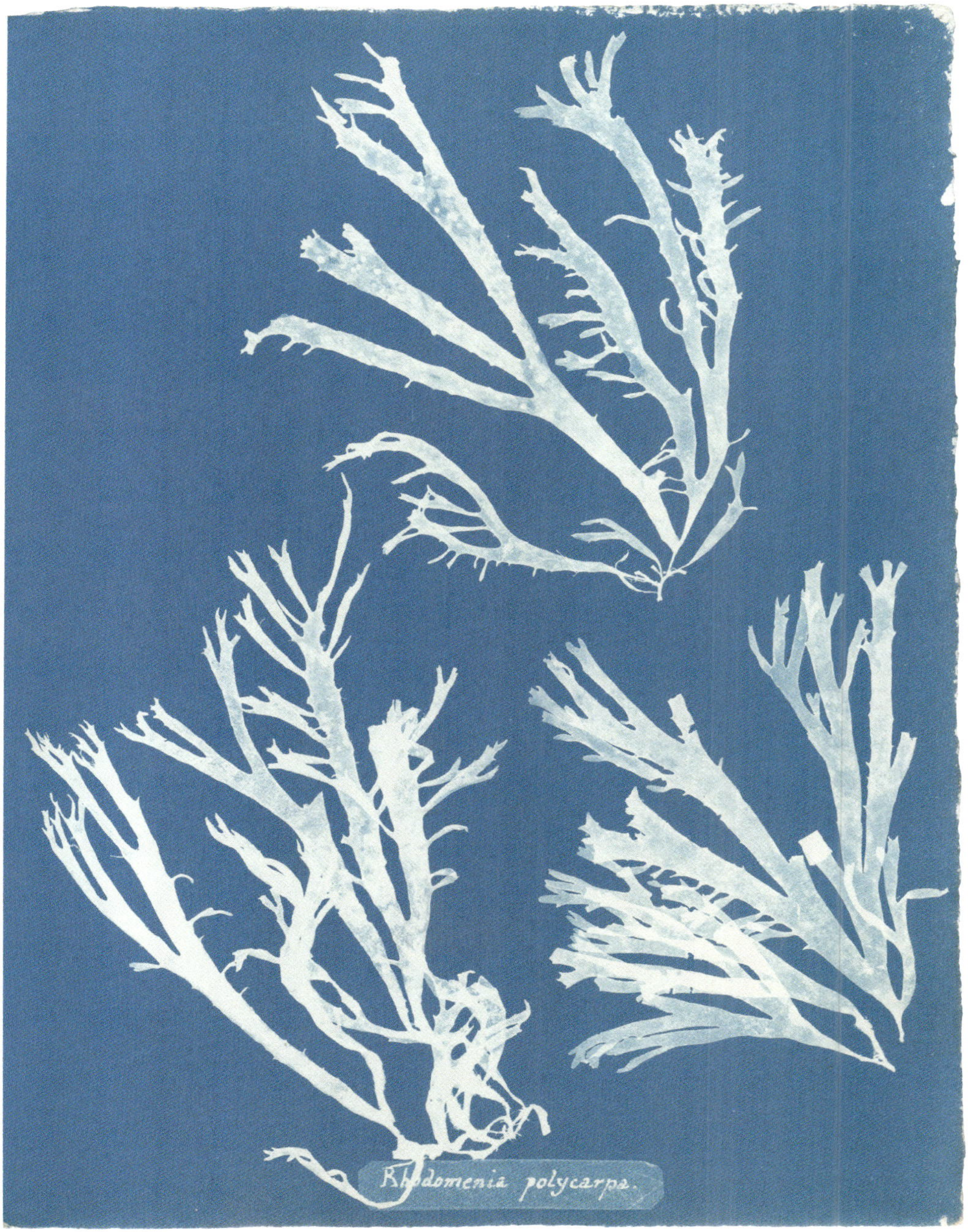

Plate 406. *Rhodomenia polycarpa*

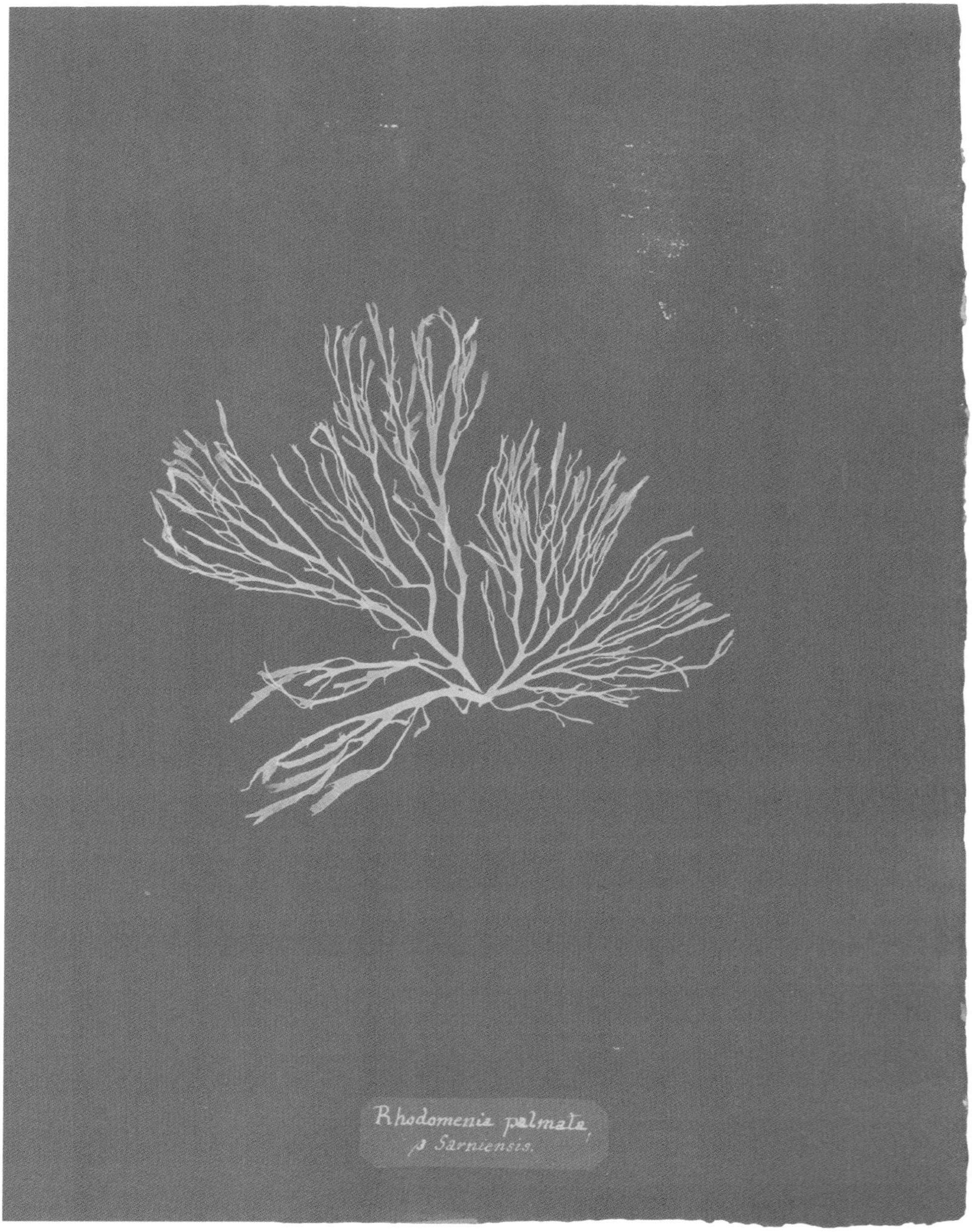

Plate 407. *Rhodomenia palmata* β *sarniensis*

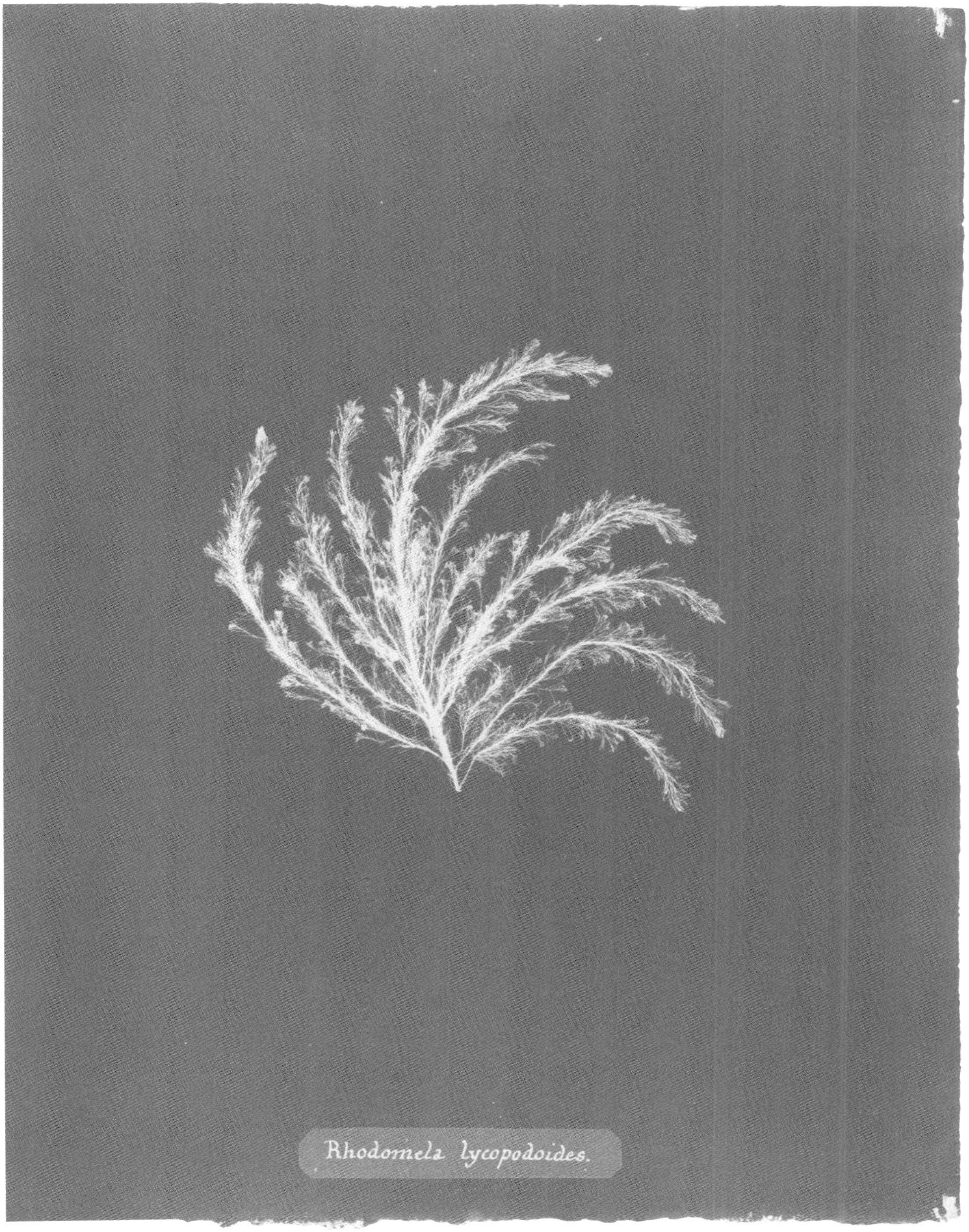

Plate 408. *Rhodomela lycopodoides*

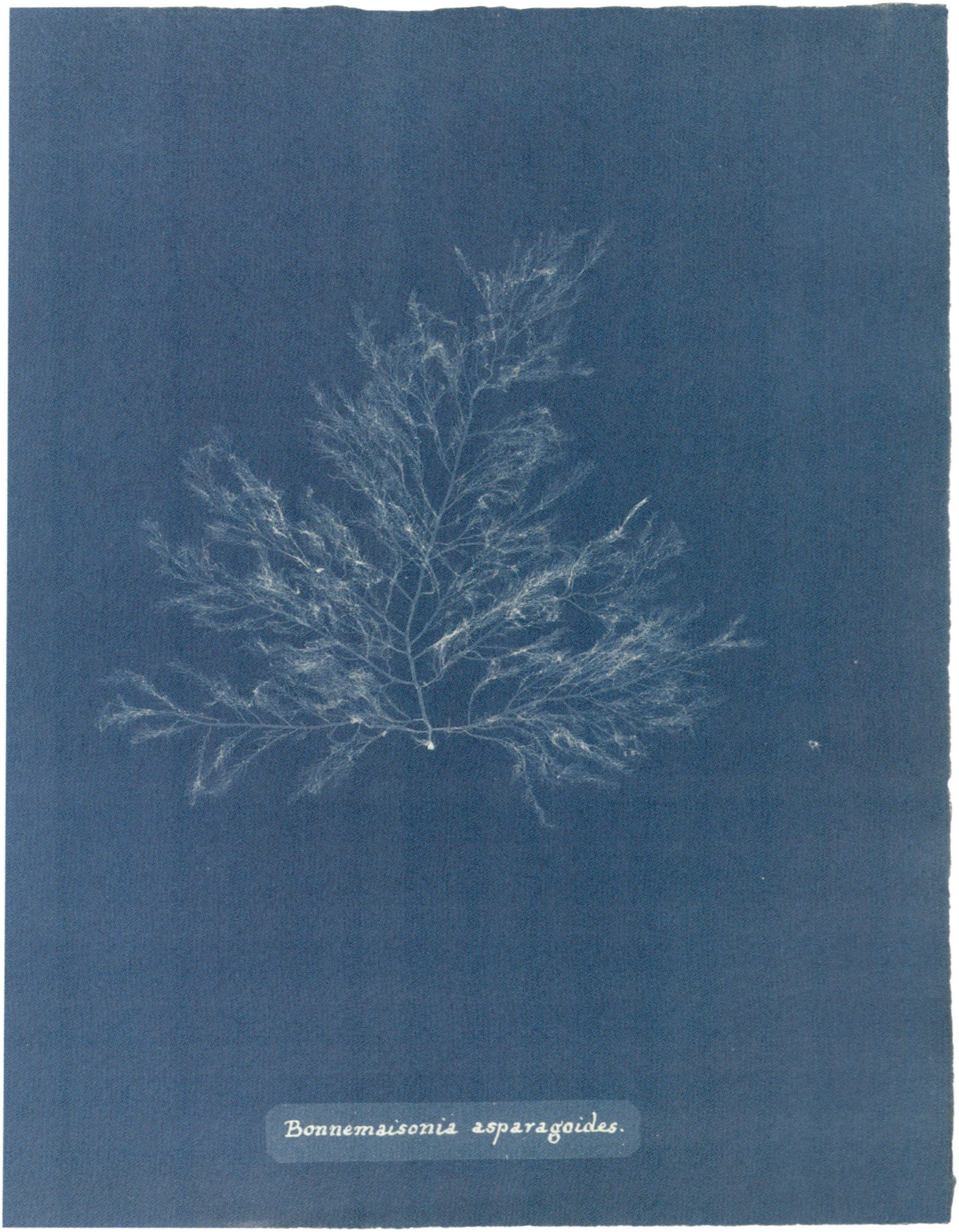

Plate 409. *Bonnemaisonia asparagoides*

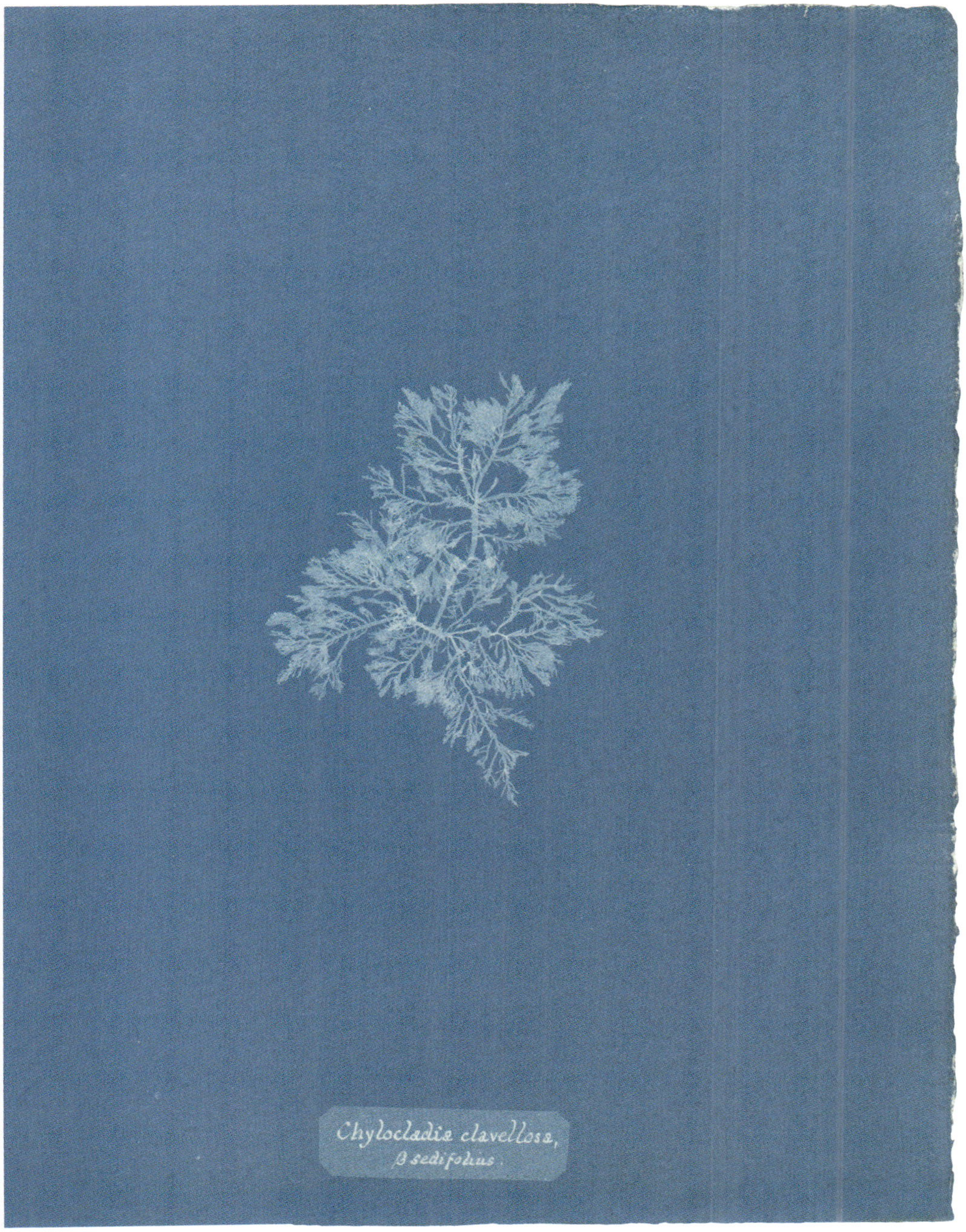

Plate 410. *Chylocladia clavellosa* β *sedifolius*

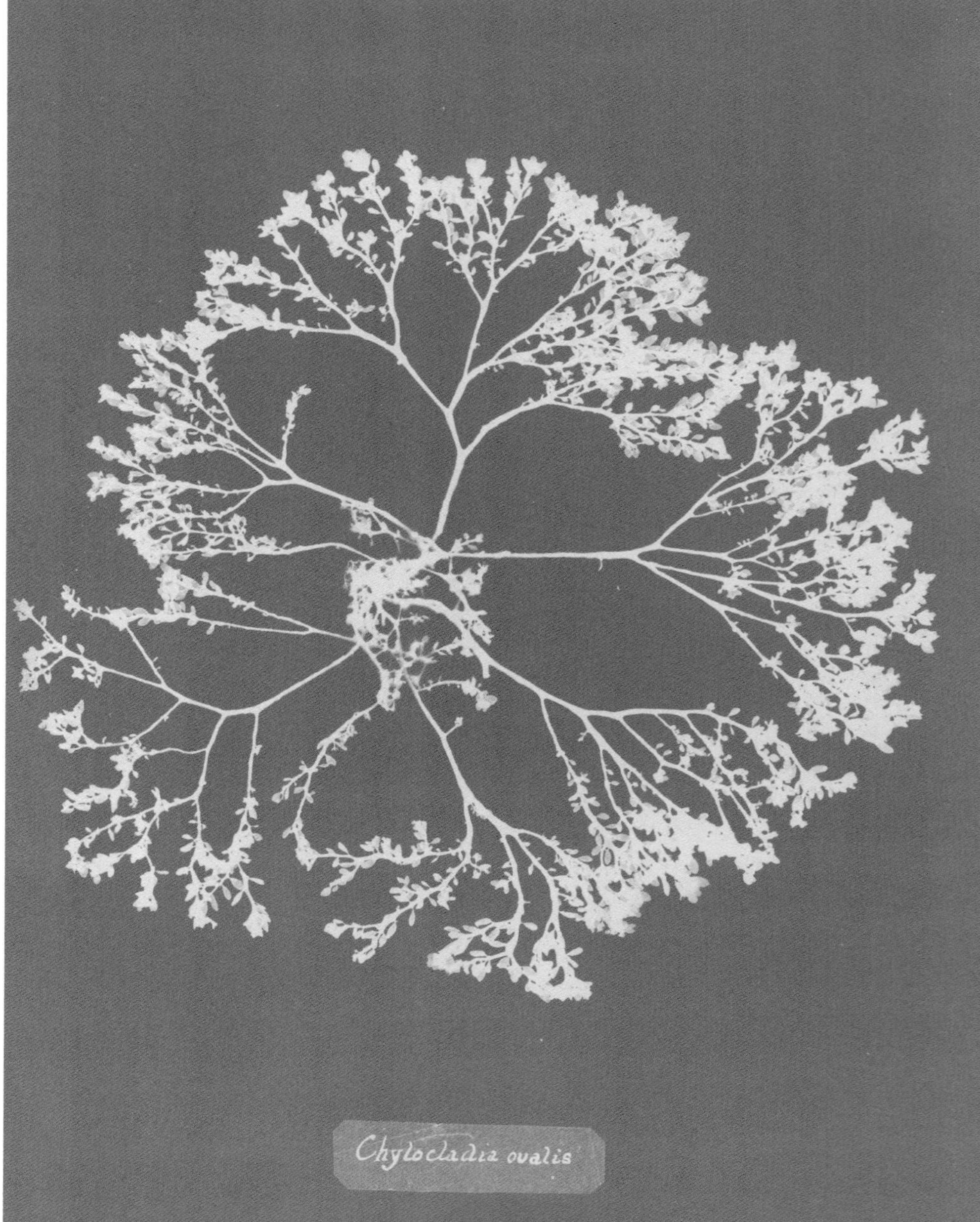

Plate 411. *Chylocladia ovalis*

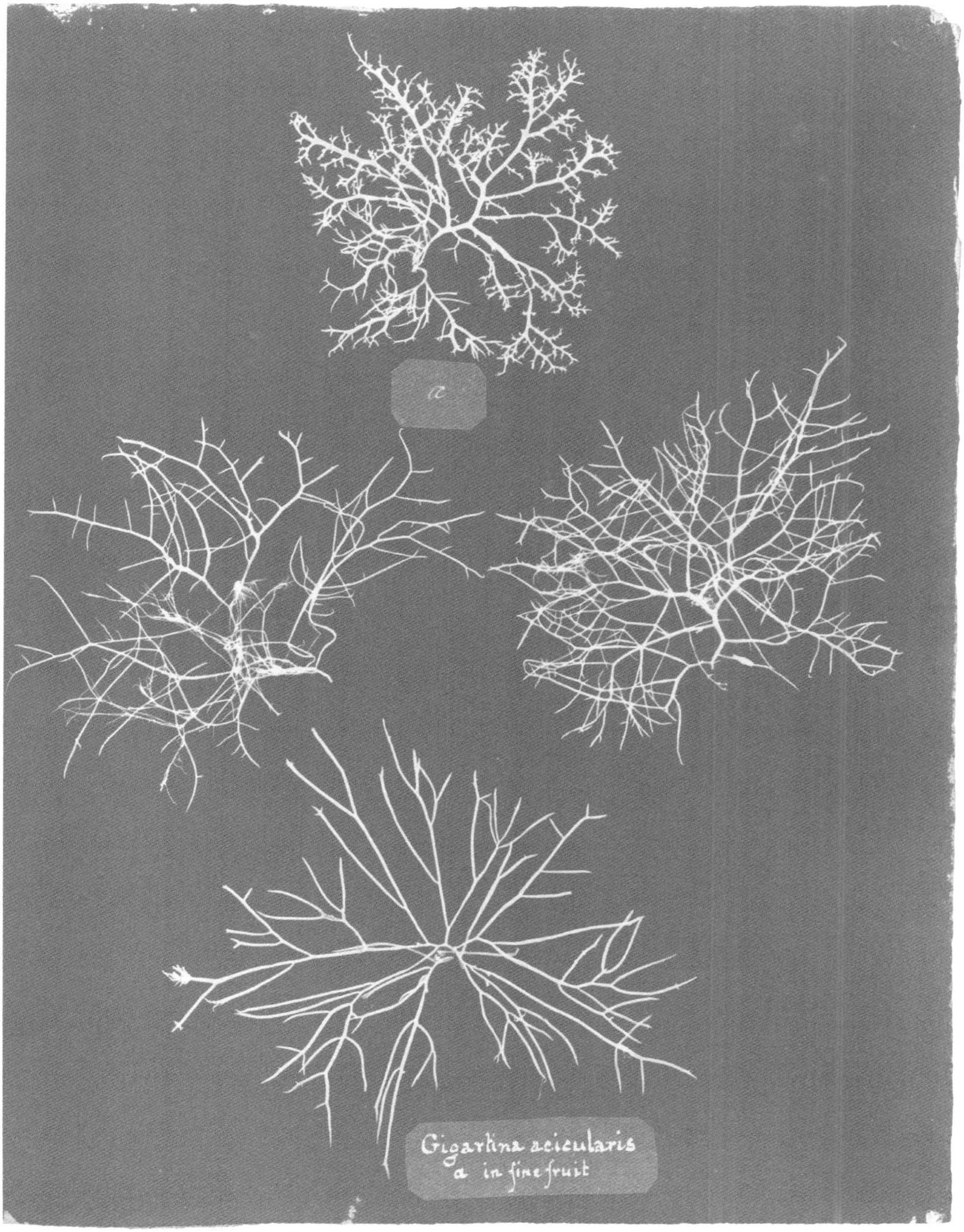

Plate 412. *Gigartina acicularis*, a. in fine fruit

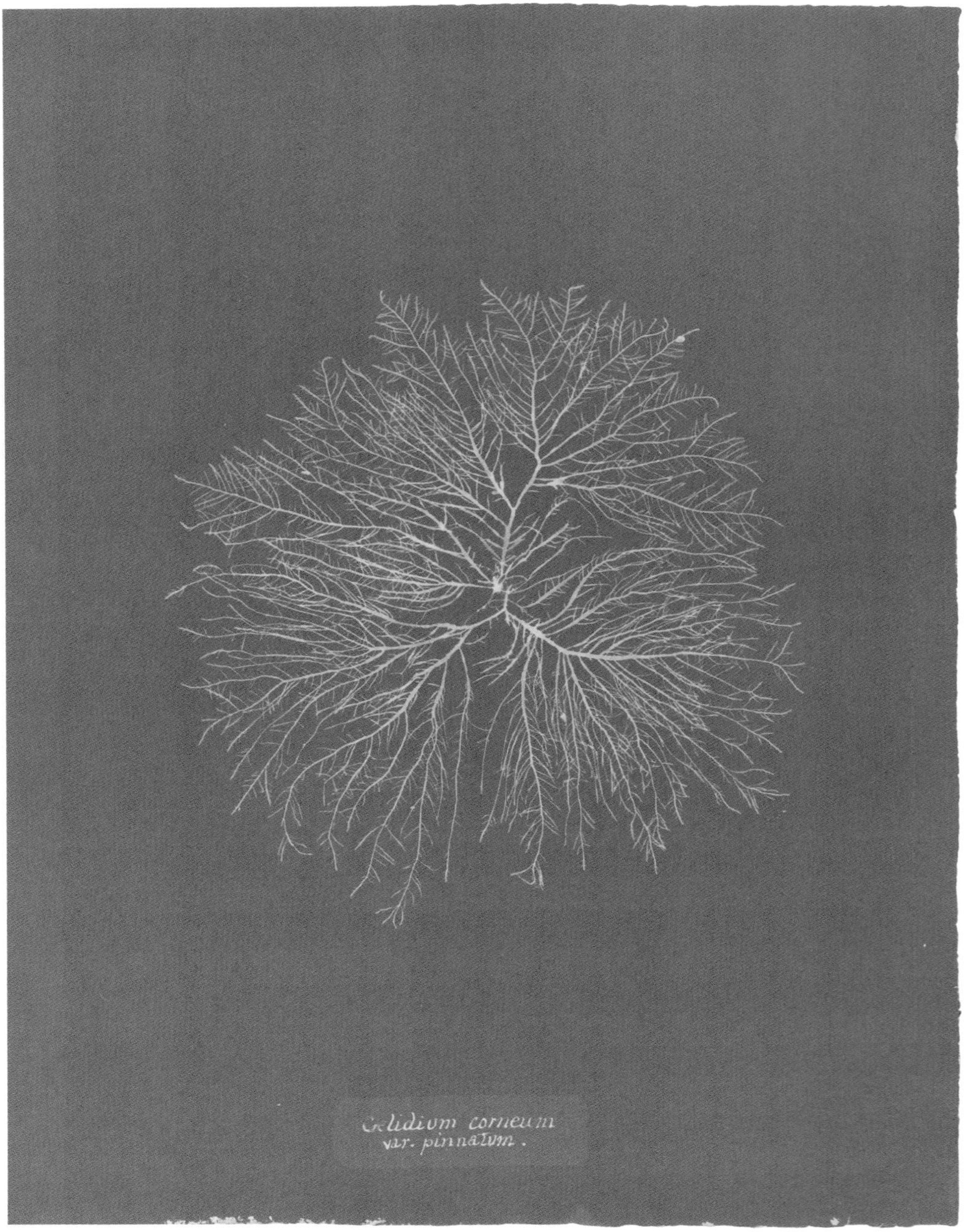

Plate 413. *Gelidium corneum* var. *pinnatum*

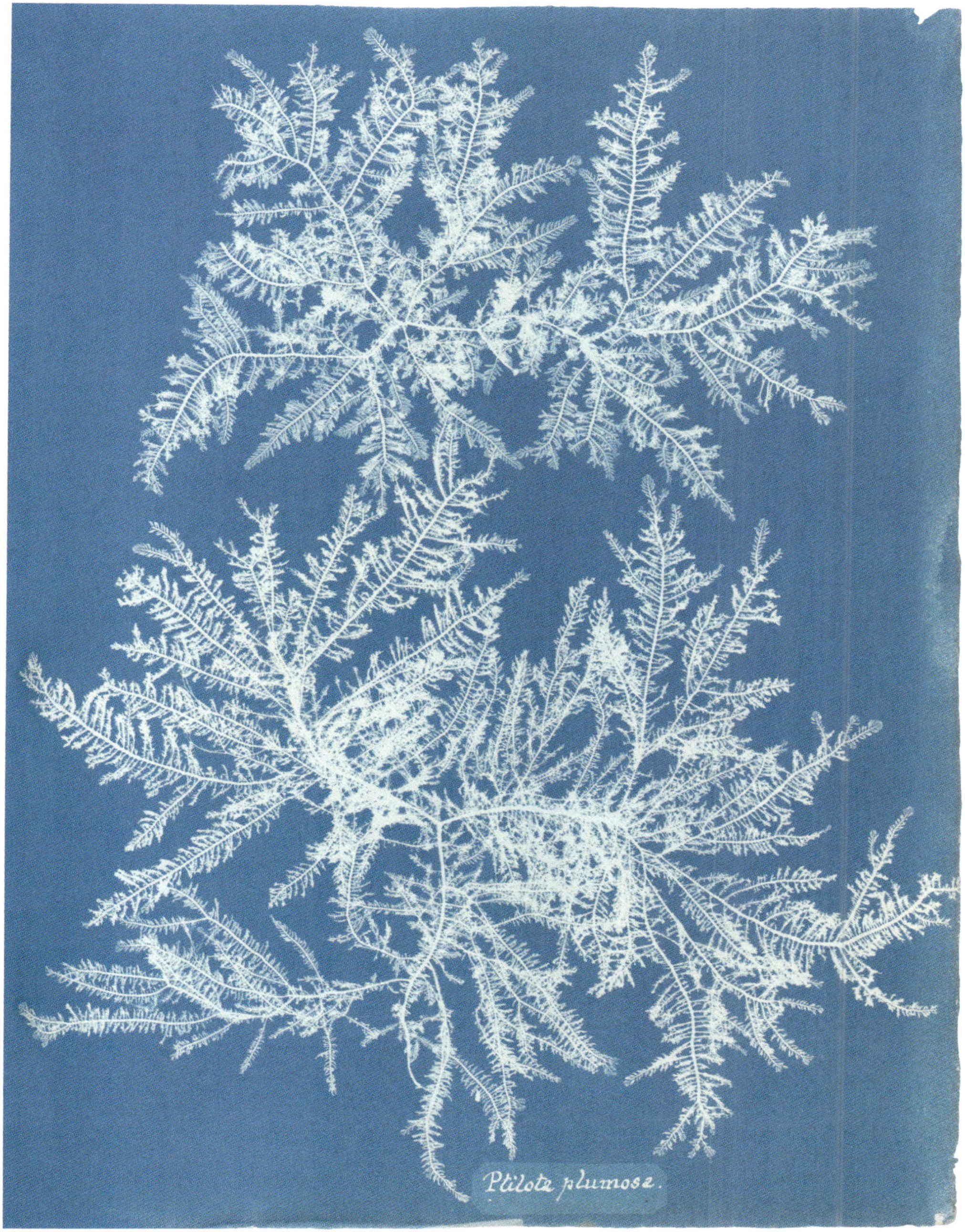

Plate 416. *Ptilota plumosa*

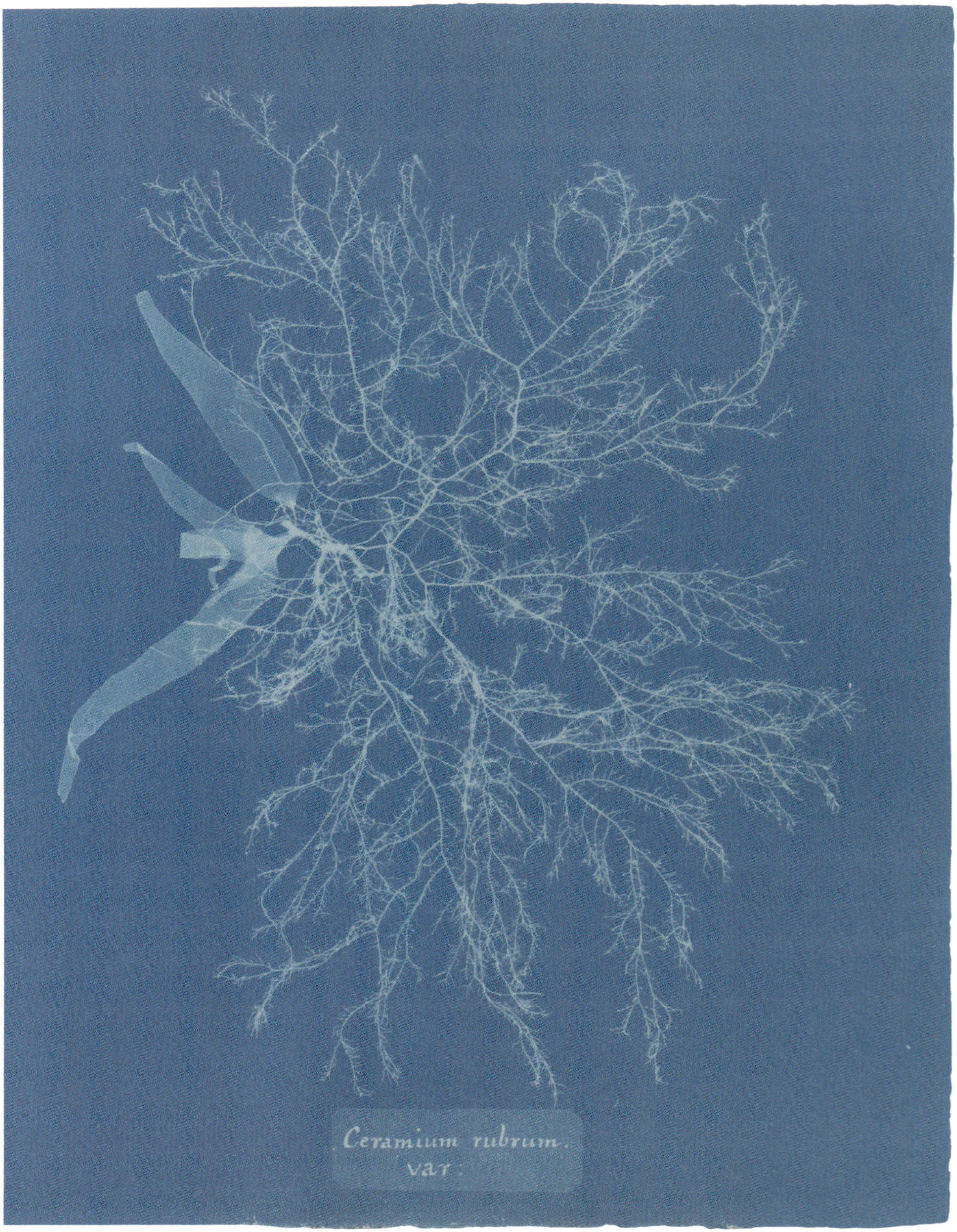

Plate 419. *Ceramium rubrum*, var.

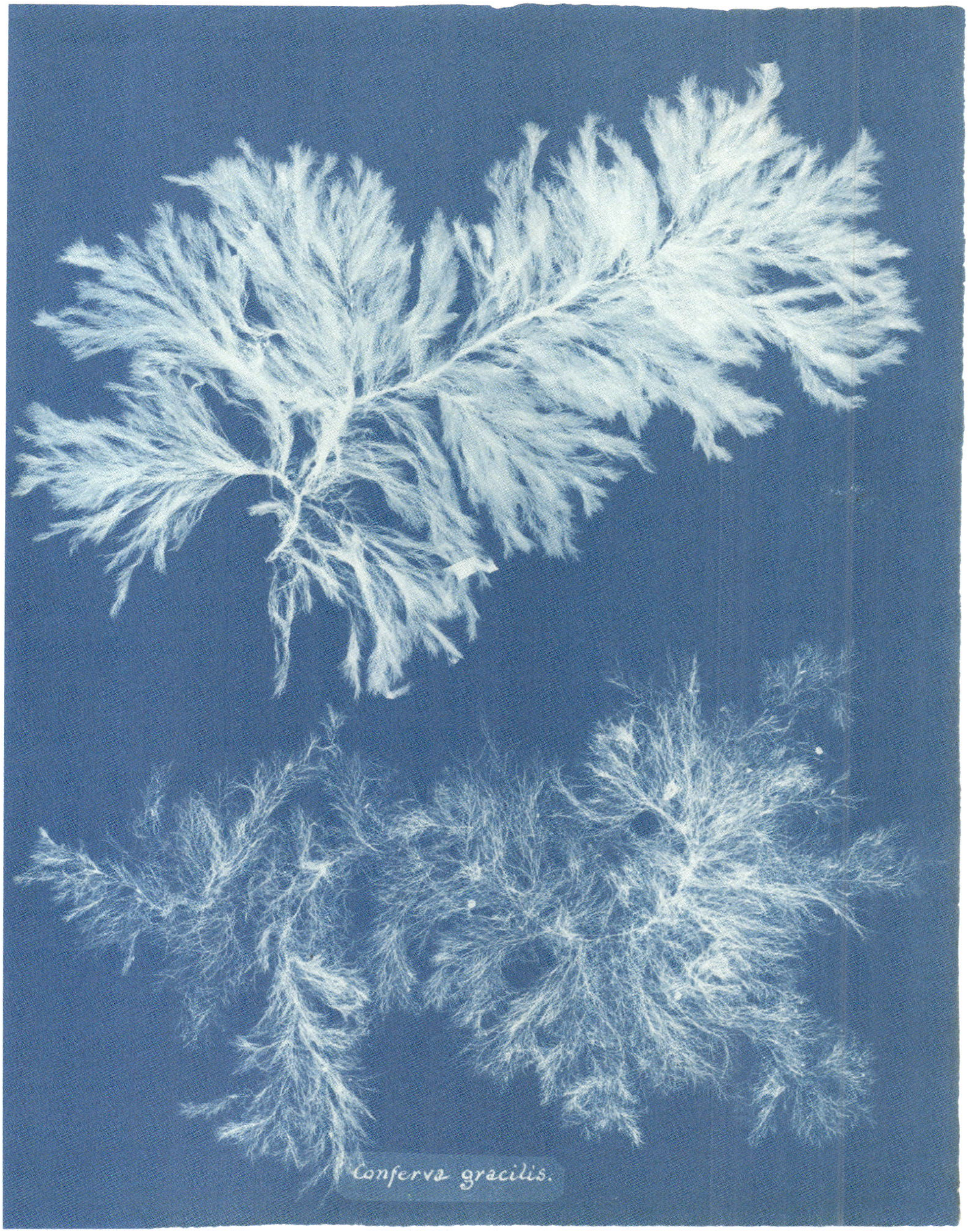

Plate 428. *Conferva gracilis*

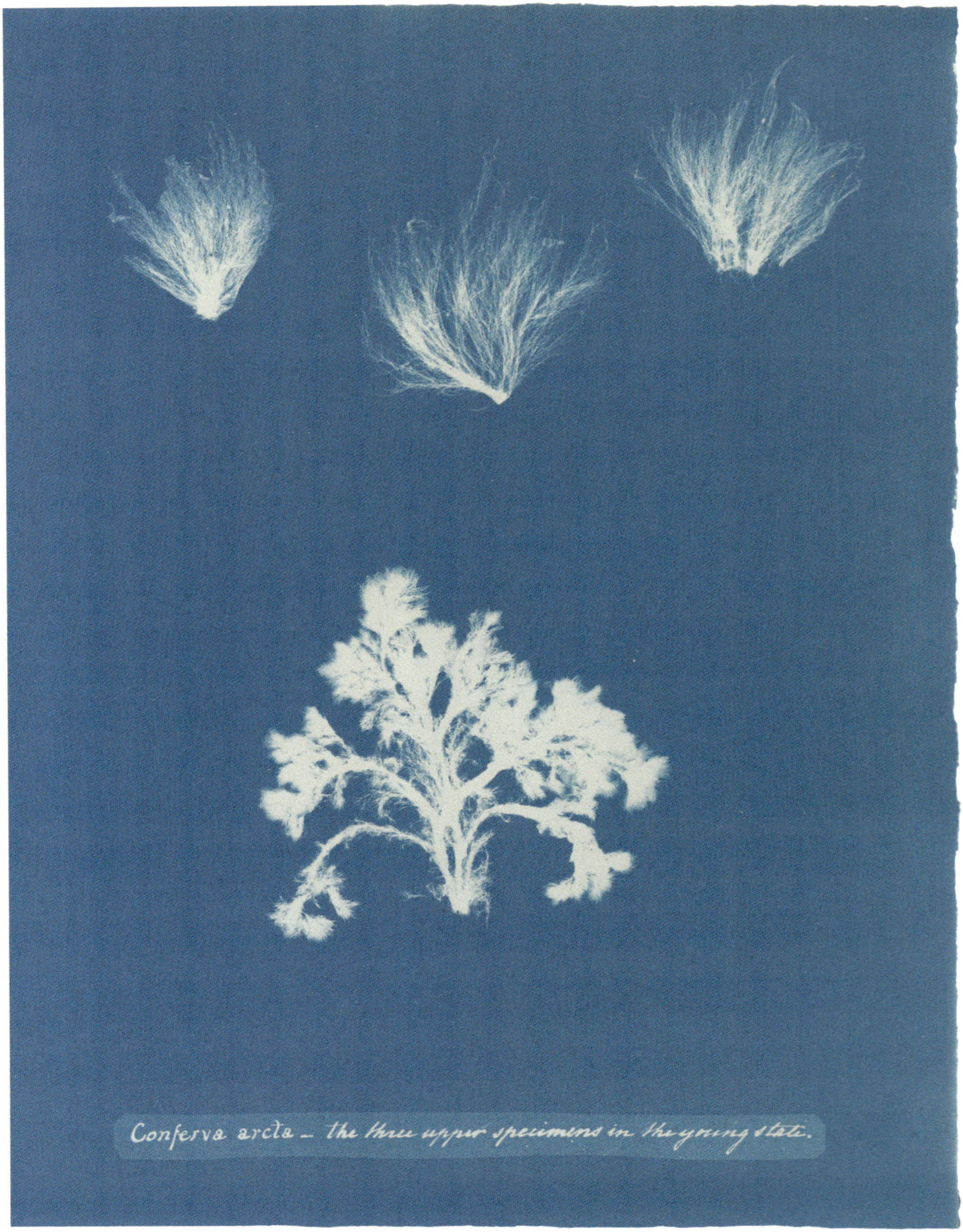

Plate 429. *Conferva arcta* – the three upper specimens in the young state

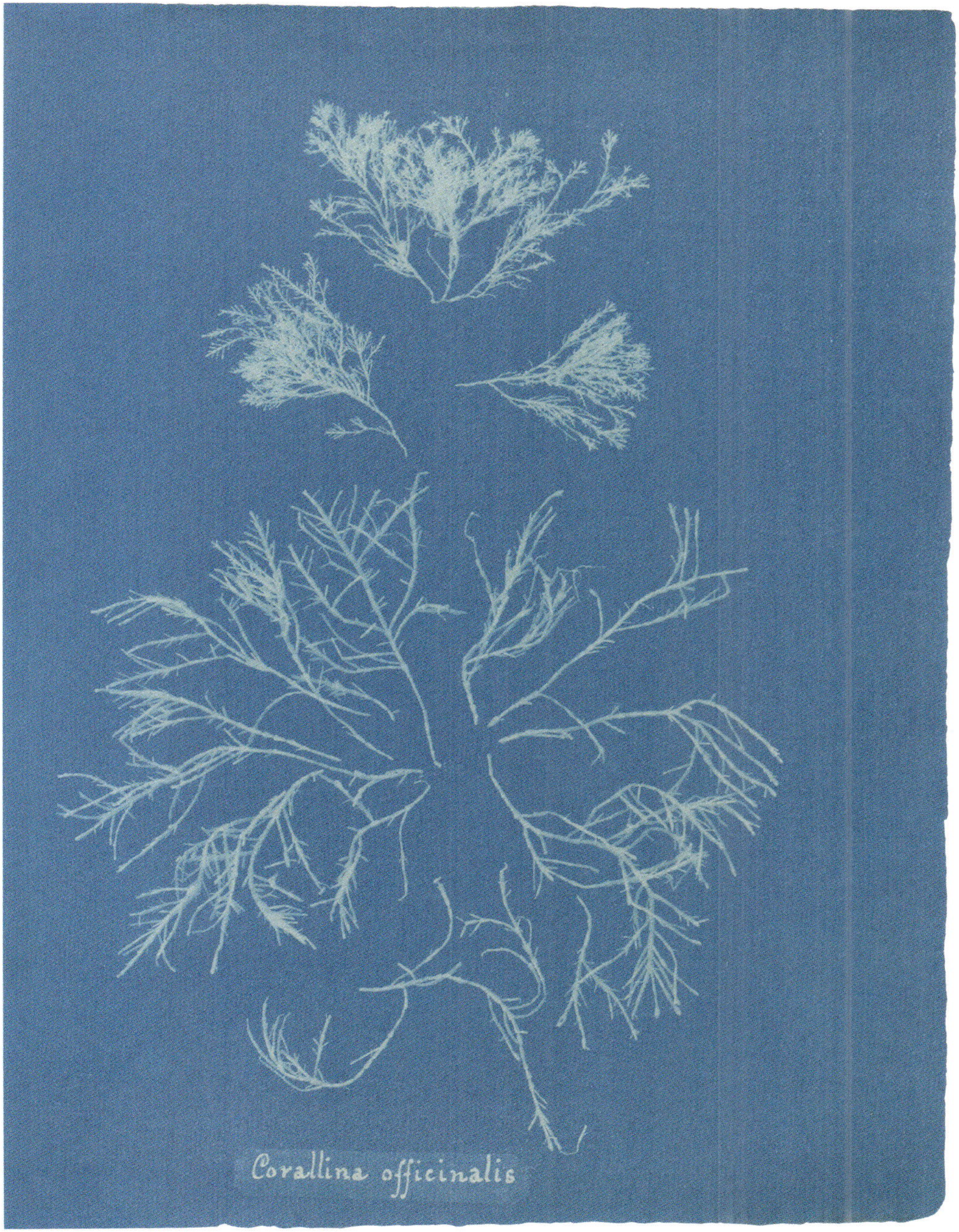

Plate 430. *Corallina officinalis*

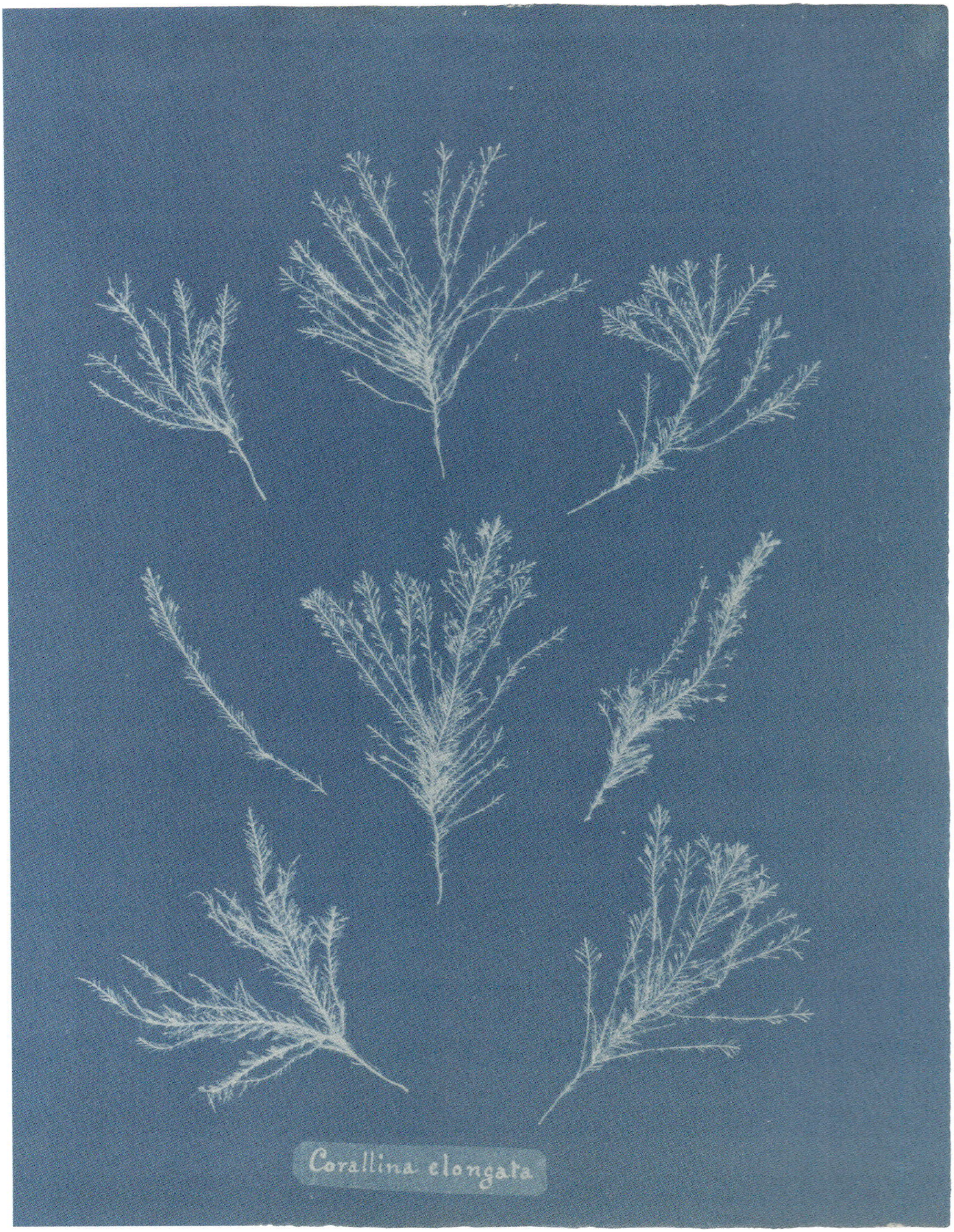

Plate 431. *Corallina elongata*

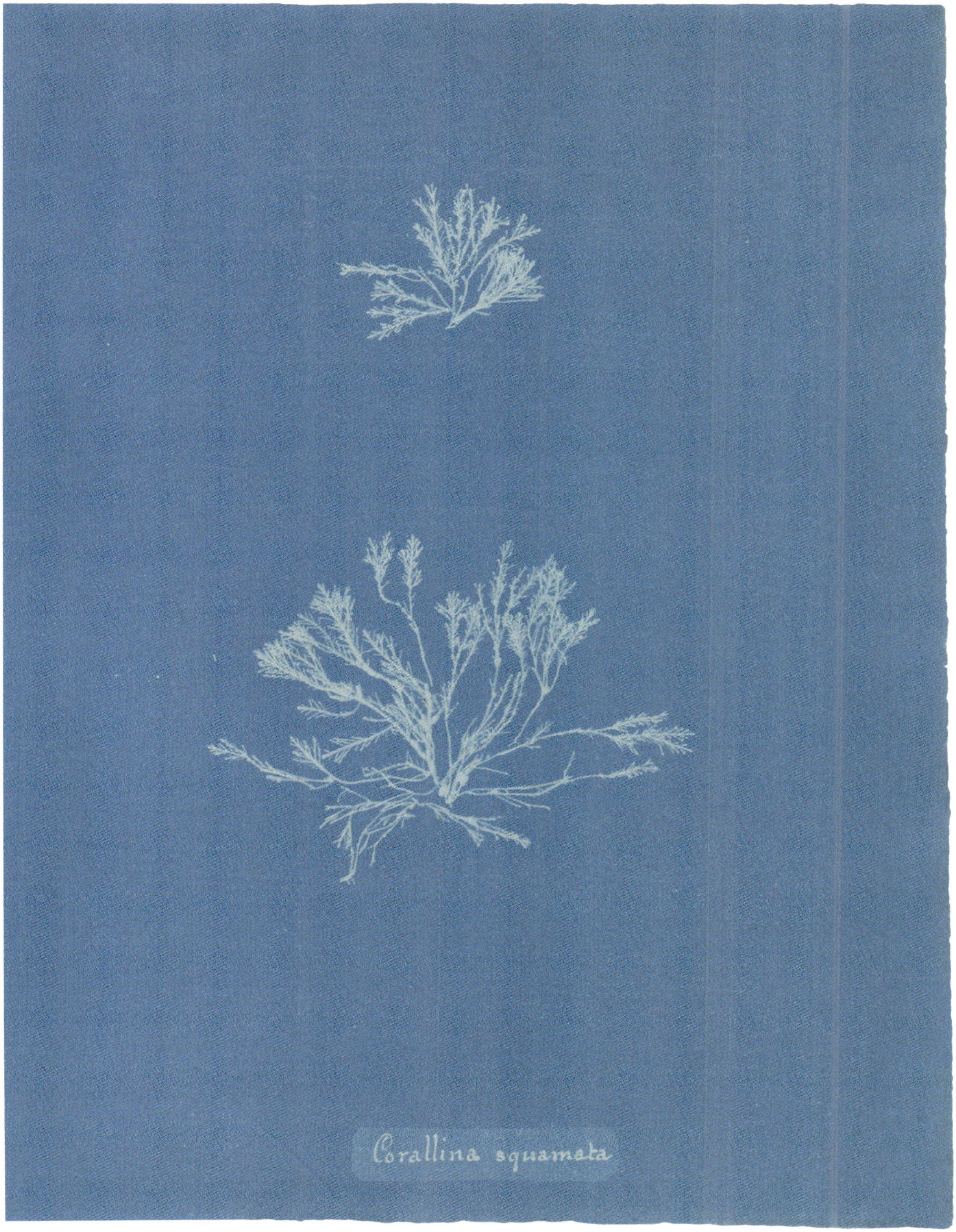

Plate 432. *Corallina squamata*

The Art of Botanical Illustration

The European tradition of botanical illustration began with a widespread desire to share antiquity's knowledge of natural history. Encyclopedic works such *Naturalis historia* by Pliny the Elder (AD 23 or 24–79) or *Materia Medica* by the Greek physician Pedanius Dioscorides (1st century AD) have been released since the end of the Greco-Roman period in richly illustrated editions. Particularly splendid is *Materia Medica* as it appears in the Vienna Dioscorides. Dated around AD 512, this is an inventory of medical plants with hundreds of miniatures of herbal remedies.

Until the High Middle Ages, plants were represented in book illustrations and architecture, mostly as symbols and decorative ornamentation. Even though examples of largely realistic plants can be found in early Netherlandish panel painting or the works of the French court painter Jean Bourdichon (ca. 1456/57–1520/21), they always appear surrounded by mystico-religious symbolism. By contrast, 15th-century artists such as Martin Schongauer (ca. 1445/50–1491) and Leonardo da Vinci (1452–1519) began to study plants of all kinds in their own right.

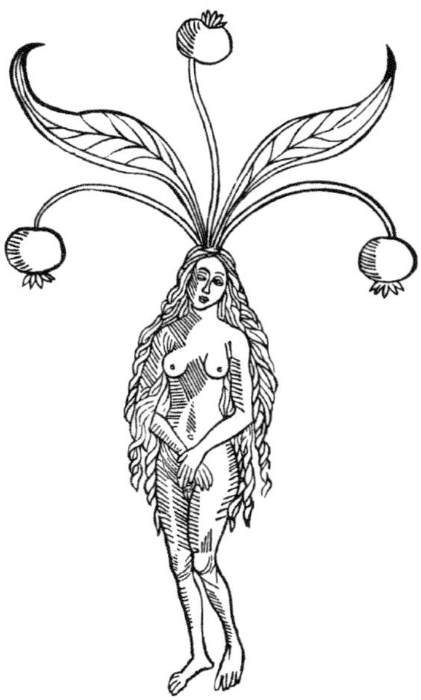

The letterpress technique opened up new possibilities for illustration. In 1477 the Nuremberg-based printer Anton Koberger (1440–1513) reintroduced the ancient tradition of herbal books by printing an extract from the *Book of Nature* by Konrad von Megenberg (1309–1374). One of the most influential works of this kind, however, was *Gart der Gesundheit* (1485) by Johann Wonnecke von Kaub (ca. 1430–1503/04). The book contains 379 woodcuts of early-flowering plants.

Whether plants were presented as symbolic and ornamental or mostly true to nature depended on the context of the illustration. This was especially true in the case of herbals, which were used as medical reference books, as artists' renditions increasingly resembled plants' natural shapes. Around 1530 the artist Hans Weiditz (ca. 1500–1536) made his woodcuts for the herbals by the humanist and botanist Otto Brunfels (1488–1534) in much greater detail, the images revealing every withering leaf and every trace of feeding activity. As templates, he used watercolours of living plants observed and painted in the open air.

No less detailed were the drawings by Albrecht Meyer (ca. 1510–after 1561), created as prototypes for more than 500 woodcuts for inclusion in a herbal by the botanist Leonhart Fuchs (1501–1566). Fuchs was the first to commit the flora of the Americas to writing and illustration. The Swiss physician and naturalist Conrad Gessner (1516–1565) also had a talent for drawing. For his *Historia Plantarum*, which remained unfinished – Gessner died of the Plague – he collected some 1,500 plant drawings, most of them his own work.

With herbals already structured according to the plants' medicinal effectiveness, and specimens drawn in order to make them easily recognizable, the 17th century saw the emergence of a new genre, the florilegium. The readership of this anthology of all things floral in book form came from among well-to-do plant-lovers, scholars and the nobility. Florilegia were not about medicinal or botanical uses of plants. Instead, they focused on how illustrations demanded true artistry to enable wealthy readers to identify plants in their own gardens. Instead of wild native plants, the florilegium presented mostly decorative, exotic blooms.

In the first French book of flowers, *Le Jardin du roy tres chrestien Henry IV* (1608), the botanical artist Pierre Vallet (ca. 1575–1657) printed a selection of the most beautiful plants from a Parisian physician's private garden. Flowers were ordered according to their flowering season, so that, as readers browsed, they were guided through the seasons. Sometimes, florilegia served as an illustrated catalogue of an existing collection of plants, but they were also used as templates or pattern books for interior designs and ornaments.

The art of botanical illustration gained further momentum thanks to the business interests of flower growers, especially in Holland and France. After tulips were introduced to the Netherlands, the early 17th century witnessed the development of a brisk trade in plants. Tulip bulbs, in particular, were a subject of speculation. As early as 1612 the florist Emanuel Sweerts (1552–1612) published a florilegium that functioned as a kind of mail-order catalogue of its time. It contained 110 copperplates, including 32 illustrations of different tulip bulbs. Soon there began to appear "tulip books" which specialized in this particular flower. In 1637 the speculative tulip bubble burst, resulting in the first stock market crash in economic history.

At that time, flower painting was gaining importance, especially in Italy and the Netherlands. As well as producing paintings and decorations for furnishing castles, country houses and urban palaces, painters often provided templates for plant illustrations in florilegia. Meanwhile, the publication on behalf of the newly founded Paris Academy of Sciences in 1676 of *Mémoires pour servir à l'histoire des plantes* (1676) by Denis Dodart (1634–1707) described and depicted plants on a scientific, rational basis.

All books of this kind were ostentatious, expensive, and in no way appropriate as a botanical guidebook for use in the great outdoors. In the early days of botanophilia, enthusiasts were obliged to make do with handbooks without illustrations, thus giving greater importance to Linnaeus'

Hans Weiditz
Female mandrake / Alraunen-Frau / Mandragore femelle
From: Johann Wonnecke von Kaub, *Gart der Gesundheit*, Mainz, 1485
London, Wellcome Collection

simplified botanical classification. Even so, people still longed to be able to identity wild plants with the help of pictures. One way or another, solutions of varying complexity were sought and found. In this way, in order to supplement the texts with illustrations, herbariums were produced on request from original specimens. Alternatively, the plant itself might be coated with paint and used as a printing block, although this meant that fewer impressions could be produced. Later, higher print-runs became possible in nature printing through lithographic processes and the use of lead or copper plates.

The invention of photography aroused great expectations that one had finally found a way to mass-produce illustrations. Initially, such hopes were dashed since the proven definition, dynamics and durability of such imagery were still way beyond the reach of early photographic methods.

Today's photographs, combined with high levels of printing technology, can capture the rich nuances of the plants' shapes and colours. Nonetheless, the art of botanical illustration remains alive and well, since only this medium is equipped to combine scientific demands of accurate representation with subjective questions of aesthetics.

Emanuel Sweerts
Daffodils / Narzissen / Jonquilles
Hand-coloured copper plate engraving
From: *Florilegium amplissimum et selectissimum*, Frankfurt, 1612–1614
Private collection

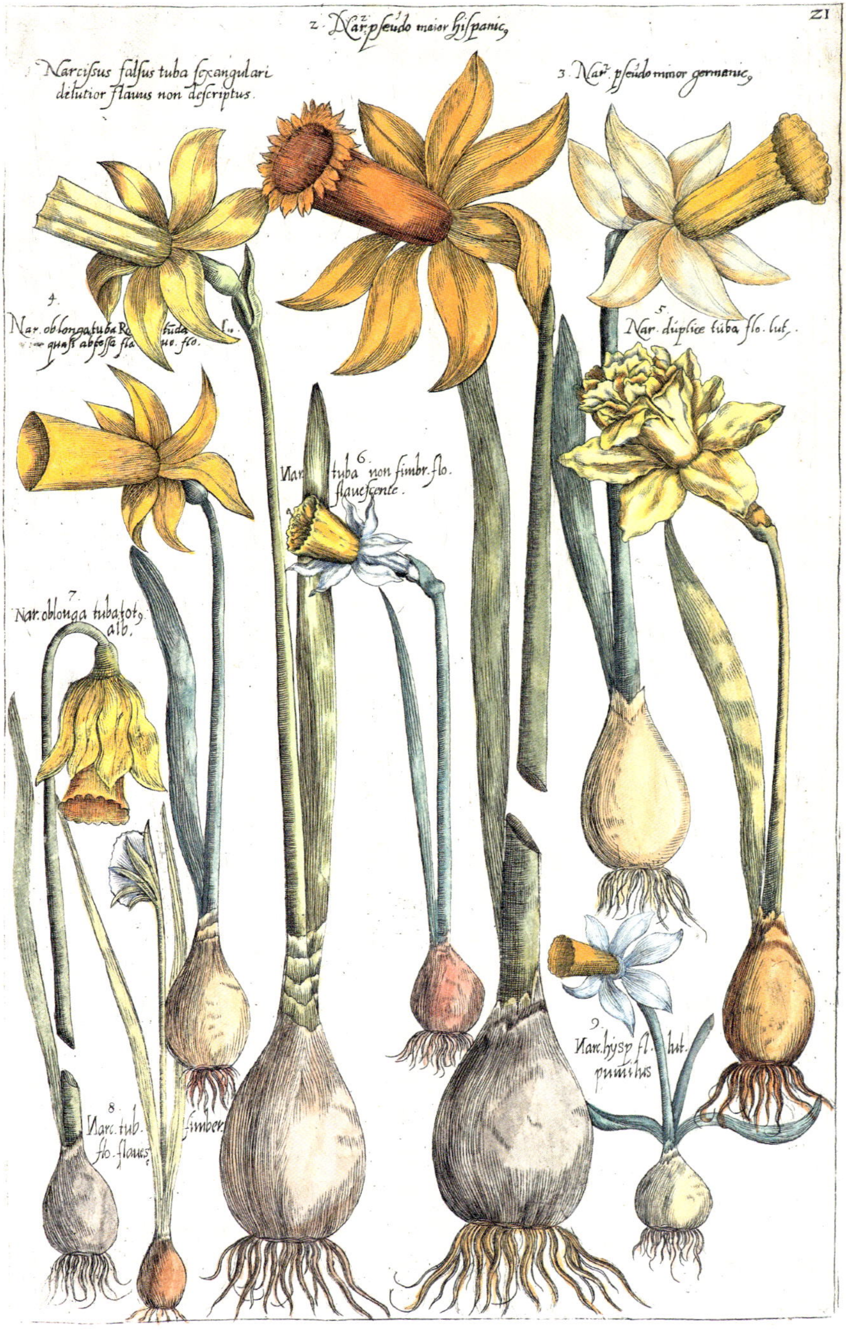
21
2. Nar. pseudo maior hispanic.
Narcisus falsus tuba sexangulari
dilutior flauus non descriptus.
3. Nar. pseudo minor germanic.
5. Nar. duplice tuba flo. lut.
7. Nar. oblonga tuba tot. alb.
9. Narc. hysp fl. lut. pumilus

Die Kunst der botanischen Illustration

In Europa entwickelt sich die Tradition botanischer Illustrationen anfänglich mit der Aneignung antiken naturkundlichen Wissens. Werke wie die Enzyklopädie *Naturalis historia* von Plinius dem Älteren (23 oder 24–79 n. Chr.) oder die *Materia Medica* des griechischen Arztes Pedanios Dioskurides (1. Jh. n. Chr.) erscheinen seit dem Ausgang der Antike in reich illustrierten Ausgaben. Besonders prachtvoll ist der Wiener Codex der *Materia Medica* aus der Zeit um 512, der ein Kräuterbuch mit Hunderten Miniaturen von Heilpflanzen enthält.

Bis in das Hochmittelalter hinein werden Pflanzen in der Buchkunst und der Architektur vor allem in Form symbolhafter Bezüge und schmückender Ornamente dargestellt. Auch wenn sich etwa in Werken der altniederländischen Tafelmalerei oder des französischen Hofmalers Jean Bourdichon (um 1456/57–1520/21) weitgehend wirklichkeitsgetreue Pflanzendarstellungen finden, stehen sie doch stets im Kontext einer mystisch-religiösen Symbolik. Dagegen beginnen während des 15. Jahrhunderts Künstler wie Martin Schongauer (um 1445/50–1491) und Leonardo da Vinci (1452–1519), Pflanzen aller Art um ihrer selbst willen zu studieren.

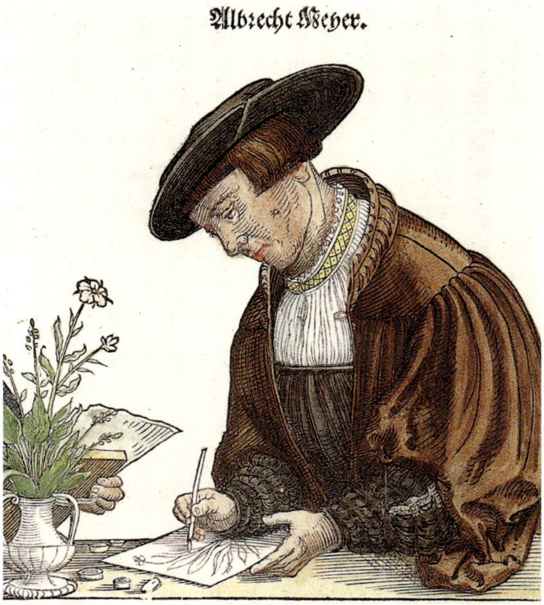

Die Technik des Buchdrucks eröffnet neue Möglichkeiten für die Illustration. 1477 setzt der Nürnberger Buchdrucker Anton Koberger (1440–1513) die Tradition antiker Kräuterbücher mit einem Auszug aus *Buch der Natur* von Konrad von Megenberg (1309–1374) fort. Zum einflussreichsten Werk dieses Genres wird jedoch der *Gart der Gesundheit* (1485) des Johann Wonnecke von Kaub (um 1430–1503/04). Das Buch enthält 379 Holzschnitte von Frühblühern.

Ob die Pflanzen eher symbolhaft und ornamental oder weitgehend naturgetreu dargestellt werden, hängt vom Kontext der Illustration ab. Vor allem in den Kräuterbüchern, die als medizinische Nachschlagewerke genutzt werden, nähern sich die Künstler zunehmend der natürlichen

Gestalt der Pflanzen. Um 1530 fertigt der Graphiker Hans Weiditz (um 1500–1536) Holzschnitte für die Kräuterbücher des Humanisten und Botanikers Otto Brunfels (1488–1534) von hoher Detailtreue an. Auf den Bildern sieht man jedes welke Blatt und jede Fraßspur. Als Vorlagen dienen ihm dabei Aquarelle von Pflanzen, die er nach Beobachtung in der Natur gemalt hat.

Nicht minder detailliert sind die Zeichnungen Albrecht Meyers (um 1510–nach 1561), die als Vorlage für über 500 Holzschnitte im Kräuterbuch des Botanikers Leonhart Fuchs (1501–1566) dienten. Fuchs präsentiert zum ersten Mal die Pflanzenwelt Amerikas in Text und Bild. Der Schweizer Arzt und Naturforscher Conrad Gessner (1516–1565) verfügt selbst über ein hohes Zeichentalent. Für seine unvollendet gebliebene *Historia Plantarum* – Gessner stirbt an der Pest – sammelt er etwa 1.500 Pflanzenzeichnungen, von denen er die meisten selbst anfertigt.

Waren die Kräuterbücher nach medizinischen Nützlichkeitserwägungen geordnet und die Pflanzen so gezeichnet, dass sie leicht zu erkennen sind, kommt im 17. Jahrhundert ein neues Genre auf, das Florilegium. Diese Blumensammlungen in Buchform entstehen im Umkreis von vermögenden Pflanzenliebhabern, von Gelehrten und Fürsten. In den Florilegien geht es nicht um den medizinischen oder botanischen Nutzen in der Darstellung der Pflanzen, sondern vor allem um den künstlerischen Anspruch der Illustration, der auf das Repräsentationsbedürfnis des Besitzers zielt. So werden statt wildwachsender einheimischer Pflanzen vorwiegend exotische und dekorative Gewächse gezeigt.

Im ersten französischen Blumenbuch, *Le Jardin du roy tres chrestien Henry IV* (1608), präsentiert Pierre Vallet (um 1575–1657) eine Auswahl der schönsten Pflanzen aus dem Privatgarten eines Pariser Mediziners. Geordnet sind die Pflanzen nach dem Zeitpunkt ihrer Blüte, sodass sich beim Blättern ein Durchgang durch die Jahreszeiten ergibt. Zuweilen dienen die Florilegien als illustrierte Kataloge einer bestehenden Sammlung von Pflanzen, sie werden aber auch als Vorlagen- oder Musterbücher für Dekorationsentwürfe und Ornamente genutzt.

Einen weiteren Impuls erhält die Kunst der botanischen Illustration durch die wirtschaftlichen Interessen der Blumenzüchter vor allem in Holland und Frankreich. Nachdem man in den Niederlanden begonnen hat, Tulpen zu importieren und zu züchten, entwickelt sich im frühen 17. Jahrhundert ein reger Handel mit den Pflanzen. Die Tulpenzwiebel wird zum Spekulationsobjekt. Bereits 1612 erscheint mit dem Florilegium des Blumenhändlers Emanuel Sweerts (1552–1612) ein Buch, das als Katalog für den Versandhandel angelegt ist. Es enthält 110 Kupfertafeln, darunter 32 Abbildungen verschiedener Tulpenblüten. Bald erscheinen ganz auf Tulpen spezialisierte „Tulpenbücher". 1637 platzt die Spekulationsblase um die Tulpenzwiebeln und führt zum ersten Börsencrash der Wirtschaftsgeschichte.

Vor allem in Italien und den Niederlanden erlangt die Blumenmalerei in dieser Zeit Bedeutung. Neben Gemälden und Dekorationen für die Ausstattung der Schlösser, Landhäuser und Stadtpaläste schaffen die Maler häufig auch Vorlagen für die Pflanzenillustrationen in den Florilegien. Zugleich

Albrecht Meyer
Self-portrait / Selbstporträt / Autoportrait (detail)
Coloured wood engraving
From: Leonard Fuchs, *De Historia Stirpium*, German edition: *New Kreüter-Buch*, Basel, 1543
Ulm, Stadtbibliothek

entsteht mit den *Mémoires pour servir à l'histoire des plantes* (1676) des Denis Dodart (1634–1707) im Auftrag der gerade gegründeten Pariser Akademie der Wissenschaften auch ein Werk, in dem die Pflanzen auf naturwissenschaftlich-rationalistischer Grundlage beschrieben und abgebildet werden.

Alle diese Bücher sind aufwendig, teuer und als Bestimmungsbücher für den Gebrauch in der freien Natur nicht geeignet. In der Frühzeit der Botanophilie setzt man daher auf Handbücher, die ohne Illustrationen auskommen müssen.

Umso wichtiger ist die Vereinfachung der botanischen Nomenklatur durch Linné. Der Wunsch, die Pflanze in der Natur nach ihrem Abbild bestimmen zu können, bleibt dennoch lebendig. Man sucht und findet dafür Lösungen, die mit unterschiedlichem Aufwand verbunden sind. So werden, um die Textkompendien mit Illustrationen zu ergänzen, auf Bestellung Herbarien aus Originalpräparaten hergestellt. Oder man nutzt die Pflanze selbst als Druckstock, indem man sie mit Farbe bestreicht. Damit lässt sich jedoch nur eine kleine Zahl von Abzügen drucken. Später erreicht man höhere Auflagen im „Naturselbstdruck" durch lithographische Verfahren und die Nutzung von Druckplatten aus Blei oder Kupfer.

Die Erfindung der Fotografie weckt zunächst große Hoffnungen, nun endlich ein Mittel für die massenhafte Reproduktion von Illustrationen gefunden zu haben. Diese Erwartungen werden in der Anfangszeit jedoch enttäuscht, denn im Hinblick auf den Reproduktionsaufwand sowie auf Schärfe, Dynamik und Haltbarkeit der Bilder kann die frühe Fotografie mit den bewährten Illustrationsverfahren nicht mithalten.

Heute liefern Fotografien im Verbund mit einem hohen drucktechnischen Niveau ein in Gestalt und Farbe reich nuanciertes Abbild der Pflanze. Dennoch lebt die Kunst botanischer Illustration fort, da nur sie geeignet ist, wissenschaftliche Ansprüche an die Genauigkeit der Darstellung mit ästhetischer Subjektivität zu verbinden.

Pierre Valet
Plate from / Tafel aus / Planche de
Le Jardin du roy tres chrestien Henry IV, Paris, 1608
Paris, Bibliothèque nationale de France

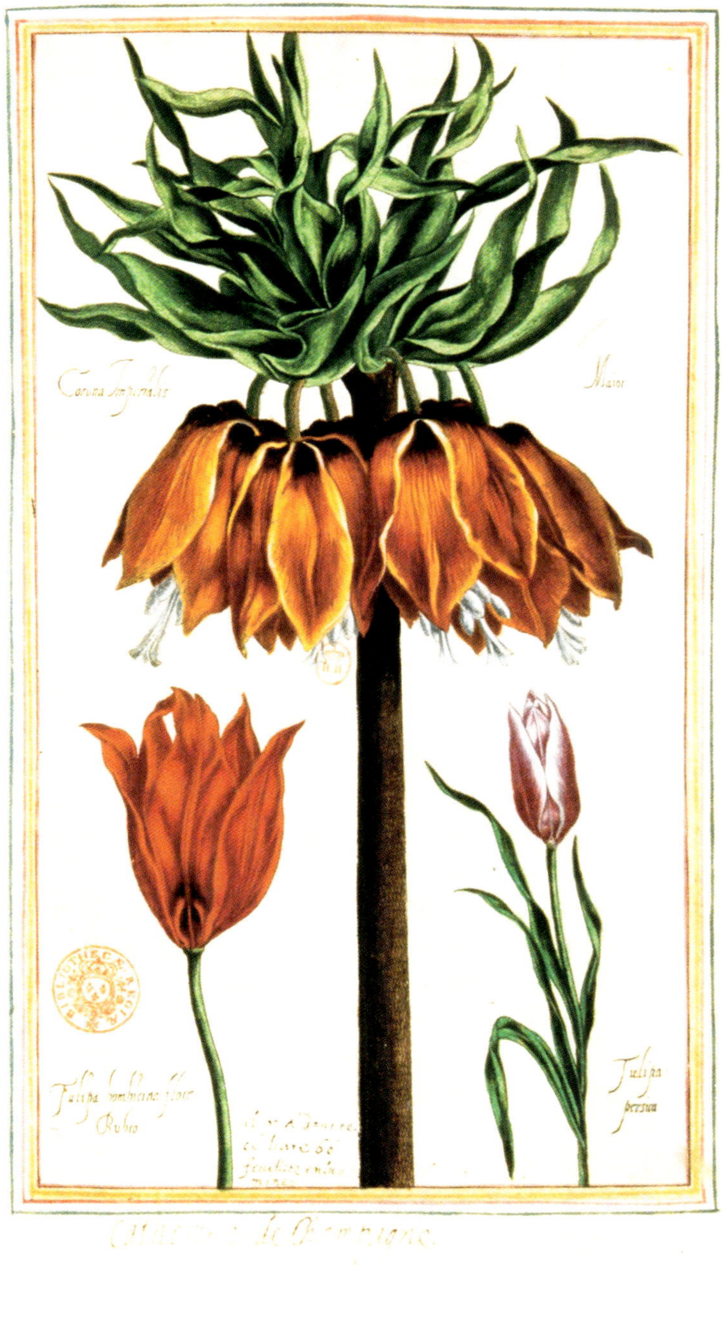

L'art de l'illustration botanique

En Europe, la tradition de l'illustration botanique débute avec l'appropriation des connaissances des sciences naturelles de l'Antiquité. Après la fin de l'Antiquité, des ouvrages comme l'*Histoire naturelle* de Pline l'Ancien (23 ou 24–79 apr. J.-C.) ou le *Traité de matière médicale* de Dioscoride (Pedanios Dioskoridês, Ier siècle apr. J.-C.) font l'objet de manuscrits richement illustrés. Particulièrement splendide est le codex viennois de *De materia medica* (vers 512), qui contient un herbier comptant des centaines de miniatures de plantes médicinales.

Jusqu'au haut Moyen Âge, les plantes sont présentées essentiellement dans l'enluminure et l'architecture, en l'occurrence sous forme de références symboliques et d'ornements décoratifs. Même si les œuvres des primitifs hollandais ou du peintre de la cour de France Jean Bourdichon (vers 1456/57–1520/21) contiennent des représentations de plantes largement fidèles à la réalité, celles-ci n'en sont pas moins toujours placées dans le contexte d'une symbolique mystique et religieuse. Vers la fin du XVe siècle en revanche, des artistes comme Martin Schongauer (vers 1445/50–1491) et Léonard de Vinci (1452–1519), commencent à étudier toutes sortes de plantes pour elles-mêmes.

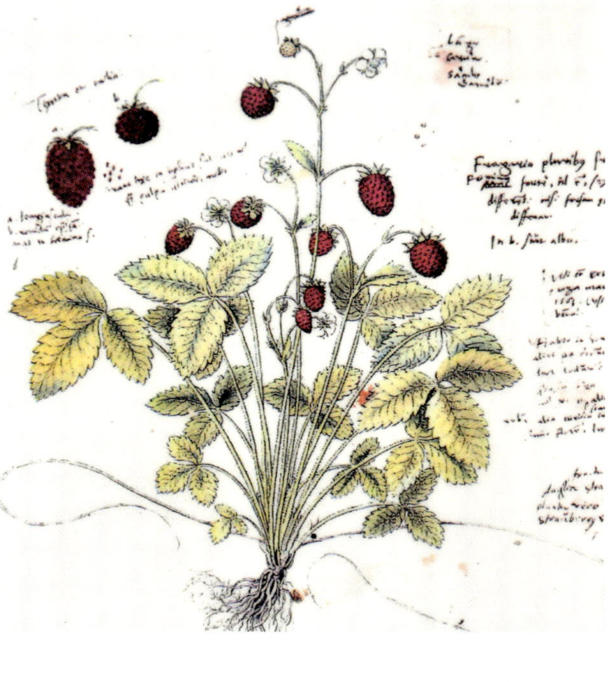

L'imprimerie ouvre de nouvelles possibilités à l'illustration. En 1477, l'imprimeur nurembergeois Anton Koberger (1440–1513) poursuit la tradition des herbiers antiques en imprimant l'extrait de l'ouvrage *Das Buch der Natur* de Konrad von Megenberg (1309–1374). Un des ouvrages les plus influents de ce domaine sera toutefois le *Gart der Gesundheit* (1485) de Johannes Wonnecke von Kaub, dit Jean de Cuba (vers 1430–1503/04), qui contient 379 xylographies de plantes à floraison précoce.

Que les plantes soient représentées sur un mode symbolique, ornemental ou largement fidèle au modèle naturel, dépend du contexte de l'illustration. C'est surtout dans les herbiers utilisés comme ouvrages de référence en médecine que les artistes se rapprochent de plus en plus de l'aspect naturel des plantes. Vers 1530, Hans Weiditz (vers 1500–1536) grave sur bois, pour l'herbier de l'humaniste et botaniste Otto Brunfels (1488–1534), des illustrations qui présentent une grande fidélité aux détails. Ses images montrent la moindre feuille fanée et la moindre trace de grignotement. Pour les illustrations de cet herbier, Weiditz s'est appuyé sur des aquarelles de plantes qu'il a lui-même peintes dans le cadre de ses observations naturelles.

Non moins détaillés sont les dessins d'Albrecht Meyer (vers 1510–apr. 1561) qui ont servi de modèle à plus de 500 xylographies de l'herbier du botaniste Leonhart Fuchs (1501–1566). Fuchs présente pour la première fois la flore d'Amérique par le texte et par l'image. Le médecin suisse et naturaliste Conrad Gessner (1516–1565) dispose lui-même d'un grand talent de dessinateur. Pour son *Historia plantarum* restée inachevée – il meurt de la peste –, Gessner put réunir quelque 1 500 dessins de plantes dont la majorité sont de sa main.

Si les herbiers sont jusqu'alors organisés en fonction de spéculations sur leur valeur médicinale et les plantes dessinées de manière à être aisément identifiables, le XVIIe siècle voit apparaître un genre nouveau, le florilège. Ces collections de fleurs sous forme de livres voient le jour dans l'entourage des amateurs de plantes fortunés, des savants et des princes. Dans le florilège, le propos de la représentation ne porte pas sur l'utilité médicinale ou botanique des plantes, mais avant tout sur l'ambition artistique de l'illustration, qui cible le besoin de représentation de son propriétaire. Ainsi, plutôt que des plantes autochtones sauvages, le florilège présente essentiellement des plantes exotiques et décoratives.

Dans le premier livre de fleurs français, le *Jardin du roy tres chrestien Henry IV* (1608), Pierre Vallet (vers 1575–1657) présente une sélection des plus belles plantes du jardin privé d'un médecin parisien. Les plantes sont classées dans l'ordre de leur floraison, et feuilleter le livre revient donc à une promenade au fil des saisons. Si les florilèges se présentent parfois comme des catalogues illustrés de telle ou telle collection de plantes constituée, ils servent aussi de livres de modèles ou de motifs pour des projets décoratifs et des ornements.

L'art de l'illustration botanique reçoit une nouvelle impulsion dans le cadre des intérêts économiques des floriculteurs principalement hollandais et français. Après l'introduction des tulipes aux Pays-Bas, un fort commerce des plantes se développe, et le bulbe de tulipe devient objet de spéculation. Dès 1612 paraît le florilège du floriculteur Emanuel Sweerts (1552–1612), conçu comme un catalogue de vente par correspondance. Il contient 110 planches gravées sur cuivre, dont 32 représentations de différentes fleurs de tulipe. Bientôt paraissent des « livres de tulipes » spécialisés dans ces fleurs. En 1637, la bulle spéculative autour des bulbes de tulipes éclate et conduit au premier krach boursier de l'histoire économique.

À l'époque, c'est surtout en Italie et aux Pays-Bas que la peinture de fleurs prend de l'importance. À côté de peintures et de décors réalisés pour orner les châteaux, les maisons de campagne et les palais

Conrad Gessner
Wild strawberries / Walderdbeere / Fraises des bois
From: *Historia plantarum*, Nuremberg, 1754
Ethnographic Museum of the University of Zurich

de ville, les peintres créent souvent aussi des modèles pour les illustrations des florilèges. En même temps, les *Mémoires pour servir à l'histoire des plantes* (1676) que Denis Dodart (1634–1707) réalise suite à une commande de la toute jeune Académie des sciences, est aussi un ouvrage dans lequel les plantes sont décrites et représentées en termes scientifiques et rationalistes.

Tous ces livres sont luxueusement dotés, chers et impropres à l'utilisation dans la nature. Aux premiers temps de la botanophilie, on mise donc sur des manuels qui doivent se passer d'illustrations. La simplification de la nomenclature botanique par Linné revêt dès lors une importance d'autant plus grande. Le désir de pouvoir identifier la plante dans la nature d'après son image n'en reste pas moins vivace. L'on cherche et trouve pour cela des solutions qui entraînent des coûts variables. Ainsi, pour compléter les compendiums purement textuels par des illustrations, des herbiers composés à partir de préparations originales sont créés sur commande. Ou bien l'on utilise comme cliché la plante elle-même enduite de peinture, sachant que ce procédé n'autorise qu'un tirage extrêmement réduit. L'on atteindra plus tard des tirages plus importants par « auto-impression naturelle » grâce aux procédés lithographiques et à l'utilisation de plaques d'imprimerie en plomb ou en cuivre.

Dans un premier temps, la découverte de la photographie suscite l'immense espoir d'avoir enfin trouvé un moyen de reproduction de masse pour l'illustration. Ces attentes sont toutefois bien vite déçues, car en termes de coûts de reproduction, de niveau de netteté, de dynamique et de durabilité des images, la photographie naissante ne peut concurrencer les procédés d'illustration éprouvés. Aujourd'hui, les photographies associées à une haute technicité de l'imprimerie fournissent une image de la plante richement nuancée en termes de formes et de couleurs. L'art de l'illustration botanique n'en survit pas moins, car lui seul permet de concilier exactitude scientifique et subjectivité esthétique de la représentation.

Emanuel Sweerts
Plate from / Tafel aus / Planche de
Florilegium amplissimum et selectissimum, Frankfurt, 1612–1614
Universitätsbibliothek Erlangen-Nürnberg

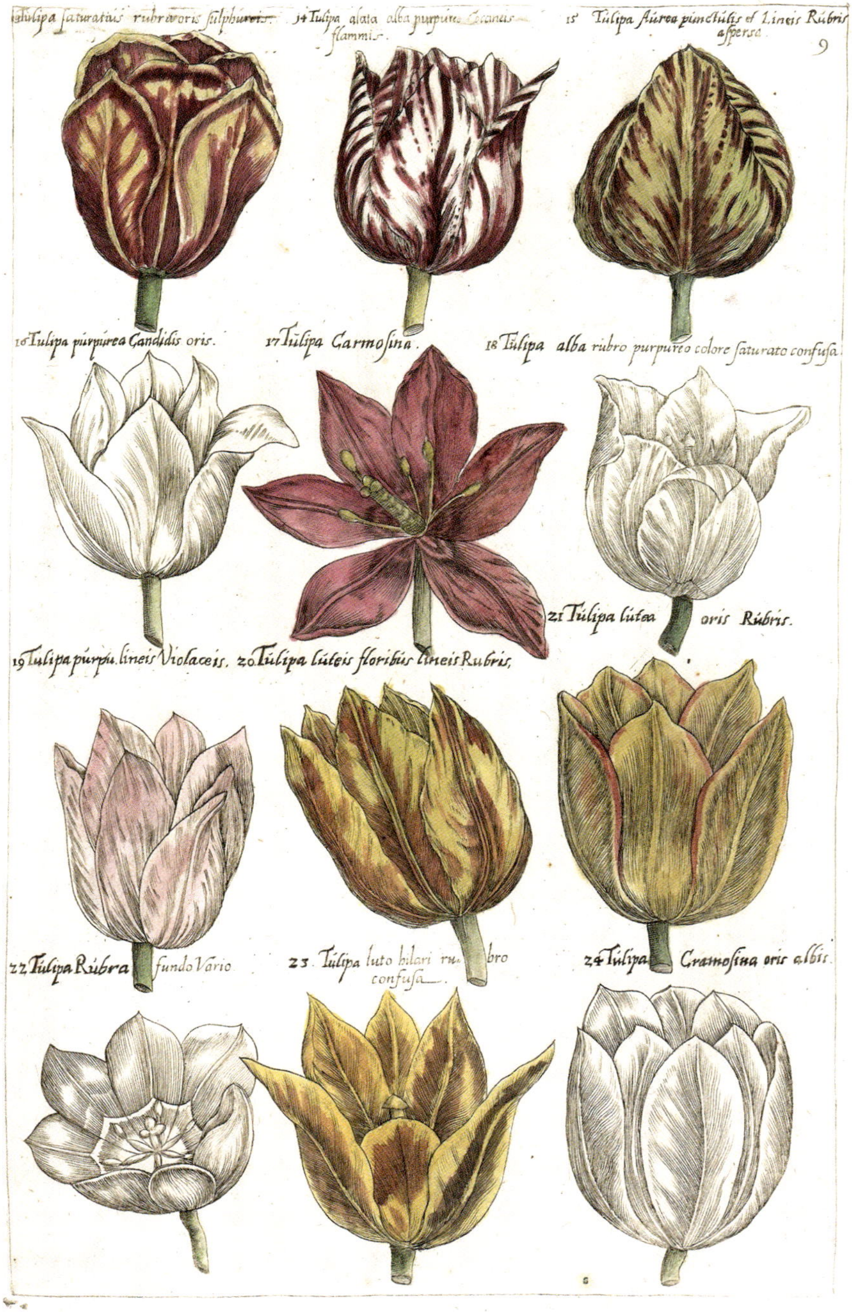
Tulipa saturatius rubra oris sulphureis.
14 Tulipa alata alba purpure. Coccineis flammis.
15 Tulipa Aurea punctulis et Lineis Rubris aspersa.
9
16 Tulipa purpurea Candidis oris.
17 Tulipa Carmosina.
18 Tulipa alba rubro purpureo colore saturato confusa
21 Tulipa lutea oris Rubris.
19 Tulipa purpu. lineis Violaceis.
20 Tulipa luteis floribus lineis Rubris.
22 Tulipa Rubra fundo Vario
23 Tulipa luto hilari rubro confusa.
24 Tulipa Cramosina oris albis.

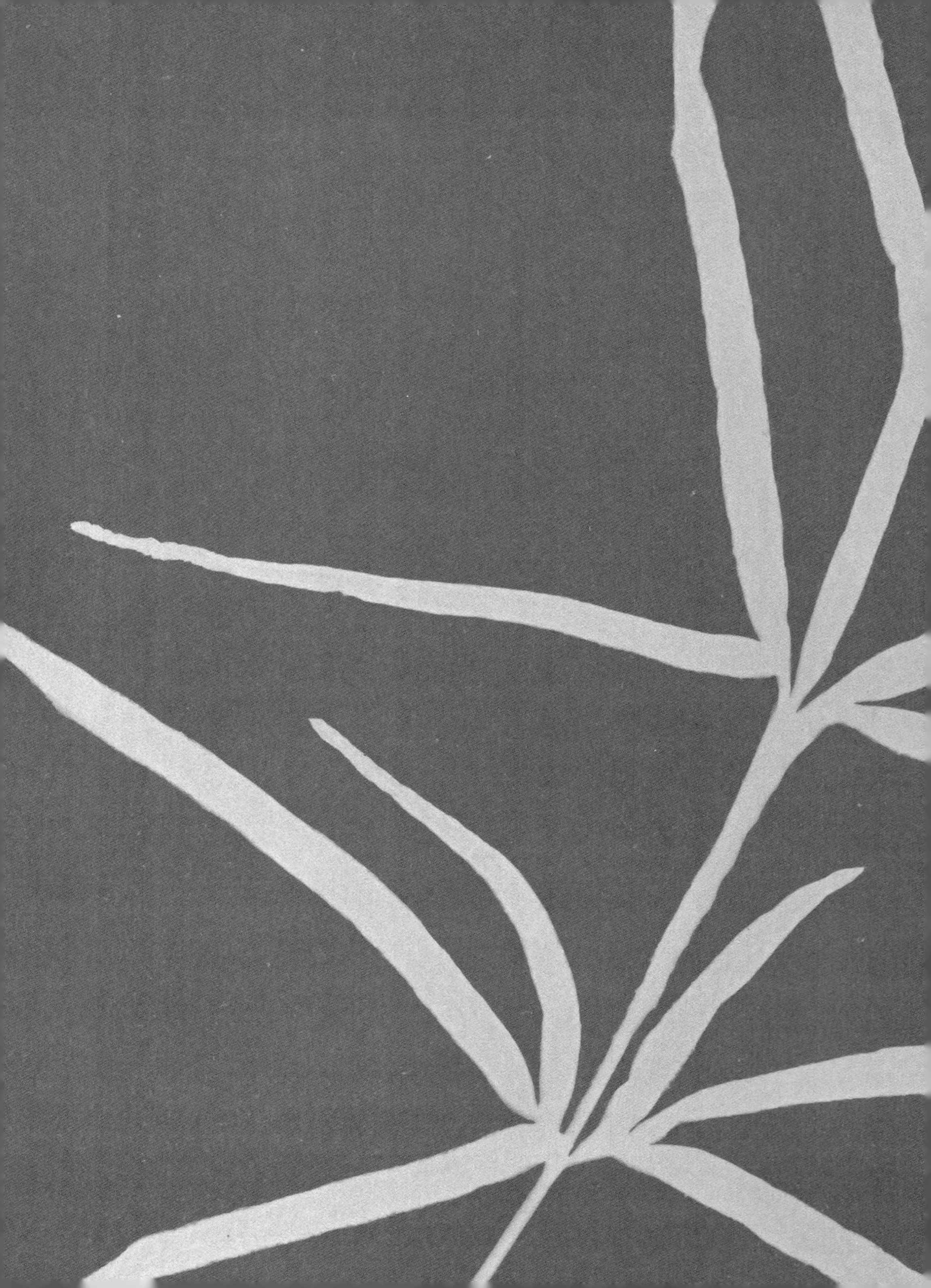

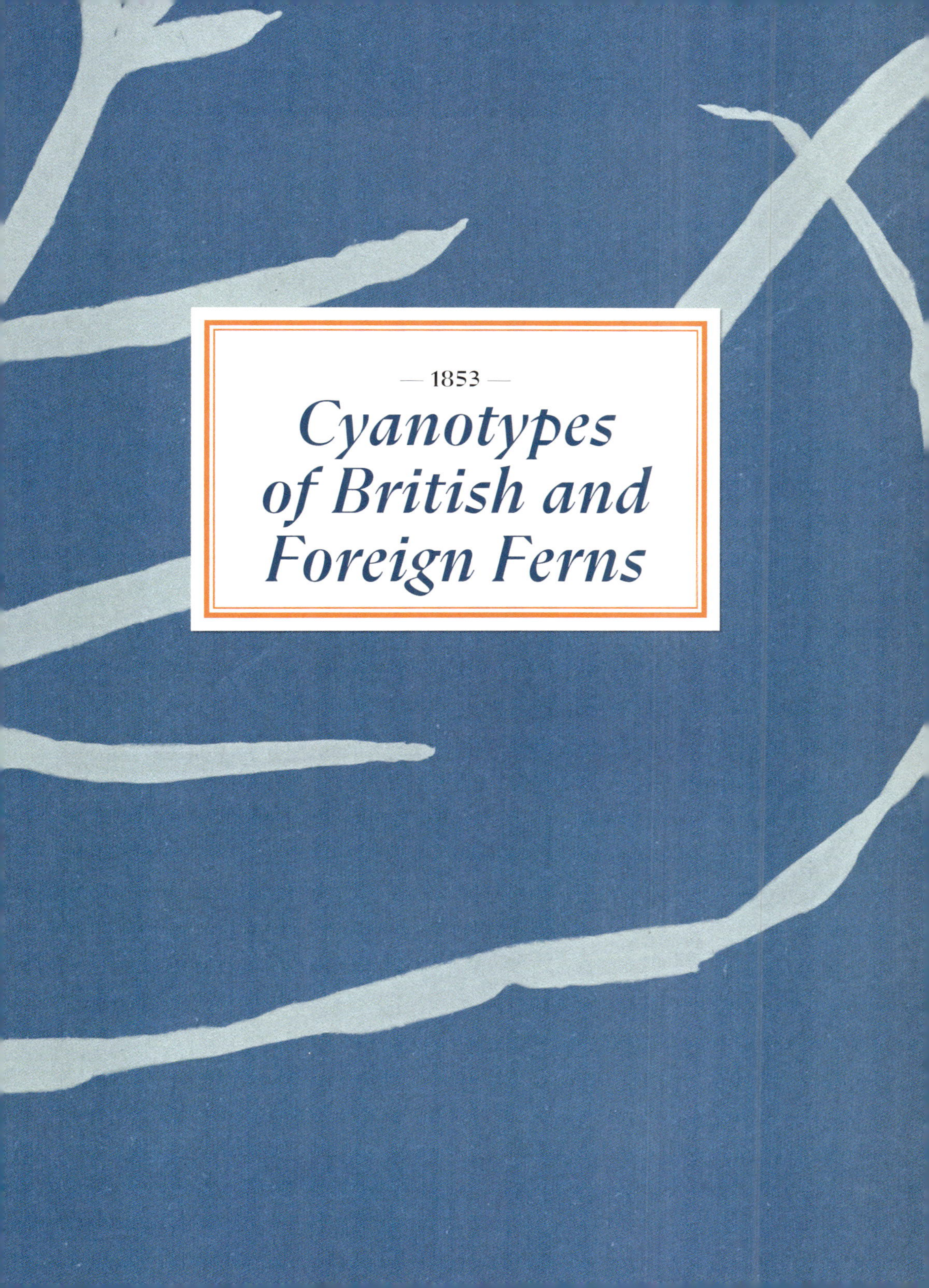

— 1853 —

Cyanotypes of British and Foreign Ferns

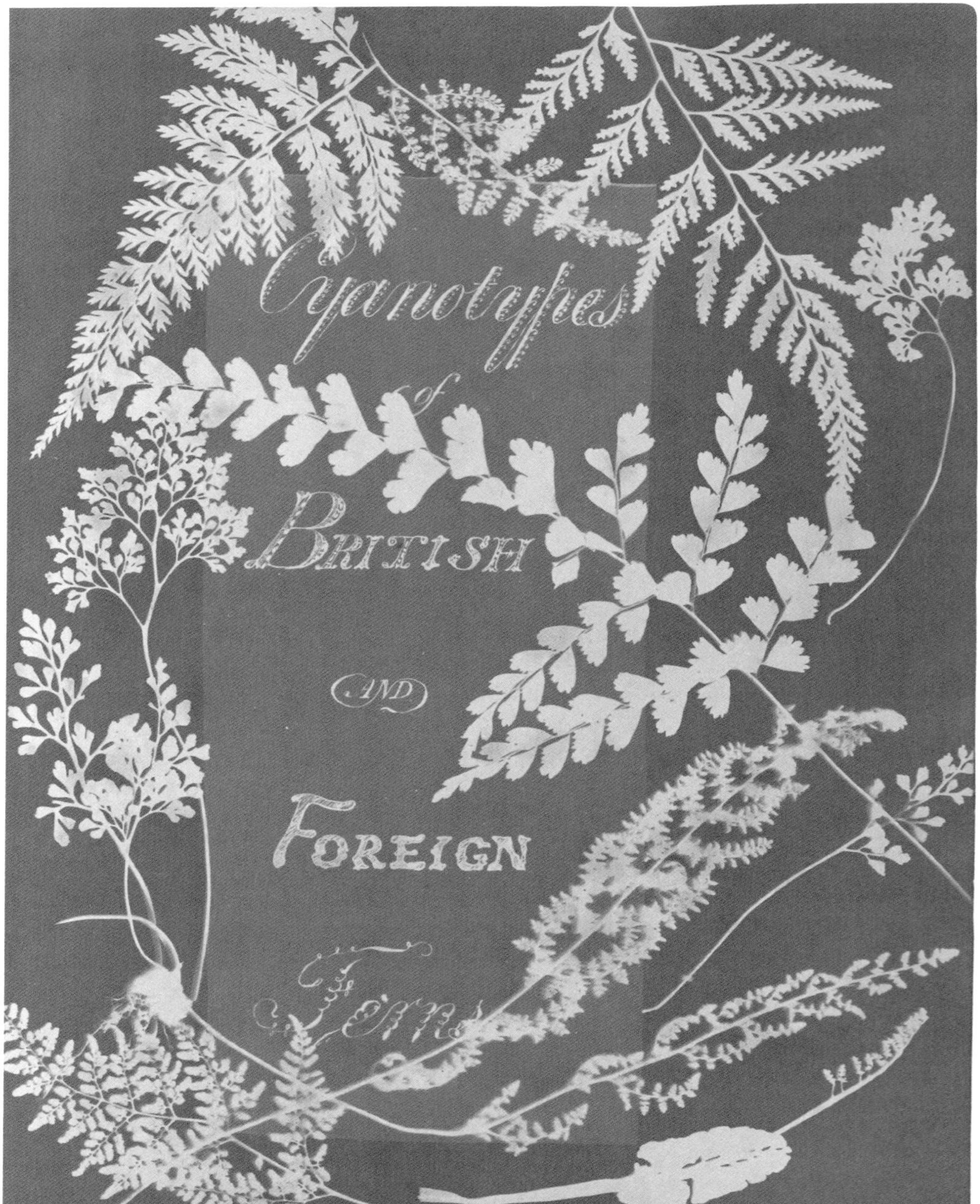

Title Page

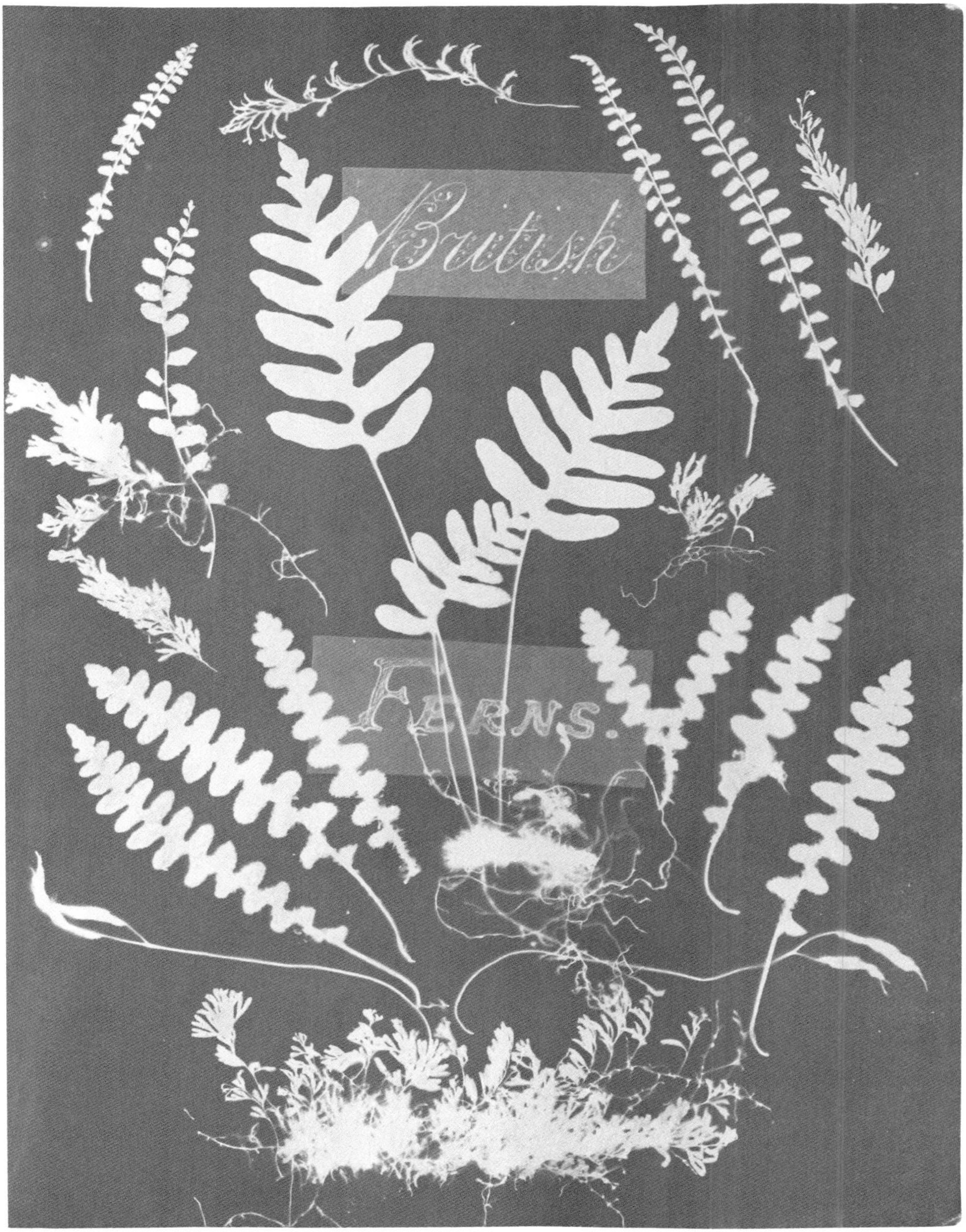

Title Page

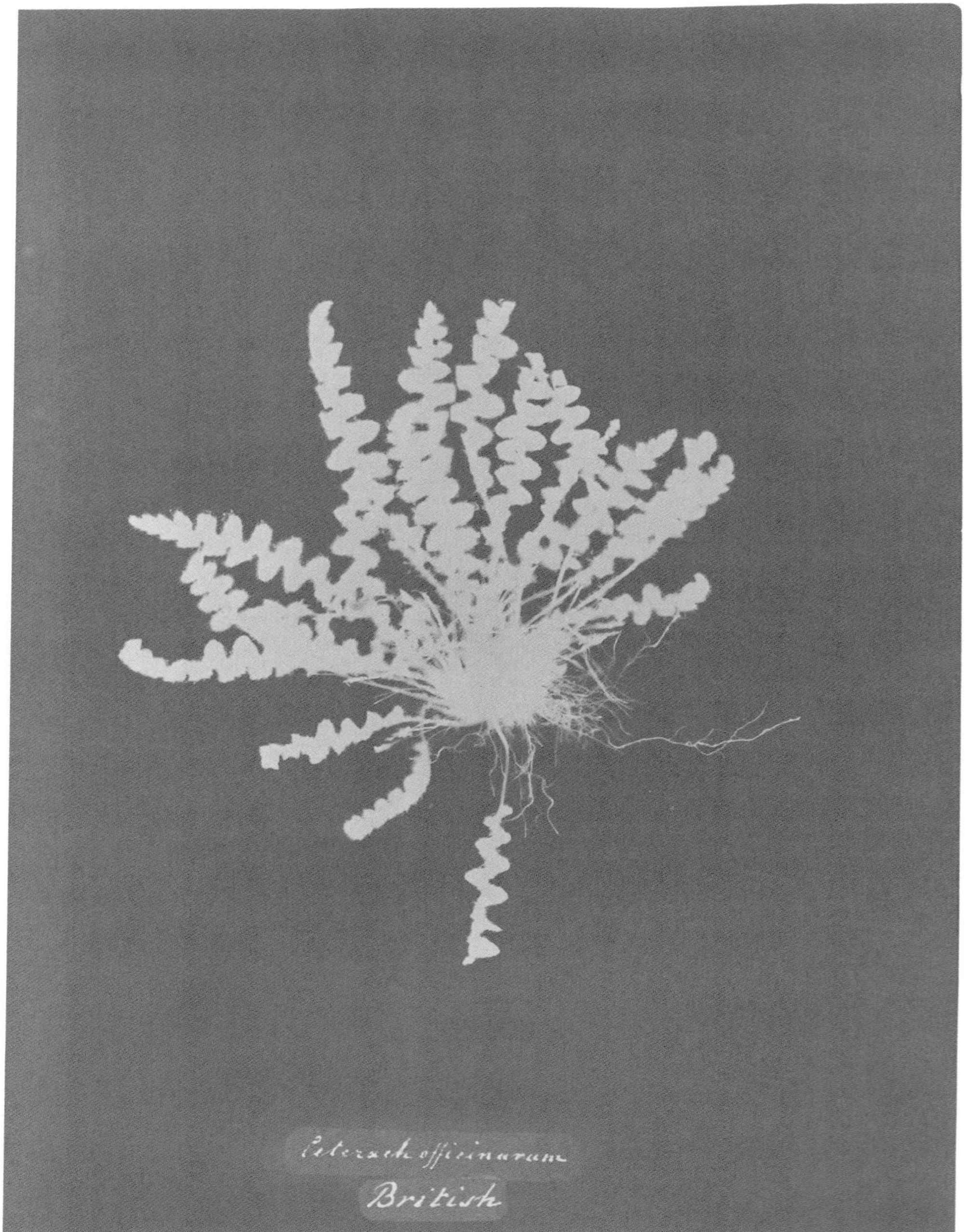

Plate 434. *Ceterach officinarum*, British

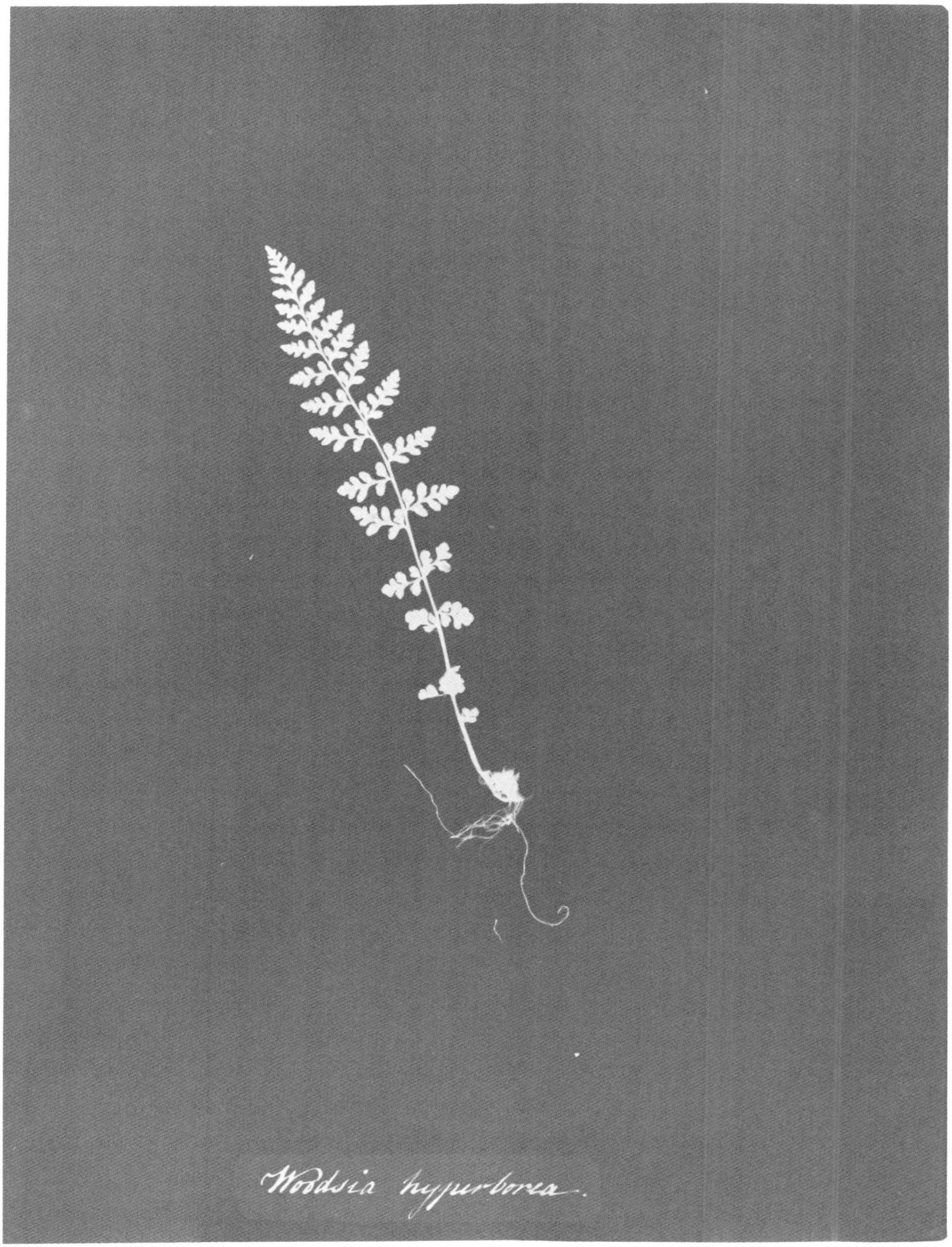

Plate 435. *Woodsia hyperborea*

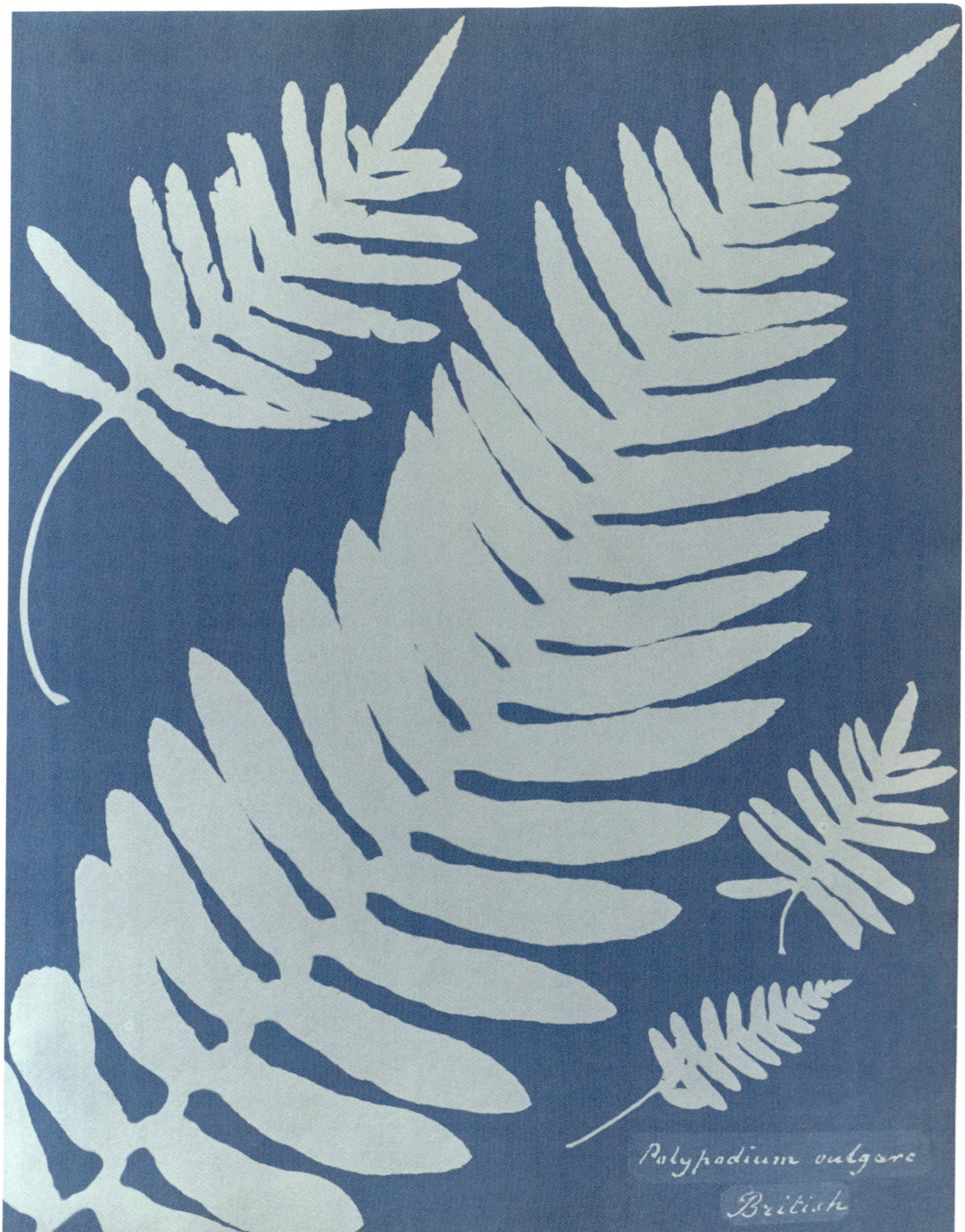

Plate 436. *Polypodium vulgare*, British

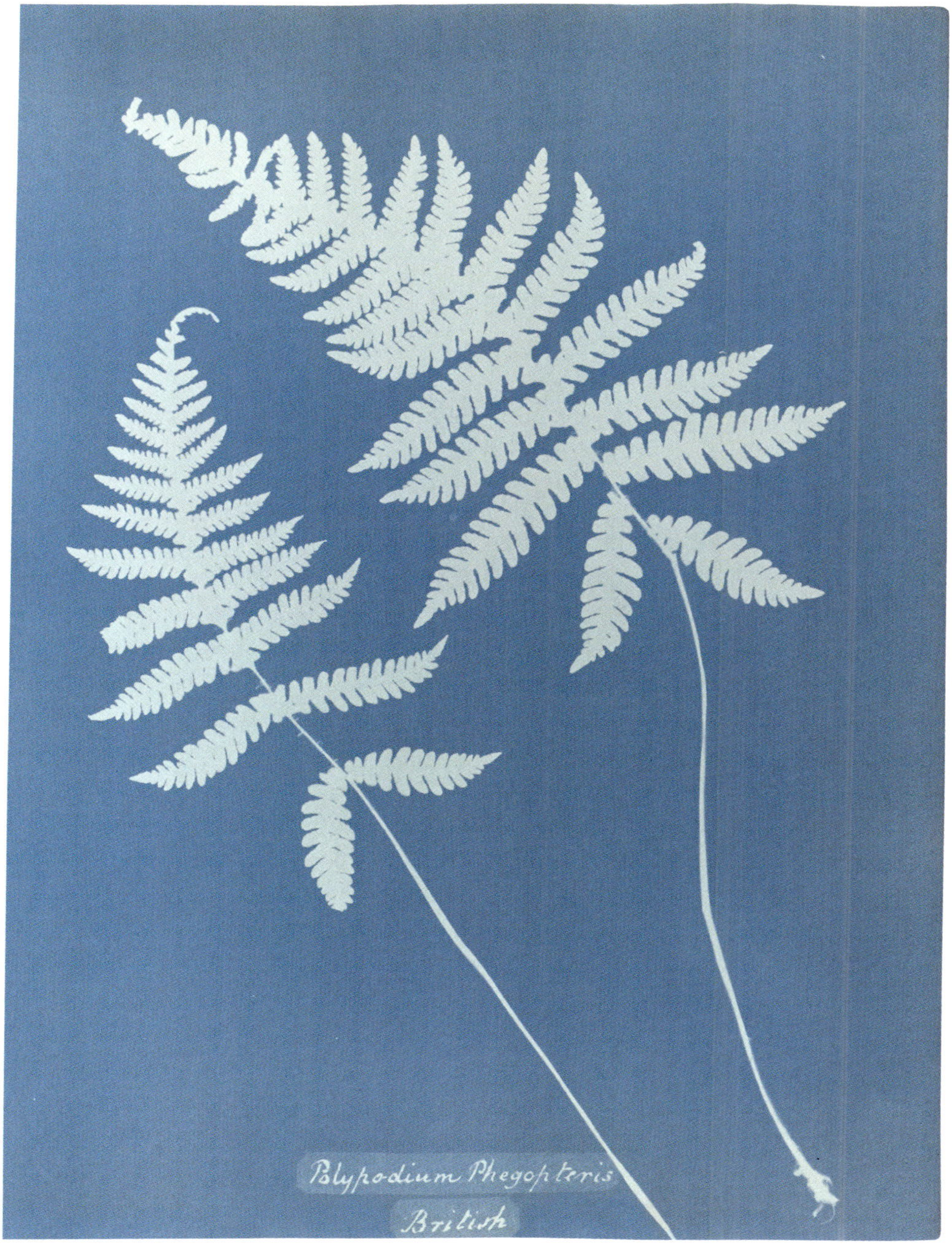

Plate 437. *Polypodium phegopteris*, British

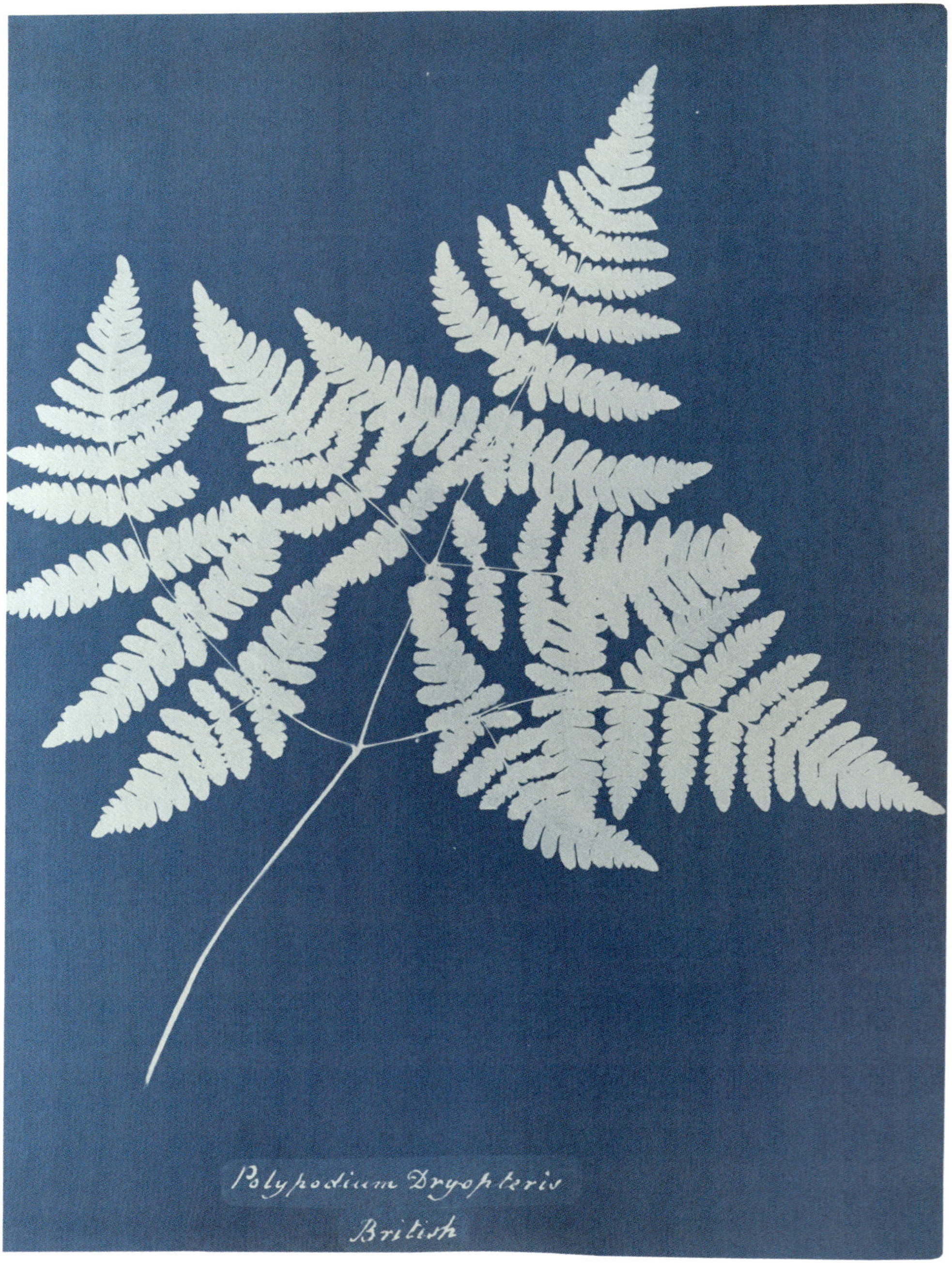

Plate 438. *Polypodium dryopteris*, British

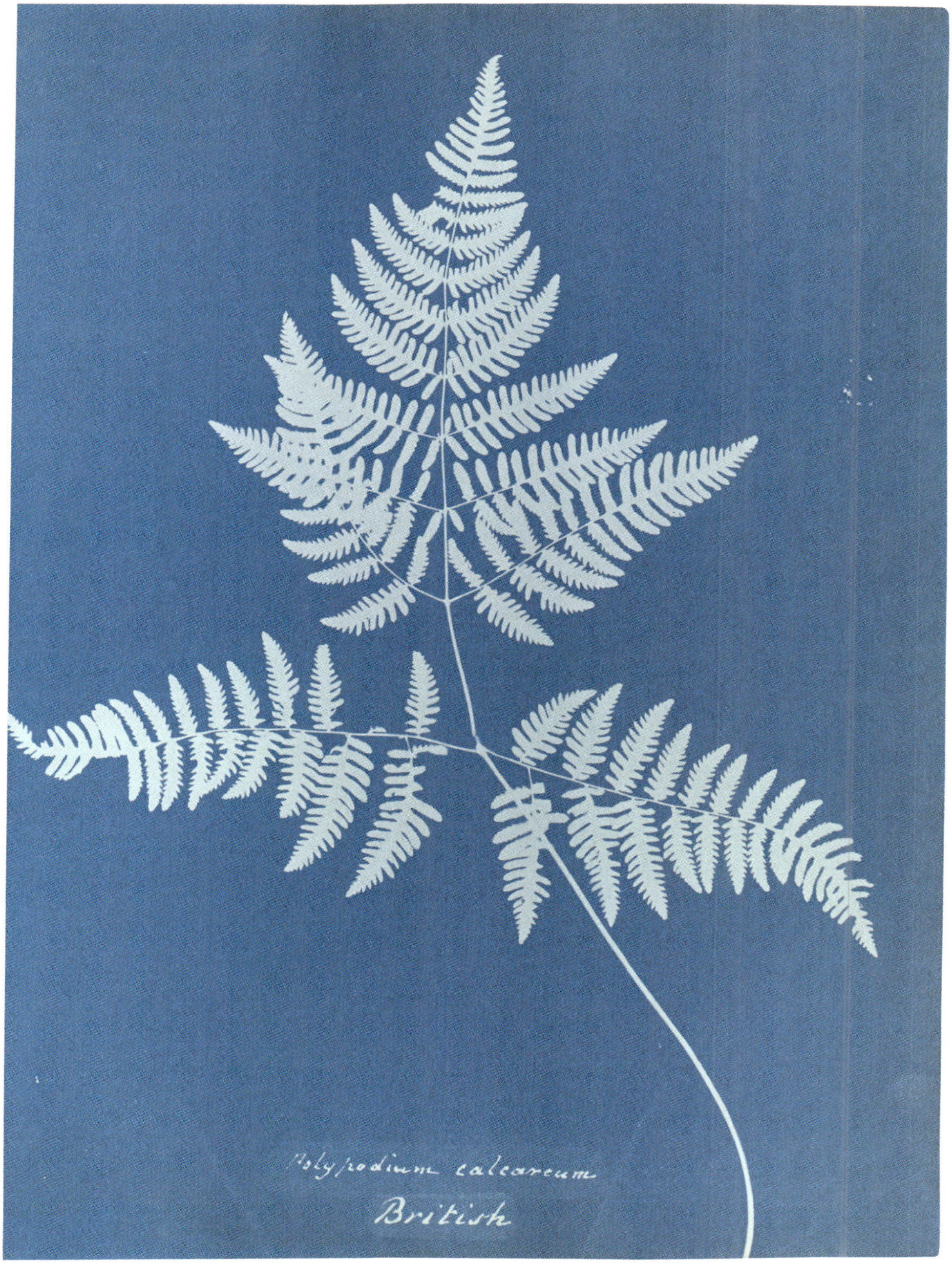

Plate 439. *Polypodium calcareum*, British

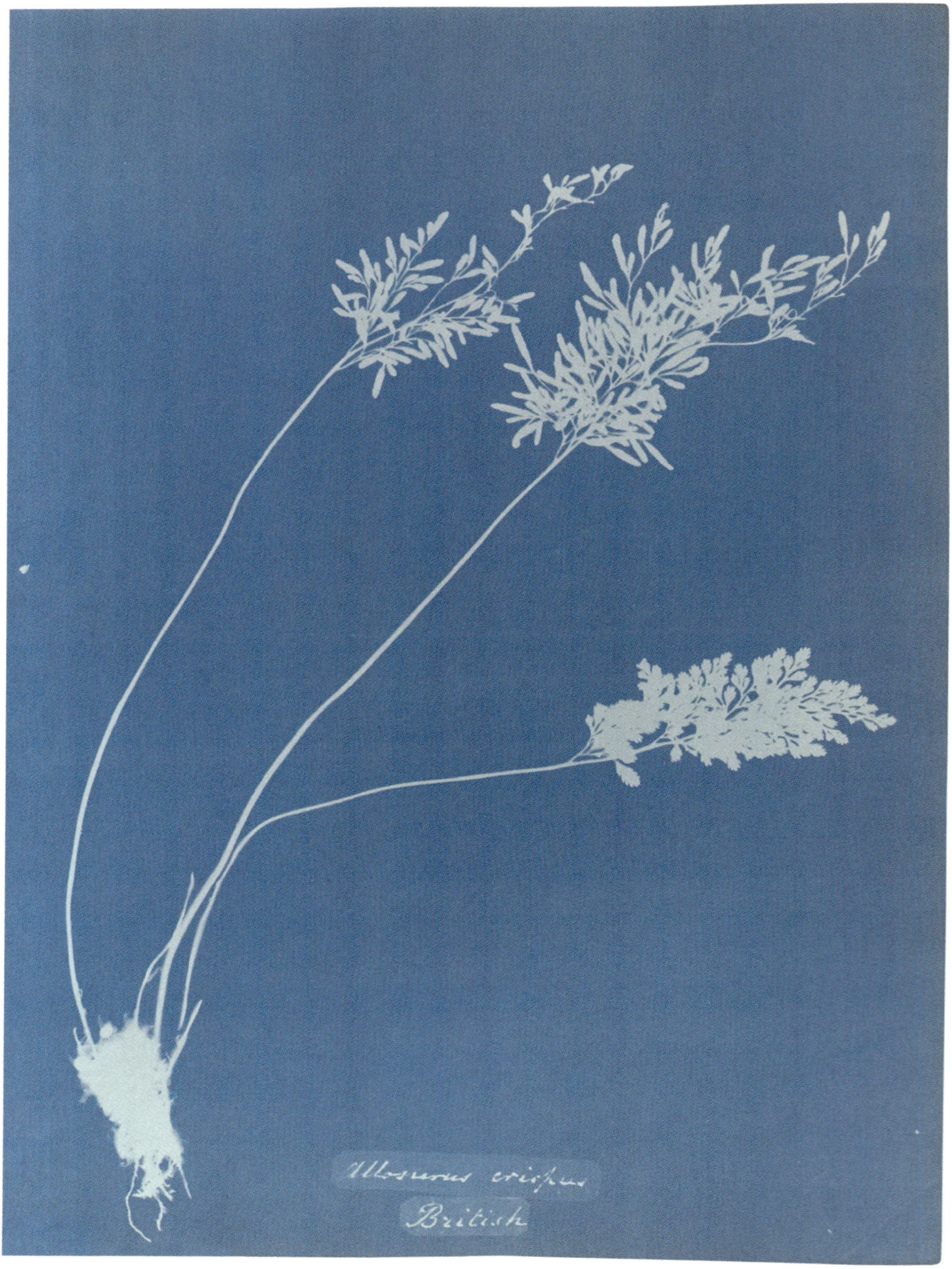

Plate 440. *Allosorus crispus*, British

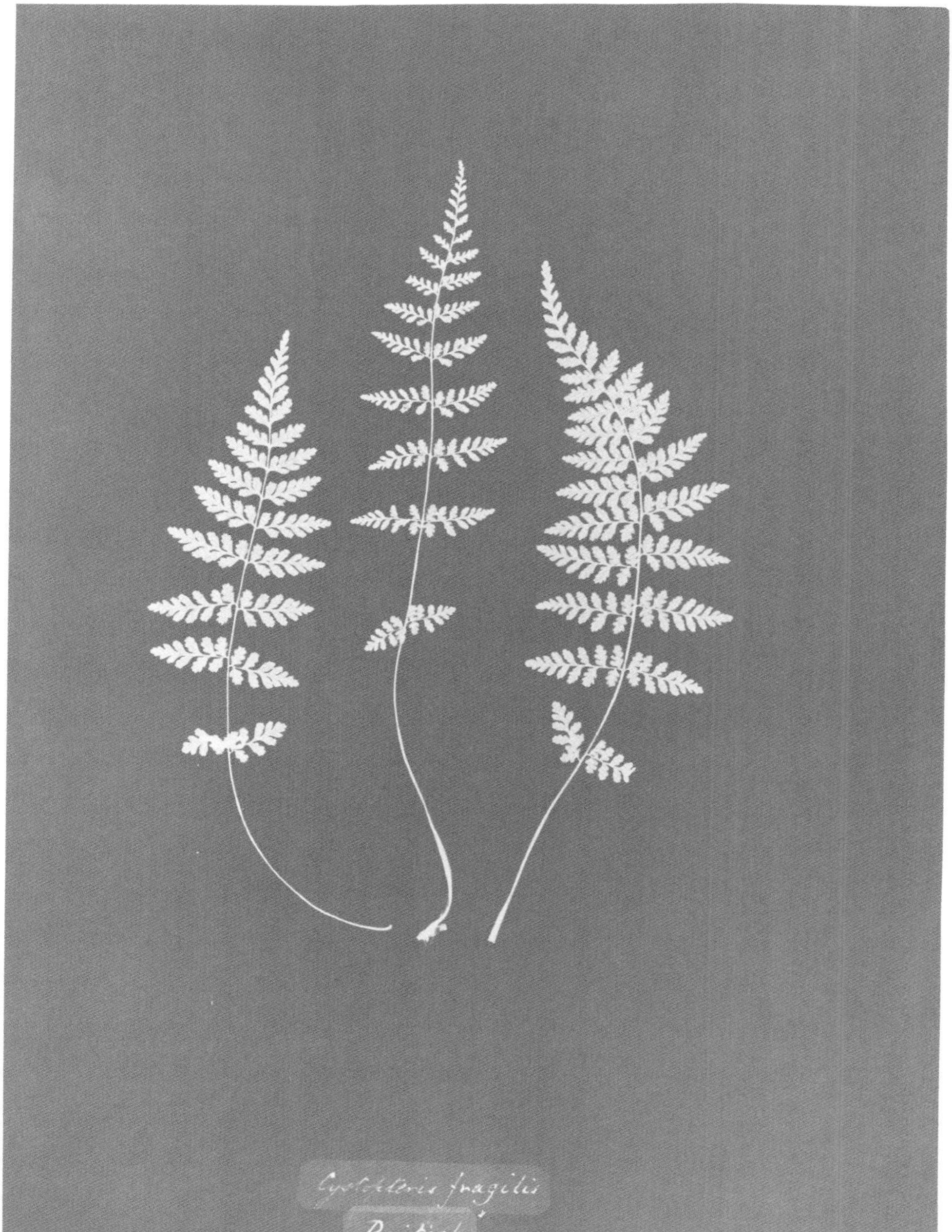

Plate 441. *Cystopteris fragilis*, British

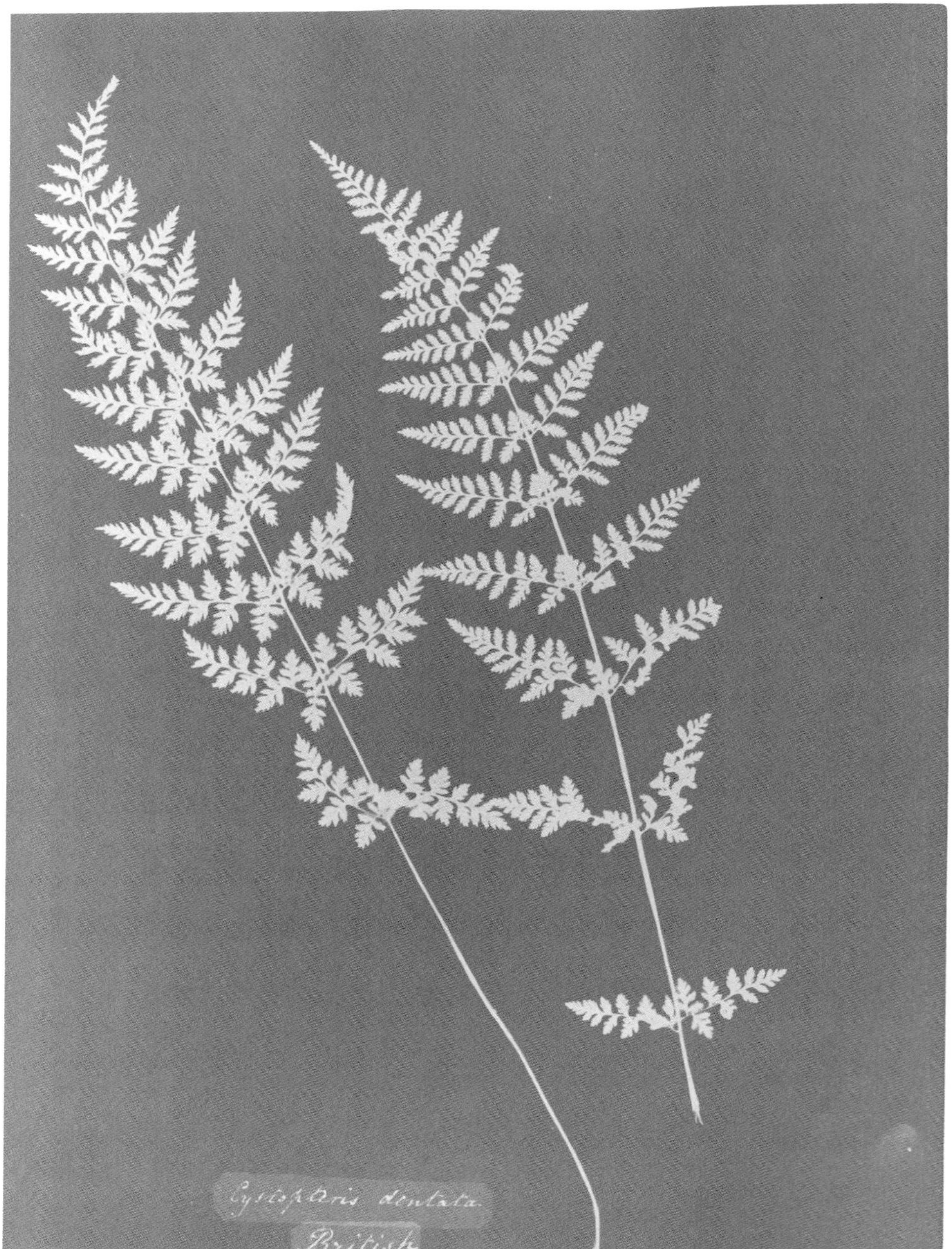

Plate 442. *Cystopteris dentata*, British

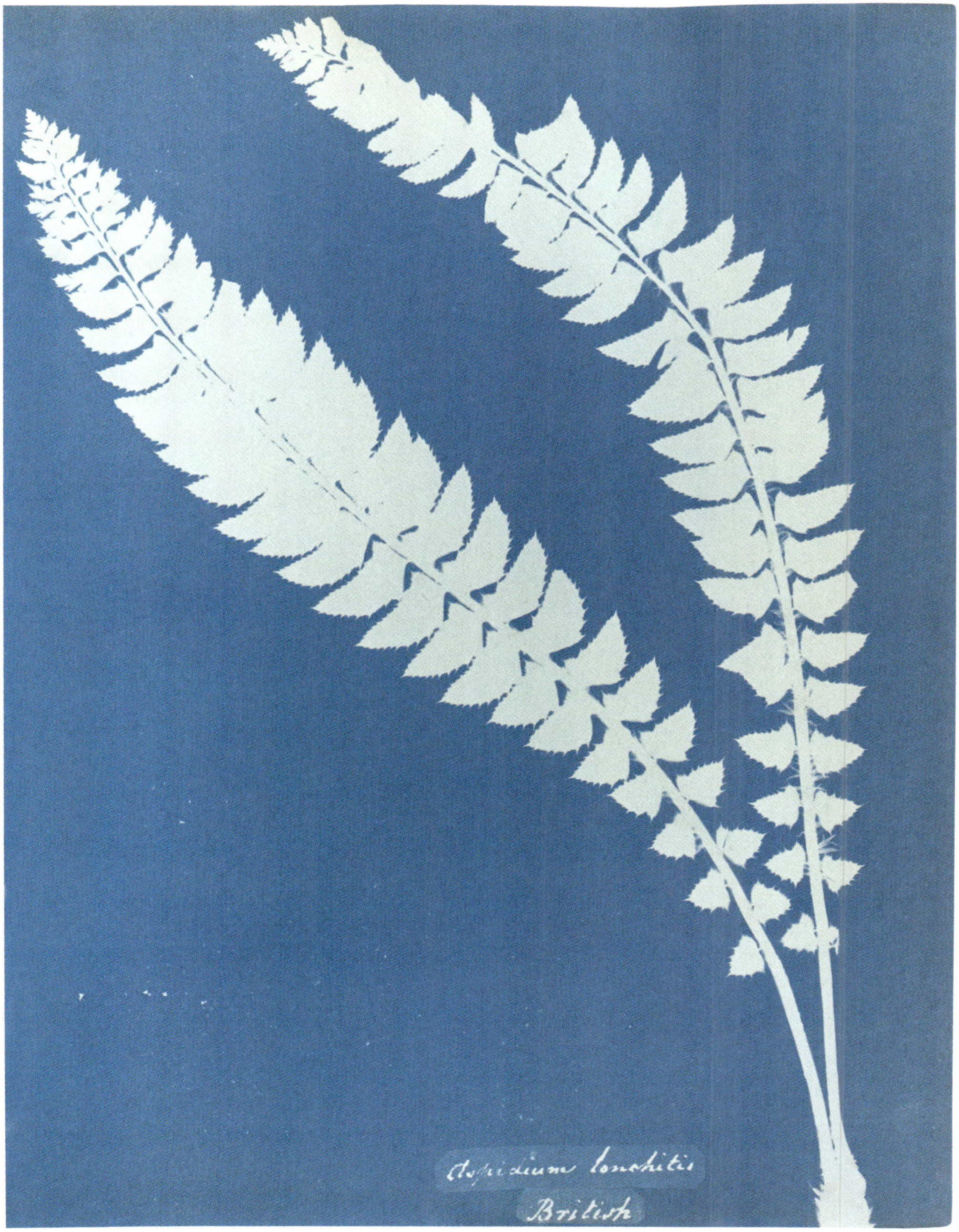

Plate 443. *Asplenium lonchitis*, British

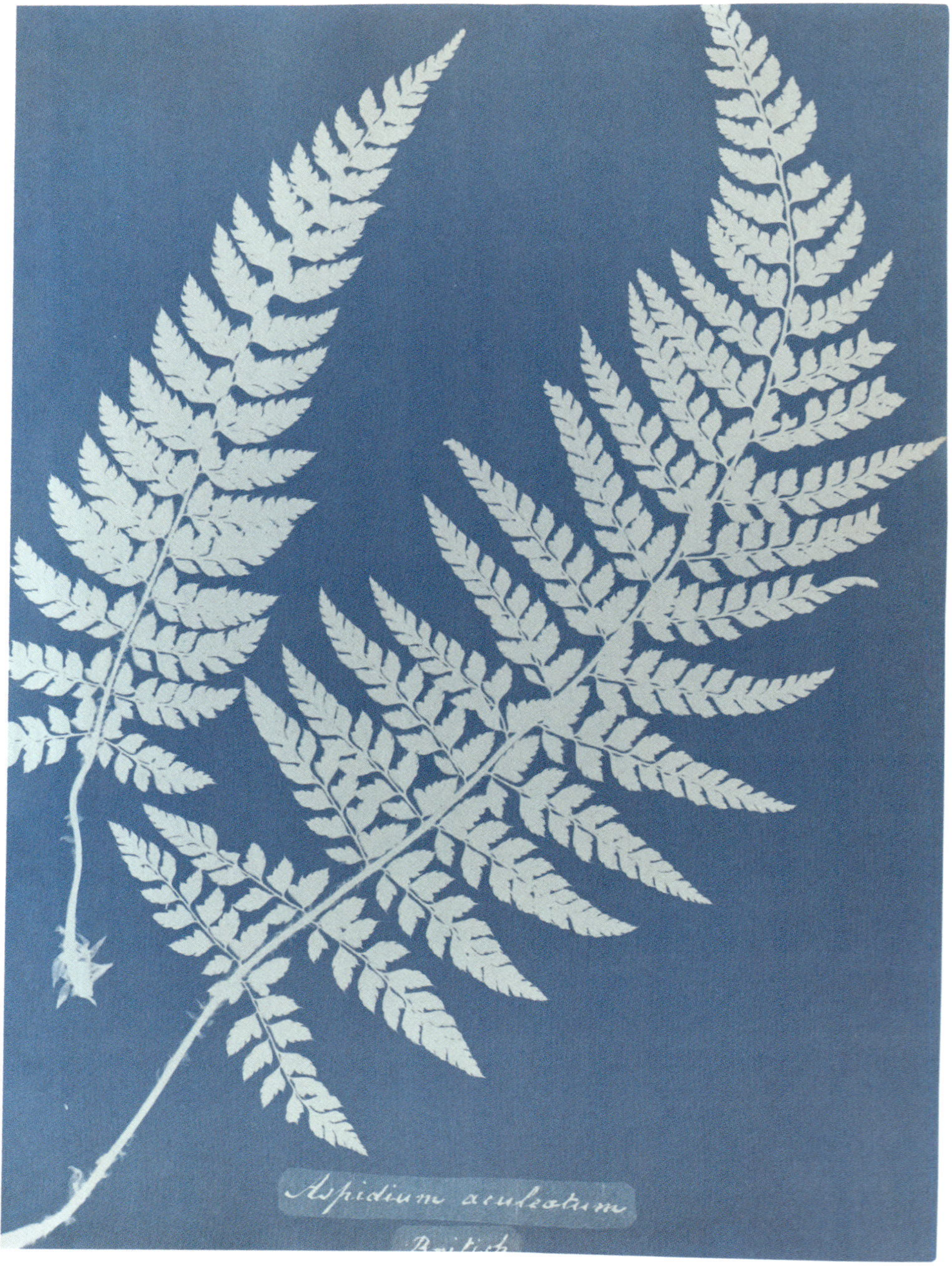

Plate 444. *Aspidium aculeatum*, British

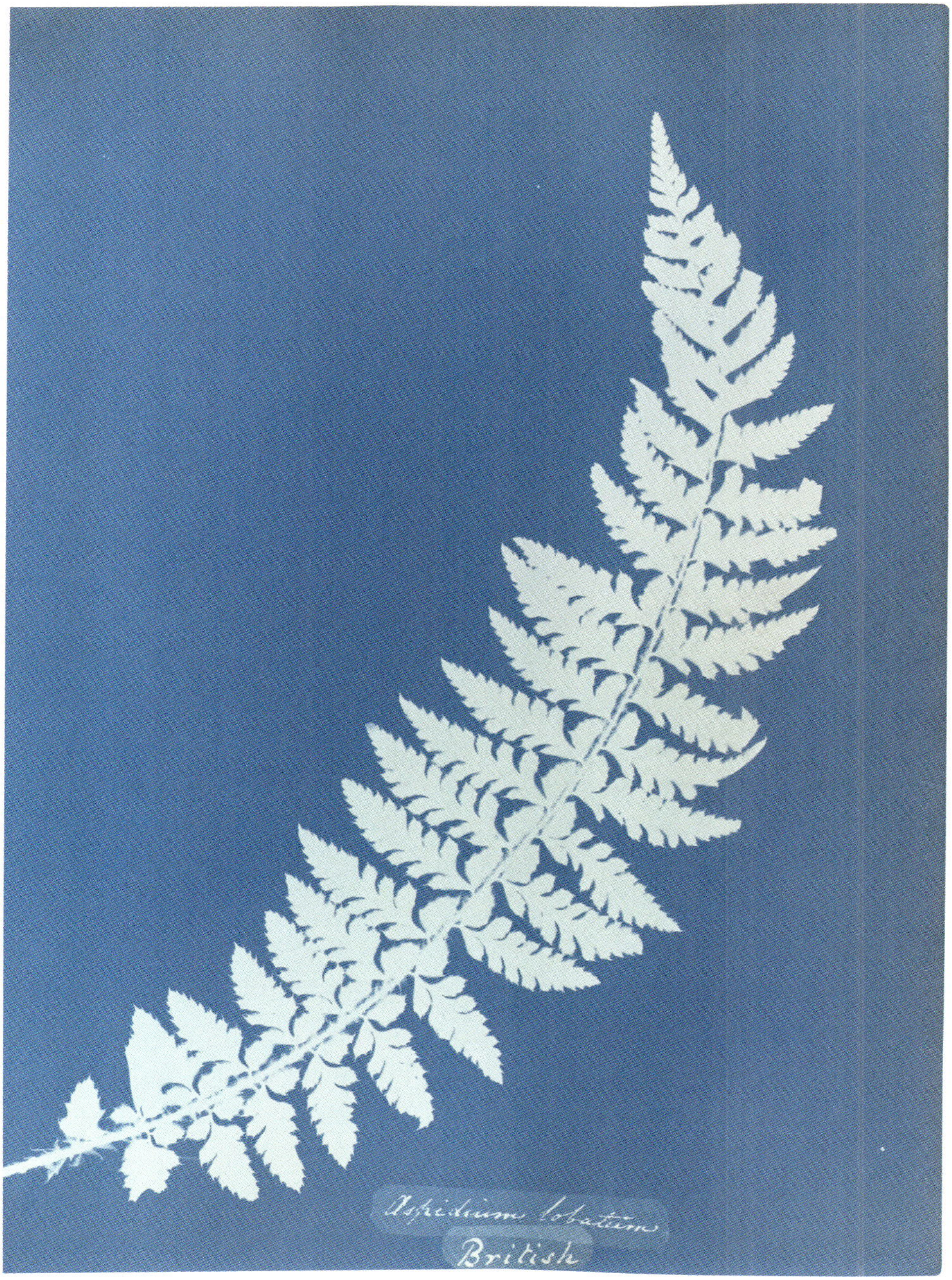

Plate 445. *Aspidium lobatum*, British

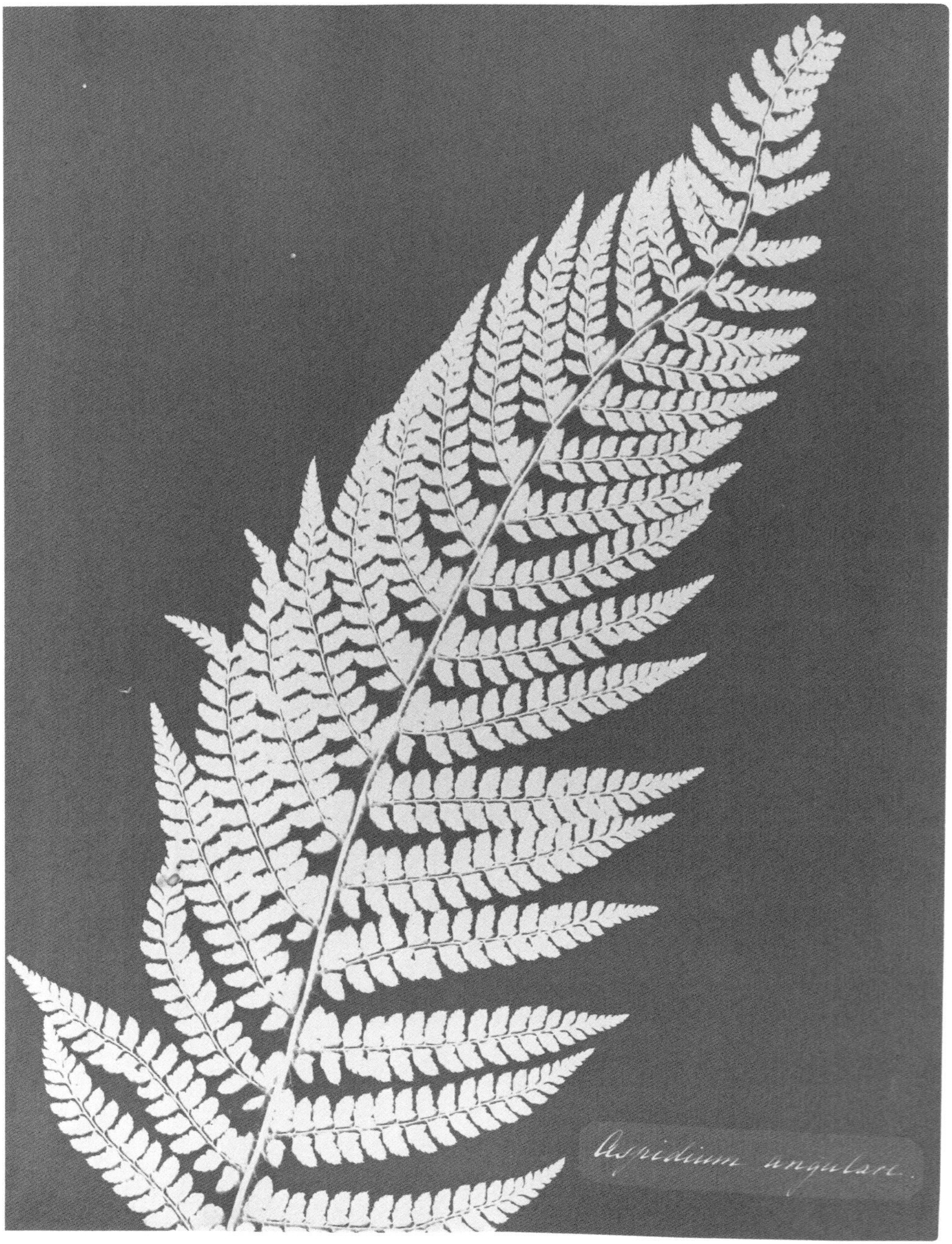

Plate 446. *Aspidium angulare*

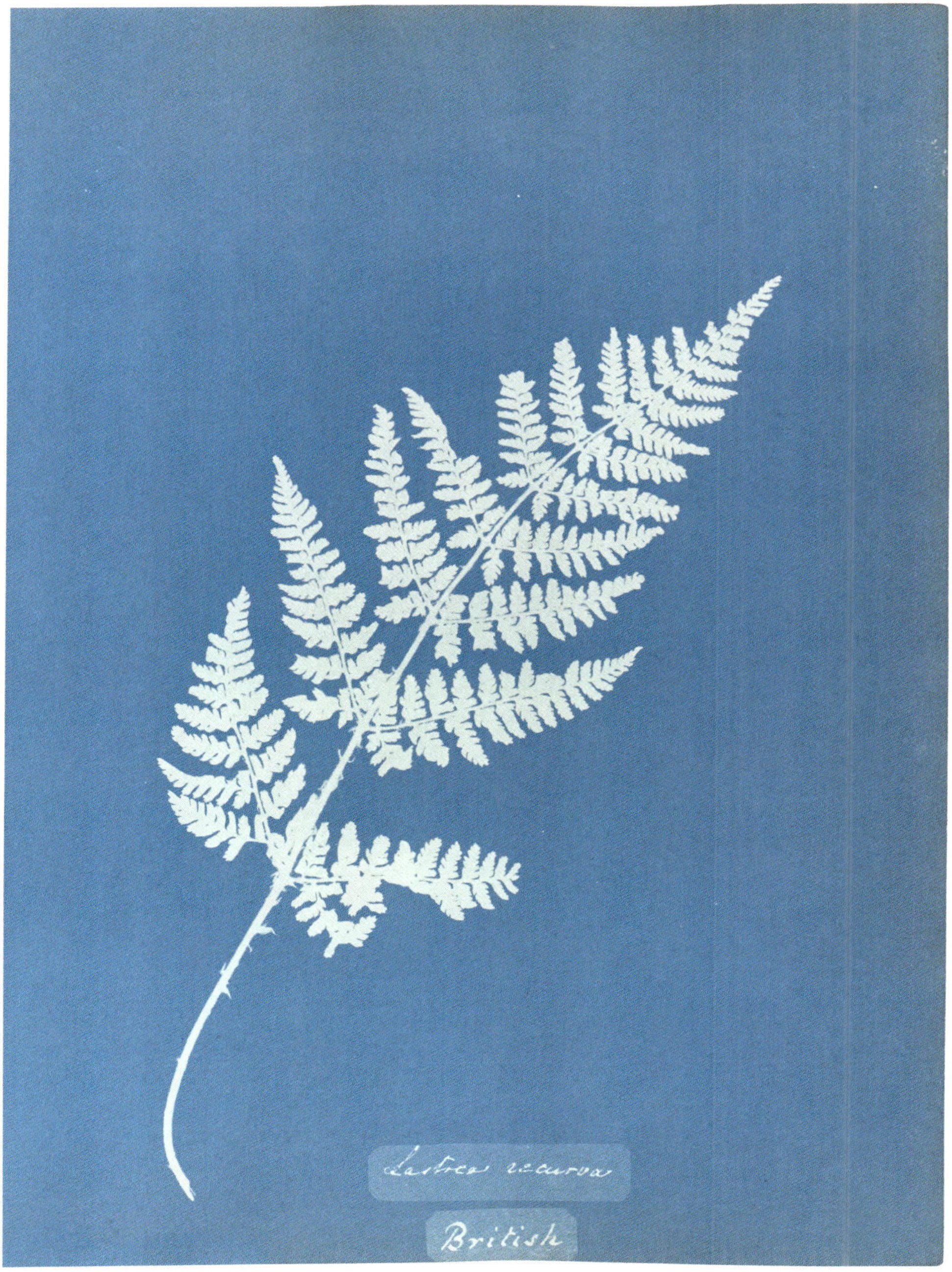

Plate 447. *Lastrea recurva*, British

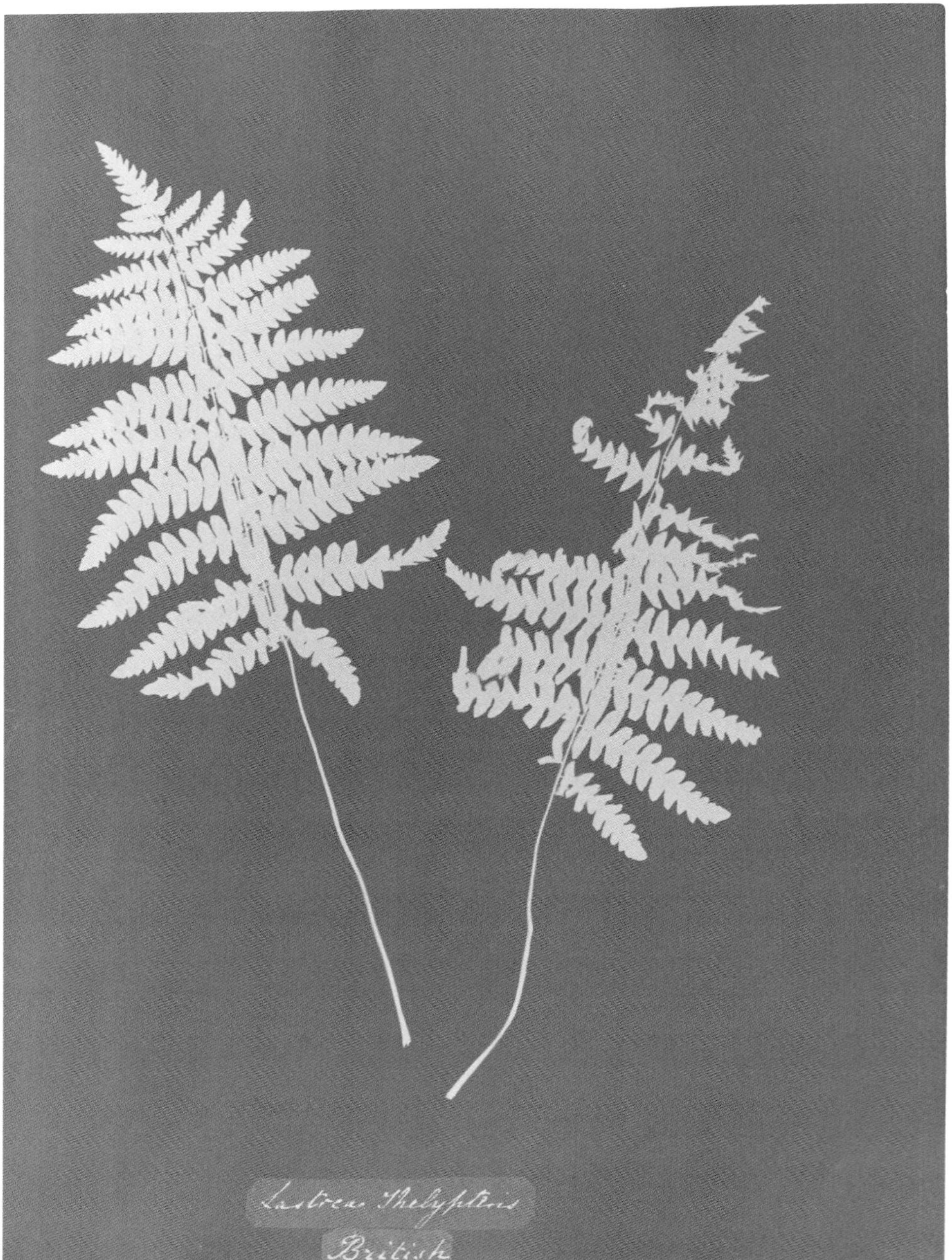

Plate 448. *Lastrea thelypteris*, British

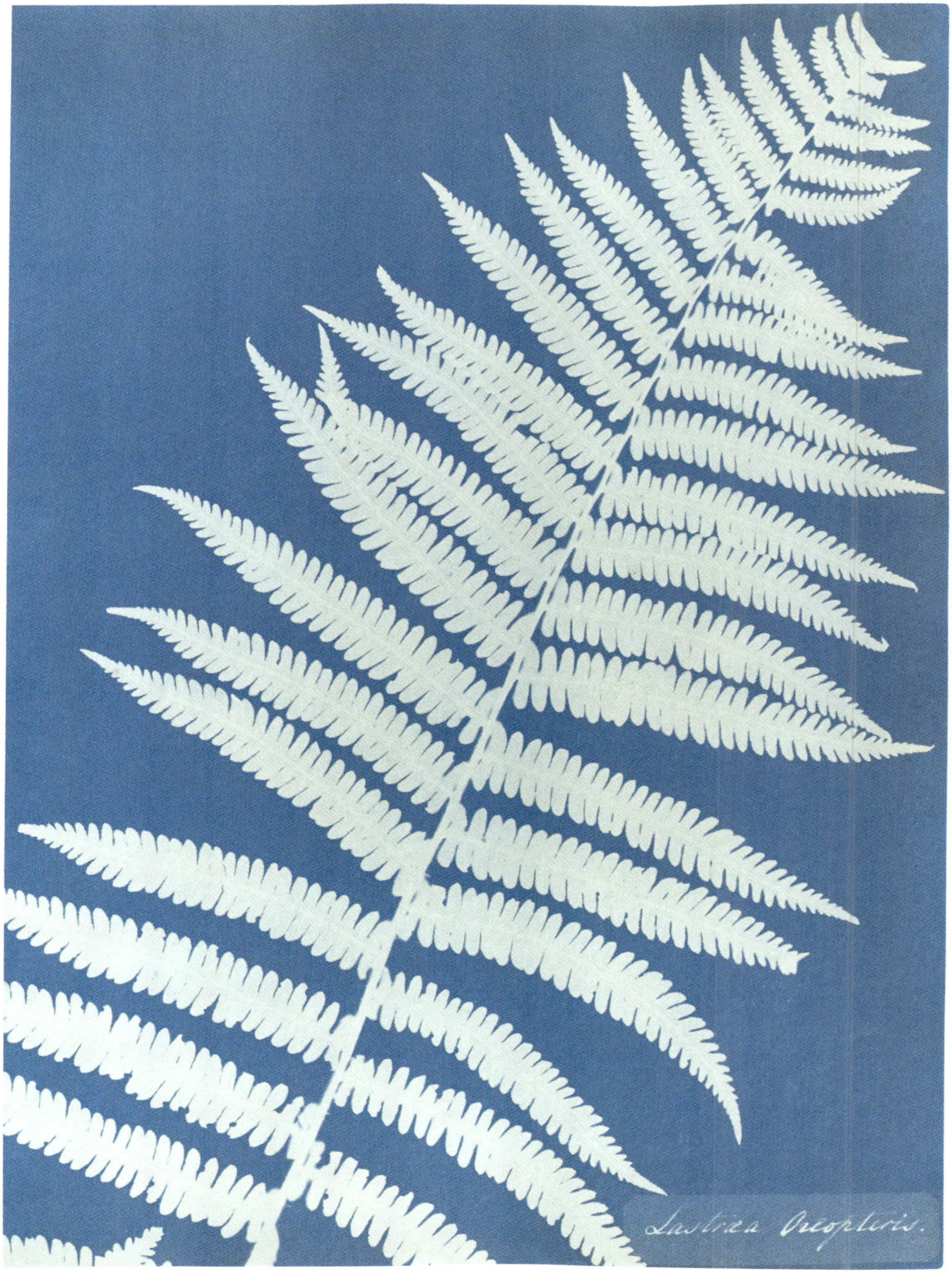

Plate 449. *Lastrea oreopteris*

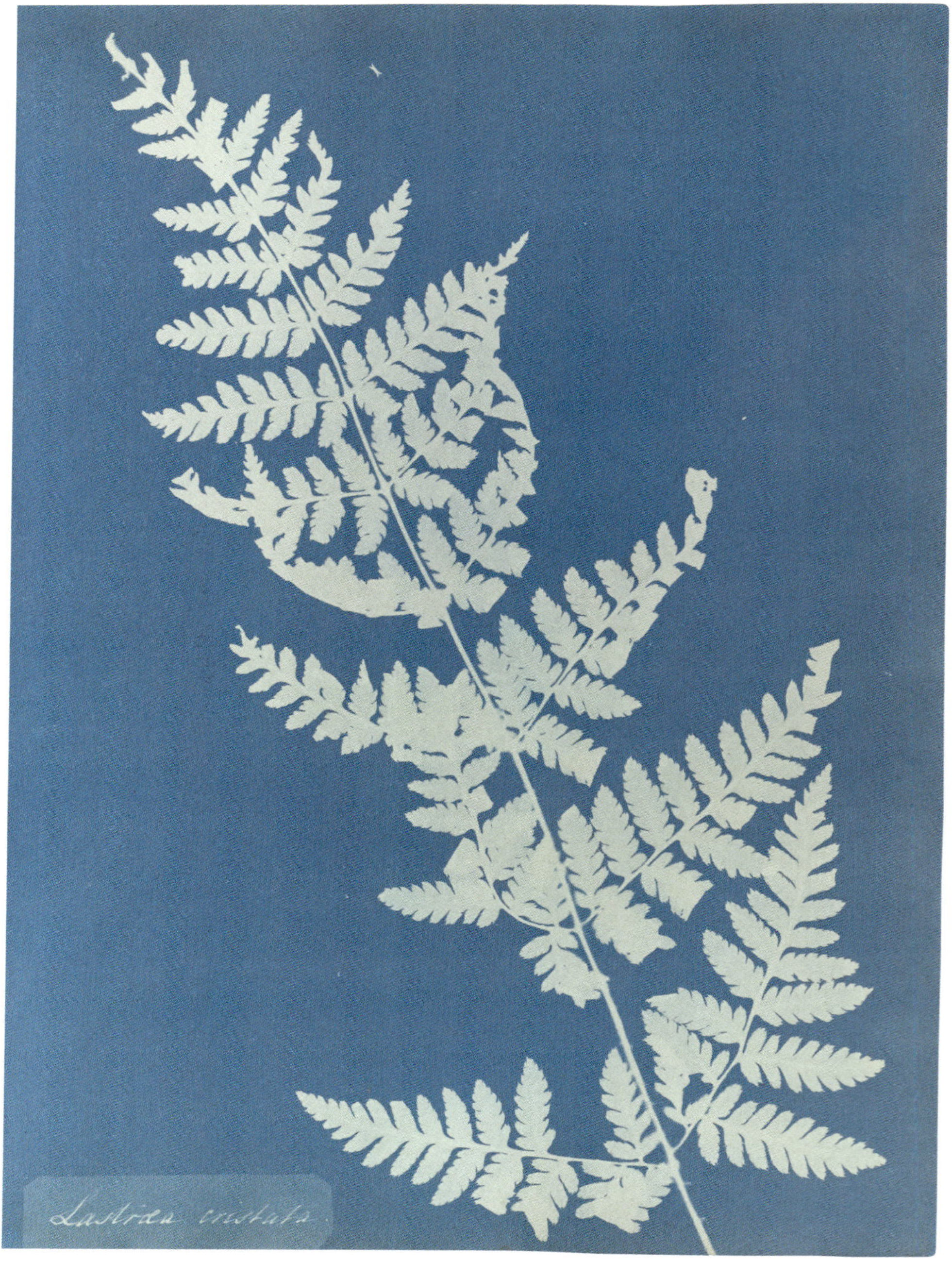

Plate 450. *Lastrea cristata*

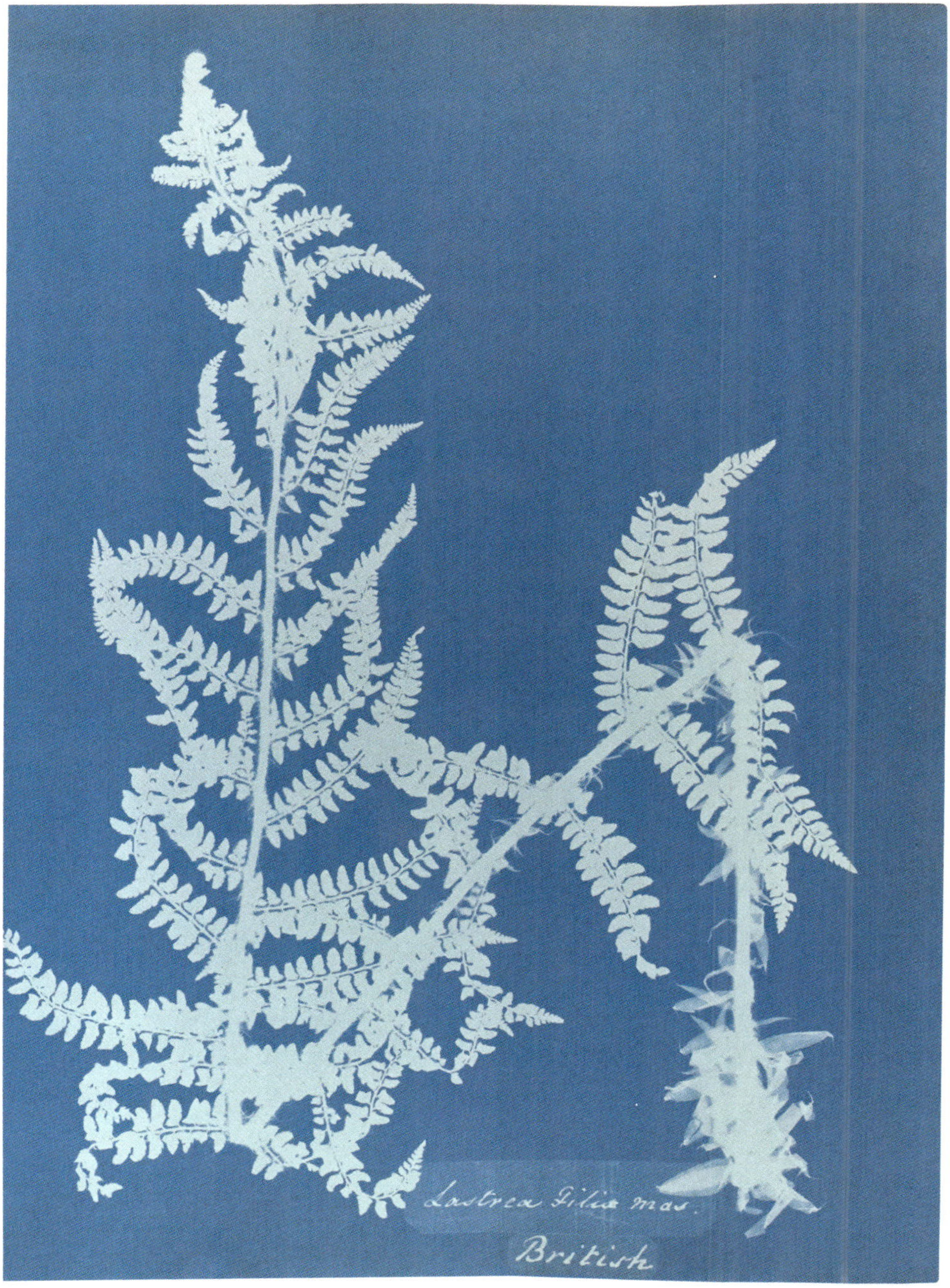

Plate 451. *Lastrea filix-mas*, British

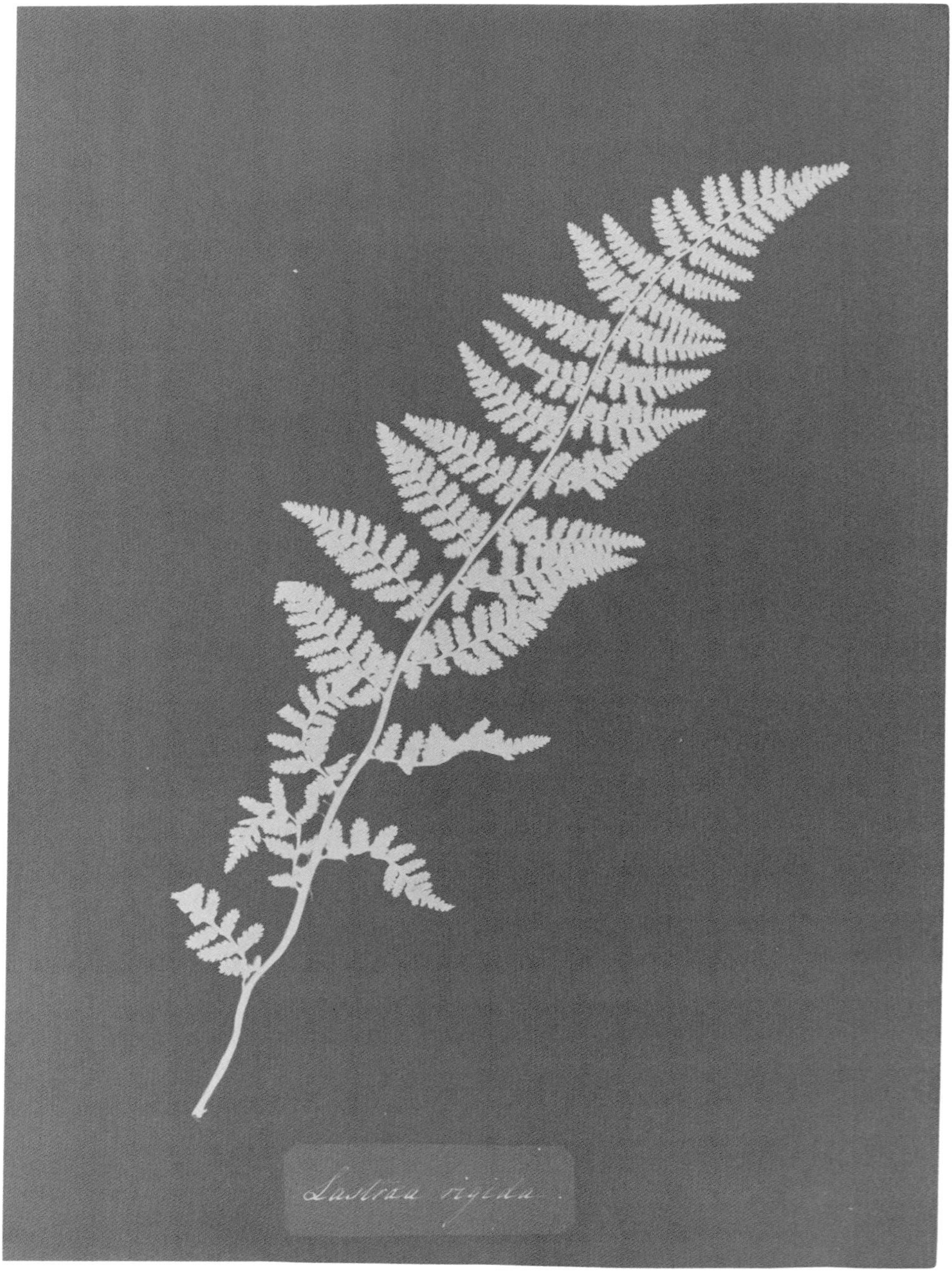

Plate 452. *Lastrea rigida*

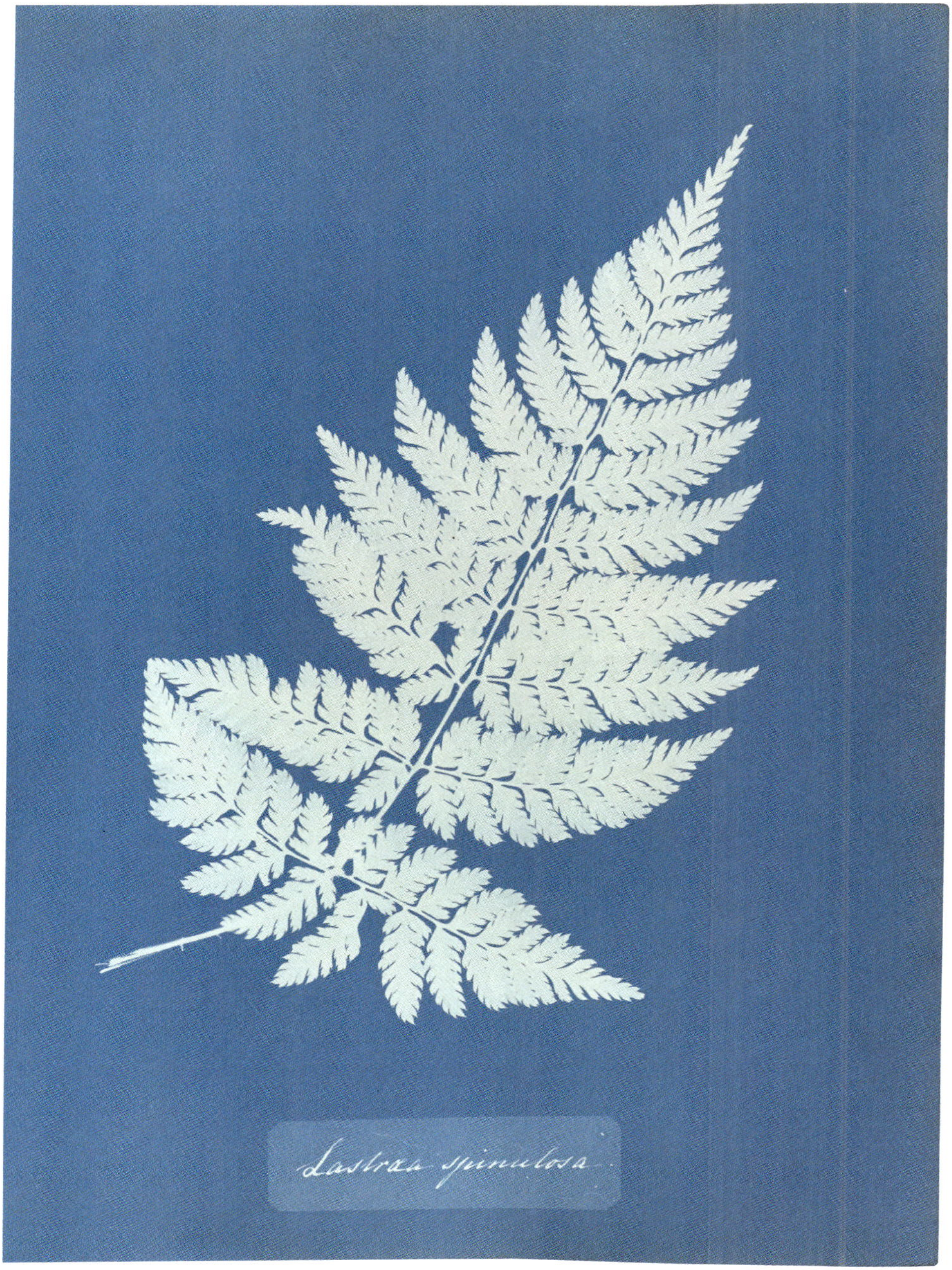

Plate 453. *Lastrea spinulosa*

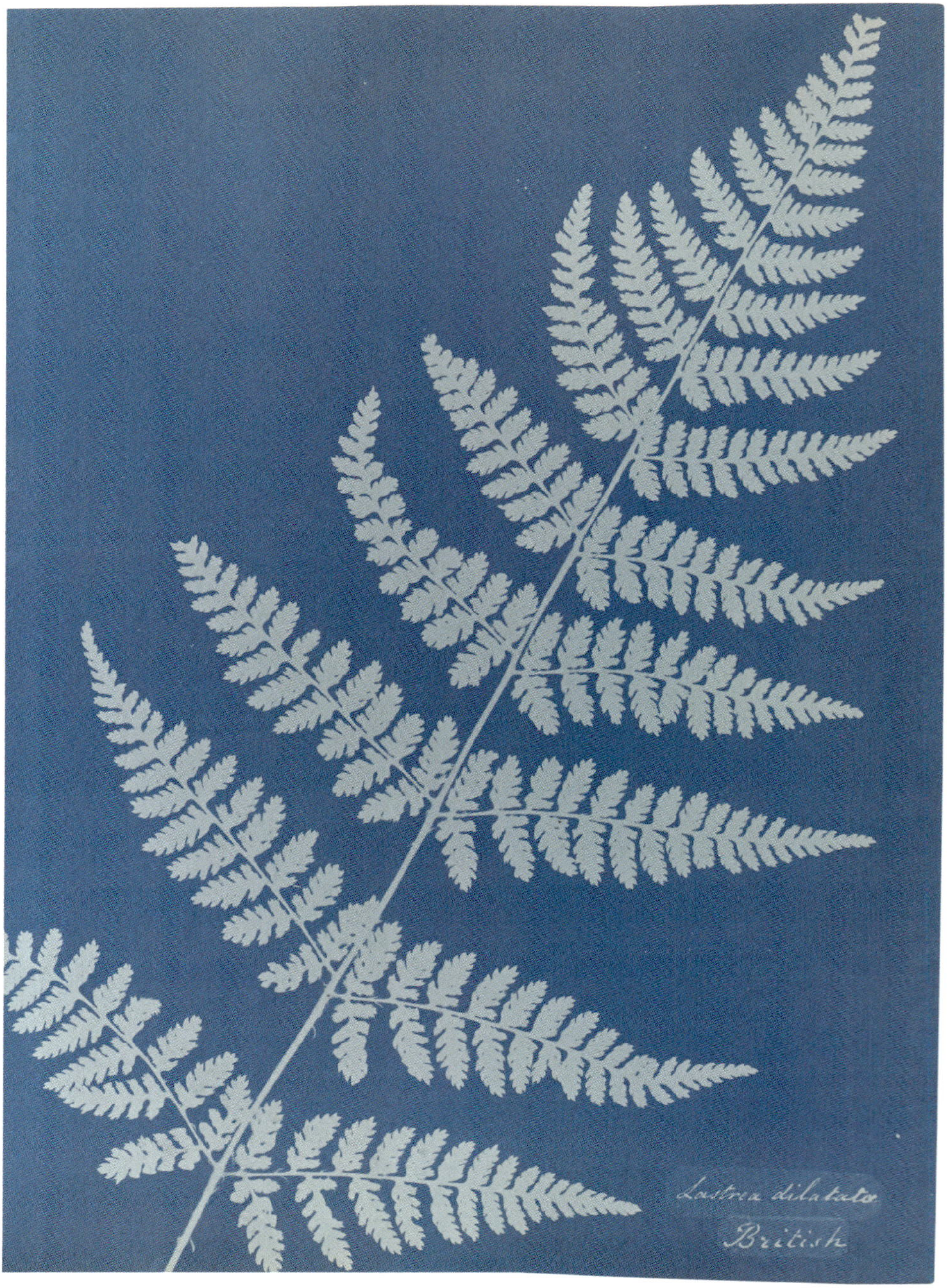

Plate 454. *Lastrea dilatato*, British

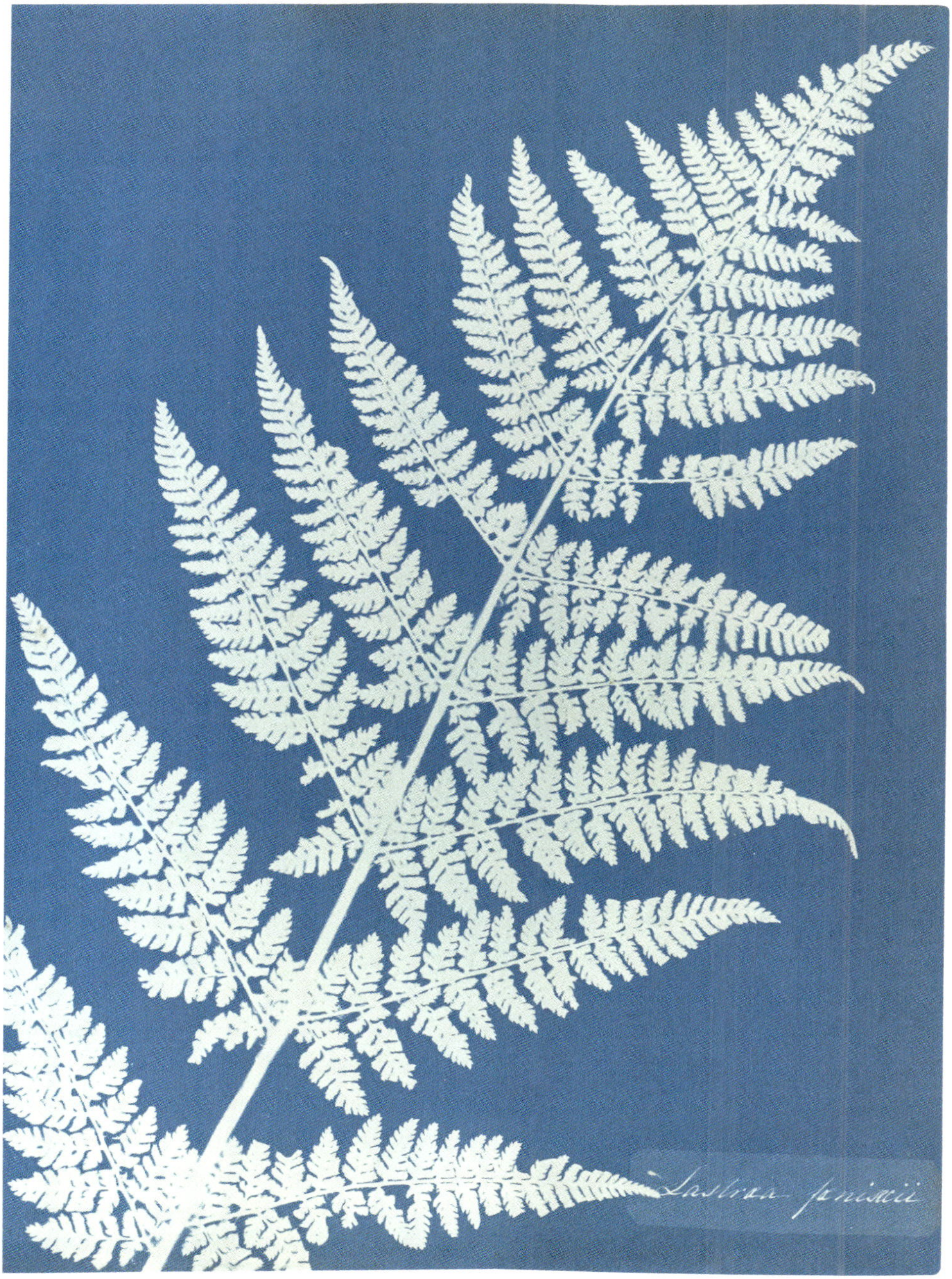

Plate 455. *Lastrea foenisecii*

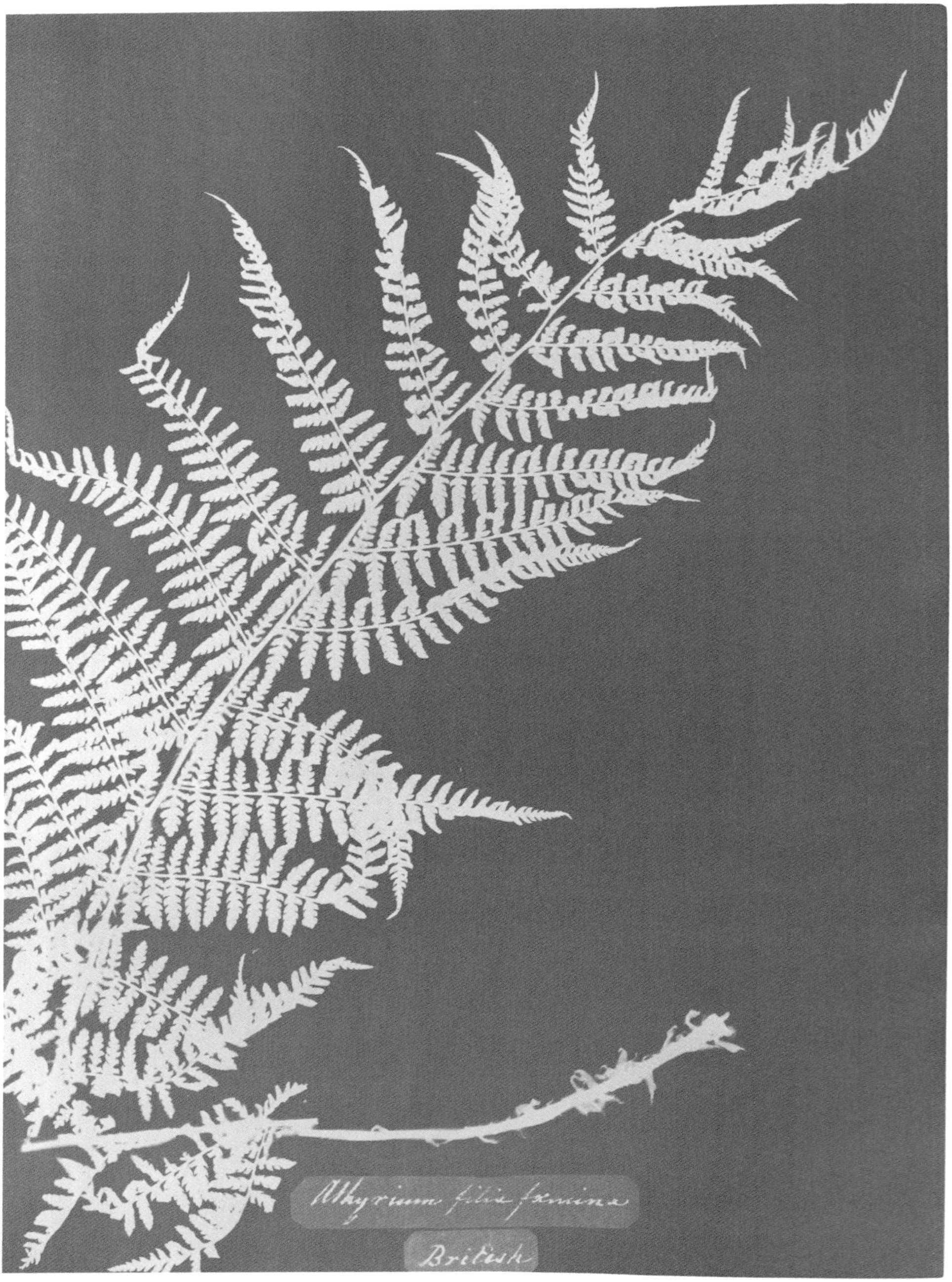

Plate 456. *Athyrium filix-femina*, British

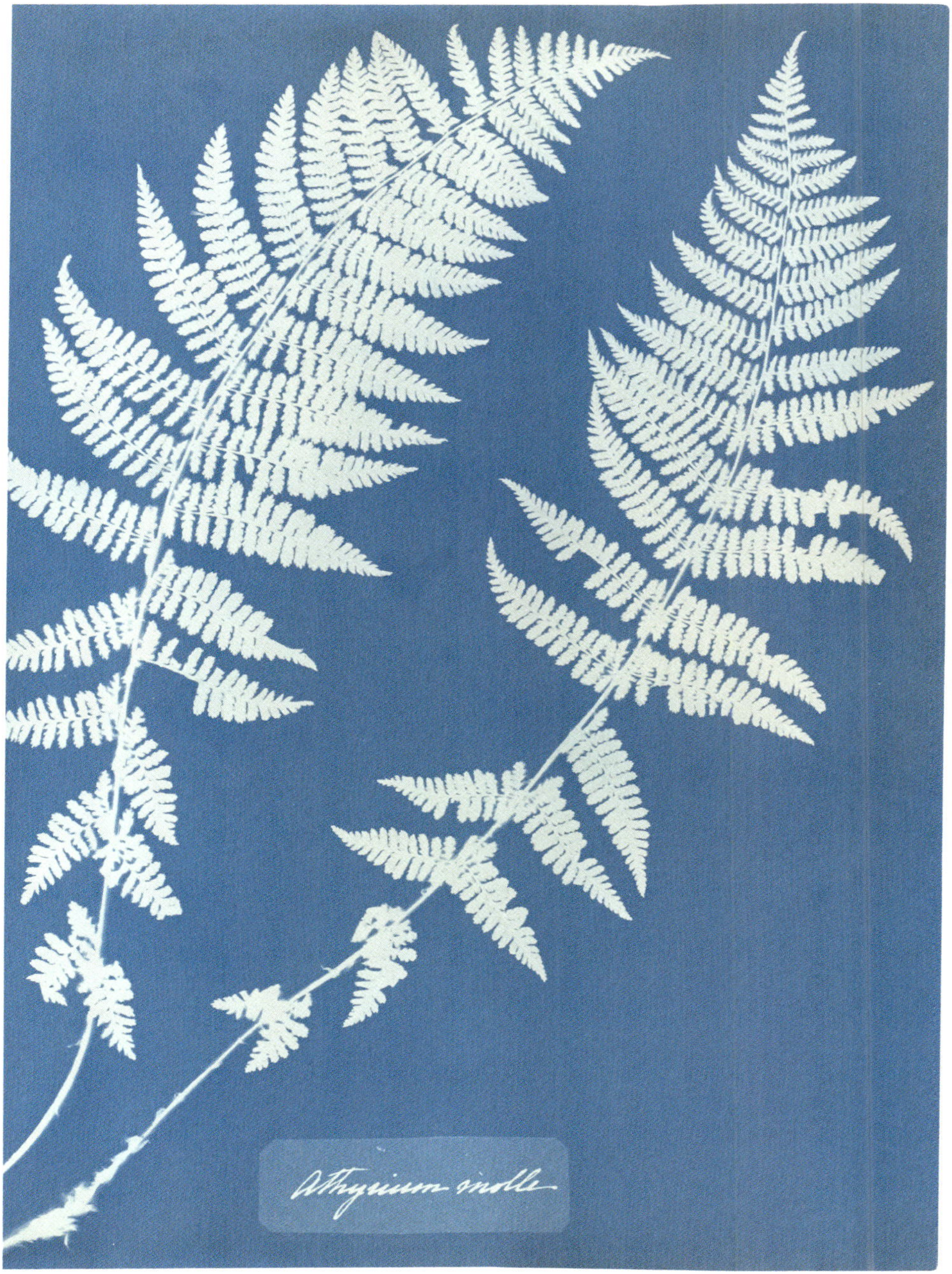

Plate 457. *Athyrium molle*

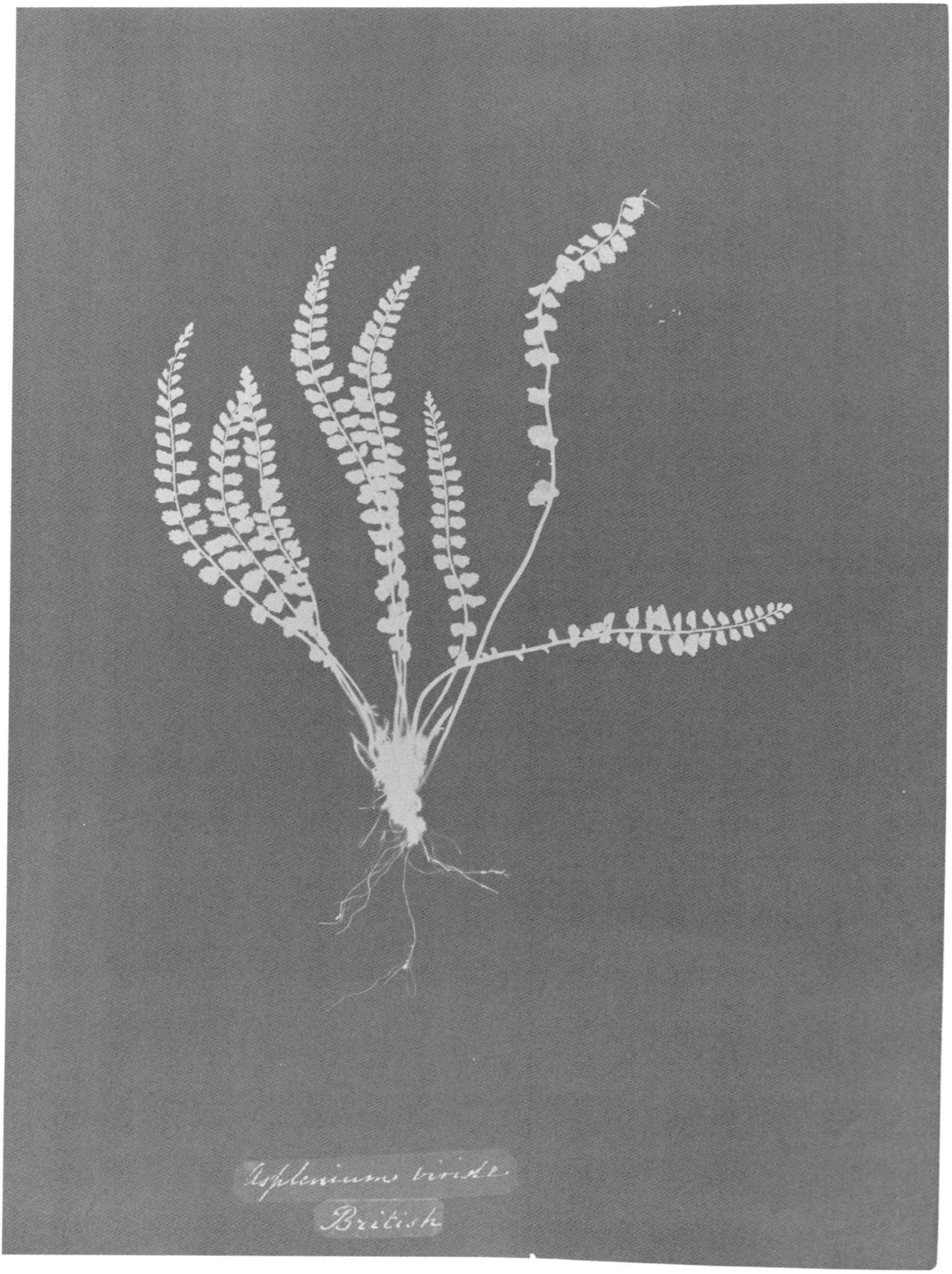

Plate 458. *Asplenium viride*, British

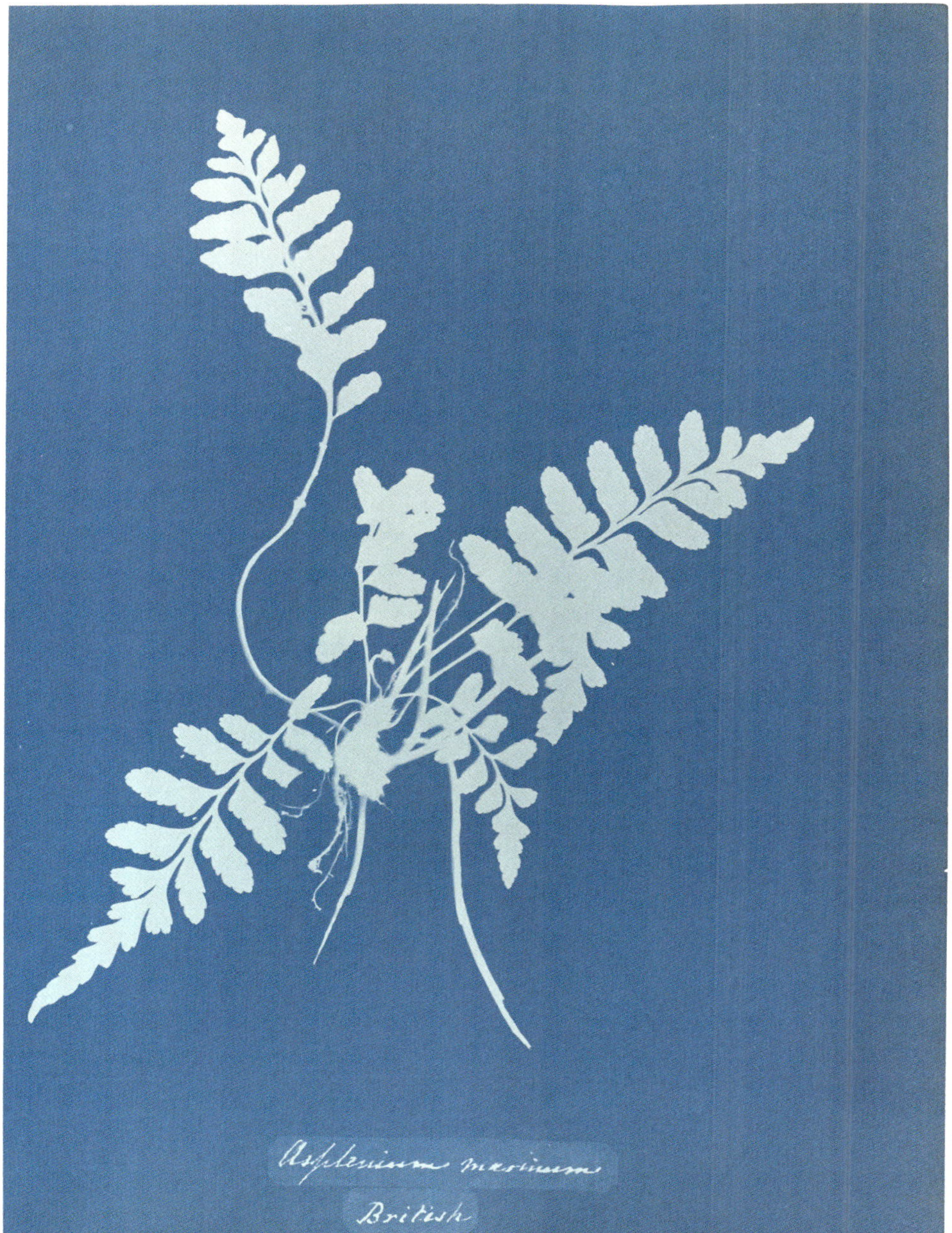

Plate 460. *Asplenium marinum*, British

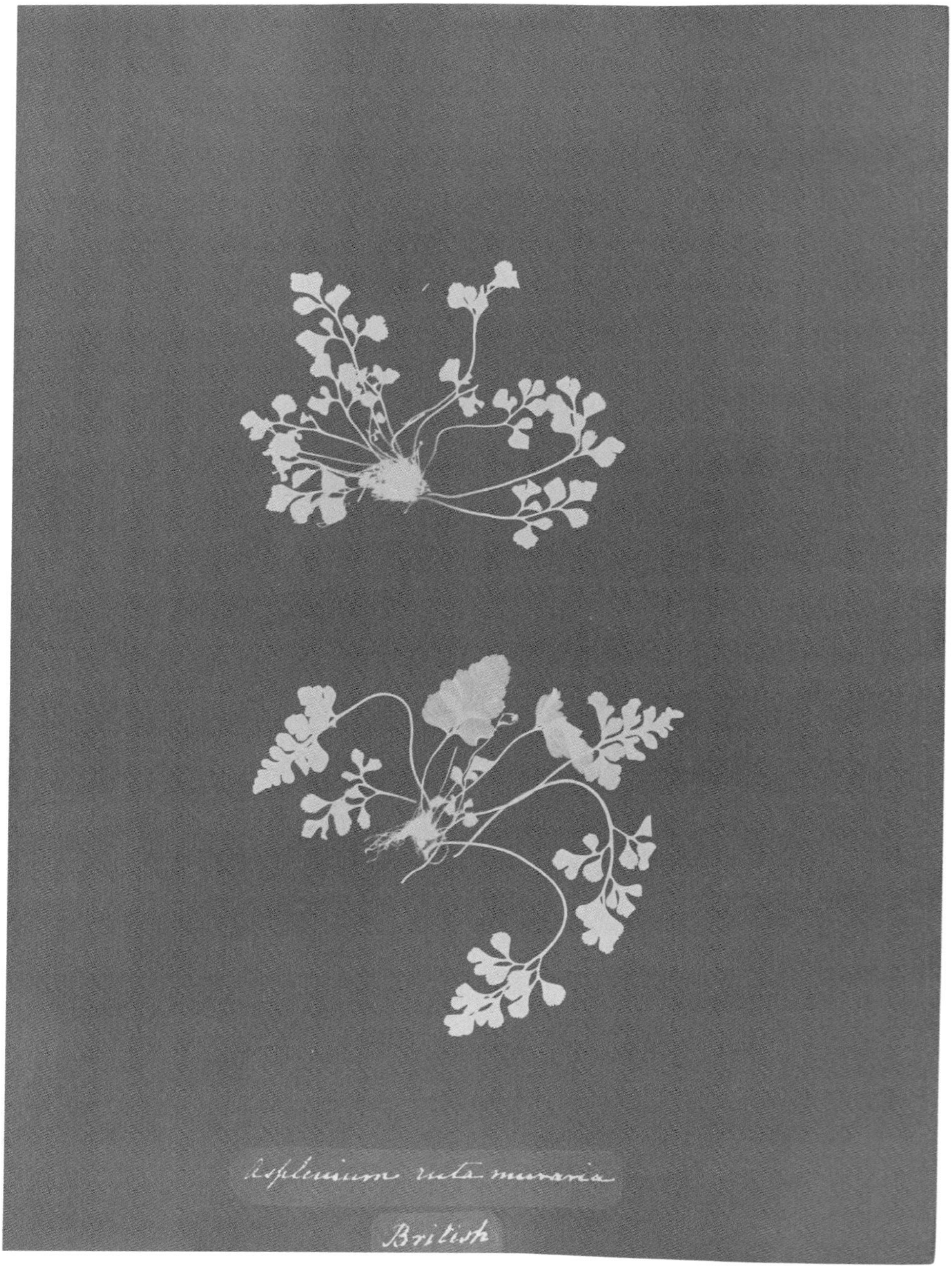

Plate 463. *Asplenium ruta muraria*, British

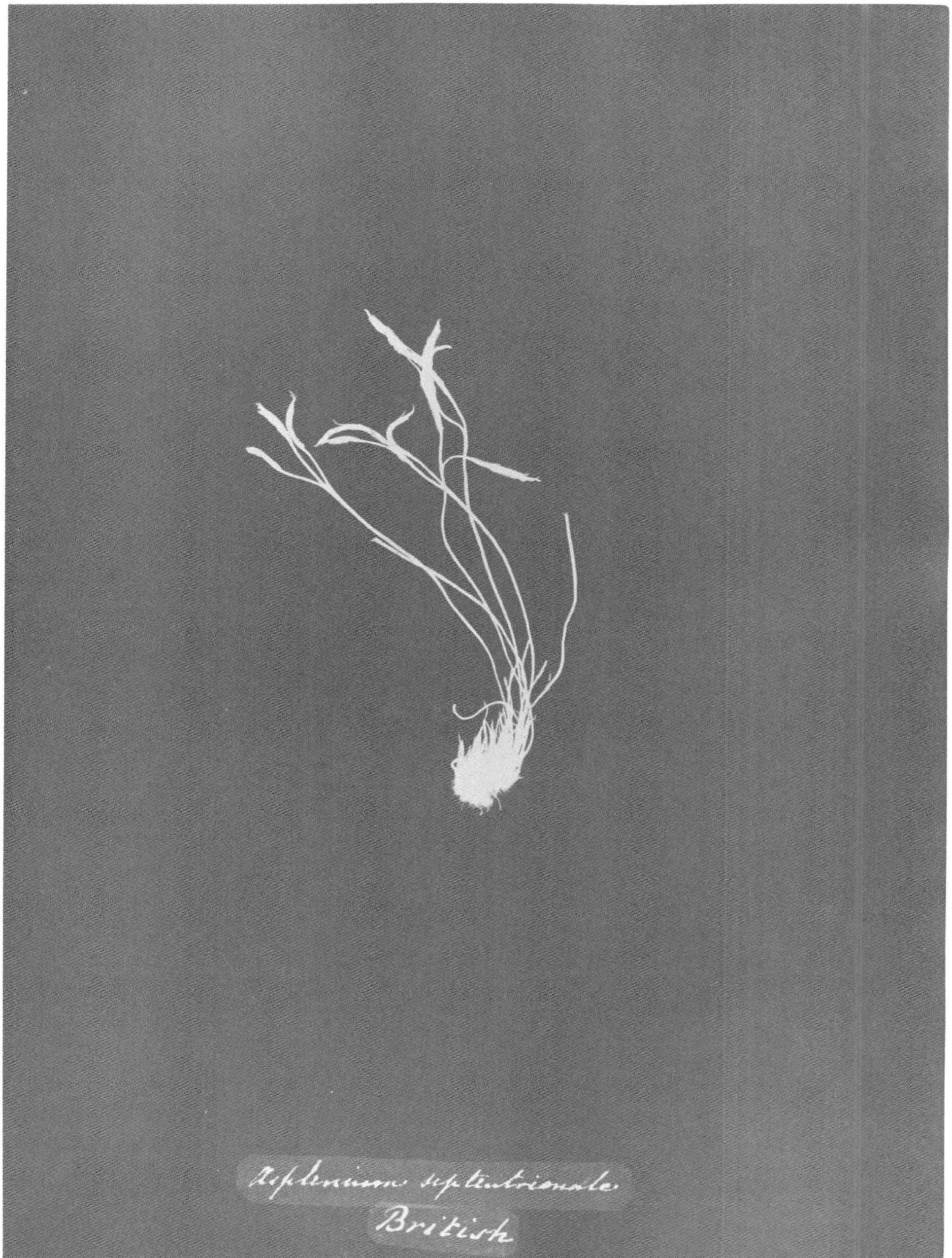

Plate 464. *Asplenium septentrionale*, British

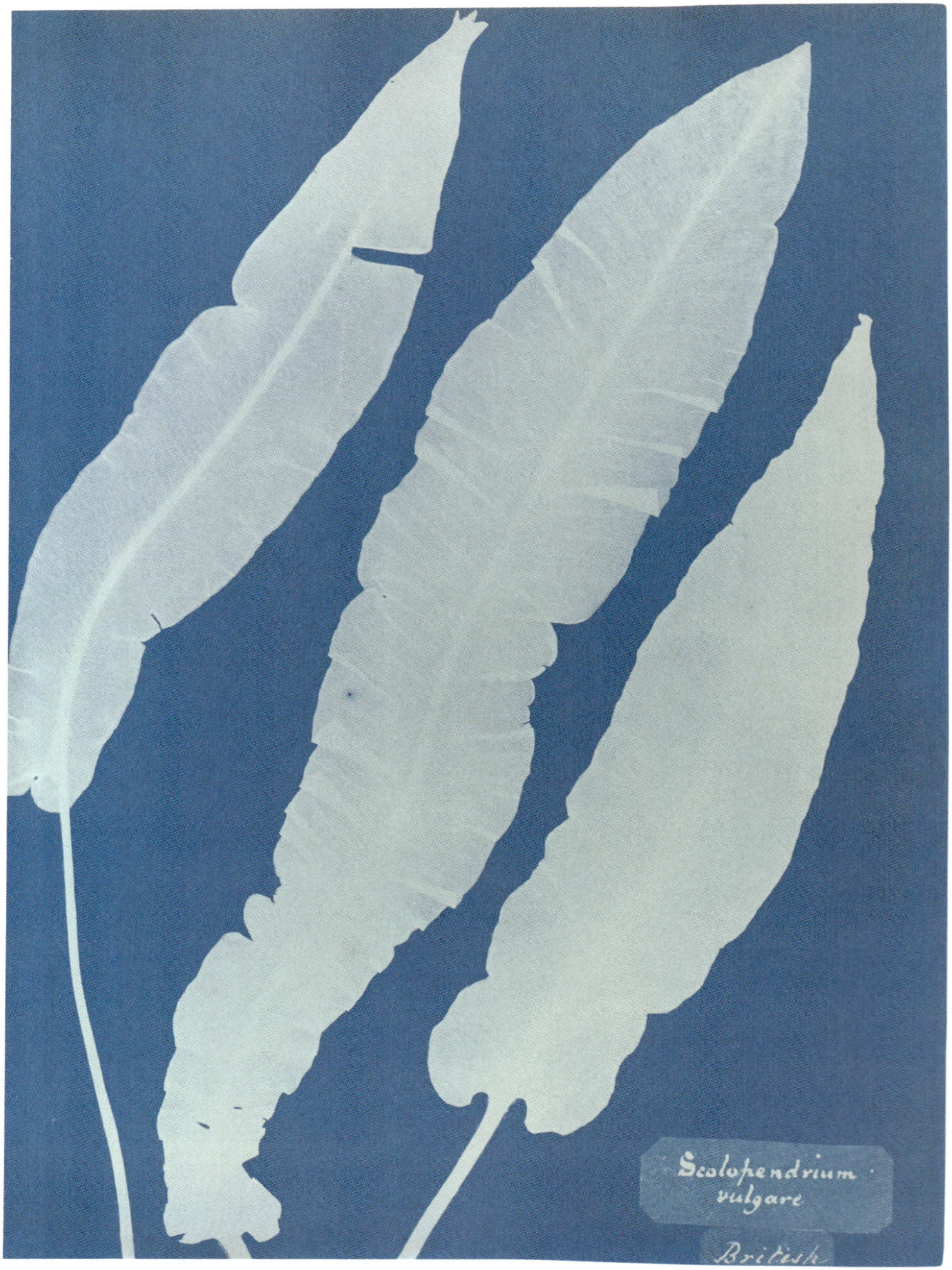

Plate 466. *Scolopendrium vulgare*, British

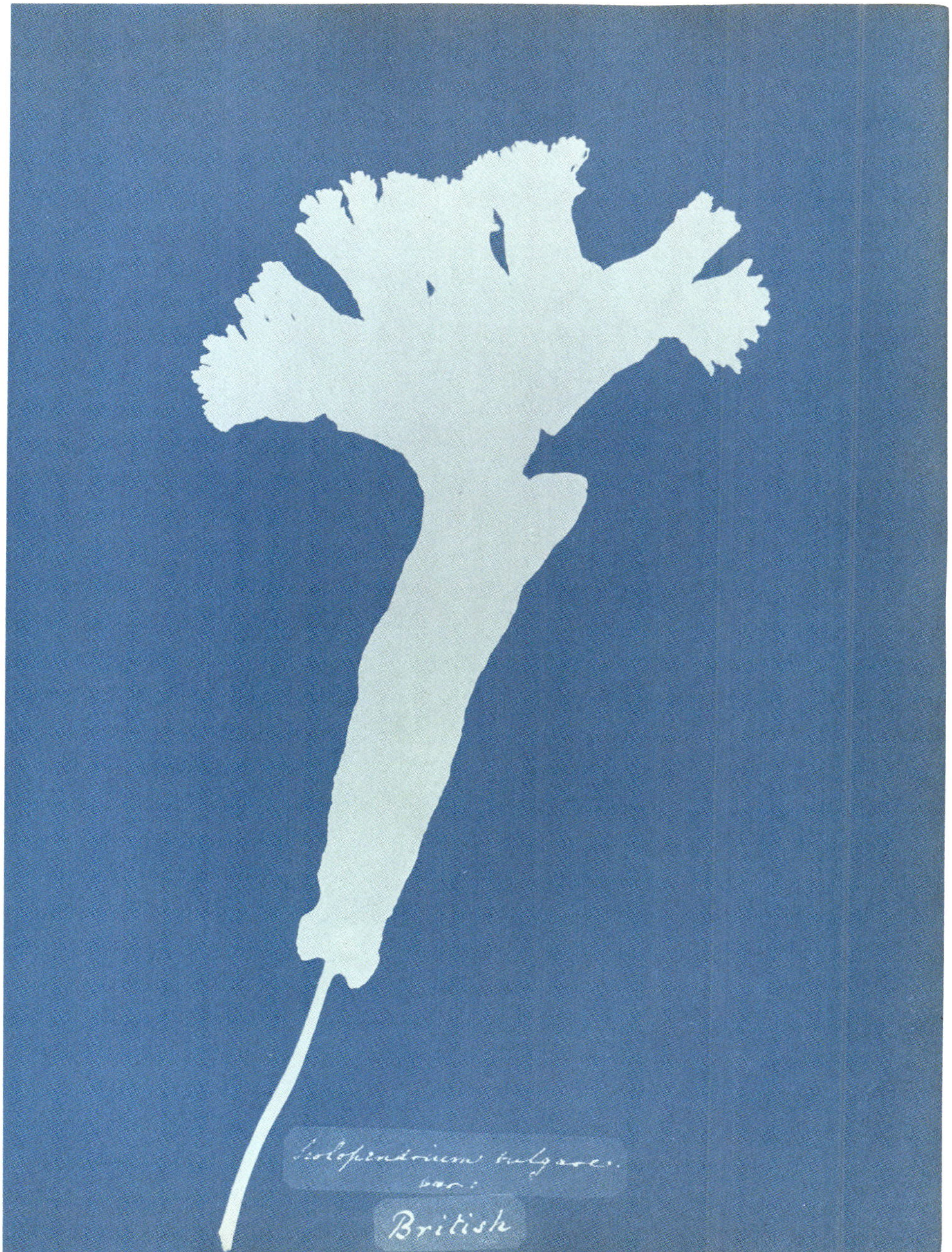

Plate 467. *Scolopendrium vulgare*, var. British

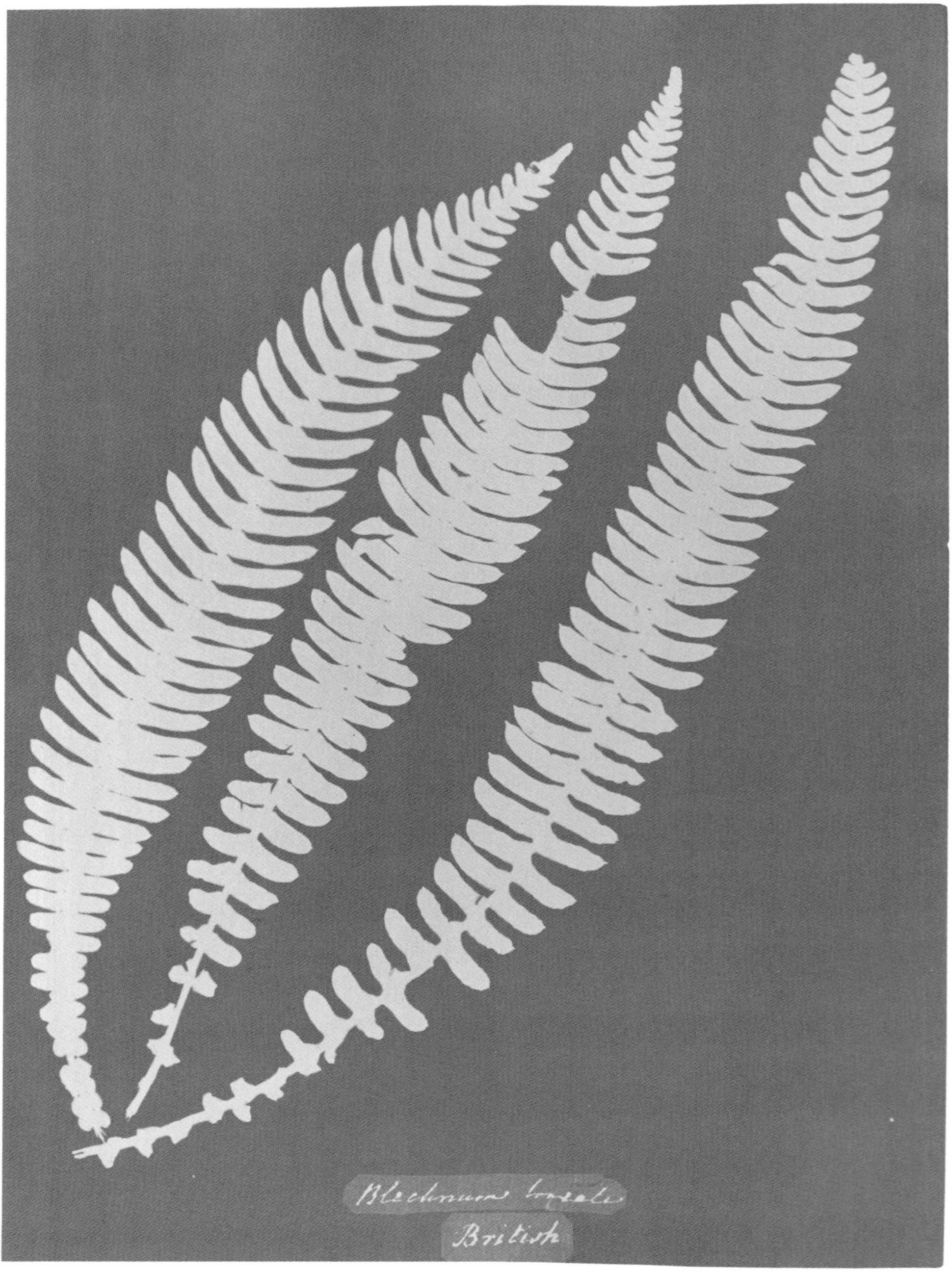

Plate 468. *Blechnum boreale*, British

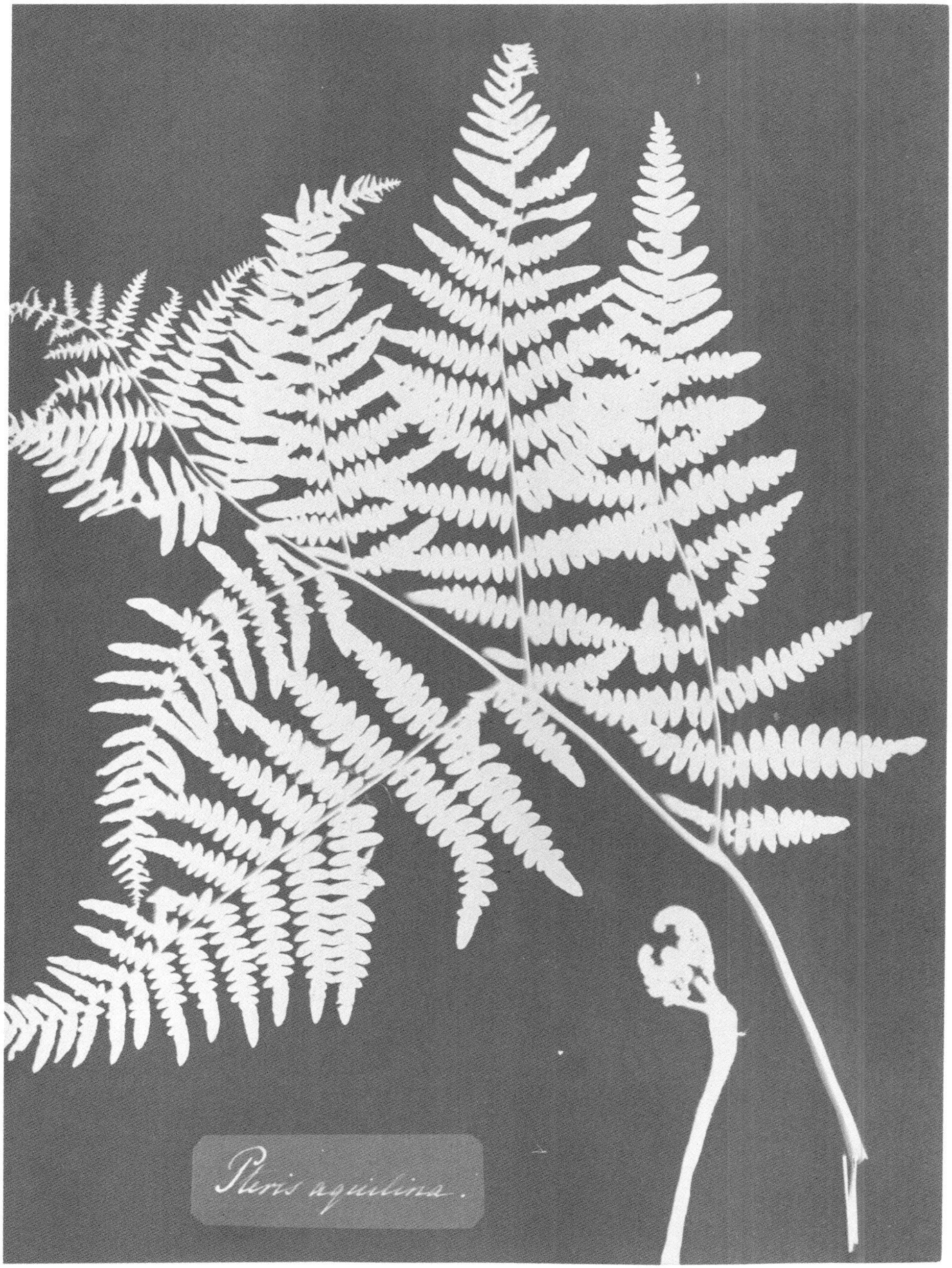

Plate 469. *Pteris aquilina*

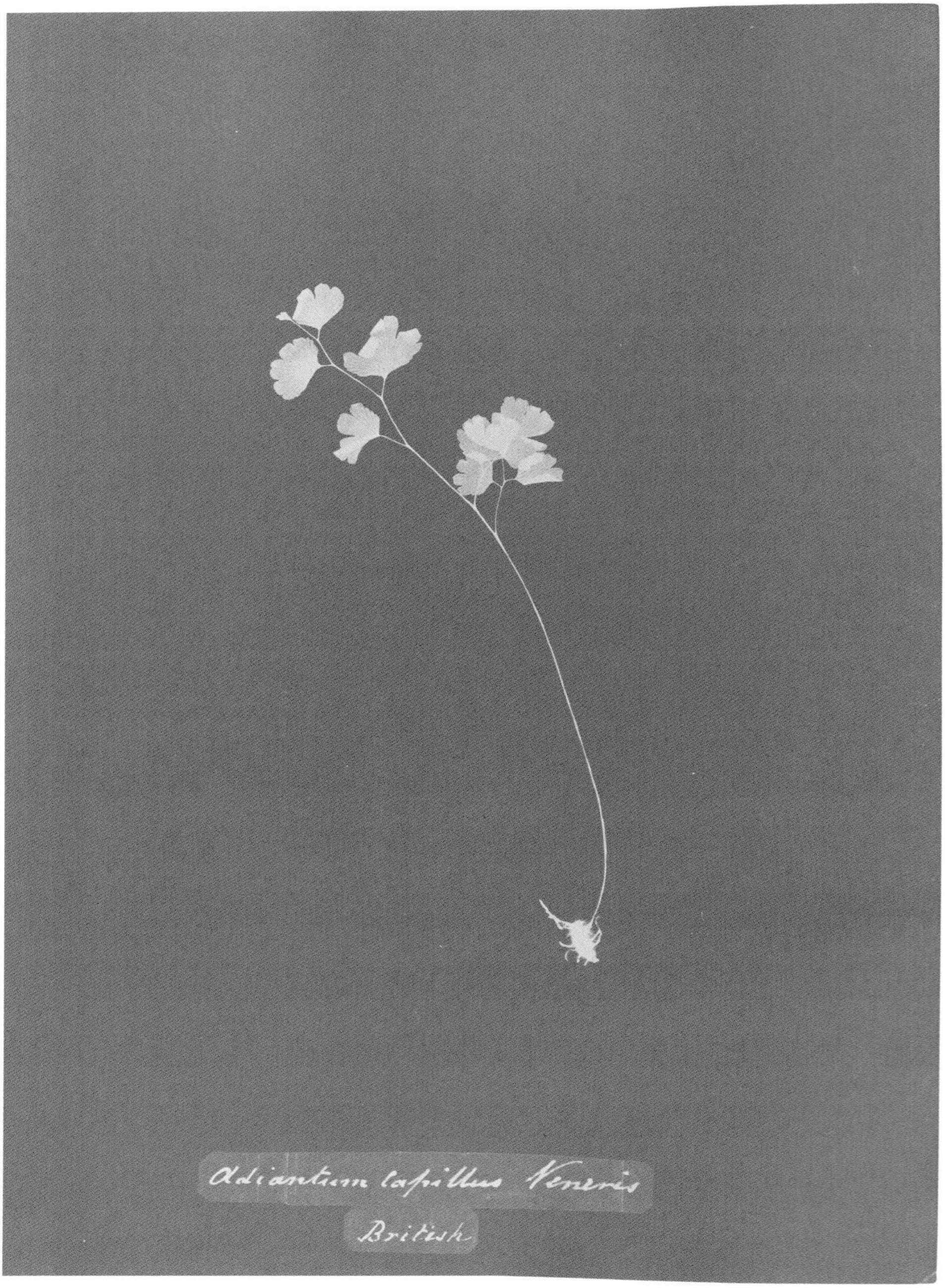

Plate 470. *Adiantum capillus veneris*, British

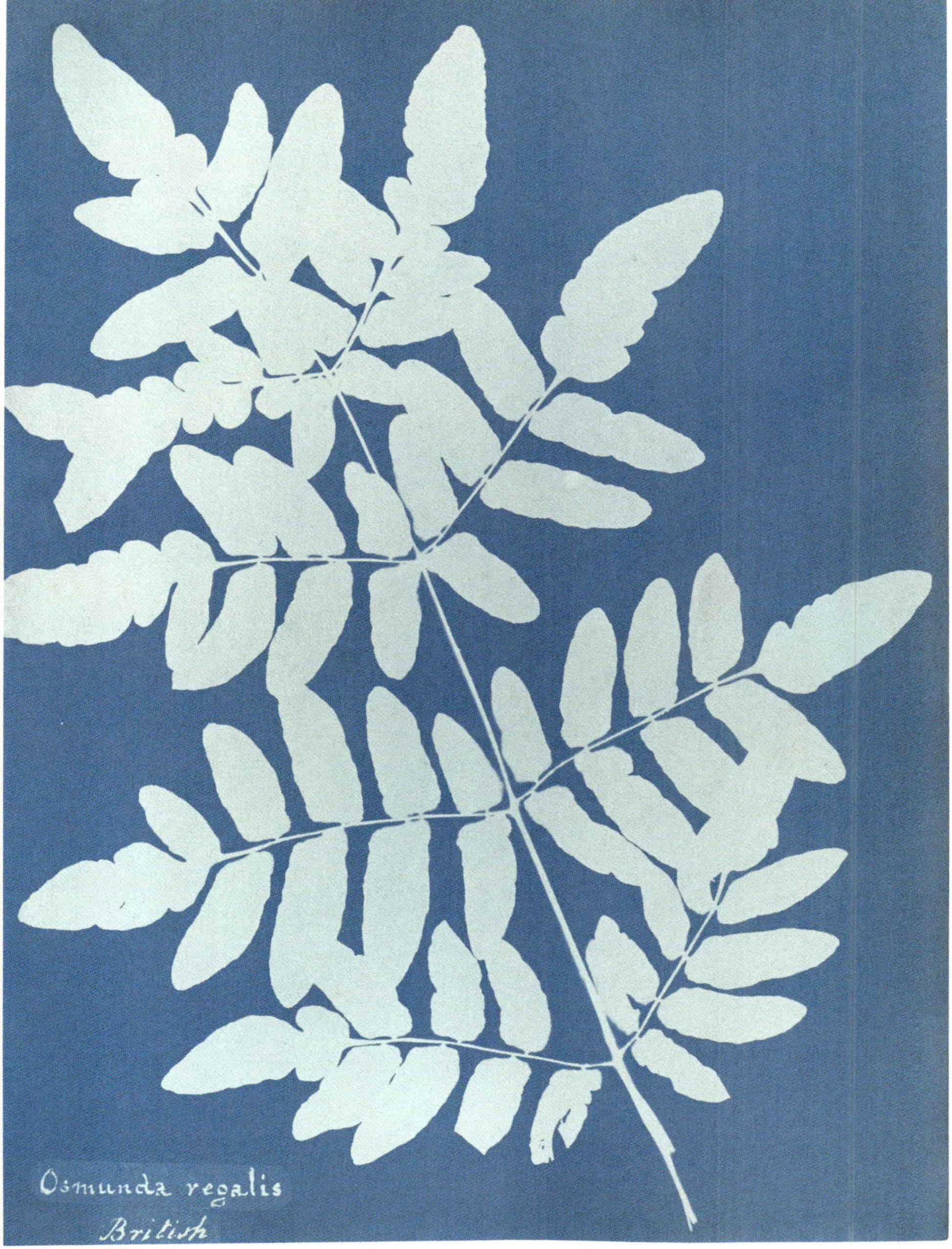

Plate 473. *Osmunda regalis*, British

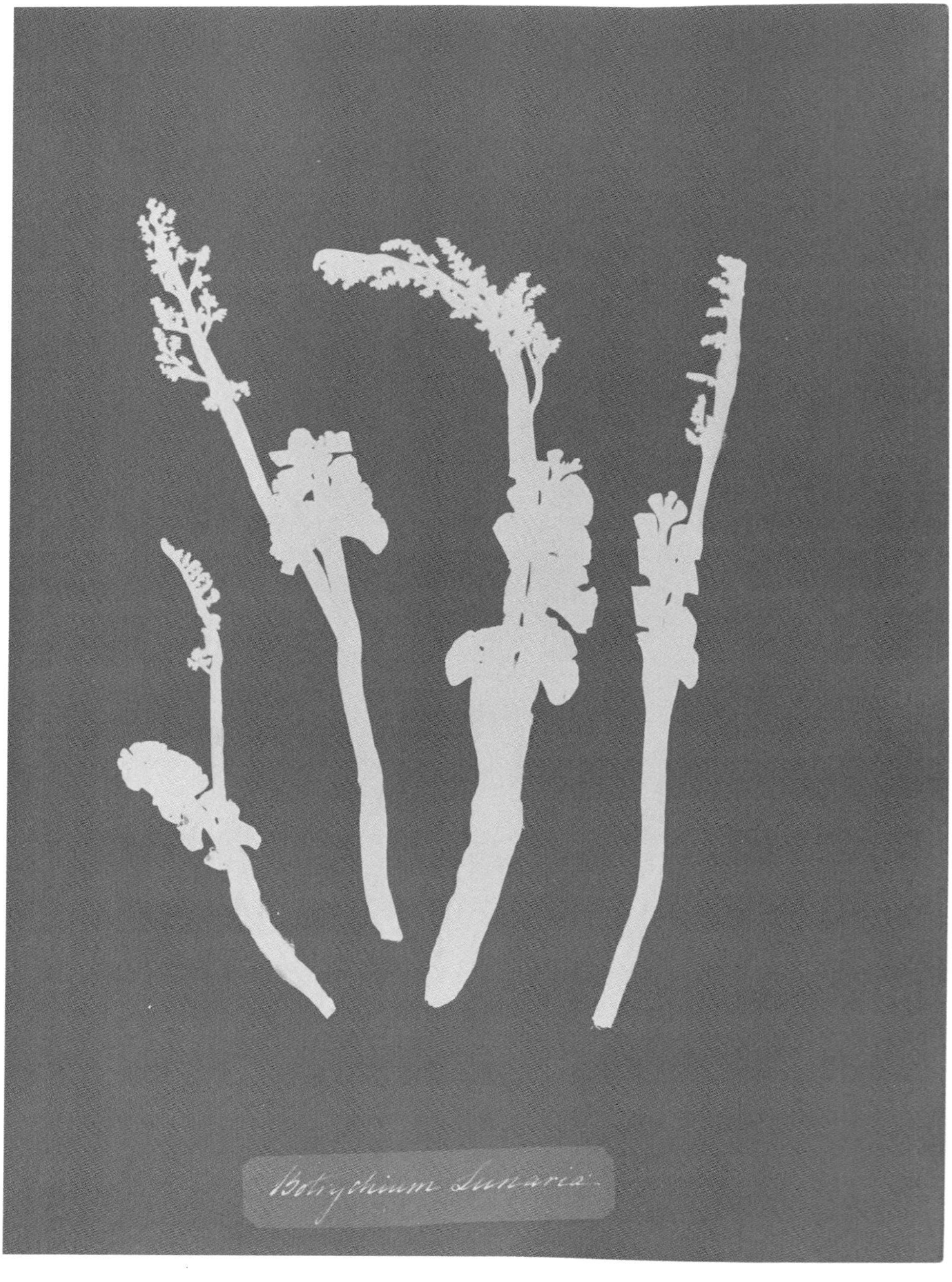

Plate 474. *Botrychium lunaria*

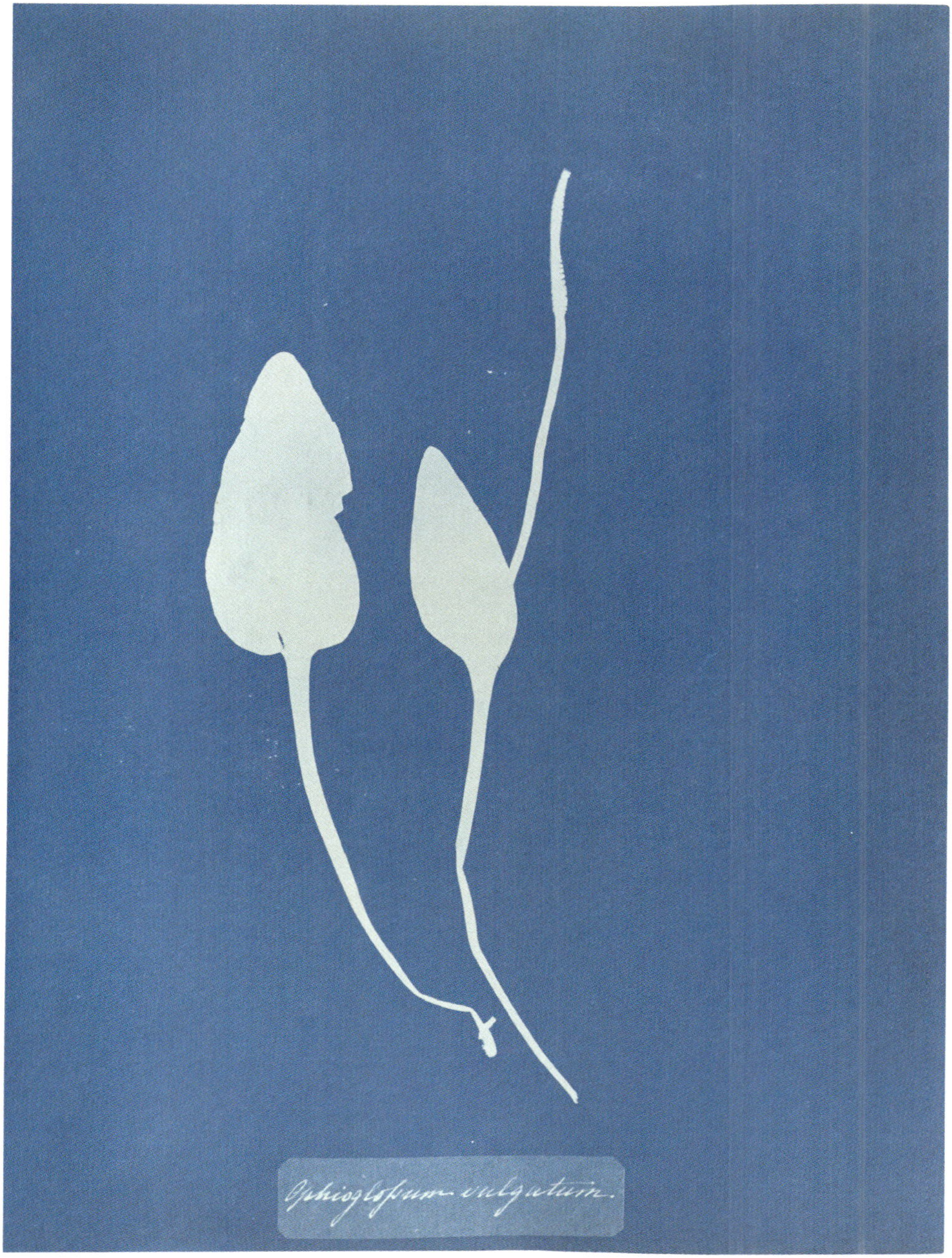

Plate 475. *Ophioglossum vulgatum*

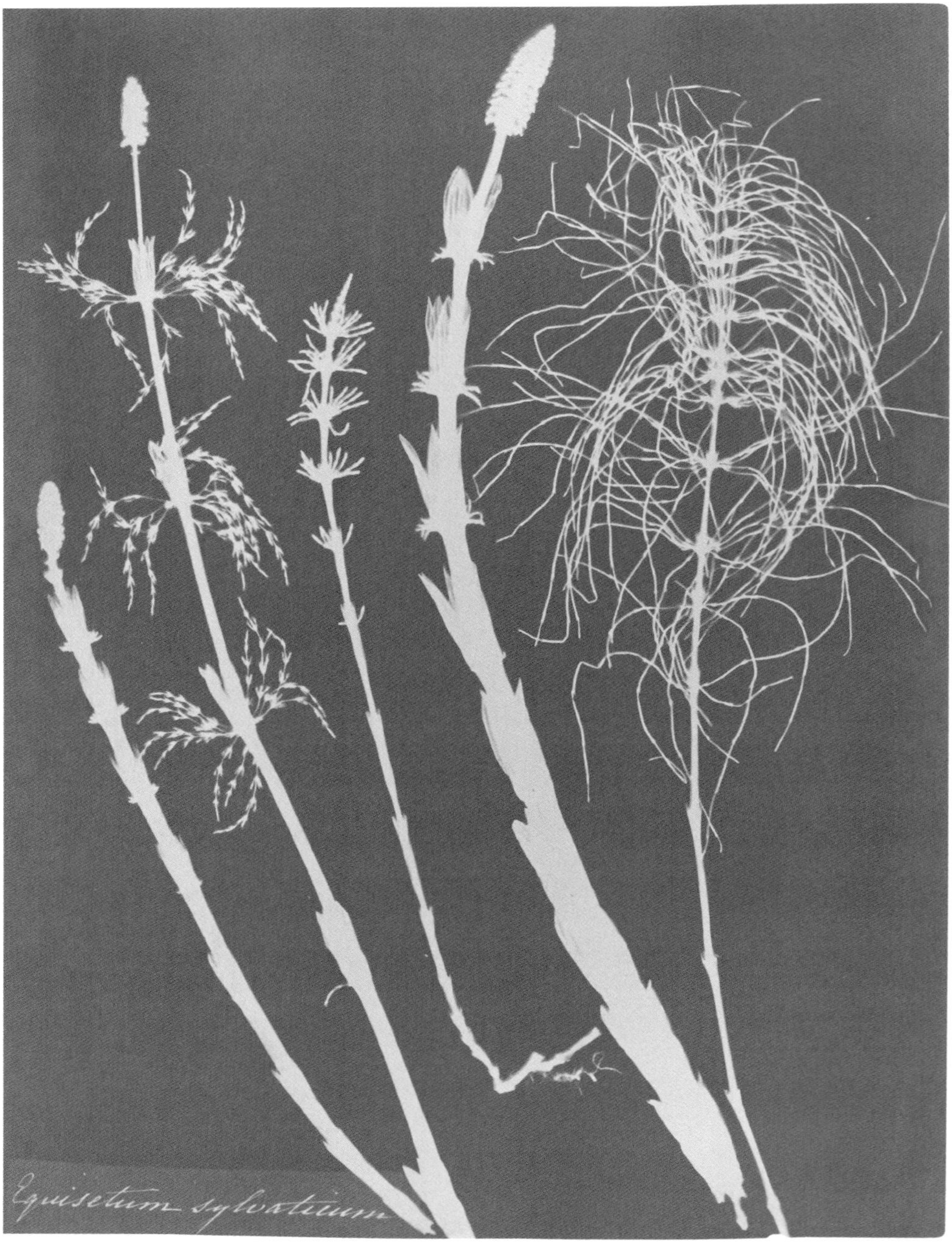

Plate 476. *Equisetum sylvaticum*

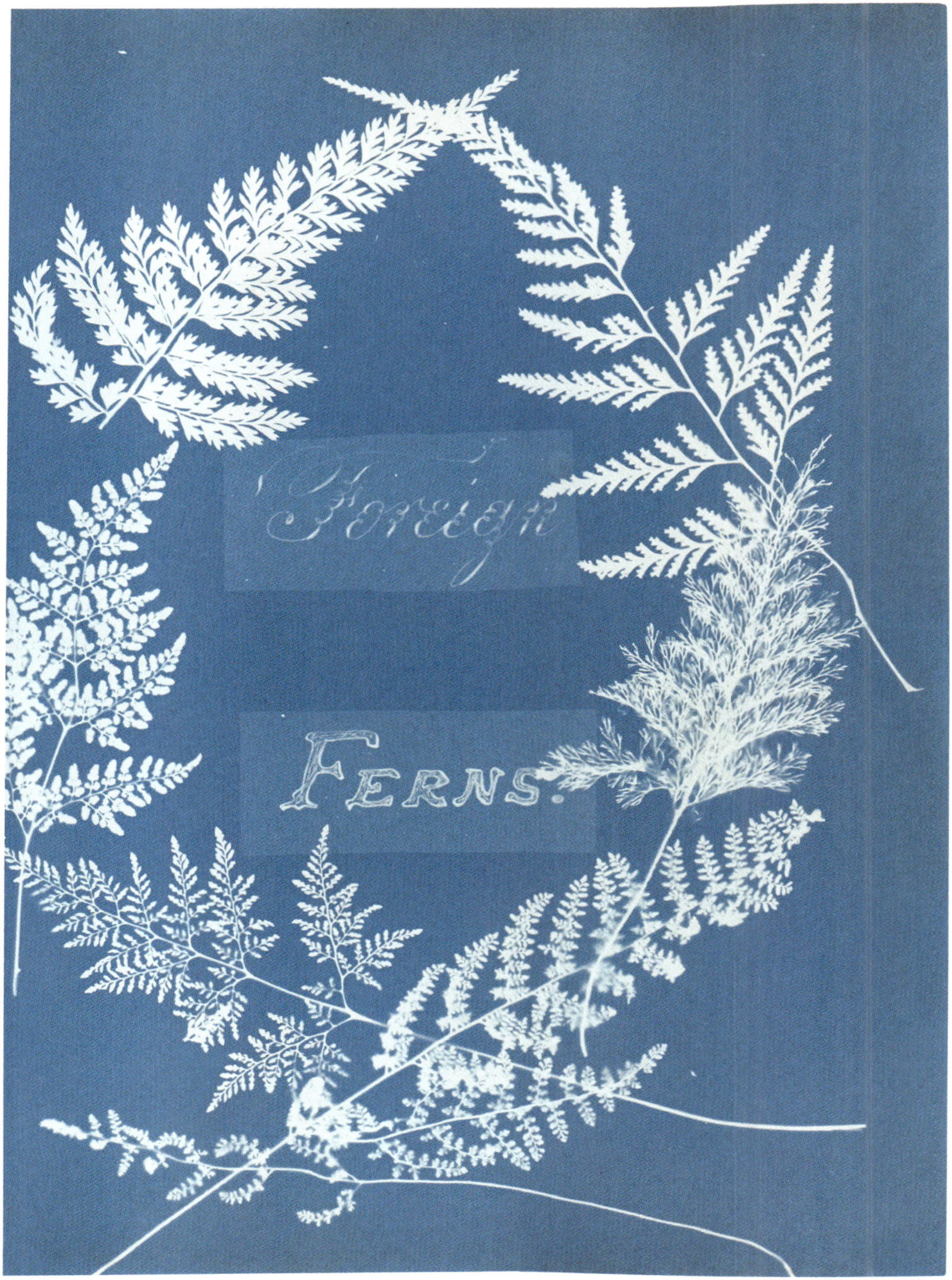

Title Page

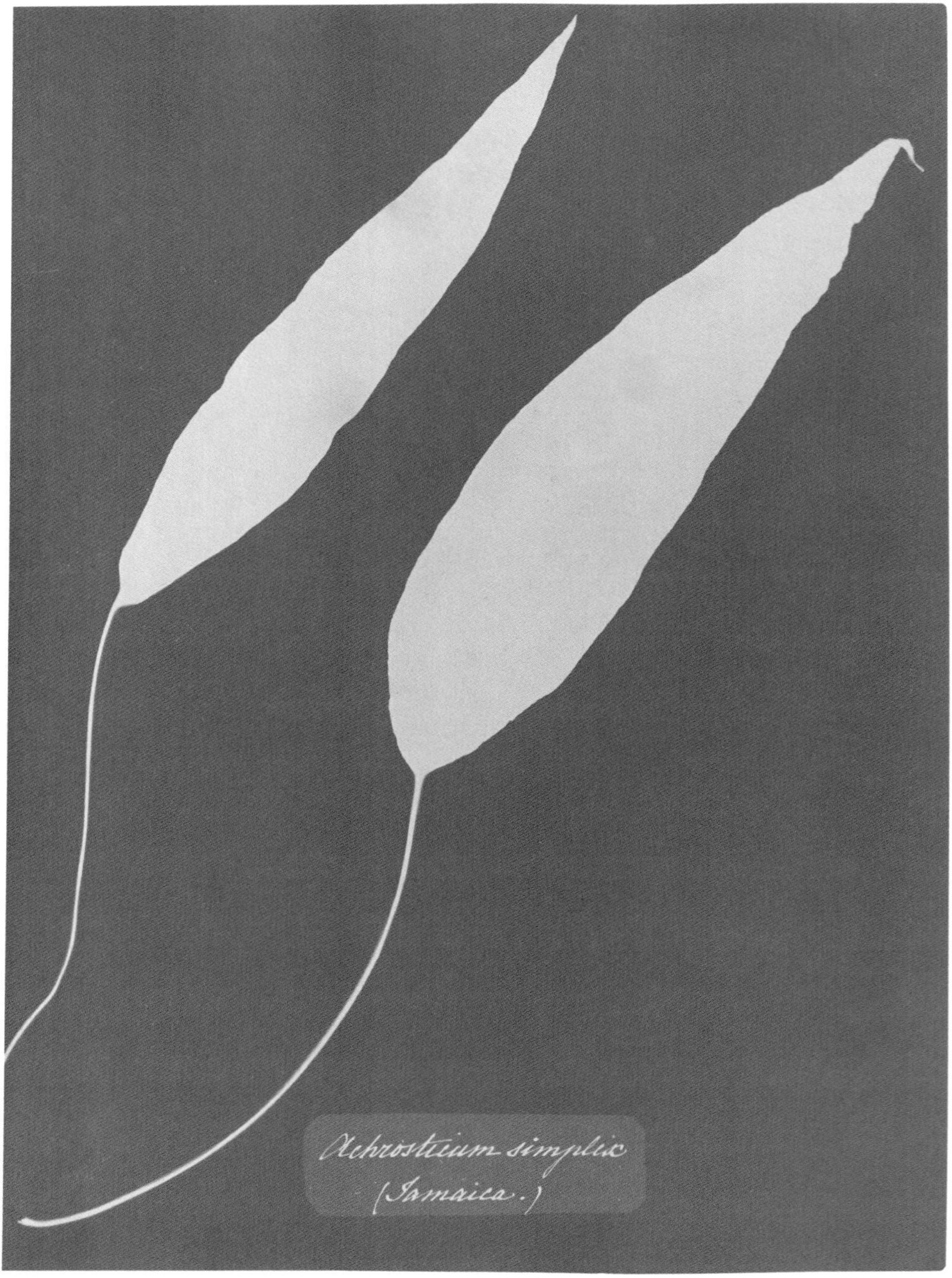

Plate 477. *Achrosticum simplex* (Jamaica)

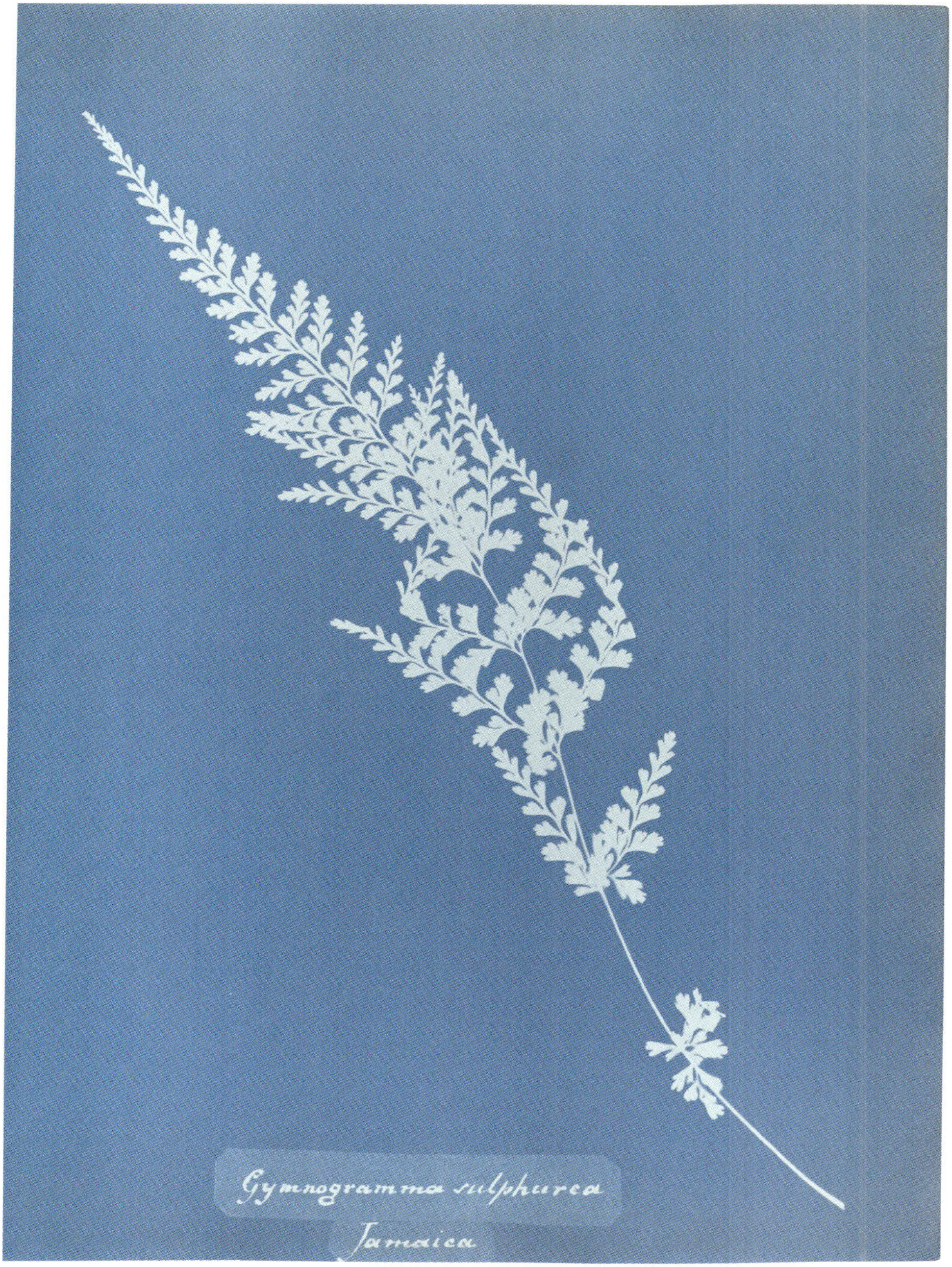

Plate 478. *Gymnogramma sulphurea*, Jamaica

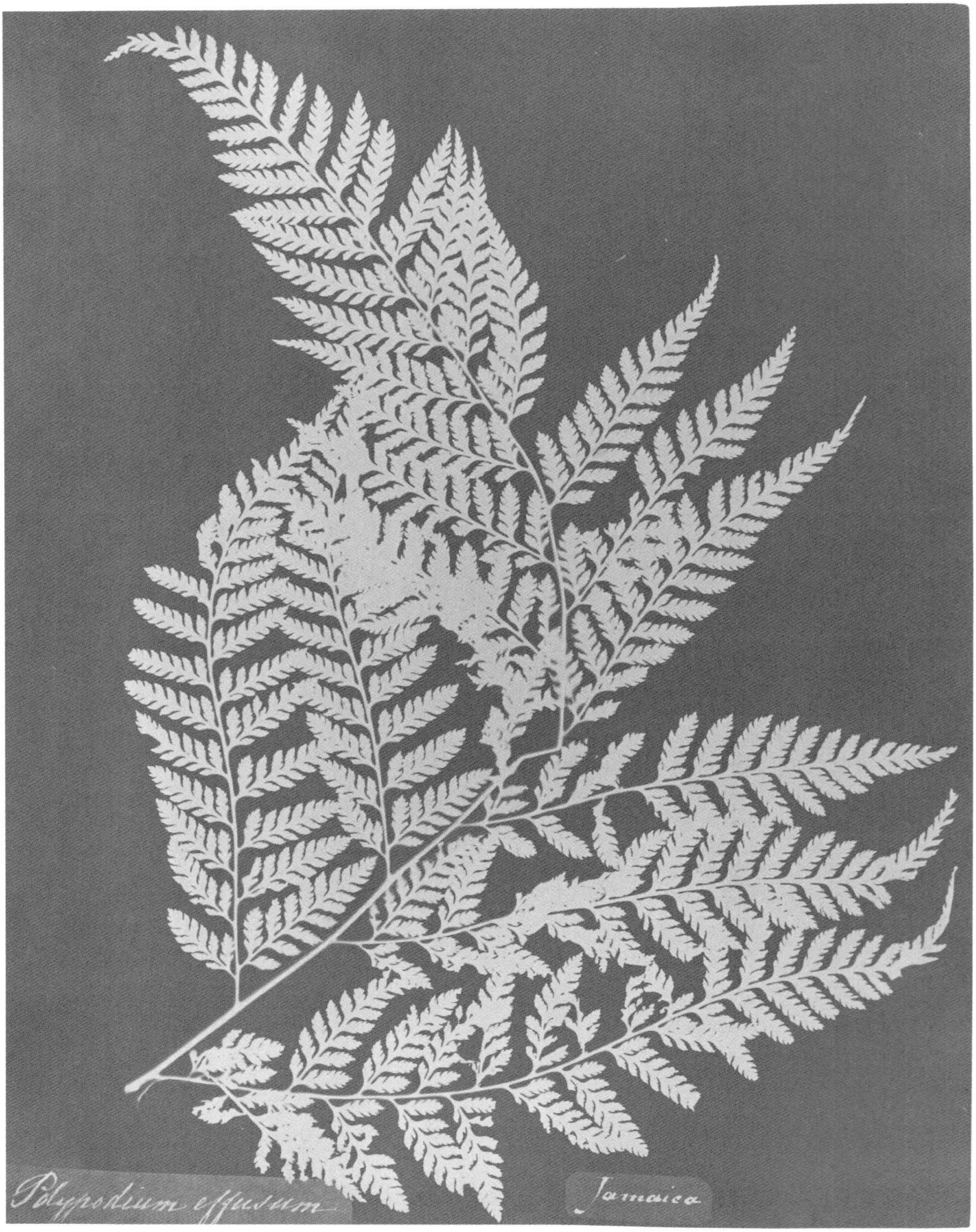

Plate 479. *Polypodium effusum*, Jamaica

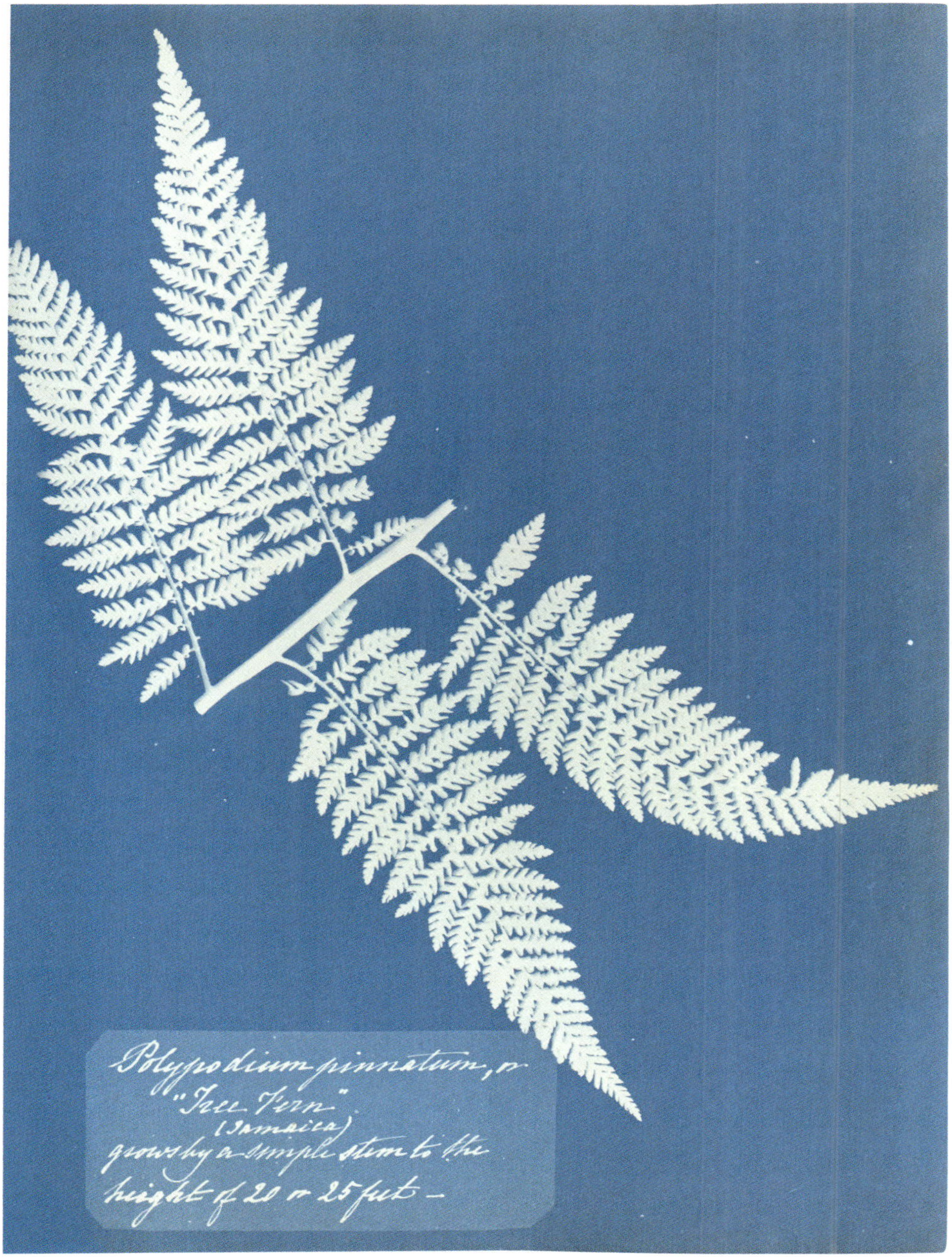

Plate 480. *Polypodium pinnatum*, Jamaica.
"Tree Fern" (Jamaica), grows by a simple stem to the height of 20 or 25 feet

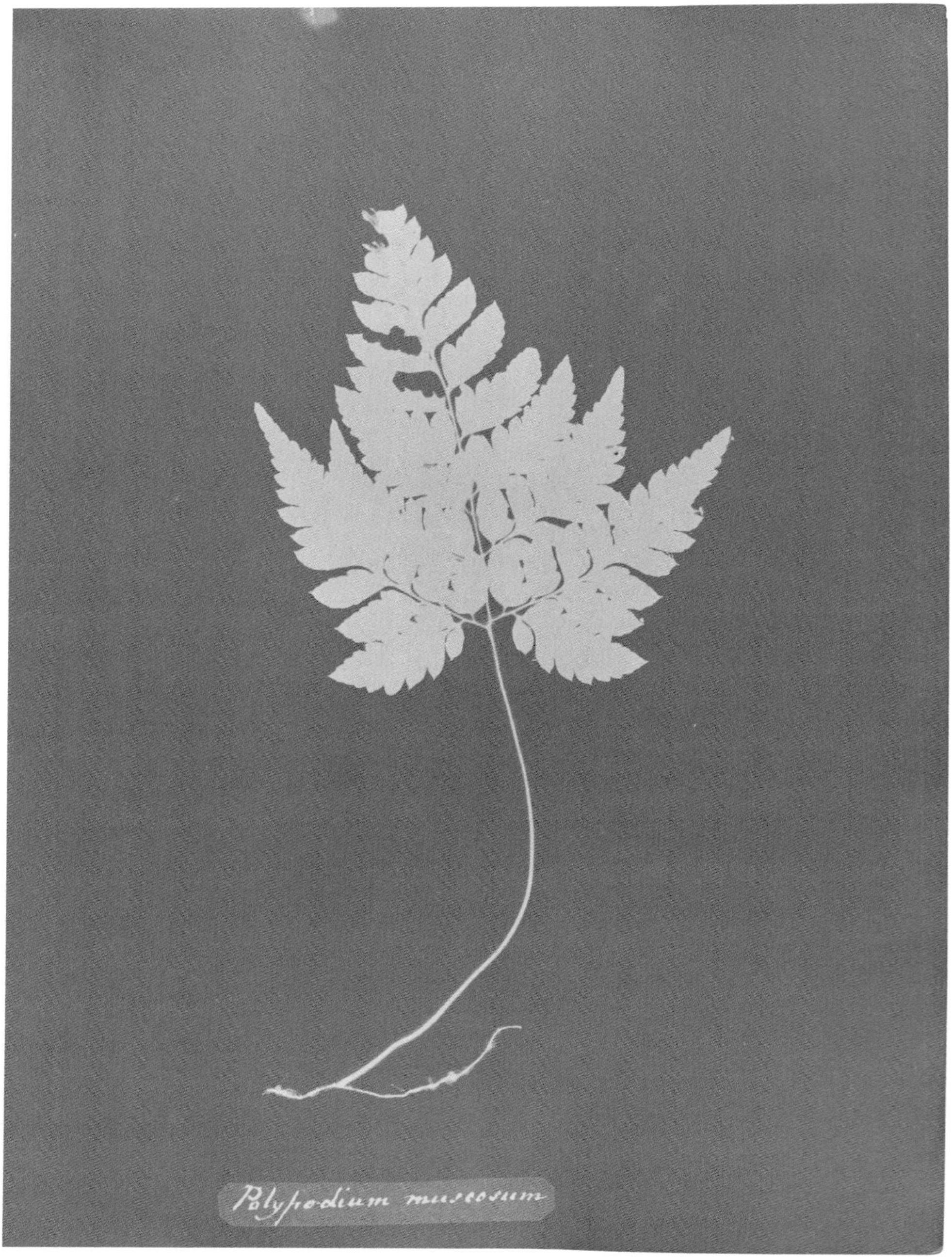

Plate 481. *Polypodium muscosum*

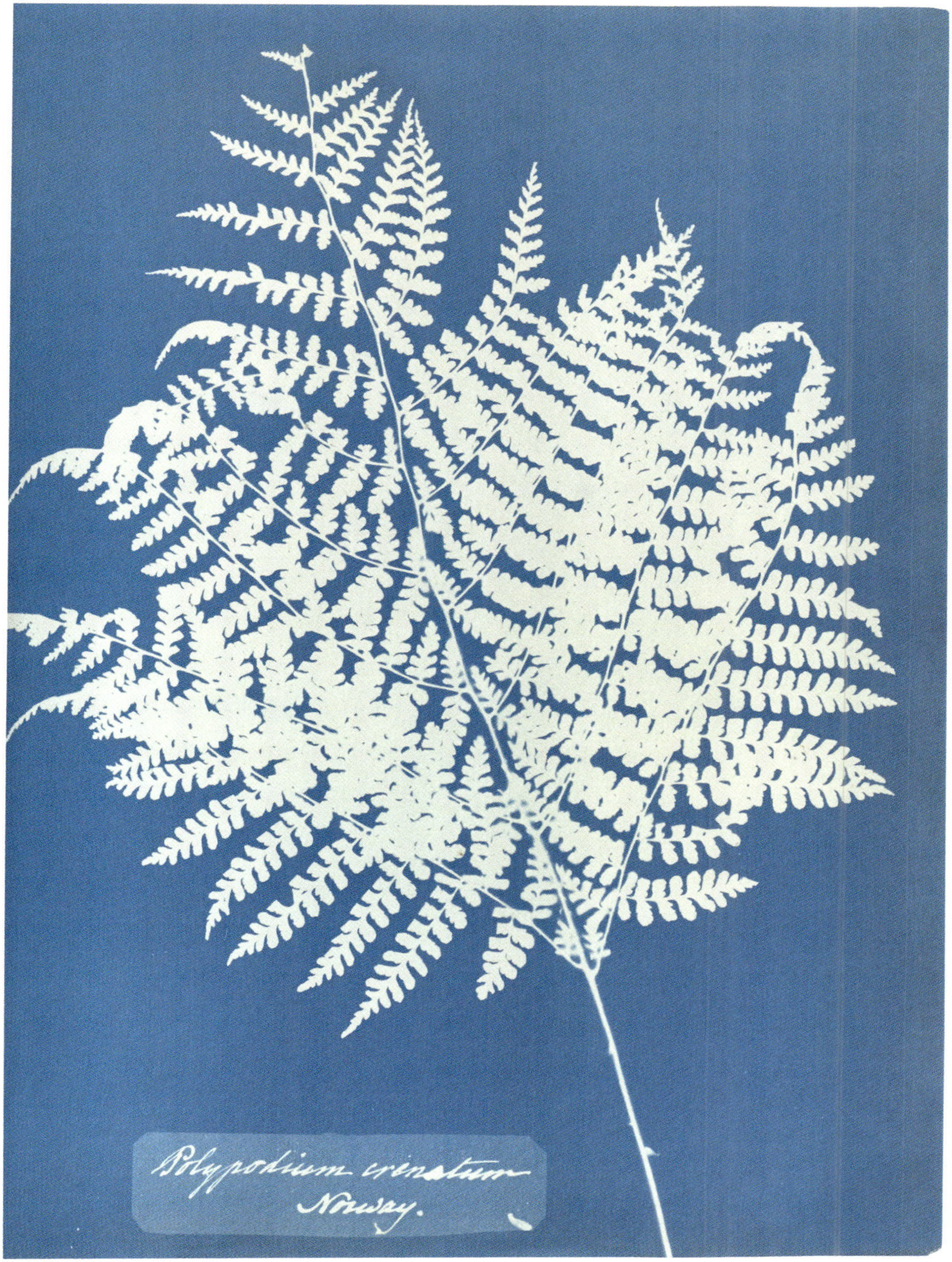

Plate 482. *Polypodium crenatum*, Norway

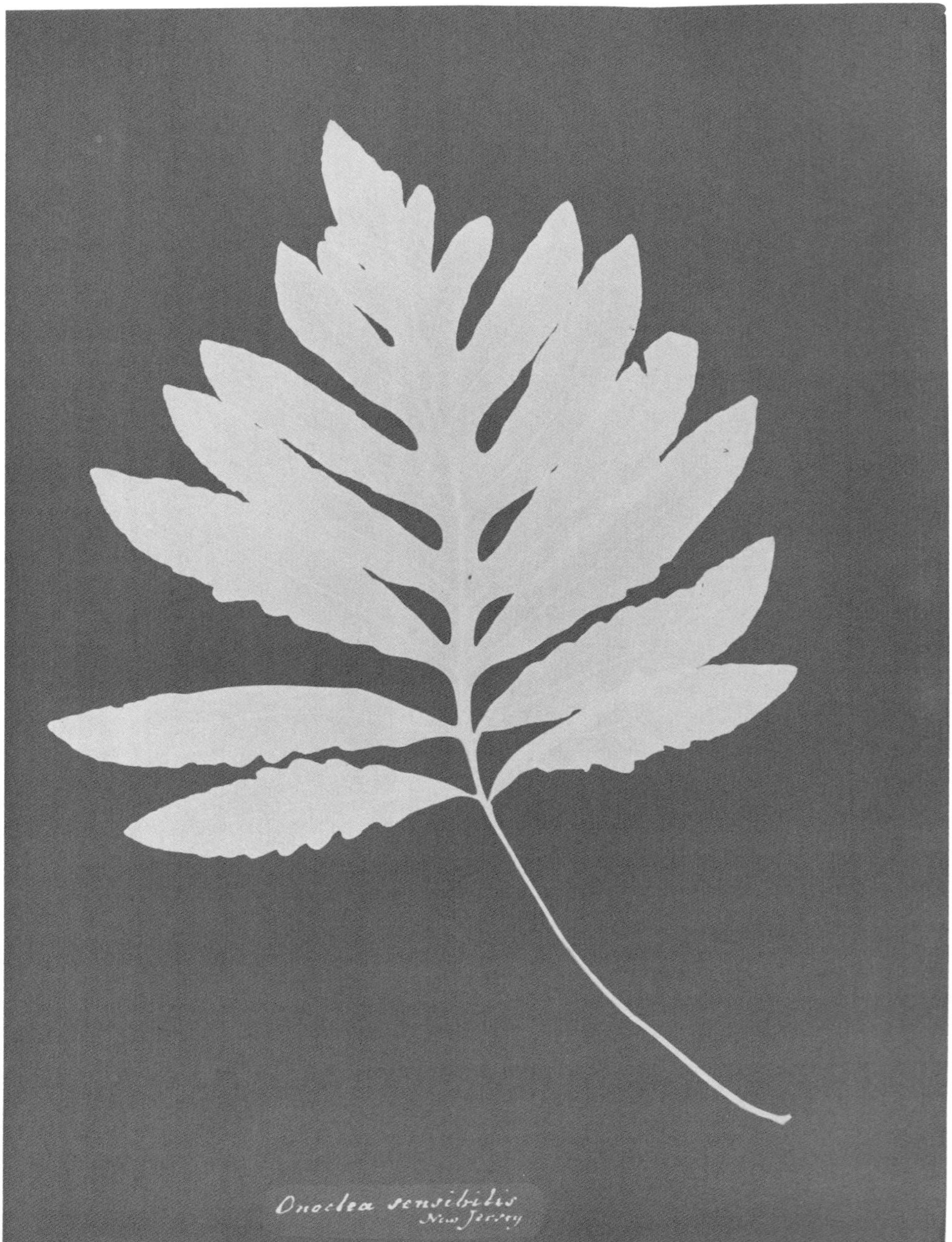

Plate 483. *Onoclea sensibilis*, New Jersey

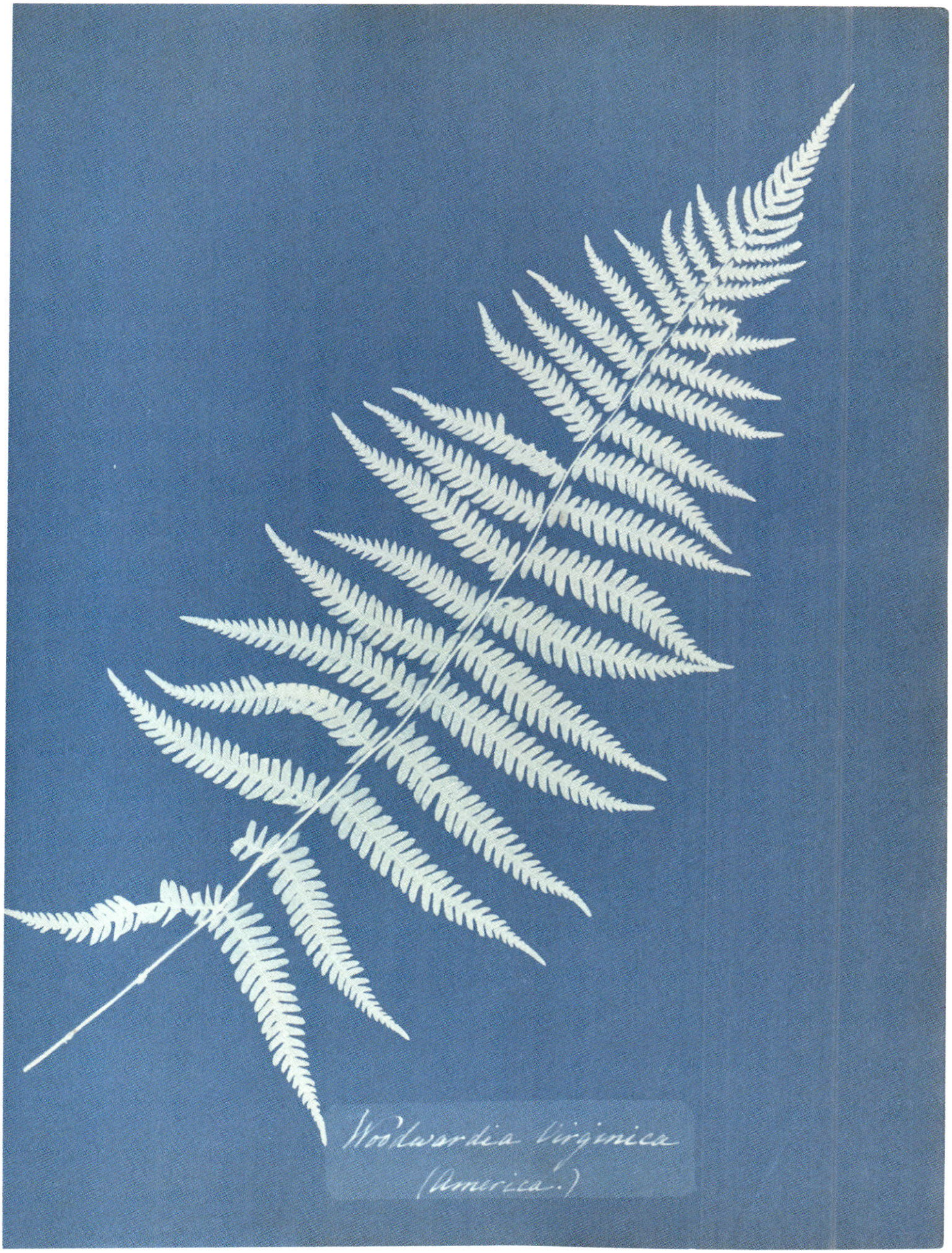

Plate 484. *Woodwardia virginica* (America)

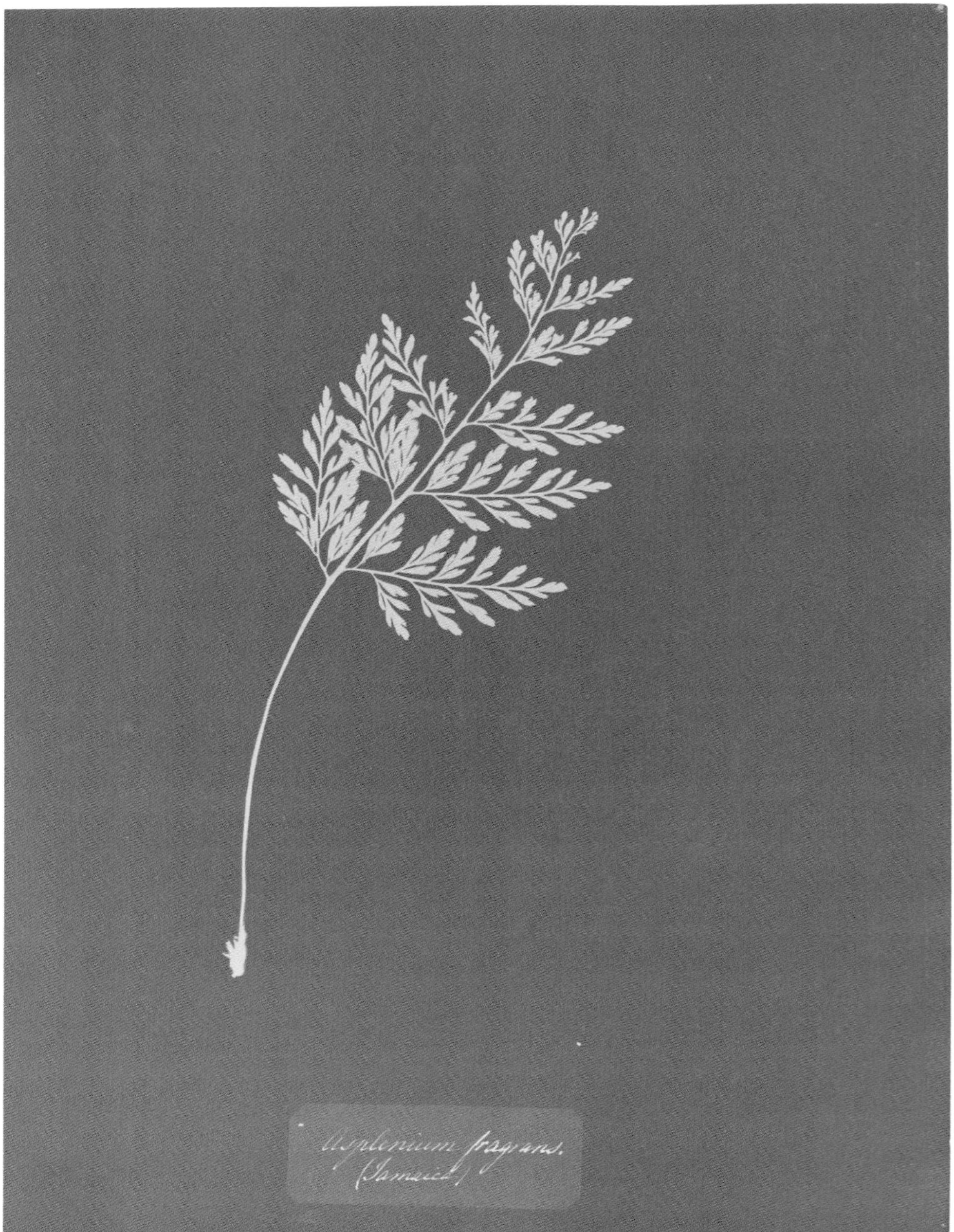

Plate 485. *Asplenium fragrans* (Jamaica)

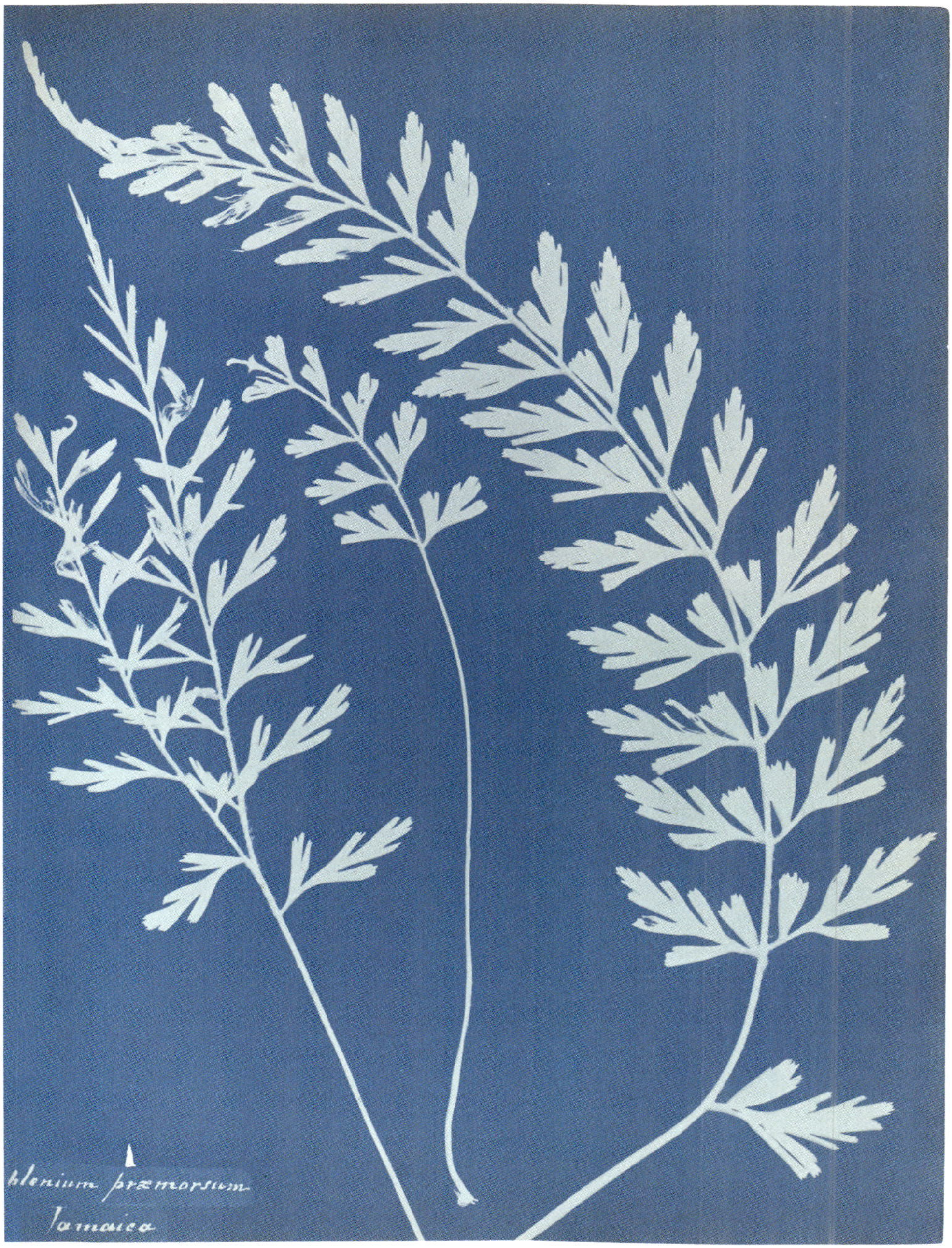

Plate 486. *Asplenium praemorsum*, Jamaica

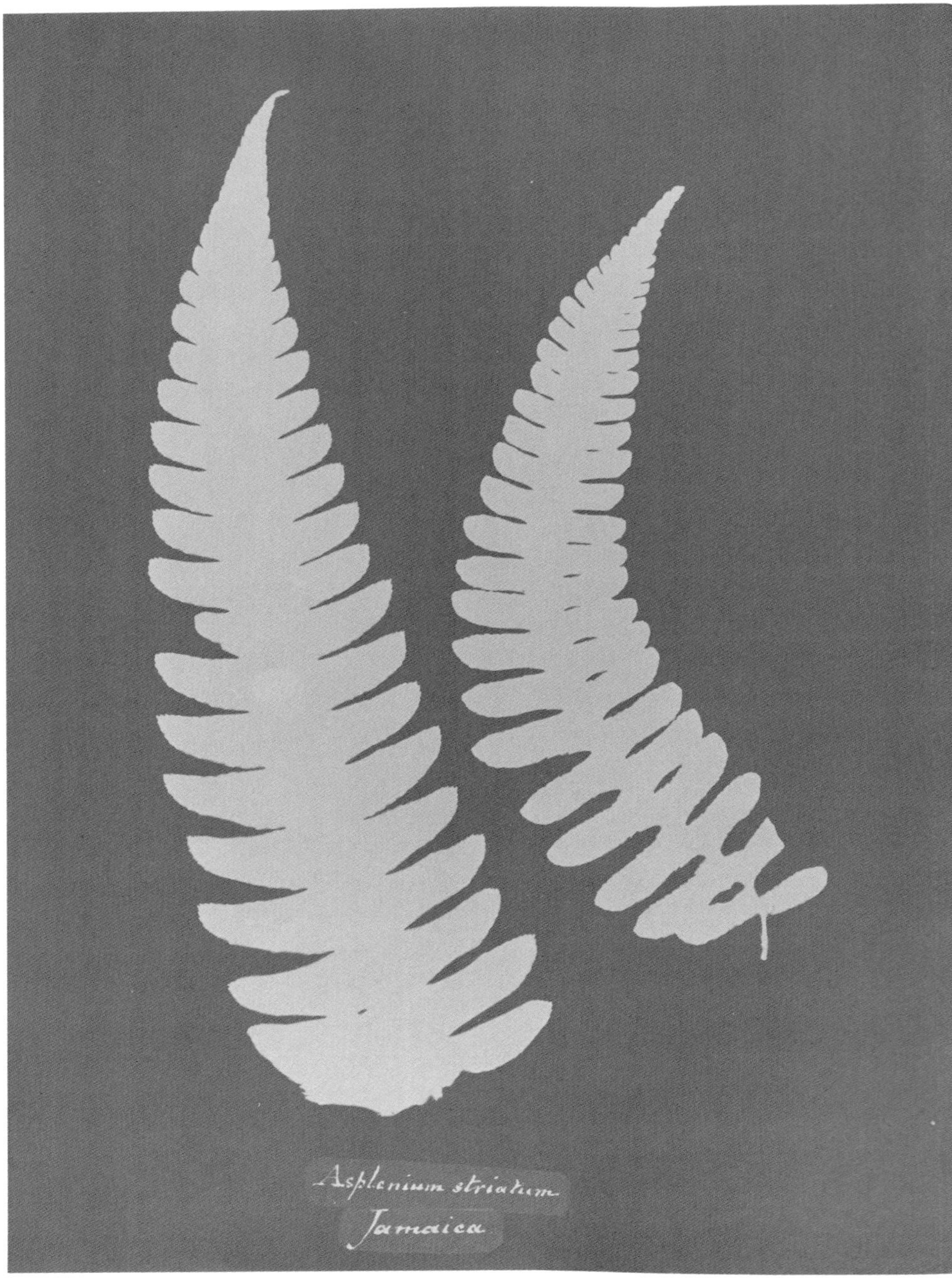

Plate 487. *Asplenium striatum*, Jamaica

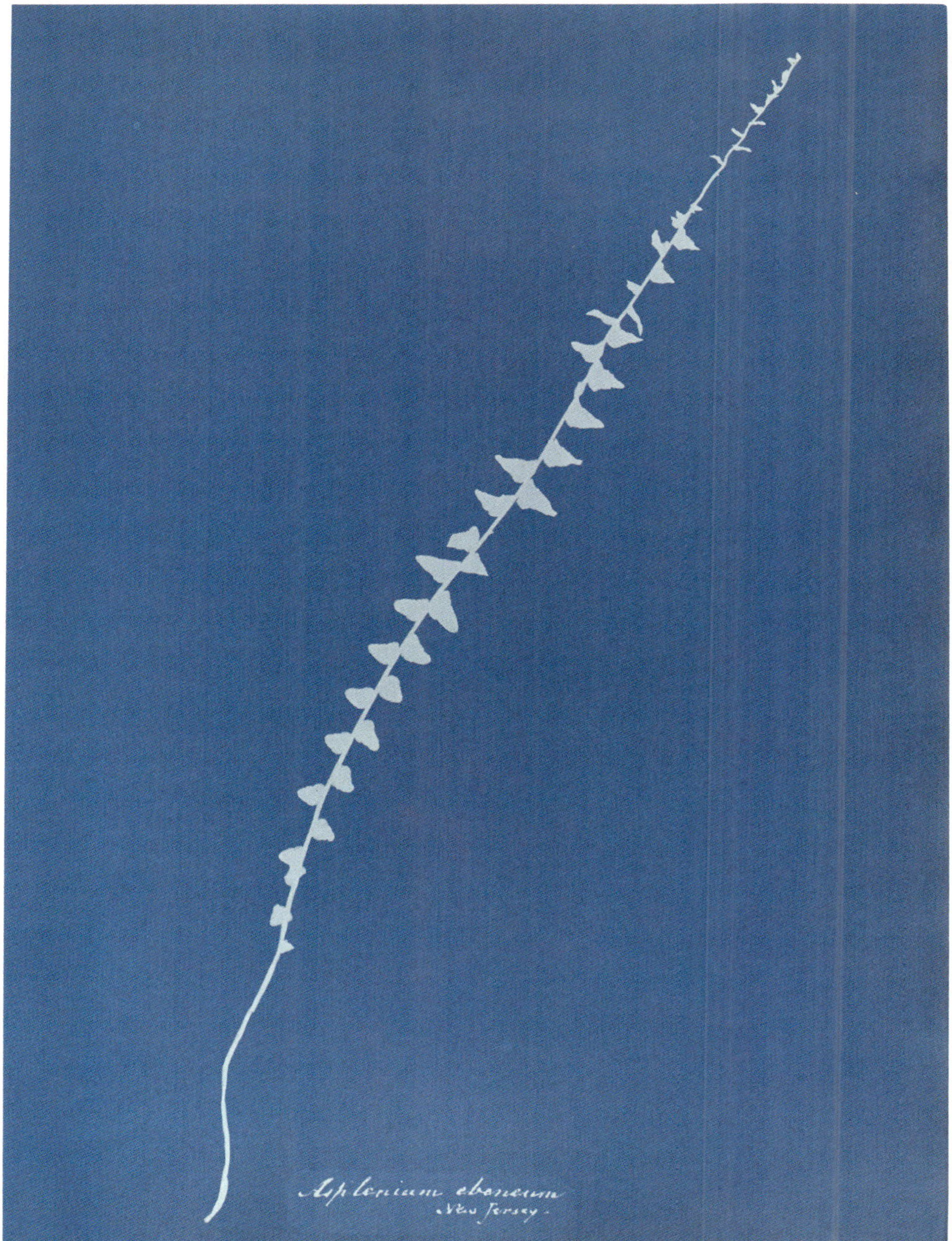

Plate 488. *Asplenium ebenum*, New Jersey

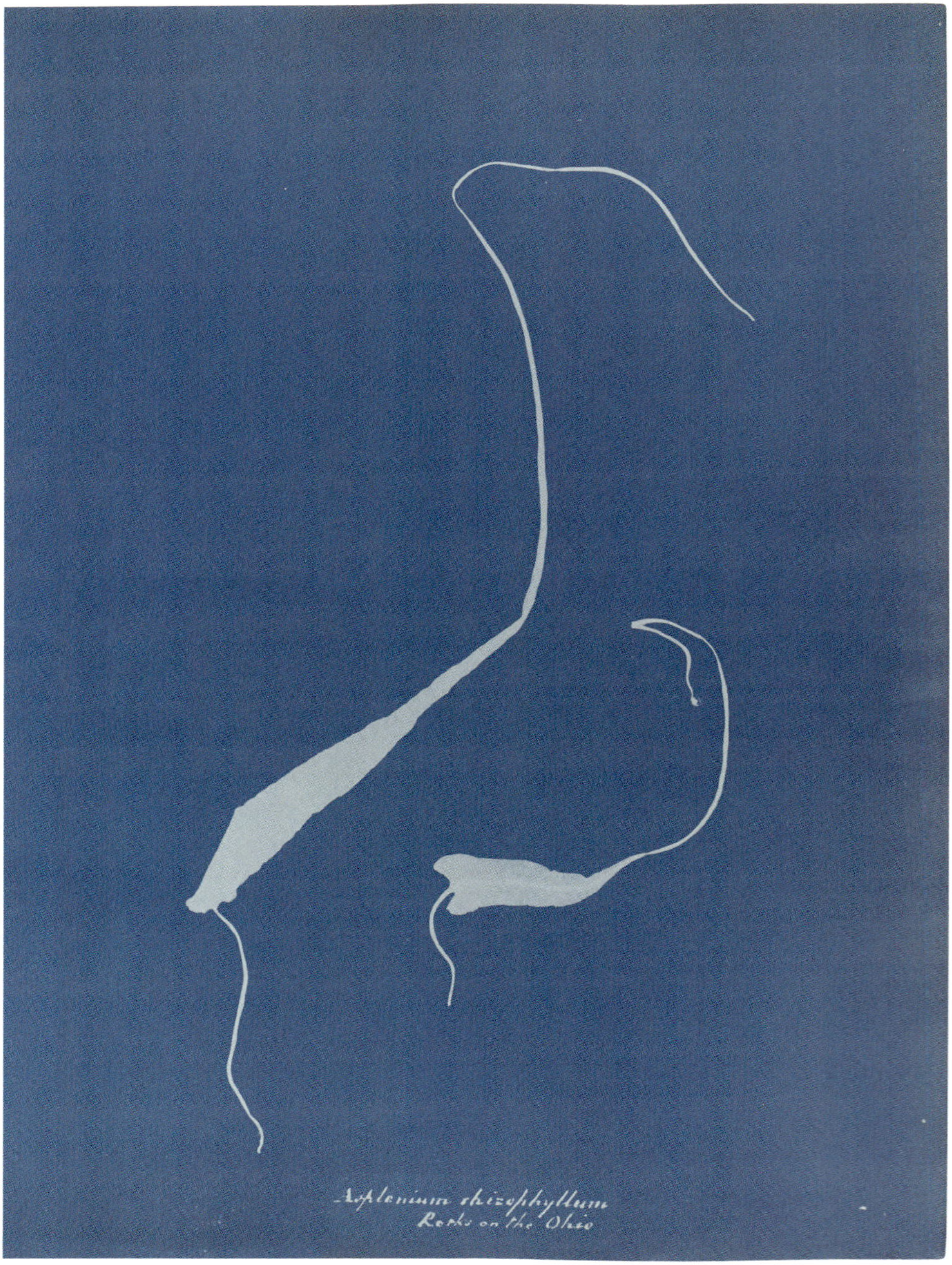

Plate 489. *Asplenium rhizophyllum*, Rocks on the Ohio

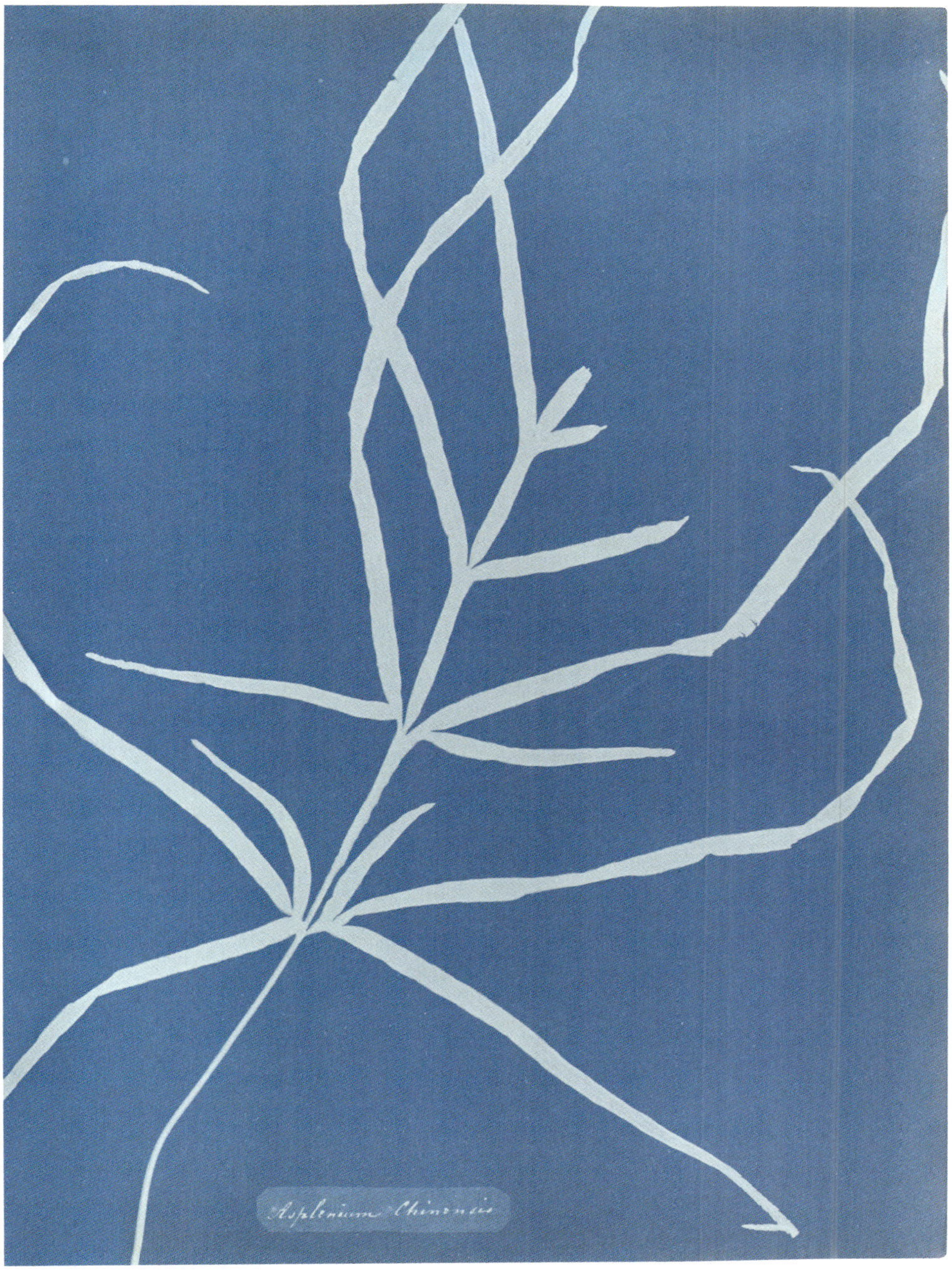

Plate 490. *Asplenium chinensis*

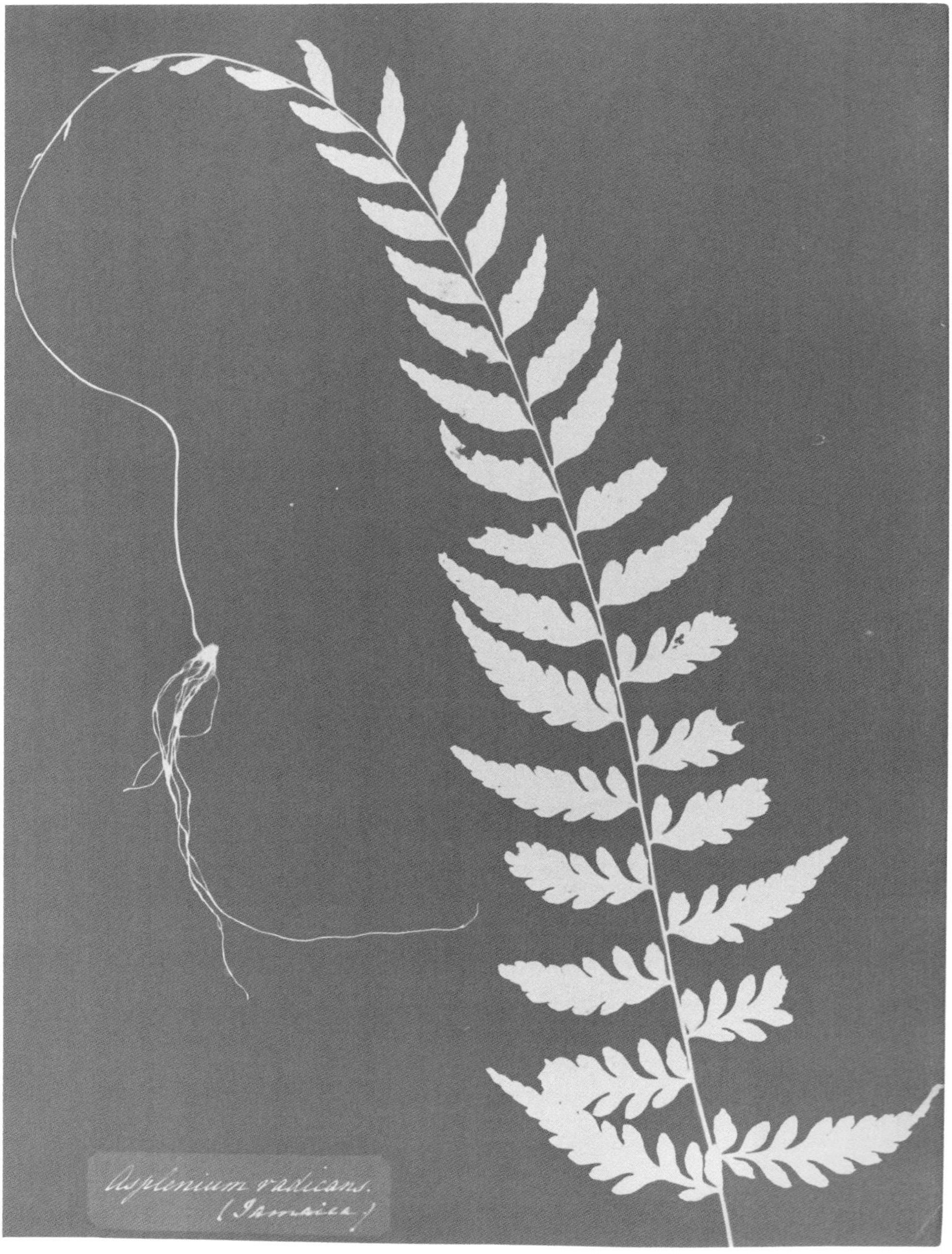

Plate 491. *Asplenium radicans* (Jamaica)

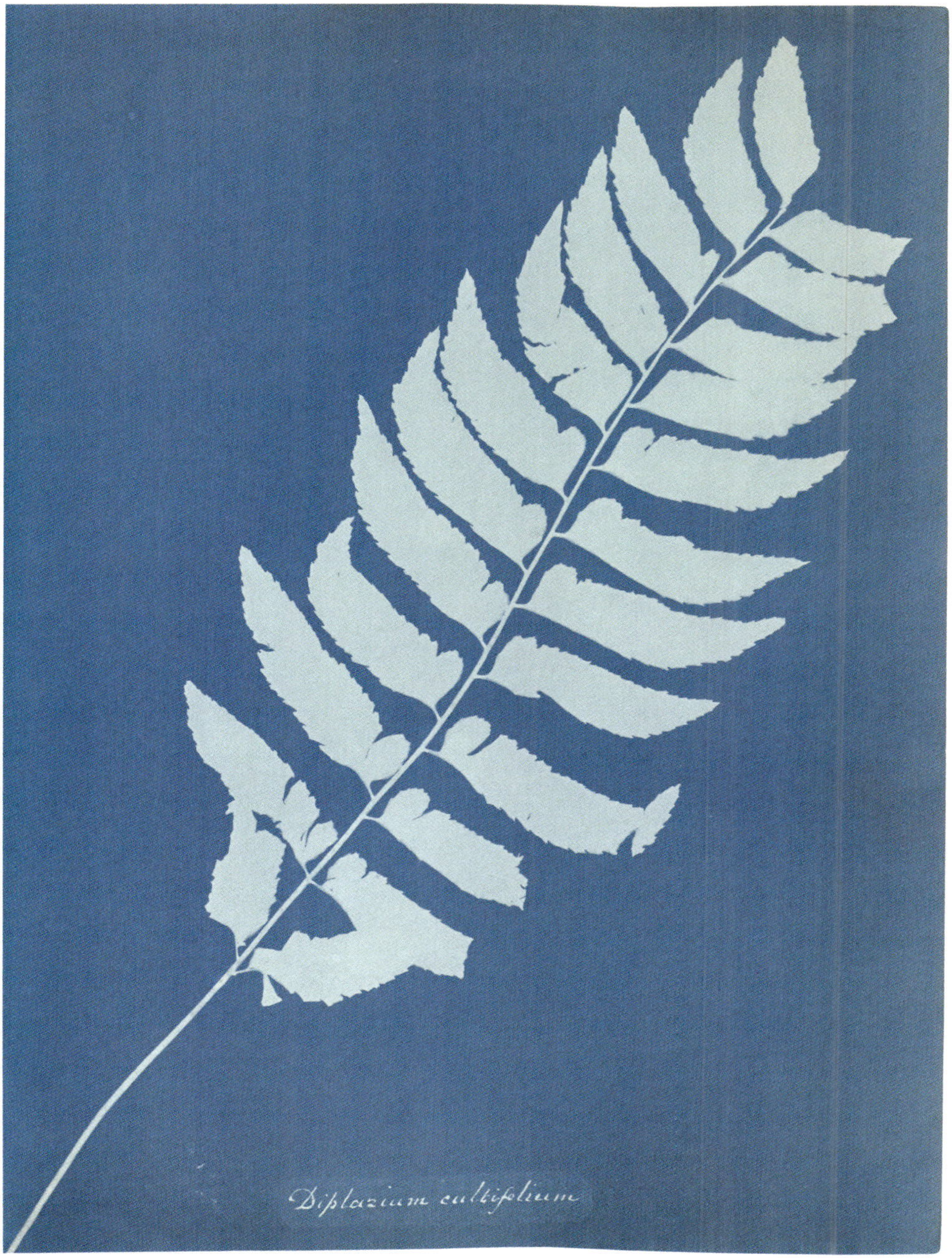

Plate 492. *Diplazium cultifolium*

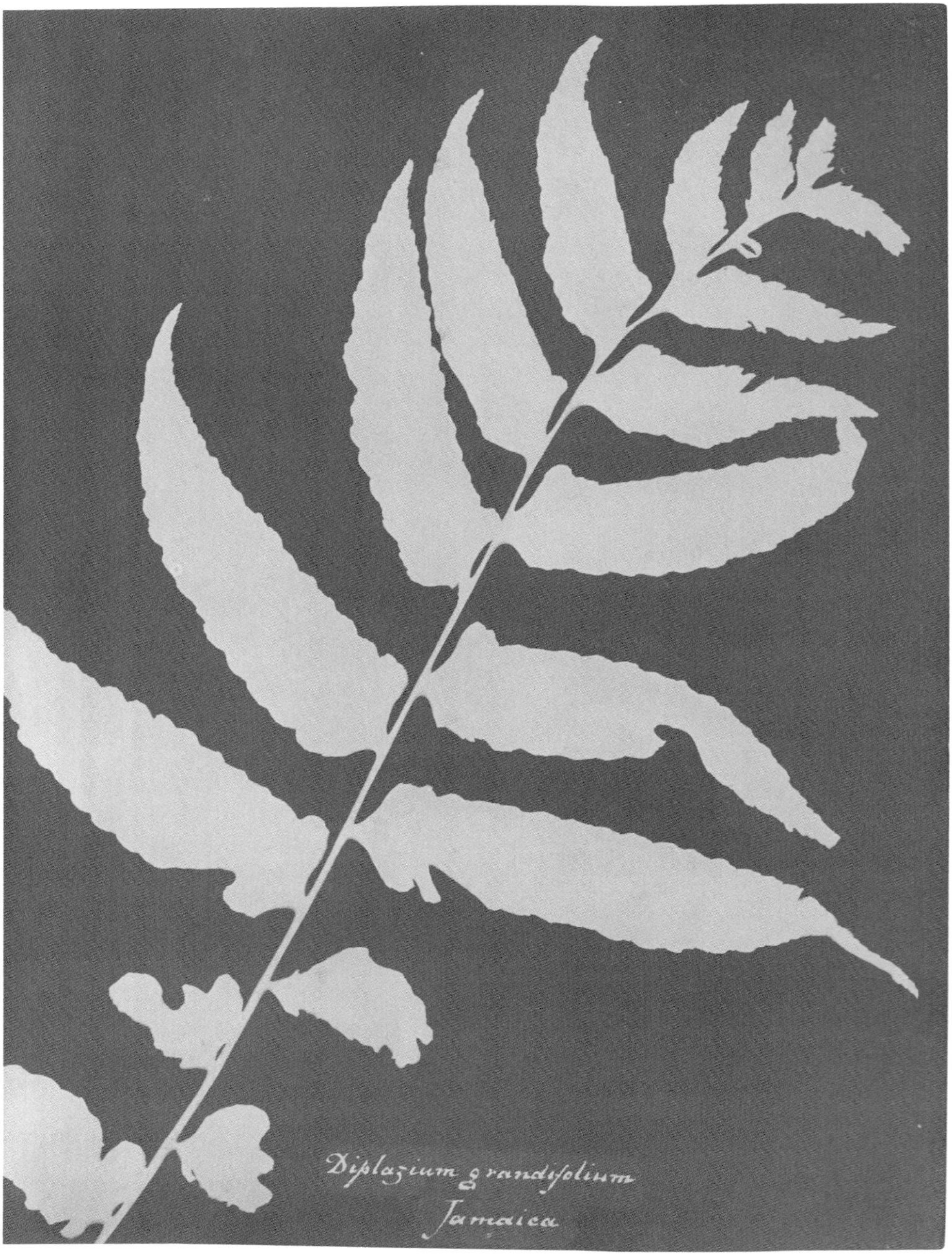

Plate 493. *Diplazium grandifolium*, Jamaica

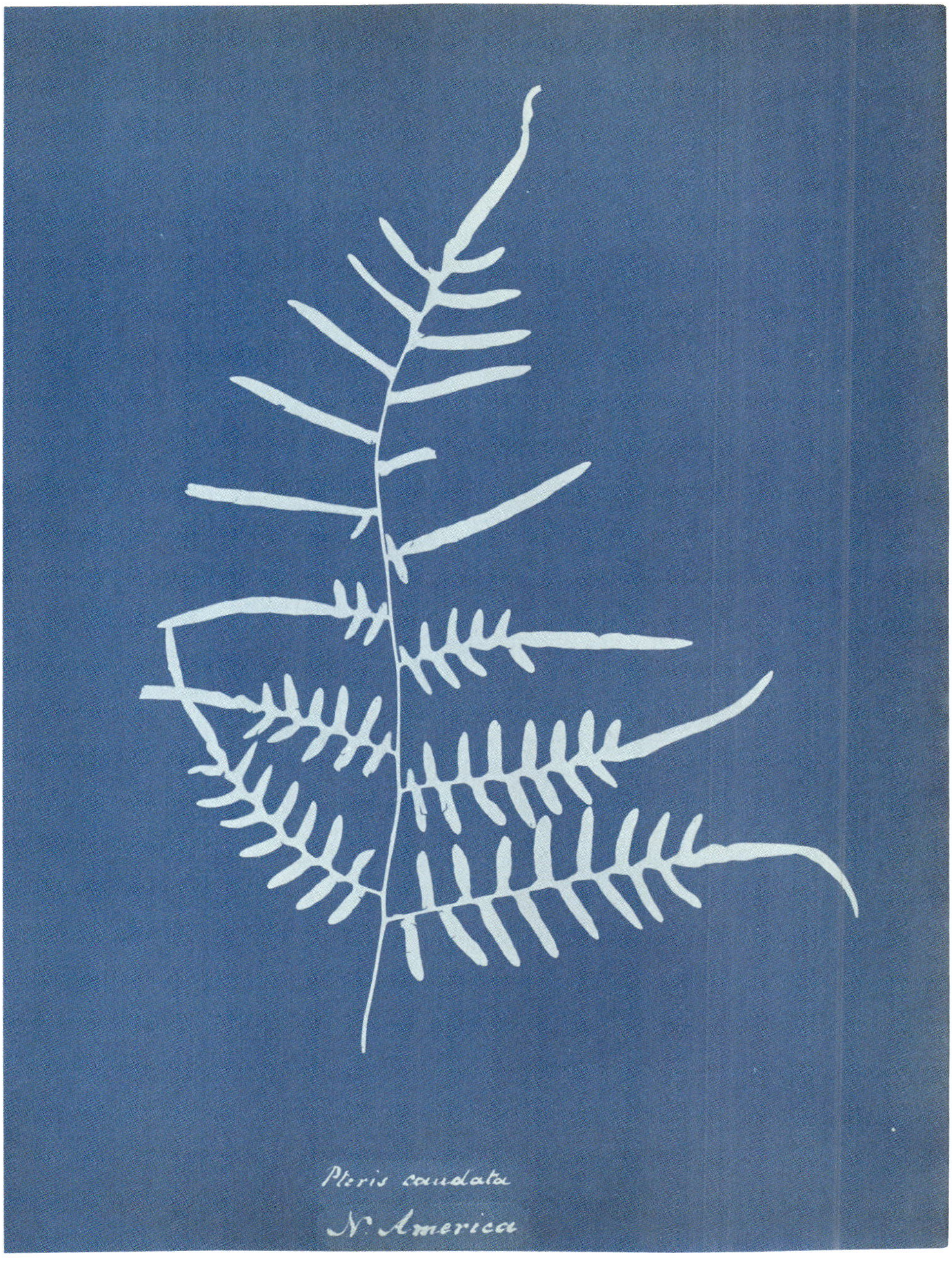

Plate 494. *Pteris caudata*, North America

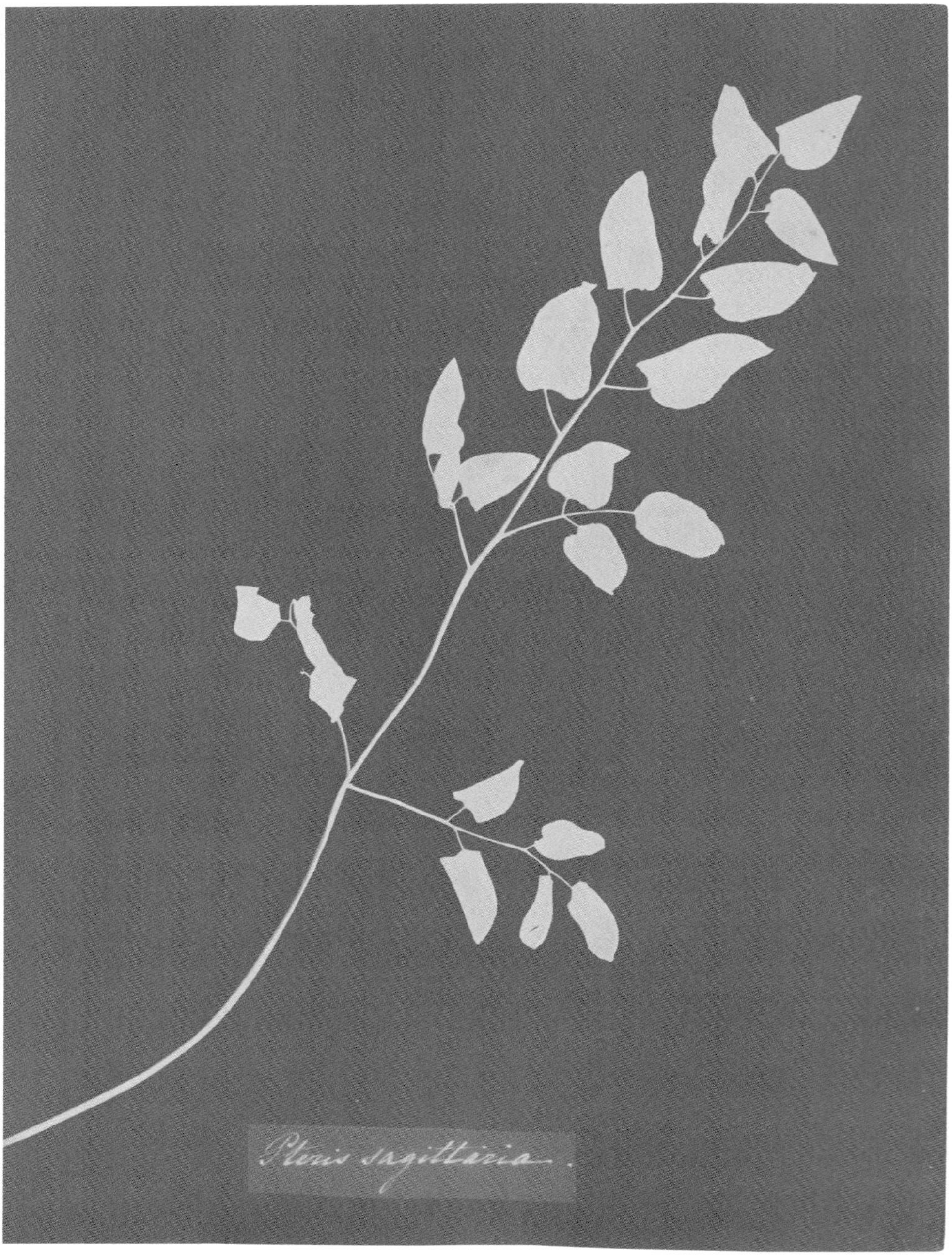

Plate 495. *Pteris sagittaria*

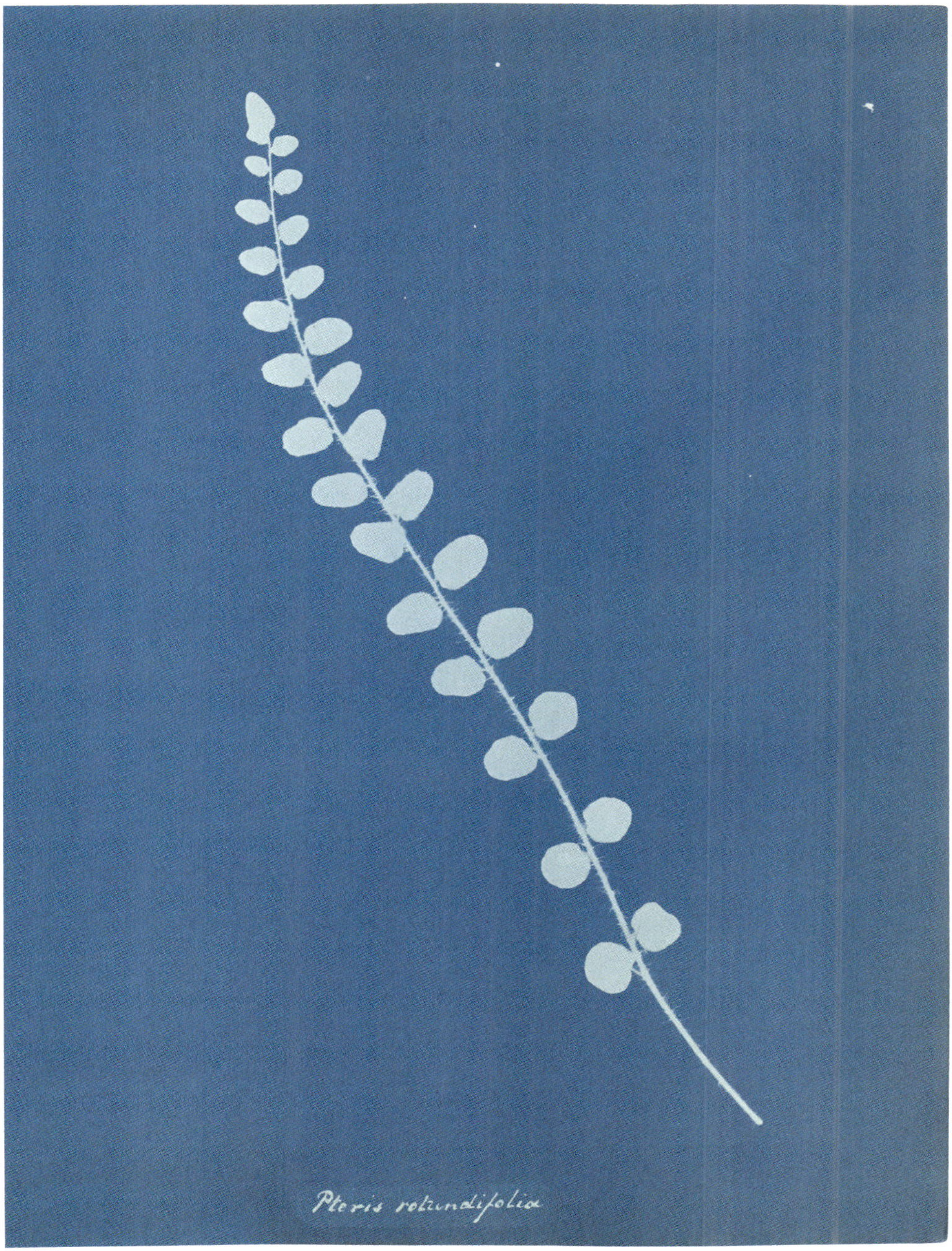

Plate 496. *Pteris rotundifolia*

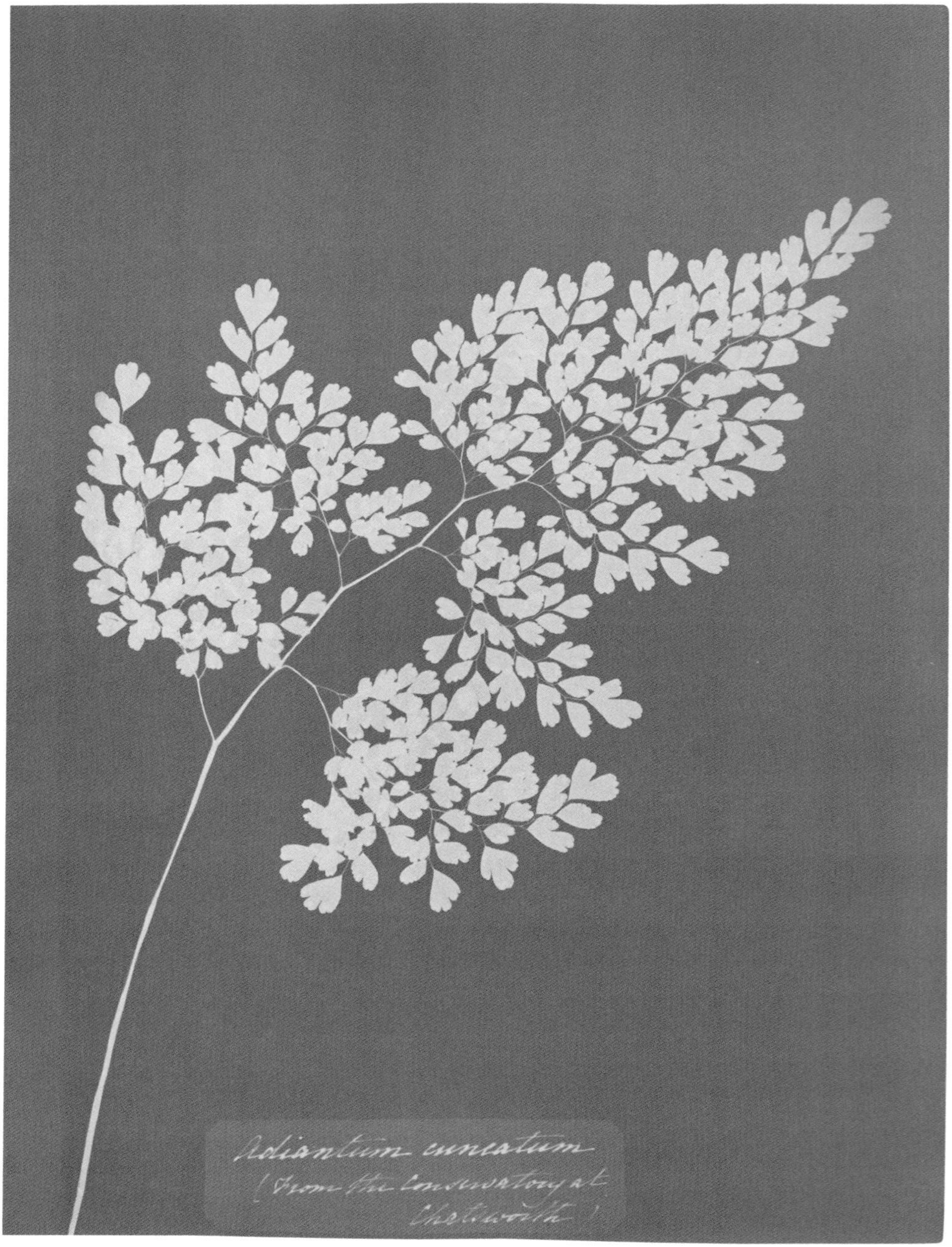

Plate 497. *Adiantum cuneatum* (From the Conservatory at Chatsworth)

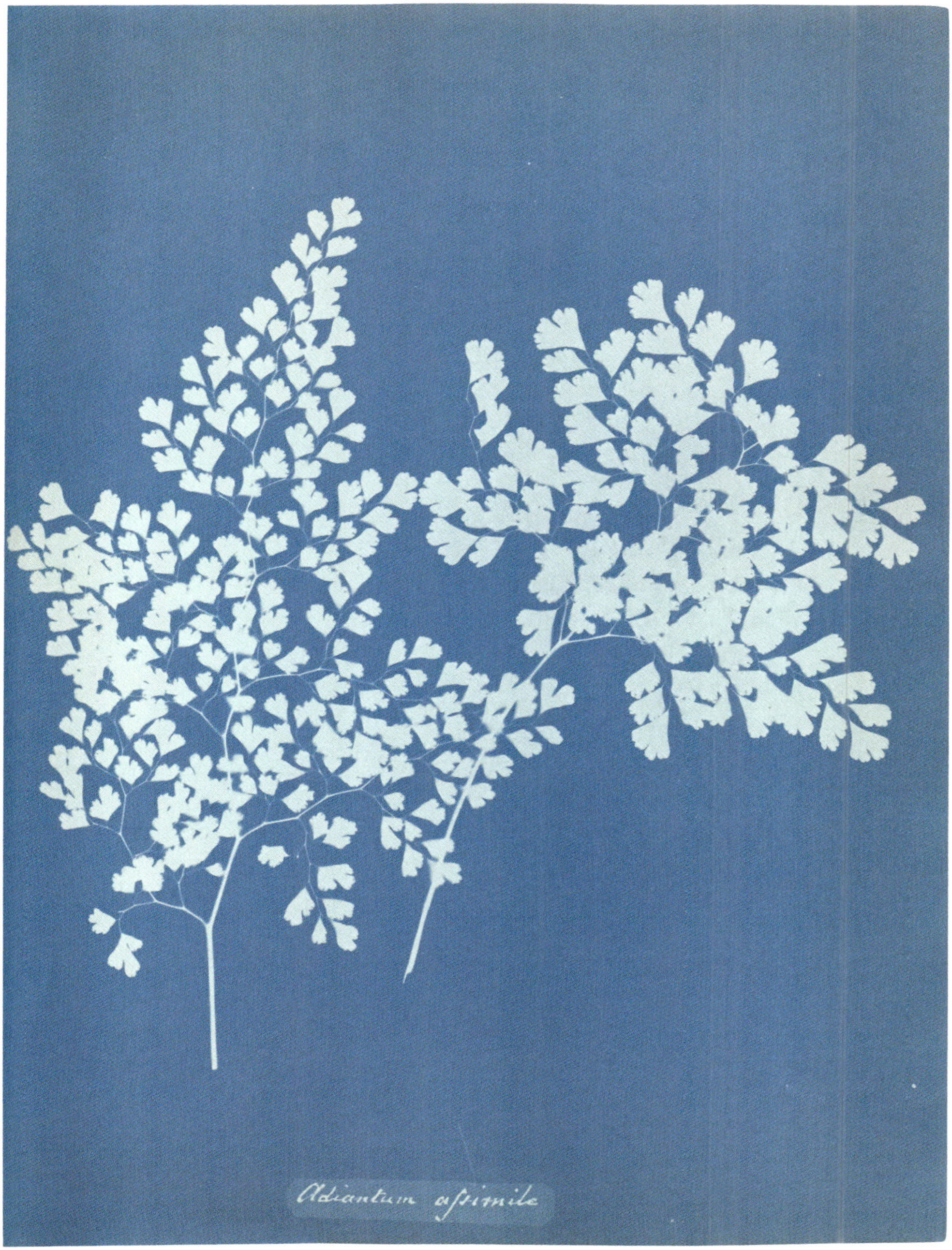

Plate 498. *Adiantum assimile*

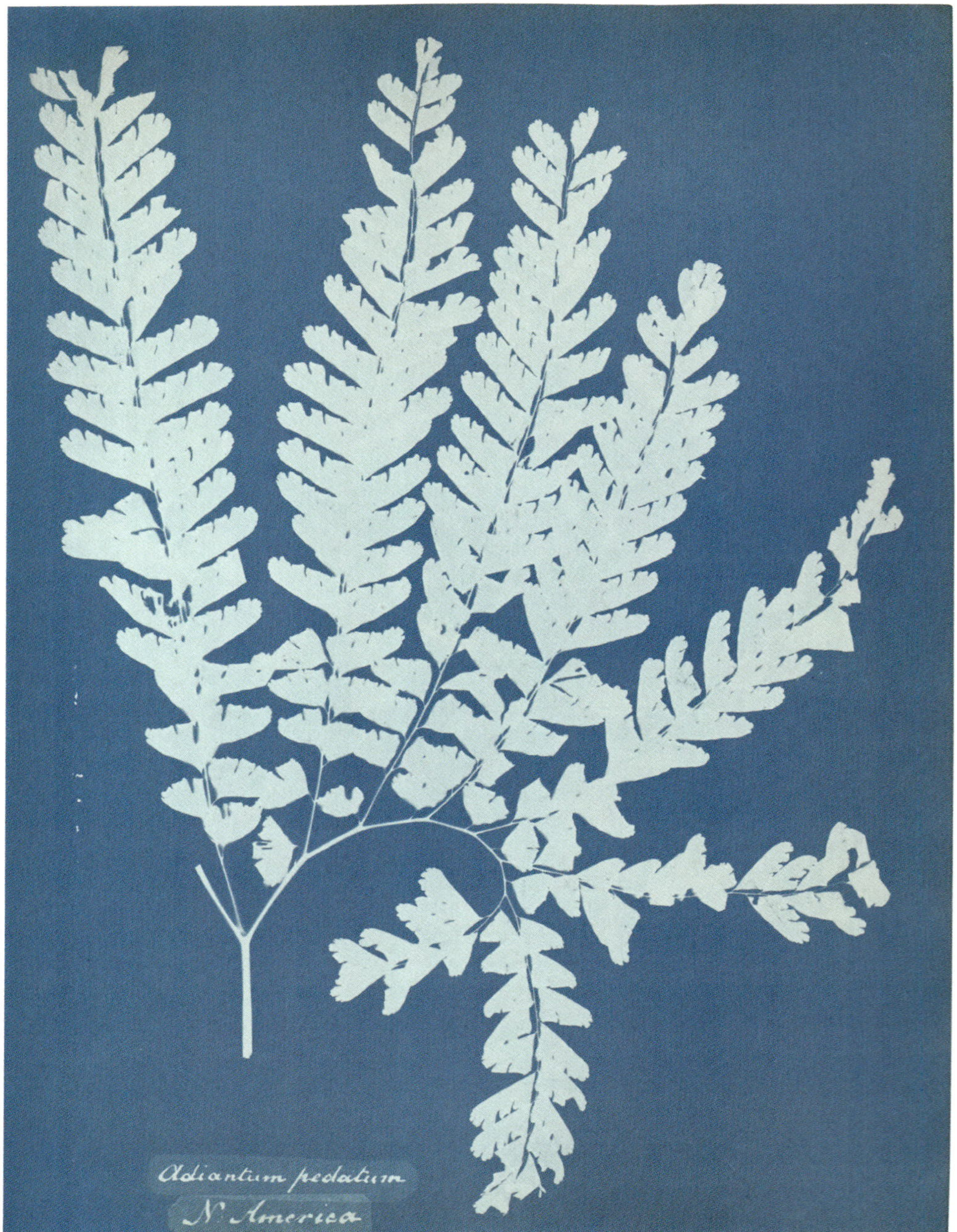

Plate 499. *Adiantum pedatum*, North America

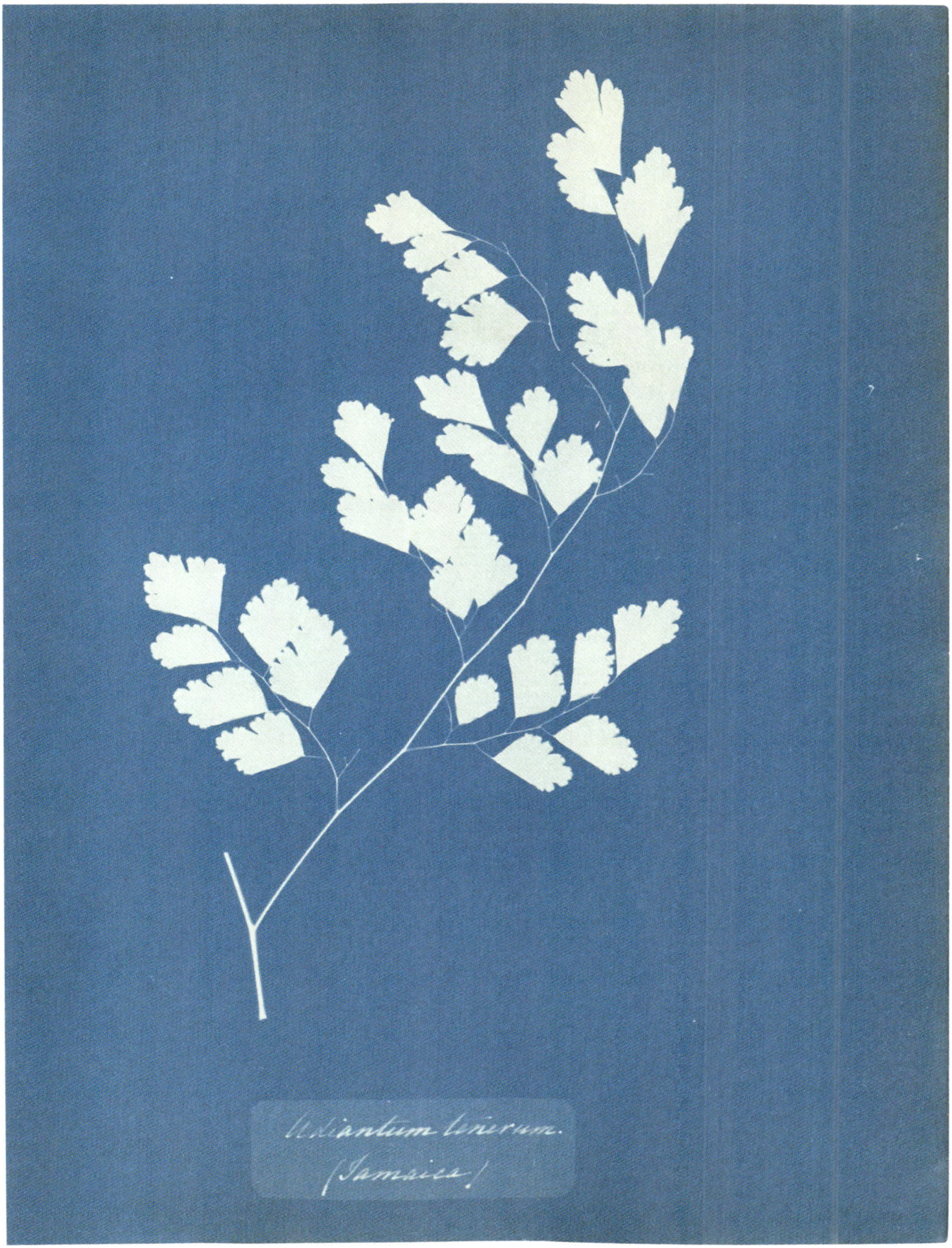

Plate 500. *Adiantum tenerum*, Jamaica

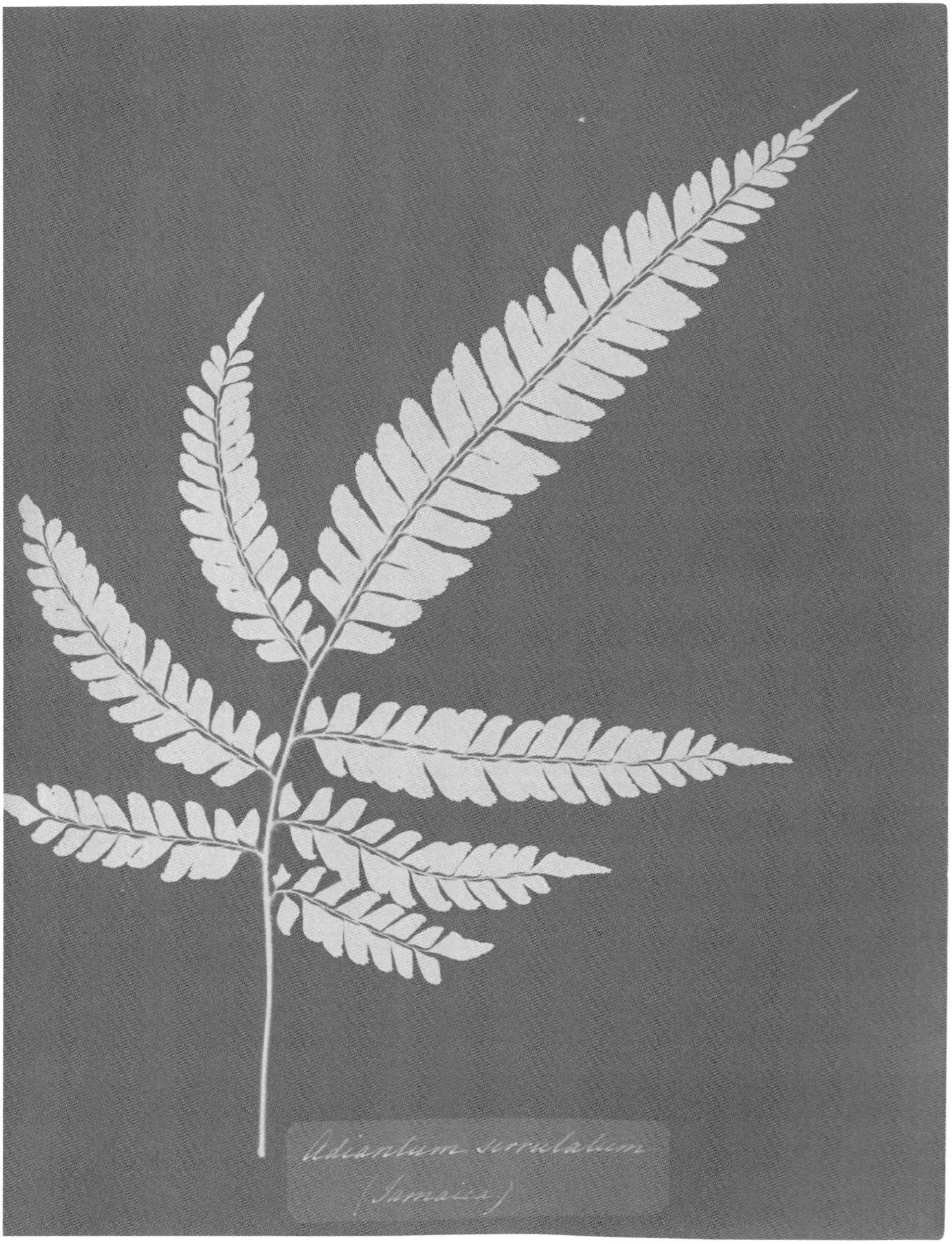

Plate 501. *Adiantum serrulatum* (Jamaica)

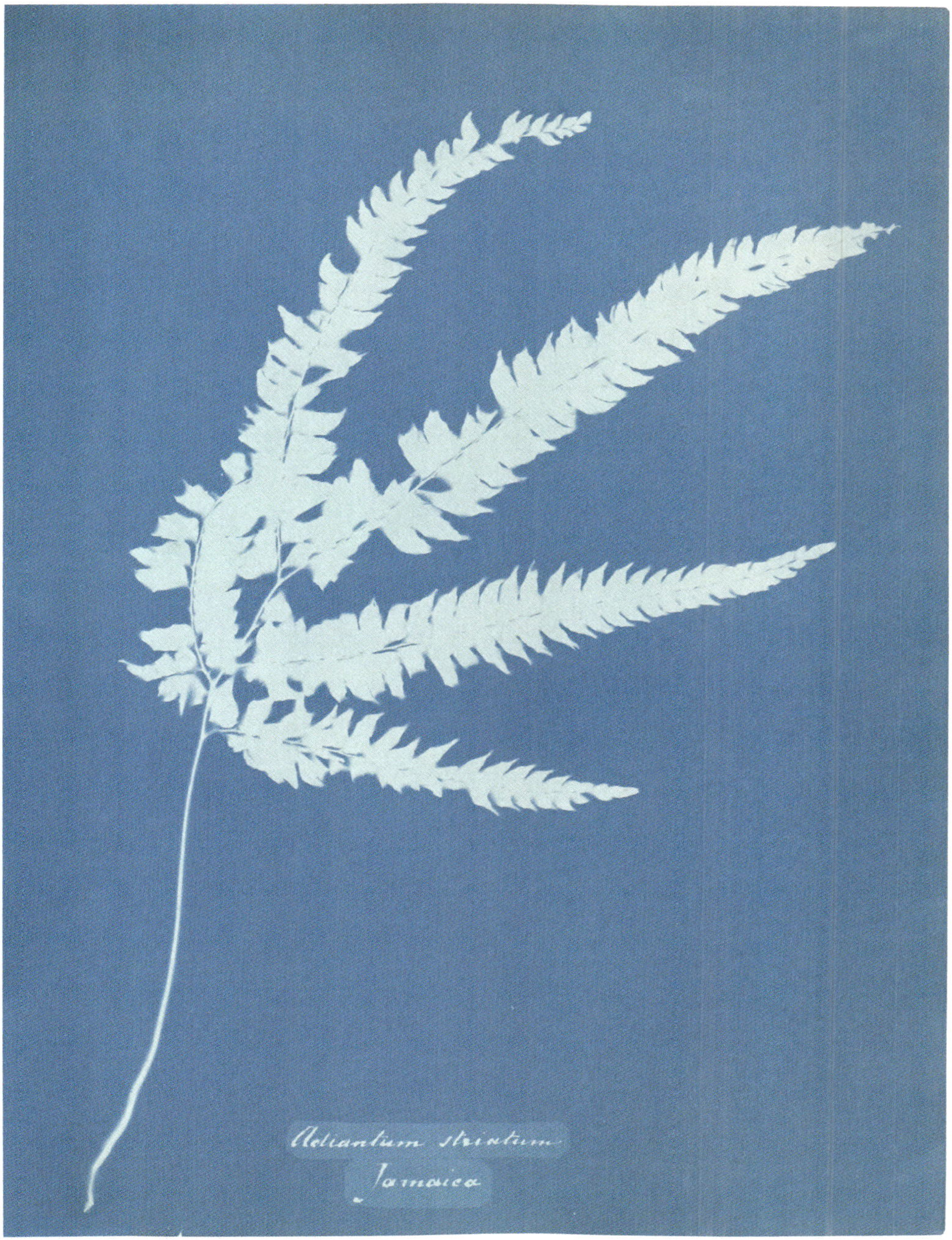

Plate 502. *Adiantum striatum*, Jamaica

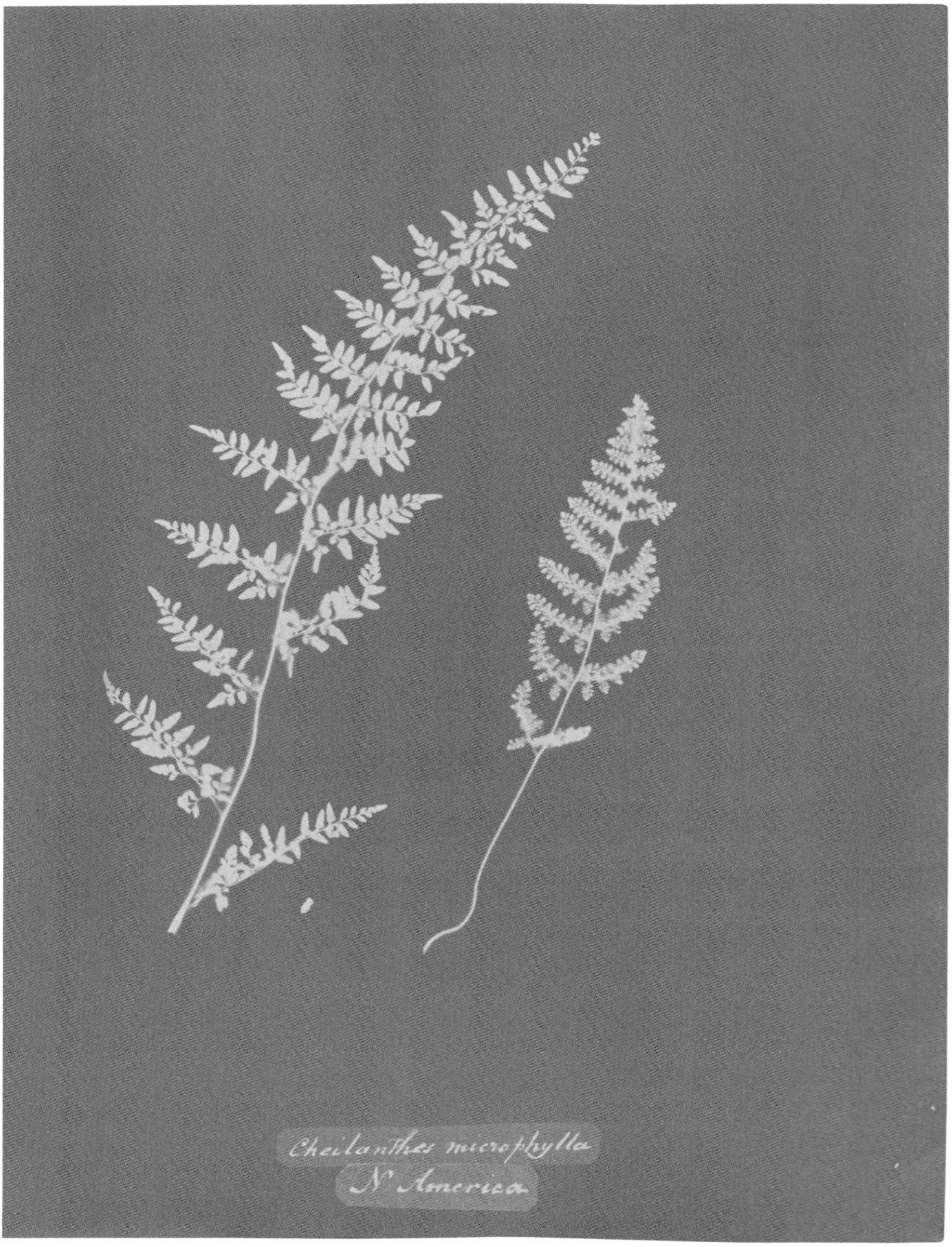

Plate 503. *Cheilanthes microphylla*, North America

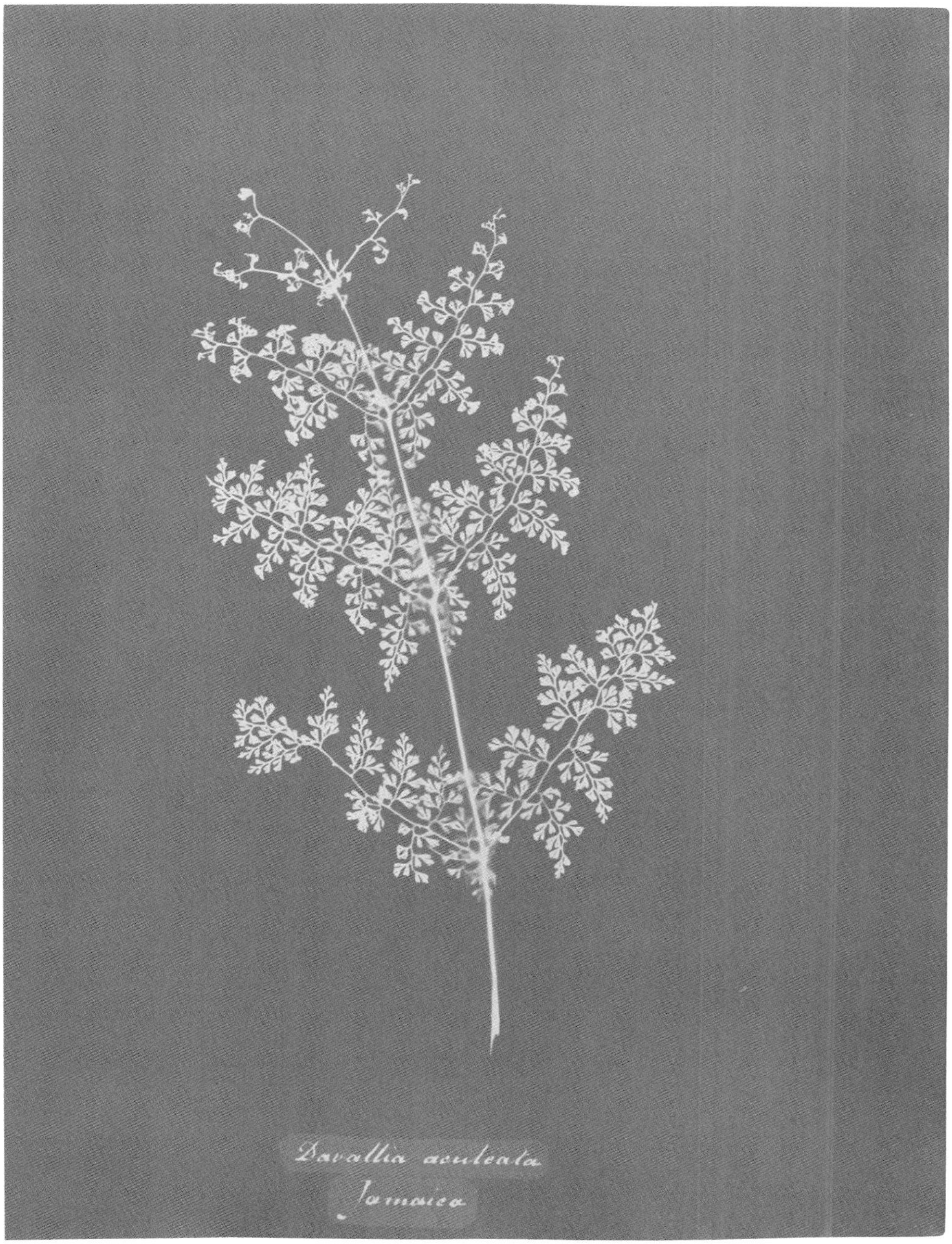

Plate 504. *Davallia aeuleata*, Jamaica

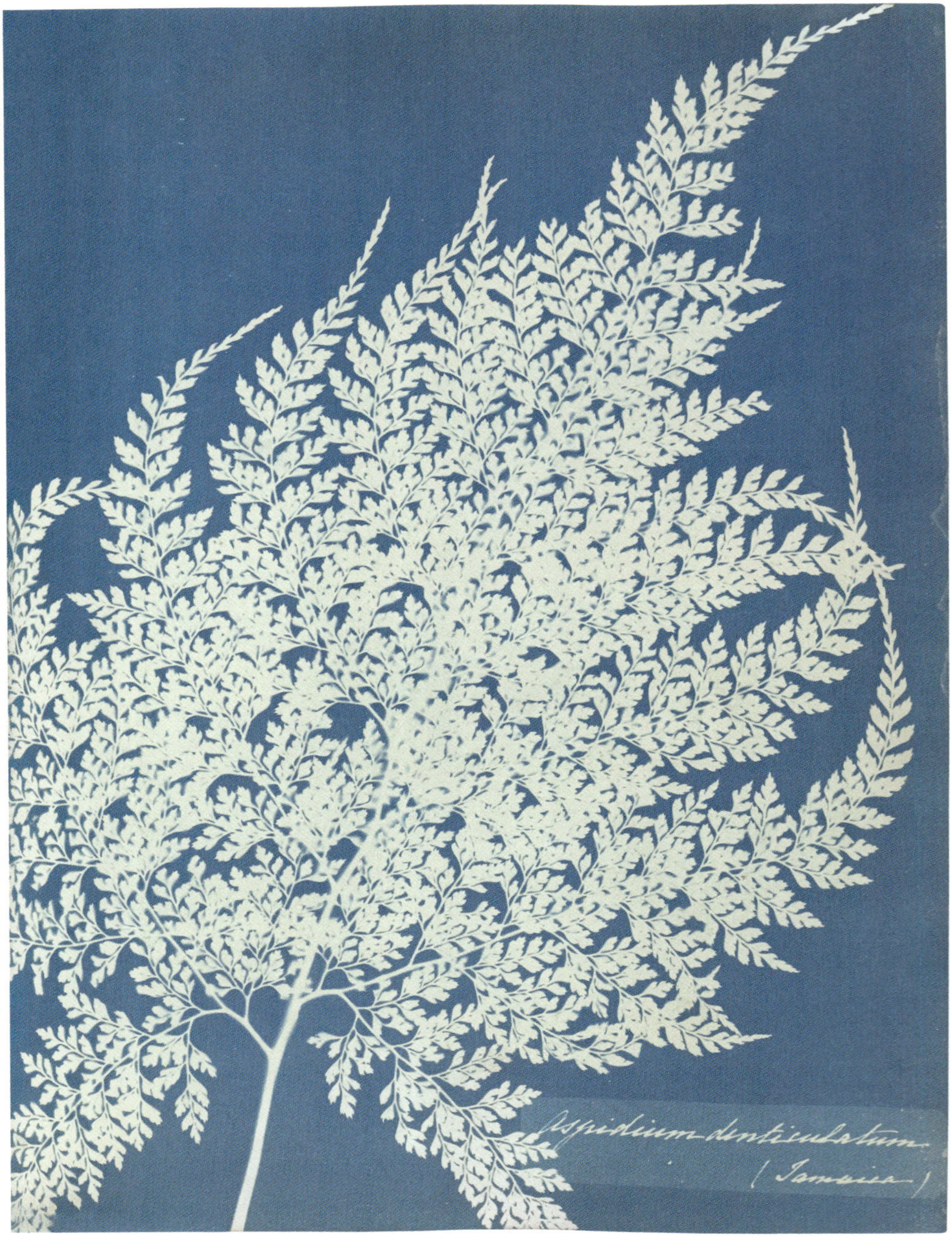

Plate 505. *Aspidium denticulatum* (Jamaica)

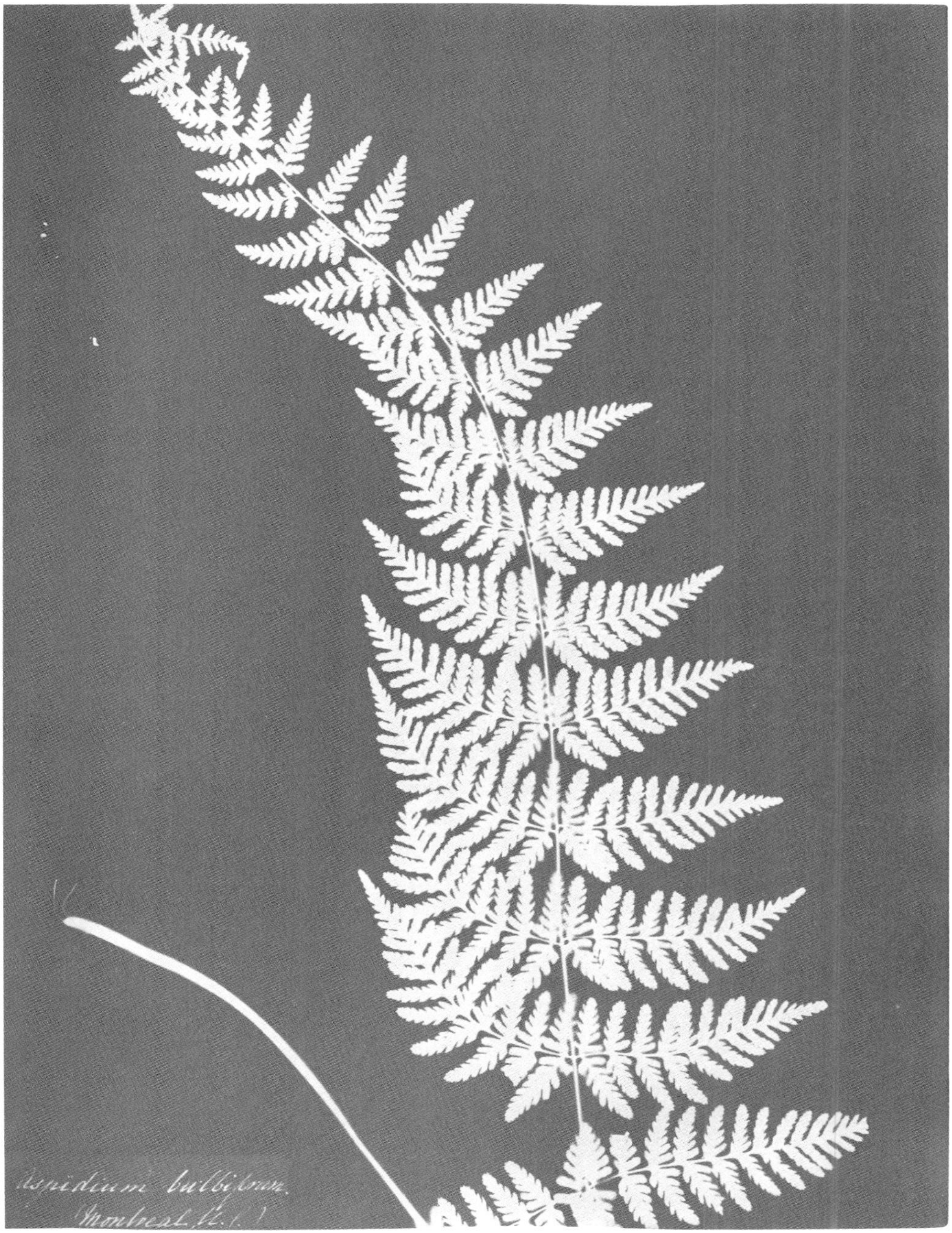

Plate 506. *Aspidium bulbiferum* (Montreal)

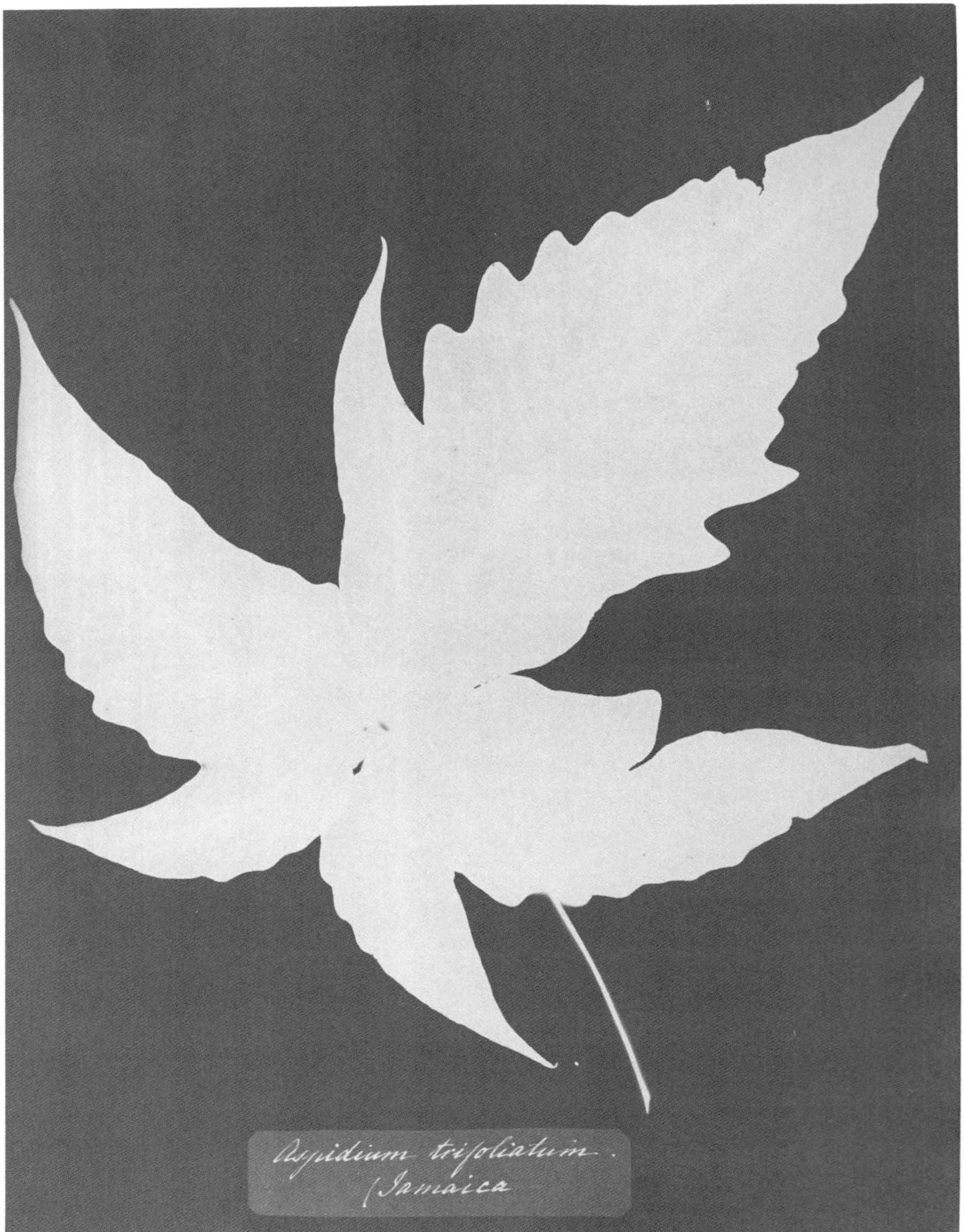

Plate 507. *Aspidium trifoliatum* (Jamaica)

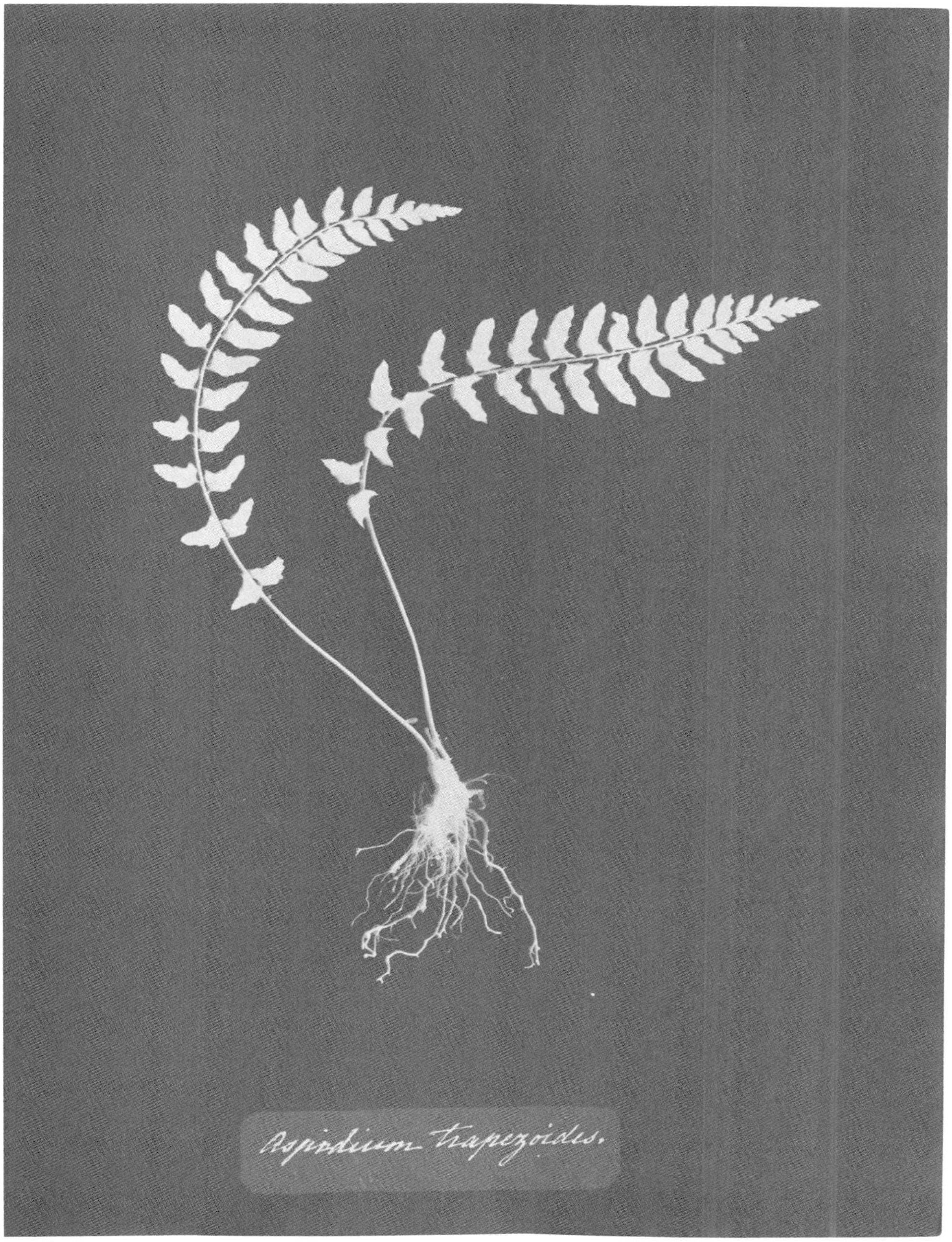

Plate 508. *Aspidium trapezoides*

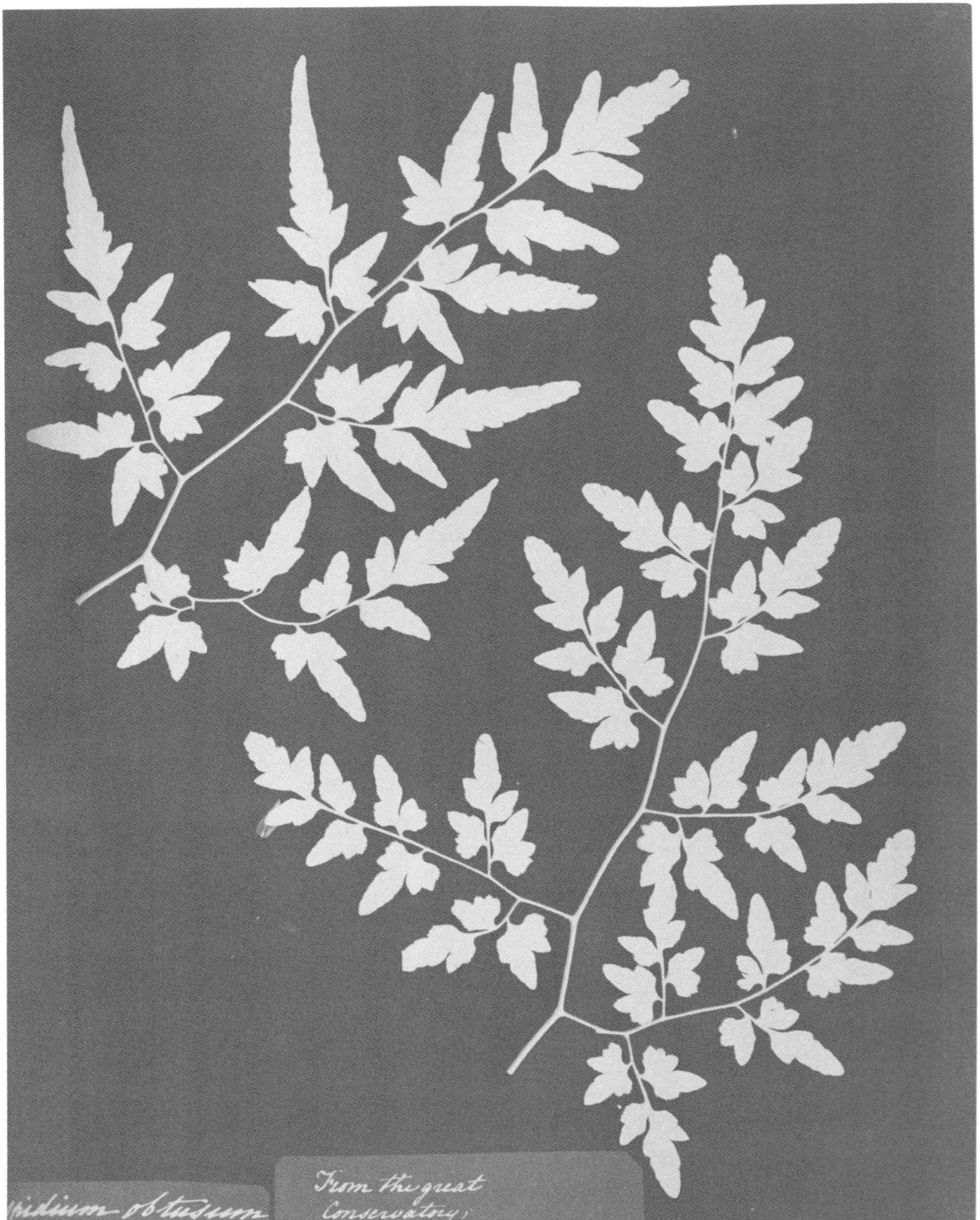

Plate 509. *Aspidium obtusium*. From the great Conservatory, Chatsworth, Aug. 26th 1851

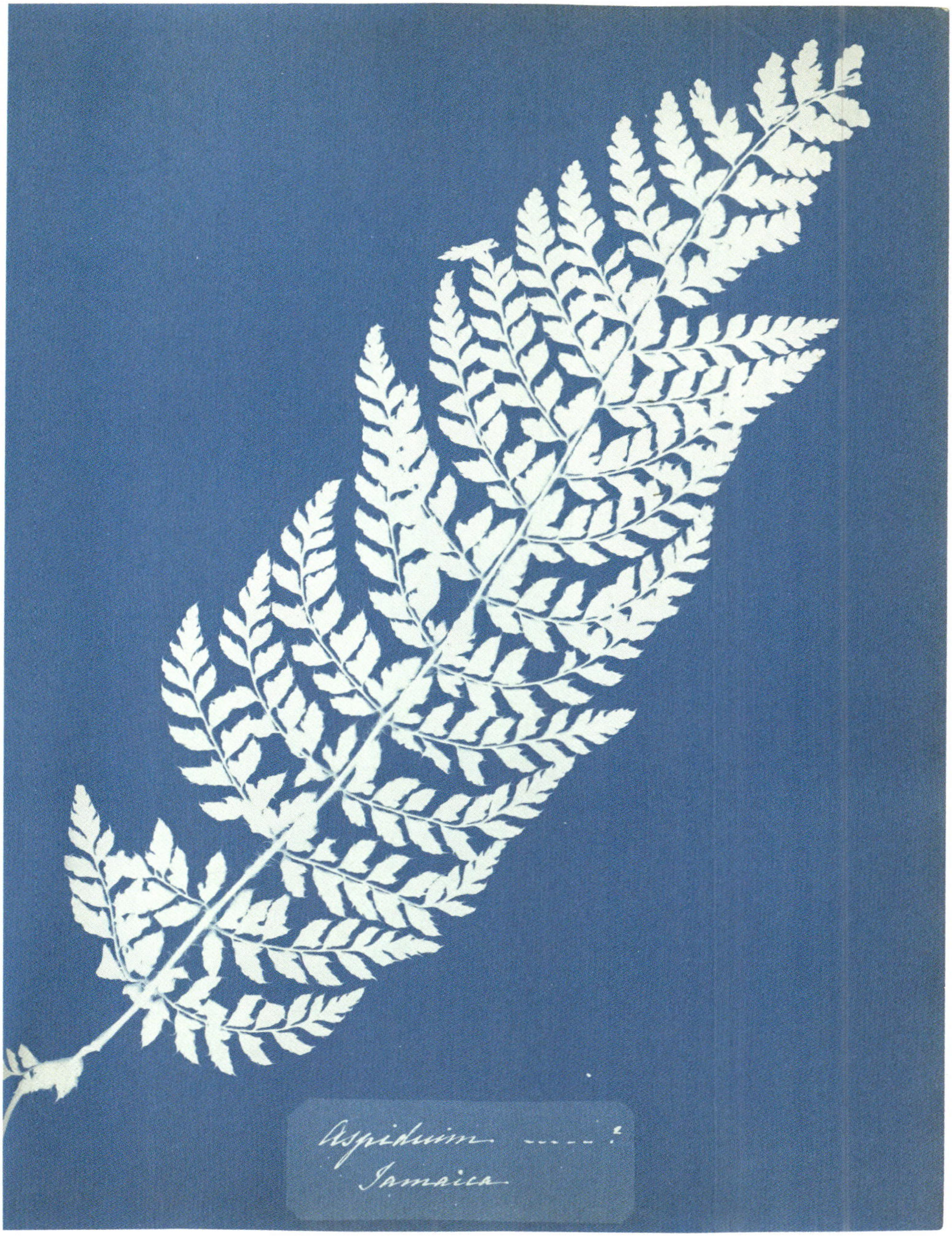

Plate 510. *Aspidium ... ?*, Jamaica

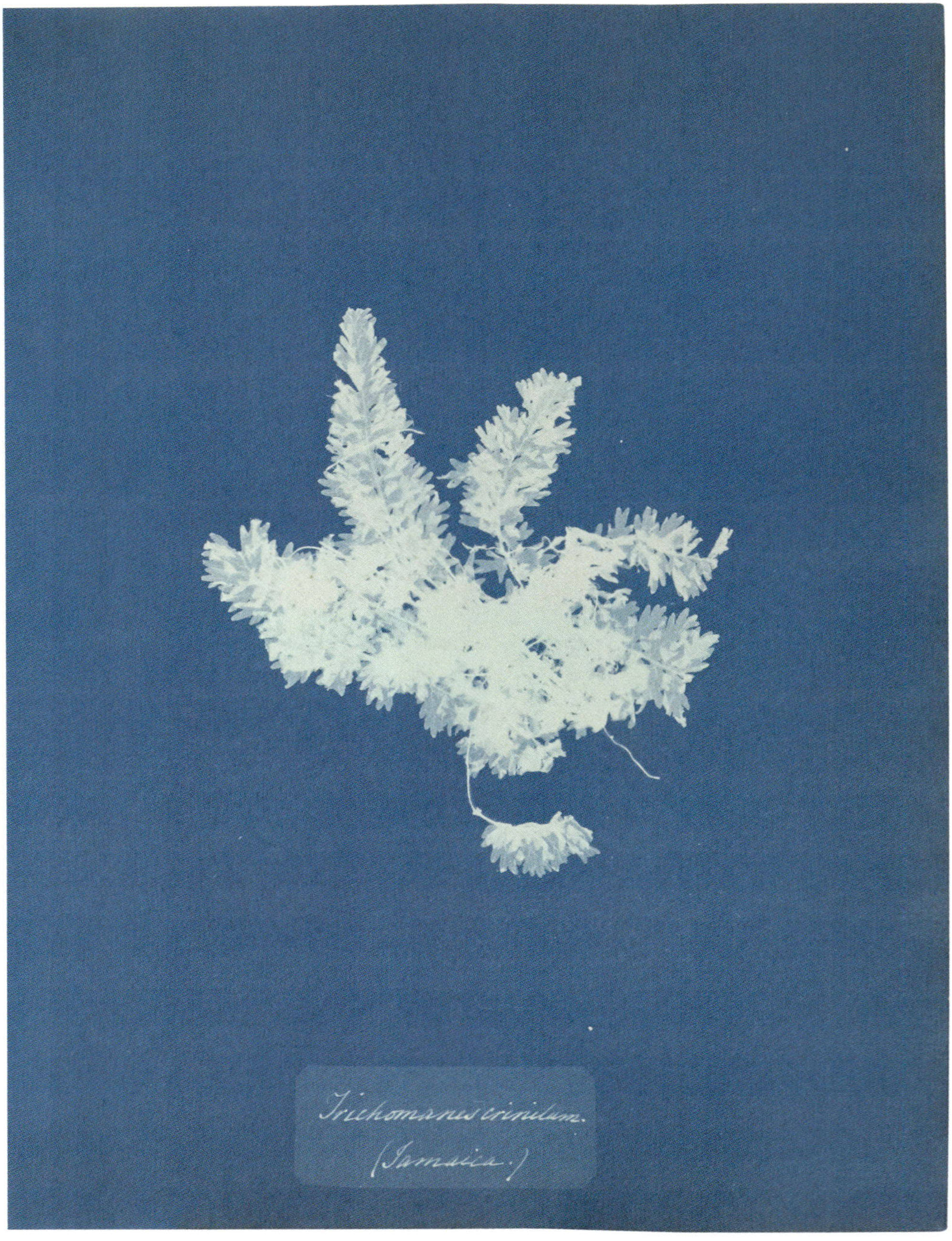

Plate 511. *Trichomanes crinitum* (Jamaica)

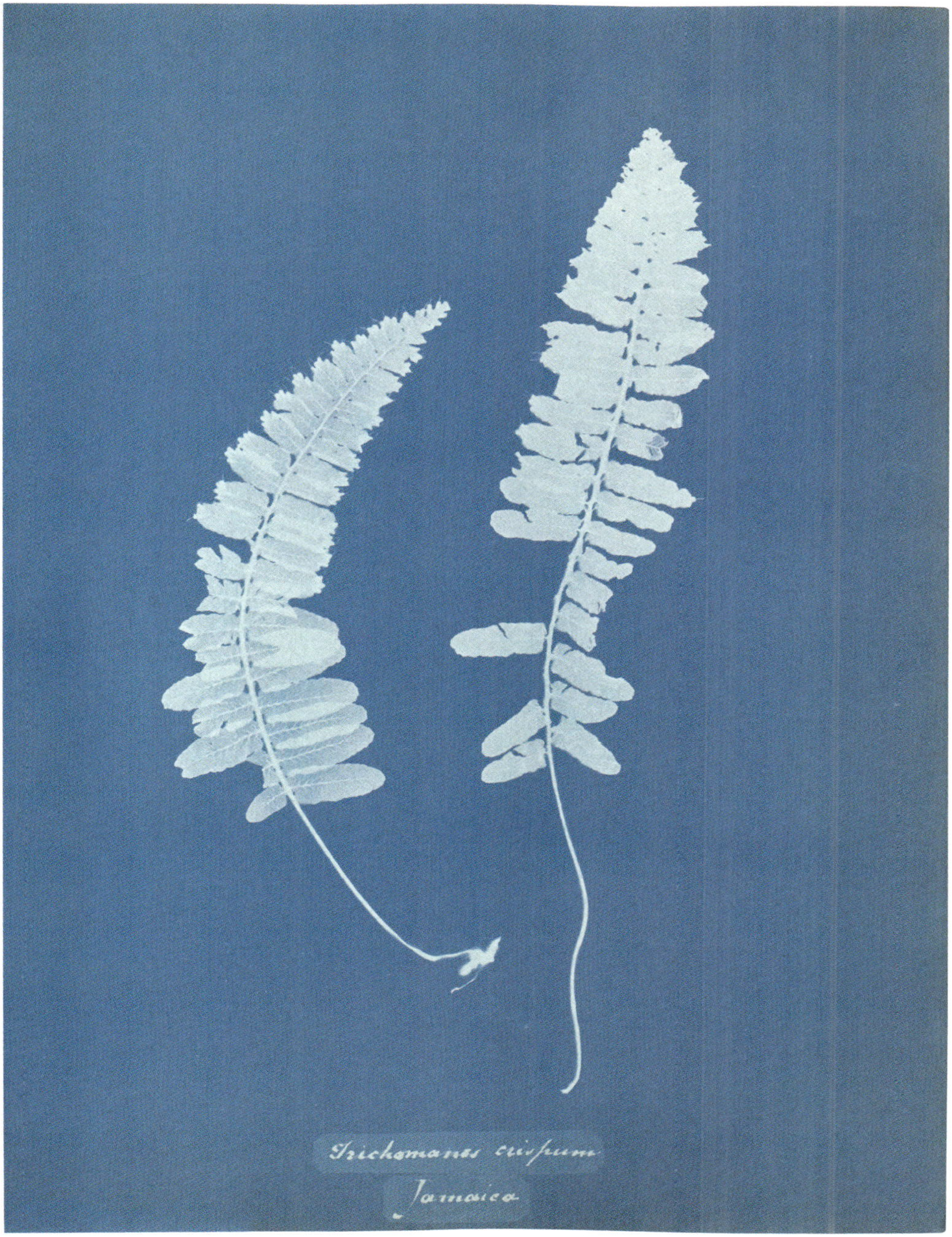

Plate 512. *Trichomanes crispum*, Jamaica

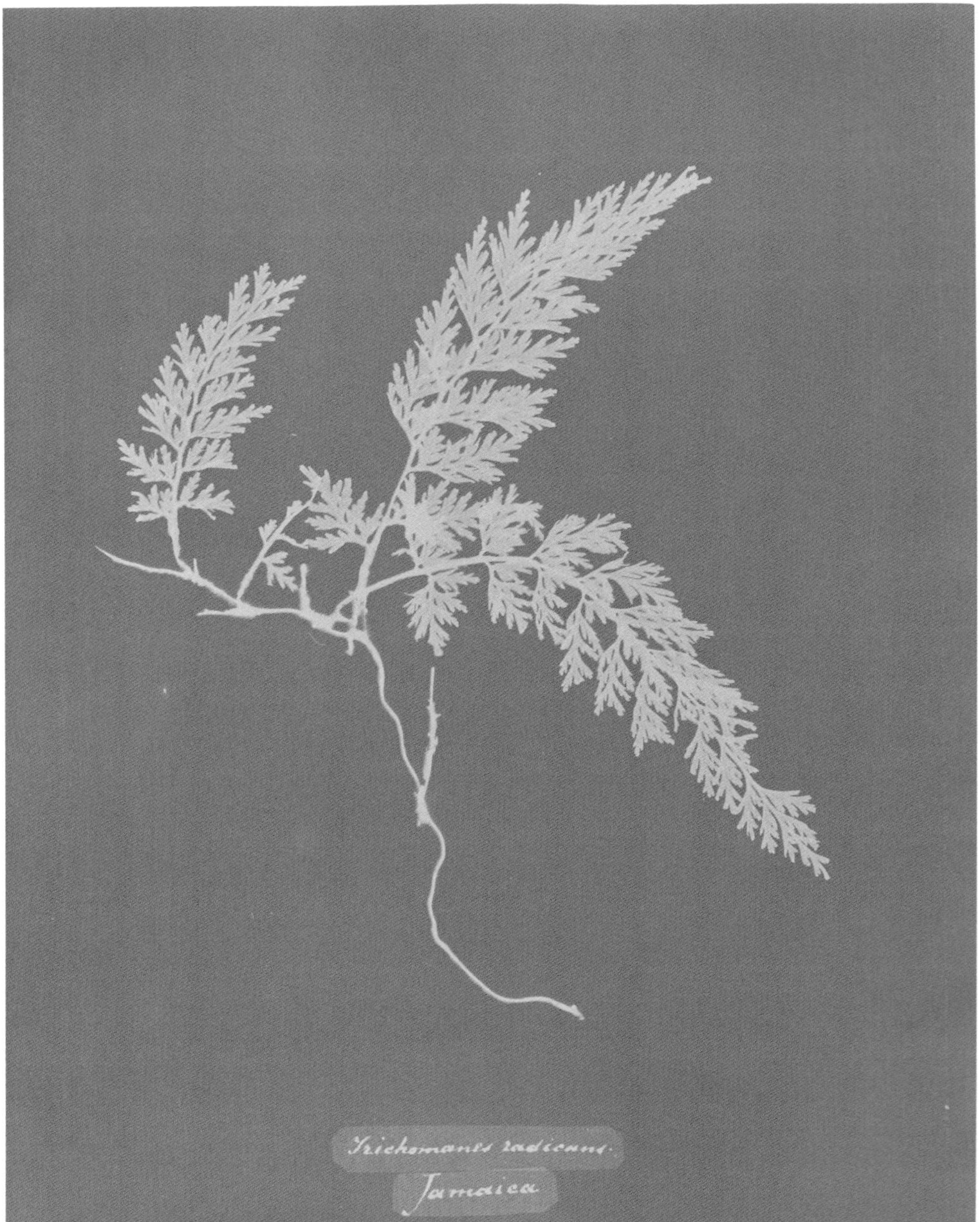

Plate 513. *Trichomanes radicans*, Jamaica

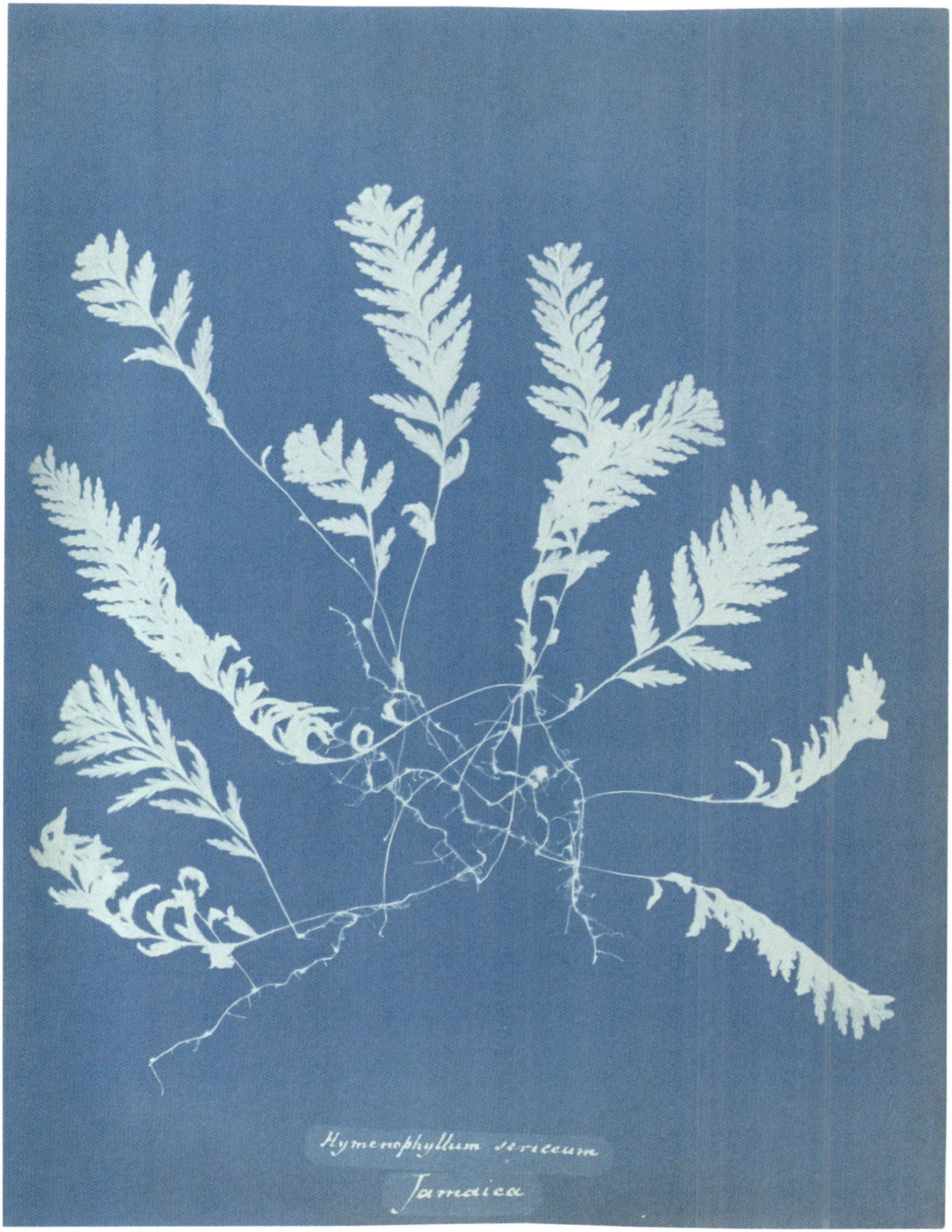

Plate 514. *Hymenophyllum sericeum*, Jamaica

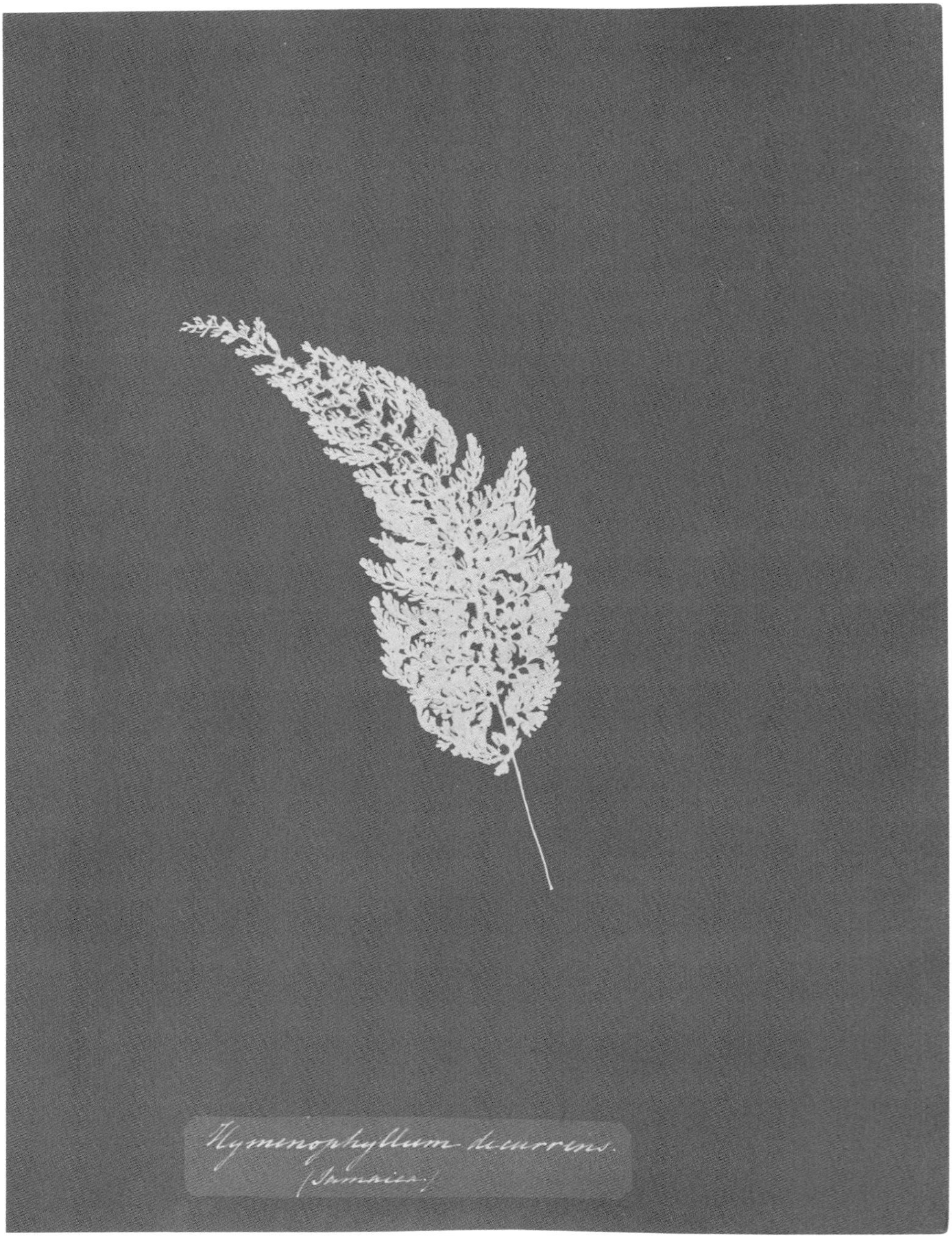

Plate 515. *Hymenophyllum decurrens* (Jamaica)

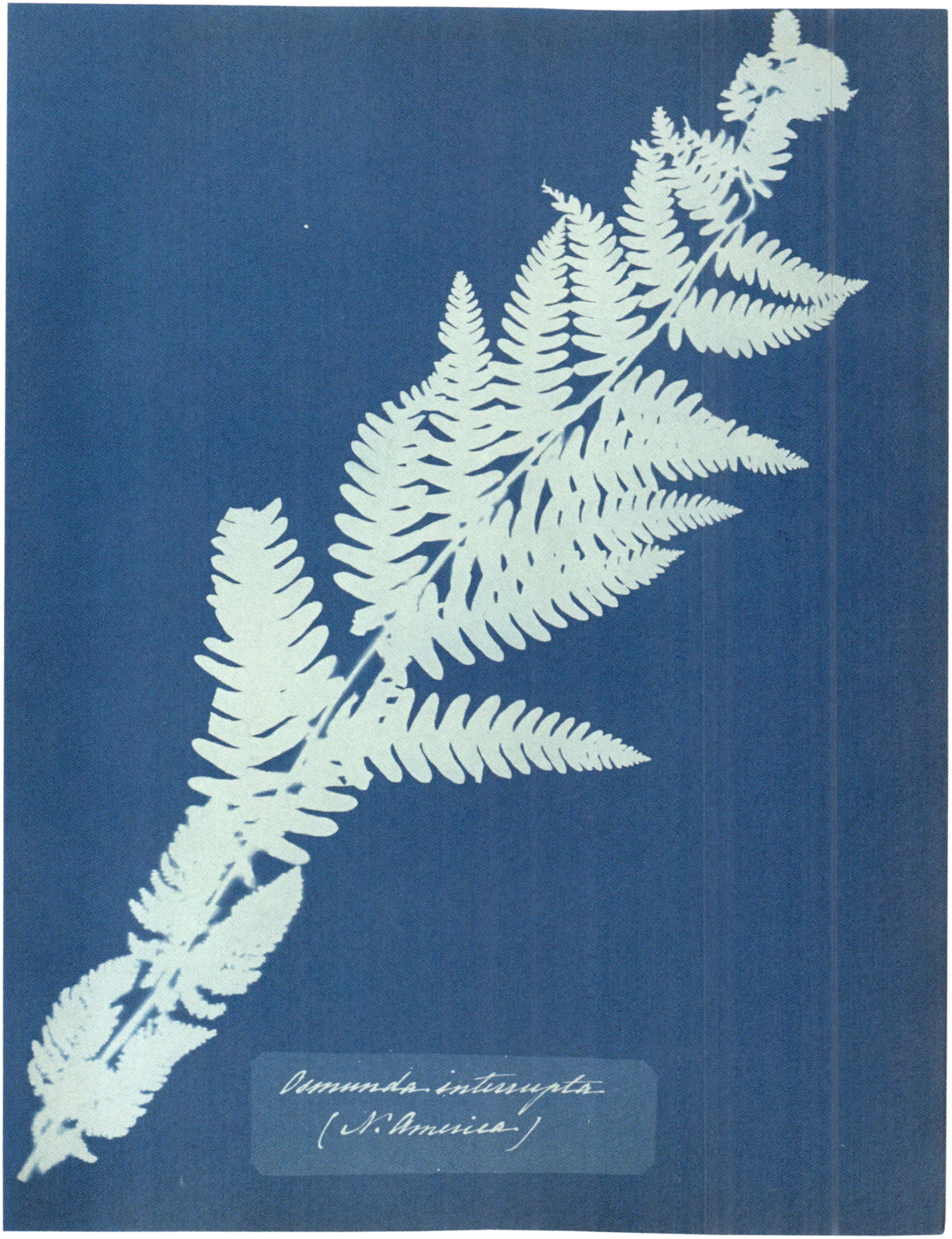

Plate 516. *Osmunda interrupta* (North America)

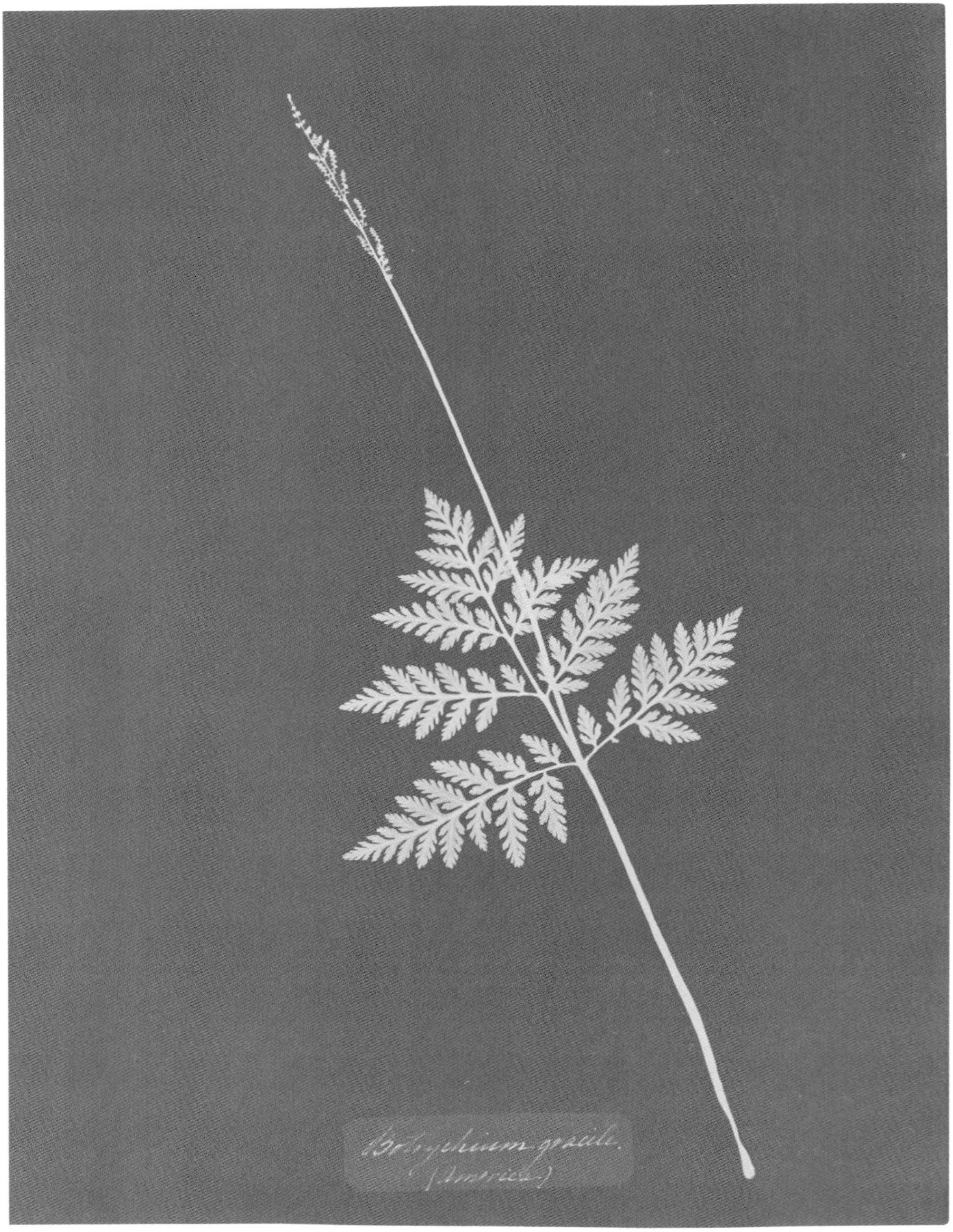

Plate 519. *Botrychium gracile* (America)

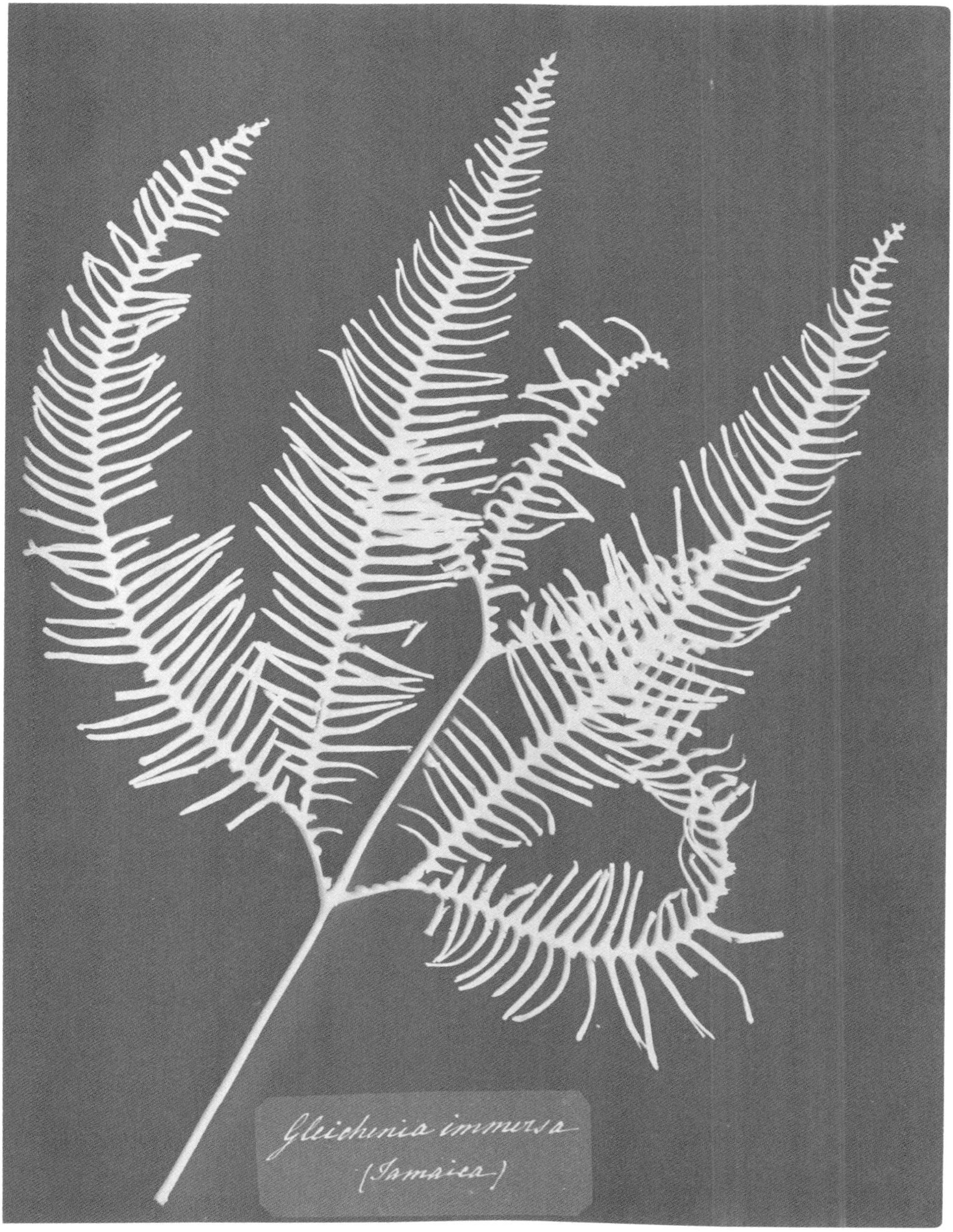

Plate 520. *Gleichenia immersa* (Jamaica)

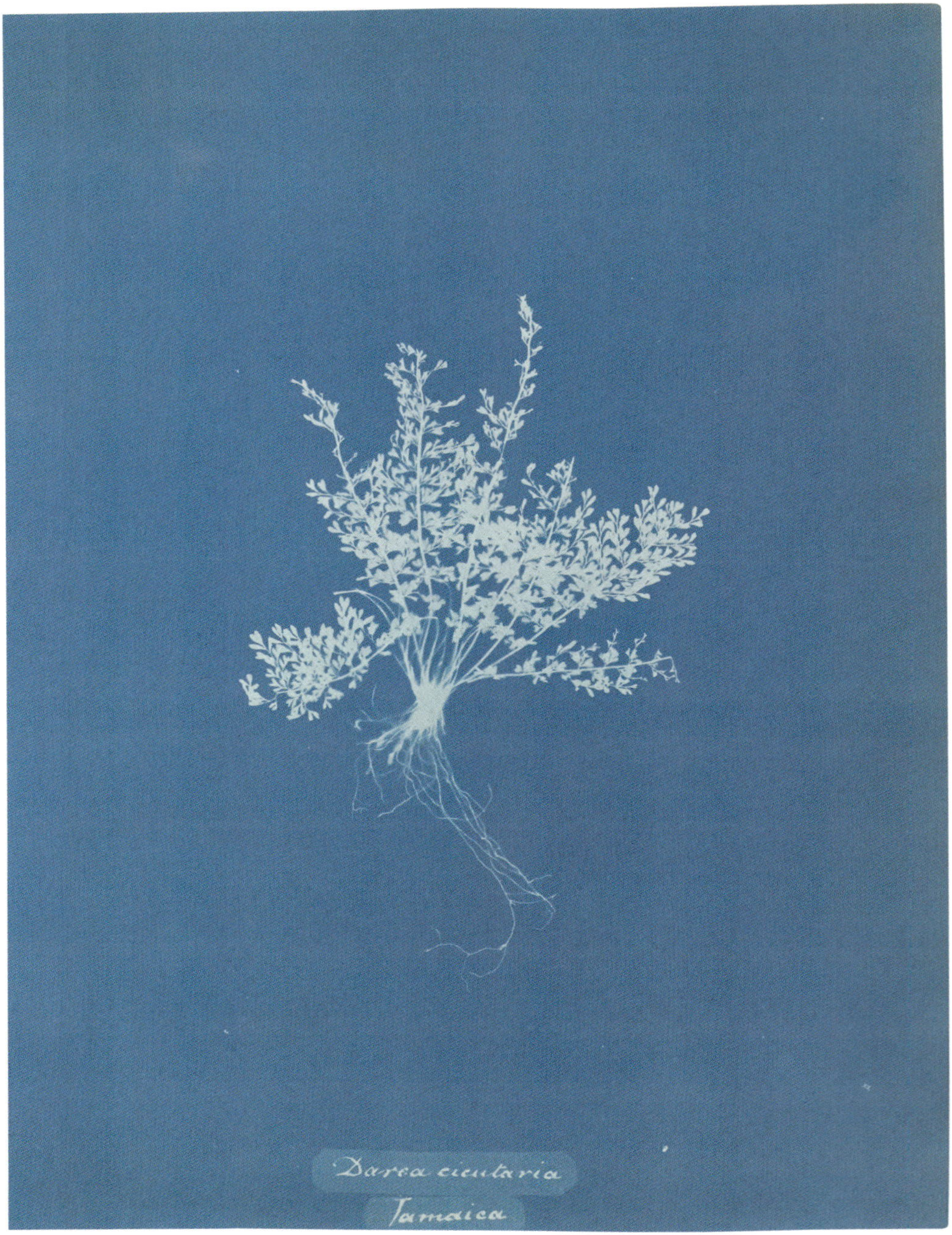

Plate 521. *Darea cicutaria*, Jamaica

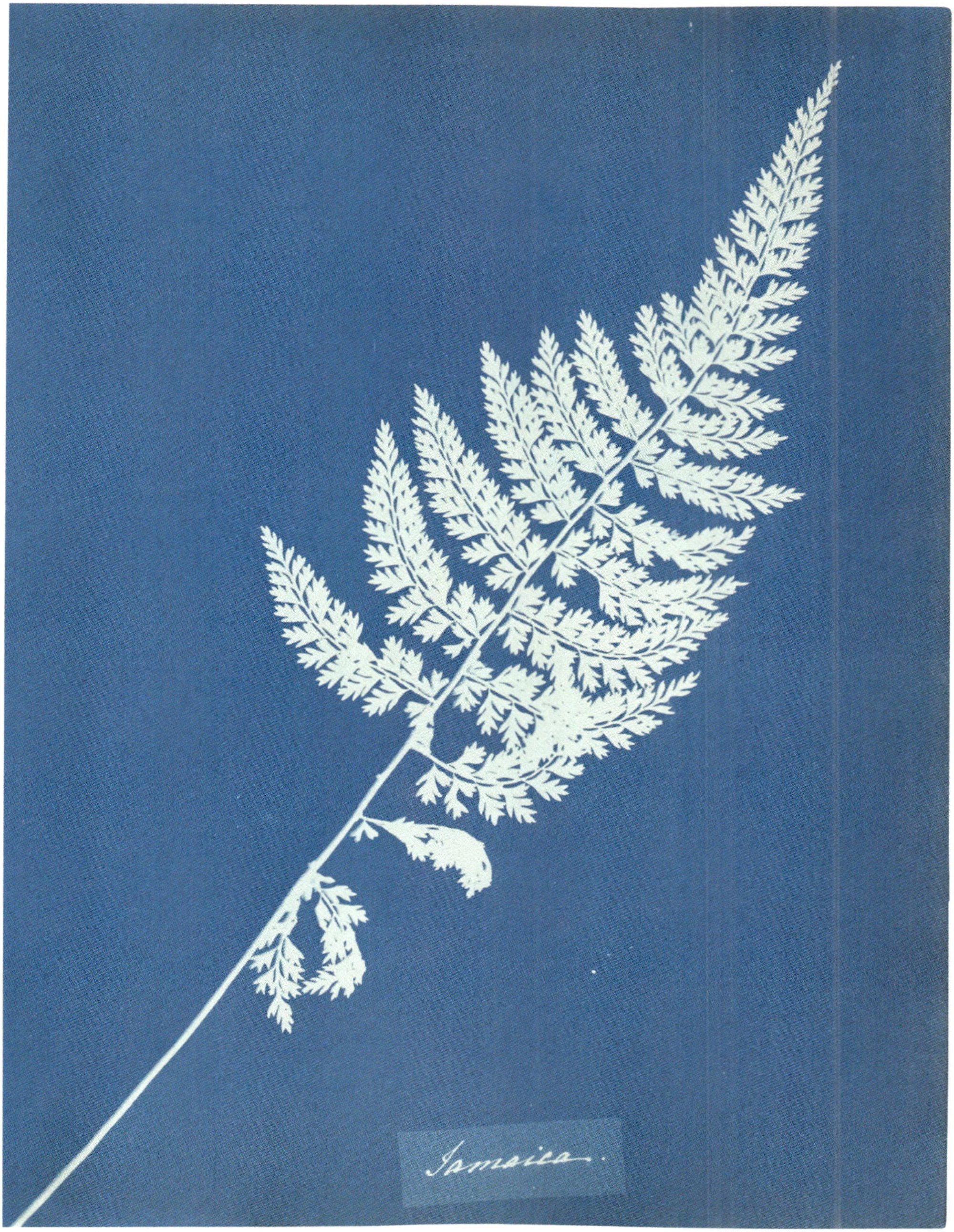

Plate 522. Jamaica

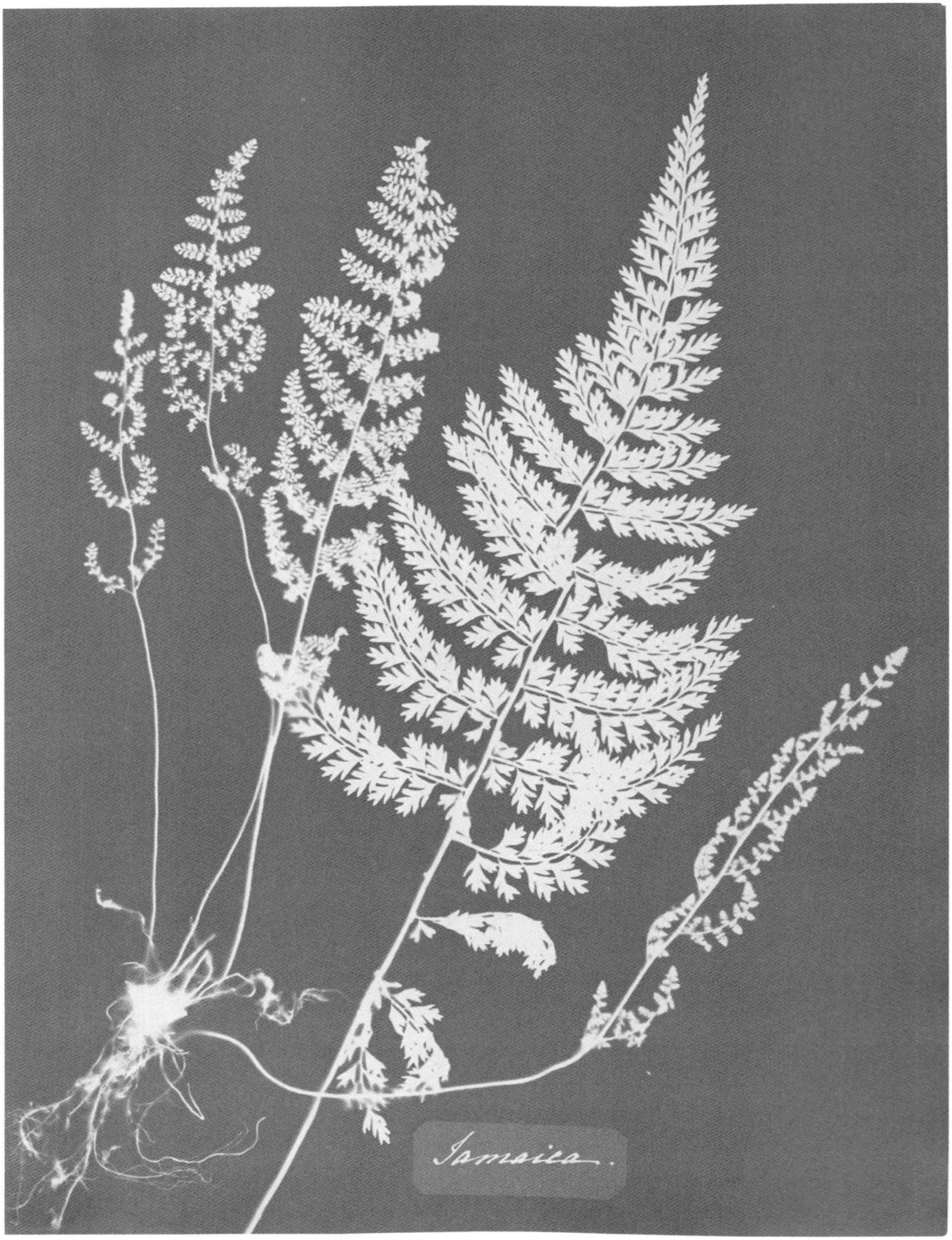

Plate 523. Jamaica

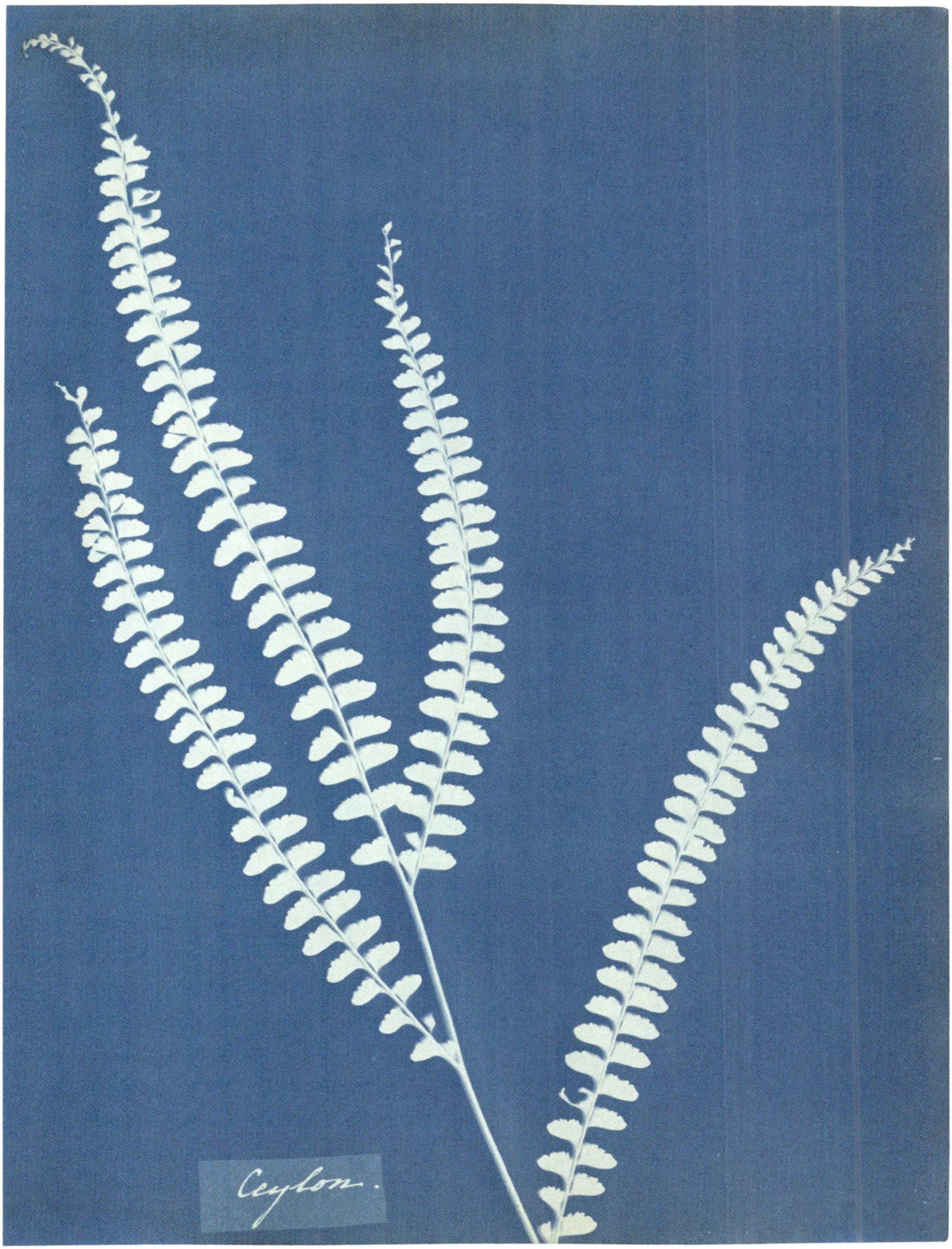

Plate 524. Ceylon

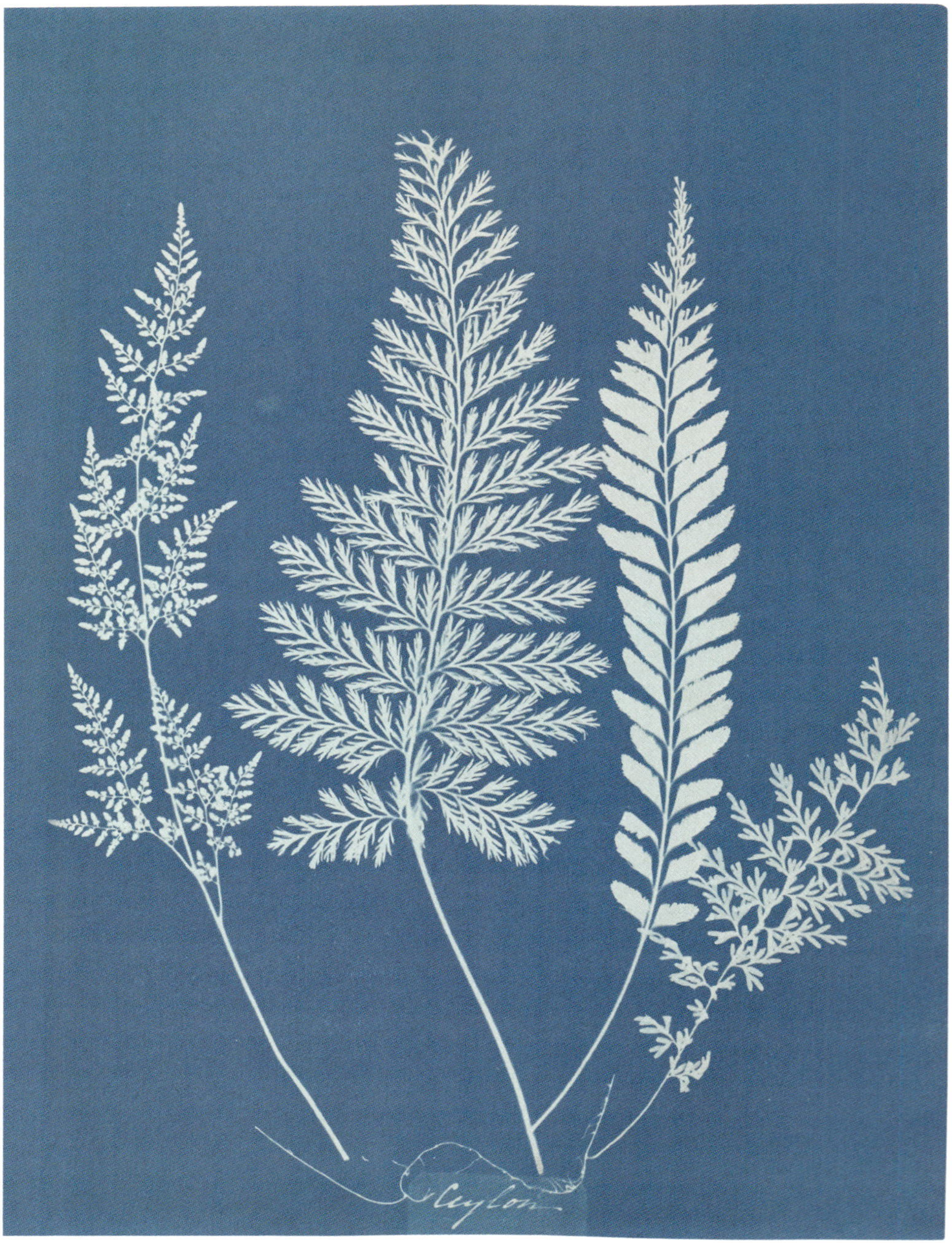

Plate 525. Ceylon

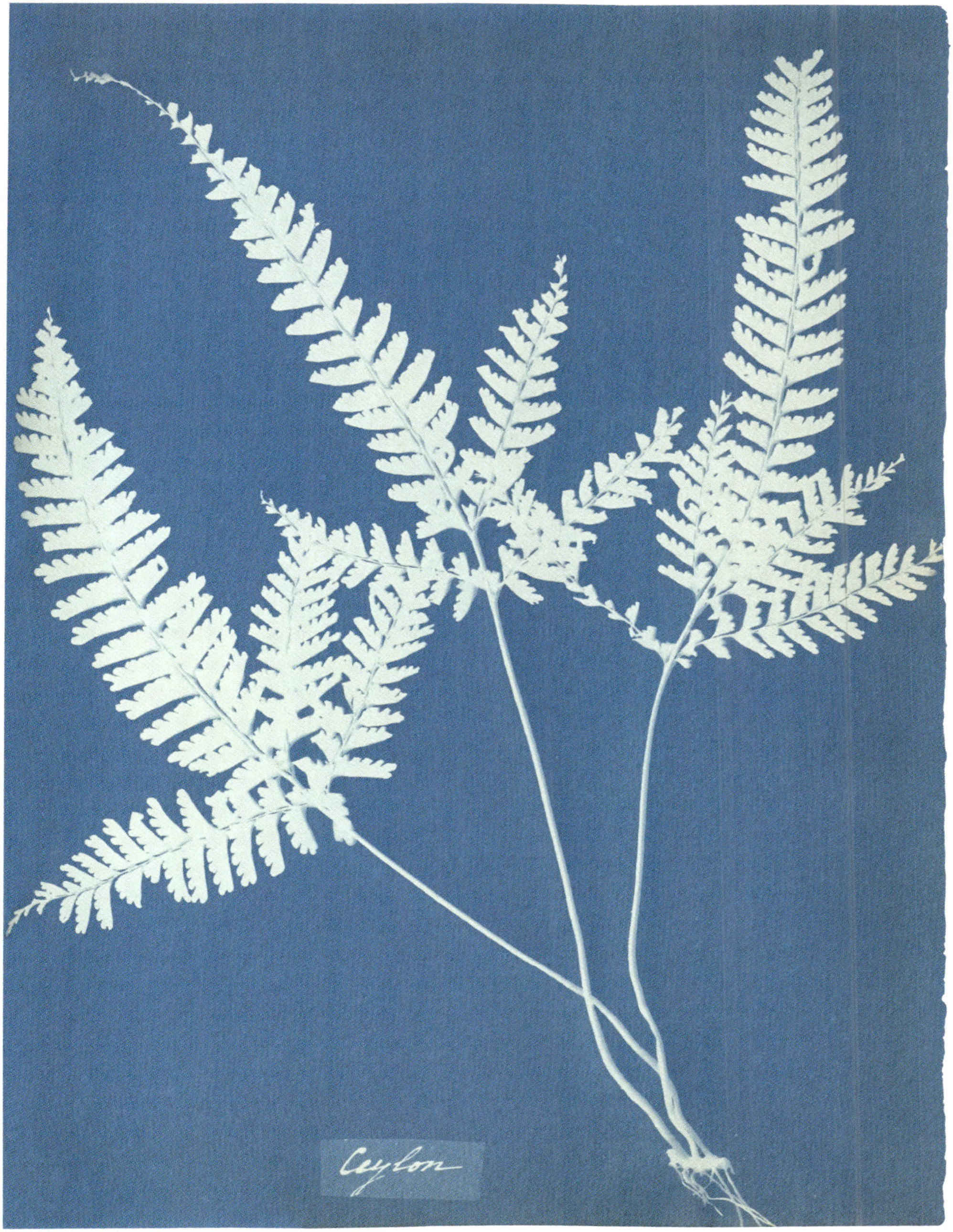

Plate 526. Ceylon

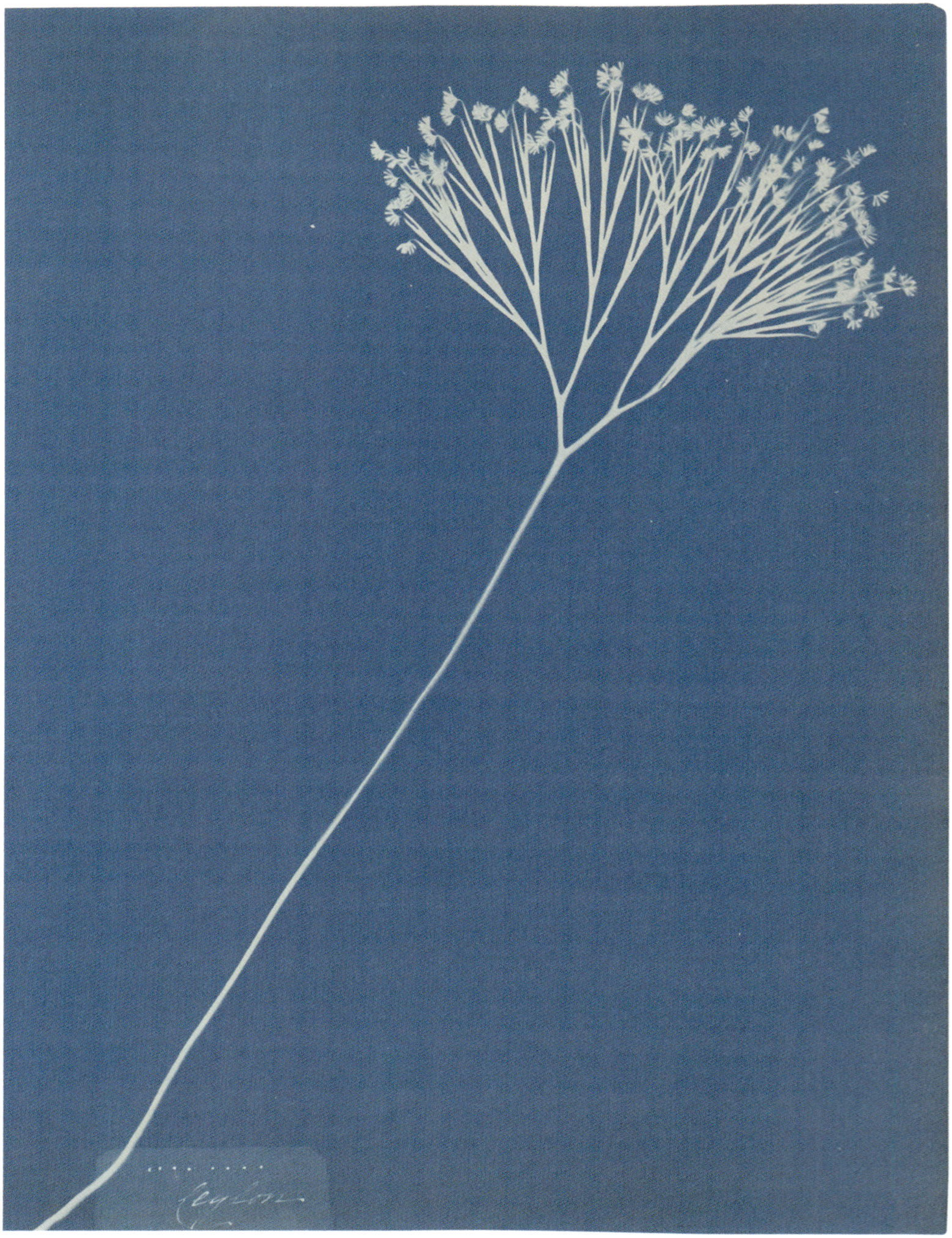

Plate 527. Ceylon

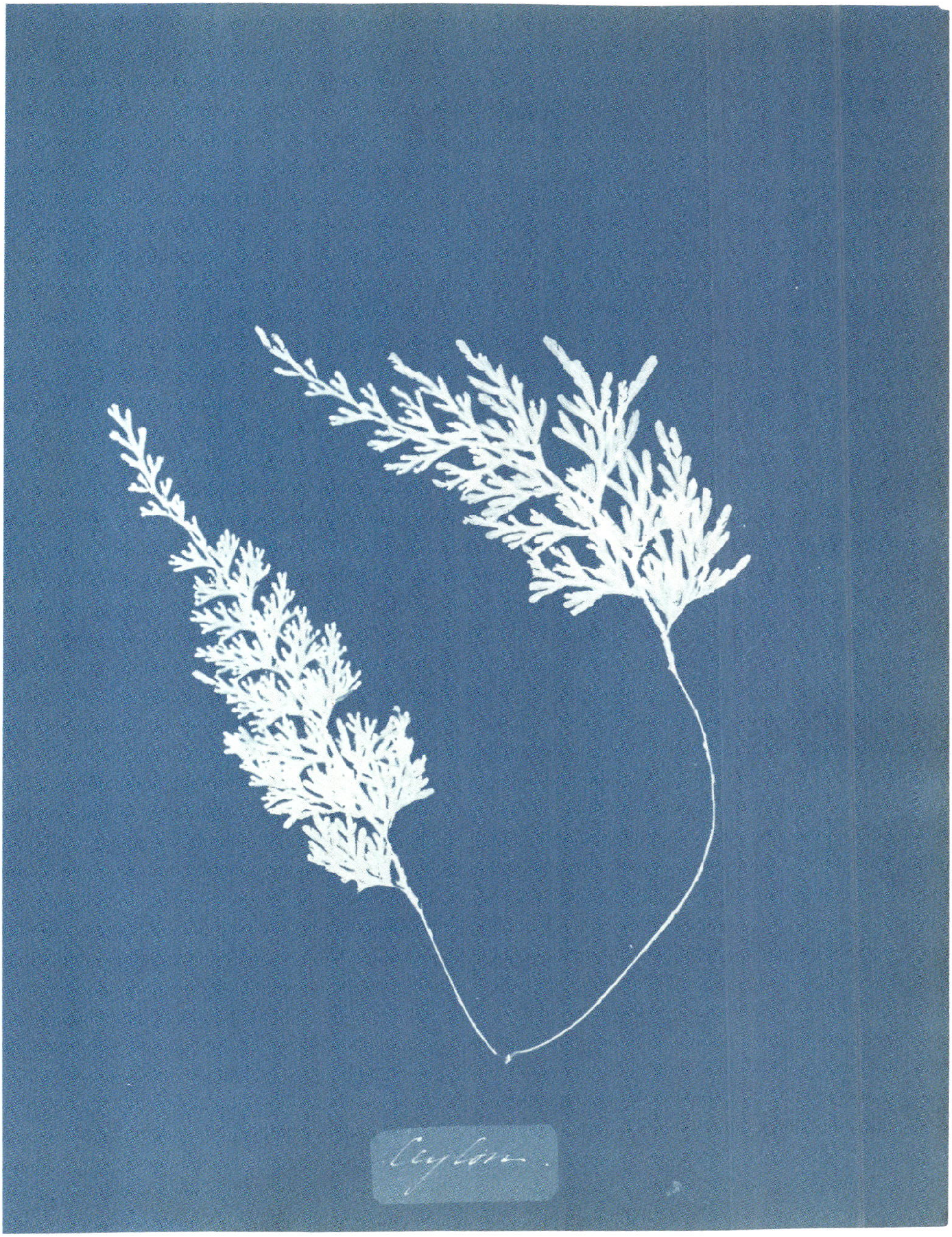

Plate 528. Ceylon

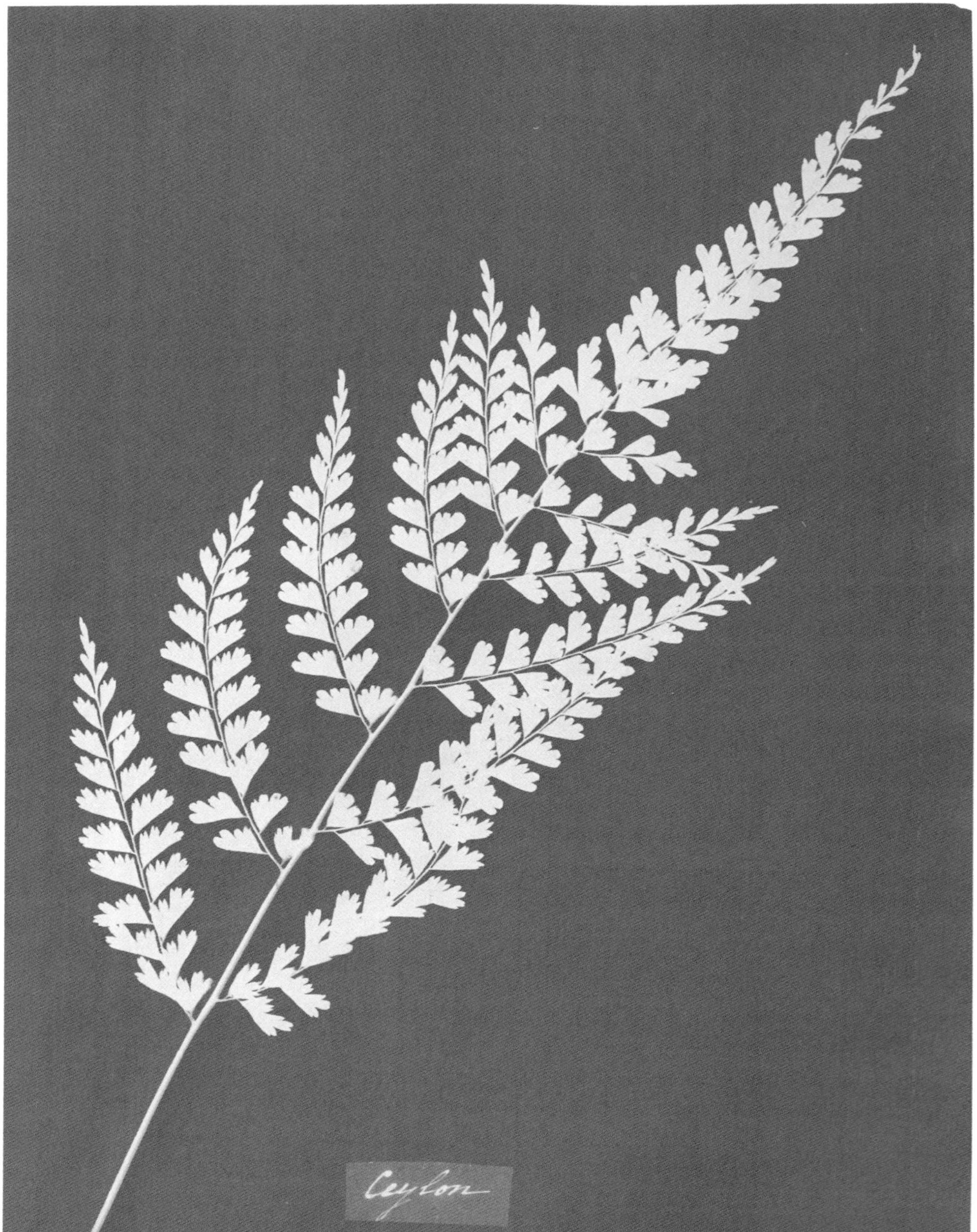

Plate 529. Ceylon

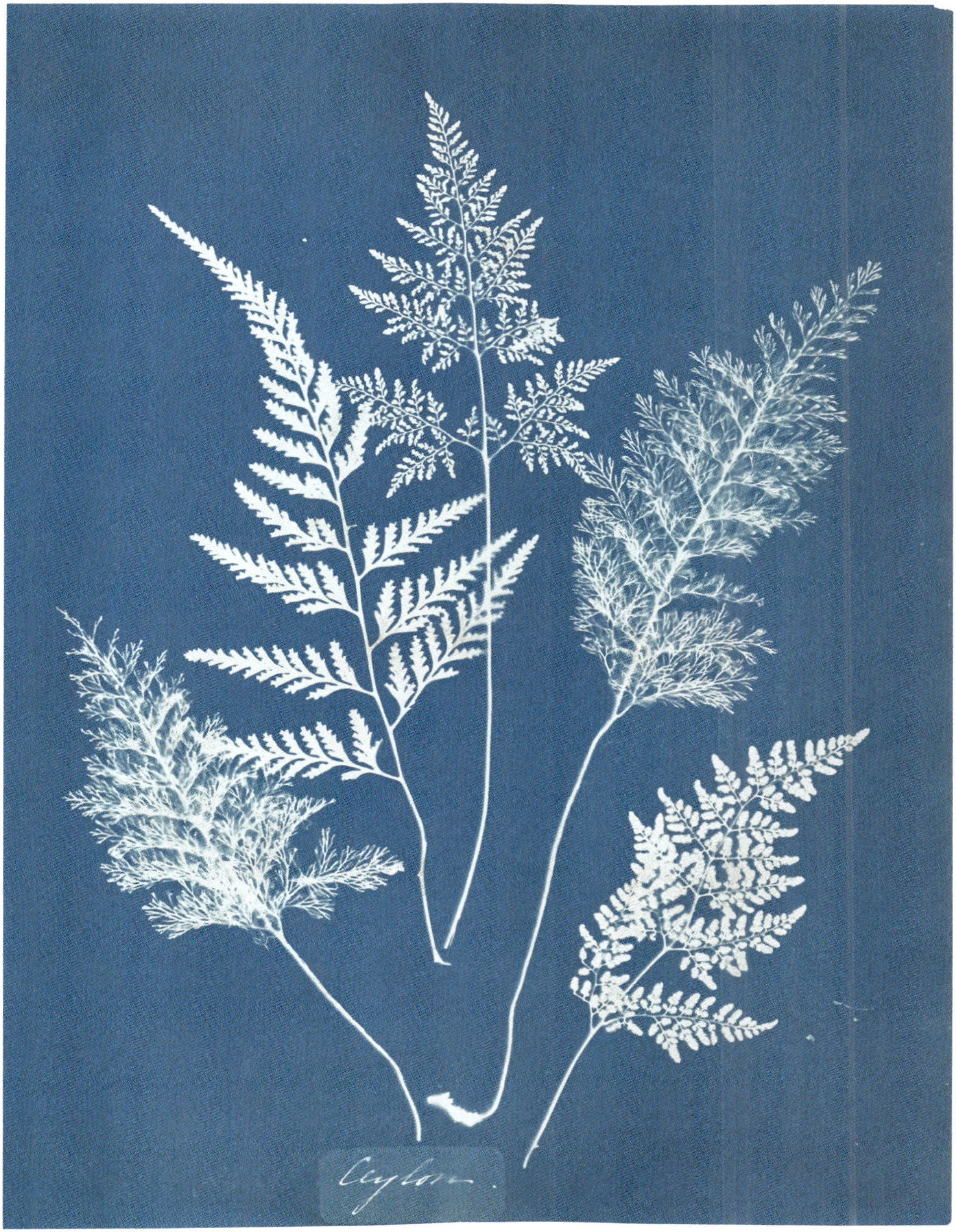

Plate 530. Ceylon

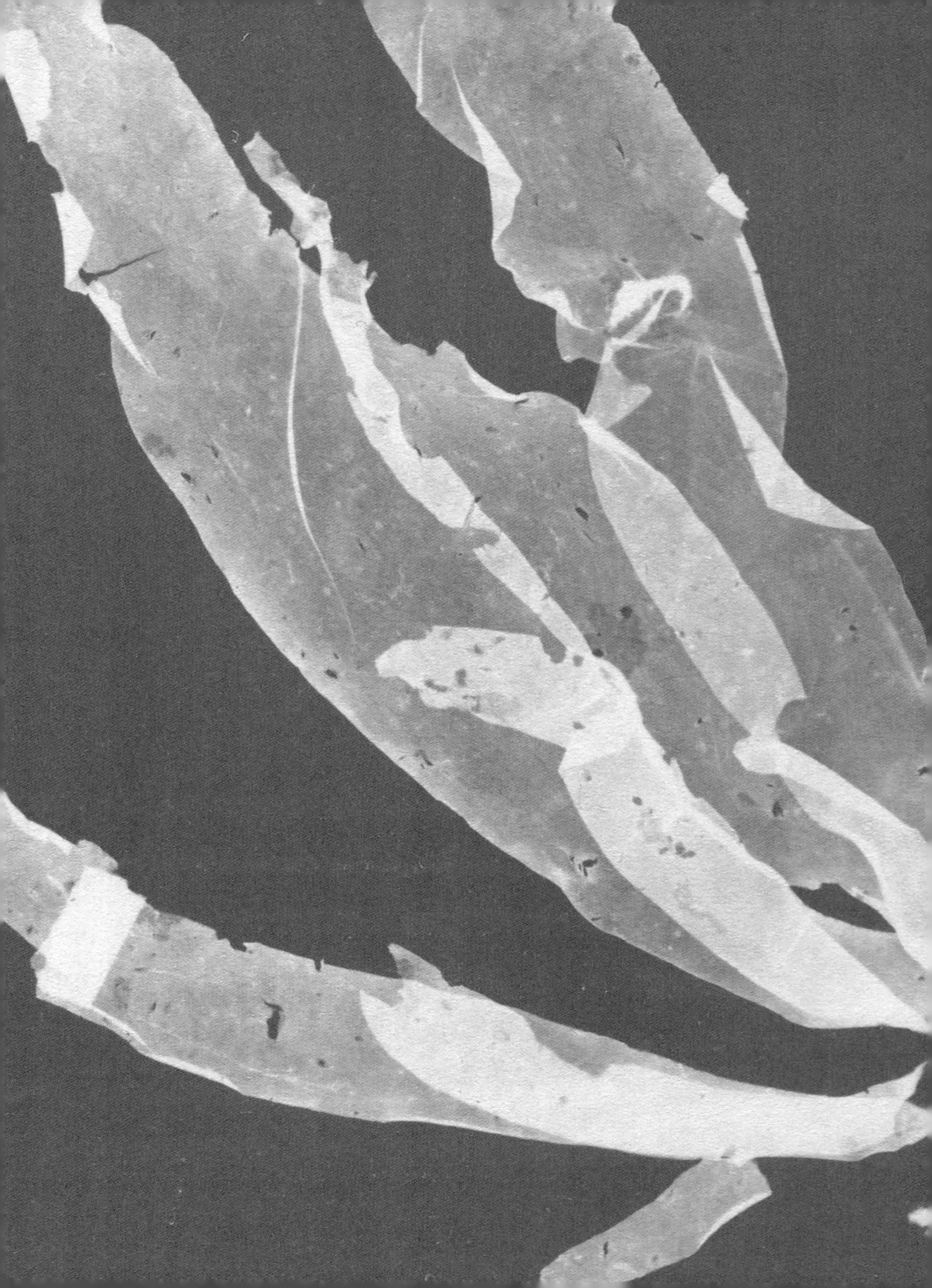

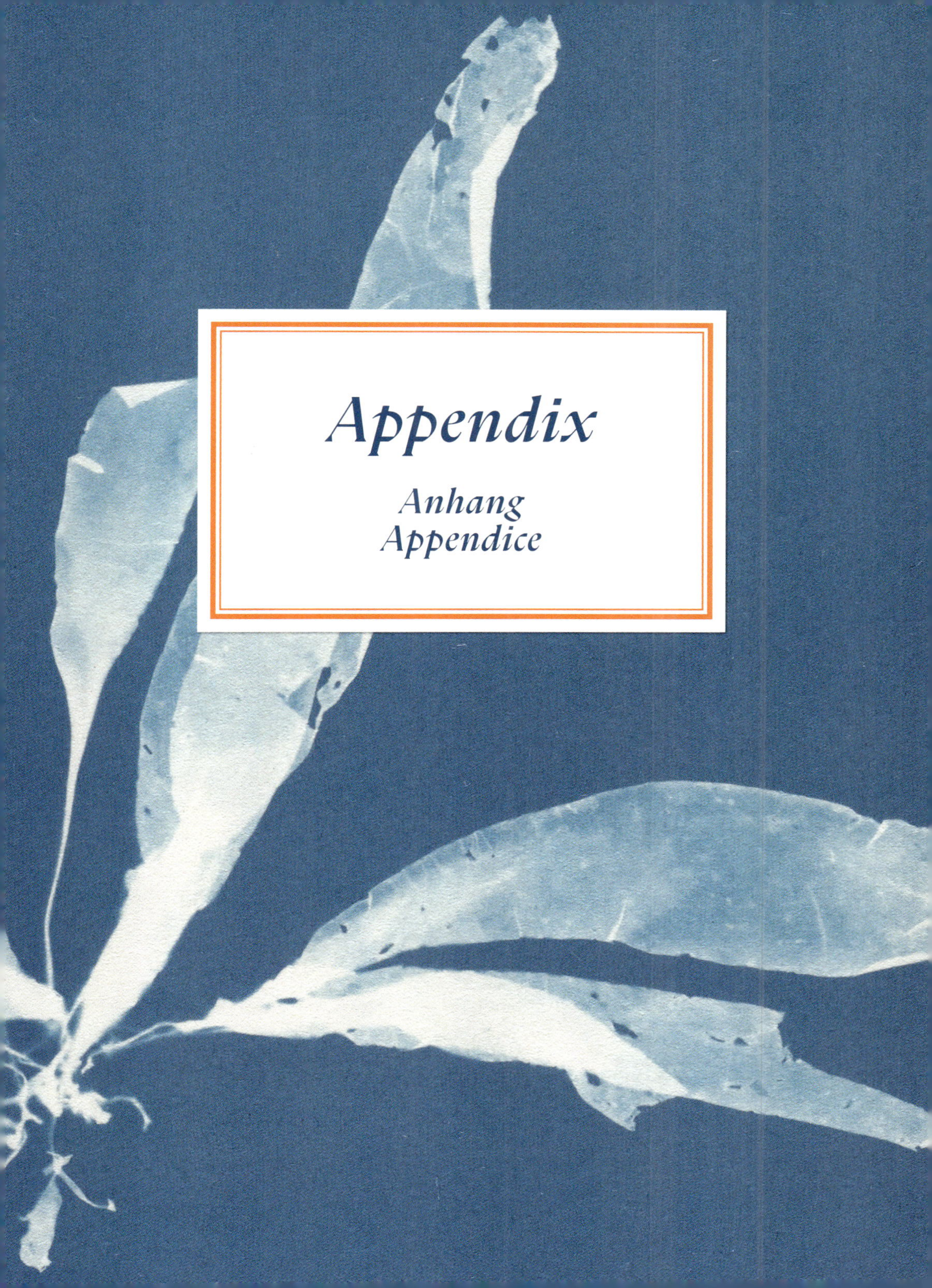

Appendix

Anhang
Appendice

Editorial Notes

British Algae
The copy of *British Algae* once the property of John Herschel, purchased by the New York Public Library in 1985, consists of 12 parts and two volumes, with Part IV handed down in two versions. In 2016 the New York Public Library acquired Volume III from another source. In total, the collection includes 310 illustrative plates and 23 text plates. These form the basic stock of plates from *British Algae* depicted here. For Part IV, the version was chosen that, according to Anna Atkins' wishes, was to replace the previously issued version of Part IV.

Part III of *British Algae*, missing from the Herschel edition, was bequeathed to the Metropolitan Museum of Art, New York, from the collection of Philip B. Mason.

Volume II of *British Algae*, which was also missing from the Herschel copy, was reconstructed from the collection in the Rijksmuseum, Amsterdam, where the plates were not arranged as originally intended but set in alphabetical order. The provenance of this copy, acquired in 2017, remains unclear. The surviving specimens at the Glasgow Museums Resource Centre and in the British Library were used to help establish the correct sequence of Volume II.

Some plates intended for Volume II, however, had already been included in previous instalments (Part XI) of the Herschel copy or were allocated to Volume III. To avoid duplication, these cyanotypes are reproduced in their appropriate place within the Herschel edition rather than in Volume II.

Cyanotypes of British and Foreign Ferns
The cyanotypes pictured in the album entitled *Cyanotypes of British and Foreign Ferns* once belonged to Anne Dixon's nephew, Henry Dixon. The album remained with the family of Dixon's sister Caroline and was bought in 1984 by the J. Paul Getty Museum, Los Angeles.

Original Formats
The original formats of the copies used for this reprint are as follows:

British Algae:
New York Public Library:
26 × 20 cm (10 ¼ × 7 ⅞ in.)
The Metropolitan Museum of Art, New York:
25.3 × 20 cm (10 × 7 ⅞ in.)
Natural History Museum, London:
26 × 19.7 cm (10 ¼ × 7 ¾ in.)
Rijksmuseum, Amsterdam:
25 × 20 cm (9 ⅞ × 7 ⅞ in.)

Cyanotypes of British and Foreign Ferns:
J. Paul Getty Museum, Los Angeles:
25.4 × 19.4 cm (10 × 7 ⅝ in.)

The number of plates in this edition has been adapted and is different from the original publication (TASCHEN, 2023); however, the original arrangement has been retained.

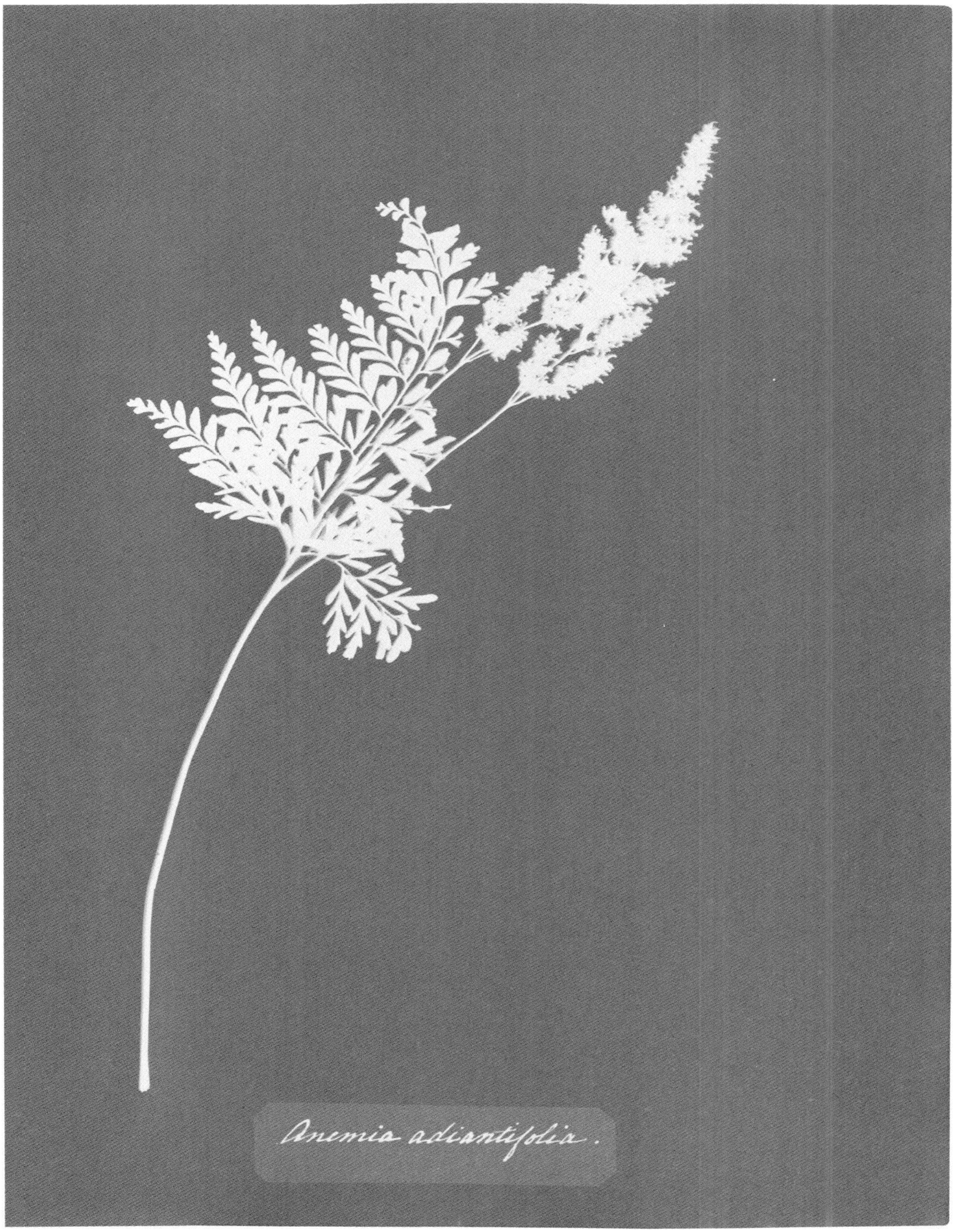
Anemia adiantifolia.

British Algae
Das 1985 von der New York Public Library angekaufte, aus dem Besitz von John Herschel stammende Exemplar der *British Algae* besteht aus 12 Teilen und 2 Bänden; Teil IV ist in zwei Varianten überliefert. 2016 konnte die New York Public Library Band III aus einer anderen Provenienz erwerben. Insgesamt umfasst die Sammlung 310 Bildtafeln und 23 Texttafeln. Sie bildet den Grundbestand der hier abgebildeten Tafeln aus *British Algae*. Von Teil IV wurde die Variante gewählt, die nach dem Willen von Anna Atkins den früher zuvor ausgelieferten Teil IV ersetzen sollte.

Der im Herschel-Exemplar fehlende Teil III der *British Algae* wurde nach dem im Metropolitan Museum of Art, New York, überlieferten Exemplar aus dem ehemaligen Besitz von Philip B. Mason ergänzt.

Der im Herschel-Exemplar ebenfalls fehlende Band II der *British Algae* wurde aus dem Exemplar des Rijksmuseums in Amsterdam rekonstruiert, in dem die Tafeln ohne Bezug zur ursprünglich vorgesehenen Struktur in alphabetischer Ordnung eingebunden sind. Die Provenienz dieses 2017 erworbenen Exemplars ist ungeklärt. Zur Festlegung der Reihenfolge von Band II wurden die im Glasgow Museums Resource Centre und in der British Library überlieferten Exemplare herangezogen.

Einige der für Band II vorgesehenen Tafeln waren jedoch schon in früheren Lieferungen (Teil XI) des Herschel-Exemplars enthalten oder dort Band III zugeordnet. Um Doubletten zu vermeiden, wurden jene Cyanotypien, die sowohl Bestandteil des in der New York Public Library überlieferten Herschel-Exemplars als auch des im Rijksmuseum befindlichen Exemplars sind, nicht in Band II übernommen, sondern an entsprechender Stelle im Herschel-Exemplar wiedergegeben.

Cyanotypes of British and Foreign Ferns
Die hier abgebildeten Cyanotypien des Albums *Cyanotypes of British and Foreign Ferns* stammen aus dem ehemaligen Besitz des Neffen von Anne Dixon, Henry Dixon. Das Album verblieb in der Familie von Dixons Schwester Caroline und wurde 1984 vom J. Paul Getty Museum in Los Angeles angekauft.

Original-Formate
Die Original-Formate der für diesen Nachdruck verwendeten Exemplare sind wie folgt:

British Algae:
New York Public Library: 26 × 20 cm
The Metropolitan Museum of Art, New York: 25,3 × 20 cm
Natural History Museum, London: 26 × 19,7 cm
Rijksmuseum, Amsterdam: 25 × 20 cm

Cyanotypes of British and Foreign Ferns:
J. Paul Getty Museum, Los Angeles: 25,4 × 19,4 cm

Für diese Edition wurde der Umfang der Tafeln gegenüber der Originalausgabe (TASCHEN, 2023) reduziert; die ursprüngliche Anordnung ist unverändert.

British Algae
L'exemplaire des *British Algae*, acquis en 1985 par la New York Public Library et ayant appartenu à John Herschel, se compose de 12 parties et deux volumes. La partie IV est conservée en deux variantes. En 2016, la New York Public Library a acquis le volume III d'une autre provenance. L'ensemble comprend 310 planches illustrées et 23 planches de textes. Elles constituent le corpus des planches des *British Algae* reproduites dans le présent ouvrage. Pour la partie IV, la variante retenue est celle qui, selon la volonté d'Anna Atkins, devait remplacer la version précédemment diffusée.

La partie III des *British Algae*, absente de l'exemplaire Herschel, a été complétée d'après l'exemplaire conservé au Metropolitan Museum of Art, New York, issu de la collection de Philip B. Mason.

Le volume II des *British Algae*, également absent de l'exemplaire Herschel, a été reconstitué à partir de l'exemplaire conservé au Rijksmuseum d'Amsterdam, dans lequel les planches ont été reliées par ordre alphabétique, sans tenir compte de la structure initialement prévue. La provenance de cet exemplaire, acquis en 2017, demeure inconnue. Afin d'établir l'ordre du volume II, les exemplaires conservés au Glasgow Museums Resource Centre et à la British Library ont été consultés.

Certaines planches destinées au volume II figuraient toutefois déjà dans des livraisons antérieures (partie XI) de l'exemplaire Herschel ou avaient été intégrées au volume III. Afin d'éviter toute duplication, ces cyanotypes n'ont pas été reproduits dans le présent volume II, mais figurent à leur emplacement correspondant dans l'exemplaire Herschel.

Cyanotypes of British and Foreign Ferns
Les cyanotypes de l'album *Cyanotypes of British and Foreign Ferns* reproduits ici proviennent de l'ancienne collection d'Henry Dixon, neveu d'Anne Dixon. L'album en question est resté dans la famille de Caroline Dixon, sa sœur, avant d'être acquis en 1984 par le J. Paul Getty Museum, Los Angeles.

Formats originaux
Les formats originaux des exemplaires utilisés pour la présente réimpression sont les suivants :

British Algae :
New York Public Library : 26 × 20 cm
The Metropolitan Museum of Art, New York : 25,3 × 20 cm
Natural History Museum, Londres : 26 × 19,7 cm
Rijksmuseum, Amsterdam : 25 × 20 cm

Cyanotypes of British and Foreign Ferns :
J. Paul Getty Museum, Los Angeles : 25,4 × 19,4 cm

Pour la présente édition, le nombre de planches a été réduit par rapport à l'édition originale (TASCHEN, 2023). Toutefois, l'organisation initiale des planches reste inchangée.

Bibliography

Easterby-Smith, Sarah, *Cultivating Commerce. Cultures of Botany in Britain and France, 1760–1815*, Cambridge, Cambridge University Press, 2017.

Ex. cat. Biel: *Pflanzen, Blüten, Früchte. Botanische Illustrationen in Kunst und Wissenschaft*, Gerd-Helge Vogel (Ed.), Berlin, Lukas Verlag, 2014.

Ex. cat. New York: Schaaf, Larry J., *Sun gardens: cyanotypes by Anna Atkins*, New York, Prestel, 2018.

Ex. cat. Stuttgart: *Blütenpracht und Farbenzauber. Illustrierte Pflanzenbücher des 18. und 19. Jahrhunderts aus den Sammlungen der Württembergischen Landesbibliothek Stuttgart*, Peter Amelung (Ed.), Stuttgart, Württembergische Landesbibliothek, 1993.

Nissen, Claus, *Die botanische Buchillustration. Ihre Geschichte und Bibliographie*, 3 vols, Stuttgart, Hiersemann, 1966.

O'Malley, Therese, and Meyers, Amy R. W. (Eds.), *The Art of Natural History. Illustrated Treatises and Botanical Paintings 1400–1850*, New Haven, Yale University Press, 2008 (Studies in History of Art, vol. 69).

Ruppel, Sophie, *Botanophilie. Mensch und Pflanze in der aufklärerisch-bürgerlichen Gesellschaft um 1800*, Vienna, Böhlau, 2019.

Sachsse, Rolf, *Anna Atkins. Blue Prints*, Munich, Hirmer, 2021.

Shteir, Ann B., *Cultivating Women, Cultivating Science. Flora's daughters and botany in England 1760–1860*, Baltimore, Johns Hopkins University Press, 1996.

Steidl, Katharina, *Am Rande der Fotografie. Eine Medialitätsgeschichte des Fotogramms im 19. Jahrhundert*, Berlin, Boston, De Gruyter, 2019.

Steidl, Katharina, "Meeresblaue Abdrucke. Anna Atkins' Cyanotypien als visuelle Medien- und Klassifikationskritik", in *Aquatische Bilder. Die Fotografie und das Meer*, Franziska Brons (Ed.), Weimar, 2020 (Fotogeschichte 40/2020, 156), pp. 7–18.

Ware, Mike, *Cyanomicon. The History, Science and Art of Cyanotype. Photographic Printing in Prussian Blue*, London, Science Museum of London, 1999 (online publication, 2020).

Whittingham, Sarah, *Fern Fever. The Story of Pteridomania*, London, Frances Lincoln, 2012.

Williams, Roger L., *Botanophilia in Eighteenth-Century France. The Spirit of Enlightenment*, Dordrecht, Springer, 2001 (Archives Internationales d'Histoire des Idées/International Archives of the History of Ideas, 179).

Acknowledgements

For their many contributions regarding the book's content, as well as their logistical and organizational support towards the realization of this book, the author would like to thank Mark Ballard (Kent History and Library Centre), Colin Harding (Bradford), Katrin Korch (Baden-Baden), Ed Miller (Ferring History Group, Sussex), Ines Otschik (Museum der Stadt Aschaffenburg), Maria Smit (Rijksmuseum, Amsterdam) and Desré Stead (Brenthurst Library, Johannesburg).

Photo Credits

We are much indebted to the museums, libraries, archives and all other institutions cited for their kind assistance and contributions towards the publication of this volume.

The Cyanotypes

British Algae:

Metropolitan Museum of Art, New York, Accession Number: 2005.100.557. Gilman Collection, Purchase, The Horace W. Goldsmith Foundation Gift, through Joyce and Robert Menschel, 2005: plates 21–31.

Natural History Museum, London: pp. 256–258 (Vol. II, title page and table of contents).

New York Public Library, Spencer Coll. Eng. 1843 93-440. NYPL catalog ID (B-number): b11861683: plates 1–19, 35–210, 336–432.

Rijksmuseum, Amsterdam, Object number RP-F-2016-133-47. Purchased with the support of the BankGiro Lottery, the Familie W. Cordia/Rijksmuseum Funds and the Paul Huf Funds/Rijksmuseum Funds: plates 211–334.

Cyanotypes of British and Foreign Ferns:

J. Paul Getty Museum, Los Angeles, Object number 84.XO.227. Digital image courtesy of the Getty's Open Content Program: plates 434–530.

Further Image Material

Bibliothèque nationale de France, Paris: p. 405.

Brenthurst Library, Johannesburg: p. 36.

Brigham Young University, Provo, Utah: p. 54.

Den Kongelige Kobberstiksamling, Copenhagen: p. 12.

Ethnographic Museum of the University of Zurich: p. 406.

Ferring History Group, Sussex, Courtesy of Ed Miller: p. 56.

Gerstein Science Information Centre, University of Toronto Library: p. 187.

J. Paul Getty Museum, Los Angeles: pp. 17, 24, 34, 40, 46, 247, 248, 251, 333.

Kahle/Austin Foundation, San Francisco: p. 53.

Library of Congress, Washington, D. C.: p. 244.

Marine Biological Library, Woods Hole Oceanographic Institution: p. 30.

Musée national d'Art moderne, Centre Pompidou, Paris: p. 327.

Museum der Stadt Aschaffenburg: p. 324.

Museum of the History of Science, Oxford: p. 35.

National Portrait Gallery, London: p. 8.

National Science & Media Museum, Bradford, West Yorkshire / Science & Society Picture Library: pp. 16, 50.

Natural History Museum, London: pp. 23, 39, 51.

New York Public Library: pp. 18/19, 45, 49, 184.

Nurstead Court Archives, Kent: pp. 11, 27.

Photography © The Art Institute of Chicago: p. 328.

Private collections: pp. 29, 181, 401.

© Rijksmuseum, Amsterdam: p. 507.

© Robert Rauschenberg Foundation / VG Bild-Kunst, Bonn 2026: p. 255.

Royal Collection Trust, London: p. 15.

The Royal Photographic Society, Yorkshire: p. 55.

Stadtbibliothek Ulm: p. 402.

Universitätsbibliothek Erlangen-Nürnberg, 2 TREW.C 685/686, Tab. 9: p. 409.

University of California Library, Berkeley: p. 179.

© 2021 University of New Hampshire, Lotte Jacobi Collection: p. 330.

Wellcome Collection, London: pp. 33, 176, 398.

Imprint

EACH AND EVERY TASCHEN BOOK PLANTS A SEED!
Each year, we offset our annual carbon emissions with carbon credits at the Instituto Terra, a reforestation program in Minas Gerais, Brazil, founded by Lélia and Sebastião Salgado. To find out more about this ecological partnership, please check: www.taschen.com/institutoterra.
Inspiration: unlimited.
Carbon footprint: (almost) zero.

Want to see more? Visit taschen.com to view our current publications, browse our latest magazine, and subscribe to our newsletter.

© 2026 TASCHEN GmbH
Hohenzollernring 53, D–50672 Köln
www.taschen.com

Project management: Mahros Allamezade, Tom Pitt-Brooke, Cologne
English translation: Isabel Varea-Riley for Grapevine Publishing Services, London
French translation: Wolf Fruhtrunk, Paris
Design: Andy Disl, Los Angeles; Claudia Frey, Cologne

Printed in Bosnia-Herzegovina
ISBN 978-3-7544-0122-4

Front cover: Ceylon
From: *Cyanotypes of British and Foreign Ferns; Foreign Ferns* (plate 530)

Back cover: *Sargassum plumosum*
From: *British Algae*, Volume I (plate 142)

Endpapers: *Chorda filum* and *Cladostephus verticillatus*
From: *British Algae*, Part III (plates 27 and 28)

Page 1: *British Algae*, title page

Pages 2 and 4: *Cyanotypes of British and Foreign Ferns*, title pages

Pages 58/59: *Dictyota dichotoma*, in the young state, and in fruit
From: *British Algae*, Part XI (detail from plate 118)

Pages 188/189: *Ulva latissima*
From: *British Algae*, Volume III (detail from plate 362)

Pages 410/411: *Asplenium chinensis*
From: *Cyanotypes of British and Foreign Ferns; Foreign Ferns* (detail from plate 490)

Pages 504/505: *Laminaria phyllitis*
From: *British Algae*, Part V (detail from plate 48)

Pages 507: *Anemia adiantifolia*
From: *Cyanotypes of British and Foreign Ferns; Foreign Ferns* (plate 518)